The Handbook of Alzheimer's Disease and Other Dementias

Wiley-Blackwell Handbooks of Behavioral Neuroscience

The rapidly expanding field of behavioral neuroscience examines neurobiological aspects of behavior, utilizing techniques from molecular biology, neuropsychology, and psychology. This series of handbooks provides a cutting-edge overview of classic research, current scholarship, and future trends in behavioral neuroscience. The series provides a survey of representative topics in this field, suggesting implications for basic research and clinical applications.

Series editor: David Mostofsky, Boston University

The Handbook of Stress: Neuropsychological Effects on the Brain
Edited by Cheryl D. Conrad

The Handbook of Alzheimer's Disease and Other Dementias
Edited by Andrew E. Budson and Neil W. Kowall

The Handbook of the Neuropsychology of Language (2 Volumes)
Edited by Miriam Faust

The Handbook of Alzheimer's Disease and Other Dementias

Edited by Andrew E. Budson and
Neil W. Kowall

WILEY-BLACKWELL

A John Wiley & Sons, Ltd., Publication

Library of Congress Cataloging-in-Publication Data

The handbook of Alzheimer's disease and other dementias / edited by Andrew E.
Budson and Neil W. Kowall.
   p. ; cm. – (Wiley-Blackwell handbooks of behavioral neuroscience)
   Includes bibliographical references and index.
   ISBN 978-1-4051-6828-1 (hardcover : alk. paper)
   1. Dementia.   I. Budson, Andrew E.   II. Kowall, Neil W.   III. Series:
Wiley-Blackwell handbooks of behavioral neuroscience.
   [DNLM: 1.   Dementia.   WM 220]
   RC521.H34 2011
   616.8'3–dc22

                                                    2011010575

A catalogue record for this book is available from the British Library.

This book is published in the following electronic formats: ePDFs 9781444344080;
Wiley Online Library 9781444344103; ePub 9781444344097
Set in 10.5/13 pt Minion by Toppan Best-set Premedia Limited
Printed and bound in Singapore by Markono Print Media Pte Ltd

1   2011

We wish to dedicate this book to our families:

Amy, Leah, and Danny

And

Miriam, Elisheva, Charlotte, Jenny, Mischa, and Jonah

Contents

Contributors

Carmela R. Abraham Department of Biochemistry & Alzheimer's Disease Center, Boston University School of Medicine, Boston, MA, USA

Brandon A. Ally Departments of Neurology, Psychiatry, and Psychology, Vanderbilt University, Nashville, TN, USA

Stacy L. Andersen New England Centenarian Study, Boston University School of Medicine, Boston, MA USA

Adam L. Boxer Memory and Aging Center, Department of Neurology, University of California, San Francisco, CA, USA

Marina Boziki 3rd Department of Neurology, Aristotle University of Thessaloniki, Greece

Andrew E. Budson Department of Neurology & Alzheimer's Disease Center, Boston University School of Medicine, Boston, MA, USA; Center for Translational Cognitive Neuroscience and Geriatric Research Education Clinical Center, VA Boston Healthcare System, Boston, MA, USA; Memory Disorders Unit, Division of Cognitive and Behavioral Neurology, Department of Neurology, Brigham & Women's Hospital, Boston, MA, USA; Harvard Medical School, Boston, MA, USA

Alice Cronin-Golomb Department of Psychology, Boston University, Boston, MA, USA

Bradford C. Dickerson Department of Neurology, Athinoula A. Martinos Center for Biomedical Imaging, and the Alzheimer's Disease Research Center, Massachusetts General Hospital, Boston, MA, USA; Memory Disorders Unit, Division of Cognitive and Behavioral Neurology, Department of Neurology, Brigham & Women's Hospital, Boston, MA, USA; Harvard Medical School, Boston, MA, USA

Tamara G. Fong Aging Brain Center, Hebrew SeniorLife, Boston, MA. USA; Department of Neurology, Beth Israel Deaconess Medical Center, Boston, MA. USA; Harvard Medical School, Boston, MA. USA

Brandon E. Gavett   Department of Neurology & Alzheimer's Disease Center, Boston University School of Medicine, Boston, MA, USA

Amanda M. Gentile   Department of Neurology & Alzheimer's Disease Center, Boston University School of Medicine, Boston, MA, USA

Robert C. Green   Division of Genetics, Department of Medicine, Brigham and Women's Hospital, Boston, MA. USA; Harvard Medical School, Boston, MA. USA

Murray Grossman   Department of Neurology, University of Pennsylvania School of Medicine, Philadelphia, PA, USA

David G. Harper   Department of Psychiatry, Harvard Medical School, Boston, MA, USA; Department of Psychology, McLean Hospital, Belmont, MA, USA

Paul Hollingworth   Medical Research Council (MRC) Centre for Neuropsychiatric Genetics and Genomics, Department of Psychological Medicine and Neurology, School of Medicine, Cardiff University, Cardiff, UK

Angela L. Jefferson   Department of Neurology & Alzheimer's Disease Center, Boston University School of Medicine, Boston, MA, USA

Ravi Kahlon   Department of Neurology & Alzheimer's Disease Center, Boston University School of Medicine, Boston, MA, USA

Ronald J. Killiany   Department of Anatomy and Neurobiology, Laboratory for Cognitive Neurobiology, Center for Biomedical Imaging, Boston University School of Medicine, Boston, MA, USA

Neil W. Kowall   Departments of Neurology and Pathology & Alzheimer's Disease Center, Boston University School of Medicine, Boston, MA, USA; Neurology Service and Geriatric Research Education Clinical Center, VA Boston Healthcare System, Boston, MA, USA; Harvard Medical School, Boston, MA, USA

Alan M. Mandell   Departments of Neurology and Psychiatry, and Alzheimer's Disease Center, Boston University School of Medicine, Boston, MA, USA; Geriatric Research Education Clinical Center, Bedford VA Hospital, Bedford, MA, USA

Ann C. McKee   Departments of Neurology and Pathology, Alzheimer's Disease Center, Boston University School of Medicine, Boston, MA, USA; Geriatric Research Education Clinical Center, Bedford VA Hospital, Bedford, MA, USA

Peter J. Morin   Department of Neurology & Alzheimer's Disease Center, Boston University School of Medicine, Boston, MA, USA; Geriatric Research Education Clinical Center, Bedford VA Hospital, Bedford, MA, USA

Vassilis Papaliagkas   3rd Department of Neurology, Aristotle University of Thessaloniki, Greece

Maija Pihlajamäki   Department of Neurology, Kuopio University Hospital, Kuopio, Finland

Daniel Z. Press   Department of Neurology, Beth Israel Deaconess Medical Center, Boston, MA, USA; Harvard Medical School, Boston, MA, USA

Jamie Reilly   Department of Speech, Language, and Hearing Sciences, University of Florida, Gainesville, FL, USA

Reisa A. Sperling   Department of Neurology, Brigham and Women's Hospital, Boston, MA, USA; Harvard Medical School, Boston, MA, USA

Robert A. Stern   Department of Neurology & Alzheimer's Disease Center, Boston University School of Medicine, Boston, MA, USA

Joshua Troche   Department of Speech, Language, and Hearing Sciences, University of Florida, Gainesville, FL, USA

Magda Tsolaki   3rd Department of Neurology, Aristotle University of Thessaloniki, Greece

Julie Williams   Medical Research Council (MRC) Centre for Neuropsychiatric Genetics and Genomics, Department of Psychological Medicine and Neurology, School of Medicine, Cardiff University, Cardiff, UK

Christopher I. Wright   Laboratory of Aging and Emotion, Department of Psychiatry, Athinoula A. Martinos Center for Biomedical Imaging, Massachusetts General Hospital, Charlestown, MA, USA; Division of Cognitive and Behavioral Neurology, Department of Neurology, Brigham and Women's Hospital, Boston, MA, USA; Harvard Medical School, Boston, MA, USA

Foreword

In 1903, Emil Kraeplin recruited Alois Alzheimer to join his department at the Nervenklinik in Munich. Kraeplin challenged Alzheimer, who was known for his clinical and pathological research, to uncover the biological basis of mental illness. In 1906, Alzheimer hit pay dirt, when he described the neuritic plaques and neurofibrillary tangles in the brain of Auguste D., his 53-year-old patient with dementia. Alzheimer's presentation at the 37th Assembly of Southwest German Psychiatrists in Tubingen apparently generated very little interest from the attendees, who included such prominent figures as Nissl, Jung, and Binswanger; the *Tubinger Chronik* newspaper carried a single line on the case in reporting the meeting. Kraeplin's influential textbook eventually accepted this condition of pre-senile dementia and proposed the name Alzheimer's disease. Growing from this single case report, Alzheimer's disease is now widely recognized as one of the most common neurological diseases, but it was not always so.

Between 1906 and 1966, there was very little clinical or research interest in Alzheimer's disease as it was widely viewed as a rare form of pre-senile dementia. Neurology textbooks rarely allotted it more than a page or two, there were only a handful of papers published in the literature, and almost nothing heard at the annual neurology meetings.

Interest began to pick up with Sir Martin Roth's report in 1966 that neuritic plaques occurred in brains of the elderly, and that their number roughly correlated with the extent of dementia severity. In 1976, Robert Katzman's seminal article on the epidemiology of Alzheimer's disease stressed that pre-senile and senile dementia were similar pathologically. His conclusion that we faced a silent epidemic of staggering proportions was a stunning wake-up call to action. Three other events occurred in the 1970s that catalyzed the modern era wave of clinical and scientific research into the causes, mechanisms, and treatment of Alzheimer's disease and related dementias. The first of these was establishing the National Institute on Aging at the National Institutes of Health, and the strategic plan for Alzheimer's disease under the direction of the Institute's first director, Robert Butler and the associate director Zaven Khachaturian. This Institute cast Alzheimer's disease as a priority on the national health stage, and provided federal funds for research. The second important step was led by Jerry Stone, who founded the Alzheimer's Disease and Related Disorders Association (now renamed the Alzheimer's Association). This private foundation spread from its base in Chicago to establish chapters across the country dedicated to raising awareness about Alzheimer's disease and raising money to support research. The third event was a scientific breakthrough: Indices of acetylcholine metabolism, a neurotransmitter in the brain linked to memory capacities, were decreased in brains of patients with Alzheimer's disease. This advance was crucial because it opened a new approach to Alzheimer's disease that justified expenditure of public and private dollars for research. Further, this discovery sparked hope for a cure because drugs can be developed that alter the neurochemical milieu of the brain, whereas the anatomic pathological features of Alzheimer's disease – the neuritic plaques and tangles – have always seemed immutably fixed. Indeed, this discovery paved the way for developing acetylcholinesterase inhibitors, the first class of drugs approved by the FDA for treating Alzheimer's disease. In 1984, the first clinical criteria for the diagnosis of Alzheimer's disease was published, and the first five Alzheimer's Disease Research Centers were established with funding from the National Institute on Aging. These Centers, which now number 30 across the United States, are the focal point for much of the clinical and scientific research conducted on Alzheimer's disease. This volume highlights many of the advances generated by investigators in these Centers and underscores the multidisciplinary approach in clinical science that is the hallmark of modern dementia research.

Alzheimer's disease is the most prevalent cause of dementia, but not the only cause. Dementia due to multiple strokes has always been appreciated, but clinicians now routinely diagnose degenerative conditions such as frontal temporal dementia and diffuse Lewy body disease that were previously lumped with Alzheimer's disease. As pointed out in chapters of this volume, these related neurodegenerative diseases have clinical and neuropsychological features that aid in the diagnosis and that distinguish them from Alzheimer's disease. In this sense, the field of cognitive neuroscience has improved the diagnosis of dementia syndromes; in turn, the study of neurodegenerative diseases has helped boost neuropsychological research. Neuroimaging also helps distinguish Alzheimer's disease, frontal temporal dementia, and dementia with Lewy bodies, as brain scans in each of these conditions have a typical anatomic, functional and molecular signature. Their separate identities are reinforced by neuropathological findings that confirm the clinical diagnoses, and that also drive scientific research into the causes of each disease. Advances in this area now permit molecular classification of diseases due to accumulation of misfolded proteins in brain that are distinctive for each condition. Thus, we speak of Alzheimer's disease as an "amyloidopathy"; some cases of frontal temporal dementia as a "tauopathy"; and dementia with Lewy bodies as an "alpha-syncleinopathy." Uncovering the molecular signature of these diseases is as important to the field now as the discovery of acetylcholine deficiency was in the 1970s, as research into the cellular mechanisms leading to accumulation of toxic protein fragments may hold the key to developing protective and even curative therapies.

John H. Growdon, M.D.
Professor of Neurology, Harvard Medical School
Massachusetts Alzheimer's Disease Research Center
Massachusetts General Hospital, Boston, MA USA

Preface

This book provides a comprehensive review of Alzheimer's disease and other dementias from both basic and clinical neuroscience perspectives. Scientists and medical professionals will find both a broad introduction and an up-to-date review of important scientific advances in a single volume. Those working in the areas of Alzheimer's disease and dementia will find this book of interest, including physicians, medical students, psychologists, scientists, graduate students, and allied health professionals including nurses, social workers, and therapists. Part I, "Common Dementias," is designed to provide an overview of Alzheimer's disease and other dementias including a brief discussion of pathology, pathophysiology, clinical manifestations, diagnosis, and treatment. It also provides background for later chapters. Part II, "Pathogenesis and Disease Mechanisms," provides an update on the current genetic risk factors and pathophysiological mechanisms related to dementia. Part III, "Cognitive and Behavioral Dysfunction," reviews the disruption of different cognitive and other functions, including emotion and sleep. Part IV, "Neuroimaging in Dementia," provides an update on this exciting and fast-paced field. The book is designed such that readers can either peruse a chapter of interest or read the book cover to cover. In either case, we believe that you will find this book a useful tool for school, research, or clinical practice.

We would like to thank all of our authors for their excellent contributions and the series editor Professor Mostofsky for his constant encouragement. It is they who deserve the credit for the value in this book; any errors contained herein are our fault alone. Lastly, we would like to note that this book was completed entirely on our own time, during late nights, early mornings, weekends, and vacations.

Andrew E. Budson and Neil W. Kowall
Boston MA

Acknowledgments: Preparation of this book was supported, in part, by P30-AG13846 (Boston University Alzheimer's Disease Core Center) and the Department of Veterans Affairs GRECC program and Research Service.

Part I
Common Dementias

1

Alzheimer's Disease
Alan M. Mandell and Robert C. Green

History

In 1871, over 30 years before Alois Alzheimer published his seminal cases, James Crichton-Browne may have been among the first physicians to remark upon the relationship between "brain wasting" and "premature dotage" in a letter to Charles Darwin (Snyder & Pearn, 2007). Age-related mental deterioration as an entity had been recognized virtually for recorded history (Boller et al., 2007; Mandell & Albert, 1990). Emil Kraepelin, however, was one of the few 19th-century giants of medicine who recognized the connection between brain pathology and mental dissolution in the elderly (Stam, 1985). He referred to "Morbus Alzheimer" as early as 1908 and used the eponym in the 1910 edition of his textbook (Kraepelin, 1910). Over the next century plus, Alzheimer's disease (AD) has become the focus of one of the most intensive investigations in medical history. A Google search for AD now generates over 18 million hits.

Alzheimer examined 51-year-old Auguste D. in 1901 (Graeber, 2006). Her husband had noted a relatively sudden change in her behavior, dominated by panic, terror and suspicions of his having an affair with a neighbor. She neglected her housework, hid objects and fumbled in the kitchen. Over the next several months, she became increasingly restless and a disturbance to their neighbors. By the time of her admission to hospital, which she never left, she suffered from "weakening of memory, persecution mania, sleeplessness, restlessness," had an "amnestic writing disorder," was unable to perform any mental or physical work and was "rarely free from fear and agitation." Periods of calm cooperation alternated with physical aggression towards other patients, "groping their faces as if she were blind" (Page & Fletcher, 2006).

Alzheimer was met with silence when he first presented his case (Alzheimer, 1906) of "a distinct disease process" (Nair & Green, 2006). Following his initial publication

The Handbook of Alzheimer's Disease and Other Dementias, First Edition.
Edited by Andrew E. Budson, Neil W. Kowall.
© 2011 Blackwell Publishing Ltd. Published 2011 by Blackwell Publishing Ltd.

of 1907 (Alzheimer, 1907), he issued his classic review article in 1911 (Alzheimer, 1911).

With a few exceptions and for several reasons (Nair & Green, 2006), "Alzheimer's disease" for roughly the next 50 years denoted "presenile" dementia and differed from the "normal" senility associated with old age, despite Alzheimer's assertion that there were no significant pathological differences between older and younger cases (Spielmeyer, 1916). Kraepelin as well opined that this illness is "a peculiar disease process that is largely independent of age" (Kraepelin, 1910).

Alzheimer described the now familiar distinctive pathology in his original 1907 article. Slides from two patients were rediscovered in 1992 and 1997, and those from Auguste D. clearly demonstrate numerous characteristic cortical plaques and tangles (Graeber, 2006).

Epidemiology of Dementia and AD

In virtually all developed countries, the oldest segments of society are increasing at the fastest rate and an epidemic of age-related diseases is already upon us. The dementia syndrome is largely a provenance of the elderly and is a major part of a looming public health crisis. The global prevalence of dementia of any cause in 2005 was about 24 million with yearly incidence of almost 5 million, tantamount to adding a new case every 7 seconds (Ferri et al., 2005).

AD accounts for about 55–70% of adult-onset dementia in the industrialized world (Lim et al., 1999), is the fifth leading cause of death in Americans older than 65, and, in contrast to the decreasing death toll attributable to other major diseases, that due to AD is on the rise (Mebane-Sims & Alzheimer's Association, 2009) (Figure 1.1).

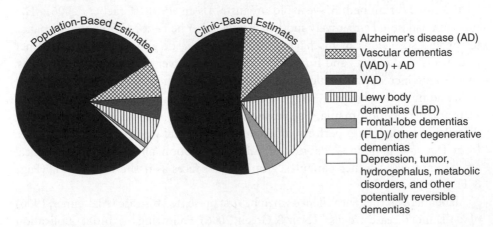

Figure 1.1   Population-based vs. clinic-based estimates of dementia
Source: Modified from Green, R.C. (2005). *Diagnosis and Management of Alzheimer's Disease and Other Dementias* (2nd edn.). Caddo, OK: Professional Communications, Inc., by permission

AD incidence is age related and doubles about every 5 years from age 65 through the 90s (Bachman et al., 1993; Berlau, 2007). The exact prevalence of AD is difficult to determine because, among other reasons, death certificates of people with end-stage AD often list infection or "cardiopulmonary arrest" as the proximate cause. Currently, over 5 million Americans have AD with incidence of a new case about every 70 seconds. In the United States, there will be at least 8.5 million people with AD by the year 2030, about 13 to 25 million in 2050 (a new case every 33 seconds) (Hebert et al., 2003; Mebane-Sims & Alzheimer's Association, 2009) plus an unknown number with other dementias. National direct and indirect monetary costs of caring for people with Alzheimer's disease alone is already at least $100 billion annually in the United States (Koppel, 2003), where nursing home cost per patient currently hovers around $50,000 per year, and over $300 billion per annum globally (Dartigues, 2009). We therefore need hardly emphasize the current and growing economic impact of AD, the "coming plague of the 21st century," on health systems worldwide. More specific epidemiological data are discussed in this and other chapters.

Dementia

Definition, evaluation, management, and treatment

Symptoms common to most dementias include forgetfulness, language deterioration, mood changes, impaired judgment, and loss of initiative. There is nevertheless no universally accepted definition of "dementia," which has been broadly characterized as a syndrome, as shorthand for unsuccessful aging, and as a specific diagnosis (Green, 2005), that is, as a synonym for AD. Within its multitude of definitions, diagnostic criteria have routinely included memory impairment, decline in social or occupational function (American Psychiatric Association, 2000), progressive deterioration, incurability, and irreversibility. Clinicians must nevertheless be aware that pathological processes underlying many causes of dementia are static and that a few are treatable. Furthermore, while the association between dementia and memory disorder is almost ubiquitous, significant amnesia is not a salient feature of every dementing disease. Evidence of *functional decline*, e.g., in personal hygiene, bill paying, housecleaning, personality, etc., is, at least for research purposes, currently the clinical marker separating "possible dementia" and "normal aging" from "dementia." Many factors can nevertheless mask or delay occupational or social incompetence and we favor a somewhat broader definition.

"Dementia," as used in this chapter, is a syndrome of *acquired persistent* intellectual impairments characterized by deterioration in at least three of the following domains: memory, language, visuospatial skills, personality or behavior, and manipulation of acquired knowledge (including executive function) (Cummings, 2004; Cummings & Benson, 1992; Cummings & Mega, 2003). According to this definition, mental retardation and acute confusional states (ACS; delirium) do not qualify, the former because it is not acquired, the latter because multiple cognitive impairments associated with it by definition are temporary (see subsequent discussion of the ACS). The presence of a dementia is *supported* by a combination of a carefully obtained history, physical and mental status examinations, significant impairment on neuropsychological tests corrected for age and education, and a *change* in test scores over a 6–12-month interval (Mesulam, 2000).

This definition, like all the others, is not perfect. Persons with superior pre-morbid intellect and greater cognitive reserve (Roe et al., 2007) may suffer decline in occupational performance which nevertheless escapes even the most detailed clinical assessment and which results in no other objective functional impairment (Cummings, 2005a; Strub & Black, 2000). Some ultimately dementing disorders (Benson et al., 1988; Dubois et al., 2007; Mesulam, 2003) may manifest for years as gradual deterioration limited to a single cognitive domain which in turn can influence execution and interpretation of other cognitive functions (Mesulam, 2000).

"Dementia of the Alzheimer type" (DAT) refers to the *clinical syndrome* which by far is that most commonly associated with autopsy-proven (*pathologic*) AD.

Recognition and differential diagnosis of the dementia syndrome

Management and treatment of dementia begins with its recognition, which is reasonably straightforward either when the patient or an independent historian expressly raises cognitive (or behavioral) deterioration as an issue, or it becomes obvious in context with other medical issues (e.g., following hospital admission). Recognition is a not inconsiderable concern, however, because cognition and behavior are indeed not issues for many "community dwelling elderly" who are nevertheless already demented and just one fall, infection, change of address or assault of a spouse away from health system entry for these issues (Albert et al., 1991).

Recognition is further hindered because widespread neuropsychological testing, imaging and laboratory screening for asymptomatic elderly people is not economically feasible. Furthermore, many health professionals as well as lay people persist in believing that cognitive loss is an inevitable and "natural" consequence of aging rather than a reflection of brain damage. Although there is some longitudinal evidence that general cognition "normally" recedes in a person's mid-70s (Brayne et al., 1999), much of the decline previously attributed to age alone probably reflects the effect of mild unrecognized dementia. Studies of optimally healthy older adults who are evaluated each year suggest that overall cognitive function may slow somewhat but does not reflect a significant longitudinal decline for these persons (Schaie, 1989). Therefore, in the absence of disease, older adults can reasonably expect stable overall cognitive function and little or no interference with performance of everyday activity (Rowe & Kahn, 1987). This requires a fundamental shift in the approach to the aging patient, in that clinicians should not automatically attribute memory or cognitive problems that interfere with everyday activities to normal aging, and this should be communicated to the patient's family.

Among adults over 85 years of age, the definition of "normal" cognition is much more difficult to establish. Many neuropsychological tests have not been validated for this group of the "oldest old," and vision and hearing problems often interfere with assessment. Apparently unimpaired individuals over 85 are nonetheless at high risk of cognitive decline (Crystal et al., 2000; Howieson et al., 2003).

Most clinicians do not routinely test mental status in older individuals unless they receive complaints either from the patient or the patient's family. Many demented patients do not, however, so-complain and, on average, most family members do not seek medical attention for the patient until several years after onset of symptoms (if the dementia is progressive). Most patients with DAT, therefore, escape early diagnosis, particularly in primary care settings (Callahan et al., 1995; Cummings, 2004; Cummings & Mega, 2003; Dartigues, 2009; Petrovitch et al., 2001). Cognitive symptoms that are not associated with obvious functional impairment may be dismissed or minimized.

The prevalence of truly curable dementia in the community has been debated (Clarfield, 1995; Weytingh et al., 1995). The probability of finding a reversible cause for dementia has nevertheless likely declined greatly in the past 20 years (Clarfield, 2003; Mok et al., 2004). Prompt recognition of dementia remains important all the same because emerging diagnostic techniques and increasingly effective therapeutic interventions are altering the definition of "treatable" (Fagan et al., 2007). Advantages of an early-as-possible diagnosis of dementia are listed in Table 1.1.

Differential diagnosis of the dementia syndrome

Dementia is a syndrome of multiple possible causes. Like anemia, dementia is a differential diagnostic, not a diagnostic term. In other words, even though AD would for most demented persons be a correct diagnosis, the clinician should systematically consider other disorders. Drugs (polypharmacy!), depression, and

Table 1.1 Advantages of early diagnosis in dementing conditions

For every case
• Provide a diagnostic answer and education for the patient and/or family
For patients with reversible or static diseases (e.g., depression, stroke)
• Relieve the fear of an irreversible or progressive disease
• Treat the underlying disease
• Initiate prevention and/or rehabilitation strategies
For patients with irreversible and progressive diseases (e.g., Alzheimer's disease)
• Treat cognitive and behavioral symptoms
• Plan legal and financial future while patient is still competent
• Initiate management strategies that will postpone dependence and institutionalization

Source: Green, R. C. (2005). *Diagnosis and management of Alzheimer's disease and other dementias* (2nd edn.). Caddo, OK: Professional Communications. Professional Communications, Inc, by permission

metabolic disturbances are relatively common causes of the dementia syndrome (alone or in combination with AD) and are at least partially treatable if not frequently fully reversible (Clarfield, 1988). Important categories and diseases to consider are summarized in Table 1.2, many of which are further discussed in this and other volumes (Cummings & Benson, 1992; Cummings & Mega, 2003; Lerner & Whitehouse, 1994; Mesulam, 2000).

Depression, a very common ailment of the elderly, is worthy of special mention. Disturbances of thinking and memory frequently accompany depression and have led to the use of the misleading term "pseudodementia." Since depression can cause authentic, often but not always reversible functional cognitive impairment, a more appropriate designation would be the dementia syndrome of depression (DSD).

Application of the differential diagnosis assumes the examiner's clinical skills, competence and perseverance in gathering information, and recognizing patterns of neuropsychological impairments. A detailed mental status examination tutorial is beyond the present scope but following is a summary, and further guidance can be found elsewhere (Mandell, 2010; Strub & Black, 2000).

Dementia evaluation

The evaluation process includes physical and mental status examinations, ancillary studies and, most importantly, *history*. We cannot overemphasize the requirement for an *independent, reliable* historian, that is, someone other than the patient. Easily emphasized, this requirement is often not practical because elderly patients often live alone or are otherwise socially isolated. Furthermore, there is no guarantee that family members' or friends' histories are more reliable than that of the patient. For example, family members sometimes attribute actual cause to triggers such as fever, minor surgery, new stresses or a disorienting vacation because subtler symptoms have previously been missed or ignored. Some informants, including spouses, may be embarrassed or otherwise less than forthcoming about alcoholism, physical aggression or sexual indiscretions in the patient's presence; for this reason it's often helpful to interview the informant, particularly a spouse, separately. Other informants, including family members and business associates, may lie.

History taking often illuminates obvious functional impairments. Sometimes, however, there has been no significant activities of daily living (ADL) or occupational deterioration. The examiner should therefore attempt to determine whether the patient has had any consistent decline from his or her *usual* level of competence. For example, a university professor may complain that he or she can no longer teach a familiar class without notes, while someone working with fewer high-level cognitive demands may not notice problems in the workplace but may neglect paying the bills. A problem with evaluating the former is that of "ceiling effect": limited sensitivity to change by any test in very mildly impaired subjects. That is, even extensive neuropsychological testing may fail to detect significant deficits. Such people would not be classified as "demented" by most current criteria. Highly educated persons with minimal or no cognitive symptoms or signs may nevertheless harbor high plaque and tangle counts, enough to satisfy current pathological criteria

Table 1.2 Differential diagnosis of the dementia syndrome

Disease category	Important examples
Infections	Prion diseases, syphilis, Lyme disease, chronic meningidites, PML, HIV, Whipple's disease, hydrocephalus
Neoplasms	Primary or metastatic tumors, (particularly of the frontal lobe), paraneoplastic encephalitis, disseminated intravascular lymphoma, hydrocephalus
Traumatic brain disease	Chronic subdural hematoma, contusions, diffuse axonal injury, hydrocephalus, dementia pugilistica
Autoimmune diseases	Multiple sclerosis, primary CNS angiitis, lupus and other vasculidites, sarcoid
Metabolic disorders	Renal and hepatic failure, hyper/hypo-thyroidism/calcemia/natremia, Wilson's disease, metachromatic/adrenoleukodystrophy
	GM_2 and other gangliosidoses
	Pantothenate kinase deficiency
Toxic disorders	POLYPHARMACY
	Drugs: antidepressants, anxiolytics, sedatives, hypnotics, anticholingergics, neuroleptics, multiple cardiac and antihypertensive drugs, narcotics, lithium, antineoplastics, antiepileptics
	Metals (arsenic, thallium, lead, manganese)
	Industrial agents (CCl_4, CS_2, TCE, organophosphides)
	Radiation encephalopathy
	Alcohol and other drugs of abuse
Nutritional/Deprivation	B12/Folate and other vitamin deficiencies
	Wernicke–Korsakoff syndrome
"Degenerative" dementias	Alzheimer's disease
	Frontotemporal and Parkinsonian dementias
	Huntington's disease
	Neuronal ceroid lipofuscinosis
Vascular dementias	Multiple infarct dementia
	"Binswanger's disease"
	"Small vessel ischemic disease"
	CADASIL
Psychiatric disorders	Schizophrenia
	Dementia syndrome of depression
	Bipolar disorder
	Malingering
	Obsessive compulsive disorder

CCl_4 = carbon tetrachloride; CS_2 = carbon disulfide; CADASIL = cerebral autosomal dominant arteriopathy with subcortical infarcts and leukoencephalopathy; CNS = central nervous system; HIV = human immunodeficiency virus; PML = progressive multi-focal leukoencephalopathy; TCE = trichlorethylene; pantothenate kinase deficiency = Hallervorden–Spatz disease

for AD. Their substantial "cognitive reserve" allows them to remain relatively asymptomatic despite extensive pathology although once (if) symptoms develop, they endure shorter duration of disease before death (Portet et al., 2009; Roe et al., 2008; Roe et al., 2007). Persons with limited education, in less demanding jobs, or those who were already significantly impaired prior to the onset of the dementing illness, in contrast, are vulnerable to "floor effect," a similar test insensitivity to change leading to overestimation of cognitive impairment.

If adequate information acquisition is possible, the following should be included:

- Present history – sudden versus insidious onset; precipitating event; relatively steady decline or remarkable fluctuations or prolonged periods of return to "normal" function; social skills, work, driving, hobbies, community activities, hygiene and eating behavior, housekeeping; sleep (nocturnal behavior; daytime somnolence).
- Past/Social history – alcohol or other substance abuse including tobacco; *all* current medications (including vitamin supplements); head trauma; psychiatric illness (particularly depression); surgical procedures; stroke and other vascular disease; cancer; sleep disorders.
- Family history – dementia; "senility"; "trouble with memory loss like his/hers when older"; "hardening of the arteries" and depression in any first-degree relative, if known.

Office testing of cognitive function should be performed on every person over the age of 65 in an attempt to distinguish demented from nondemented persons and thus inaugurate evaluation of the former. What constitutes "office testing" is often determined by the realities of practice type, time constraints and reimbursement. Many brief cognitive rating scales have been published in response to these realities, through which it is possible to get a reasonable notion of cognitive capacity ("mental status") (Mandell, 2010). These tests are simple to administer, require relatively little training, are in general valid for the functions being assessed, and usually boast good inter-rater and test–retest reliability.

Screening tests

All screening tests have their pros and cons since all are surrogates for more extensive neuropsychological testing. Some are highly verbal thus penalizing patients with relatively more profound language impairment or limited education. Some are directed to the patient, others are informant-based (generally more sensitive) (Tierney et al., 1996), some are dual purpose and all can be combined with elements from other tests to increase sensitivity and specificity (Galvin, Roe, & Morris, 2007), albeit at the expense of additional administration time. In general, all are relatively insensitive to mild cognitive and behavioral impairments and many are subject to educational, racial, cultural, and age biases. Some investigators have even recommended against screening in the absence of truly effective treatments for AD (Boustani et al., 2003).

The most commonly used brief rating scale is the Mini-Mental State Examination (MMSE) (Albert, 2008; Folstein et al., 1975; Mandell et al., 1994). Its advantages are its brevity, ease of administration, and accuracy in detecting moderate dementia. Used sequentially over several years, moreover, scores, in general, track cognitive decline, if any, reasonably accurately. Nevertheless, the MMSE suffers from insensitivity and both floor and ceiling effects, is very language dependent, culturally insensitive, and has limited value as a method to mark cognitive changes in people with AD in short clinical trials (Bowie et al., 1999; Clark et al., 1999).

A published brief informant-based test, the AD8 (Galvin et al., 2005), appears to distinguish dementia from nondementia reasonably well and may also be useful as a self-assessment tool in the absence of an informant, at least when dementia is mild (Galvin et al., 2007).

Other popular instruments include the Short Portable Mental Status Questionnaire (Pfeiffer, 1975), the Montreal Cognitive Assessment (www.mocatest.org) and 7-Minute Screen (Solomon et al., 1998).

Mental status testing

If you are the clinician to whom a patient has been referred specifically for neurobehavioral issues, however, these scales often are inadequate and office or bedside mental status evaluation, tempered in consideration of the patient's educational and cultural background, should include at least brief assessments of attention, language, praxis, visuospatial, memory, and executive functions. Assessment of attention is particularly important because the remainder of the mental status examination will be nonspecifically impaired by inattention. Also recognize that all of these domains are functionally interdependent. Copying a clock face, for example, requires sequencing ("executive") skill and attention as well as visuoperception. Selected tests include:

- Attention: digit span forwards, reciting months of the year in reverse, serial subtractions.
- Language: object and body part naming, assessment of spontaneous conversation (fluent or non-fluent speech), at least *auditory* comprehension, preferably reading comprehension as well; word-list generation and repetition (Green, 2005; Jorm et al., 2007; Knopman & Ryberg, 1989).
- Praxis: three or four transitive limb actions (hair combing, screw driving, teeth brushing, hammering, coin flipping), which are somewhat more sensitive than intransitive actions (waving goodbye, saluting) (Rapcsak, Croswell, & Rubens, 1989).
- Visuospatial: copy an analog clock face or a complex line drawing.
- Executive: clock drawing to command, proverb interpretation, similarities (e.g., between an apple and a grape, or a poem and a statue), coin switch test, cursive alternate writing of the letters "m" and "n" (Mandell, 2010).
- Memory: while assessment of orientation, delayed recall of several unrelated words, current events and verifiable biographical information are fine for overtly demented patients, we recommend adding the relatively brief drilled word span

and Three Words–Three Shapes (TWTS) (Weintraub, 2000) tests to mental status testing to capture more subtle memory deficits in dubious cases. Either adds several minutes to the encounter, but the information derived usually justifies the effort. The TWTS test is particularly useful because it assesses incidental learning (affected early in AD), both verbal and nonverbal episodic memory, and enhances encoding by minimizing the effect of inattention.

For descriptions and details of other brief cognitive tests, see Lezak (1995), Hebben (2002), Weintraub (2000) and other chapters in this book.

Ancillary testing for dementia

Time constraint, type or lack of insurance, availability of ancillary testing, and patient or family cooperation are important issues. A combination of neuropsychological, serologic, and spinal fluid testing is often employed, but these services are out of reach for many patients. Even when available, which tests should be performed depends on the source of the recommendation. Full batteries of laboratory tests and at least one brain magnetic resonance (MR) scan are recommended by many (Blennow et al., 2006; Cummings & Benson, 1992; Green, 2005; Knopman et al., 2001); others argue that this is a costly shotgun approach unlikely to determine a treatable cause in the vast majority (Clarfield, 1988; Siu, 1991).

Including B12, folate, and TSH levels, for example, is a point of some contention. Treatment of B12 encephalopathy, if instituted early, improves some functions, but not others, including memory (Freidenberg & Drake, 1990). Furthermore, high-dose B vitamin supplementation fails to slow cognitive decline in patients with presumed AD (Aisen et al., 2008). The American Academy of Neurology (AAN) Practice Parameter (Knopman et al., 2001), acknowledging that the association of B12 deficiency and hypothyroidism with dementia is not clear and that treatment of same in cognitively impaired people often yields no improvement, nevertheless recommends B12 (and TSH) measurement at *guideline* level.

If ancillary testing is available (and allowed), most clinicians still check, and we recommend: CBC, B12, TSH, liver and renal function. We also recommend brain MRI or, if not possible, at least a noncontrast brain CT scan (Knopman et al., 2001). MRIs in the elderly often demonstrate nonspecific "atrophy" and equally nonspecific scattered bright T2 white matter signals (leukoaraiosis; "microvascular white matter ischemic changes"). The aim of clinical neuroimaging is two-fold:

- to rule out (or in) significant abnormalities that are themselves treatable (e.g., chronic subdural hematoma, meningioma) or indicative of correctible underlying disorders (hypertension);
- to identify such specific perturbations as neoplasms, small or large infarcts, focal atrophy, infections which one could reasonably implicate as a cause of cognitive decline.

Serological testing for syphilis is recommended only if a patient has some specific risk factor or resides in an endemic area (Knopman et al., 2001). Consider additional tests (e.g., antiphospholipid antibodies; HIV) if history, physical examination or other studies warrant them.

Routine electroencephalography (EEG) in general is not useful in the routine dementia evaluation except when Creutzfeldt–Jakob disease (CJD) or subclinical seizures are strongly suspected, deterioration is rapid, or possibly in young (less than 60 years) persons. In AD, once clinically established, the EEG is diffusely but nonspecifically abnormal (Smith, 2005).

Occasionally, older patients with obstructive sleep apnea (OSA) can present with cognitive impairment or a confusional state, which may be reversible with proper treatment (Naegele et al., 1995). This underscores the importance of asking about the patient's sleeping habits, particularly daytime somnolence. Consider overnight polysomnography when OSA or other parasomnia is suspected from the history.

Lumbar puncture (LP) is indicated when data suggest neurosyphilis, CJD, any type of meningitis or vasculitis, demyelinating disease, or, again, when deterioration seems rapid. In general, LP is not useful for routine dementia evaluation. Cerebrospinal fluid (CSF) analysis is, however, assuming more importance in the specific diagnosis of AD (Li et al., 2007b), as we discuss later in the chapter.

Communication with the patient and family/caregivers

If you have diagnosed any type of dementia, should you inform the patient? One needs to consider each case individually, but in general, the answer is "yes," and this includes involved family members who collectively, in effect, become "the patient" (Mittelman et al., 2006). Patients and families must preferably be informed, if deterioration is expected, when the patient's comprehension and reasoning are optimal and he/she may be more willing to accept help with managing social needs, or consider therapeutic clinical trials. Driving can also be raised as an issue at this time (see later section). When patients have no support system, try to assist the patient in establishing support networks and relevant services (Grossberg & Desai, 2003).

Alzheimer's Disease

The conventional understanding of AD may be summarized:

- a degenerative brain disorder characterized by progressive intellectual and behavioral deterioration;
- symptomatically almost always heralded, and usually dominated by, memory disorder, with prominent visuospatial and language impairment in the context, at least early in the course, of preserved social skills;

- association with several neuropathological markers, the most distinctive of which are amyloid plaques and neurofibrillary tangles which appear initially in medial temporal limbic structures and then spread to neocortex (Braak & Braak, 1991);
- broad age range of clinical onset but usually after age 65;
- life span after diagnosis generally about 10 years, but can be as long as 20 years;
- motor and primary sensory disturbances are either not present or are late manifestations.

Diagnosis

Emerging diagnostic techniques for identifying persons prior to development of *any* symptoms are discussed later in this chapter and elsewhere in the book. In the absence of fully reliable biological markers for AD, major issues in clinical diagnosis are the trade off between sensitivity (the proportion of persons with AD-specific pathology who are accurately diagnosed in life as having the disease) and specificity (the proportion of persons without the disease who are accurately diagnosed as *not* having the disease), and what is meant by "disease."

As we go to press, AD remains a clinical diagnosis which for years has been based on criteria from the *Diagnostic and Statistical Manual of Mental Disorders*, 4th edition (DSM IV) (American Psychiatric Association, 2000) and the National Institute of Neurological and Communicative Disorders and Stroke-Alzheimer's Disease and Related Disorders Association (NINCDS-ADRDA) (McKhann et al., 1984). As noted previously, the former require both memory disorder and deterioration in social function or in ADL. The latter do not require ADL debasement but specify insidious onset and demonstrable absence of other systemic or neurological diseases that might account for the cognitive deficits. NINCDS-ADRDA criteria designate AD as definite (clinical diagnosis with pathological confirmation), probable (typical syndrome without histopathology) and possible (atypical clinical features, no pathology but no other apparent diagnosis).

The good news is that when compared with histopathological gold standards (Braak & Braak, 1991; Consensus recommendations for the postmortem diagnosis of Alzheimer's disease. The National Institute on Aging, and Reagan Institute Working Group on Diagnostic Criteria for the Neuropathological Assessment of Alzheimer's Disease, 1997; Mirra et al., 1991), NINCDS-ADRDA criteria for probable AD are very good (over 90% sensitivity) (Galasko et al., 1994), even in early stages of the disease (Salmon et al., 2002). This means that when brains of demented patients are burdened with sufficient AD pathology, well-trained clinicians are almost always correct when matching clinical diagnosis with pathology. However, high sensitivity is paid for by low (~20–80%) specificity, which is even lower for the "possible AD" diagnosis (Varma et al., 1999).

Many Alzheimer brains prove not to have "pure" plaque and tangle pathology; most have significant vascular disease and many have abundant cortical Lewy bodies even when parkinsonism was absent in life (Lim et al., 1999; Lopez et al., 2002; Olde Rikkert et al., 2006). Furthermore, most patients with pathologically proven non-Alzheimer frontotemporal lobar degenerations also fulfill NINCDS-ADRDA criteria (Varma et al., 1999). In other words, the criteria are better at predicting the presence of Alzheimer-type pathology (higher sensitivity), particularly as dementia worsens, than at accurately identifying patients with co-morbid pathologies (lower specificity) (Chui, 2002; Cummings, 2005b; Jellinger, 2002; Knopman et al., 2001; Strub & Black, 2000). For these reasons, major revision of the NINCDS-ADRDA criteria has been proposed (Dubois et al., 2007). For the present, since most cases incorrectly diagnosed as "just" AD have equally irreversible diseases, high sensitivity may be more important than high specificity as long as clinicians do not miss the minority of reversible disorders. The health consequences and economic costs of making false-positive or false-negative diagnostic errors will dictate whether higher sensitivity, higher specificity, or high values for both are required for a test or procedure to be clinically useful.

AD risk and protective factors

In epidemiological studies, the terms "risk factor" and "protective factor" should be interpreted cautiously since the observed risk or benefit can actually be due to known or unknown confounders. Several factors have nevertheless been consistently associated with greater or lesser risk of developing AD.

- Aging confers the greatest risk for dementia in general and AD in particular.
- Family history: No clear genetic pattern is evident in the vast majority (over 95%) of patients, who are said to have "sporadic" AD. Family history of AD increases relative risk three- to fourfold (at least up to age 80). An important figure for clinicians to know when they are asked by a family member about his or her own risk is this: The cumulative incidence of AD in first-degree relatives of individuals with AD is 41% by the ninth decade of life for white Americans, with even higher risks for dementia in African Americans (Cupples et al., 2004; Green et al., 2002) (Figure 1.2).
- Susceptibility genes: The genetics of heightened risk in sporadic cases has yet to be fully elucidated. Risk has been associated with at least 250 susceptibility (non-deterministic) genes, including *SORL1* (Bertram et al., 2007; Blacker & Tanzi, 1998; Rogaeva et al., 2007). The most robust risk by far is that associated with the APOE polymorphism on chromosome 19. This tri-allelic ($\epsilon2$, $\epsilon3$, $\epsilon4$) gene codes for apolipoprotein E (ApoE), a remarkable protein involved in multiple normal physiological functions. The apoE2 isoform has been shown in multiple studies to confer at least some degree of protection against developing AD (Talbot et al., 1994). Possession of ApoE4, in contrast, increases risk for AD and several other disorders, including multiple sclerosis and obstructive sleep apnea (Gozal et al., 2007; Mahley et al., 2006), and to enhance other AD risk factors (e.g., head

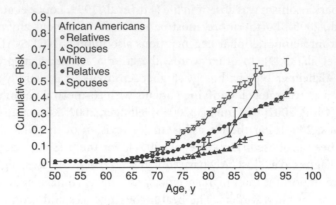

Figure 1.2 Cumulative risk of dementia in first-degree biological relatives and in spouses of probands, stratified by ethnicity of probands error bars indicate standard error (SE) Source: Green, R. C., Cupples, L. A., Go, R., Benke, K. ., Edeki, T., Griffith, P. A., et al. (2002). Risk of dementia among white and African American relatives of patients with Alzheimer disease. *Journal of the American Medical Association, 287*(3), 329–336.

trauma). Inheritance of the ε4 allele significantly increases risk (3× for a hetero-zygote, about 15× for a homozygote) of developing AD, and at an earlier age.

Roughly 50% of sporadic AD victims do not possess the ε4 allele (Auguste D. was homozygous ε3) (Graeber et al., 1998), clearly indicating that other factors are involved (Hayden et al., 2009), and the strength of the association appears to vary in different ethnic groups (Farrer et al., 1997). For this and other reasons, APOE genotyping is currently not recommended for risk assessment except within controlled research studies (Green, 2002).

- Deterministic autosomal dominant transmission of AD resulting from multiple mutations on chromosomes 1, 14, 21 and likely others occurs in less than 5% of AD patients, in whom symptoms typically emerge quite young, sometimes as early as the third decade.

- Other putative, established, and in some cases *still-debated* risk factors include: traumatic brain injury (Guo et al., 2000); muscle weakness in old age (Boyle et al., 2009); systemic inflammatory activity (Holmes et al., 2009; Tan et al., 2007); low bone density in women but not men (Tan et al., 2005); midlife depression (Green et al., 2003; Ownby et al., 2006; Wilson et al., 2003); female gender; low serum docosahexaenoic acid (DHA) (Schaefer et al., 2006); isoflurane anesthesia (Xie et al., 2007); metabolic syndrome (Razay et al., 2007); low folate intake (Luchsinger, Tang et al., 2007); low thyroid stimulating hormone level (van Osch et al., 2004); obesity (Jagust et al., 2005; Kivipelto et al., 2005); obesity in younger but not older persons (Luchsinger, Patel et al., 2007); weight loss in women but not in men (Knopman et al., 2007); weight loss in the elderly (Fitzpatrick et al., 2009); vascular risk factors including hypertension (Launer et al., 2000; Petrovitch et al., 2000), smoking (Ford et al., 1996; Reitz et al., 2007; Rinne, 1989; Shalat et al., 1987; Swan & Lessov-Schlaggar, 2007), not smoking (Ott et al., 1998), diabetes mellitus (Arvanitakis et al., 2004; Luchsinger et al., 2001), hyperhomocysteinemia (McMahon et al., 2006; Nilsson et al., 2002); low cerebral perfusion (Bradley et al., 2002); low educational achievement (Cummings, 2005b; Ngandu et al., 2007; Snowdon et al., 1996; Stern et al., 1994; Strub & Black, 2000); poor performance on verbal, visual memory and other learning tests (Blacker et al., 2007; Green, 2005; Jorm et al., 2007; Knopman & Ryberg, 1989); chronic psychological stress (Wilson et al., 2005); apathy (Bottiglieri et al., 1990; Robert et al., 2006; Starkstein et al., 2006); alcohol consumption (Paul et al., 2008) and many others.

- Possible protective factors include "mental exercise" (i.e., learning new skills in middle age and beyond) (Wilson et al., 2007); physical exercise (Boyle et al., 2009); *modest* alcohol consumption (Solfrizzi et al., 2007; Solfrizzi et al., 2009), especially red wine; caffeine consumption (women) (Ritchie et al., 2007); "healthy" diet including antioxidants (Galvin, 2007; Qin, Yang et al., 2006); increased physical activity (Mattson, 2008; Weuve et al., 2004); and diabetes (slower rate of cognitive decline) (Sanz et al., 2009).

Pathophysiology – The amyloid hypothesis

The cause of AD is not fully understood. By way of introduction, the "amyloid cascade" hypothesis is now generally accepted as at least a very important contributor, if not the sole explanation. In brief, both autosomal dominant and sporadic forms of AD likely result from the generation and accumulation of toxic fragments known as beta amyloid or amyloid beta (Aβ). Aβ fragments accumulate extracellularly, oligomerize and damage neuronal synapses, then precipitate eventually into misfolded neuritic plaques, which in turn seem to provoke inflammation, free radical formation, and, likely very early on, oxidative stress (Nunomura et al., 2001). This process kills neurons and disrupts neuronal networks.

Autosomal dominant AD is a consequence of several mutations that generate abnormal species of *secretases,* which in turn cause aberrant cleavages of the transmembrane amyloid precursor protein (APP) into Aβ, particularly its very toxic 42 amino acid isoform. This may be an important mechanism as well for sporadic AD.

Aβ may also interfere with microtubule-associated proteins (MAPs) causing clumping of phosphorylated tau filaments into neurofibrillary tangles.

Dementia severity correlates more with tangle than with plaque load, leading some to claim that AD is primarily a tauopathy rather than an amyloidopathy. Another explanation for this correlation is that Aβ deposition reaches a "ceiling" early in the disease process, while tangle formation, synaptic loss and gliosis continue throughout the course (Giannakopoulos et al., 2003).

The exact role of amyloid accumulation in the pathogenesis of AD remains to be fully elucidated (Duara et al., 2009; Killiany, 2009), and there is increasing speculation that a variety of exogenous factors, particularly infection by a variety of organisms, might ultimately underlie inflammation, oxidative stress, and other proposed pathogenetic mechanisms (Honjo et al., 2009; Kamer et al., 2008).

Pathology

In brief: The brain is grossly atrophic, most profoundly in frontal, parietal and temporal gyri, particularly entorhinal cortex and hippocampus, with commensurate ventricular enlargement. Brain weight and volume are usually markedly reduced. The major histopathological hallmarks of AD are:

- *Extracellular* neuritic (amyloid) plaques (NP), composed of neuronal and glial processes and Aβ, and distributed primarily throughout the association and limbic cortex as well as basal forebrain, substantia nigra, raphe nuclei, and locus ceruleus. Amyloid is also deposited in cerebral arterioles. AD is thus one of several disorders associated with cerebral amyloid angiopathy (Pardridge et al., 1987), a risk factor for lobar hemorrhage.
- *Intracellular* neurofibrillary tangles (NFT). Tangles can be found in the brains of nondemented older people and are a feature of other neurodegenerative diseases, but in AD have a relatively distinctive paired helical structure and are quantitatively highly correlated with dementia severity. The major components of NFTs are the hyperphosphorylated MAP *tau, and ubiquitin.* The intracellular deposition of tau and its disruption of the normal cytoskeletal architecture may be an important factor in neuronal death and is the target of several therapies discussed below (Iqbal et al., 2003).
- Widespread cortical neuronal loss and synaptic destruction. This loss is characteristically most obvious in hippocampus, temporal neocortex and in basal forebrain nuclei (nucleus basalis), but is also prominent in several subcortical structures including substantia nigra. Synaptic degeneration may be the major proximate cause of early cognitive decline.

Clinical features

AD is the prototypical "cortical dementia." Benson et al. formulated the cortical/subcortical dementia dichotomy in 1981 (Benson, 1983; Cummings, 1982). Controversy regarding the usefulness of this terminology notwithstanding (Brown & Marsden, 1988; Mandell & Albert, 1990; Mayeux et al., 1983), cortical dementia is code for a neuropsychological *pattern* suggesting multi-focal cortical damage, including amnesia, aphasia, agnosia, apraxia, prominent visuospatial impairment, and dysexecutive symptoms but, until late in disease course, normal gait, muscle tone, posture, speech volume and articulation, and lack of movement disorder (Cummings & Benson, 1992; Huber, 1990). Cortical dementias usually conform to

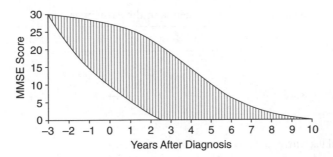

Figure 1.3 Deterioration in Mini-Mental State Examination scores over time
Source: Modified from Green, R.C. (2005). *Diagnosis and Management of Alzheimer's Disease and Other Dementias* (2nd edn.). Caddo, OK: Professional Communications, Inc., by permission

one of four "profiles" described by Mesulam (2000). These profiles reflect their dominant clinical features and include progressive language, comportmental/executive, and visual syndromes. Each clinical profile differs in its probability of association with specific underlying pathology.

Pathological AD has ultimately been associated with all of these profiles, but its signature syndrome is that of "progressive amnestic dysfunction" (sometimes referred to as progressive amnestic dementia), which henceforth will be referred to as "dementia of the Alzheimer type" (DAT). It is the most common dementia profile affecting the elderly. Although early executive, behavioral, visuospatial and language impairments are common in what proves to be pathological AD (Neary et al., 1986), until reliable biomarkers are readily available, lack of early and prominent memory impairment, that is, a non-DAT pattern, should raise at least some doubt regarding the diagnosis of AD (Mesulam, 2003).

The cognitive decline of DAT in general is inexorable (Figure 1.3): indolent in early stages, accelerating with disease progression (Morris et al., 1993), but can plateau (Bozoki et al., 2009).

DAT has for years been described as progressing through "stages." The staging formula relies on the relatively stereotypical evolution of symptoms and signs through three clinical phases variously termed initial, early, *mild* or stage I; intermediate, *moderate* or stage II; and advanced, *severe*, final or stage III disease (Table 1.3) (Cummings & Benson, 1992; Green, 2005; Hodges, 2006; Mesulam, 2000). Each stage denotes a characteristic *pattern* of functional losses (language, memory, social engagement) and abnormal gains (delusions, wandering, agitation), which collectively equate to severity.

There is nevertheless variation in time course of each stage among individual patients with DAT. One or more stages may be relatively prolonged for one patient compared with another, and for any given patient, duration of stages also is variable (Grady et al., 1988). There is overlap even when disease progression is orderly. The memory impairment usually ascribed to moderate stage disease, for example, may

Alan M. Mandell and Robert C. Green

Table 1.3 Clinical characteristics of dementia of the Alzheimer type

	MCI	Mild	Moderate	Severe
Memory				
Working	–	–/+	++	+++
Anterograde episodic	++	+++	+++	+++
Remote	–/+	–/+	++	+++
Semantic	–/+	+	+++	+++
Attention and executive	–/+	++	++	+++
Language	–	–/+	+	++
Visuospatial and perceptual	–	–/+	++	++
Praxis	–	–	++	++

– = absent; + = present; –/+ = variable; MCI = mild cognitive impairment
Source: Hodges, J.R. (2006). Alzheimer's centennial legacy: Origins, landmarks and the current status of knowledge concerning cognitive aspects. *Brain, 129*(Pt 11), 2811–2822. By permission of Oxford University Press

associate with language deficit more characteristic of mild stage (Storandt et al., 1986). Furthermore, day-to-day variability even in early DAT is common and dependent on factors such as intrinsic circadian rhythm (Volicer et al., 2001), blood glucose, pain severity (if any), sleep adequacy, drugs, and social stressors.

Once ADL dependence is fully established, worsening tends to accelerate. More severe memory impairment combines with fluent (usually) aphasia, apraxia, multimodal agnosias, attentional and reasoning disturbances, incontinence, and a variety of behavioral changes including wandering and pacing. Later, patients slow down, cognitive function cannot be assessed, communication becomes impossible, primitive reflexes often appear, and weight loss usually is prominent. In late stage, ambulation ceases, patients become bedridden, cachectic, and susceptible to infection. End of life is spent for months, sometimes for years, in a mute, tetraplegia-in-flexion state (Cummings & Benson, 1992).

Clinical neuropsychology of DAT

Following is a discussion of clinically pertinent neuropsychological features of DAT. Expanded analyses of domain-specific (frontal-executive, visuospatial, language, memory) functions and their clinical assessment are covered elsewhere in this book.

Memory
By definition, DAT is characterized primarily by progressive memory dysfunction. Clinically, memory impairment is manifest initially as inconsistent but more-than-before forgetfulness, particularly of names, phone numbers and recent conversa-

tions, and misplacement of personal belongings. Missing appointments and "forgetting to remember" events and tasks to occur in the future (prospective memory) is another very early feature (Huppert & Beardsall, 1993). Functional memory impairments nevertheless usually are few in mild-stage DAT. For example, housekeeping, most social and sporting activities, driving and, depending on the job, professional responsibilities are *usually* reasonably well maintained, particularly if other people "cover" for diminished capacity. At this point, clues, cues, and multiple choices usually improve retrieval and recognition of forgotten items. With worsening, forgetting becomes more persistent, resulting in repetitive iterations of the same questions and statements, often accompanied by irritable insistence that he/she is doing no such thing.

Memory deficit sufficient to constrict ADL signals moderate stage DAT. By this point, patients can neither store new information for more than a few minutes nor maintain a coherent stream of thought (Mesulam, 2000). The result is increasing dependence on a spouse or friend, who has by this time become a *caregiver*. Memory is difficult to characterize, much less to test, in severe DAT because of multiple other cognitive impairments. At this stage, even the most overlearned memories are starting to be lost or inaccessible, including recognition of close family or even of personal identity.

Many patients initially are acutely aware of their memory impairment and develop compensatory strategies such as list keeping, dependence on speed dialing, and asking a spouse for names in anticipation of personal encounters. Many become depressed about their forgetfulness and seek professional assessment. Not infrequently, however, they vociferously deny any cognitive problem, including memory, a consequence of anosognosia (lack of awareness of deficits), which at some point is virtually universal, although not always absolute (Grut et al., 1993; McGlynn & Kaszniak, 1991).

Neuropsychological testing demonstrates a variety of memory problems, the dissolution reflecting involvement of relatively distinct anatomical systems. Episodic memory, the ability to encode, retain and recall at will specific events and items, particularly those recently acquired, is the earliest and most affected, before behavior and language impairments become clinically manifest. If a patient can be tested at the earliest stage of DAT, intentional acquisition (encoding) of small amounts of new information is variable but fairly normal (Schachter & Kihlstrom, 1989). In contrast, poor delayed free recall even of subspan (two or three items) word lists after seconds-lasting distracting tasks is often apparent (Kopelman, 1985; Welsh et al., 1991), as is impairment of incidental learning (learning without awareness of doing so). Brief stories and nonverbal material also, in general, are poorly recalled (Weintraub, 2000) and soon become impervious to most cuing techniques and to repetition (Lezak, 1995). Recognition formats may show improvement over free recall but even then performance in most cases is significantly below established norms for age. Patients tend to contaminate their responses with irrelevant items from other lists or previous tests.

In contrast to recent memory, remote general and autobiographical information is *relatively* preserved (Piolino et al., 2003): "I can remember what I did in the army, but I can't remember what I ate for breakfast." Patients therefore tend to become preoccupied with the past. The dissociation between "recent" and "remote" memory preservation has, however, been exaggerated. Proper testing can demonstrate that, in mild DAT, patients perform poorly on tests even of autobiographical memory and that deficient naming, ostensibly a "language" impairment, likely has a semantic memory basis (Albert, 2008; Warrington, 1975). Implicit (unconscious) learning, including "procedural memory," at least for simple tasks, is usually spared well into the illness (Eslinger & Damasio, 1986; Harrison et al., 2007). The practical effect on ADL of a curious "rebound phenomenon," the ability of some early AD patients to recall stimuli better after three days' delay than at one day (Freed et al., 1989), is not clear.

Working memory (WM) is that needed for integrating the beginning of this sentence with its end, and for mentally manipulating small bits of information over several seconds. WM likely degrades with normal aging (Gazzaley et al., 2005). At least as assessed routinely by digit span testing, WM is spared in early DAT, as noted above, but acquisition of supraspan lists dwindles shortly after onset of overt memory disorder. Even in mild disease, working memory is demonstrably defective with tests of complex and divided attention (Becker, 1988; Grady et al., 1989; Perry & Hodges, 1999). Some early stage patients show significant deficits in all aspects of information acquisition (Lezak, 1995).

As a mater of differential diagnosis, the memory loss of DAT for years has been distinguished from that associated with microvascular ischemic disease ("vascular cognitive impairment"). This differentiation has recently been challenged (Reed et al., 2007).

Visuospatial and perceptual deficits
Associative visual cortex is an early locus of AD pathology (McKee et al., 2006, 2007). Not surprisingly, visuospatial dysfunction is an important component of DAT. It occurs early but in general is not clinically apparent until memory and attentional disturbances are fully established. The more subtle the deficit, the more rigorous the testing required to evoke it. For example, patients having little difficulty copying the MMSE intersecting pentagons may fail utterly when attempting to copy more complex line drawings (Rey, 1941) or to perform a block design test. Equally unsurprising, by the time perceptual deficits become a functional problem, differentiating "pure" visuospatial impairment from accompanying attentional, memory and executive perturbations is difficult. As with nondemented patients with other structural brain lesions (e.g., stroke), visuospatial dysfunction is referable mostly to right hemispheric damage.

Once apparent, clinical manifestations include:

• environmental and geographic disorientation: getting lost in familiar locations and when driving; aimless wandering;

- dressing disturbance ("apraxia"): inability to locate shirt sleeves or pant legs or to match socks;
- impaired contrast and figure-ground discrimination(Mendez et al., 1990): consistently missing the toilet when urinating, difficulty locating misplaced objects, inability to segregate clothes properly within a closet;
- construction disturbance: defective copy even of 2-D line drawings and poor judgment of line orientation (Finton et al., 1998);
- various visual agnosias: non-recognition of common objects and their use (eating utensils) and familiar faces, including one's own ("mirror sign"), inability to discriminate among members of a given class (e.g., different car brands, animal species);
- poor clock drawing (one of several reasons for this);
- defective imaging: tasks requiring mental rotation of objects, topography;
- Unique, AD-associated cataracts, macular degeneration, and glaucoma (Valenti, 2010).

Language

Aphasia (the acquired disturbance of language secondary to brain damage) is an important feature of DAT. Progressive and isolated language dissolution occasionally is *the* dominant clinical manifestation of what proves pathologically to be AD. In general, however, language impairment either parallels or follows that of memory, but language loss is not "global" until end stage; even then some patients who are otherwise mute retain minimal verbal responsiveness to their names or other audible stimuli (Volicer et al., 1997). Language characteristics for a given patient depend upon the severity of the dementia and loss in most cases occurs in a predictable sequence. Both output (speech and writing) and input (auditory and reading comprehension) are affected. Early, some linguistic functions are clearly better preserved than others, but, again, adequate testing almost always shows preservation to be relative when compared to properly matched normals.

Word-finding difficulty during everyday discourse is usually the earliest manifestation but auditory comprehension impairment can be demonstrated in some patients as well. Patients are often quite disturbed when searching for words and attempt to remedy conveyance via circumlocution. In some cases speech initiation becomes less spontaneous. Testing at this point usually demonstrates preserved confrontation naming but, in comparison, impoverished word-list generation. As patients become less engaged in conversation, parlance becomes "empty" as first nouns and then verbs elide from their lexicon and words without clear referents such as "thing/it/this" invade content and reduce meaning. At mid-stage, patients are significantly anomic in confrontation tasks and auditory comprehension deteriorates. If a patient cannot name a proffered item, most likely he/she will not be able to define it (Hodges & Patterson, 1995). Language remains fluent with preserved repetition while semantic (whole word) and neologisitic (non-word) paraphasias litter the output, a picture resembling transcortical sensory aphasia (Cummings et al., 1985). Basic language structure is nevertheless intact, that is, "nouns are placed where nouns should go and verbs and other types of words are placed where they should go" (Bayles, 1988). Patients eventually become dysprosodic, failing both to charge speech with emotional tone and to recognize emotional content in the language of others (Allender & Kaszniak, 1989). A variety of reiterative speech disturbances such as echolalia (repeating others' words and phrases) and palilalia (repeating his/her own words and phrases) (Cummings & Benson, 1992) precedes terminal mutism; some patients become mute while still fully ambulatory.

Articulation often remains normal, basically as long as the patient speaks, although later in the course of DAT, dysarthria and stuttering are not unusual (Cummings & Benson, 1992).

Apraxia

Apraxia is a family of *cognitive* motor disorders that entail the loss or impairment of the ability to program motor systems to perform purposeful skilled movements in the absence of weakness, dystonia, tremor, other movement disorders, seizures, defects of sensory feedback or poor comprehension, agnosia or inattention (Heilman, 2003). This definition does not include entities such as constructional, dressing, and gait "apraxias" because these primarily are visuospatial or noncognitive motor disorders. Apraxia has often been described in association with DAT but its role as a symptom, that is, its clinical impact, has been confounded by imprecision of the term.

The two common types of apraxia, ideational (failure to pantomime correctly the sequence of events of a complex motor act, such as selecting and lighting a cigarette) and idiomotor (inability to do on command an act that can be performed spontaneously, such as brushing one's teeth) (Cummings & Benson, 1992) are usually demonstrable by mid-stage. Body part as tool substitution (using the index finger to brush teeth rather than pretending to hold a toothbrush) is a common manifestation of idiomotor apraxia (Rapcsak et al., 1989), but in advanced stages content errors (sawing wood instead of combing hair, or a nonsense action) also appear. Apraxia rarely can be an early disabling symptom of what proves to be AD (Green et al., 1995) but if specifically sought, it can sometimes be demonstrated even before other cognitive impairments are obvious (Heilman, 2003).

Attention

What often is referred to as "attention" is of particular interest. Like memory and language, a network of anatomical areas underlies attention, which has been described by several models and has several subcomponents: selective, sustained, and divided attention (Grady et al., 1989; Perry & Hodges, 1999). If by attention one is referring essentially to vigilance (sustained attention), it is preserved in early DAT even when new learning is clearly impaired, at least when assessed by tests such as digit span, reciting months in reverse, serial 3s or 7s subtractions or the "Trail Making A" test. In the absence of significant aphasia, poor performance on these tests should suggest another or at least additional disorder (e.g., hypoglycemia). As

DAT worsens, patients eventually become distractible and are often described as having poor concentration. We often hear patients complain that reading for pleasure has become too difficult because "I can't concentrate."

Dysexecutive syndrome

The domain of *executive* ("frontal executive") *functions* has been increasingly recognized. This term refers to a variety of abilities ranging from planning, manipulation of information, and initiation and termination or inhibition of behavioral responses, i.e., social judgment (Hebben, 2002). Lezak posits four executive components: volition; planning; purposive action; and effective performance (Lezak, 1995). All are necessary for appropriate, socially responsible adult conduct. *Dys*executive syndromes are often attributed to "frontal systems" damage, but they may result from diffuse and extra-frontal focal brain lesions (Cummings, 1993; Stokholm et al., 2006).

An entire chapter of this book is devoted to the description and testing of executive impairments. For now, a few statements are in order. Executive deficits, as with visuospatial dysfunction, are demonstrable in most DAT patients at mild stage (Albert, 2008; Stokholm et al., 2006).

Assessment of executive dysfunction is, nevertheless, not easy. The examiner usually determines the goals, directions, materials, and timing of any given test. Executive function testing, in contrast, requires transferring "goal setting, structuring, and decision making from the clinician to the subject within the structured examination" (Lezak, 1995). Although in general not an overt disabling feature of early DAT, deficits in executive function influence performance in multiple cognitive domains. "Working memory," for example, essentially is an executive function, and poor organizational strategies can affect verbal learning and impede retrieval of "remote" memories. Even a relatively simple test of language comprehension, *executing* a three-step command, demands maintenance of serial order. Executive disturbances likely, in fact, underlie the ADL impairments at a stage when memory disorder is the only obvious symptom (Grady et al., 1989; Hodges, 2006; Perry & Hodges, 1999).

Neuropsychiatric issues

Behavioral aberrations are core features of DAT, were very prominent early in Alzheimer's original patient, and eventually arise in all patients. Manifestations are protean, are roughly severity-specific, but occur earlier in some patients than in others. Once established, some evolve, some remain stable, some recede. Behavioral deterioration may be triggered suddenly by an acute systemic perturbation, a change in environment, or any other stressor. Changes range from apathy and social withdrawal ("pseudo-depressed") to disinhibition, agitation, eating disorders, and frank psychosis ("pseudopsychopathic") (Cummings, 1982).

In early DAT, personality and social behavior in general are broadly preserved (Galton et al., 2000). Subtle indifference and emotional detachment are common (Petry et al., 1988) but frequently either go unnoticed or may even be welcomed

(Mesulam, 2000). Many individuals thus continue to function well socially, leading others to underestimate or excuse memory, language or executive impairments until, for example, sudden disruption in routine leaves the patient unable to deal with a novel situation (Cummings & Benson, 1992). The tolerance for personality change, however, usually is less than that for insidious memory loss, which for most people is a "normal part of aging." Patients with overt personality change therefore are referred, or dragged into, an evaluative process soon after onset.

Apathy (lack of motivation relative to the patient's baseline state) is common in many brain disorders and is worthy of special consideration. Ranging from mild passivity and loss of interest to abulic immobilization, and difficult to evaluate, apathy is the most common neuropsychiatric manifestation of AD and a source of considerable caregiver stress (Marshall et al., 2007). Although prevalence increases with severity of cognitive impairment (Bózzola et al., 1992; Landes et al., 2005; Mega et al., 1996), noticeable apathy may appear when cognitive impairment is minimal (Onyike et al., 2007), when it can be misdiagnosed as depression. This misdiagnosis is understandable since low mood and apathy frequently go hand in hand. Apathy and depression nevertheless are separate phenomena with different neuroanatomic substrates, and at least half of apathetic DAT patients are not depressed (Geldmacher, 2007; Hodges, 2006; Levy et al., 1998). The distinction is clinically important because generally well-tolerated drugs such as selective serotonin reuptake inhibitors (SSRIs) may worsen apathy (Barnhart et al., 2004).

Apathy is a double whammy for patients and their caregivers because it is also strongly associated with anosognosia and executive dysfunction (McGlynn & Kaszniak, 1991; McPherson et al., 2002): "They don't know and they don't care." This combination underlies the poor hygiene and inappropriate dressing so common in mid-stage DAT. Apathetic patients are more ADL-dependent than those without apathy at a similar level of cognitive impairment, are more likely to manifest other abnormal behaviors (Chow et al., 2009), and, even when functional impairments are not yet an issue, have double the risk of progression to overt DAT (Starkstein et al., 2006). Apathy is difficult to treat, given the probability that the patient already will have been prescribed several other medications, but ameliorative effects of cholinesterase inhibitors have been shown (van Reekum et al., 2005; Wynn & Cummings, 2004).

Apathy very often is replaced by or mixed with a variety of disruptive behaviors as the dementia worsens. These include psychomotor agitation, aggression, resistance, delusions and hallucinations, repetitive vocalizations, shadowing, and frank psychosis. Disruptive behaviors are common and usually late manifestations of AD although agitation occurs in a significant percentage of even mildly demented patients (Cummings, 2005a). When evident early in the course, delusions and hallucinations (usually visual) in particular predict more rapid cognitive and functional decline (Scarmeas et al., 2005), are more likely to prompt institutionalization than even incontinence, and are associated with longer hospital stays (Wancata et al., 2003). Delusions are more common than hallucinations and usually are persecutory, involving fears of personal harm, property theft, and spousal infidelity. Capgras syndrome (a belief that someone, often a spouse, has been replaced by an identical imposter) and other reduplicative phenomena also occur (Rubin, 1992).

Behavioral problems in general become more common and more severe as cognitive abilities deteriorate, although the pattern changes. Delusions and hallucinations tend to decline as the disease proceeds from moderate to severe stage, while agitation, aggression, and inappropriate shouting increase (Cummings, 2005b).

There appear to be both cultural-dependent similarities and differences in behavior patterns at similar stages (Binetti et al., 1998; Ortiz et al., 2006). Particular aberrant behaviors possibly correlate with pre-morbid personality traits, although findings among various studies have been mixed (Archer et al., 2007). Persons with at least one copy of the ApoE ε4 allele may be more likely to become agitated (Craig et al., 2004). Behavioral symptoms, depending on specific type, have been correlated with both right medial frontal lobe damage (Rosen et al., 2005; Senanarong et al., 2004) and with left frontotemporal hypoperfusion, regardless of dementia etiology (Hirono et al., 2000).

Virtually every patient with a progressive dementia develops agitation, wandering, sleep difficulties, or other behavioral problems at some point in the course of the disease. The clinician should be mindful that behavioral symptoms are manifestations of an older, diseased brain that will usually be far more vulnerable to the side effects of psychiatric medications than the brain of a younger or nondemented patient. In practice, patients will often have combinations of these symptoms or linked symptoms (e.g., a patient who paces due to anxiety). Agitation and aggression, for example, are provoked by:

- confusion due to cognitive, memory, or language impairments;
- delusions;
- depression in a patient too impaired to express distress in another manner;
- sleep disturbance;
- pain (fall injury, decubitus ulcers, arthritis, renal colic, etc.);
- infections, metabolic perturbations, and drug interactions and changes;
- trivial environmental changes including recent travel and bathing (Corey-Bloom et al., 2006; Press & Alexander, 2007).

Depression often accompanies DAT. Depression is common among the elderly. It is still not clear whether DAT patients suffer depression with greater frequency compared with age-matched nondemented people (Rubin et al., 1991; Wilson et al., 2003).

Degenerative brain diseases, including AD, often coexist with depression in the same patient and symptoms overlap. Agitation, apathy, eating disorders, weight loss, and sleep disorders are common to both, rendering interpretation of these symptoms difficult (Riviere et al., 2002). Confirming depression in a patient presenting with cognitive impairment is not easy since patients may not complain of mood disturbance. Instead, they frequently present with somatic symptoms and sleep problems as well as memory difficulties. Overt depressive symptoms nevertheless can occur prior to manifest dementia and at nearly any point in DAT and are more common when there is a family history of mood disorder (Strauss & Ogrocki, 1996).

Late-onset depression without significant cognitive abnormalities is a risk factor for later development of DAT (Green et al., 2003; Reding, Haycox, & Blass, 1985) although major depression fulfilling DSM-IV criteria is unusual, and the mechanism may be independent of plaque and tangle burden (Wilson et al., 2003). In most but not all persons with DAT, depressive symptoms decrease as the dementia worsens (Teri & Wagner, 1992). Since depression in the elderly may present atypically and may worsen the cognitive impairments that are already present due to underlying neurodegenerative disease, it is not always easily recognizable and many clinicians prescribe antidepressants empirically to cognitively impaired persons with vague somatic symptoms. A six- to eight-week treatment trial of one of the serotonin reuptake inhibitors is relatively safe (but see above regarding apathy) and sometimes provides considerable and even unexpected improvement. In our clinical experience, an impressive improvement in mood or anxiety may be seen with antidepressant treatment, while the cognitive impairment remains relatively unchanged.

Other manifestations

Sleep disruption occurs in more than half of community-dwelling patients with DAT and is one of the most disturbing behavioral symptoms associated with AD, creating exhaustion and despair among caregivers (McCurry et al., 2009). In at least one study, sleep disturbances and night wandering were considered among the most intolerable of the behavioral symptoms and thus a major precipitant of institutionalization (Sanford, 1975). Several studies have demonstrated that the average nursing-home resident may never sleep for a full hour, nor be awake for a full hour, throughout the entire 24-hour day (Jacobs et al., 1989). Sleep disruption is not only a prominent behavioral problem in patients with AD and other dementias but it may also exacerbate daytime confusion or agitation.

Sundowning is a widely used term for a clinical phenomenon that is neither medically defined nor biologically well understood. In general, sundowning may be characterized by the onset or exacerbation of agitation, restlessness, panic, intensified disorientation, and verbal or physical outbursts in the afternoon or evening. In some studies, disease-related abnormalities of the sleep–wake cycle have been implicated as potential causes of sundowning, although it is clear that patient agitation may contribute to sleep problems as well (Reynolds et al., 1988).

Epilepsy can complicate DAT (Hauser et al., 1986; Hesdorffer et al., 1996). Old age is itself a risk factor for epilepsy through multiple mechanisms (most commonly, stroke), and differentiation between epileptic and non-epileptic events can be difficult among the elderly demented. Whether or not epilepsy is a complication of AD per se, independent of other risk factors, is not completely clear. Risk factors for seizures are more advanced dementia in some studies (Amatniek et al., 2006; Romanelli et al., 1990), focal EEG abnormalities, race and younger age in others (Amatniek et al., 2006; Scarmeas, Honig et al., 2009). Seizures provoked by AD pathology alone are likely uncommon, but more common compared with age-matched persons in the general population (Scarmeas, Honig et al., 2009). Recent animal studies suggest that subclinical seizures may contribute to Aβ-induced deficits (Palop et al., 2007) and may even account for some cases of wandering (Palop & Mucke, 2009).

Treatment of epilepsy in DAT doesn't differ much from that of younger patients. Enzyme-inducing drugs such as phenytoin, carbamazepine (CBZ) should be avoided, if possible, in view of their drug interactions, reduced protein binding and, in relatively younger persons, their osteopenic effect. Valproate (VPA) is often too sedating. Nevertheless, any anti-epileptic drug may interact differently within a demented host than within an otherwise normal person, so one prescribes what is ultimately necessary to control seizures with the least side effects (Palop & Mucke, 2009). CBZ and VPA may even ameliorate disruptive behaviors in a few patients.

Myoclonus, or brisk irregular involuntary muscle contractions, occurs in 5–25% of AD patients, mostly as a late manifestation (Hauser et al., 1986). Creutzfeldt–Jakob disease (CJD) is therefore not the only dementia associated with myoclonus. Since AD is much more common than CJD, it is probably a more common cause of dementia associated with myoclonus. Pathological AD has been reported to be a rare cause of the progressive myoclonus epilepsy syndrome in young adults (Melanson et al., 1997).

Sexual behavior. Actual hypersexuality or aggression almost never occurs although inappropriate sexual comments and increased interest may in some cases be early manifestations. When this occurs, redirection usually suffices in halting what for many partners has become unwelcome attention. Badgering of the spouse is unusual, but can occur. In general, sexual interest and activity are diminished (Kumar et al., 1988).

Clinical heterogeneity in AD

DAT is by far the most common manifestation of pathological AD. However, AD is phenotypically a heterogeneous disorder that doesn't always generate the DAT syndrome. The very earliest indication that something is wrong, i.e., that determined by the patient, family, or close friends to be worthy of reporting, may not be a memory problem (Galton et al., 2000; Hodges, 2006; Johnson et al., 1999; Lambon Ralph et al., 2003; Oppenheim, 1994). To the extent that autopsy can "confirm" AD, pathologically verified cases sometimes clinically don't conform to the standard DAT blueprint, and *clinically* "pure" cases, as previously noted, often harbor other, sometimes unexpected, pathologies (Lim et al., 1999; Lopez et al., 2002).

AD as pathologically defined sometimes symptomatically manifests as one of the other cortical dementia syndromes (Mesulam, 2000) and begins with isolated language, visuospatial, or, as with Auguste D., executive/comportmental deterioration. Striking focal motor, cerebellar (Piccini et al., 2007), or sensory symptoms rarely may even dominate the entire clinical course (Crystal et al., 1982; Jagust et al., 1990), particularly when AD is caused by autosomal dominant presenilin mutations (Marrosu et al., 2006). AD should therefore be considered in a wide spectrum of focal cortical syndromes, including both fluent and non-fluent progressive aphasia and progressive personality dissolution (Galton et al., 2000), but should not be the assumed cause of all cortical dementia syndromes (Tang-Wai & Mapstone, 2006). Indeed, some persons with pathological AD according to multiple established criteria show no signs of cognitive impairment prior to death (Erten-Lyons et al., 2009; Roe et al., 2007; Snowdon et al., 1997) and, rarely, brains of patients with typical DAT show no pathology at all (Crystal et al., 2000; Howieson et al., 2003).

Pathological AD, the prototypical "cortical dementia" syndrome, has been associated with a variety of motor disturbances, especially parkinsonism, which can predate the dementia and have been described in cases of mild cognitive impairment (Louis et al., 2005; Portet et al., 2009; Richards et al., 1993).

Is, therefore, AD *per se* a valid nosological concept? The received wisdom is that "Alzheimer's disease" exists, it has a recognized pathology with a recognized anatomical distribution, and this anatomical and chemical pathology leads to a characteristic clinical syndrome. What if this received wisdom is wrong? What would the alternatives be? Once this question is asked, the options open and multiply. One option is that there are different etiologies of Alzheimer's disease and they have different underlying pathophysiologies but overlapping clinical phenomenology (Grossberg & Desai, 2003; Hardy, 1997). There is little difference, for example, in plaque and tangle distribution and morphology between early-onset and late-onset Alzheimer brains. Plaque and tangle load is, however, more severe and correlates much better with dementia severity in the former versus the latter (Prohovnik et al., 2006). Pathophysiologically, early- and late-onset AD may not, in fact, represent the same, unique disease (Blennow et al., 2006; Licht et al., 2007).

One can argue that overlapping but nevertheless different clinical clusters with different natural histories represent Alzheimer "variants" (Blennow et al., 1994; Holtzer et al., 2003; Mayeux et al., 1985). One could also argue that, as fundamental neurobiological research exposes brain–behavior relationships in health and disease, the various forms and patterns of underlying mechanisms that lead to the common clinical presentation currently labeled AD will emerge, and each of these forms and patterns would thus be given its own name (Albert, 2008; Graham et al., 1996; Neary et al., 1986). The reader should keep in mind, especially when consulting older citations, that many current (and for that matter, future) staining techniques (e.g., ubiquitin, synuclein, AT8) were not available as recently as the early 1990s. The "pathological Alzheimer's" of circa 1990 and before differs in many ways from what neuropathologists are now confirming as "Alzheimer's disease" (Consensus recommendations for the postmortem diagnosis of Alzheimer's disease. The National Institute on Aging, and Reagan Institute Working Group on Diagnostic Criteria for the Neuropathological Assessment of Alzheimer's Disease, 1997).

Mild cognitive impairment

Many older adults, both those with and without cognitive complaints, enjoy substantially uncompromised ADL and do not meet DSM-IV clinical criteria for dementia, yet show impairments, if tested. The overall prevalence of this condition has been estimated at 19% up to age 75 and about 29% for age 85 or older (Lopez et al., 2003). These people have for years been described by a variety of terms such as "cognitive impairment not demented" (Di Carlo et al., 2007; Ebly et al., 1995), "age associated memory impairment" (Crook et al., 1986), "benign senescent forgetfulness," and most recently and most often by mild cognitive impairment (MCI) (Flicker et al., 1991; Negash et al., 2008; Petersen et al., 2009; Petersen, 2007; Petersen et al., 1999; Winblad et al., 2004).

MCI refers to people with subjective *and* objective cognitive symptoms "greater than expected for an individual's age and education level but that do not interfere notably with activities of daily life" (Gauthier et al., 2006; Petersen, 2007), i.e., a transitional state between "normal aging" and dementia.

MCI was originally described as isolated subjective and objective memory impairment without functional decline (Petersen, 2007; Petersen et al., 1999). Cognitive loss in other domains was added to MCI criteria in response to criticism that they were insufficiently inclusive of the non-amnestic problems that often occur in elderly persons, i.e., not sufficiently accountable for MCI heterogeneity (Winblad et al., 2004) (Figure 1.4).

Individuals with memory-only cognitive decline are a small proportion of the total MCI population (Kramer et al., 2006; Lopez et al., 2003). They are said to have the "amnestic single domain" form of MCI (aMCI), although whether or not memory is the only impaired system in these people has been questioned (Dudas et al., 2005). Most research has nevertheless been focused on this cohort of MCI patients (Guillozet et al., 2003; Markesbery et al., 2006; Petersen et al., 2006; Whitwell et al., 2007). The pathological substrate putatively reflects the entorhinal and hippocampal changes asserted frequently to be the earliest change of AD (Whitwell et al., 2007), but both this assertion and the necessary association between medial temporolimbic degeneration and memory impairment in AD have been challenged (Galluzzi et al., 2005; Lim et al., 1999; McKee et al., 2000; Nestor et al., 2006; Scheff et al., 2007; Snowdon et al., 1997; Vinters, 2006).

The reported "conversion" rate of aMCI to overt DAT ranges from 8–33% over two years (Aisen et al., 2003; Cummings, Doody, & Clark, 2007), generally about 15% for patients evaluated in specialized memory clinics (Tuokko et al., 2003), which is much higher than the incidence rate of DAT in the general population.

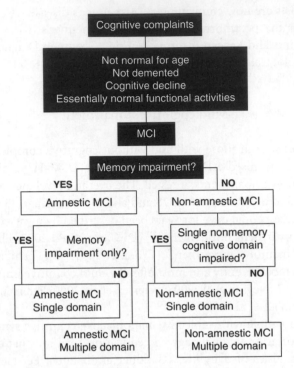

Figure 1.4   Flow chart of decision process for making diagnosis of subtypes of mild cognitive impairment
Source: Petersen, R.C. (2004). Mild cognitive impairment. *Continuum, 10*, 9–28. Taylor & Francis

If MCI is applied to non-(overtly) demented patients with a clear history of progressive memory impairment, the one- and two-year conversion rates are 41% and 64%, respectively (Geslani et al., 2005). Nevertheless, in a study having interpretive implications of therapeutic trials, 30% of aMCI patients who "converted" did not meet neuropathological criteria for AD (Jicha et al., 2006): not all patients with deteriorating MCI turn out to have AD. As of this writing, there is no clear evidence that pharmacological treatment of MCI has any efficacy (Doody et al., 2009).

Discrepancies in conversion rates, that is, the heterogeneity of prognosis, are reflective of the heterogeneity of MCI (Albert, 2008; Chetelat & Baron, 2003). Variability is due to the manner in which patients are recruited to studies, the use of different testing measures to operationalize the MCI construct, differing outcome measures and statistical modeling, quality of information (i.e., history) available to clinicians and researchers, and insufficient consideration of co-morbid conditions that can affect cognition (Cummings, Doody et al., 2007; Dubois et al., 2007; Geslani et al., 2005; Lopez et al., 2003; Petersen, 2007). Some people with MCI do not worsen significantly over time, a minority improve, and persons with non-amnestic MCI (naMCI) can develop DAT as well as other types of dementia (Mesulam, 2000).

Of those who do convert from MCI to DAT, risk factors for so doing have been addressed. ApoE ε4 carrier status very likely is important (Blacker et al., 2007; Petersen et al., 1995; Tervo et al., 2004). Some studies indicate that those with amnestic-multiple domain MCI (aMCI-MD), rather than those with pure aMCI, are at highest risk, likely because such people have more advanced pathological AD (Chen et al., 2000; Tabert et al., 2006; Whitwell et al., 2007). Others conclude that conversion to clinical DAT (Storandt et al., 2006) or even other dementing disorders is independent of MCI "type" (Fischer et al., 2007).

Poor prognostic conversion indicators of variable strength and specificity also include neuropsychiatric symptoms (Copeland et al., 2003; Palmer et al., 2007), lack of awareness of subtle functional impairments (Tabert et al., 2002), subjective complaints versus no complaints (Geerlings et al., 1999; Reisberg et al., 2005), suboptimal performance on a variety of cognitive measures (Arnaiz et al., 2004; Blacker et al., 2007; Fleisher et al., 2007; Galvin, Roe, & Morris, 2007; Petersen, 2007), particularly delayed recall (Arnaiz et al., 2004; Ivanoiu et al., 2005), and MRI atrophy of limbic and association cortices (Whitwell et al., 2007; Whitwell et al., 2008).

Many dementia experts accept MCI as a useful concept, and its inclusion into DSM V is under consideration (Negash et al., 2008). Others continue to debate its validity (Gauthier et al., 2006; Gauthier & Touchon, 2005), *to the extent that MCI has been eliminated in the proposed revision of the NINCDS-ADRDA research criteria for AD* (Dubois et al., 2007). For Petersen and Morris (2005) "mild cognitive impairment is an evolving construct" but "the heterogeneity reflects a refinement of the entity rather than a weakness."

Indeed, it is now evident that the pathogenetic processes underlying AD begin decades before development of any clinically recognizable symptoms. *Subjective* impairments, for example, remembering names and recalling where one has placed things, in the absence of any objective cognitive deficit, have collectively been termed "subjective cognitive impairment" (SCI) (Reisberg et al., 2008). This ultimately is the focus of large biomarker research trials such as the Alzheimer's Disease Neuroimaging Initiative (ADNI), and others listed below, and the National Institute on Aging Alzheimer's Disease Centers Program for the Uniform Data Set (Jagust, 2008; Mueller et al., 2005).

MCI is a concept in transition, a subject of intense investigation and competing models of characterization (Gauthier & Touchon, 2005; Grundman et al., 2004; Petersen & Morris, 2005).

DAT without MCI

Recognizable DAT is almost always preceded by MCI, but sometimes AD and other dementing diseases are akin to a falling tree heard by no one until its crash. That is, for a significant cohort of "community dwelling elderly," in which multiple systemic illnesses, multiple causes of dementia (Schneider et al., 2007), and polypharmacy are common, and in whom cognitive reserve has about been exhausted, the trigger for entry into the health care system may not be MCI or equivalent. Rather, such people, either having lived alone or been assisted by ever more attentive associates, often present to emergency departments in an acute confusional state (ACS; delirium). A declaration, "he was sharp as a tack until . . ." is not uncommon (Dembner, 2007).

The core feature of the ACS, which has a differential diagnosis as diverse as that of the dementia syndrome (Lipowski, 1987), is impairment of attention, which disrupts all other cognitive domains. Markedly reduced digit span and inappropriate responses to extraneous stimuli are salient characteristics, which often are accompanied by some combination of delusions, hallucinations, myoclonus, asterixis, and disturbances of the sleep–wake cycle. The gross disturbance of attention of the ACS should facilitate its differentiation from otherwise uncomplicated DAT, in which, at least in mild stage, attention as commonly assessed is preserved. However, about 25% of elderly patients admitted with a delirium harbor an underlying dementing disease, often pathological AD with or without significant cerebrovascular disease. The message: a dementing process should be suspected in elderly people in an ACS, and dementing diseases, including AD, render persons more vulnerable to developing it (Jackson et al., 2004). In such cases, even when underlying causes are identified and treated, recovery to baseline is usually slow, frequently incomplete, in part genetically determined (Ely et al., 2007), and associated with prolonged hospital stays (Erkinjuntti et al., 1986).

Emerging Developments in the Diagnosis of AD

Recall that recommendations from the preceding paragraphs reflect many years of clinical practice. Clinical evaluation remains the gold standard of diagnosis, differential diagnosis, and assessment of the success of therapeutic interventions but has several disadvantages, including insensitivity to pathology during the preclinical phase and the variability of the host (cognitive reserve) in which the disease process occurs (Cummings, 2005a; Deary et al., 2004; Strub & Black, 2000). Principal goals of AD research have been to develop methods for diagnosis, predicting risk, and tracking effects of therapy. We are at the threshold of realizing these goals in the form of reliable biomarkers and their employment in a proposed revision of the NINCDS-ADRDA criteria (Craig-Schapiro et al., 2009; Duara et al., 2009; Dubois et al., 2007).

A biomarker is a characteristic that is objectively measured and evaluated as an indicator of normal biological processes, pathogenic processes, or pharmacological responses to therapy (Cummings, 2005b; Strub & Black, 2000) and comes in three varieties (Fox & Growdon, 2004):

• State markers – also known as diagnostic markers, reflect intensity of disease process and indicate that the pathology of concern (in this case, of AD) indeed is present. In general, these suffer from suboptimal specificity, i.e., distinguishing AD from other causes of the dementia syndrome (Blennow & Hampel, 2003).

- Rate or stage markers (surrogate endpoints) – track disease progression or detect response (or lack thereof) to therapeutic interventions. Quantitative measurement of hippocampal and other medial temporal atrophy, and rating scales are examples.
- Trait (genetic) markers – predict likelihood of developing a disease or indicate susceptibility to it, e.g., APOE genotype or presenilin mutations.

Biomarkers for AD can also be classified as direct (e.g., measuring Aβ in CSF or with neuroimaging) or indirect (quantifying cerebral atrophy, clinical assessment), according to which step in the putative pathophysiological cascade they are associated with (isoprostanes Π oxidation; PIB PET Π Aβ plaque burden) (Cummings, 2005a; Strub & Black, 2000), and by which body compartment (CSF, brain, serum) is scrutinized. Biomarkers also include a variety of neuroimaging techniques, particularly positron emission tomography (Jagust et al., 2007), which are covered in detail in other chapters of this book.

The ideal biomarker should be convenient, safe, non-invasive, inexpensive, at least 80% sensitive and specific even in preclinical AD (the population for which biomarkers are mostly intended), feasible to perform, and validated by neuropathology (Borroni et al., 2006; Silver et al., 1998). Currently available biomarkers satisfy many of these requirements, but remaining limitations render them not yet ready for clinical use. Most of them require measurement at research or custom laboratories and there is insufficient standardization of assays and collection procedures (e.g., type of conveyance into which specimens are collected). Effects of circadian rhythms on biomarkers, likely an important factor, have not been well studied. It is, moreover, difficult, time consuming, and very expensive to follow a cohort of asymptomatic or minimally symptomatic individuals, even those enriched with higher-at-risk persons, long enough to associate the biomarker with subsequent development of DAT (Borroni et al., 2006; Fagan et al., 2005; Galasko, 2005). For the foreseeable future, no single biomarker is likely to fulfill all ideal criteria. The real, as yet untapped, potentials for biomarkers are in pre-symptomatic identification of at-risk individuals and in tracking persons with DAT in clinical therapeutic trials. Once they are readily available, convenient and precise, combinations of several CSF, plasma and neuroimaging markers likely will prove useful (Hansson et al., 2006). Several biomarkers have been chosen for the ADNI study (Mueller et al., 2005). The usefulness of which biomarkers, in which combinations, have yet to be determined (Frisoni et al., 2009).

Biomarkers are discussed in detail in many recent reviews (Blennow & Hampel, 2003; Borroni et al., 2006; Craig-Schapiro et al., 2009; Cummings, 2005a; Fagan et al., 2005; Strub & Black, 2000). In summary:

- Plasma biomarkers: High plasma Aβ$_{42}$ levels are found in *some* cognitively normal first-degree relatives of AD patients (Ertekin-Taner et al., 2007), and are a risk factor for developing AD, but this marker is still insufficiently sensitive and specific for reliable early diagnosis. Plasma $A\beta_{42}/A\beta_{40}$ ratio may be a better indicator (Graff-Radford et al., 2007).

Platelet APP isoform ratio (130 kDa band/110 kDa band) is reduced in persons with clinically diagnosed AD, correlates with declining MMSE scores (Baskin et al., 2000), and may predict conversion from MCI to DAT. This ratio, in combination with measurement of platelet β and α-secretase may increase accuracy of early diagnosis (Borroni et al., 2006).

• CSF biomarkers: Low $A\beta_{42}$ level appears to predict conversion of MCI to DAT but reduced level is also found in many other neurological diseases, and CSF $A\beta$ levels appear to be time of day and activity dependent (Bateman et al., 2007).

The same is true for increased total CSF tau (t-tau); high CSF phosphorylated tau (p-tau) is more specific for AD but does not distinguish those with and without cortical Lewy bodies (Sjogren et al., 2001).

Measuring CSF $A\beta_{42}$/t-tau or $A\beta_{42}$/p-tau[181 and/or 231] ratio has improved diagnostic sensitivity and specificity in some but not all studies.

Low CSF $A\beta_{42}$/p-tau[181] ratio nonetheless has accurately predicted conversion not only from MCI to DAT but also from normal (CDR 0) cognition to dementia, and correlated with PIB-PET brain amyloid burden (Fagan et al., 2007). Abnormal CSF $A\beta_{42}$ and p-tau[181] concentrations in cognitively intact middle-aged persons also correlate with FDG-PET hypometabolic areas known to be affected in early AD (Petrie et al., 2009).

F2-isoprostanes, a marker of oxidative stress, are elevated in CSF, blood and urine in early AD and are potentially useful for monitoring effects of antioxidant therapy but, again, there is discrepancy among studies regarding sensitivity and specificity (Flirski & Sobow, 2005; Ringman et al., 2008).

Many other fluid biological markers, including CSF cytokines, as well as techniques employing mass spectrometry (proteomics) are in various stages of development and validation (Craig-Schapiro et al., 2009; Cummings, 2005a; Ma et al., 2009; Strub & Black, 2000).

Treatment

We begin with a discussion of the pharmacological treatment of DAT. We stress, however, that DAT is a family-systems disease, causing tremendous upheaval and morbidity for the patient and for everyone in the patient's family. At every stage of the disease, the patient's deterioration requires increasing resources. At every stage of the disease, the family requires new information and access to new services. The focus of care must expand from diagnosis and specific management to include the patient's caregiver, and supportive care ideally begins at the time of diagnosis (Cummings & Benson, 1992). Nonpharmacological assistance is addressed in a subsequent section.

The therapeutic goal ultimately, of course, is intervention with disease-modifying agents at multiple points within the pathophysiological cascade during the years-lasting *preclinical* phase of AD, when pathological burden is low (primary prevention). Once symptoms have developed, however, one should expect that early and persistent pharmacotherapy for AD will result in less behavioral, functional, and cognitive deterioration over a period of time than one would expect in the absence of pharmacotherapy (secondary prevention). Thus, treatment success includes not only short-term improvement of symptoms but also less decline over the long term (Geldmacher et al., 2006).

Identifying these phases is *the* challenge to effective treatment and is addressed later in this chapter, elsewhere in this book, and in other articles (Cummings, Doody et al., 2007). Distinguishing, for example, between a substantial epoch of "natural" memory stability in MCI (Smith et al., 2007) and treatment effects (when memory change is a principal outcome measure) may prove very difficult.

In this chapter, we distinguish among symptomatic therapies, such as the cholinesterase inhibitors (ChEIs) and *N*-methyl-D-aspartate (NMDA) receptor antagonists (Figure 1.5, left), disease-modifying therapies (DMT) that may prevent the onset or slow the progression of the disease, such as antioxidant drugs (Figure 1.5, right), and adjunctive medications for neuropsychiatric symptoms (Table 1.4).

The confounding problems of clinical trials in need of overcoming include accurate detection of placebo responses, the difficulty of differentiating between symptomatic and disease-modifying effects, especially for drugs that harbor both

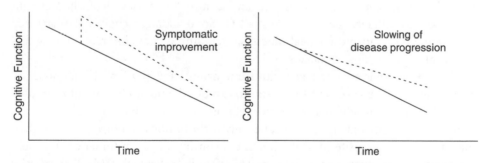

Figure 1.5   These figures suggest how different pharmacological treatments may affect the downward course of symptoms of AD and show the distinction between a treatment that improves symptoms and one that slows disease progress. The ChEIs have been shown in many studies to provide symptomatic improvement but not to modify disease progression. As discussed in the text, several new possibly disease-modifying compounds are in phase III trials

Source: Modified from Green, R.C. (2005). *Diagnosis and management of Alzheimer's disease and other dementias* (2nd edn.). Caddo, OK: Professional Communications, Inc., by permission

Table 1.4   Pharmacological treatment of Alzheimer's disease

DISEASE SPECIFIC Symptomatic		*ADJUNCTIVE* Disease-modifying
ChEIs	Immunotherapy	Antipsychotics
Memantine	Secretase inhibitors	Antidepressants
Herbals	Selective Aβ lowering drugs	Opioids
Muscarinic receptor agonists	Anti-Aβ aggregation agents	Anti-epileptics
Nicotinc receptor agonists	Hormonals	β-Blockers
	NSAIDs	Anxiolytics
	Statins	Tau inhibitors
	Metal chelators	Diet/Nutrition
	Antioxidants	NMDA receptor antagonists?
	Small peptides	

properties, and circumventing insufficient trial durations (Cummings, 2009; Doody, 2008; Kennedy et al., 2007). Furthermore, the people who take these drugs are likely to have other age-related medical disorders that directly (in the case of vascular disease) or indirectly influence symptoms and treatment. It is common, for example, for patients with DAT also to be taking a variety of anticholinergic medications for bladder control, "dizziness," insomnia, and, particularly, depression (tricyclics). These often worsen cognition and precipitate neuropsychiatric symptoms and should be avoided. Confusional states are associated with many cardiovascular agents (calcium channel and beta-blockers, amiodarone, ACE inhibitors) and particularly with narcotics, benzodiazepines and sedative-hypnotics, all of which should be prescribed with circumspection, if at all. Optimal management of polypharmacy and frequent co-morbid medical illnesses, including depression, remain a significant challenge for most clinicians.

There have been separate trials with some drugs (donepezil, anti-inflammatory agents, hormone replacement therapies) to explore the possibility of both symptomatic and disease-modifying properties (Hashimoto et al., 2005). DMT and symptomatic treatments may not, in fact, be fully dichotomous (Doody, 2008). Rather, they may reflect opposite ends of a treatment continuum: symptomatic drugs possibly alleviating downstream effects (neurotransmitter deficits), DMT theoretically disrupting early events such as $A\beta_{42}$ or hyperphosphorylated tau overproduction. If by 2012 drugs could delay the onset of AD by about seven years, its prevalence would decline by approximately 40% by 2050 (Sloane et al., 2002), reducing the national cost by trillions of dollars.

The distinction between symptomatic and DMT is frequently misunderstood by both clinicians and families, leading to unrealistic expectations. Since every medication choice weighs the anticipated benefits against the side effects and financial costs of that therapy, it is particularly important that clinicians inform patients accurately. Providing accurate information is a key step in the treatment protocol for the use of pharmacological therapies in AD. Ideally, one should expect that the patient who is treated early and persistently with medication for AD will show less evidence of behavioral, functional, and cognitive deterioration over a period of time than one would expect in the absence of pharmacotherapy.

What, precisely, "accurate information" is, is still unsettled. ChEIs, for example, are currently the standard of care for the treatment of mild, moderate, and severe AD (Doody et al., 2001). We use them, and believe that they are underutilized and that every patient/family should have access to them. We have, furthermore, previously referred to several articles and studies indicating that ChEIs provide real symptomatic benefit to patients with DAT. There are nonetheless issues relating to their use.

A recent meta-analysis concluded that the scientific evidence for their use is highly questionable (Kaduszkiewicz et al., 2005). The National Institute for Health and Clinical Excellence in the UK (Technology Appraisal TA 111, 2006) argues that the modest benefits of ChEIs for mild dementia do not justify their cost (Corey-Bloom et al., 2006), an opinion that has been challenged by the drug companies (Dyer, 2007). There is both supportive and contrary evidence (Birks & Flicker, 2006; Feldman et al., 2007; Petersen & Morris, 2005) that cholinesterase inhibition delays progression of MCI to manifest DAT.

Symptomatic treatment

The AD pathophysiological process affects nearly all neurotransmitter systems, including noradrenergic neurons in the locus ceruleus, serotonergic cells in the dorsal raphe, and glutamate, dopaminergic and multiple polypeptide networks necessary for normal synaptic function (Coyle et al., 1983). Current treatment, however, rests mostly on the "cholinergic hypothesis": a central nervous system (CNS) drug-induced cholinergic blockade causes reversible cognitive impairment. Degeneration in AD of presynaptic cholinergic neurons in the basal forebrain results in widespread cortical and hippocampal depletion of acetylcholine (ACh). Several studies support an association between memory and other cognitive impairments on the one hand and basal forebrain cholinergic neuronal loss and virtual absence of cortical choline acetyltransferace in AD brains on the other (Terry & Buccafusco, 2003). In theory, cholinergic replenishment would partly counteract the insufficiency associated with AD neuropathology. Other studies indicate lack of such an association (Kaduszkiewicz et al., 2005). Disappointing results in many cases with cholinergic therapy are not particularly surprising.

Therapeutic trials commenced in the 1980s with ACh muscarinic precursors such as lethicin and oral choline. All studies concluded with either too small drug versus placebo differences or high incidences of side effects. More recent research has focused on cholinergic muscarinic and and nicotinic agonists. Either side effects, lack of efficacy, or conflicting and insufficient evidence render the role of these drugs presently unclear, and none is commercially available.

Acetylcholinesterase inhibitors

ChEIs are FDA-approved and are recommended by the American Academy of Neurology as standard (Doody et al., 2001) for the symptomatic treatment of mild-to-moderate AD. These drugs block, through a variety of mechanisms, the degradation of ACh at surviving presynaptic neuronal terminals, thereby prolonging its action and partially compensating for postsynaptic ACh depletion.

ChEIs have all shown measurable but modest improvements in cognition and ADL function. When treatment has been discontinued in many ChEI trials, cognitive and global ratings for the treatment groups have rapidly declined to levels that were not significantly different from those of the placebo group, suggesting that the beneficial effects of ChEIs rely upon continued administration. Hake (2007) suggests as prolonged a trial as possible, with ChEIs and with memantine, because "no difference" in fact could reflect benefit in view of the progressive nature of the disease, although improvement, if any is noticed, occurs mostly within three months.

The average cost of ChEI treatment is $1200–$1800 per year and pharmaco-economic studies suggest that, if initiated early and continued for two years, the drug cost can be recouped by savings through reduced care costs (transportation, daycare, remunerated private supervision) and delayed nursing home placement (Cummings, 2003). Cost has also been justified in custodial settings (Volicer, 2001). Nevertheless, these and most other pharmacological treatments remain financially out of reach for many patients and their families (Matthews et al., 2006).

Few studies have focused upon when to begin these treatments, how to choose optimal dosing, when and how to change drugs, and how long to continue treatment. Reliable data are not yet available on the long-term efficacy of ChEIs after one year, although there is evidence that donepezil transiently slows the deterioration of cognitive function in amnestic MCI patients for at least one year (Petersen et al., 2005) and stabilizes severely demented patients with DAT (Black et al., 2007). No distinctive subpopulations (age, gender, APOE genotype) of patients have been identified that show greater benefit with ChEIs than others. Many of the trials evaluating ADL, caregiver burden, and patient behavior were either not randomized or were uncontrolled.

To repeat, the actual benefits, duration (anywhere from six months to five years) of meaningful improvement or clinical stability of these drugs, even when started early, and their effects on severely demented patients, remain to be firmly established (Blennow et al., 2006; Corey-Bloom et al., 2006; Cummings, 2004). Whatever their effect, most studies are in agreement that any benefit wanes over time. Our bias nonetheless is to encourage their use when finances are not a significant issue.

Three approved ChEIs are currently available: donepezil, rivastigmine, and galantamine. They differ in their structure, mode (competitive or noncompetitive), and specificity (CNS vs. GI) of inhibition, metabolism, half-life, and duration of action.

All are indicated for mild-to-moderate DAT. Only donepezil is FDA approved for severe DAT. All three have pretty much the same efficacy. Nevertheless, in the event of clear non-efficacy (worsening) or of side effects, switching from one ChEI to another is a reasonable strategy and can be done without a washout period for those who have not responded to the first ChEI, or with a washout period of five to seven days for those who had significant side effects on the first ChEI. Donepezil 10 mg/day and galantamine extended release (ER) 16 mg/day, are, for example, equivalent.

Having hopefully established realistic expectations for treatment benefits and side effects, there are two approaches to long-term continuation:

- Continue therapy until the patient's quality of life is too impaired to justify the potential benefit or financial cost.
- Continue as long as function appears to be stabilized. If cognition declines, reduce the dose of the ChEI and observe for accelerating deterioration. If yes, restart ChEI. If discontinuing treatment has no effect, ChEI can be stopped (Green, 2005).

Words of caution regarding "stabilization": as if there were no other management conundrums, caregivers and clinicians must be circumspect and take into account length of observation period before concluding that any given treatment is ineffective. As previously discussed in the Clinical Manifestations section, cognitive and behavioral deterioration tend to accelerate over time, but there is considerable variation in rate of change both among patients and within individuals even in the absence of intercurrent illnesses, drug side effects, environmental effects, etc. Reports from caregivers of "good days" (or even weeks) and "bad days" for mildly or moderately demented patients are not unusual. Reliability of reported change increases in proportion to the length of the observation. This underlies the importance of developing and accessing reliable surrogate endpoints (Cummings et al., 2008).

Practically, the main differences among the ChEIs are in their titration schedule and dosing regimen (Corey-Bloom et al., 2006), and, to a certain extent, their tendency to cause adverse effects. Administration is summarized in Table 1.5.

As with any drug, multiple side effects and drug interactions are possible. Overall, ChEIs are safe and well tolerated. Side effects generally are limited to gastrointestinal symptoms, in roughly this order of frequency: nausea, anorexia, dyspepsia, diarrhea, and vomiting. Uncommon side effects include insomnia, vivid dreams and nightmares, leg cramps, diaphoresis, headache, confusion, rarely seizures. The FDA has issued an alert concerning galantamine, for which there is a small risk of increased mortality (www.fda.gov/cder/drug/InfoSheets/HCP/galantamineHCP.htm).

Donepezil should be used with caution in patients with significant liver or renal disease; it may adversely interact with paroxetine (Dooley & Lamb, 2000), and can worsen patients with frontotemporal dementia (if AD diagnosis is incorrect)

Table 1.5 Prescription of cholinesterase inhibitors

	Donepezil (Aricept®)	Rivastigmine (Exelon®)	Galantamine (Razadyne®) IR	Galantamine (Razadyne®) ER
Doses per day	1	2	2	1
How supplied	5 mg, 10 mg, 23 mg tablets. (5 & 10 mg oral disintegrating tablets available)	1.5 mg, 3 mg, 4.5 mg, 6 mg tablets. Also available as patch 4.6 mg/24 hr, 9.5 mg/24hr	4 mg, 8 mg, 12 mg tablets	8 mg, 16 mg, 24 mg capsules
Initial daily dose/ titration schedule	5 mg per day HS or AM/Increase to 10 mg after one month (23 mg for select patients with severe AD after 3 months on 10 mg)	1.5 mg B.I.D./Increase each dose by 1.5 mg every month 4.6 mg/24hr to 9.5 mg/24hr after 1 month	4 mg BID/Increase each dose by 4 mg every month	8 mg AM/Increase by 8 mg every month
Recommended daily dose	10 mg per day, HS or AM	6 mg B.I.D.	12 mg B.I.D.	24 mg AM
Take with food	Unnecessary	Yes	Yes	Yes

HS = bedtime

(Mendez et al., 2007). Usually taken at bedtime, morning administration is indicated for patients experiencing nightmares or insomnia. In our experience, gastrointestinal intolerance is most likely with oral rivastigmine but we have nevertheless successfully switched some patients intolerant to donepezil or galantamine to rivastigmine. Rivastigmine differs somewhat from the other ChEIs in that its metabolism does not require the cytochrome P450 system; theoretically this means less possibility of drug interactions. A rivastigmine trans-dermal patch, which may improve treatment efficacy and compliance, is commercially available (Cummings, Lefevre et al., 2007). Galantamine ER 24 mg might confer additional benefits (over, for example, donepezil 10 mg/day), if tolerated.

NMDA receptor antagonism

The rationale for using NMDA receptor antagonists rests on the theory that "excitotoxicity" plays a pathogenetic role in AD. Glutamate, a major excitatory neurotransmitter, acts on the NMDA receptor. Sustained NMDA stimulation, possibly resulting from NMDA receptor/Aβ interaction (Mattson & Rychlik, 1990), leads to prolonged calcium ion influx which can then trigger a cascade of neuronal injury and death. NMDA antagonism theoretically blocks low, tonic levels of glutamate-mediated excitation ("noise") while still allowing at least some normal NMDA responses ("signal").

Memantine is a low affinity NMDA receptor antagonist. It is approved for mild and late stage DAT. The biological basis for its therapeutic effect is not well understood. Large-scale, double-blind, six-month placebo-controlled trials of memantine in patients with moderate-to-severe dementia (Wilcock et al., 2002; Winblad & Poritis, 1999) and moderate-to-severe DAT (Reisberg et al., 2003) have demonstrated significant but modest improvements in cognition, but its effects on ADL have been inconsistent.

Memantine has a long history of extensive use in Europe and has been available in the United States since 2004. It has no significant drug interactions and improves patients with moderate-to-severe DAT who are already on a stable donepezil dose (Tariot et al., 2004). It can be taken with or without food and, in clinical trials, was not associated with any greater discontinuation of drug or any more side effects than seen in the placebo arms. Among patients who stop memantine because of side effects, the most common are headache, confusion, dizziness, and hallucinations, although these tend to dissipate with continued treatment. Recommended initial dosage is 5 mg per day, then increase the dose by 5 mg increments at least one week apart to the target dose of 10 mg B.I.D. Memantine is clinically used in conjunction with ChEIs besides donepezil.

Numerous other transmitter modulators are either in clinical or pre-clinical development, some already with discouraging results (Chappell et al., 2007; Jacobsen et al., 2005). Each is anticipated similarly to provide more symptomatic than disease-modifying effect.

Disease-modifying treatment (DMT)

The most fruitful areas for pharmacological treatment concern compounds that prevent AD in cognitively normal persons, or slow the progression of mild cases, such as those with MCI. Despite a wealth of epidemiological evidence about drugs or lifestyle interventions that might be helpful, the trials necessary to demonstrate clear efficacy are arduous and expensive. This is a rapidly moving field, but no treatments currently are available that either unequivocally protect normal individuals against developing AD or significantly slow the degenerative process. All agents discussed in this section are still in the investigative stage.

DMT is an attempt either to translate the advances in the molecular pathogenesis of AD into therapeutic strategies or to develop pharmacological treatments based on epidemiology. The former is represented mostly by drugs aimed at preventing and/or reducing accumulated brain $A\beta$ or tau, the latter essentially by putatively neuroprotective agents. The success of most of these agents depends ultimately on the extent to which the amyloid cascade hypothesis is correct and whether transgenic mouse models are suitable in vivo surrogates for AD. Keep in mind that treatments successful in markedly reducing brain $A\beta$ burden in murine models do not necessarily improve cognitive function in patients with DAT or MCI (Blennow et al., 2006). Other review articles relating to DMT are available (Davis et al., 2008; Doody, 2008; Duara et al., 2009; Salloway et al., 2008), as are summaries of ongoing and completed phase II and III trials (Sabbagh, 2009; Schneider & Sano, 2009).

Neuroprotection

So far, neuroprotective approaches, as reflected in multiple primary prevention studies, have been disappointing (Kaye, 2009). Following is a brief discussion of those that have generated most interest.

1 Anti-inflammatory drugs. This strategy is based on observations that AD plaques are routinely accompanied by inflammatory changes (McGeer & McGeer, 1995), on increasing evidence that CNS inflammation may precede or even promote the development of neuritic plaques (NPs) and neurofibrillary tangles (NFTs) (Rosenberg, 2005; Tan et al., 2007), and on animal (van Groen & Kadish, 2005) and epidemiological studies indicating reduced incidence of AD in chronic users of nonsteroidal anti-inflammatory drugs (NSAIDS) (in 't Veld et al., 2001; Szekely et al., 2004). In animals, ibuprofen reduces microglial activation and production of $A\beta_{42}$ peptides (Lim et al., 1999), suggesting an effect at an early stage of plaque development. These drugs may safely promote a shift from $A\beta_{42}$ to less toxic $A\beta_{40}$ production (Weggen et al., 2001).

   Clinical trials with rofecoxib and naproxen and with prednisone, however, have either not substantiated significant amelioration of cognitive decline (Aisen et al.,

2000; Aisen et al., 2003), or were hampered by unacceptable gastrointestinal or cardiac toxicity (Burns et al., 2006) due to their inhibition of cyclooxygenase 1 (COX 1).

A large multicenter primary prevention trial testing the efficacy and safety of naproxen and celecoxib for the primary prevention of DAT, the ADAPT study (Martin et al., 2002), was suspended due to cardiovascular safety concerns. Primary analyses have now shown no effect on the incidence of milder cognitive syndromes and an inconclusive trend toward *increased* DAT incidence with either NSAID (Group et al., 2007). One explanation for inefficacy in all trials is that NSAID consumption was tardy with respect to the putative inflammatory mechanisms. It is possible that NSAIDs may, in fact, be effective but only when taken many years before onset of symptoms, particularly for those who have one or both ApoE ε4 alleles (Hayden et al., 2007). Another reason for failure is that naproxen and celecoxib do not lower $A\beta_{42}$ production; the wrong drugs may have been chosen! Mechanisms other than their anti-inflammatory properties may explain their still-possible neuroprotective effect. With few exceptions, clinical evidence currently does not support routine prescription of anti-inflammatory agents for the prevention and treatment of DAT. Continued masked follow-up of the ADAPT cohort is necessary.

2 Antioxidants. There is evidence that oxidative damage may be the earliest event in the pathogenesis of AD (Nunomura et al., 2001). Free radicals, the byproducts of metabolic processes such as oxidative metabolism, may accumulate, leading to excessive lipid peroxidation, nitration, and free carbonyls (Pratico et al., 2002). Observational and case-control studies suggest that supplemental intake of antioxidants such as vitamins E and C, or MAO inhibitors, can reduce risk, that is, act as neuroprotectors (Zandi et al., 2004). Most supplement studies have focused on vitamin E. Sano et al. (1997) conducted a large, randomized placebo-controlled study of large dose vitamin E and the MAO inhibitor selegiline. Neither drug yielded cognitive improvement over two years, although all treated groups, after statistical adjustment to equate initial severity of dementia, showed less decline on an ADL scale when compared with placebo. More vitamin E patients suffered falls.

Other trials have shown no effect of supplemental vitamin E either on delay of symptoms or rate of progression in MCI (Petersen et al., 2005), and increased mortality with this and other antioxidants (Bjelakovic et al., 2007).

There is now little to support vitamin E as either prevention or therapy of DAT although some authors believe that the *form* of vitamin E is as important as the dose, that further studies are justified (Dunn et al., 2007), and, as with the NSAIDs, results of an adequate (i.e., early-enough) prevention trial could be very different from the results of a treatment trial.

Ginkgo biloba, available widely as an "herbal supplement" is also believed to act as an antioxidant. Again, the data are mixed. Some studies have shown modest cognitive improvement in patients with DAT (Le Bars et al., 1997), but it is likely ineffective (DeKosky et al., 2008; Doody et al., 2001). Questions regarding this treatment, and, more importantly, the stucture and design of all primary preven-tion trials, nevertheless remain (Kaye, 2009).

Curcumin, a component of tumeric, has antioxidant and anti-inflammatory properties and inhibits formation of amyloid fibrils in vitro (Kennedy et al., 2007).

As of this writing, evidence is insufficient to recommend antioxidants as treatment for or prevention of AD and there are warrants against it (Burns et al., 2006).

3 Hormonal treatment (HRT). Estrogen and testosterone therapy have both been advocated for prevention and treatment of DAT on the basis of epidemiological studies. Here again the data are inconsistent (Burns et al., 2006). Although one small study showed possible benefit for young, fertile women (Henderson et al., 2005), several controlled estrogen trials with both normal and cognitively impaired post-menopausal women, with and without progesterone, have shown either no benefit, increased risk of dementia, or worsening of dementia (Henderson et al., 2000; Mulnard et al., 2000; Shumaker et al., 2003). There is evidence that age-related increase in leutenizing hormone (LH) "may be a fundamental instiga-tor responsible for the aberrant reactivation of the cell cycle that is seen in AD" (Casadesus et al., 2006). This has prompted clinical trials with leuprolide acetate, a gonadotropin-releasing hormone agonist that lowers LH levels (Casadesus et al., 2006; Christensen, 2007). The preponderance of the evidence at present indicates that estrogen therapy is ineffective and should not be used.

Testosterone levels and cognition seem to be correlated in healthy older men (Yaffe et al., 2002). The benefits of testosterone supplementation for prevention or treatment of MCI and DAT are at present not clear. Some studies have shown no change, others, modest but measurable improvements in quality of life, if not cognition (Lu et al., 2006). Future trials may yet indicate testosterone treatment for DAT, but as of now this also cannot be recommended unless there are other indications for treatment.

4 Statins. Statins (HMG-CoA reductase inhibitors) are effective treatments, among those that tolerate them, of hyperlipidemia and are effective for the prevention of stroke and heart disease. Some case-control epidemiological studies have sug-gested that statins, at least some of them, may reduce the risk of developing DAT (Green et al., 2006; Rockwood et al., 2002; Wolozin, 2004; Wolozin et al., 2000), independently of their cholesterol-lowering property. Atorvastatin (80 mg/day) slowed rate of cognitive decline but did not affect other outcome measures in a recent one-year study of patients with mild to moderate DAT (Sparks et al., 2005). Activation of the α-secretase pathway, inhibition of tau phophrylation, and mod-eration of inflammatory cascades have been proposed as mechanisms (Kennedy et al., 2007; Li et al., 2007). More recent prospective trials have not supported significant risk reduction, or changes in plasma or CSF $A\beta_{42}$ (Arvanitakis et al., 2008; Hoglund et al., 2005; Zandi et al., 2005). As with the NSAIDs, early treat-ment, before significant neuronal degeneration has occurred, may abate one or

more pathological processes leading to clinical AD (Li et al., 2007). Additional long-term trials are in progress.

5 Diet. There is increasing evidence that "healthy" eating, e.g., Mediterranean diets (Scarmeas et al., 2006; Scarmeas, Stern et al., 2009; Solfrizzi et al., 2006), any diet high in omega-3 fatty acids, or even calorie restriction (Qin, Chachich et al., 2006) reduces risk of all types of dementia, and may even reduce mortality in AD (Scarmeas et al., 2007). Multiple possible mechanisms are possible, including antioxidant effects. Additional nutritional studies are ongoing. Diet and other risk-factor modification seems, not surprisingly, a promising avenue of primary prevention at least for dementia, if not specifically for AD (Middleton & Yaffe, 2009).

6 Other investigational DMTs. An enormous number of strategies are under investigation for their potential as treatment or preventive agents in persons with or at risk for AD. Drugs have included opiate antagonists, GM_1 ganglioside, clonidine, thiamine, somatostatin replacement, and guanfacine. All have proven disappointing. Nerve growth factor treatment is promising but it does not cross the blood–brain barrier, so an effective, non-invasive delivery system is an important issue (Christensen, 2007).

Treatments directed at amyloid and tau

The likely role of Aβ and tau in the pathogenesis of AD has led to many novel therapeutic strategies targeting the mechanisms of plaque and tangle formation. Some of the most promising therapies are those designed to alter the production, deposition, or clearance of Aβ. These include the APP β and γ secretase inhibitors, Aβ vaccine, selective Aβ lowering and anti-aggregation agents, and drugs directed at tau protein. The hope is that one or more of these compounds will slow or stop the neurodegeneration characteristic of DAT.

Aβ immunotherapy

Active immunization of older transgenic mice with aggregated $A\beta_{42}$ both reduces amyloid plaque burden and improves function (Schenk et al., 1999). Multiple studies have suggested several possible mechanisms for these effects (Klafki et al., 2006; Walker et al., 2005). These comprised the rationale for trials with the Aβ vaccine AN1792. A phase II trial was halted because 18 of 300 patients developed meningoencephalitis. T-cell attack on the C-terminal of the Aβ peptide (Nicoll et al., 2003; Schenk et al., 2004) and polysorbate supplementation of the vaccine (Gilman et al., 2005) may have been responsible. Autopsies on several study participants suggested reduced neocortical Aβ plaque and dystrophic neurite burden, but no change in NFT concentration or amyloid angiopathy (Bombois et al., 2007; Klafki et al., 2006).

About 20% of patients mounted an antibody response. In general, differences in cognition or functional ability were not great between antibody responders and nonresponders, but response correlated with improvement on some memory subscales, and mean total CSF tau concentration was lower in responders than in the placebo group. Conversely, responders with high antibody titers showed whole-brain volume reduction and ventricular enlargement compared to nonresponders and those with less robust antibody production (Koepsell et al., 2007), although these effects did not correlate with cognitive decline (Gilman et al., 2005). A recent animal study raises further concern that $A\beta_{42}$ immunization increases vascular amyloid and microhemorrhages (Wilcock et al., 2007).

The upshot is that results have been encouraging enough to warrant additional studies, including trials of $A\beta$ immunoconjugates composed of its N-terminal part in the hope of producing a more specific antibody response (Schenk et al., 2004).

Passive immunotherapy, which bypasses the need for active antibody formation, is also under evaluation. This approach may be more beneficial for older patients, whose immune response is relatively impaired. Anti-$A\beta$ fragments to APP, monoclonal antibodies, and human intravenous immunoglobulin in several trials have all shown promise and reasonable safety and are in various stages of development (Kennedy et al., 2007; Klafki et al., 2006). Most interest is now focused on the humanized monoclonal antibody bapineuzumab. A phase II trial has not shown efficacy in primary outcomes (Salloway et al., 2009). We and others are in the midst of a large phase III trial (ICARA). The human immune system likely represents significant untapped potential in the treatment of DAT (Mohajeri, 2007).

Secretase modulators

Elucidation of the roles of APP α-, β-, and γ-secretases in the pathogenesis of AD has spurred development of agents targeting them as therapeutic substrates. The goal is either to augment α-secretase or to inhibit β- and γ-secretase activity, safely.

The promise of anti-β-secretase treatment derives from the observation that BACE1 (β-secretase converting enzyme) knock-out transgenic mice produce only very small amounts of $A\beta$ yet have no apparent behavioral or cognitive impairments (Roberds et al., 2001). The difficulties with β-secretase inhibitors are that they are large molecules that do not cross the blood–brain barrier and the relationship between their activity and $A\beta$ formation is nonlinear. The first difficulty has encouraged synthesis of so-called "natural binding partners," such as reticulons, that would allow β-secretase inhibition in vivo. Reticulons negatively modulate BACE1, decreasing both $A\beta_{42}$ and $A\beta_{40}$ secretion in a dose-dependent manner without changing their intracellular ratio (Bornebroek & Kumar-Singh, 2004). However, BACE1 inhibition may as well disrupt peripheral nerve function (Willem et al., 2006). As with many of the other investigational agents, additional preclinical studies are necessary (Skovronsky & Lee, 2000).

Stimulating α-secretase activity in the hope of shifting APP processing toward the non-amyloidogenic pathway (see *Pathogenesis* section) is another approach. Clinical development of this type of drug has also proven difficult because of concern that α-secretase might also increase peripheral $A\beta_{42}$, which can then be taken into the brain via receptor-mediated uptake from the vascular compartment (Bornebroek & Kumar-Singh, 2004). Clinical trials are nevertheless underway with several agents. The anticancer drug, bryostatin, a protein kinase C activator, enhances α-secretase activity and reduces $A\beta_{42}$ concentration in transgenic mice (Blennow et al., 2006; Etcheberrigaray et al., 2004).

Finally, the search is on for safe and effective γ-secretase inhibitors. Animal studies have demonstrated that they lower CSF $A\beta_{42}$, and that this reflects lowering of brain oligomeric Aβ (Barten et al., 2005). Phase I and II testing of mild to moderate AD patients with the drug LY450139 has so far been disappointing. CSF Aβ dropped in both active drug and placebo patients but cognitive effects were not impressive (Siemers et al., 2006). Safety is also an issue because γ-secretase inhibitors are nonspecific. In addition to blocking APP processing, they also block physiologically essential substrates, notably the Notch signaling protein, which modulates many cellular functions including proliferation of T cells and gastrointestinal goblet cells (Christensen, 2007; Gandy, 2005; Kennedy et al., 2007). A multicenter phase III study (the IDENTITY study) to demonstrate safety, CNS specificity, and efficacy is ongoing. This drug class nevertheless remains an attractive therapeutic strategy.

Selective Aβ lowering agents

Another means of modifying the disease process, if not to interfere with AD pathogenesis, involves selective $A\beta_{42}$ lowering agents (SALAs). These drugs lessen $A\beta_{42}$ production by allosterically altering the active core of γ-secretase, "in essence moving the site of action on APP to produce shorter, less toxic Aβ fragments" (Kennedy et al., 2007). These drugs do not *inhibit* γ-secretase, therefore do not interfere with essential substrates such as Notch.

Tarenflurbil (Flurizan®), the pure R-enantiomer of flurbiprofen, was the first SALA to enter clinical trials. It has no significant COX I or II activity and is therefore virtually devoid of gastrointestinal side effects. It reduces plaque burden and preserves learning and normal behavior in Alzheimer transgenic mice and lowers $A\beta_{42}$ levels in human cell lines. In a phase II trial, a subgroup of patients with mild AD (MMSE 20–26) declined more slowly in ADL and global function, and showed a trend toward cognitive improvement in those treated with a higher dose (800 mg twice daily). The patents with the highest R-flurbiprofen levels deteriorated least (Christensen, 2007; Kennedy et al., 2007).

In yet another demonstration of the necessity of circumspection when extending results of animal trials to humans, however, final results of a very large and well-conducted phase III trial of tarenflurbil on patients with mild DAT confirmed inefficacy – at any drug dose – on either cognitive or ADL primary endpoints (Green et al., 2009).

The disappointment with tarenflurbil hopefully will be tempered by results of an ongoing phase III study of docosahexaenoic acid (DHA), a deriviative of fish oil, which itself has been the subject of multiple investigational trials (Cunnane et al., 2009). Low plasma DHA levels are clearly associated with cognitive decline in elders, although its association with AD specifically is less robust (Cunnane et al., 2009; Schaefer et al., 2006). In various animal models and using a variety of experimental protocols, DHA exerts a protective effect against neuropathological signs of AD, including Aβ accumulation, synaptic marker loss, and hyperphosphorylation of tau. It appears also to have anti-inflammatory activity and may reduce oxidative stress.

Anti-Aβ aggregation agents

Aβ-derived diffusible ligands (small oligomers) are likely just as toxic as deposited Aβ, if not more so (Lambert et al., 1998; Walsh & Selkoe, 2004) and are associated with very early cognitive impairments (Lacor et al., 2004). There is increasing evidence that, if the amyloid hypothesis is at all correct, brain damage occurs well before plaque formation (Gandy et al., 2007; Kaye et al., 2007). Preventing aggregation of Aβ fibrils into plaques, or enhancing clearance of soluble Aβ, is another anti-amyloid treatment in development and has shown modest promise. Strategies include small molecule inhibition, glycosaminoglycan mimetics, proline-rich polypeptides, and copper chelators.

Small peptides can interfere with the conformational change of soluble Aβ to β-sheet structure but in general lack sufficient steric bulk to prevent interactions between larger peptides. Small peptides can, however, bind with larger "chaperone" molecules which can still bind with Aβ and increase their anti-aggregation power (Gestwicki et al., 2004; Kelly, 2005). They have been the subject mostly of animal studies.

An exception is dimebolin hydrochloride (latrepirdine) (Dimebon), an orally active small molecule originally marketed in Russia as a nonspecific antihistamine. Dimebon appears to act through a variety of mechanisms, including neuroprotection, anti-amyloid, serotonergic, adrenergic and NMDA receptor blockade, mitochondrial permeability, and inhibition of butyrylcholinesterase and acetylcholinesterase (Bachurin et al., 2001). On the basis of several studies showing improvement in several outcome measures in AD patients (Doody et al., 2008), Dimebon was the subject of an ongoing phase III efficacy and safety study (CONCERT) (Hung, 2008) that was recently suspended due to lack of efficacy (March 2010).

Sulfated glycosaminoglycan (GAG) binds to Aβ and allows polymerization into amyloid plaques. GAG mimetics compete for GAG binding sites, hinders fibril formation, and may reduce soluble Aβ. Preclinical studies with tramiprosate (3-amino-1-propanesulfonic acid [3APS]; Alzhemed®), a GAG mimetic competing for Aβ binding sites, reduced plaque burden in animals but yielded no clear cognitive or behavioral improvements. In phase II trials 3APS significantly lowered CSF Aβ although there were no significant clinical effects after three months (Aisen et al., 2004; Aisen et al., 2006). A phase III trial showed no effect compared with placebo (Sabbagh, 2009) and development of the drug was discontinued.

Colostrinin (O-CLN), another Aβ anti-aggregant, is a proline-rich polypeptide complex (PRP) from sheep pre-milk colostrum. Colostrinin and other PRPs are cytokine-like molecules that induce interferon gamma, regulate the secretion of cytokines, and inhibit nitric oxide and apoptosis in cell cultures (Bacsi et al., 2007; Leszek et al., 2002; Zablocka et al., 2005).) Limited (phase I and II) testing with several doses so far indicates reasonably good tolerance with modest but unsustained cognitive improvement.

Putative DMTs

Pioglitazone and peroxisome proliferators-activated receptor-gamma (PPAR-gamma) antagonists, are prescribed for type II diabetes although safety issues are a significant concern (Home et al., 2007). They reduce $A\beta$, plaque deposition, and microglial-mediated inflammation in transgenic mice. Phase II studies of several daily doses administered to mild–moderate AD patients over six months discerned no differences in cognition or global function between active drug and placebo groups. However, ApoE ε4 negative patients receiving rosiglitazone 8 mg per day showed significant improvement in cognitive testing scores whereas ApoE ε4 carriers did not improve and some even declined (Risner et al., 2006). Pioglitazone trials in animals have yet to suggest any utility. More studies are needed.

Metal chelators have been used previously for the treatment of AD with findings of interest (Crapper McLachlan et al., 1991). Clioquinol (PBT-1), a quinolone antibacterial and antifungal agent, interferes with copper and zinc homeostasis. Copper is enriched in amyloid plaque and is bound by APP. Clioquinol apparently reduces extracellular copper availability, interrupting $A\beta_{42}$ production and facilitating the clearance of soluble $A\beta$. A phase II trial showed marginal cognitive improvements in moderately severe AD patients (Ritchie et al., 2003) but further clinical trials have been halted because of toxic impurities during production. Clinical trials with a similar drug (PBT-2) are in progress (Blennow et al., 2006). In general, side effects associated with metal chelators prohibit their widespread use.

Lithium and valproate, drugs not particularly useful for neuropsychiatric symptoms of DAT (Sink et al., 2005), have been investigated as disease-modifying agents in preclinical studies. Lithium limits formation of hyperphosphorylated tau by inhibiting glycogen synthase kinase-3 (GSK-3β) (Iqbal et al., 2005; Noble et al., 2005). Inhibition of a single kinase is probably insufficient to reverse tau hyperphosphorylation since this process is regulated by the balance between multiple kinases and phosphates (Blennow et al., 2006). Both lithium and valproate modify $A\beta$ processing (Su et al., 2004) and tau hyperphosphorylation can also be limited by their increasing the activity of phosphatases such as protein phosphatase 2A (Bornebroek & Kumar-Singh, 2004). Limited clinical studies of both drugs have yet to yield particularly promising results.

On the horizon is the isolation and restoration of enzymes, likely deficient in Alzheimer brains, that degrade $A\beta$ (Press & Alexander, 2007; Yamin et al., 2007). Table 1 in the article by Jacobsen et al. summarizes many of the studies currently underway with these and other drugs (Jacobsen et al., 2005). Many promising drugs other than those specifically discussed above are in clinical development.

Pharmacotherapy for behavioral problems

Cholinesterase inhibitors
For most patients with access to adequate health care, ChEIs are not the initial drugs of choice for behavioral symptoms since they likely have already been prescribed for cognitive deterioration. Several studies nonetheless indicate that ChEIs may improve or delay onset of neuropsychiatric symptoms for patients with mild AD (Gauthier & Touchon, 2005; Suh et al., 2004; Terry & Buccafusco, 2003; Trinh et al., 2003). Effects generally are modest (Ballard et al., 2005). If cost is not an issue, a trial is not unreasonable. The same assertions are valid for memantine (Ballard et al., 2005; Cummings et al., 2008; Cummings et al., 2006).

Antipsychotic drugs
As the incidence of disruptive behaviors increases with disease progression, so does prescription of antipsychotic drugs, which are administered to at least 25% of nursing home patients, the majority of whom are demented (Katz et al., 1992). Pharmacological treatment of neuropsychiatric disorders is expensive, accounting for about 30% of the direct costs of caring for AD patients (Beeri et al., 2002).

It is now generally agreed, if not universally practiced, that older ("typical") antipsychotics (butyrophenones, phenothiazines) should be avoided. These agents are more likely than other adjunctive drugs to cause side effects (Lee et al., 2004), representing for many patients and caregivers a cure worse than the disease. Side effects, in part dependent on the specific drug, include sometimes irreversible parkinsonism, acute and tardive dyskinesias, dystonias, sedation, orthostasis, gait disturbance, weight gain, and falling. Worsened agitation, cognition, and confusion are also particularly common, even at low doses, for neuroleptics with anticholinergic properties.

Are they effective? Differences in methodologies and quality among the few controlled studies of these drugs account for variable conclusions. For example, one controlled study indicated that haloperidol, especially at higher doses, reduces agitation (Devanand et al., 1998), another demonstrated amelioration of both agitation and aggression (Allain et al., 2000), and another clearly showed improvement in psychosis (albeit at a cost of increased "anergy") (Tariot et al., 2006). A Cochrane review, however, concluded that haloperidol might alleviate aggression but not agitation or other neuropsychiatric symptoms (Lonergan et al., 2002). Studies with other typical antipsychotics have likewise indicated improvements in some but not other disruptive behaviors, but practically all have also shown that side effects are a significant cost of any improvement, and there is no conclusive evidence that any one of these drugs is better than the others (Sink et al., 2005; Teri et al., 2000).

The fact, however, is that symptoms such as pervasive shadowing, aggression, and persistent yelling are very stressful to caregivers and usually so resistant to other strategies (pharmacological and nonpharmacological) that antipsychotic drugs may

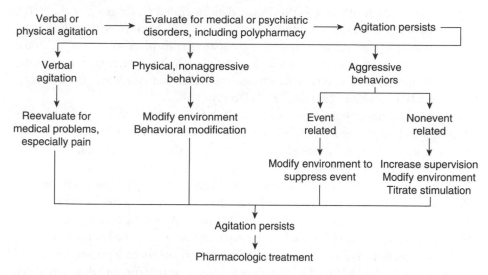

Figure 1.6 Diagnosis and treatment of agitation in the demented elderly
Source: Modified from Green, R.C. (2005). *Diagnosis and management of Alzheimer's disease and other dementias* (2nd edn.). Caddo, OK: Professional Communications, Inc., by permission

represent the only alternative, and we use them judiciously. As is the case with any other treatment, risk/benefit analysis is essential. Analysis requires data. Whether the patient is living in the community or in an institution, there is no substitute for collecting a careful history of the behavioral symptoms prior to formulating treatment (Figure 1.6). Determine, whenever possible, whether:

- the caregiver's complaint truly reflects the patient's behavior;
- the behavior in question is an isolated occurrence or a frequent event;
- some fundamental feature of the patient's environment or health has changed;
- the behavior represents a danger to the patient or to those caring for the patient.

For patients who are unable to communicate adequately, the clinician should specifically consider coincident medical conditions causing increased confusion or pain, particularly occult infections, constipation, hunger, or discomfort from falls.

"Atypical" neuroleptics are the current agents of choice for severe disruptive behaviors and are widely used although they are not FDA-approved for use in demented patients. Particularly when patient behavior is dangerous to him/herself or to others, a trial is reasonable once risks and limited expectations are discussed with family or other caregivers.

Does efficacy override a drug's known side effects? Again, quality of trials and conflicting results are issues. The atypicals (risperidone, quetiapine, olanzapine, clozapine, aripiprazole, ziprasidone) are in general perceived as better tolerated than older neuroleptics and a recent cohort study suggests that cognitive deterioration may not be as much of a risk as previously demonstrated (Livingston et al., 2007). Studies have shown modest reduction in psychotic behaviors with risperidone, aripiprazole, quetiapine, and olanzapine compared with placebo (Lee et al., 2004; Schneider et al., 2006; Sink et al., 2005). Experts vary in their preferences for specific drugs. On the basis of several small trials, the American Academy of Neurology recommends atypicals at *guideline* level (Doody et al., 2001).

Atypicals are nevertheless far from problem-free and for many patients, risks ultimately outweigh their possible benefits. Potential adverse effects are multiple, common, and in general dose-related (Lee et al., 2004; Sink et al., 2005). Table 3 from Schneider et al. (2006) summarizes side effects associated with three commonly prescribed atypicals. Quetiapine is less likely to cause parkinsonism than the others and for this reason is the favored agent for many practitioners, but inconsistent efficacy is likewise an issue (Tariot et al., 2006). A principal side effect of the atypical neuroleptics is sedation, but this may in some cases be useful in treating nighttime agitation. We avoid using clozapine because of its epileptic potential and the risk of agranulocytosis, which requires frequent monitoring of white blood cell counts.

Like typical antipsychotics, atypicals are associated with increased mortality (Ellul et al., 2007; Schneider et al., 2005) on account of which they are under an advisory by the FDA. Several but not all studies report increased risk of stroke (Brodaty et al., 2003; Sink et al., 2005). In the aggregate, trials so far suggest that for a majority of patients with DAT, there is no significant clinical benefit from atypical antipsychotics compared with placebo and that side effects limit their overall effectiveness (Ballard et al., 2005; Kurlan et al., 2007; Schneider, 2007; Schneider et al., 2005; Schneider et al., 2006; Sink et al., 2005).

Antipsychotic drugs are clearly effective, however, for some patients. If these drugs are prescribed and are salutary, the goal is short-term treatment with the lowest possible dose and their indication should frequently be reassessed. No response after two to four weeks is an indication for discontinuing treatment or switching to another drug. In the absence of greatly effective DMT, clinicians quite rightly desire adjunctive drugs that reliably alleviate psychotic behavior with minimal side effects. No such "magic pills" are currently available (Sink et al., 2005).

Antidepressants

As previously noted, depression is common in the elderly, it coexists or is part and parcel of many dementing diseases in which it may have "atypical" features, and it may initially be the salient symptom of AD. If depression is evident clinically, pharmacotherapy is often effective. SSRIs are generally safe, even in older persons, and can be quite effective for elevating or stabilizing depressed or labile mood. It is often helpful to initiate antidepressant treatment in the face of fragmentary symptoms of depression even if the full syndrome is not present. We initiate these drugs at the lowest starting dosage recommended (or lower) and gradually increase to a typical, but low, antidepressant dosage. For example, we often start a patient on sertraline

12.5 mg daily, very gradually increasing to 50 mg daily, and if necessary, increasing further to 100 mg per day. Citalopram, escitalopram, and duloxetine are reasonable alternatives. Some practitioners regard agitation and aggressiveness as surrogate behaviors for underlying depression, but with the possible exception of citalopram, these drugs have not shown particular efficacy against neuropyschiatric symptoms other than relatively clear-cut depression (Sink et al., 2005).

We have had success with trazodone for the treatment of agitation, particularly if sleep problems are involved although one controlled study failed to demonstrate its efficacy (Teri et al., 2000). We typically begin with a low dose of 50 mg at bedtime and increase slowly, up to 100 mg b.i.d. We add the morning dose only to impact daytime agitation, and if the problem is largely restricted to nighttime, increase only the evening dose. Trazodone can in most cases be combined safely with other SSRIs.

All of these medications have potential side effects, including gastrointestinal distress, sexual dysfunction, sedation, and orthostasis. While generally well tolerated, for some patients antidepressants are not necessarily safer than neuroleptics (Rabins & Lyketsos, 2005; Schneider, 2007).

We avoid tricyclics and paroxetine because of their anticholinergic properties, and fluoxetine because of its long half-life and many drug interactions. Venlafaxine, mirtazapine, and bupropion may also be useful but information regarding their efficacy and safety in DAT is scant, and they may interfere with sleep.

Other drugs

Benzodiazepines, mood stabilizers (including antiepileptic drugs), beta-adrenergic blocking agents, and buspirone have all been used as adjuncts for neuropsychiatric symptoms. Valproate (long or short acting) is possibly useful for short-term use (Porsteinsson et al., 2001) and has been advocated in review articles (Corey-Bloom et al., 2006; Rabins & Lyketsos, 2005), but a contemporaneous review (Sink et al., 2005) and a comprehensive placebo-controlled trial in nursing home patients (Tariot et al., 2005) indicate that it is not effective. Evidence is insufficient to recommend carbamazepine, an enzyme-inducing drug that should be avoided whenever possible, as well as gabapentin, lamotrigine, and levetiracetam. Beta-blockers, particularly propranolol and pindolol, have also been used with some success to treat physical aggressiveness and motor restlessness in demented patients, but efficacy is less well documented and the risk of adverse effects makes these a less favorable choice (Peskind et al., 2005).

Opioids have been reported to control agitation (Manfredi et al., 2003; Sink et al., 2005), and melatonin for the treatment of sleep disruption (Singer et al., 2003). Some clinicians use benzodiazepines (e.g., short-acting lorazepam) for acute agitation. They may be useful for severely demented institutionalized patients. We typically avoid them as they are not only sedating but also can lower inhibitions, worsen gait, and add to confusion and agitation. Buspirone, in general better tolerated than benzodiazepines, may be useful for repetitive and stereotyped behaviors (Helvink & Holroyd, 2006).

Nonpharmacological treatment

Nonpharmacological strategies (Gray, 2004; Teri et al., 2002) should always be considered prior to using medication, but bear in mind that timing is an important issue. An important lesson of DAT management is that, practically, it's a very different disease at different stages and management approach must be tailored accordingly. Once the patient is dependent on the caregiver (if there is one), general recommendations for reducing the impact of cognitive impairment include: providing predictable routines; dressing patient in his/her own clothing; explaining procedures many times, in simple language; simplifying all tasks as much as possible and providing instructions for each step. For neuropsychiatric disorders, the following recommendations are often useful:

- determine precipitating factors;
- avoid environmental triggers;
- don't make significant changes to the environment (e.g., moving furniture);
- use distraction and redirection for problem situations;
- if possible, anticipate unmet needs.

Successful interventions are often symptom specific. Consider the stress associated with bathing demented people. There are several strategies one can employ, for example, using "person-centered bathing" (Corey-Bloom et al., 2006): provide sponge baths when the patient is strongly averse to bathing; raise room temperature and have towels ready in advance to create a warm environment; offer a favorite food after the bath; and play soothing background music that the patient likes. Whatever the symptoms, pharmacotherapy in general is unwarranted if the behavior is not disturbing to either the patient or the caregiver(s). When drugs are employed, nonpharmacological strategies should be continued.

Caregiver issues may be, as previously noted, depression, anxiety, loss of autonomy, and their own deteriorating health. Other common caregiver problems include unease over role reversal, helplessness, guilt about even considering nursing home placement, anger and frustration with the patient's ever increasing limitations, and concern about continuation or lack of sexual relationship (Cummings & Benson, 1992).

Typically, families look to their primary medical clinician to be their interpreter and referral source – someone to prioritize and guide them through the maze of issues they may be facing for the first time.

The often-frustrating management of DAT begins with an alliance between clinicians and family members and other caregivers responsible for the patient (Cummings, 2004). Some families are unprepared for a diagnosis of AD and may refuse offers of assistance, or may be unwilling to share their difficulties during an office interview. This reaction impedes the clinician's ability to get an accurate assessment of the patient's functional status and makes recommendations for supportive measures difficult. Most families and caregivers, however, are grateful for appropriate referrals to education and support services and the clinician's coordination of information with other medical specialists.

Caregivers should receive:

- An explanation of the diagnostic process and the disease itself, i.e., what to expect at each stage of the illness including possible behavioral symptoms and increasing levels of dependency.
- A general description of the prognosis and what to expect in terms of cognitive decline, possible behavioral symptoms, and increasing levels of dependency.
- An overview of available pharmacological treatments, including their medical benefits, financial costs, and possible side effects and a treatment recommendation.
- Referral to the local Alzheimer's Association for further education and caregiver support and introduction to educational materials.
- Information about local social workers, lawyers specializing in the management of elders with cognitive impairment, and home-based care services.
- Encouragement to caregivers to take care of their own emotional and health needs. Neglecting their own health reduces their ability to care for the patient and renders them more vulnerable to depression.

Family education and reducing caregiver burden

Nonpharmacological and supportive interventions are extremely important to patient management, if they can actually be executed. In most families, a spouse or adult child assumes the role of the primary caregiver, an unanticipated and demanding job that often continues even after nursing home placement. Almost 90% of caregivers interviewed in one study reported fatigue, anger, and depression as a consequence of caring for a demented family member (Rabins et al., 1982). Younger, less financially secure, and more poorly educated caregivers are at especial risk of depression (Covinsky et al., 2003). The majority of caregivers of patients are female family members who provide care informally, with little outside assistance, and without pay ("no salary, benefits, sick days, or vacations") (Cummings & Benson, 1992). Men are more likely to delegate duties and use professional services for both household and patient management (Corcoran, 1992). The needs of both the patient and the caregivers should at least be addressed, if not totally satisfied.

"Burden" refers to the extent to which caregivers perceive their emotional or physical health, social life, and financial status as suffering as a result of caring for their demented friend or relative. The level of caregiver burden is not directly related to the degree of patient impairment (Hadjistavropoulos et al., 1994). Availability of social support, caregiver finances, and coping are important co-determinants. Burden is lessened when other family members share in the caregiving and facilitate respite periods for the primary caregiver (Cummings & Benson, 1992).

Recommendations are easy enough to print, but, for an increasing number of involved individuals, difficult to execute. Evidence that education programs and community support services reduce caregiver perception of burden and depression, enhance well-being, and sometimes delay nursing home placement, is mixed. Examples of interventions include structured interactions between the caregiver(s) and an AD expert, short-term community occupational therapy (Graff et al., 2006), counseling, and intensive long-term education and support programs (Doody et al., 2001). Families who have had formal instruction in custodial care and recommendations for simple home modifications to encourage independent patient function may need less assistance within the home (Gitlin et al., 2005). Professional counseling in management of behavioral problems may also aid the caregiver (Guerriero Austrom et al., 2004; Mittelman et al., 2004), but pharmacotherapy, in itself problematic, usually also is necessary (Weiner et al., 2002).

These services are often effective for those with access to them, and should be offered. However, they are time consuming and for many families not readily available (Graff et al., 2006; Mittelman et al., 2006), particularly in underprivileged communities. It is not clear, for example, whether interventions that have been designed for primarily white populations attending AD specialist clinics are as effective for minority families who receive their care, if at all, mostly in a primary care setting, and who are more inclined to rely on extended networks of family and friends (Dilworth-Anderson, 2001; Green, 2005; Guerriero Austrom et al., 2006; White-Means & Thornton, 1990). Many minority individuals perceive even the screening process, during a regularly scheduled primary care visit, as harmful (Guerriero Austrom et al., 2006).

Specific issues

Safety   Almost any behavior can pose a risk to a demented individual. Examples of potentially dangerous events include leaving the house alone, wandering, dressing inappropriately for the cold, becoming lost, using a toaster or a stove improperly, and eating spoiled food. Even when the demented person can perform routine activities without difficulty, confusion may hamper his or her ability to respond appropriately to an unexpected or dangerous situation, such as an electrical problem in the home or a simple fall. Persons with cognitive impairment can easily become the victims of financial scams or be taken advantage of by unscrupulous family members. As the dementia worsens, the simplest, but sometimes most difficult, intervention is to increase direct supervision. A few key safeguards should always be considered:

- reducing fire hazards by putting timers on stoves and ovens;
- reducing medication errors by counting pills into pillboxes;
- ample lighting, locks on cabinets and ovens, unplugging dangerous appliances;
- reducing falls by adding handrails and changing loose rugs;
- reducing and stopping patient driving.

Incontinence   Along with disruptive behaviors, sleep disturbances, and withdrawal of a paid caregiver, incontinence is a major precipitator of institutionalization.

Urinary incontinence occurs in about half of ambulatory dementia patients and fecal incontinence is common among those with frequent urinary incontinence (Cummings & Benson, 1992). As with hallucinations and agitation, there are multiple noncognitive causes including fecal impaction, drugs, urinary tract infection, hyperglycemia, restricted mobility, and age-related and pathological (e.g., prostatism, surgical injury) changes in sphincter anatomy, all of which are potentially treatable. Cognitive causes are inability to recognize when they need to go to the bathroom, forgetting where the bathroom is, delusions, and visuospatial impairments (agnosia, defective contrast discrimination). Drugs that are often effective for nondemented patients (anticholinergics, α-adrenegic antagonists, baclofen, dantrolene, opioid antagonists) are sometimes useful but frequently worsen memory or exacerbate behavioral problems. Donepezil can cause urinary incontinence (Hashimoto et al., 2000) but all ChEIs may precipitate or exacerbate this problem.

Nonpharmacological methods, while time consuming and labor intensive, are usually more effective, at least in early to mid-stage disease. These include prompted voiding and scheduled toileting, wearing incontinence pads, reducing evening fluid intake, and external collection devices when possible. The Alzheimer's Association website (www.alz.org/living_with_alzheimers_personal_care.asp#3) has additional useful suggestions.

Wandering and pacing Walking provides several health benefits for demented persons: preventing the consequences of deconditioning and muscle weakness; reducing the risk of urinary tract infections and pneumonia; and encouraging an experience of independence. Wandering refers to "aimless or purposeful motor activity that leads to getting lost, leaving a safe environment or intruding in inappropriate places" (Cummings & Benson, 1992). It occurs in about one-third of community-dwelling dementia patients and 10% of nursing home residents. Risks are traffic accidents, assault, exposure, and falling. Wandering implies casual or random walking. Pacing is a more driven, nearly constant walking and generally is a more intrusive and troublesome behavior.

As with other aberrant behaviors, specific causes and treatments are usually elusive, but precipitants nevertheless should be sought. Neuroleptic-induced akathisia, sedative hypnotics, some antibiotics, antidepressants, and anti-hypertensive agents are all possibilities. Reducing or discontinuing any drug not demonstrably necessary may be helpful. Anxiety, delusions, hallucinations, and sleep disturbances, on the other hand, are also important causes and are reasons for drug administration in the first place. Finding the correct balance between drug and non-drug treatment may require prolonged observation, therapeutic trial (and error) and, ultimately, lots of patience. Wandering behavior for those patients still at home can be diminished with the installation of complex door locks or in-house alarms or bells. Patient identification bracelets may help minimize the hazardous consequences of wandering (Yaari & Corey-Bloom, 2007). The Safe Return program is a nationwide service sponsored by the Alzheimer's Association to help police and private citizens identify, locate, and return people with dementia (www.alz.org/we_can_help_safe_return.asp).

In the 1970s, many nursing homes established special-care units that segregate demented residents from the mainstream residents. Ideally, residential units that specialize in the care of dementia patients should provide comfortable, less clinical environments, focused activities, and staffing patterns to promote the functional abilities of demented residents; environmental designs that allow residents to wander safely; and opportunities for the active involvement of family members. Nursing homes adopting a "sheltered freedom" approach (Cummings & Benson, 1992) provide indoor and outdoor structure that allows pacing, wandering, and exploration in a relatively uninhibited but safe environment.

Driving   Restricting the driving privileges of patients with dementia deserves special mention because it is such an emotionally charged issue in many families. Regardless of what patients and their families may claim, as a group, persons with even mild dementia drive more poorly and have a greater risk of accidents than persons without dementia. Yet, in the very earliest stages of dementia, when memory problems are the only detectable deficits, many patients appear to drive safely on familiar streets, and the symbolic impact of reducing a patient's independence by preventing the patient from driving can be distressing and divisive within a family (Ott et al., 2008).

The decision to restrict or forbid driving on the basis of cognitive impairment is best made jointly by the family and the clinician since patients routinely resist surrendering this privilege, even when they are obviously too impaired to drive safely. The discussion should include:

• patient's capacity and competence
• patient's driving history;
• current driving patterns;
• potential alternative means for transportation.

There are no rules to help clinicians judge when to restrict patient driving and the neuropsychological heterogeneity of a disease like AD means that mildly impaired patients with visuospatial problems may be more dangerous on the road than patients with severe, but more straightforward, memory problems. A history of getting lost, misjudging distances, inappropriate speed, missing signs or signals, accidents or near misses should be documented. However, our clinical experience and some published literature suggest that problems are underreported by caregivers and that many mildly demented people are not safe drivers when directly observed. In questionable cases, a standardized driving evaluation may help determine some aspects of driver competence, although these assessments routinely cost hundreds of dollars and a substantial portion of mildly demented persons pass performance tests. Many rehabilitation hospitals offer formal driving evaluation programs that give a more sophisticated assessment of the patient's driving ability than the state motor vehicle department or commercial driving schools. But in progressive dementias, such a snapshot does not accurately reflect what the patient will be like several months later, or even the next day, since there is such day-to-day fluctuation in concentration of impaired patients. Serial testing, at least every six months, essentially is mandatory. The AAN driving practice parameter offers specific suggestions based on the patient's cognitive status (Dubinsky et al., 2000), although these in part have been challenged as possibly too restrictive (Ott et al., 2008).

When the impairments are mild, the clinician can wean the patient from driving by encouraging the family to find alternatives and gradually begin using them well before driving must be terminated. When driving privileges must be restricted suddenly, a carefully worded statement implying that the loss of privilege will be temporary ("I'm afraid you will need to stop driving while we work on ways to help your memory problem") is not entirely honest but often softens the blow. The clinician can also relieve pressure within the family by accepting the blame for the restriction, since amnestic patients often quickly forget the conversation. These recommendations should also be applied to patients who operate heavy machinery or who possess guns or other potentially harmful equipment in the home (Green, 2005).

Elder abuse

Abuse and neglect of AD patients by family, friends, telemarketers, and professional caregivers is an unfortunate reality for which the health professional should be on the lookout (Lachs et al., 1997). Evidence includes malnutrition, decubitus ulcers, poor hygiene, and repetitive trauma. This is a very difficult issue, particularly since behavioral disturbances, if present, are clearly impediments to proper care. Counseling, family psychotherapy, respite, and alternative living arrangements, if possible, may be helpful but the physician needs to know the particular state's law on reporting of suspected elder abuse.

Placement/Hospice

Roughly 90% of AD victims are institutionalized before death (Smith et al., 2000). The threshold for custodial placement depends on patient (disruptive behaviors, incontinence) and caregiver (finances, his/her own medical problems) characteristics. When possible, planned nursing home care is preferable to unplanned admissions and clinicians should introduce the possibility of long-term care as a contingency well before it is necessary. Medicare does not pay for nursing home care. When money is an issue (as it is for most), the patient must qualify on the basis of financial need for enrollment in a Medicaid nursing home. Before choosing a long-term care facility, the family should access www.medicare.gov for reports of deficiencies in state inspections. Every family must individually negotiate the challenges of finding suitable placement and the traumas of moving the patient out of the home, sometimes in the face of bitter opposition and accusations.

A hospice may be an option for patients with life expectancy of less than six months. Hospice care must be prescribed by a physician for either home or institutional care.

Conclusion

AD is rapidly evolving as the predominant chronic illness of the new millennium. The past decade has brought unprecedented progress in understanding the genetics, pathophysiology, and natural history of AD. The clinical care of AD patients is still in relative infancy but is rapidly evolving, with important new advances in diagnosis and pharmacological and nonpharmocological management. We are at the dawn of more effective care and treatment of AD and related degenerative dementias. "The future looks bright" is something we'd all like to say to our next patient and his or her family. It is our expectation that this will be possible within the next decade.

Note: The authors wish to thank Martin Albert, M.D., Ph.D., for his thoughtful reflections and comments.

References

Aisen, P. S., Davis, K. L., Berg, J. D., Schafer, K., Campbell, K., Thomas, R. G., et al. (2000). A randomized controlled trial of prednisone in Alzheimer's disease: Alzheimer's Disease Cooperative Study. *Neurology, 54*(3), 588–593.

Aisen, P. S., Mehran, M., Poole, R., et al. (2004). *Clinical data on Alzhemed after 12 months of treatment in patients with mild to moderate Alzheimer's disease.* Paper presented at the 9th International Conference on Alzheimer's disease and Related Disorders, Philadelphia, PA, July 18, 2004.

Aisen, P. S., Saumier, D., Briand, R., Laurin, J., Gervais, F., Tremblay, P., et al. (2006). A Phase II study targeting amyloid-β with 3APS in mild-to-moderate Alzheimer disease. *Neurology, 67*, 1757–1763.

Aisen, P. S., Schafer, K. A., Grundman, M., Pfeiffer, E., Sano, M., Davis, K. L., et al. (2003). Effects of rofecoxib or naproxen vs. placebo on Alzheimer disease progression: A randomized controlled trial. *Journal of the American Medical Association 289*(21), 2819–2826.

Aisen, P. S., Schneider, L. S., Sano, M., Diaz-Arrastia, R., van Dyck, C. H., Weiner, M. F., et al. (2008). High-dose B vitamin supplementation and cognitive decline in Alzheimer disease: A randomized controlled trial. *Journal of the American Medical Association, 300*(15), 1774–1783.

Albert, M. (2008). Neuropsychology of Alzheimer's disease. In G. Goldenberg & B. Miller (Eds.), *Neuropsychology and Behavioral Neurology* (pp. 511–525). Amsterdam: Elsevier.

Albert, M., Smith, L. A., Scherr, P. A., Taylor, J. O., Evans, D. A., & Funkenstein, H. H. (1991). Use of brief cognitive tests to identify individuals in the community with clinically diagnosed Alzheimer's disease. *International Journal of Neuroscience, 57*, 167–178.

Allain, H., Dautzenberg, P. H., Maurer, K., Schuck, S., Bonhomme, D., & Gerard, D. (2000). Double blind study of tiapride versus haloperidol and placebo in agitation and aggressiveness in elderly patients with cognitive impairment. *Psychopharmacology, 148*, 361–366.

Allender, J., & Kaszniak, A. W. (1989). Processing of emotional cues in patients with dementia of the Alzheimer's type. *International Journal of Neuroscience, 46*(3–4), 147–155.

Alzheimer, A. (1906). *Über einen eigenartigen, schweren Erkrankungsprozess der Hirnrinde.* Paper presented at the Assembly of Southwest German Psychiatrists.

Alzheimer, A. (1907). Uber eine eigenartige Erkrankung der Hirnrinde. *Allgemeine Zeitschrift für Psychiatrie, 64,* 146.

Alzheimer, A. (1911). Über eigenartige Krankheitsfälle des späteren Alters. *Zeitschrift für die gesamte Neurologie und Psychiatrie, 4,* 356–385.

Amatniek, J. C., Hauser, W. A., DelCastillo-Castaneda, C., Jacobs, D. M., Marder, K., Bell, K., et al. (2006). Incidence and predictors of seizures in patients with Alzheimer's disease. *Epilepsia, 47*(5), 867–872.

American Psychiatric Association. (2000). *Diagnostic and statistical manual of mental disorders, fourth edition-text revision (DSMIV-TR).* Washington, DC: American Psychiatric Publishing.

Archer, N., Brown, R. G., Reeves, S. J., Boothby, H., Nicholas, H., Foy, C., et al. (2007). Premorbid personality and behavioral and psychological symptoms in probable Alzheimer disease. *American Journal of Geriatric Psychiatry, 15*(3), 202–213.

Arnaiz, E., Almkvist, O., Ivnik, R. J., Tangalos, E. G., Wahlund, L. O., Winblad, B., et al. (2004). Mild cognitive impairment: A cross-national comparison. *Journal of Neurology, Neurosurgery & Psychiatry, 75*(9), 1275–1280.

Arvanitakis, Z., Schneider, J. A., Wilson, R. S., Bienias, J. L., Kelly, J. F., Evans, D. A., et al. (2008). Statins, incident Alzheimer disease, change in cognitive function, and neuropathology. *Neurology, 70*(19 Pt 2), 1795–1802.

Arvanitakis, Z., Wilson, R. S., Bienias, J. L., Evans, D. A., & Bennett, D. A. (2004). Diabetes mellitus and risk of Alzheimer disease and decline in cognitive function. *Archives of Neurology, 61*(5), 661–666.

Bachman, D. L., Wolf, P. A., Linn, R. T., Knoefel, J. E., Cobb, J. L., Belanger, A. J., et al. (1993). Incidence of dementia and probable Alzheimer's disease in a general population: The Framingham study. *Neurology, 43*(3), 515–519.

Bachurin, S., Bukatina, E., Lermontova, N., Tkachenko, S., Afanasiev, A., Grigoriev, V., et al. (2001). Antihistamine agent Dimebon as a novel neuroprotector and a cognition enhancer. *Annals of the New York Academy of Sciences, 939,* 425–435.

Bacsi, A., Woodberry, M., Kruzel, M. L., & Boldogh, I. (2007). Colostrinin delays the onset of proliferative senescence of diploid murine fibroblast cells. *Neuropeptides, 41*(2), 93–101.

Ballard, C., Margallo-Lana, M., Juszczak, E., Douglas, S., Swann, A., Thomas, A., et al. (2005). Quetiapine and rivastigmine and cognitive decline in Alzheimer's disease: Randomised double blind placebo controlled trial. *British Medical Journal, 330*(7496), 874.

Barnhart, W. J., Makela, E. H., & Latocha, M. J. (2004). SSRI-induced apathy syndrome: A clinical review. *Journal of Psychiatric Practice, 10*(3), 196–199.

Barten, D. M., Guss, V. L., Corsa, J. A., Loo, A., Hansel, S. B., Zheng, M., et al. (2005). Dynamics of {beta}-amyloid reductions in brain, cerebrospinal fluid, and plasma of {beta}-amyloid precursor protein transgenic mice treated with a {gamma}-secretase inhibitor. *Journal of Pharmacology and Experimental Therapeutics, 312*(2), 635–643.

Baskin, F., Rosenberg, R. N., Iyer, L., Hynan, L., & Cullum, C. M. (2000). Platelet APP isoform ratios correlate with declining cognition in AD. *Neurology, 54*(10), 1907–1909.

Bateman, R. J., Wen, G., Morris, J. C., & Holtzman, D. M. (2007). Fluctuations of CSF amyloid-beta levels: implications for a diagnostic and therapeutic biomarker. *Neurology, 68*(9), 666–669.

Bayles, K. (1988). Dementia: The clinical perspective. *Seminars in Speech and Language, 9,* 149–165.

Becker, J. T. (1988). Working memory and secondary memory deficits in Alzheimer's disease. *Journal of Clinical and Experimental Neuropsychology, 10*(6), 739–753.

Beeri, M. S., Werner, P., Davidson, M., & Noy, S. (2002). The cost of behavioral and psychological symptoms of dementia (BPSD) in community dwelling Alzheimer's disease patients. *International Journal of Geriatric Psychiatry, 17*(5), 403–408.

Benson, D. F. (1983). Subcortical dementia: A clinical approach. In R. Mayeux & W. G. Rosen (Eds.), *Advances in neurology* (Vol. 38, pp. 185–194). New York: Raven Press.

Benson, D. F., Davis, R. J., & Snyder, B. D. (1988). Posterior cortical atrophy. *Archives of Neurology, 45,* 789–793.

Berlau, D. J., Corrada, M., Paganini-Hill, A., Brookmeyer, R., & Kawas C. (2007). Incidence of dementia continues to increase after age 90: Results from the 90+ study. *Neurology, 68*(*Suppl 1*), 83.

Bertram, L., McQueen, M. B., Mullin, K., Blacker, D., & Tanzi, R. E. (2007). Systematic meta-analyses of Alzheimer disease genetic association studies: The AlzGene database. *Nature Genetics, 39*(1), 17–23.

Binetti, G., Mega, M. S., Magni, E., Padovani, A., Rozzini, L., Bianchetti, A., et al. (1998). Behavioral disorders in Alzheimer disease: A transcultural perspective. *Archives of Neurology, 55*(4), 539–544.

Birks, J., & Flicker, L. (2006). Donepezil for mild cognitive impairment. *Cochrane Database System Reviews, 3,* CD006104.

Bjelakovic, G., Nikolova, D., Gluud, L. L., Simonetti, R. G., & Gluud, C. (2007). Mortality in randomized trials of antioxidant supplements for primary and secondary prevention: Systematic review and meta-analysis. *Journal of the American Medical Association, 297*(8), 842–857.

Black, S. E., Doody, R., Li, H., McRae, T., Jambor, K. M., Xu, Y., et al. (2007). Donepezil preserves cognition and global function in patients with severe Alzheimer disease. *Neurology, 69*(5), 459–469.

Blacker, D., Lee, H., Muzikansky, A., Martin, E. C., Tanzi, R., McArdle, J. J., et al. (2007). Neuropsychological measures in normal individuals that predict subsequent cognitive decline. *Archives of Neurology, 64*(6), 862–871.

Blacker, D., & Tanzi, R. (1998). The genetics of Alzheimer disease: Current status and future prospects. *Archives of Neurology, 55,* 294–296.

Blennow, K., de Leon, M. J., & Zetterberg, H. (2006). Alzheimer's disease. *Lancet, 368*(9533), 387–403.

Blennow, K., & Hampel, H. (2003). CSF markers for incipient Alzheimer's disease. *Lancet Neurology, 2*(10), 605–613.

Blennow, K., Wallin, A., & Gottfries, C. (1994). Clinical subgroups of Alzheimer's disease. In E. Emerey et al. (Ed.), *Dementia: Presentations, differential diagnosis, and nosology* (pp. 95–107). Baltimore: Johns Hopkins University Press.

Boller, F., Bick, K., & Duyckaerts, C. (2007). They have shaped Alzheimer disease: The protagonists, well known and less well known. *Cortex, 43*(4), 565–569.

Bombois, S., Maurage, C. A., Gompel, M., Deramecourt, V., Mackowiak-Cordoliani, M. A., Black, R. S., et al. (2007). Absence of beta-amyloid deposits after immunization in Alzheimer disease with Lewy body dementia. *Archives of Neurology, 64*(4), 583–587.

Bornebroek, M., & Kumar-Singh, S. (2004). A novel drug target in Alzheimer's disease. *Lancet, 364*(9447), 1738–1739.

Borroni, B., Di Luca, M., & Padovani, A. (2006). Predicting Alzheimer dementia in mild cognitive impairment patients. Are biomarkers useful? *European Journal of Pharmacology, 545*(1), 73–80.

Bottiglieri, T., Godfrey, P., Flynn, T., Carney, M. W., Toone, B. K., & Reynolds, E. H. (1990). Cerebrospinal fluid S-adenosylmethionine in depression and dementia: Effects of treatment with parenteral and oral S-adenosylmethionine. *Journal of Neurology, Neurosurgery & Psychiatry, 53*(12), 1096–1098.

Boustani, M., Peterson, B., Hanson, L., Harris, R., & Lohr, K. N. (2003). Screening for dementia in primary care: A summary of the evidence for the U. S. Preventive Services Task Force. *Annals of Internal Medicine, 138*(11), 927–937.

Bowie, P., Branton, T., & Holmes, J. (1999). Should the Mini Mental State Examination be used to monitor dementia treatments? *Lancet, 354*(9189), 1527–1528.

Boyle, P. A., Buchman, A. S., Wilson, R. S., Leurgans, S. E., & Bennett, D. A. (2009). Association of muscle strength with the risk of Alzheimer disease and the rate of cognitive decline in community-dwelling older persons. *Archives of Neurology, 66*(11), 1339–1344.

Bozoki, A. C., An, H., Bozoki, E. S., & Little, R. J. (2009). The existence of cognitive plateaus in Alzheimer's disease. *Alzheimer's & Dementia, 5*(6), 470–478.

Bózzola, F. G., Gorelick, P. B., & Freels, S. (1992). Personality changes in Alzheimer's disease. *Archives of Neurology, 49*, 297–300.

Braak, H., & Braak, E. (1991). Neuropathological staging of Alzheimer-related changes. *Acta Neuropathologica, 82*, 239–259.

Bradley, K. M., O'Sullivan, V. T., Soper, N. D., Nagy, Z., King, E. M., Smith, A. D., et al. (2002). Cerebral perfusion SPET correlated with Braak pathological stage in Alzheimer's disease. *Brain, 125*(Pt 8), 1772–1781.

Brayne, C., Spiegelhalter, D. J., Dufouil, C., Chi, L. Y., Dening, T. R., Paykel, E. S., et al. (1999). Estimating the true extent of cognitive decline in the old old. *Journal of the American Geriatric Society, 47*(11), 1283–1288.

Brodaty, H., Ames, D., Snowdon, J., Woodward, M., Kirwan, J., Clarnette, R., et al. (2003). A randomized placebo-controlled trial of risperidone for the treatment of aggression, agitation, and psychosis of dementia. *Journal of Clinical Psychiatry, 64*(2), 134–143.

Brown, R., & Marsden, C. (1988). Subcortical dementia: The neuropsychological evidence. *Neuroscience, 25*, 363–387.

Burns, A., O'Brien, J., Auriacombe, S., Ballard, C., Broich, K., Bullock, R., et al. (2006). Clinical practice with anti-dementia drugs: A consensus statement from British Association for Psychopharmacology. *Journal of Psychopharmacology, 20*(6), 732–755.

Callahan, C., Hendrie, H. C., & Tierney, W. M. (1995). Documentation and evaluation of cognitive impairment in elderly primary care patients. *Annals of Internal Medicine, 122*, 422–429.

Casadesus, G., Garrett, M. R., Webber, K. M., Hartzler, A. W., Atwood, C. S., Perry, G., et al. (2006). The estrogen myth: Potential use of gonadotropin-releasing hormone agonists for the treatment of Alzheimer's disease. *Drugs in R&D, 7*(3), 187–193.

Chappell, A. S., Gonzales, C., Williams, J., Witte, M. M., Mohs, R. C., & Sperling, R. (2007). AMPA potentiator treatment of cognitive deficits in Alzheimer disease. *Neurology, 68*(13), 1008–1012.

Chen, P., Ratcliff, G., Belle, S. H., Cauley, J. A., DeKosky, S. T., & Ganguli, M. (2000). Cognitive tests that best discriminate between presymptomatic AD and those who remain non-demented. *Neurology, 55*(12), 1847–1853.

Chetelat, G., & Baron, J. C. (2003). Early diagnosis of Alzheimer's disease: contribution of structural neuroimaging. *Neuroimage, 18*(2), 525–541.

Chow, T. W., Binns, M. A., Cummings, J. L., Lam, I., Black, S. E., Miller, B. L., et al. (2009). Apathy symptom profile and behavioral associations in frontotemporal dementia vs. dementia of Alzheimer type. *Archives of Neurology, 66*(7), 888–893.

Christensen, D. D. (2007). Alzheimer's disease: progress in the development of anti-amyloid disease-modifying therapies. *CNS Spectrums, 12*(2), 113–116, 119–123.

Chui, H. (2002). Clinical criteria for dementia subtypes. In S. L. Qizilbash et al. (Ed.), *Evidence-based dementia practice* (pp. 106–119). Oxford: Blackwell.

Clarfield, A. M. (1988). The reversible dementias: Do they reverse? *Annals of Internal Medicine, 109*(6), 476–486.

Clarfield, A. M. (1995). Reversible dementia. *Neurology, 45*(3 Pt 1), 601.

Clarfield, A. M. (2003). The decreasing prevalence of reversible dementias: An updated meta-analysis. *Archives of Internal Medicine, 163*, 2219–2229.

Clark, C. M., Sheppard, L., Fillenbaum, G. G., Galasko, D., Morris, J. C., Koss, E., et al. (1999). Variability in annual Mini-Mental State Examination score in patients with probable Alzheimer disease: A clinical perspective of data from the Consortium to Establish a Registry for Alzheimer's Disease. *Archives of Neurology, 56*(7), 857–862.

Consensus recommendations for the postmortem diagnosis of Alzheimer's disease. The National Institute on Aging, and Reagan Institute Working Group on Diagnostic Criteria for the Neuropathological Assessment of Alzheimer's Disease. (1997). *Neurobiology and Aging, 18*(4 Suppl), S1–S2.

Copeland, M. P., Daly, E., Hines, V., Mastromauro, C., Zaitchik, D., Gunther, J., et al. (2003). Psychiatric symptomatology and prodromal Alzheimer's disease. *Alzheimer Disease and Associated Disorders, 17*(1), 1–8.

Corcoran, M. A. (1992). Gender differences in dementia management plans of spousal caregivers: Implications for occupational therapy. *American Journal of Occupational Therapy, 46*(11), 1006–1012.

Corey-Bloom, J., Yaari, R., & Weisman, D. (2006). Managing patients with Alzheimer's disease. *Practical Neurology, 6*(2), 78–89.

Covinsky, K. E., Newcomer, R., Fox, P., Wood, J., Sands, L., Dane, K., et al. (2003). Patient and caregiver characteristics associated with depression in caregivers of patients with dementia. *Journal of General Internal Medicine, 18*(12), 1006–1014.

Coyle, J. R., Price, D. L., & DeLong, M. R. (1983). Alzheimer's disease: A disorder of cortical cholinergic innervation. *Science, 219*, 1184–1190.

Craig, D., Hart, D. J., McCool, K., McIlroy, S. P., & Passmore, A. P. (2004). Apolipoprotein E e4 allele influences aggresive behaviour in Alzheimer's disease. *Journal of Neurology, Neurosurgery & Psychiatry, 75*(9), 1327–1330.

Craig-Schapiro, R., Fagan, A. M., & Holtzman, D. M. (2009). Biomarkers of Alzheimer's disease. *Neurobiology of Disease, 35*(2), 128–140.

Crapper McLachlan, D. R., Dalton, A. J., Kruck, T. P., Bell, M. Y., Smith, W. L., Kalow, W., et al. (1991). Intramuscular desferrioxamine in patients with Alzheimer's disease. *Lancet, 337*(8753), 1304–1308.

Crook, T., Bartus, R. T., Ferris, S. H., Whitehouse, P., Cohen, G. D., & Gershon, S. (1986). Age-Associated Memory Impairment: Proposed diagnostic criteria and measures of clinical change – Report of a National Institute of Mental Health Work Group. *Developmental Neuropsychology*, 2(4), 261–276.

Crystal, H. A., Dickson, D., Davies, P., Masur, D., Grober, E., & Lipton, R. B. (2000). The relative frequency of "dementia of unknown etiology" increases with age and is nearly 50% in nonagenarians. *Archives of Neurology*, 57(5), 713–719.

Crystal, H. A., Horoupian, D. S., Katzman, R., & Jotkowitz, S. (1982). Biopsy-proved Alzheimer disease presenting as a right parietal lobe syndrome. *Annals of Neurology*, 12, 186–188.

Cummings, J. L. (1982). Cortical dementias. In B. D. Benson (Ed.), *Psychiatric aspects of neurologic disease* (Vol. 2, pp. 93–121). New York: Grune & Stratton.

Cummings, J. L. (1993). Frontal-subcortical circuits and human behavior. *Archives of Neurology*, 50, 873–880.

Cummings, J. L. (2003). Use of cholinesterase inhibitors in clinical practice: Evidence-based recommendations. *American Journal of Geriatric Psychiatry*, 11(2), 131–145.

Cummings, J. L. (2004). Alzheimer's disease. *New England Journal of Medicine*, 351, 56–67.

Cummings, J. L. (2005a). Clinical evaluation as a biomarker for Alzheimer's disease. *Journal of Alzheimer's Disease*, 8(4), 327–337.

Cummings, J. L. (2005b). Neuropsychiatric and behavioral alterations and their management in moderate to severe Alzheimer disease. *Neurology*, 65(Suppl 3), S18–S24.

Cummings, J. L. (2009). Defining and labeling disease-modifying treatments for Alzheimer's disease. *Alzheimer's & Dementia*, 5(5), 406–418.

Cummings, J. L., & Benson, D. F. (1992). *Dementia: A clinical approach* (2nd edn.). Boston: Butterworth-Heinemann.

Cummings, J. L., Benson, D. F., Hill, M. A., & Read, S. (1985). Aphasia in dementia of the Alzheimer type. *Neurology*, 35(3), 394–397.

Cummings, J. L., Doody, R., & Clark, C. (2007). Disease-modifying therapies for Alzheimer disease: Challenges to early intervention. *Neurology*, 69(16), 1622–1634.

Cummings, J. L., Lefevre, G., Small, G., & Appel-Dingemanse, S. (2007). Pharmacokinetic rationale for the rivastigmine patch. *Neurology*, 69(4 Suppl 1), S10–S13.

Cummings, J. L., Mackell, J., & Kaufer, D. (2008). Behavioral effects of current Alzheimer's disease treatments: A descriptive review. *Alzheimer's & Dementia*, 4(1), 49–60.

Cummings, J. L., & Mega, M. S. (2003). *Neuropsychiatry and behavioral neuroscience*. New York: Oxford University Press.

Cummings, J. L., Schneider, E., Tariot, P. N., & Graham, S. M. (2006). Behavioral effects of memantine in Alzheimer disease patients receiving donepezil treatment. *Neurology*, 67(1), 57–63.

Cunnane, S. C., Plourde, M., Pifferi, F., Begin, M., Feart, C., & Barberger-Gateau, P. (2009). Fish, docosahexaenoic acid and Alzheimer's disease. *Progress in Lipid Research*, 48(5), 239–256.

Cupples, L. A., Farrer, L., Sadovnick, D., Relkin, N., Whitehouse, P., & Green, R. C. (2004). Estimating risk curves for first-degree relatives of patients with Alzheimer's disease: The REVEAL Study. *Genetic Medicine*, 6(4), 192–196.

Dartigues, J. F. (2009). Alzheimer's disease: A global challenge for the 21st century. *Lancet Neurology*, 8(12), 1082–1083.

Davis, J., Bountra, C., & Richardson, J. (2008). Perspectives of Alzheimer's disease treatments. In C. Duyckaerts & I. Litvan (Eds.), *Dementias* (pp. 273–290). Amsterdam: Elsevier.

Deary, I. J., Whiteman, M. C., Starr, J. M., Whalley, L. J., & Fox, H. C. (2004). The impact of childhood intelligence on later life: Following up the Scottish Mental Surveys of 1932 and 1947. *Journal of Personality and Social Psychology, 86,* 130–147.

DeKosky, S. T., Williamson, J. D., Fitzpatrick, A. L., Kronmal, R. A., Ives, D. G., Saxton, J. A., et al. (2008). Ginkgo biloba for prevention of dementia: A randomized controlled trial. *Journal of the American Medical Association, 300*(19), 2253–2262.

Dembner, A. (February 1, 2007). An end's beginning. *Boston Globe,* pp. C1–2.

Devanand, D. P., Marder, K., Michaels, K. S., Sackeim, H. A., Bell, K., Sullivan, M. A., et al. (1998). A randomized, placebo-controlled dose-comparison trial of haloperidol for psychosis and disruptive behaviors in Alzheimer's disease. *American Journal of Psychiatry, 155*(11), 1512–1520.

Di Carlo, A., Lamassa, M., Baldereschi, M., Inzitari, M., Scafato, E., Farchi, G., et al. (2007). CIND and MCI in the Italian elderly: Frequency, vascular risk factors, progression to dementia. *Neurology, 68*(22), 1909–1916.

Dilworth-Anderson, P. (2001). Family issues and the care of persons with Alzheimer's disease. *Aging and Mental Health, 5*(Suppl 1), S49–S51.

Doody, R. S. (2008). We should not distinguish between symptomatic and disease-modifying treatments in Alzheimer's disease drug development. *Alzheimer's & Dementia, 4*(1 Suppl 1), S21–S25.

Doody, R. S., Ferris, S. H., Salloway, S., Sun, Y., Goldman, R., Watkins, W. E., et al. (2009). Donepezil treatment of patients with MCI: A 48-week randomized, placebo-controlled trial. *Neurology, 72*(18), 1555–1561.

Doody, R. S., Gavrilova, S. I., Sano, M., Thomas, R. G., Aisen, P. S., Bachurin, S. O., et al. (2008). Effect of dimebon on cognition, activities of daily living, behaviour, and global function in patients with mild-to-moderate Alzheimer's disease: A randomised, double-blind, placebo-controlled study. *Lancet, 372*(9634), 207–215.

Doody, R. S., Stevens, J. C., Beck, C., Dubinsky, R. M., Kaye, J. A., Gwyther, L., et al. (2001). Practice parameter: Management of dementia (an evidence-based review). Report of the Quality Standards Subcommittee of the American Academy of Neurology. *Neurology, 56,* 1154–1166.

Dooley, M., & Lamb, H. M. (2000). Donepezil: A review of its use in Alzheimer's Disease. *Drugs & Aging, 16*(3), 199–226.

Duara, R., Barker, W., Loewenstein, D., & Bain, L. (2009). The basis for disease-modifying treatments for Alzheimer's disease: The Sixth Annual Mild Cognitive Impairment Symposium. *Alzheimer's & Dementia, 5*(1), 66–74.

Dubinsky, R. M., Stein, A. C., & Lyons, K. (2000). Practice parameter: Risk of driving and Alzheimer's disease (an evidence-based review): Report of the quality standards sub-committee of the American Academy of Neurology. *Neurology, 54*(12), 2205–2011.

Dubois, B., Feldman, H. H., Jacova, C., Dekosky, S. T., Barberger-Gateau, P., Cummings, J., et al. (2007). Research criteria for the diagnosis of Alzheimer's disease: Revising the NINCDS-ADRDA criteria. *Lancet Neurology, 6*(8), 734–746.

Dudas, R. B., Clague, F., Thompson, S. A., Graham, K. S., & Hodges, J. R. (2005). Episodic and semantic memory in mild cognitive impairment. *Neuropsychologia, 43*(9), 1266–1276.

Dunn, J. E., Weintraub, S., Stoddard, A. M., & Banks, S. (2007). Serum alpha-tocopherol, concurrent and past vitamin E intake, and mild cognitive impairment. *Neurology, 68*(9), 670–676.

Dyer, C. (2007). NICE faces legal challenge over Alzheimer's drug. *British Medical Journal*, *334*(7595), 654–655.

Ebly, E. M., Hogan, D. B., & Parhad, I. M. (1995). Cognitive impairment in the nondemented elderly. Results from the Canadian Study of Health and Aging. *Archives of Neurology*, *52*(6), 612–619.

Ellul, J., Archer, N., Foy, C. M., Poppe, M., Boothby, H., Nicholas, H., et al. (2007). The effects of commonly prescribed drugs in patients with Alzheimer's disease on the rate of deterioration. *Journal of Neurology, Neurosurgery & Psychiatry*, *78*(3), 233–239.

Ely, E. W., Girard, T. D., Shintani, A. K., Jackson, J. C., Gordon, S. M., Thomason, J. W., et al. (2007). Apolipoprotein E4 polymorphism as a genetic predisposition to delirium in critically ill patients. *Critical Care Medicine*, *35*(1), 112–117.

Erkinjuntti, T., Wikstrom, J., Palo, J., & Autio, L. (1986). Dementia among medical inpatients: Evaluation of 2000 consecutive admissions. *Archives of Internal Medicine*, *146*, 1923–1926.

Ertekin-Taner, N., Younkin, L. H., Yager, D. M., Parfitt, F., Baker, M. C., Asthana, S., et al. (2008). Plasma amyloid {beta} protein is elevated in late-onset Alzheimer disease families. *Neurology*, *70*(8), 596–606.

Erten-Lyons, D., Woltjer, R. L., Dodge, H., Nixon, R., Vorobik, R., Calvert, J. F., et al. (2009). Factors associated with resistance to dementia despite high Alzheimer disease pathology. *Neurology*, *72*(4), 354–360.

Eslinger, P. J., & Damasio, A. R. (1986). Preserved motor learning in Alzheimer's disease: Implications for anatomy and behavior. *Journal of Neuroscience*, *6*(10), 3006–3009.

Etcheberrigaray, R., Tan, M., Dewachter, I., Kuiperi, C., Van der Auwera, I., Wera, S., et al. (2004). Therapeutic effects of PKC activators in Alzheimer's disease transgenic mice. *Proceedings of the National Academy of Sciences USA*, *101*(30), 11141–11146.

Fagan, A. M., Csernansky, C. A., Morris, J. C., & Holtzman, D. M. (2005). The search for antecedent biomarkers of Alzheimer's disease. *Journal of Alzheimer's Disease*, *8*(4), 347–358.

Fagan, A. M., Roe, C. M., Xiong, C., Mintun, M. A., Morris, J. C., & Holtzman, D. M. (2007). Cerebrospinal fluid tau/beta-amyloid42 ratio as a prediction of cognitive decline in nondemented older adults. *Archives of Neurology*, *64*.

Farrer, L. A., Cupples, L. A., Haines, J. L., Hyman, B., Kukull, W. A., Mayeux, R., et al. (1997). Effects of age, sex and ethnicity on the association between apolipoprotein E genotype and Alzheimer's disease: A meta-analysis. *Journal of the American Medical Association*, *278*(16), 1349–1356.

Feldman, H. H., Ferris, S., Winblad, B., Sfikas, N., Mancione, L., He, Y., et al. (2007). Effect of rivastigmine on delay to diagnosis of Alzheimer's disease from mild cognitive impairment: The InDDEx study. *Lancet Neurology*, *6*(6), 501–512.

Ferri, C. P., Prince, M., Brayne, C., Brodaty, H., Fratiglioni, L., Ganguli, M., et al. (2005). Global prevalence of dementia: A Delphi consensus study. *Lancet*, *366*(9503), 2112–2117.

Finton, M. J., Lucas, J. A., Graff-Radford, N. R., & Uitti, R. J. (1998). Analysis of visuospatial errors in patients with Alzheimer's disease or Parkinson's disease. *Journal of Clinical and Experimental Neuropsychology*, *20*(2), 186–193.

Fischer, P., Jungwirth, S., Zehetmayer, S., Weissgram, S., Hoenigschnabl, S., Gelpi, E., et al. (2007). Conversion from subtypes of mild cognitive impairment to Alzheimer dementia. *Neurology*, *68*(4), 288–291.

Fitzpatrick, A. L., Kuller, L. H., Lopez, O. L., Diehr, P., O'Meara, E. S., Longstreth, W. T., Jr., et al. (2009). Midlife and late-life obesity and the risk of dementia: cardiovascular health study. *Archives of Neurology*, 66(3), 336–342.

Fleisher, A. S., Sowell, B. B., Taylor, C., Gamst, A. C., Petersen, R. C., & Thal, L. J. (2007). Clinical predictors of progression to Alzheimer disease in amnestic mild cognitive impairment. *Neurology*, 68(19), 1588–1595.

Flicker, C., Ferris, S. H., & Reisberg, B. (1991). Mild cognitive impairment in the elderly: Predictors of dementia. *Neurology*, 41, 1006–1009.

Flirski, M., & Sobow, T. (2005). Biochemical markers and risk factors of Alzheimer's disease. *Current Alzheimer Research*, 2(1), 47–64.

Folstein, M. F., Folstein, S. E., & McHugh, P. R. (1975). "Mini-Mental State": A practical method for grading the cognitive state of patients for the clinician. *Journal of Psychiatric Research*, 12, 189–198.

Ford, A. B., Mefrouche, Z., Friedland, R. P., & Debanne, S. M. (1996). Smoking and cognitive impairment: A population-based study. *Journal of the American Geriatric Society*, 44(8), 905–909.

Fox, N., & Growdon, J. (2004). Biomarkers and surrogates. *NeuroRx*, 1(April), 181.

Freed, D. M., Corkin, S., Growdon, J. H., & Nissen, M. J. (1989). Selective attention in Alzheimer's disease: Characterizing cognitive subgroups of patients. *Neuropsychologia*, 27, 325–339.

Freidenberg, D. L., & Drake M. E. (1990). Vitamin B12 deficiency syndrome: Selective recovery of mental functions after treatment. *Neuropsychiatry, Neuropsychology, and Behavioral Neurology*, 3(3), 226–235.

Frisoni, G. B., Prestia, A., Zanetti, O., Galluzzi, S., Romano, M., Cotelli, M., et al. (2009). Markers of Alzheimer's disease in a population attending a memory clinic. *Alzheimer's & Dementia*, 5(4), 307–317.

Galasko, D. (2005). Biomarkers for Alzheimer's disease – Clinical needs and application. *Journal of Alzheimer's Disease*, 8(4), 339–346.

Galasko, D., Hansen, L. A., Katzman, R., Wiederholt, W., Masliah, E., Terry, R., et al. (1994). Clinical-neuropathological correlations in Alzheimer's disease and related dementias. *Archives of Neurology*, 51(9), 888–895.

Galluzzi, S., Sheu, C. F., Zanetti, O., & Frisoni, G. B. (2005). Distinctive clinical features of mild cognitive impairment with subcortical cerebrovascular disease. *Dementia and Geriatric Cognitive Disorders*, 19(4), 196–203.

Galton, C. J., Patterson, K., Xuereb, J. H., & Hodges, J. R. (2000). Atypical and typical presentations of Alzheimer's disease: A clinical, neuropsychological, neuroimaging and pathological study of 13 cases. *Brain*, 123(Pt 3), 484–498.

Galvin, J. E. (2007). Pass the grain; spare the brain. *Neurology*, 69(11), 1072–1073.

Galvin, J. E., Roe, C. M., Coats, M. A., & Morris, J. C. (2007). Patient's rating of cognitive ability: Using the AD8, a brief informant interview, as a self-rating tool to detect dementia. *Archives of Neurology*, 64(5), 725–730.

Galvin, J. E., Roe, C. M., & Morris, J. C. (2007). Evaluation of cognitive impairment in older adults: Combining brief informant and performance measures. *Archives of Neurology*, 64(5), 718–724.

Galvin, J. E., Roe, C. M., Powlishta, K. K., Coats, M. A., Muich, S. J., Grant, E., et al. (2005). The AD8: A brief informant interview to detect dementia. *Neurology*, 65(4), 559–564.

Gandy, S. (2005). The role of cerebral amyloid beta accumulation in common forms of Alzheimer disease. *Journal of Clinical Investigation, 115*(5), 1121–1129.

Gandy, S., Lah, J., Walker, L., Kufahamu, T., Pedrini, S., Gieringer, T., et al. (2007). Plaque amyloid per se plays no detectable role in timing of onset or initial severity of cognitive dysfunction in a mouse model of Alzheimer's. *Neurology 68*(Suppl 1), 188.

Gauthier, S., Reisberg, B., Zaudig, M., Petersen, R. C., Ritchie, K., Broich, K., et al. (2006). Mild cognitive impairment. *Lancet, 367*(9518), 1262–1270.

Gauthier, S., & Touchon, J. (2005). Mild cognitive impairment is not a clinical entity and should not be treated. *Archives of Neurology, 62*(7), 1164–1166; discussion 1167.

Gazzaley, A., Cooney, J. W., Rissman, J., & D'Esposito, M. (2005). Top-down suppression deficit underlies working memory impairment in normal aging. *Nature Neuroscience, 8*(10), 1298–300.

Geerlings, M. I., Schmand, B., Jonker, C., Lindeboom, J., & Bouter, L. M. (1999). Education and incident Alzheimer's disease: A biased association due to selective attrition and use of a two-step diagnostic procedure? *International Journal of Epidemiology, 28*, 492–497.

Geldmacher, D. S. (2007). What if the patient doesn't care? *Practical Neurology, 7*, 14–15.

Geldmacher, D. S., Frolich, L., Doody, R. S., Erkinjuntti, T., Vellas, B., Jones, R. W., et al. (2006). Realistic expectations for treatment success in Alzheimer's disease. *Journal of Nutrition, Health & Aging, 10*(5), 417–429.

Geslani, D. M., Tierney, M. C., Herrmann, N., & Szalai, J. P. (2005). Mild cognitive impairment: An operational definition and its conversion rate to Alzheimer's disease. *Dementia and Geriatric Cognitive Disorders, 19*(5–6), 383–389.

Gestwicki, J. E., Crabtree, G. R., & Graef, I. A. (2004). Harnessing chaperones to generate small-molecule inhibitors of amyloid beta aggregation. *Science, 306*(5697), 865–869.

Giannakopoulos, P., Herrmann, F. R., Bussiere, T., Bouras, C., Kovari, E., Perl, D. P., et al. (2003). Tangle and neuron numbers, but not amyloid load, predict cognitive status in Alzheimer's disease. *Neurology, 60*(9), 1495–1500.

Gilman, S., Koller, M., Black, R. S., Jenkins, L., Griffith, S. G., Fox, N. C., et al. (2005). Clinical effects of Abeta immunization (AN1792) in patients with AD in an interrupted trial. *Neurology, 64*(9), 1553–1562.

Gitlin, L. N., Hauck, W. W., Dennis, M. P., & Winter, L. (2005). Maintenance of effects of the home environmental skill-building program for family caregivers and individuals with Alzheimer's disease and related disorders. *Journal of Gerontology Series A: Biological Sciences and Medical Sciences, 60*(3), 368–374.

Gozal, D., Capdevila, O. S., Kheirandish-Gozal, L., & Crabtree, V. M. (2007). ApoE epsilon 4 allele, cognitive dysfunction, and obstructive sleep apnea in children. *Neurology, 69*(3), 243–249.

Grady, C. L., Grimes, A. M., Patronas, N., Sunderland, T., Foster, N. L., & Rapoport, S. I. (1989). Divided attention, as measured by dichotic speech performance, in dementia of the Alzheimer type. *46*, 317–321.

Grady, C. L., Haxby, J. V., Horwitz, B., Sundaram, M., Berg, G., Schapiro, M., et al. (1988). Longitudinal study of early neuropsychological and cerebral metabolic changes in dementia of the Alzheimer's type. *Journal of Clinical and Experimental Neuropsychology, 10*, 576–596.

Graeber, M. B. (2006). Alois Alzheimer (1864–1915). Available at: http://www.ibro.info.

Graeber, M. B., Kosel, S., Grasbon-Frodl, E., Moller, H. J., & Mehraein, P. (1998). Histopathology and APOE genotype of the first Alzheimer disease patient, Auguste D. *Neurogenetics, 1*(3), 223–228.

Graff, M. J., Vernooij-Dassen, M. J., Thijssen, M., Dekker, J., Hoefnagels, W. H., & Rikkert, M. G. (2006). Community based occupational therapy for patients with dementia and their care givers: Randomised controlled trial. *British Medical Journal, 333*(7580), 1196.

Graff-Radford, N. R., Crook, J. E., Lucas, J., Boeve, B. F., Knopman, D. S., Ivnik, R. J., et al. (2007). Association of low plasma Abeta42/Abeta40 ratios with increased imminent risk for mild cognitive impairment and Alzheimer disease. *Archives of Neurology, 64*(3), 354–362.

Graham, J. E., Mitnitski, A. B., Mogilner, A. J., Gauvreau, D., & Rockwood, K. (1996). Symptoms and signs in dementia: Synergy and antagonism. *Dementia, 7*(6), 331–335.

Gray, K. F. (2004). Managing agitation and difficult behavior in dementia. *Clinical Geriatric Medicine, 20*, 69–82.

Green, R. C. (2002). Risk assessment for Alzheimer's disease with genetic susceptibility testing: Has the moment arrived? *Alzheimer's Care Quarterly, 3*(3), 208–214.

Green, R. C. (2005). *Diagnosis and management of Alzheimer's disease and other dementias* (2nd edn.). Caddo, OK: Professional Communications.

Green, R. C., Cupples, L. A., Go, R., Edeki, T., Griffith, P., Williams, M. P., et al. (2002). Risk of dementia among White and African American relatives of Alzheimer's disease patients. *Journal of the American Medical Association, 287*(3), 329–336.

Green, R. C., Cupples, L. A., Kurz, A., Auerbach, S., Go, R., Sadovnick, D., et al. (2003). Depression as a risk factor for Alzheimer's disease: The MIRAGE Study. *Archives of Neurology, 60*(5), 753–759.

Green, R. C., Goldstein, F. C., Mirra, S. S., Alazraki, N. P., Baxt, J. L., & Bakay, R. A. E. (1995). Slowly progressive apraxia in Alzheimer's disease. *Journal of Neurology, Neurosurgery & Psychiatry, 59*, 312–315.

Green, R. C., McNagny, S. E., Jayakumar, P., Cupples, L. A., Benke, K., & Farrer, L. A. (2006). Statin use and the risk of Alzheimer's disease. *Alzheimer's & Dementia, 2*, 96–103.

Green, R. C., Schneider, L., Amato, D., Beelen, A., Wilcock, G., Swabb, E., et al. (2009). Effect of tarenflurbil on cognitive decline and activities of daily living in patients with mild Alzheimer disease. A randomized controlled trial. *Journal of the American Medical Association, 302*(23), 2557–2564.

Grossberg, G. T., & Desai, A. K. (2003). Management of Alzheimer's disease. *Journals of Gerontology Series A: Biological Sciences and Medical Sciences, 58*(4), 331–353.

Group, A. R., Lyketsos, C. G., Breitner, J. C., Green, R. C., Martin, B. K., Meinert, C., et al. (2007). Naproxen and celecoxib do not prevent AD in early results from a randomized controlled trial. *Neurology, 68*(21), 1800–1808.

Grundman, M., Petersen, R. C., Ferris, S. H., Thomas, R. G., Aisen, P. S., Bennett, D. A., et al. (2004). Mild cognitive impairment can be distinguished from Alzheimer disease and normal aging for clinical trials. *Archives of Neurology, 61*(1), 59–66.

Grut, M., Fratiglioni, L., Forsell, Y., Viitanen, M., & Winblad, B. (1993). Memory complaints of elderly people in a population survey: Variation according to dementia stage and depression. *Journal of the American Geriatric Society, 139*, 1295–1300.

Guerriero Austrom, M., Damush, T. M., Hartwell, C. W., Perkins, T., Unverzagt, F., Boustani, M., et al. (2004). Development and implementation of nonpharmacologic protocols for the management of patients with Alzheimer's disease and their families in a multiracial primary care setting. *Gerontologist, 44*(4), 548–553.

Guerriero Austrom, M., Hartwell, C., Patricia Moore, P., Perkins, A., Damush, T., Unverzagt, F., et al. (2006). An integrated model of comprehensive care for people with Alzheimer's disease and their caregivers in a primary care setting. *Dementia, 5*, 339–352.

Guillozet, A. L., Weintraub, S., Mash, D. C., & Mesulam, M.-M. (2003). Neurofibrillary tangles, amyloid, and memory in aging and mild cognitive impairment. *Archives of Neurology, 60*, 729–736.

Guo, Z., Cupples, L. A., Kurz, A., Auerbach, S. H., Volicer, L., Chui, H., et al. (2000). Head injury and the risk of Alzheimer disease in the MIRAGE study. *Neurology, 54*(6), 1316–1323.

Hadjistavropoulos, T., Taylor, S., Tuokko, H., & Beattie, B. L. (1994). Neuropsychological deficits, caregivers' perception of deficits and caregiver burden. *Journal of the American Geriatric Society, 42*(3), 308–314.

Hake, A. (2007). Achieving proper balance in combination therapy for Alzheimer's. *Practical Neurology, 6*(1), 46–48.

Hansson, O., Zetterberg, H., Buchhave, P., Londos, E., Blennow, K., & Minthon, L. (2006). Association between CSF biomarkers and incipient Alzheimer's disease in patients with mild cognitive impairment: A follow-up study. *Lancet Neurology, 5*(3), 228–234.

Hardy, J. (1997). The Alzheimer family of diseases: Many etiologies, one pathogenesis? *Proceedings of the National Academy of Sciences USA, 94*(6), 2095–2097.

Harrison, B. E., Son, G. R., Kim, J., & Whall, A. L. (2007). Preserved implicit memory in dementia: A potential model for care. *American Journal of Alzheimer's Disease & Other Dementias, 22*(4), 286–293.

Hashimoto, M., Imamura, T., Tanimukai, S., Kazui, H., & Mori, E. (2000). Urinary incontinence: An unrecognised adverse effect with donepezil. *Lancet, 356*(9229), 568

Hashimoto, M., Kazui, H., Matsumoto, K., Nakano, Y., Yasuda, M., & Mori, E. (2005). Does donepezil treatment slow the progression of hippocampal atrophy in patients with Alzheimer's disease? *American Journal of Psychiatry, 162*(4), 676–682.

Hauser, W., Morris, M., Heston, L., & Anderson, V. (1986). Seizures and myoclonus in patients with Alzheimer's disease. *Neurology, 36*, 1226–1230.

Hayden, K. M., Zandi, P. P., Khachaturian, A. S., Szekely, C. A., Fotuhi, M., Norton, M. C., et al. (2007). Does NSAID use modify cognitive trajectories in the elderly? The Cache County study. *Neurology, 69*(3), 275–282.

Hayden, K. M., Zandi, P. P., West, N. A., Tschanz, J. T., Norton, M. C., Corcoran, C., et al. (2009). Effects of family history and apolipoprotein E epsilon4 status on cognitive decline in the absence of Alzheimer dementia: The Cache County Study. *Archives of Neurology, 66*(11), 1378–1383.

Hebben, N. M. W. (2002). *Essentials of neuropsychological assessment.* New York: John Wiley & Sons.

Hebert, L. E., Scherr, P. A., Bienias, J. L., Bennett, D. A., & Evans, D. A. (2003). Alzheimer disease in the US population: Prevalence estimates using the 2000 census. *Archives of Neurology, 60*(8), 1119–1122.

Heilman, K. M. (2003). Apraxia. In E. Valenstein & K. M. Heilman (Eds.), *Clinical neuropsychology* (4th edn.). New York: Oxford University Press.

Helvink, B., & Holroyd, S. (2006). Buspirone for stereotypic movements in elderly with cognitive impairment. *Journal of Neuropsychiatry and Clinical Neurosciences, 18*(2), 242–244.

Henderson, V. W., Benke, K., Green, R. C., Cupples, L. A., & Farrer, L. A. (2005). Postmenopausal hormone therapy and Alzheimer's disease risk: Interaction with age. *Journal of Neurology, Neurosurgery & Psychiatry, 76*(1), 103–105.

Henderson, V. W., Paganini-Hill, A., Miller, B. L., Elble, R. J., Reyes, P. F., Shoupe, D., et al. (2000). Estrogen for Alzheimer's disease in women: Randomized, double-blind, placebo-controlled trial. *Neurology, 54*, 295–301.

Hesdorffer, D. C., Hauser, W. A., Annegers, J. F., Kokmen, E., & Rocca, W. A. (1996). Dementia and adult-onset unprovoked seizures. *Neurology, 46*(3), 727–730.

Hirono, N., Mega, M. S., Dinov, I. D., Mishkin, F., & Cummings, J. L. (2000). Left frontotemporal hypoperfusion is associated with aggression in patients with dementia. *Archives of Neurology, 57*(6), 861–866.

Hodges, J. R. (2006). Alzheimer's centennial legacy: Origins, landmarks and the current status of knowledge concerning cognitive aspects. *Brain, 129*(Pt 11), 2811–2822.

Hodges, J. R., & Patterson, K. (1995). Is semantic memory consistently impaired early in the course of Alzheimer's disease? Neuroanatomical and diagnostic implications. *Neuropsychologia, 33*(4), 441–459.

Hoglund, K., Thelen, K. M., Syversen, S., Sjogren, M., von Bergmann, K., Wallin, A., et al. (2005). The effect of simvastatin treatment on the amyloid precursor protein and brain cholesterol metabolism in patients with Alzheimer's disease. *Dementia and Geriatric Cognitive Disorders, 19*(5–6), 256–265.

Holmes, C., Cunningham, C., Zotova, E., Woolford, J., Dean, C., Kerr, S., et al. (2009). Systemic inflammation and disease progression in Alzheimer disease. *Neurology, 73*(10), 768–774.

Holtzer, R., Tang, M. X., Devanand, D. P., Albert, S. M., Wegesin, D. J., Marder, K., et al. (2003). Psychopathological features in Alzheimer's disease: Course and relationship with cognitive status. *Journal of the American Geriatrics Society, 51*(7), 953–960.

Home, P. D., Pocock, S. J., Beck-Nielsen, H., Gomis, R., Hanefeld, M., Jones, N. P., et al. (2007). Rosiglitazone evaluated for cardiovascular outcomes – An interim analysis. *New England Journal of Medicine, 357*(1), 28–38.

Honjo, K., van Reekum, R., & Verhoeff, N. P. (2009). Alzheimer's disease and infection: Do infectious agents contribute to progression of Alzheimer's disease? *Alzheimer's & Dementia, 5*(4), 348–360.

Howieson, D. B., Camicioli, R., Quinn, J., Silbert, L. C., Care, B., Moore, M. M., et al. (2003). Natural history of cognitive decline in the old old. *Neurology, 60*(9), 1489–1494.

Huber, S. J. (1990). Neuropsychological assessment of subcortical dementia. In J. L. Cummings (Ed.), *Subcortical dementia*. New York: Oxford University Press.

Hung, D. (2008). Dimebon: A phase 3 investigational agent for Alzheimer's disease with a novel mitochondrial mechanism of action. *Alzheimer's & Dementia, 4*(Suppl 1), T182–T183.

Huppert, F. A., & Beardsall, L. (1993). Prospective memory impairment as an early indicator of dementia. *Journal of Clinical and Experimental Neuropsychology, 15*(5), 805–821.

in 't Veld, B. A., Ruitenberg, A., Hofman, A., Launer, L. J., van Duijn, C. M., Stijnen, T., et al. (2001). Nonsteroidal anti-inflammatory drugs and the risk of Alzheimer's disease. *New England Journal of Medicine, 345*(21), 1515–1521.

Iqbal, K., Alonso Adel, C., Chen, S., Chohan, M. O., El-Akkad, E., Gong, C. X., et al. (2005). Tau pathology in Alzheimer disease and other tauopathies. *Biochimica et Biophysica Acta, 1739*(2–3), 198–210.

Iqbal, K., Alonso Adel, C., El-Akkad, E., Gong, C. X., Haque, N., Khatoon, S., et al. (2003). Alzheimer neurofibrillary degeneration: Therapeutic targets and high-throughput assays. *Journal of Molecular Neuroscience, 20*(3), 425–429.

Ivanoiu, A., Adam, S., Van der Linden, M., Salmon, E., Juillerat, A. C., Mulligan, R., et al. (2005). Memory evaluation with a new cued recall test in patients with mild cognitive impairment and Alzheimer's disease. *Journal of Neurology, 252*(1), 47–55.

Jackson, J. C., Gordon, S. M., Hart, R. P., Hopkins, R. O., & Ely, E. W. (2004). The association between delirium and cognitive decline: A review of the empirical literature. *Neuropsychological Reviews, 14*(2), 87–98.

Jacobs, D., Ancoli-Israel, S., Parker, L., & Kripke, D. F. (1989). Twenty-four-hour sleep-wake patterns in a nursing home population. *Psychology and Aging, 4*(3), 352–356.

Jacobsen, J. S., Reinhart, P., & Pangalos, M. N. (2005). Current concepts in therapeutic strategies targeting cognitive decline and disease modification in Alzheimer's disease. *NeuroRx, 2*(4), 612–626.

Jagust, W. (2008). Is amnestic mild cognitive impairment always AD? *Neurology, 70*(7), 502–503.

Jagust, W., Harvey, D., Mungas, D., & Haan, M. (2005). Central obesity and the aging brain. *Archives of Neurology, 62*(10), 1545–1548.

Jagust, W., Reed, B., Mungas, D., Ellis, W., & Decarli, C. (2007). What does fluorodeoxyglucose PET imaging add to a clinical diagnosis of dementia? *Neurology, 69*(9), 871–877.

Jagust, W. J., Davies, P., Tiller-Borcich, J. K., & Reed, B. R. (1990). Focal Alzheimer's disease. *Neurology, 40*(1), 14–19.

Jellinger, K. A. (2002). Accuracy of clinical criteria for AD in the Honolulu-Asia Aging Study, a population-based study. *Neurology, 58*(6), 989–990; author reply 990.

Jicha, G. A., Parisi, J. E., Dickson, D. W., Johnson, K., Cha, R., Ivnik, R. J., et al. (2006). Neuropathological outcome of mild cognitive impairment following progression to clinical dementia. *Archives of Neurology, 63*(5), 674–681.

Johnson, J. K., Head, E., Kim, R., Starr, A., & Cotman, C. W. (1999). Clinical and pathological evidence for a frontal variant of Alzheimer disease. *Archives of Neurology, 56*(10), 1233–1239.

Jorm, A. F., Mather, K. A., Butterworth, P., Anstey, K. J., Christensen, H., & Easteal, S. (2007). APOE genotype and cognitive functioning in a large age-stratified population sample. *Neuropsychology, 21*(1), 1–8.

Kaduszkiewicz, H., Zimmermann, T., Beck-Bornholdt, H. P., & van den Bussche, H. (2005). Cholinesterase inhibitors for patients with Alzheimer's disease: Systematic review of randomised clinical trials. *British Medical Journal, 331*(7512), 321–327.

Kamer, A. R., Craig, R. G., Dasanayake, A. P., Brys, M., Glodzik-Sobanska, L., & de Leon, M. J. (2008). Inflammation and Alzheimer's disease: Possible role of periodontal diseases. *Alzheimer's & Dementia, 4*(4), 242–250.

Katz, I. R., Rovner, B. W., & Schneider, L. (1992). Use of psychoactive drugs in nursing homes. *New England Journal of Medicine, 327*(19), 1392–1393.

Kaye, J. (2009). Ginkgo biloba prevention trials: More than an ounce of prevention learned. *Archives of Neurology, 66*(5), 652–654.

Kaye, J., Vorobik, R., Nixon, R., & Montine, T. (2007). Factors associated with high Alzheimer neuropathology burdens at death, but normal ante-mortem cognitive function. *Neurology 68*(Suppl 1), 235.

Kelly, J. W. (2005). Attacking amyloid. *New England Journal of Medicine, 352*(7), 722–723.

Kennedy, G. J., Golde, T. E., Tariot, P. N., & Cummings, J. L. (2007). Amyloid-based interventions in Alzheimer's disease. *CNS Spectrums, 12*(12 Suppl 1), 1–14.

Killiany, R. J. (2009). Isn't amyloid more than just a marker for Alzheimer disease? *Neurology, 73*(15), 1174–1175.

Kivipelto, M., Ngandu, T., Fratiglioni, L., Viitanen, M., Kareholt, I., Winblad, B., et al. (2005). Obesity and vascular risk factors at midlife and the risk of dementia and Alzheimer disease. *Archives of Neurology, 62*(10), 1556–1560.

Klafki, H. W., Staufenbiel, M., Kornhuber, J., & Wiltfang, J. (2006). Therapeutic approaches to Alzheimer's disease. *Brain, 129*(Pt 11), 2840–2855.

Knopman, D. S., & Ryberg, S. (1989). A verbal memory test with high predictive accuracy for dementia of the Alzheimer type. *Archives of Neurology, 46*, 141–145.

Knopman, D. S., DeKosky, S. T., Cummings, J. L., Chui, H., Corey-Bloom, J., Relkin, N., et al. (2001). Practice parameter: Diagnosis of dementia (an evidence-based review). Report of the Quality Standards Subcommittee of the American Academy of Neurology. *Neurology, 56*(9), 1143–1153.

Knopman, D. S., Edland, S. D., Cha, R. H., Petersen, R. C., & Rocca, W. A. (2007). Incident dementia in women is preceded by weight loss by at least a decade. *Neurology, 69*(8), 739–746.

Koepsell, T. D., Chi, Y. Y., Zhou, X. H., Lee, W. W., Ramos, E. M., & Kukull, W. A. (2007). An alternative method for estimating efficacy of the AN1792 vaccine for Alzheimer disease. *Neurology, 69*(19), 1868–1872.

Kopelman, M. D. (1985). Rates of forgetting in Alzheimer-type dementia and Korsakoff's syndrome. *Neuropsychologia, 23*(5), 623–638.

Koppel, R. (2003). Alzheimer's disease: The costs to U. S. businesses in 2002. Alzheimer's Association. Available from www.alz.org/alzheimers_disease_publications.asp.

Kraepelin, E. (1910). *Psychiatrie. Ein Lehrbuch für Studierende und Aertze.* Leipzig.

Kramer, J. H., Nelson, A., Johnson, J. K., Yaffe, K., Glenn, S., Rosen, H. J., et al. (2006). Multiple cognitive deficits in amnestic mild cognitive impairment. *Dementia and Geriatric Cognitive Disorders, 22*(4), 306–311.

Kumar, A., Koss, E., Metzler, D., Moore, A., & Friedland, R. P. (1988). Behavioral symptomatology in dementia of the Alzheimer type. *Alzheimer Disease and Associated Disorders, 2*(4), 363–365.

Kurlan, R., Cummings, J., Raman, R., & Thal, L. (2007). Quetiapine for agitation or psychosis in patients with dementia and parkinsonism. *Neurology, 68*(17), 1356–1363.

Lachs, M. S., Williams, C., O'Brien, S., Hurst, L., & Horwitz, R. (1997). Risk factors for reported elder abuse and neglect: A nine-year observational cohort study. *Gerontologist, 37*(4), 469–474.

Lacor, P. N., Buniel, M. C., Chang, L., Fernandez, S. J., Gong, Y., Viola, K. L., et al. (2004). Synaptic targeting by Alzheimer's-related amyloid beta oligomers. *Journal of Neuroscience, 24*(45), 10191–10200.

Lambert, M. P., Barlow, A. K., Chromy, B. A., Edwards, C., Freed, R., Liosatos, M., et al. (1998). Diffusible, nonfibrillar ligands derived from A-beta(1–42) are potent central nervous system neurotoxins. *Proceedings of the National Academy of Sciences USA, 95*, 6448–6453.

Lambon Ralph, M. A., Patterson, K., Graham, N., Dawson, K., & Hodges, J. R. (2003). Homogeneity and heterogeneity in mild cognitive impairment and Alzheimer's disease: A cross-sectional and longitudinal study of 55 cases. *Brain, 126*(Pt 11), 2350–2362.

Landes, A. M., Sperry, S. D., & Strauss, M. E. (2005). Prevalence of apathy, dysphoria, and depression in relation to dementia severity in Alzheimer's disease. *Journal of Neuropsychiatry and Clinical Neurosciences, 17*(3), 342–349.

Launer, L. J., Ross, G. W., Petrovitch, H., Masaki, K., Foley, D., White, L. R., et al. (2000). Midlife blood pressure and dementia: The Honolulu-Asia aging study. *Neurobiology and Aging, 21*(1), 49–55.

Le Bars, P. L., Katz, M. M., Berman, N., Itil, T. M., Freedman, A. M., & Schatzberg, A. F. (1997). A placebo-controlled, double-blind, randomized trial of an extract of Ginkgo Biloba for dementia. *Journal of the American Medical Association, 278*(16), 1327–1332.

Lee, P. E., Gill, S. S., Freedman, M., Bronskill, S. E., Hillmer, M. P., & Pochon, P. A. (2004). Atypical antipsychotic drugs in the treatment of behavioural and psychological symptoms of dementia: Systematic review. *British Medical Journal, 329*, 75.

Lerner, A., & Whitehouse, P. J. (1994). Primary dementias. In M. L. Albert (Ed.), *Clinical neurology of aging* (p. 364). New York: Oxford University Press.

Leszek, J., Inglot, A. D., Janusz, M., Byczkiewicz, F., Kiejna, A., Georgiades, J., et al. (2002). Colostrinin proline-rich polypeptide complex from ovine colostrums – A long-term study of its efficacy in Alzheimer's disease. *Medical Science Monitor, 8*(10), PI93–PI96.

Levy, M. L., Cummings, J. L., Fairbanks, L. A., Masterman, D., Miller, B. L., Craig, A. H., et al. (1998). Apathy is not depression. *Journal of Neuropsychiatry and Clinical Neurosciences, 10*(3), 314–319.

Lezak, M. D. (1995). *Neuropsychological assessment* (3rd edn.). New York: Oxford University Press.

Li, G., Larson, E. B., Sonnen, J. A., Shofer, J. B., Petrie, E. C., Schantz, A., et al. (2007). Statin therapy is associated with reduced neuropathological changes of Alzheimer disease. *Neurology, 69*(9), 878–885.

Li, G., Sokai, I., Quinn, J. F., Leverenz, J. B., Schellenberg, G. D., Kaye, J. A., et al. (2007b). CSF tau/Abeta42 ratio for increased risk of mild cognitive impairment: A follow-up study. *Neurology, 69*(7), 631–639.

Licht, E., McMurtray, A. M., Saul, R. E., Mendez, M. E. (2007). Cognitive differences between early- and late-onset Alzheimer's disease. *American Journal of Alzheimer's Disease & Other Dementias, 22*(3), 218–222.

Lim, A., Tsuang, D., Kukull, W. A., Nochlin, D., Leverenz, J., McCormick, W., et al. (1999). Clinico-neuropathological correlation of Alzheimer's disease in a community-based case series. *Journal of the American Geriatrics Society, 47*(5), 564–569.

Lipowski, Z. J. (1987). Delirium (acute confusional states). *Journal of the American Medical Association, 258*(13), 1789–1792.

Livingston, G., Walker, A. E., Katona, C. L., & Cooper, C. (2007). Antipsychotics and cognitive decline in Alzheimer's disease: the LASER-Alzheimer's disease longitudinal study. *Journal of Neurology, Neurosurgery & Psychiatry, 78*(1), 25–29.

Lonergan, E., Luxenberg, J., & Colford, J. (2002). Haloperidol for agitation in dementia. *Cochrane Database System Reviews* (2), CD002852.

Lopez, O. L., Becker, J. T., Kaufer, D. I., Hamilton, R. L., Sweet, R. A., Klunk, W., et al. (2002). Research evaluation and prospective diagnosis of dementia with Lewy bodies. *Archives of Neurology, 59*(1), 43–46.

Lopez, O. L., Jagust, W. J., DeKosky, S. T., Becker, J. T., Fitzpatrick, A., Dulberg, C., et al. (2003). Prevalence and classification of mild cognitive impairment in the Cardiovascular Health Study cognition study. *Archives of Neurology, 60*(10), 1385–1389.

Louis, E. D., Schupf, N., Manly, J., Marder, K., Tang, M. X., & Mayeux, R. (2005). Association between mild Parkinsonian signs and mild cognitive impairment in a community. *Neurology, 64*(7), 1157–1161.

Lu, P. H., Masterman, D. A., Mulnard, R., Cotman, C., Miller, B., Yaffe, K., et al. (2006). Effects of testosterone on cognition and mood in male patients with mild Alzheimer disease and healthy elderly men. *Archives of Neurology, 63*(2), 177–185.

Luchsinger, J. A., Patel, B., Tang, M. X., Schupf, N., & Mayeux, R. (2007). Measures of adiposity and dementia risk in elderly persons. *Archives of Neurology, 64*(3), 392–398.

Luchsinger, J. A., Tang, M. X., Miller, J., Green, R., & Mayeux, R. (2007). Relation of higher folate intake to lower risk of Alzheimer disease in the elderly. *Archives of Neurology, 64*(1), 86–92.

Luchsinger, J. A., Tang, M. X., Stern, Y., Shea, S., & Mayeux, R. (2001). Diabetes mellitus and risk of Alzheimer's disease and dementia with stroke in a multiethnic cohort. *American Journal of Epidemiology, 154*, 635–641.

Ma, Q. L., Galasko, D. R., Ringman, J. M., Vinters, H. V., Edland, S. D., Pomakian, J., et al. (2009). Reduction of SorLA/LR11, a sorting protein limiting beta-amyloid production, in Alzheimer disease cerebrospinal fluid. *Archives of Neurology, 66*(4), 448–457.

Mahley, R. W., Weisgraber, K. H., & Huang, Y. (2006). Apolipoprotein E4: A causative factor and therapeutic target in neuropathology, including Alzheimer's disease. *Proceedings of the National Academy of Sciences USA, 103*(15), 5644–5651.

Mandell, A. M. (2010). Mental status examination in the elderly. In M. L. Albert, & J. E. Knoefel (Eds.), *Clinical Neurology of Aging*, 3rd Edition. New York: Oxford University Press.

Mandell, A., & Albert, M. L. (1990). History of subcortical dementia. In J. Cummings (Ed.), *Subcortical dementia*. New York: Oxford University Press.

Manfredi, P. L., Breuer, B., Wallenstein, S., Stegmann, M., Bottomley, G., & Libow, L. (2003). Opioid treatment for agitation in patients with advanced dementia. *International Journal of Geriatric Psychiatry, 18*(8), 700–705.

Markesbery, W. R., Schmitt, F. A., Kryscio, R. J., Davis, D. G., Smith, C. D., & Wekstein, D. R. (2006). Neuropathological substrate of mild cognitive impairment. *Archives of Neurology, 63*(1), 38–46.

Marrosu, M. G., Floris, G., Costa, G., Schirru, L., Spinicci, G., Cherchi, M. V., et al. (2006). Dementia, pyramidal system involvement, and leukoencephalopathy with a presenilin 1 mutation. *Neurology, 66*(1), 108–111.

Marshall, G. A., Monserratt, L., Harwood, D., Mandelkern, M., Cummings, J. L., & Sultzer, D. L. (2007). Positron emission tomography metabolic correlates of apathy in Alzheimer disease. *Archives of Neurology, 64*(7), 1015–1020.

Martin, B. K., Meinert, C. L., & Breitner, J. C. (2002). Double placebo design in a prevention trial for Alzheimer's disease. *Controlled Clinical Trials, 23*(1), 93–99.

Matthews, F. E., McKeith, I., Bond, J., & Brayne, C. (2006). Reaching the population with dementia drugs: What are the challenges? *International Journal of Geriatric Psychiatry, 22*(7), 627–631.

Mattson, M. P. (2008). Hormesis defined. *Ageing Research Reviews, 7*(1), 1–7.

Mattson, M. P., & Rychlik, B. (1990). Glia protect hippocampal neurons against excitatory amino acid-induced degeneration: Involvement of fibroblast growth factor. *International Journal of Developmental Neuroscience, 8*(4), 399–415.

Mayeux, R., Stern, Y., & Spanton, S. (1985). Heterogeneity in dementia of the Alzheimer type: Evidence of subgroups. *Neurology, 35*, 453–461.

Mayeux, R., Stern, Y., Rosen, J., & Benson, F. (1983). Is "subcortical dementia" a recognizable clinical entity? *Annals of Neurology, 14*(3), 278–283.

McCurry, S., Gibbons, L., Logsdon, R., Vitiello, M., & Teri, L. (2009). Insomnia in caregivers of persons with dementia: Who is at risk and what can be done about it? In K. Lichstein (Ed.), *Adult behavioral sleep medicine* (Vol. 4, pp. 519–526). Amsterdam: Elsevier.

McGeer, P. L., & McGeer, E. G. (1995). The inflammatory response system of brain: Implications for therapy of Alzheimer and other neurodegenerative disorders. *Brain Research Reviews, 21*, 195–218.

McGlynn, S. M., & Kaszniak, A. W. (1991). When metacognition fails: Impaired awareness of deficit in Alzheimer's disease. *Journal of Cognitive Neuroscience, 3*, 183–189.

McKee, A., Seshadri, S., An, R., Kase, C. S., Kowall, N., & Wolf, P. A. (2000). Cognitively normal very elderly brain donors in the Framingham Study do not show evidence of definite Alzheimer's disease. *Neurology, 54*, A324.

McKhann, G. M., Drachman, D., Folstein, M. F., Katzman, R., Price, D., & Stadlan, E. M. (1984). Clinical diagnosis of Alzheimer's disease: Report of the NINCDS-ADRDA work group. *Neurology, 34*, 939–944.

McMahon, J. A., Green, T. J., Skeaff, C. M., Knight, R. G., Mann, J. I., & Williams, S. M. (2006). A controlled trial of homocysteine lowering and cognitive performance. *New England Journal of Medicine, 354*(26), 2764–2772.

McPherson, S., Fairbanks, L., Tiken, S., Cummings, J. L., & Back-Madruga, C. (2002). Apathy and executive function in Alzheimer's disease. *Journal of the International Neuropsychological Society, 8*(3), 373–381.

Mebane-Sims, I., & Alzheimer's Association (2009). 2009 Alzheimer's disease facts and figures. *Alzheimer's & Dementia, 5*(3), 234–270.

Mega, M. S., Cummings, J. L., Fiorello, T., & Gornbein, J. (1996). The spectrum of behavioral changes in Alzheimer's disease. *Neurology, 46*, 130–135.

Melanson, M., Nalbantoglu, J., Berkovic, S., Melmed, C., Andermann, E., Roberts, L. J., et al. (1997). Progressive myoclonus epilepsy in young adults with neuropathological features of Alzheimer's disease. *Neurology, 49*(6), 1732–1733.

Mendez, M. F., Mendez, M. A., Martin, R., Smyth, K. A., & Whitehouse, P. J. (1990). Complex visual disturbances in Alzheimer's disease. *Neurology, 40*, 439–443.

Mendez, M. F., Shapira, J. S., McMurtray, A., & Licht, E. (2007). Preliminary findings: Behavioral worsening on donepezil in patients with frontotemporal dementia. *American Journal of Geriatric Psychiatry, 15*(1), 84–87.

Mesulam, M.-M. (2000). Aging, Alzheimer's disease and dementia. In M.-M. Mesulam (Ed.), *Principles of behavioral and cognitive neurology* (2nd edn.). New York: Oxford University Press.

Mesulam, M.-M. (2003). Primary progressive aphasia – A language-based dementia. *New England Journal of Medicine, 349*(16), 1535–1542.

Middleton, L. E., & Yaffe, K. (2009). Promising strategies for the prevention of dementia. *Archives of Neurology, 66*(10), 1210–1215.

Mirra, S. S., Heyman, A., McKeel, D., Sumi, S. M., Crain, B. J., Brownlee, L. M., et al. (1991). The consortium to establish a registry for Alzheimer's disease (CERAD): Part II standardization of the neuropathological assessment of Alzheimer's disease. *Neurology, 41*, 479–486.

Mittelman, M. S., Haley, W. E., Clay, O. J., & Roth, D. L. (2006). Improving caregiver well-being delays nursing home placement of patients with Alzheimer disease. *Neurology, 67*(9), 1592–1599.

Mittelman, M. S., Roth, D. L., Haley, W. E., & Zarit, S. H. (2004). Effects of a caregiver intervention on negative caregiver appraisals of behavior problems in patients with Alzheimer's disease: Results of a randomized trial. *Journal of Gerontology Series A: Psychological Sciences and Social Sciences, 59*(1), P27–P34.

Mohajeri, M. H. (2007). The underestimated potential of the immune system in prevention of Alzheimer's disease pathology. *Bioessays, 29*(9), 927–932.

Mok, W., Chow, T. W., Zheng, L., Mack, W. J., & Miller, C. (2004). Clinicopathological concordance of dementia diagnoses by community versus tertiary care clinicians. *American Journal of Alzheimer's Disease and Other Dementias, 19*(3), 161–165.

Morris, J. C., Edland, S., Clark, C., Galasko, D., Koss, E., Mohs, R., et al. (1993). The Consortium to Establish a Registry for Alzheimer's Disease (CERAD). Part IV. Rates of cognitive change in the longitudinal assessment of probable Alzheimer's disease. *Neurology, 43*, 2457–2465.

Mueller, S. G., Weiner, M. W., Thal, L. J., Petersen, R. C., Jack, C. R., Jagust, W., et al. (2005). Ways toward an early diagnosis in Alzheimer's disease: The Alzheimer's Disease Neuroimaging Initiative (ADNI). *Alzheimer's & Dementia, 1*(1), 55–66.

Mulnard, R. A., Cotman, C. W., Kawas, C., van Dyck, C. H., Sano, M., Doody, R., et al. (2000). Estrogen replacement therapy for treatment of mild to moderate Alzheimer disease: A randomized controlled trial. *Journal of the American Medical Association, 283*, 1007–1015.

Naegele, B., Thouvard, V., Pepin, J. L., Levy, P., Bonnet, C., Perret, J. E., et al. (1995). Deficits of cognitive executive functions in patients with sleep apnea syndrome. *Sleep, 18*(1), 43–52.

Nair, A. K., & Green, R. C. (2006). A century of Alzheimer's: Progress and pitfalls. *Practical Neurology, 5*(9), 22–29.

Neary, D., Snowden, J. S., Bowen, D. M., Sims, N. R., Mann, D. M., Benton, J. S., et al. (1986). Neuropsychological syndromes in presenile dementia due to cerebral atrophy. *Journal of Neurology, Neurosurgery & Psychiatry, 49*, 163–174.

Negash, S., Geda, Y., & Petersen, R. (2008). Neuropsychological characterization of mild cognitive impairment. In G. Goldenberg & B. Miller (Eds.), *Handbook of clinical neurology* (pp. 499–509). Amsterdam: Elsevier.

Nestor, P. J., Fryer, T. D., & Hodges, J. R. (2006). Declarative memory impairments in Alzheimer's disease and semantic dementia. *Neuroimage, 30*(3), 1010–1020.

Ngandu, T., von Strauss, E., Helkala, E. L., Winblad, B., Nissinen, A., Tuomilehto, J., et al. (2007). Education and dementia: What lies behind the association? *Neurology, 69*(14), 1442–1450.

Nicoll, J. A., Wilkinson, D., Holmes, C., Steart, P., Markham, H., & Weller, R. O. (2003). Neuropathology of human Alzheimer disease after immunization with amyloid-beta peptide: A case report. *Nature Medicine, 9*(4), 448–452.

Nilsson, K., Gustafson, L., & Hultberg, B. (2002). Relation between plasma homocysteine and Alzheimer's disease. *Dementia and Geriatric Cognitive Disorders, 14*(1), 7–12.

Noble, W., Planel, E., Zehr, C., Olm, V., Meyerson, J., Suleman, F., et al. (2005). Inhibition of glycogen synthase kinase-3 by lithium correlates with reduced tauopathy and degeneration in vivo. *Proceedings of the National Academy of Sciences USA, 102*(19), 6990–6995.

Nunomura, A., Perry, G., Aliev, G., Hirai, K., Takeda, A., Balraj, E. K., et al. (2001). Oxidative damage is the earliest event in Alzheimer disease. *Journal of Neuropathology and Experimental Neurology, 60*(8), 759–767.

Olde Rikkert, M. G., van der Flier, W. M., de Leeuw, F. E., Verbeek, M., Jansen, R. W., Verhey, F., et al. (2006). Multiple diagnostic tests are needed to assess multiple causes of dementia. *Archives of Neurology, 63*(1), 144–146.

Onyike, C. U., Sheppard, J. M., Tschanz, J. T., Norton, M. C., Green, R. C., Steinberg, M., et al. (2007). Epidemiology of apathy in older adults: the Cache County Study. *American Journal of Geriatric Psychiatry, 15*(5), 365–375.

Oppenheim, G. (1994). The earliest signs of Alzheimer's disease. *Journal of Geriatric Psychiatry and Neurology, 7*, 188–192.

Ortiz, F., Fitten, L. J., Cummings, J. L., Hwang, S., & Fonseca, M. (2006). Neuropsychiatric and behavioral symptoms in a community sample of Hispanics with Alzheimer's disease. *American Journal of Alzheimer's Disease and Other Dementias, 21*(4), 263–273.

Ott, A., Slooter, A. J. C., Hofman, A., van Harskamp, F., Witteman, J. C. M., van Broeckhoven, C., et al. (1998). Smoking and the risk of dementia and Alzheimer's disease in a population-based cohort study: The Rotterdam Study. *Lancet, 351*, 1840–1843.

Ott, B. R., Heindel, W. C., Papandonatos, G. D., Festa, E. K., Davis, J. D., Daiello, L. A., et al. (2008). A longitudinal study of drivers with Alzheimer disease. *Neurology, 70*(14), 1171–1178.

Ownby, R. L., Crocco, E., Acevedo, A., John, V., & Loewenstein, D. (2006). Depression and risk for Alzheimer disease: Systematic review, meta-analysis, and metaregression analysis. *Archives of General Psychiatry, 63*(5), 530–538.

Page, S., & Fletcher, T. (2006). Auguste D: One hundred years on: "The person not the case." *Dementia, 5*, 571–583.

Palmer, K., Berger, A. K., Monastero, R., Winblad, B., Backman, L., & Fratiglioni, L. (2007). Predictors of progression from mild cognitive impairment to Alzheimer disease. *Neurology, 68*(19), 1596–602.

Palop, J. J., & Mucke, L. (2009). Epilepsy and cognitive impairments in Alzheimer disease. *Archives of Neurology, 66*(4), 435–440.

Palop, J. J., Chin, J., Roberson, E. D., Wang, J., Thwin, M. T., Bien-Ly, N., et al. (2007). Aberrant excitatory neuronal activity and compensatory remodeling of inhibitory hippocampal circuits in mouse models of Alzheimer's disease. *Neuron, 55*(5), 697–711.

Pardridge, W. M., Vinters, H. V., Yang, J., Eisenberg, J., Choi, T. B., Tourtellotte, W. W., et al. (1987). Amyloid angiopathy of Alzheimer's disease: Amino acid composition and partial sequence of a 4,200-dalton peptide isolated from cortical microvessels. *Journal of Neurochemistry, 49*(5), 1394–1401.

Paul, C. A., Au, R., Fredman, L., Massaro, J. M., Seshadri, S., Decarli, C., et al. (2008). Association of alcohol consumption with brain volume in the Framingham study. *Archives of Neurology, 65*(10), 1363–1367.

Perry, R. J., & Hodges, J. R. (1999). Attention and executive deficits in Alzheimer's disease. A critical review. *Brain, 122*(Pt 3), 383–404.

Peskind, E. R., Tsuang, D. W., Bonner, L. T., Pascualy, M., Riekse, R. G., Snowden, M. B., et al. (2005). Propranolol for disruptive behaviors in nursing home residents with probable or possible Alzheimer disease: A placebo-controlled study. *Alzheimer Disease and Associated Disorders, 19*(1), 23–28.

Petersen, R. C. (2004). Mild cognitive impairment. *Continuum, 10*, 9–28.

Petersen, R. C. (2007). Mild cognitive impairment: Current research and clinical implications. *Seminars in Neurology, 27*(1), 22–31.

Petersen, R. C., & Morris, J. C. (2005). Mild cognitive impairment as a clinical entity and treatment target. *Archives of Neurology, 62*(7), 1160–3; discussion 1167.

Petersen, R. C., Parisi, J. E., Dickson, D. W., Johnson, K. A., Knopman, D. S., Boeve, B. F., et al. (2006). Neuropathological features of amnestic mild cognitive impairment. *Archives of Neurology, 63*(5), 665–672.

Petersen, R. C., Roberts, R., Knopman, D., Boeve, B., Geda, Y., Ivnik, R., et al. (2009). Mild cognitive impairment: Ten years later. *Archives of Neurology, 66*(12), 1447–1455.

Petersen, R. C., Smith, G. E., Ivnik, R. J., Tangalos, E. G., Schaid, D. J., Thibodeau, S. N., et al. (1995). Apolipoprotein E status as a predictor of the development of Alzheimer's disease in memory-impaired individuals. *Journal of the American Medical Association, 273*, 1274–1278.

Petersen, R. C., Smith, G. E., Waring, S. C., Ivnik, R. J., Tangalos, E. G., & Kokmen, E. (1999). Mild cognitive impairment. Clinical characterization and outcome. *Archives of Neurology, 56*, 303–308.

Petersen, R. C., Thomas, R. G., Grundman, M., Bennett, D. A., Doody, R., Ferris, S., et al. (2005). Vitamin E and donepezil for the treatment of mild cognitive impairment. *New England Journal of Medicine, 352*.

Petrie, E. C., Cross, D. J., Galasko, D., Schellenberg, G. D., Raskind, M. A., Peskind, E. R., et al. (2009). Preclinical evidence of Alzheimer changes: Convergent cerebrospinal fluid biomarker and fluorodeoxyglucose positron emission tomography findings. *Archives of Neurology, 66*(5), 632–637.

Petrovitch, H., White, L. R., Izmirilian, G., Ross, G. W., J. H. R., Markesbery, W. R., et al. (2000). Mid-life blood pressure and neuritic plaues, neurofibrillary tangles and brain weight and death: The HAAS. *Neurobiology of Aging, 21*, 57–62.

Petrovitch, H., White, L. R., Ross, G. W., Steinbhorn, S. C., Li, C. Y., Masaki, K. H., et al. (2001). Accuracy of clinical criteria for AD in the Honolulu-Asia Aging Study, a population-based study. *Neurology, 57*, 226–234.

Petry, S., Cummings, J. L., Hill, M. A., & Shapira, J. (1988). Personality alterations in dementia of the Alzheimer type. *Archives of Neurology, 45*, 1187–1190.

Pfeiffer, E. (1975). A short portable mental status questionnaire for the assessment of organic brain deficit in elderly patients. *Journal of the American Geriatric Society, 23*(10), 433–441.

Piccini, A., Zanusso, G., Borghi, R., Noviello, C., Monaco, S., Russo, R., et al. (2007). Association of a presenilin 1 S170F mutation with a novel Alzheimer disease molecular phenotype. *Archives of Neurology, 64*(5), 738–745.

Piolino, P., Desgranges, B., Belliard, S., Matuszewski, V., Lalevee, C., De la Sayette, V., et al. (2003). Autobiographical memory and autonoetic consciousness: Triple dissociation in neurodegenerative diseases. *Brain, 126*(Pt 10), 2203–2219.

Porsteinsson, A. P., Tariot, P. N., Erb, R., Cox, C., Smith, E., Jakimovich, L., et al. (2001). Placebo-controlled study of divalproex sodium for agitation in dementia. *American Journal of Geriatric Psychiatry, 9*, 58–66.

Portet, F., Scarmeas, N., Cosentino, S., Helzner, E. P., & Stern, Y. (2009). Extrapyramidal signs before and after diagnosis of incident Alzheimer disease in a prospective population study. *Archives of Neurology, 66*(9), 1120–1126.

Pratico, D., Clark, C. M., Liun, F., Rokach, J., Lee, V. Y., & Trojanowski, J. Q. (2002). Increase of brain oxidative stress in mild cognitive impairment: A possible predictor of Alzheimer disease. *Archives of Neurology, 59*(6), 972–976.

Press, D., & Alexander, M. (2007). Treatment of behavioral symptoms related to dementia. Retrieved April 24, 2007 from www.uptodat.com.

Prohovnik, I., Perl, D. P., Davis, K. L., Libow, L., Lesser, G., & Haroutunian, V. (2006). Dissociation of neuropathology from severity of dementia in late-onset Alzheimer disease. *Neurology, 66*(1), 49–55.

Qin, W., Chachich, M., Lane, M., Roth, G., Bryant, M., de Cabo, R., et al. (2006). Calorie restriction attenuates Alzheimer's disease type brain amyloidosis in Squirrel monkeys (Saimiri sciureus). *Journal of Alzheimer's Disease, 10*(4), 417–422.

Qin, W., Yang, T., Ho, L., Zhao, Z., Wang, J., Chen, L., et al. (2006). Neuronal SIRT1 activation as a novel mechanism underlying the prevention of Alzheimer disease amyloid neuropathology by calorie restriction. *Journal of Biological Chemistry, 281*(31), 21745–21754.

Rabins, P. V., & Lyketsos, C. G. (2005). Antipsychotic drugs in dementia: What should be made of the risks? *Journal of the American Medical Association, 294*(15), 1963–1965.

Rabins, P. V., Mace, N. L., & Lucas, M. J. (1982). The impact of dementia on the family. *Journal of the American Medical Association, 248*(3), 333–335.

Rapcsak, S. Z., Croswell, S. C., & Rubens, A. B. (1989). Apraxia in Alzheimer's disease. *Neurology, 39*, 664–668.

Razay, G., Vreugdenhil, A., & Wilcock, G. (2007). The metabolic syndrome and Alzheimer disease. *Archives of Neurology, 64*(1), 93–96.

Reding, M., Haycox, J., & Blass, J. (1985). Depression in patients referred to a dementia clinic: A three-year prospective study. *Archives of Neurology, 42*, 894–896.

Reed, B. R., Mungas, D. M., Kramer, J. H., Ellis, W., Vinters, H. V., Zarow, C., et al. (2007). Profiles of neuropsychological impairment in autopsy-defined Alzheimer's disease and cerebrovascular disease. *Brain, 130*(Pt 3), 731–739.

Reisberg, B., Doody, R., Stoffler, A., Schmitt, F., Ferris, S., Mobius, H. J., et al. (2003). Memantine in moderate-to-severe Alzheimer's disease. *New England Journal of Medicine, 348*, 1333–1341.

Reisberg, B., Ferris, S., de Leon, M., Torossian, C., Kadiyala, S., & Zhu, W. (2005). Subjective cognitive impairment: the pre-mild cognitive impairment stage of brain degeneration-longitudinal outcome after a mean of 7 years follow-up. *Neuropsychopharmacology, 30* (Suppl 1), S81.

Reisberg, B., Prichep, L., Mosconi, L., John, E. R., Glodzik-Sobanska, L., Boksay, I., et al. (2008). The pre-mild cognitive impairment, subjective cognitive impairment stage of Alzheimer's disease. *Alzheimer's & Dementia, 4*(1 Suppl 1), S98–S108.

Reitz, C., den Heijer, T., van Duijn, C., Hofman, A., & Breteler, M. M. (2007). Relation between smoking and risk of dementia and Alzheimer disease: The Rotterdam Study. *Neurology, 69*(10), 998–1005.

Rey, A. (1941). L'examen psychologie dans les cas d'encephalopathie traumatique. *Archives de Psychologie, 28*, 286–340.

Reynolds, C. F., Hoch, C. C., Stack, J., & Campbell, D. (1988). The nature and management of sleep/wake disturbance in Alzheimer's dementia. *Psychopharmacology Bulletin, 24*(1), 43–48.

Richards, M., Stern, Y., & Mayeux, R. (1993). Subtle extrapyramidal signs can predict the development of dementia in elderly individuals. *Neurology, 43*, 2184–2188.

Ringman, J. M., Younkin, S. G., Pratico, D., Seltzer, W., Cole, G. M., Geschwind, D. H., et al. (2008). Biochemical markers in persons with preclinical familial Alzheimer disease. *Neurology, 71*(2), 85–92.

Rinne, U. K. (1989). Lisuride, a dopamine agonist in the treatment of early Parkinson's disease. *Neurology, 39*, 336–339.

Risner, M. E., Saunders, A. M., Altman, J. F., Ormandy, G. C., Craft, S., Foley, I. M., et al. (2006). Efficacy of rosiglitazone in a genetically defined population with mild-to-moderate Alzheimer's disease. *Pharmacogenomics Journal*, 1–9.

Ritchie, C. W., Bush, A. I., Mackinnon, A., Macfarlane, S., Mastwyk, M., MacGregor, L., et al. (2003). Metal-protein attenuation with iodochlorhydroxyquin (clioquinol) targeting Abeta amyloid deposition and toxicity in Alzheimer disease: A pilot phase 2 clinical trial. *Archives of Neurology, 60*(12), 1685–1691.

Ritchie, K., Carriere, I., de Mendonca, A., Portet, F., Dartigues, J. F., Rouaud, O., et al. (2007). The neuroprotective effects of caffeine: A prospective population study (the Three City Study). *Neurology, 69*(6), 536–545.

Riviere, S., Gillette-Guyonnet, S., Andrieu, S., Nourhashemi, F., Lauque, S., Cantet, C., et al. (2002). Cognitive function and caregiver burden: Predictive factors for eating behaviour disorders in Alzheimer's disease. *International Journal of Geriatric Psychiatry, 17*(10), 950–955.

Roberds, S. L., Anderson, J., Basi, G., Bienkowski, M. J., Branstetter, D. G., Chen, K. S., et al. (2001). BACE knockout mice are healthy despite lacking the primary beta-secretase activity in brain: Implications for Alzheimer's disease therapeutics. *Human Molecular Genetics, 10*(12), 1317–1324.

Robert, P. H., Berr, C., Volteau, M., Bertogliati, C., Benoit, M., Sarazin, M., et al. (2006). Apathy in patients with mild cognitive impairment and the risk of developing dementia of Alzheimer's disease: A one-year follow-up study. *Clinical Neurology and Neurosurgery, 108*(8), 733–736.

Rockwood, K., Kirkland, S., Hogan, D. B., MacKnight, C., Merry, H., Verreault, R., et al. (2002). Use of lipid-lowering agents, indication bias, and the risk of dementia in community-dwelling elderly people. *Archives of Neurology, 59*(2), 223–227.

Roe, C. M., Mintun, M. A., D'Angelo, G., Xiong, C., Grant, E. A., & Morris, J. C. (2008). Alzheimer disease and cognitive reserve: Variation of education effect with carbon 11-labeled Pittsburgh Compound B uptake. *Archives of Neurology, 65*(11), 1467–1471.

Roe, C. M., Xiong, C., Miller, J. P., & Morris, J. C. (2007). Education and Alzheimer disease without dementia: Support for the cognitive reserve hypothesis. *Neurology, 68*(3), 223–228.

Rogaeva, E., Meng, Y., Lee, J. H., Gu, Y., Kawarai, T., Zou, F., et al. (2007). The neuronal sortilin-related receptor SORL1 is genetically associated with Alzheimer disease. *Nature Genetics, 39*(2), 168–177.

Romanelli, M. F., Morris, J. C., Ashkin, K., & Coben, L. A. (1990). Advanced Alzheimer's disease is a risk factor for late-onset seizures. *Archives of Neurology, 47*, 847–850.

Rosen, H. J., Allison, S. C., Schauer, G. F., Gorno-Tempini, M. L., Weiner, M. W., & Miller, B. L. (2005). Neuroanatomical correlates of behavioural disorders in dementia. *Brain, 128*(Pt 11), 2612–2625.

Rosenberg, P. B. (2005). Clinical aspects of inflammation in Alzheimer's disease. *International Reviews of Psychiatry, 17*(6), 503–514.

Rowe, J., & Kahn, R. (1987). Human aging: Usual and successful. *Science, 237*, 143–149.

Rubin, E. (1992). Psychosis in neurologic diseases: Delusions as part of Alzheimer's disease. *Neuropsychiatry, Neuropsychology, and Behavioral Neurology, 5*(2), 108–113.

Rubin, E., Kinscherf, D., Grant, E., & Storandt, M. (1991). The influence of major depression on clinical and psychometric assessment of senile dementia of the Alzheimer type. *American Journal of Psychiatry, 148,* 1164–1171.

Sabbagh, M. N. (2009). Drug development for Alzheimer's disease: Where are we now and where are we headed? *American Journal of Geriatric Pharmacotherapy, 7*(3), 167–185.

Salloway, S., Mintzer, J., Weiner, M. F., & Cummings, J. L. (2008). Disease-modifying therapies in Alzheimer's disease. *Alzheimer's & Dementia, 4*(2), 65–79.

Salloway, S., Sperling, R., Gilman, S., Fox, N. C., Blennow, K., Raskind, M., et al. (2009). A phase 2 multiple ascending dose trial of bapineuzumab in mild to moderate Alzheimer disease. *Neurology, 73*(24), 2061–2070.

Salmon, D. P., Thomas, R. G., Pay, M. M., Booth, A., Hofstetter, C. R., Thal, L. J., et al. (2002). Alzheimer's disease can be accurately diagnosed in very mildly impaired individuals. *Neurology, 59*(7), 1022–1028.

Sanford, J. R. A. (1975). Tolerance of debility in elderly dependents by supporters at home: Its significance for hospital practice. *British Medical Journal, 3,* 471–473.

Sano, M., Ernesto, C., Thomas, R. G., Klauber, M. R., Schafer, K., Grundman, M., et al. (1997). A controlled trial of selegiline, alpha-tocopherol, or both as treatment for Alzheimer's disease. *New England Journal of Medicine, 336*(17), 1216–1222.

Sanz, C., Andrieu, S., Sinclair, A., Hanaire, H., & Vellas, B. (2009). Diabetes is associated with a slower rate of cognitive decline in Alzheimer disease. *Neurology, 73*(17), 1359–1366.

Scarmeas, N., Brandt, J., Albert, M., Hadjigeorgiou, G., Papadimitriou, A., Dubois, B., et al. (2005). Delusions and hallucinations are associated with worse outcome in Alzheimer disease. *Archives of Neurology, 62*(10), 1601–1608.

Scarmeas, N., Honig, L. S., Choi, H., Cantero, J., Brandt, J., Blacker, D., et al. (2009). Seizures in Alzheimer disease: Who, when, and how common? *Archives of Neurology, 66*(8), 992–997.

Scarmeas, N., Stern, Y., Mayeux, R., & Luchsinger, J. (2007). Mediterranean diet (MeDi) and longevity in Alzheimer's disease (AD) course. *Neurology, 68*(Suppl 1), 169.

Scarmeas, N., Stern, Y., Mayeux, R., & Luchsinger, J. A. (2006). Mediterranean diet, Alzheimer disease, and vascular mediation. *Archives of Neurology, 63*(12), 1709–1717.

Scarmeas, N., Stern, Y., Mayeux, R., Manly, J. J., Schupf, N., & Luchsinger, J. A. (2009). Mediterranean diet and mild cognitive impairment. *Archives of Neurology, 66*(2), 216–225.

Schachter, D. L., & Kihlstrom, J. F. (1989). Models of memory and the understanding of memory disorders. In P. R. Yanagihara (Ed.), *Memory disorders: Research and clinical practice.* New York: Marcel Dekker.

Schaefer, E. J., Bongard, V., Beiser, A. S., Lamon-Fava, S., Robins, S. J., Au, R., et al. (2006). Plasma phosphatidylcholine docosahexaenoic acid content and risk of dementia and Alzheimer disease: The Framingham Heart Study. *Archives of Neurology, 63*(11), 1545–1550.

Schaie, K. W. (1989). The hazards of cognitive aging. *Gerontologist, 29*(4), 484–493.

Scheff, S. W., Price, D. A., Schmitt, F. A., DeKosky, S. T., & Mufson, E. J. (2007). Synaptic alterations in CA1 in mild Alzheimer disease and mild cognitive impairment. *Neurology, 68*(18), 1501–1508.

Schenk, D., Barbour, R., Dunn, W., et al. (1999). Immunization with amyloid-beta attenuates Alzheimer-disease-like pathology in the PDAPP mouse. *Nature, 400,* 173–177.

Schenk, D., Hagen, M., & Seubert, P. (2004). Current progress in beta-amyloid immuno-therapy. *Current Opinions in Immunology, 16*(5), 599–606.

Schneider, J. A., Arvanitakis, Z., Bang, W., & Bennett, D. A. (2007). Mixed brain pathologies account for most dementia cases in community-dwelling older persons. *Neurology, 69*(24), 2197–2204.

Schneider, L. S. (2007). Author's reply. *New England Journal of Medicine, 356,* 416–418.

Schneider, L. S., & Sano, M. (2009). Current Alzheimer's disease clinical trials: methods and placebo outcomes. *Alzheimer's & Dementia, 5*(5), 388–397.

Schneider, L. S., Dagerman, K. S., & Insel, P. (2005). Risk of death with atypical antipsychotic drug treatment for dementia: Meta-analysis of randomized placebo-controlled trials. *Journal of the American Medical Association, 294*(15), 1934–1943.

Schneider, L. S., Tariot, P. N., Dagerman, K. S., Davis, S. M., Hsiao, J. K., Ismail, M. S., et al. (2006). Effectiveness of atypical antipsychotic drugs in patients with Alzheimer's disease. *New England Journal of Medicine, 355*(15), 1525–1538.

Senanarong, V., Cummings, J. L., Fairbanks, L., Mega, M., Masterman, D. M., O'Connor, S. M., et al. (2004). Agitation in Alzheimer's disease is a manifestation of frontal lobe dysfunction. *Dementia and Geriatric Cognitive Disorders, 17*(1–2), 14–20.

Shalat, S. L., Seltzer, B., Pidcock, C., & Baker, E. L., Jr. (1987). Risk factors for Alzheimer's disease: A case-control study. *Neurology, 37*(10), 1630–1633.

Shumaker, S., Legault, C., & Rapp, S. (2003). The effects of estrogen plus progestin on the incidence of dementia and mild cognitive impairment in postmenopausal women: The Women's Health Initiative Memory Study. *Journal of the American Medical Association, 289,* 2651–2662.

Siemers, E. R., Quinn, J. F., Kaye, J., Farlow, M. R., Porsteinsson, A., Tariot, P., et al. (2006). Effects of a gamma-secretase inhibitor in a randomized study of patients with Alzheimer disease. *Neurology, 66*(4), 602–604.

Silver, M., Newell, K., Hyman, B., Growdon, J., Hedley-Whyte, E. T., & Perls, T. (1998). Unraveling the mystery of cognitive changes in old age: Correlation of neuropsychological evaluation with neuropathological findings in the extreme old. *International Psychogeriatrics, 10*(1), 25–41.

Singer, C., Tractenberg, R. E., Kaye, J., Schafer, K., Gamst, A., Grundman, M., et al. (2003). A multicenter, placebo-controlled trial of melatonin for sleep disturbance in Alzeimer's disease. *Sleep, 26*(7), 893–901.

Sink, K. M., Holden, K. F., & Yaffe, K. (2005). Pharmacological treatment of neuropsychiatric symptoms of dementia: A review of the evidence. *Journal of the American Medical Association, 293*(5), 596–608.

Siu, A. (1991). Screening for dementia and investigating its causes. *Annals of Internal Medicine, 115,* 122–132.

Sjogren, M., Davidsson, P., Tullberg, M., Minthon, L., Wallin, A., Wikkelso, C., et al. (2001). Both total and phosphorylated tau are increased in Alzheimer's Disease. *Journal of Neurology, Neurosurgery & Psychiatry, 70,* 624–630.

Skovronsky, D. M., & Lee, V. M. (2000). Beta-secretase revealed: Starting gate for race to novel therapies for Alzheimer's disease. *Trends in Pharmacological Science, 21*(5), 161–163.

Sloane, P. D., Zimmerman, S., Suchindran, C., Reed, P., Wang, L., Boustani, M., et al. (2002). The public health impact of Alzheimer's disease, 2000–2050: Potential implication of treatment advances. *Annual Review of Public Health, 23,* 213–231.

Smith, G. E., Kokmen, E., & O'Brien, P. C. (2000). Risk factors for nursing home placement in a population-based dementia cohort. *Journal of the American Geriatric Society, 48*(5), 519–525.

Smith, G. E., Pankratz, V. S., Negash, S., Machulda, M. M., Petersen, R. C., Boeve, B. F., et al. (2007). A plateau in pre-Alzheimer memory decline: Evidence for compensatory mechanisms? *Neurology, 69*(2), 133–139.

Smith, S. J. (2005). EEG in neurological conditions other than epilepsy: When does it help, what does it add? *Journal of Neurology, Neurosurgery & Psychiatry, 76*(Suppl 2), ii8–12.

Snowdon, D., Greiner, L., Mortimer, J., Riley, K., Greiner, P., & Markesbery, W. (1997). Brain infarction and the clinical expression of Alzheimer disease. The Nun Study. *Journal of the American Medical Association, 277*, 813–817.

Snowdon, D. A., Kemper, S. J., Mortimer, J. A., Greiner, L. H., Wekstein, D. R., & Markesbury, W. R. (1996). Linguistic ability in early life and cognitive function and Alzheimer's disease in late life: Findings from the nun study. *Journal of the American Medical Association, 275*(7), 528–532.

Snyder, P. J., & Pearn, A. M. (2007). Historical note on Darwin's consideration of early-onset dementia in older persons, thirty-six years before Alzheimer's initial case report. *Alzheimer's & Dementia, 3*(3), 137–142.

Solfrizzi, V., Colacicco, A. M., D'Introno, A., Capurso, C., Torres, F., Rizzo, C., et al. (2006). Dietary intake of unsaturated fatty acids and age-related cognitive decline: A 8. 5-year follow-up of the Italian Longitudinal Study on Aging. *Neurobiology and Aging, 27*(11), 1694–1704.

Solfrizzi, V., D'Introno, A., Colacicco, A. M., Capurso, C., Del Parigi, A., Baldassarre, G., et al. (2007). Alcohol consumption, mild cognitive impairment, and progression to dementia. *Neurology, 68*(21), 1790–1799.

Solfrizzi, V., Frisardi, V., Capurso, C., D'Introno, A., Colacicco, A. M., Vendemmiale, G., et al. (2009). Moderate alcohol consumption, apolipoprotein E, and neuroprotection. *Archives of Neurology, 66*(4), 541–542.

Solomon, P. R., Hirschoff, A., Kelly, B., Relin, M., Brush, M., DeVeaux, R. D., et al. (1998). A 7 minute neurocognitive screening battery highly sensitive to Alzheimer's disease. *Archives of Neurology, 55*, 349–355.

Sparks, D. L., Sabbagh, M. N., Connor, D. J., Lopez, J., Launer, L. J., Browne, P., et al. (2005). Atorvastatin for the treatment of mild to moderate Alzheimer Disease: Preliminary results. *Archives of Neurology, 62*, 753–757.

Spielmeyer, W. (1916). Alzheimer's Lebenswerk. *Zeitschrift für die gesamte Neurologie und Psychiatrie, 33*, 1–44.

Stam, F. (1985). Senile dementia and senile involution of the brain. In J. A. M. Fredericks (Ed.), *Neurobehavioral disorders* (pp. 283–288). Amsterdam: Elsevier Science.

Starkstein, S. E., Jorge, R., Mizrahi, R., & Robinson, R. G. (2006). A prospective longitudinal study of apathy in Alzheimer's disease. *Journal of Neurology, Neurosurgery & Psychiatry, 77*(1), 8–11.

Stern, Y., Gurland, B., Tatemichi, T. K., Tang, M. X., Wilder, D., & Mayeux, R. (1994). Influence of education and occupation on the incidence of Alzheimer's disease. *Journal of the American Medical Association, 271*, 1004–1010.

Stokholm, J., Vogel, A., Gade, A., & Waldemar, G. (2006). Heterogeneity in executive impairment in patients with very mild Alzheimer's disease. *Dementia and Geriatric Cognitive Disorders, 22*(1), 54–59.

Storandt, M., Botwinick, J., & Danziger, W. (1986). Longitudinal changes: Patients with mild SDAT and matched healthy controls. In L. Poon (Ed.), *Handbook of clinical memory assessment for older adults* (pp. 227–284). Washington, DC: American Psychological Association.

Storandt, M., Grant, E. A., Miller, J. P., & Morris, J. C. (2006). Longitudinal course and neuropathological outcomes in original vs. revised MCI and in pre-MCI. *Neurology, 67*(3), 467–473.

Strauss, M. E., & Ogrocki, P. K. (1996). Confirmation of an association between family history of affective disorder and the depressive syndrome in Alzheimer's disease. *American Journal of Psychiatry, 153*, 1340–1342.

Strub, R. L., & Black, F. W. (2000). *The Mental Status Examination in neurology* (4th edn.). Philadelphia: F. A. Davis.

Su, Y., Ryder, J., Li, B., Wu, X., Fox, N., Solenberg, P., et al. (2004). Lithium, a common drug for bipolar disorder treatment, regulates amyloid-beta precursor protein processing. *Biochemistry, 43*(22), 6899–6908.

Suh, D. C., Arcona, S., Thomas, S. K., Powers, C., Rabinowicz, A. L., Shin, H., et al. (2004). Risk of antipsychotic drug use in patients with Alzheimer's disease treated with rivastigmine. *Drugs & Aging, 21*(6), 395–403.

Swan, G. E., & Lessov-Schlaggar, C. N. (2007). The effects of tobacco smoke and nicotine on cognition and the brain. *Neuropsychological Review, 17*(3), 259–273.

Szekely, C. A., Thorne, J. E., Zandi, P. P., Ek, M., Messias, E., Breitner, J. C., et al. (2004). Nonsteroidal anti-inflammatory drugs for the prevention of Alzheimer's disease: A systematic review. *Neuroepidemiology, 23*, 159–169.

Tabert, M. H., Albert, S. M., Borukhova-Milov, L., Camacho, Y., Pelton, G., Liu, X., et al. (2002). Functional deficits in patients with mild cognitive impairment: Prediction of AD. *Neurology, 58*(5), 758–764.

Tabert, M. H., Manly, J. J., Liu, X., Pelton, G. H., Rosenblum, S., Jacobs, M., et al. (2006). Neuropsychological prediction of conversion to Alzheimer disease in patients with mild cognitive impairment. *Archives of General Psychiatry, 63*(8), 916–924.

Talbot, C., Lendon, C., Craddock, N., Shears, S., Morris, J. C., & Goate, A. (1994). Protection against Alzheimer's disease with ApoE epsilon2. *Lancet, 343*, 1432–1433.

Tan, Z. S., Beiser, A. S., Vasan, R. S., Roubenoff, R., Dinarello, C. A., Harris, T. B., et al. (2007). Inflammatory markers and the risk of Alzheimer disease: The Framingham Study. *Neurology, 68*(22), 1902–1908.

Tan, Z. S., Seshadri, S., Zhang, Y., Beiser, A., Felson, D., Hannan, M. T., et al. (2005). Bone mineral density and the risk of Alzheimer's disease. *Archives of Neurologyogy, 62*(1), 107–111.

Tang-Wai, D., & Mapstone, M. (2006). What are we seeing? Is posterior cortical atrophy just Alzheimer disease? *Neurology, 66*(3), 300–301.

Tariot, P. N., Farlow, M. R., Grossberg, G. T., Graham, S. M., McDonald, S., & Gergel, I. (2004). Memantine treatment in patients with moderate to severe Alzheimer disease already receiving donepezil: A randomized controlled trial. *Journal of the American Medical Association, 291*, 317–324.

Tariot, P. N., Raman, R., Jakimovich, L., Schneider, L., Porsteinsson, A., Thomas, R., et al. (2005). Divalproex sodium in nursing home residents with possible or probable Alzheimer Disease complicated by agitation: A randomized, controlled trial. *American Journal of Geriatric Psychiatry, 13*(11), 942–949.

Tariot, P. N., Schneider, L., Katz, I. R., Mintzer, J. E., Street, J., Copenhaver, M., et al. (2006). Quetiapine treatment of psychosis associated with dementia: A double-blind, randomized, placebo-controlled clinical trial. *American Journal of Geriatric Psychiatry, 14*(9), 767–776.

Technology Appraisal TA 111 [Electronic (2006). Version]. *National Institute for Health and Clinical Excellence*. Retrieved November 11, 2007 from www.nice.org.uk/guidance/TA111.

Teri, L., & Wagner, A. (1992). Alzheimer's disease and depression. *Journal of Consulting and Clinical Psychology, 60*(3), 379–391.

Teri, L., Logsdon, R. G., & McCurry, S. M. (2002). Nonpharmacologic treatment of behavioral disturbance in dementia. *Medical Clinics of North America, 86*(3), 641–656.

Teri, L., Logsdon, R. G., Peskind, E., Raskind, M., Weiner, M., Tractenberg, R. E., et al. (2000). Treatment of agitation in AD: A randomized, placebo controlled clinical trial. *Neurology, 55*(9), 1271–1278.

Terry, A. V., Jr., & Buccafusco, J. J. (2003). The cholinergic hypothesis of age and Alzheimer's disease-related cognitive deficits: Recent challenges and their implications for novel drug development. *Journal of Pharmacology and Experimental Therapeutics, 306*(3), 821–827.

Tervo, S., Kivipelto, M., Hanninen, T., Vanhanen, M., Hallikainen, M., Mannermaa, A., et al. (2004). Incidence and risk factors for mild cognitive impairment: A population-based three-year follow-up study of cognitively healthy elderly subjects. *Dementia and Geriatric Cognitive Disorders, 17*(3), 196–203.

Tierney, M. C., Szalai, J. P., Snow, W. G., & Fisher, R. H. (1996). The prediction of Alzheimer disease. The role of patient and informant perceptions of cognitive deficits. *Archives of Neurology, 53*(5), 423–427.

Trinh, N. H., Hoblyn, J., Mohanty, S., & Yaffe, K. (2003). Efficacy of cholinesterase inhibitors in the treatment of neuropsychiatric symptoms and functional impairment in Alzheimer disease: A meta-analysis. *Journal of the American Medical Association, 289*(2), 210–216.

Tuokko, H., Frerichs, R., Graham, J., Rockwood, K., Kristjansson, B., Fisk, J., et al. (2003). Five-year follow-up of cognitive impairment with no dementia. *Archives of Neurology, 60*(4), 577–582.

Valenti, D. (2010). Alzheimer's disease: Visual system review. *Optometry – Journal of the American Optometric Association 81*(1), 12–21.

van Groen, T., & Kadish, I. (2005). Transgenic AD model mice, effects of potential anti-AD treatments on inflammation and pathology. *Brain Research Reviews, 48*(2), 370–378.

van Osch, L. A., Hogervorst, E., Combrinck, M., & Smith, A. D. (2004). Low thyroid-stimulating hormone as an independent risk factor for Alzheimer disease. *Neurology, 62*(11), 1967–1971.

van Reekum, R., Stuss, D. T., & Ostrander, L. (2005). Apathy: Why care? *Journal of Neuropsychiatry and Clinical Neurosciences, 17*(1), 7–19.

Varma, A. R., Snowden, J. S., Lloyd, J. J., Talbot, P. R., Mann, D. M., & Neary, D. (1999). Evaluation of the NINCDS-ADRDA criteria in the differentiation of Alzheimer's disease and frontotemporal dementia. *Journal of Neurology, Neurosurgery & Psychiatry, 66*(2), 184–188.

Vinters, H. V. (2006). Neuropathology of amnestic mild cognitive impairment. *Archives of Neurology, 63*(5), 645–646.

Volicer, L. (2001). Alzheimer's disease treatment in the VHA: Why cholinesterase inhibitors are worth the cost. *Federal Practitioner* (April), 25, 32, 35.

Volicer, L., Berman, S. A., Cipolloni, P. B., & Mandell, A. (1997). Persistent vegetative state in Alzheimer disease – Does it exist? *Archives of Neurology, 54*, 1382–1384.

Volicer, L., Harper, D. G., Manning, B. C., Goldstein, R., & Statlin, A. (2001). Sundowning and circadian rhythms in Alzheimer's disease. *American Journal of Psychiatry, 158*, 5.

Walker, L. C., Ibegbu, C. C., Todd, C. W., Robinson, H. L., Jucker, M., & LeVine, H. (2005). Emerging prospects for the disease-modifying treatment of Alzheimer's disease. *Biochemical Pharmacology, 69*(7), 1001–1008.

Walsh, D. M., & Selkoe, D. J. (2004). Deciphering the molecular basis of memory failure in Alzheimer's disease. *Neuron, 44*(1), 181–193.

Wancata, J., Windhaber, J., Krautgartner, M., & Alexandrowicz, R. (2003). The consequences of non-cognitive symptoms of dementia in medical hospital departments. *International Journal of Psychiatry in Medicine, 33*(3), 257–271.

Warrington, E. K. (1975). The selective impairment of semantic memory. *Quarterly Journal of Experimental Psychology, 27*(4), 635–657.

Weggen, S., Eriksen, J. L., & Das, P. (2001). A subset of NSAIDs lower amyloidgenic Abeta42 independently of cyclooxygenase activity. *Nature, 414*, 212–216.

Weiner, M. F., Tractenberg, R. E., Sano, M., Logsdon, R. G., Teri, L., Galasko, D., et al. (2002). No long-term effect of behavioral treatment on psychotropic drug use for agitation in Alzheimer's Disease patients. *Journal of Geriatric Psychiatry and Neurology, 15*(2), 95–98.

Weintraub, S. (2000). Neuropsychological assessment of mental state. In M.-M. Mesulam (Ed.), *Principles of behavioral and cognitive neurology* (pp. 121–173). New York: Oxford University Press.

Welsh, K., Butters, N., Hughes, J., Mohs, R., & Heyman, A. (1991). Detection of abnormal memory decline in mild cases of Alzheimer's disease using CERAD neuropsychological measures. *Archives of Neurology, 48*, 278–281.

Weuve, J., Kang, J. H., Manson, J. E., Breteler, M. M. B., Ware, J. H., & Grodstein, F. (2004). Physical activity, including walking, and cognitive function in older women. *Journal of the American Medical Association, 292*(12), 1454–1461.

Weytingh, M. D., Bossuyt, P. M., & van Crevel, H. (1995). Reversible dementia: More than 10% or less than 1%? A quantitative review. *Journal of Neurology, 242*(7), 466–471.

White-Means, S., & Thornton, M. C. (1990). Ethnic differences in the production of informal home health care. *The Gerontologist, 30*, 758–768.

Whitwell, J. L., Petersen, R. C., Negash, S., Weigand, S. D., Kantarci, K., Ivnik, R. J., et al. (2007). Patterns of atrophy differ among specific subtypes of mild cognitive impairment. *Archives of Neurology, 64*(8), 1130–1138.

Whitwell, J. L., Shiung, M. M., Przybelski, S. A., Weigand, S. D., Knopman, D. S., Boeve, B. F., et al. (2008). MRI patterns of atrophy associated with progression to AD in amnestic mild cognitive impairment. *Neurology, 70*(7), 512–520.

Wilcock, D. M., Jantzen, P. T., Li, Q., Morgan, D., & Gordon, M. N. (2007). Amyloid-beta vaccination, but not nitro-nonsteroidal anti-inflammatory drug treatment, increases vascular amyloid and microhemorrhage while both reduce parenchymal amyloid. *Neuroscience, 144*(3), 950–960.

Wilcock, G., Mobius, H., & Sotffler, A. (2002). A double-blind, placebo-controlled multicentre study of memantine in mild to moderate vascular dementia (MMM500). *International Clinical Physchoparmacology, 17*(6), 297–305.

Willem, M., Garratt, A. N., Novak, B., Citron, M., Kaufmann, S., Rittger, A., et al. (2006). Control of peripheral nerve myelination by the β-secretase BACE1. *Science, 314*, 664–666.

Wilson, R. S., Barnes, L. L., Bennett, D. A., Li, Y., Bienias, J. L., Mendes de Leon, C. F., et al. (2005). Proneness to psychological distress and risk of Alzheimer disease in a biracial community. *Neurology, 64*(2), 380–382.

Wilson, R. S., Scherr, P. A., Schneider, J. A., Tang, Y., & Bennett, D. A. (2007). Relation of cognitive activity to risk of developing Alzheimer disease. *Neurology, 69*(20), 1911–1920.

Wilson, R. S., Schneider, J. A., Bienias, J. L., Arnold, S. E., Evans, D. A., & Bennett, D. A. (2003). Depressive symptoms, clinical AD, and cortical plaques and tangles in older persons. *Neurology, 61*(8), 1102–1107.

Winblad, B., & Poritis, N. (1999). Memantine in severe dementia: Results of the M-BEST Study (Benefit and Efficacy in Severely Demented Patients During Treatment with Memantine). *International Journal of Geriatric Psychiatry, 14*, 135–146.

Winblad, B., Palmer, K., & Kivipelto, M., et al. (2004). Mild cognitive impairment: Beyond controversies, toward a consensus: Report of the international working group on mild cognitive impairment. *Journal of Internal Medicine, 256*, 240–246.

Wolozin, B. (2004). Cholestesterol and the biology of Alzheimer's disease. *Neuron, 41*, 7–10.

Wolozin, B., Kellman, W., Ruosseau, P., Celesia, G. G., & Siegel, G. (2000). Decreased prevalence of Alzheimer disease associated with 3-hydroxy-3methyglutaryl coenzyme A reductase inhibitors. *Archives of Neurology, 57*, 1439–1443.

Wynn, Z. J., & Cummings, J. L. (2004). Cholinesterase inhibitor therapies and neuropsychiatric manifestations of Alzheimer's disease. *Dementia and Geriatric Cognitive Disorders, 17*(1–2), 100–108.

Xie, Z., Dong, Y., Maeda, U., Moir, R. D., Xia, W., Culley, D. J., et al. (2007). The inhalation anesthetic isoflurane induces a vicious cycle of apoptosis and amyloid beta-protein accumulation. *Journal of Neuroscience, 27*(6), 1247–1254.

Yaari, R., & Corcy-Bloom, J. (2007). Alzheimer's disease. *Seminars in Neurology, 27*(1), 32–41.

Yaffe, K., Lui, L. Y., Zmuda, J., & Cauley, J. (2002). Sex hormones and cognitive function in older men. *Journal of the American Geriatric Society, 50*(4), 707–712.

Yamin, R., Bagchi, S., Hildebrant, R., Scaloni, A., Widom, R. L., & Abraham, C. R. (2007). Acyl peptide hydrolase, a serine proteinase isolated from conditioned medium of neuroblastoma cells, degrades the amyloid-beta peptide. *Journal of Neurochemistry, 100*(2), 458–467.

Zablocka, A., Janusz, M., Macala, J., & Lisowski, J. (2005). A proline-rich polypeptide complex and its nonapeptide fragment inhibit nitric oxide production induced in mice. *Regulatory Peptides, 125*(1–3), 35–39.

Zandi, P. P., Anthony, J. C., Khachaturian, A. S., Stone, S. V., Gustafson, D., Tschanz, J. T., et al. (2004). Reduced risk of Alzheimer disease in users of antioxidant vitamin supplements: The Cache County Study. *Archives of Neurology, 61*(1), 82–88.

Zandi, P. P., Sparks, D. L., Khachaturian, A. S., Tschanz, J. T., Norton, M., Steinberg, M., et al. (2005). Do statins reduce risk of incident dementia and Alzheimer Disease? The Cache County Study. *Archives of General Psychiatry, 62*, 217–224.

2

Vascular Dementia

Angela L. Jefferson, Amanda M. Gentile, and Ravi Kahlon

Introduction

The impact of vascular disease on cognition has been of interest to scientists and clinicians for over a century. Early 19th-century French neurologists speculated that postmortem region-specific vascular lesions were responsible for cognitive decline (Paul et al., 2005). In 1894, Swiss neurologist, Otto Binswanger, reported an association between atherosclerosis, reduction in cerebral perfusion, and cognitive decline in older adults (Binswanger, 1894; Paul et al., 2005). Since Binswanger's initial investigations, research of how vascular disease impacts central nervous system integrity has yielded considerable advances, but many mechanistic aspects remain unclear.

The concept of vascular-related brain injury has assumed many diagnostic labels over the years, emphasizing different etiological nuances. One of the first labels for what is now referred to as vascular dementia (VaD) was "senile dementia," a common term for various forms of dementia associated with older age in the early 20th century (Torack, 1983). In some cases, senile dementia was used to describe dementia due to hardening of the arteries, suggesting dementia of a vascular origin (Torack, 1983). The term "multi-infarct dementia" was introduced in 1975 to describe a pattern of cognitive decline associated with multiple and diffuse strokes (Hachinski et al., 1975). By 1985, VaD had replaced the multi-infarct dementia label, as the field began to recognize that vascular pathologies aside from stroke, such as subcortical microvascular disease, were related to dementia (Loeb & Meyer, 1996). More recently, vascular cognitive impairment (VCI) has been applied to the spectrum of mild to severe cognitive deficits presumed to be caused by

The Handbook of Alzheimer's Disease and Other Dementias, First Edition.
Edited by Andrew E. Budson, Neil W. Kowall.
© 2011 Blackwell Publishing Ltd. Published 2011 by Blackwell Publishing Ltd.

cerebrovascular disease, including cortical infarcts, subcortical infarcts, silent infarcts, strategic infarcts, small vessel disease, and lacunes (Iemolo et al., 2009; Thomas et al., 2003).

This chapter focuses on the diagnosis, pathophysiology, risk factors, and current treatment of dementia due to cerebrovascular injury. Our literature review is drawn from a combination of clinical, neuroimaging, postmortem, referral-based, and epidemiological studies. Because this textbook focuses on dementia, the content presented below is restricted to dementia due to cerebrovascular injury, rather than the entire VCI spectrum. The term "VaD" is used broadly throughout the chapter, and when specific studies are referenced, the relevant diagnostic group label will be referred to in a manner consistent with the original reference.

VaD Incidence and Prevalence

Though there is a clear need for advancing our understanding of the mechanisms underlying VaD and corresponding prevention and treatment strategies, diagnostic issues (Cosentino et al., 2004; Lopez et al., 2005; Mathias & Burke, 2009; Verhey et al., 1996) discussed below make it difficult to determine the exact incidence and prevalence of VaD. Identifying pure VaD is also difficult because of the neuropathological and clinical overlap between VaD and Alzheimer's disease (AD) (Heyman et al., 1998; Snowdon et al., 1997).

With these limitations in mind, some epidemiological studies rank VaD as the second most common form of dementia worldwide (Roman, 2004). In China and Japan, epidemiological studies estimate that VaD makes up nearly 50% of all dementia cases (Ikeda et al., 2001), while the ratio of AD to VaD in North America is 2 : 1 (Chen, 2004). Epidemiological studies also note that the incidence of VaD increases with the presence of certain VaD risk factors, including age (Ott et al., 1995), hypertension (Hayden et al., 2006; Posner et al., 2002), diabetes (Hayden et al., 2006; Ott et al., 1996; Peila et al., 2002; Posner et al., 2002), metabolic syndrome (Raffaitin et al., 2009), and stroke (Barba et al., 2000). Overall, epidemiological evidence of the incidence and prevalence of VaD suggests that VaD is a major public health issue necessitating effective prevention and treatment methods to improve quality of life for a significant portion of elders suffering from dementia.

VaD Diagnosis and Clinical Features

VaD is the most inclusive and widely used term to describe dementia resulting from vascular-related brain injury. However, due to its etiological ambiguity, there are other terms currently used to reference a similar pattern of cognitive decline and dementia. Ischemic vascular dementia (IVD) and subcortical vascular dementia (SVD) are two interchangeable terms for VaD that have emerged in the literature.

IVD is a subtype of VaD that emphasizes the purported ischemic nature of cerebral infarcts. Cerebral ischemia refers to narrowing and degeneration of tissue due to hypoperfusion. Cerebrovascular disease is implicated as the underlying cause of most ischemia in VaD. SVD is similar to IVD in that lesions of an ischemic nature are also implicated in this subtype of VaD, but lesions are confined to the subcortical regions of the brain. A third term used less frequently in the VaD literature collapses SVD and IVD into a category referred to as subcortical ischemic vascular dementia (SIVD). Though each of these three terms focuses on a specific etiological trait of VaD, all three definitions share a common assertion that cerebrovascular damage can result in a dementia syndrome.

VCI was introduced in 1995 (Bowler & Hachinski, 1995) to describe a broad spectrum of mild to severe cognitive impairment due to all causes of ischemic cerebrovascular disease, excluding large-vessel stroke. VCI offers an umbrella term that includes early cognitive changes associated with vascular disease, VaD, and mixed dementia in which AD coexists (Moorhouse & Rockwood, 2008). Similarly, the term vascular cognitive disorder (VCD) was introduced in 1999 to replace VaD and its aliases (Sachdev, 1999). VCD conceptualizes VaD as a set of related disorders sharing similar vascular etiology and progressive cognitive decline. However, it was introduced to shift the emphasis away from memory dysfunction (which is emphasized in the diagnostic features of VaD) (American Psychiatric Association, 2000; Roman et al., 1993; World Health Organization, 1992) toward early markers of VaD, such as executive dysfunction (Roman et al., 2004; Sachdev, 1999).

Consistent with the etiological ambiguity of VaD, numerous clinical classification schemes are widely used, posing a major diagnostic challenge. The four most common schemes include the Diagnostic and Statistical Manual-IV, Text Revision (DSM-IV TR) (American Psychiatric Association, 2000), the International Classification of Diseases, 10th Edition (ICD-10) (World Health Organization, 1992), the Alzheimer's Disease Diagnostic and Treatment Centers (ADDTC) criteria (Chui et al., 1992), and the National Institute of Neurological Disorders and Stroke with the Association Internationale pour la Recherché et l'Enseignement en Neurosciences (NINDS-AIREN) criteria (Roman et al., 1993). These diagnostic schemes share some overlapping features, including a history of clinical stroke or neurological evidence of cerebrovascular disease, clinical dementia, and a temporal association between the vascular insult and onset of dementia symptoms (Cosentino et al., 2004). However, differences exist within the diagnostic features of these schemes, such as required neuroimaging evidence of focal or diffuse lesions or the presence of a memory deficit. Indeed, attempts to compare these diagnostic schemes have yielded varied results, as only a few patients diagnosed with VaD by one classification system overlap with those diagnosed with VaD by another system (Gold et al., 2002; Lopez et al., 2005; Pohjasvaara et al., 2000; Wetterling et al., 1996). Table 2.1 summarizes the diagnostic criteria within each of these four major classification systems. The sections below describe the neuropsychological, neuroimaging, functional, pathophysiological, and neuropathological aspects of VaD that set it apart from other forms of dementia, including AD.

Table 2.1 Clinical diagnostic criteria for VaD: Four classification systems

Criterion	DSM-IV-TR	ADDTC	NINDS-AIREN	ICD-10
Neurological signs	Focal neurological and pathological evidence of cerebrovascular disease, such as gait abnormality and exaggerated deep tendon reflexes	Neurological evidence of two or more ischemic strokes OR a single ischemic stroke temporally related to dementia onset	Neurological evidence of stroke, such as lower facial weakness, dysarthria, or sensory deficit. MUST be associated with neuroimaging findings of cerebrovascular disease	Neurological evidence of focal brain injury, such as unilaterally increased tendon reflexes, extensor plantar response, or pseudobulbar palsy
Neuroimaging evidence	Not required	CT or MRI evidence of one or more infarcts outside the cerebellum	Evidence of cerebrovascular disease such as large vessel infarcts, basal ganglia lacunes, or white matter lesions. MUST be associated with neurological evidence of cerebrovascular disease	Not required
Cognitive deficits	Memory impairment AND (1) executive dysfunction OR (2) one or more of the following: aphasia, agnosia, or apraxia. Neuropsychological testing is NOT required for diagnosis	Deterioration in multiple cognitive domains. MUST be supported by bedside mental status testing or necropsychological examination results	Memory deficit AND deficit in two or more cognitive domains. MUST be documented by neuropsychological testing	Unequal distribution of impairment of higher order cognitive functions. MUST include memory impairment
Functional impairments	Significant impairment of daily social and occupational functioning that represents a significant decline from previous level of functioning	Broad impairment of daily functioning that is a significant decline from previous level	Impaired activities of daily living, with a significant decline in previous functioning INDEPENDENT of cerebrovascular-related physical disturbances, such as gait disturbance	Functional impairments set out under the general criteria for dementia and cerebrovascular disease

DSM-IV TR = *Diagnostic and Statistical Manual-IV, Text Revision* (American Psychiatric Association, 2000); ADDTC = Alzheimer's Disease Diagnostic and Treatment Centers Criteria (Chui et al., 1992); NINDS-AIREN = National Institute of Neurological Disorders and Stroke with the Association Internationale pour la Recherché et l'Enseignement en Neurosciences (Roman et al., 1993); ICD-10 = *International Classification of Diseases, 10th Edition* (World Health Organization, 1992)

Neuropsychological features

The neuropsychological profile of VaD is diverse and encompasses several cognitive domains, including learning and memory (Libon, Mattson et al., 1996; Tierney et al., 2001), executive functioning (Kertesz & Clydesdale, 1994; Kramer et al., 2002; Padovani et al., 1995; Yuspeh et al., 2002), language (Lukatela et al., 2000; Paul, Moser et al., 2001; Traykov et al., 2002), visuoperceptual (Kertesz & Clydesdale, 1994; Libon, Malamut et al., 1996; Paul, Cohen et al., 2001), and psychomotor abilities (Almkvist et al., 1993; Kertesz & Clydesdale, 1994; Paul, Moser et al., 2001). Most diagnostic criteria for VaD require memory impairment in addition to impairment in other cognitive domains (American Psychiatric Association, 2000; Roman et al., 1993; World Health Organization, 1992). The discussion below addresses the pattern, underlying neural substrates, and possible cognitive confounds associated with neuropsychological deficits in VAD. Consistent with the literature, the content below addresses aspects of each domain that differentiate VaD patients from AD patients.

VaD diagnostic criteria (with the exception of the ADDTC criteria) (Chui et al., 1992) require significant memory decline from pre-morbid levels (American Psychiatric Association, 2000; Roman et al., 1993; World Health Organization, 1992). Therefore, declarative memory problems are an essential feature of the VaD neuropsychological profile, including difficulties learning, encoding, and retrieving novel information. Memory impairment may be one of the earliest features of cognitive decline in VaD. A longitudinal study of an elderly cohort found that compared to controls, patients who eventually developed clinical VaD and AD showed impairment on tests of episodic memory three years before diagnosis (Laukka et al., 2004). Neuropsychological studies of VaD suggest the typical memory impairment seen in VaD is characterized by a disproportionate problem retrieving versus encoding new material (Traykov et al., 2002; Yuspeh et al., 2002). For example, compared to patients with AD and other forms of dementia, VaD patients perform better with a forced-choice recognition paradigm (Grober et al., 2008; Lafosse et al., 1997; Libon, Mattson et al., 1996; Poore et al., 2006; Tierney et al., 2001). The pattern of memory impairment seen in VaD may be due to disruptions of prefrontal metabolic processes, as evidenced by functional neuroimaging analysis of memory impairment in patients with stroke-induced cognitive impairment (Reed et al., 2000). These findings are supported by the results of a cross-sectional study of patients with clinically diagnosed IVD and AD, which found that IVD patients' performances on verbal memory tests were associated with lesions of the frontal-subcortical circuitry (Lafosse et al., 1997).

Though not explicitly specified in any of the VaD diagnostic schemes, executive dysfunction appears to be the most salient cognitive impairment in VaD (Cannata et al., 2002; Jefferson et al., 2002; Looi & Sachdev, 2000). Generally speaking, executive function refers to a set of cognitive skills involved in the conceptualization of a task and subsequent transition from conceptualization to behavior (Lezak et al.,

2004). Examples of executive function abilities include planning, mental set-shifting, sequencing, generation, inhibition, reasoning, and abstraction. The executive functioning umbrella often broadly includes attention and information-processing speed (Lezak et al., 2004). Executive dysfunction sometimes appears in the prodromal phase of VaD (Kramer et al., 2002), suggesting that it might be one of the earliest clinical indicators of evolving VaD neuropathology. Patients with VaD routinely perform poorly compared to controls on executive function measures of sequencing (Boyle et al., 2002), generation (Boyle et al., 2002; Graham et al., 2004), and inhibition (Graham et al., 2004). In studies differentiating neuropsychological characteristics between VaD and AD, VaD patients routinely have comparable performance across most cognitive domains, except executive function (Graham et al., 2004; Villardita, 1993), particularly tests of attention (Graham et al., 2004; Villardita, 1993), planning (Villardita, 1993), and mental flexibility (Graham et al., 2004; Oguro et al., 2006). Not only does executive dysfunction appear early in VaD, but it may also confound performance in other cognitive domains, such as memory (Padovani et al., 1995; Yuspeh et al., 2002) and visuoconstruction (Freeman et al., 2000). In one study, VaD patients' scores on a test of mental flexibility were associated with performance on a measure of visuoconstruction abilities, such that impaired mental flexibility was associated with poor visuoconstruction ability (Freeman et al., 2000). However, as VaD progresses and the underlying cerebrovascular pathology becomes more diffuse, impairments in memory or visuoconstruction abilities become more prominent, independent of underlying executive dysfunction (Paul, Moser et al., 2001).

Language skills include comprehension, repetition, and naming (also referred to as lexical retrieval). Unfortunately, there is a paucity of research addressing these specific skills in VaD samples with the majority of relevant literature to date emphasizing auditory comprehension (Traykov et al., 2002; Vuorinen et al., 2000) and naming abilities (Lukatela et al., 2000; Paul, Moser et al., 2001; Vuorinen et al., 2000). Naming difficulties are typical of the neuropsychological profile of VaD and worsen as VaD progresses (Paul, Moser et al., 2001). Compared to controls, VaD patients in one study made more semantic naming errors than control subjects (Lukatela et al., 1998). The same study reported that AD patients made significantly more naming errors than their VaD counterparts (Lukatela et al., 1998), a common trend in the literature (Vuorinen et al., 2000).

Visuoperceptual abilities synthesize one's perception and interaction with the environment and include acquisition and mental manipulation of basic perceptual information (e.g., shape discrimination) as well as more complex visual processing tasks (e.g., object perception, facial recognition, spatial localization). Visuoconstruction, a complex visuoperceptual task requiring motor planning and integration of multiple spatial aspects, is commonly affected in VaD (Paul, Cohen et al., 2001). VaD patients are significantly impaired relative to normative data on visual organization tasks (Paul, Cohen et al., 2001), and patients with IVD perform significantly worse than their AD counterparts on visuoconstruction tasks (Jefferson et al., 2002).

In the early stage of VaD, it is speculated that visuoconstructional deficits are most likely attributable to frontal lobe disturbances (Libon et al., 1994) versus damage to neural networks underlying pure visuospatial function (Desimone et al., 1984; Kurylo et al., 1996).

One last cognitive domain impacted by VaD is psychomotor function. Psychomotor function reflects speeded motor responses that frequently require fine motor coordination, which often integrate motor and information-processing abilities. VaD patients perform poorly on tests of psychomotor speed relative to normative data (Paul, Moser et al., 2001). When dichotomized into mild and severe dementia categories, patients with severe VaD perform significantly more poorly on psychomotor speed tests than their mild VaD counterparts (Paul, Moser et al., 2001), suggesting that psychomotor function worsens with disease severity. While both AD and VaD patients present with psychomotor deficits, VaD patients perform significantly worse on tests of psychomotor speed (Almkvist et al., 1993; Kertesz & Clydesdale, 1994; Traykov et al., 2002). Neuroimaging studies of cognitive deficits in VaD show a significant association between performance on tests of psychomotor function and prevalence of subcortical white matter hyperintensities as determined by structural magnetic resonance imaging (MRI) (Cohen et al., 2002; Moser et al., 2001). These studies support the notion that subcortical white matter disruption is one potential underlying neuropathological mechanism of psychomotor impairment in VaD.

Neuroimaging features

Neuroimaging is an especially useful tool that helps clinicians diagnose and monitor the neuropathological progression of VaD. Many neuroimaging techniques developed and refined over the last two decades, including computed tomography (CT) and MRI, have helped advance our understanding of the neuropathological correlates of dementia. With the emergence of CT as a medical tool in the early 1970s (for review, see Sedvall & Pauli, 2002), it became possible to visualize hemorrhagic stroke location and size even in the absence of clinical symptoms. Advances in CT imaging, including angiography and perfusion imaging, greatly enriched our ability to examine the evolution and estimate the progression of VaD through improved understanding of stroke severity and the status of post-stroke cerebral blood flow (Schramm et al., 2004).

In 1973, not long after the introduction of CT, MRI technology was introduced. MRI, with increased resolution, enhanced visualization of soft tissue, and multiple sequence options, has facilitated the development of more sophisticated scanning methods and image post-processing that have advanced our understanding of VaD. Diffusion-weighted imaging (DWI), perfusion-weighted imaging (PWI), diffusion tensor imaging (DTI), and arterial spin labeling (ASL) are four MRI modalities that provide rich information about vascular dynamics and allow for the examination of associations between clinical symptomology and physiological changes in the cerebral vasculature. DWI quantifies the natural movement of water molecules within biological tissues providing valuable information regarding injury and edema associated with stroke. DWI has been used to examine associations between cognition and cerebrovascular disease (O'Sullivan et al., 2004), as a means of differentiating acute versus chronic subcortical infarcts (Singer et al., 1998), and as a tool for documenting the progression of microvascular infarcts in VaD (Choi et al., 2000). PWI directly assesses cerebral perfusion, so it has been applied as a method for determining the success of cerebral reperfusion following stroke (Hillis et al., 2004). DTI techniques are similar to DWI and work by quantifying the multiple directional components of water diffusion, which can then be used to project the probable trajectory of white matter pathways. DTI appears to be more valuable than conventional T2-weighted MRI in imaging white matter damage (Cassol et al., 2004; O'Sullivan et al., 2001) and is extremely useful in examining connectivity within the subcortical white matter (Melhem et al., 2002). In fact, recent evidence suggests DTI markers of white matter connectivity may be useful in differentiating VaD from AD (Lee et al., 2009; Zarei et al., 2009). ASL is a non-invasive MRI technique that directly analyzes cerebral blood flow by imaging the difference between the magnetization of blood and the magnetization of static tissue. Cerebral blood flow changes due to cerebrovascular disease can be quantified via ASL (Wolf et al., 2003), making it a viable means for detecting blood flow changes in VaD.

One of the most salient neuroradiological features of VaD visualized by CT or MRI is white matter hyperintensities (WMHs), also referred to as *white matter signal abnormalities* (see Figure 2.1 for an example, plate section) (Bigler et al., 2003; Cohen et al., 2002). Though the exact etiology of WMHs is controversial (Kozachuk et al., 1990; Schmidt, Schmidt, Kapeller et al., 2002), evidence suggests that these hyperintensities represent areas of ischemic damage, microvascular infarction, and arteriosclerosis (Fazekas et al., 1993). Both positron emission tomography (Hatazawa et al., 1997) and PWI (Marstrand et al., 2002) data suggest that reduced cerebral blood flow is associated with WMHs but not areas of normal appearing white matter, suggesting a vascular basis for WMHs. The presence of WMHs is a useful predictor of the risk of future stroke (Jeerakathil et al., 2004) and post-stroke conversion to VaD (Debette et al., 2007; Meyer et al., 2007), suggesting WMHs have clinical significance. As such, WMHs have been used as a neuroimaging marker of cerebrovascular disease (Longstreth et al., 1996; Pico et al., 2002; Pohjasvaara et al., 1999) and VaD (Erkinjuntti et al., 1987). In fact, the NINDS-AIREN clinical classification of VaD requires that at least 25% of the white matter should have clear neuroradiologically documented WMHs (Roman et al., 1993). The potential diagnostic usefulness of WMHs in VaD is also seen in an MRI analysis of the metabolic processes in areas of WMHs in AD, IVD, and control subjects. For example, recent MR spectroscopy results revealed that in IVD and AD subjects, metabolic processes in areas of WMHs were different from those of the surrounding normal-appearing white matter (Constans et al., 1995). Furthermore, the nature of this metabolic change was different in IVD subjects' regions of WMHs from that seen in AD subjects (Constans et al., 1995), suggesting that metabolic neuroimaging in regions of WMHs may be valuable in differentiating VaD from AD.

The presence of lacunes on CT or MRI is also a prominent neuroradiological feature of VaD. Lacunes are small, perivascular cavities located primarily in the subcortical and deep structures of the brain. These lesions are a neuroimaging and neuropathological marker of cerebrovascular disease. Though research has not yet directly addressed the specific impact of lacunes on cognitive status in patients with VaD, studies based on other samples demonstrate a strong inverse relation between lacunes and cognition. For example, in an older cohort of individuals free of dementia, the presence of subcortical lacunes as determined by volumetric MRI techniques was inversely associated with performance on tests of executive function (Carey et al., 2008). Among a heterogeneous cohort, including cognitively normal elders and persons with MCI and dementia (both AD and VaD), MRI evidence suggests that the number of lacunes and white matter lesions are directly associated with dorsolateral prefrontal cortex metabolism (Reed et al., 2004). Subsequently, this decreased prefrontal cortex metabolism was associated with executive dysfunction (Reed et al., 2004).

Diffuse atrophy is one last neuroradiological feature of VaD. MRI-evidenced hippocampal (Fein et al., 2000; Laakso et al., 1996) and global cortical atrophy (Fein et al., 2000) have been observed in patients with VaD. Other MRI studies note patterns of medial temporal lobe atrophy in VaD, specifically in the case of VaD with neuroradiologically confirmed macrovascular disease (Bastos-Leite et al., 2007). In general, neuroimaging studies in VaD suggest that underlying cerebrovascular pathology is related to general cortical atrophy (Staekenborg et al., 2008). However, atrophy in VaD lacks specificity as compared to the other neuroradiological features discussed above because the pattern of atrophy seen in VaD is comparable to that seen in AD (Fein et al., 2000; Laakso et al., 1996).

Overall, neuroimaging serves as an important tool in visualizing the neuropathology of VaD. The continued evolution of neuroimaging and post-processing techniques will advance diagnostic specificity and determinations about progression for patients with VaD.

Functional impairment

Functional decline secondary to cognitive impairment is a necessary criterion for the diagnosis of dementia. Activities of daily living (ADLs) are generally dichotomized into two categories, including instrumental (IADLs) and basic activities of daily living (BADLs). IADLs facilitate independent living and include shopping, meal preparation, medication management, telephone use, financial management, housekeeping, laundry, and driving or traveling. BADLs are basic, self-care tasks that are habitual in nature, such as ambulating, feeding, toileting, bathing, grooming, and dressing. Assessing functional capacities of patients with VaD is clinically important, as functional decline is associated with patient institutionalization (Juva et al., 1997; Knopman et al., 1988), decreased patient quality of life (Knopman et al., 1988), increased caregiver burden (DeBettignies et al., 1990), and increased healthcare costs (DeBettignies et al., 1990). Assessment and quantification of ADLs and understanding the clinical and neuropathological correlates of functional decline in dementia has clinical utility for diagnostic and prognostic clinical purposes (Jefferson et al., 2008; Jefferson, Paul et al., 2006).

Despite significant interest in understanding functional decline in dementia, few studies have focused on VaD cohorts (Boyle et al., 2002; Boyle, Paul et al., 2003; Boyle et al., 2004; Jefferson, Cahn-Weiner et al., 2006; Okazaki et al., 2009). Longitudinal studies assessing the rate of functional progression suggest that IADL impairment in VaD is slower than that seen in AD, but progressive nevertheless (Boyle et al., 2004; Nyenhuis et al., 2002). One study reported that over a 12-month period, VaD patients experienced a 15% decline in IADLs, which translated into the loss of one complete IADL, such as medication management or food preparation (Boyle et al., 2004). Consistent with models of functional deterioration (Kempen & Suurmeijer, 1990; Lawton, 1972; Lawton & Brody, 1969), BADL impairment in VaD does not appear until after significant IADL impairment evolves (Boyle et al., 2002).

Because cognitive decline contributes to functional deterioration in dementia, several studies have related neuropsychological measures to functional status in VaD samples. It is not surprising that cognitive impairment predicts functional impairment in VaD (Boyle, Paul et al., 2003; Boyle et al., 2004; Jefferson, Cahn-Weiner et al., 2006); however, determining the specific cognitive correlates of functional decline is less straightforward. Baseline executive function performance predicts IADL decline over a 12-month period in patients with VaD (Boyle et al., 2004; Jefferson, Cahn-Weiner et al., 2006), a finding supported by studies of community-dwelling elders (Carlson et al., 1999; Grigsby et al., 1998) and other dementia subtypes (Boyle, Malloy et al., 2003). IADLs are heterogeneous and complex, requiring organization, sequencing, inhibition, and planning, all of which are features of executive functioning (Jefferson, Paul et al., 2006). Therefore, findings relating executive functioning to IADL decline are theoretically supported. Memory impairment also contributes to functional changes seen in VaD, but this relation appears to be specific for BADLs rather than IADLs. In particular, longitudinal data among patients with VaD suggests memory performance changes over a 12-month period are associated with a decline in BADLs (Jefferson, Cahn-Weiner et al., 2006).

Neuroimaging studies provide evidence for specific neuroanatomical correlates of functional impairment in dementia; however, few studies have emphasized VaD samples. One exception is a study reporting an association between IADL impairment and prevalence of subcortical WMHs (Boyle, Paul et al., 2003), a neuroanatomic correlate of executive dysfunction (Gunning-Dixon & Raz, 2003). The evidence suggests that WMHs may mediate relations between executive dysfunction and IADL impairment in VaD. Future studies of functional impairment in dementia should include neuroimaging to further understand neuroanatomical markers of functional decline.

Biomarker correlates of VaD

Biomarkers are quantifiable and detectable biological agents that serve as indicators of a normal biological process, pathogenic process, or pharmacological response to an intervention. Identifying and applying biomarkers as diagnostic and prognostic markers of neurodegenerative disease is becoming increasingly important to aid in early identification and intervention.

In VaD, identifying useful biomarkers is difficult due to the heterogeneous nature of VaD pathology and the frequent overlap between AD and VaD pathology (Utter et al., 2008; Yip et al., 2005). The majority of potential biomarkers for VaD include inflammatory markers. Inflammation is strongly linked to cerebrovascular disease (Nencini et al., 2003; Palasik et al., 2005; van Dijk et al., 2005), an important pathophysiological aspect of VaD (Bastos-Leite et al., 2007; Staekenborg et al., 2008). As such, inflammatory markers are a viable means of detecting the presence of vascular-related inflammation. Epidemiological evidence suggests that serum levels of C-reactive protein (CRP), an acute phase reactant associated with cerebrovascular disease (Montaner et al., 2006; van Dijk et al., 2005), precede the onset of VaD and increase with VaD progression (Schmidt, Schmidt, Curb et al., 2002). Increased cerebrospinal fluid (CSF) (Wada-Isoe et al., 2004) and plasma levels (Engelhart et al., 2004) of interleukin-6 (IL-6), an inflammatory cytokine, have also been reported in VaD samples. Elevations in CSF tumor necrosis factor-alpha (TNF-α), an inflammatory cytokine implicated in demyelination, have been reported in patients with SVD (Tarkowski et al., 1999; Tarkowski et al., 2003a). Collectively, these inflammatory markers may be sensitive to the presence of VaD pathology; however, they are frequently associated with other forms of neurodegeneration, questioning their specificity for VaD. Future work should explore in more detail the prognostic utility of these markers.

In addition to inflammatory markers, two CSF-measured biological agents are implicated in the pathology of VaD include sulfatide (Fredman et al., 1992; Tarkowski et al., 2003a) and lipoprotein(a) (Urakami et al., 1987). In patients with VaD, sulfatide, a glycolipid subtype in demyelination processes, is elevated (Fredman et al., 1992). Such elevations typically correspond to elevated TNF-α levels (Tarkowski et al., 2003a), as both of these markers are associated with demyelination (Tarkowski et al., 2003b). Sulfatide may be a unique biomarker for VaD, as levels of sulfatide are elevated in patients with VaD but markedly lower in patients with AD (Fredman et al., 1992; Han et al., 2003; Jeste et al., 2007). Lipoprotein(a) is also a promising biomarker for VaD, due to its association with cerebrovascular disease (Jurgens et al., 1995; Peng et al., 1999; Urakami et al., 1987; Zenker et al., 1986) and its genetic link to VaD (Emanuele et al., 2004).

Lipoprotein(a) is a lipoprotein involved in cholesterol metabolism and is regulated by the apolipoprotein(a) gene. Smaller apolipoprotein(a) isoforms are associated with increased plasma lipoprotein(a) levels (Panza et al., 2006), the combination of which is associated with heritable cerebrovascular disease (Jurgens et al., 1995). There is an indirect association between apolipoprotein(a) polymorphism size and VaD prevalence as compared to prevalence of AD or stroke, and increased serum levels of lipoprotein(a) are associated with VaD (Emanuele et al., 2004). As in VaD, smaller apolipoprotein(a) polymorphism size is associated with prevalence of AD, but this association is not as statistically strong (Emanuele et al., 2004). Collectively, these findings suggest that apolipoprotein(a) phenotype and elevated serum levels of lipoprotein(a) may predict the incidence of heritable VaD and post-stroke dementia (Emanuele et al., 2004).

Although the inflammatory (Hull et al., 1996; Maes et al., 1999; Yasojima et al., 2000) and non-inflammatory (Emanuele et al., 2004; Zeng & Han, 2008) biomarkers discussed here are associated with AD, they may be useful in making prognostic and diagnostic decisions in VaD. Future research may identify VaD biomarkers that do not overlap with other neurodegenerative conditions to increase the prognostic and diagnostic usefulness of VaD-specific biomarkers.

Neuropathological Findings in VaD

Unlike AD and other neurodegenerative disorders, there is no definitive set of pathological criteria for VaD. Difficulties forming a consensus for the neuropathological classification of VaD are comparable to those challenges in forming a consensus for the clinical diagnosis of VaD. The underlying cerebrovascular pathology of VaD is expansive and results in a diffuse pattern of brain injury, making it difficult to define a gold standard for the neuropathological diagnosis of VaD. Despite the lack of widely accepted neuropathological criteria, key neuropathological features have been put forth. Postmortem investigations of VaD typically quantify neuropathological signs of large and small vessel disease, white matter lesions, infarcts, and lacunes. Microvascular and white matter changes due to arteriosclerotic pathologies, such as those discussed below in the pathophysiology section, are common neuropathological findings in VaD (see Figure 2.2, plate section). The absence of confounding pathologies, such as neurofibrillary tangles, amyloid plaques, and Lewy bodies (Gold et al., 2002; Knopman, Parisi et al., 2003), is also an important characteristic of the neuropathological classification of VaD. The following discussion addresses the general trends in the neuropathological classification of VaD and the various neuropathological findings of postmortem studies of VaD.

White matter lesions are an important neuropathological feature of VaD. Clinicopathological studies of VaD include white matter lesions as an essential feature of the neuropathological classification of VaD (Erkinjuntti et al., 1996; Erkinjuntti et al., 1988; Molsa et al., 1985). White matter lesions in VaD are frequently referred to as leukoariosis, leukoencephalopathy, leukomalacia, and Binswanger's disease. Because of the heterogeneity of VaD pathophysiology, white matter lesions in VaD neuropathology are varied and diffuse. White matter lesions in VaD include diffuse demyelination (see Figure 2.2d, plate section), infarction (including microinfarcts and large, strategic infarcts), and lacunes (Erkinjuntti et al., 1996; Jellinger, 2002). Figures 2.3b and 2.3c (plate section) show the diffuse pattern of subcortical white matter infarction and presence of lacunes typical of VaD. The presence of lacunes in frontal, parietal, and occipital white matter and periventricular white matter regions is a common neuropathological finding in VaD (Jellinger, 2006). Microinfarcts of the subcortical and cortical white matter are also a hallmark of VaD neuropathological investigations (Jellinger, 2002).

Infarcts and lacunes are not confined to the white matter in VaD. Both lacunar and non-lacunar infarction of the thalamus (Gold et al., 2005; Hulette et al., 1997), hippocampus (Jellinger & Attems, 2007), and basal ganglia (Gold et al., 2005; Hulette et al., 1997; Jellinger & Attems, 2007) are frequent findings upon neuropathological investigation of VaD. In terms of neuropathological classification of VaD, the specific role of infarcts varies. In one neuropathological study investigating the validity of several clinical criteria for VaD, neuropathological confirmation of VaD included lacunar infarction of at least three neocortical regions at the exclusion of the primary and secondary visual cortex (Gold et al., 2002). This particular study also discounted lesions located in subcortical brain regions (Gold et al., 2002). In contrast, other neuropathological investigations of VaD involve a more inclusive criterion with respect to infarction, as many clinico-pathological investigations in VaD require postmortem cortical and subcortical infarctions (including lacunar and non-lacunar infarctions) (Erkinjuntti et al., 1988; Pohjasvaara et al., 2000).

Neuropathological signs of cerebrovascular disease essential to confirmation of VaD should occur in the absence of confounding pathology, including neurofibrillary tangles and amyloid plaques as seen in AD (Roman et al., 1993). However, the presence of some AD pathology is a relatively common postmortem finding in patients with clinically and neuropathologically confirmed VaD (Hulette et al., 1997; Knopman, Parisi et al., 2003). In a postmortem analysis of patients clinically diagnosed with VaD, 87% of patients were determined to have AD neuropathology, 42% of whom had concomitant AD and VaD neuropathology (Nolan et al., 1998). These findings emphasize the significance of mixed dementia. Clinico-pathological studies note that AD patients with extensive cerebrovascular neuropathology (comparable to that seen in VaD patients) present with greater clinical impairment (Snowdon et al., 1997), suggesting that mixed pathology contributes to worse clinical outcome. Generally speaking, the differentiation between pure VaD and mixed dementia is defined as the presence of senile plaques and neurofibrillary tangles at or above Braak stage IV (Kalaria et al., 2004). Standardizing the neuropathological criteria for different forms of VaD may help clarify the postmortem examination of VaD and allow for greater neuropathological classification accuracy.

Pathophysiology of VaD

The primary pathophysiological feature of VaD is cerebrovascular disease. Cerebrovascular disease is associated with cerebral hypoperfusion (Baird et al., 1997; Shaw et al., 1984) and neurodegeneration (Bots et al., 1993), and is an essential component of the pathogenesis of VaD (Bastos-Leite et al., 2007; Staekenborg et al., 2008). Cerebrovascular disease refers to the diseased state of blood vessels in the brain, both large and small, in which vascular function is disrupted by any number of pathologies. These pathologies are etiologically unique, yet often overlapping, and include large and small vessel stroke and cerebral arteriosclerotic changes. The following sections address how specific forms of cerebrovascular disease are associated with VaD neuropathology.

Stroke

Stroke is a broad concept used to describe the clinical impact of an acute disruption of cerebral blood flow, either by an ischemic or hemorrhagic event. Ischemic stroke occurs when a major cerebral blood vessel or a series of small cerebral blood vessels are occluded due to thickening of the vascular wall or acute blockage of the vessel due to embolism. Hemorrhagic stroke occurs when large or small cerebral blood vessels rupture, causing blood to leak out of the vessel onto surrounding tissue. The post-stroke development of VaD appears to be equally frequent following ischemic and hemorrhagic stroke (Barba et al., 2000). The discussion below addresses the risk of developing VaD following two major forms of stroke (i.e., large and small vessel stroke). These stroke types differentially impact cerebrovascular and neuronal health with unique contributions to the pathophysiology of VaD.

Large vessel stroke, also referred to as large vessel disease, is a common form of cerebrovascular disease implicated in the pathogenesis of VaD (Staekenborg et al., 2008). Large vessel stroke occurs when one or more of the major arteries supplying blood to the brain rupture or experience blockage due to cardiac emboli or atherosclerosis. Vessel occlusion leads to hypoperfusion, exposes the cerebrovasculature to thromboembolic agents, and causes damage to blood vessels and subsequent infarction of the tissue. While therapeutic interventions can partially reverse large vessel ischemic stroke (Hill et al., 2002), the clinical and neuropathological ramifications of acute arterial blockage are often chronic (Smith et al., 2006). In a large cross-sectional neuroimaging study of 706 patients with VaD, large vessel disease based on MRI findings and medical histories was identified in 126 (18%) patients (Staekenborg et al., 2008). Among these patients, lesions were most common in areas adjacent to the medial cerebral artery and carotid artery (Staekenborg et al., 2008). These findings suggest that the placement, not the volume, of lesions resulting from large vessel stroke is a key factor in VaD due to large vessel disease.

Small vessel stroke, also referred to as lacunar stroke or small vessel disease, results from blockage of the cerebral microvessels by thromboembolic, atherosclerotic, or microangiopathic changes and is strongly associated with hypertension (Andin et al., 2005; Staekenborg et al., 2008). Unlike large vessel stroke, the cerebrovascular damage characteristic of small vessel stroke is much more diffuse. Compared to large vessel stroke, small vessel stroke is more frequently associated with VaD (Jellinger, 2002; Ross et al., 1999; Vinters et al., 2000). WMHs and lacunar infarcts are two prominent structural MRI findings in small vessel disease. In the aforementioned cross-sectional neuroimaging study of 706 patients with VaD, 74% of patients had neuroimaging findings consistent with small vessel disease, including WMHs in one-fourth of the total white matter (Staekenborg et al., 2008). Additionally, these patients had lacunar infarcts in multiple brain regions, including the periventricular white matter, basal ganglia, and frontal white matter (Staekenborg et al., 2008). The diffuse anatomical location of lacunar infarcts and WMHs, as demonstrated by these findings, suggests that microvascular injury may account for the diffuse pattern of cognitive impairment seen in patients with VaD. Arteriosclerosis, the most common form of small vessel disease in VaD, is discussed in greater detail in the following section.

Cerebrovascular arteriosclerosis

Arteriosclerosis refers to any process involved in small vessel stenosis (see Figure 2.2b, plate section) and loss of vasoelasticity. Stenosis of cerebral microvessels can result in vessel occlusion, bulging (aneurism), or rupture and leakage. Subsequently, arteriosclerotic pathologies often lead to white matter changes, such as myelin degeneration (see Figure 2.2d, plate section) and the formation of lacunes and infarcts in both white and gray matter. Cerebral amyloid angiopathy (CAA) and cerebrovascular atherosclerosis are two arteriosclerotic pathologies implicated in VaD. The most frequent form of cerebrovascular arteriosclerosis implicated in VaD is cerebrovascular atherosclerosis (see Figure 2.3a, plate section), which serves as a major pathway of cerebrovascular and neuronal injury. While atherosclerosis occurs in both large and small cerebral blood vessels, the present discussion focuses on microvascular changes resulting from atherosclerosis of the small blood vessels. The mechanism underlying atherosclerosis involves accumulation of fatty proteins along the vessel wall, which form hard plaques that interfere with endothelial function (Zeiher et al., 1991). Cerebrovascular atherosclerosis results in narrowing of the vascular pathway, predisposing the vessel to occlusion. Cerebrovascular and subsequent neuronal changes due to atherosclerosis are a common feature of postmortem neuropathological findings in VaD (Hulette et al., 1997; Pantoni et al., 1996).

CAA is a form of arteriosclerotic cerebrovascular disease in which amyloid deposits develop within the vessel wall (see Figure 2.2a, plate section), causing the wall to grow thick and rigid. As in non-amyloid angiopathy, stenosis of the vessel wall predisposes the vessel to occlusion, subsequently causing tissue death in the perivascular region (see Figure 2.2c, plate section). While amyloid pathology is one of the hallmark characteristics of AD, the vascular mechanism of CAA makes it a viable feature of VaD. The role and prevalence of CAA in VaD is not yet well known. In one neuropathological study of patients clinically diagnosed with VaD, 8 of 26 patients presented with CAA pathology (Haglund et al., 2006). Furthermore, retrospective analysis revealed that these 8 patients were more neurologically impaired than their non-CAA counterparts, suggesting CAA may exacerbate the clinical presentation of VaD or be a subtype of VaD (Haglund et al., 2006). Evidence for a CAA subtype of VaD is supported by postmortem data revealing that 6 of 11 subjects clinically diagnosed with VaD had CAA neuropathology, and this neuropathology was more severe than that found in the AD cases (Haglund et al., 2004).

Risk Factors for VaD

Understanding risk factors for dementia, particularly those amenable to intervention, is important for formulation of prevention and treatment strategies. In this section, we review data supporting several risk factors for VaD, including age, genetics, and vascular factors, such as hypertension, diabetes, smoking, and obesity.

Age

In adults 55 years and older, the chances of developing VaD increase steeply with age (Ott et al., 1995). There are several reasons why age may be a risk factor for VaD, including age-related increases in the prevalence of vascular risk factors for VaD, (i.e., hypertension (Hajjar & Kotchen, 2003) and diabetes (Wanless et al., 1987)), cerebrovascular disease (Wolf et al., 1991), and cerebrovasculature fragility (Henry-Feugeas et al. 2008).

Genetics

The genetics of VaD are not well understood with the exception of one rare hereditary form of microvascular disease known as cerebral autosomal dominant arteriopathy with subcortical infarcts and leukoencephalopathy (CADASIL) (Chabriat et al., 2009). The known genetic mutations associated with CADASIL involve point mutations in the Notch3 gene (Viitanen & Kalimo, 2000). These mutations are the catalyst for a chain of cellular dysregulation that ultimately results in granular osmiophilic material (GOM) accumulation in the medial smooth muscle layer of the vascular wall (Viitanen & Kalimo, 2000). GOM accumulation is unique to

CADASIL and results in disruption of endothelial function and increased permeability of the vessel wall, making the vessel more susceptible to further granule deposition and other forms of maladaptive protein accumulation (Brulin et al., 2002; Ruchoux & Maurage, 1998; Viitanen & Kalimo, 2000). Deep and periventricular white matter changes are associated with CADASIL, as evidenced by WMHs on structural MRI (Viitanen & Kalimo, 2000). CADASIL frequently results in VaD (Thomas et al., 2000), as persons with CADASIL experience transient ischemic attacks and stroke, and working memory impairments and executive dysfunction are often present in these patients prior to and following ischemic events (Amberla et al., 2004).

Vascular risk factors

Many vascular factors are implicated as risks for VaD, including metabolic syndrome (Raffaitin et al., 2009) and many of its components, such as hypertension (Hayden et al., 2006; Posner et al., 2002), diabetes (Hayden et al., 2006; Ott et al., 1996; Peila et al., 2002; Posner et al., 2002), and obesity (Chiang et al., 2007; Whitmer et al., 2007), as well as smoking (Anstey et al., 2007; Chiang et al., 2007; Juan et al., 2004)). Among these variables, hypertension and diabetes are two of the strongest risk factors for VaD (Craft & Watson, 2004; Papademetriou, 2005; Posner et al., 2002). Though the clinical literature is inconsistent (Posner et al., 2002), population-based studies suggest hypertension is a risk factor of VaD, independent of other vascular factors (Hayden et al., 2006). When combined with prevalent heart disease, hypertension increases the risk of VaD by threefold (Posner et al., 2002). Two potential pathways accounting for the risk that hypertension confers for VaD include cerebral hypoperfusion (Nobili et al., 1993) and endothelial dysfunction (Ferro & Webb, 1997).

Diabetes, a common co-morbidity of hypertension (Craft & Watson, 2004), is also strongly implicated in VaD (Hayden et al., 2006; Ott et al., 1996; Peila et al., 2002; Posner et al., 2002). In longitudinal population-based studies, the development of diabetes in midlife was associated with an increased incidence of VaD (Peila et al., 2002; Yamada et al., 2003). Epidemiological evidence from the Rotterdam Study suggests that insulin-dependent diabetes is more strongly associated with VaD than other forms of dementia, including AD (Ott et al., 1996). There are multiple mechanisms that purportedly account for these associations. Through impaired insulin production, hyperglycemia, and metabolic dysregulation, diabetes affects the cerebrovasculature by impacting cerebral perfusion (Keymeulen et al., 1995; Tkac et al., 2001) and endothelial function (Fulesdi et al., 1997) and promoting atherosclerosis in the macrovasculature and microvasculature (Reed et al., 1988).

Smoking is a purported risk factor for both cardiovascular (Ambrose & Barua, 2004) and cerebrovascular disease (Lindenstrom et al., 1993; Shinton & Beevers, 1989). Though some longitudinal data suggest that there is a weak correlation between smoking and risk for VaD (Anstey et al., 2007; Reitz et al., 2007), there appears to be a higher incidence of VaD in current smokers compared to persons who never smoked (Anstey et al., 2007; Juan et al., 2004). The link between smoking and VaD risk has been attributed to data suggesting chronic smoking affects cerebral blood flow, resulting in the evolution of silent cerebral infarcts (Cruickshank et al., 1989).

Obesity may also be a risk factor for VaD. Independent of vascular risk factors, including cardiovascular disease and diabetes, a high body mass index and greater amount of adiposity, indicating obesity, was related to a fivefold increase in the risk of VaD (Whitmer et al., 2007). One case-control study of midlife risk factors for dementia found that the combination of cigarette smoking and increased body mass index increased incidence of VaD (Chiang et al., 2007). The link between obesity and VaD may be due to the impact of adiposity on the vasculature via the secretion of hormonal compounds from adipose tissue, which has been related to multiple dementia subtypes, including VaD (Gustafson, 2006).

Cardiovascular disease

Research shows that the burden of cardiovascular disease has shifted to the elderly (Lloyd-Jones et al., 2010), emphasizing the importance of investigating the relation between cardiovascular health and dementia. Consistent with some vascular risk factors for VaD, cardiovascular diseases are amenable to intervention. Therefore, identifying the risk that cardiovascular disease poses for dementia in general, and VaD in particular, is critical. This section reviews several processes involved in the pathogenesis of heart disease, neurological damage, and subsequent VaD, including atrial fibrillation, myocardial infarction, and heart failure.

Atrial fibrillation is a cardiac arrhythmia characterized by an irregular rhythm and loss of effective atrial contraction. Changes in heart rhythm related to atrial fibrillation contribute to reduced cardiac efficiency, cardiac output, and cerebral blood flow (Petersen et al., 1989), and increased thromboembolic risk (Barber et al., 2004), thus contributing to cognitive impairment and dementia. Atrial fibrillation is linked to cognitive decline and dementia through a number of mechanisms, including shared risk factors, decreased cardiac output and efficiency (Petersen et al., 1989), and silent (Ezekowitz et al., 1995) or clinical stroke (Wolf et al., 1987). Epidemiological data from the Rotterdam Study demonstrates that after statistically adjusting for prevalent cardiovascular disease, VaD and AD were more than twice as common in elders with atrial fibrillation than those elders without (Ott et al., 1997). These data suggest that even though atrial fibrillation is often a consequence of existing heart disease (including myocardial infarction, heart failure, and valvular heart disease), the association between atrial fibrillation and dementia may be independent of underlying cardiovascular disease.

Myocardial infarctions occur when atherosclerotic plaques rupture and thrombose, leading to an acute limitation of coronary artery blood flow and myocardial tissue death. The underlying substrates for an acute coronary event frequently include inflammation and progressive atherosclerosis. Myocardial infarction is thought to contribute to low cardiac output, reduction in cerebral blood flow, and microembolism. Pathological data suggest relations between atherosclerotic plaques and maladaptive cognitive decline, such as VaD. In one neuropathological series, portmortem intracranial atherosclerosis was significantly more severe in individuals diagnosed in vivo with dementia, including VaD, as compared to participants without dementia (Beach et al., 2007). Among a small clinical referral sample, myocardial infarction was related to risk of vascular-mediated dementia. Tresch and colleagues (1985) reported that patients with multi-infarct dementia were more likely to have a history of myocardial infarction compared to patients with AD. In a case-control study of Japanese men, Watanabe et al. (2004) demonstrated that men with VaD had significantly more atherosclerotic plaques and increased carotid intima-media thickness compared to men with AD. These findings were extended when the same authors reported that the presence of atherosclerosis was significantly increased in both Japanese men and women with VaD relative to their dementia-free peers (Ban et al., 2006). Epidemiological studies support the association between myocardial infarction, atherosclerosis, and VaD. The Honolulu-Asia Aging Study reported that coronary heart disease was associated with an increased risk for VaD (Ross et al., 1999). Cross-sectional epidemiological data from the Rotterdam Study has linked increased carotid and leg vessel atherosclerosis to VaD and AD, as the odds ratios for both dementia types increased as the burden of atherosclerosis increased (Hofman et al., 1997). These findings suggest that a history of myocardial infarction and vascular atherosclerosis are associated with increased risk for VaD. Relations between prior myocardial infarction and VaD may be partially accounted for by the atherosclerotic burden leading to the initial myocardial infarction and changes in cardiac function following myocardial infarction.

Heart failure is due to abnormal ventricular contracting (systolic heart failure) or relaxing (diastolic heart failure), leading to reductions in the heart's ability to pump blood efficiently to the body and brain. The relation between heart failure and vascular brain injury is theoretically due to impairments in blood flow to the brain, a model that is supported by data documenting that restoration of normal heart function following cardiac transplant results in substantial cerebral blood flow increases (Gruhn et al., 2001). However, additional pathways accounting for relations between heart failure and vascular brain injury may include neurohumoral factors (Felder et al., 2003), thromboemboli (Freudenberger & Massie, 2005), and oxidative stress (Mariani et al., 2005). Recent epidemiological data have linked heart failure to dementia. In a population-based Swedish cohort, Qiu et al. (2006) found that heart failure was associated with an 80% increased risk of dementia over a nine-year follow-up period. Further research is warranted to determine if heart failure is a unique risk factor for VaD over other types of dementia.

Treatment and Intervention of VaD

For reasons that remain unknown, patients with VaD have a higher rate of mortality compared to other dementia populations (Knopman, Rocca et al., 2003). Additionally, research shows that delaying the onset of dementia by just five years can decrease the prevalence of dementia by nearly 50% (Brookmeyer et al., 1998), emphasizing the importance of identifying effective prevention and intervention strategies. VaD is often referred to as a "preventable" form of dementia because many of the risk factors for VaD can be avoided with a healthy lifestyle (e.g., low-fat diet and regular exercise) or treated with pharmacological interventions. This section specifically addresses management and prevention of vascular risk factors, methods of stroke prevention, and pharmacological intervention for the cognitive decline seen in VaD.

Vascular risk factor prevention and management

Behavioral and pharmacological interventions are efficacious in the prevention and management of vascular risk factors for VaD, including obesity, hypertension, hypercholesterolemia, and diabetes. With regard to behavioral intervention, prevention of vascular risk factors is most effectively achieved with a low-fat diet and regular exercise. Such behavioral methods prevent or manage obesity, which greatly reduces the risk of other vascular risk factors, such as hypertension (Zanella et al., 2001), hypercholesterolemia (Tremblay et al., 1991; Tremblay et al., 1999), and diabetes (Sjostrom et al., 2000; Zanella et al., 2001). Behavioral prevention methods are also effective in managing vascular risk factors in non-obese adults with hypertension (Whelton et al., 2002), hypercholesterolemia (Hellenius et al., 1993), and diabetes (Lindstrom et al., 2006).

In addition to lifestyle modifications, pharmacological interventions are effective in managing vascular risk factors and disease. Angiotensin converting enzyme (ACE) inhibitors and beta-blockers are the two major classes of antihypertensive medications. ACE inhibitors work to increase cardiac output and vasorelaxation by regulating angiotensin II production via regulation of ACE. Beta-blockers work differently, binding to beta-adrenoceptors to therapeutically reduce heart rate and smooth muscle. The importance of managing hypertension has been illustrated by one recent study in which antihypertensive medication successfully lowered the risk for VaD (Frishman, 2002).

Statins are effective in managing hypercholesterolemia, as they work to decrease high-density lipoprotein cholesterol and increase low-density lipoprotein cholesterol. A population-based case-control study of the prevalence of dementia (including VaD) with respect to statin use noted a significant decrease in all subtypes of dementia prevalence among statin users (Hajjar et al., 2002). Additionally, patients with co-morbid VaD and hypercholesterolemia who were using statins had significantly less impaired cognition than their counterparts not using statins (Hajjar et al., 2002), suggesting that statin use may be a viable means of treating VaD.

Diabetes management includes stimulating insulin production (non-insulin dependent diabetes) and the administration of synthetic insulin (insulin-dependent diabetes). A population-based study suggests that well-controlled diabetes (i.e., fasting glucose levels within healthy limits or between 70 to 100 milligrams of glucose per deciliter of blood), is associated with decreased incidence of stroke (Kuusisto et al., 1994), a precursor to some forms of VaD. While VaD is typically a late-life disease, lifelong management of vascular risk factors is essential in avoiding vascular complications leading to VaD.

Stroke prevention

Several risk factors for stroke cannot be prevented, such as age or genetics. However, there are significant lifestyle and biomedical risk factors associated with stroke that are amenable to behavioral and pharmacological intervention. Specifically, three behavioral risk factors for stroke include cigarette smoking (Shinton & Beevers, 1989), lack of exercise (Sacco et al., 1998), and a diet high in saturated fat (Sasaki et al., 1995) and lacking in fruits and vegetables (Joshipura et al., 1999). Avoiding or cessation of cigarette smoking can improve an individual's chances of evading a stroke (Kawachi et al., 1993; Wannamethee et al., 1995) and subsequent VaD (Anstey et al., 2007). Regular physical exercise and a low-fat diet are also effective behavioral interventions for the prevention of stroke (Boden-Albala & Sacco, 2000). For instance, just one serving of fruits and vegetables per day is sufficient to significantly lower the risk of ischemic stroke among middle and older aged adults (Joshipura et al., 1999).

Stroke prevention also includes managing medical risk factors, such as hypertension, diabetes, hypercholesterolemia, and cardiovascular disease (Wolf et al., 1991). Research suggests effectively monitoring and controlling hypertension is efficacious in the prevention of stroke among patients with vascular co-morbidities, such as diabetes and metabolic syndrome (Rothwell, 2005). As mentioned above, pharmacological management of non-insulin dependent diabetes is implicated in reduced risk for stroke (Kuusisto et al., 1994). The use of statins is perhaps the most effective method for stroke prevention in adults with vascular risk factors, as findings from a meta-analysis suggest statin use lowered the risk for stroke across all vascular risk factor categories (i.e., hypertension and hypercholesterolemia) (Amarenco et al., 2004). Among patients with atrial fibrillation, chronic use of anticoagulants, such as warfarin or aspirin, appears to prevent stroke (Hart, 1998).

Pharmacological intervention for VaD

Similar to other forms of dementia, there is no present cure for VaD. However, there are several pharmacological interventions targeted to slow the progression of VaD and ameliorate the cognitive, behavioral, and physical characteristics of VaD. The primary pathway for pharmacological intervention in VaD is the modulation of abnormal neurotransmitter function, including cholinergic and glutamatergic systems (Paul et al., 2005).

Injury to the cholinergic system occurs as a result of ischemic injury to the basal forebrain nuclei and cholinergic pathways (Erkinjuntti et al., 2004). Cholinesterase inhibitors, which reduce the action of cholinesterase and increase acetylcholine levels in the brain, increase cerebral perfusion (specifically in the frontal lobes) in VaD patients (Lojkowska et al., 2003). Other longitudinal studies have demonstrated that cholinesterase inhibitors improve VaD patients' performance on tests of executive functioning (Moretti et al., 2002), a behavioral correlate of frontal lobe integrity (Cummings, 1993). Donepezil (known commercially as Aricept), a cholinesterase inhibitor used to treat AD, has been shown to be efficacious in VaD (Black et al., 2003; Passmore et al., 2005). In a randomized, double-blind placebo-controlled clinical trial of 603 patients with VaD, global cognition significantly improved after 24 weeks in the patients receiving donepezil compared to the patients receiving the placebo (see Figure 2.4a) (Black et al., 2003). Other cholinesterase inhibitors, including galantamine (Erkinjuntti et al., 2002) and rivastigmine (Moretti et al., 2002), have also proven to be a safe means of treating cognitive decline in VaD.

The glutamatergic system is also implicated in the pathogenesis of VaD because its dysregulation results in the neurotoxic build up of glutamate, which plays a significant role in learning, memory, and neuronal death in dementia. Medications, such as memantine (known commercially as Namenda), regulate the glutamatergic pathway by binding to N-methyl-D-aspartate receptors and blocking the action of glutamate. Clinical trials of memantine have had promising results. One randomized, double-blind placebo-controlled clinical trial of 288 patients with VaD showed that memantine significantly improved global cognitive function as compared to the placebo (see Figure 2.4b) (Orgogozo et al., 2002). These findings were supported by another 28-week, double-blind randomized controlled clinical trial of memantine in a VaD cohort (Wilcock et al., 2002) and replicated in additional studies (Mobius & Stoffler, 2003), suggesting that memantine is a safe method of treating cognitive decline in VaD. Despite multiple studies demonstrating the efficacy of cholinesterase inhibitors and glutamatergic antagonists in treating patients with VaD, these agents are not yet approved by the Federal Drug Administration for management of VaD.

Future Directions

In this chapter, we have reviewed the clinical features, pathophysiology, neuropathology, risk factors, and treatment of VaD. Our review draws from a combination of clinical, neuroimaging, postmortem, referral-based, and epidemiological studies. There are several key areas for future research directions in VaD, the greatest of

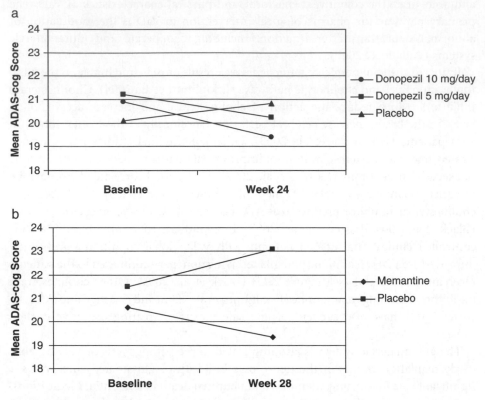

Figure 2.4 Cognitive improvement following pharmacological treatment of VaD. (a) Results of Black et al. (2003) clinical trial of donepezil in VaD. Mean ADAS-cog score at week 24 reflects least squares mean change from baseline mean score; (b) Results of Orgogozo et al. (2002) clinical trial of memantine in VaD. Mean ADAS-cog score at week 28 reflects mean change from baseline mean score
ADAS-cog = Alzheimer's Disease Assessment Scale, cognitive subscale (Rosen et al., 1984); higher scores reflect worse performance.

which includes better understanding preclinical disease and the mild end of the VCI spectrum (Iemolo et al., 2009). Similarly, identification of subclinical risk factors and examination of the effects of early intervention and proper risk factor management are major areas for future research focus because of implications for stroke prevention, cardiovascular risk factor management, and prevention of cardiovascular disease. Many adults do not effectively manage their vascular risk factors, such as hypertension (Hajjar & Kotchen, 2003) and hypercholesterolemia (Ford et al., 2003). Therefore, early identification and management of subclinical vascular risk factors is a critical next step to prevention of VaD, as it may offer an opportunity for early intervention. Past research suggests that interventions targeted at managing cardiovascular risk factors, such as hypertension, can result in a substantial reduction in dementia cases. For example, a clinical trial targeted at managing hypertension yielded a 50% reduction in the incidence of dementia over a five-year follow-up period (Forette et al., 1998). These data emphasize that identifying and managing vascular risk factors for dementia has strong potential for improving health and reducing functional disability through dementia prevention. As advances in medicine increase the average life expectancy rates worldwide by enhancing medical management of vascular risk factors, it will become more important to flesh out the diagnostic criteria of VaD so that effective prevention and treatment approaches can be developed.

While there has been some progress in understanding the genetic risk factors associated with VaD, the identification of new genetic risk factors and understanding how these factors confer risk for vascular disease is a critical area of future research emphasis. Multiple studies are underway to provide opportunities for studying genetic risk factors for complex diseases like dementia, such as the SNP-Health Association Resource (SHARe) study. These large, multi-site, collaborative projects involving candidate gene and genome-wide association studies will shed light on genetic risk factors for VaD, shared genetic risk factors between heart disease and VaD, and the complex interaction between genetic and environmental factors in the expression of cognitive decline and VaD.

Acknowledgments

Preparation of this chapter was supported, in part, by AG022773 (ALJ), AG027480 (ALJ), AG030962 (Paul B. Beeson Career Development Award in Aging; ALJ), IIRG-08-88733 (Alzheimer's Association, ALJ), and P30-AG13846 (Boston University Alzheimer's Disease Core Center). The authors wish to thank Dr. David Tate and Dr. Ann McKee for their insightful comments on an earlier draft.

References

Almkvist, O., Backman, L., Basun, H., & Wahlund, L. O. (1993). Patterns of neuropsychological performance in Alzheimer's disease and vascular dementia. *Cortex, 29*(4), 661–673.

Amarenco, P., Labreuche, J., Lavallee, P., & Touboul, P. J. (2004). Statins in stroke prevention and carotid atherosclerosis: Systematic review and up-to-date meta-analysis. *Stroke, 35*(12), 2902–2909.

Amberla, K., Waljas, M., Tuominen, S., Almkvist, O., Poyhonen, M., Tuisku, S., et al. (2004). Insidious cognitive decline in CADASIL. *Stroke, 35*(7), 1598–1602.

Ambrose, J. A., & Barua, R. S. (2004). The pathophysiology of cigarette smoking and cardiovascular disease: An update. *Journal of the American College of Cardiology, 43*(10), 1731–1737.

American Psychiatric Association (2000). *Diagnostic and statistical manual of mental disorders, Fourth Edition, Text Revision* (Vol. IV).

Andin, U., Gustafson, L., Passant, U., & Brun, A. (2005). A clinico-pathological study of heart and brain lesions in vascular dementia. *Dementia and Geriatric Cognitive Disorders, 19*(4), 222–228.

Anstey, K. J., von Sanden, C., Salim, A., & O'Kearney, R. (2007). Smoking as a risk factor for dementia and cognitive decline: A meta-analysis of prospective studies. *American Journal of Epidemiology, 166*(4), 367–378.

Baird, A. E., Benfield, A., Schlaug, G., Siewert, B., Lovblad, K. O., Edelman, R. R., et al. (1997). Enlargement of human cerebral ischemic lesion volumes measured by diffusion-weighted magnetic resonance imaging. *Annals of Neurology, 41*(5), 581–589.

Ban, Y., Watanabe, T., Miyazaki, A., Nakano, Y., Tobe, T., Idei, T., et al. (2007). Impact of increased plasma serotonin levels and carotid atherosclerosis on vascular dementia. *Atherosclerosis, 195*(1), 153–159.

Barba, R., Martinez-Espinosa, S., Rodriguez-Garcia, E., Pondal, M., Vivancos, J., & Del Ser, T. (2000). Poststroke dementia: Clinical features and risk factors. *Stroke, 31*(7), 1494–1501.

Barber, M., Tait, R. C., Scott, J., Rumley, A., Lowe, G. D., & Stott, D. J. (2004). Dementia in subjects with atrial fibrillation: Hemostatic function and the role of anticoagulation. *Journal of Thrombosis and Haemostasis, 2*(11), 1873–1878.

Bastos-Leite, A. J., van der Flier, W. M., van Straaten, E. C., Staekenborg, S. S., Scheltens, P., & Barkhof, F. (2007). The contribution of medial temporal lobe atrophy and vascular pathology to cognitive impairment in vascular dementia. *Stroke, 38*(12), 3182–3185.

Beach, T. G., Wilson, J. R., Sue, L. I., Newell, A., Poston, M., Cisneros, R., et al. (2007). Circle of Willis atherosclerosis: Association with Alzheimer's disease, neuritic plaques and neurofibrillary tangles. *Acta Neuropathologica (Berlin), 113*(1), 13–21.

Bigler, E. D., Lowry, C. M., Kerr, B., Tate, D. F., Hessel, C. D., Earl, H. D., et al. (2003). Role of white matter lesions, cerebral atrophy, and APOE on cognition in older persons with and without dementia: The Cache County, Utah, study of memory and aging. *Neuropsychology, 17*(3), 339–352.

Binswanger, O. (1894). Die abgrenzung der allgemeinen progressiven paralyse. *Berl Klin Wochenschr, 49; 50; 52,* 1103–1105; 1137–1139; 1180–1186.

Black, S., Roman, G. C., Geldmacher, D. S., Salloway, S., Hecker, J., Burns, A., et al. (2003). Efficacy and tolerability of donepezil in vascular dementia: positive results of a 24-week, multicenter, international, randomized, placebo-controlled clinical trial. *Stroke, 34*(10), 2323–2330.

Boden-Albala, B., & Sacco, R. L. (2000). Lifestyle factors and stroke risk: Exercise, alcohol, diet, obesity, smoking, drug use, and stress. *Current Atherosclerosis Reports, 2*(2), 160–166.

Bots, M. L., van Swieten, J. C., Breteler, M. M., de Jong, P. T., van Gijn, J., Hofman, A., et al. (1993). Cerebral white matter lesions and atherosclerosis in the Rotterdam Study. *Lancet, 341*(8855), 1232–1237.

Bowler, J. V., & Hachinski, V. (1995). Vascular cognitive impairment: A new approach to vascular dementia. *Bailliere's Clinical Neurology, 4*(2), 357–376.

Boyle, P. A., Cohen, R. A., Paul, R., Moser, D., & Gordon, N. (2002). Cognitive and motor impairments predict functional declines in patients with vascular dementia. *International Journal of Geriatric Psychiatry, 17*(2), 164–169.

Boyle, P. A., Malloy, P. F., Salloway, S., Cahn-Weiner, D. A., Cohen, R., & Cummings, J. L. (2003). Executive dysfunction and apathy predict functional impairment in Alzheimer disease. *American Journal of Geriatric Psychiatry, 11*(2), 214–221.

Boyle, P. A., Paul, R. H., Moser, D. J., & Cohen, R. A. (2004). Executive impairments predict functional declines in vascular dementia. *Clinical Neuropsychologist, 18*(1), 75–82.

Boyle, P. A., Paul, R., Moser, D., Zawacki, T., Gordon, N., & Cohen, R. (2003). Cognitive and neurologic predictors of functional impairment in vascular dementia. *American Journal of Geriatric Psychiatry, 11*(1), 103–106.

Brookmeyer, R., Gray, S., & Kawas, C. (1998). Projections of Alzheimer's disease in the United States and the public health impact of delaying disease onset. *American Journal of Public Health, 88*(9), 1337–1342.

Brulin, P., Godfraind, C., Leteurtre, E., & Ruchoux, M. M. (2002). Morphometric analysis of ultrastructural vascular changes in CADASIL: Analysis of 50 skin biopsy specimens and pathogenic implications. *Acta Neuropathologica, 104*(3), 241–248.

Cannata, A. P., Alberoni, M., Franceschi, M., & Mariani, C. (2002). Frontal impairment in subcortical ischemic vascular dementia in comparison to Alzheimer's disease. *Dementia and Geriatric Cognitive Disorders, 13*(2), 101–111.

Carey, C. L., Kramer, J. H., Josephson, S. A., Mungas, D., Reed, B. R., Schuff, N., et al. (2008). Subcortical lacunes are associated with executive dysfunction in cognitively normal elderly. *Stroke, 39*(2), 397–402.

Carlson, M. C., Fried, L. P., Xue, Q. L., Bandeen-Roche, K., Zeger, S. L., & Brandt, J. (1999). Association between executive attention and physical functional performance in community-dwelling older women. *Journals of Gerontology. Series B, Psychological Sciences and Social Sciences, 54*(5), S262–S270.

Cassol, E., Ranjeva, J. P., Ibarrola, D., Mckics, C., Manelfe, C., Clanet, M., et al. (2004). Diffusion tensor imaging in multiple sclerosis: A tool for monitoring changes in normal-appearing white matter. *Multiple Sclerosis, 10*(2), 188–196.

Chabriat, H., Joutel, A., Dichgans, M., Tournier-Lasserve, E., & Bousser, M. G. (2009). Cadasil. *Lancet Neurology, 8*(7), 643–653.

Chen, C. P. (2004). Transcultural expression of subcortical vascular disease. *Journal of Neurological Science, 226*(1–2), 45–47.

Chiang, C. J., Yip, P. K., Wu, S. C., Lu, C. S., Liou, C. W., Liu, H. C., et al. (2007). Midlife risk factors for subtypes of dementia: A nested case-control study in Taiwan. *American Journal of Geriatric Psychiatry, 15*(9), 762–771.

Choi, S. H., Na, D. L., Chung, C. S., Lee, K. H., Na, D. G., & Adair, J. C. (2000). Diffusion-weighted MRI in vascular dementia. *Neurology, 54*(1), 83–89.

Chui, H. C., Victoroff, J. I., Margolin, D., Jagust, W., Shankle, R., & Katzman, R. (1992). Criteria for the diagnosis of ischemic vascular dementia proposed by the State of California Alzheimer's Disease Diagnostic and Treatment Centers. *Neurology, 42*(3 Pt 1), 473–480.

Cohen, R. A., Paul, R. H., Ott, B. R., Moser, D. J., Zawacki, T. M., Stone, W., et al. (2002). The relationship of subcortical MRI hyperintensities and brain volume to cognitive function in vascular dementia. *Journal of the International Neuropsychological Society, 8*(6), 743–752.

Constans, J. M., Meyerhoff, D. J., Gerson, J., MacKay, S., Norman, D., Fein, G., et al. (1995). H-1 MR spectroscopic imaging of white matter signal hyperintensities: Alzheimer disease and ischemic vascular dementia. *Radiology, 197*(2), 517–523.

Cosentino, S. A., Jefferson, A. L., Carey, M., Price, C. C., Davis-Garrett, K., Swenson, R., et al. (2004). The clinical diagnosis of vascular dementia: A comparison among four classification systems and a proposal for a new paradigm. *Clinical Neuropsychologist, 18*(1), 6–21.

Craft, S., & Watson, G. S. (2004). Insulin and neurodegenerative disease: Shared and specific mechanisms. *Lancet Neurology, 3*(3), 169–178.

Cruickshank, J. M., Neil-Dwyer, G., Dorrance, D. E., Hayes, Y., & Patel, S. (1989). Acute effects of smoking on blood pressure and cerebral blood flow. *Journal of Human Hypertension, 3*(6), 443–449.

Cummings, J. L. (1993). Frontal-subcortical circuits and human behavior. *Archives of Neurology, 50*(8), 873–880.

Debette, S., Bombois, S., Bruandet, A., Delbeuck, X., Lepoittevin, S., Delmaire, C., et al. (2007). Subcortical hyperintensities are associated with cognitive decline in patients with mild cognitive impairment. *Stroke, 38*(11), 2924–2930.

DeBettignies, B. H., Mahurin, R. K., & Pirozzolo, F. J. (1990). Insight for impairment in independent living skills in Alzheimer's disease and multi-infarct dementia. *Journal of Clinical and Experimental Neuropsychology, 12*(2), 355–363.

Desimone, R., Albright, T. D., Gross, C. G., & Bruce, C. (1984). Stimulus-selective properties of inferior temporal neurons in the macaque. *Journal of Neuroscience, 4*(8), 2051–2062.

Emanuele, E., Peros, E., Tomaino, C., Feudatari, E., Bernardi, L., Binetti, G., et al. (2004). Relation of apolipoprotein(a) size to Alzheimer's disease and vascular dementia. *Dementia and Geriatric Cognitive Disorders, 18*(2), 189–196.

Engelhart, M. J., Geerlings, M. I., Meijer, J., Kiliaan, A., Ruitenberg, A., van Swieten, J. C., et al. (2004). Inflammatory proteins in plasma and the risk of dementia: The Rotterdam Study. *Archives of Neurology, 61*(5), 668–672.

Erkinjuntti, T., Benavente, O., Eliasziw, M., Munoz, D. G., Sulkava, R., Haltia, M., et al. (1996). Diffuse vacuolization (spongiosis) and arteriolosclerosis in the frontal white matter occurs in vascular dementia. *Archives of Neurology, 53*(4), 325–332.

Erkinjuntti, T., Haltia, M., Palo, J., Sulkava, R., & Paetau, A. (1988). Accuracy of the clinical diagnosis of vascular dementia: a prospective clinical and post-mortem neuropathological study. *Journal of Neurology, Neurosurgery & Psychiatry, 51*(8), 1037–1044.

Erkinjuntti, T., Ketonen, L., Sulkava, R., Sipponen, J., Vuorialho, M., & Iivanainen, M. (1987). Do white matter changes on MRI and CT differentiate vascular dementia from Alzheimer's disease? *Journal of Neurology, Neurosurgery & Psychiatry, 50*(1), 37–42.

Erkinjuntti, T., Kurz, A., Gauthier, S., Bullock, R., Lilienfeld, S., & Damaraju, C. V. (2002). Efficacy of galantamine in probable vascular dementia and Alzheimer's disease combined with cerebrovascular disease: A randomised trial. *Lancet, 359*(9314), 1283–1290.

Erkinjuntti, T., Roman, G., & Gauthier, S. (2004). Treatment of vascular dementia-evidence from clinical trials with cholinesterase inhibitors. *Neurological Research, 26*(5), 603–605.

Ezekowitz, M. D., James, K. E., Nazarian, S. M., Davenport, J., Broderick, J. P., Gupta, S. R., et al. (1995). Silent cerebral infarction in patients with nonrheumatic atrial fibrillation. The Veterans Affairs Stroke Prevention in Nonrheumatic Atrial Fibrillation Investigators. *Circulation, 92*(8), 2178–2182.

Fazekas, F., Kleinert, R., Offenbacher, H., Schmidt, R., Kleinert, G., Payer, F., et al. (1993). Pathologic correlates of incidental MRI white matter signal hyperintensities. *Neurology, 43*(9), 1683–1689.

Fein, G., Di Sclafani, V., Tanabe, J., Cardenas, V., Weiner, M. W., Jagust, W. J., et al. (2000). Hippocampal and cortical atrophy predict dementia in subcortical ischemic vascular disease. *Neurology, 55*(11), 1626–1635.

Felder, R. B., Francis, J., Zhang, Z. H., Wei, S. G., Weiss, R. M., & Johnson, A. K. (2003). Heart failure and the brain: New perspectives. *American Journal of Physiology. Regulatory, Integrative, & Comparative Physiology, 284*(2), R259–R276.

Ferro, C. J., & Webb, D. J. (1997). Endothelial dysfunction and hypertension. *Drugs, 53*(Suppl 1), 30–41.

Ford, E. S., Mokdad, A. H., Giles, W. H., & Mensah, G. A. (2003). Serum total cholesterol concentrations and awareness, treatment, and control of hypercholesterolemia among US adults: Findings from the National Health and Nutrition Examination Survey, 1999 to 2000. *Circulation, 107*(17), 2185–2189.

Forette, F., Seux, M. L., Staessen, J. A., Thijs, L., Birkenhager, W. H., Babarskiene, M. R., et al. (1998). Prevention of dementia in randomised double-blind placebo-controlled Systolic Hypertension in Europe (Syst-Eur) trial. *Lancet, 352*(9137), 1347–1351.

Fredman, P., Wallin, A., Blennow, K., Davidsson, P., Gottfries, C. G., & Svennerholm, L. (1992). Sulfatide as a biochemical marker in cerebrospinal fluid of patients with vascular dementia. *Acta Neurologica Scandinavica, 85*(2), 103–106.

Freeman, R. Q., Giovannetti, T., Lamar, M., Cloud, B. S., Stern, R. A., Kaplan, E., et al. (2000). Visuoconstructional problems in dementia: Contribution of executive systems functions. *Neuropsychology, 14*(3), 415–426.

Freudenberger, R. S., & Massie, B. M. (2005). Silent cerebral infarction in heart failure: Vascular or thromboembolic? *Journal of Cardiac Failure, 11*(7), 490–491.

Frishman, W. H. (2002). Are antihypertensive agents protective against dementia? A review of clinical and preclinical data. *Heart Disease, 4*(6), 380–386.

Fulesdi, B., Limburg, M., Bereczki, D., Michels, R. P., Neuwirth, G., Legemate, D., et al. (1997). Impairment of cerebrovascular reactivity in long-term type 1 diabetes. *Diabetes, 46*(11), 1840–1845.

Gold, G., Bouras, C., Canuto, A., Bergallo, M. F., Herrmann, F. R., Hof, P. R., et al. (2002). Clinicopathological validation study of four sets of clinical criteria for vascular dementia. *American Journal of Psychiatry, 159*(1), 82–87.

Gold, G., Kovari, E., Herrmann, F. R., Canuto, A., Hof, P. R., Michel, J. P., et al. (2005). Cognitive consequences of thalamic, basal ganglia, and deep white matter lacunes in brain aging and dementia. *Stroke, 36*(6), 1184–1188.

Graham, N. L., Emery, T., & Hodges, J. R. (2004). Distinctive cognitive profiles in Alzheimer's disease and subcortical vascular dementia. *Journal of Neurology, Neurosurgery & Psychiatry, 75*(1), 61–71.

Grigsby, J., Kaye, K., Baxter, J., Shetterly, S. M., & Hamman, R. F. (1998). Executive cognitive abilities and functional status among community-dwelling older persons in the San Luis Valley Health and Aging Study. *Journal of the American Geriatrics Society, 46*(5), 590–596.

Grober, E., Hall, C., Sanders, A. E., & Lipton, R. B. (2008). Free and cued selective reminding distinguishes Alzheimer's disease from vascular dementia. *Journal of the American Geriatric Society, 56*(5), 944–946.

Gruhn, N., Larsen, F. S., Boesgaard, S., Knudsen, G. M., Mortensen, S. A., Thomsen, G., et al. (2001). Cerebral blood flow in patients with chronic heart failure before and after heart transplantation. *Stroke, 32*(11), 2530–2533.

Gunning-Dixon, F. M., & Raz, N. (2003). Neuroanatomical correlates of selected executive functions in middle-aged and older adults: A prospective MRI study. *Neuropsychologia, 41*(14), 1929–1941.

Gustafson, D. (2006). Adiposity indices and dementia. *Lancet Neurology, 5*(8), 713–720.

Hachinski, V. C., Iliff, L. D., Zilhka, E., Du Boulay, G. H., McAllister, V. L., Marshall, J., et al. (1975). Cerebral blood flow in dementia. *Archives of Neurology, 32*(9), 632–637.

Haglund, M., Passant, U., Sjobeck, M., Ghebremedhin, E., & Englund, E. (2006). Cerebral amyloid angiopathy and cortical microinfarcts as putative substrates of vascular dementia. *International Journal of Geriatric Psychiatry, 21*(7), 681–687.

Haglund, M., Sjobeck, M., & Englund, E. (2004). Severe cerebral amyloid angiopathy characterizes an underestimated variant of vascular dementia. *Dementia and Geriatric Cognitive Disorders, 18*(2), 132–137.

Hajjar, I., & Kotchen, T. A. (2003). Trends in prevalence, awareness, treatment, and control of hypertension in the United States, 1988–2000. *Journal of the American Medical Association, 290*(2), 199–206.

Hajjar, I., Schumpert, J., Hirth, V., Wieland, D., & Eleazer, G. P. (2002). The impact of the use of statins on the prevalence of dementia and the progression of cognitive impairment. *Journals of Gerontology. Series A, Biological Sciences and Medical Sciences, 57*(7), M414–M418.

Han, X., Fagan, A. M., Cheng, H., Morris, J. C., Xiong, C., & Holtzman, D. M. (2003). Cerebrospinal fluid sulfatide is decreased in subjects with incipient dementia. *Annals of Neurology, 54*(1), 115–119.

Hart, R. G. (1998). Intensity of anticoagulation to prevent stroke in patients with atrial fibrillation. *Annals of Internal Medicine, 128*(5), 408.

Hatazawa, J., Shimosegawa, E., Satoh, T., Toyoshima, H., & Okudera, T. (1997). Subcortical hypoperfusion associated with asymptomatic white matter lesions on magnetic resonance imaging. *Stroke, 28*(10), 1944–1947.

Hayden, K. M., Zandi, P. P., Lyketsos, C. G., Khachaturian, A. S., Bastian, L. A., Charoonruk, G., et al. (2006). Vascular risk factors for incident Alzheimer disease and vascular dementia: The Cache County study. *Alzheimer Disease and Associated Disorders, 20*(2), 93–100.

Hellenius, M. L., de Faire, U., Berglund, B., Hamsten, A., & Krakau, I. (1993). Diet and exercise are equally effective in reducing risk for cardiovascular disease. Results of a randomized controlled study in men with slightly to moderately raised cardiovascular risk factors. *Atherosclerosis, 103*(1), 81–91.

Henry-Feugeas, M. C., Onen, F., & Claeys, E. S. (2008). Classifying late-onset dementia with MRI: Is arteriosclerotic brain degeneration the most common cause of Alzheimer's syndrome? *Clinical Interventions in Aging, 3*(1), 187–199.

Heyman, A., Fillenbaum, G. G., Welsh-Bohmer, K. A., Gearing, M., Mirra, S. S., Mohs, R. C., et al. (1998). Cerebral infarcts in patients with autopsy-proven Alzheimer's disease: CERAD, part XVIII. Consortium to Establish a Registry for Alzheimer's Disease. *Neurology, 51*(1), 159–162.

Hill, M. D., Barber, P. A., Demchuk, A. M., Newcommon, N. J., Cole-Haskayne, A., Ryckborst, K., et al. (2002). Acute intravenous–intra-arterial revascularization therapy for severe ischemic stroke. *Stroke, 33*(1), 279–282.

Hillis, A. E., Wityk, R. J., Beauchamp, N. J., Ulatowski, J. A., Jacobs, M. A., & Barker, P. B. (2004). Perfusion-weighted MRI as a marker of response to treatment in acute and subacute stroke. *Neuroradiology, 46*(1), 31–39.

Hofman, A., Ott, A., Breteler, M. M., Bots, M. L., Slooter, A. J., van Harskamp, F., et al. (1997). Atherosclerosis, apolipoprotein E, and prevalence of dementia and Alzheimer's disease in the Rotterdam Study. *Lancet, 349*(9046), 151–154.

Hulette, C., Nochlin, D., McKeel, D., Morris, J. C., Mirra, S. S., Sumi, S. M., et al. (1997). Clinical-neuropathologic findings in multi-infarct dementia: A report of six autopsied cases. *Neurology*, *48*(3), 668–672.

Hull, M., Strauss, S., Berger, M., Volk, B., & Bauer, J. (1996). The participation of interleukin-6, a stress-inducible cytokine, in the pathogenesis of Alzheimer's disease. *Behavioural Brain Research*, *78*(1), 37–41.

Iemolo, F., Duro, G., Rizzo, C., Castiglia, L., Hachinski, V., & Caruso, C. (2009). Pathophysiology of vascular dementia. *Immunity & Ageing*, 6, 13.

Ikeda, M., Hokoishi, K., Maki, N., Nebu, A., Tachibana, N., Komori, K., et al. (2001). Increased prevalence of vascular dementia in Japan: A community-based epidemiological study. *Neurology*, *57*(5), 839–844.

Jeerakathil, T., Wolf, P. A., Beiser, A., Massaro, J., Seshadri, S., D'Agostino, R. B., et al. (2004). Stroke risk profile predicts white matter hyperintensity volume: The Framingham Study. *Stroke*, *35*(8), 1857–1861.

Jefferson, A. L., Byerly, L. K., Vanderhill, S., Lambe, S., Wong, S., Ozonoff, A., et al. (2008). Characterization of activities of daily living in individuals with mild cognitive impairment. *American Journal of Geriatric Psychiatry*, *16*(5), 375–383.

Jefferson, A. L., Cahn-Weiner, D., Boyle, P., Paul, R. H., Moser, D. J., Gordon, N., et al. (2006). Cognitive predictors of functional decline in vascular dementia. *International Journal of Geriatric Psychiatry*, *21*(8), 752–754.

Jefferson, A. L., Cosentino, S. A., Ball, S. K., Bogdanoff, B., Leopold, N., Kaplan, E., et al. (2002). Errors produced on the mini-mental state examination and neuropsychological test performance in Alzheimer's disease, ischemic vascular dementia, and Parkinson's disease. *Journal of Neuropsychiatry and Clinical Neurosciences*, *14*(3), 311–320.

Jefferson, A. L., Paul, R. H., Ozonoff, A., & Cohen, R. A. (2006). Evaluating elements of executive functioning as predictors of instrumental activities of daily living (IADLs). *Archives of Clinical Neuropsychology*, *21*(4), 311–320.

Jellinger, K. A. (2006). Clinicopathological analysis of dementia disorders in the elderly – An update. *Journal of Alzheimer's Disease*, *9*(3 Suppl), 61–70.

Jellinger, K. A. (2002). The pathology of ischemic-vascular dementia: An update. *Journal of the Neurological Sciences*, *203–204*, 153–157.

Jellinger, K. A., & Attems, J. (2007). Neuropathological evaluation of mixed dementia. *Journal of the Neurological Sciences*, *257*(1–2), 80–87.

Jeste, D. V., Palmer, B. W., Appelbaum, P. S., Golshan, S., Glorioso, D., Dunn, L. B., et al. (2007). A new brief instrument for assessing decisional capacity for clinical research. *Archives of General Psychiatry*, *64*(8), 966–974.

Joshipura, K. J., Ascherio, A., Manson, J. E., Stampfer, M. J., Rimm, E. B., Speizer, F. E., et al. (1999). Fruit and vegetable intake in relation to risk of ischemic stroke. *Journal of the American Medical Association*, *282*(13), 1233–1239.

Juan, D., Zhou, D. H., Li, J., Wang, J. Y., Gao, C., & Chen, M. (2004). A 2-year follow-up study of cigarette smoking and risk of dementia. *European Journal of Neurology*, *11*(4), 277–282.

Jurgens, G., Taddei-Peters, W. C., Koltringer, P., Petek, W., Chen, Q., Greilberger, J., et al. (1995). Lipoprotein(a) serum concentration and apolipoprotein(a) phenotype correlate with severity and presence of ischemic cerebrovascular disease. *Stroke*, *26*(10), 1841–1848.

Juva, K., Makela, M., Sulkava, R., & Erkinjuntti, T. (1997). One-year risk of institutionalization in demented outpatients with caretaking relatives. *International Psychogeriatrics*, *9*(2), 175–182.

Kalaria, R. N., Kenny, R. A., Ballard, C. G., Perry, R., Ince, P., & Polvikoski, T. (2004). Towards defining the neuropathological substrates of vascular dementia. *Journal of the Neurological Sciences*, *226*(1–2), 75–80.

Kawachi, I., Colditz, G. A., Stampfer, M. J., Willett, W. C., Manson, J. E., Rosner, B., et al. (1993). Smoking cessation and decreased risk of stroke in women. *Journal of the American Medical Association*, *269*(2), 232–236.

Kempen, G. I., & Suurmeijer, T. P. (1990). The development of a hierarchical polychotomous ADL-IADL scale for noninstitutionalized elders. *The Gerontologist*, *30*(4), 497–502.

Kertesz, A., & Clydesdale, S. (1994). Neuropsychological deficits in vascular dementia vs. Alzheimer's disease. Frontal lobe deficits prominent in vascular dementia. *Archives of Neurology*, *51*(12), 1226–1231.

Keymeulen, B., Jacobs, A., de Metz, K., de Sadeleer, C., Bossuyt, A., & Somers, G. (1995). Regional cerebral hypoperfusion in long-term type 1 (insulin-dependent) diabetic patients: Relation to hypoglycaemic events. *Nuclear Medicine Communications*, *16*(1), 10–16.

Knopman, D. S., Kitto, J., Deinard, S., & Heiring, J. (1988). Longitudinal study of death and institutionalization in patients with primary degenerative dementia. *Journal of the American Geriatrics Society*, *36*(2), 108–112.

Knopman, D. S., Parisi, J. E., Boeve, B. F., Cha, R. H., Apaydin, H., Salviati, A., et al. (2003). Vascular dementia in a population-based autopsy study. *Archives of Neurology*, *60*(4), 569–575.

Knopman, D. S., Rocca, W. A., Cha, R. H., Edland, S. D., & Kokmen, E. (2003). Survival study of vascular dementia in Rochester, Minnesota. *Archives of Neurology*, *60*(1), 85–90.

Kozachuk, W. E., DeCarli, C., Schapiro, M. B., Wagner, E. E., Rapoport, S. I., & Horwitz, B. (1990). White matter hyperintensities in dementia of Alzheimer's type and in healthy subjects without cerebrovascular risk factors. A magnetic resonance imaging study. *Archives of Neurology*, *47*(12), 1306–1310.

Kramer, J. H., Reed, B. R., Mungas, D., Weiner, M. W., & Chui, H. C. (2002). Executive dysfunction in subcortical ischaemic vascular disease. *Journal of Neurology, Neurosurgery & Psychiatry*, *72*(2), 217–220.

Kurylo, D. D., Corkin, S., Rizzo III, J. F., & Growdon, J. H. (1996). Greater relative impairment of object recognition than of visuospatial abilities in Alzheimer's disease. *Neuropsychology*, *10*(1), 74–81.

Kuusisto, J., Mykkanen, L., Pyorala, K., & Laakso, M. (1994). Non-insulin-dependent diabetes and its metabolic control are important predictors of stroke in elderly subjects. *Stroke*, *25*(6), 1157–1164.

Laakso, M. P., Partanen, K., Riekkinen, P., Lehtovirta, M., Helkala, E. L., Hallikainen, M., et al. (1996). Hippocampal volumes in Alzheimer's disease, Parkinson's disease with and without dementia, and in vascular dementia: An MRI study. *Neurology*, *46*(3), 678–681.

Lafosse, J. M., Reed, B. R., Mungas, D., Sterling, S. B., Wahbeh, H., & Jagust, W. J. (1997). Fluency and memory differences between ischemic vascular dementia and Alzheimer's disease. *Neuropsychology*, *11*(4), 514–522.

Laukka, E. J., Jones, S., Small, B. J., Fratiglioni, L., & Backman, L. (2004). Similar patterns of cognitive deficits in the preclinical phases of vascular dementia and Alzheimer's disease. *Journal of the International Neuropsychological Society, 10*(3), 382–391.

Lawton, M. P. (1972). Assessing the competence of older people. In D. P. Kent, R. Kastenbaum & S. Sherwood (Eds.), *Research planning & action for the elderly: The power & potential of social science* (pp. 122–143). New York: Behavioral Publications, Inc.

Lawton, M. P., & Brody, E. M. (1969). Assessment of older people: Self-maintaining and instrumental activities of daily living. *The Gerontologist, 9*(3), 179–186.

Lee, D. Y., Fletcher, E., Martinez, O., Ortega, M., Zozulya, N., Kim, J., et al. (2009). Regional pattern of white matter microstructural changes in normal aging, MCI, and AD. *Neurology, 73*(21), 1722–1728.

Lezak, M. D., Howieson, D. B., & Loring, D. W. (2004). *Neuropsychological assessment* (4th edn.). New York: Oxford University Press.

Libon, D. J., Glosser, G., Malamut, B. L., Kaplan, E., Goldberg, E., Swenson, R., et al. (1994). Age, executive functions, and visuospatial functioning in healthy older adults. *Neuropsychology, 8*(1), 38–43.

Libon, D. J., Malamut, B. L., Swenson, R., Sands, L. P., & Cloud, B. S. (1996). Further analyses of clock drawings among demented and nondemented older subjects. *Archives of Clinical Neuropsychology, 11*(3), 193–205.

Libon, D. J., Mattson, R. E., Glosser, G., Kaplan, E., Malamut, B. L., Sands, L. P., et al. (1996). A nine-word dementia version of the California Verbal Learning Test. *The Clinical Neuropsychologist, 10*(3), 237–244.

Lindenstrom, E., Boysen, G., & Nyboe, J. (1993). Lifestyle factors and risk of cerebro-vascular disease in women. The Copenhagen City Heart Study. *Stroke, 24*(10), 1468–1472.

Lindstrom, J., Peltonen, M., Eriksson, J. G., Louheranta, A., Fogelholm, M., Uusitupa, M., et al. (2006). High-fibre, low-fat diet predicts long-term weight loss and decreased type 2 diabetes risk: The Finnish Diabetes Prevention Study. *Diabetologia, 49*(5), 912–920.

Lloyd-Jones, D., Adams, R.J., Brown, T.M., Carnethon, M., Dai, S., De Simone, G. et al. (2010). Heart disease and stroke statistics: 2010 update: A report from the American Heart Association. *Circulation, 121*(7), e46–e215.

Loeb, C., & Meyer, J. S. (1996). Vascular dementia: Still a debatable entity? *Journal of the Neurological Sciences, 143*(1–2), 31–40.

Lojkowska, W., Ryglewicz, D., Jedrzejczak, T., Minc, S., Jakubowska, T., Jarosz, H., et al. (2003). The effect of cholinesterase inhibitors on the regional blood flow in patients with Alzheimer's disease and vascular dementia. *Journal of the Neurological Sciences, 216*(1), 119–126.

Longstreth, W. T., Jr., Manolio, T. A., Arnold, A., Burke, G. L., Bryan, N., Jungreis, C. A., et al. (1996). Clinical correlates of white matter findings on cranial magnetic resonance imaging of 3301 elderly people. The Cardiovascular Health Study. *Stroke, 27*(8), 1274–1282.

Looi, J. C., & Sachdev, P. S. (2000). Vascular dementia as a frontal subcortical system dysfunction. *Psychological Medicine, 30*(5), 997–1003.

Lopez, O. L., Kuller, L. H., Becker, J. T., Jagust, W. J., DeKosky, S. T., Fitzpatrick, A., et al. (2005). Classification of vascular dementia in the Cardiovascular Health Study Cognition Study. *Neurology, 64*(9), 1539–1547.

Lukatela, K., Malloy, P., Jenkins, M., & Cohen, R. (1998). The naming deficit in early Alzheimer's and vascular dementia. *Neuropsychology, 12*(4), 565–572.

Lukatela, K. A., Cohen, R. A., Kessler, H. A., Jenkins, M. A., Moser, D. J., Stone, W. F., et al. (2000). Dementia rating scale performance: A comparison of vascular and Alzheimer's dementia. *Journal of Clinical and Experimental Neuropsychology, 22*(4), 445–454.

Maes, M., DeVos, N., Wauters, A., Demedts, P., Maurits, V. W., Neels, H., et al. (1999). Inflammatory markers in younger vs elderly normal volunteers and in patients with Alzheimer's disease. *Journal of Psychiatric Research; 33*(5), 397–405.

Mariani, E., Polidori, M. C., Cherubini, A., & Mecocci, P. (2005). Oxidative stress in brain aging, neurodegenerative and vascular diseases: An overview. *Journal of Chromatography. B, Analytical Technologies in the Biomededical & Life Sciences, 827*(1), 65–75.

Marstrand, J. R., Garde, E., Rostrup, E., Ring, P., Rosenbaum, S., Mortensen, E. L., et al. (2002). Cerebral perfusion and cerebrovascular reactivity are reduced in white matter hyperintensities. *Stroke, 33*(4), 972–976.

Mathias, J. L., & Burke, J. (2009). Cognitive functioning in Alzheimer's and vascular dementia: A meta-analysis. *Neuropsychology, 23*(4), 411–423.

Melhem, E. R., Mori, S., Mukundan, G., Kraut, M. A., Pomper, M. G., & van Zijl, P. C. (2002). Diffusion tensor MR imaging of the brain and white matter tractography. *American Journal of Roentgenology, 178*(1), 3–16.

Meyer, J. S., Huang, J., & Chowdhury, M. H. (2007). MRI confirms mild cognitive impairments prodromal for Alzheimer's, vascular and Parkinson–Lewy body dementias. *Journal of Neurological Science, 257*(1–2), 97–104.

Mobius, H. J., & Stoffler, A. (2003). Memantine in vascular dementia. *International Psychogeriatrics, 15*(Suppl 1), 207–213.

Molsa, P. K., Paljarvi, L., Rinne, J. O., Rinne, U. K., & Sako, E. (1985). Validity of clinical diagnosis in dementia: A prospective clinicopathological study. *Journal of Neurology, Neurosurgery & Psychiatry, 48*(11), 1085–1090.

Montaner, J., Fernandez-Cadenas, I., Molina, C. A., Ribo, M., Huertas, R., Rosell, A., et al. (2006). Poststroke C-reactive protein is a powerful prognostic tool among candidates for thrombolysis. *Stroke, 37*(5), 1205–1210.

Moorhouse, P., & Rockwood, K. (2008). Vascular cognitive impairment: Current concepts and clinical developments. *Lancet Neurology, 7*(3), 246–255.

Moretti, R., Torre, P., Antonello, R. M., Cazzato, G., & Bava, A. (2002). Rivastigmine in subcortical vascular dementia: An open 22-month study. *Journal of the Neurological Sciences, 203–204*, 141–146.

Moser, D. J., Cohen, R. A., Paul, R. H., Paulsen, J. S., Ott, B. R., Gordon, N. M., et al. (2001). Executive function and magnetic resonance imaging subcortical hyperintensities in vascular dementia. *Neuropsychiatry, Neuropsychology, and Behavioral Neurology, 14*(2), 89–92.

Nencini, P., Sarti, C., Innocenti, R., Pracucci, G., & Inzitari, D. (2003). Acute inflammatory events and ischemic stroke subtypes. *Cerebrovascular Diseases, 15*(3), 215–221.

Nobili, F., Rodriguez, G., Marenco, S., De Carli, F., Gambaro, M., Castello, C., et al. (1993). Regional cerebral blood flow in chronic hypertension. A correlative study. *Stroke, 24*(8), 1148–1153.

Nolan, K. A., Lino, M. M., Seligmann, A. W., & Blass, J. P. (1998). Absence of vascular dementia in an autopsy series from a dementia clinic. *Journal of the American Geriatrics Society, 46*(5), 597–604.

Nyenhuis, D. L., Gorelick, P. B., Freels, S., & Garron, D. C. (2002). Cognitive and functional decline in African Americans with VaD, AD, and stroke without dementia. *Neurology*, *58*(1), 56–61.

Oguro, H., Yamaguchi, S., Abe, S., Ishida, Y., Bokura, H., & Kobayashi, S. (2006). Differentiating Alzheimer's disease from subcortical vascular dementia with the FAB test. *Journal of Neurology*, *253*(11), 1490–1494.

Okazaki, M., Kasai, M., Meguro, K., Yamaguchi, S., & Ishii, H. (2009). Disturbances in everyday life activities and sequence disabilities in tool use for Alzheimer disease and vascular dementia. *Cognitive and Behavioral Neurology*, *22*(4), 215–221.

Orgogozo, J. M., Rigaud, A. S., Stoffler, A., Mobius, H. J., & Forette, F. (2002). Efficacy and safety of memantine in patients with mild to moderate vascular dementia: A randomized, placebo-controlled trial (MMM 300). *Stroke*, *33*(7), 1834–1839.

O'Sullivan, M., Morris, R. G., Huckstep, B., Jones, D. K., Williams, S. C., & Markus, H. S. (2004). Diffusion tensor MRI correlates with executive dysfunction in patients with ischaemic leukoaraiosis. *Journal of Neurology, Neurosurgery & Psychiatry*, *75*(3), 441–447.

O'Sullivan, M., Summers, P. E., Jones, D. K., Jarosz, J. M., Williams, S. C., & Markus, H. S. (2001). Normal-appearing white matter in ischemic leukoaraiosis: A diffusion tensor MRI study. *Neurology*, *57*(12), 2307–2310.

Ott, A., Breteler, M. M., de Bruyne, M. C., van Harskamp, F., Grobbee, D. E., & Hofman, A. (1997). Atrial fibrillation and dementia in a population-based study. The Rotterdam Study. *Stroke*, *28*(2), 316–321.

Ott, A., Breteler, M. M., van Harskamp, F., Claus, J. J., van der Cammen, T. J., Grobbee, D. E., et al. (1995). Prevalence of Alzheimer's disease and vascular dementia: Association with education. The Rotterdam study. *British Medical Journal*, *310*(6985), 970–973.

Ott, A., Stolk, R. P., Hofman, A., van Harskamp, F., Grobbee, D. E., & Breteler, M. M. (1996). Association of diabetes mellitus and dementia: The Rotterdam Study. *Diabetologia*, *39*(11), 1392–1397.

Padovani, A., Di Piero, V., Bragoni, M., Iacoboni, M., Gualdi, G. F., & Lenzi, G. L. (1995). Patterns of neuropsychological impairment in mild dementia: A comparison between Alzheimer's disease and multi-infarct dementia. *Acta Neurologica Scandinavica*, *92*(6), 433–442.

Palasik, W., Fiszer, U., Lechowicz, W., Czartoryska, B., Krzesiewicz, M., & Lugowska, A. (2005). Assessment of relations between clinical outcome of ischemic stroke and activity of inflammatory processes in the acute phase based on examination of selected parameters. *European Neurology*, *53*(4), 188–193.

Pantoni, L., Garcia, J. H., & Brown, G. G. (1996). Vascular pathology in three cases of progressive cognitive deterioration. *Journal of the Neurological Sciences*, *135*(2), 131–139.

Panza, F., D'Introno, A., Colacicco, A. M., Capurso, C., Pichichero, G., Capurso, S. A., et al. (2006). Lipid metabolism in cognitive decline and dementia. *Brain Research Reviews*, *51*(2), 275–292.

Papademetriou, V. (2005). Hypertension and cognitive function. Blood pressure regulation and cognitive function: A review of the literature. *Geriatrics*, *60*(1), 20–22.

Passmore, A. P., Bayer, A. J., & Steinhagen-Thiessen, E. (2005). Cognitive, global, and functional benefits of donepezil in Alzheimer's disease and vascular dementia: Results from large-scale clinical trials. *Journal of the Neurological Sciences*, *229–230*, 141–146.

Paul, R., Cohen, R., Moser, D., Ott, B., Zawacki, T., & Gordon, N. (2001). Performance on the Hooper Visual Organizational Test in patients diagnosed with subcortical vascular dementia: Relation to naming performance. *Neuropsychiatry, Neuropsychology, and Behavioral Neurology, 14*(2), 93–97.

Paul, R., Cohen, R., Ott, B. R., & Salloway, S. (2005). *Vascular dementia: Cerebrovascular mechanisms and clinical management.* Totowa, NJ: Humana Press.

Paul, R., Moser, D., Cohen, R., Browndyke, J., Zawacki, T., & Gordon, N. (2001). Dementia severity and pattern of cognitive performance in vascular dementia. *Applied Neuropsychology, 8*(4), 211–217.

Peila, R., Rodriguez, B. L., & Launer, L. J. (2002). Type 2 diabetes, APOE gene, and the risk for dementia and related pathologies: The Honolulu-Asia Aging Study. *Diabetes, 51*(4), 1256–1262.

Peng, D. Q., Zhao, S. P., & Wang, J. L. (1999). Lipoprotein (a) and apolipoprotein E epsilon 4 as independent risk factors for ischemic stroke. *Journal of Cardiovascular Risk, 6*(1), 1–6.

Petersen, P., Kastrup, J., Videbaek, R., & Boysen, G. (1989). Cerebral blood flow before and after cardioversion of atrial fibrillation. *Journal of Cerebral Blood Flow & Metabolism, 9*(3), 422–425.

Pico, F., Dufouil, C., Levy, C., Besancon, V., de Kersaint-Gilly, A., Bonithon-Kopp, C., et al. (2002). Longitudinal study of carotid atherosclerosis and white matter hyperintensities: The EVA-MRI cohort. *Cerebrovascular Diseases, 14*(2), 109–115.

Pohjasvaara, T., Mantyla, R., Aronen, H. J., Leskela, M., Salonen, O., Kaste, M., et al. (1999). Clinical and radiological determinants of prestroke cognitive decline in a stroke cohort. *Journal of Neurology, Neurosurgery & Psychiatry, 67*(6), 742–748.

Pohjasvaara, T., Mantyla, R., Ylikoski, R., Kaste, M., & Erkinjuntti, T. (2000). Comparison of different clinical criteria (DSM-III, ADDTC, ICD-10, NINDS-AIREN, DSM-IV) for the diagnosis of vascular dementia. National Institute of Neurological Disorders and Stroke-Association Internationale pour la Recherche et l'Enseignement en Neurosciences. *Stroke, 31*(12), 2952–2957.

Poore, Q. E., Rapport, L. J., Fuerst, D. R., & Keenan, P. (2006). Word list generation performance in Alzheimer's disease and vascular dementia. *Neuropsychology, development, and cognition. Section B, Aging, neuropsychology and cognition, 13*(1), 86–94.

Posner, H. B., Tang, M. X., Luchsinger, J., Lantigua, R., Stern, Y., & Mayeux, R. (2002). The relationship of hypertension in the elderly to AD, vascular dementia, and cognitive function. *Neurology, 58*(8), 1175–1181.

Qiu, C., Winblad, B., Marengoni, A., Klarin, I., Fastbom, J., & Fratiglioni, L. (2006). Heart failure and risk of dementia and Alzheimer disease: A population-based cohort study. *Archives of Internal Medicine, 166*(9), 1003–1008.

Raffaitin, C., Gin, H., Empana, J. P., Helmer, C., Berr, C., Tzourio, C., et al. (2009). Metabolic syndrome and risk for incident Alzheimer's disease or vascular dementia: The Three-City Study. *Diabetes Care, 32*(1), 169–174.

Reed, B. R., Eberling, J. L., Mungas, D., Weiner, M. W., & Jagust, W. J. (2000). Memory failure has different mechanisms in subcortical stroke and Alzheimer's disease. *Annals of Neurology, 48*(3), 275–284.

Reed, B. R., Eberling, J. L., Mungas, D., Weiner, M. W., Kramer, J. H., & Jagust, W. J. (2004). Effects of white matter lesions and lacunes on cortical function. *Archive of Neurology, 61*(10), 1545–1550.

Reed, D. M., Resch, J. A., Hayashi, T., MacLean, C., & Yano, K. (1988). A prospective study of cerebral artery atherosclerosis. *Stroke, 19*(7), 820–825.

Reitz, C., den Heijer, T., van Duijn, C., Hofman, A., & Breteler, M. M. (2007). Relation between smoking and risk of dementia and Alzheimer disease: The Rotterdam Study. *Neurology, 69*(10), 998–1005.

Roman, G. C. (2004). Facts, myths, and controversies in vascular dementia. *Journal of Neurological Science, 226*(1–2), 49–52.

Roman, G. C., Sachdev, P., Royall, D. R., Bullock, R. A., Orgogozo, J. M., Lopez-Pousa, S., et al. (2004). Vascular cognitive disorder: A new diagnostic category updating vascular cognitive impairment and vascular dementia. *Journal of the Neurological Sciences, 226*(1–2), 81–87.

Roman, G. C., Tatemichi, T. K., Erkinjuntti, T., Cummings, J. L., Masdeu, J. C., Garcia, J. H., et al. (1993). Vascular dementia: Diagnostic criteria for research studies. Report of the NINDS-AIREN International Workshop. *Neurology, 43*(2), 250–260.

Rosen, W. G., Mohs, R. C., & Davis, K. L. (1984). A new rating scale for Alzheimer's disease. *American Journal of Psychiatry, 141*(11), 1356–1364.

Ross, G. W., Petrovitch, H., White, L. R., Masaki, K. H., Li, C. Y., Curb, J. D., et al. (1999). Characterization of risk factors for vascular dementia: The Honolulu-Asia Aging Study. *Neurology, 53*(2), 337–343.

Rothwell, P. M. (2005). Prevention of stroke in patients with diabetes mellitus and the metabolic syndrome. *Cerebrovascular Diseases, 20*(Suppl 1), 24–34.

Ruchoux, M. M., & Maurage, C. A. (1998). Endothelial changes in muscle and skin biopsies in patients with CADASIL. *Neuropathology and Applied Neurobiology, 24*(1), 60–65.

Sacco, R. L., Gan, R., Boden-Albala, B., Lin, I. F., Kargman, D. E., Hauser, W. A., et al. (1998). Leisure-time physical activity and ischemic stroke risk: The Northern Manhattan Stroke Study. *Stroke, 29*(2), 380–387.

Sachdev, P. (1999). Vascular cognitive disorder. *International Journal of Geriatric Psychiatry, 14*(5), 402–403.

Sasaki, S., Zhang, X. H., & Kesteloot, H. (1995). Dietary sodium, potassium, saturated fat, alcohol, and stroke mortality. *Stroke, 26*(5), 783–789.

Schmidt, R., Schmidt, H., Curb, J. D., Masaki, K., White, L. R., & Launer, L. J. (2002). Early inflammation and dementia: A 25-year follow-up of the Honolulu-Asia Aging Study. *Annals of Neurology, 52*(2), 168–174.

Schmidt, R., Schmidt, H., Kapeller, P., Enzinger, C., Ropele, S., Saurugg, R., et al. (2002). The natural course of MRI white matter hyperintensities. *Journal of the Neurological Sciences, 203–204*, 253–257.

Schramm, P., Schellinger, P. D., Klotz, E., Kallenberg, K., Fiebach, J. B., Kulkens, S., et al. (2004). Comparison of perfusion computed tomography and computed tomography angiography source images with perfusion-weighted imaging and diffusion-weighted imaging in patients with acute stroke of less than 6 hours' duration. *Stroke, 35*(7), 1652–1658.

Sedvall, G., & Pauli, S. (2002). *Brain imaging research in psychiatry.* Chichester, UK: John Wiley & Sons Ltd.

Shaw, T. G., Mortel, K. F., Meyer, J. S., Rogers, R. L., Hardenberg, J., & Cutaia, M. M. (1984). Cerebral blood flow changes in benign aging and cerebrovascular disease. *Neurology, 34*(7), 855–862.

Shinton, R., & Beevers, G. (1989). Meta-analysis of relation between cigarette smoking and stroke. *British Medical Journal, 298*(6676), 789–794.

Singer, M. B., Chong, J., Lu, D., Schonewille, W. J., Tuhrim, S., & Atlas, S. W. (1998). Diffusion-weighted MRI in acute subcortical infarction. *Stroke, 29*(1), 133–136.

Sjostrom, C. D., Peltonen, M., Wedel, H., & Sjostrom, L. (2000). Differentiated long-term effects of intentional weight loss on diabetes and hypertension. *Hypertension, 36*(1), 20–25.

Smith, W. S., Tsao, J. W., Billings, M. E., Johnston, S. C., Hemphill, J. C., 3rd, Bonovich, D. C., et al. (2006). Prognostic significance of angiographically confirmed large vessel intracranial occlusion in patients presenting with acute brain ischemia. *Neurocritical Care, 4*(1), 14–17.

Snowdon, D. A., Greiner, L. H., Mortimer, J. A., Riley, K. P., Greiner, P. A., & Markesbery, W. R. (1997). Brain infarction and the clinical expression of Alzheimer disease. The Nun Study. *Journal of the American Medical Association, 277*(10), 813–817.

Staekenborg, S. S., van Straaten, E. C., van der Flier, W. M., Lane, R., Barkhof, F., & Scheltens, P. (2008). Small vessel versus large vessel vascular dementia: Risk factors and MRI findings. *Journal of Neurology, 255*(11), 1644–1651.

Tarkowski, E., Blennow, K., Wallin, A., & Tarkowski, A. (1999). Intracerebral production of tumor necrosis factor-alpha, a local neuroprotective agent, in Alzheimer disease and vascular dementia. *Journal of Clinical Immunology, 19*(4), 223–230.

Tarkowski, E., Tullberg, M., Fredman, P., & Wikkelso, C. (2003a). Correlation between intrathecal sulfatide and TNF-alpha levels in patients with vascular dementia. *Dementia and Geriatric Cognitive Disorders, 15*(4), 207–211.

Tarkowski, E., Tullberg, M., Fredman, P., & Wikkelso, C. (2003b). Normal pressure hydrocephalus triggers intrathecal production of TNF-alpha. *Neurobiology of Aging, 24*(5), 707–714.

Thomas, A. J., O'Brien, J. T., Barber, R., McMeekin, W., & Perry, R. (2003). A neuropathological study of periventricular white matter hyperintensities in major depression. *Journal of Affective Disorders, 76*(1–3), 49–54.

Thomas, N. J., Morris, C. M., Scaravilli, F., Johansson, J., Rossor, M., De Lange, R., et al. (2000). Hereditary vascular dementia linked to notch 3 mutations. CADASIL in British families. *Annals of the New York Academy of Sciences, 903*, 293–298.

Tierney, M. C., Black, S. E., Szalai, J. P., Snow, W. G., Fisher, R. H., Nadon, G., et al. (2001). Recognition memory and verbal fluency differentiate probable Alzheimer disease from subcortical ischemic vascular dementia. *Archives of Neurology, 58*(10), 1654–1659.

Tkac, I., Troscak, M., Javorsky, M., Petrik, R., & Tomcova, M. (2001). Increased intracranial arterial resistance in patients with type 2 diabetes mellitus. *Wien Klin Wochenschr, 113*(22), 870–873.

Torack, R. (1983). The history of senile dementia. In B. Reisberg (Ed.), *Alzheimer's disease* (pp. 23–28). New York: The Free Press.

Traykov, L., Baudic, S., Thibaudet, M. C., Rigaud, A. S., Smagghe, A., & Boller, F. (2002). Neuropsychological deficit in early subcortical vascular dementia: Comparison to Alzheimer's disease. *Dementia and Geriatric Cognitive Disorders, 14*(1), 26–32.

Tremblay, A., Despres, J. P., Maheux, J., Pouliot, M. C., Nadeau, A., Moorjani, S., et al. (1991). Normalization of the metabolic profile in obese women by exercise and a low fat diet. *Medicine & Science in Sports & Exercise, 23*(12), 1326–1331.

Tremblay, A., Doucet, E., Imbeault, P., Mauriege, P., Despres, J. P., & Richard, D. (1999). Metabolic fitness in active reduced-obese individuals. *Obesity Research, 7*(6), 556–563.

Tresch, D. D., Folstein, M. F., Rabins, P. V., & Hazzard, W. R. (1985). Prevalence and significance of cardiovascular disease and hypertension in elderly patients with dementia and depression. *Journal of the American Geriatric Society, 33*(8), 530–537.

Urakami, K., Mura, T., & Takahashi, K. (1987). Lp(a) lipoprotein in cerebrovascular disease and dementia. *Japanese Journal of Psychiatry and Neurology, 41*(4), 743–748.

Utter, S., Tamboli, I. Y., Walter, J., Upadhaya, A. R., Birkenmeier, G., Pietrzik, C. U., et al. (2008). Cerebral small vessel disease-induced apolipoprotein E leakage is associated with Alzheimer disease and the accumulation of amyloid beta-protein in perivascular astrocytes. *Journal of Neuropathology and Experimental Neurology, 67*(9), 842–856.

van Dijk, E. J., Prins, N. D., Vermeer, S. E., Vrooman, H. A., Hofman, A., Koudstaal, P. J., et al. (2005). C-reactive protein and cerebral small-vessel disease: The Rotterdam Scan Study. *Circulation, 112*(6), 900–905.

Verhey, F. R., Lodder, J., Rozendaal, N., & Jolles, J. (1996). Comparison of seven sets of criteria used for the diagnosis of vascular dementia. *Neuroepidemiology, 15*(3), 166–172.

Viitanen, M., & Kalimo, H. (2000). CADASIL: Hereditary arteriopathy leading to multiple brain infarcts and dementia. *Annals of the New York Academy of Sciences, 903*, 273–284.

Villardita, C. (1993). Alzheimer's disease compared with cerebrovascular dementia. Neuropsychological similarities and differences. *Acta Neurologica Scandinavica, 87*(4), 299–308.

Vinters, H. V., Ellis, W. G., Zarow, C., Zaias, B. W., Jagust, W. J., Mack, W. J., et al. (2000). Neuropathologic substrates of ischemic vascular dementia. *Journal of Neuropathology and Experimental Neurology, 59*(11), 931–945.

Vuorinen, E., Laine, M., & Rinne, J. (2000). Common pattern of language impairment in vascular dementia and in Alzheimer disease. *Alzheimer Disease and Associated Disorders, 14*(2), 81–86.

Wada-Isoe, K., Wakutani, Y., Urakami, K., & Nakashima, K. (2004). Elevated interleukin-6 levels in cerebrospinal fluid of vascular dementia patients. *Acta Neurologica Scandinavica, 110*(2), 124–127.

Wanless, R. B., Anand, I. S., Gurden, J., Harris, P., & Poole-Wilson, P. A. (1987). Regional blood flow and hemodynamics in the rabbit with adriamycin cardiomyopathy: Effects of isosorbide dinitrate, dobutamine and captopril. *Journal of Pharmacology & Experimental Therapeutics, 243*(3), 1101–1106.

Wannamethee, S. G., Shaper, A. G., Whincup, P. H., & Walker, M. (1995). Smoking cessation and the risk of stroke in middle-aged men. *Journal of the American Medical Association, 274*(2), 155–160.

Watanabe, T., Koba, S., Kawamura, M., Itokawa, M., Idei, T., Nakagawa, Y., et al. (2004). Small dense low-density lipoprotein and carotid atherosclerosis in relation to vascular dementia. *Metabolism, 53*(4), 476–482.

Wetterling, T., Kanitz, R. D., & Borgis, K. J. (1996). Comparison of different diagnostic criteria for vascular dementia (ADDTC, DSM-IV, ICD-10, NINDS-AIREN). *Stroke, 27*(1), 30–36.

Whelton, P. K., He, J., Appel, L. J., Cutler, J. A., Havas, S., Kotchen, T. A., et al. (2002). Primary prevention of hypertension: Clinical and public health advisory from The National High Blood Pressure Education Program. *Journal of the American Medical Association, 288*(15), 1882–1888.

Whitmer, R. A., Gunderson, E. P., Quesenberry, C. P., Jr., Zhou, J., & Yaffe, K. (2007). Body mass index in midlife and risk of Alzheimer disease and vascular dementia. *Current Alzheimer Research, 4*(2), 103–109.

Wilcock, G., Mobius, H. J., & Stoffler, A. (2002). A double-blind, placebo-controlled multi-centre study of memantine in mild to moderate vascular dementia (MMM500). *International Clinical Psychopharmacology, 17*(6), 297–305.

Wolf, P. A., Abbott, R. D., & Kannel, W. B. (1987). Atrial fibrillation: A major contributor to stroke in the elderly. The Framingham Study. *Archives of Internal Medicine, 147*(9), 1561–1564.

Wolf, P. A., D'Agostino, R. B., Belanger, A. J., & Kannel, W. B. (1991). Probability of stroke: A risk profile from the Framingham Study. *Stroke, 22*(3), 312–318.

Wolf, R. L., Alsop, D. C., McGarvey, M. L., Maldjian, J. A., Wang, J., & Detre, J. A. (2003). Susceptibility contrast and arterial spin labeled perfusion MRI in cerebrovascular disease. *Journal of Neuroimaging, 13*(1), 17–27.

World Health Organization (1992). *The ICD-10 Classification of Mental and Behavioral Disorders.* Geneva.

Yamada, M., Kasagi, F., Sasaki, H., Masunari, N., Mimori, Y., & Suzuki, G. (2003). Association between dementia and midlife risk factors: The Radiation Effects Research Foundation Adult Health Study. *Journal of the American Geriatric Society, 51*(3), 410–414.

Yasojima, K., Schwab, C., McGeer, E. G., & McGeer, P. L. (2000). Human neurons generate C-reactive protein and amyloid P: Upregulation in Alzheimer's disease. *Brain Research, 887*(1), 80–89.

Yip, A. G., McKee, A. C., Green, R. C., Wells, J., Young, H., Cupples, L. A., et al. (2005). APOE, vascular pathology, and the AD brain. *Neurology, 65*(2), 259–265.

Yuspeh, R. L., Vanderploeg, R. D., Crowell, T. A., & Mullan, M. (2002). Differences in executive functioning between Alzheimer's disease and subcortical ischemic vascular dementia. *Journal of Clinical and Experimental Neuropsychology, 24*(6), 745–754.

Zanella, M. T., Kohlmann, O., Jr., & Ribeiro, A. B. (2001). Treatment of obesity hypertension and diabetes syndrome. *Hypertension, 38*(3 Pt 2), 705–708.

Zarei, M., Damoiseaux, J. S., Morgese, C., Beckmann, C. F., Smith, S. M., Matthews, P. M., et al. (2009). Regional white matter integrity differentiates between vascular dementia and Alzheimer disease. *Stroke, 40*(3), 773–779.

Zeiher, A. M., Drexler, H., Wollschlager, H., & Just, H. (1991). Modulation of coronary vasomotor tone in humans. Progressive endothelial dysfunction with different early stages of coronary atherosclerosis. *Circulation, 83*(2), 391–401.

Zeng, Y., & Han, X. (2008). Sulfatides facilitate apolipoprotein E-mediated amyloid-beta peptide clearance through an endocytotic pathway. *Journal of Neurochemistry, 106*(3), 1275–1286.

Zenker, G., Koltringer, P., Bone, G., Niederkorn, K., Pfeiffer, K., & Jurgens, G. (1986). Lipoprotein(a) as a strong indicator for cerebrovascular disease. *Stroke, 17*(5), 942–945.

3

Dementia with Lewy Bodies
Tamara G. Fong and Daniel Z. Press

Dementia with Lewy bodies (DLB) shares features with Parkinson's disease and Alzheimer's disease, but is a distinct and common cause of dementia. DLB is a neurodegenerative disorder characterized by a classic triad of fluctuating cognitive impairment, visual hallucinations, and extrapyramidal features. There can also be falls and syncope due to involvement of the autonomic nervous system. The clinical and pathological features of DLB overlap with idiopathic Parkinson's disease (PD) and Alzheimer's disease (AD), but key features distinguish it as a separate entity.

DLB and Parkinson's disease with dementia (PDD) are descriptive labels that describe the time course of symptoms. DLB should be used if the dementia occurs before or at the onset of parkinsonism, whereas PDD should be used to describe patients who develop dementia 12 months or longer after development of idiopathic PD. Age of onset tends to be later for DLB than PDD and co-morbid Alzheimer's disease is less common in PDD, but there are few other distinctions between DLB and PDD. The cognitive profile, performance on attentional tasks, neuropsychiatric features, associated sleep disorders, autonomic involvement, severity of parkinsonism, and response to medications are similar. Thus, these definitions of DLB and PDD are best suited for clinical use; the generic term of Lewy body dementias may be more useful in other situations, including clinical, where the two phenotypes of DLB and PDD can be considered as different points along a spectrum of pathological abnormalities (see Figure 3.1).

The prevalence of DLB has not been fully determined. Estimates range from 10% to 25% of all dementias, which would make it the second most common cause of dementia in the elderly following AD. Diagnostic criteria for DLB with good specificity have been established (see Table 3.1), but the sensitivity of these criteria is

The Handbook of Alzheimer's Disease and Other Dementias, First Edition.
Edited by Andrew E. Budson, Neil W. Kowall.
© 2011 Blackwell Publishing Ltd. Published 2011 by Blackwell Publishing Ltd.

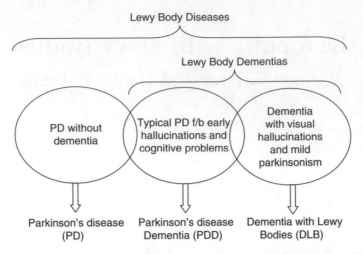

Figure 3.1   The spectrum of Lewy body disorders. The underlying pathophysiology of these conditions includes abnormal accumulation of alpha-synuclein protein in Lewy bodies

suboptimal. Thus, patients with DLB often receive initial misdiagnoses of AD, and under-diagnosis of DLB is probably common. In spite of these difficulties, many patients present in a characteristic manner and in these cases the clinician can be fairly confident in the diagnosis and can consider specific treatments.

Pathophysiology

Lewy bodies were first described in the brainstem of patients with idiopathic Parkinson's disease nearly a century ago. However, the role of Lewy bodies in the pathophysiology of both DLB and PD remains a mystery. Lewy bodies are intracytoplasmic, spherical eosinophilic neuronal inclusions (see Figure 3.3, plate section) that are the neuropathological signature of idiopathic PD. They contain a number of proteins including ubiquitin and alpha-synuclein. Lewy bodies are typically found in subcortical nuclei such as the substantia nigra, where they are easily visualized with routine stains. In contrast, cortical Lewy bodies are difficult to visualize by routine stains. Specialized stains for ubiquitin and alpha-synuclein have aided greatly in the identification of cortical Lewy bodies and in the development of pathological criteria for the diagnosis of DLB. Alpha-synuclein immunohistochemistry is the most sensitive and specific method for detecting Lewy bodies and alpha-synuclein containing Lewy neurites.

The Lewy body diseases are part of a spectrum of neurodegenerative disorders including DLB, PD, and the multiple systems atrophies (MSAs), which share a common pathophysiology of dysregulation and aggregation of alpha-synuclein. These disorders are often referred to as "synucleinopathies," to distinguish them from disorders of the proteins tau (tauopathies) and amyloid (amyloidopathies).

Table 3.1 Criteria for the clinical diagnosis of dementia with Lewy bodies

1 **Progressive cognitive decline** (*central feature*) sufficient to interfere with normal social or occupational function. Deficits in attention, executive function, and visuospatial function are early and prominent. Memory is variably impaired but becomes evident with progression.

2 **Recurrent visual hallucinations** (*core feature*) which are typically well formed and detailed.

3 **Parkinsonism** (*core feature*), which is not induced by medications, including rigidity, bradykinesia (slowness of movements) and variable degree of rest tremor.

4 **Fluctuations in cognition** (*core feature*) with marked variations in attention and alertness.

5 **Suggestive features:**
  (a) REM sleep behavior disorder;
  (b) severe neuroleptic sensitivity;
  (c) low dopamine transporter uptake in basal ganglia with SPECT or PET imaging.

6 **Supportive features** (often present but not diagnostic):
  (a) repeated falls and syncope;
  (b) severe autonomic dysfunction with orthostatic hypotension and bladder incontinence;
  (c) systematized delusions, including Capgras syndrome;
  (d) hallucinations in nonvisual modalities;
  (e) depression;
  (f) relative preservation of medial temporal lobe structures on MRI;
  (g) generalized low uptake on SPECT/PET perfusion imaging with reduced occipital lobe activity;
  (h) prominent slow wave activity on EEG with temporal lobe transient sharp waves.

7 **Temporal sequence of symptoms:** DLB is diagnosed when dementia occurs before or concurrent to parkinsonism. The term Parkinson's disease dementia (PDD) should be used if dementia occurs in context of established Parkinson's disease. In practice, the distinction is somewhat arbitrary, but for research the existing one-year rule between the onset of dementia and parkinsonism is recommended for consistency.

Two core features in addition to the central feature are sufficient for probable DLB, one for possible DLB. If one core feature is present then the addition of suggestive features is sufficient for diagnosis of probable DLB. In the absence of core features, then the presence of suggestive features is sufficient for diagnosis of possible DLB

Source: Adopted from McKeith, I.G., Dickson, D.W., Lowe, J., Emre, M., O'Brien, J.T., Feldmen, H. et al. (2005). Diagnosis and management of dementia with Lewy bodies. Third report of the DLB consortium. *Neurology, 65,* 1863–1872

With careful pathological review, nearly all patients with cortical Lewy bodies also have some Lewy bodies in subcortical regions and vice versa. But the regional distribution of Lewy bodies can vary, likely correlating with the symptomatology. In patients with brainstem predominant disease, including the substantia nigra, motor symptoms prevail; in patients with limbic and neocortical Lewy bodies, cognitive deficits are the primary clinical feature. At autopsy, DLB patients who had experienced visual hallucinations have increased numbers of Lewy bodies in the anterior and inferior temporal lobe and amygdala.

The number of cortical Lewy bodies does not correlate with the severity and duration of the dementia in DLB. Whether the Lewy bodies themselves cause neuronal dysfunction or are a protective mechanism for sequestering toxic synuclein aggregates is an area of controversy. The presence of cortical Lewy bodies is necessary but not sufficient for the diagnosis of DLB. Some patients with PD without dementia also have large numbers of cortical Lewy bodies at postmortem examination. Lewy body pathology has also been found in cognitively normal elderly subjects who have no clinical evidence for DLB or PD.

To complicate nosological and pathological matters further, the majority of cases of DLB, but not PDD, will have some degree of concomitant Alzheimer's changes. Amyloid plaques are more common than neurofibrillary tangles. The extent of AD changes is quite variable and a subgroup of cases exists without any plaques or tangles, confirming that "pure" DLB is sufficient to cause dementia. These patients with "pure" DLB are highly likely to have the core features of the disease. The presence of neurofibrillary cortical tangles makes it less likely for core features to be present, and instead, the clinical presentation includes more significant memory problems and a cognitive profile more characteristic for AD. Various names have been proposed in an attempt to express the frequent overlap of AD and DLB, including "Lewy body variant AD." Lewy body variant AD tends to have a more rapidly progressive course than "pure" AD. One way of sorting these mixed disorders is to view DLB as existing along two spectra, one being the degree of Alzheimer's changes and the other the degree of cortical vs. subcortical Lewy bodies (see Figure 3.2). While these distinctions are useful in theory, distinguishing among the groups antemortem is not yet possible.

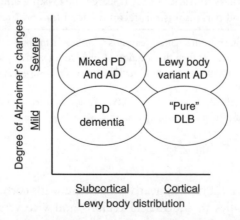

Figure 3.2	A schematic overview categorizing the overlap between Lewy body disorders and Alzheimer's disease based on the severity of the Alzheimer's pathology and the relative distribution of the Lewy bodies. Lewy body dementias is the inclusive term
PD = Parkinson's disease; AD = Alzheimer's disease; DLB = dementia with Lewy bodies

Deficits in cholinergic and dopaminergic neurotransmission occur in DLB. Loss of striatal dopaminergic innervation is severe enough to produce extrapyramidal motor symptoms essentially identical to PD. Mild extrapyramidal signs can also be present in advanced AD, but they differ in being primarily gait related, without bradykinesia (a progressive slowing of movements with repetition) or "cogwheel" rigidity (a ratchet-like stiffness to passive movements). Post-synaptic dopamine D2 receptors are also significantly reduced in DLB, and may explain why DLB patients often show severe sensitivity to "typical" neuroleptics, which selectively block D2 receptors.

Postmortem neurochemical studies in DLB patients have identified a cholinergic deficit in the temporal and parietal cortices, and this deficit is greater than that found in AD. DLB patients who suffer from visual hallucinations have significantly lower choline acetyltransferase (ChAT) levels than those who do not, and this can predict better response to cholinesterase inhibitors (ChEIs). Early clinical trials of ChEIs in AD found that patients who responded well to treatment had DLB pathology at autopsy.

Diagnosis

Consensus guidelines for the clinical and pathological diagnosis of DLB were first published in 1996. Validation studies have confirmed that the clinical criteria outlined in these guidelines have high specificity in predicting the presence of Lewy body pathology, but sensitivity was low and highly variable. The guidelines were revised in 1999 and again in 2003, and most recently published in 2005 (see Table 3.1). Criteria include features that are suggestive of a DLB diagnosis (occurring more commonly in DLB than other types of dementia) or supportive of a DLB diagnosis (occurs commonly but with lower specificity).

For a diagnosis of DLB, progressive cognitive decline that interferes with normal social or occupational functioning must be present, along with one or more additional features: fluctuations in cognition and alertness; recurrent formed visual hallucinations; or motor features of parkinsonism (see Table 3.1). DLB is also strongly associated with REM sleep behavior disorder (RBD – see below) and the presence of RBD is suggestive of a diagnosis of DLB. Other suggestive features include a severe sensitivity to neuroleptics. There are currently no serological markers for the disorder. The ApoE4 genotype occurs in higher frequency in both DLB and AD, but is not clinically useful for diagnosis. The clinical criteria are as follows.

Progressive cognitive decline (central feature)

The cognitive profile of DLB has similarities to AD. Both diseases impair memory, naming, visuospatial function, and executive/frontal lobe function. However, there are some potentially useful clinical distinctions. Patients with DLB often have more severe deficits in attention, verbal fluency, visuospatial ability, and frontosubcortical performance, and disproportionate cognitive slowing on timed tasks. Compared with other dementias, performance on the Mini-Mental State Examination (MMSE) is relatively preserved in DLB. Memory usually fails at the retrieval stage (i.e., there is preserved recognition of items that are not recalled spontaneously) in DLB as compared to the failure of storage (i.e., complete loss of information leading to failure of both recall and recognition) in AD. Confrontation naming is often preserved in DLB. In general, the rate of progression of dementia in DLB is slightly faster than AD, but there is a great deal of overlap.

Fluctuations in cognition and alertness (core feature)

Identifying cognitive fluctuation is often challenging. Patients with DLB frequently show marked variations in cognitive performance and level of alertness that can be discerned by caregivers, and by formal rating scales such as the Clinician Assessment of Fluctuation, for use by experienced clinicians, and the One-Day Fluctuation Assessment Scale, which can be completed by interviewing caregivers. Fluctuation occurs early in the course of the disease and is often a prominent symptom, affecting 80–90% of patients at some point. Fluctuations can occur rapidly, over a minutes to hours, or very gradually over days to weeks. The depth of the fluctuations can range from episodes of simple daytime sleepiness or mild impairments in concentration to episodes of wakeful unresponsiveness, or "going blank." The short-term fluctuations in cognition and in level of arousal have recently been shown to correlate closely with rapid changes (over seconds) in the EEG background frequency. These fluctuations are likely due to damage to brainstem alerting and arousal systems.

Parkinsonism (core feature)

Estimates on the rate of extrapyramidal signs in DLB range from 45% to 100%, with differences likely due to variability in ascertainment and definition. In autopsy-confirmed cases of DLB, up to 25% of cases did not have any evidence of parkinsonism. When parkinsonian signs are present in DLB, they closely mirror those of idiopathic Parkinson's disease. However, postural instability, hypomimia, and gait difficulty are more common with DLB and PDD, whereas rest tremor is less common. Progression of extrapyramidal symptoms occurs at an average annual rate of 10%. Rigidity and bradykinesia are present in approximately 90% of both PD and DLB. Rest tremor is somewhat less common in DLB, present in 55% as compared to 85% of PD subjects. The motor symptoms of DLB are usually mild. These symptoms are levodopa-responsive but generally do not require treatment and patients are at high risk for developing visual hallucinations when treated.

Parkinsonism can be seen in other neurodegenerative disorders including AD, frontotemporal dementia, and vascular dementia (see Table 3.2). The presence of tremor and the treatment responsiveness favor the diagnosis of DLB from the other non-PD parkinsonian syndromes. DLB patients with parkinsonism tend to have an earlier age of disease onset.

Neuropsychiatric features (core feature)

Approximately 80% of patients with DLB have visual hallucinations, and typically these occur early in the disease course. Visual hallucinations are very rare in AD in the absence of ocular causes, and their presence is highly suggestive of DLB. The hallucinations are often vivid, colorful, three-dimensional images of mute people or animals and resemble those seen as a side effect of excessive dopaminergic stimulation in idiopathic PD patients. Some degree of insight into the nature of the hallucinations is generally present, but this recedes over the course of the disease. The hallucinations are not typically threatening and may upset the caregiver more than the patient. Hallucinations are occasionally associated with either paranoid delusions or delusional beliefs that loved ones have been replaced by imposters (Capgras syndrome), or of paranoid delusions of theft or persecution. Delusions and hallucinations resulting in agitation or other behavioral problems can lead to early nursing home admission and require immediate treatment. Apathy, anxiety, and depression can also occur in DLB. Neuropsychiatric symptoms of DLB tend to persist throughout the course of the disease.

Sleep disorders (suggestive feature)

In REM sleep behavior disorder (RBD) the normal atonia of REM sleep does not occur, allowing movements, often vigorous, during REM periods, as if acting out dreams. Visual dream images can be vivid, although patients often do not recall them. The best clinical assessment for RBD is to ask a patient's bed partner if there are abnormal, even violent, movements during sleep. RBD can also be diagnosed by polysomnography. RBD is a frequent precursor of PD, with one study finding that 38% of RBD patients will develop a parkinsonian disorder. RBD is often associated with dementia, much more commonly with the synucleinopathies though sometimes with Alzheimer's disease or frontotemporal dementia. Ninety per cent of patients with diagnoses of dementia and RBD meet clinical criteria for DLB. In the few cases that have come to autopsy, the diagnosis of DLB has been confirmed pathologically. RBD can precede the associated neurodegenerative condition by many years.

Table 3.2 Comparison of Alzheimer's disease (AD), diffuse Lewy body disease (DLB) and Parkinson's disease (PD)

	AD	DLB	PD
Cognitive features			
Neuoropsychology	Early impairment of declarative memory	Early impairment in attention and visual-spatial skills	Impaired executive functioning
Cognitive fluctuation	+	+++ Can be prominent, severe, and early in disease course	–
Neuropsychiatric features			
Visual hallucinations	+	+++ Persistent and early in disease course	++ Late in disease course
Delusions	++	+++	+
Depression	++	+++	+++
Apathy	++	+++	+
Extrapyramidal motor symptoms			
Tremor	–	++	+++
Rigidity	+	+++	+++
Bradykinesia	+	+++	+++
	Rare, usually mild, appears late in disease course	Pronounced rigidity and bradykinesia; may be similar severity to PD	Initial manifestation of disease, often unilateral
Neuropathology			
Senile plaque density	+++	++	–
Neurofibrillary tangle density	+++	+	–
Subcortical Lewy bodies	–	++	+++
Cortical Lewy bodies	–	+++	+
Cholinergic deficit	++	+++	++
Dopaminergic deficit	–	++	+++
Neuroimaging			
Global atrophy	++	++	–
Medial temporal lobe atrophy	+++	–	–
Occipital hypoperfusion	–	+++	+
Impaired dopaminergic activity	–	+++	+++

+++ = typical finding; ++ = usually present; + = present, – = unusual finding

Source: Modified from Mosimann, U.P., & McKeith, I.G. (2003). Dementia with Lewy bodies – Diagnosis and treatment. *Swiss Medical Weekly, 133*, 131–142

Neuroimaging (supportive/suggestive feature)

Routine neuroimaging with MRI or CT is not clinically definitive in separating DLB from either AD or PD, but is essential to rule out vascular dementia and normal pressure hydrocephalus, both of which have parkinsonian features and dementia. Distinguishing DLB from AD is more of a challenge. An absence of medial temporal lobe atrophy on structural MRI suggests DLB rather than AD, but if medial temporal lobe atrophy is present, either diagnosis is possible. Functional neuroimaging methods show promise for identifying biomarkers that would improve diagnostic sensitivity (Figure 3.3, plate section). SPECT studies of striatal dopamine transporters, or nigrostriatal dopamine function with 18F-fluorodopa PET scanning may separate DLB from AD, but these techniques have not been validated and are generally not clinically available. Recent studies with an amyloid-binding PET ligand, PiB, demonstrate uptake in the majority of DLB patients but in fewer PDD patients, confirming pathological data that co-morbid AD is more common in DLB. Others have proposed that reduction of postganglionic sympathetic cardiac innervation, as measured by I-123 MIBG scintigraphy, putaminal atrophy, or occipital atrophy, hypoperfusion or hypometabolism, are helpful in the diagnosis of DLB. Such findings measured by functional imaging are included in the most recent consensus criteria as suggestive or supportive features of the disease (see Table 3.1).

Treatment

Treatment is focused on management of functionally impairing symptoms of the disease, and is summarized in Table 3.3.

Disease modifying therapies

There is no treatment to slow the progression of the neurodegeneration in DLB. A single randomized, placebo-controlled study has shown that large doses of vitamin E (alpha-tocopherol), 1000 IU twice daily, may slow the progression of moderate AD, and because a large subset of DLB patients have concomitant Alzheimer's changes, predominantly amyloid plaques, use in DLB may also be of benefit. However, meta-analysis data suggest that high-dose vitamin E may carry an increased risk of mortality. In the future, agents that either specifically prevent alpha-synuclein deposition in Lewy bodies or prevent amyloid deposition in plaques would be worthwhile agents to investigate.

Treatment of cognitive symptoms

The cholinergic deficit in DLB is often even more severe than that of AD, and in direct comparison studies, treatment with cholinesterase inhibitors (ChEIs) resulted

Table 3.3 Treatment for DLB

	Cholinesterase inhibitors	Neuroleptics	Antidepressants	Dopamine agonists
Indication	Cognitive impairment, neuropsychiatric symptoms	Visual hallucinations, delusions	Depression, anxiety, aggression	Extrapyramidal motor symptoms
Drug choice	Donepezil 5–10 mg/day; or rivastigmine 9–12 mg/day via pill or patch; or galantamine 8–24 mg/day	Quetiapine 25–150 mg/day; clozapine 6.25–37.5 mg/day; olanzapine 2.5–5 mg/day	SSRI (citalopram, sertraline, paroxitine) or multi-receptor (nefazodone, mirtazapine, venlafaxine)	Levodopa
Avoid		High D2 affinity antagonists (i.e., haloperidol) or drugs with anticholinergic side effects (i.e., promethazine)	Agents with high anticholinergic activity (i.e., tricyclic antidepressants)	Anticholinergics, antimuscarinics (benzatropine)
Side effects	Nausea, vomiting, diarrhea, bradycardia	Increased rigidity, immobility, confusion, sedation, and falls	Gastrointestinal upset, hypo- or hypertension	Visual hallucinations, delusions, orthostatic hypotension, gastrointestinal upset
Comments	Worsening of extrapyramidal motor symptoms (rare)	Risk of neuroleptic malignant syndrome (higher with typical antipsychotics)		

Source: Modified from Mosimann, U.P., & McKeith, I.G. (2003). Dementia with Lewy bodies – Diagnosis and treatment. *Swiss Medical Weekly, 133,* 131–142

in greater improvement on MMSE scores and attentional tasks in DLB patients compared to AD patients. Multiple case reports and open-label trials confirm that treatment with ChEIs result in a reduction in neuropsychiatric symptoms including sundowning, apathy, anxiety, delusions, and hallucinations. ChEI treatment also results in objective improvement on neuropsychological test performance including measures of attention, working memory, and episodic memory in patients with DLB. The agents currently available are donepezil (Aricept), rivastigmine (Exelon), and galantamine (Razadyne), and they appear to be equally effective. Only rivastigmine has been studied in multi-centered, placebo-controlled studies for use in treatment of DLB or PDD, which has been approved by the United States Food and Drug Administration for PDD. Side effects from ChEIs are due primarily to cholinomimetic properties (nausea, vomiting, headaches, hypersalivation, postural hypotension, and excessively vivid dreams). Rivastigmine is available in a topical, patch form, which may improve tolerability.

Use of ChEIs in combination with antiparkinsonian or atypical antipsychotics, although commonly used in clinical practice, has not been studied formally. Anecdotal reports have been published describing worsening of confusion and agitation with the use of the NMDA antagonist memantine; however, in a single double-blind, placebo-controlled multi-center study, treatment with memantine resulted in improvement on a global measure of cognitive function in a small number of subjects with DLB or PDD. This was comparable to the effect of ChEI in PDD or AD, and memantine was well tolerated.

Treatment of extrapyramidal motor symptoms

The parkinsonism in DLB will respond to dopaminergic agents, but these drugs may worsen neuropsychiatric features of the disease. Levodopa is less likely than dopamine agonists to worsen hallucinations. Anticholinergics should be avoided because of the possibility of marked worsening of cognitive symptoms. Levodopa should only be used when motor symptoms are functionally limiting, and used at the lowest effective dose (generally 150–300 mg of levodopa divided t.i.d.). If hallucinations worsen during treatment, there are two options: lower or discontinue the dopaminergic agent, or introduce a low dose of an atypical neuroleptic.

Treatment of neuropsychiatric symptoms

Visual hallucinations occur in DLB even without the provocation of levodopa. Whether provoked or spontaneous, visual hallucinations can often be managed without medication. The onset of hallucinations can often signal an underlying illness or infection, particularly if it coincides with worsening attention or signs of delirium. A medical evaluation is indicated to diagnose and treat any inciting illness (see Figure 3.4). Visual hallucinations often occur in patients with impaired vision

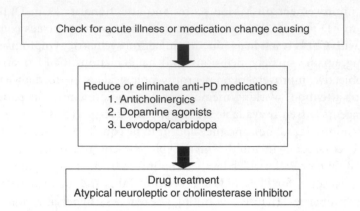

Figure 3.4 Pathway for management of visual hallucinations in Lewy body dementias. The first step is to determine if a superimposed illness such as a urinary tract infection or a change in medications, particularly addition of an anticholinergics medication, has triggered hallucinations. If this fails, then medications to treat motor symptoms should be reduced, beginning with anticholinergics medications, then dopamine agonists and finally reducing levodopa, as possible. If hallucinations continue, or patient is not receiving medications for motor symptoms, then either an atypical neuroleptic or a cholinesterase inhibitor should be introduced

so efforts to maximize visual acuity such as keeping rooms well lit and treating any primary visual problem are helpful. Low levels of arousal and attention can also worsen the visual hallucinations, so strategies to increase social interactions and introduction to novelty may also be of benefit. If the hallucinations are not disturbing to the patient, then educating the family in how to adapt to them may be sufficient. If the hallucinations are disturbing or debilitating to either the patient or the family, then a trial of an atypical neuroleptic is warranted. Very low doses of clozapine (6.25–37.5 mg) have been demonstrated to treat hallucinations in PD without exacerbating the parkinsonism. Potential side effects including agranulocytosis, excessive sedation, and lowering of seizure threshold makes this agent less practical clinically. Low doses of quetiapine may be more practical, though results in studies have been mixed, and other atypical antipsychotics ziprasidone and aripiprazole have not been investigated for their use in this population. Risperidone is often considered an atypical neuroleptic but clearly worsens parkinsonism in patients with dementia and should be avoided. Typical neuroleptics can induce profound, even fatal worsening of the parkinsonism with impaired consciousness, and should be avoided in any subject where DLB is a diagnostic consideration.

While depression is common in DLB, treatment of these symptoms has not been formally studied. Currently selective serotonin reuptake inhibitors (SSRIs) and selective norepinephrine reuptake inhibitors (SNRIs) are the preferred drugs of choice (Table 3.3). REM behavior disorder (RBD) can be treated with clonazepam

0.25 mg or melatonin 3 mg at bedtime. Quetiapine 12.5 mg or higher may also be effective in RBD.

Because confusion, hallucinations, sleep disturbance and delusions may appear early and repeatedly in the course of DLB, home care of patients with DLB is often very difficult for caregivers. The symptoms of DLB often lead to nursing home placement, regardless of the underlying diagnosis. Efforts to support families through the course of the disease are crucial. The assistance of well-trained social workers should be sought early in the course of the disease. Preparation will allow for a much smoother transfer if nursing home care becomes necessary.

Prognosis

The rate of progression of DLB is somewhat quicker than either PD or AD. The mean survival from diagnosis for DLB is generally between 6 and 9 years as compared to 8 to 11 years for both PD and AD.

Summary

Many of the manifestations of DLB reflect the underlying pathology of cortical Lewy bodies and frequently co-occurring Alzheimer's type changes. A number of fundamental questions about the pathophysiology and the nosology of Lewy body disease remain. The accurate clinical diagnosis is predicated on specific features including parkinsonism, dementia, visual hallucinations, and fluctuating levels of attention. Symptomatic treatment is available but side effects often limit the therapeutic benefit. Cholinesterase inhibitors are an exception and can improve both the cognitive and the neuropsychiatric symptoms. DLB likely represents more than just the manifestations of the pathological overlap of two common disorders, PD and AD. Clarification will require a better understanding of the pathophysiology of cortical Lewy bodies and the ability to clinically discern the degree of AD changes and Lewy body changes in patients antemortem.

Selected Readings

Aarsland, D., Ballard, C., Walker, Z., Bostrom, F., Alves, G., Kossakowski, K., et al. (2010). Memantine in patients with Parkinson's disease dementia or dementia with Lewy bodies: A double-blind, placebo-controlled multicentre trial. *Lancet Neurology, 8,* 613–618.

Barber, R., Gholkar, A., Scheltens, P, Ballard, C., McKeith, I. G., & O'Brien, J. T. (1999). Medial temporal lobe atrophy on MRI in dementia with Lewy bodies. *Neurology, 52,* 1153–1158.

Boeve, B. F., Silber, M. H., Ferman, T. J., Kokmen, E., Smith, G. E., Ivnik, R. J., et al. (1998). REM sleep behavior disorder and degenerative dementia: An association likely reflecting Lewy body disease. *Neurology, 51,* 363–370.

Hu, X. S., Okamura, N., Arai, H., Higuchi, M., Matsui, T., Tashiro, M., et al. (2000). 18F-fluorodopa PET study of striatal dopamine uptake in the diagnosis of dementia with Lewy bodies. *Neurology, 55,* 1575–1577.

Lennox, G. (1998). Dementia with Lewy bodies. In J. Growdon, & M. Rossor (Eds.), *The dementias* (vol. 19, pp. 67–79). Boston, MA: Butterworth Heinemann.

Louis, E. D., Klatka, L. A., Liu, Y., & Fahn, S. (1997). Comparison of extrapyramidal features in 31 pathologically confirmed cases of diffuse Lewy body disease and 34 pathologically confirmed cases of Parkinson's disease. *Neurology, 48,* 376–380.

Luis, C. A., Barker, W. W., Gajaraj, K., Harwood, D., Petersen, R., Kashuba, A., et al. (1999). Sensitivity and specificity of three clinical criteria for dementia with Lewy bodies in an autopsy-verified sample. *International Journal of Geriatric Psychiatry,14,* 526–533.

Markesbery, W. R., Jicha, G. A., Liu, H., & Schmitt, F. A. (2009). Lewy body pathology in normal elderly subjects. *Journal of Neuropathology and Experimental Neurology, 68,* 816–822.

McKeith, I. G., Dickson, D. W., Lowe, J., Emre, M., O'Brien, J. T., Feldmen, H., et al. (2005). Diagnosis and management of dementia with Lewy bodies. Third report of the DLB consortium. *Neurology, 65,* 1863–1872.

McKeith, I. G., Galasko, D., Kosaka, K., Perry, E. K., Dickson, D. W., Hansen, L. A., et al. (1996). Consensus guidelines for the clinical and pathologic diagnosis of dementia with Lewy bodies (DLB): Report of the consortium on DLB international workshop. *Neurology, 47,* 1113–1124.

McKeith, I. G., Grace, J. B., Walker, Z., Byrne, E. J., Wilkinson, D., Stevens, T., et al. (2000). Rivastigmine in the treatment of dementia with Lewy bodies: Preliminary findings from an open trial. *International Journal of Geriatric Psychiatry, 15,* 387–392.

McKeith, I. G., Mintzer, J., Aarsland, D., Burn, D., Chiu, H., Cohen-Mansfield, J., et al. (2004). Dementia with Lewy bodies. *Lancet Neurology, 3,* 19–28.

McKeith, I. G., Perry, E. K., & Perry, R. H. (1999). Report of the second dementia with Lewy body international workshop: Diagnosis and treatment. Consortium on dementia with Lewy bodies. *Neurology, 53,* 902–905.

Mosimann, U. P., & McKeith, I. G. (2003). Dementia with Lewy bodies – Diagnosis and treatment. *Swiss Medical Weekly, 133,* 131–142.

Nelson, P. T., Kryscio, R. J., Jicha, G. A., Abner, E. L., Schmitt, F. A., Xu, L. O., et al. (2009). Relative preservation of MMSE scores in autopsy-proven dementia with Lewy bodies. *Neurology, 73,* 1127–1133.

Salmon, D. P., Galasko, D., Hansen, L. A., Masliah, E., Butters, N., Thal, L. J., et al. (1996). Neuropsychological deficits associated with diffuse Lewy body disease. *Brain and Cognition, 31,* 148–165.

Walker, M. P., Ayre, G. A., Cummings, J. L., Wesnes, K., McKeith, I. G., O'Brien, J. T., et al. (2000). Quantifying fluctuation in dementia with Lewy bodies, Alzheimer's disease, and vascular dementia. *Neurology, 54,* 1616–1625.

4

Frontotemporal Dementia
Adam L. Boxer

What was once called Pick's disease has three major anatomical variants. With all three, frontotemporal brain is selectively injured while posterior cortical regions are spared. These three clinical patterns include a bifrontal, slightly asymmetric subtype with more involvement of the right frontotemporal region called frontotemporal dementia (FTD) or the frontal variant of FTD, a temporal-predominant subtype called the temporal variant of FTD or semantic dementia, and a left frontal-predominant subtype called progressive non-fluent aphasia. The three anatomical groups help to classify distinctive clinical syndromes with unique features. This chapter will primarily describe the clinical, pathologic, and neuroimaging features of the frontal and temporal variants of FTD.

Careful study of these subtypes of frontotemporal dementia, using combinations of new quantitative neuroimaging, behavioral, and physiological measures are yielding important information about the functioning of the brain's frontal and temporal regions. As we come to better understand the biological basis for the three FTD clinical syndromes, new classification schemas may emerge, but our current clinical criteria serve as a strong guide to the diagnosis and separation of FTD from Alzheimer's disease (AD) and other dementias.

Introduction

Frontotemporal dementia (FTD) or frontotemporal lobar degeneration (FTLD), formerly called Pick's disease, is a progressive neurodegenerative dementia that is

The Handbook of Alzheimer's Disease and Other Dementias, First Edition.
Edited by Andrew E. Budson, Neil W. Kowall.
© 2011 Blackwell Publishing Ltd. Published 2011 by Blackwell Publishing Ltd.

associated with focal atrophy of the frontal and/or temporal lobes. FTD encompasses a spectrum of clinical phenotypes that lead to different combinations of social and behavioral abnormalities, cognitive deficits, and motor dysfunction. These clinical phenotypes frequently overlap three other neurodegenerative diseases: motor neuron disease (FTD-MND); corticobasal syndrome (CBS); and progressive supranuclear palsy (PSP) (Boeve et al., 2003). Although FTD patients often present with features of one clinical syndrome, with time, features of other FTD clinical syndromes often emerge, leading some authors to suggest that FTD and related disorders should be grouped together as a Pick complex (Kertesz et al., 2007; Kertesz et al., 2005).

Each FTD clinical syndrome is associated with a variety of histopathological diagnoses at autopsy. Currently neuropathological criteria for FTD list seven distinct diagnostic categories, many of which may be associated with a variety of clinical FTD syndromes (Cairns et al., 2007). Although a few clinical FTD syndromes are strongly correlated with one neuropathological diagnosis, such as FTD-amyotrophic lateral sclerosis (FTD-ALS) with FTD-motor neuron disease (FTD-MND), the majority of clinical syndromes have multiple neuropathological correlates, and the majority of neuropathological diagnoses have multiple clinical correlates. This multi-level diagnostic heterogeneity can create confusion due to similarities in nomenclature between certain clinical and neuropathological diagnoses, such as clinical corticobasal degeneration syndrome (CBS) and corticobasal degeneration pathology (CBD). Here I review the core FTD clinical syndromes, the frontal lobe or behavioral/dysexecutive variant of FTD (bvFTD), the temporal lobe variant of FTD, which often presents as a fluent aphasia referred to as semantic dementia (SD), and progressive non-fluent aphasia (PNFA). In this chapter I will emphasize bvFTD and SD; additional information on PNFA can be found in other chapters.

History

The first case of what is now called frontotemporal dementia (FTD) was described by Arnold Pick in 1892 (Pick, 1892). His subsequent description of six similar patients emphasized a language impairment, which he termed "amnestic aphasia," and a focal pattern of brain atrophy involving the temporal and/or frontal lobes. A lack of senile plaques and tangles in the brains of similar patients was noted by Alzheimer in 1911 (Alzheimer, 1911). He and Altman provided the first histopathological description of argyrophilic inclusions (later termed Pick bodies) and swollen achromatic cells (later termed Pick cells) (Altman, 1923). Onari and Spatz, two of Pick's students, later introduced the term Pick's disease to describe cases of circumscribed atrophy lacking plaques and tangles (Onari & Spatz, 1926). The later insistence by some researchers that a diagnosis of Pick's disease require the presence of Pick bodies on histopathology led to an underestimation of FTLD cases and most likely hindered research into this disorder.

Constantinidis et al. (1974) documented three types of histopathology in cases clinically defined as having Pick's disease. The first group of patients had classic Pick bodies and Pick cells. The second group of patients had pathology similar to what is now called corticobasal ganglionic degeneration (CBD). The last group was more heterogeneous, and would include what is now termed dementia lacking distinctive histopathology. The recognition that it was difficult to distinguish histological subtypes of Pick's disease eventually led to a focus on clinical symptoms associated with circumscribed lobar atrophy.

In the late 1980s, Arne Brun and Lars Gustafson, working in Lund, Sweden, and David Neary and Julie Snowden working in Manchester, England began studying non-Alzheimer's degenerative dementias. Both groups described clinical, neuroimaging, and histopathological features of dementia patients with progressive frontal lobar degeneration (Snowden et al., 1996a). Although the patients studied by both groups clinically resembled those originally described by Pick, most lacked classic Pick bodies. Instead, Brun noted the presence of prominent astrocytic gliosis and spongiosis of layers I–III in the frontal cortex in typical cases, without the plaques and tangles found in AD (Brun, 1987). He suggested the name *frontal dementia of the non-Alzheimer type* for these patients, while Neary coined the term *dementia of the frontal type* (Miller, Boone et al., 1998). In 1994, the Lund and Manchester groups published consensus research criteria for what they termed frontotemporal dementia (FTD) ("Clinical and neuropathological criteria for frontotemporal dementia. The Lund and Manchester Groups", 1994).

Also during the 1980s, Mesulam described a group of patients who developed a progressive aphasia with few other cognitive symptoms, which he termed primary progressive aphasia (Mesulam, 1982). He noted that there were two subtypes of patients, one with a primary non-fluent aphasia associated with atrophy of the left frontal lobe, and a second type with a primary fluent aphasia associated with degeneration of the left anterior temporal lobe. This latter group was similar to the original patients described by Pick. The majority of patients in both groups lacked Alzheimer's pathology, and instead showed neuropathological features similar to the frontal disease described by Brun. During the same period of time, Snowden and colleagues described the linguistic deficits of patients with left anterior temporal lobe degeneration (Snowden et al., 1992). These patients also lacked AD pathology and instead resembled FTD. Because the language disorder was primarily due to a loss of semantic information in these patients, the disorder was later termed semantic dementia (Hodges et al., 1992).

Taking into account the clinical and pathological similarities between frontotemporal dementia, semantic dementia and primary progressive aphasia, the Lund–Manchester criteria were further refined by Neary et al. in 1998 to provide descriptions of these three common clinical presentations of FTD, which was renamed frontotemporal lobar degeneration (FTLD) (Neary et al., 1998). The confusing nomenclature associated with FTLD has led to the proposal that clinical variants of FTLD be referred to as frontotemporal dementia (FTD) (Kertesz et al., 2003). Evidence of pathological and genetic overlap between FTD and corticobasal degeneration (CBD) suggested to Kertesz and colleagues that these clinical syndromes may be one pathological entity (Kertesz, Martinez-Lage et al., 2000). The most recent clinicopathological criteria for FTD reflect this association, as well as the overlap between FTD and amyotrophic lateral sclerosis (ALS) or motor neuron disease (MND) (McKhann et al., 2001).

Clinical Features

Clinical presentation

Clinically, FTD presents either with changes in personality, behavioral problems and/or executive impairment, or as a primary progressive aphasia syndrome (PPA) (Figure 4.1). The behavioral presentation of FTD is often referred to as "frontal variant" FTD (fvFTD) or "behavioral variant" FTD (bvFTD). The PPA associated with FTD pathology may be further subdivided into a fluent aphasia and a non-fluent aphasia. The fluent PPA has been referred to as semantic dementia (SD), reflecting a primary loss of knowledge about the world as the etiology of the aphasia, or as "temporal variant" FTD, reflecting the prominent anterior temporal lobe atrophy associated with this clinical FTD subtype. The non-fluent aphasia has been termed progressive non-fluent aphasia (PNFA) (Neary et al., 1998). As the disease progresses, motor impairments often arise in subjects who are destined to develop motor neuron disease (FTD-MND), corticobasal degeneration (CBD), or progressive supranuclear palsy (PSP).

Motor impairment often indicates a worse prognosis in FTD. Motor neuron disease (amyotrophic lateral sclerosis [ALS]), most commonly with prominent bulbar symptoms, is associated with FTD in approximately 10% of patients (Miller, Cummings et al., 1995). In a series of 36 patients with FTD, five met clinical criteria for ALS, and an additional 11 patients had at least one clinical sign of ALS (Lomen-Hoerth et al., 2002). Likewise, almost one-third of a series of 100 ALS patients were

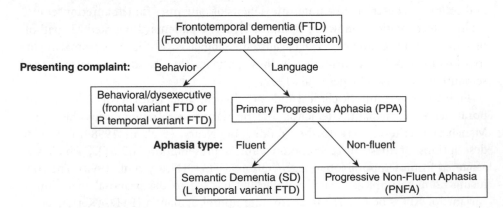

Figure 4.1   Frontotemporal dementia subtypes

found to meet clinical criteria for FTD (Lomen-Hoerth et al., 2003). Accumulating evidence suggests that there is a spectrum of cognitive impairment in motor neuron disease. Some individuals have little impairment, whereas others meet criteria for a full-blown FTD. Even in individuals who do not meet criteria for FTD, the presence of FTD-related cognitive and behavioral impairments in ALS makes management of such individuals considerably more difficult (Olney et al., 2005; Rippon et al., 2006).

Epidemiology

FTD is a common cause of dementia in patients who are younger than 65 (Ratnavalli et al., 2002); and in patients who are less than 60 years of age, FTD may be more common than AD (Grossman, 2001; Knopman et al., 2004). The prevalence of FTD in patients aged 45 to 64 in Cambridgeshire, England was 15 (95% CI: 8.4 to 27) per 100,000 and identical to the prevalence of early-onset AD in the same population (Ratnavalli et al., 2002). The mean age of onset for FTD is between 52 to 56 years old (Miller, Boone, et al., 1998), however, a study of pre-symptomatic family members of patients with an autosomal dominant FTD syndrome suggests that subtle cognitive and/or behavioral abnormalities may begin in childhood or adolescence in some FTD patients (Geschwind et al., 2001). Of the different clinical FTD syndromes, the frontal or behavioral/dysexecutive variant is the most common, accounting for approximately 50% of cases in some series (Josephs, Petersen et al., 2006). bvFTD progresses to death faster than AD (median survival from symptom onset, 8.7 ± 1.2 vs. 11.8 ± 0.6 years), whereas SD progresses to death at a rate comparable to AD (11.9 ± 0.2 years) (Roberson et al., 2005). One explanation for the faster progression to death in FTD is the frequent coexistence of motor neuron disease (MND) pathology. While the median survival of all FTD patients in one series was 6.1 ± 1.1 years, those with FTD-MND survived only 3 ± 0.4 years (Hodges et al., 2003).

Differentiation from AD

Historically, many cases of pathologically-verified FTD were diagnosed with AD during life (Mendez et al., 1993). Studies of pathologically-verified cases of FTD have identified clinical and neuropsychological features which differentiate FTD from AD. The presence of a social conduct disorder, hyperorality or akinesia, and the absence of amnesia or a perceptual disorder correctly classified 93% of patients with FTD in one series of 30 autopsy-proven cases of FTD and 30 of AD (Rosen, Hartikainen et al., 2002). Patients with autopsy-proven FTD performed worse on letter and category fluency tests, but better on the Mattis Dementia Rating Scale memory subscale, block design test, and clock drawing test than patients with AD (Rascovsky et al., 2002).

The first symptom of disease can be helpful in differentiating FTD from AD. Disinhibition, social awkwardness, passivity, and loss of executive function are more common in FTD, while memory loss is more common in AD (Ikeda et al., 2002; Lindau et al., 2000). FTD patients tend to have less insight into their deficits than AD patients, and frequently overestimate their positive qualities (Rankin et al., 2005). FTD patients also show larger deficits in online error-monitoring in certain cognitive tasks than AD patients (O'Keeffe et al., 2007). FTD patients show a unique pattern of deficits on tests of everyday function, such as the Disability Assessment for Dementia (DAD), particularly involving initiation, planning and execution, that may help to differentiate them from AD (Mioshi et al., 2007).

Analysis of brain atrophy patterns helps to distinguish FTD from AD. One recent study examined clinical variants of PPA, and found that the FTD subtypes SD and PNFA were associated with anterior temporal lobe and left frontal lobe atrophy, respectively, while the fluent PPA that is likely due to AD (supported by a high prevalence of ApoE4 alleles in this series) is associated with parietal lobe atrophy (Gorno-Tempini et al., 2004). The presence of cinguloparietal atrophy on MRI scans in AD separates AD from SD with a high degree of accuracy (Boxer et al., 2003).

Clinical Subtypes

Behavioral/dysexecutive FTD (behavioral variant; bvFTD; Figure 4.2)

The insidious onset of personality changes and behavioral abnormalities is initially the most prominent feature of bvFTD. Poor insight, loss of personal awareness, loss

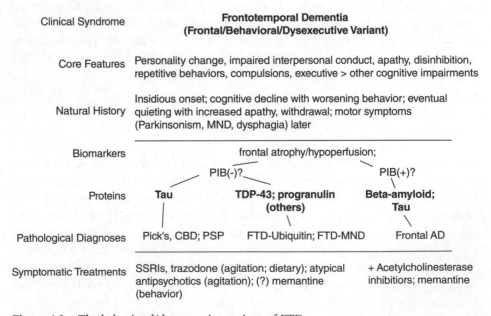

Figure 4.2   The behavioral/dysexecutive variant of FTD

of social awareness, and blunting of affect are common behavioral changes that are seen early in bvFTD. Patients may deny the existence of deficits and often show a lack of concern about their illness (Rosen et al., 2000). Increased submissiveness, a lack of empathy, self-centeredness, emotional coldness, and decreased concern about family and friends is also common (Rankin et al., 2003). Patients with evidence of right brain involvement on neuroimaging studies tend to have the most severe behavioral symptoms (Mychack et al. 2001). These patients may undergo dramatic changes in beliefs, attitudes and/or religious sentiment, leading to the emergence of a new personality as the disease progresses (Miller et al., 2001).

Orbitobasal (ventromedial) frontal lobe dysfunction leads to disinhibition, poor impulse control, antisocial behavior, and stereotyped behaviors. Disinhibition or distractibility may manifest as restlessness, pressured speech, impulsivity, irritability, aggressiveness, violent outbursts, or excessive sentimentality (Rosen et al., 2000). Damage to orbitofrontal structures also leads to a decrease in patients' "agreeableness," a construct which encompasses the traits of trust, straightforwardness, altruism, compliance, modesty, and tender-mindedness (Rankin et al., 2004).

Verbally inappropriate sexual comments and gestures are common in FTD. Despite these inappropriate behaviors, sexual drive is often reduced with impotence common in the FTD prodrome in men (Miller, Darby et al., 1995). Other socially inappropriate behaviors sometimes seen in FTD include theft, assault, inappropriate or offensive speech, and public urination or masturbation (Miller, Cummings et al., 1995). Many FTD patients exhibit stereotyped or perseverative behaviors such as repetitive cleaning, pacing, organizing objects into groups, use of catchphrases, impulse buying, hoarding, and counting. Features of obsessive-compulsive disorder are very common in bvFTD, and some patients may initially be given this psychiatric diagnosis (Ames et al., 1994). Compulsions were presenting symptoms in 30–60% of patients in three clinical series of FTD patients (Perry & Miller, 2001). Delusions are common in bvFTD, and tend to be jealous, somatic, religious or bizarre, but are rarely persecutory. Euphoric symptoms, such as elevated mood, inappropriate jocularity, and exaggerated self-esteem were found in 30% of FTD patients in one clinical series (Levy et al., 1996).

Apathy is frequently seen in patients with bvFTD who have involvement of the anterior cingulate and medial frontal lobes (Liu et al., 2004). This may be mistaken for depression in some patients, however, unlike in AD, depression is uncommon in bvFTD. Increased apathy may be related to caregivers' ratings of submissiveness in bvFTD (Rankin et al., 2003). Apathy and emotional withdrawal are often punctuated with outbursts of disinhibited behavior (Swartz, Miller, Lesser, Booth et al., 1997). With more advanced disease, many patients develop language dysfunction, with features of progressive non-fluent aphasia (see below) if disease involves left frontal/insular cortex, and/or akinetic mutism with progressive medial frontal/cingulate cortex involvement.

Dietary changes, especially cravings for sweets, are common in FTD (Miller, Derby et al., 1995). Decreased satiety and food cravings often lead to a weight gain in many patients. As the disease progresses, features of the Kluver–Bucy syndrome, such as hyperorality and oral exploratory behaviors may arise.

Impairments on tests of executive function or working memory are the most common deficits in bvFTD. Memory and visuospatial function are relatively spared and screening tests such as the Mini-Mental State Examination may remain normal even after patients require nursing home care (Gregory et al., 1999). This is in striking contrast to AD, where there is early impairment of memory and visuospatial function (Perry & Hodges, 2000). Patients may have difficulty with set shifting, concept formation, abstraction and reasoning, inhibition of over-learned responses, response generation, organization, planning, self-monitoring, and using feedback to guide behavior (Rosen et al., 2000). Tasks such as the Wisconsin Card Sorting Test, Trailmaking Test, Stroop Category Test, verbal and design fluency, and proverb interpretation are sensitive to frontal executive dysfunction in patients with bvFTD (Hodges, 2001). FTD patients have profoundly impaired insight into their deficits (O'Keeffe et al., 2007), leading to overestimates of strengths and underestimates of weaknesses on a variety of measures (Rankin et al., 2005).

Semantic dementia (temporal lobe variant FTD or SD)

Semantic dementia (SD) is a syndrome of progressive loss of semantic knowledge, or knowledge about people, objects, facts, and words (Snowden et al., 1996b). The most common presenting complaint in SD involves language, and is often described as a loss of memory for words or a loss of word meaning that results in a fluent progressive aphasia (Figure 4.3) (Adlam et al., 2006). While SD patients are aware of their expressive deficits, they are often unaware of their comprehension difficulties (Hodges, 2001). Speech is fluent, but there are frequent semantic paraphasias, and use of substitute phrases such as "thing" or "stuff." Repetition, prosody, syntax, and verb generation are preserved. Associative agnosia may lead to difficulty with object recognition. This may manifest as misuse of or an inability to recognize household items such as a can-opener or pliers. Patients with more significant right temporal lobe damage may present with prosopagnosia, but more commonly with behavioral abnormalities such as irritability, impulsiveness, bizarre alterations in dress, and mental rigidity (Edwards-Lee et al., 1997; Evans et al., 1995; Seeley et al., 2005). Early on, these right temporal lobe-predominant FTD cases can be difficult to differentiate from bvFTD.

Many of the disinhibited and compulsive behaviors seen in bvFTD are also present in SD, as both groups have measurable damage to the orbitofrontal cortex (Liu et al., 2004). Patients with right-sided disease tend to have more severe behavioral abnormalities than patients with left-sided disease (Edwards-Lee et al., 1997). As SD patients are often less apathetic than bvFTD patients, compulsive behaviors may be more prominent in SD than bvFTD. SD patients have deficits in emotion comprehension, especially for emotions with negative valence, such as sadness, anger, and fear (Rosen, Perry et al., 2002). These deficits in emotion recognition

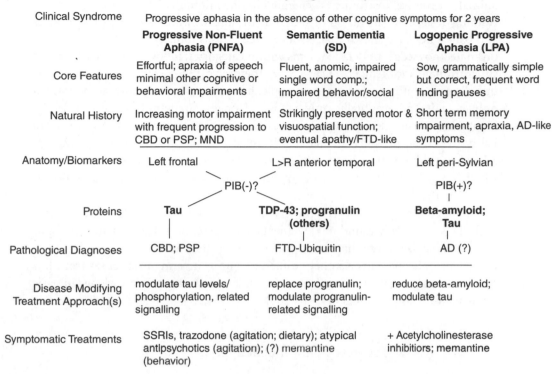

Primary Progressive Aphasia

	Progressive Non-Fluent Aphasia (PNFA)	Semantic Dementia (SD)	Logopenic Progressive Aphasia (LPA)
Clinical Syndrome	Progressive aphasia in the absence of other cognitive symptoms for 2 years		
Core Features	Effortful; apraxia of speech minimal other cognitive or behavioral impairments	Fluent, anomic, impaired single word comp.; impaired behavior/social	Sow, grammatically simple but correct, frequent word finding pauses
Natural History	Increasing motor impairment with frequent progression to CBD or PSP; MND	Strikingly preserved motor & visuospatial function; eventual apathy/FTD-like	Short term memory impairment, apraxia, AD-like symptoms
Anatomy/Biomarkers	Left frontal	L>R anterior temporal	Left peri-Sylvian
	PIB(-)?		PIB(+)?
Proteins	**Tau**	**TDP-43; progranulin (others)**	**Beta-amyloid; Tau**
Pathological Diagnoses	CBD; PSP	FTD-Ubiquitin	AD (?)
Disease Modifying Treatment Approach(s)	modulate tau levels/ phosphorylation, related signalling	replace progranulin; modulate progranulin-related signalling	reduce beta-amyloid; modulate tau
Symptomatic Treatments	SSRIs, trazodone (agitation; dietary); atypical antIpsychotics (agitation); (?) memantine (behavior)		+ Acetylcholinesterase inhibitiors; memantine

Figure 4.3 Primary progressive aphasia variants of FTD

may in part explain caregivers' reports of increased interpersonal coldness in SD (Rankin et al., 2003).

An emergence of artistic talent has been observed in some patients with SD who have significant language impairment, but preserved visuospatial skills (Miller, Cummings et al., 1998). Emergence of other visual talents, including an increased interest in or ability to play games or sports involving eye–hand coordination, such as tennis or ping-pong has also been reported. These abilities may arise in part from strikingly preserved visual attention and oculomotor function in SD, as compared to other forms of dementia, coupled with an emergence of compulsive behaviors (Boxer et al., 2006).

Due to their language difficulties, patients with SD may score poorly on bedside screening measures such as the Mini-Mental State Examination. More detailed testing reveals a loss of semantic knowledge, with relatively preserved episodic memory for recent events (Graham et al., 2000). In contrast to AD, recent memory tends to be preserved early in the course of SD, while many autobiographical events are lost. Thus in SD, some suggest that there is a reversal of the temporal gradient of memory impairment that is observed in AD (Hodges & Graham, 2001).

Patients are most impaired on tests such as category fluency (i.e., the number of animals or musical instruments generated in one minute), picture naming (Boston Naming Test), and generation of verbal definitions of words and pictures. Hodges and colleagues have shown that errors on these tasks initially reflect a loss of sub-ordinate knowledge, or detailed items within categories, followed by a loss of more superordinate knowledge (the categories, themselves). For example, a patient may initially misidentify an orange as an apple, however, with time, both are identified only as fruit, and eventually, only as food (Hodges, Graham, & Patterson, 1995). Nonverbal semantic knowledge may be assessed with tests such as the Pyramids and Palm Trees Test, in which the subject is asked to judge which of two pictures is related to a third picture. For example, a pyramid is shown, and the subject is asked whether a picture of a pine tree or a palm tree best goes with the pyramid (Bozeat et al., 2000).

Language testing in SD reveals preserved phonology and syntax. However, surface dyslexia is commonly found in SD patients, and presents as difficulty in reading or spelling irregular words that sound different than they are spelled ("pint" read as hint or lint). SD patients also have difficulty with generating past tenses from low frequency verbs, which has implications for the role of semantic knowledge in basic linguistic functions (Patterson et al., 2001).

Progressive non-fluent aphasia (PNFA)

Patients present with changes in fluency, pronunciation, or word-finding difficulty. Anomia in PNFA is more significant for verbs than for nouns, and this type of deficit has been associated with pathology involving Brodman's areas 44 and 45 (Bak et al., 2001). Unlike bvFTD and SD, PNFA patients do not display typical behavioral abnormalities until later in the disease (Neary et al., 1998). Insight and personal awareness can be exquisitely preserved, while depression and social withdrawal are common. PNFA is a frequent presenting complaint in patients who ultimately develop CBD or PSP (Josephs, Duffy et al., 2006; Kertesz, Martinez-Lage et al., 2000) and, less commonly, MND (Caselli et al., 1993; Rakowicz & Hodges, 1998).

Episodic memory, semantic memory, and visuospatial function are preserved in PNFA. Executive function and working memory are often impaired. Language difficulties include agrammatism, phonemic paraphasias and anomia. Agrammatism is defined as the presence of grammatical errors in speech, such as the omission or incorrect usage of articles ("cow jumped over moon"), prepositions ("dog walk bridge"), or verbs ("cat eated mouse"). Phonemic paraphasias are errors involving use of the incorrect phoneme ("head" instead of "bed") or transpo-sition of a phoneme ("efelant" for "elephant") (Hodges, 2001). Other language problems may include stuttering, impaired repetition, apraxia of speech, alexia, and agraphia.

Genetics

A strong genetic component can be identified in many cases of FTD. Approximately 29–45% of patients with FTD have a positive family history of dementia, and it has been estimated that first-degree relatives of patients with FTD are at a 3.5 times higher risk of developing dementia than the general population (Stevens et al., 1998). An autosomal dominant inheritance pattern can be found in approximately 80% of familial cases (Chow et al., 1999). A strong family history or autosomal dominant pattern of inheritance is most frequently found in FTD-ALS and least frequently found in SD (Goldman et al., 2005).

In 1998 mutations in the tau (MAPT) gene were first identified as a cause of autosomal dominant FTD and related syndromes in a number of pedigrees. Since then, three other genes, valosin containing-protein (VCP), charged multivesicular body protein 2b (CHMP2B), and progranulin (PGRN) have been identified as causes of FTD in other autosomal dominant FTD families (Table 4.1). An association between autopsy-confirmed Pick's disease with AD pathology and the G183V presenilin 1 gene mutation has been described (Dermaut et al., 2004), however, most FTD-associated PSEN1 cases have been found to harbor PGRN mutations, which suggests that PSEN1 mutations are not truly a cause of FTD (Boeve et al., 2006; Pickering-Brown et al., 2006). Currently, MAPT mutations and PGRN mutations are thought to be the most common identifiable cause of FTD, accounting for approximately 5% of all FTD cases each (Roberson, 2006). An as yet unidentified gene linked to FTD-ALS on chromosome 9p may account for a substantial percentage of additional familial FTD cases (Hosler et al., 2000; Morita et al., 2006; Vance et al., 2006).

Tau (MAPT)

Advances in the molecular biology of the tau protein have led to a better understanding of the molecular pathogenesis and histopathology of FTD (Hutton, 2001). Tau is a neuronal protein that binds to microtubules, and is thought to be involved in assembly, and maintaining the stability of these cytoskeletal structural elements. In the normal adult human brain, tau is a soluble protein that is expressed as six major protein isoforms that are generated by alternative splicing of the tau gene. The alternative splicing of exon 10 controls the number of microtubule binding domains. If exon 10 is included in the mRNA (exon10+), there will be four microtubule-binding domains in the translated protein (4R tau). If exon 10 is excluded in the mRNA (exon 10–), there will be three microtubule-binding domains (3R tau). In the normal adult human brain, there is an approximately 1:1 ratio of 3R tau to 4R tau.

Table 4.1 Frontotemporal dementia associated genes

Gene	Location	Clinical syndromes	Neuropathology	References
Tau (*MAPT*)	Chr 17q21–22	FTDP-17 (can resemble: bvFTD, tvFTD, CBS, PSP)	Tau (+) inclusions	Cairns et al., 2007; Clark et al., 1998; Hong et al., 1998; Hutton, 2001; Hutton et al., 1998; Reed et al., 2001
Progranulin (*PGRN*)	Chr 17q21	bvFTD, tvFTD, FTD-ALS PPA, CBS; rarely ALS alone	FTLD-U/ TDP-43(+) inclusions	Ahmed et al., 2007; Baker et al., 2006; Cruts et al., 2006; Huey, Grafman, et al., 2006; Josephs et al., 2007; Mackenzie et al., 2006; Spina et al., 2007
Valosin-containing protein (*VCP*)	Chr 9p12–13	tvFTD, PPA with inclusion body myopathy and Paget's disease of bone (IBMPFD)	FTLD-U/TDP-43(+) inclusions; sparing dentate gyrus	Forman, Mackenzie et al., 2006; Guyant-Marechal et al., 2006; Neumann et al., 2007; Watts et al., 2004
Charged mulitvesicular body protein 2B (*CHMP2B*)	Pericentromeric Chr 3	bvFTD, FTD-ALS; sporadic ALS	FTLD-U; TDP-43(–) inclusions	Cairns et al., 2007; Gydesen et al., 2002; Parkinson et al., 2006; Skibinski et al., 2005; Yancopoulou et al., 2003
Presenilin 1 (*PSEN1*)	Chr 14	FTD	Pick's disease (G183V mutant); most other cases found to harbor *PGRN* mutations	Dermaut et al. (2004) but see also Pickering-Brown et al. (2006)
Unidentified	Chr 9p13.3– 21.3	FTD-ALS	FTLD-U/TDP-43(+) inclusions	Morita et al., 2006; Vance et al., 2006

bvFTD = behavioral variant FTD; FTD-ALS = frontotemporal dementia with amyotrophic lateral sclerosis; CBS = clinical corticobasal syndrome; PSP = clinical progressive supranuclear palsy syndrome; PPA = primary progressive aphasia; FTLD-U = frontotemporal lobar degeneration–ubiquitin pathology

The tau gene is found on chromosome 17q21. Mutations in the tau gene lead to FTD and parkinsonism linked to chromosome 17, termed FTDP-17. Most patients with tau gene mutations develop an autosomal dominantly inherited syndrome with features of FTLD. Analysis of tau mutations found in FTDP-17 has provided insight into the pathogenesis of FTLD. Tau gene mutations that produce this clinical syndrome are clustered around exon 10, and alter the microtubule binding affinity of the translated protein (missense mutations in exon 10) or the ratio of 3R to 4R tau (splice site mutations flanking exon 10) that is expressed (Hong et al., 1998). Changes in tau isoform expression are thought to eventually result in the formation of insoluble protein aggregates, which in turn lead to neuronal dysfunction and death.

Biochemical analysis of tau protein extracted from brains with histopathologically diagnosed Pick's shows that Pick bodies consist of deposits of predominantly 3R tau. Ballooned neurons found in Pick's and CBD are thought to contain predominantly 4R tau, as are tau deposits identified in the brains of patients with PSP. Neurofibrillary tangles in AD contain an equal mixture of 3R and 4R tau. Other disorders, such as post-encephalitic parkinsonism (Bussiere et al., 1999), neurofibrillary tangle dementia (Reed et al., 1997), Lytico-bodig disease (Hof et al., 1994), and Niemann Pick C disease (Love et al., 1995) also produce insoluble protein aggregates containing equal ratios of 3R and 4R tau.

FTD and other primary neurodegenerative disorders with prominent tau pathology were previously grouped together as "tauopathies," to distinguish them from other protein aggregate diseases such as Parkinson's and Lewy body disease, which display protein aggregates composed of alpha synuclein (Hardy & Gwinn-Hardy, 1998). With the discovery of progranulin, and non-tau FTD pathologies, this diagnostic designation has fallen somewhat out of favor. Recent consensus statements on clinical and pathological diagnosis of FTD emphasized the composition of insoluble tau deposits found in brains at autopsy (Cairns et al., 2007; McKhann et al., 2001).

In addition to *MAPT* mutations, the chromosome 17q21 region is associated with two conserved haplotypes, termed H1 and H2 which also play a role in determining FTD-related pathology. The presence of the H1 haplotype, which may reflect a polymorphism in the *MAPT* promoter region (Rademakers et al., 2005), has been associated with PSP and CBD (Houlden et al., 2001). These haplotypes may affect the level of tau expression or/as well as the alternative splicing to 3R and 4R forms.

Progranulin (PGRN)

Along with MAPT, PGRN mutations are relatively common among identifiable mutations causing FTD. Mutations in the gene encoding for progranulin were identified in a number of families who had autosomal dominant FTD linked to chromosome 17q21, in the vicinity of MAPT, but who did not have tau pathology at autopsy and in whom no MAPT mutation could be identified (Kertesz, Kawarai et al., 2000; Rosso et al., 2001). A decrease in progranulin gene expression due to premature termination and nonsense mutations in one copy of the PGRN gene leads to haploinsufficiency of progranulin protein (Baker et al., 2006; Cruts et al., 2006; Yu et al., 2010). Progranulin is thought to act as growth factor and/or mediator of inflammation, which provides a potential mechanism for PGRN-related FTD due to a loss of trophic support for neurons and/or glia within FTD-related neuronal networks (Ahmed et al., 2007). A variety of FTD clinical phenotypes have been found in association with PGRN mutations, however, only rarely FTD-ALS (Behrens et al., 2007; Boeve et al., 2006; Huey, Grafman et al., 2006; Leverenz et al., 2007; Mesulam et al., 2007; Mukherjee et al., 2006; Pickering-Brown et al., 2006; Schymick et al., 2007; Spina et al., 2007). All PGRN mutations lead to TDP-43 pathology (FTLD-U).

Valosin-containing protein (VCP)

Mutations in the VCP protein, located on chromosome 9p13-12, have been identified in a number of families who have a rare syndrome consisting of inclusion body myopathy, Paget's disease of bone and FTD, termed IBMPFD (Watts et al., 2004). In these families FTD is only about 30% penetrant, possibly because individuals die of their musculoskeletal disease before the FTD becomes symptomatic (Kimonis & Watts, 2005). At autopsy, IBMPFD individuals have FTLD-U pathology without evidence of tau deposition, similar to individuals with PGRN mutations (Cairns et al., 2007).

Charged multivesicular protein 2B (CHMP2B)

Mutations in CHMP2B, located in the peri-centromeric region of chromosome 3, were identified in a large, autosomal dominant FTD cohort from Denmark (Skibinski et al., 2005). This protein plays a role in sorting proteins within the endosomal/lysosomal transport system. Clinically, affected individuals frequently resemble typical bvFTD. Screening of other autosomal dominant FTD kindreds suggests that *CHMP2B* mutations are rare causes of FTD (Cannon et al., 2006; Lindquist et al., 2008).

Neuropathology of FTD

Pattern of vulnerability

Focal brain atrophy is apparent both macroscopically and microscopically in FTLD brains. Severe brain atrophy may result in postmortem brain weights as low as 750 grams (Dickson, 2001). Quantitative volumetric assessments of brain atrophy have demonstrated tissue loss in the frontal lobes, the anterior, medial and inferior temporal lobes, including the amygdala and hippocampus, the insula, and variably in subcortical structures such as the caudate, putamen, thalamus and substantia nigra (Mann & South, 1993). Of these regions, the frontal and anterior temporal lobes usually show the largest volume losses. Based on patterns of brain atrophy measured at autopsy in patients with bvFTD, four stages of disease severity have been proposed: (i) mild atrophy of the orbital and superior medial frontal cortices and hippocampus; (ii) progression of mild atrophy to the anterior frontal and temporal cortices and basal ganglia; (iii) progression of mild atrophy to other cortical regions; and (iv) severe, cortical atrophy (Broe et al., 2003).

Selective vulnerability of a phylogenetically recent type of neuron, termed von Economo neurons (VENs) after the neuroanatomist who first described them, and found in frontal lobe regions thought to be involved in social behavior, has recently been documented in FTD (Seeley et al., 2006). If VENs are key components of brain social function networks, their early and prominent damage in FTD may explain the frequent, early, and severe impairments in social interactions in these patients.

Histopathological Subtypes of FTD

Tau versus TDP-43 (formerly ubiquitin)

The histopathology of FTD is a rapidly evolving field that has benefited from advances in FTD genetics as well as biochemical analysis of autopsy specimens. With the identification of new FTD-related proteins, and immunohistochemical stains directed against them, the most common pathological correlates of FTD have been successively redefined. Whereas once, many cases of FTD were thought to harbor no distinctive protein deposits (such as the plaques or tangle in Alzheimer's disease), a finding termed dementia lacking distinctive histopathology (DLDH) (Knopman et al., 1990), new immunostains have allowed for the identification of a distinctive set of proteins that are commonly deposited intracellularly in neurons and glia in FTD. The current consensus neuropathological criteria for FTD focus on two main types of immunohistochemically defined deposits, those that contain the protein tau or those that contain the protein ubiquitin (Table 4.2) (Cairns et al., 2007). The chief protein constituent of protein deposits that contain ubiquitin has recently been identified to be TAR DNA-binding protein 43 kDa (TDP-43) (Neumann et al., 2006). Most protein deposits in FTD brains with ubiquitin-staining deposits (FTLD-U) and/or ALS stain also stain for TDP-43. It is not yet understood what role TDP-43 plays in the pathogenesis of FTD but mutations of TDP-43 have been recently associated with FTD without ALS (Borroni et al., 2009), as well as ALS without FTD.

A number of large clinicopathological series have demonstrated that there is a relatively weak correlation between pathological FTD diagnosis and clinical FTD

Table 4.2 Neuropathologic diagnoses associated with frontotemporal dementia

General pathological diagnosis	Includes specific pathological diagnoses	Commonly associated clinical syndromes
Tau-associated proteinopathies		
Tauopathy with predominantly 3R tau insoluble deposits	Pick's disease	FTD, PPA, SD, CBS, PSP, Frontotemporal dementia with parkinsonism linked to chromosome 17 (FTDP-17) FTDP-17
	Frontotemporal dementia with *MAPT* mutation	
Tauopathy with predominantly 4R tau insoluble deposits	Corticobasal degeneration (CBD)	PPA, CBS, PSP, FTD, SD, FTDP-17
	Progressive supranuclear palsy (PSP)	
	Argyrophilic grain disease (AGD)	
	Frontotemporal dementia with *MAPT* mutation	
Tauopathy with predominantly both 3R and 4R tau insoluble deposits	Neurofibrillary tangle dementia	FTD, AD
	Frontotemporal dementia with *MAPT* mutation	
Ubiquitin-associated proteinopathies		
TDP-43 proteinopathy with motor neuron disease (MND)-type inclusions; tau-negative	FTLD–ubiquitin (U) with MND	FTD, SD, FTD-ALS, PPA
	FTLD-U without MND	
	FTLD-U with *PGRN* mutation	
	FTLD-U with *VCP* mutation	
	FTLD-U linked to Chr 9p	
Frontotemporal neuronal loss and gliosis with ubiquitin(+), TDP-43(-) inclusions; tau-negative	FTLD-U with *CHMP2B* mutation	FTD, PPA, FTD-ALS
	Basophilic inclusion body disease (BIBD)	
Frontotemporal neuronal loss and gliosis with ubiquitin(+), alpha-internexin (+) inclusions	Neuronal intermediate filament inclusion disease (NIFID)	FTD, CBS, FTD-ALS
Other, non-tau, non-ubiquitin associated		
Dementia lacking distinctive histopathology (DLDH)	Dementia lacking distinctive histopathology (DLDH)	FTD, SD; others

Source: Cairns, N.J., Bigio, E.H., Mackenzie, I.R., Neumann, M., Lee, V.M., Hatanpaa, K.J., et al. (2007). Neuropathologic diagnostic and nosologic criteria for fronto-temporal lobar degeneration. Consensus of the Consortium for Frontotemporal Lobar Degeneration. *Acta Neuropathologicaogica (Berlin)*, 114(1), 5–22

syndrome (Forman, Farmer et al., 2006; Hodges et al., 2004; Josephs, Duffy et al., 2006; Josephs, Petersen et al., 2006). That is, starting with a histopathological FTD-associated diagnosis, it is very difficult to predict what clinical syndrome was present during life. There is somewhat better predictive value of certain clinical FTD syndromes for certain histopathological diagnoses. The strongest association exists between clinical FTD-ALS and FTLD-U (TDP-43) pathology at autopsy. Another strong association exists between the progressive non-fluent aphasia subtype of FTD and autopsy diagnoses with tau deposits, either PSP or CBD. bvFTD has been associated with both tau and FTLD-U (TDP-43) pathology with relatively similar frequency, however, SD is more commonly associated with FTLD-U (TDP-43) than tau pathology (Davies et al., 2005). Importantly, most clinical FTD series are found to contain a small percentage of Alzheimer's disease cases at autopsy. These cases may represent frontal or other focal variants of AD (Johnson et al., 1999; Kramer & Miller, 2000).

Discussed below are the most common FTD-associated pathological diagnoses. The reader is referred to the recent consensus pathological criteria for FTD, summarized in Table 4.2, for a more complete discussion of all FTD-associated neuropathological diagnoses (Cairns et al., 2007).

Tau-Related FTD Pathologies

Pick's disease (Predominantly 3R tau)

A minority of patients who are clinically diagnosed with FTD will be found to have classic Pick's disease pathology. Microscopically, areas of cortex most severely affected in Pick's disease show a severe loss of large pyramidal neurons with diffuse spongiosis and gliosis. Pick cells, ballooned neurons that stain weakly with silver stains, are found in the deeper cortical layers. These ballooned neurons are filled with granulofilamentous material that is best demonstrated with antibodies to phosphorylated neurofilament, low molecular weight stress protein, $\alpha\beta$-crystallin, and ubiquitin hydrolase. Focal tau and/or ubiquitin hydrolase immunoreactivity is sometimes present in ballooned neurons (Dickson, 2001).

In Pick's disease, superficial cortical layers in affected areas contain small neurons with round inclusions that are intensely argyrophilic on silver stains called Pick bodies. Brain regions rich in Pick bodies show extensive loss of large neurons as well as evidence of synapse loss as demonstrated by loss of synaptophysin immunoreactivity (Masliah et al., 1990). Pick bodies are most commonly found in limbic, paralimbic, and ventral temporal lobe cortex. Smaller numbers of Pick bodies are found in the anterior frontal and dorsal temporal lobes, and are rarely found elsewhere. Like the neurofibrillary tangles found in AD, the hippocampus and amygdala have the largest numbers of Pick bodies. Unlike the neurofibrillary tangles in AD, which spare the dentate gyrus, Pick bodies are frequently found there. Also in contrast to AD, the nucleus basalis of Meynert is relatively spared in Pick's disease.

Consistent with this observation, cholinergic markers are relatively preserved in Pick's disease (Wood et al., 1983). In contrast, dopaminergic neurons in the substantia nigra are frequently affected in Pick's disease.

Pick bodies stain with antibodies to the paired helical filaments (PHF) that make up the neurofibrillary tangles observed in AD and PSP, although ultrastructurally the arrangement of tau filaments is different. Pick bodies are composed of randomly arranged filaments of tau, as opposed to PHF (Pollock et al., 1986). The most sensitive stain for Pick bodies is the anti-tau antibody (Dickson, 2001). Western blot analysis of hyperphosphorylated tau protein in Pick's brains demonstrates a different pattern of abnormal variants than in AD. In Pick's disease, there are two abnormal bands that migrate at 55 and 66 kDa, whereas in AD there are three bands: 55, 66, and 69 kDa.

Corticobasal degeneration (CBD) (Predominantly 4R tau)

CBD brains have ballooned neurons similar to classic Pick's brains, however, there are no Pick bodies. Atrophy and ballooned neurons are found throughout the neocortex, and are most abundant in the superior frontal and parietal lobes, unlike Pick's disease, which tends to spare these regions. Unlike Pick's disease, ballooned cells may be found in primary motor or sensory cortex. There is prominent neuronal loss and gliosis in areas most affected by CBD pathology. In many cases, there is significant involvement of basal ganglia structures. Astrocytic plaques, ballooned neurons and coiled bodies that stain with anti-tau antibodies are a hallmark of CBD (Dickson et al., 2002).

Progressive supranuclear palsy (PSP) (Predominantly 4R tau)

The histological hallmarks of PSP are subcortical, globose neurofibrillary tangles and tufted astrocytes that stain for the protein tau (Dickson, 1999). Cortical atrophy and white matter pathology is frequently less severe in PSP than in CBD. PSP pathology may be found concurrently with AD pathology, especially in older individuals. A recent clinicopathological series of PSP cases suggests that autopsy-defined cases do not correspond to the typical PSP clinical syndrome during life (Williams et al., 2005).

Ubiquitin-Related FTD Pathologies (FTLD-U)

TDP-43 proteinopathy

This is currently believed to be the most common form of neuropathology found in FTD. Immunohistochemical staining for ubiquitin or TDP-43 reveals protein deposits in neurons, glia, and oligodenrocytes that may fall into one of four common patterns that correlates with clinical and genetic features (Cairns et al., 2007). The clinical FTD and FTD-ALS syndromes strongly correlate with TDP-43(+) pathology.

Demential lacking distinctive histopathology (DLDH)

DLDH was previously considered to be a common pathological finding in patients with the clinical symptoms of sporadic FTD (Bird & Schellenberg, 2001; Knopman et al., 1990). There is a variable pattern of brain involvement in DLDH. These patients have significant neuronal loss and gliosis, without Pick bodies, ballooned neurons, neurofibrillary tangles, or other inclusion bodies. There may be spongiform changes in the superficial cortical layers. With stains directed against ubiquitin and TDP-43, most DLDH cases have been reclassified as FTLD-U affected areas of cerebral cortex, as well as in anterior horn cells.

Imaging

Frontotemporal dementia (bvFTD)

Functional neuroimaging of blood flow abnormalities using Tc_{99}-hexamethylylpropylencamine (HMPAO) SPECT shows bilateral frontal hypoperfusion early in the course of bvFTD, and reliably differentiates patients with FTD from patients with AD (McMurtray et al., 2005; Miller et al., 1991; Miller & Gearhart, 1999; Miller et al., 1997). Fluorodeoxy glucose (FDG)-PET demonstrates frontal hypometabolism in patients with FTD (Hoffman et al., 2000). Unbiased analysis of T1-weighted MRI scans from patients with bvFTD has identified regions of significant cortical atrophy in the ventromedial frontal cortex, the posterior orbital frontal regions bilaterally, the insula bilaterally, the left anterior cingulate cortex, the right dorsolateral frontal cortex, and the left premotor cortex as compared with controls and patients with SD (Cardenas et al., 2007; Du et al., 2007; (Rosen, Gorno-Tempini et al., 2002); (see also Figure 4.4).

Longitudinal measurements of MRI scans of patients with bvFTD show faster rates of frontal atrophy (4.1–4.5% per year), and similar rates of parieto-occipital atrophy (2.2–2.4% per year) as compared to patients with AD (2.4–2.8% per year, globally) (Chan, Fox, Jenkins et al., 2001). Statistically significant atrophy of frontal and temporal lobe gray matter structures can be measured in annual MRI scans in relatively small groups of bvFTD or SD patients, using new methods such as tensor-based morphometry (TBM; Brambati, Rankin et al., 2007; Brambati, Renda et al., 2007). These findings suggest that longitudinal measurements of brain volume may be useful outcome measures in future clinical trials of potential disease-modifying FTD therapies. Parkinsonism in FTD has been associated with reduced uptake of

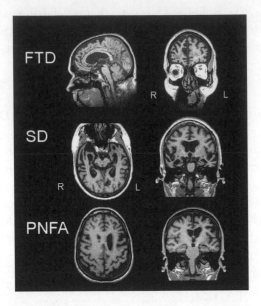

Figure 4.4   MRI findings in FTD
FTD: Parasagittal and coronal images from T1-weighted MRI scan of a patient with fronto-temporal dementia. Note asymmetric right frontal atrophy on coronal image, and lack of significant atrophy posterior to frontal lobe on saggital image
SD: Axial and coronal images from a patient with semantic dementia. Note that atrophy is most severe anteriorly and involves both medial and lateral temporal lobe structures
PNFA: Axial and coronal images from a patient with progressive non-fluent aphasia. Note asymmetric left frontal atrophy with minimal temporal lobe involvement

the dopamine transporter ligand [^{11}C]CFT in the caudate and putamen on PET imaging (Rinne et al., 2002).

Semantic dementia (SD)

SD patients often have severe, bilateral, but asymmetric atrophy of anterior temporal lobe ("knife edge atrophy") as well as medial temporal lobe structures (Figure 4.4). These findings may be preceded by hypoperfusion on HMPAO-SPECT (Edwards-Lee et al., 1997; Garrard & Hodges, 2000). Anterior temporal lobe atrophy is easily appreciated on MRI scans, and visual inspection may be sufficient to accurately differentiate SD from AD patients (Galton, Gomez-Anson et al., 2001). More detailed volumetric measurements of temporal lobe structures have demonstrated that hippocampal atrophy is often more severe in SD than in AD patients, but is usually more asymmetric, and accompanied by more severe atrophy of the amygdala, temporal pole, fusiform, and inferolateral temporal gyri (Chan, Fox, Scahill et al., 2001; Galton, Patterson et al., 2001). Unbiased measurements of T1-

weighted MRI scans suggest that atrophy in SD is much more significant in temporal than extra-temporal brain regions (Mummery et al., 2000; Rosen, Gorno-Tempini et al., 2002). FDG-PET studies during semantic memory tasks in SD patients show brain activation changes outside the areas of brain atrophy, suggesting that neuronal networks involving the temporal lobes are disrupted in SD (Mummery et al., 1999).

Amyloid imaging

The advent of amyloid-sensitive PET ligands, such as Pittsburgh Compound-B (PiB) (Klunk et al., 2004), may be useful for differentiation of FTD from AD, and particularly in identifying individuals with a clinical FTD syndrome caused by underlying AD pathology. Although most cases of clinically defined FTD syndromes show no PIB uptake, a small percentage may display cerebral amyloid levels comparable to those seen in AD (Rabinovici et al., 2007; Rowe et al., 2007). Most likely, these individuals will be found to have unusual (often frontal) variants of AD (Johnson et al., 1999), however, it is also possible that some of these cases will have both concurrent FTD– and AD– pathology (Behrens et al., 2007). A definitive answer awaits the results of autopsy studies of PiB(+) FTD individuals.

Treatment

Although there are currently no FDA-approved medications indicated for the treatment of FTD, a number of pharmacological interventions may ameliorate or suppress disinhibition, poor impulse control, sexually inappropriate and stereotyped behaviors in bvFTD. Selective serotonin reuptake inhibitors (SSRIs; fluoxetine, fluvoxamine, sertraline or paroxetine) are often used as first-line agents for management of disinhibited, repetitive, sexually inappropriate behaviors and dietary changes in FTD (Chow, 2005; Moretti, Torre, Antonello, Cazzato, & Bava, 2003; Swartz, Miller, Lesser, & Darby, 1997). Most descriptions of SSRI effects in FTD are based on open-label experience or cases series. The few randomized placebo-controlled trials that have been performed have produced mixed results. For example, although open-label experience suggests that paroxetine may be helpful for symptomatic management of FTD (Moretti, Torre, Antonello, Cazzato, & Bava, 2003), a randomized placebo-controlled trial failed to show efficacy (Deakin et al., 2004). Trazadone has also been shown to be effective in treating the behavioral symptoms of FTD in a randomized, placebo-controlled trial (Lebert et al., 2004), however, somnolence associated with trazadone use may limit its usefulness in some individuals. A meta-analysis of SSRI and trazodone effects on the Neuropsychiatric Inventory (NPI) (Cummings, 1997), a measure of behavioral impairment in FTD, demonstrated a mean reduction (improvement) of 15.4 points in bvFTD (Huey,

Putnam et al., 2006) supporting the use of these drugs as first-line agents for the management of behavioral symptoms in FTD.

Behavioral symptoms refractory to SSRI treatment are often responsive to atypical antipsychotic agents, although side effects including somnolence, weight gain, and emergence of parkinsonism may limit efficacy (Moretti, Torre, Antonello, Cazzato et al., 2003; Pijnenburg et al., 2003). FTD patients may be particularly susceptible to extrapyramidal side effects of atypical antipsychotic agents (Pijnenburg et al., 2003). Delusions are common in bvFTD, and tend to be jealous, somatic, religious or bizarre, but are rarely persecutory. Euphoric symptoms, such as elevated mood, inappropriate jocularity, and exaggerated self-esteem were found in 30% of FTD patients in one clinical series (Levy et al., 1996). When severe, such behaviors may also be suppressed by treatment with an atypical antipsychotic agent.

An open-label study with the acetylcholinesterase inhibitor, rivastigmine, reported modest improvements in mood and behavior in bvFTD (Moretti et al., 2004). However, the lack of cholinergic deficit in FTD (Huey, Putnam et al., 2006) and a recent case series documented worsening disinhibition and compulsions after donepezil treatment that resolved with medication withdrawal suggest that acetylcholinesterase inhibitors should not routinely be used in FTD (Mendez et al., 2007). A preliminary study of methylphenidate in FTD suggests a possible beneficial effect on risk-taking behavior (Rahman et al., 2006). More studies with this and similar medications are needed to assess the long-term safety and potential benefits of stimulant medications in FTD.

Symptomatic pharmacotherapy for all three subtypes of FTD is most frequently initiated when behavioral symptoms become intolerable to caregivers. With time, neuropsychiatric symptoms, such as agitation, aggressiveness, verbally and socially inappropriate behaviors, obsessive and compulsive symptoms, and sweet cravings eventually manifest in many FTD patients regardless of the initial clinical syndrome (Kertesz et al., 2005). Such behavioral abnormalities often reach a peak during the middle-to late stages of disease and depending on the rate of disease progression (which in turn may be dependent on the underlying neuropathology), symptomatic pharmacotherapy may be indicated for many years. However, as disease pathology progressively destroys medial frontal lobe structures involved in motivation (Broe et al., 2003; Rosen et al., 2005), many patients exhibit increasing apathy, become more withdrawn, and display fewer difficult-to-manage behaviors. Motor impairments, including atypical parkinsonism or weakness due to motor neuron involvement, are commonly observed with more advanced disease (Kertesz et al., 2007). These motor impairments may limit the expression of aberrant behaviors, and may allow for the withdrawal of symptomatic treatments such as atypical antipsychotics. Since FTD patients may be sensitive to extrapyramidal side effects of antipsychotic medications (Pijnenburg et al., 2003), clinicians should have a low threshold to reduce antipsychotic dose or stop such medications altogether in patients with worsening parkinsonism, particularly those with more advanced disease.

Behavioral symptoms, lack of empathy, poor insight, and communication difficulties create a unique constellation of stressors for the caregivers of FTD patients that are different from the stressors experienced by AD caregivers. Caregiver distress is associated with earlier nursing home placement of dementia patients (Litvan, 2001), and thus an important role of the physician is to support the caregiver as well as the patient. Caregivers should be educated about FTD and given anticipatory guidance as to what problems will likely arise with time. Efforts to increase detection of caregiver depression, and to treat psychiatric morbidity in caregivers with support groups, psychiatric referrals, and respite care may delay patient institutionalization and improve the quality of life for both patients and caregivers (Talerico & Evans, 2001). Environmental, behavioral, and psychosocial strategies have been developed to aid in management of FTD both at home and if institutionalization becomes necessary (Talerico & Evans, 2001).

The lack of randomized, placebo-controlled data on most symptomatic treatments for FTD limits clinicians' ability to determine the optimal therapy for this disorder. The data that is available is limited by the variable clinical criteria for subject enrollment and the variable outcome measures used in each study. Clearly, more clinical trials of currently available symptomatic agents for the treatment of dementia are needed. New therapies directed at tau protein aggregation may eventually lead to disease-modifying therapy (Trojanowski et al., 2008). Such studies should use outcome measures that are sensitive to the cognitive and behavioral deficits associated with FTD, such as the Neuropsychiatric Inventory (Cummings, 1997), Frontal Behavioral Inventory (Kertesz et al., 1997), Executive Interview (Royall et al., 1992), and others (Freedman, 2007). As suggested by Freedman, a greater consensus among investigators as to the optimal criteria for inclusion of FTD subjects, as well as the most appropriate outcome measures to measure treatment efficacy, would greatly improve the validity of future studies and the ability to develop evidence-based treatment recommendations for FTD (Freedman, 2007).

References

Adlam, A. L., Patterson, K., Rogers, T. T., Nestor, P. J., Salmond, C. H., Acosta-Cabronero, J., et al. (2006). Semantic dementia and fluent primary progressive aphasia: Two sides of the same coin? *Brain, 129*(Pt 11), 3066–3080.

Ahmed, Z., Mackenzie, I. R., Hutton, M. L., & Dickson, D. W. (2007). Progranulin in frontotemporal lobar degeneration and neuroinflammation. *Journal of Neuroinflammation, 4*, 7.

Altman, E. (1923). Uber die eigenartige Krankheitsfalle des spateren Alters. *Zeitscrift fur die Gesamte Neurologie und Psychiatrie, 4*, 356–385.

Alzheimer, A. (1911). Uber eigenartige Krankheitsfalle des spateren Alters. *Zeitscrift fur die Gesamte Neurologie und Psychiatrie, 4*, 7–44.

Ames, D., Cummings, J. L., Wirshing, W. C., Quinn, B., & Mahler, M. (1994). Repetitive and compulsive behavior in frontal lobe degenerations. *Journal of Neuropsychiatry and Clinical Neurosciences, 6*(2), 100–113.

Bak, T. H., O'Donovan, D. G., Xuereb, J. H., Boniface, S., & Hodges, J. R. (2001). Selective impairment of verb processing associated with pathological changes in Brodmann areas 44 and 45 in the motor neurone disease- dementia-aphasia syndrome. *Brain*, *124*(Pt 1), 103–120.

Baker, M., Mackenzie, I. R., Pickering-Brown, S. M., Gass, J., Rademakers, R., Lindholm, C., et al. (2006). Mutations in progranulin cause tau-negative frontotemporal dementia linked to chromosome 17. *Nature*, *442*(7105), 916–919.

Behrens, M. I., Mukherjee, O., Tu, P. H., Liscic, R. M., Grinberg, L. T., Carter, D., et al. (2007). Neuropathologic heterogeneity in HDDD1: a familial frontotemporal lobar degeneration with ubiquitin-positive inclusions and progranulin mutation. *Alzheimer Disease & Associated Disorders*, *21*(1), 1–7.

Bird, T. D., & Schellenberg, G. D. (2001). The case of the missing tau, or, why didn't the mRNA bark? *Annals of Neurology*, *49*(2), 144–145.

Boeve, B. F., Baker, M., Dickson, D. W., Parisi, J. E., Giannini, C., Josephs, K. A., et al. (2006). Frontotemporal dementia and parkinsonism associated with the IVS1+1G->A mutation in progranulin: A clinicopathologic study. *Brain*, *129*(Pt 11), 3103–3114.

Boeve, B. F., Lang, A. E., & Litvan, I. (2003). Corticobasal degeneration and its relationship to progressive supranuclear palsy and frontotemporal dementia. *Annals of Neurology*, *54*(Suppl 5), S15–S19.

Borroni, B., Bonvicini, C., Alberici, A., Buratti, E., Agosti, C., Archetti, S., et al. (2009). Mutation within TARDBP leads to frontotemporal dementia without motor neuron disease. *Human Mutation*, *30*(11), E974–E983.

Boxer, A. L., Garbutt, S., Rankin, K. P., Hellmuth, J., Neuhaus, J., Miller, B. L., et al. (2006). Medial versus lateral frontal lobe contributions to voluntary saccade control as revealed by the study of patients with frontal lobe degeneration. *Journal of Neuroscience*, *26*(23), 6354–6363.

Boxer, A. L., Rankin, K. P., Miller, B. L., Schuff, N., Weiner, M., Gorno-Tempini, M. L., et al. (2003). Cinguloparietal atrophy distinguishes Alzheimer disease from semantic dementia. *Archives of Neurology*, *60*(7), 949–956.

Bozeat, S., Gregory, C. A., Ralph, M. A., & Hodges, J. R. (2000). Which neuropsychiatric and behavioural features distinguish frontal and temporal variants of frontotemporal dementia from Alzheimer's disease? *Journal of Neurology, Neurosurgery & Psychiatry*, *69*(2), 178–186.

Brambati, S. M., Rankin, K. P., Narvid, J., Seeley, W. W., Dean, D., Rosen, H. J., et al. (2007). Atrophy progression in semantic dementia with asymmetric temporal involvement: A tensor-based morphometry study. *Neurobiology of Aging*, ePub, July 2.

Brambati, S. M., Renda, N. C., Rankin, K. P., Rosen, H. J., Seeley, W. W., Ashburner, J., et al. (2007). A tensor based morphometry study of longitudinal gray matter contraction in FTD. *Neuroimage*, *35*(3), 998–1003.

Broe, M., Hodges, J. R., Schofield, E., Shepherd, C. E., Kril, J. J., & Halliday, G. M. (2003). Staging disease severity in pathologically confirmed cases of frontotemporal dementia. *Neurology*, *60*(6), 1005–1011.

Brun, A. (1987). Frontal lobe degeneration of non-Alzheimer type. I. Neuropathology. *Archives of Gerontology and Geriatrics*, *6*(3), 193–208.

Bussiere, T., Hof, P. R., Mailliot, C., Brown, C. D., Caillet-Boudin, M. L., Perl, D. P., et al. (1999). Phosphorylated serine422 on tau proteins is a pathological epitope found in several diseases with neurofibrillary degeneration. *Acta Neuropathologica (Berlin)*, *97*(3), 221–230.

Cairns, N. J., Bigio, E. H., Mackenzie, I. R., Neumann, M., Lee, V. M., Hatanpaa, K. J., et al. (2007). Neuropathologic diagnostic and nosologic criteria for frontotemporal lobar degeneration: Consensus of the Consortium for Frontotemporal Lobar Degeneration. *Acta Neuropathologica (Berlin)*, *114*(1), 5–22.

Cannon, A., Baker, M., Boeve, B., Josephs, K., Knopman, D., Petersen, R., et al. (2006). CHMP2B mutations are not a common cause of frontotemporal lobar degeneration. *Neuroscience Letters*, *398*(1–2), 83–84.

Cardenas, V. A., Boxer, A. L., Chao, L. L., Gorno-Tempini, M. L., Miller, B. L., Weiner, M. W., et al. (2007). Deformation-based morphometry reveals brain atrophy in frontotemporal dementia. *Archives of Neurology*, *64*(6), 873–877.

Caselli, R. J., Windebank, A. J., Petersen, R. C., Komori, T., Parisi, J. E., Okazaki, H., et al. (1993). Rapidly progressive aphasic dementia and motor neuron disease. *Annals of Neurology*, *33*(2), 200–207.

Chan, D., Fox, N. C., Jenkins, R., Scahill, R. I., Crum, W. R., & Rossor, M. N. (2001). Rates of global and regional cerebral atrophy in AD and frontotemporal dementia. *Neurology*, *57*, 1756–1763.

Chan, D., Fox, N. C., Scahill, R. I., Crum, W. R., Whitwell, J. L., Leschziner, G., et al. (2001). Patterns of temporal lobe atrophy in semantic dementia and Alzheimer's disease. *Annals of Neurology*, *49*(4), 433–442.

Chow, T. W. (2005). Treatment approaches to symptoms associated with frontotemporal degeneration. *Current Psychiatry Reports*, *7*(5), 376–380.

Chow, T. W., Miller, B. L., Hayashi, V. N., & Geschwind, D. H. (1999). Inheritance of frontotemporal dementia. *Archives of Neurology*, *56*(7), 817–822.

Clark, L. N., Poorkaj, P., Wszolek, Z., Geschwind, D. H., Nasreddine, Z. S., Miller, B., et al. (1998). Pathogenic implications of mutations in the tau gene in pallido-ponto-nigral degeneration and related neurodegenerative disorders linked to chromosome 17. *Proceedings of the National Academy of Sciences USA*, *95*(22), 13103–13107.

Clinical and neuropathological criteria for frontotemporal dementia. The Lund and Manchester Groups. (1994). *Journal of Neurology, Neurosurgery & Psychiatry*, *57*(4), 416–418.

Constantinidis, J., Richard, J., & Tissot, R. (1974). Pick's disease. Histological and clincial correlations. *European Neurology*, *11*, 208–217.

Cruts, M., Gijselinck, I., van der Zee, J., Engelborghs, S., Wils, H., Pirici, D., et al. (2006). Null mutations in progranulin cause ubiquitin-positive frontotemporal dementia linked to chromosome 17q21. *Nature*, *442*(7105), 920–924.

Cummings, J. L. (1997). The Neuropsychiatric Inventory: Assessing psychopathology in dementia patients. *Neurology*, *48*(5 Suppl 6), S10–S16.

Davies, R. R., Hodges, J. R., Kril, J. J., Patterson, K., Halliday, G. M., & Xuereb, J. H. (2005). The pathological basis of semantic dementia. *Brain*, *128*(Pt 9), 1984–1995.

Deakin, J. B., Rahman, S., Nestor, P. J., Hodges, J. R., & Sahakian, B. J. (2004). Paroxetine does not improve symptoms and impairs cognition in frontotemporal dementia: A double-blind randomized controlled trial. *Psychopharmacology (Berlin)*, *172*(4), 400–408.

Dermaut, B., Kumar-Singh, S., Engelborghs, S., Theuns, J., Rademakers, R., Saerens, J., et al. (2004). A novel presenilin 1 mutation associated with Pick's disease but not beta-amyloid plaques. *Annals of Neurology*, *55*(5), 617–626.

Dickson, D. W. (1999). Neuropathologic differentiation of progressive supranuclear palsy and corticobasal degeneration. *Journal of Neurology*, *246*(Suppl 2), 116–115.

Dickson, D. W. (2001). Neuropathology of Pick's disease. *Neurology*, *56*(Suppl 4), S16–S20.

Dickson, D. W., Bergeron, C., Chin, S. S., Duyckaerts, C., Horoupian, D., Ikeda, K., et al. (2002). Office of Rare Diseases neuropathologic criteria for corticobasal degeneration. *Journal of Neuropathology & Experimental Neurology, 61*(11), 935–946.

Du, A. T., Schuff, N., Kramer, J. H., Rosen, H. J., Gorno-Tempini, M. L., Rankin, K., et al. (2007). Different regional patterns of cortical thinning in Alzheimer's disease and frontotemporal dementia. *Brain, 130*(Pt 4), 1159–1166.

Edwards-Lee, T., Miller, B. L., Benson, D. F., Cummings, J. L., Russell, G. L., Boone, K., et al. (1997). The temporal variant of frontotemporal dementia. *Brain, 120*(Pt 6), 1027–1040.

Evans, J. J., Heggs, A. J., Antoun, N., & Hodges, J. R. (1995). Progressive prosopagnosia associated with selective right temporal lobe atrophy. A new syndrome? *Brain, 118*(Pt 1), 1–13.

Forman, M. S., Farmer, J., Johnson, J. K., Clark, C. M., Arnold, S. E., Coslett, H. B., et al. (2006). Frontotemporal dementia: Clinicopathological correlations. *Annals of Neurology, 59*(6), 952–962.

Forman, M. S., Mackenzie, I. R., Cairns, N. J., Swanson, E., Boyer, P. J., Drachman, D. A., et al. (2006). Novel ubiquitin neuropathology in frontotemporal dementia with valosin-containing protein gene mutations. *Journal of Neuropathology & Experimental Neurology, 65*(6), 571–581.

Freedman, M. (2007). Frontotemporal dementia: recommendations for therapeutic studies, designs, and approaches. *Canadian Journal of the Neurological Sciences, 34*(Suppl 1), S118–S124.

Galton, C. J., Gomez-Anson, B., Antoun, N., Scheltens, P., Patterson, K., Graves, M., et al. (2001). Temporal lobe rating scale: application to Alzheimer's disease and frontotemporal dementia. *Journal of Neurology, Neurosurgery & Psychiatry, 70*(2), 165–173.

Galton, C. J., Patterson, K., Graham, K., Lambon-Ralph, M. A., Williams, G., Antoun, N., et al. (2001). Differing patterns of temporal atrophy in Alzheimer's disease and semantic dementia. *Neurology, 57*(2), 216–225.

Garrard, P., & Hodges, J. R. (2000). Semantic dementia: clinical, radiological and pathological perspectives. *Journal of Neurology, 247*(6), 409–422.

Geschwind, D. H., Robidoux, J., Alarcon, M., Miller, B. L., Wilhelmsen, K. C., Cummings, J. L., et al. (2001). Dementia and neurodevelopmental predisposition: Cognitive dysfunction in presymptomatic subjects precedes dementia by decades in frontotemporal dementia. *Annals of Neurology, 50*(6), 741–746.

Goldman, J. S., Farmer, J. M., Wood, E. M., Johnson, J. K., Boxer, A., Neuhaus, J., et al. (2005). Comparison of family histories in FTLD subtypes and related tauopathies. *Neurology, 65*(11), 1817–1819.

Gorno-Tempini, M. L., Dronkers, N. F., Rankin, K. P., Ogar, J. M., Phengrasamy, L., Rosen, H. J., et al. (2004). Cognition and anatomy in three variants of primary progressive aphasia. *Annals of Neurology, 55*(3), 335–346.

Graham, K. S., Simons, J. S., Pratt, K. H., Patterson, K., & Hodges, J. R. (2000). Insights from semantic dementia on the relationship between episodic and semantic memory. *Neuropsychologia, 38*(3), 313–324.

Gregory, C. A., Serra-Mestres, J., & Hodges, J. R. (1999). Early diagnosis of the frontal variant of frontotemporal dementia: how sensitive are standard neuroimaging and neuropsychologic tests? *Neuropsychiatry, Neuropsychology, & Behavioral Neurology, 12*(2), 128–135.

Grossman, M. (2001). A multidisciplinary approach to Pick's disease and frontotemporal dementia. *Neurology*, *56*(S4), S1–S2.

Guyant-Marechal, L., Laquerriere, A., Duyckaerts, C., Dumanchin, C., Bou, J., Dugny, F., et al. (2006). Valosin-containing protein gene mutations: Clinical and neuropathologic features. *Neurology*, *67*(4), 644–651.

Gydesen, S., Brown, J. M., Brun, A., Chakrabarti, L., Gade, A., Johannsen, P., et al. (2002). Chromosome 3 linked frontotemporal dementia (FTD-3). *Neurology*, *59*(10), 1585–1594.

Hardy, J., & Gwinn-Hardy, K. (1998). Genetic classification of primary neurodegenerative disease. *Science*, *282*(5391), 1075–1079.

Hodges, J. R. (2001). Frontotemporal dementia (Pick's disease): Clinical features and assessment. *Neurology*, *56*(11 Suppl 4), S6–S10.

Hodges, J. R., Davies, R., Xuereb, J., Kril, J., & Halliday, G. (2003). Survival in frontotemporal dementia. *Neurology*, *61*(3), 349–354.

Hodges, J. R., Davies, R. R., Xuereb, J. H., Casey, B., Broe, M., Bak, T. H., et al. (2004). Clinicopathological correlates in frontotemporal dementia. *Annals of Neurology*, *56*(3), 399–406.

Hodges, J. R., & Graham, K. S. (2001). Episodic memory: insights from semantic dementia. *Philosophical Transactions of the Royal Society B: Biological Sciences*, *356*(1413), 1423–1434.

Hodges, J. R., Graham, N., & Patterson, K. (1995). Charting the progression in semantic dementia: Implications for the organisation of semantic memory. *Memory*, *3*(3–4), 463–495.

Hodges, J. R., Patterson, K., Oxbury, S., & Funnell, E. (1992). Semantic dementia. Progressive fluent aphasia with temporal lobe atrophy. *Brain*, *115*(Pt 6), 1783–1806.

Hof, P. R., Nimchinsky, E. A., Buee-Scherrer, V., Buee, L., Nasrallah, J., Hottinger, A. F., et al. (1994). Amyotrophic lateral sclerosis/parkinsonism-dementia complex of Guam: Quantitative neuropathology, immunohistochemical analysis of neuronal vulnerability, and comparison with related neurodegenerative disorders. *Acta Neuropathologica*, *88*(5), 397–404.

Hoffman, J. M., Welsh-Bohmer, K. A., Hanson, M., Crain, B., Hulette, C., Earl, N., et al. (2000). FDG PET imaging in patients with pathologically verified dementia. *Journal of Nuclear Medicine*, *41*(11), 1920–1928.

Hong, M., Zhukareva, V., Vogelsberg-Ragaglia, V., Wszolek, Z., Reed, L., Miller, B. I., et al. (1998). Mutation-specific functional impairments in distinct tau isoforms of hereditary FTDP-17. *Science*, *282*(5395), 1914–1917.

Hosler, B. A., Siddique, T., Sapp, P. C., Sailor, W., Huang, M. C., Hossain, A., et al. (2000). Linkage of familial amyotrophic lateral sclerosis with frontotemporal dementia to chromosome 9q21-q22. *Journal of the American Medical Association*, *284*(13), 1664–1669.

Houlden, H., Baker, M., Morris, H. R., MacDonald, N., Pickering-Brown, S., Adamson, J., et al. (2001). Corticobasal degeneration and progressive supranuclear palsy share a common tau haplotype. *Neurology*, *56*(12), 1702–1706.

Huey, E. D., Grafman, J., Wassermann, E. M., Pietrini, P., Tierney, M. C., Ghetti, B., et al. (2006). Characteristics of frontotemporal dementia patients with a Progranulin mutation. *Annals of Neurology*, *60*(3), 374–380.

Huey, E. D., Putnam, K. T., & Grafman, J. (2006). A systematic review of neurotransmitter deficits and treatments in frontotemporal dementia. *Neurology*, *66*(1), 17–22.

Hutton, M. (2001). Missense and splice site mutations in tau associated with FTDP-17: Multiple pathogenic mechanisms. *Neurology, 56*(11 Suppl 4), S21–S25.

Hutton, M., Lendon, C. L., Rizzu, P., Baker, M., Froelich, S., Houlden, H., et al. (1998). Association of missense and 5'-splice-site mutations in tau with the inherited dementia FTDP-17. *Nature, 393*(6686), 702–705.

Ikeda, M., Brown, J., Holland, A. J., Fukuhara, R., & Hodges, J. R. (2002). Changes in appetite, food preference, and eating habits in frontotemporal dementia and Alzheimer's disease. *Journal of Neurology, Neurosurgery & Psychiatry, 73*(4), 371–376.

Johnson, J. K., Head, E., Kim, R., Starr, A., & Cotman, C. W. (1999). Clinical and pathological evidence for a frontal variant of Alzheimer disease. *Archives of Neurology, 56*(10), 1233–1239.

Josephs, K. A., Ahmed, Z., Katsuse, O., Parisi, J. F., Boeve, B. F., Knopman, D. S., et al. (2007). Neuropathologic features of frontotemporal lobar degeneration with ubiquitin-positive inclusions with progranulin gene (PGRN) mutations. *Journal of Neuropathology and Experimental Neurology, 66*(2), 142–151.

Josephs, K. A., Duffy, J. R., Strand, E. A., Whitwell, J. L., Layton, K. F., Parisi, J. E., et al. (2006). Clinicopathological and imaging correlates of progressive aphasia and apraxia of speech. *Brain, 129*(Pt 6), 1385–1398.

Josephs, K. A., Petersen, R. C., Knopman, D. S., Boeve, B. F., Whitwell, J. L., Duffy, J. R., et al. (2006). Clinicopathologic analysis of frontotemporal and corticobasal degenerations and PSP. *Neurology, 66*(1), 41–48.

Kertesz, A., Blair, M., McMonagle, P., & Munoz, D. G. (2007). The diagnosis and course of frontotemporal dementia. *Alzheimer Disease & Associated Disorders, 21*(2), 155–163.

Kertesz, A., Davidson, W., & Fox, H. (1997). Frontal Behavioral Inventory: Diagnostic criteria for frontal lobe dementia. *Canadian Journal of the Neurological Sciences, 24*, 29–36.

Kertesz, A., Kawarai, T., Rogaeva, E., St George-Hyslop, P., Poorkaj, P., Bird, T. D., et al. (2000). Familial frontotemporal dementia with ubiquitin-positive, tau-negative inclusions. *Neurology, 54*(4), 818–827.

Kertesz, A., Martinez-Lage, P., Davidson, W., & Munoz, D. G. (2000). The corticobasal degeneration syndrome overlaps progressive aphasia and frontotemporal dementia. *Neurology, 55*(9), 1368–1375.

Kertesz, A., McMonagle, P., Blair, M., Davidson, W., & Munoz, D. G. (2005). The evolution and pathology of frontotemporal dementia. *Brain, 128*(Pt 9), 1996–2005.

Kertesz, A., Munoz, D. G., & Hillis, A. (2003). Preferred terminology. *Annals of Neurology, 54*(Suppl 5), S3–S6.

Kimonis, V. E., & Watts, G. D. (2005). Autosomal dominant inclusion body myopathy, Paget disease of bone, and frontotemporal dementia. *Alzheimer Disease & Associated Disorders, 19*(Suppl 1), S44–S47.

Klunk, W. E., Engler, H., Nordberg, A., Wang, Y., Blomqvist, G., Holt, D. P., et al. (2004). Imaging brain amyloid in Alzheimer's disease with Pittsburgh Compound-B. *Annals of Neurology, 55*(3), 306–319.

Knopman, D. S., Mastri, A. R., Frey, W. H., 2nd, Sung, J. H., & Rustan, T. (1990). Dementia lacking distinctive histologic features: A common non- Alzheimer degenerative dementia. *Neurology, 40*(2), 251–256.

Knopman, D. S., Petersen, R. C., Edland, S. D., Cha, R. H., & Rocca, W. A. (2004). The incidence of frontotemporal lobar degeneration in Rochester, Minnesota, 1990 through 1994. *Neurology, 62*(3), 506–508.

Kramer, J. H., & Miller, B. L. (2000). Alzheimer's disease and its focal variants. *Seminars in Neurology*, *20*(4), 447–454.

Lebert, F., Stekke, W., Hasenbroekx, C., & Pasquier, F. (2004). Frontotemporal dementia: A randomised, controlled trial with trazodone. *Dementia and Geriatric Cognitive Disorders*, *17*(4), 355–359.

Leverenz, J. B., Yu, C. E., Montine, T. J., Steinbart, E., Bekris, L. M., Zabetian, C., et al. (2007). A novel progranulin mutation associated with variable clinical presentation and tau, TDP43 and alpha-synuclein pathology. *Brain*, *130*(Pt 5), 1360–1374.

Levy, M. L., Miller, B. L., Cummings, J. L., Fairbanks, L. A., & Craig, A. (1996). Alzheimer disease and frontotemporal dementias. Behavioral distinctions. *Archives of Neurology*, *53*(7), 687–690.

Lindau, M., Almkvist, O., Kushi, J., Boone, K., Johansson, S. E., Wahlund, L. O., et al. (2000). First symptoms–frontotemporal dementia versus Alzheimer's disease. *Dementia and Geriatric Cognitive Disorders*, *11*(5), 286–293.

Lindquist, S. G., Braedgaard, H., Svenstrup, K., Isaacs, A. M., & Nielsen, J. E. (2008). Frontotemporal dementia linked to chromosome 3 (FTD-3) – Current concepts and the detection of a previously unknown branch of the Danish FTD-3 family. *European Journal of Neurology*, *15*(7), 667–670.

Litvan, I. (2001). Therapy and management of frontal lobe dementia patients. *Neurology*, *56*(11 Suppl 4), S41–S45.

Liu, W., Miller, B. L., Kramer, J. H., Rankin, K., Wyss-Coray, C., Gearhart, R., et al. (2004). Behavioral disorders in the frontal and temporal variants of frontotemporal dementia. *Neurology*, *62*(5), 742–748.

Lomen-Hoerth, C., Anderson, T., & Miller, B. (2002). The overlap of amyotrophic lateral sclerosis and frontotemporal dementia. *Neurology*, *59*(7), 1077–1079.

Lomen-Hoerth, C., Murphy, J., Langmore, S., Kramer, J. H., Olney, R. K., & Miller, B. (2003). Are amyotrophic lateral sclerosis patients cognitively normal? *Neurology*, *60*(7), 1094–1097.

Love, S., Bridges, L. R., & Case, C. P. (1995). Neurofibrillary tangles in Niemann-Pick disease type C. *Brain*, *118*(Pt 1), 119–129.

Mackenzie, I. R., Baker, M., Pickering-Brown, S., Hsiung, G. Y., Lindholm, C., Dwosh, E., et al. (2006). The neuropathology of frontotemporal lobar degeneration caused by mutations in the progranulin gene. *Brain*, *129*(Pt 11), 3081–3090.

Mann, D. M., & South, P. W. (1993). The topographic distribution of brain atrophy in frontal lobe dementia. *Acta Neuropathologicaogica (Berlin)*, *85*(3), 334–340.

Masliah, E., Terry, R. D., Alford, M., & DeTeresa, R. (1990). Quantitative immunohistochemistry of synaptophysin in human neocortex: An alternative method to estimate density of presynaptic terminals in paraffin sections. *Journal of Histochemistry and Cytochemistry*, *38*(6), 837–844.

McKhann, G. M., Albert, M. S., Grossman, M., Miller, B., Dickson, D., & Trojanowski, J. (2001). Clinical and pathological diagnosis of frontotemporal dementia. *Archives of Neurology*, *58*, 1803–1809.

McMurtray, A., Clark, D. G., Christine, D., & Mendez, M. F. (2005). Early-onset dementia: Frequency and causes compared to late-onset dementia. *Dementia and Geriatric Cognitive Disorders*, *21*(2), 59–64.

Mendez, M. F., Selwood, A., Mastri, A. R., & Frey, W. H., 2nd. (1993). Pick's disease versus Alzheimer's disease: A comparison of clinical characteristics. *Neurology*, *43*(2), 289–292.

Mendez, M. F., Shapira, J. S., McMurtray, A., & Licht, E. (2007). Preliminary findings: Behavioral worsening on donepezil in patients with frontotemporal dementia. *American Journal of Geriatric Psychiatry, 15*(1), 84–87.

Mesulam, M. M. (1982). Slowly progressive aphasia without generalized dementia. *Annals of Neurology, 11*(6), 592–598.

Mesulam, M. M., Johnson, N., Krefft, T. A., Gass, J. M., Cannon, A. D., Adamson, J. L., et al. (2007). Progranulin mutations in primary progressive aphasia: the PPA1 and PPA3 families. *Archives of Neurology, 64*(1), 43–47.

Miller, B. L., Boone, K., Mishkin, F., Swartz, J. R., Koras, N., & Kushii, J. (1998). Clinical and neuropsychological features of frontotemporal dementia. In A. Kertesz & D. Munoz (Eds.), *Pick's disease and Pick complex* (pp. 23–33). New York: Wiley-Liss.

Miller, B. L., Cummings, J., Boone, K., Chang, L., Schuman, S., Pahan, N., et al. (1995). Clinical and neurobehavioral characteristics of fronto-temporal dementia and Alzheimer disease. *Neurology, 45*, A318.

Miller, B. L., Cummings, J., Mishkin, F., Boone, K., Prince, F., Ponton, M., et al. (1998). Emergence of artistic talent in frontotemporal dementia. *Neurology, 51*(4), 978–982.

Miller, B. L., Cummings, J. L., Villanueva-Meyer, J., Boone, K., Mehringer, C. M., Lesser, I. M., et al. (1991). Frontal lobe degeneration: Clinical, neuropsychological, and SPECT characteristics. *Neurology, 41*(9), 1374–1382.

Miller, B. L., Darby, A. L., Swartz, J. R., Yener, G. G., & Mena, I. (1995). Dietary changes, compulsions and sexual behavior in frontotemporal degeneration. *Dementia, 6*(4), 195–199.

Miller, B. L., & Gearhart, R. (1999). Neuroimaging in the diagnosis of frontotemporal dementia. *Dementia and Geriatric Cognitive Disorders, 10*(Suppl 1), 71–74.

Miller, B. L., Ikonte, C., Ponton, M., Levy, M., Boone, K., Darby, A., et al. (1997). A study of the Lund–Manchester research criteria for frontotemporal dementia: Clinical and single-photon emission CT correlations. *Neurology, 48*(4), 937–942.

Miller, B. L., Seeley, W. W., Mychack, P., Rosen, H. J., Mena, I., & Boone, K. (2001). Neuroanatomy of the self: Evidence from patients with frontotemporal dementia. *Neurology, 57*(5), 817–821.

Mioshi, E., Kipps, C. M., Dawson, K., Mitchell, J., Graham, A., & Hodges, J. R. (2007). Activities of daily living in frontotemporal dementia and Alzheimer disease. *Neurology, 68*(24), 2077–2084.

Moretti, R., Torre, P., Antonello, R. M., Cattaruzza, T., Cazzato, G., & Bava, A. (2004). Rivastigmine in frontotemporal dementia: An open-label study. *Drugs & Aging, 21*(14), 931–937.

Moretti, R., Torre, P., Antonello, R. M., Cazzato, G., & Bava, A. (2003). Frontotemporal dementia: Paroxetine as a possible treatment of behavior symptoms. A randomized, controlled, open 14-month study. *European Neurology, 49*(1), 13–19.

Moretti, R., Torre, P., Antonello, R. M., Cazzato, G., Griggio, S., & Bava, A. (2003). Olanzapine as a treatment of neuropsychiatric disorders of Alzheimer's disease and other dementias: A 24-month follow-up of 68 patients. *American Journal of Alzheimer's Disease & Other Dementias, 18*(4), 205–214.

Morita, M., Al-Chalabi, A., Andersen, P. M., Hosler, B., Sapp, P., Englund, E., et al. (2006). A locus on chromosome 9p confers susceptibility to ALS and frontotemporal dementia. *Neurology, 66*(6), 839–844.

Mukherjee, O., Pastor, P., Cairns, N. J., Chakraverty, S., Kauwe, J. S., Shears, S., et al. (2006). HDDD2 is a familial frontotemporal lobar degeneration with ubiquitin-positive, tau-negative inclusions caused by a missense mutation in the signal peptide of progranulin. *Annals of Neurology, 60*(3), 314–322.

Mummery, C. J., Patterson, K., Price, C. J., Ashburner, J., Frackowiak, R. S., & Hodges, J. R. (2000). A voxel-based morphometry study of semantic dementia: Relationship between temporal lobe atrophy and semantic memory. *Annals of Neurology, 47*(1), 36–45.

Mummery, C. J., Patterson, K., Wise, R. J. S., Vandenbergh, R., Price, C. J., & Hodges, J. R. (1999). Disrupted temporal lobe connections in semantic dementia. *Brain, 122,* 61–73.

Mychack, P., Kramer, J. H., Boone, K. B., & Miller, B. L. (2001). The influence of right frontotemporal dysfunction on social behavior in frontotemporal dementia. *Neurology, 56*(11 Suppl 4), S11–S15.

Neary, D., Snowden, J. S., Gustafson, L., Passant, U., Stuss, D., Black, S., et al. (1998). Frontotemporal lobar degeneration: A consensus on clinical diagnostic criteria. *Neurology, 51*(6), 1546–1554.

Neumann, M., Mackenzie, I. R., Cairns, N. J., Boyer, P. J., Markesbery, W. R., Smith, C. D., et al. (2007). TDP-43 in the ubiquitin pathology of frontotemporal dementia with VCP gene mutations. *Journal of Neuropathology & Experimental Neurology, 66*(2), 152–157.

Neumann, M., Sampathu, D. M., Kwong, L. K., Truax, A. C., Micsenyi, M. C., Chou, T. T., et al. (2006). Ubiquitinated TDP-43 in frontotemporal lobar degeneration and amyotrophic lateral sclerosis. *Science, 314*(5796), 130–133.

O'Keeffe, F. M., Murray, B., Coen, R. F., Dockree, P. M., Bellgrove, M. A., Garavan, H., et al. (2007). Loss of insight in frontotemporal dementia, corticobasal degeneration and progressive supranuclear palsy. *Brain, 130*(Pt 3), 753–764.

Olney, R. K., Murphy, J., Forshew, D., Garwood, E., Miller, B. L., Langmore, S., et al. (2005). The effects of executive and behavioral dysfunction on the course of ALS. *Neurology, 65*(11), 1774–1777.

Onari, K., & Spatz, H. (1926). Anatomische Beitrage zur Lehre von der Pickschen umschriebene-Grosshirnriden-Atrophie ('Picksche Krankheit'). *Zeitscrift fur die Gesamte Neurologie und Psychiatrie, 101,* 470–511.

Parkinson, N., Ince, P. G., Smith, M. O., Highley, R., Skibinski, G., Andersen, P. M., et al. (2006). ALS phenotypes with mutations in CHMP2B (charged multivesicular body protein 2B). *Neurology, 67*(6), 1074–1077.

Patterson, K., Lambon Ralph, M. A., Hodges, J. R., & McClelland, J. L. (2001). Deficits in irregular past-tense verb morphology associated with degraded semantic knowledge. *Neuropsychologia, 39*(7), 709–724.

Perry, R. J., & Hodges, J. R. (2000). Differentiating frontal and temporal variant frontotemporal dementia from Alzheimer's disease. *Neurology, 54*(12), 2277–2284.

Perry, R. J., & Miller, B. L. (2001). Behavior and treatment in frontotemporal dementia. *Neurology, 56*(11 Suppl 4), S46–S51.

Pick, A. (1892). Uber die Beziehungen der senilen Hirnantropie zur aphasie. *Prager Medizinishe Wochenscrift, 17,* 165–167.

Pickering-Brown, S. M., Baker, M., Gass, J., Boeve, B. F., Loy, C. T., Brooks, W. S., et al. (2006). Mutations in progranulin explain atypical phenotypes with variants in MAPT. *Brain, 129*(Pt 11), 3124–3126.

Pijnenburg, Y. A., Sampson, E. L., Harvey, R. J., Fox, N. C., & Rossor, M. N. (2003). Vulnerability to neuroleptic side effects in frontotemporal lobar degeneration. *International Journal of Geriatric Psychiatry*, *18*(1), 67–72.

Pollock, N. J., Mirra, S. S., Binder, L. I., Hansen, L. A., & Wood, J. G. (1986). Filamentous aggregates in Pick's disease, progressive supranuclear palsy, and Alzheimer's disease share antigenic determinants with microtubule-associated protein, tau. *Lancet*, *2*(8517), 1211.

Rabinovici, G. D., Furst, A. J., O'Neil, J. P., Racine, C. A., Mormino, E. C., Baker, S. L., et al. (2007). 11C-PIB PET imaging in Alzheimer disease and frontotemporal lobar degeneration. *Neurology*, *68*(15), 1205–1212.

Rademakers, R., Melquist, S., Cruts, M., Theuns, J., Del-Favero, J., Poorkaj, P., et al. (2005). High-density SNP haplotyping suggests altered regulation of tau gene expression in progressive supranuclear palsy. *Human Molecular Genetics*, *14*(21), 3281–3292.

Rahman, S., Robbins, T. W., Hodges, J. R., Mehta, M. A., Nestor, P. J., Clark, L., et al. (2006). Methylphenidate ('Ritalin') can ameliorate abnormal risk-taking behavior in the frontal variant of frontotemporal dementia. *Neuropsychopharmacology*, *31*(3), 651–658.

Rakowicz, W. P., & Hodges, J. R. (1998). Dementia and aphasia in motor neuron disease: An underrecognised association? *Journal of Neurology, Neurosurgery & Psychiatry*, *65*(6), 881–889.

Rankin, K. P., Baldwin, E., Pace-Savitsky, C., Kramer, J. H., & Miller, B. L. (2005). Self awareness and personality change in dementia. *Journal of Neurology, Neurosurgery & Psychiatry*, *76*(5), 632–639.

Rankin, K. P., Kramer, J. H., Mychack, P., & Miller, B. L. (2003). Double dissociation of social functioning in frontotemporal dementia. *Neurology*, *60*(2), 266–271.

Rankin, K. P., Rosen, H. J., Kramer, J. H., Schauer, G. F., Weiner, M. W., Schuff, N., et al. (2004). Right and left medial orbitofrontal volumes show an opposite relationship to agreeableness in FTD. *Dementia and Geriatric Cognitive Disorders*, *17*(4), 328–332.

Rascovsky, K., Salmon, D. P., Ho, G. J., Galasko, D., Peavy, G. M., Hansen, L. A., et al. (2002). Cognitive profiles differ in autopsy-confirmed frontotemporal dementia and AD. *Neurology*, *58*(12), 1801–1808.

Ratnavalli, E., Brayne, C., Dawson, K., & Hodges, J. R. (2002). The prevalence of frontotemporal dementia. *Neurology*, *58*(11), 1615–1621.

Reed, L. A., Grabowski, T. J., Schmidt, M. L., Morris, J. C., Goate, A., Solodkin, A., et al. (1997). Autosomal dominant dementia with widespread neurofibrillary tangles. *Annals of Neurology*, *42*(4), 564–572.

Reed, L. A., Wszolek, Z. K., & Hutton, M. (2001). Phenotypic correlations in FTDP-17. *Neurobiology of Aging*, *22*(1), 89–107.

Rinne, J. O., Laine, M., Kaasinen, V., Norvasuo-Heila, M. K., Nagren, K., & Helenius, H. (2002). Striatal dopamine transporter and extrapyramidal symptoms in frontotemporal dementia. *Neurology*, *58*(10), 1489–1493.

Rippon, G. A., Scarmeas, N., Gordon, P. H., Murphy, P. L., Albert, S. M., Mitsumoto, H., et al. (2006). An observational study of cognitive impairment in amyotrophic lateral sclerosis. *Archives of Neurology*, *63*(3), 345–352.

Roberson, E. D. (2006). Frontotemporal dementia. *Current Neurology and Neuroscience Reports*, *6*(6), 481–489.

Roberson, E. D., Hesse, J. H., Rose, K. D., Slama, H., Johnson, J. K., Yaffe, K., et al. (2005). Frontotemporal dementia progresses to death faster than Alzheimer disease. *Neurology*, *65*(5), 719–725.

Rosen, H. J., Allison, S. C., Schauer, G. F., Gorno-Tempini, M. L., Weiner, M. W., & Miller, B. L. (2005). Neuroanatomical correlates of behavioural disorders in dementia. *Brain*, *128*(11), 2612–2625.

Rosen, H. J., Gorno-Tempini, M. L., Goldman, W. P., Perry, R. J., Schuff, N., Weiner, M., et al. (2002). Patterns of brain atrophy in frontotemporal dementia and semantic dementia. *Neurology*, *58*, 198–208.

Rosen, H. J., Hartikainen, K. M., Jagust, W., Kramer, J. H., Reed, B. R., Cummings, J. L., et al. (2002). Utility of clinical criteria in differentiating frontotemporal lobar degeneration (FTLD) from AD. *Neurology*, *58*(11), 1608–1615.

Rosen, H. J., Lengenfelder, J., & Miller, B. (2000). Frontotemporal dementia. *Neurologic Clinics*, *18*(4), 979–992.

Rosen, H. J., Perry, R. J., Murphy, J., Kramer, J. H., Mychack, P., Schuff, N., et al. (2002). Emotion comprehension in the temporal variant of frontotemporal dementia. *Brain*, *125*(Pt 10), 2286–2295.

Rosso, S. M., Kamphorst, W., de Graaf, B., Willemsen, R., Ravid, R., Niermeijer, M. F., et al. (2001). Familial frontotemporal dementia with ubiquitin-positive inclusions is linked to chromosome 17q21-22. *Brain*, *124*(Pt 10), 1948–1957.

Rowe, C. C., Ng, S., Ackermann, U., Gong, S. J., Pike, K., Savage, G., et al. (2007). Imaging beta-amyloid burden in aging and dementia. *Neurology*, *68*(20), 1718–1725.

Royall, D. R., Mahurin, R. K., & Gray, K. F. (1992). Bedside assessment of executive cognitive impairment: the executive interview. *Journal of the American Geriatrics Society*, *40*(12), 1221–1226.

Schymick, J., Yang, Y., Andersen, P., Vonsattel, J., Greenway, M., Momeni, P., et al. (2007). Progranulin mutations and ALS or ALS-FTD phenotypes. *Journal of Neurology, Neurosurgery & Psychiatry*, *78*, 754–756.

Seeley, W. W., Bauer, A. M., Miller, B. L., Gorno-Tempini, M. L., Kramer, J. H., Weiner, M., et al. (2005). The natural history of temporal variant frontotemporal dementia. *Neurology*, *64*(8), 1384–1390.

Seeley, W. W., Carlin, D. A., Allman, J. M., Macedo, M. N., Bush, C., Miller, B. L., et al. (2006). Early frontotemporal dementia targets neurons unique to apes and humans. *Annals of Neurology*, *60*(6), 660–667.

Skibinski, G., Parkinson, N. J., Brown, J. M., Chakrabarti, L., Lloyd, S. L., Hummerich, H., et al. (2005). Mutations in the endosomal ESCRTIII-complex subunit CHMP2B in frontotemporal dementia. *Nature Genetics*, *37*(8), 806–808.

Snowden, J. S., Neary, D., & Mann, D. M. A. (1996a). Fronto-temporal dementia. In J. S. Snowden, D. Neary, & D. M. A. Mann (Eds.), *Fronto-temporal lobar degeneration* (pp. 1–41). New York: Churchill Livingstone.

Snowden, J. S., Neary, D., & Mann, D. M. A. (1996b). Semantic dementia. In J. S. Snowden, D. Neary & D. M. A. Mann (Eds.), *Fronto-temporal lobar degeneration* (pp. 91–114). New York: Churchill Livingstone.

Snowden, J. S., Neary, D., Mann, D. M., Goulding, P. J., & Testa, H. J. (1992). Progressive language disorder due to lobar atrophy. *Annals of Neurology*, *31*(2), 174–183.

Spina, S., Murrell, J. R., Huey, E. D., Wassermann, E. M., Pietrini, P., Baraibar, M. A., et al. (2007). Clinicopathologic features of frontotemporal dementia with progranulin sequence variation. *Neurology*, *68*(11), 820–827.

Stevens, M., van Duijn, C. M., Kamphorst, W., de Knijff, P., Heutink, P., van Gool, W. A., et al. (1998). Familial aggregation in frontotemporal dementia. *Neurology*, *50*(6), 1541–1545.

Swartz, J. R., Miller, B. L., Lesser, I. M., Booth, R., Darby, A., Wohl, M., et al. (1997). Behavioral phenomenology in Alzheimer's disease, frontotemporal dementia, and late-life depression: A retrospective analysis. *Journal of Geriatric Psychiatry and Neurology, 10*(2), 67–74.

Swartz, J. R., Miller, B. L., Lesser, I. M., & Darby, A. L. (1997). Frontotemporal dementia: Treatment response to serotonin selective reuptake inhibitors. *Journal of Clinical Psychiatry, 58*(5), 212–216.

Talerico, K. A., & Evans, L. K. (2001). Responding to safety issues in frontotemporal dementias. *Neurology, 56*(11 Suppl 4), S52–S55.

Trojanowski, J. Q., Duff, K., Fillit, H., Koroshetz, W., Kuret, J., Murphy, D., et al. (2008). New directions for frontotemporal dementia drug discovery. *Alzheimer's & Dementia, 4*(2), 89–93.

Vance, C., Al-Chalabi, A., Ruddy, D., Smith, B. N., Hu, X., Sreedharan, J., et al. (2006). Familial amyotrophic lateral sclerosis with frontotemporal dementia is linked to a locus on chromosome 9p13. 2–21. 3. *Brain, 129*(Pt 4), 868–876.

Watts, G. D., Wymer, J., Kovach, M. J., Mehta, S. G., Mumm, S., Darvish, D., et al. (2004). Inclusion body myopathy associated with Paget disease of bone and frontotemporal dementia is caused by mutant valosin-containing protein. *Nature Genetics, 36*(4), 377–381.

Williams, D. R., de Silva, R., Paviour, D. C., Pittman, A., Watt, H. C., Kilford, L., et al. (2005). Characteristics of two distinct clinical phenotypes in pathologically proven progressive supranuclear palsy: Richardson's syndrome and PSP-parkinsonism. *Brain, 128*(Pt 6), 1247–1258.

Wood, P. L., Etienne, P., Lal, S., Nair, N. P., Finlayson, M. H., Gauthier, S., et al. (1983). A post-mortem comparison of the cortical cholinergic system in Alzheimer's disease and Pick's disease. *Journal of the Neurological Sciences, 62*(1–3), 211–217.

Yancopoulou, D., Crowther, R. A., Chakrabarti, L., Gydesen, S., Brown, J. M., & Spillantini, M. G. (2003). Tau protein in frontotemporal dementia linked to chromosome 3 (FTD-3). *Journal of Neuropathology & Experimental Neurology, 62*(8), 878–882.

Yu, C. E., Bird, T. D., Bekris, L. M., Montine, T. J., Leverenz, J. B., Steinbart, E., et al. (2010). The spectrum of mutations in progranulin: A collaborative study screening 545 cases of neurodegeneration. *Arch Neurol, 67*(2), 161–170.

5

Other Dementias

Peter Morin

Introduction

One of the most common questions posed in the clinic is, "what is the difference between Alzheimer's and dementia?" Dementia results from encephalopathy, or cerebral dysfunction, and has many causes that produce numerous overlapping syndromes. A patient presenting with symptoms of memory dysfunction and one other sign of cognitive impairment that interferes with normal performance meets the DSM-IV cognitive criteria for the diagnosis of dementia. While these criteria establish the minimal symptoms required for the diagnosis of dementia, they do so without reference to the distinguishing features and underlying pathologies of the many dementia syndromes. The DSM criteria, for example, do not distinguish between dementias due to head injury and Parkinson's disease, though few clinicians would have difficulty resolving these conditions. Most dementias are syndromic clinical entities recognizable by a concurrence of symptoms and, in some cases, laboratory tests. While the majority of dementias afflicting the aged population are caused by Alzheimer's disease (~60%), dementia with Lewy bodies (~15%), and ischemic brain injury (~15%), a long list of etiologies accounts for the remaining cases of encephalopathy. Resolving these less common disorders from the highly prevalent dementias is an important contribution of the neurologist, neuropsychologist, geriatric and neuro-psychiatrist, geriatrician, and, indeed, many primary care physicians. This chapter will review the major clinical and pathological features of the less common dementia syndromes.

The Handbook of Alzheimer's Disease and Other Dementias, First Edition.
Edited by Andrew E. Budson, Neil W. Kowall.
© 2011 Blackwell Publishing Ltd. Published 2011 by Blackwell Publishing Ltd.

The term "dementia" is increasingly reserved for chronic, progressive, and irreversible syndromes of cognitive deterioration (Table 5.1), of which Alzheimer's disease is the prototype. There are relatively few causes of acute-onset degenerative dementia (Table 5.2). Aside from Creutzfeldt–Jakob disease, most cases of acute-onset cognitive impairment result from trauma, stroke, or one of several potentially reversible conditions. A careful history is important to resolve those cases of "acute dementia" that are actually acutely recognized chronic conditions. The term "reversible dementia" is often used to describe reversible encephalopathies (Table 5.3), but is somewhat misleading due to the connotations associated with the term "demen-

Table 5.1 Chronic degenerative dementias

Alzheimer's disease
Frontotemporal dementia
Lewy body dementia
Parkinson's disease
Progressive supranuclear palsy
Corticobasalganglionic degeneration
Multiple system atrophy
Multiple sclerosis
Huntington's disease
Amyotrophic lateral sclerosis
Mitochondrial disorders

Table 5.2 Acute dementias

Creutzfeldt–Jakob disease
Traumatic brain injury
Vascular events/syndromes
Neurotoxin exposure
Infectious disease
Reversible encephalopathies

Table 5.3 Reversible encephalopathies

Toxic/metabolic
Hypertensive
Thyroidism
B12 deficiency
Infectious
Interictal
Sleep disorders
Polypharmacy

tia." Irreversible, *non*progressive cognitive impairment defines the static encephalopathy, such as that associated with limited brain trauma, stroke, or neurotoxin exposure. In many cases, a reversible encephalopathy is superimposed on a chronic or static condition (acute-on-chronic encephalopathy). In practice, the distinction between dementia and reversible encephalopathy includes proof of reversibility by effective treatment of the underlying cause. In general, the aim of the clinician is to sort out the historical factors, cognitive deficits, and associated clinical features with the goal of identifying and treating the underlying cause(s) of encephalopathy. This method requires a good deal of clinical skill and a sound appreciation of the myriad causes and clinical features of encephalopathy.

Irreversible Encephalopathies

Progressive supranuclear palsy (PSP)

Progressive supranuclear palsy (Steele–Richardson–Olszewski syndrome) was classically defined as a parkinsonian disorder due to prominent extrapyramidal signs and symptoms. Like idiopathic Parkinson's disease, onset is in the sixth and seventh decade and the symptoms include parkinsonism, but key clinical features distinguish PSP in most cases. These include cognitive/behavioral symptoms, increased axial tone, early bulbar symptoms, and supranuclear gaze palsy. Unlike the Parkinson's disease patient, the PSP patient may exhibit early signs of frontal systems dysfunction, including impaired executive function and disinhibited behavior. Bulbar symptoms (including dysphagia) are common at presentation. The supranuclear gaze palsy typically affects vertical gaze disproportionately, and is a reliable sign when present. Unlike the Parkinson's patient, who exhibits a flexed axial posture, the PSP patient often exhibits an extended posture with pronounced axial rigidity. This posture, coupled with the vertical gaze palsy and cerebellar pathology, leads to multiple falls and lower extremity bruising (so called "PSP knees"). Appendicular rigidity is more likely to be bilateral in PSP than in idiopathic Parkinson's disease. No diagnostic tests are available, although mid-brain atrophy and subthalamic nuclear degeneration are sometimes apparent on magnetic resonance (MR) images. Importantly, the response to levodopa is nominal in the PSP patient. Once a suitable challenge of L-dopa (1200 mg/day) has been deemed a failure, further treatment with dopaminergic agents is unwarranted, and management is focused on management of psychiatric symptoms and comfort.

Corticobasalganglionic degeneration (CBD)

CBD is an unusual neurodegenerative disorder with onset in the sixth and seventh decades that may include parkinsonism. The clinical presentation can be difficult to distinguish from idiopathic Parkinson's disease, since early signs may include asymmetric limb dystonia (akinetic rigidity). Distinguishing motor features include involuntary limb movements (alien limb) and myoclonus. The former often includes involuntary choreoform, semi-purposeful movements that are dysphoric. Most patients will not report these movements unless asked specifically by the clinician. Parkinsonism per se may not appear early in the course, making a clinical diagnosis difficult. Importantly, neuropsychological deficits are more weighted toward ideomotor dyspraxia and global cognitive impairment than the dysexecutive syndromes seen in other parkinsonian conditions, although pronounced disinhibition may occur especially late in the course. The clinical course is highly variable, with most reports suggesting a slower progression than idiopathic Parkinson's disease and many anecdotal reports of rapid, inexorable progression. These are no diagnostic tests available, although mid-brain atrophy and subthalamic nuclear degeneration are sometimes apparent on MR images along with subcortical white matter changes that correlate with typical CBD neurodegeneration. Like PSP, the response to levodopa is nominal in the CBD patient. Once a suitable challenge of L-dopa (1200 mg/day) has been deemed a failure, further treatment with dopaminergic agents is unwarranted, and management is focused on management of psychiatric symptoms and comfort.

Primary progressive aphasia (PPA)

PPA is a clinical syndrome that has been associated with the early stages of several neurodegenerative diseases beginning, on average, early in the seventh decade of life. The language disturbance can take the form of fluent or non-fluent aphasia, or word comprehension difficulties. Many patients arrive in the clinic frustrated as a result of their complaints being repeatedly dismissed as "stress-related" symptoms, as dysphasia represents an atypical symptom of onset for neurodegenerative diseases. By (arbitrary) definition, PPA exists when gradually progressive (nonspecific) language impairment is present for two years in the absence of impairment of executive function, visuospatial skills, and memory. In this sense, the PPA patient is more of a "mild cognitive impairment" (MCI) than a dementia. Rates of progression to full-blown dementia of one type or another have not been established, and careful testing may reveal a memory deficit that is mild in comparison to the language disturbance. One might expect that rates of progression would be comparable to those for amnestic MCI, even if language cortex is statistically less likely to be the first symptomatic locus of cortical disease.

The clinical features of the PPA syndromes correlate with regional pathology in the dominant hemisphere, mostly due to frontotemporal dementia (FTD). With non-fluent dysphasia, the syndrome is most often associated with lobar degeneration involving the dominant frontal lobe. The neuropathology lacks distinctive histology in many cases, but tau-positive FTDs, CBD, Alzheimer's disease, and other neurodegenerative conditions have been reported in various proportions. Clinically, the language disturbance consists of agrammatical, effortful speech, and phonemic paraphasic errors. Patients often present with complaints of frustration, which compounds their language difficulties. With fluent aphasias, there is more uncertainty surrounding the nature of the cognitive impairment, since a posterior language (comprehension) deficit can be difficult to distinguish from a verbal memory disorder (semantic dementia). Unlike the non-fluent aphasias, the semantic dementias may be more often associated with ubiquitin-positive inclusions in the temporal lobe and progranulin mutations. Patients who pause due to word-finding difficulty (logopenic variant) may have a higher incidence of underlying Alzheimer's disease, but this has not been confirmed in autopsy series. On the whole, PPA is another good example of the clinical heterogeneity of neurodegenerative disorders. How the regional anatomical predilections of these disorders are related to intrinsic (genetic) and extrinsic (environmental, vascular, or historical factors) mechanisms is an important, but little researched feature of neurodegenerative disease.

Multiple system atrophy

In the current nosology of neurodegenerative disorders, the relationships between striatonigral degeneration, olivopontocerebellar degeneration, and Multiple system atrophy remain controversial. For the most part, these conditions cause disability on the basis of dysfunction of motor and autonomic systems in the central nervous system (CNS). Involvement of pyramidal, extrapyramidal, cerebellar, and autonomic systems is variable, resulting in diagnostic ambiguity. Neuropathologically, the conditions are linked to Lewy body dementia and Parkinson's disease by the presence of alpha-synuclein inclusions. In some cases, a subcortical dementia, characterized by cognitive slowing and inattention, has been ascribed to these conditions. But in general the cognitive concomitants of these neurodegenerative disorders remain poorly characterized. Development of biomarkers for these disorders is long overdue, and would allow for cleaner clinical parsing and genetic research.

Creutzfeldt–Jakob disease (CJD)

Spongiform encephalopathy is a rapidly progressive and uniformly fatal degenerative disease that is transmitted by abnormal prion protein. The course of the disease, from the onset of symptoms to death, rarely exceeds one year. Prominent early symptoms include ataxia, exaggerated startle response, myoclonus, delusions, and behavioral changes (sometimes bizarre). With progression, pyramidal and extrapyramidal symptoms emerge and progress rapidly, along with severe cognitive deterioration and sensory disturbances that are sometimes painful. Seizures, when they occur, can be intractable. Characteristic electroencephalographic changes (periodic sharp wave complexes) may evolve as the disease progresses, and these are the only reliable aid to clinical diagnosis. Magnetic resonance imaging (MRI) may demonstrate subcortical abnormalities (T2- and diffusion-weighted signal in the basal ganglia). Brain biopsy is generally considered to be unwarranted, since no treatments are available. The neuropathology of the spongiform encephalopathies reflects, as the name implies, the severely destructive consequences of aggregates of the prion protein in the brain. This phenomenon is related to abnormal folding and aggregation of the zeta isoform of the 14-3-3 protein. Misfolding is also associated with numerous known point mutations in the 14-3-3 protein gene. Such hereditary forms of CJD are to be distinguished from the more common sporadic variety, which is acquired from exposure to infectious (misfolded) forms of the prion protein in food, prosthetics, or contaminated medical equipment. The disease is rarely, if ever, communicated by contact with affected individuals during life, though careful attention to handling affected patients and their bodily secretions is prudent nevertheless.

CJD occurs in all human populations at a rate of approximately $1:10^6$, probably reflecting the incidence of disease-causing mutations in the prion gene. Clinical classification systems are based on initial symptoms of: (i) cortical blindness/visual hallucinations (Heidenhain variant); (ii) ataxia without visual symptoms (Oppenheimer–Brownell variant); (iii) dementia without visual symptoms or ataxia (cognitive variant); (iv) depression, mania, or mood lability (affective variant); or (v) cognitive symptoms plus ataxia without visual or affective symptoms (classic CJD). Cerebrospinal fluid (CSF) is positive for 14-3-3 protein in all variants and periodic sharp complexes are seen in all but the Oppenheimer–Brownell variant. The affective variant is associated with the youngest average age at onset (~60 years) and the longest survival time (just over one year). The cognitive variant is the most prevalent and about two-thirds of cases occur in male patients. Beginning in 1995, an outbreak of over 100 variant cases of unusually protracted duration has been observed in younger patients, mostly in Europe. Variant CJD (vCJD) is now recognized as a spongiform encephalopathy associated with the bovine prion protein, which causes bovine spongiform encephalopathy (BSE, mad cow disease, or scrapie). Since prion diseases can incubate asymptomatically for up to 40 years, additional bovine-derived cases are expected.

Gerstmann–Straussler–Scheinker disease (GSS)

Prion disease is also inheritable as an autosomal dominant mutation in the epsilon isoform of the 14-3-3 protein with an incidence of not more than $1:10^7$. The most common mutation is a prorin for leution substitution at position 102 (P102L). The clinical syndrome begins with ataxia, dysesthesia, and lower extremity hyporeflexia, often as early as the third decade of life. In some cases, the MRI brain shows high intensity lesions in cortex. A "mosaic" pattern of perfusion defects, seen on a SPECT scan may be a more reliable early marker.

Progressive multifocal leukoencephalopathy (PML)

PML results from recrudescence of the JC virus in the setting of immunodeficiency. Evidence suggests that JC virus DNA resides in a dormant state in glial cells in most, if not all, human beings. Immunosuppression resulting from oncologic, infectious, or iatrogenic causes can be permissive to active CNS infection. In recent years, PML has been found to be associated with some humanized monoclonal antibody therapies, such as natalizumab (Tysabri) and rituximab (Rituxan). Once started, progression is inexorable and uniformly fatal. Presenting symptoms are more often motor than cognitive, but cognitive impairment inevitably emerges as a prominent feature of disease progression. Diagnosis is made by history, neuroimaging, and, occasionally, brain biopsy. While no treatments are effective, progression in some cases reflects immunological reactivity to JC virus following recovery from the underlying immunosuppressive insult, as in the immune reconstitution inflammatory syndrome (IRIS). Inflammation in such cases may respond to corticosteroids, which provide some clinical benefit.

Normal pressure hydrocephalus (NPH)

Communicating hydrocephalus with normal CSF pressure results in symptoms associated with ventricular expansion. Some studies suggest that abnormal resorption of CSF is the primary cause, and results in incremental, but small, increases in CSF pressure that remain within the normal range. Deformation of periventricular structures account for the symptoms. Vulnerable white matter tracts include frontopontocerebellar fibers, descending motor fibers (including detrusor tracts), and limbic connections surrounding the lateral ventricle. The contribution of neuronal dysfunction from gray matter distortion is unknown. The radiological appearance is that of hydrocephalus with normal cerebral volume. In some cases, periventricular exudation of CSF is apparent as a rim of bright signal around the lateral ventricles on FLAIR images, but this finding is neither diagnostic nor required for the diagnosis. The symptoms of NPH are often described as a triad of gait disorder, mental status changes, and urinary incontinence. In practice, these symptoms are highly variable and the complete triad is rarely encountered. When severe, memory and executive function impairment may dominate the cognitive changes. The gait disorder can include ataxic, magnetic, or parkinsonian features. Since alterations of gait, cognition, and urological functions are ubiquitous with advancing age, mild cases are difficult to assess. Serial evaluations demonstrating progression that correlates with ventricular expansion may be the most reliable diagnostic approach. Reversal of symptoms following removal of CSF by lumbar puncture is sometimes possible but benefits are usually temporary. It is often said of NPH that the diagnosis and treatment are one in the same, namely placement of a ventriculoperitonial shunt. Even with careful case selection, confirmation of suspected NPH by successful shunt placement occurs only about 50% of the time. In the frail geriatric population, the prudent clinician will have a high threshold for neurosurgical referral.

Multiple sclerosis (MS)

Multiple sclerosis is characterized by immunologically mediated destruction of myelin within the brain and cervical spinal cord. The primary cause of this autoimmunity is unknown, but epidemiological and clinical data suggest both genetic and environmental components. MS occurs disproportionately in females between the ages of 15 and 50 and has been associated with virtually every known neurological symptom. In the clinic, far and away the most common cognitive complaints relate to memory and concentration. While sometimes difficult to separate from the extreme fatigue associated with MS and depression, these complaints are borne out by neuropsychological studies. The neuropsychological deficits found in MS do not always correlate with plaque distribution, and this may reflect the contributions of demyelination within gray matter and/or cerebral atrophy. The clinical and radiological features of MS render accurate diagnosis straightforward in most cases according to the McDonald criteria. A variety of disease-modifying treatments are currently available for the treatment of MS, and the interested reader is referred to the specialty literature for more information.

Other multifocal diseases

A variety of infectious, parainfectious, paraneoplastic, and autoimmune processes can cause diffuse or multifocal meningeoencephalitic conditions that are associated with cognitive dysfunction. The most common viral encephalitis is herpes simplex virus (HSV) 1 infection, which is associated with subacute onset of limbic encephalopathy that is often accompanied by seizures. The clinical diagnosis, on the basis of memory disturbance and/or behavioral changes accompanied by CSF pleocytosis and MRI abnormalities in limbic structures, can be confirmed by detection of viral DNA in CSF. HSV infections respond well to antiviral treatment, but damage caused prior to the initiation of treatment is often associated with substantial morbidity. Paraneoplastic limbic encephalitis typically produces a similar clinical picture with a more indolent course. A variety of parainfectious and paraneoplastic syndromes have been described and these are thought to reflect inappropriate immune system activity within the CNS based on antigens shared by specific brain regions and the corresponding infectious agent or neoplasm. Acute demyelinating encephalomyelitis (ADEM) may also produce a multifocal brain injury based on immune-mediated CNS attack provoked by an unidentified primary insult, though in most cases the primary insult is thought to be infectious in nature. When progressive or severe, corticosteroid treatment becomes necessary to arrest a destructive inflammatory process. The clinical picture depends entirely on the location of the pathology within the CNS and diagnosis is strictly clinical.

Neuro-rheumatological conditions may be associated with identical neurological syndromes. However, these conditions are often associated with systemic vasculitis, peculiar connective tissue symptoms, and sometimes diagnostic tests. Neuro-Behcet's disease may produce cognitive symptoms (memory and attention) in association with neutrophilic or lymphocytic CSF pleocytosis, subcortical lesions on MRI, or intracranial hypertension. These are accompanied by a constellation of dermatological (genital ulcers), ophthalmic (uveitis), and gastroenterological (oral aphtae) symptoms, and often additional signs of general rheumatological disease. Neuro-Sjogren's disease may produce similar cognitive impairment with associated lymphocytic pleocytosis, subcortical or periventricular lesions on MRI, or temporal lobe hypoperfusion on SPECT. These are always accompanied by sicca syndrome (dry eyes and mouth) and diagnosis can be made on the basis of evidence of parotid gland dysfunction, including biopsy, and the presence of anti-Ro antibodies on serology. Aggressive immunomodulatory treatment, including steroids and chemotherapy, is often warranted. CNS lupus erythematosis may produce similar cognitive impairment with associated seizures, gray matter lesions on MRI, and characteristic serologies. The diagnosis of CNS lupus, like neurosarcoidosis, is most often suggested by systemic disease.

Genetic conditions

This broad category includes conditions that develop with age or are not recognized during childhood.

Huntington's disease

First described in 1872 by Dr. George Huntington, Huntington's chorea results from the presence of greater than 40 trinucleotide (CAG) repeats in the coding region of the Huntingtin gene, located on the short arm of chromosome 4. Fewer than 30 trinucleotide repeats are found in the unaffected population; with increasing repeats, disease severity increases and age of onset decreases. The diagnosis can be made, and predicted, by genetic testing for trinucleotide repeat expansion, and a family history of neurological disease is most often present. The mechanism of neurodegeneration that is associated with trinucleotide repeats in the Huntington protein, and other trinucleotide repeat disorders, remains unknown. Profound striatal atrophy, especially of the caudate nucleus, is the hallmark of Huntington's disease, and is thought to be associated with the adventitious movements that invariably accompany a progressive syndrome of cognitive and motor deterioration. Involuntary movements are often incorporated into normal behaviors, giving rise to peculiar, sometimes bizarre distortions of speech and gait. Truncal choreoform movements, especially those involving the neck, are often striking. With progression, the excessive movements give way to a parkinsonian-like rigidity. Cognitive impairment evolves in concert with the motor manifestations, and is usually characterized by executive dysfunction, affective lability, and psychiatric symptoms. These symptoms correlate with the widespread neuronal loss and cerebral atrophy that is evident by neuropathological evaluation. Treatment is symptomatic, and neuroleptics are helpful in reducing the intensity of involuntary movements when severe, even if they exacerbate parkinsonian symptoms.

Leukodystrophy

Late-onset metachromatic leukodystrophy (MLD) results from deficiency of aryl-sulfatase A or its activator, saposin B. The majority of cases begin during infancy or childhood, but milder deficiencies can present as a late-life dementia. The major pathophysiological features include marked reduction of oligodendrocytes and inclusions containing sulfated lipids and sphingolipids within neurons and Schwann cells. The sulfated lipid inclusions turn from blue to red (hence metachromatic) when stained with toluidine blue and cresyl violet. Demyelination in the central and peripheral nervous systems, with sparing of cortical U-fibers, is detectable by MRI and electrophysiological studies. These findings are associated with progressive cognitive and motor impairment. Cognitive impairment is more likely to be the presenting feature in older patients, and some patients exhibit schizophreniform disorders as they progress to dementia. Seizures and blindness, in addition to progressive spastic quadriplegia, are common. The diagnosis is made by detection of deficient aryl-sulfatase activity and sequencing of the Aryl-sulfatase gene. Bone marrow transplant has shown some benefit when applied early in the course of this disorder.

Wilson's disease

Wilson's disease is a progressive motor and cognitive syndrome associated with abnormal copper metabolism. Onset is between age 5 and 40 in most cases, but insidious onset in the fifth or sixth decade has been described. About half of patients, especially the young, present with hepatitis with or without hemolytic anemia; older patients may present with neurological symptoms. These range from insidious psychiatric symptoms to cerebellar and extrapyramidal signs. Lytic lesions in the basal ganglia and cortical atrophy are apparent on MRI, and Kaiser–Fleischer rings, resulting from accumulation of copper in Descemet's membrane in the cornea, always accompany neurological involvement. Laboratory findings include reduced urinary and biliary excretion of copper and reduced serum ceruloplasmin, but these do not correlate well with disease progression. Over 300 mutations in the ATP7B gene, a P-type ATPase copper transporter, have been associated with Wilson's disease, but the precise role of the Cu-ATPase in copper homeostasis remains unknown. Pathological findings in the CNS include diffuse hyperplasia of Alzheimer's type II astrocytes and Opalski cells, but the relationship between these findings and copper metabolism are not clear. Chelation therapy with D-Penicillamine can be helpful.

Mitochondrial disorders

The syndrome of mitochondrial encephalopathy, lactic acidosis, and stroke (MELAS) may be associated with progressive cognitive impairment and dementia. The presence of stroke-like episodes and seizures, along with systemic symptoms, onset of symptoms prior to age 35, hearing loss, and myopathy symptoms, generally alert the physician that they are not dealing with a common neurodegenerative disease. The course is highly variable, and the majority of symptoms may be non-neurological. MELAS is not infrequently mistaken for systemic vasculitis. Calcifications in the basal ganglia (and cerebellum) and, when present, ragged red fibers on muscle biopsy, are useful clinical findings. Definitive diagnosis is made by sequencing of mitochondrial tRNA, and the most common mutation is tRNA^{LEU} A3243G. Treatment is symptomatic (e.g., for seizures). Dietary supplementation with co-enzyme Q, carnitine, and other metabolic co-enzymes may be useful.

Reversible Encephalopathy

Reversible cerebral dysfunction is an expected concomitant of numerous medical conditions, especially in the elderly. The higher cortical functions are dependent upon intact cortical circuitry and a stable biochemical milieu. Each of these is susceptible to even minor fluctuations, a fact that is easily appreciated by noting the profound cognitive and behavioral changes that can be induced by well-placed focal lesions or by drugs, toxins, and metabolic derangements. Metabolic challenges associated with organ dysfunction (e.g., renal, cardiopulmonary) generate a diffuse stress on neural circuitry. Under these circumstances, higher order cortical functions are disproportionately affected and primary sensory and motor function is relatively preserved. The reason for this susceptibility is unclear, but may be related to the relative complexity or sensitivity of neuronal networks associated with executive function. From a neuropsychological perspective, the primary deficit of a generalized encephalopathy is attentional. The first abnormalities detectable by bedside testing are tests of working memory and attention, such as spelling words or giving the months backwards. When moderately severe, it becomes impossible to reliably test other cortical functions. Once relieved of the ability to refocus the attention with agility, a patient may be unable to participate in tests of language, praxis, or even advanced motor skills. The encephalopathic patient can perceive the pieces of the environment, but cannot assemble a coherent whole from the parts, and hence does not appreciate context. This impairment generates anxiety, which is often manifested as hyper vigilance. When mild, the result is simply confusion. When severe, the result is delirium, which can be accompanied by abnormalities of sensory information processing (hallucinations) in addition to profound inattention with associated confusion and agitation. Attempts to evaluate cortical function under these circumstances often results in identification of numerous "abnormalities" related to disparate cortical regions and must be interpreted with caution. In many instances, the medical history and laboratory investigations are more informative than the details of cognitive dysfunction. Neuroimaging is generally indicated to exclude structural abnormalities (subdural hematoma, abscess, etc.) as focal deficits may be obscured by attentional deficits.

Cyanocobolamin (B12) deficiency

Deficiency of vitamin B12 (pernicious anemia) can cause irreversible neurological injury and may be found in up to 10% of aged individuals. However, dietary supplementation does not improve cognition in normal or cognitively impaired patients in the absence of symptomatic deficiency. Cognitive symptoms from B12 deficiency overlap with, but are distinguishable from, the most common deficits of early Alzheimer's disease. B12 deficient patients exhibit, on average, more impairment of attention, working memory, and executive function. Prominent psychiatric symptoms, including depression, hypomania, psychosis, and the Capgras syndrome have also been reported. Evidence for a relationship between serum B12 levels and episodic memory performance is scant. The severity of symptoms does not correlate well with the degree of deficiency. Depressed deep tendon reflexes, mild macrocytic anemia, and T2-hyperintense white matter lesions on MRI are useful clinical signs. In severe cases of "combined systems degeneration," demyelination may also be seen in the spinal cord posterior columns and is associated with both cognitive impairment and ataxia (due to proprioceptive loss). Diagnosis is made by measuring the levels of serum B12 and methylmalonic acid, the latter being elevated when B12 deficiency is severe. The treatment is parenteral or oral B12 replacement.

Thyroidism

Thyroid hormones regulate many genes involved in neuronal metabolism and synaptic plasticity. Thyroid dysfunction is associated with profound cognitive and motor symptoms that are often overlooked because of gradual emergence. Perhaps the most common of these is parkinsonism, which can occur in both the hypo- and hyper-thyroid state. Thyroid-associated parkinsonism can be asymmetric and include a tremor, making distinction from idiopathic Parkinson's disease difficult without laboratory testing. Thyroid-associated parkinsonism is, however, notably refractory to levodopa therapy and reversible with thyroid treatment. Autoimmune thyroiditis may produce fluctuating thyroid hormone levels and be associated with subacute encephalopathy, seizures, and stroke-like events (Hashimoto's encephalopathy). Neurological symptoms may be severe and do not correlate with the magnitude (or direction) of thyroid dysfunction. Some evidence suggests that anti-thyroid antibodies may be associated with an underlying vasculitis and positron emission tomography shows reversible multifocal cerebral hypometabolism. The diagnosis is generally made by detecting anti-thyroid antibodies in serum and acute symptoms respond to steroids in most cases.

The cognitive symptoms of thyroid deficiency include deficits in working memory and executive function, in addition to affective symptoms. The symptoms of thyroidism thus overlap with the symptoms of the major dementias, making thyroid screening an important component of a dementia workup. That being said, the number of dementia cases that are attributable to thyroidism are small in most series. Like pseudodementia related to depression, it is often unclear whether the presenting cognitive symptoms are related to thyroidism alone or to a progressive cognitive impairment that is secondarily complicated by thyroid disease. When isolated, the cognitive deficits of hypothyroidism can resolve slowly over the course of several months or longer, during which time the patient (and clinician) remain nervous regarding the correct diagnosis. Patients undergoing thyroid replacement should be carefully monitored for steady improvement. If no improvement is seen within 4–6 months, additional dementia workup is advisable.

Metabolic encephalopathy

There is considerable variation in the cognitive impairment associated with the metabolic encephalopathies. Most are characterized by impairment of attention and executive functions. The degree of confusion, hypervigilance, agitation, and other symptoms may vary from hour to hour such that caregivers may report very different impressions over time. Disruption of circadian rhythm is common. Most patients exhibit more intense symptoms late in the day, or at night, when they are fatigued and the sensorium is relatively deprived. Clinical assessment includes review of the history, careful clinical examination to identify focal brain injury and defined clinical syndromes, and laboratory testing. The uremic patient is more likely to have pronounced myoclonus; the hepatic patient may be jaundiced; the hypoxic patient may be in respiratory distress. Reviews of the patient's drug use (including medications), social and psychiatric history, and family medical history are necessary to identify idiosyncratic conditions. Neuroimaging is indicated in most patients because of the severity of neurological symptoms and signs and the difficulty of cognitive testing in the inattentive patient. A full metabolic workup will generally identify the source of the problem. Treatment consists of correcting the underlying disorder, if possible. Psychotropic medications often complicate the course of encephalopathy, but are sometimes necessary for patient and staff safety.

Toxic encephalopathy

Confusional states arising from infectious disease are ubiquitous and follow the same general course outlined above for metabolic derangements. The symptoms resolve when the underlying infection is successfully treated. In elderly and especially demented patients, complete resolution can take several days, or even weeks or months after the infection is treated. If a source of infection is readily identifiable, then neuroimaging is not necessary unless pronounced focal signs are present. Problems arise when the usual sources of infection are not present, despite all of the usual signs of infectious disease. In such cases, a lumbar puncture is indicated to evaluate primary CNS infection.

Hypertensive encephalopathy (HTE)

Acute elevation of diastolic blood pressure may produce cerebral edema in the posterior circulation and associated acute confusional state. Balint's syndrome is not rare in HTE, although a wide variety of visual processing deficits may be observed including cortical blindness. The retina is also affected, which complicates the identification of cortical signs. Agitation and seizures are common and many patients report headaches prior to the onset of cerebral symptoms. The diagnosis of HTE depends on the presence of retinal hemorrhages, elevated blood pressure (which may not be severe), and cortical edema on MRI. When the encephalopathy is mild-moderate, the edema is limited to the posterior circulation and is completely reversible. Management includes restoration of normal blood pressure and treatment of seizures if necessary. Severe cases may be associated with significant cerebral and renal injury.

Polypharmacy

It is not unusual to find elderly patients taking more than a dozen medications. Even with sophisticated information technologies that screen for drug–drug interactions, encephalopathy resulting from excessive medication can occur. This is especially true for psychotropic medications: even if each and every medication is useful, the sum can be more than the parts in terms of cognitive side effects. Prudent tapering and simplification of medical regimens can be accomplished on an outpatient basis, except in extreme circumstances.

Interictal

An uncommon, but treatable cause of cognitive dysfunction is that associated with interictal encephalopathy. Every dementia workup should include queries designed to expose the erratic nature of cognitive impairment (primarily memory loss) that is associated with interictal cerebral dysfunction. In elderly patients, the most common causes of new onset seizures are stroke and cortical diseases (such as Alzheimer's disease). When occult seizures are identified, the clinician's work thus includes both a stroke workup and follow-up cognitive testing to ensure that the problem has been solved with treatment.

Infectious disease

Subacute onset of infectious signs and encephalopathy should raise concern for meningitis. Chronic meningititides are more difficult to diagnose, and can masquerade as early dementia. A history of gastrointestinal symptoms and neuro-ophthalmic signs (ophthalmoplegia) should prompt consideration of Whipple's disease, which is confirmed by identification of *Tropheryma whippelii* in CSF by polymerase chain reaction (PCR). Herpetic encephalitis often presents with subacute behavioral changes (sometimes bizarre) accompanied by fever, with or without seizures. A history of HIV infection should alert the clinician to the high risk of opportunistic infection and primary HIV encephalitis. Aggressive evaluation of CSF is indicated in all patients with unexplained encephalopathy and systemic signs of infectious disease. Many authorities recommend routine screening for tertiary syphilis in the workup of dementia, but the American Academy of Neurology has dropped this recommendation.

Sleep disorders

Sleep deprivation as a common cause of cognitive dysfunction in middle-aged and elderly persons has been increasingly recognized over the past several years. The typical patient, a slightly heavy, dysthymic patient brought to clinic by their partner, will not spontaneously report a history of sleep disruption in the memory clinic; the history must be actively extracted. A formal sleep study should be a routine component of cognitive evaluation of persons under 60 years of age who are at risk on the basis of body habitus. Obstructive sleep apnea and restless leg syndrome are the most common culprits, but more complex parasomnias are not rare in this population and may be associated with Parkinson's disease or dementia with Lewy bodies. Even in the absence of underlying neurodegenerative disease, many patients do not fully recover from a cognitive standpoint for months after the sleep disorder is corrected.

Part II

Pathogenesis and Disease Mechanisms

6

Genetic Risk Factors for Dementia

Paul Hollingworth and Julie Williams

Introduction

A variety of conditions result in dementia. Alzheimer's disease (AD) is the most common form of dementia (Nussbaum & Ellis, 2003). It is estimated that 15 million individuals worldwide have AD (Fratiglioni et al., 1999), with 4.5 million individuals with AD in the United States alone (Hebert et al., 2003). Hebert and colleagues (2003) estimated that, baring a cure, AD in the United States will increase almost threefold by 2050, to over 13 million people. Numerous genes and hundreds of gene variants that affect the risk of developing dementia have been identified and the biological systems they implicate are now beginning to be understood. But more genes remain to be found, especially for the common dementias, which have complex genetic patterns of susceptibility involving many genes. This chapter will focus on the genetics of Alzheimer's disease, vascular dementia, and frontotemporal dementia.

Alzheimer's Disease

Historically, AD genetics has been split into two broad categories. First, rare autosomal dominant forms of the disease, typically of early onset (<65 years); and second, the more common form of late-onset AD. Much of the initial work on the molecular genetics of AD stemmed from studies of early-onset AD families. Early-onset AD occurs primarily in rare families, in which the disease is usually transmitted in an autosomal dominant fashion and clinical symptoms usually present before

The Handbook of Alzheimer's Disease and Other Dementias, First Edition.
Edited by Andrew E. Budson, Neil W. Kowall.

65 years of age. Rare mutations in three genes (e.g., APP, PSEN1, and PSEN2) have been shown to cause early-onset AD, and will be discussed later in this chapter. Autosomal dominant early-onset AD only accounts for around 13% of early-onset AD and less than 0.01% of all AD (Campion et al., 1999). The majority of AD cases usually occur after 65 years of age (late-onset Alzheimer's disease (LOAD)). Although LOAD does not typically show a Mendelian pattern of inheritance, epidemiological studies have shown that it still has a strong genetic component.

Early-onset Alzheimer's disease

Initial attempts to understand the genetic underpinnings of AD began in the early 1980s and focused on the familial, autosomal dominant, fully penetrant forms of the disease, which typically occur before the age of 65 years. The identification of mutations in three genes that cause early-onset AD has already had a major impact on the understanding of the pathogenesis of AD.

The amyloid precursor gene and Alzheimer's disease

The search for genes responsible for AD began when the APP gene was cloned and localized to the long arm of chromosome 21 (for a review of early APP linkage and localization studies see Hardy et al., 1989). Initially, it was believed that familial AD was a homogeneous disorder, consequently early reports of linkage to chromosome 21 were contradictory. However, the confusion was resolved when it became apparent that only a proportion of early-onset AD families showed linkage to the APP locus.

Interest in the APP gene heightened when mutations within exon 17 of the gene were shown to cause hereditary cerebral hemorrhage with amyloidosis, Dutch type (HCHWA-D) (discussed later in this chapter), which together with exon 16 encode the beta amyloid (Aβ) peptide (Levy et al., 1990; Van Broeckhoven et al., 1990) – the major component of beta amyloid in AD. Consequently exon 17 was sequenced in members of a large British pedigree with familial AD that showed clear linkage to the APP locus. Affected members were shown to carry a C to T transition causing a valine to isoleucine substitution at amino acid 717 (V717I) (Goate et al., 1991). Subsequently, over 20 missense mutations in APP have been definitively associated with AD. The V717I mutation has been identified in early-onset AD families around the world, whereas other mutations have typically only been reported in single AD pedigrees (for details of pathogenic APP mutations see: www.ncbi.nlm.nih.gov/entrez/dispomim.cgi?id=104760 and www.molgen.ua.ac.be/ADMutations).

All known mutations in APP lie within, or close to β- or γ-secretase cleavage sites and have been shown in cell culture studies and transgenic mice to enhance cleavage at these sites (Lendon et al., 1997), which leads to an increased production of Aβ and Aβ42, the most amyloidogenic form of the peptide (Citron et al., 1992; Suzuki et al., 1994). Amyloid plaques, one of the pathological hallmarks of AD, consist of extracellular deposits of Aβ peptide. The role of Aβ in the pathogenesis of AD is also discussed in Chapters 1 and 8 of this book.

More recently, focus has shifted toward elucidation of the role of APP in the more common late-onset form of the disease. Linkage studies of LOAD have implicated a region on chromosome 21, containing the APP gene, in the development of AD among the very elderly (Olson et al., 2001). Three mutations, with functional impact on gene transcription have been associated with AD patients from the Netherlands and Belgium, with an age of disease onset ≤70 years of age (−369C/G, −479C/T, −534G/A) (Theuns et al., 2006). A subsequent study failed to replicate the association with two of these mutations (−479C/T, −534G/A), but did find evidence of association with two further variants in the APP gene promoter region (−1023T/C and −3102G/C) (Guyant-Marechal et al., 2007). However, others have generally failed to find evidence linking common variants in APP with LOAD. Nowotny and colleagues (2007) performed a dense screen of the APP gene in large case-control series of 738 AD cases and 657 healthy controls, reporting that AD was not associated with any of the single nucleotide polymorphisms (SNPs), or common haplotypes in APP. Similarly, others have reported negative association with SNPs in the promoter region of APP (Athan et al., 2002; Theuns et al., 2000).

Presenilin genes and Alzheimer's disease
Despite the identification of several pathogenic mutations in APP, it soon became clear that APP mutations accounted for a very small proportion of early-onset AD. The majority of "non-chromosome 21" linked familial early-onset AD families were shown to be linked to a locus on chromosome 14q and positional cloning led to the identification and isolation of the presenilin 1 (PSEN1) gene (Sherrington et al., 1995). Similarly, evidence for a locus on chromosome 1q was reported in several kindreds of German-Russian origin with multiple cases of autosomal dominant early-onset AD (Levy-Lahad, Lahad et al., 1995). Subsequently, the presenilin 2 gene (PSEN2) was identified based mainly on its high degree of homology to PSEN1 (Levy-Lahad, Wasco et al., 1995; Rogaeva et al., 1995). Since then over 150 pathogenic mutations have been identified in PSEN1, and a further nine have been reported in PSEN2 (see www.molgen.ua.ac.be/ADMutations).

Mutations in the presenilin genes are predominantly located in highly conserved transmembrane domains and are presumed to distort the precise conformation of the molecule within the membrane. The effect of these mutations again seems to be the enhanced production of Aβ42 (Borchelt et al., 1996; Wolfe et al., 1999), which appears to lead to AD. It is noteworthy that around one-third of dominantly inherited AD cases are not associated with known mutations in either the APP or PSEN genes, which implies the existence of further disease loci (Campion et al., 1999).

Furthermore, mutations in the PSEN genes do not appear to influence susceptibility to LOAD. In 1996 Wragg and colleagues reported that one SNP in intron 8 of PSEN1 was associated with the more common, late-onset form of AD, finding that it accounted for about half as much risk for LOAD as the APOE ε4 allele (Wragg et al., 1996). Subsequently, PSEN1 has been the focus of intense scrutiny, with studies performed in a variety of ethnic groups reporting widely contradictory findings. Meta-analysis of the available published data, including 5410 AD cases and 5179 controls, suggests that the intron 8 SNP is weakly, but significantly, associated with AD (OR ~1.07, p −0.02) (Bertram et al., 2007), which implies PSEN1 is unlikely to play a major role in contributing to the common form of AD. Both early- and late-onset forms of the disease are characterized by the pathological accumulation of Aβ within the brain. It is therefore interesting that the known genetic mutations in APP, PSEN1, and PSEN2, which cause early-onset AD, do not appear to effect susceptibility to the more common late-onset form of the disease. This suggests that early- and late-onset forms of AD are etiologically heterogeneous.

Late-onset Alzheimer's disease

Genetic epidemiology

Twin studies in Alzheimer's disease Twin studies have been performed to determine the genetic heritability of late-onset AD. The majority of studies has been of Scandinavian origin and has arisen from well-established population-based twin registers. Raiha and colleagues (1996) performed a population-based study using Finnish twins. Among 13,888 pairs, they found that the pairwise concordance among monozygotic (MZ) twins was 31% compared to 9% among dizygotic (DZ) pairs. In a Norwegian study, data from 23,000 cognitively impaired individuals were matched to 26,000 individuals on the Norwegian Twin Register (Bergem et al., 1997). The concordance rates for AD were 87% and 46% between MZ and DZ twins, respectively, corresponding to a heritability estimate of around 58%.

Perhaps the most comprehensive studies were based upon the well-established Swedish twin registry. The Swedish Study of Dementia in Twins reported data from twins who were reared apart, and a similar number of pairs who were reared together (Gatz et al., 1997). The concordance rate for MZ twins for AD was 67% compared to 22% among DZ twins, resulting in a heritability estimate of between 75% and 85%. Gatz and colleagues have recently extended this work, reporting analyses from the HARMONY study (Gatz et al., 2006). They incorporated data from over 4000 twin pairs, aged over 65, who had completed at least basic telephone cognitive screening. The heritability of AD was estimated to be between 58% and 79%. They also reported that AD concordance was higher in female twins compared to male twins; however, this is likely to reflect increased longevity among females.

A number of other twin studies have been performed (Breitner et al., 1995; Nee et al., 1987), but issues relating to sample size, incomplete ascertainment, low sample age, and inaccurate case detection make it difficult to draw conclusions from their data. Perhaps the best evidence comes from the large population-based studies of Scandinavian origin (Bergem et al., 1997; Gatz et al., 1997; Gatz et al., 2006; Raiha et al., 1996), which generally support a heritability estimate of between 60% and 80%.

Family studies in AD   In addition to twin research, a number of studies have attempted to elucidate the proportion of AD risk attributable to genetic factors by assessing the familial aggregation of the disease. However, before further consideration it is important to acknowledge that such studies have a number of complications. First, they may be susceptible to issues of incomplete case ascertainment and issues surrounding diagnosis, particularly for more distant family members. Also, they cannot differentiate between shared environment and genetic effects as increased familial risk could be attributable to environmental conditions common to members of the same family. Despite these limitations, family studies do have the particular advantage that a greater proportion of the population can be ascertained, providing more powerful samples for hypothesis testing.

The evidence to date is largely consistent, suggesting a combination of environmental and genetic risk factors increase susceptibility to late-onset AD. Early family studies noted increase rates of dementia among first-degree relatives of AD probands (Heston et al., 1981; Larsson et al., 1963; Sjogren et al., 1952). Since then, studies of familial clustering of AD have largely relied on standardized clinical and neuropathological criteria for AD, such as the National Institute of Neurological and Communicative Disorders and Stroke – Alzheimer's Disease and Related Disorders Association (NINCDS-ADRDA) criteria for probable AD (McKhann et al., 1984). In general, the risk to first-degree relatives of AD probands has been found to be between 32% and 49%, approximately two to four times the risk attributable to first-degree relatives of controls (Breitner et al., 1988; Canadian Study of Health and Aging 1994; Farrer et al., 1989; Fratiglioni et al., 1993; Heston et al., 1981; Martin et al., 1988; Zubenko et al., 1988). In addition to investigating the risk among family members of AD probands and unaffected control subjects, others have investigated the epidemiology of dementia in genetically isolated populations. For example, Sleegers and colleagues (2004) reported that AD patients from a genetically isolated Dutch population were more closely related than healthy individuals.

The role of genetic factors in AD appears to vary across the life span, with a number of studies reporting that the genetic risk to first-degree relatives decreases with increasing onset ages among AD probands (Huff et al., 1988; Li et al., 1995; Silverman et al., 2003; Silverman et al., 2005; van Duijn et al., 1991; Wu et al., 1998). Silverman and colleagues (2005) performed the largest investigation of this hypothesis reported to date, assessing over 12,000 first-degree relatives of AD probands and elderly probands without dementia. They found that the risk to relatives of those with AD increased with age, until around 85–90 years of age, but was decreased among relatives of AD probands with later ages of disease onset.

Apolipoprotein E and late-onset AD
Apolipoprotein E (ApoE) is a protein with roles in lipid metabolism and tissue repair. ApoE has three major isoforms (ApoE2, ApoE3, and ApoE4), which differ in

amino acid sequence at two sites, codon 112 and 158. These isoforms are coded for by three alleles of the apolipoprotein gene (APOE): ε2, ε3, and ε4. In most populations the ε3 allele is the most frequent, while ε4 occurs slightly more often than ε2 (Hendrie, 1998). To date, APOE located on chromosome 19 is the only widely acknowledged susceptibility gene for late-onset AD. The association was first reported in a series of publications in 1993. A group, headed by Alan Roses at Duke University, North Carolina, noted that the frequency in AD patients, at 0.3–0.5, was greater than the frequency in age-matched population controls (Strittmatter et al., 1993). Similar findings were reported by Saunders and colleagues (1993) who found an association between the APOE ε4 allele and AD using a small prospective series of sporadic AD cases and spouse controls, which then replicated in a sample of autopsy-confirmed cases. Authors from the same group reported that the APOE ε4 allele was associated with both late-onset familial and sporadic forms of AD, increasing risk of disease from 20% to 90% and reducing the age at onset from 94 to 68 years with increasing ε4 alleles (Corder et al., 1993). They concluded that homozygosity for the APOE ε4 allele was almost sufficient to cause AD by 80 years of age. Around the same time, the same group also identified an association with the ε4 allele and increased Aβ deposition in senile plaques, the major neuropathological feature of AD (Schmechel et al., 1993). Taken together, these findings provided strong evidence that the APOE gene was implicated in the development of late-onset AD. Since then, hundreds of studies, using divergent populations have demonstrated an association between AD and the pathogenic ε4 allele. The findings have been remarkably consistent, with only a few failing to find an association, largely in selective populations.

The largest study of APOE and AD incorporated data from 43 studies, providing information from 5930 AD cases and 8607 controls without dementia (Farrer et al., 1997). A dose-dependent increase in risk of AD with increasing ε4 alleles was reported (odds ratios (OR) compared to ε3 homozygotes: 2.6, 3.2, and 14.9 in those with ε2/ε4 or ε3/ε4, and ε4/ε4 genotype, respectively). The effect was weaker among African Americans and Hispanics, and stronger in Japanese subjects. A summary of these results can be seen in Table 6.1. These findings have also been confirmed in a more recent meta-analysis, using largely overlapping data taken from the AlzGene database (Bertram et al., 2007). Despite being nearly as common as the ε4 allele in the general population, there are relatively few AD patients studied with the APOE ε2 allele (Raber et al., 2004), which has led some to conclude that it is protective against the development of dementia (Farrer et al., 1997; Talbot et al., 1994).

The strength of the relationship varies among epidemiological studies, however, the APOE ε4 allele is generally found to be neither necessary nor sufficient to cause AD. For example, in the Framingham study cohort, comprising 1030 elderly individuals, Myers and colleagues (1996) reported that 45% of ε4 homozygotes had not developed dementia by the age of 80. In their cohort about 50% of AD was not attributable to APOE genotype. Likewise, in a further population-based study, Evans and colleagues (1997) found that APOE only accounted for a small proportion of the incidence of AD. Indeed, they reported that if the allele did not exist or had no

Table 6.1 Odds ratios of APOE genotypes in four populations

Genoty	Odds Ratio (95% Confidence Interval)			
	Caucasian	African-Americans	Hispanic	Japanese
ε3/ε3*	–	–	–	–
ε2/ε2	0.6 (0.2–2.0)	2.4 (0.3–22.7)	2.6 (0.2–33.3)	1.1 (0.1–17.2)
ε2/ε3	0.6 (0.5–0.8)	0.6 (0.4–1.7)	0.6 (0.3–1.3)	0.9 (0.4–2.5)
ε2/ε4	2.6 (1.6–4.0)	1.8 (0.4–8.1)	3.2 (0.9–11.6)	2.4 (0.4–15.4)
ε3/ε4	3.2 (2.8–3.8)	1.1 (0.7–1.8)	2.2 (1.3–3.4)	5.6 (3.9–8)
ε4/ε4	14.9 (10.8–20.6)	5.7 (2.3–14.1)	2.2 (0.7–6.7)	33.1 (13.6–80.5)

*ε3/ε3 = reference group
Source: adapted from Farrer, L. A., Cupples L. A., et al. (1997). Effects of age, sex, and ethnicity on the association between apolipoprotein E genotype and Alzheimer disease. A meta-analysis. APOE and Alzheimer Disease Meta Analysis Consortium. *Journal of the American Medical Association, 278*(16), 1349–1356

effect on disease risk, the incidence would be reduced by only 13.7%. In general, estimates of population risk attributable to APOE are between 20% to 57% (Nalbantoglu et al., 1994; Seshadri et al., 1995; Slooter et al., 1998).

The APOE effect has been shown to decrease with increasing age (Corder et al., 1996; Roses, 1998). Numerous studies have reported a lower age at onset among those with increasing numbers of APOE ε4 alleles in both sporadic (Corder et al., 1993; Lucotte et al., 1994) and familial AD (Levy-Lahad, Lahad et al., 1995). This has led some to conclude that APOE does not influence whether subjects will develop AD, but rather *when* susceptible individuals will develop the disease. This hypothesis has been investigated in detail in the Cache County study using data from 3308 elderly individuals (Khachaturian et al., 2004). APOE genotype had no meaningful difference in 100-year lifetime incidence of AD; however, the ε4 allele was associated with a substantial acceleration of AD onset, particularly among homozygotes. Others have reported contradictory findings, for example, Skoog and colleagues (1998) reported the APOE ε4 allele remained predictive of AD in a case-control sample that consisted solely of individuals aged over 85 years of age.

In addition to the ε2 and ε4 alleles, polymorphisms in the APOE promoter region have been implicated in disease susceptibility, however, the results of these associations have so far been inconclusive (Bullido et al., 1998; Lambert et al., 2002; Parker et al., 2005; Song et al., 1998; Wang et al., 2000). It is generally assumed that the association between the APOE locus and AD is explained almost entirely by APOE ε4. However, it remains possible that other polymorphisms and regulatory elements within the linkage disequilibrium (LD) region surrounding APOE may influence disease expression. Genetic and cell biology data could support the hypothesis that multiple loci within the LD block including the APOE gene influence mitochondrial function and consequently AD pathogenesis (Roses et al., 2007). TOMM40, which is in LD with APOE, has shown strong evidence of association with AD (Grupe et al., 2007). TOMM40 forms mitochondrial import channels that accumulate APP and result in mitochondrial dysfunction, potentially triggering the caspase apoptotic cascade (Devi et al., 2006). More detailed speculation on the specific function of APOE is beyond the scope of this chapter, interested readers should see Saunders et al. (2000) or Huang (2006) for detailed reviews.

Identifying other genes for late-onset AD

Linkage studies of AD Despite the robust association between APOE and AD, the ε4 allele is neither necessary nor sufficient to cause the disease. Several studies have indicated that a number of other genes are implicated in the development of late-onset AD (Daw et al., 2000; Jarvik et al., 1996; Martinez et al., 1998; Steffens et al., 2000). Tremendous effort has been put into identifying these genes. Linkage analysis offered a means of identifying regions of the genome, which were likely to contain disease loci. A number of chromosomal regions have been identified which are likely to harbor susceptibility genes for LOAD, with the strongest and most consistent evidence found on chromosomes 9 (Blacker et al., 2003; Curtis et al., 2001; Farrer et al., 2003; Hamshere et al., 2007; Kehoe et al., 1999; Myers et al., 2002; Olson et al., 2002; Pericak-Vance et al., 2000; Scott et al., 2003) and 10 (Blacker et al., 2003; Curtis et al., 2001; Farrer et al., 2003; Hamshere et al., 2007; Kehoe et al., 1999; Li et al., 2002; Myers et al., 2002; Olson et al., 2002).

Linkage to chromosome 10q was first reported in a two-stage genome scan involving 429 affected sibling pairs (ASPs) with probable or definite AD (Kehoe et al., 1999; Myers et al., 2000). Evidence for linkage to this region has since been reported in studies of various AD phenotypes, including familial AD (Bertram et al., 2000; Blacker et al., 2003; Lee et al., 2004); age at disease onset (Li et al., 2002); plasma amyloid β42 peptide (Ertekin-Taner et al., 2000); and AD in genetically isolated populations (Farrer et al., 2003). The linked regions in these studies span over 50 centiMorgan (cM) and are largely split between the 10q21 region and a more distal locus around 10q25. Methodological or sampling differences across studies could be responsible for discrepant localization of the two linkage peaks, which could be caused by the same gene, indeed varying results from linkage analyses were similarly reported on chromosome 19 prior to the identification of APOE as a risk factor for AD (Liu et al., 1996). In an attempt to assess the strength of the evidence for linkage and to obtain the best indication of the location of susceptibility genes, Hamshere and colleagues (2007) have recently amalgamated three large samples, from published genome screens (Bassett et al., 2002; Blacker et al., 2003; Kehoe et al., 1999; Myers et al., 2002), providing the largest linkage study of late-onset AD to date. Their study included data from 635 markers (average marker spacing: 6 cM) on 723 affected relative pairs, with increased marker density on chromosome 10 (average marker spacing: 4 cM). Significant evidence for a susceptibility locus was identified on chromosome 10q21.2, with the most likely location of a risk gene at 78 cM. The study also showed strong evidence that this locus operates in a number of populations. In addition, the study by Hamshere and colleagues did not find evidence for a second locus on chromosome 10q25-26 as implied elsewhere (Blacker et al., 2003; Lee et al., 2004; Li et al., 2002). However, it should be noted that this study cannot exclude a second chromosome 10q locus, as differentiating between one or two loci in close proximity would require larger samples with higher genetic information content and resolution (e.g., using SNP genotypes). Therefore, it remains possible that two or more genes on chromosome 10 may influence disease susceptibility and/or age at disease onset.

Linkage to chromosome 9 was first reported by Pericak-Vance and colleagues (2000). They found a high multipoint LOD score (i.e., the likeliness of two gene loci being near each other) of 4.3 around 9p22.1 when restricting their analysis to sibling pairs with autopsy-confirmed AD. They later extended this work by performing ordered subsets linkage analysis, reporting that linkage to this region is strongest in families with a minimum age of onset between 60–75 years (Scott et al., 2003). Empirical support for this region has been mixed. Two studies have reported some evidence for a gene (or genes) in this region (Farrer et al., 2003; Kehoe et al., 1999; Myers et al., 2000), while others have not (Blacker et al., 2003; Lee et al., 2004; Sillen et al., 2006). In a combined analyses reported by Hamshere and colleagues, genome-wide suggestive linkage was reported on chromosome 9q22.33 (LOD 2.5) and a separate independent peak was identified on 9q21.3 (LOD 1.2). Linkage evidence at the 9q22.33 was found exclusively in pedigrees ascertained in the United States as part of the National Institute of Mental Health's (NIMH) AD genetics initiative, whereas evidence from the smaller linkage signal around 9q21.3 was derived from pedigrees ascertained by the NIMH, National Institute on Aging, and in the United Kingdom.

A number of authors have reanalyzed the available genetic data including information about pertinent disease characteristics as covariates. Most notably, analyses have included data regarding age at disease onset. It is hoped that if genetic mechanisms that influence age at disease onset can be identified, it may be possible to modify their processes to prevent or delay disease onset, which is of particular importance for late-onset disorders such as AD. Interestingly, Olson and colleagues (2001) reported linkage to a region close to the APP gene on chromosome 21 which may be implicated in AD among groups of cases with very late age of onset (>80 years). Support for this finding has also been reported in an overlapping sample of affected sibling pairs with late-onset AD (Holmans et al., 2005). Olson and colleagues extended this work and also reported significant age-at-onset effects on chromosomes 9, 14, and 20 (Olson et al., 2002). Finally, a number of recent reports have performed linkage analysis of AD pedigrees conditioning on the presence or absence of psychotic symptoms, which commonly occur during the disease and show evidence for clustering within families (Avramopoulos et al., 2005; Bacanu et al., 2005; Hollingworth et al., 2007). Perhaps the most interesting finding is that of linkage to markers located on chromosome 6q21 (Bacanu et al., 2002; Hollingworth et al., 2007). This finding is particularly intriguing as it has been widely implicated in studies of schizophrenia (Cao et al., 1997; Levinson et al., 2000;

Martinez et al., 1999) and bipolar disorder (Dick et al., 2003; Lambert et al., 2005; McQueen et al., 2005; Pato et al., 2004; Schumacher et al., 2005; Venken et al., 2005), both of which have prominent psychotic features. This could implicate a gene in this region in the development of psychiatric symptoms in the presence of other neurological illness.

Reviewing linkage findings provides an illustration of the difficulties in replicating linkage and in estimating the location of genes underlying complex disorders. A total of 16 regions on 11 chromosomes show evidence of linkage to late-onset AD across at least two studies. Figures 6.1(a) and (b) depict chromosomal regions, which have been linked to late-onset AD through linkage studies. Like studies of many complex disorders, issues of power were a persistent problem for linkage studies of late-onset AD. Adequate family-based samples are difficult and costly to ascertain and in the current context, where genome-wide association studies are now viable, the focus has shifted toward susceptibility gene identification through large-scale testing for direct or indirect association.

Large scale genome-wide association studies of AD　　Prior to 2009, thousands of genetic association studies had been published claiming or refuting association between AD and hundreds of genes. These studies are summarized on the Alzgene database (www.alzgene.org). However, results were often inconsistent as most studies were insufficiently powered to detect the small genetic effects conferred by common risk alleles. More recently focus has shifted toward large-scale Genome-wide Association (GWA) studies. Rapid improvements in genotyping technology and analysis now permit genotyping and analysis of hundreds of thousands, or even millions, of well-chosen genetic variants, providing >80% coverage of common variation in the human genome (Barrett & Cardon, 2006). GWA studies have heralded the most prolific period of discovery in human genetics (Hirschhorn, 2009) identifying common genetic variants which show replicated association with a wide range of polygenic traits.

Initial GWAS studies of AD typically included <1000 subjects and, with the exception of APOE, failed to identify loci which have been consistently replicated in independent samples. It rapidly became clear that, given the stringent criteria for genome-wide significance, sample sizes in the order of thousands, or tens of thousands, would be required to detect true risk loci (Wang et al., 2005). The first such studies, including one by our group, were published in the same edition of *Nature Genetics* in September 2009 (Harold et al., 2009; Lambert et al., 2009). Our initial GWAS utilized the Genetic and Environmental Risk in AD Consortium 1 (GERAD1) sample, which comprised 3941 AD cases and 7848 controls, with replication in an independent sample of 2023 cases and 2340 controls. This study identified two genome-wide significant susceptibility loci: *CLU* ($P = 8.5 \times 10^{-10}$) and *PICALM* ($P = 1.3 \times 10^{-9}$). Remarkably, the Lambert et al. GWAS, performed using the European Alzheimer's Disease Initiative (EADI) sample, showed genome-wide significant evidence for association with same SNP in *CLU* ($P = 7.5 \times 10^{-9}$). Lambert and colleagues also observed genome-wide significant association with *CR1*

a

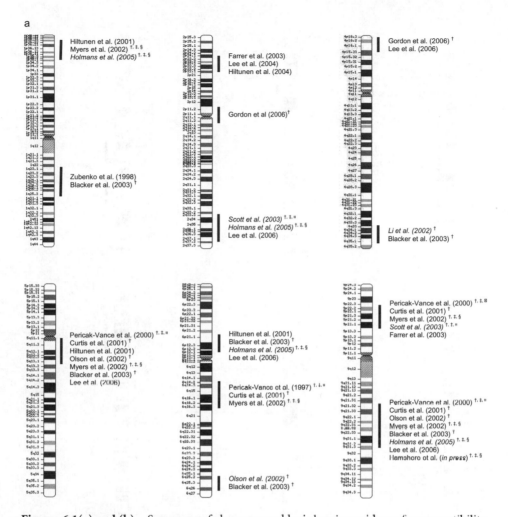

Figures 6.1(a) and (b) Summary of chromosomal loci showing evidence for susceptibility genes for late-onset Alzheimer's disease. A number of these studies have been conducted using samples that show partial or complete overlap. Studies marked [†], [‡], [§] and [‖] incorporated data from samples obtained from the National Institute of Mental Health AD Genetics Initiative, the Indiana Alzheimer's Disease Research Center National Cell Repository, United Kingdom affected sibling pair collection and the Collaborative Alzheimer Project, respectively. Studies in italics have found linkage evidence in the corresponding region when conditioning on age at disease onset, age at assessment, age at death, or rate of disease progression. Results from studies by Kehoe et al. (1999) and Lee et al. (2004) are not shown as they have subsequently been extended by Myers et al. (2002) and Lee et al. (2006), respectively

b

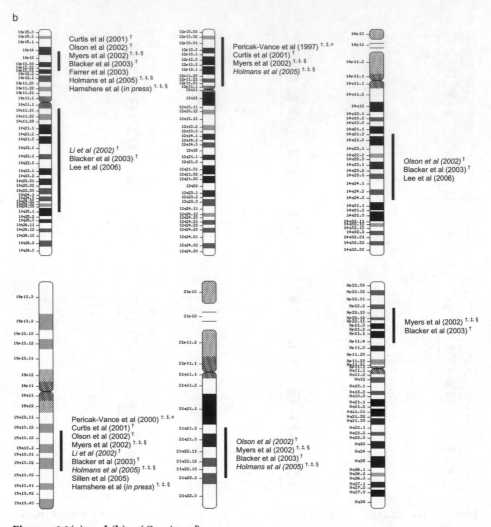

Figures 6.1(a) and (b)　　(*Continued*)

($P = 3.7 \times 10^{-9}$), and support for *PICALM* ($P = 3 \times 10^{-3}$). The associations in *CLU*, *PICALM*, and *CR1* have since been replicated in several independent datasets (Carrasquillo et al., 2010; Corneveaux et al., 2010; Naj et al., 2011; Seshadri et al., 2010) and shown relationships with neurodegenerative processes underlying disease (Biffi et al., 2010). Harold and colleagues observed more SNPs showing "sub-threshold" association ($P < 1 \times 10^{-5}$) with AD than expected by chance, providing strong evidence that several genes associated with AD remained to be identified. Included amongst these "sub-threshold" SNPs were variants 5' to the bridging integrator 1 (BIN1) gene (rs744373). Seshadri and colleagues have since reported genome-wide significant evidence for association for this SNP ($P = 1.6 \times 10^{-11}$) when combining GERAD1 and EADI data with data from the Cohorts for Heart and Aging Research in Genomic Epidemiology (CHARGE) (Seshadri et al., 2010).

Table 6.2 Summary of the confirmed AD risk loci in the GERAD+ and ADGC GWAS studies

SNP	Gene	CHR	MAF	GERAD+ (Hollingworth et al., 2011)		ADGC (Naj et al., 2011)		GERAD+ & ADGC Meta-analysis	
				OR	P	OR	P	OR	P
rs2075650	TOMM40/APOE	19	0.20	2.72	7.8×10^{-266}*	2.68	6.2×10^{-184}	NA	NA
rs11136000	CLU	9	0.39	0.83	2.0×10^{-16}*	0.91	1.1×10^{-4}	NA	NA
rs3851179	PICALM	11	0.36	0.87	7.2×10^{-10}*	0.88	1.7×10^{-7}	NA	NA
rs3818361	CR1	1	0.19	1.18	3.7×10^{-14}†	1.18	1.5×10^{-8}	NA	NA
rs744373	BIN1	2	0.29	1.17	2.6×10^{-14}†	1.18	3.0×10^{-10}	NA	NA
rs3764650	ABCA7	19	0.10	1.23	4.5×10^{-17}‡	1.20	8.3×10^{-6}	1.23	5.0×10^{-21}
rs610932	MS4A6A	11	0.42	0.90	1.8×10^{-14}‡	0.90	2.6×10^{-5}	0.91	1.2×10^{-16}
rs670139	MS4A4E	11	0.41	1.09	1.4×10^{-9}‡	1.05	1.5×10^{-2}	1.08	1.1×10^{-10}
rs9349407	CD2AP	6	0.29	1.11	8.0×10^{-4}**	1.12	1.0×10^{-6}	1.11	8.6×10^{-9}
rs11767557	EPHA1	7	0.21	0.90	3.4×10^{-4}**	0.87	2.4×10^{-7}	0.9	6.0×10^{-10}
rs3865444	CD33	19	0.31	0.89	2.2×10^{-4}**	0.89	1.1×10^{-7}	0.91	1.6×10^{-9}

CHR = chromosome; MAF = minor allele frequency;

* = genotyped in GERAD+ Stage 1 samples: GERAD1, EADI1, ADNI, & TGEN1 <6688 cases, 13685 controls;

† = genotyped in GERAD+ Stage 2 samples: Stage 1 + GERAD2, deCODE, AD-IG: 11584 AD cases, 18588 controls;

‡ = genotyped in GERAD+ Stage 3 samples: Stage 1 + Stage 2 + EADI2, CHARGE, Mayo2 <19,870 AD cases, 39846 controls;

** = genotyped in GERAD1, EADI1, deCODE, AD-IG up to 6992 cases and 13472 controls

Following our initial GWA study we reported an extended three-stage study (GERAD+), which included 19 870 AD cases and 39 846 controls and identified genome-wide evidence for association at the *ABCA7* locus ($P = 5.0 \times 10^{-21}$) and the *MS4A* gene cluster ($P = 1.2 \times 10^{-16}$) (Hollingworth et al., 2011). The American Alzheimer's Disease Genetic Consortium (ADGC) also reported significant evidence at the *MS4A* gene cluster and further support for *ABCA7* in a GWA study comprising 8309 AD cases and 7366 controls (Naj et al., 2011). Furthermore, they reported suggestive evidence for association with SNPs at the *CD33*, *CD2AP*, *ARID5B*, and *EPHA1* loci. When combining data from ADGC and GERAD+ SNPs at *CD33* ($P = 1.6 \times 10^{-9}$), *CD2AP* ($P = 8.6 \times 10^{-9}$), and *EPHA1* ($P = 6.0 \times 10^{-10}$) exceeded criteria for genome-wide significant association with AD. Finally, meta-analysis of GWAS (including data from our group) and non-GWAS data has provided evidence that variants in the *SORL1* gene are associated with AD (Reitz et al., 2011).

Together these studies have provided compelling evidence for association with 10 novel risk loci, representing the first new confirmed susceptibility genes for the common form of AD since the detection of *APOE* in 1993. What is clear about the susceptibility genes thus identified is that they are not random, as argued by some (Goldstein, 2009), but show patterns of putative functional relationships. Five of the recently identified AD susceptibility loci *CLU, CR1, ABCA7, CD33* and *EPHA1* have putative functions in the immune system; *PICALM, BIN1, CD33, CD2AP* are involved in processes at the cell membrane, including endocytosis and *APOE, CLU* and *ABCA7* in lipid processing. Processes related to cholesterol metabolism and the innate immune response are further implicated by pathway of analyses of both the GERAD and EADI GWAS datasets (Jones et al., 2010). These findings therefore provide new impetus for focused studies aimed at understanding the pathogenesis of AD and provide new targets for novel and existing therapeutic approaches. A more detailed discussion of the likely function of each of these loci is beyond the scope of this chapter, however, several excellent reviews are available elsewhere (Bertram et al., 2010; Hollingworth et al., in press; Jones et al., 2010; Morgan, 2011).

Conclusions

AD is governed by rare autosomal dominant mutations (*APP, PSEN1, PSEN2*), a common variant with moderate to large effect (*APOE*) and common variants of smaller effect (*CLU, PICALM, CR1, BIN1, ABCA7, MS4A, CD33, CD2AP, EPHA1, SORL1*). In contrast to other complex disorders (Hirschhorn & Lettre, 2009; Lettre & Rioux, 2008; Mohlke et al., 2008), the genes known to be responsible for Mendelian early-onset AD appear to have little or no effect on susceptibility to common late-onset AD. Current findings have already refined previous ideas and defined new putative disease mechanisms including: amyloid clearance from the brain; lipid processing; endocytosis/trafficking; and innate/adaptive immunity. Despite this the identified genetic risk factors for the common form of AD are likely to have little clinical utility in predicting disease risk. Even APOE, which has a relatively large effect, has little predictive utility and simulation studies suggest that as many as 100 loci with allele frequencies similar to those of *CLU* would be required to reach discriminative accuracy of ~70% (van der Net et al., 2009). It therefore seems that accurate disease prediction will not be possible without the elucidation of more genetic risk loci, along with a comprehensive knowledge of gene–gene and gene–environment interactions.

The current genetic data are providing new avenues for exploration, but also highlight the potential for gene discovery when larger samples are analyzed, using ever more sophisticated methods. To this end the GERAD, EADI, ADGC, and CHARGE consortium have begun the International Genomics of AD Project (IGAP). IGAP aims to combine GWAS data from 18 600 cases and 41 370 controls and follow up the most interesting results in up to 30 000 independent samples. Others are seeking to identify new risk loci by analyzing refined disease phenotypes characterized by behavioral symptoms which show evidence of heritability in AD, such as psychosis (Hollingworth et al., 2007), depression and age at disease onset. GWAS data also offers exciting opportunity to compare and combine data from AD subjects with those suffering other neurological disorders such as Parkinson's disease or amyloid lateral sclerosis. It is clear that the coming years will be an exciting time for AD genetics as we move closer and closer to completely unravelling the genetic architecture of the disease.

Vascular Dementia

Cognitive impairment attributable to vascular disease is generally believed to be the second-most common form of dementia and is an escalating public health concern (Leblanc et al., 2006). Around one-third of stroke survivors go on to develop dementia within three months (Barba et al., 2000; Pohjasvaara et al., 1997), while postmortem studies show that a substantial proportion of dementia cases display significant vascular pathology (Leblanc et al., 2006). There are a number of autosomal dominantly inherited forms of vascular dementia (VaD), in which causative genetic mutations have been identified. Aside from rare autosomal dominant forms of the disease, the genetic risk factors for VaD are essentially drawn from two classes. First, genes that govern susceptibility to major vascular disease, where VaD could simply be viewed as a long-term complication of vascular disease. Second, genes that determine tissue responses to vascular disease. The search for genes for VaD presents a number of challenges. Perhaps none more problematic than choosing the study population (Leblanc et al., 2006), as the cerebrovascular pathologies that cause dementia are heterogeneous, a problem that is further compounded by the limitations of the diagnostic criteria for VaD (Pohjasvaara et al., 2000; Wetterling et al., 1996).

Autosomal dominant forms of VaD

There are a number of autosomal dominantly inherited forms of VaD in which causative mutations have been identified.

Cerebral autosomal dominant arteriopathy with subcortical infarcts and leukoencephalopathy (CADASIL)

Cerebral autosomal dominant arteriopathy with subcortical infarcts and leukoencephalopathy (CADASIL) manifests as subcortical small vessel disease accompanied by recurrent transient ischemic attacks (TIAs), lacunar strokes, migraine, neuropsychiatric complications, and dementia (Tournier-Lasserve et al., 1993). CADASIL can affect individuals of both sexes from their twenties upwards. Sufferers display prominent signal abnormalities on brain MRI, including white matter abnormalities and small subcortical infarcts, which can often be observed prior to the first stroke.

In 1993, genetic linkage analysis of two unrelated families mapped CADASIL to chromosome 19q12 (Tournier-Lasserve et al., 1993). Subsequent studies refined the region of interest to a 2cM interval on chromosome 19p13.1 (Ducros et al., 1996; Sabbadini et al., 1995). Mutations in the Notch3 gene, located in the linkage region on chromosome 19, were later identified, which segregated with the disease within families (Joutel et al., 1996; Joutel et al., 1997). Notch3 is normally expressed in vascular smooth muscle cells and perictyes, including those of the cerebral vasculature (Joutel et al., 2000; Prakash et al., 2002). The Notch3 gene contains 33 exons encoding a Notch3 protein of 2321 amino acids with a single transmembrane domain. The extracellular portion of Notch3 comprises 34 epidermal growth factor (EDF) domains followed by three notch/lin-12 repeats. The cytoplasmic portion of Notch3 consists of six cdc10/ankyrin repeats. CADASIL results primarily from missense mutations within the EGF repeats of Notch3.

Heritable cerebral hemorrhage with amyloidosis (HCHWA)

Heritable cerebral hemorrhage with amyloidosis (HCHWA) is characterized primarily by hemorrhagic strokes and dementia (Bornebroek et al., 1996; Maat-Schieman et al., 1996), which are often accompanied by migraines and psychiatric problems. There are at least two forms of HCHWA: the "Icelandic type" and "Dutch type." The "Dutch type" is characterized by multiple cerebral hemorrhages, starting around the ages of 40 to 50 years, which progress to increased neurological deficit, dementia, and ultimately death. The disease is caused, and passed onto subsequent generations, by mutations in the APP gene (Levy et al., 1990; Van Broeckhoven et al., 1990), which, as previously discussed, also contains variants responsible for some cases of familial AD. The mutations in APP lead to the abnormal deposition of amyloid in the walls of the leptomeningeal arteries and cortical arterioles (Herzig et al., 2004; Levy et al., 1990). The Icelandic type occurs in those of Icelandic origin and is also characterized by recurrent cerebral hemorrhages, usually in the absence of hypertension. Icelandic patients, on average, suffer their first stroke in their mid-20s, some

25 years before the mean age at first stroke among those with the Dutch mutation (van Duinen et al., 1987). Rather than APP, the Icelandic type HCHWA is caused by a mutation in the cystatin C gene (*CST3*) (Abrahamson et al., 1987), which results in the deposition of a mutated form of the protease inhibitor cystatin C in the walls of the cerebral blood vessels.

Genetics of non-autosomal dominant VaD

Sporadic and common forms of VaD are thought to result from a combination of genetic and environmental influences. A number of twin studies have sought to estimate the heritability of VaD. In a study of Finnish twins, using hospital discharge records, the probandwise concordance rates for VaD was 31% in MZ versus 12.5% in DZ twins (Raiha et al., 1996), supporting a genetic component. In contrast the Norwegian register-based study of elderly twins, in which participants were inter-viewed and clinically examined, found identical probandwise concordance rates of 29% in MZ and DZ twins (Bergem et al., 1997). Despite being the smaller of the two studies, the study by Bergem et al. (1997) is probably the most methodologically sound and suggests that environmental influences dominate in VaD.

Genes that do affect VaD may share susceptibility with other diseases, such as cerebrovascular disease (CVD) and stroke, where genes are thought to play an important role. In a review of 11 epidemiological studies, Hademenos and col-leagues reported an increased risk of CVD to offspring of parents affected by CVD (Hademenos et al., 2001). The genetic basis of stroke, a strong predictor of VaD, has been well researched. The evidence to date is not always consistent, with some studies reporting family history of stroke as a risk factor (Meschia et al., 2006; van Rijn et al., 2005), while others do not (Wiklund et al., 2007). Flossmann and col-leagues (2004) provided a systematic review of 39 published twin and family history studies, which investigated the familial risk of stroke (Flossmann et al., 2004). Meta-analyses found a moderate genetic component for stroke, despite substantial hetero-geneity between studies. They also found that the heritability of ischemic and hemorrhagic stroke might differ. This finding has been investigated in a large Swedish population study (Sundquist et al., 2006), which found that ischemic stroke was associated only with a family history of ischemic stroke (OR 2.14), while hem-orrhagic stroke was only associated with a family history of hemorrhagic stroke (OR 1.82), suggesting that ischemic and hemorrhagic stroke are not under the same genetic influence. Two genome-wide linkage studies of common stroke have been published. The first reported significant linkage evidence on chromosome 5q12 (Gretarsdottir et al., 2002), which subsequently led to the positive association between the phosphodiesterase 4D gene (PDE4D), located within the linked region, and stroke. PDE4D, a cyclic nucleotide phosphodiesterase, selectively degrades second messenger cyclic AMP (cAMP). Reduced cAMP levels are associated with increased smooth muscle cell proliferation and migration, key events in atheroscle-rosis, making an association with stroke pathophysiologically plausible. However, the validity of the original association remains unclear, as a number of replication studies have reported contradictory findings (Rosand et al., 2006). A more recent linkage study has provided additional support for the chromosome 5 locus, but did not identify any new major stroke loci (Nilsson-Ardnor et al., 2007). A number of other vascular risk factors for VaD have been shown to have an underlying genetic component, and varying progress has been made in identifying susceptibility genes. For example, aneurysmal subarachnoid hemorrhage (SAH) and intracranial aneurysms (IAs) show evidence of clustering within families (Teasdale et al., 2005), and linkage studies have reported numerous suggestive (Yamada et al., 2004) and significant (Nahed et al., 2005; Roos et al., 2004) linkage regions. However, causative mutations have yet to be identified (Markus & Alberts, 2006).

Less attention has been paid to genes that influence the brain's susceptibility to injury following vascular insult (Leblanc et al., 2006). So, do genes exist which influence tissue response to cerebrovascular disease? It is well established that those with similar levels of vascular pathology have widely differing levels of cognitive impairment, ranging from no impairment to severely cognitive impaired (de Groot et al., 2001; Price et al., 1997; Vermeer et al., 2003; White et al., 2002). Evidence that genetic factors affect cellular responses to cerebrovascular pathology can be derived from twin studies of white matter hyperintensities (WMHs). WMHs can be observed via MRI and are more prevalent and severe in individuals with CVD and CVD risk factors (Meyer et al., 1992). There is evidence that WMHs are a highly heritable trait, with heritable estimates of between 0.51 and 0.73 (Atwood et al., 2004; Carmelli et al., 1998; Lunetta et al., 2007). However, these findings do not appear to be directly due to the heritability of underlying CVD. For example in the Framingham Heart Study, the heritability of WMHs remained high among individuals with low prevalence of cerebrovascular brain injury (Atwood et al., 2004), suggesting that there are genetic factors affecting cellular responses to cerebrovascular pathology that are different from those that cause cerebrovascular pathology itself.

To date, relatively little is known about genes that influence tissue response to CVD. The AD genes, including APOE, APP, and the presenilins are known to be involved in the VaD disease pathway. For example, mutations at different loci in the APP gene lead to the development of either autosomal dominant forms of AD or HCHWA "Dutch type." The presenilins, mutations of which cause AD, have been shown to interact directly with Notch3 proteins, which can lead to CADASIL (Sisodia & St George-Hyslop, 2002). There is also evidence linking APOE to both susceptibility to CVD and VaD. Further evidence that AD and VaD share pathological pathways can be gleaned from clinical studies of vascular pathology and AD. For example, the Nun study (Snowdon et al., 1997), and others (Petrovitch et al., 2005; Riekse et al., 2004), have shown that those with both AD and cerebrovascular pathology generally show more severe cognitive impairment. A number of other genes, outside the AD pathway, have been shown to influence outcomes post vascular accident, including genes for α-fibrinogen (Carter et al., 1999), but not specifically with regard to the development of dementia.

APOE and vascular dementia

APOE, which is strongly associated with AD, has a complex relationship with car-diovascular disease and vascular dementia. APOE genotype has been associated with a number of factors linked to VaD, including cholesterol metabolism (Eichner et al., 2002), hypertension (Hirono et al., 2000), intracerebral hemorrhage (Rosand et al., 2000; Woo et al., 2002), ischemic heart disease (Song et al., 2004), and cerebral amyloid angiopathy (McCarron et al., 2000). APOE has been hypothesized to influence the risk of stroke. A recent meta-analysis by Sudlow and colleagues (2006) incorporated data from 31 studies, including data from 5961 stroke sufferers and 17,965 healthy controls. Small relationships were noted between the APOE ε4 allele and ischemic stroke and subarachnoid hemorrhage, but not with intracerebral hemorrhage, which was associated with ε2 genotypes.

Others have sought to directly investigate the association between APOE and VaD. Probably the best evidence has come from large population-based studies. For example, a study of the Framingham cohort, involving over 1000 individuals aged between 70 and 100 years old, found that the APOE ε4 allele was associated with both dementia following stroke and multi-infarct dementia (Myers et al., 1996). Likewise, Slooter et al (1997) reported that VaD and mixed VaD and AD were both increased among APOE ε4 carriers (Slooter et al., 1997). Given the well-established and strong association between APOE and AD (Farrer et al., 1997), investigations of VaD are likely to be complicated by issues of diagnosis, as dementia sufferers often exhibit mixed AD and vascular pathology (Blacker & Lovestone, 2006). Indeed, the Gothenburg longitudinal study found that the APOE ε4 allele was associated with an increased risk of AD and mixed dementia, but not pure VaD (Skoog et al., 1998). This issue can be addressed by studies performed in samples of dementia sufferers whose diagnosis has been confirmed at postmortem. Polvikoski and colleagues established the prevalence of neuropathologically defined AD and other dementias, together with APOE genotype, in 88% of the 85 years old and older residents of Vantaa, Finland (Polvikoski et al., 2001). They noted a strong relationship between APOE and both clinically diagnosed VaD and AD. However, neuropathological analyses showed that over half of those with clinically diagnosed VaD demonstrated AD pathology. This study suggests that the association between APOE ε4 and VaD probably results from an association with underlying and undiagnosed AD. Indeed, other autopsy studies of VaD have either found no association with VaD and APOE, or an association only in cases of mixed VaD and AD (Betard et al., 1994; Saunders et al., 1993).

Frontotemporal Dementia

Frontotemporal dementia (FTD) is a pathologically heterogeneous disease, which can be subdivided into three types based on the presence of protein inclusions in the brain: those with tau-positive inclusions; those with ubiquitin-positive, tau-negative inclusions; and those lacking distinctive histopathology (Mackenzie, Shi et al., 2006). Most cases of FTD are sporadic, however, studies suggest that 25–50% of disease sufferers have a first-degree relative with FTD (Poorkaj et al., 2001; Rosso et al., 2003), with a substantial proportion of these patients reporting a family history of disease consistent with autosomal dominant inheritance. Around 30% of familial FTD cases are caused by mutations in the tau gene and are characterized by tau pathology (Morris et al., 2001; Rosso et al., 2003). However, a substantial proportion of hereditary FTD does not result from mutations in the tau gene (Tolnay & Probst, 2002), and further susceptibility loci have been identified.

Frontotemporal dementia and parkinsonism linked to chromosome 17

Frontotemporal dementia and parkinsonism linked to chromosome 17 (FTDP-17) is an autosomal dominantly inherited disease, which probably accounts for less than 5% of all dementias. FTDP-17 can largely be categorized into two major types: predominant-dementia or predominant-parkinsonism (van Swieten & Spillantini, 2007). However, both dementia- and parkinsonism-predominant FTD can occur in families carrying the same mutations (Yasuda et al., 1999). The dementia phenotype is commonly characterized by cognitive difficulties, including problems with memory and language, and marked personality changes, including disinhibition and apathy (Neary et al., 2005). Those with the parkinsonism-predominant subtype usually experience gait impairment, rigidity, bradykinesia, and resting tremor (Arima et al., 2000). In contrast to AD, those with FTDP-17 have relatively intact episodic memory and have fewer difficulties with orientation. Rather, they present with deficits in verbal fluency, abstract thinking, attention, and executive function (see Hodges & Miller, 2001, for a review of the neuropsychology of FTD).

Spillantini and colleagues (Spillantini, Bird et al. 1998) first reported linkage to chromosome 17q21-22 in families with FTD and parkinsonism. Further analysis of this region revealed mutations in the gene encoding the microtubule-associated tau protein (MAPT) located within a region of overlapping linkage, caused symptoms of FTD (Clark et al., 1998; Hutton et al., 1998; Goedert et al., 1999; Poorkaj et al., 1998). Since then 40 MAPT disease mutations have been reported across 113 families (see www.molgen.ua.ac.be/FTDMutations/). FTDP-17 is now used as a collective term for primarily autosomal dominant conditions linked to chromosome 17. Historically, several of these conditions have been referred to as different nosological entities, e.g., Pick's disease, familial subcorticol gliosis, and autosomal dominant dementia with widespread neurofibrillary tangles (Foster et al., 1997; Lee et al., 2001; Spillantini et al., 1997; Spillantini, Bird et al., 1998). FTDP-17 shows a primarily dominant mode of inheritance, although recessive forms have also been described (Nicholl et al., 2003; Rademakers et al., 2002). MAPT mutations are found in between 10% and 30% of FTD patients with a positive family history of the disease and up to 70% of cases from families exhibiting an autosomal dominant mode of disease transmission (Bird et al., 2003; Poorkaj et al., 2001; Rizzu et al., 1999).

Tau is involved in microtubule assembly and stabilization. In normal nerve cells there are six tau isoforms, which are produced by alternate mRNA splicing of exons 9, 10, 11, and 12 (Goedert et al., 1989). They differ first in terms of the inclusion of certain N-terminal domains and secondly in the inclusion of three or four repeat domains within the carboxy-terminal region of the molecule (Lee et al., 2001). The repeat domains are important because they act as the microtubule-binding domains of tau and thus play a precise role in the maintenance of microtubule structure within the cell. If either of the three- or four- repeat isoforms fail to function, or if the ratio of the two alters within the cell, microtubule formation and stability become compromised. Additionally, unused tau of either form can be bundled into a tangle, which can impair cell function (Lee et al., 2001; Neary et al., 2005). MAPT mutations can be largely grouped according to their position in the gene, which defines their effect on tau mRNA and protein, which in turn influences the type of resultant pathology. The majority of tau mutations occur within the C-terminal region of the gene and most within or adjacent to the microtubule-binding domains between exons 9 and 12, or close to exon 13. Intronic mutations, close to exon 10, are also common and act to increase splicing of exon 10 (Hutton et al., 1998; Poorkaj et al., 1998). Others have reported mutations in exon 1 of the MAPT gene (Hayashi et al., 2002; Poorkaj et al., 2002). Intronic mutations and some mutations that affect splicing regulatory elements manifest at the level of mRNA splicing, which leads to altered expressions of tau isoforms (Clark et al., 1998; Hutton et al., 1998; Spillantini, Murrell et al., 1998; van Swieten et al., 2007). Generally, tau mutations either affect tau–microtubule interactions and/or fibril formation or affect exon 10 splicing However, some mutations have multiple effects.

The clinical presentation of FTDP-17 varies, to some extent, according to the type and location of the tau mutation. For example, some mutations lead to very similar age of onset both within and between families, even among families from different continents (Arima et al., 2000; Delisle et al., 1999; Kodama et al., 2000). Some mutations are associated with disease onset in mid to late adulthood (e.g., P301L (van Swieten et al., 1999)), whereas others can lead to an onset of clinical symptoms between 20 and 30 years of age (e.g., P301S (Bugiani et al., 1999; Sperfeld et al., 1999); L315R (van Herpen et al., 2003); G335S (Sperfeld et al., 1999)). Disease onset after the age of 70 years is less common but is sometimes observed in those with R5H (Hayashi et al., 2002) and 1260V (Grover et al., 2003) mutations.

Despite the robust association between tau mutations, tau pathology, and FTDP-17, mutations in MAPT do not appear to be a common cause of general dementia. Studies have generally reported no, or weak, association with AD (Mukherjee et al., 2007; Myers et al., 2005; Roks et al., 1999), Parkinson's disease (Zabetian et al., 2007; Zhang et al., 2005), or sporadic FTD (Bernardi et al., 2006; Verpillat et al., 2002).

These findings are particularly interesting as a number of other dementias, including AD, are associated with extensive tau pathology (Lee et al., 2001).

Non-tau frontotemporal dementia

A family history of similar neurodegenerative disease may be present in up to 50% of individuals with FTD, however, a substantial proportion of hereditary FTD does not result from mutations in the tau gene (Tolnay & Probst, 2002). A number of loci and mutations in genes other than tau have been shown to be associated with FTD. The disease often appears with pathological ubiquitin inclusions, in the absence of tau pathology (FTD-TDP) (Forman et al., 2006). Two independent studies reported linkage to chromosome 17q21-22, which was not attributable to known mutations in the MAPT gene (Rademakers et al., 2002; Rosso, Kamphorst et al., 2001). Mackenzie, Baker et al. (2006) later identified several mutations in the progranulin gene (*GRN*), located 1.7 Mb centromeric of *MAPT* on chromosome 17q21.3, that segregated with FTD-TDP in eight families. Cruts et al. (2006) have also found mutations in *GRN* in a Belgian family with autosomal dominantly inherited FTD-TDP (Cruts et al., 2006). Furthermore, they reported that *GRN* mutations were over three times more frequent than mutations in MAPT, emphasizing their primary role in FTD.

Further, autosomal dominant risk loci have been identified including *CHMPB2* (Parkinson et al., 2006; Skibinski et al., 2005), *FUS* (Kwiatkowski, Bosco et al. 2009) and *VCP* (Schroder et al., 2005; Watts et al., 2004). However, only around 11% of FTD cases (or 29% of familial cases) are explained by autosomal dominant mutations in these genes (van der Zee and Van Broeckhoven, in press), suggesting further loci remain to be identified. Even those with known mutations show wide variation in terms of age at disease onset and other clinical characteristics, which is likely to be under genetic and environmental control. Wide clinical and pathological differences between FTD sufferers have caused some concerns about applying GWAS approaches, which assume aetiological homogeneity, to FTD. Despite this, Van Deerlin and colleagues reported the first GWAS study of FTD in March 2010 (Van Deerlin, Sleiman et al., 2010). They formed an international collaboration to compare a sample of 515 individuals with FTD-TDP with 2509 control individuals. They identified association with several SNPs mapping to a single LD block on chromosome 7p21, which contains the gene *TMEM106B* (top SNP rs1990622, $P = 1.08 \times 10^{-11}$, OR = 0.61). This has since replicated in independent samples comprising those with FTD-TDP (van der Zee & Van Broeckhoven, in press) and those diagnosed clinical with FTD (van der Zee, Van Langenhove et al. 2011). A number of interesting sub-threshold hits were reported in the GWAS and have since been followed up by Rollinson and colleagues (Rollinson, Mead et al., 2011). Although none of these loci replicated in clinical cohort of 470 patients, convincing evidence for association was found on chromosome 9 in a subgroup of 84 patients with FTD amyloid lateral sclerosis.

Conclusions and Future Directions

Identifying genes that contribute to disease risk is focusing research on biological pathways affecting the development of different dementias. Some of these may develop, as suggested, by the influence of variation in the *APOE* gene. Many mutations can result in devastating illness, mostly of early onset. However, it does not always follow that the genes implicated in early-onset familial disease influence susceptibility of the more common forms of dementia. For example, the three genes that cause mainly early-onset AD – APP, PSEN1, and PSEN2 – do not show strong evidence of having a major impact on susceptibility to late-onset AD. Genes for common forms of dementia are now beginning to be identified. These findings have refined previous ideas and defined new putative disease mechanisms, providing new impetus for focused studies aimed at understanding AD pathogenesis. A substantial proportion of heritability also remains unaccounted for. Further research using more powerful GWA and whole genome sequencing approaches is likely to define more of the genetic architecture of AD.

References

Abrahamson, M., Grubb, A., Olafsson, I., & Lundwall, A. (1987). Molecular cloning and sequence analysis of cDNA coding for the precursor of the human cysteine proteinase inhibitor cystatin C. *FEBS Letters*, *216*(2), 229–233.

Arima, K., Kowalska, A., Hasegawa, M., Mukoyama, M., Watanabe, R., Kawai, M., et al. (2000). Two brothers with frontotemporal dementia and parkinsonism with an N279K mutation of the tau gene. *Neurology*, *54*(9), 1787–1795.

Athan, E. S., Lee, J. H., Arriaga, A., Mayeux, R. P., & Tycko, B. (2002). Polymorphisms in the promoter of the human APP gene: Functional evaluation and allele frequencies in Alzheimer disease. *Archives of Neurology*, *59*(11), 1793–1799.

Atwood, L. D., Wolf, P. A., Heard-Costa, N. L., Massaro, J. M., Beiser, A., D'Agostino, R. B., et al. (2004). Genetic variation in white matter hyperintensity volume in the Framingham Study. *Stroke*, *35*(7), 1609–1613.

Avramopoulos, D., Fallin, M. D., & Bassett, S. S. (2005). Linkage to chromosome 14q in Alzheimer's disease (AD) patients without psychotic symptoms. *American Journal of Medical Genetics, B NeuroPsychiatric Genetics*, *132*(1), 9–13.

Bacanu, S. A., Devlin, B., Chowdari, K. V., DeKosky, S. T., Nimgaonkar, V. L., & Sweet, R. A. (2002). Linkage analysis of Alzheimer disease with psychosis. *Neurology*, *59*(1), 118–120.

Bacanu, S. A., Devlin, B., Chowdari, K. V., DeKosky, S. T., Nimgaonkar, V. L., & Sweet, R. A. (2005). Heritability of psychosis in Alzheimer disease. *American Journal of Geriatric Psychiatry*, *13*(7), 624–627.

Barba, R., Martinez-Espinosa, S., Rodriguez-Garcia, E., Pondal, M., Vivancos, J., & Del Ser, T. (2000). Poststroke dementia: Clinical features and risk factors. *Stroke*, *31*(7), 1494–1501.

Barrett, J. C. & Cardon. L. R. (2006). Evaluating coverage of genome-wide association studies. *Nature Genetics*, *38*(6), 659–662.

Bassett, S. S., Avramopoulos, D., & Fallin, D. (2002). Evidence for parent of origin effect in late-onset Alzheimer disease. *American Journal of Medical Genetics, 114*(6), 679–686.

Bergem, A. L., Engedal, K., & Kringlen, E. (1997). The role of heredity in late-onset Alzheimer disease and vascular dementia. A twin study. *Archives of General Psychiatry, 54*(3), 264–270.

Bernardi, L., Maletta, R. G., Tomaino, C., Smirne, N., Di Natale, M., Perri, M., et al. (2006). The effects of APOE and tau gene variability on risk of frontotemporal dementia. *Neurobiology of Aging, 27*(5), 702–709.

Bertram, L., Blacker, D., Mullin, K., Keeney, D., Jones, J., Basu, S., et al. (2000). Evidence for genetic linkage of Alzheimer's disease to chromosome 10q. *Science, 290*(5500), 2302–2303.

Bertram, L., Lill, C. M., et al. (2010). The genetics of Alzheimer disease: Back to the future. *Neuron, 68*(2), 270–281.

Betard, C., Robitaille, Y., Gee, M., Tiberghien, D., Larrivee, D., Roy, P., et al. (1994). Apo E allele frequencies in Alzheimer's disease, Lewy body dementia, Alzheimer's disease with cerebrovascular disease and vascular dementia. *Neuroreport, 5*(15), 1893–1896.

Biffi, A., Anderson, C. D., et al. (2010). Genetic variation and neuroimaging measures in Alzheimer disease. *Archives of Neurology, 67*(6), 677–685.

Bird, T., Knopman, D., VanSwieten, J., Rosso, S., Feldman, H., Tanabe, H., et al. (2003). Epidemiology and genetics of frontotemporal dementia/Pick's disease. *Annals of Neurology, 54*(Suppl 5), S29–S31.

Blacker, D., Bertram, L., Saunders, A. J., Moscarillo, T. J., Albert, M. S., Wiener, H., et al. (2003). Results of a high-resolution genome screen of 437 Alzheimer's disease families. *Human Molecular Genetics, 12*(1), 23–32.

Blacker, D., & Lovestone, S. (2006). Genetics and dementia nosology. *Journal of Geriatric Psychiatry and Neurology, 19*(3), 186–191.

Borchelt, D. R., Thinakaran, G., Eckman, C. B., Lee, M. K., Davenport, F., Ratovitsky, T., et al. (1996). Familial Alzheimer's disease-linked presenilin 1 variants elevate Abeta1-42/1-40 ratio in vitro and in vivo. *Neuron, 17*(5), 1005–1013.

Bornebroek, M., Haan, J., Maat-Schieman, M. L., Van Duinen, S. G., & Roos, R. A. (1996). Hereditary cerebral hemorrhage with amyloidosis-Dutch type (HCHWA-D), I – A review of clinical, radiologic and genetic aspects. *Brain Pathology, 6*(2), 111–114.

Breitner, J. C., Silverman, J. M., Mohs, R. C., & Davis, K. L. (1988). Familial aggregation in Alzheimer's disease: Comparison of risk among relatives of early-and late-onset cases, and among male and female relatives in successive generations. *Neurology, 38*(2), 207–212.

Breitner, J. C., Welsh, K. A., Gau, B. A., McDonald, W. M., Steffens, D. C., Saunders, A. M., et al. (1995). Alzheimer's disease in the National Academy of Sciences-National Research Council Registry of Aging Twin Veterans. III. Detection of cases, longitudinal results, and observations on twin concordance. *Archives of Neurology, 52*(8), 763–771.

Bugiani, O., Murrell, J. R., Giaccone, G., Hasegawa, M., Ghigo, G., Tabaton, M., et al. (1999). Frontotemporal dementia and corticobasal degeneration in a family with a P301S mutation in tau. *Journal of Neuropathology & Experimental Neurology, 58*(6), 667–677.

Bullido, M. J., Artiga, M. J., Recuero, M., Sastre, I., Garcia, M. A., Aldudo, J., et al. (1998). A polymorphism in the regulatory region of APOE associated with risk for Alzheimer's dementia. *Nature Genetics, 18*(1), 69–71.

Campion, D., Dumanchin, C., Hannequin, D., Dubois, B., Belliard, S., Puel, M., et al. (1999). Early-onset autosomal dominant Alzheimer disease: Prevalence, genetic heterogeneity, and mutation spectrum. *American Journal of Human Genetics, 65*(3), 664–670.

Canadian Study of Health and Aging (1994). The Canadian Study of Health and Aging: Risk factors for Alzheimer's disease in Canada. *Neurology, 44*(11), 2073–280.

Cao, Q., Martinez, M., Zhang, J., Sanders, A. R., Badner, J. A., Cravchik, A., et al. (1997). Suggestive evidence for a schizophrenia susceptibility locus on chromosome 6q and a confirmation in an independent series of pedigrees. *Genomics, 43*(1), 1–8.

Carmelli, D., DeCarli, C., Swan, G. E., Jack, L. M., Reed, T., Wolf, P. A., et al. (1998). Evidence for genetic variance in white matter hyperintensity volume in normal elderly male twins. *Stroke, 29*(6), 1177–1181.

Carrasquillo, M. M., Belbin, O., et al. (2010). Replication of CLU, CR1, and PICALM associations with Alzheimer disease. *Archives of Neurology, 67*(8), 961–964.

Carter, A. M., Catto, A. J., & Grant, P. J. (1999). Association of the alpha-fibrinogen Thr312Ala polymorphism with poststroke mortality in subjects with atrial fibrillation. *Circulation, 99*(18), 2423–2426.

Citron, M., Oltersdorf, T., Haass, C., McConlogue, L., Hung, A. Y., Seubert, P., et al. (1992). Mutation of the beta-amyloid precursor protein in familial Alzheimer's disease increases beta-protein production. *Nature, 360*(6405), 672–674.

Clark, L. N., Poorkaj, P., Wszolek, Z., Geschwind, D. H., Nasreddine, Z. S., Miller, B., et al. (1998). Pathogenic implications of mutations in the tau gene in pallido-ponto-nigral degeneration and related neurodegenerative disorders linked to chromosome 17. *Proceedings of the National Academy of Sciences USA, 95*(22), 13103–13107.

Corder, E. H., Basun, H., Lannfelt, L., Viitanen, M., & Winblad, B. (1996). Attenuation of apolipoprotein E Epsilon4 allele gene dose in late age. *Lancet, 347*(9000), 542.

Corder, E. H., Saunders, A. M., Strittmatter, W. J., Schmechel, D. E., Gaskell, P. C., Small, G. W., et al. (1993). Gene dose of apolipoprotein E type 4 allele and the risk of Alzheimer's disease in late onset families. *Science, 261*(5123), 921–923.

Corneveaux, J. J., Myers, A. J., et al. (2010). Association of CR1, CLU and PICALM with Alzheimer's disease in a cohort of clinically characterized and neuropathologically verified individuals. *Human Molecular Genetics, 19*(16), 3295–3301.

Cruts, M., Gijselinck, I., van der Zee, J., Engelborghs, S., Wils, H., Pirici, D., et al. (2006). Null mutations in progranulin cause ubiquitin-positive frontotemporal dementia linked to chromosome 17q21. *Nature, 442*(7105), 920–924.

Curtis, D., North, B. V., & Sham, P. C. (2001). A novel method of two-locus linkage analysis applied to a genome scan for late onset Alzheimer's disease. *Annals of Human Genetics, 65*(Pt 5), 473–481.

Daw, E. W., Payami, H., Nemens, E. J., Nochlin, D., Bird, T. D., Schellenberg, G. D., et al. (2000). The number of trait loci in late-onset Alzheimer disease. *American Journal of Human Genetics, 66*(1), 196–204.

de Groot, J. C., de Leeuw, F. E., Oudkerk, M., Hofman, A., Jolles, J., & Breteler, M. M. (2001). Cerebral white matter lesions and subjective cognitive dysfunction: The Rotterdam Scan Study. *Neurology, 56*(11), 1539–1545.

Delisle, M. B., Murrell, J. R., Richardson, R., Trofatter, J. A., Rascol, O., Soulages, X., et al. (1999). A mutation at codon 279 (N279K) in exon 10 of the Tau gene causes a tauopathy with dementia and supranuclear palsy. *Acta Neuropathologica (Berlin), 98*(1), 62–77.

Devi, L., Prabhu, B. M., Galati, D. F., Avadhani, N. G., & Anandatheerthavarada, H. K. (2006). Accumulation of amyloid precursor protein in the mitochondrial import channels of human Alzheimer's disease brain is associated with mitochondrial dysfunction. *Journal of the Neurosciences, 26*(35), 9057–9068.

Dick, D. M., Foroud, T., Flury, L., Bowman, E. S., Miller, M. J., Rau, N. L., et al. (2003). Genomewide linkage analyses of bipolar disorder: A new sample of 250 pedigrees from the National Institute of Mental Health Genetics Initiative. *American Journal of Human Genetics, 73*(1), 107–114.

Ducros, A., Nagy, T., Alamowitch, S., Nibbio, A., Joutel, A., Vahedi, K., et al. (1996). Cerebral autosomal dominant arteriopathy with subcortical infarcts and leukoencephalopathy, genetic homogeneity, and mapping of the locus within a 2-cM interval. *American Journal of Human Genetics, 58*(1), 171–181.

Eichner, J. E., Dunn, S. T., Perveen, G., Thompson, D. M., Stewart, K. E., & Stroehla, B. C. (2002). Apolipoprotein E polymorphism and cardiovascular disease: A HuGE review. *American Journal of Epidemiology, 155*(6), 487–495.

Ertekin-Taner, N., Graff-Radford, N., Younkin, L. H., Eckman, C., Baker, M., Adamson, J., et al. (2000). Linkage of plasma Abeta42 to a quantitative locus on chromosome 10 in late-onset Alzheimer's disease pedigrees. *Science, 290*(5500), 2303–2304.

Evans, D. A., Beckett, L. A., Field, T. S., Feng, L., Albert, M. S., Bennett, D. A., et al. (1997). Apolipoprotein E epsilon4 and incidence of Alzheimer disease in a community population of older persons. *Journal of the American Medical Association, 277*(10), 822–824.

Farrer, L. A., Bowirrat, A., Friedland, R. P., Waraska, K., Korczyn, A. D., & Baldwin, C. T. (2003). Identification of multiple loci for Alzheimer disease in a consanguineous Israeli-Arab community. *Human Molecular Genetics, 12*(4), 415–422.

Farrer, L. A., Cupples, L. A., Haines, J. L., Hyman, B., Kukull, W. A., Mayeux, R., et al. (1997). Effects of age, sex, and ethnicity on the association between apolipoprotein E genotype and Alzheimer disease. A meta-analysis. APOE and Alzheimer Disease Meta Analysis Consortium. *Journal of the American Medical Association, 278*(16), 1349–1356.

Farrer, L. A., O'Sullivan, D. M., Cupples, L. A., Growdon, J. H., & Myers, R. H. (1989). Assessment of genetic risk for Alzheimer's disease among first-degree relatives. *Annals of Neurology, 25*(5), 485–493.

Flossmann, E., Schulz, U. G., & Rothwell, P. M. (2004). Systematic review of methods and results of studies of the genetic epidemiology of ischemic stroke. *Stroke, 35*(1), 212–227.

Forman, M. S., Farmer, J., Johnson, J. K., Clark, C. M., Arnold, S. E., Coslett, H. B., et al. (2006). Frontotemporal dementia: Clinicopathological correlations. *Annals of Neurology, 59*(6), 952–962.

Foster, N. L., Wilhelmsen, K., Sima, A. A., Jones, M. Z., D'Amato, C. J., & Gilman, S. (1997). Frontotemporal dementia and parkinsonism linked to chromosome 17: A consensus conference. Conference Participants. *Annals of Neurology, 41*(6), 706–715.

Fratiglioni, L., Ahlbom, A., Viitanen, M., & Winblad, B. (1993). Risk factors for late-onset Alzheimer's disease: A population-based, case-control study. *Annals of Neurology, 33*(3), 258–266.

Fratiglioni, L., De Ronchi, D., & Aguero-Torres, H. (1999). Worldwide prevalence and incidence of dementia. *Drugs, & Aging, 15*(5), 365–375.

Gatz, M., Pedersen, N. L., Berg, S., Johansson, B., Johansson, K., Mortimer, J. A., et al. (1997). Heritability for Alzheimer's disease: The study of dementia in Swedish twins.

Journals of Gerontology Series A: Biological Sciences and Medical Sciences, 52(2), M117–M125.

Gatz, M., Reynolds, C. A., Fratiglioni, L., Johansson, B., Mortimer, J. A., Berg, S., et al. (2006). Role of genes and environments for explaining Alzheimer disease. *Archives of General Psychiatry, 63*(2), 168–174.

Goate, A., Chartier-Harlin, M. C., Mullan, M., Brown, J., Crawford, F., Fidani, L., et al. (1991). Segregation of a missense mutation in the amyloid precursor protein gene with familial Alzheimer's disease. *Nature, 349*(6311), 704–706.

Goedert, M., Spillantini, M. G., Crowther, R. A., Chen, S. G., Parchi, P., Tabaton, M., et al. (1999). Tau gene mutation in familial progressive subcortical gliosis. *Nature Medicine, 5*(4), 454–457.

Goedert, M., Spillantini, M. G., Jakes, R., Rutherford, D., & Crowther, R. A. (1989). Multiple isoforms of human microtubule-associated protein tau: Sequences and localization in neurofibrillary tangles of Alzheimer's disease. *Neuron, 3*(4), 519–526.

Goldstein, D. B. (2009). Common genetic variation and human traits. *New England Journal of Medicine, 360*(17), 1696–1698.

Gretarsdottir, S., Sveinbjornsdottir, S., Jonsson, H. H., Jakobsson, F., Einarsdottir, E., Agnarsson, U., et al. (2002). Localization of a susceptibility gene for common forms of stroke to 5q12. *American Journal of Human Genetics, 70*(3), 593–603.

Grover, A., England, E., Baker, M., Sahara, N., Adamson, J., Granger, B., et al. (2003). A novel tau mutation in exon 9 (1260V) causes a four-repeat tauopathy. *Experimental Neurology, 184*(1), 131–140.

Guyant-Marechal, L., Rovelet-Lecrux, A., Goumidi, L., Cousin, E., Hannequin, D., Raux, G., et al. (2007). Variations in the APP gene promoter region and risk of Alzheimer disease. *Neurology, 68*(9), 684–687.

Hademenos, G. J., Alberts, M. J., Awad, I., Mayberg, M., Shepard, T., Jagoda, A., et al. (2001). Advances in the genetics of cerebrovascular disease and stroke. *Neurology, 56*(8), 997–1008.

Hamshere, M. L., Holmans, P. A., Dimitrios Avramopoulos, D., Bassett, S. S., Blacker, D., Bertram, L., et al. (2007). Genome-wide linkage analysis of 723 affected relative pairs with late-onset Alzheimer's Disease. *Human Molecular Genetics, 16*(22), 2703–2712.

Hardy, J. A., Owen, M. J., Goate, A. M., James, L. A., Haynes, A. R., Rossor, M. N., et al. (1989). Molecular genetics of Alzheimer's disease. *Biochemical Society Transactions, 17*(1), 75–76.

Harold, D., Abraham, R., et al. (2009). Genome-wide association study identifies variants at CLU and PICALM associated with Alzheimer's disease. *Nature Genetics, 41*(10), 1088–1093.

Hayashi, S., Toyoshima, Y., Hasegawa, M., Umeda, Y., Wakabayashi, K., Tokiguchi, S., et al. (2002). Late-onset frontotemporal dementia with a novel exon 1 (Arg5His) tau gene mutation. *Annals of Neurology, 51*(4), 525–530.

Hebert, L. E., Scherr, P. A., Bienias, J. L., Bennett, D. A., & Evans, D. A. (2003). Alzheimer disease in the US population: Prevalence estimates using the 2000 census. *Archives of Neurology, 60*(8), 1119–1122.

Hendrie, H. C. (1998). Epidemiology of dementia and Alzheimer's disease. *American Journal of Geriatric Psychiatry, 6*(2 Suppl 1), S3–S18.

Herzig, M. C., Winkler, D. T., Burgermeister, P., Pfeifer, M., Kohler, E., Schmidt, S. D., et al. (2004). Abeta is targeted to the vasculature in a mouse model of hereditary cerebral hemorrhage with amyloidosis. *Nature Neuroscience, 7*(9), 954–960.

Heston, L. L., Mastri, A. R., Anderson, V. E., & White, J. (1981). Dementia of the Alzheimer type. Clinical genetics, natural history, and associated conditions. *Archives of General Psychiatry, 38*(10), 1085–1090.

Hirono, N., Yasuda, M., Tanimukai, S., Kitagaki, H., & Mori, E. (2000). Effect of the apolipoprotein E epsilon4 allele on white matter hyperintensities in dementia. *Stroke, 31*(6), 1263–1268.

Hirschhorn, J. N. (2009). Genome-wide Association Studies – Illuminating biologic pathways. *New England Journal of Medicine, 360*(17), 1699–1701.

Hirschhorn, J. N. & Lettre, G. (2009). Progress in genome-wide association studies of human height. *Hormone Research, 71*(Suppl 2), 5–13.

Hodges, J. R., & Miller, B. (2001). The neuropsychology of frontal variant frontotemporal dementia and semantic dementia. Introduction to the special topic papers: Part II. *Neurocase, 7*(2), 113–121.

Hollingworth, P., Hamshere, M. L., et al. (2007). Increased familial risk and genome-wide significant linkage for Alzheimer's disease with psychosis. *American Journal of Medical Genetics B: Neuropsychiatric Genetics, 144B*(7), 841–848.

Hollingworth, P., Hamshere, M. L., Holmans, P. A., O'Donovan, C., Sims, M. R., Powell, J., et al. (2007). Increased familial risk and genomewide significant linkage for Alzheimer's disease with psychosis. *American Journal of Medical Genetics, B NeuroPsychiatric Genetics, 144B*(7), 841–848.

Hollingworth, P., Harold, D., et al. (2010). Alzheimer's disease genetics: Current knowledge and future challenges. *International Journal of Geriatric Psychiatry.*

Hollingworth, P., Harold, D., et al. (2011). Common variants at ABCA7, MS4A6A/MS4A4E, EPHA1, CD33 and CD2AP are associated with Alzheimer's disease. *Nature Genetics, 43*(5), 429–435.

Holmans, P., Hamshere, M., Hollingworth, P., Rice, F., Tunstall, N., Jones, S., et al. (2005). Genome screen for loci influencing age at onset and rate of decline in late onset Alzheimer's disease. *American Journal of Medical Genetics, B NeuroPsychiatric Genetics, 135*(1), 24–32.

Huang, Y. (2006). Molecular and cellular mechanisms of apolipoprotein E4 neurotoxicity and potential therapeutic strategies. *Current Opinion in Drug Discovery & Development, 9*(5), 627–641.

Huff, F. J., Auerbach, J., Chakravarti, A., & Boller, F. (1988). Risk of dementia in relatives of patients with Alzheimer's disease. *Neurology, 38*(5), 786–790.

Hutton, M., Lendon, C. L., Rizzu, P., Baker, M., Froelich, S., Houlden, H., et al. (1998). Association of missense and 5'-splice-site mutations in tau with the inherited dementia FTDP-17. *Nature, 393*(6686), 702–705.

Jones, L., Harold, D., et al. (2010). Genetic evidence for the involvement of lipid metabolism in Alzheimer's disease. *Biochimica et Biophysica Acta, 1801*(8), 754–761.

Jones, L., Holmans, P. A., et al. (2010). Genetic evidence implicates the immune system and cholesterol metabolism in the aetiology of Alzheimer's disease. *PLoS One, 5*(11), e13950.

Joutel, A., Andreux, F., Gaulis, S., Domenga, V., Cecillon, M., Battail, N., et al. (2000). The ectodomain of the Notch3 receptor accumulates within the cerebrovasculature of CADASIL patients. *Journal of Clinical Investigation, 105*(5), 597–605.

Joutel, A., Corpechot, C., Ducros, A., Vahedi, K., Chabriat, H., Mouton, P., et al. (1996). Notch3 mutations in CADASIL, a hereditary adult-onset condition causing stroke and dementia. *Nature, 383*(6602), 707–710.

Joutel, A., Vahedi, K., Corpechot, C., Troesch, A., Chabriat, H., Vayssiere, C., et al. (1997). Strong clustering and stereotyped nature of Notch3 mutations in CADASIL patients. *Lancet, 350*(9090), 1511–1515.

Kehoe, P., Wavrant-De Vrieze, F., Crook, R., Wu, W. S., Holmans, P., Fenton, I., et al. (1999). A full genome scan for late onset Alzheimer's disease. *Human Molecular Genetics, 8*(2), 237–245.

Khachaturian, A. S., Corcoran, C. D., Mayer, L. S., Zandi, P. P., & Breitner, J. C. (2004). Apolipoprotein E epsilon4 count affects age at onset of Alzheimer disease, but not lifetime susceptibility: The Cache County Study. *Archives of General Psychiatry, 61*(5), 518–524.

Kodama, K., Okada, S., Iseki, E., Kowalska, A., Tabira, T., Hosoi, N., et al. (2000). Familial frontotemporal dementia with a P301L tau mutation in Japan. *Journal of the Neurological Sciences, 176*(1), 57–64.

Kwiatkowski, T. J., Jr., Bosco, D. A., et al. (2009). Mutations in the FUS/TLS gene on chromosome 16 cause familial amyotrophic lateral sclerosis. *Science, 323*(5918), 1205–1208.

Lambert, D., Middle, F., Hamshere, M. L., Segurado, R., Raybould, R., Corvin, A., et al. (2005). Stage 2 of the Wellcome Trust UK-Irish bipolar affective disorder sibling-pair genome screen: Evidence for linkage on chromosomes 6q16–q21, 4q12–q21, 9p21, 10p14–p12 and 18q22. *Molecular Psychiatry, 10*(9), 831–841.

Lambert, J. C., Araria-Goumidi, L., Myllykangas, L., Ellis, C., Wang, J. C., Bullido, M. J., et al. (2002). Contribution of APOE promoter polymorphisms to Alzheimer's disease risk. *Neurology, 59*(1), 59–66.

Lambert, J. C., Heath, S., et al. (2009). Genome-wide association study identifies variants at CLU and CR1 associated with Alzheimer's disease. *Nature Genetics, 41*(10), 1094–1099.

Larsson, J. F., Weissman, M. M., Prusoff, B. A., Caruso, K. A., Merikangas, K. & Pauls, D. (1963). Senile dementia: A clinical, sociomedical and genetic study. *Acta Psychiatrica Scandinavica*, Suppl. *167*, 39.

Leblanc, G. G., Meschia, J. F., Stuss, D. T., & Hachinski, V. (2006). Genetics of vascular cognitive impairment: The opportunity and the challenges. *Stroke, 37*(1), 248–255.

Lee, J. H., Cheng, R., Santana, V., Williamson, J., Lantigua, R., Medrano, M., et al. (2006). Expanded genomewide scan implicates a novel locus at 3q28 among Caribbean hispanics with familial Alzheimer disease. *Archives of Neurology, 63*(11), 1591–1598.

Lee, J. H., Mayeux, R., Mayo, D., Mo, J., Santana, V., Williamson, J., et al. (2004). Fine mapping of 10q and 18q for familial Alzheimer's disease in Caribbean Hispanics. *Molecular Psychiatry, 9*(11), 1042–1051.

Lee, V. M., Goedert, M., & Trojanowski, J. Q. (2001). Neurodegenerative tauopathies. *Annual Review of Neuroscience, 24*, 1121–1159.

Lendon, C. L., Ashall, F., & Goate, A. M. (1997). Exploring the etiology of Alzheimer disease using molecular genetics. *Journal of the American Medical Association, 277*(10), 825–831.

Lendon, C. L., Lynch, T., Norton, J., McKeel, Jr. D. W., Busfield, F., Craddock, N., et al. (1998). Hereditary dysphasic disinhibition dementia: a frontotemporal dementia linked to 17q21–22. *Neurology, 50*(6), 1546–1555.

Lettre, G. & Rioux, J. D. (2008). Autoimmune diseases: Insights from genome-wide association studies. *Human Molecular Genetics, 17*(R2), R116–R121.

Levinson, D. F., Holmans, P., Straub, R. E., Owen, M. J., Wildenauer, D. B., Gejman, P. V., et al. (2000). Multicenter linkage study of schizophrenia candidate regions on chromosomes 5q, 6q, 10p, and 13q: schizophrenia linkage collaborative group III. *American Journal of Human Genetics, 67*(3), 652–663.

Levy, E., Carman, M. D., Fernandez-Madrid, I. J., Power, M. D., Lieberburg, I., van Duinen, S. G., et al. (1990). Mutation of the Alzheimer's disease amyloid gene in hereditary cerebral hemorrhage, Dutch type. *Science, 248*(4959), 1124–1126.

Levy-Lahad, E., Lahad, A., Wijsman, E. M., Bird, T. D., & Schellenberg, G. D. (1995). Apolipoprotein E genotypes and age of onset in early-onset familial Alzheimer's disease. *Annals of Neurology, 38*(4), 678–680.

Levy-Lahad, E., Wasco, W., Poorkaj, P., Romano, D. M., Oshima, J., Pettingell, W. H., et al. (1995b). Candidate gene for the chromosome 1 familial Alzheimer's disease locus. *Science, 269*(5226), 973–977.

Li, G., Silverman, J. M., Smith, C. J., Zaccario, M. L., Schmeidler, J., Mohs, R. C., et al. (1995). Age at onset and familial risk in Alzheimer's disease. *American Journal of Psychiatry, 152*(3), 424–430.

Li, Y. J., Scott, W. K., Hedges, D. J., Zhang, F., Gaskell, P. C., Nance, M. A., et al. (2002). Age at onset in two common neurodegenerative diseases is genetically controlled. *American Journal of Human Genetics, 70*(4), 985–993.

Liu, L., Forsell, C., Lilius, L., Axelman, K., Corder, E. H., & Lannfelt, L. (1996). Allelic association but only weak evidence for linkage to the apolipoprotein E locus in late-onset Swedish Alzheimer families. *American Journal of Medical Genetics, 67*(3), 306–311.

Lucotte, G., Turpin, J. C., & Landais, P. (1994). Apolipoprotein E-epsilon 4 allele doses in late-onset Alzheimer's disease. *Annals of Neurology, 36*(4), 681–682.

Lunetta, K. L., Erlich, P. M., Cuenco, K. T., Cupples, L. A., Green, R. C., Farrer, L. A., et al. (2007). Heritability of magnetic resonance imaging (MRI) traits in Alzheimer disease cases and their siblings in the MIRAGE study. *Alzheimer Disease and Associated Disorders, 21*(2), 85–91.

Maat-Schieman, M. L., van Duinen, S. G., Bornebroek, M., Haan, J., & Roos, R. A. (1996). Hereditary cerebral hemorrhage with amyloidosis-Dutch type (HCHWA-D), II – A review of histopathological aspects. *Brain Pathology, 6*(2), 115–120.

Mackenzie, I. R., Baker, M., West, G., Woulfe, J., Qadi, N., Gass, J., et al. (2006). A family with tau-negative frontotemporal dementia and neuronal intranuclear inclusions linked to chromosome 17. *Brain, 129*(Pt 4), 853–867.

Mackenzie, I. R., Shi, J., Shaw, C., Duplessis, D., Neary, D., Snowden, J. S., et al. (2006). Dementia lacking distinctive histology (DLDH) revisited. *Acta Neuropathologica (Berlin), 112*(5), 551–559.

Markus, H. S., & Alberts, M. J. (2006). Update on genetics of stroke and cerebrovascular disease 2005. *Stroke, 37*(2), 288–290.

Martin, R. L., Gerteis, G. & Gabrielli, Jr., W. F. (1988). A family-genetic study of dementia of Alzheimer type. *Archives of General Psychiatry, 45*(10), 894–900.

Martinez, M., Campion, D., Brice, A., Hannequin, D., Dubois, B., Didierjean, O., et al. (1998). Apolipoprotein E epsilon4 allele and familial aggregation of Alzheimer disease. *Archives of Neurology, 55*(6), 810–816.

Martinez, M., Goldin, L. R., Cao, Q., Zhang, J., Sanders, A. R., Nancarrow, D. J., et al. (1999). Follow-up study on a susceptibility locus for schizophrenia on chromosome 6q. *American Journal of Medical Genetics, 88*(4), 337–343.

McCarron, M. O., Muir, K. W., Nicoll, J. A., Stewart, J., Currie, Y., Brown, K., et al. (2000). Prospective study of apolipoprotein E genotype and functional outcome following ischemic stroke. *Archives of Neurology, 57*(10), 1480–1484.

McKhann, G., Drachman, D., Folstein, M., Katzman, R., Price, D., & Stadlan, E. M. (1984). Clinical diagnosis of Alzheimer's disease: Report of the NINCDS-ADRDA Work Group under the auspices of Department of Health and Human Services Task Force on Alzheimer's Disease. *Neurology, 34*(7), 939–944.

McQueen, M. B., Devlin, B., Faraone, S. V., Nimgaonkar, V. L., Sklar, P., Smoller, J. W., et al. (2005). Combined analysis from eleven linkage studies of bipolar disorder provides strong evidence of susceptibility loci on chromosomes 6q and 8q. *American Journal of Human Genetics, 77*(4), 582–595.

Meschia, J. F., Kissela, B. M., Brott, T. G., Brown, Jr., R. D., Worrall, B. B., Beck, J., et al. (2006). The Siblings with Ischemic Stroke Study (SWISS), a progress report. *Clinical Medicine & Research, 4*(1), 12–21.

Meyer, J. S., Kawamura, J., & Terayama, Y. (1992). White matter lesions in the elderly. *Journal of the Neurological Sciences, 110*(1–2), 1–7.

Mohlke, K. L., Boehnke, M., et al. (2008). Metabolic and cardiovascular traits: An abundance of recently identified common genetic variants. *Human Molecular Genetics, 17*(R2), R102–R108.

Morgan, K. (2011). Commentary: The three new pathways leading to Alzheimer's disease. *Neuropathology and Applied Neurobiology*.

Morris, H. R., Khan, M. N., Janssen, J. C., Brown, J. M., Perez-Tur, J., Baker, M., et al. (2001). The genetic and pathological classification of familial frontotemporal dementia. *Archives of Neurology, 58*(11), 1813–1816.

Mukherjee, O., Kauwe, J. S., Mayo, K., Morris, J. C., & Goate, A. M. (2007). Haplotype-based association analysis of the MAPT locus in late onset Alzheimer's disease. *BMC Genetics, 8*, 3.

Myers, A., Holmans, P., Marshall, H., Kwon, J., Meyer, D., Ramic, D., et al. (2000). Susceptibility locus for Alzheimer's disease on chromosome 10. *Science, 290*(5500), 2304–2305.

Myers, A., Wavrant De-Vrieze, F., Holmans, P., Hamshere, M., Crook, R., Compton, D., et al. (2002). Full genome screen for Alzheimer disease: Stage II analysis. *American Journal of Medical Genetics, 114*(2), 235–244.

Myers, A., Kaleem, M., Marlowe, L., Pittman, A. M., Lees, A. J., Fung, H. C., et al. (2005). The H1c haplotype at the MAPT locus is associated with Alzheimer's disease. *Human Molecular Genetics, 14*(16), 2399–2404.

Myers, R. H., Schaefer, E. J., Wilson, P. W., D'Agostino, R., Ordovas, J. M., Espino, A., et al. (1996). Apolipoprotein E epsilon4 association with dementia in a population-based study: The Framingham study. *Neurology, 46*(3), 673–677.

Nahed, B. V., Seker, A., Guclu, B., Ozturk, A. K., Finberg, K., Hawkins, A. A., et al. (2005). Mapping a Mendelian form of intracranial aneurysm to 1p34. 3-p36. 13. *American Journal of Human Genetics, 76*(1), 172–179.

Naj, A. C., Jun, G. et al. (2011). Common variants at MS4A4/MS4A6E, CD2AP, CD33 and EPHA1 are associated with late-onset Alzheimer's disease. *Nature Genetics, 43*(5), 436–441.

Nalbantoglu, J., Gilfix, B. M., Bertrand, P., Robitaille, Y., Gauthier, S., Rosenblatt, D. S., et al. (1994). Predictive value of apolipoprotein E genotyping in Alzheimer's disease: Results of an autopsy series and an analysis of several combined studies. *Annals of Neurology,* *36*(6), 889–895.

Neary, D., Snowden, J., & Mann, D. (2005). Frontotemporal dementia. *Lancet Neurology,* *4*(11), 771–780.

Nee, L. E., Eldridge, R., Sunderland, T., Thomas, C. B., Katz, D., Thompson, K. E., et al. (1987). Dementia of the Alzheimer type: Clinical and family study of 22 twin pairs. *Neurology,* *37*(3), 359–363.

Nicholl, D. J., Greenstone, M. A., Clarke, C. E., Rizzu, P., Crooks, D., Crowe, A., et al. (2003). An English kindred with a novel recessive tauopathy and respiratory failure. *Annals of* *Neurology, 54*(5), 682–686.

Nilsson-Ardnor, S., Janunger, T., Wiklund, P. G., Lackovic, K., Nilsson, A. K., Lindgren, P., et al. (2007). Genome-wide linkage scan of common stroke in families from northern Sweden. *Stroke, 38*(1), 34–40.

Nowotny, P., Simcock, X., Bertelsen, S., Hinrichs, A. L., Kauwe, J. S., Mayo, K., et al. (2007). Association studies testing for risk for late-onset Alzheimer's disease with common variants in the beta-amyloid precursor protein (APP). *American Journal of Medical* *Genetics, B NeuroPsychiatric Genetics, 144*(4), 469–474.

Olson, J. M., Goddard, K. A.,, & Dudek, D. M. (2001). The amyloid precursor protein locus and very-late-onset Alzheimer disease. *American Journal of Human Genetics, 69*(4), 895–899.

Olson, J. M., Goddard, K. A.,, & Dudek, D. M. (2002). A second locus for very-late-onset Alzheimer disease: A genome scan reveals linkage to 20p and epistasis between 20p and the amyloid precursor protein region. *American Journal of Human Genetics, 71*(1), 154–161.

Parker, G. R., Cathcart, H. M., Huang, R., Lanham, I. S., Corder, E. H., & Poduslo, S. E. (2005). Apolipoprotein gene E4 allele promoter polymorphisms as risk factors for Alzheimer's disease. *Psychiatric Genetics, 15*(4), 271–275.

Pato, C. N., Pato, M. T., Kirby, A., Petryshen, T. L., Medeiros, H., Carvalho, C., et al. (2004). Genome-wide scan in Portuguese Island families implicates multiple loci in bipolar disorder: Fine mapping adds support on chromosomes 6 and 11. *American Journal of* *Medical Genetics, 127B*(1), 30–34.

Pericak-Vance, M. A., Bass, M. P., Yamaoka, L. H., Gaskell, P. C., Scott, W. K., Terwedow, H. A., et al. (1997). Complete genomic screen in late-onset familial Alzheimer disease. Evidence for a new locus on chromosome 12. *Journal of the American Medical Association,* *278*(15), 1237–1241.

Pericak-Vance, M. A., Grubber, J., Bailey, L. R., Hedges, D., West, S., Santoro, L., et al. (2000). Identification of novel genes in late-onset Alzheimer's disease. *Experimental Gerontology,* *35*(9–10), 1343–1352.

Petrovitch, H., Ross, G. W., Steinhorn, S. C., Abbott, R. D., Markesbery, W., Davis, D., et al. (2005). AD lesions and infarcts in demented and non-demented Japanese-American men. *Annals of Neurology, 57*(1), 98–103.

Pohjasvaara, T., Erkinjuntti, T., Vataja, R., & Kaste, M. (1997). Dementia three months after stroke. Baseline frequency and effect of different definitions of dementia in the Helsinki Stroke Aging Memory Study (SAM) cohort. *Stroke, 28*(4), 785–792.

Pohjasvaara, T., Mantyla, R., Ylikoski, R., Kaste, M., & Erkinjuntti, T. (2000). Comparison of different clinical criteria (DSM-III, ADDTC, ICD-10, NINDS-AIREN, DSM-IV) for the diagnosis of vascular dementia. National Institute of Neurological Disorders and

Stroke-Association Internationale pour la Recherche et l'Enseignement en Neurosciences. *Stroke, 31*(12), 2952–2957.

Polvikoski, T., Sulkava, R., Myllykangas, L., Notkola, I. L., Niinisto, L., Verkkoniemi, A., et al. (2001). Prevalence of Alzheimer's disease in very elderly people: A prospective neuropathological study. *Neurology, 56*(12), 1690–1696.

Poorkaj, P., Bird, T. D., Wijsman, E., Nemens, E., Garruto, R. M., Anderson, L., et al. (1998). Tau is a candidate gene for chromosome 17 frontotemporal dementia. *Annals of Neurology, 43*(6), 815–825.

Poorkaj, P., Grossman, M., Steinbart, E., Payami, H., Sadovnick, A., Nochlin, D., et al. (2001). Frequency of tau gene mutations in familial and sporadic cases of non-Alzheimer dementia. *Archives of Neurology, 58*(3), 383–387.

Poorkaj, P., Muma, N. A., Zhukareva, V., Cochran, E. J., Shannon, K. M., Hurtig, H., et al. (2002). An R5L tau mutation in a subject with a progressive supranuclear palsy phenotype. *Annals of Neurology, 52*(4), 511–516.

Prakash, N., Hansson, E., Betsholtz, C., Mitsiadis, T., & Lendahl, U. (2002). Mouse Notch 3 expression in the pre- and postnatal brain: Relationship to the stroke and dementia syndrome CADASIL. *Experimental Cell Research, 278*(1), 31–44.

Price, T. R., Manolio, T. A., Kronmal, R. A., Kittner, S. J., Yue, N. C., Robbins, J., et al. (1997). Silent brain infarction on magnetic resonance imaging and neurological abnormalities in community-dwelling older adults. The Cardiovascular Health Study. CHS Collaborative Research Group. *Stroke, 28*(6), 1158–1164.

Raber, J., Huang, Y., & Ashford, J. W. (2004). ApoE genotype accounts for the vast majority of AD risk and AD pathology. *Neurobiology of Aging, 25*(5), 641–650.

Rademakers, R., Cruts, M., Dermaut, B., Sleegers, K., Rosso, S. M., Van den Broeck, M., et al. (2002). Tau negative frontal lobe dementia at 17q21: Significant finemapping of the candidate region to a 4. 8 cM interval. *Molecular Psychiatry, 7*(10), 1064–1074.

Raiha, I., Kaprio, J., Koskenvuo, M., Rajala, T., & Sourander, L. (1996). Alzheimer's disease in Finnish twins. *Lancet, 347*(9001), 573–578.

Reitz, C., Cheng, R. et al. (2011). Meta-analysis of the association between variants in SORL1 and Alzheimer disease. *Archives of Neurology, 68*(1), 99–106.

Riekse, R. G., Leverenz, J. B., McCormick, W., Bowen, J. D., Teri, L., Nochlin, D., et al. (2004). Effect of vascular lesions on cognition in Alzheimer's disease: a community-based study. *Journal of the American Geriatric Society, 52*(9), 1442–1448.

Rizzu, P., Van Swieten, J. C., Joosse, M., Hasegawa, M., Stevens, M., Tibben, A., et al. (1999). High prevalence of mutations in the microtubule-associated protein tau in a population study of frontotemporal dementia in the Netherlands. *American Journal of Human Genetics, 64*(2), 414–421.

Rogaeva, E. I., Sherrington, R., Rogaeva, E. A., Levesque, G., Ikeda, M., Liang, Y., et al. (1995). Familial Alzheimer's disease in kindreds with missense mutations in a gene on chromosome 1 related to the Alzheimer's disease type 3 gene. *Nature, 376*(6543), 775–778.

Roks, G., Dermaut, B., Heutink, P., Julliams, A., Backhovens, H., Van de Broeck, M., et al. (1999). Mutation screening of the tau gene in patients with early-onset Alzheimer's disease. *Neuroscience Letters, 277*(2), 137–139.

Rollinson, S., Mead, S., et al. (2011). Frontotemporal lobar degeneration genome wide association study replication confirms a risk locus shared with amyotrophic lateral sclerosis. *Neurobiology of Aging, 32*(4), 751–758.

Roos, Y. B., Pals, G., Struycken, P. M., Rinkel, G. J., Limburg, M., Pronk, J. C., et al. (2004). Genome-wide linkage in a large Dutch consanguineous family maps a locus for intracranial aneurysms to chromosome 2p13. *Stroke, 35*(10), 2276–2781.

Rosand, J., Bayley, N., Rost, N., & de Bakker, P. I. (2006). Many hypotheses but no replication for the association between PDE4D and stroke. *Nature Genetics, 38*(10), 1091–1092; author reply 1092–1093.

Rosand, J., Hylek, E. M., O'Donnell, H. C., & Greenberg, S. M. (2000). Warfarin-associated hemorrhage and cerebral amyloid angiopathy: a genetic and pathologic study. *Neurology, 55*(7), 947–951.

Roses, A. D. (1998). Alzheimer diseases: A model of gene mutations and susceptibility polymorphisms for complex psychiatric diseases. *American Journal of Medical Genetics, 81*(1), 49–57.

Roses, A. M., Saunders, A. M., Huang, Y., Strum, J., Weisgraber, K. H., & Mahley, R. W. (2007). Complex disease-associated pharmacogenetics: Drug efficacy, drug safety, and confirmation of a pathogenetic hypothesis (Alzheimer's disease). *Pharmacogenomics Journal, 7*(1), 10–28.

Rosso, S. M., Donker Kaat, L., Baks, T., Joosse, M., de Koning, I., Pijnenburg, Y., et al. (2003). Frontotemporal dementia in The Netherlands: Patient characteristics and prevalence estimates from a population-based study. *Brain, 126*(Pt 9), 2016–2022.

Rosso, S. M., Kamphorst, W., Graaf, B., de Willemsen, R., Ravid, R., Niermeijer, M. F., et al. (2001). Familial frontotemporal dementia with ubiquitin-positive inclusions is linked to chromosome 17q21–22. *Brain, 124*(Pt 10), 1948–1957.

Rosso, S. M., Kamphorst, W., et al. (2001). Familial frontotemporal dementia with ubiquitin-positive inclusions is linked to chromosome 17q21–22. *Brain, 124*(Pt 10), 1948–1957.

Sabbadini, G., Francia, A., Calandriello, L., Di Biasi, C., Trasimeni, G., Gualdi, G. F., et al. (1995). Cerebral autosomal dominant arteriopathy with subcortical infarcts and leucoencephalopathy (CADASIL). Clinical, neuroimaging, pathological and genetic study of a large Italian family. *Brain, 118*(Pt 1), 207–215.

Saunders, A. M., Strittmatter, W. J., Schmechel, D., George-Hyslop, P. H., Pericak-Vance, M. A., Joo, S. H., et al. (1993). Association of apolipoprotein E allele epsilon 4 with late-onset familial and sporadic Alzheimer's disease. *Neurology, 43*(8), 1467–1472.

Saunders, A. M., Trowers, M. K., Shimkets, R. A., Blakemore, S., Crowther, D. J., Mansfield, T. A., et al. (2000). The role of apolipoprotein E in Alzheimer's disease: Pharmacogenomic target selection. *Biochimica et Biophysica Acta, 1502*(1), 85–94.

Schmechel, D. E., Saunders, A. M., Strittmatter, W. J., Crain, B. J., Hulette, C. M., Joo, S. H., et al. (1993). Increased amyloid beta-peptide deposition in cerebral cortex as a consequence of apolipoprotein E genotype in late-onset Alzheimer disease. *Proceedings of the National Academy of Sciences USA, 90*(20), 9649–9653.

Schroder, R., Watts, G. D., Mehta, S. G., Evert, B. O., Broich, P., Fliessbach, K., et al. (2005). Mutant valosin-containing protein causes a novel type of frontotemporal dementia. *Annals of Neurology, 57*(3), 457–461.

Schumacher, J., Kaneva, R., Jamra, R. A., Diaz, G. O., Ohlraun, S., Milanova, V., et al. (2005). Genomewide scan and fine-mapping linkage studies in four European samples with bipolar affective disorder suggest a new susceptibility locus on chromosome 1p35-p36 and provides further evidence of loci on chromosome 4q31 and 6q24. *American Journal of Human Genetics, 77*(6), 1102–1111.

Scott, W. K., Hauser, E. R., Schmechel, D. E., Welsh-Bohmer, K. A., Small, G. W., Roses, A. D., et al. (2003). Ordered-subsets linkage analysis detects novel Alzheimer disease loci on chromosomes 2q34 and 15q22. *American Journal of Human Genetics, 73*(5), 1041–1051.

Seshadri, S., Drachman, D. A., & Lippa, C. F. (1995). Apolipoprotein E epsilon 4 allele and the lifetime risk of Alzheimer's disease. What physicians know, and what they should know. *Archives of Neurology, 52*(11), 1074–1079.

Seshadri, S., Fitzpatrick, A. L., et al. (2010). Genome-wide analysis of genetic loci associated with Alzheimer disease. *Journal of the American Medical Association, 303*(18), 1832–1840.

Sherrington, R., Rogaev, E. I., Liang, Y., Rogaeva, E. A., Levesque, G., Ikeda, M., et al. (1995). Cloning of a gene bearing missense mutations in early-onset familial Alzheimer's disease. *Nature, 375*(6534), 754–760.

Sillen, A., Forsell, C., Lilius, L., Axelman, K., Bjork, B. F., Onkamo, P., et al. (2006). Genome scan on Swedish Alzheimer's disease families. *Molecular Psychiatry, 11*(2), 182–186.

Silverman, J. M., Ciresi, G., Smith, C. J., Marin, D. B., & Schnaider-Beeri, M. (2005). Variability of familial risk of Alzheimer disease across the late life span. *Archives of General Psychiatry, 62*(5), 565–573.

Silverman, J. M., Smith, C. J., Marin, D. B., Mohs, R. C., & Propper, C. B. (2003). Familial patterns of risk in very late-onset Alzheimer disease. *Archives of General Psychiatry, 60*(2), 190–197.

Sisodia, S. S., & St George-Hyslop, P. H. (2002). Gamma-secretase, Notch, Abeta and Alzheimer's disease: Where do the presenilins fit in? *Nature Reviews Neuroscience, 3*(4), 281–290.

Sjogren, T., Sjogren, H. & Lindgren, A. G. (1952). Morbus Alzheimer and morbus Pick: A genetic, clinical and patho-anatomical study. *Acta Psychiatrica Scandinavica, Suppl. 82*, 1–152.

Skoog, I., Hesse, C., Aevarsson, O., Landahl, S., Wahlstrom, J., Fredman, P., et al. (1998). A population study of apoE genotype at the age of 85: Relation to dementia, cerebrovascular disease, and mortality. *Journal of Neurology, Neurosurgery & Psychiatry, 64*(1), 37–43.

Sleegers, K., Roks, G., Theuns, J., Aulchenko, Y. S., Rademakers, R., Cruts, M., et al. (2004). Familial clustering and genetic risk for dementia in a genetically isolated Dutch population. *Brain, 127*(Pt 7), 1641–1649.

Slooter, A. J., Cruts, M., Kalmijn, S., Hofman, A., Breteler, M. M., Van Broeckhoven, C., et al. (1998). Risk estimates of dementia by apolipoprotein E genotypes from a population-based incidence study: The Rotterdam Study. *Archives of Neurology, 55*(7), 964–968.

Slooter, A. J., Tang, M. X., van Duijn, C. M., Stern, Y., Ott, A., Bell, K., et al. (1997). Apolipoprotein E epsilon4 and the risk of dementia with stroke. A population-based investigation. *Journal of the American Medical Association, 277*(10), 818–821.

Snowdon, D. A., Greiner, L. H., Mortimer, J. A., Riley, K. P., Greiner, P. A., & Markesbery, W. R. (1997). Brain infarction and the clinical expression of Alzheimer disease. The Nun Study. *Journal of the American Medical Association, 277*(10), 813–817.

Song, Y., Stampfer, M. J., & Liu, S. (2004). Meta-analysis: Apolipoprotein E genotypes and risk for coronary heart disease. *Annals of Internal Medicine, 141*(2), 137–147.

Song, Y., Rogaeva, E., Premkumar, S., Brindle, N., Kawarai, T., Orlacchio, A., et al. (1998). Absence of association between Alzheimer disease and the -491 regulatory region polymorphism of APOE. *Neuroscience Letters*, *250*(3), 189–192.

Sperfeld, A. D., Collatz, M. B., Baier, H., Palmbach, M., Storch, A., Schwarz, J., et al. (1999). FTDP-17: An early-onset phenotype with parkinsonism and epileptic seizures caused by a novel mutation. *Annals of Neurology*, *46*(5), 708–715.

Spillantini, M. G., Bird, T. D., & Ghetti, B. (1998). Frontotemporal dementia and parkinsonism linked to chromosome 17: A new group of tauopathies. *Brain Pathology*, *8*(2), 387–402.

Spillantini, M. G., Goedert, M., Crowther, R. A., Murrell, J. R., Farlow, M. R., & Ghetti, B. (1997). Familial multiple system tauopathy with presenile dementia: a disease with abundant neuronal and glial tau filaments. *Proceedings of the National Academy of Sciences USA*, *94*(8), 4113–4118.

Spillantini, M. G., Murrell, J. R., Goedert, M., Farlow, M. R., Klug, A., & Ghetti, B. (1998). Mutation in the tau gene in familial multiple system tauopathy with presenile dementia. *Proceedings of the National Academy of Sciences USA*, *95*(13), 7737–7741.

Steffens, D. C., Plassman, B. L., Helms, M. J., Welsh-Bohmer, K. A., Newman, T. T., & Breitner, J. C. (2000). APOE and AD concordance in twin pairs as predictors of AD in first-degree relatives. *Neurology*, *54*(3), 593–598.

Strittmatter, W. J., Weisgraber, K. H., Huang, D. Y., Dong, L. M., Salvesen, G. S., Pericak-Vance, M., et al. (1993). Binding of human apolipoprotein E to synthetic amyloid beta peptide: Isoform-specific effects and implications for late-onset Alzheimer disease. *Proceedings of the National Academy of Sciences USA*, *90*(17), 8098–8102.

Sudlow, C., Martinez Gonzalez, N. A., Kim, J., & Clark, C. (2006). Does apolipoprotein E genotype influence the risk of ischemic stroke, intracerebral hemorrhage, or subarachnoid hemorrhage? Systematic review and meta-analyses of 31 studies among 5961 cases and 17,965 controls. *Stroke*, *37*(2), 364–370.

Sundquist, K., Li, X., & Hemminki, K. (2006). Familial risk of ischemic and hemorrhagic stroke: A large-scale study of the Swedish population. *Stroke*, *37*(7), 1668–1673.

Suzuki, T., Oishi, M., Marshak, D. R., Czernik, A. J., Nairn, A. C.,, & Greengard, P. (1994). Cell cycle-dependent regulation of the phosphorylation and metabolism of the Alzheimer amyloid precursor protein. *EMBO Journal*, *13*(5), 1114–1122.

Talbot, C., Lendon, C., Craddock, N., Shears, S., Morris, J. C., & Goate, A. (1994). Protection against Alzheimer's disease with apoE epsilon 2. *Lancet*, *343*(8910), 1432–1443.

Teasdale, G. M., Wardlaw, J. M., White, P. M., Murray, G., Teasdale, E. M., & Easton, V. (2005). The familial risk of subarachnoid haemorrhage. *Brain*, *128*(Pt 7), 1677–1685.

Theuns, J., Brouwers, N., Engelborghs, S., Sleegers, K., Bogaerts, V., Corsmit, E., et al. (2006). Promoter mutations that increase amyloid precursor-protein expression are associated with Alzheimer disease. *American Journal of Human Genetics*, *78*(6), 936–946.

Theuns, J., & Van Broeckhoven, C. (2000). Transcriptional regulation of Alzheimer's disease genes: Implications for susceptibility. *Human Molecular Genetics*, *9*(16), 2383–2394.

Tolnay, M., & Probst, A. (2002). Frontotemporal lobar degeneration – Tau as a pied piper? *Neurogenetics*, *4*(2), 63–75.

Tournier-Lasserve, E., Joutel, A., Melki, J., Weissenbach, J., Lathrop, G. M., Chabriat, H., et al. (1993). Cerebral autosomal dominant arteriopathy with subcortical infarcts and leukoencephalopathy maps to chromosome 19q12. *Nature Genetics*, *3*(3), 256–259.

Van Broeckhoven, C., Haan, J., Bakker, E., Hardy, J. A., Van Hul, A., Wehnert, A., et al. (1990). Amyloid beta protein precursor gene and hereditary cerebral hemorrhage with amyloidosis (Dutch). *Science, 248*(4959), 1120–1122.

Van Deerlin, V. M., Sleiman, P. M., et al. (2010). Common variants at 7p21 are associated with frontotemporal lobar degeneration with TDP-43 inclusions. *Nature Genetics, 42*(3), 234–239.

van der Net, J. B., Janssens, A. C., et al. (2009). Value of genetic profiling for the prediction of coronary heart disease. *American Heart Journal, 158*(1), 105–110.

van der Zee, J. & Van Broeckhoven, C. (2011). TMEM106B: A novel risk factor for frontotemporal lobar degeneration. *Journal of Molecular Neuroscience.*

van der Zee, J., Van Langenhove, T., et al. (2011). TMEM106B is associated with frontotemporal lobar degeneration in a clinically diagnosed patient cohort. *Brain, 134*(Pt 3), 808–815.

van Duijn, C. M., Clayton, D., Chandra, V., Fratiglioni, L., Graves, A. B., Heyman, A., et al. (1991). Familial aggregation of Alzheimer's disease and related disorders: A collaborative re-analysis of case-control studies. EURODEM Risk Factors Research Group. *International Journal of Epidemiology, 20*, S13–S20.

van Duinen, S. G., Castano, E. M., Prelli, F., Bots, G. T., Luyendijk, W., & Frangione, B. (1987). Hereditary cerebral hemorrhage with amyloidosis in patients of Dutch origin is related to Alzheimer disease. *Proceedings of the National Academy of Sciences USA, 84*(16), 5991–5994.

van Herpen, E., Rosso, S. M., Serverijnen, L. A., Yoshida, H., Breedveld, G., van de Graaf, R., et al. (2003). Variable phenotypic expression and extensive tau pathology in two families with the novel tau mutation L315R. *Annals of Neurology, 54*(5), 573–581.

van Rijn, M. J., Slooter, A. J., Schut, A. F., Isaacs, A., Aulchenko, Y. S., Snijders, P. J., et al. (2005). Familial aggregation, the PDE4D gene, and ischemic stroke in a genetically isolated population. *Neurology, 65*(8), 1203–1209.

van Swieten, J., & Spillantini, M. G. (2007). Hereditary frontotemporal dementia caused by Tau gene mutations. *Brain Pathology, 17*(1), 63–73.

van Swieten, J. C., Bronner, I. F., Azmani, A., Severijnen, L. A., Kamphorst, W., Ravid, R., et al. (2007). The DeltaK280 mutation in MAP tau favors exon 10 skipping in vivo. *Journal of Neuropathology & Experimental Neurology, 66*(1), 17–25.

van Swieten, J. C., M. Stevens, S. M. Rosso, P. Rizzu, M. Joosse, I. de Koning, et al. (1999). Phenotypic variation in hereditary frontotemporal dementia with tau mutations. *Annals of Neurology, 46*(4), 617–626.

Venken, T., Claes, S., Sluijs, S., Paterson, A. D., van Duijn, C., Adolfsson, R., et al. (2005). Genomewide scan for affective disorder susceptibility loci in families of a northern Swedish isolated population. *American Journal of Human Genetics, 76*(2), 237–248.

Vermeer, S. E., Prins, N. D., den Heijer, T., Hofman, A., Koudstaal, P. J., & Breteler, M. M. (2003). Silent brain infarcts and the risk of dementia and cognitive decline. *New England Journal of Medicine, 348*(13), 1215–1222.

Verpillat, P., Camuzat, A., Hannequin, D., Thomas-Anterion, C., Puel, M., Belliard, S., et al. (2002). Association between the extended tau haplotype and frontotemporal dementia. *Archives of Neurology, 59*(6), 935–939.

Wang, J. C., Kwon, J. M., Shah, P., Morris, J. C., & Goate, A. (2000). Effect of APOE genotype and promoter polymorphism on risk of Alzheimer's disease. *Neurology, 55*(11), 1644–1649.

Wang, W. Y., Barratt, B. J., et al. (2005). Genome-wide association studies: theoretical and practical concerns. *Nature Review Genetics, 6*(2), 109–118.

Watts, G. D., Wymer, J., Kovach, M. J., Mehta, S. G., Mumm, S., Darvish, D., et al. (2004). Inclusion body myopathy associated with Paget disease of bone and frontotemporal dementia is caused by mutant valosin-containing protein. *Nature Genetics, 36*(4), 377–381.

Wetterling, T., Kanitz, R. D., & Borgis, K. J. (1996). Comparison of different diagnostic criteria for vascular dementia (ADDTC, DSM-IV, ICD-10, NINDS-AIREN). *Stroke, 27*(1), 30–36.

White, L., Petrovitch, H., Hardman, J., Nelson, J., Davis, D. G., Ross, G. W., et al. (2002). Cerebrovascular pathology and dementia in autopsied Honolulu-Asia Aging Study participants. *Annals of the New York Academy of Sciences, 977*, 9–23.

Wiklund, P. G., Brown, W. M., Brott, T. G., Stegmayr, B., Brown, Jr., R. D., Nilsson-Ardnor, S., et al. (2007). Lack of aggregation of ischemic stroke subtypes within affected sibling pairs. *Neurology, 68*(6), 427–431.

Wolfe, M. S., Xia, W., Ostaszewski, B. L., Diehl, T. S., Kimberly, W. T., & Selkoe, D. J. (1999). Two transmembrane aspartates in presenilin-1 required for presenilin endoproteolysis and gamma-secretase activity. *Nature, 398*(6727), 513–517.

Woo, D., Sauerbeck, L. R., Kissela, B. M., Khoury, J. C., Szaflarski, J. P., Gebel, J., et al. (2002). Genetic and environmental risk factors for intracerebral hemorrhage: Preliminary results of a population-based study. *Stroke, 33*(5), 1190–1195.

Wragg, M., Hutton, M., & Talbot, C. (1996). Genetic association between intronic polymorphism in presenilin-1 gene and late-onset Alzheimer's disease. Alzheimer's Disease Collaborative Group. *Lancet, 347*(9000), 509–512.

Wu, Z., Kinslow, C., Pettigrew, K. D., Rapoport, S. I., & Schapiro, M. B. (1998). Role of familial factors in late-onset Alzheimer disease as a function of age. *Alzheimer Disease and Associated Disorders, 12*(3), 190–197.

Yamada, S., Utsunomiya, M., Inoue, K., Nozaki, K., Inoue, S., Takenaka, K., et al. (2004). Genome-wide scan for Japanese familial intracranial aneurysms: Linkage to several chromosomal regions. *Circulation, 110*(24), 3727–3733.

Yasuda, M., Kawamata, T., Komure, O., Kuno, S., D'Souza, I., Poorkaj, P., et al. (1999). A mutation in the microtubule-associated protein tau in pallido-nigro-luysian degeneration. *Neurology, 53*(4), 864–868.

Zabetian, C. P., Hutter, C. M., Factor, S. A., Nutt, J. G., Higgins, D. S., Griffith, A., et al. (2007). Association analysis of MAPT H1 haplotype and subhaplotypes in Parkinson's disease. *Annals of Neurology, 62*(2), 137–144.

Zhang, J., Song, Y., Chen, H., & Fan, D. (2005). The tau gene haplotype h1 confers a susceptibility to Parkinson's disease. *European Neurology, 53*(1), 15–21.

Zubenko, G. S., Huff, F. J., Beyer, J., Auerbach, J., & Teply, I. (1988). Familial risk of dementia associated with a biologic subtype of Alzheimer's disease. *Archives of General Psychiatry, 45*(10), 889–893.

7

The Neuropathology of the Dementing Disorders

Ann C. McKee and Brandon E. Gavett

Alzheimer's Disease

Alzheimer's disease (AD) is the most common dementing disorder in the United States (Hebert et al., 2004). Current figures from the Alzheimer's Association and the United States Census Bureau indicate that 2% of Americans aged 65–74 have AD. The incidence of AD roughly doubles with every additional five years of age to an estimated 42% of those 85 years of age and older (Hebert et al., 2004). Aging is the major risk factor for AD, but other important risk factors are the presence of apolipoprotein E (APOE) ε4 alleles, a positive family history, a history of head injury, low educational achievement, as well as multiple vascular risk factors including diabetes, hypercholesterolemia, hypertension, hyperhomocysteinemia, high dietary saturated fats, high cholesterol, atrial fibrillation, and atherosclerotic disease (Luchsinger & Mayeux, 2007). Moderate alcohol consumption, particularly red wine, may lessen the risk (Luchsinger & Mayeux, 2004). Mutations of amyloid precursor protein (APP) (Goate et al., 1991), presenilin 1 and presenilin 2 (PS1 and PS2) genes (Rogaeva et al., 2007; Sherrington et al., 1995) account for most familial early-onset cases of AD by enhancing amyloid beta (Aß) production. Some cases of late-onset AD are associated with variants in genes that result in increased Aß, including the ε4 allele of the APOE gene (Strittmatter & Roses, 1996), and more recently, the SORL1 gene that directs trafficking of APP into Aß-generating compartments (Rogaev et al., 1995).

The neuropathological hallmarks of AD, namely the neurofibrillary tangle (NFT) and the senile plaque (SP), were described in 1906 by Alois Alzheimer using the

The Handbook of Alzheimer's Disease and Other Dementias, First Edition.
Edited by Andrew E. Budson, Neil W. Kowall.
© 2011 Blackwell Publishing Ltd. Published 2011 by Blackwell Publishing Ltd.

Bielschowsky silver method, a histological method that continues to be widely used for the diagnosis of AD. In his original report in 1906, Alzheimer documented his findings of a 51-year-old woman who developed rapidly progressive memory loss, confusion and paranoia, progressing to complete apathy, incontinence, and confinement to bed in a fetal position by the time of her death 4.5 years later. Postmortem neuropathological examination showed generalized cerebral atrophy, and Bielschowsky's silver preparation of brain tissue sections demonstrated tangled bundles of neurofibrils within the nerve cells of the cerebral cortex. Alzheimer also observed "miliar foci... of a peculiar substance" distributed throughout the cerebral cortex. These miliary foci were later termed senile plaques (SPs) by Simchowicz, who described large numbers of plaques in patients with senile dementia (Graeber & Mehraein, 1999).

Macroscopic appearance of the brain in AD

In most cases of Alzheimer's disease, the gross weight of the brain is usually decreased and there is generalized cerebral atrophy, although neither the brain weight nor the distribution of atrophy is consistently helpful in distinguishing AD from other neurodegenerative dementing disorders (Figure 7.1, plate section). The cerebral atrophy in AD usually involves the frontal, parietal, temporal, and occipital lobes in a bilaterally symmetrical fashion. In some cases, the atrophy is most pronounced in the frontal and temporal lobes, however, the atrophy of AD is characteristically diffuse and symmetrical, without the distinct lobar boundaries that typify the frontotemporal degenerations. In addition, there are cases of AD in which the brain is diffusely miniaturized with a generalized diminution of all cortical, subcortical, and white matter structures, as well as cases with very little apparent gross atrophy.

On coronal sectioning, the cortical ribbon is thinned and slightly irregular, especially in areas of severe atrophy. The gray matter, which is translucent in young and neurologically normal elderly individuals, is often opaque in AD, and the white matter, normally a dense, vigorous white, becomes reduced in volume and may be discolored yellowish-gray. The medial temporal lobe structures, specifically the hippocampus, entorhinal cortex, and amygdala, are conspicuously atrophic. The frontal and temporal horns of the lateral ventricles are expanded; the third ventricle and occipital horns are enlarged. In general, the basal ganglia are not affected, except for the flattening of the contour of the caudate that accompanies marked ventricular expansion. Elsewhere in the brain, the only other consistent macroscopic finding is pallor of the locus ceruleus. Depigmentation of the locus ceruleus is found in other neurodegenerative conditions including Parkinson's disease, Lewy body disease, and progressive supranuclear palsy, however, AD is distinguished from these disorders by a normally pigmented substantia nigra. In summary, diffuse (or frontotemporal) cerebral atrophy and medial temporal atrophy, in association with pallor of the locus ceruleus and a normally pigmented substantia nigra, is very suggestive of the diagnosis of AD.

Microscopic features of the brain in AD

The microscopic hallmarks of AD are NFTs, intraneuronal filaments composed of aggregated hyperphosphorylated tau protein; and SPs, extracellular accumulations of amyloid beta (Aβ) protein (Blennow et al., 2006).

Senile plaques (SPs)

The Aβ protein contained in SPs consists of a 39–43 amino acid peptide that is derived from a larger transmembrane precursor protein, amyloid precursor protein (APP), containing 695–770 amino acids. Aβ peptide is derived by sequential proteolytic cleavage of APP by β-secretase and presenilin dependent γ-secretase to yield $A\beta_{42}$ and $A\beta_{40}$ (Walsh & Selkoe, 2007).

SPs are best visualized by silver stains, including Bielschowsky's silver stain, or by immunostaining for Aβ. SPs exist in two principal forms: diffuse and neuritic plaques. Diffuse plaques have an amorphous, irregular shape, stain with Bielschowsky's silver method, and are Aβ immunoreactive. They do not stain with Congo red as the Aβ protein in diffuse plaques is not in β-pleated sheet conformation. Diffuse plaques are usually not associated with reactive astroglia or microglia. Ultrastructurally, the neuropil is normal in appearance and there are few, if any, amyloid fibrils. Neuritic plaques, also referred to as cored or compacted plaques, are composed of a central amyloid core surrounded by a halo of distorted neurites, reactive astrocytes, and microglia. Neuritic plaques are positively stained by Bielschowsky's silver stain as well as Aβ immunostain. The dystrophic neurites that surround neuritic plaques are typically argyrophilic and immunoreactive for phosphorylated tau protein. In addition, neuritic SPs are also associated with a variety of brain and serum-derived proteins, including heparan sulfate proteoglycans, complement proteins, protease inhibitors, ApoE, and advanced glycation end-products (Markesbery, 1998).

The presence of Aβ deposits in the brain is not specific for AD. Aβ deposition in the walls of small blood vessels and in the parenchyma as SPs is commonly found in cognitively normal elderly adults. The brains of individuals with trisomy 21, who are at high risk for AD, develop intraneuronal Aβ as early as one year of age, diffuse Aβ plaques in the late teenage years, and neuritic plaques in the early 20s, decades before the development of neocortical NFTs (and consequently cognitive impairment and full-blown AD) in the 40s (Gyure et al., 2001). In the Boston University Alzheimer's Disease Center (BU ADC) Brain Bank, which collects brains from many cognitively intact and cognitively impaired individuals from the Framingham Heart Study (FHS) as well as the BU ADC patient registry, we find Aβ deposition as SPs and vascular amyloid deposits 85% of cognitively intact subjects over the age of 65 years. Furthermore, 37% of cognitively intact subjects over the age of 65 have moderate numbers of neuritic SP throughout their neocortex. In subjects with mild cognitive impairment and mild AD, the density of diffuse and neuritic SPs is increased over cognitively intact subjects, but in the moderate and advanced stages of AD, the density of SPs reaches a plateau that is not significantly increased from mild AD (Gyure et al., 2001). Elevated levels of Aβ 40 and Aβ 42 are also found in the brain prior to the development of any SP or tau pathology and have been shown to correlate with cognitive decline (Näslund et al., 2000). These findings indicate that Aβ deposition precedes neurofibrillary tangle formation in AD and suggest that Aβ may play an initial role in the pathogenesis of AD dementia.

Staging of senile plaque deposition and the Consortium to Establish a Registry for Alzheimer's Disease (CERAD)

In 1990, the Consortium to Establish a Registry for Alzheimer's Disease (CERAD) presented a protocol for the neuropathological diagnosis of AD (Mirra et al., 1991). The CERAD criteria involve a semi-quantitative assessment of neuritic plaques designated as sparse, moderate, or frequent in the cortex. An age-related plaque score is assigned based on the semi-quantitative plaque density and the patient's age, and a level of certainty of the diagnosis of AD is generated using the age-related plaque score, the presence or absence of other neuropathological lesions associated with dementia, and clinical evidence of dementia. The CERAD criteria for the diagnosis of AD have important shortcomings, namely: there is an inherent circular reliance on the clinical diagnosis; and NFTs are not assessed. However, the CERAD criteria for evaluating semi-quantitative neuritic plaque density as sparse, moderate, and frequent (with supporting cartoons) are widely used by many Alzheimer's disease centers and are a key component of the NIA-Reagan criteria for the diagnosis of AD.

Neurofibrillary tangles (NFTs)

The neurofibrillary pathology of AD takes three forms: NFTs; neuropil threads (NTs); and dystrophic neurites surrounding neuritic plaques. All three forms represent intracellular accumulations of paired helical filaments (PHF), one of the basic components of which is phosphorylated tau protein. Ultrastructurally, PHF have a diameter of ~20 nm and a periodicity of ~80 nm. Neuropil threads initially form in the proximal neurites of degenerating neurons where they appear as discontinuous short fibers, and simultaneously or shortly thereafter form in the perikaryon and apical dendrite, as NFTs. NFTs accumulate in the neuronal cytoplasm, displacing the nucleus, until the neuron dies; the NFTs that remain in the tissue after the neuronal cytoplasm and nucleus disappears are referred to as "ghost" or "tombstone" tangles. Ghost tangles are extracellular and stain differently than intracellular NFTs, in addition, they tend to lose the PHF conformation and become thicker straight filaments. NTs resemble NFTs in their staining and immunocytochemical characteristics and both are found in a laminar distribution in the neocortex, generally most dense in cortical layers III and V. It has been repeatedly shown that NFT and neuropil threads correlate with the severity of dementia in AD (Arriagada et al., 1992; McKee et al., 2006).

The regional distribution of NFTs

The regional brain distribution of NFTs evolves in a generally predictable hierarchical pattern in AD, delineated by Braak and Braak in their analysis of 83 brains from individuals ranging from cognitively intact to severely demented (Braak & Braak, 1997). In stages I and II, the transentorhinal stages, NFTs are restricted to the transentorhinal cortex, entorhinal cortex, and CA1 of the hippocampus. In stage III, the limbic stage, the transentorhinal and entorhinal cortex, and hippocampus CA1, are severely affected, ghost tangles first appear in the entorhinal cortex, and the amygdala displays NFTs. The neocortex is considered to be unaffected during stage III although small numbers of NFTs may be found in the inferior temporal cortex. Stage IV is characterized by increasing NFTs in the neocortex and the appearance of ghost tangles in transentorhinal and entorhinal cortex and hippocampus. In stages V and VI, the neocortical stages, the entorhinal, transentorhinal, and hippocampal regions are severely involved, increasing numbers of NFTs are found in the neocortex; the primary sensory areas tend to remain resistant to NFT until the most advanced stage, stage VI.

Our work characterizing the neuropathological alterations of cognitively intact elderly subjects from the FHS provides evidence that there may be modifications from the traditional Braak hierarchical staging scheme for NFTs in early, preclinical stages of AD. We have shown that 40–50% of cognitively intact elderly individuals show dense neurofibrillary pathology in the visual association cortex, BA 19 and 37, very posterior regions of the temporal and occipital lobe, in subjects with early Braak stages I–III (McKee et al., 1991). We have also found similar posterior pathology in a cognitively intact 79-year-old man at high risk for AD, as his monozygotic twin developed classical AD, confirmed by postmortem neuropathology, at age 60.

Additional credence to this modified Braak scheme is found in Braak's own monograph, depicting moderate numbers of NFTs and NTs in the parastriate cortex in Braak stage III disease (Braak & Braak, 1997). Early focal NFT degeneration in the posterior association areas of the brain is compatible with imaging studies in preclinical AD, including SPECT, PET, and fMRI that found initial changes in blood flow, metabolic defects, and activation latencies localized to the posterior temporoparietal and occipital cortices (Buckner, 2004; Buckner et al., 2004; Chételat et al., 2003; Ober et al., 1991).

The NIA-Reagan criteria for AD

In 1997, the National Institute on Aging and the Ronald and Nancy Reagan Institute of the Alzheimer's Association (NIA-Reagan) Working Group proposed the current criteria for the neuropathological diagnosis of AD (Hyman & Trojanowski, 1997). The NIA-Reagan criteria incorporate the Braak staging of NFTs and the CERAD criteria for semi-quantitative analysis of SPs, and are currently the most widely used criteria for the neuropathological diagnosis of AD.

The NIA-Reagan criteria are as follows:

> There is a high likelihood of a diagnosis of AD if there are frequent neuritic plaques by CERAD criteria and a high Braak stage of NFTs (V/VI). There is an intermediate likelihood of AD if there is a moderate density of neuritic SPs and NFTs in a limbic distribution (i.e., a "moderate" CERAD neuritic plaque score, and Braak NFT stage III/IV). A low likelihood of AD corresponds to a scarce distribution of SPs and NFTs (i.e., a "sparse" CERAD neuritic plaque score, and Braak stage I/II).

Cerebral amyloid angiopathy

Since the beginning of the century, it has been recognized that Aβ is also deposited in the walls of small and medium arterioles in elderly intact individuals as well as in persons with AD. Our results from the BU ADC and FHS show that 60% of all cognitively intact subjects over 60 years have some degree of vascular Aβ deposition. Amyloid angiopathy affects small diameter arteries of the cortex and meninges; in arteries that penetrate the white matter, only the portion of the vessel that courses through the gray matter shows amyloid deposition. Amyloid angiopathy is most pronounced in the posterio parieto-occipital region and least pronounced in the temporal lobe. The distribution and severity of vascular amyloid is unrelated to the severity of the Alzheimer changes, the duration of the disease, and is not required for the diagnosis of AD. A common complication of amyloid angiopathy is spontaneous intracerebral hemorrhage, a complication that occurs earlier and more often in individuals who have inherited an apolipoprotein E ε2 or ε4 allele (Nicoll et al., 1996). There is also experimental evidence to suggest that age and cerebrovascular disease may reduce the elimination of Aβ along the perivascular interstitial fluid drainage pathways and lead to the deposition of Aβ in vascular walls (Weller & Kaas, 1983).

Dementia with Lewy Bodies (DLB)

Dementia with Lewy bodies (DLB) is the second-most common neurodegenerative cause of dementia after AD (McKeith et al., 1996; McKeith et al., 2005). DLB was first described in 1961, when Okazaki and colleagues described two elderly patients with a severe dementing illness accompanied by rigidity (Okazaki et al., 1961) whose cerebral cortex contained large numbers of intracytoplasmic inclusions that closely resembled Lewy bodies (LBs). Since that time, DLB has been increasingly recognized as a distinct pathological entity, whose frequency of diagnosis was greatly enhanced by the discovery of positive ubiquitin immunostaining of LBs in 1988 (Kuzuhara et al., 1988) and later, by a-synuclein immnuostaining in 1997 (Spillantini et al., 1998). In DLB, LBs are found in widespread cortical structures, particularly in the amygdala, transentorhinal and entorhinal cortex, cingulate gyrus, insular cortex, and frontotemporal cortex, in addition to the brainstem, basal forebrain, and diencephalic sites involved in Parkinson's disease (PD) (McKee et al., 1998). The dementia in DLB is likely due to the combination of LB pathology, Alzheimer pathology, neuronal loss, and neurochemical deficits, although most studies indicate that density of Lewy bodies and Lewy neurites in the cerebral cortex is more strongly associated with the cognitive changes than the Alzheimer changes (Samuel et al., 1996). Neocortical Lewy body counts correlate with dementia in the Lewy body variant of Alzheimer's (Apaydin et al., 2002). In 1996, the Dementia with Lewy Bodies International Workshop established that a single brainstem and cortical LB were the only criteria essential to the pathological diagnosis of DLB (McKeith et al., 2005). With the passage of time, these criteria were considered too inclusive and were revised in 2005 to include a semi-quantitative grading of LB density and a regional pattern of LB involvement (McKee et al., 1998). DLB is often found in association with AD and was considered a subset of AD by some authors (the Lewy body variant of AD) (Hansen et al., 1989). However, the prevailing opinion, first championed by Kosaka (Kosaka et al., 1984) is that DLB is part of a spectrum of Lewy body disorders with PD at one end and DLB at the other (see Chapter 3). In PD, LBs are primarily restricted to the brainstem, basal forebrain and diencephalon, while DLB is characterized by significant numbers of LBs in widespread limbic and neocortical structures, in addition to the subcortical structures. Lewy body disorders may be divided into three subtypes: brainstem predominant; limbic or transitional; or neocortical, based on the relative severity of LB density and the pattern of regional involvement. Other pathological findings in DLB include spongiform changes in the neuropil and Lewy neurites in CA2-3 of the hippocampus (Dickson et al., 1991). In 2005, the DLB consortium revised criteria for the clinical and pathological diagnosis of DLB incorporating new information about core clinical features and also proposing a new scheme for the pathological assessment of LBs and Lewy neurites using α-synuclein immunocytochemistry and semi-quantitative grading of lesion density, with the regional pattern of involvement being more important than total LB count. The new criteria take into account both Lewy-related and AD pathology to allocate a defined probability that these pathologies are associated with the clinical DLB syndrome (McKeith et al., 2005).

The Lewy body

Lewy bodies are intracytoplasmic, eosinophilic, neuronal inclusion bodies that are classically spherical but may be multilocular or fusiform in shape. LBs with a dense spherical hyaline core and a clear peripheral halo are found in the brainstem and basal forebrain (brainstem LBs). Ultrastructurally, brainstem LBs have a dense osmiophilic core consisting of granular and vesicular material and a concentric, peripheral rim of radiating, haphazardly arranged fibrils, 8–10 nm diameter. Contributing to their peculiar appearance is the admixture of neuromelanin, lipofuscin, mitochondria, dense core vesicles, other organelles, and amorphous material. The halo, or rings of lamination, sets the LB apart from other axonal swellings or cytoplasmic inclusions. Cortical LBs are less discrete, rounded inclusions typically found in the deeper cortical layers in small to medium-sized non-pyramidal cortical neurons. Cortical LBs are similar to brainstem LBs ultrastructurally, although the fibrils are arranged more loosely and there is no distinct core. A third body, the pale body, is a larger, granular, eosinophilic, intraneuronal inclusion lacking a halo that is also found in brainstem neurons and probably represents a precursor to the brainstem LB. LBs and Lewy neurites are primarily composed of aggregates of α-synuclein, although other proteins including neurofilament proteins, ubiquitin, UHC-L1 or ubiquitin C terminal hydrolase, have also been found (Nussbaum & Polymeropoulos, 1997) and UHC-L1 (Leroy et al., 1998). The identification of full-length as well as truncated and insoluble aggregates of α-synuclein in LBs suggests that alterations in α-synuclein, its processing, ubiquitination, and/or its interaction with neurofilaments may lead to neuronal degeneration in PD and DLB (Baba et al., 1998).

Macroscopic appearance of the brain in PD and DLB

The brain weight is typically normal in PD and often in DLB, unless there is coexistent AD. The key distinguishing gross features of PD and DLB are the loss of pigmentation in the substantia nigra and the absence of significant cortical atrophy. As concomitant AD is found in as many as 60% of cases of DLB, the presence of medial temporal atrophy or generalized cortical atrophy in association with depigmentation of the nigra and locus ceruleus is strongly suggestive of the combined diagnoses of DLB or PD and AD.

Microscopic appearance of the brain in the LB disorders

Brainstem LBs are easily detected with routine hematoxylin and eosin (H&E) staining, although cortical LBs, which are less discretely defined, may be overlooked. LBs are most easily and reliably identified with α-synuclein immunocytochemistry. Ubiquitin also unequivocally stains LBs and Lewy neurites, but since ubiquitin also stains NFTs and neuropil threads, as well as a number of other intracellular inclusions, positive ubiquitin immunostaining can be difficult to interpret in the presence of AD or other neurodegenerative changes.

Staging of brain pathology in Parkinson's disease and Lewy body disease

In 2003, Braak and colleagues analyzed the regional LB pathology of 41 cases of sporadic Parkinson's disease (Braak et al., 2003) and devised a six-tiered staging system. Stage I is characterized by Lewy neurites and LBs in the dorsal IX/X motor nucleus and intermediate reticular zone of the medulla; brains with slightly greater involvement showed Lewy pathology in the caudal raphe nuclei, magnocellular reticular nucleus, locus ceruleus and anterior olfactory nucleus are stage II. With intermediate disease, stage III, Lewy pathology is found in the midbrain, including the pars compacta of the substantia nigra and basal forebrain. Stage IV disease is characterized by involvement of other mesencephalic nuclei, hypothalamus, thalamus, stria terminalis, accessory and central nuclei of the amygdala, and ventral claustrum. Cortical involvement is restricted to the transentorhinal and CA2 region of the hippocampus. In stage V disease, the degree of neuronal loss and LB pathology is increased in all structures previously affected, the olfactory areas and high order sensory association areas of the neocortex and prefrontal neocortex are involved as well. In the most severe stage, stage VI, the pathology advances to involve the sensory, premotor, and motor neocortex.

Recently, this staging was confirmed in younger patients with a long disease course by Halliday and colleagues who longitudinally followed 69 patients with the clinical diagnosis of PD confirmed by autopsy (Halliday, 2008). They also found two other clinicopathological subtypes: older onset PD patients with a shorter survival and more complex disease course and more varied pathology; and a third group with an early-onset malignant dementia-dominant syndrome with severe neocortical LB disease (Halliday, 2008).

Frontotemporal Lobar Degeneration (FTLD)

The term FTLD encompasses a group of degenerative diseases that demonstrate the most severe pathology in the frontal and temporal lobes, but may involve other cortical and subcortical regions (Cairns et al., 2007; Forman et al., 2006; Josephs et al., 2007; Kwong et al., 2008; Mackenzie et al., 2007; Mackenzie et al., 2010; McKhann et al., 2001; Neary et al., 1998; Snowden et al., 2007; Van Deerlin, et al., 2010). After AD and DLB, FTLD is the third-most common neurodegenerative dementia, accounting for approximately 5–15% of dementia cases. FTLD most often presents as a behavioral disorder, with disinhibition and changes in personality and social conduct, usually associated with the gradual disturbance of language. Some patients with FTLD develop parkinsonian symptoms or motor neuron disease, usually in the later stages of the disease.

FTLD is often an early-onset dementia, with a peak incidence between 50–65 years, and age at onset ranging from 20–100 years. The FTLDs include the tauopathies, such as Pick's disease, corticobasal degeneration, progressive supranuclear palsy, neurofibrillary tangle dementia, argyrophilic grain dementia, and frontotemporal dementia with microtubule-associated tau (MAPT) gene mutation (also called FTD with parkinsonism linked to chromosome 17), as well as tau-negative disease including FTLD with ubiquitin-positive inclusions (FTLD-U) with or without motor neuron disease, and FTLD with no distinctive histopathology.

Macroscopic appearance of the brain in FTLD

The brain in FTLD is generally atrophic, with the greatest atrophy found in the frontal and temporal lobes. The atrophy may be extremely pronounced, and is very often strikingly focal and asymmetric. There is often an abrupt line of demarcation between affected and unaffected brain. The cortical mantle is reduced in volume, the underlying white matter is yellowed and atrophied, and the cerebral ventricles are correspondingly enlarged. The substantia nigra may show loss of pigmentation.

Microscopic appearance of the brain in FTLD

In most forms of FTLD, there is microvacuolation of the cerebral cortex, most marked in layer II, associated with neuronal loss. In severely affected cases there is microvacuolation of all cortical layers associated with marked neuronal loss and astrocytic gliosis. The white matter often shows marked myelin and axonal loss that parallels the cortical neuronal loss. Some cases also show substantial neuronal loss in the basal ganglia and substantia nigra.

FTLD is subdivided into tau-positive and tau-negative disorders according to whether there are tau-immunoreactive neuronal and glial inclusions by immunohistochemistry and abnormal tau isoforms biochemically. In normal adult brain, there are six isoforms of the microtubule-associated protein tau: three isoforms with zero, one, or two inserts contain three microtubule-binding repeats (3R tau); three isoforms, also with zero, one, or two repeats, contain four microtubule-binding repeats (4R tau). The tauopathies are distinct biochemically, the tau protein is relatively insoluble, and the insoluble species can be detected by tau fractionation methods and characterized by the pattern of tau isoforms. In AD, all six isoforms are abnormally hyperphosphorylated; treatment with alkaline phosphatase reveals six bands (3R and 4R). In Pick's disease, the tau is predominantly 3R tau, whereas in CBD, PSP, and argyrophilic grain disease primarily 4R is present, and in NFT-only dementia, tau is a mixture of 3R and 4R tau.

Tau-positive FTLD

Pick's disease

In 1892, Arnold Pick described circumscribed atrophy of the anterior forebrain in an aphasic, demented patient. The microscopic hallmarks of the disease, namely rounded argyrophilic intraneuronal inclusions, or Pick bodies, and ballooned achromasic neurons, or Pick cells, were described nearly two decades later by Alois Alzheimer. The cortical atrophy of Pick's disease is usually severe; the brain weight is often reduced to less than 1000 grams. The atrophy may be strikingly restricted in its distribution, with normal appearing cortex immediately adjacent to extremely atrophic gyri. The atrophy is usually most pronounced in the frontal and temporal lobes, often abruptly ending at the frontal precentral gyrus and sparing the posterior two-thirds of the superior temporal gyrus. The atrophy is asymmetrical in over half the cases, the left hemisphere is more often more atrophic than the right. Rare cases show focal involvement of the parietal lobes or pancortical atrophy. The white matter is reduced in parallel with the cortical atrophy; there may be marked atrophy of the caudate, putamen, globus pallidus, and pars reticulata of the substantia nigra. Microscopically, severe neuronal loss, marked gliosis, Pick bodies and Pick cells are found. Pick bodies are clearly delineated, round or oval arygrophilic inclusions in the neuronal cytoplasm, readily identified by the Bielschowsky or other silver stains, as well as antibodies to phosphorylated tau, 3 repeat tau, ubiquitin, and phosphorylated nerofilaments. Pick bodies are most frequent in the granule cells of the dentate gyrus and hippocampal pyramidal neurons, as well as cortical layers II and VI. Pick cells are pale-staining, enlarged neurons, often with an eccentric nucleus, most often found in cortical layers III and V and immunoreactive for alpha beta-crystallin (Kato et al., 1992).

Corticobasal degeneration

The gross features of corticobasal degeneration are not sufficiently consistent or distinctive to qualify as diagnostic features of the condition (Dickson et al., 2002; Gibb et al., 1989; Rebeiz et al., 1968). There is often atrophy of the posterior aspect of the frontal lobes in a parasagittal distribution, with less severe involvement of the inferior and middle frontal lobes, frontal operculum, and cingulate gyrus. There also may be circumscribed atrophy of the anterior parietal lobes, while the temporal and occipital lobes tend to be spared. The atrophy may be asymmetric. The corpus callosum and subcortical white matter are generally reduced in size. Pallor of the substantia nigra is the only invariable macroscopic finding, in contrast to normal pigmentation of the locus ceruleus. Brainstem atrophy, a characteristic of progressive supranuclear palsy, is unusual in corticobasal degeneration. The diagnosis of corticobasal degeneration rests on the microscopic findings. The cortical ribbon is thinned in affected areas, with neuronal loss and astrocytosis. Astrocytosis is particularly prominent at the gray-white junction. The white matter shows myelin loss. Ballooned, achromasic neurons lacking apparent Nissl substance are scattered in cortical layers III, V, and VI. Ballooned neurons demonstrate immunoreactivity for alpha-beta-crystallin, phosphorylated neurofilaments, and occasionally ubiquitin and tau. Tau immunostaining (4 repeat tau) demonstrates diffuse or granular positivity in scattered neurons of the upper cortical layers and globose neurofibrillary tangles in the substantia nigra and locus ceruleus. Extensive tau immunoreactive threadlike structures are found in the gray and white matter of the affected cortices, as well as basal ganglia, thalamus and rostral brainstem. In addition, there are tau-positive argyrophilic inclusions in oligodendroglia, and widespread tau-positive plaque-like structures termed "astrocytic plaques."

Progressive supranuclear palsy

The macroscopic features of progressive supranuclear palsy are atrophy of the globus pallidus, subthalamic nucleus, midbrain, and pontine tegmentum (Hauw et al., 1994; Steele et al., 1964). Microscopically, there are tau immunoreactive neurofibrillary tangles, neuropil threads, tufted astrocytes and oligodendroglial inclusions. The tau abnormalities (primarily 4 repeat tau) are found in the neocortex and subcortical white matter, entorhinal cortex, hippocampus, striatum, globus pallidus, subthalamic nucleus, substantia nigra, oculomotor nuclei, red nucleus, pontine nuclei, inferior olives, cerebellar dentate nuclei, and dorsal horns of the spinal cord.

Neurofibrillary tangle dementia

The macroscopic pathology of neurofibrillary tangle dementia usually shows generalized cerebral atrophy (Iseki et al., 2006; Jellinger & Bancher, 1998). Microscopically the disease is characterized by abundant NFTs, ghost tangles, and neuropil threads largely restricted to the transentorhinal, entorhinal cortex, hippocampus, and amygdala with only rare involvement of other neocortical sites. NFTs are also found in the nucleus basalis of Meynert and locus ceruleus, but the remainder of the brainstem and basal ganglia are not involved. The tau protein in NFTs is composed of both 3 and 4 repeat tau. Neuritic plaques and amyloid deposits are scarce or absent.

Argyrophilic grain disease

Argrophilic grain disease (AGD) is a common neuropathological finding in cognitively normal as well as demented elderly subjects, with a reported frequency of 6–9% in unselected autopsy series. In clinically demented individuals it is found in up to 35–43% of individuals (Jicha et al., 1997), usually in association with other neurodegenerative conditions such as AD, LBD, PD, other tauopathies, and hippocampal sclerosis. In AGD, tau-positive (primarily 4-repeat tau) and Gallyas silver positive grains are found in the limbic regions, including the transentorhinal, entorhinal cortex, hippocampus, and amygdala (Braak & Braak, 1998). With advancing disease severity, argyrophilic grains are also found in the anterior medial temporal lobe, insula, anterior cingulate gyrus, septal nuclei, and hypothalamus. Scattered ballooned neurons may also be present in the limbic regions.

Frontotemporal dementia with microtubule-associated tau (MAPT)
gene mutation
FTLD-MAPT (also called FTD with parkinsonism linked to chromosome 17) is a clinically and neuropathologically heterogeneous condition, with more than 40 mutations reported in the MAPT gene (Spillantini et al., 2000). The neuronal and glial tau pathology often runs the entire spectrum between the 3 repeat, 4 repeat and combined 3 and 4 repeat tauopathies described above. Rarely, this condition occurs in the absence of a family history and without identifiable mutations in tau.

Tau-negative FTLD

The tau-negative FTLDs are a heterogeneous group of disorders with ubiquitin-positive, but tau- and synuclein-negative, neuronal inclusions.

FTLD with ubiquitin-positive inclusions (FTLD-U) with or
without motor neuron disease
FTLD with ubiquitin-positive inclusions (FTLD-U) with or without motor neuron disease is the most common underlying pathology in FTLD. TAR DNA-binding protein 43 (TDP-43), a nuclear protein implicated in transcription regulation, was recently identified as a major protein of the ubiquitin-immunoreactive inclusions characteristic of FTLD-U, with and without MND, as well as in sporadic ALS (Arai et al., et al., 2006; Baker et al., 2006, Cairns et al., 2007; Josephs et al., 2007; Neumann et al., 2006). The neuropathology of FTLD-U is characterized by cerebral atrophy, predominantly in a frontotemporal distribution, striatal atrophy (most marked in the caudate), and pallor of the substantia nigra. Ubiquitin- and TDP-43 positive neuronal intranuclear and cytoplasmic inclusions, dystrophic neurites, and glial cytoplasmic inclusions are found, most commonly in the dentate gyrus of the hippocampus, striatum, and frontotemporal neocortex. Variability in the morphology and distribution of the neuronal inclusions has led to a proposed classification into four subtypes of FTLD-U. Mutations in the progranulin gene (PGRN) were recently reported in chromosome 17-linked FTLD-U, mutations that lead to a process referred to as nonsense-mediated decay, characterized by truncated or no messenger RNA, and no RNA translation. FTLD-U with PGRN mutations (PGRN +) has more cortical and striatal atrophy than FTLD-U without PGRN mutations (PGRN −). There is also more nigral degeneration and a higher density of cortical neuronal inclusions (Beck et al., 2008).

Hippocampal Sclerosis

Hippocampal sclerosis is characterized by neuronal loss and gliosis in CA1 and subiculum of the hippocampus and is associated with memory decline and dementia (Amador-Ortiz & Dickson, 2008; Amador-Ortiz et al., 2007). Hippocampal sclerosis occurs in 2.8–13% of demented patients (Amador-Ortiz & Dickson, 2008) and in as many as 10–18% of convenience autopsy series (BU ADC) (Chui et al., 2006). Hippocampal sclerosis is heterogeneous in etiology, and may be caused by hypoxia – ischemia or neurodegeneration. Indeed, recent evidence suggests that the majority of hippocampal sclerosis is neurodegenerative, most commonly associated with FTLD-U (Amador-Ortiz & Dickson, 2008), tauopathy (Probst et al., 2007), AD, and DLB (Attems & Jellinger, 2006; Beach et al., 2003). In a recent series of 21 cases of hippocampal sclerosis, 71% showed immunoreactivity for TDP-43; another series reported that tau-positive neuronal and glial pretangles in the dentate gyrus and the CA fields were the predominant finding. When hippocampal sclerosis is found as an isolated finding and is not associated with other degenerative pathology in cases of dementia, it is referred to as hippocampal sclerosis dementia (HSD). HSD occurs in 0.4–2% of dementia cases, is more common with advanced age, and may be associated with greater neuronal and synaptic loss, reactive gliosis and corpora amylacea (Amador-Ortiz & Dickson, 2008).

Chronic Traumatic Encephalopathy

Chronic traumatic encephalopathy (CTE) is a progressive tau immunoreactive neurofibrillary degeneration of the brain and spinal cord with distinctive clinical and pathological features (Figure 7.2, plate section). In all cases of CTE reported in the medical literature, it has occurred after repetitive closed head injury. Although CTE is best known in association with boxing, it may also occur in association with the play of many contact sports, including professional football, soccer, hockey, and wrestling. CTE is clinically characterized by subtle deterioration in the 40s and 50s with memory loss, inattention, confusion, irritability and short temper, outbursts of anger or aggression, worsening of organization and planning skills, and depression. As the disease advances, usually occurs over decades, there is further decline in cognition and memory, attention, executive function and language skills. Pathologically, CTE is unique from other neurodegenerative diseases (McKee et al., 2009); the widespread distribution of NFTs and glial tangles in the frontal, insular and temporal cortices, white matter, thalamus, hypothalamic nuclei, mammillary bodies, substantia innominata, midbrain tegmentum, substantia nigra, medullary reticular formation, and spinal cord is considerably more extensive than that found in AD. Furthermore, the pattern of the neurofibrillary abnormalities (their irregularity, the superficial and perivascular distribution, the focal deposits greatest at the depths of the sulci, and the pronounced tau immunoreactive astrocytic tangles) is entirely distinct from AD or any other tauopathy, including the many types of frontotemporal degeneration (McKee et al., 2009)). Notably, β-amyloid protein deposits, as either senile plaques or amyloid angiopathy, are not a characteristic of CTE, although in some cases small numbers of diffuse plaques may be found in the frontal and temporal cortex.

Vascular Dementia

The prevalence of vascular dementia (VaD) in autopsy series varies widely; in the United States it ranges from 2–58%; in countries such as England, Switzerland, Austria, Sweden, Finland, and Norway, it ranges from 5–34%; while in Japan, it is seen in 22–35% of autopsies (Barclay et al., 1985; Esiri & Wilcock, 1986; Jellinger & Attems, 2006; Markesbery, 1998; Tomlinson et al., 1970). In the oldest age groups, vascular dementia may predominate over all other causes of dementia (Skoog et al., 1993). Part of the difficulty in assessing the prevalence of vascular dementia lies in its heterogeneity, the neuropathological substrate of vascular cognitive impairment and vascular dementia is highly variable, it often coexists with other degenerative pathologies, and no clear diagnostic criteria for vascular dementia are available. In a prospective study of VaD in a dementia clinic, it was found that 87% had AD, either alone (58%) or in combination with vascular disease (42%) (Nolan et al., 1998). Various forms of vascular lesions are found in 60–90% of AD cases (Kalaria, 2000) and if microvascular lesions, such as amyloid angiopathy and white matter lesions are included, nearly all cases of AD show some degree of vascular pathology. Concomitant vascular lesions are thought to accelerate the clinical expression of dementia in persons with AD (Esiri et al., 1997; Heyman et al., 1998; Jellinger, 2002; Nagy et al., 1997; Snowden et al. 2007; Zekry et al., 2003), particularly in the early stages (Esiri, 2000; Jellinger, 2001). Many pathological studies analyzing the overlap between AD and cerebrovascular injury have emphasized large vessel pathology, such as infarcts and hemorrhages, and large volume small vessel lesions, such as lacunes (Bowling & Beal, 1995; Heyman et al., 1998; Lee et al., 2000; Olichney et al., 1997; Skoog et al., 1993; Snowden et al. 2007; Zekry et al., 2002). More recently, microvascular pathology has been recognized as a major substrate of dementia in the elderly (Esiri et al., 1997; Esiri et al., 1999; Kalaria et al., 1993; Kövari et al., 2007; Sonnen et al., 2007; Thal et al., 2003; White et al., 2002; Zekry et al., 2003). An additional type of pathology that may contribute to cognitive decline especially among the very elderly, is hippocampal sclerosis (Dickson et al., 1994), although there is debate as to how often isolated hippocampal sclerosis (hippocampal sclerosis dementia) is caused by ischemic disease, as discussed above the most recent literature favors a predominantly neurodegenerative origin (Amador-Ortiz & Dickson, 2008; Probst et al., 2007).

The major types of vascular lesions associated with cognitive impairment are as follows (modified from Jellinger, 2007; Kalaria et al., 2004; Román et al., 1993).

1 Multiple large infarcts, affecting the cerebral hemispheres or basal ganglia, also referred to as multi-infarct dementia, and usually affecting more than 50–100 ml of tissue (Ince & Fernando, 2003; Tomlinson et al., 1970).
2 Small vessel disease, either as multiple lacunar infarcts, white matter lesions including subcortical arteriosclerotic leukoencephalopathy (Binswanger's disease), multiple micro-infarcts or cerebral amyloid angiopathy (CAA).

3 Strategic infarct dementia, usually consisting of small or medium-sized infarcts in functionally important brain regions, such as the thalamus, hippocampus, and basal forebrain.
4 Cerebral hypoperfusion, either as hippocampal sclerosis, pseudolaminar cortical laminar necrosis, post-ischemic, usually in arterial border zones, or borderzone infarcts.
5 Cerebral hemorrhages (lobar, intracerebral, or subarachnoid hemorrhage).
6 Mixed dementia, usually cerebrovascular disease with AD, but may be any other degenerative process plus vascular lesions

Multiple large vessel infarcts

Single or multiple infarcts involving major cerebral artery territories most commonly result from atherosclerosis and thromboembolism. Atherothromboembolism accounts for approximately 50% of all ischemic strokes (Kalimo et al., 2002). Other causes of large cerebral infarcts are cardiac emboli, including those associated with atrial fibrillation and myocardial infarction. Less common causes of cerebral infarcts include hematological conditions, vasculitides, and CADASIL (autosomal dominant arteriopathy wth subcortical infarcts and leukoencephalopathy), all of which usually result in multiple subcortical and cortical lesions.

Small vessel disease

Lacunes
Small vessel disease, either as multiple lacunar infarcts, subcortical arteriosclerotic leukoencephalopathy (Binswanger's disease), or multiple micro-infarcts is the most common cause of VaD (Esiri et al., 1997; Esiri et al., 1999; Kalaria et al., 1993; Kövari et al., 2007; Sonnen et al., 2007; Thal et al., 2003; White et al., 2002; Zekry et al., 2003). Among Japanese American men in the Honolulu Asia Aging Study, small vessel disease accounted for 50% of VaD, while large vessel disease accounted for 23% and mixed-vessel disease for 16% of VaD (Román, 2002). Furthermore, in the subsample with small vessel disease, multiple lacunes were found in 85% and Binswanger syndrome was found in 15%. Lacunes are small cavitating infarcts up to 1.5 cm in diameter, visible to the eye on gross inspection, and usually confined to the cerebral white matter, thalamus, pons and cerebellar white matter. Lacunes are the most frequent type of cerebrovascular lesion, occurring in 27–42% of patients studied (Gorelick et al., 1992; Ishii et al., 1986; Jellinger, 2007; Jellinger & Attems, 2006). Cognitive decline is associated with multiple lacunes (Gold et al., 2007; Kövari et al., 2004; van der Flier et al., 2005). In an autopsy study of 30 subjects with VaD, dementia was found in subjects with 6–24 lacunes (mean 12) plus incomplete white matter infarctions (Kövari et al., 2004). Other studies suggest that the

brain region affected may be more important than the number of lacunes in producing dementia. Early reports indicate that the most common site of lacunar infarcts in VaD is the periventricular white matter around the anterior horns of the lateral ventricles, at the head of the caudate nucleus and putamen (Kövari et al., 2004; Markesbery, 1998). Whereas a more recent clinicopathological study of 72 subjects (mean age of 83.4 years) with no macroscopic ischemic lesions other than lacunes and no significant neurofibrillary tangle pathology (Braak stages I and II), the location of lacunes in the thalamus and basal ganglia significantly predicted cognitive function (van der Flier et al., 2005). There was no relationship between deep white matter lacunes in frontal, temporal and parietal areas and cognition (Fisher, 1989; van der Flier et al., 2005).

White matter lesions

The importance of small vessel disease of the cerebral white matter with infarction and demyelination has been recognized as a cause of dementia for over a century (Akisaki et al., 2006; Binswanger, 1894). Neuroimaging studies have further emphasized white matter lesions and their relationship to cognitive impairment (Fernando et al., 2004; Gold et al., 2007; Gorelick et al., 1992). White matter lesions may be variously referred to as leukoariosis, leukoencephalopathy, leukomalacia, and if severe, and confluent, Binswanger's disease or subcortical arteriolosclerotic encephalopathy. White matter lesions and lacunes often coexist, and each has been shown to correlate with cognitive impairment (Fisher, 1989; Ogata, 1999). Neuropathologically, white matter lesions consist of demyelination, axonal loss and lacunar infarcts in the frontal, parietal and occipital white matter and periventricular regions (Jellinger & Attems, 2006). The myelin degeneration usually has a patchy distribution that spares the subcortical U-fibers and, in severe cases, is associated with multiple cavitary and non-cavitary infarctions

Micro-infarcts

Esiri and colleagues in their study of demented and nondemented elderly subjects without significant AD pathology, found that severe cribriform change and micro-infarcts in the subcortical white matter and deep nuclei were associated with dementia and suggested that microvascular lesions might represent a critical source of cerebral damage relevant to vascular dementia (Esiri et al., 1999). White et al. (2002) studied a group of 285 elderly men of Japanese descent and observed that the proportion of demented individuals with micro-infarcts in the neocortex and basal ganglia was nearly equal to that of demented individuals with AD lesions, signifying that the role of microvascular injury in the pathogenesis of dementia might be approximately equal to that of AD. Ogata found two-thirds of 25 cases of vascular dementia were associated with small vessel disease and associated subcortical leukoencephalopathy (Ogata, 1999); and Vinters similarly stressed the importance of widespread small ischemic lesions as a basis for vascular dementia in his series of 20 subjects (Vinters et al., 2000). In addition, in Ballard's series of vascular dementia associated with small volume macro-infarction, over 70% of subjects had microvascular lesions and white matter pathology as well (Ballard et al., 2000). The importance of microvascular pathology as a major contributor to dementia is not without its detractors. Although the MRC Optima study found microvascular pathology to be the most common vascular lesion in its neuropathological study of 209 brains, the severity of microvascular disease did not distinguish demented from nondemented subjects (Neuropathology Group. Medical Research Council Cognitive Function and Aging Study, 2001). Zekry and colleagues also found no significant correlation between microscopic lesions and neuropsychological assessment in their analysis of the brains of 33 subjects, apart from the correlation between the severity of amyloid angiopathy and the severity of cognitive impairment (Zekry et al., 2002; Zekry et al., 2003). Similarly, the neuropathological analysis of 101 non-demented and mildly demented elderly subjects conducted by Xuereb and colleagues found that while vascular amyloid and white matter pallor were associated with dementia, micro-infarcts were not (Xuereb et al., 2000).

Cerebral amyloid angiopathy

Another form of small vessel disease that contributes to cognitive loss is cerebral amyloid angiopathy (CAA) or the deposition of Aβ in the walls of small vessels within the brain parenchyma and leptomeninges. CAA is associated with lobar, intraparenchymal and subarachnoid hemorrhage, ischemic infarcts, white matter lesions, micro-infarcts, micro-bleeds and a granulomatous vasculitis; it is also an independent risk factor for cognitive decline and dementia (Attems, 2005; Jellinger, 2007; Greenberg et al., 1992; Haglund et al., 2006; Ogata, 1999; Yoshimura et al., 1992; Zekry et al., 2002). CAA occurs in 70–98% of individuals with AD as well as 2–100% of nondemented elderly (Attems, 2005). Progressive white matter lesions, detectable with MRI, are associated with CAA, although fibrohyalinosis of the deep white matter vessels likely plays a far greater role in promoting their development than CAA (Chen et al., 2006; Tomimoto et al., 1999). Micro-infarcts, a well-recognized substrate of vascular cognitive impairment, are significantly correlated with CAA, suggesting that these microscopic ischemic lesions may also contribute to the pathological substrate of dementia in subjects with CAA (Haglund et al., 2006). Another microscopic vascular lesion, micro-bleeds, minute hemorrhages detectable by MRI, are associated with CAA in AD although their contribution to cognitive impairment is unclear (Nakata-Kudo et al., 2006).

Strategic infarct dementia

Focal ischemic lesions, usually consisting of small or medium-sized infarcts in functionally important brain regions, such as dominant angular gyrus, anterior cerebral artery territory, unilateral or bilateral medial thalamus, bilateral hippocampus, dominant caudate nucleus and basal forebrain, may produce a dementia syndrome often in association with other prominent neurological impairments (Jellinger, 2007; Markesbery, 1998; Tatemichi et al., 1992).

Cerebral hypoperfusion

Cerebral hypoperfusion injuries result in a variety of cerebrovacuar lesions, but the most common are hippocampal sclerosis, borderzone infarction, or pseudolaminar cortical laminar necrosis

Ischemic hippocampal sclerosis, consisting of neuronal and gliosis in CA1 and the subiculum of the hippocampus differs morphologically from neurodegenerative hippocampal sclerosis by showing greater neuronal and synaptic loss and greater reactive astrocytosis and less immunoreactivity for TDP-43 (Amador-Ortiz & Dickson, 2008; Attems & Jellinger, 2006; Jellinger, 2007). Recent evidence suggests that most of hippocampal sclerosis is neurodegenerative although ischemic origins are also well recognized and may account for a greater proportion of hippocampal sclerosis cases occurring in the very elderly (>80 years) (Dickson et al., 1994). Watershed or borderzone infarcts may occur in circulatory borderzones between the branches of the anterior cerebral artery (ACA), middle cerebral artery (MCA) and posterior cerebral arteries (PCA) secondary to reduced cerebral blood flow or showers of micro-emboli. These infarcts generally occur in individuals with severe atherosclerosis and prolonged periods of hypotension. The infarcts are generally most severe in the superior frontal region between the distal end-fields of the ACA and MCA or in the posterior parieto-occipital region involving the end artery territories of the ACA, MCA, and PCA. The hippocampal CA fields, anteromedial thalamus, and the lateral caudate and putamen may also be affected (Jellinger, 2007). Pseudolaminar necrosis is patchy cortical neuronal ischemia that occurs in the setting of global cerebral ischemia or hypoxia that accompanies cardiac or respiratory arrest. It typically affects arterial border zones, may be associated with diffuse white matter and cerebellar damage, and is associated with cognitive impairment (Jellinger, 2007).

References

Akisaki, T., Sakurai, T., Takata, T., et al. (2006). Cognitive dysfunction associates with white matter hyperintensities and subcortical atrophy on magnetic resonance imaging of the elderly diabetes mellitus Japanese elderly diabetes intervention trial (J-EDIT). *Diabetes/Metabolism Research and Reviews, 22*(5), 376–384.

Amador-Ortiz, C., & Dickson, D. W. (2008). *Neuropathology* of hippocampal sclerosis. *Handbook of Clinical Neurology, 89,* 569–572.

Amador-Ortiz, C., Lin, W. L., Ahmed, Z, et al. (2007). TDP-43 immunoreactivity in hippocampal sclerosis and Alzheimer's disease. *Annals of Neurology, 61*(5), 435–445.

Apaydin, H., Ahlskog, J., Parisi, J., Boeve, B., & Dickson, D. (2002). Parkinson disease neuropathology, later-developing dementia and loss of the levodopa response. *Archives of Neurology*, *59*(1), 102–112.

Arai, T., Hasegawa, M., Akiyama, H., et al. (2006). TDP-43 is a component of ubiquitin-positive tau-negative inclusions in frontotemporal lobar degeneration and amyotrophic lateral sclerosis. *Biochemical and Biophysical Research Communications*, *351*(3), 602–611.

Arriagada, P.V., Marzloff, K., & Hyman, B.T. (1992). Distribution of Alzheimer-type pathologic changes in nondemented elderly individuals matches the pattern in Alzheimer's disease. *Neurology*, *42*(9), 1681–1688.

Attems, J. (2005). Sporadic cerebral amyloid angiopathy: Pathology, clinical implications, and possible pathomechanisms. *Acta Neuropathologica*, *110*(4), 345–359.

Attems, J., & Jellinger, K. A. (2006). Hippocampal sclerosis in Alzheimer disease and other dementias. *Neurology*, *66*(5), 775.

Baba, M., Nakajo, S., Tu, P., et al. (1998). Aggregation of alpha-synuclein in Lewy bodies of sporadic Parkinson's disease and dementia with Lewy bodies. *American Journal of Pathology*, *152*(4), 879–884.

Baker, M., Mackenzie, I. R., Pickering-Brown, S. M., et al. (2006). Mutations in progranulin cause tau-negative frontotemporal dementia linked to chromosome 17. *Nature*, *442*(7105), 916–919.

Ballard, C,. McKeith, I., O'Brien, J., et al. (2000). Neuropathological substrates of dementia and depression in vascular dementia, with a particular focus on cases with small infarct volumes. *Dementia and Geriatric Cognitive Disorders*, *11*(2), 59–65.

Barclay, L. L., Zemcov, A., Blass, J. P., & McDowell, F. H. (1985). Factors associated with duration of survival in Alzheimer's disease. *Biological Psychiatry*, *20*(1), 86–93.

Beach, T. G., Sue, L., Scott, S., et al. (2003). Hippocampal sclerosis dementia with tauopathy. *Brain Pathology (Zurich)*, *13*(3), 263–278.

Beck, J., Rohrer, J. D., Campbell, T., et al. (2008). A distinct clinical, neuropsychological and radiological phenotype is associated with progranulin gene mutations in a large UK series. *Brain*, *131*(Pt 3), 706–720.

Binswanger, O. (1894). Die Abgrenzung der allgemeinen progressiven Paralyse. *Berliner Klin Wochenschr*, *31*, 1103–1105, 1137–1139, 1180–1186.

Blennow, K., de Leon, M., & Zetterberg, H. (2006). Alzheimer's disease. *Lancet*, *368*(9533), 387–403.

Bowling, A., & Beal, M. (1995). Bioenergetic and oxidative stress in neurodegenerative diseases. *Life Sciences*, *56*(14), 1151–1171.

Braak, H., & Braak, E. (1997). Staging of Alzheimer-related cortical destruction. *International Psychogeriatrics*, *9*(Suppl 1), 257–261; discussion 269–272.

Braak, H., & Braak, E. (1998). Argyrophilic grain disease: Frequency of occurrence in different age categories and neuropathological diagnostic criteria. *Journal of Neural Transmission*, *105*(8–9), 801-819.

Braak, H., Del Tredici, K., Rüb, U., de Vos, R. A. I., Jansen Steur, E. N. H., & Braak, E. (2003). Staging of brain pathology related to sporadic Parkinson's disease. *Neurobiology of Aging*, *24*(2), 197–211.

Buckner, R.L. (2004). Memory and executive function in aging and AD, multiple factors that cause decline and reserve factors that compensate. *Neuron*, *44*(1), 195–208.

Buckner, R.L., Head, D., Parker, J., et al. (2004). A unified approach for morphometric and functional data analysis in young, old, and demented adults using automated atlas-based head size normalization, reliability and validation against manual measurement of total intracranial volume. *NeuroImage, 23*(2), 724–738.

Cairns, N. J., Bigio, E. H., Mackenzie, I. R., et al. (2007). Neuropathologic diagnostic and nosologic criteria for frontotemporal lobar degeneration: consensus of the Consortium for Frontotemporal Lobar Degeneration. *Acta Neuropathologica, 114*(1), 5–22.

Chen, Y. W., Gurol, M. E., Rosand, J., et al. (2006). Progression of white matter lesions and hemorrhages in cerebral amyloid angiopathy. *Neurology, 67*(1), 83–87.

Chételat, G., Desgranges, B., de la Sayette, V., Viader, F., Eustache, F., & Baron, J.C. (2003). Mild cognitive impairment. Can FDG-PET predict who is to rapidly convert to Alzheimer's disease? *Neurology, 60*(8), 1374–1377.

Chui, H. C., Zarow, C., Mack, W. J., et al. (2006). Cognitive impact of subcortical vascular and Alzheimer's disease pathology. *Annals of Neurology, 60*(6), 677–687.

Dickson, D. W., Bergeron, C., Chin, S. S., et al. (2002). Office of Rare Diseases neuropathologic criteria for corticobasal degeneration. *Journal of Neuropathology & Experimental Neurology, 61*(11), 935–946.

Dickson, D. W., Davies, P., Bevona, C., et al. (1994). Hippocampal sclerosis: A common pathological feature of dementia in very old (> or = 80 years of age) humans. *Acta Neuropathologica, 88*(3), 212–221

Dickson, D., Ruan, D., Crystal, H. et al. (1991). Hippocampal degeneration differentiates diffuse Lewy body disease (DLBD) from Alzheimer's disease, light and electron microscopic immunocytochemistry of CA2-3 neurites specific to DLBD. *Neurology, 41*(9), 1402–1409.

Esiri, M. (2000). Which vascular lesions are of importance in vascular dementia? *Annals of the New York Academy of Sciences, 903*, 239–243.

Esiri, M. M., & Wilcock, G. K. (1986). Cerebral amyloid angiopathy in dementia and old age. *Journal of Neurology, Neurosurgery & Psychiatry, 49*(11), 1221–1226.

Esiri, M., Nagy, Z., Smith, M., Barnetson, L., & Smith, A. (1999). Cerebrovascular disease and threshold for dementia in the early stages of Alzheimer's disease. *Lancet, 354*(9182), 919–920.

Esiri, M., Wilcock, G., & Morris, J. (1997). Neuropathological assessment of the lesions of significance in vascular dementia. *Journal of Neurology, Neurosurgery & Psychiatry, 63*(6), 749–753.

Fernando, M. S., O'Brien, J. T., Perry, R. H., et al. (2004). Comparison of the pathology of cerebral white matter with post-mortem magnetic resonance imaging (MRI) in the elderly brain. *Neuropathology and Applied Neurobiology, 30*(4), 385–395.

Fisher, C. M. (1989). Binswanger's encephalopathy: A review. *Journal of Neurology, 236*(2), 65–79.

Forman, M. S., Mackenzie, I. R., Cairns, N. J., et al. (2006). Novel ubiquitin neuropathology in frontotemporal dementia with valosin-containing protein gene mutations. *Journal of Neuropathology & Experimental Neurology, 65*, 571–581.

Gibb, W. R., Luthert, P. J., & Marsden, C.D. (1989). Corticobasal degeneration. *Brain, 112* (Pt 5), 1171–1192.

Goate, A., Chartier-Harlin, M., Mullan, M. et al. (1991). Segregation of a missense mutation in the amyloid precursor protein gene with familial Alzheimer's disease. *Nature, 349*(6311), 704–706.

Gold, G., Giannakopoulos, P., Herrmann, F. R., Bouras, C., & Kövari, E. (2007). Identification of Alzheimer and vascular lesion thresholds for mixed dementia. *Brain, 130*(Pt 11), 2830–2836.

Gorelick, P. B., Chatterjee, A., Patel, D., Flowerdew, G., Dollear, W., Taber, J., et al. (1992). Cranial computed tomographic observations in multi-infarct dementia. A controlled study. *Stroke, 23*(6), 804–811.

Graeber, M.B., & Mehraein, P. (1999). Reanalysis of the first case of Alzheimer's disease. *European Archives of Psychiatry and Clinical Neuroscience, 249*(Suppl 3), 10–13.

Greenberg, S., Davies, P., Schein, J., & Binder, L. (1992). Hydrofluoric acid-treated tau PHF proteins display the same biochemical properties as normal tau. *Journal of Biological Chemistry, 267*(1), 564–569.

Gyure, K., Durham, R., Stewart, W., Smialek, J., & Troncoso, J. (2001). Intraneuronal abeta-amyloid precedes development of amyloid plaques in Down syndrome. *Archives of Pathology & Laboratory Medicine, 125*(4), 489–492.

Haglund, M., Passant, U., Sjöbeck, M., Ghebremedhin, E., & Englund, E. (2006). Cerebral amyloid angiopathy and cortical microinfarcts as putative substrates of vascular dementia. *International Journal of Geriatric Psychiatry, 21*(7), 681–687.

Halliday, G. (2008). Clarifying the pathological progression of Parkinson's disease. *Acta Neuropathologica, 115*(4), 377–378.

Hansen, L., Masliah, E., Terry, R., & Mirra, S. (1989). A neuropathological subset of Alzheimer's disease with concomitant Lewy body disease and spongiform change. *Acta Neuropathologica (Berlin), 78*(2), 194–201.

Hauw, J. J., Daniel, S. E., Dickson, D., et al. (1994). Preliminary NINDS neuropathologic criteria for Steele-Richardson-Olszewski syndrome (progressive supranuclear palsy). *Neurology, 44*(11), 2015–2019.

Hebert, L.E., Scherr, P.A., Bienias, J.L., Bennett, D.A., & Evans, D.A. (2004). State-specific projections through 2025 of Alzheimer disease prevalence. *Neurology, 62*(9), 1645.

Heyman, A., Fillenbaum, G. G., Welsh-Bohmer, K. A., et al. (1998). Cerebral infarcts in patients with autopsy-proven Alzheimer's disease: CERAD, part XVIII. Consortium to Establish a Registry for Alzheimer's Disease. *Neurology, 51*(1), 159–162.

Hyman, B., & Trojanowski, J. (1997). Consensus recommendations for the postmortem diagnosis of Alzheimer disease from the National Institute on Aging and the Reagan Institute Working Group on diagnostic criteria for the neuropathological assessment of Alzheimer disease. *Journal of Neuropathology aAnd Experimental Neurology, 56*(10), 1095–1097.

Ince, P. G., & Fernando, M. S. (2003). Neuropathology of vascular cognitive impairment and vascular dementia. *International Psychogeriatrics, 15*(Suppl 1), 71–75.

Iseki, E., Yamamoto, R., Murayama, N., et al. (2006). Immunohistochemical investigation of neurofibrillary tangles and their tau isoforms in brains of limbic neurofibrillary tangle dementia. *Neuroscience Letters, 405*(1–2), 29–33.

Ishii, N., Nishihara, Y., & Imamura, T. (1986). Why do frontal lobe symptoms predominate in vascular dementia with lacunes? *Neurology, 36*(3), 340–345.

Jellinger, K. A. (2001). Neuropathologic substrates of ischemic vascular dementia. *Journal of Neuropathology & Experimental Neurology, 60*(6), 658–659.

Jellinger, K. A. (2002). Vascular-ischemic dementia: An update. *Journal of Neural Transmissions, 62*, 1–23.

Jellinger, K. A. (2007). The enigma of vascular cognitive disorder and vascular dementia. *Acta Neuropathologica, 113*(4), 349–388.

Jellinger, K. A., & Attems, J. (2006). Prevalence and impact of cerebrovascular pathology in Alzheimer's disease and parkinsonism. *Acta Neurologica Scandinavica, 114*(1), 38–46.

Jellinger, K. A., & Bancher, C. (1998). Senile dementia with tangles (tangle predominant form of senile dementia). *Brain Pathology, 8*(2), 367–376.

Jicha, G., Bowser, R., Kazam, I., & Davies, P. (1997). Alz-50 and MC-1, a new monoclonal antibody raised to paired helical filaments, recognize conformational epitopes on recombinant tau. *Journal of Neuroscience Research, 48*(2), 128–132.

Josephs, K. A., Ahmed, Z., Katsuse, O., Parisi, J. F., Boeve, B. F., Knopman, D. S., et al. (2007). Neuropathologic features of frontotemporal lobar degeneration with ubiquitin-positive inclusions with progranulin gene (PGRN) mutations. *Journal of Neuropathology & Experimental Neurology, 66*, 142–151.

Kalaria, R. N. (2000). The role of cerebral ischemia in Alzheimer's disease. *Neurobiology of Aging, 21*(2), 321–330.

Kalaria, R. N., Bhatti, S., Lust, W., & Perry, G. (1993). The amyloid precursor protein in ischemic brain injury and chronic hypoperfusion. *Annals of the New York Academy of Sciences, 695*, 190–193.

Kalaria, R. N., Kenny, R. A., Ballard, C. G., Perry, R., Ince, P., Polvikoski. T. (2004). Towards defining the neuropathological substrates of vascular dementia. *Journal of the Neurological Sciences, 226*(1–2), 75–80.

Kalimo, H., Kaste, M., & Haltia, M. (2002). Vascular diseases. In D. Graham & P. Lantos (Eds.), *Greenfield's neuropathology* (pp. 281–355). Arnold Press.

Kato, S., Hirano, A., Umahara, T., Llena, J. F., Herz, F., & Ohama, E. (1992). Ultrastructural and immunohistochemical studies on ballooned cortical neurons in Creutzfeldt-Jakob disease: Expression of alpha B-crystallin, ubiquitin and stress-response protein 27. *Acta Neuropathologica, 84*(4), 443–448.

Kosaka, K., Yoshimura, M., Ikeda, K., & Budka, H. (1984). Diffuse type of Lewy body disease, progressive dementia with abundant cortical Lewy bodies and senile changes of varying degree – A new disease? *Clinical Neuropathology, 3*(5), 185–192.

Kövari, E., Gold, G., Herrmann, F. R., et al. (2004). Cortical microinfarcts and demyelination significantly affect cognition in brain aging. *Stroke, 35*(2), 410–414.

Kövari, E., Gold, G., Herrmann, F. R., et al. (2007). Cortical microinfarcts and demyelination affect cognition in cases at high risk for dementia. *Neurology, 68*(12), 927–931.

Kuzuhara, S., Mori, H., Izumiyama, N., Yoshimura, M., & Ihara, Y. (1988). Lewy bodies are ubiquitinated. A light and electron microscopic immunocytochemical study. *Acta Neuropathologica (Berlin), 75*(4), 345–353.

Kwong, L. K., Uryu, K., Trojanowski, J. Q., & Lee, V. M. Y. (2008). TDP-43 proteinopathies: Neurodegenerative protein misfolding diseases without amyloidosis. *Neuro-Signals, 16*(1), 41–51.

Lee, J., Olichney, J., Hansen, L., Hofstetter, C., & Thal, L. (2000). Small concomitant vascular lesions do not influence rates of cognitive decline in patients with Alzheimer disease. *Archives of Neurology, 57*(10), 1474–1479.

Leroy, E., Boyer, R., Auburger, G., et al. (1998). The ubiquitin pathway in Parkinson's disease. *Nature, 395*(6701), 451–452.

Luchsinger, J.A., & Mayeux, R. (2004). Dietary factors and Alzheimer's disease. *Lancet Neurology, 3*(10), 579–587.

Luchsinger, J.A., & Mayeux, R. (2007). Adiposity and Alzheimer's disease. *Current Alzheimer Research, 4*(2), 127–134.

Mackenzie, I. R. A., Bigio, E. H., Ince, P. G., et al. (2007). Pathological TDP-43 distinguishes sporadic amyotrophic lateral sclerosis from amyotrophic lateral sclerosis with SOD1 mutations. *Annals of Neurology, 61*(5), 427–434.

Mackenzie, I.R., Neumann, M., Bigio, E.H., et al. (2010). Nomenclature and nosology for neuropathologic subtypes of frontotemporal lobar degeneration: An update. *Acta Neuropathoogical, 119*(1), 1–4.

Markesbery, W.R. (1998). *Neuropathology of dementing disorders?* London: Edward Arnold.

McKee, A., Au, R., Cabral, H. et al. (2006). Visual association pathology in preclinical Alzheimer disease. *Journal of Neuropathology and Experimental Neurology, 65*(6), 621–630.

McKee, A., Cantu, R. C., Nowinski, C. J., et al. (2009). Chronic traumatic encephalopathy in athletes: Progressive tauopathy after repetitive head injury. *Journal of Neuropathology & Experimental Neurology, 68*(7), 709–735.

McKee, A., Kosik, K., & Kowall, N. (1991). Neuritic pathology and dementia in Alzheimer's disease. *Annals of Neurology, 30*(2), 156–165.

McKee, A., Kowall, N., Schumacher, J., & Beal, M. (1998). The neurotoxicity of amyloid beta protein in aged primates. *Amyloid, 5*(1), 1–9.

McKeith, I. G., Dickson, D. W., Lowe, J. et al. (2005). Diagnosis and management of dementia with Lewy bodies, third report of the DLB Consortium. *Neurology, 65*(12), 1863–1872.

McKeith, I. G., Galasko, D., Kosaka, K. et al. (1996). Consensus guidelines for the clinical and pathologic diagnosis of dementia with Lewy bodies (DLB), report of the consortium on DLB international workshop. *Neurology, 47*(5), 1113–1124.

McKhann, G. M., Albert, M. S., Grossman, M., et al. (2001). Clinical and pathological diagnosis of frontotemporal dementia: Report of the Work Group on Frontotemporal Dementia and Pick's Disease. *Archives of Neurology, 58*(11), 1803–1809

Mirra, S.S., Heyman, A., McKeel, D. et al. (1991). The Consortium to Establish a Registry for Alzheimer's Disease (CERAD). Part II. Standardization of the neuropathologic assessment of Alzheimer's disease. *Neurology, 41*(4), 479–486.

Nagy, Z., Vatter-Bittner, B., Braak, H., et al. (1997). Staging of Alzheimer-type pathology: An interrater-intrarater study. *Dementia and Geriatric Cognitive Disorders, 8*(4), 248–251.

Nakata-Kudo, Y., Mizuno, T., Yamada, K., et al. (2006). Microbleeds in Alzheimer disease are more related to cerebral amyloid angiopathy than cerebrovascular disease. *Dementia and Geriatric Cognitive Disorders, 22*(1), 8–14.

Näslund, J., Haroutunian, V., Mohs, R. et al. (2000). Correlation between elevated levels of amyloid beta-peptide in the brain and cognitive decline. *Journal of the American Medical Association, 283*(12), 1571–1577.

Neary, D., Snowden, J. S., Gustafson, L., et al. (1998). Frontotemporal lobar degeneration: A consensus on clinical diagnostic criteria. *Neurology, 51*(6), 1546–1554.

Neumann, M., Sampathu, D. M., Kwong, L. K., et al. (2006). Ubiquitinated TDP-43 in frontotemporal lobar degeneration and amyotrophic lateral sclerosis. *Science, 314*(5796), 130–133.

Neuropathology Group. Medical Research Council Cognitive Function and Aging Study. (2001). Pathological correlates of late-onset dementia in a multicentre, community-based population in England and Wales. Neuropathology Group of the Medical Research

Council Cognitive Function and Ageing Study (MRC CFAS). *Lancet, 357*(9251), 169–175.

Nicoll, J.A., Burnett, C., Love, S., Graham, D.I., Ironside, J.W., & Vinters, H.V. (1996). High frequency of apolipoprotein E epsilon 2 in patients with cerebral hemorrhage due to cerebral amyloid angiopathy. *Annals of Neurology, 39*(5), 682–683.

Nolan, K. A., Lino, M. M., Seligmann, A. W., & Blass, J. P. (1998). Absence of vascular dementia in an autopsy series from a dementia clinic. *Journal of the American Geriatrics Society, 46*(5), 597–604.

Nussbaum, R., & Polymeropoulos, M. (1997). Genetics of Parkinson's disease. *Human Molecular Genetics, 6*(10), 1687–1691.

Ober, B.A., Jagust, W.J., Koss, E., Delis, D.C., & Friedland, R.P. (1991). Visuoconstructive performance and regional cerebral glucose metabolism in Alzheimer's disease. *Journal of Clinical and Experimental Neuropsychology, 13*(5), 752–772.

Ogata, J. (1999). Vascular dementia: The role of changes in the vessels. *Alzheimer Disease and Associated Disorders, 13*(Suppl 3), S55–S58.

Okazaki, H., Lipkin, L., & Aronson, S. (1961). Diffuse intracytoplasmic ganglionic inclusions (Lewy type) associated with progressive dementia and quadriparesis in flexion. *Journal of Neuropathology and Experimental Neurology, 20*, 237–244

Olichney, J. M, Ellis, R. J, Katzman, R., Sabbagh, M. N., & Hansen, L. (1997). Types of cerebrovascular lesions associated with severe cerebral amyloid angiopathy in Alzheimer's disease. *Annals of the New York Academy of Sciences, 826*, 493–497.

Probst, A., Taylor, K. I., & Tolnay, M. (2007). Hippocampal sclerosis dementia: A reappraisal. *Acta Neuropathologica, 114*(4), 335–345.

Rebeiz, J. J., Kolodny, E. H., & Richardson, E. P. (1968). Corticodentatonigral degeneration with neuronal achromasia. *Archives of Neurology, 18*(1), 20–33.

Rogaev, E., Sherrington, R., Rogaeva, E. et al. (1995). Familial Alzheimer's disease in kindreds with missense mutations in a gene on chromosome 1 related to the Alzheimer's disease type 3 gene. *Nature, 376*(6543), 775–778.

Rogaeva, E., Meng, Y., Lee, J., et al. (2007). The neuronal sortilin-related receptor SORL1 is genetically associated with Alzheimer disease. *Nature Genetics, 39*(2), 168–177.

Román, G. C. (2002). On the history of lacunes, etat criblé, and the white matter lesions of vascular dementia. *Cerebrovascular Diseases (Basel, Switzerland), 13*(Suppl 2), 1–6.

Román, G. C., Tatemichi, T. K., Erkinjuntti, T., et al. (1993). Vascular dementia: Diagnostic criteria for research studies. Report of the NINDS-AIREN International Workshop. *Neurology, 43*(2), 250–260.

Samuel, W., Galasko, D., Masliah, E., & Hansen, L. (1996). Neocortical Lewy body counts correlate with dementia in the Lewy body variant of Alzheimer's disease. *Journal of Neuropathology and Experimental Neurology, 55*(1), 44–52.

Sherrington, R., Rogaev, E., Liang, Y., et al. (1995). Cloning of a gene bearing missense mutations in early-onset familial Alzheimer's disease. *Nature, 375*(6534), 754–760.

Skoog, I., Nilsson, L., Palmertz, B., Andreasson, L. A., & Svanborg, A. (1993). A population-based study of dementia in 85-year-olds. *New England Journal of Medicine, 328*(3), 153–158.

Snowden, J., Neary, D., & Mann D. (2007). Frontotemporal lobar degeneration: Clinical and pathological relationships. *Acta Neuropathologica, 114*(1), 31–38.

Sonnen, J. A., Larson, E. B., Crane, P. K., et al. (2007). Pathological correlates of dementia in a longitudinal, population-based sample of aging. *Annals of Neurology, 62*(4), 406–413.

Spillantini, M., Crowther, R., Jakes, R., Hasegawa, M., & Goedert, M. (1998). alpha-Synuclein in filamentous inclusions of Lewy bodies from Parkinson's disease and dementia with Lewy bodies. *Proceedings of the National Academy of Sciences USA*, *95*(11), 6469–6473.

Spillantini, M., Van Swieten, J. C., & Goedert, M. (2000). Tau gene mutations in frontotemporal dementia and parkinsonism linked to chromosome 17 (FTDP-17). *Neurogenetics*, *2*(4), 193–205.

Steele, J. C., Richardson, J. C., & Olszewski, J. (1964). Progressive supranuclear palsy. A heterogeneous degenration involving the brain stem, basal ganglia and cerebellum with vertical gaze and pseudobulbar palsy, nuchal dystonia and dementia. *Archives of Neurology*, *10*, 333–359.

Strittmatter, W.J., & Roses, A.D. (1996). Apolipoprotein E and Alzheimer's disease. *Annual Review of Neuroscience*, *19*, 53–57.

Tatemichi, T. K., Desmond, D. W., Mayeux, R., et al. (1992). Dementia after stroke: Baseline frequency, risks, and clinical features in a hospitalized cohort. *Neurology*, *42*(6), 1185–1193.

Thal, D., Ghebremedhin, E., Orantes, M., & Wiestler, O. (2003). Vascular pathology in Alzheimer disease: Correlation of cerebral amyloid angiopathy and arteriosclerosis/lipohyalinosis with cognitive decline. *Journal of Neuropathology & Experimental Neurology*, *62*(12), 1287–1301.

Tomimoto, H., Akiguchi, I., Akiyama, H., et al. (1999). Vascular changes in white matter lesions of Alzheimer's disease. *Acta Neuropathologica*, *97*(6), 629–634.

Tomlinson, B. E., Blessed, G., & Roth, M. (1970). Observations on the brains of demented old people. *Journal of the Neurological Sciences*, *11*(3), 205–242.

Van Deerlin, V.M., Sleiman, P.M., Martinez-Lage, M., et al. (2010). Common variants at 7p21 are associated with frontotemporal lobar degeneration with TDP-43 inclusions. *Nature Genetics*, *42*(3), 234–239.

van der Flier, W. M., van Straaten, E. C., Barkhof, F., et al. (2005). Small vessel disease and general cognitive function in nondisabled elderly: The LADIS study. *Stroke*, *36*(10), 2116–2120.

Vinters, H. V., Ellis, W. G., Zarow, C., et al. (2000). Neuropathologic substrates of ischemic vascular dementia. *Journal of Neuropathology & Experimental Neurology*, *59*(11), 931–945.

Walsh, D.M., & Selkoe, D.J. (2007). A beta oligomers – A decade of discovery. *Journal of Neurochemistry*, *101*(5), 1172–1184.

Weller, R., & Kaas, J. (1983). Retinotopic patterns of connections of area 17 with visual areas V-II and MT in macaque monkeys. *Journal of Comparative Neurology*, *220*(3), 253–279.

White, L., Petrovitch, H., Hardman, J., et al. (2002). Cerebrovascular pathology and dementia in autopsied Honolulu-Asia Aging Study participants. *Annals of the New York Academy of Sciences*, *977*, 9-23.

Xuereb, J. H., Brayne, C., Dufouil, C., et al. (2000). Neuropathological findings in the very old. Results from the first 101 brains of a population-based longitudinal study of dementing disorders. *Annals of the New York Academy of Sciences*, *903*, 490–496.

Yoshimura, M., Yamanouchi, H., Kuzuhara, S., et al. (1992). Dementia in cerebral amyloid angiopathy: a clinicopathological study. *Journal of Neurology*, *239*(8), 441–450.

Zekry, D., Duyckaerts, C., Belmin, J., et al. (2003). The vascular lesions in vascular and mixed dementia: The weight of functional neuroanatomy. *Neurobiology og Aging, 24*(2), 213–219.

Zekry, D., Duyckaerts, C., Belmin, J., Geoffre, C., Moulias, R., & Hauw, J. (2002). Alzheimer's disease and brain infarcts in the elderly. Agreement with neuropathology. *Journal of Neurology, 249*(11), 1529–1534.

8

Amyloid Beta Peptide and the Amyloid Cascade Hypothesis

Carmela R. Abraham

Introduction

In 1907, Alois Alzheimer was the first to describe the clinical symptoms and neu-ropathological changes of a disease, which now bears his name. He observed plaques and tangles in the brain of a 51-year-old patient suffering from progressive demen-tia. He wrote: "Dispersed over the entire cortex . . . miliary foci could be found which represented the sites of deposition of a peculiar substance in the cerebral cortex" (Alzheimer, 1907). We know today that the "peculiar substance" is the amyloid beta (Aβ) peptide. The next seminal discovery was the isolation of the Aβ peptide and partial elucidation of its sequence by George Glenner in 1984 (Glenner & Wong, 1984). Based on the Aβ sequence, the Aβ precursor protein (APP) was cloned in 1987 (Goldgaber et al., 1987; Kang et al., 1987; Robakis et al., 1987; Tanzi et al., 1987). Cloning of APP opened a plethora of research directions that lead to a rich body of information and potential treatments.

Alzheimer's disease (AD) is the major cause of dementia in the elderly and perhaps the fourth-leading cause of death in the United States, following heart attack, stroke, and cancer. On neuropathological examination, brains of AD victims contain intraneuronal neurofibrillary tangles and extracellular amyloid deposits in parenchymal plaques and in the cerebral microvasculature. Whether the amyloid plaques or the tangles are the primary causes or the effects of the neurodegenera-tion seen in AD has been debated at numerous conferences over the years. However, genetic and biochemical advances allowed for the identification of genes that invar-iably cause early-onset AD and strengthens considerably the role of amyloid β peptide in the hereditary, as well as in the sporadic form of the disease. Studies on

The Handbook of Alzheimer's Disease and Other Dementias, First Edition.
Edited by Andrew E. Budson, Neil W. Kowall.
© 2011 Blackwell Publishing Ltd. Published 2011 by Blackwell Publishing Ltd.

members of families who inherit the disease in an autosomal dominant manner have led to the discovery of three genes that cause early-onset AD. These genes code for APP, presenilin 1 (PS1), and presenilin 2 (PS2). APP is the precursor of Aβ, the major protein in plaques and vascular deposits. Convincing evidence exists that both presenilins play a crucial role in the formation of Aβ. Mutations in APP or either of the presenilins cause an increased formation of a particularly hydrophobic and potentially neurotoxic form of Aβ. Moreover, the APP gene is found on chromosome 21, and patients with Down syndrome (trisomy 21), who possess three copies of this chromosome, develop AD-type dementia and neuropathological changes, including Aβ plaques, if they live past the age of 40. Finally, AD patients have been identified who possess a duplication of the APP gene (Rovelet-Lecrux et al., 2006). In early-onset familial AD, Aβ peptide accumulates as a direct consequence of the mutations in APP and presenilin leading to aberrant APP processing, while in sporadic AD Aβ appears to accumulate as a result of decreased clearance.

The apolipoprotein E4 (ApoE4) allele of ApoE, a lipid transport protein, has been identified as a major risk factor affecting the age of onset of AD. ApoE, too, has a role in Aβ deposition in the brain: it increases the levels of plaque and vascular Aβ deposits. Thus, all four genes currently implicated as causes of inherited AD increase Aβ levels or deposition or both.

The second neuropathological hallmark of AD, the neurofibrillary tangle (NFT), is composed primarily of abnormally phosphorylated tau, an axonal microtubule associated protein. When tau is phosphorylated at its microtubule-binding domains, it can no longer stabilize the microtubules and they de-polymerize. Because tau plays an important role in axonal transport, the hyperphosphorylation leads to its accumulation and aggregation in the neuronal cell bodies and dendrites as neurofibrillary tangles. The tangles are devastating to neuronal function. Interestingly, mutations in tau do not cause AD, but another type of dementia called frontotemporal dementia or FTD. For more details on FTD, see Chapter 4.

When analyzing the sequence of events culminating in the appearance of tangles in Down syndrome, where both AD neuropathologies occur, tangles appear up to 10 years after amyloid deposits are first identified (Lemere et al., 1996). Furthermore, transgenic mouse models of AD that co-express both mutant human APP and mutant human tau provide additional evidence that tangles are a consequence of Aβ accumulation. Taken together, the above findings support the "amyloid hypothesis of AD," which posits that cerebral accumulation of the Aβ peptide is the initiating event leading to the development of AD. Based on current knowledge, efforts are being made toward designing compounds that would reduce the levels of Aβ in brain, in the hope of delaying or preventing AD (Hardy, 2009; Hardy & Selkoe, 2002; Sisodia & St George-Hyslop, 2002).

However, several other genes and their cognate proteins are being considered as potential risk factors for AD and are under intensive investigation. In addition, new genes are being sought as causes of familial AD. Nonetheless, most AD cases appear to be "sporadic," although a combination of multiple predisposing genes could play a role in initiating the development of the disease in some individuals. For a list of all the genes associated with AD and related references, please visit www.alzforum.org/res/com/gen/alzgene/default.asp.

The Beta Amyloid Precursor Protein (APP) and Beta Amyloid (Aβ) Peptide

The cloning of the APP gene revealed that its translation product, APP, is a type I transmembrane glycoprotein with a long extracellular N-terminal domain and a short intracellular (cytoplasmic) C-terminal domain (Figure 8.1) (Kang et al., 1987). APP is the precursor of the amyloid β peptide (Aβ), a cytotoxic peptide that plays an important role in the pathogenesis of AD (Selkoe & Kopan, 2003). APP is constitutively expressed in many cell types and evolutionarily conserved. A plethora of functions have been attributed to APP including cell adhesion, cell growth and survival, neuroprotection (Mucke et al., 1995), synaptotrophism (Mucke et al., 1995), axonal transport (Kamal et al., 2000; Koo et al., 1990), apoptosis (Chen et al., 2003; Rohn et al., 2000), neuronal migration during development (Young-Pearse et al., 2007), protease inhibition (Van Nostrand et al., 1990), and involvement in transcription (Cao & Sudhof, 2004; Hass & Yankner, 2005; Kimberly et al., 2001). Some of these functions occur as a result of the interaction of APP with extracellular proteins such as the heparan sulfate proteoglycans; homodimerization of transmembrane APP on two adjacent cells, heterodimerization of APP with the other two APP family members, APLP1 and APLP2 (Soba et al., 2005); while others represent the interaction of APP with intracellular proteins such as Fe65, X11, and kinesin (reviewed in De Strooper & Annaert, 2000). Our group has identified Notch as an APP-interacting protein (Oh et al., 2005)., and we have recently provided evidence that in cell culture APP affects Notch signaling (Oh et al., 2010). However, as of now, the mechanisms by which APP exerts its multiple functions remain elusive.

The Aβ peptides, which are 39–43 amino acids long with the predominant lengths being Aβ40 and Aβ42, are derived from APP by the proteolytic action of two proteinases termed β- and γ-secretases. β-secretase creates the N-terminus of Aβ, whereas γ-secretase creates the C-terminus by cleaving in a region that is embedded in cell membranes (the transmembrane domain) (see Figure 8.1). All cells generate Aβ, but for as yet unknown reasons, Aβ accumulates only in brain. The normal physiological ratio between the Aβ42 and Aβ40 peptides is 1:10. This ratio is increased in familial AD (see below). A growing body of evidence suggests that oligomeric forms of Aβ1–42 are the most toxic Aβ forms (Haass, 2010; Selkoe, 2008). APP is also proteolytically processed via a non-amyloidogenic pathway in which scissions by α- and γ-secretase lead to the production of a fragment of Aβ (called p3) that is unlikely to be involved in plaque formation. Furthermore, the non-amyloidogenic processing of APP also results in the secretion of the extracel-

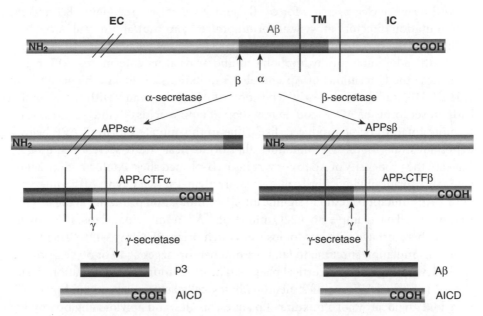

Figure 8.1 Diagram of the APP molecule and its proteolytic processing. In the non-amyloidogenic pathway APP is cleaved by α-secretase to generate APPsα and APP-CTF-α and then CTF-α is cleaved by γ-secretase to produce P3 and AICD. In the amyloidogenic and pathogenic pathway, APP is cleaved by β-secretase to create APPsβ and APP-CTF-β, which in turn is cleaved by γ-secretase to generate Aβ and AICD EC = extracellular domain; TM = transmembrane domain; IC = intracellular domain; CTF = C-terminal fragment; AICD = APP-intracellular domain

lular form of APP (APPsα) that has been shown to be neuroprotective (Masliah et al., 1997; Stein et al., 2004).

In recent years, β-secretase has been identified as a membrane-anchored aspartic protease named BACE (for β-site APP-cleaving enzyme) (Vassar et al., 1999). There are two forms of BACE: BACE 1 and BACE 2. BACE 1 is the major β-secretase in brain, because the levels of BACE 2 mRNA and protein in brain are low. So far, no association has been made between BACE and the inheritance of AD. γ-Secretase has an intriguing activity, because the site of cleavage in APP resides in the transmembrane domain, that is, in the hydrophobic lipid bilayer. Based on experimental data, Wolfe and Selkoe suggested in 1999 that the presenilins might actually serve as the proteolytic activity of γ-secretase (see below and Wolfe et al., 1999).

Three major isoforms, APP695, APP751, and APP770, arise from APP by differential mRNA splicing. Although APP is a ubiquitous protein found in all cells, the 695-residue isoform is expressed predominantly in neurons. Interestingly, mutations in APP that cause early-onset AD and related disorders cluster in the Aβ region of APP near the cleavage sites for α-, β-, and γ-secretases (see Figure 8.1 and the APP mutation directory at www.alzforum.org/res/com/mut/app/default.asp).

Between the two major forms of Aβ, Aβ42 has a higher tendency to aggregate due to the additional two hydrophobic amino acids at its C-terminus. APP mutations near the C-terminus of Aβ and all PS mutations result in a higher ratio of Aβ42/Aβ40, leading to the early deposition of Aβ in the brains with these familial early-onset forms of AD. A double mutation at amino acids −1 and −2 of Aβ leads to more total Aβ being produced, likely due to this mutated form of APP being a better substrate for BACE. Mutations that occur near the α-secretase site of Aβ increase the propensity of Aβ to convert into a β-pleated sheet conformation, aggregate, and form amyloid fibrils more readily than the wild type Aβ. Some such "intra-Aβ" mutations result in significant Aβ accumulation primarily in the cerebral vasculature. For example an E22Q mutation (Aβ numbering) causes hereditary cerebral hemorrhage with amyloidosis of Dutch origin (HCHWA-D). Patients carrying this mutation succumb to fatal cerebral hemorrhages at 40 or 50 years of age, while developing only few cortical plaques. The other four known mutations inside the Aβ region of APP manifest neuropathologically as vascular amyloid primarily (amyloid angiopathy) or a mixture of plaques, tangles, and amyloid angiopathy. For a detailed description of intra-Aβ mutations and the disorders associated with them visit www.alzforum.org/new/detail.asp?id=666.

In addition to overproduction, another possible reason for the accumulation of Aβ is inadequate degradation of the peptide. Several proteinases have been identified that degrade Aβ in the brain or in cell culture. The two most studied are neprilysin and insulin-degrading enzyme (IDE) (Eckman & Eckman, 2005). For a comprehensive review of other Aβ-degrading enzymes see Miners et al. (2008). Our group has identified a novel Aβ-degrading enzyme, acyl peptide hydrolase, which prefers to degrade dimers and trimers, the most toxic species of Aβ reported so far (Yamin et al., 2007; Yamin et al., 2009). A failure to degrade Aβ might occur as a result of: (i) a change of Aβ to a β-pleated sheet conformation that is more resistant to degradation; (ii) the association of Aβ with "pathological chaperons" such as $alpha_1$-antichymotrypsin and ApoE, that could block the accessibility of Aβ to proteinases (Abraham et al., 1988; Mucke et al., 2000; Nilsson et al., 2004); (iii) oxidation or cross-linking of Aβ that could again block the scissile bonds (Smith et al., 2007); (iv) a primary genetic defect in an Aβ-degrading proteinase; or (v) an age-related or disease-related reduction in one or more Aβ-degrading proteinases (Miners et al., 2008).

How does Aβ exert its toxicity? There is evidence for several mechanisms by which Aβ is neurotoxic and by which it could induce tau modifications. (i) Aβ can form ion channels that are heterogeneous in size, selectivity, blockade and gating. They admit Ca^{2+}, Na^+, K^+, Cs^+, Li^+ and possibly Cl^-. For a review see Kagan et al. (2002). (ii) Aβ may drive tau pathology by activating specific kinases leading to tau hyperphosphorylation and NFT formation. (iii) In the AD brain, Aβ also triggers a massive inflammatory response and pro-inflammatory cytokines can in turn indirectly modulate tau phosphorylation. (iv) Aβ may also inhibit tau degradation via the proteasome. (v) Aβ and tau may indirectly interact at the level of axonal transport. For a review see Blurton-Jones and Laferla (2006). (vi) Aβ oligomers are toxic to synapses by modulating an NMDA-type glutamate receptor-dependent signaling pathway (Shankar et al., 2007).

Recently, new polymorphisms in the Sorl1 gene have been shown to be associated with late-onset AD (Rogaeva et al., 2007). Sorl1 functions to traffic the APP molecule intracellularly, and variations in Sorl1 have been proposed to preferentially traffic APP into the amyloidogenic pathway leading to elevated Aβ amounts (Rogaeva et al., 2007).

The Presenilins (PSs)

The PS1 gene was identified in a region of chromosome 14 that had been previously associated with a major risk of developing AD (Schellenberg et al., 1992; Sorbi et al., 1995; St George-Hyslop et al., 1992). Shortly afterward, a homologous gene, PS2, was discovered on chromosome 1 (Levy-Lahad et al., 1996). PS1 and PS2 are nine-pass transmembrane proteins. For a diagram of the presenilin structure and the location of mutations, please visit www.alzforum.org/res/com/mut/pre/ diagram2006.asp. Since their discovery, over 100 mutations have been identified in PS1, and six in PS2. A majority of early-onset (<60 years) AD cases seems to be caused by PS1 mutations. For a diagram of PS1 and the AD-causing mutations see www.alzforum.org/res/com/mut/prc/diagram1.asp. For a diagram of PS2 and the AD-causing mutations see www.alzforum.org/res/com/mut/pre/diagram2.asp. For more information and references on PS1 and PS2 visit www.alzforum.org/res/com/ mut/pre/default.asp.

Because mutations in PSs affect the processing of the C-terminus of Aβ, favoring a cleavage at position 42 of Aβ, it has been suggested that PS is either γ-secretase itself or is necessary for the γ-secretase cleavage. Moreover, inhibitor studies have shown that γ-secretase is an aspartic protease. The active site of aspartic proteases consists of two crucial aspartic acids that participate in the catalytic event. These findings prompted investigators to determine whether PS itself is γ-secretase. These researchers identified two aspartic acids in two of the transmembrane domains of PS1. Substituting either one of these aspartic acids with alanine caused a complete loss of γ-secretase activity (Wolfe et al., 1999). Two separate groups then succeeded in labeling PS1 using specific irreversible inhibitors of aspartic proteases. Recent accumulating evidence suggests that PS1 forms complexes with several proteins and that only the intact complex has full γ-secretase activity. The proteins associated with PS1 in the active complex that have been identified so far are nicastrin, Aph-1, and Pen-2 (Francis et al., 2002).

In addition to being involved in γ-secretase processing of APP, another known substrate of γ-secretase is the Notch protein. Notch is a type I transmembrane receptor protein crucial to dorsal axis embryonic development but also important in hematopoiesis and many other cell development pathways in the adult. Similarly to APP, the Notch receptor is cleaved by γ-secretase in its transmembrane domain after Notch binds its ligands such as delta. From both APP and Notch, a cytoplasmic domain, termed AICD or NICD, respectively, is released. NICD is translocated to the nucleus, and has been shown to play a role in transcriptional regulation. AICD is also involved in transcription but its localization to the nucleus is still controversial. Thus, γ-secretase appears to be a founding example of the phenomenon of regulated intramembrane proteolysis (RIP). The generation of nuclear signaling proteins by RIP is a new paradigm of signal transduction (Ebinu & Yankner, 2002).

Several groups reported recently that a number of other proteins are substrates for PS/γ-secretase. Among these are ErbB4, a transmembrane receptor tyrosine kinase that regulates cell proliferation and differentiation, syndecan 3, CD44, Delta 1, Jagged 1, and deleted in colon cancer (DCC). In summary, γ-secretase is a transmembrane proteolytic complex that cleaves transmembrane substrates, with PS1 or PS2 apparently being the catalytic executors. The fact that presenilins have so many substrates makes them a less likely drug target for inhibition although major efforts are still being invested in γ-secretase inhibitors.

The Amyloid Cascade Hypothesis

The cloning of APP, PS1, and the discovery that mutations in these genes contribute to overproduction of Aβ and to familial AD, led researchers to formulate the amyloid hypothesis (Hardy & Higgins, 1992; Selkoe, 1991). Below is a list of reasons why many scientists believe that the APP metabolite, Aβ, is an initiating factor in the development of AD (adapted from a lecture by D.J. Selkoe; also see Hardy & Selkoe, 2002):

1 All four genes now known to cause AD have been shown to increase Aβ production (APP, PS1, PS2) or Aβ deposition (ApoE4).
2 All AD patients have many amyloid deposits containing degenerating nerve endings; their plaque count far exceeds that found in normal aging.
3 The amount of Aβ in "thinking" regions of the brain correlates with the degree of impairment.
4 Down syndrome patients, who invariably develop classical AD pathology by age 50, produce too much Aβ from birth and begin to get amyloid plaques as early as age 12, long before they get tangles and other AD lesions.
5 ApoE4, the major genetic risk factor for AD, leads to excess amyloid buildup in the brain before AD symptoms arise. Thus, Aβ deposition *precedes* clinical AD.
6 Aβ polymers reproducibly damage cultured neurons and activate brain inflammatory cells (microglia). Blocking Aβ polymer formation prevents this toxicity.

7 Transgenic mice solely expressing a mutant human APP gene develop first diffuse and then fibrillary Aβ plaques associated with neuronal and microglial changes. Mouse models reproduce the major features of AD.

8 In other amyloidoses, blocking the production of the responsible amyloid protein can successfully treat these diseases.

9 Rigorous evidence for an alternate basis for AD (virus, toxin, loss of trophic factor, etc.) has not emerged during more than 20 years of intensive research on AD.

The amyloid cascade hypothesis can explain both dominantly inherited forms of AD and nondominant forms of AD, which include the so-called " sporadic" AD. The first steps of the cascade are different for the two types of AD but then they merge into a single cascade (see Figure 8.2). The familial, dominantly inherited AD is caused by missense mutations in the APP or PS1 or PS2 genes. These mutations cause an increased Aβ42 production throughout life leading to early-onset AD. On the other hand, in nondominant AD, a failure in Aβ clearance leads to a gradual Aβ accumulation in the brain. Aβ can accumulate due to the inheritance of the ApoE4 allele, due to faulty Aβ degradation by local proteinases or due to aberrant transport from brain to blood. When the balance between production and clearance of Aβ is

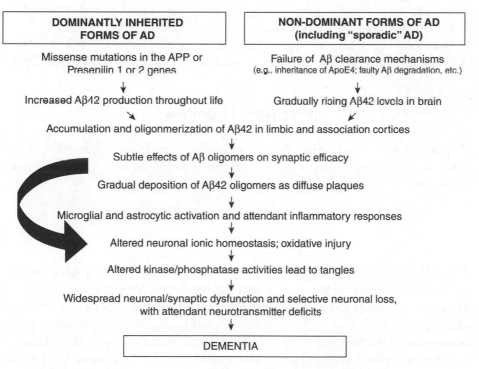

Figure 8.2 The amyloid cascade hypothesis in Alzheimer's disease Source: Courtesy of D. J. Selkoe

tilted, Aβ starts to accumulate and oligomerize in limbic and association cortices, the thinking and memory regions of the brain. These Aβ oligomers have a negative effect on synaptic efficacy. In parallel, Aβ oligomers continue to gradually deposit into diffuse plaques. In addition to its detrimental effects on synapses, Aβ also has been shown to cause microglial and astrocytic activation. When these immune cells of the brain are activated they start to produce and secrete a variety of cytokines, reactive oxygen species and acute phase proteins such as α1-antichymotrypsin, leading to neuroinflammation and oxidative injury to nearby neurons. Thus, Aβ could be directly toxic to neurons, or exert its neurotoxicity indirectly via the activation of microglia and astrocytes. The altered ionic homeostasis of neurons leads to activation of kinases or inactivation of phosphatases resulting in a net hyperphosphorylation of tau. This abnormally modified tau causes microtubule depolymerization and neurofibrillary tangle formation in neuronal cell bodies and neurites. The compromised axonal transport due to tau alterations together with the direct Aβ-induced damage to synapses leads to neuronal and synaptic dysfunction and selective neuronal loss. Many neurotransmitter abnormalities in AD have been attributed to this neuronal loss or dysfunction, the most common of which being the cholinergic neurons. It is hypothesized that these aforementioned brain changes culminate in dementia. With so many Aβ lowering drugs currently in clinical studies, the amyloid hypothesis will be proven or disproven in the very near future.

To read more about the amyloid hypothesis please visit www.alzforum.org/res/adh/cur/knowntheamyloidcascade.asp.

In a recent review article Golde and colleagues describe in more detail the various Aβ assemblies and their roles in the amyloid cascade hypothesis (Golde et al., 2006).

Alternative Hypotheses

Scientists, who strongly believe that other proteins or pathways initiate AD and that Aβ is merely a consequence of other pathological processes, have formulated other hypotheses.

Tau

Neurofibrillary tangles and amyloid plaques are the chief neuropathological hallmarks of AD. Since they have been described, researchers favored one or another as the causative factors in the disease, even before tau or Aβ had been identified and characterized as the major protein components of tangles and plaques. Since tangles accumulate in neurons and some tangles are found extracellularly as "ghost tangles," it is easy to envision that such abnormal protein accumulations could incapacitate or kill the neuron. However, since tau mutations do not cause AD, but different neurodegenerative diseases, collectively named tauopathies, and because tangles appear later than Aβ, the number of "tauists," or those that favor tau as an initiating factor in AD, is decreasing rapidly. Nevertheless, because hyperphosphorylated tau is toxic to neurons, compounds that would inhibit the kinases such as GSK3β, which abnormally phosphorylate tau, are being developed as potential drugs for AD.

Presenilin (PS)

Several investigators have been supporting the idea that either due to mutations or abnormal function, the loss of essential functions of PS could better explain neurodegeneration and dementia in AD independently of Aβ (Shen & Kelleher, 2007). The presenilin hypothesis was prompted by studies on conditional PS knockout mice. These mice reproduce the central features of AD including synaptic plasticity impairments and neurodegeneration. In another study Baki, Robakis and colleagues found that PS1 FAD mutations inhibit the PS1-dependent PI3K/Akt activation, thus promoting GSK-3 activity and tau overphosphorylation at AD-related residues. Their data raise the possibility that PS1 may prevent development of AD pathology by activating the PI3K/Akt signaling pathway. In contrast, FAD mutations may promote AD pathology by inhibiting this pathway (Baki et al., 2004).

Inflammation

Eikelenboom and colleagues support the hypothesis that inflammation plays a crucial role in the early stage of AD pathology, particularly in Aβ metabolism and deposition (Eikelenboom et al., 2006). They suggest that the amyloid plaque is the nidus of a non-immune mediated chronic inflammatory response locally induced by fibrillar Aβ deposits. Albeit early, the neuroinflammation appears to be secondary to Aβ accumulation. Nevertheless, reducing this inflammatory state could be beneficial for AD patients.

Other hypotheses

Several more unconventional hypotheses have been formulated to explain the development of AD. Among them, the pathogen hypothesis, which posits that microorganisms may cause AD. For a list of additional hypotheses please visit www.alzforum.org/res/adh/hyp/default.asp.

Future Treatments for AD

The only way to prove the amyloid cascade hypothesis is to show that lowering the Aβ load in the brain is beneficial and can prevent or slow the clinical and neuropathological features of AD. In cell cultures and in transgenic models of AD, it has been shown that Aβ reduction by various means is advantageous. One way to reduce Aβ is to inhibit either one of the secretases that produce it: β- and γ-secretase. Because γ-secretase cleaves many proteins other than APP, its inhibition could be deleterious. For example the inhibition of Notch cleavage affects the maturation of many cell types. Less is known about β-secretase substrates, although recently Haass and colleagues demonstrated that neuregulin, an important white matter growth factor, is also a substrate for BACE (Willem et al., 2006). The activation of the non-amyloidogenic pathway could also prove beneficial as an Aβ-lowering intervention since that approach would decrease the amount of APP available for BACE cleavage. However, the known α-secretases ADAM10 and ADAM17 are highly regulated due to their crucial functions and, thus, difficult and potentially dangerous to manipulate.

A completely novel idea of preventing Aβ deposits from forming, or even reducing them once formed, was introduced with the concept of an anti-Aβ vaccine. The Aβ vaccine was extremely successful in transgenic mice (Schenk et al., 1999), but so far results from human clinical studies using an active Aβ vaccine were less promising because the initial clinical trial had to be stopped due to ~6% of patients developing unacceptable side effects. The proponents of Aβ immunotherapy needed to optimize the immunogen, the adjuvant, and the immunization protocol. Today over 10 clinical trials with Aβ vaccines are being performed worldwide including passive immunization using humanized mouse anti-Aβ antibodies. Perhaps the design of a safer vaccine will prove beneficial in the near future. For a review on immunotherapy see Lemere (2009). For more on therapeutics see Chapter 10.

If the reduction of the toxic oligomeric forms of Aβ improves the clinical outcome of AD patients, the amyloid hypothesis will have been proven. If not, we have to create a new hypothesis and start all over.

References

Abraham, C. R., Selkoe, D. J., & Potter, H. (1988). Immunochemical identification of the serine protease inhibitor alpha 1-antichymotrypsin in the brain amyloid deposits of Alzheimer's disease. *Cell, 52*(4), 487–501.

Alzheimer, A. (1907). Ueber eine eigenartige Erkrankung der hirnrinde. *Zeitschrift fuer Psychiatrie und Psychisch-Gerichtliche Mediz, 64,* 146–148.

Baki, L., Shioi, J., Wen, P., Shao, Z., Schwarzman, A., Gama-Sosa, M., et al. (2004). PS1 activates PI3K thus inhibiting GSK-3 activity and tau overphosphorylation: Effects of FAD mutations. *EMBO Journal, 23*(13), 2586–2596.

Blurton-Jones, M., & Laferla, F. (2006). Pathways by which Abeta facilitates tau pathology. *Current Alzheimer Research, 3*(5), 437–448.

Cao, X., & Sudhof, T. C. (2004). Dissection of amyloid-beta precursor protein-dependent transcriptional transactivation. *Journal of Biological Chemistry, 279*(23), 24601–24611.

Chen, Y., Liu, W., McPhie, D. L., Hassinger, L., & Neve, R. L. (2003). APP-BP1 mediates APP-induced apoptosis and DNA synthesis and is increased in Alzheimer's disease brain. *Journal of Cell Biology, 163*(1), 27–33.

De Strooper, B., & Annaert, W. (2000). Proteolytic processing and cell biological functions of the amyloid precursor protein. *Journal of Cell Science, 113*(Pt 11), 1857–1870.

Ebinu, J. O., & Yankner, B. A. (2002). A RIP tide in neuronal signal transduction. *Neuron, 34*(4), 499–502.

Eckman, E. A., & Eckman, C. B. (2005). Abeta-degrading enzymes: Modulators of Alzheimer's disease pathogenesis and targets for therapeutic intervention. *Biochemical Society Transactions, 33*(Pt 5), 1101–1105.

Eikelenboom, P., Veerhuis, R., Scheper, W., Rozemuller, A. J., van Gool, W. A., & Hoozemans, J. J. (2006). The significance of neuroinflammation in understanding Alzheimer's disease. *Journal of Neural Transmission, 113*(11), 1685–1695.

Francis, R., McGrath, G., Zhang, J., Ruddy, D. A., Sym, M., Apfeld, J., et al. (2002). aph-1 and pen-2 are required for Notch pathway signaling, gamma-secretase cleavage of betaAPP, and presenilin protein accumulation. *Developmental Cell, 3*(1), 85–97.

Glenner, G. G., & Wong, C. W. (1984). Alzheimer's disease and Down's syndrome: Sharing of a unique cerebrovascular amyloid fibril protein. *Biochemical and Biophysical Research Communications, 122*(3), 1131–1135.

Golde, T. E., Dickson, D., & Hutton, M. (2006). Filling the gaps in the abeta cascade hypothesis of Alzheimer's disease. *Current Alzheimer Research, 3*(5), 421–430.

Goldgaber, D., Lerman, M. I., McBride, O. W., Saffiotti, U., & Gajdusek, D. C. (1987). Characterization and chromosomal localization of a cDNA encoding brain amyloid of Alzheimer's disease. *Science, 235*(4791), 877–880.

Hardy, J. (2009). The amyloid hypothesis for Alzheimer's disease: A critical reappraisal. *Journal of Neurochemistry, 110*(4), 1129–1134.

Hardy, J. A., & Higgins, G. A. (1992). Alzheimer's disease: The amyloid cascade hypothesis. *Science, 256*(5054), 184–185.

Hardy, J., & Selkoe, D. J. (2002). The amyloid hypothesis of Alzheimer's disease: Progress and problems on the road to therapeutics. *Science, 297*(5580), 353–356.

Haass, C. (2010). Initiation and propagation of neurodegeneration. *Nature Medicine, 16*(11), 1201–1204.

Hass, M. R., & Yankner, B. A. (2005). A gamma-secretase independent mechanism of signal transduction by the amyloid precursor protein. *Journal of Biological Chemistry, 280*(44), 36895-36904.

Kagan, B. L., Hirakura, Y., Azimov, R., Azimova, R., & Lin, M. C. (2002). The channel hypothesis of Alzheimer's disease: current status. *Peptides, 23*(7), 1311–1315.

Kamal, A., Stokin, G. B., Yang, Z., Xia, C. H., & Goldstein, L. S. (2000). Axonal transport of amyloid precursor protein is mediated by direct binding to the kinesin light chain subunit of kinesin-I. *Neuron, 28*(2), 449–459.

Kang, J., Lemaire, H. G., Unterbeck, A., Salbaum, J. M., Masters, C. L., Grzeschik, K. H., et al. (1987). The precursor of Alzheimer's disease amyloid A4 protein resembles a cell-surface receptor. *Nature, 325*(6106), 733–736.

Kimberly, W. T., Zheng, J. B., Guenette, S. Y., & Selkoe, D. J. (2001). The intracellular domain of the beta-amyloid precursor protein is stabilized by Fe65 and translocates to the nucleus in a notch-like manner. *Journal of Biological Chemistry, 276*(43), 40288–40292.

Koo, E. H., Sisodia, S. S., Archer, D. R., Martin, L. J., Weidemann, A., Beyreuther, K., et al. (1990). Precursor of amyloid protein in Alzheimer disease undergoes fast anterograde axonal transport. *Proceedings of the National Academy of Sciences USA*, *87*(4), 1561–1565.

Lemere, C. A. (2009). Developing novel immunogens for a safe and effective Alzheimer's disease vaccine. *Progress in Brain Research*, *175*, 83–93.

Lemere, C. A., Blusztajn, J. K., Yamaguchi, H., Wisniewski, T., Saido, T. C., & Selkoe, D. J. (1996). Sequence of deposition of heterogeneous amyloid beta-peptides and APO E in Down syndrome: Implications for initial events in amyloid plaque formation. *Neurobiology of Disease*, *3*(1), 16–32.

Levy-Lahad, E., Poorkaj, P., Wang, K., Fu, Y. H., Oshima, J., Mulligan, J., et al. (1996). Genomic structure and expression of STM2, the chromosome 1 familial Alzheimer disease gene. *Genomics*, *34*(2), 198–204.

Masliah, E., Westland, C. E., Rockenstein, E. M., Abraham, C. R., Mallory, M., Veinberg, I., et al. (1997). Amyloid precursor proteins protect neurons of transgenic mice against acute and chronic excitotoxic injuries in vivo. *Neuroscience*, *78*(1), 135–146.

Miners, J. S., Baig, S., Palmer, J., Palmer, L. E., Kehoe, P. G., & Love, S. (2008). Abeta-degrading enzymes in Alzheimer's disease. *Brain Pathology*, *18*(2), 240–252.

Mucke, L., Abraham, C. R., Ruppe, M. D., Rockenstein, E. M., Toggas, S. M., Mallory, M., et al. (1995). Protection against HIV-1 gp120-induced brain damage by neuronal expression of human amyloid precursor protein. *Journal of Experimental Medicine*, *181*(4), 1551–1556.

Mucke, L., Yu, G. Q., McConlogue, L., Rockenstein, E. M., Abraham, C. R., & Masliah, E. (2000). Astroglial expression of human alpha(1)-antichymotrypsin enhances alzheimer-like pathology in amyloid protein precursor transgenic mice. *American Journal of Pathology*, *157*(6), 2003–2010.

Nilsson, L. N., Arendash, G. W., Leighty, R. E., Costa, D. A., Low, M. A., Garcia, M. F., et al. (2004). Cognitive impairment in PDAPP mice depends on ApoE and ACT-catalyzed amyloid formation. *Neurobiology of Aging*, *25*(9), 1153–1167.

Oh, S. Y., Ellenstein, A., Chen, C. D., Hinman, J. D., Berg, E. A., Costello, C. E., et al. (2005). Amyloid precursor protein interacts with notch receptors. *Journal of Neuroscience Research*, *82*(1), 32–42.

Oh, S. Y., Chen, C. D., & Abraham, C. R. (2010). Cell-type dependent modulation of Notch signaling by the amyloid precursor protein. *Journal of Neurochemistry*, *113*(1), 262–274.

Robakis, N. K., Ramakrishna, N., Wolfe, G., & Wisniewski, H. M. (1987). Molecular cloning and characterization of a cDNA encoding the cerebrovascular and the neuritic plaque amyloid peptides. *Proceedings of the National Academy of Sciences USA*, *84*(12), 4190–4194.

Rogaeva, E., Meng, Y., Lee, J. H., Gu, Y., Kawarai, T., Zou, F., et al. (2007). The neuronal sortilin-related receptor SORL1 is genetically associated with Alzheimer disease. *Nature Genetics*, *39*(2), 168–177.

Rohn, T. T., Ivins, K. J., Bahr, B. A., Cotman, C. W., & Cribbs, D. H. (2000). A monoclonal antibody to amyloid precursor protein induces neuronal apoptosis. *Journal of Neurochemistry*, *74*(6), 2331–2342.

Rovelet-Lecrux, A., Hannequin, D., Raux, G., Le Meur, N., Laquerriere, A., Vital, A., et al. (2006). APP locus duplication causes autosomal dominant early-onset Alzheimer disease with cerebral amyloid angiopathy. *Nature Genetics*, *38*(1), 24–26.

Schellenberg, G. D., Bird, T. D., Wijsman, E. M., Orr, H. T., Anderson, L., Nemens, E., et al. (1992). Genetic linkage evidence for a familial Alzheimer's disease locus on chromosome 14. *Science, 258*(5082), 668–671.

Schenk, D., Barbour, R., Dunn, W., Gordon, G., Grajeda, H., Guido, T., et al. (1999). Immunization with amyloid-beta attenuates Alzheimer-disease-like pathology in the PDAPP mouse. *Nature, 400*(6740), 173–177.

Selkoe, D. J. (1991). The molecular pathology of Alzheimer's disease. *Neuron, 6*(4), 487–498.

Selkoe, D. J. (2008). Soluble oligomers of the amyloid beta-protein impair synaptic plasticity and behavior. *Behavioral Brain Research, 192*(1), 106–113.

Selkoe, D. J. & Kopan, R. (2003). Notch and presenilin: Regulated intramembrane proteolysis links development and degeneration. *Annual Review of Neuroscience, 26*, 565–597.

Shankar, G. M., Bloodgood, B. L., Townsend, M., Walsh, D. M., Selkoe, D. J., & Sabatini, B. L. (2007). Natural oligomers of the Alzheimer amyloid-beta protein induce reversible synapse loss by modulating an NMDA-type glutamate receptor-dependent signaling pathway. *Journal of Neuroscience, 27*(11), 2866–2875.

Shen, J., & Kelleher, R. J., 3rd. (2007). The presenilin hypothesis of Alzheimer's disease: Evidence for a loss-of-function pathogenic mechanism. *Proceedings of the National Academy of Sciences USA, 104*(2), 403–409.

Sisodia, S. S., & St George-Hyslop, P. H. (2002). gamma-Secretase, Notch, Abeta and Alzheimer's disease: Where do the presenilins fit in? *Nature Reviews Neuroscience, 3*(4), 281–290.

Smith, D. G., Cappai, R., & Barnham, K. J. (2007). The redox chemistry of the Alzheimer's disease amyloid beta peptide. *Biochimica et Biophysica Acta, 1768*(8), 1976–1990.

Soba, P., Eggert, S., Wagner, K., Zentgraf, H., Siehl, K., Kreger, S., et al. (2005). Homo- and heterodimerization of APP family members promotes intercellular adhesion. *EMBO Journal, 24*(20), 3624–3634.

Sorbi, S., Nacmias, B., Forleo, P., Piacentini, S., Sherrington, R., Rogaev, E., et al. (1995). Missense mutation of S182 gene in Italian families with early-onset Alzheimer's disease. *Lancet, 346*(8972), 439–440.

St George-Hyslop, P., Haines, J., Rogaev, E., Mortilla, M., Vaula, G., Pericak-Vance, M., et al. (1992). Genetic evidence for a novel familial Alzheimer's disease locus on chromosome 14. *Nature Genetics, 2*(4), 330–334.

Stein, T. D., Anders, N. J., DeCarli, C., Chan, S. L., Mattson, M. P., & Johnson, J. A. (2004). Neutralization of transthyretin reverses the neuroprotective effects of secreted amyloid precursor protein (APP) in APPSW mice resulting in tau phosphorylation and loss of hippocampal neurons: Support for the amyloid hypothesis. *Journal of Neuroscience, 24*(35), 7707–7717.

Tanzi, R. E., Gusella, J. F., Watkins, P. C., Bruns, G. A., St George-Hyslop, P., Van Keuren, M. L., et al. (1987). Amyloid beta protein gene: cDNA, mRNA distribution, and genetic linkage near the Alzheimer locus. *Science, 235*(4791), 880–884.

Van Nostrand, W. E., Wagner, S. L., Farrow, J. S., & Cunningham, D. D. (1990). Immunopurification and protease inhibitory properties of protease nexin-2/amyloid beta-protein precursor. *Journal of Biological Chemistry, 265*(17), 9591–9594.

Vassar, R., Bennett, B. D., Babu-Khan, S., Kahn, S., Mendiaz, E. A., Denis, P., et al. (1999). Beta-secretase cleavage of Alzheimer's amyloid precursor protein by the transmembrane aspartic protease BACE. *Science, 286*(5440), 735–741.

Willem, M., Garratt, A. N., Novak, B., Citron, M., Kaufmann, S., Rittger, A., et al. (2006). Control of peripheral nerve myelination by the beta-secretase BACE1. *Science*, *314*(5799), 664–666.

Wolfe, M. S., Xia, W., Ostaszewski, B. L., Diehl, T. S., Kimberly, W. T., & Selkoe, D. J. (1999). Two transmembrane aspartates in presenilin-1 required for presenilin endoproteolysis and gamma-secretase activity. *Nature*, *398*(6727), 513–517.

Yamin, R., Bagchi, S., Hildebrant, R., Scaloni, A., Widom, R. L., & Abraham, C. R. (2007). Acyl peptide hydrolase, a serine proteinase isolated from conditioned medium of neuroblastoma cells, degrades the amyloid-beta peptide. *Journal of Neurochemistry*, *100*(2), 458–467.

Yamin, R., Zhao, C., O'Connor, P. B., McKee, A. C., & Abraham, C. R. (2009). Acyl peptide hydrolase degrades monomeric and oligomeric amyloid-beta peptide. *Molecular Neurodegeneration*, *4*, 33.

Young-Pearse, T. L., Bai, J., Chang, R., Zheng, J. B., LoTurco, J. J., & Selkoe, D. J. (2007). A critical function for beta-amyloid precursor protein in neuronal migration revealed by in utero RNA interference. *Journal of Neuroscience*, *27*(52), 14459–14469.

9

Other Mechanisms of Neurodegeneration

Neuronal Cell Death and Neuroprotection in Alzheimer's Disease

Marina Boziki, Vassilis Papaliagkas, and Magda Tsolaki

Introduction

Alzheimer's disease (AD) is the most common cause of cognitive decline and dementia in the elderly (Querfurth & LaFerla, 2010). The definitive diagnosis of AD requires postmortem brain examination. Senile plaques (SPs) and neurofibrillary tangles (NFTs) are the two major pathological hallmarks of AD (Braak & Braak, 1985; McKee et al., 1991) and their widespread presence in the cerebral neurocortex is diagnostic of AD. Both of these pathological changes are hypothesized to reflect key steps in a series of linked events that begin with beta amyloid deposition and culminate in synaptic loss and neuronal death – the so-called "amyloid cascade" (Hardy & Higgins, 1992; Huse & Doms, 2000; Pimplikar, 2009). However, the amyloid cascade hypothesis may not fully encompass the broad spectrum of mechanisms leading to neuronal cell death. Our lack of knowledge with respect to the underlying mechanisms responsible for neuronal damage in AD has hampered our progress toward better pharmacological treatments. Currently, medications that are available are only partially effective in improving the symptoms of the disease and delaying its progression. It is hoped that through the further elucidation of cell death mechanisms that novel pharmaceutical targets for the prevention and therapy of AD can be identified. The development of more effective treatments will likely depend on the acquisition of more detailed knowledge concerning the cellular pathways affected in AD. In this chapter we review the major pathways of neurotoxicity and neuronal death known to be relevant to AD and describe some of the neuroprotective factors currently being investigated as potential treatments for AD.

The Handbook of Alzheimer's Disease and Other Dementias, First Edition.
Edited by Andrew E. Budson, Neil W. Kowall.
© 2011 Blackwell Publishing Ltd. Published 2011 by Blackwell Publishing Ltd.

Neuronal Cell Death Pathways in AD

Apoptotic and necrotic cell death pathways are biochemically and morphologically distinct and either may result from endogenous or exogenous signals. Typically apoptosis leads to the formation of apoptotic bodies that are eventually phagocytized, while necrosis triggers oxidative stress and inflammation leading to more widespread damage which may affect neighboring neurons.

Although many in vivo and in vitro studies indicate that apoptosis occurs in AD, there is considerable evidence that necrotic cell death may also contribute to neurodegeneration in AD (Behl, 2000).

Apoptosis

Apoptosis is a tightly regulated mechanism responsible for cell death. It is crucial for normal development in terms of maintaining the balance between proliferation and cell death (Behl, 2000; Han et al., 2008). Apoptosis is referred to as programmed cell death because it occurs as a consequence of the physiological cell cycle. Intra- and extracellular stimuli can lead in activation of the downstream cascade that promotes cell death. Programmed cell death can take place following either accumulation of damaged organelles' derivatives, or ligation of respective molecules to death receptors. A toxic substance in the cell environment may interfere with mitochondrial function, thus promoting the production of cytochrome c. Cytochrome c is an effector molecule, implicated in several pathways of cell death. It participates in the formation of a complex named Apaf (apoptosis protease activating factor-1), which is responsible for the further activation of specific mediators of apoptotic cell death, the caspases. Activation of death receptors in the cell surface also results in interaction and accumulation of caspases in the cytosol, via a distinct pathway. Fas (CD95) and its ligand (Fas/L) are representative of death receptors, the ligation promoting formation of caspase 8 and other pro-apoptotic molecules. Other death receptors are bound into TNF-family molecules, such as TNF-RI and TNF-RII, which bind TNF-alpha and TNF-beta, respectively (Figure 9.1). Irrespective of the trigger that initiates intracellular response, all pro-apoptotic pathways are consequently linked with cytosolic accumulation of active caspase-3, a key molecule that mediates apoptosis. Caspases, a term used to describe a broad family of cysteine proteases that serve as downstream molecules, are key factors contributing to apoptosis. Caspases mediate apoptosis through cleavage of specific intracellular substrates at aspartate residues, thus eventually provoking DNA fragmentation. The process is further regulated by co-stimulatory molecules in the Bcl-2 protein family. Members of this family are either pro-apoptotic (Bak, Bok, Bit3, Bad-like protein, Bid, Bik, Bim, Hrk) or anti-apoptotic (Bcl-2, Bcl-xl, Ced-9, Bcl-w, Mcl-1) molecules. Bcl-2, Bcl-xl, and Bcl-xs prevent the egress of cytochrome-c

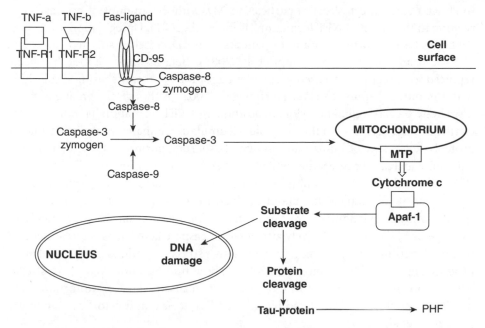

Figure 9.1 Signal transduction for apoptosis. The Fas ligand is a representative of death factors that act as inducers of apoptosis. It binds to the Fas receptor causing a subsequent cascade of secondary messages. Caspase 3 is activated by caspase 8. Caspase 8 cleaves Bid, a pro-apoptotic member of Bcl-2, which translocates to mitochondria to release cytochrome C into the cytosol. Bcl-2 or Bcl-xL, anti-apoptotic members of the Bcl-2 family, inhibits the release of cytochrome C. Subsequently, cytochrome C activates Apaf-1, a factor that mediates cleavage of cell substrates, such as protein and DNA

from mitochondria, while their expression is dependent on the JNK–kinase pathway (Li et al., 2009). The sensitivity of cells to apoptotic stimuli may depend on the balance of pro- and anti-apoptotic Bcl-2 proteins. Caspase-3 is a key mediator of apoptosis in all mammalian cells including neurons. Recent evidence suggests that caspase activation may cleave tau to initiate tangle formation and that truncated tau may then recruit normal tau to misfold and form tangles (Calignon et al., 2010).

A third, intrinsic, apoptotic pathway seems to be independent of extracellular triggers, such as death receptor ligands and toxins. It is induced by oxidative stress within the cell, initially affecting endoplasmic reticulum (ER). The specific pathway is described as ER stress and is mediated by caspase 12.

The potential contribution of apoptotic cell death to the pathogenesis of AD has been extensively studied. The neuropathological hallmarks of the AD, extracellular beta amyloid deposits and intracellular NFTs consisting of paired helical filaments (PHFs), made of hyperphosphorylated microtubule-associated protein tau, have been implicated in caspase-linked cell death processes. Caspases have been reported to cleave neuronal cytoskeleton particles in AD, with the amount of cleavage correlating to the extent of NFT formation (Rohn et al., 2001). Upregulation of caspase genes has been reported in brains of patients with AD, closely associated with both NFTs and amyloid burden (Pompl et al., 2003). Beta amyloid peptide has been reported to upregulate caspase-8-dependent apoptotic pathway sharing similarities with Fas-induced apoptosis (Wei, Norton et al., 2002). Although the linking mechanism between extracellular amyloid deposition and NFT formation has not yet been clarified, it has been shown that amyloid accumulation enhances caspase-mediated proteolytic cleavage of human tau protein at aspartate positions. Proteolytic products show increased aggregation potential, thereby contributing to NFT formation (Gamblin et al., 2003). By combining anti-tau immunohistochemistry and TUNEL techniques, it was shown that apoptosis load in AD is positively correlated with specific phosphorylation sites of tau protein (Kobayashi et al., 2003). Proteolytic cleavage of PHF-tau is exclusively attributed to caspase activity, as pretreatment of neuronal cells under excitotoxicity or oxidative stress conditions in vitro failed to produce similar results (Kang et al., 2005). These findings, however, contrast to a study reporting that beta amyloid fragments caused classical mitochondrial-mediated apoptosis characterized by elevated Bcl-2, Bax, and cytochrome c levels (Tamagno et al., 2003).

Apart from mitochondria, beta amyloid also affects ER, thereby inducing so-called "ER stress". The process is mediated by caspase-4, a homologous molecule to caspase-12, localized in the ER membrane, cleaved in reaction to ER stress-inducing reagents. Cleavage of caspase-4 is not affected by the presence of Bcl-2, thereby implying that caspase-4 is primarily activated in ER stress-induced apoptosis, in contrast to mitochondria-induced apoptosis which is associated with Bcl-family upregulation (Hitomi et al., 2004).

Necrosis

Necrotic cell death may be triggered by changes in the permeability of cell surface ion channels that activate intracellular mediators leading to elevated cytosolic Ca+. Ca+ gathers in the cytosol either through cell membrane channels, or by release from the ER. In turn, cysteine calcium-dependent proteases, "calpains," are activated leading to lysosome rupture and the release of lysosomal cysteine proteases, "cathepsins," which cause DNA fragmentation and cell death (Vaisid et al., 2008) (Figure 9.2). Depletion of the endogenous calpain inhibitor calpastatin (CAST) from AD neurons is accompanied by activation of the signaling pathways of several kinases, leading to NFT hyperphosphorylation and subsequent neuronal death, an effect that is attenuated in neurons overexpressing CAST (Rao et al., 2008). Calpains act sequentially with aspartyl proteases to facilitate cell death. Production of reactive oxygen species (ROS), another critical step in necrotic neuron cell death, also results in lysosome rupture. Although calpains mobilize pro-apoptotic factors, their activation is not mediated by caspase activation (Takano et al., 2005).

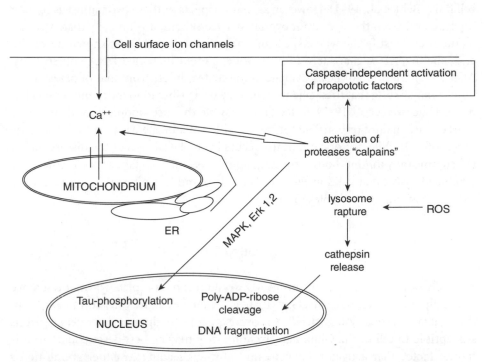

Figure 9.2 Signal transduction for necrosis. Many diverse initiating conditions that trigger necrosis may provoke a net increase in the cytoplasmic calcium concentration, either by stimulating uptake of extracellular calcium or by facilitating the release of calcium stores from the endoplasmic reticulum. Increased calcium influx induces activation of "calpains." Calpains act sequentially with cathepsin aspartyl proteases, downstream of cytoplasmic calcium elevation, to facilitate cell death. Calpains have also been implicated in the activation of pro-apoptotic caspase proteases

In AD, proteases play crucial roles in neuron degeneration by exerting both regulatory and catabolic functions. Calpain activation occurs concomitantly with elevations of intracellular calcium, the most ubiquitous feature of neuronal death. Calpains and lysosomal catabolic aspartyl proteases play key roles in the necrotic death of neurons (Artal-Sanz et al., 2005). Specifically, calpains are capable of converting cdk5 activator protein p35 to a C-terminal fragment p25 and this conversion promotes a deregulation of cdk5 activity. As cdk5 is a kinase responsible partially for tau phosphorylation, pathological activation plays a role in abnormal phosphorylation of tau in AD (Nath et al., 2000). It has been suggested that necrosis, rather than apoptosis, appears to be the crucial component of the damage to the nervous system during neurodegeneration (Yamashima, 2004). Cortical primary cultures exposed to beta amyloid 25–35 revealed immediate cellular damage such as vacuolization of the cytoplasm, breakdown of Golgi apparatus and other membrane systems, and neuritis disintegration, followed by total collapse of the cytoplasm and cell lysis (Behl et al., 1994). However, as many aspects of these two pathways remain unclear, and given the significant overlap between them, it is unlikely that only one of them can justify the whole spectrum of pathology in AD. As shown by *in situ* end labeling, AD is characterized by area-dependent increased DNA vulnerability. Also the distribution of DNA damage in the cortex differs from that of plaques and tangles, suggesting that these phenomena may be attributed to independent mechanisms (Lucassen et al., 1997). In fact, it is possible that pro-apoptotic and apoptotic markers are mainly responsible for neuronal lesions in the early and intermediate stages of AD, while necrotic cell death occurs in the late stages of the disease. Bcl-X (L) significantly inhibits both early-stage apoptosis and late-stage apoptosis/necrosis produced by beta amyloid in PC12 cells in vitro and it exhibits both anti-necrotic as well as anti-apoptotic roles (Tan et al., 1999).

Excitotoxicity

A review of cell death mechanisms in AD would not be complete without reference to the glutamate excitotoxicity. Glutamate is a major excitatory neurotransmitter in the central nervous system (CNS) yet overexposure to glutamate renders neurons susceptible to cell death. Glutamate excitotoxicity may be best described as an initiating factor that activates downstream pathways leading to either apoptotic or necrotic cell death. Experimental evidence links excitotoxicity to acute CNS damage in both traumatic brain injury (TBI) and ischemia as well as in chronic CNS neurodegenerative diseases, including AD.

There are three major categories of glutamate receptors: the N-methyl-D-aspartate receptor (NMDAR); the AMPA (-amino-3-hydroxy-5-methyl-4-isoxazole propionic acid)/kainate receptors; and the metabotropic glutamate receptors (mGlyR). The NMDA receptor is the most thoroughly studied so far and the only type targeted for pharmacological intervention. Activation of NMDAR is a complex requiring not only ligation of glutamate and other potential ligands, but also cell membrane depolarization and the presence of glycine as a co-stimulatory factor. The result of NMDAR activation is excessive calcium influx into the cytosol that originates from the extracellular environment. Activation of AMPA/kainate receptors produces a similar effect, in contrast to mGluR activation that leads to calcium mobilization primarily from mitochondria. Increased intracellular calcium selectively triggers a variety of downstream events, many of which are potentially toxic to the cell with excessive activation. Other consequences include nitric oxide (NO) production, Ca+ dependent cysteine protease (calpain) activation, production of ROS, protein kinase c activation, and activation of Ca dependent DNAase and Ca dependent phospholipase (Lynch & Guttmann, 2002).

Experiments using transgenic mouse models of AD and human cortical neurons showed that increased production of amyloid beta-peptide (1–42/43) results in gene dosage-dependent vulnerability to excitotoxicity. Neurons exhibit enhanced calcium responses to glutamate and increased oxyradical production and mitochondrial dysfunction (Guo et al., 1999; Mattson et al., 1992). Because of its potential neuro-toxicity, clearance of glutamate from the synaptic cleft is also critical for neuronal survival. In AD, glutamate transporters are inhibited by oxidative damage caused by ROS and lipid peroxidation products such as 4-hydroxy-2-nonenal (HNE). Beta amyloid (1–42) was found to increase HNE conjugation to the glutamate trans-porter, thereby linking oxidative damage and excitotoxicity in AD (Lauderback et al., 2001). Moreover, beta amyloid directly downregulates glutamate uptake in astrocytes by inhibiting glutamate transporter-1 (GLT-1) and glutamate-aspartate transporter (GLAST), through a MAP–kinase-dependent pathway (Matos et al., 2008). Evidence of glutamate-induced NMDA dependent excitotoxicity has been well demonstrated in AD in association with apoptosis markers in neuronal cells (Fang et al., 2005). This effect is mainly attributed to extrasynaptic NMDA receptors whose stimulation causes loss of mitochondrial membrane potential (an early marker for glutamate induced neuronal damage) and cell death, whereas synaptic NMDA receptors seem to have anti-apoptotic activity (Giles et al., 2002). Furthermore, peroxynitrite, a reaction product of NO and superoxide radicals, has been implicated in NMDA-mediated excitotoxic damage. Nitration of tyrosine resi-dues in proteins, mediated by peroxynitrite breakdown, is a consequence of oxidative damage that links oxidative stress and glutamate excitotoxicity to the pathogenesis of cell death in AD (Good et al., 1996; Mamelak, 2007). High levels of extracellular glutamate inhibit the import of cysteine, resulting in glutathione depletion and a form of cellular injury termed oxidative glutamate toxicity, which may play a role in the pathogenesis of AD independent of excitotoxicity. This NMDA receptor-independent process is inhibited by a variety of reagents that block oxidative gluta-mate toxicity (Schubert & Piasecki, 2001). Since many neurological disorders, including AD, have been proposed to have excitotoxic components, development of NMDA receptor antagonists is a major area of pharmaceutical investigation. Signal transduction pathways related to excitotoxicity are summarized in Figure 9.3.

Beta amyloid was recently shown to exert a direct excitotoxic effect (Gong et al., 2010) resulting in the synaptic loss that is prominent in AD brains, possibly through the SNK–SPAR signaling pathway. Spine-associated Rap GTPase activating protein (SPAR) forms a complex with NMDAR located in the dendritic spines of neurons. As SPAR is a protein associated with the actin cytoskeleton, it is believed that SPAR, and serum-induced kinase (SNK), a kinase that is upregulated by neuronal activity, cause SPSR degradation and synaptic loss. Administration of beta amyloid (1–40) in vivo was shown to provoke excitotoxic damage and synaptic loss in rat brain by downregulating SPAR expression, while SNK expression was upregulated.

Apart from beta amyloid, other metabolites also have been implicated in excito-toxic neuronal damage, such as homocysteine, which may be an independent risk factor of AD (Kuszczyk et al., 2009). Nicotinamide, a known neuroprotective factor, was found to protect rat cerebellar granule cells from homocysteine-induced exci-totoxicity (Slomka et al., 2008).

Glutamate-mediated excitotoxicity has also been linked with the second patho-logical "hallmark" of AD, that is, NFT, which consist of hyperphosphorylated tau

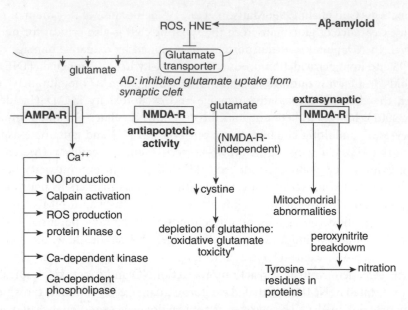

Figure 9.3   Signal transduction for excitotoxicity. Overstimulation of both non-NMDA and NMDA receptors with glutamate results in large influx of calcium into the cell. This can result in a series of calcium-dependent enzymes, which are normally suppressed, being activated. When these enzymes, such as lipid peroxidase, nitric oxide synthetase and xanthine oxidase, are activated, they cause the production of free radicals and nitric oxide, cytoskeletal breakdown, failure to generate ATP, lipid peroxidation and nucleic acid fragmentation, which lead to neuronal death

protein. In a mouse model of acute excitotoxicity a significant increase in the amount of abnormally phosphorylated tau protein has been described (Liang et al., 2009).

Neuroprotective Strategies in AD

Recent advances in elucidating the underlying molecular pathogenic mechanisms have suggested the possibility of novel therapeutic approaches. One such treatment strategy would target pathogenic pathways upstream of neuronal death, i.e., at the stage of neuronal injury or synaptic failure but prior to neuronal death.

Neuroprotection against apoptosis

Inhibitors of cytochrome c translocation
As previously mentioned, oxidative damage triggers the release of cytochrome c by mitochondria, which binds to Apaf-1 and recruits caspase 9, to form the apopto-

some, an apoptosis-mediating molecule. *Stereoisomers of pramipexole (PPX)*, a free radical scavenger, inhibit the opening of mitochondrial transition pore (MTP), thus interfering with the release of cytochrome c to the cytosol. In vitro studies showed that PPX stereoisomers may prevent caspase activation and restore calcium accumulation through this mechanism (Abramova et al., 2002). *Flavopiridol* is another agent that inhibits both the release of cytochrome c and the activation of caspase-3. Flavopiridol was developed as a drug for cancer therapy because it is able to inhibit cell cycle progression by targeting cyclin-dependent kinases (CDKs) (Jorda et al., 2003). *Estrogens, 17-beta-estradiol (17b-E2)* in particular, were also shown to prevent glutamate-induced translocation of cytochrome c from mitochondria to cytosol, and the accompanied upregulation of caspase-3, in rat primary cortical cells (Zhang & Bhavnani, 2005). Additionally, *17-alpha-estradiol*, an isomer of E2, was discovered to be as equally cytoprotective as E2, yet >200-fold less active as a hormone. Novel estrogen analogs may stabilize mitochondria under Ca(2+) loading otherwise sufficient to collapse membrane potential and thereby prevent mitochondrial degeneration in AD (Simpkins et al., 2005). Calcineurin inhibitors are also novel agent that prevent beta amyloid-induced loss of mitochondrial membrane potential thereby reducing mitochondrial cytochrome c release and caspase-3 activation, which is regulated by calcineurin-mediated BAD dephosphorylation (Cardoso & Oliveira, 2005).

Bcl-family modulators

As already mentioned, Bcl-2 is a well-demonstrated anti-apoptotic protein, however, the mechanisms of anti-apoptotic action of Bcl-2 in beta amyloid-induced neuronal cell death are not fully understood. Moreover, other molecules in the Bcl-family have been proven to trigger pro-apoptotic pathways, such as Bcl-xs and Bax. The potential role of Bcl-2 overexpression in preventing beta amyloid-induced cell death through the inhibition of of p38 MAP kinase and NF-kappaB in vitro activation has been reported (Song et al., 2004). Estrogen also significantly increases the expression of the anti-apoptotic protein Bcl-xL (Pike, 1999). Bcl-w, a novel member of the Bcl-2 family may also promote cell survival, as indicated by its increased expression in AD neurons and its ultrastructural localization in mitochondria and neurofibrillary pathology (Zhu et al., 2004).

Caspase inhibitors

Since caspases are critical executioners of the apoptotic cell death program, apoptosis can be blocked by agents that inhibit caspase activity. A number of *caspase inhibitors* have been being tested for potential therapeutic effects in AD models (Charriaut-Marlangue, 2004). One of the first caspase inhibitors identified was L-carnitine, which inhibits apoptosis induced by Fas ligation. L-carnitine also inhibits the activity of recombinant caspases 3, 7, and 8 (Mutomba et al., 2000). Caspase inhibitors act by binding to the active site of caspases and form either a reversible or an irreversible linkage. For example, treatment of basal forebrain cholinergic cells of AD young rats with a pan-caspase synthesis inhibitor, z-Val-Ala-Asp

(OMe)-fluoromethyl ketone (zVAD), significantly decreased the levels of caspases 3, 8, and 9 (Wenk et al., 2000). Caspase-3 activity was also attenuated in vitro after co-treatment of rat pheochromocytoma cell lines with propentofylline, a phosphodiesterase inhibitor that has previously demonstrated neuroprotective activity in stroke models and is a current potential candidate for therapeutic treatment in neurodegenerative diseases (Wirtz-Brugger & Giovanni, 2000). Interestingly, nonsteroidal anti-inflammatory drug therapy was shown to attenuate the toxicity of the inflammation upon cholinergic cells and to reduce caspase 3, 8, and 9 activity in the caudate/putamen of rat basal forebrain (Wenk et al., 2000). Moreover, 17b-E2 seems to prevent caspase-6-mediated neuronal cell death by inducing a caspase inhibitory factor (CIF) which prevents neuronal apoptosis. This process involves mitogen-activated protein kinase activation and is induced through a receptor-mediated non-genomic pathway, providing an additional mechanism for the neuroprotective action of 17b-E2 (Zhang et al., 2001). Finally, since age-related tissue zinc deficiency is thought to contribute to apoptosis in AD, the effects of increasing the levels of intracellular labile zinc on apoptosis have been studied in vitro. Zinc may reduce apoptosis by stabilizing the cytoskeleton, which is severely damaged by caspase-induced protein cleavage, rather than by the inhibition of caspase activation (Ho et al., 2000).

Antioxidants

Although inflammatory processes and oxidative stress generated by ROS are thought to primarily mediate necrotic cell death, a significant overlap with apoptotic cell death has been discovered. Vitamin E, a known antioxidant agent, has long been regarded as a potential neuroprotective candidate because it suppresses cell death and caspase-3 activation. Pycnogenol (PYC), a potent antioxidant and ROS scavenger, was recently shown not only to suppress the generation of ROS, but also to attenuate caspase-3 activation, DNA fragmentation, PARP cleavage, and eventually to protect against beta amyloid-induced apoptosis (Peng et al., 2002). Another well-known antioxidant agent, water-soluble Coenzyme Q10 (CoQ10), inhibited ROS generation when neuroblastoma cells were pretreated before paraquat exposure. Pretreatment with CoQ10 also seemed to significantly reduce the number of apoptotic cells and DNA fragmentation (McCarthy et al., 2004).

Nuclear factor-kappa B (NF-kB)

The transcription factor NF-kB can be activated in response to a variety of insults, including oxidative stress. NF-kB activation after beta amyloid (25–35) or (1–40) treatment prevented caspase activation in neuroblastoma cells while NF-kB inhibition induced increased caspase-3 and caspase-6 activation. Furthermore, NF-kB activation has been reported to prevent beta amyloid peptide neurotoxicity by increasing superoxide dismutase (SOD)expression (Cardoso & Oliveira, 2003). It has been suggested that the neuroprotective effects of corticotrophin release hormone (CRH) are mediated by CRH-R1 (CRH-receptor type 1) and the suppression of NF-kB. The role of CRH as an endogenous anti-oxidant neuropeptide may be in part mediated by the inactivation of NF-kB (Lezoualc'h et al., 2000).

Kinases inhibitors

Caspase activation leads to both protein cleavage and nuclear cytoskeleton damage. Tau protein is a component of the cytoskeleton and NFTs composed of hyperphosphorylated tau protein are one of the neuropathological hallmarks of AD. Since neuronal deregulation of kinase activity plays a key role in tau protein hyperphosphorylation, modulation of various kinase pathways may be a significant target for neuroprotective strategies.

Phosphatidyl inositol-3 (PI-3) kinase (PI-3k/Akt) Phosphatidyl inositol (PI) kinase and PI phosphate (PIP) kinase activities were measured in postmortem samples of AD patients' brain tissue and were found to be reduced by 50% in prefrontal cortex, temporal cortex, and parietal cortex; and by 40% in precentral gyrus, compared to nondemented control subjects (Jolles et al., 1992). This finding was confirmed by other researchers (Bothmer et al., 1994; Zubenko et al., 1999). Furthermore, it was suggested that beta amyloid (25–35) inhibits PI-3 kinase, resulting in the activation of TPK I/GSK-3 pathway, the phosphorylation of tau, and resultant neuronal death in rat hippocampal neurons (Takashima et al., 1996). Therefore, it has been proposed that increased levels of Akt phosphorylation through the well-described PI-3K/Akt axis could result in neuroprotective effects. Indeed, the above-described pathway is the mechanism by which neurotrophin-3 (NT-3) protects neurons against beta amyloid toxicity. In cultured primary cortical neurons, NT-3 reduced beta amyloid-induced apoptosis by limiting caspase-8, caspase-9, and caspase-3 cleavage. This neuroprotective effect was accompanied by increased Akt phosphorylation and was abolished by an inhibitor of PI-3K (Lesne et al., 2005). Alpha-synuclein (alpha-SN), a ubiquitous protein localized in the human brain, was found to protect neurons against serum deprivation, oxidative stress, and excitotoxicity through the PI3/Akt signaling pathway at nanomolar concentrations. At both low micromolar concentrations, however, alpha-SN in cytotoxic due to decreased Bcl-xL and increased Bax expression, which lead to cytochrome c release and caspase activation (Seo et al., 2002). Other agents have been found to exhibit neuroprotective action through induction of the PI-3K/Akt axis, including tauroursodeoxycholic acid (TUDCA), an endogenous bile acid (Sola et al., 2003), and insulin-like growth factor 1 (IGF-1), which likely protect neuroblastoma cells against beta amyloid toxicity by strongly activating the ERK and Akt pathways and by blocking JNK activation in a PI3K-dependent manner (Wei, Wang et al., 2002).

c-Jun N-terminal kinase (JNK) The c-Jun N-terminal kinase (JNK) can mediate various neurotoxic signals, including beta amyloid neurotoxicity (Hashimoto et al.,

2003). It has already been mentioned that IGF-1 exerts its neuroprotective action by blocking JNK activation in a PI3K-dependent manner. The survival promoting activity of CEP-1347, an inhibitor of the stress-activated/c-jun N-terminal (SAPK/JNK) kinase pathway, against beta amyloid-induced cortical neuron death in vitro, has also been evaluated (Bozyczko-Coyne et al., 2001).

Glycogen synthase kinase-3 (GSK-3)   Elevated endogenous GSK-3 beta kinase activity has been described in familial AD presenilin lymphoblast cells (Ryder et al., 2004). Estrogen exerts many of its receptor-mediated neuroprotective functions through modulation of several intracellular signal transduction pathways, including the phosphorylation and inactivation of GSK-3 beta. Estrogen affects basal tau phosphorylation at a site known to be phosphorylated by GSK-3 beta, further supporting efforts to target estrogen receptor modulation for AD therapeutics (Goodenough et al., 2005). Similar in vitro results were reported using lithium chloride, which inhibits GSK-3 (Li et al., 2006; Noble et al., 2005). Valproate is another GSK inhibitor with neuroprotective potential that is under investigation (Kim et al., 2005).

Cyclin-dependent kinase 5 (Cdk5)   Cdk5 and JNK activation have been put forth as early events leading to beta amyloid-induced cell death. Butyrolactone I, a Cdk5 inhibitor, showed protective effects against beta amyloid toxicity in a neuroblastoma cell line (Wei, Wang et al., 2002). At therapeutic doses, flavopiridol almost completely prevents colchicine-induced apoptosis in cerebellar granule neurons by inhibiting both the release of cytochrome c and the activation of caspase-3. Flavopiridol may have therapeutic potential in diseases such as AD where cytoskeleton alteration mediated by Cdk5 activation has been demonstrated (Jorda et al., 2003).

Protein kinase C (PKC)   Simultaneous inhibition of PI3K and PKC can induce GSK-3 overactivation, and increase Alzheimer-like tau hyperphosphorylation in neuroblastoma cells (Xu et al., 2005). Estrogen activates PKC in a variety of cell types – 17-beta-estradiol E2 rapidly increases PKC activity in primary cultures of rat cerebrocortical neurons (Cordey et al., 2003).

Neuroprotection against necrosis

Calcium (Ca) reduction

The pivotal role of increased cytosolic calcium in necrotic cell death has been well described. Calcium translocation is mediated both through mitochondrial membrane and cell surface ion channels. Treatment with a voltage-operated L-type Ca^{2+} channel blocker, such as nimodipine, might therefore have positive therapeutic effects in AD (Fu et al., 2006). Nicotine suppresses beta amyloid-induced free radical production and increased of intracellular free calcium, at least partly through nicotinic receptors in vitro (Liu & Zhao, 2004). Xestospongin C, 2-aminoethoxydiphenyl borate, and FK506 only partially attenuate beta amyloid peptide neurotoxicity in primary cortical neurons in culture suggesting that by modulating ER calcium release may have limited therapeutic effects (Suen et al., 2003).

Calpain inhibitors

Several calpain inhibitors have been tested for their efficacy to mediate neuroprotection in models of AD. Calpain inhibitors have been found to restore synaptic function in hippocampal cultures and slices from APP mice (Trinchese et al., 2008) and to inhibit tau protein cleavage (Sinjoanu et al., 2008). In rat hippocampal slices acutely exposed to glutamate, treatment with the calpain inhibitor calpeptin significantly restored intracellular levels of b-catenin, a transcriptional co-activator of the Wnt-cell-survival pathway (Lee et al., 2008). It has also been shown that neurofilament hyperphosphorylation in neocortical pyramidal neurons is accompanied by activation of both Erk1,2 and calpain. Under conditions of calcium injury in neurons, calpains are upstream activators of Erk1,2 signaling and are likely to mediate in part the hyperphosphorylation of neurofilaments and tau. Calpeptin blocks both Erk1,2 activation and neurofilament hyperphosphorylation at concentrations that inhibit calpain-mediated cleavage of brain spectrin, a protein that, along with tau protein, plays a key role in cytoskeleton stability (Veeranna et al., 2004).

Cathepsin inhibitors

Cathepsins are proteases released by lysososmal rupture that results from calpain activation during cell necrosis. Beta amyloid increases the activity of cathepsin-L and promotes transient increased cytosolic expression of cathepsin-L in cultured cortical neurons. The selective cathepsin-L inhibitor Z-FF-FMK prevents beta amyloid-induced activation of caspase-3 and DNA fragmentation due to cleavage of the DNA repair enzyme poly-ADP ribose polymerase (Boland & Campbell, 2004). Cathepsin B, a recently investigated beta amyloid-degrading enzyme, was found to partially regulate soluble beta amyloid concentrations in the extracellular matrix (Mueller-Steiner et al., 2006; Nagai et al., 2005). Genetic ablation of the endogenous cathepsin B inhibitor cystatin C (CysC) in a transgenic mouse model of AD significantly lowered soluble beta amyloid brain load and improved cognitive and behavioral deficits (Sun et al., 2008). Contrary to these findings, exogenous administration of synthetic B cathepsin inhibitors in APP mice improved memory performance by reducing brain beta amyloid burden in transgenic mice (Hook et al., 2008). Notably, this effect was reported only in mice expressing the wild-type beta-secretase site of APP, not the Swedish-mutant beta-secretase site. The dual role of cathepsins points to the complexity of cell survival and cell death equilibrium in the pathogenesis of AD.

Neuroprotection against excitotoxicity

Modulation of glutamate receptors: NMDAR and AMPAR antagonists
One of the first recognized potential targets of pharmacological intervention against excitotoxicity was NMDAR. Only a few, however, were subject to clinical trials because of serious adverse events (reviewed by Lau & Tymianski, 2010). Memantine is the only NMDAR antagonist now in clinical use. It is approved for the treatment of moderate to severe AD. Co-administration of memantine with antioxidant and anti-inflammatory agents enhances positive effects in an experimental model of excitotoxicity (Chen et al., 2008). Memantine attenuates beta amyloid-induced toxicity by preventing tau protein and associated kinase phosphorylation (Song et al., 2008). NMDAR antagonists preferentially targeting the GluN2B NMDAR subunit have proved to be beneficial in preventing beta amyloid-mediated excitotoxicity in hippocampal slices in vivo (Hu et al., 2009). It has already been mentioned that Ca+ dependent cysteine protease (calpain) activation is triggered by intracellular Ca+ influx, which is partially responsible for excitotoxic cell death. Calpain inhibitors, such as A-705253, have been used to decrease excitotoxic effects (Nimmrich et al., 2010).

Modulation of AMPAR/kainate receptors has received less attention as a potential pathway to neuroprotection in AD. Beneficial effects of AMPAR inhibition have been described by omega-3 polyunsaturated fatty acids. Treatment of rat hippocampal slices with docosahexanoic acid (DHA) restored CA1 neurons from AMPA-mediated glutamate excitotoxicity (Menard et al., 2009).

Modulating extracellular glutamate burden: strategies to reduce glutamate release/increase glutamate uptake
Glutamate-release inhibitors that decrease glutamate release into the synaptic cleft have primarily been used to treat epilepsy. It is unlikely that anti-epileptic drugs, such as lamotrigine, phenytoin and gabapentin, will produce benefits beyond those achieved using memantine (Rammes et al., 2008). Modulation of glutamate uptake and transport from the extracellular space by excitatory amino acid transporter (EAAT-2), a molecule mainly expressed by astrocytes, may be therapeutically useful. Ceftriaxone, a beta-lactam-antibiotic, upregulates EAAT-2 expression in primary human fetal astrocytes through an NF-kB dependent mechanism and provides neuroprotection by increasing extracellular glutamate uptake by astrocytes.

Statins
Statins are HMG-CoA reductase inhibitors which modulate lipid metabolism and lower blood cholesterol. Beneficial effects in AD may be mediated by their anti-inflammatory or antioxidative actions. Statins were shown to protect cortical neurons against glutamate-mediated excitotoxicity (Dolga et al., 2008). This protection was dependent on the presence of TNF receptor 2, and mediated by the NF-kB and PKB/Akt signaling pathways.

Strategies to restore cell energy homeostasis

It has been argued that the final step in glutamate-mediated excitotoxic damage is the disruption of cellular energy homeostasis and the bioenergetic breakdown. Several interventions to increase cell energy homeostatis are currently under investigation. Nicotinamide, an NAD+ precursor molecule, has been used to restore levels of intracellular NAD+ by attenuating poly (ADP-ribose) polymerase-1 (PARP-1), an enzyme responsible for NAD+ depletion downstream its production step. Treatment of rat cortical neurons prevented glutamate-induced excitotoxicity by restoring intracellular NAD+ levels (Liu et al., 2009).

Other neuroprotective agents targeting excitotoxicity

Derangements in AMPA receptor mediated synaptic transmission may contribute to neurological and neurodegenerative diseases and could be a target for therapeutic intervention (Yamada, 2000). Two *N*-alkylglycine trimers appear to efficiently prevent excitotoxic neurodegeneration in vitro and in vivo. Because they do not seem to block the NMDA receptor channel, attenuate glutamate-induced increase of Ca^{2+}, or affect the glutamate–nitric oxide–cGMP pathway, it has been hypothesized that they may have fewer side effects than NMDA receptor antagonists (Montoliu et al., 2002). Activation of GABA receptors may decrease neuronal vulnerability to excitotoxic damage. Taurine, a β-amino acid found in high concentrations in the brain, protected cultured chick retinal neurons from excitotoxicity and beta amyloid neurotoxicity. The protective effects of taurine are not mediated by glutamate receptors but is blocked by picrotoxin, a GABA receptor antagonist. GABAergic transmission may therefore represent a promising target for the treatment of AD (Louzada et al., 2004). Equine estrogens such as 17b-E2 significantly protect cortical cells against glutamate-induced excitotoxicity by a mechanism that appears to be independent of Ca^{2+} influx (Perrella & Bhavnani, 2005). Vasoactive intestinal peptide protects cultured cortical neurons from excitotoxic injury but the exact mechanism remain to be determined (Said et al., 1998).

Neuroprotective properties of currently used anti-dementia drugs

Cholinesterase inhibitor (ChEI) therapy enhances performance of activities of daily living, reduces behavioral disturbances, stabilizes cognitive impairment, decreases caregiver stress, and delays nursing home placement (Standridge, 2004). Recent evidence from preclinical studies suggests that ChEIs may attenuate neuronal damage and death from cytotoxic insults (Francis et al., 2005). There is substantial evidence that galantamine upregulates Bcl-2 via alpha7 nicotinic acetylcholine receptors (Geerts, 2005). Others have showed that galantamine and donepezil-mediated neuroprotection is linked to alpha7 nicotinic receptors and the PI3K-Akt pathway (Arias et al., 2005; Takada et al., 2003). Clinical data also suggest the potential of disease-modifying properties by galantamine and donepezil. Two pilot studies (Nordberg et al., 2000; Tune et al., 2003) suggested that regional brain glucose metabolism stabilizes after treatment with both drugs, as shown by positron emission tomography. Moreover, donepezil has recently been shown to significantly increase cerebral blood flow as measured by Tc-hexamethylpropylene amine oxime single photon emission tomography imaging. Donepezil treatment was associated with significantly increased concentrations of *N*-acetylaspartate in two brain regions and less reduction in hippocampal volume, compared to placebo (Krishnan et al., 2003). The mechanisms responsible are uncertain. In vitro evidence suggests that ChEIs enhance the release of nonamyloidogenic, neurotrophic/neuroprotective amyloid precursor protein and decrease the formation of amyloidogenic amyloid precursor protein. Tacrine and donepezil, at clinically relevant concentrations, attenuated beta amyloid (25–35)-induced toxicity in rat PC12 cells (Svensson & Nordberg, 1998) indicating that attenuation of amyloid toxicity may slow the neurodegenerative process and thus stabilize hippocampal volume.

Memantine has been shown to benefit cognition, function, and global outcome in patients with moderate to severe AD and, more recently, in patients with earlier stages of disease (Molinuevo et al., 2005). The combination of memantine and ChEI therapy was reported to be more efficacious than ChEI therapy alone (Dantoine et al., 2006).

Conclusion

Although much progress has been made, there are currently no clinically approved interventions for AD that are disease modifying or neuroprotective. There are a large number of compounds currently being investigated that have produced encouraging results in experimental systems but translating these hopeful findings to human trials has been very challenging Because of the extremely complex nature of the neurodegenerative process, it may be that a combination of neuroprotective agents will be needed. Moreover, until the initiators of the neurodegenerative process are identified, it is likely that progress towards effective new therapies will be uncertain. Even if a potent neuroprotective compound is identified, the challenges of determining human pharmacokinetics and bioavailability could be a further barrier to achieving clinical efficacy. Environment may play a significant role in phenotypic manifestations and disease progression. Socioeconomic status and diet, as well as stressful experiences, are examples of environmental factors that could interfere with the results of randomized clinical trials. Outcomes of clinical trials are further hampered by the limitations of clinical criteria and currently available biomarkers. The definition of early clinical stages of AD and mild cognitive impairment may also confound the interpretation of clinical trials (Gauthier et al., 2006).

References

Abramova, N. A., Cassarino, D. S., Khan, S. M., Painter, T. W., & Bennett, Jr., J. P. (2002). Inhibition by R (+) or S(−) pramipexole of caspase activation and cell death induced by methylpyridinium ion or beta amyloid peptide in SH-SY5Y neuroblastoma. *Journal of Neuroscience Research, 67*(4), 494–500.

Arias, E., Gallego-Sandin, S., Villarroya, M., Garcia, A. G., & Lopez, M. G. (2005). Unequal neuroprotection afforded by the acetylcholinesterase inhibitors galantamine, donepezil, and rivastigmine in SH-SY5Y neuroblastoma cells: Role of nicotinic receptors. *Journal of Pharmacology and Experimental Therapeutics, 315*(3), 1346–1353.

Artal-Sanz, M., & Tavernarakis, N. (2005). Proteolytic mechanisms in necrotic cell death and neurodegeneration. *FEBS Letters, 579*(15), 3287–3296.

Behl, C. (2000). Apoptosis and Alzheimer's disease. Lovastatin induces neuroprotection through tumor necrosis factor receptor 2 signaling pathways. *Journal of Neural Transmission, 107*(11), 1325–1344.

Behl, C., Davis, J. B., Klier, F. G., & Schubert, D. (1994). Amyloid beta peptide induces necrosis rather than apoptosis. *Brain Research, 645*(1–2), 253–264.

Boland, B., & Campbell, V. (2004). Beta amyloid-mediated activation of the apoptotic cascade in cultured cortical neurones: a role for cathepsin-L. *Neurobiology of Aging, 25*(1), 83–91.

Bothmer, J., Markerink, M., & Jolles, J. (1994). Evidence for a selective decrease in type 1 phosphatidylinositol kinase activity in brains of patients with Alzheimer's disease. *Dementia, 5*(1), 6–11.

Bozyczko-Coyne, D., O'Kane, T. M., Wu, Z. L., Dobrzanski, P., Murthy, S., Vaught, J. L., et al. (2001). CEP-1347/KT-7515, an inhibitor of SAPK/JNK pathway activation, promotes survival and blocks multiple events associated with beta amyloid-induced cortical neuron apoptosis. *Journal of Neurochemistry, 77*(3), 849–863.

Braak, H., & Braak, E. (1985). On areas of transition between entorhinal allocortex and temporal isocortex in the human brain. Normal morphology and lamina-specific pathology in Alzheimer's disease. *Acta Neuropathologica (Berlin), 68*(4), 325–332.

Calignon, A., Fox, L. M., Pitstick, R., Carlson, G. A., Bacskai, B. J., Spires-Jones, T. L. et al. (2010). Caspase activation precedes and leads to tangles. *Nature, 464*(7292), 1201–1204.

Cardoso, S. M., & Oliveira, C. R. (2003). Inhibition of NF-kB renders cells more vulnerable to apoptosis induced by amyloid beta peptides. *Free Radical Research, 37*(9), 967–973.

Cardoso, S. M., & Oliveira, C. R. (2005). The role of calcineurin in beta amyloideta-peptides-mediated cell death. *Brain Research, 1050*(1–2), 1–7.

Charriaut-Marlangue, C. (2004). Apoptosis: a target for neuroprotection. *Therapie, 59*(2), 185–190.

Chen, C. M., Lin, J. K., Liu, S. H., & Lin-Shiau, S. Y. (2008). Novel regimen through combination of memantine and tea polyphenol for neuroprotection against brain excitotoxicity. *Journal of Neuroscience Research, 86*(12), 2696–2704.

Cordey, M., Gundimeda, U., Gopalakrishna, R., & Pike, C. J. (2003). Estrogen activates protein kinase C in neurons: role in neuroprotection. *Journal of Neurochemistry, 84*(6), 1340–1348.

Dantoine, T., Auriacombe, S., Sarazin, M., Becker, H., Pere, J. J., & Bourdeix, I. (2006). Rivastigmine monotherapy and combination therapy with memantine in patients with moderately severe Alzheimer's disease who failed to benefit from previous cholinesterase inhibitor treatment. *International Journal of Clinical Practice, 60*(1), 110–118.

Dolga, A. M., Nijholt, I. M., Ostroveanu, A., Ten Bosch, Q., Luiten, P. G., & Eisel, U. L. (2008). Lovastatin induces neuroprotection through tumor necrosis factor receptor 2 signaling pathways. *Journal of Alzheimer's Disease, 13*(2), 111–122.

Fang, M., Li, J., Tiu, S. C., Zhang, L., Wang, M., & Yew, D. T. (2005). N-methyl-D-aspartate receptor and apoptosis in Alzheimer's disease and multiinfarct dementia. *Journal of Neuroscience Research, 81*(2), 269–274.

Francis, P. T., Nordberg, A., & Arnold, S. E. (2005). A preclinical view of cholinesterase inhibitors in neuroprotection: Do they provide more than symptomatic benefits in Alzheimer's disease? *Trends in Pharmacological Sciences, 26*(2), 104–111.

Fu, H., Li, W., Lao, Y., Luo, J., Lee, N. T., Kan, K. K., et al. (2006). Bis(7)-tacrine attenuates beta amyloid-induced neuronal apoptosis by regulating L-type calcium channels. *Journal of Neurochemistry, 98*(5), 1400–1410.

Gamblin, T. C., Chen, F., Zambrano, A., Abraha, A., Lagalwar, S., Guillozet, A. L., et al. (200e). Caspase cleavage of tau: Linking amyloid and neurofibrillary tangles in Alzheimer's disease. *Proceedings of the National Academy of Sciences USA, 100*(17), 10032–10037.

Gauthier, S., Reisberg, B., Zaudig, M., Petersen, R. C., Ritchie, K., Broich, K., et al. (2006). International Psychogeriatric Association Expert Conference on mild cognitive impairment. Mild cognitive impairment. *Lancet, 367*(9518), 1262–1270.

Geerts, H. (2005). Indicators of neuroprotection with galantamine. *Brain Research Bulletin, 64*(6), 519–524.

Giles, E. H., Fukunaga, Y., & Bading, H. (2002). Extrasynaptic NMDARs oppose synaptic NMDARs by triggering CREB shut-off and cell death pathways. *Nature Neuroscience, 5*, 405–414.

Gong, X., Lu, X., Zhan, L., Sui, H., Qi, X., Ji, Z., et al. (2010). Role of the SNK-SPAR pathway in the development of Alzheimer's disease. *IUBMB Life, 62*(3), 214–221.

Good, P. F., Werner, P., Hsu, A., Olanow, C. W., & Perl, D. P. (1996). Evidence of neuronal oxidative damage in Alzheimer's disease. *American Journal of Pathology, 149*(1), 21–28.

Goodenough, S., Schleusner, D., Pietrzik, C., Skutella, T., & Behl, C. (2005). Glycogen synthase kinase 3beta links neuroprotection by 17beta-estradiol to key Alzheimer processes. *Neuroscience, 132*(3), 581–589.

Guo, Q., Sebastian, L., Sopher, B. L., Miller, M. W., Glazner, G. W., Ware, C. B., et al. (1999). Neurotrophic factors (activity-dependent neurotrophic factor (ADNF) and basic fibroblast growth factor (bFGF)) interrupt excitotoxic neurodegenerative cascades promoted by a PS1 mutation. *Proceedings of the National Academy of Sciences USA, 96*(7), 4125–4130.

Han, S. I., Kim, Y. S., & Kim, T. H. (2008). Role of apoptotic and necrotic cell death under physiologic conditions. *BMB Reports, 41*(1), 1–10.

Hardy, J. A., & Higgins, G. A. (1992). Alzheimer's disease: The amyloid cascade hypothesis. *Science, 256*(5054), 184–185.

Hashimoto, Y., Tsuji, O., Niikura, T., Yamagishi, Y., Ishizaka, M., Kawasumi, M., et al. (2003). Involvement of c-Jun N-terminal kinase in amyloid precursor protein-mediated neuronal cell death. *Journal of Neurochemistry, 84*, 864–877.

Hitomi, J., Katayama, T., Eguchi, Y., Kudo, T., Taniguchi, M., Koyama, Y., et al. (2004). Involvement of caspase-4 in endoplasmic reticulum stress-induced apoptosis and Beta amyloid-induced cell death. *Journal of Cell Biology, 165*(3), 347–356.

Ho, L. H., Ratnaike, R. N., & Zalewski, P. D. (2000). Involvement of intracellular labile zinc in suppression of DEVD-caspase activity in human neuroblastoma cells. *Biochemical and Biophysical Research Communications, 268*(1), 148–154.

Hook, V. Y., Kindy, M., & Hook, G. (2008). Inhibitors of cathepsin B improve memory and reduce beta-amyloid in transgenic Alzheimer disease mice expressing the wild-type, but not the Swedish mutant, beta-secretase site of the amyloid precursor protein. *Journal of Biological Chemistry, 283*(12), 7745–7753.

Hu, N. W., Klyubin, I., Anwy, R., & Rowan, M. J. (2009). GluN2B subunit-containing NMDA receptor antagonists prevent beta amyloid-mediated synaptic plasticity disruption in vivo. *Proceedings of the National Academy of Sciences USA, 106*(48), 20504–20509.

Huse, J. T., & Doms, R. W. (2000). Closing in on the amyloid cascade: Recent insights into the cell biology of Alzheimer's disease. *Molecular Neurobiology, 22*(1–3), 81–98.

Jolles, J., Bothmer, J., Markerink, M., & Ravid, R. (1992). Phosphatidylinositol kinase is reduced in Alzheimer's disease. *Journal of Neurochemistry, 58*(6), 2326–2329.

Jorda, E. G., Verdaguer, E., Canudas, A. M., Jimenez, A., Bruna, A., Caelles, C., et al. (2003). Neuroprotective action of flavopiridol, a cyclin-dependent kinase inhibitor, in colchicine-induced apoptosis. *Neuropharmacology, 45*(5), 672–683.

Kang, H. J., Yoon, W. J., Moon, G. J., Kim, D. Y., Sohn, S., Kwon, H. J., et al. (2005). Caspase-3-mediated cleavage of PHF-1 tau during apoptosis irrespective of excitotoxicity and oxidative stress: An implication to Alzheimer's disease. *Neurobiology of Disease, 18*(3), 450–458.

Kim, A., Shi, Y., Austin, R., & Werstuck, G. (2005). Valproate protects cells from ER stress-induced lipid accumulation and apoptosis by inhibiting glycogen synthase kinase-3. *Journal of Cell Science, 118*(Pt 1), 89–99.

Kobayashi, K., Nakano, H., Hayashi, M., Shimazaki, M., Fukutani, Y., Sasaki, K., et al. (2003). Association of phosphorylation site of tau protein with neuronal apoptosis in Alzheimer's disease. *Journal of the Neurological Sciences, 208*(1–2), 17–24.

Krishnan, K. R., Charles, H. C., Doraiswamy, P. M., Mintzer, J., Weisler, R., Yu, X., et al. (2003). Randomized, placebo-controlled trial of the effects of donepezil on neuronal markers and hippocampal volumes in Alzheimer's disease. *American Journal of Psychiatry, 160*(11), 2003–2011.

Kuszczyk, M., Gordon-Krajcer, W., & Lazarewicz, J. W. (2009). Homocysteine-induced acute excitotoxicity in cerebellar granule cells in vitro is accompanied by PP2A-mediated dephosphorylation of tau. *Neurochemistry International, 55*(1–3), 174–180.

Lau, A., & Tymianski, M. (2010). Glutamate receptors, neurotoxicity and neurodegeneration. Pflugers Archiv, March 14.

Lauderback, C. M., Hackett, J. M., Huang, F. F., Keller, J. N., Szweda, L. I., Markesbery, W. R., et al. (2001). The glial glutamate transporter, GLT-1, is oxidatively modified by 4-hydroxy-2-nonenal in the Alzheimer's disease brain: The role of beta amyloid1–42. *Journal of Neurochemistry, 78*(2), 413–416.

Lee, S. G., Su, Z. Z., Emdad, L., Gupta, P., Sarkar, D., Borjabad, A., et al. (2008). Mechanism of ceftriaxone induction of excitatory amino acid transporter-2 expression and glutamate uptake in primary human astrocytes. *Journal of Biological Chemistry, 283*(19), 13116–13123.

Lesne, S., Gabriel, C., Nelson, D. A., White, E., Mackenzie, E. T., Vivien, D., et al. (2005). Akt-dependent expression of NAIP-1 protects neurons against amyloid-{beta} toxicity. *Journal of Biological Chemistry, 280*(26), 24941–24947.

Lezoualc'h, F., Engert, S., Berning, B., & Behl, C. (2000). Corticotropin-releasing hormone-mediated neuroprotection against oxidative stress is associated with the increased release of non-amyloidogenic amyloid beta precursor protein and with the suppression of nuclear factor-kappaB. *Molecular Endocrinology, 14*(1), 147–159.

Li, X., Lu, F., Tian, Q., Yang, Y., Wang, Q., & Wang, J. Z. (2006). Activation of glycogen synthase kinase-3 induces Alzheimer-like tau hyperphosphorylation in rat hippocampus slices in culture. *Journal of Neural Transmissions, 113*(1), 93–102.

Li, C., Xing, G., Dong, M., Zhou, L., Li, J., Wang, G, et al. (2010). Beta-asarone protection against beta-amyloid-induced neurotoxicity in PC12 cells via JNK signaling and modulation of Bcl-2 family proteins. *European Journal of Pharmacology*, March 20.

Liang, Z., Liu, F., Iqbal, K., Grundke-Iqbal, I., & Gong, C. X. (2009). Dysregulation of tau phosphorylation in mouse brain during excitotoxic damage. *Journal of Alzheimer's Disease, 17*(3), 531–539.

Liu, Q., & Zhao, B. (2004). Nicotine attenuates beta-amyloid peptide-induced neurotoxicity, free radical and calcium accumulation in hippocampal neuronal cultures. *British Journal of Pharmacology, 141*(4), 746–754.

Liu, D., Gharavi, R., Pitta, M., Gleichmann, M., & Mattson, M. P. (2009). Nicotinamide prevents NAD+ depletion and protects neurons against excitotoxicity and cerebral ischemia: NAD+ consumption by SIRT1 may endanger energetically compromised neurons. *Neuromolecular Medicine, 11*(1), 28–42.

Louzada, P., Lima, A., Mendonça-Silva, D., Noël, F., De Mello, F., & Ferreira, S. (2004). Taurine prevents the neurotoxicity of β-amyloid and glutamate receptor agonists: Activation of GABA receptors and possible implications for Alzheimer's disease and other neurological disorders. *FASEB Journal, 18*, 511–518.

Lucassen, P. J., Chung, W. C., Kamphorst, W., & Swaab, D. F. (1997). DNA damage distribution in the human brain as shown by in situ end labeling: Area-specific differences in aging and Alzheimer disease in the absence of apoptotic morphology. *Journal of Neuropathology & Experimental Neurology, 56*(8), 887–900.

Lynch, D. R., & Guttmann, R. P. (2002). Excitotoxicity: Perspectives based on N-methyl-D-aspartate receptor subtypes. *Journal of Pharmacology and Experimental Therapeutics, 300*(3), 717–723.

Mamelak, M. (2007). Alzheimer' s disease, oxidative stress and gammahydroxybutyrate. *Neurobiology of Aging, 28*(9), 1340–1360. Epub 2006 Jul 11.

Matos, M., Augusto, E., Oliveira, C. R., & Agostinho, P. (2008). Beta amyloid beta peptide decreases glutamate uptake in cultured astrocytes: Involvement of oxidative stress and mitogen-activated protein kinase cascades. *Neuroscience, 156*(4), 898–910.

Mattson, M. P., Cheng, B., Davis, D., Bryant, K., Lieberburg, I., & Rydel, R. E. (1992). Beta-amyloid peptides destabilize calcium homeostasis and render human cortical neurons vulnerable to excitotoxicity. *Journal of Neuroscience, 12*(2), 376–389.

McCarthy, S., Somayajulu, M., Sikorska, M., Borowy-Borowski, H., & Pandey, S. (2004). Paraquat induces oxidative stress and neuronal cell death: Neuroprotection by water-soluble Coenzyme Q10. *Toxicology and Applied Pharmacology, 201*(1), 21–31.

McKee, A. C., Kosik, K. S., & Kowall, N. W. (1991). Neuritic pathology and dementia in Alzheimer's disease. *Annals of Neurology, 30*(2), 156–165.

Menard, C., Patenaude, C., Gagné, A. M., & Massicotte, G. (2009). AMPA receptor-mediated cell death is reduced by docosahexaenoic acid but not by eicosapentaenoic acid in area CA1 of hippocampal slice cultures. *Journal of Neuroscience Research, 87*(4), 876–886.

Molinuevo, J. L., Llado, A., & Rami, L. (2005). Memantine: Targeting glutamate excitotoxicity in Alzheimer's disease and other dementias. *American Journal of Alzheimer's Disease & Other Dementias, 20*(2), 77–85.

Montoliu, C., Humet, M., Canales, J., Burda, J., Planells-Cases, R., Sánchez-Baeza, F., et al. (2002). Prevention of in vivo excitotoxicity by a family of trialkylglycines, a novel class of neuroprotectants. *Pharmacology, 301*, 29–36.

Mueller-Steiner, S., Zhou, Y., Arai, H., Roberson, E. D., Sun, B., Chen, J., et al. (2006). Antiamyloidogenic and neuroprotective functions of cathepsin B: implications for Alzheimer's disease. *Neuron, 51*,703–714.

Mutomba, M. C., Yuan, H., Konyavko, M., Adachi, S., Yokoyama, C. B., Esser, V., et al. (2000). Regulation of the activity of caspases by L-carnitine and palmitoylcarnitine. *FEBS Letters, 478*(1–2), 19–25.

Nagai, A., Ryu, J. K., Terashima, M., Tanigawa, Y., Wakabayashi, K., McLarnon, J. G., et al. (2005). Neuronal cell death induced by cystatin C in vivo and in cultured human CNS neurons is inhibited with cathepsin B. *Brain Research, 1066*(1–2), 120–128.

Nath, R., Davis, M., Probert, A. W., Kupina, N. C., Ren, X., Schielke, G. P., et al. (2000). Processing of cdk5 activator p35 to its truncated form (p25) by calpain in acutely injured neuronal cells. *Biochemical and Biophysical Research Communications, 274*(1), 16–21.

Nimmrich, V., Reymann, K. G., Strassburger, M., Schöder, U. H., Gross, G., Hahn, A., et al. (2010). Inhibition of calpain prevents NMDA-induced cell death and beta-amyloid-induced synaptic dysfunction in hippocampal slice cultures. *British Journal of Pharmacology, 159*(7), 1523–1531.

Noble, W., Planel, E., Zehr, C., Olm, V., Meyerson, J., Suleman, F., et al. (2005). Inhibition of glycogen synthase kinase-3 by lithium correlates with reduced tauopathy and degeneration in vivo. *Proceedings of the National Academy of Sciences USA, 102*(19), 6990–6995.

Nordberg, A., Almkvist, O., Wall, A. et al. (2000). Maintained cerebral glucose metabolism after one-year rivastigmine treatment in AD patients. Poster presentation at the 6th International Stockholm/Springfield Symposium on Advances in Alzheimer Therapy. April 5–8, Stockholm, Sweden.

Peng, Q. L., Buz'Zard, A. R., & Lau, B. H. (2002). Pycnogenol protects neurons from beta amyloideta peptide-induced apoptosis. *Molecular Brain Research, 104*(1), 55–65.

Perrella, J., & Bhavnani, B. R. (2005). Protection of cortical cells by equine estrogens against glutamate-induced excitotoxicity is mediated through a calcium independent mechanism. *BMC Neuroscience, 6*(1), 34.

Pike, C. J. (1999). Estrogen modulates neuronal Bcl-xL expression and beta-amyloid-induced apoptosis: Relevance to Alzheimer's disease. *Journal of Neurochemistry, 72*(4), 1552–1563.

Pimplikar, S. W. (2009). Reassessing the amyloid cascade hypothesis of Alzheimer's disease. *International Journal of Biochemistry & Cell Biology, 41*(6), 1261–1268.

Pompl, P. N., Yemul, S., Xiang, Z., Ho, L., Haroutunian, V., Purohit, D., et al. (2003). Caspase gene expression in the brain as a function of the clinical progression of Alzheimer disease. *Archives of Neurology, 60*(3), 369–376.

Querfurth, H. W., & LaFerla, F. M. (2010). Alzheimer's disease. *New England Journal of Medicine, 362*(4), 329–344.

Rammes, G., Zieglgänsberger, W., & Parsons, C. G. (2008). The fraction of activated N-methyl-D-aspartate receptors during synaptic transmission remains constant in the presence of the glutamate release inhibitor riluzole. *Journal of Neural Transmission, 115*(8), 1119–1126.

Rao, M. V., Mohan, P. S., Peterhoff, C. M., Yang, D. S., Schmidt, S. D., Stavrides, P. H., et al. (2008). Marked calpastatin (CAST) depletion in Alzheimer's disease accelerates cytoskeleton disruption and neurodegeneration: Neuroprotection by CAST overexpression. *Journal of Neuroscience, 28*(47), 12241–12254.

Rohn, T. T., Head, E., Su, J. H., Anderson, A. J., Bahr, B. A., Cotman, C. W. et al. (2001). Correlation between caspase activation and neurofibrillary tangle formation in Alzheimer's disease. *American Journal of Pathology, 158*(1), 189–198.

Ryder, J., Su, Y., & Ni, B. (2004). Akt/GSK3beta serine/threonine kinases: Evidence for a signalling pathway mediated by familial Alzheimer's disease mutations. *Cellular Signalling, 16*(2), 187–200.

Said, S. I., Dickman, K., Dey, R. D., Bandyopadhyay, A., De Stefanis, P., Raza, S., et al. (1998). Glutamate toxicity in the lung and neuronal cells: Prevention or attenuation by VIP and PACAP. *Annals of the NY Academy of Science, 865*, 226–237.

Schubert, D., & Piasecki, D. (2001). Oxidative glutamate toxicity can be a component of the excitotoxicity cascade. *Journal of Neuroscience, 21*(19), 7455–7462.

Seo, J. H., Rah, J. C., Choi, S. H., Shin, J. K., Min, K., Kim, H. S., et al. (2002). Alpha-synuclein regulates neuronal survival via Bcl-2 family expression and PI3/Akt kinase pathway. *FASEB Journal, 16*(13), 1826–1828.

Simpkins, J. W., Wang, J., Wang, X., Perez, E., Prokai, L., & Dykens, J. A. (2005). Mitochondria play a central role in estrogen-induced neuroprotection. *Current Drug Targets – CNS & Neurological Disorders, 4*(1), 69–83.

Sinjoanu, R. C., Kleinschmidt, S., Bitner, R. S., Brioni, J. D., Moeller, A., & Ferreira, A. (2008). The novel calpain inhibitor A-705253 potently inhibits oligomeric beta-amyloid-induced dynamin 1 and tau cleavage in hippocampal neurons. *Neurochemistry International, 53*(3–4), 79–88.

Slomka, M., Zieminska, E., & Lazarewicz, J. (2008). Nicotinamide and 1-methylnicotinamide reduce homocysteine neurotoxicity in primary cultures of rat cerebellar granule cells. *Acta Neurobiologiae Experimentalis (Wars), 68*(1), 1–9.

Sola, S., Castro, R. E., Laires, P. A., Steer, C. J., & Rodrigues, C. M. (2003). Tauroursodeoxycholic acid prevents beta amyloideta peptide-induced neuronal death via a phosphatidylinositol 3-kinase-dependent signaling pathway. *Molecular Medicine, 9*(9–12), 226–234.

Song, Y. S., Park, H. J., Kim, S. Y., Lee, S. H., Yoo, H. S., Lee, H. S., et al. (2004). Protective role of Bcl-2 on beta-amyloid-induced cell death of differentiated PC12 cells: reduction of NF-kappaB and p38 MAP kinase activation. *Neuroscience Research, 49*(1), 69–80.

Song, M. S., Rauw, G., Baker, G. B., & Kar, S. (2008). Memantine protects rat cortical cultured neurons against beta-amyloid-induced toxicity by attenuating tau phosphorylation. *European Journal of Neuroscience, 28*(10), 1989–2002.

Standridge, J. B. (2004). Pharmacotherapeutic approaches to the treatment of Alzheimer's disease. *Clinical Therapeutics, 26*(5), 615–630.

Suen, K. C., Lin, K. F., Elyaman, W., So, K. F., Chang, R. C., & Hugon, J. (2003). Reduction of calcium release from the endoplasmic reticulum could only provide partial neuroprotection against beta-amyloid peptide toxicity. *Journal of Neurochemistry, 87*(6), 1413–1426.

Sun, B., Zhou, Y., Halabisky, B., Lo, I., Cho, S. H., Mueller-Steiner, S., et al. (2008). Cystatin C-cathepsin B axis regulates amyloid beta levels and associated neuronal deficits in an animal model of Alzheimer's disease. *Neuron, 60*(2), 247–257.

Svensson, A. L., & Nordberg, A. (1998). Tacrine and donepezil attenuate the neurotoxic affect of A beta(25–35) in rat PC12 cells. *Neuroreport, 9*, 1519–1522.

Takada, Y., Yonezawa, A., Kume, T., Katsuki, H., Kaneko, S., Sugimoto, H., et al. (2003). Nicotinic acetylcholine receptor-mediated neuroprotection by donepezil against gluta-mate neurotoxicity in rat cortical neurons. *Journal of Pharmacology and Experimental Therapeutics, 306*(2), 772–777.

Takano, J., Tomioka, M., Tsubuki, S., Higuchi, M., Iwata, N., Itohara, S. et al. (2005). Calpain mediates excitotoxic DNA fragmentation via mitochondrial pathways in adult brains. *Journal of Biological Chemistry, 280*(16), 16175–16184.

Takashima, A., Noguchi, K., Michel, G., Mercken, M., Hoshi, M., Ishiguro, K., et al. (1996). Exposure of rat hippocampal neurons to amyloid beta peptide (25–35) induces the inactivation of phosphatidyl inositol-3 kinase and the activation of tau protein kinase I/glycogen synthase kinase-3 beta. *Neuroscience Letters, 203*(1), 33–36.

Tamagno, E., Parola, M., Guglielmotto, M., Santoro, G., Bardini, P., Marra, L., et al. (2003). Multiple signaling events in amyloid beta-induced, oxidative stress-dependent neuronal apoptosis. *Free Radical Biology and Medicine, 35*(1), 45–58.

Tan, J., Town, T., Placzek, A., Kundtz, A., Yu, H., & Mullan, M. (1999). Bcl-X(L) inhibits apoptosis and necrosis produced by Alzheimer's beta-amyloid1-40 peptide in PC12 cells. *Neuroscience Letters, 272*(1), 5–8.

Trinchese, F., Fa', M., Liu, S., Zhang, H., Hidalgo, A., Schmidt, S. D., et al. (2008). Inhibition of calpains improves memory and synaptic transmission in a mouse model of Alzheimer disease. *Journal of Clinical Investigation, 118*(8), 2796–2807.

Tune, L., Tiseo, P. J., Ieni, J., Perdomo, C., Pratt, R. D., Votaw, J. R., et al. (2003). Donepezil HCl (E2020) maintains functional brain activity in patients with Alzheimer disease: Results of a 24-week, double-blind, placebo-controlled study. *American Journal of Geriatric Psychiatry, 11*(2), 169–177.

Vaisid, T., Kosower, N. S., Elkind, E., & Barnoy, S. (2008). Amyloid beta peptide toxicity in differentiated PC12 cells: calpain-calpastatin, caspase, and membrane damage. *Journal of Neuroscience Research, 86*(10), 2314–2325.

Veeranna, K. T, Boland, B., Odrljin, T., Mohan, P., Basavarajappa, B. S., et al. (2004). Calpain mediates calcium-induced activation of the erk1,2 MAPK pathway and cytoskeletal phosphorylation in neurons: Relevance to Alzheimer's disease. *American Journal of Pathology, 165*(3), 795–805.

Wei, W., Norton, D. D., Wang, X., & Kusiak, J. W. (2002). Beta amyloid 17–42 in Alzheimer's disease activates JNK and caspase-8 leading to neuronal apoptosis. *Brain, 125*(Pt 9), 2036–2043.

Wei, W., Wang, X., & Kusiak, J. W. (2002). Signaling events in amyloid beta-peptide-induced neuronal death and insulin-like growth factor I protection. *Journal of Biological Chemistry, 277*(20), 17649–17656.

Wenk, G. L., McGann, K., Mencarelli, A., Hauss-Wegrzyniak, B., Del Soldato, P., & Fiorucci, S. (2000). Mechanisms to prevent the toxicity of chronic neuroinflammation on fore-brain cholinergic neurons. *European Journal of Pharmacology, 402*(1–2), 77–85.

Wirtz-Brugger, F., & Giovanni, A. (2000). Guanosine 3',5'-cyclic monophosphate mediated inhibition of cell death induced by nerve growth factor withdrawal and beta-amyloid: Protective effects of propentofylline. *Neuroscience, 99*(4), 737–750.

Xu, G. G., Deng, Y. Q., Liu, S. J., Li, H. L., & Wang, J. Z. (2005). Prolonged Alzheimer-like tau hyperphosphorylation induced by simultaneous inhibition of phosphoinositol-3 kinase and protein kinase C in N2a cells. *Acta Biochimica et Biophysica Sinica (Shanghai)*, *37*(5), 349–354.

Yamada, K. A. (2000). Therapeutic potential of positive AMPA receptor modulators in the treatment of neurological disease. *Expert Opinion on Investigational Drugs*, *9*(4), 765–778.

Yamashima T. (2004). Ca2+-dependent proteases in ischemic neuronal death: A conserved calpain-cathepsin cascade from nematodes to primates. *Cell Calcium*, *36*(3–4), 285–293.

Zhang, Y., Tounekti, O., Akerman, B., Goodyer, C. G., & LeBlanc, A. (2001). 17-beta-estradiol induces an inhibitor of active caspases. *Journal of Neuroscience*, *21*(20), RC176.

Zhang, Y., & Bhavnani, B. R. (2005). Glutamate-induced apoptosis in primary cortical neurons is inhibited by equine estrogens via down-regulation of caspase-3 and prevention of mitochondrial cytochrome c release. *BMC Neuroscience*, *6*(1), 13.

Zhu, X., Wang, Y., Ogawa, O., Lee, H. G., Raina, A. K., Siedlak, S. L., et al. (2004). Neuroprotective properties of Bcl-w in Alzheimer disease. *Journal of Neurochemistry*, *89*(5), 1233–1240.

Zubenko, G. S., Stiffler, J. S., Hughes, H. B., & Martinez, A. J. (1999). Reductions in brain phosphatidylinositol kinase activities in Alzheimer's disease. *Biological Psychiatry*, *45*(6), 731–736.

10

Rational Therapeutics for Alzheimer's Disease and Other Dementias

Neil W. Kowall

Introduction

The first decade of the 21st century has been an exciting yet frustrating time as many candidate therapies for Alzheimer's disease (AD) have failed to live up to their early promise. Even though the only FDA-approved treatments for AD in April 2011 were cholinesterase inhibitors and memantine, ClinicalTrials.gov listed 255 clinical trials actively recruiting volunteers for studies. Hopefully some of these novel pharmaceuticals in late-stage clinical trials will prove to be efficacious and be approved for clinical use in the near future (Sabbagh, 2009; Strobel, 2009).

A great deal has been learned about the pathogenesis of AD in the last 20 years and in 2011 it can be safely stated that Alzheimer therapeutics is a "target-rich" environment (Burns & Iliffe, 2009; Grundman, 2008; Neugroschl & Sano, 2010; Querfurth & LaFerla, 2010; Rafii & Aisen, 2009). As discussed elsewhere in this volume, it is generally but not universally acknowledged that beta amyloid deposition likely plays a key role in the pathogenesis of neuronal degeneration in AD. The origin and fate of beta amyloid is now known in considerable detail and the several points of pharmacological attack have been identified that either reduce its production or enhance its degradation including enzyme inhibitors, immunotherapy, and DNA vaccines as discussed further below. It is also well established that AD brains show evidence of inflammation and oxidative injury so several agents that reduce inflammation and/or oxidative injury are being tested for therapeutic efficacy. Activation of signal transduction cascades, growth factors, and cell death pathways possibly related to oxidative and/or inflammatory processes have also been extensively documented in AD. Here as well pharmacological approaches have been

The Handbook of Alzheimer's Disease and Other Dementias, First Edition.
Edited by Andrew E. Budson, Neil W. Kowall.
© 2011 Blackwell Publishing Ltd. Published 2011 by Blackwell Publishing Ltd.

developed and are being tested. Mitochondrial abnormalities have also been postu-
lated to contribute to AD pathogenesis and, recently, epigenetic modifications of
DNA and histones have been recognized as a key pathway to neurodegeneration.
High profile phase 3 clinical trial failures of drugs targeting beta amyloid have led
some to question whether beta amyloid is the preferred target for AD treatment.
One common feature found in several neurodegenerative diseases is abnormal
protein aggregation and in AD both beta amyloid and tau protein aggregate and
may therefore be therapeutic targets. Early reports suggest that inhibiting tau aggregation in particular could be therapeutically useful. Other molecular pathways
potentially implicated include cell cycle components and cholesterol and/or insulin
metabolism. Finally a growing body of evidence implicates vascular abnormalities
in the pathogenesis of AD. In this chapter I will review some of the candidate therapies that may be made available by the FDA in the near future to treat AD and
related disorders.

Approved Treatments for Alzheimer's Disease and Other Dementias (2011)

Two classes of medications have been approved for the treatment of AD as of April,
2011 (Waldemar et al., 2007). Cholinesterase inhibitors have been FDA approved
for use since 1993. Their effects amount to "turning the clock back" on the progression of clinical dementia in AD and other disorders, and are modest but clinically
significant in some cases. Tacrine was the first drug in this class, but the development of liver toxicity in up to half of patients limited its widespread acceptance and
use. In 1996 donepezil was approved and today is the most widely used cholinesterase inhibitor. Its once-daily dosing and favorable side-effects profile have contrib-
uted to its wide usage. As with other drugs in its class, the most frequent side effects
are gastrointestinal (nausea, vomiting, diarrhea). Initially approved for use in mild
to moderate AD, in 2006 it became approved for use in all stages of AD. About a
third of patients show discernible improvement. Rivastigmine and galantamine are
the other drugs currently available in this class. Rivastigmine inhibits both acetyl-
and butyryl-cholinesterases and has been claimed to be more effective in late-stage
disease and in patients with prominent hallucinations or delusions. It is also
approved for use in Parkinson's disease dementia (PDD). In 2007 a slow-release
transdermal patch preparation became available. Galantamine has additional direct
effects on nicotinic cholinergic receptors that have been claimed to increase its
efficacy but this has not been definitively established. A once-daily extended-release
form of galantamine is now available. All have similar efficacy and side-effects profiles and all may be useful in AD, PDD, and vascular dementia. Specific circumstances may favor individual agents such as the desire for transdermal therapy
(rivastigmine) or once-daily dosing (donepezil or extended-release galantamine).
In 2006 it was reported that cholinesterase inhibitors might increase risk of myocardial infarction (MI) and stroke. The benefit : risk ratio in AD probably favors use

but probably not in patients with normal cognition or minimal impairment of memory.

Memantine is an NMDA receptor antagonist approved for use in moderate to severe AD by the FDA in 2004 (Reisberg et al., 2003). Side effects are minimal, but include drowsiness and confusion that, interestingly, tend to be worse in milder patients. Some patients become "overactivated" and irritable necessitating discontinuation of the drug. Combination therapy with memantine and cholinesterase inhibitors may be superior to treatment with cholinesterase inhibitors alone for patients with moderate to severe disease (Lopez et al., 2009). About two-thirds of patients will have a positive response in overall function and/or cognition. Recent studies suggest that memantine might also be helpful in the treatment of earlier stages of AD. A prospective double-blind cooperative multicenter trial testing combination therapy and vitamin E in mild to moderate AD is currently underway at several sites in the VA healthcare system (Cooperative Studies Program trial #546, Principal Investigator: Maurice Dysken, MD).

Prevention and Secondary Prevention versus Treatment

It is important to differentiate preventative interventions from disease treatment when evaluating therapeutic agents for AD. Lack of efficacy in a prevention trial does not preclude efficacy in an intervention trial and vice versa. For example, estrogen has been clearly shown to lack efficacy in slowing the progression of established AD in a randomized blinded prospective clinical trial (Henderson et al., 2000; Mulnard et al., 2000), but its efficacy as a preventative intervention is still debated (Pike et al., 2009).

Risk Factor Modification

A large and growing body of evidence links a heart-healthy lifestyle to brain health (Scarmeas et al., 2009). Vascular risk factor control may prevent or delay the development of clinical dementia (Middleton & Yaffe, 2009). Exercise and dietary modifications are potentially effective strategies (Scarmeas et al., 2009). Hypertension has been linked to reduced cognitive function (Qiu et al., 2005). Insulin excess is linked to AD pathogenesis and diabetes is a risk factor (Kopf & Frolich, 2009).

Failed Therapies

The ultimate goal of AD therapeutics is the discovery of a therapy that arrests or reverses the inexorable and irreversible course of AD (Salloway et al., 2008). Only a well-designed randomized prospective clinical trial can definitively establish effectiveness. These trials are expensive and difficult to initiate so it is likely that definitive conclusions regarding the efficacy of many interventions will remain elusive. Unfortunately, several agents that looked promising in smaller phase 2 studies have failed in large-scale phase 3 efficacy trials. Notable examples of recent failures in late-stage trials include tarenflurbil (Green et al., 2009) and Dimebon (press release from Pfizer Inc. and Medivation Inc., March 3, 2010). Despite the potential importance of inflammation in the pathogenesis of AD, corticosteroids have not been shown to be effective (Aisen et al., 2000). Ginko Biloba is also probably not effective (Snitz et al., 2009) and high-dose B vitamins had no positive clinical effects (Aisen et al., 2008).

Towards an Effective Therapy for AD

Targeting beta amyloid or its precursor

As discussed elsewhere in this volume, it is widely believed that beta amyloid (Aβ) generated from its precursor, APP, is neurotoxic, especially when it forms oligomers. Based on this theory, drugs have been designed to specifically target Aβ production, aggregation, and degradation. This hypothesis has lost some of its luster because recent therapeutic trials focused on reducing brain Aβ have had disappointing results including phase 3 trials of tarenflurbil and tramiprosate (Alzhemed) (Carlsson, 2008). Nevertheless several compounds continue to be tested in clinical trials.

Reducing Aβ production
The APP degrading enzymes BACE (beta site APP cleaving enzyme) and gamma-secretase that generate Aβ from APP are potential candidates for inhibition (Marks & Berg, 2010). Developing small-molecule BACE inhibitors that cross the blood–brain barrier has been challenging and BACE inhibition may have serious consequences on memory and behavior because of its involvement in other important metabolic pathways (Vassar et al., 2009). Because of this limitation only one compound, CTS-21166, has been subject to early clinical trials. Trials using gamma-secretase inhibitors have progressed further (Serneels et al., 2009). One agent, semagacestat (Eli-Lilly), is in phase 3 clinical trials. Gastrointestinal toxicity and immune system side effects have been noted. Two other gamma-secretase inhibitors are in phase 2 clinical trials and two others have completed phase 1 studies (late 2009). Recently, attempts to increase the activity of alpha-secretase, which cleaves APP in the Aβ domain, have been developed and two agents are in phase 2 clinical trials (Panza et al., 2009).

Increasing Aβ clearance
Activation of the immune system either actively or passively with Aβ antibodies increases Aβ clearance from the brain. This has been directly confirmed using

imaging beta amyloid in living AD patients passively immunized against Aβ with bapineuzumab (Rinne et al., 2010). Initial trials using Aβ as an immunogen caused fatal autoimmune encephalitis in some cases leading to the suspension of that clinical trial in 2002 (Lemere, 2009). A postmortem histological study on subjects enrolled in that trial showed that immunization efficiently cleared beta amyloid containing senile plaques from brain but, despite this, patients died with dementia (Nicoll et al., 2003). This observation does not necessarily prove that beta amyloid is not the cause of neuronal degeneration in AD. Ongoing neurodegeneration could be due to other APP-derived fragments or invisible beta amyloid oligomers that are still present and killing neurons. Other immunogens have been developed and are now being tested in preclinical trials (Lemere, 2009; Wilcock & Colton, 2008). Preclinical trials using the DNA vaccine approach are being tested (Lambracht-Washington et al., 2009). Phase 2 trials with the monoclonal Aβ antibody bapineuzumab did not show efficacy but there was a suggestion that a subset of ApoE4 negative subjects could be responders (Salloway et al., 2009). A phase 2 study of intravenous immunoglobulin (IVIG) has been completed and a large-scale clinical trial is underway (Relkin et al., 2009). IVIG infusions increased anti-beta amyloid antibody and beta amyloid peptides in plasma and decreased beta amyloid peptides in cerebrospinal fluid compared with values prior to treatment (Hughes et al., 2009).

Inhibiting Aβ aggregation

Because it is widely held that beta amyloid toxicity is increased by aggregation into oligomers, one therapeutic approach has been to inhibit oligomer formation (Ondrejcak et al., 2010; Panza et al., 2009; Querfurth & LaFerla, 2010). The most promising agent tested, tramiprosate (Alzhemed), ultimately failed in phase 3 clinical trials (Amijee & Scopes, 2009). Scyllo-Inositol (ELND005), another agent that reduces Aβ oligomer formation, also successfully completed a phase 1 trial. In December 2009, Elan and Transition Therapeutics, Inc. announced modifications to the ongoing ELND005 Phase 2 trial because of serious adverse affects including some deaths in patients receiving higher doses. Only the lowest dose, 250 mg twice daily, will be tested. A direct relationship between ELND005 and these deaths was not established.

Targeting tau protein aggregation and NFT formation

The microtubule-associated protein tau is the major constituent of the neurofibrillary tangles (NFT) that accumulate within neurons in AD (Querfurth & LaFerla, 2010). Aggregated tau, like aggregated beta amyloid, is thought to be neurotoxic (Meraz-Rios et al., 2009; Querfurth & LaFerla, 2010). Based on this notion, Wischik and colleagues performed a placebo-controlled double-blind study on 332 subjects with probable AD using methylthioninium chloride (methylene blue, Rember, MTC), which has been shown to interfere with tau aggregation in in vitro studies and in animal models (ICAD 2008, abstract number O3-04-07). This preliminary report, which has not been reported in the peer-reviewed literature, showed that MTC produced a significant improvement relative to placebo and stabilized disease progression over 50 weeks in both mild and moderate AD. MTC has other actions aside from its effect on tau aggregation including antioxidant and mitochondrial effects that could contribute to its potential efficacy. MTC and related derivatives and other tau-directed interventions may represent a new avenue for AD therapeutics (Brunden et al., 2009).

Targeting inflammatory mechanisms

Inflammation may be a key contributor to AD pathogenesis (Ray & Lahiri, 2009). Indirect evidence suggests nonsteroidal anti-inflammatory drugs (NSAIDs) may reduce AD risk but prospective treatment trials to date have been disappointing (Green et al., 2009). NSAIDs such as ibuprofen and naproxen may delay the onset of AD (Breitner et al., 2009). The large AD anti-inflammatory prevention trial (ADAPT) was suspended because of concerns regarding the toxicity of long-term NSAID use but the study is being restarted because data gathered from participants followed since the suspension of the study suggest that chronic use of naproxen may significantly reduce the risk of developing AD. A striking report suggested that intrathecal infusion of etanercept caused rapid reversal of cognitive defects in patients with AD but this observation has not yet been replicated or tested in a controlled clinical trial (Tobinick & Gross, 2008). Oral drugs such as impiramine, which inhibit TNF alpha, may be candidates for future clinical trials (Chavant et al., 2010).

Targeting oxidative mechanisms, signal transduction, growth factors, and cell death pathways

The antioxidant vitamin E was shown to slow the progression of moderate to severe AD and delay nursing home placement by six months. Since the use of vitamin E has been associated with increased rates of cardiac death, it is generally viewed that its use in cognitively normal individuals is not warranted. The efficacy of vitamin E in mild to moderate AD is being tested at part of a national VA cooperative study (Cooperative Studies Program trial #546, Principal Investigator: Maurice Dysken, MD). A small pilot of intranasal insulin has been shown to have positive short-term cognitive effects in mild AD (Reger et al., 2008). Insulin signal transduction pathway has also been an area of interest. The c-Jun N-terminal kinase (JNK) plays a major role in the regulation of these downstream pathways. Beta amyloid oligomers activate JNK in a transgenic mouse model of AD while treatment with curcumin and the omega-3 fatty acid docosahexanoic acid (DHA) reduce JNK activation (Ma et al., 2009). Curcumin has been tested in pilot studies but definitive controlled clinical trials demonstrating efficacy have yet to be reported (Mancuso & Barone, 2009; Ray & Lahiri, 2009). Cell death pathways are activated by a number of insults and may represent a final common pathway leading to cell death in AD as discussed by Tsolaki and colleagues elsewhere in this volume. This knowledge has not yet translated into therapeutic trials but there are a number of potential directions for future clinical trials. For example, cyclin-dependent kinase 5 (Cdk5), which is primarily active in postmitotic neurons, phosphorylates tau, induces the cell cycle induction, and triggers apoptotic cell death in postmitotic neurons exposed to beta amyloid in vivo. An orally active cdk5 inhibitor, roscovitine, is currently being studied in phase 2 clinical trials for lung cancer (Leitch et al., 2010). The phytoalexin Resveratrol, which may be the active protective moiety in red wine, has been shown to protect against beta amyloid toxicity in animal models of AD. Resveratol activates the sirtuin 1, an important deacetylase whose substrates include p53, PPAR gamma, and histones (Albani et al., 2010). A clinical trial of Resveratrol on 60 patients with AD is underway at Mount Sinai and the Bronx VA in New York (Neugroschl & Sano, 2010). There is substantial evidence suggesting that omega 3 fatty acid supplementation might prevent or slow the development of AD but clinical trials to date have been disappointing. An 18-month Alzheimer Disease Cooperative Studies (ADCS) treatment trial on 402 people with mild to moderate AD did not slow progression. Advocates suggest that earlier intervention in subsets of patients who are ApoE4 negative may yield positive results (Cole & Frautschy, 2010). Recently vitamin D supplementation has been identified as a potential intervention or preventative measure for a number of diseases including Alzheimer's disease because low vitamin D levels are associated with dementia, Alzheimer's disease, and stroke (Buell et al., 2010; Evatt et al., 2008).

Alternative Medicine for Alzheimer's Disease

Many herbal and alternative medicine-based approaches have been suggested as potential treatments for AD. A recent systemic review of Chinese herbs including Ginko Biloba, Huperzine A, and Ginseng concluded that evidence in support of the use of Chinese herbs in AD is inconclusive or inadequate. High-dose B vitamins have not been shown to be helpful (Aisen et al., 2008). Tea may be helpful but evidence is weak (Bastianetto et al., 2006).

Future Directions for Drug Development

Millions of patients and their families, clinicians, and the research community have suffered repeated disappointments but remain hopeful. Recent trials suggest that focusing on subsets of patients, such as those who do not carry the ApoE4 genotype, may identify patients who might be more responsive to therapy. Once effective therapies are identified, combination therapy using drugs with different mechanisms of action may lead to further improvements in treatment. In 2009 a European group proposed a Multidomain Alzheimer Preventive Trial (MAPT) study based on the idea that multiple factors may contribute to the development of AD. The plan is to perform a three-year, randomized, controlled trial to assess the efficacy of nutritional, physical, and cognitive training combined with omega 3 supplementation in the prevention of cognitive decline in frail elderly persons (Gillette-Guyonnet et al., 2009). Studies that are part of the genome-wide association study (GWAS) led to the discovery of new susceptibility genes related to late-onset AD including a locus on chromosome 12 near the vitamin D receptor, a gene on chromosome 1 associated with schizophrenia, and a chromosome 19 gene independent of ApoE (Sleegers et al., 2010). A genome-wide, whole-brain approach to investigate genetic effects on neuroimaging phenotypes ("endophenotype") for identifying quantitative trait loci was recently reported (Shen et al., 2010). These and other similar new findings will likely point the way to new therapeutic directions in the years ahead.

References

Aisen, P. S., Davis, K. L., Berg, J. D., Schafer, K., Campbell, K., Thomas, R. G., et al. (2000). A randomized controlled trial of prednisone in Alzheimer's disease. Alzheimer's Disease Cooperative Study. *Neurology, 54*(3), 588–593.

Aisen, P. S., Schneider, L. S., Sano, M., Diaz-Arrastia, R., van Dyck, C. H., Weiner, M. F., et al. (2008). High-dose B vitamin supplementation and cognitive decline in Alzheimer disease: A randomized controlled trial. *Journal of the American Medical Association, 300*(15), 1774–1783.

Albani, D., Polito, L., & Forloni, G. (2010). Sirtuins as novel targets for Alzheimer's disease and other neurodegenerative disorders: Experimental and genetic evidence. *Journal of Alzheimer's Disease, 19*(1), 11–26.

Amijee, H., & Scopes, D. I. (2009). The quest for small molecules as amyloid inhibiting therapies for Alzheimer's disease. *Journal of Alzheimer's Disease, 17*(1), 33–47.

Bastianetto, S., Yao, Z. X., Papadopoulos, V., & Quirion, R. (2006). Neuroprotective effects of green and black teas and their catechin gallate esters against beta-amyloid-induced toxicity. *European Journal of Neuroscience, 23*(1), 55–64.

Breitner, J. C., Haneuse, S. J., Walker, R., Dublin, S., Crane, P. K., Gray, S. L., et al. (2009). Risk of dementia and AD with prior exposure to NSAIDs in an elderly community-based cohort. *Neurology, 72*(22), 1899–1905.

Brunden, K. R., Trojanowski, J. Q., & Lee, V. M. (2009). Advances in tau-focused drug discovery for Alzheimer's disease and related tauopathies. *Nature Reviews Drug Discovery, 8*(10), 783–793.

Buell, J. S., Dawson-Hughes, B., Scott, T. M., Weiner, D. E., Dallal, G. E., Qui, W. Q., et al. (2010). 25-Hydroxyvitamin D, dementia, and cerebrovascular pathology in elders receiving home services. *Neurology, 74*(1), 18–26.

Burns, A., & Iliffe, S. (2009). Alzheimer's disease. *British Medical Journal, 338*, b158.

Carlsson, C. M. (2008). Lessons learned from failed and discontinued clinical trials for the treatment of Alzheimer's disease: Future directions. *Journal of Alzheimer's Disease, 15*(2), 327–338.

Chavant, F., Deguil, J., Pain, S., Ingrand, I., Milin, S., Fauconneau, B., et al. (2010). Imipramine, in part through tumor necrosis factor alpha inhibition, prevents cognitive decline and beta-amyloid accumulation in a mouse model of Alzheimer's disease. *Journal of Pharmacology and Experimental Therapeutics, 332*(2), 505–514.

Cole, G. M., & Frautschy, S. A. (2010). DHA May Prevent Age-Related Dementia. *Journal of Nutrition, 140*(4), 869–874.

Evatt, M. L., Delong, M. R., Khazai, N., Rosen, A., Triche, S., & Tangpricha, V. (2008). Prevalence of vitamin D insufficiency in patients with Parkinson disease and Alzheimer disease. *Archives of Neurology, 65*(10), 1348–1352.

Gillette-Guyonnet, S., Andrieu, S., Dantoine, T., Dartigues, J. F., Touchon, J., & Vellas, B. (2009). Commentary on "A roadmap for the prevention of dementia II. Leon Thal Symposium 2008." The Multidomain Alzheimer Preventive Trial (MAPT): A new approach to the prevention of Alzheimer's disease. *Alzheimer's & Dementia, 5*(2), 114–121.

Green, R. C., Schneider, L. S., Amato, D. A., Beelen, A. P., Wilcock, G., Swabb, E. A., et al. (2009). Effect of tarenflurbil on cognitive decline and activities of daily living in patients with mild Alzheimer disease: A randomized controlled trial. *Journal of the American Medical Association, 302*(23), 2557–2564.

Grundman, M. (2008). A quarter century of advancing treatment for Alzheimer's disease with Leon J. Thal. *Alzheimer's & Dementia, 4*(1 Suppl 1), S51–S55.

Henderson, V. W., Paganini-Hill, A., Miller, B. L., Elble, R. J., Reyes, P. F., Shoupe, D., et al. (2000). Estrogen for Alzheimer's disease in women: Randomized, double-blind, placebo-controlled trial. *Neurology, 54*(2), 295–301.

Hughes, R. A., Dalakas, M. C., Cornblath, D. R., Latov, N., Weksler, M. E., & Relkin, N. (2009). Clinical applications of intravenous immunoglobulins in neurology. *Clinical & Experimental Immunology, 158*(Suppl 1), 34–42.

Kopf, D., & Frolich, L. (2009). Risk of incident Alzheimer's disease in diabetic patients: A systematic review of prospective trials. *Journal of Alzheimer's Disease, 16*(4), 677–685.

Lambracht-Washington, D., Qu, B. X., Fu, M., Eagar, T. N., Stuve, O., & Rosenberg, R. N. (2009). DNA beta-amyloid(1-42) trimer immunization for Alzheimer disease in a wild-type mouse model. *Journal of the American Medical Association, 302*(16), 1796–1802.

Leitch, A. E., Riley, N. A., T, A. S., Festa, M., Fox, S., Duffin, R., et al. (2010). The cyclin-dependent kinase inhibitor R-roscovitine down-regulates Mcl-1 to override pro-inflammatory signalling and drive neutrophil apoptosis. *European Journal of Immunology, 40*(4), 1127–1138.

Lemere, C. A. (2009). Developing novel immunogens for a safe and effective Alzheimer's disease vaccine. *Progress in Brain Research, 175*, 83–93.

Lopez, O. L., Becker, J. T., Wahed, A. S., Saxton, J., Sweet, R. A., Wolk, D. A., et al. (2009). Long-term effects of the concomitant use of memantine with cholinesterase inhibition in Alzheimer disease. *Journal of Neurology, Neurosurgery & Psychiatry, 80*(6), 600–607.

Ma, Q. L., Yang, F., Rosario, E. R., Ubeda, O. J., Beech, W., Gant, D. J., et al. (2009). Beta-amyloid oligomers induce phosphorylation of tau and inactivation of insulin receptor substrate via c-Jun N-terminal kinase signaling: Suppression by omega-3 fatty acids and curcumin. *Journal of Neuroscience, 29*(28), 9078–9089.

Mancuso, C., & Barone, E. (2009). Curcumin in clinical practice: myth or reality? *Trends in Pharmacological Sciences, 30*(7), 333–334.

Marks, N., & Berg, M. J. (2010). BACE and gamma-secretase characterization and their sorting as therapeutic targets to reduce amyloidogenesis. *Neurochemical Research, 35*(2), 181–210.

Meraz-Rios, M. A., Lira-De Leon, K. I., Campos-Pena, V., De Anda-Hernandez, M. A., & Mena-Lopez, R. (2009). Tau oligomers and aggregation in Alzheimer's disease. *Journal of Neurochemistry, 112*(6), 1353–67.

Middleton, L. E., & Yaffe, K. (2009). Promising strategies for the prevention of dementia. *Archives of Neurology, 66*(10), 1210–1215.

Mulnard, R. A., Cotman, C. W., Kawas, C., van Dyck, C. H., Sano, M., Doody, R., et al. (2000). Estrogen replacement therapy for treatment of mild to moderate Alzheimer disease: A randomized controlled trial. Alzheimer's Disease Cooperative Study. *Journal of the American Medical Association, 283*(8), 1007–1015.

Neugroschl, J., & Sano, M. (2010). Current treatment and recent clinical research in Alzheimer's disease. *Mount Sinai Journal of Medicine, 77*(1), 3–16.

Nicoll, J. A., Wilkinson, D., Holmes, C., Steart, P., Markham, H., & Weller, R. O. (2003). Neuropathology of human Alzheimer disease after immunization with amyloid-beta peptide: A case report. *Nature Medicine, 9*(4), 448–452.

Ondrejcak, T., Klyubin, I., Hu, N. W., Barry, A. E., Cullen, W. K., & Rowan, M. J. (2010). Alzheimer's disease amyloid beta-protein and synaptic function. *NeuroMolecular Medicine, 12*(1), 13–26.

Panza, F., Solfrizzi, V., Frisardi, V., Capurso, C., D'Introno, A., Colacicco, A. M., et al. (2009). Disease-modifying approach to the treatment of Alzheimer's disease: From alpha-secretase activators to gamma-secretase inhibitors and modulators. *Drugs & Aging, 26*(7), 537–555.

Pike, C. J., Carroll, J. C., Rosario, E. R., & Barron, A. M. (2009). Protective actions of sex steroid hormones in Alzheimer's disease. *Frontiers in Neuroendocrinology, 30*(2), 239–258.

Qiu, C., Winblad, B., & Fratiglioni, L. (2005). The age-dependent relation of blood pressure to cognitive function and dementia. *Lancet Neurology, 4*(8), 487–499.

Querfurth, H. W., & LaFerla, F. M. (2010). Alzheimer's disease. *New England Journal of Medicine, 362*(4), 329–344.

Rafii, M. S., & Aisen, P. S. (2009). Recent developments in Alzheimer's disease therapeutics. *BMC Medicine, 7*, 7.

Ray, B., & Lahiri, D. K. (2009). Neuroinflammation in Alzheimer's disease: Different molecular targets and potential therapeutic agents including curcumin. *Current Opinion in Pharmacology, 9*(4), 434–444.

Reger, M. A., Watson, G. S., Green, P. S., Wilkinson, C. W., Baker, L. D., Cholerton, B., et al. (2008). Intranasal insulin improves cognition and modulates beta-amyloid in early AD. *Neurology, 70*(6), 440–448.

Reisberg, B., Doody, R., Stoffler, A., Schmitt, F., Ferris, S., & Mobius, H. J. (2003). Memantine in moderate-to-severe Alzheimer's disease. *New England Journal of Medicine, 348*(14), 1333–1341.

Relkin, N. R., Szabo, P., Adamiak, B., Burgut, T., Monthe, C., Lent, R. W., et al. (2009). 18-Month study of intravenous immunoglobulin for treatment of mild Alzheimer disease. *Neurobiology of Aging, 30*(11), 1728–1736.

Rinne, J. O., Brooks, D. J., Rossor, M. N., Fox, N. C., Bullock, R., Klunk, W. E., et al. (2010). (11)C-PiB PET assessment of change in fibrillar amyloid-beta load in patients with

Alzheimer's disease treated with bapineuzumab: A phase 2, double-blind, placebo-controlled, ascending-dose study. *Lancet Neurology, 9*(4), 363–372.

Sabbagh, M. N. (2009). Drug development for Alzheimer's disease: Where are we now and where are we headed? *American Journal of Geriatric Pharmacotherapy, 7*(3), 167–185.

Salloway, S., Mintzer, J., Weiner, M. F., & Cummings, J. L. (2008). Disease-modifying therapies in Alzheimer's disease. *Alzheimer's & Dementia, 4*(2), 65–79.

Salloway, S., Sperling, R., Gilman, S., Fox, N. C., Blennow, K., Raskind, M., et al. (2009). A phase 2 multiple ascending dose trial of bapineuzumab in mild to moderate Alzheimer disease. *Neurology, 73*(24), 2061–2070.

Scarmeas, N., Luchsinger, J. A., Schupf, N., Brickman, A. M., Cosentino, S., Tang, M. X., et al. (2009). Physical activity, diet, and risk of Alzheimer disease. *Journal of the American Medical Association, 302*(6), 627–637.

Serneels, L., Van Biervliet, J., Craessaerts, K., Dejaegere, T., Horre, K., Van Houtvin, T., et al. (2009). gamma-Secretase heterogeneity in the Aph1 subunit: Relevance for Alzheimer's disease. *Science, 324*(5927), 639–642.

Shen, L., Kim, S., Risacher, S. L., Nho, K., Swaminathan, S., West, J. D., et al. (2010). Whole genome association study of brain-wide imaging phenotypes for identifying quantitative trait loci in MCI and AD: A study of the ADNI cohort. *Neuroimage, 53*(3), 1051–1063.

Sleegers, K., Lambert, J. C., Bertram, L., Cruts, M., Amouyel, P., & Van Broeckhoven, C. (2010). The pursuit of susceptibility genes for Alzheimer's disease: Progress and prospects. *Trends in Genetics, 26*(2), 84–93.

Snitz, B. E., O'Meara, E. S., Carlson, M. C., Arnold, A. M., Ives, D. G., Rapp, S. R., et al. (2009). Ginkgo Biloba for preventing cognitive decline in older adults: A randomized trial. *Journal of the American Medical Association, 302*(24), 2663–2670.

Strobel, G. (2009). 12th International Conference on Alzheimer's Disease (ICAD), Vienna, Austria. *Journal of Alzheimer's Disease, 18*(4), 973–990.

Tobinick, E. L., & Gross, H. (2008). Rapid improvement in verbal fluency and aphasia following perispinal etanercept in Alzheimer's disease. *BMC Neurology, 8*, 27.

Vassar, R., Kovacs, D. M., Yan, R., & Wong, P. C. (2009). The beta-secretase enzyme BACE in health and Alzheimer's disease: Regulation, cell biology, function, and therapeutic potential. *Journal of Neuroscience, 29*(41), 12787–12794.

Waldemar, G., Dubois, B., Emre, M., Georges, J., McKeith, I. G., Rossor, M., et al. (2007). Recommendations for the diagnosis and management of Alzheimer's disease and other disorders associated with dementia: EFNS guideline. *European Journal of Neurology, 14*(1), e1–e26.

Wilcock, D. M., & Colton, C. A. (2008). Anti-amyloid-beta immunotherapy in Alzheimer's disease: Relevance of transgenic mouse studies to clinical trials. *Journal of Alzheimer's Disease, 15*(4), 555–569.

Part III

Cognitive and Behavioral Dysfunction

11

Memory Dysfunction in Dementia

Andrew E. Budson

Although once thought to be a simple concept, memory is now considered to be a collection of mental abilities that use different systems and components within the brain to retain information over time. Memory research that began with neuropsychological studies of patients with focal brain lesions and now includes newer methods such as positron emission tomography, functional MRI, and event-related potentials has provided the rationale for a more refined and improved classification system (Budson, 2009; Schacter et al., 2000). In this chapter a number of different memory systems and their relevance for dementia will be reviewed, including the important anatomical structures for each, and the major disorders that disrupt them (Tables 11.1 and 11.2). A greater understanding of these memory systems will help the student or researcher to learn more about dementia in addition to aiding clinicians in their diagnosis and treatment of the memory disorders of patients. This improved understanding will become increasingly important as new therapeutic interventions for memory disorders are developed.

A memory system is a way for the brain to process information that will be available for use at a later time (Schacter & Tulving, 1994). Some systems are associated with conscious awareness (explicit) and can be consciously recalled (declarative), whereas others are typically unconscious (implicit) and are instead expressed by a change in behavior (non-declarative) (Squire, 1992). Memory can also be categorized in other ways, such as the nature of the material to be remembered, verbal (Champod & Petrides, 2010; Wagner et al., 1998) versus visual (Brewer et al., 1998; Morita et al., 2010).

The Handbook of Alzheimer's Disease and Other Dementias, First Edition.
Edited by Andrew E. Budson, Neil W. Kowall.
© 2011 Blackwell Publishing Ltd. Published 2011 by Blackwell Publishing Ltd.

Table 11.1 Selected memory systems

Memory system	Examples	Awareness	Length of storage	Major anatomical structures
Episodic memory	Remembering a short story, what you had for dinner last night, and what you did on your last birthday	Explicit Declarative	Minutes to years	Medial temporal lobe, anterior thalamic nucleus, mamillary body, fornix, prefrontal cortex
Semantic memory	Knowing who was the first US President, the color of a lion, and how a fork and comb are different	Explicit Declarative	Minutes to years	Inferior lateral temporal lobes
Procedural memory	Driving a standard transmission car, and learning the sequence of numbers on a touch-tone phone without trying	Implicit Non-declarative	Minutes to years	Basal ganglia, cerebellum, supplementary motor area
Working memory	Phonological: keeping a phone number "in your head" before dialing Spatial: Mentally following a route, or rotating an object in your mind	Explicit Declarative	Seconds to minutes; information actively rehearsed or manipulated	Phonological: prefrontal cortex, Broca's area, Wernike's area. Spatial: Prefrontal cortex, visual association areas

Table 11.2 Selective memory system disruptions in common clinical disorders

Disease	Episodic memory	Semantic memory	Procedural memory	Working memory
Alzheimer's disease	+++	++	−	++
Frontotemporal dementia	++	++	−	+++
Semantic dementia	+	+++	?	−
Lewy body dementia	++	?	?	++
Vascular dementia	+	+	+	++
Parkinson's disease	+	+	+++	++
Huntington's disease	+	+	+++	+++
Progressive supranuclear palsy	+	+	++	+++
Korsakoff syndrome	+++	−	−	+/−
Multiple sclerosis	+	+/−	?	++
Transient global amnesia	+++	+/−	−	−
Hypoxic-ischemic injury	++	−	−	+/−
Head trauma	+	+	+/−	++
Depression	+	+/−	++	+/−
Anxiety	+	−	−	+/−
Obsessive compulsive disorder	+	−	++	++
Attention deficit hyperactivity disorder			?	+

+++ = Early and severe impairment; ++ = Moderate impairment; + = Mild impairment; occasional impairment or impairment in some studies but not others; − = No significant impairment; ? = Unknown

Episodic Memory

Episodic memory refers to the explicit and declarative memory system used to remember a particular episode of one's life, such as going out to dinner with a friend. This memory system is dependent upon the medial temporal lobes (including the hippocampus), as episodic memory has been largely defined by what patients with medial temporal lobe lesions cannot remember relative to healthy individuals. Other critical structures in the episodic memory system (some of which are associated with a circuit described by Papez in 1937) include the basal forebrain with the medial septum and diagonal band of Broca, the retrosplenial cortex, the presubiculum, the fornix, mammillary bodies, the mammillothalamic tract, and the anterior nucleus of the thalamus (Mesulam, 2000) (Figure 11.1, plate section). A lesion in any one of these structures may cause the impairment that is characteristic of dysfunction of the episodic memory system.

Memory loss due to dysfunction of the episodic memory system generally follows a pattern known as Ribot's law, which states that events just prior to an ictus are most vulnerable to decay, whereas remote memories are more resistant. Thus, dysfunction of the episodic memory system typically causes greatest disruption in the ability to learn new information (anterograde amnesia), moderate disruption in the

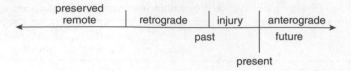

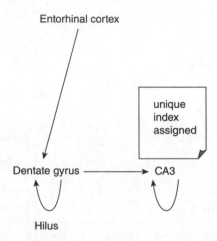

Figure 11.2   Ribot's law

Figure 11.3   Schematic of encoding in the medial temporal lobe

ability to recall recently learned information (retrograde amnesia), and the ability to recall remotely learned information is generally intact (Ribot, 1881) (Figure 11.2).

The core of the episodic memory system is the medial temporal lobe and hippocampus. The medial temporal lobes are neuroanatomically complex structures with multiple regions and subregions including the parahippocampal gyrus, presubiculum, subiculum, and hippocampus proper, including its subregions.

Although we do not completely understand how the medial temporal lobes store and retrieve memories, our current understanding from cognitive neuroscience is as follows. An individual experiences an episode of their life, such as having lunch one afternoon. The cortically distributed patterns of neural activity representing the sights, sounds, smells, tastes, emotions, and thoughts during that episode are transferred first to the parahippocampal region and then to the hippocampus proper. After being transferred to the entorhinal cortex, the information is processed in the dentate gyrus, and then transferred to the CA3 region where it is further processed (Figure 11.3). It is in this CA3 region where the critically important hippocampal index is assigned, allowing the memory to be stored in a unique way so that it can later be recalled.

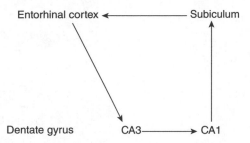

Figure 11.4   Schematic of retrieval in the medial temporal lobe

Typically memories are retrieved when a cue from the environment matches a part of the stored memory. Continuing our lunch example, years later the individual might now bite into a little cake that tastes remarkably like the one she had previously for desert during that particular lunch. This sensory cue is transferred from the cortex to the parahippocampal region and to the hippocampus. After the cue is transferred from the entorhinal cortex it now goes directly to the CA3 region where the original hippocampal index is retrieved (Figure 11.4). When found, the hippocampal index may be used to retrieve much of the original pattern of the neural activity representing the original episode stored in memory. This retrieved pattern of activity may then be transferred to the CA1 region, the subiculum, the entorhinal cortex, and then back out to the cortex – recreating all of sights, sounds, smells, tastes, emotions, and thoughts of the original memory episode.

The hippocampus remains critical for memory retrieval until a process known as *consolidation* occurs. Much research still needs to be done to better understand consolidation, but one thought is that once a memory is consolidated the distributed pattern of cortical neural activity is directly linked together, such that when a cue is encountered, the memory may be retrieved directly from cortical–cortical connections, without the need for the hippocampus. And although there are many details that need to be learned, there is much data that suggest that sleep is critical for consolidation to occur (Aly & Moscovitch, 2010; Diekelmann & Born, 2010; O'Neill et al., 2010; Stickgold, 2005, 2006).

In looking at the cognitive neuroscience model just presented of how memories are stored and retrieved, it is the CA3 region of the hippocampus that seems most critical – it is this region in which the hippocampal index is formed, and this region in which pattern matching of cues and memories occurs. Although we do not know exactly how the CA3 region is involved in these activities, a number of models using neural networks have been proposed. A simplified example of such a model is as follows. In this example we will show how an individual can find their car when they park in a parking garage over three successive days – and also why it is sometimes difficult for an individual to find their car. In this mythical parking garage there are two areas, Red and Blue, and two levels, first and second. Two weather

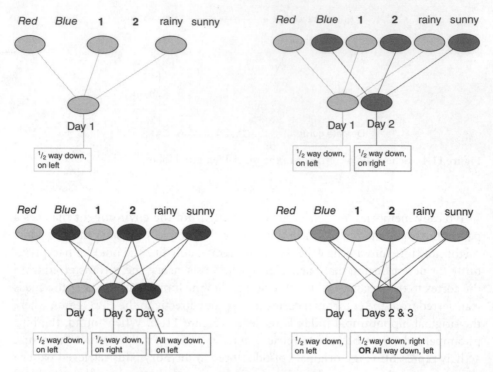

Figure 11.5   A neural network model. See text for details

states, rainy and sunny, are also shown to represent not only the weather but also other contextual details that may differ between one day and the next. On the first day the car is parked in the Red area, on the first floor, and it was a rainy day. From this distributed pattern of neural activity a hippocampal index can be formed that helps one remember that the car was parked in the Red area, on the first floor, and halfway down the aisle on the left (Figure 11.5, top left). On the second day the car is parked in the Blue area, on the second floor, and it was a sunny day. This distinct pattern of neural activity allows a unique hippocampal index to form that enables one to remember that the car was parked in the Blue area, on the second floor, and halfway down the aisle on the right (Figure 11.5, top right). On the third day the car is also parked in the Blue area, on the second floor, and it again was a sunny day (Figure 11.5, bottom left). Although one might wish that a hippocampal index will form to enable one to remember that the car was parked in the Blue area, on the second floor, and all the way down the aisle on the left – there is a problem. When there are completely overlapping patterns of neural activity a separate hippocampal index cannot form. Instead, there is a single hippocampal index which forms for both days two and three (Figure 11.5, bottom right). This hippocampal index is strengthened for the common aspects of the two memories: parking in the Blue area, on the second floor. But this index will also contain divergent aspects of the memory: halfway down the aisle on the right and all the way down the aisle on the

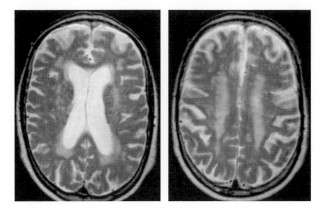

Figure 2.1 White matter hyperintensities in VCI. Periventricular WMHs in a patient with vascular cognitive impairment as visualized on T2-weighted images acquired with a 3T MRI scanner
Source: Courtesy of Dr. Angela Jefferson, Boston University School of Medicine

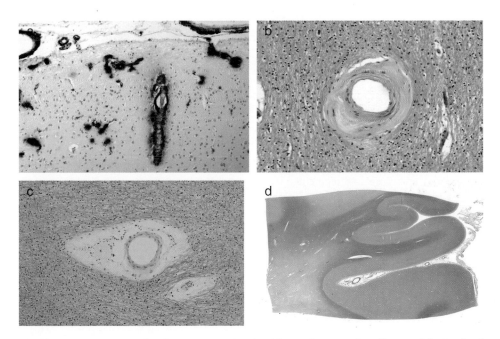

Figure 2.2 Microvascular lesions associated with cerebrovascular disease. (a) Cerebral amyloid angiopathy; (b) Stenotic vessel from arteriosclerosis; (c) Widening of perivascular spaces; (d) Myelin loss
Source: Courtesy of Dr. Ann McKee, Boston University School of Medicine

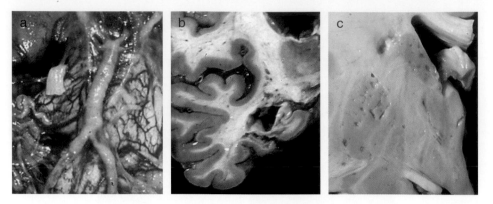

Figure 2.3 Vascular lesions evident upon gross pathological examination. (a) Atherosclerosis; (b) Infarcts; (c) Lacunes
Source: Courtesy of Dr. Ann McKee, Boston University School of Medicine

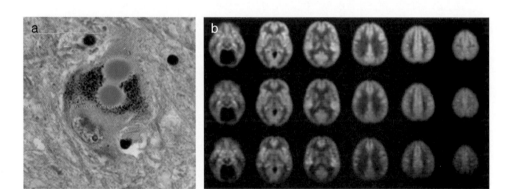

Figure 3.3 (a) On the left are two Lewy bodies, seen as spherical, eosinophilic (pink) intracellular inclusions in a pigmented neuron from the substantia nigra (picture courtesy of Dr. Jeffrey Joseph). (b) On the right is a demonstration of changes seen in perfusion MRI with arterial spin labeling in DLB. The top row represents normal perfusion imaging, the second row shows mild decreases seen in mild AD, the third row shows greater decreases seen in DLB matched for severity

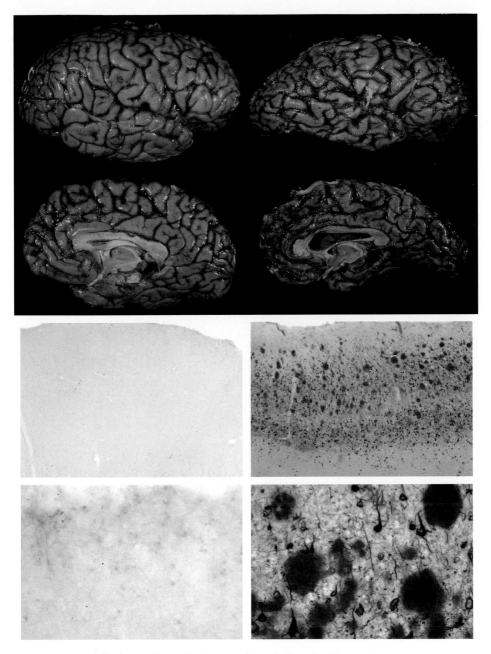

Figure 7.1 Cerebral atrophy and microscopic pathology in AD
Source: Courtesy of Dr. Ann McKee, Boston University School of Medicine

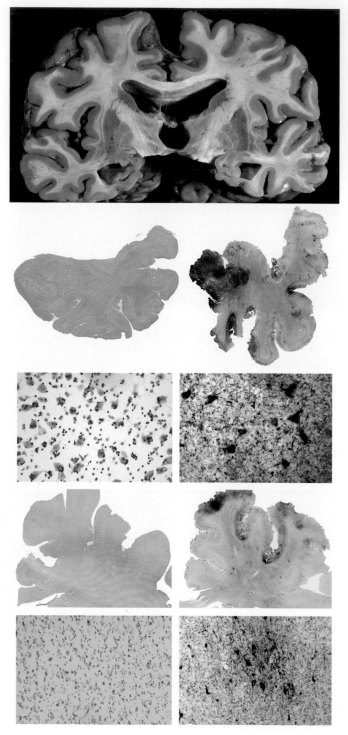

Figure 7.2   Chronic traumatic encephalopathy
Source: Courtesy of Dr. Ann McKee, Boston University School of Medicine

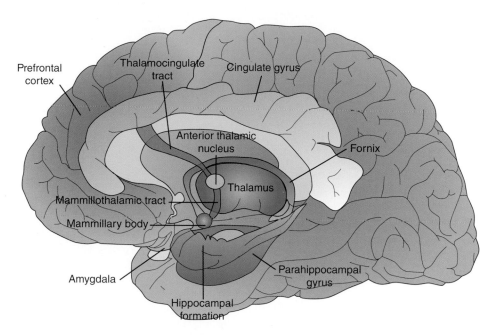

Figure 11.1 Episodic memory. The medial temporal lobes, including the hippocampus and parahippocampus, form the core of the episodic memory system. Other brain regions are also necessary for episodic memory to function correctly. In addition to being involved in episodic memory, the amygdala is also important for the autonomic conditioning

Source: From Budson, A. E., & Price, B. H. (2005). Memory dysfunction. *New England Journal of Medicine, 352,* 692–699; permission granted by the *New England Journal of Medicine*

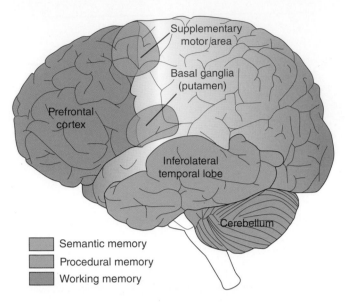

Figure 11.6 Semantic, procedural, and working memory. The inferolateral temporal lobes are important in the naming and categorization tasks by which semantic memory is typically assessed. However, in the broadest sense, semantic memory may reside in multiple and diverse cortical areas that are related to various types of knowledge. The basal ganglia, cerebellum, and supplementary motor area are critical for procedural memory. The prefrontal cortex is active in virtually all working memory tasks; other cortical and subcortical brain regions will also be active, depending on the type and complexity of the working memory task. In addition to being involved in procedural memory, the cerebellum is also important for the motoric conditioning

Source: From Budson, A. E., & Price, B. H. (2005). Memory dysfunction. *New England Journal of Medicine, 352,* 692–699; permission granted by the *New England Journal of Medicine*

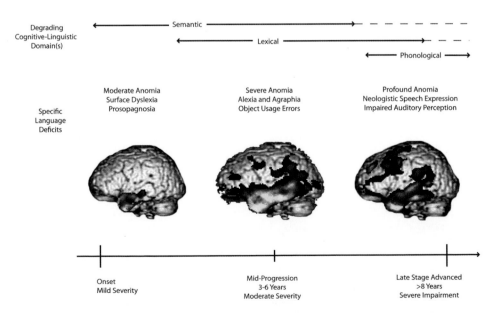

Figure 12.2 A cascade model of the cognitive-linguistic decline in semantic dementia

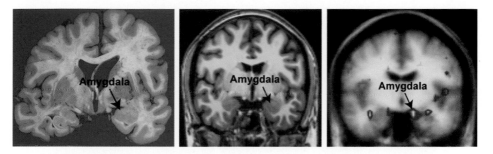

Figure 14.3 The amygdala structure and function. Coronal gross section (left), high resolution T1 weighted MRI (middle), and fMRI activation map demonstrating responses to fearful versus neutral faces

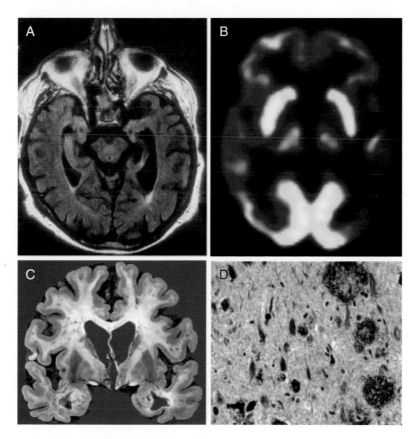

Figure 14.5 Alzheimer's disease. (A) Axial FLAIR MRI showing medial temporal lobe atrophy. (B) Axial FDG PET showing parietotemrporal hypometabolism. (C) Coronal cross-section showing medial temporal lobe atrophy. (D) Silver stained histopathological section showing plaques and tangles

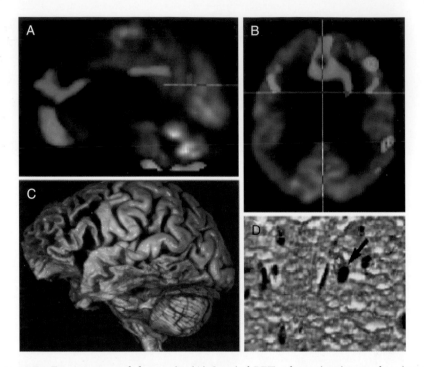

Figure 14.7 Frontotemporal dementia. (A) Saggital PET subtraction image showing areas of medial PFC hypometabolism relative to a normative database. (B) Axial PET subtraction image showing areas of medial and lateral PFC hypometabolism (courtesy of Keith Johnson). (C) Gross pathological whole-brain specimen showing frontotemporal atrophy. (D) Histopathological specimen showing Pick bodies

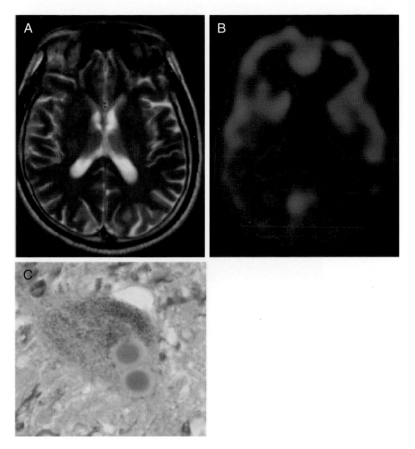

Figure 14.8 Lewy body dementia. (A) Axial T2 weighted MRI scan showing lack of atrophy in early LBD. (B) Axial PET image showing areas of occipitopatietal hypometabolism (courtesy of Keith Johnson). (C) Microscopic pathological tissue specimen showing Lewy bodies in pigmented nerve cell of substantia nigra

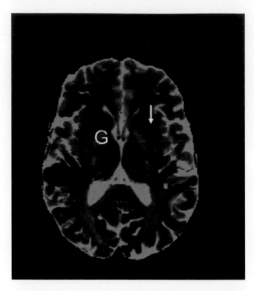

Figure 17.6 Axial T2 relaxation map from a non-demented elderly individual showing areas of T2 signal shortening in red superimposed over a corresponding T2 weighted axial scan. Certain areas of the brain such as the globus pallidus (G) are known to accumulate iron with age and this is the likely cause for the T2 signal shortening in this area. Less clear is why smaller areas of T2 signal shortening (white arrow indicates an example) can be found. These may be markers of oxidative damage

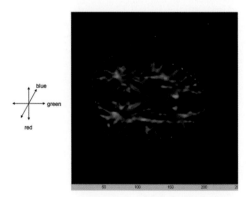

Figure 17.9 Example of an axial FA map generated by the post processing of a DTI scan. The different colors to the white matter represent the preferred direction of diffusion for each voxel with red representing the medial/lateral direction, green the rostral/caudal direction and blue the ventral/dorsal direction

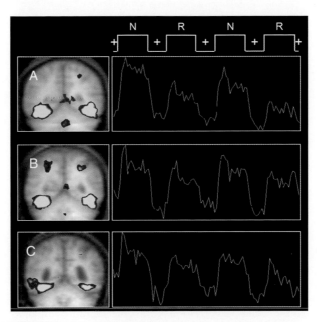

Figure 18.1 This figure illustrates typical inferotemporal BOLD fMRI responses during a "block design" memory paradigm, that is, associative encoding of Novel (N) face–name pairs compared to visual Fixation (+) in young (A) and older (B) healthy subjects and in AD patients (C). FMRI time courses also show the smaller fMRI BOLD response amplitude during blocks of Repeated (R) stimuli than during Novel blocks. P-values range from 0.0001 (in dark blue) to 0.0000001 (in yellow)

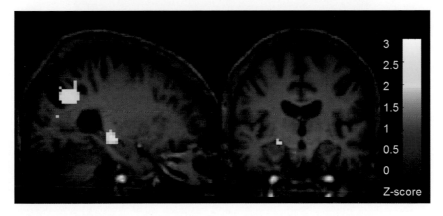

Figure 18.2 This figure shows the right hippocampal area of significantly decreased fMRI activation ($P < 0.001$) in mild AD patients compared to healthy older subjects when contrasting encoding of Novel face–name pairs to visual Fixation. Z-scores range from 0.0 (in dark red) to 3.0 (in white)

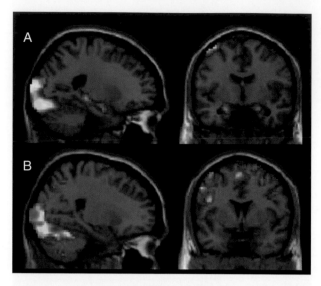

Figure 18.3 Subjects with "early" MCI (A), i.e., CDR-SB scores of 0.5–1.5, demonstrate greater task-related hippocampal activation than clinically more impaired "late" MCI subjects (B) with CDR-SB scores of 2.0–3.5 during associative encoding of Novel and Repeated face–name pairs. T-values range from 0 (in dark red) to 10 (in white)

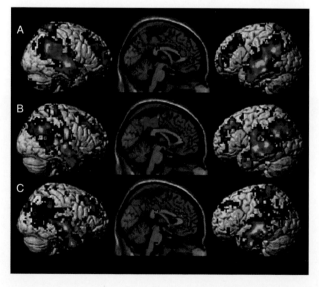

Figure 18.4 This figure shows increasingly disrupted fMRI task-induced deactivation pattern during processing of Novel and Repeated face–name pairs, as revealed by independent component analysis, across the continuum from healthy older controls (A) to MCI subjects (B) to patients with mild AD (C). T-values range from 0 (in dark blue) to 14 (in white)

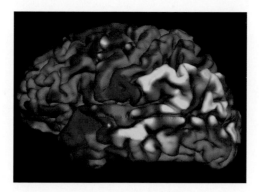

Figure 19.1 In mild Alzheimer's disease, cortical glucose metabolism is typically reduced in the temporoparietal region, as well as posterior midline and orbitofrontal regions. This now classic finding is useful clinically in differential diagnosis and may be valuable as an imaging biomarker for early detection of the metabolic signature of the disease in patients with minimal or no symptoms. This figure shows the largest reduction in metabolism in yellow, with lesser reductions in red hues from a single patient with mild AD, displayed on that patient's cortical surface as reconstructed from the anatomic MRI

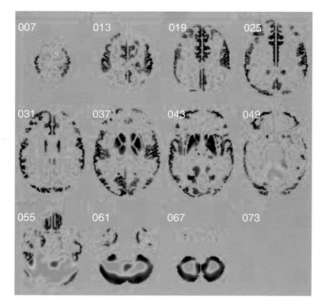

Figure 19.2 Regional brain metabolism can be used in the differential diagnosis of AD versus vascular dementia. This map shows the areas of relative hypometabolism in AD along the yellow-red end of the spectrum, including temporoparietal, posterior midline, and orbitofrontal regions, and areas of relative hypometabolism in vascular dementia along the violet-blue end of the spectrum. Areas of relative hypometabolism in vascular dementia include frontal cortex, primary sensorimotor cortices, basal ganglia, and cerebellar regions
Source: Kerrouche, N., Herholz, K., Mielke, R., Holthoff, V., & Baron, J. C. (2006). 18FDG PET in vascular dementia: Differentiation from Alzheimer's disease using voxel-based multivariate analysis. *Journal of Cerebral Blood Flow & Metabolism, 26*, 1213–1221. Figure reproduced with permission from the International Society of Cerebral Blood Flow and Metabolism

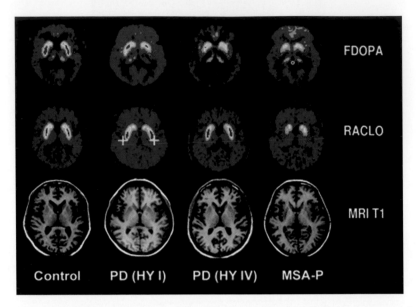

Figure 19.3 The variety of dopaminergic PET tracers highlight different abnormalities at different clinical stages of Parkinson's disease and in other movement disorders, such as multiple system atrophy (MSA-P). Top row illustrates dopamine synthesis and storage as measured by F-DOPA, middle row illustrates D2 receptor binding as measured by raclopride (RACLO). Dopamine synthesis and storage is reduced in the putamen in all conditions (red star), while D2 receptor binding is increased at an early clinical stage of PD (HY I, yellow plus sign), returns to normal in advanced PD (HY IV), and is reduced in MSA-P (red plus sign)

Source: Heiss, W.D., & Herholz, K. (2006). Brain receptor imaging. *Journal of Nuclear Medicine, 47,* 302–312. Figure reproduced with permission from the Society of Nuclear Medicine

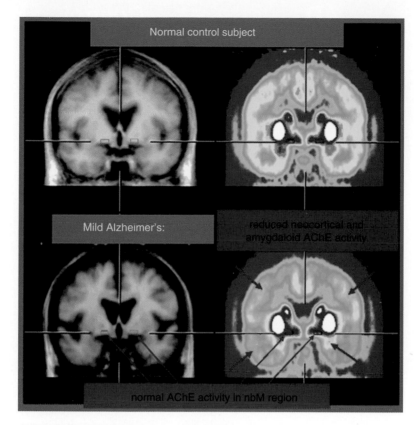

Figure 19.4 Cholinergic PET tracers highlight the reduction of acetylcholinesterase (AChE) in mild Alzheimer's disease, particularly in cortex and amygdala with relative preservation in basal forebrain (nucleus basalis of Meynert, nbM), suggesting a dying-back of cholinergic neurons rather than initial loss of cell bodies

Source: Heiss, W.D., & Herholz, K. (2006). Brain receptor imaging. *Journal of Nuclear Medicine, 47*, 302–312. Figure reproduced with permission from the Society of Nuclear Medicine

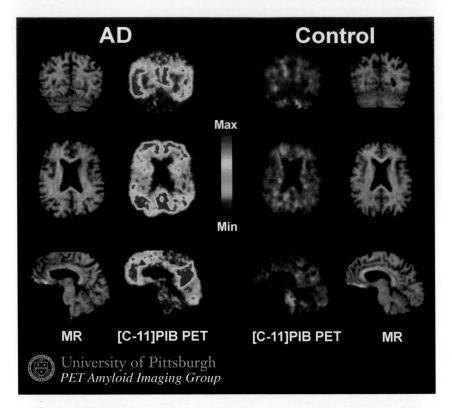

Figure 19.5 In vivo PET-based detection of beta amyloid. Increased retention of Pittsburgh Compound B (PiB) is found in frontal and temporoparietal regions in a patient with clinical AD dementia (left), compared with a control (right). PIB-PET images are shown in color with yellow-red hues indicating relatively high amyloid binding and blue indicating essentially no amyloid binding

Source: Dickerson, B. C., & Sperling, R. A. (2005). Neuroimaging biomarkers for clinical trials of disease-modifying therapies in Alzheimer's sisease. *Neurorx, 2,* 348–360. Figure courtesy of William E. Klunk, M.D., Ph.D., and reproduced with permission from Elsevier, Inc.

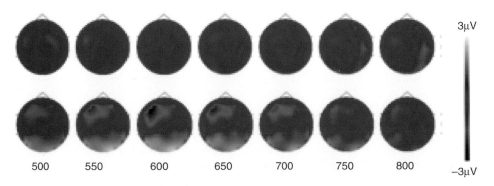

Figure 20.3 Hit–correct rejection scalp topographies during the recollection of words for patients with mild cognitive impairment and healthy older adults

left. Thus, on day three it will be easy to remember that the car is parked in the Blue area on the second floor, but it will be difficult to remember if it is parked halfway down the aisle on the right or all the way down the aisle on the left.

Over the last 15 years it has become increasingly clear that in addition to the medial temporal lobes and Papez's circuit, the frontal lobes are also important for episodic memory (Fletcher & Henson, 2001; Simons & Spiers, 2003). Whereas the medial temporal lobes are critical for the retention of information, the frontal lobes are important for the acquisition, registration, or encoding of information (Wagner et al., 1998); the retrieval of information without contextual and other cues (Manenti et al., 2010; Petrides, 2002); the recollection of the source of information (Johnson, Kounios et al., 1997); and the assessment of the temporal sequence and recency of events (Kopelman et al., 1997). One important reason why the frontal lobes are highly involved in episodic memory is that they enable the individual to focus their attention on the information to be remembered and to engage the medial temporal lobes. Also notable is that the left medial temporal and left frontal lobes are most active when a person is learning words (Wagner et al., 1998), and that the right medial temporal and right frontal lobes are most active when learning visual scenes (Brewer et al., 1998).

Dysfunction of the frontal lobes may cause a variety of memory problems, including distortions of episodic memory and false memories, such as when information becomes associated with the wrong context (Johnson, O'Connor et al., 1997) or incorrect specific details (Budson et al., 2002). Extreme memory distortions are often synonymous with confabulations, which occur when "memories" are created to be consistent with current information (Johnson, O'Connor et al., 1997), such as "remembering" that someone broke into the house and rearranged household items.

A clinically useful analogy can be used to help conceptualize the dysfunction in episodic memory that occurs due to damage to the medial temporal lobes (and Papez's circuit) versus damage to the frontal lobes (Budson & Price, 2002, 2005). The frontal lobes are analogous to the "file clerk" of the episodic memory system, the medial temporal lobes to the "recent memory file cabinet," and other cortical regions to the "remote memory file cabinet" (Table 11.3). Thus, if the frontal lobes are impaired, it is difficult – but not impossible – to get information in and out of storage. For example, getting information into storage may require stronger encoding, and getting information out of storage may require stronger cues from the environment. Additionally, when the frontal lobes are impaired the information

Table 11.3 A filing analogy of episodic memory

Brain structure	Analogy
Frontal lobes	File clerk
Medial temporal lobes	Recent memory files
Other cortical regions	Remote memory files

stored in memory may be distorted due to "improper filing" that leads to an inaccurate source, context, or sequence. If, on the other hand, the medial temporal lobes are impaired, it may be impossible for recent information to be stored. This will often lead to the patient asking for the same information again and again – perhaps 20 times in an hour. Older information that has been consolidated over months to years is likely stored in other cortical regions and will therefore be available for retrieval even when the medial temporal lobes or Papez's circuit are damaged. To illustrate this analogy we can compare the episodic memory dysfunction attributable to Alzheimer's disease versus depression. In general, patients with Alzheimer's disease have a dysfunctional "recent memory file cabinet," whereas patients with depression have a dysfunctional "file clerk."

Recent evidence has suggested that the parietal lobes also play an important role in episodic memory. In fact, in functional imaging studies the parietal lobes are more frequently associated with successful memory retrieval than either the frontal or medial temporal lobes (Simons et al., 2008). Despite this ubiquitous activation, the precise role of the parietal lobes in memory is not clear. Theories include attention to memory in both top-down and bottom-up roles (Cabeza et al., 2008), working memory's contribution to episodic memory (Berryhill & Olson, 2008), its role in retrieval and recollection (Davidson et al., 2008; Vilberg & Rugg, 2008, 2009), and the subjective memorial experience (Ally et al., 2008; Simons et al., 2010).

Evaluating episodic memory

When a disorder of episodic memory is suspected due to inability to remember recent information and experiences accurately, further evaluation is warranted. A detailed history of the memory dysfunction should be taken, with particular emphasis on the time course of the memory disorder. Speaking with a caregiver or other informant is usually critical, since the patient with memory dysfunction will invariably not remember important aspects of the history. A history of other cognitive deficits (such as deficits in attention, language, visuospatial, and executive function) should be obtained. Medical and neurological examinations should be performed, searching for signs of systemic illness, focal neurological injury, and neurodegenerative disorders.

The history, examination, and cognitive testing will suggest a differential diagnosis, which in turn will determine which laboratory and imaging studies are indicated. Brief cognitive testing may be performed by asking the patient to remember several words or a short story, or by using tools such as the Mini-Mental State Examination (MMSE; Folstein et al., 1975) – but beware of ceiling and floor effects (Franco-Marina et al., 2010), the Blessed Dementia Scale (Blessed et al., 1968), the Three Words–Three Shapes memory test (Mesulam, 2000), the word list memory test of the Consortium to Establish a Registry for Alzheimer's Disease (Welsh et al., 1992), the Drilled Word Span Test (Mesulam, 2000), the Seven-

Minute Screen (Solomon et al., 1998), and the Montreal Cognitive Assessment (www.mocatest.org). To help distinguish episodic memory dysfunction attributable to impairment of the frontal lobes versus impairment of the medial temporal lobes, difficulties in the encoding and retrieval of information should be contrasted with a primary failure of storage. When information cannot be remembered even when multiple rehearsals have maximized encoding, and retrieval demands have been minimized with the use of a multiple-choice recognition test, a primary failure of storage is present. In complex cases, a formal neuropsychological evaluation should be obtained.

Treatment depends upon the specific disorder identified. Cholinesterase inhibitors have been approved by the Food and Drug Administration (FDA) to treat Alzheimer's disease (Darreh-Shori & Jelic, 2010; Winblad et al. 2001) and Parkinson's disease dementia (Darreh-Shori & Jelic, 2010; Emre et al., 2004; Press, 2004); these medications have also been used to treat vascular dementia (Moretti et al., 2002) and dementia with Lewy bodies (McKeith et al., 2000). Memantine has been approved to treat Alzheimer's disease, with or without concomitant treatment with cholinesterase inhibitors (Tariot et al., 2004).

Episodic memory dysfunction in dementia

Episodic memory loss in degenerative diseases, such as Alzheimer's disease, dementia with Lewy bodies, and frontotemporal dementia, begins insidiously and progresses gradually (Solomon & Budson, 2003). Episodic memory in disorders that affect multiple brain regions, such as multiple sclerosis and vascular dementia, generally deteriorates in a stepwise manner. Some disorders of memory can have a more complicated and variable time course, including memory dysfunction attributable to tumors, hypoglycemia, medications, Korsakoff's syndrome, and traumatic brain injury. The cognitive profile of each disorder varies with the brain regions that are pathologically involved.

Alzheimer's disease
Alzheimer's disease pathology has a predilection for a number of particular regions of the brain. These regions include the hippocampus and amygdala, and the parietal, temporal, and frontal lobes. Alzheimer's pathology also affects subcortical nuclei that project to the cortex, such as the basal forebrain cholinergic nuclei (which produce acetylcholine), the locus ceruleus (which produces norepinephrine), the raphe nuclei (which produce serotonin), and certain nuclei of the thalamus.

Because the hippocampus and other medial temporal lobe structures are the earliest and most severely affected brain regions in Alzheimer's disease, episodic memory – and in particular the file cabinet component of episodic memory – is the earliest and most impaired cognitive function. Common symptoms include asking the same questions repeatedly, repeating the same stories, forgetting appointments, and leaving the stove on. Following Ribot's law, patients with Alzheimer's disease show *anterograde amnesia* or difficulty learning new information. They also show *retrograde amnesia* or difficulty retrieving previously learned information. However, the patients typically demonstrate preserved memory for remote information. Thus, a patient may report, "I've got short-term memory problems – I cannot remember what I did yesterday but I can still remember things from thirty years ago." Not understanding that this pattern is suggestive of the memory impairment common in Alzheimer's disease, family members may report that they feel confident that whatever the patient's problem is, that "it isn't Alzheimer's disease," because the patient can still remember what happened many years ago.

Another hallmark of the episodic memory impairment in the disease is that memory is impaired even when the learning or encoding of information is maximized by multiple rehearsals, and after retrieval demands have been minimized with the use of a multiple-choice recognition test. In other words, even when patients appear to have successfully learned new information by repeating it back over several learning trials, they are often unable to recognize this information on a multiple-choice test. This type of memory loss is often referred to as a "rapid rate of forgetting," although whether the information has been truly learned or not in the first place has been a matter of debate (e.g., Budson et al., 2007).

From a practical standpoint, this means that in very mild and mild Alzheimer's disease on the MMSE and the Blessed Dementia Scale, for example, the registration or learning of the items is usually intact, but recall is usually impaired (and although it is not part of these tests, patients are also unable to choose the registered words from a list). Similarly, on more comprehensive tests that include both recall and recognition components (such as the CERAD word list memory test (Welsh et al., 1992)), there will be a number of words successfully learned in the encoding trials, that are not recognized on the multiple-choice recognition test.

In addition to rapid forgetting, patients with Alzheimer's disease also experience distortions of memory and false memories. These distortions may include falsely remembering that they have already turned off the stove or taken their medications, leading patients to neglect performing these tasks. More dramatic distortions of memory may occur when patients substitute one person in a memory for another, combine two memories together, or think that an event that happened long ago occurred recently. Sometimes a false memory can be confused with a psychotic delusion or hallucination. For example, a patient may claim to have recently seen and spoken with a long-deceased family member. This patient is much more likely to be suffering from a memory distortion or a false memory than a true hallucination. The same is true for the patient who claims that people are breaking into the house, and moving around things. That these symptoms likely represent memory distortions rather than true hallucinations or delusions has implications when it comes time for treatment; as memory distortions are best treated with memory enhancing medications (such as cholinesterase inhibitors) rather than antipsychotic medications.

Although not as impaired as medial temporal lobes, the frontal lobes are involved in both Alzheimer's disease and mild cognitive impairment (Dickerson & Sperling, 2009; Schonknecht et al., 2009). Frontal lobe dysfunction may be one reason that patients with Alzheimer's disease experience memory distortions and false memories. That they show frontal lobe dysfunction also means that, in addition to a major impairment with their "file cabinet," patients with Alzheimer's disease also show milder but definite impairment with their "file clerk" as well. Additionally, patients with Alzheimer's disease have major pathology in parietal cortex, and this pathology may occur quite early in the disease (McKee et al., 2006). Thus, although the medial temporal lobe pathology is most relevant in the majority, patients with Alzheimer's disease have multiple components impaired in their episodic memory system.

Dementia with Lewy bodies

Because patients with dementia with Lewy bodies often have concomitant Alzheimer's disease pathology, the pattern of cognitive impairment may be identical to that which is seen in Alzheimer's disease, or it may show relatively greater impairment on measures of attention, visuospatial, and executive function with relative sparing of episodic memory. In general, however, episodic memory dysfunction in dementia with Lewy bodies is greater than that of other parkinsonian disorders such as multiple system atrophy and Parkinson's disease (Kao et al., 2009).

Vascular dementia

As vascular dementia is dementia due to multiple strokes, whether a patient experiences episodic memory dysfunction and of what quality depends upon the size, number, and location of the cerebrovascular disease. However, the most common type of vascular dementia is that due to small vessel ischemic disease (also known as subcortical ischemic vascular disease, see Chapter 2). Because small vessel ischemic disease has a predilection for the subcortical white matter, and because most of the white matter in the brain is carrying neural signals going to or from the frontal lobes, patients with vascular dementia experience a "frontal" memory disorder. In other words, because their frontal lobes are not working (or are not properly connected to the rest of the brain), they show impairment in the "file clerk" component of episodic memory. Consequently encoding is often impaired, as is free recall, whereas relative preservation is typically seen when tasks that assist in retrieval, such as cued recall and recognition, are used.

Frontotemporal dementia

Patient with frontotemporal dementia often show no impairment in episodic memory until late in the disease. If they do demonstrate early episodic memory impairment, it is generally that of a frontal memory disorder, similar to that of patient with vascular dementia.

Other disorders

Many other dementias also affect the frontal lobes and thus may also lead to a frontal episodic memory disorder. These dementias include progressive supranuclear palsy, corticobasal degeneration, multiple system atrophy, and normal pressure hydrocephalus.

Semantic Memory

Semantic memory refers to our store of conceptual and factual knowledge that is not related to any specific memory, such as the color of a banana or what a cup is used for. Like episodic memory, semantic memory is an explicit and declarative memory system. Evidence that semantic memory and episodic memory are separate memory systems has come from both neuroimaging studies (Schacter et al., 2000) and the fact that previously acquired semantic memory is spared in patients who have severe impairment of episodic memory, such as with disruption of Papez's circuit or surgical removal of the medial temporal lobes (Corkin, 1984).

In its broadest sense, semantic memory includes all our knowledge of the world not related to any specific episodic memory. It could therefore be argued that semantic memory resides in multiple cortical areas throughout the brain. For example, there is evidence that visual images are stored in nearby visual association areas (Vaidya et al., 2002). A more restrictive view of semantic memory justified in light of the naming and categorization tasks by which it is usually tested, however, localizes semantic memory to the inferolateral temporal lobes, particularly on the left (Figure 11.6, plate section) (Damasio et al., 1996; Perani et al., 1999).

Semantic memory dysfunction in dementia

The most common clinical disorder disrupting semantic memory is Alzheimer's disease (Salmon & Bondi, 2009). This disruption may be due to pathology in the inferolateral temporal lobes (Price & Morris, 1999) or to pathology in frontal cortex (Lidstrom et al., 1998), leading to poor activation and retrieval of semantic information (Balota et al., 1999). Supporting the idea that two separate memory systems are impaired in Alzheimer's disease, episodic and semantic memory decline independently of each other in this disorder (Green & Hodges, 1996).

Almost any disorder that can disrupt the inferolateral temporal lobes may cause impairment of semantic memory, including traumatic brain injury, stroke, surgical lesions, encephalitis, and tumors (Table 11.2). Patients with semantic dementia (the temporal variant of frontotemporal dementia) exhibit deficits in all functions of semantic memory, such as naming, single-word comprehension, and impaired general knowledge (such as the color of common items). Other aspects of cognition, however, are relatively preserved, including components of speech, perceptual and nonverbal problem-solving skills, and episodic memory (Hodges, 2001).

Although naming difficulties (particularly with proper nouns) are common in healthy older adults, naming difficulties may also be a sign of a disorder of semantic memory. When a disorder of semantic memory is suspected, the evaluation should include the same components as the work-up for episodic memory disorders. One of the first aspects of the history and cognitive examination that should be ascertained is whether the problem is solely one of difficulty in recalling people's names and other proper nouns (common in healthy older adults) or to a true loss of semantic information. Patients with mild dysfunction of semantic memory may show only reduced generation of words in a semantic category (for example, the number of grocery items that can be generated in one minute), whereas patients with a more severe impairment of semantic memory usually show a two-way naming deficit: they are unable to name an item when it is described, and they are also unable to describe an item when it is named. General knowledge is also impoverished in these more severely affected patients. Treatment will depend upon the specific disorder identified.

Procedural Memory

Procedural memory refers to the ability to learn cognitive and behavioral skills and algorithms that operate at an automatic, unconscious level. Procedural memory is non-declarative and implicit. Examples include learning to play the violin or drive a standard transmission automobile (Table 11.1). Because procedural memory is spared in patients who have severe deficits of the episodic memory system (such as those who have undergone surgical removal of the medial temporal lobes), it is clear that the procedural memory system is separate and distinct from the episodic memory system (Corkin, 1984; Heindel et al., 1989).

Functional imaging research has shown that a number of brain regions involved in procedural memory become active as a new task is learned, including the supplementary motor area, basal ganglia, and cerebellum (Daselaar et al., 2003) (Figure 11.6). Convergent evidence comes from studies of patients with damage to the basal ganglia or cerebellum who show impairment in learning procedural skills (Exner et al., 2002).

Procedural memory dysfunction in dementia

Because the basal ganglia and cerebellum are relatively spared in early Alzheimer's disease, despite their episodic memory deficit these patients show normal acquisition and maintenance of their procedural memory skills (Baird & Samson, 2009). Parkinson's disease is the most common disorder disrupting procedural memory (Wang et al., 2009), and thus it should not be surprising that the most common neurodegenerative disorder to disrupt procedural memory is dementia with Lewy bodies (Longworth et al., 2005). Patients in the early stages of Huntington's disease and olivopontocerebellar degeneration also show impaired procedural memory while performing nearly normally on episodic memory tests (Heindel et al., 1989; Salmon et al., 1998). Other causes of damage to the basal ganglia or cerebellum including tumors, strokes, and hemorrhages may also disrupt procedural memory. Patients with major depression also show impairment in procedural memory tasks, perhaps because depression involves dysfunction of the basal ganglia (Sabe et al., 1995).

Disruption of procedural memory should be suspected when patients show evidence of either substantial difficulties in learning new skills (compared to their baseline) or the loss of previously learned skills. For example, patients may lose the ability to perform automatic, skilled movements, such as knitting, swinging a golf club, or playing the saxophone. Although these patients may be able to relearn the fundamentals of these skills, explicit thinking becomes required for their performance. As a result, patients with damage to the procedural memory system lose the automatic, effortlessness of simple motor tasks that healthy individuals take for granted. The evaluation of disorders of procedural memory is similar to that of disorders of episodic memory; treatment depends upon the specific disease process. Lastly, it is worth noting that patients whose episodic memory has been devastated by a static disorder, such as encephalitis, have had successful rehabilitation by using procedural memory (and other non-declarative forms of memory) to learn new skills (Glisky & Schacter, 1989).

Working Memory

Bringing together the traditional fields of attention, concentration, and short-term memory, working memory refers to the ability to temporarily maintain and manipulate information that one needs to keep in mind. Requiring active and conscious participation, working memory is an explicit and declarative memory system. Working memory has traditionally been divided into three components: one that processes phonologic information (e.g., keeping a phone number "in your head"); one that processes spatial information (e.g., mentally following a route); and an executive system that allocates attentional resources (Baddeley, 1998).

Studies have demonstrated that working memory involves a network of cortical and subcortical areas, which differ depending on the particular task (Rowe et al., 2000). Participation of the prefrontal cortex, however, is involved in virtually all working memory tasks (Fletcher & Henson, 2001) (Figure 11.6). The network of cortical and subcortical areas typically includes posterior brain regions (e.g., visual association areas) that are linked with prefrontal regions to form a circuit. Research suggests that spatial working memory tends to involve more regions on the right side, and phonologic working memory tends to involve more regions on the left side of the brain. Bilateral brain activation is observed, however, in more difficult working memory tasks, regardless of the nature of the material being processed (Newman et al., 2003). Additionally, an increase in the number of brain regions activated in prefrontal cortex is observed as the complexity of the task increases (Jaeggi et al., 2003).

Working memory dysfunction in dementia

Because working memory depends upon networks which include frontal and parietal cortical regions as well as subcortical structures, most neurodegenerative diseases impair working memory. Studies have demonstrated that working memory may be impaired in patients with Alzheimer's disease, Parkinson's disease, Huntington's disease, dementia with Lewy bodies, as well as less common disorders such as progressive supranuclear palsy (Table 11.2) (Calderon et al., 2001; Gotham et al., 1988). In Alzheimer's disease spatial working memory is particularly impaired (Iachini et al., 2009). In addition to these neurodegenerative diseases, almost any disease process that disrupts the frontal lobes or their connections to posterior cortical regions and subcortical structures can interfere with working memory. Such processes include tumors, strokes, multiple sclerosis, head injury, and others (Kubat-Silman et al., 2002; Sfagos et al., 2003). Because it involves the silent rehearsal of verbal information, almost any type of aphasia may impair phonologic working memory. Disorders that diminish attentional resources, including attention deficit hyperactivity disorder, obsessive compulsive disorder, depression, and schizophrenia, can also impair working memory (Egeland et al., 2003; Klingberg et al., 2002; Purcell et al., 1998).

Disorders of working memory may present in several different ways. Often the patient will exhibit an inability to concentrate or pay attention. Impairment in performing a new task with multi-step instructions is frequently seen. Interestingly, a disorder of working memory may also present as a problem with episodic memory, because information must first be "kept in mind" by working memory in order for episodic memory to encode it (Fletcher & Henson, 2001). Such cases will therefore show a primary impairment in encoding.

The evaluation of disorders of working memory is similar to that of disorders of episodic memory. Treatment depends upon the underlying cause. Stimulants, approved by the FDA for the treatment of attention deficit hyperactivity disorder (Elia et al., 1999; Mehta et al., 2004), will often be helpful in disorders of working memory.

Conclusion

Although traditionally memory has been viewed as a simple concept, converging and complementary evidence from patient studies and more recent neuroimaging research suggest that memory is composed of separate and distinct systems. Improved understanding of these different types of memory will aid the clinician in the diagnosis and treatment of dementia and other causes of memory impairment in their patients. As more specific therapeutic strategies are developed for the treatment of diseases which cause memory dysfunction, this knowledge will become increasingly important.

References

Ally, B. A., Simons, J. S., McKeever, J. D., Peers, P. V., & Budson, A. E. (2008). Parietal contributions to recollection: Electrophysiological evidence from aging and patients with parietal lesions. *Neuropsychologia, 46*, 1800–1812.

Aly, M., & Moscovitch, M. (2010). The effects of sleep on episodic memory in older and younger adults. *Memory*, 1–8.

Baddeley, A. D. (1998). Recent developments in working memory. *Current Opinion in Neurobiology, 8*, 234–238.

Baird, A., & Samson, S. (2009). Memory for music in Alzheimer's disease: Unforgettable? *Neuropsychology Reviews, 19*, 85–101.

Balota, D. A., Watson, J. M., Duchek, J. M., & Ferraro, F. R. (1999). Cross-modal semantic and homographic priming in healthy young, healthy old, and in Alzheimer's disease individuals. *Journal of the International Neuropsychological Society, 5*, 626–640.

Berryhill, M. E., & Olson, I. R. (2008). The right parietal lobe is critical for visual working memory. *Neuropsychologia, 46*, 1767–1774.

Blessed, G., Tomlinson, B. E., & Roth, M. (1968). The association between quantitative measures of dementia and of senile change in the cerebral grey matter of elderly subjects. *British Journal of Psychiatry, 114*, 797–811.

Brewer, J. B., Zhao, Z., Desmond, J. E., Glover, G. H., & Gabrieli, J. D. (1998). Making memories: Brain activity that predicts how well visual experience will be remembered. *Science, 281*, 1185–1187.

Budson, A. E. (2009). Understanding memory dysfunction. *Neurologist, 15*, 71–79.

Budson, A. E., & Price, B. H. (2002). Memory: Clinical disorders. In *Encyclopedia of Life Sciences. Vol. 11* (pp. 529–536). New York: Macmillan.

Budson, A. E., & Price, B. H. (2005). Memory dysfunction. *New England Journal of Medicine, 352*, 692–699.

Budson, A. E., Simons, J. S., Waring, J. D., Sullivan, A. L., Hussoin, T., & Schacter, D. L. (2007). Memory for the September 11, 2001, terrorist attacks one year later in patients with Alzheimer's disease, patients with mild cognitive impairment, and healthy older adults. *Cortex, 43*, 875–888.

Budson, A. E., Sullivan, A. L., Mayer, E., Daffner, K. R., Black, P. M., & Schacter, D. L. (2002). Suppression of false recognition in Alzheimer's disease and in patients with frontal lobe lesions. *Brain, 125*, 2750–2765.

Cabeza, R., Ciaramelli, E., Olson, I. R., & Moscovitch, M. (2008). The parietal cortex and episodic memory: An attentional account. *Nature Reviews Neuroscience, 9*, 613–625.

Calderon, J., Perry, R. J., Erzinclioglu, S. W., Berrios, G. E., Dening, T. R., & Hodges, J. R. (2001). Perception, attention, and working memory are disproportionately impaired in dementia with Lewy bodies compared with Alzheimer's disease. *Journal of Neurology, Neurosurgery & Psychiatry, 70*, 157–164.

Champod, A. S., & Petrides, M. (2010). Dissociation within the frontoparietal network in verbal working memory: A parametric functional magnetic resonance imaging study. *Journal of Neuroscience, 30*, 3849–3856.

Corkin, S. (1984). Lasting consequences of bilateral medial temporal lobectomy: Clinical course and experimental findings in H.M. *Seminars in Neurology, 380*, 249–259.

Damasio, H., Grabowski, T. J., Tranel, D., Hichwa, R. D., & Damasio, A. R. (1996). A neural basis for lexical retrieval. *Nature, 380*, 499–505.

Darreh-Shori, T., & Jelic, V. (2010). Safety and tolerability of transdermal and oral rivastigmine in Alzheimer's disease and Parkinson's disease dementia. *Expert Opinion on Drug Safety, 9*, 167–176.

Daselaar, S. M., Rombouts, S. A., Veltman, D. J., Raaijmakers, J. G., & Jonker, C. (2003). Similar network activated by young and old adults during the acquisition of a motor sequence. *Neurobiology of Aging, 24*, 1013–1019.

Davidson, P. S., Anaki, D., Ciaramelli, E., Cohn, M., Kim, A. S., Murphy, K. J., et al. (2008). Does lateral parietal cortex support episodic memory? Evidence from focal lesion patients. *Neuropsychologia, 46*, 1743–1755.

Dickerson, B. C., & Sperling, R. A. (2009). Large-scale functional brain network abnormalities in Alzheimer's disease: Insights from functional neuroimaging. *Behavioral Neurology, 21*, 63–75.

Diekelmann, S., & Born, J. (2010). The memory function of sleep. *Nature Reviews Neuroscience, 11*, 114–126.

Egeland, J., Sundet, K., Rund, B. R., Asbjornsen, A., Hugdahl, K., Landro, N. I., et al. (2003). Sensitivity and specificity of memory dysfunction in schizophrenia: A comparison with major depression. *Journal of Clinical and Experimental Neuropsychology*, 79–93.

Elia, J., Ambrosini, P. J., & Rapoport, J. L. (1999). Treatment of attention-deficit-hyperactivity disorder. *New England Journal of Medicine, 340*, 780–788.

Emre, M., Aarsland, D., Albanese, A., Byrne, E. J., Deuschl, G., De Deyn, P. P., et al. (2004). Rivastigmine for dementia associated with Parkinson's disease. *New England Journal of Medicine, 351*, 2509–2518.

Exner, C., Koschack, J., & Irle, E. (2002). The differential role of premotor frontal cortex and basal ganglia in motor sequence learning: Evidence from focal basal ganglia lesions. *Learning & Memory, 9*, 376–386.

Fletcher, P. C., & Henson, R. N. A. (2001). Frontal lobes and human memory: Insights from functional neuroimaging. *Brain, 124*, 849–881.

Folstein, M. F., Folstein, S. E., & McHugh, P. R. (1975). A practical method for grading the cognitive state of patients for the clinician. *Journal of Psychiatric Research, 12*, 189–198.

Franco-Marina, F., Garcia-Gonzalez, J. J., Wagner-Echeagaray, F., Gallo, J., Ugalde, O., Sanchez-Garcia, S., et al. (2010). The Mini-Mental State Examination revisited: Ceiling and floor effects after score adjustment for educational level in an aging Mexican population. *International Psychogeriatrics, 22*, 72–81.

Glisky, E. L., & Schacter, D. L. (1989). Extending the limits of complex learning in organic amnesia: Computer training in a vocation domain. *Neuropsychologia, 27*, 173–178.

Gotham, A. M., Brown, R. G., & Marsden, C. D. (1988). "Frontal" cognitive functions in patients with Parkinson's disease "on" and "off" levodopa. *Brain, 111*, 299–321.

Green, J. D., & Hodges, J. R. (1996). Identification of famous faces and famous names in early Alzheimer's disease. Relationship to anterograde episodic and general semantic memory. *Brain, 119*, 111–128.

Heindel, W. C., Salmon, D. P., Shults, C. W., Walicke, P. A., & Butters, N. (1989). Neuropsychological evidence for multiple implicit memory systems: a comparison of Alzheimer's, Huntington's, and Parkinson's disease patients. *Journal of Neuroscience, 9*, 582–587.

Hodges, J. R. (2001). Frontotemporal dementia (Pick's disease): Clinical features and assessment. *Neurology, 56*, 6–10.

Iachini, I., Iavarone, A., Senese, V. P., Ruotolo, F., & Ruggiero, G. (2009). Visuospatial memory in healthy elderly, AD and MCI: A review. *Current Aging Science, 2*, 43–59.

Jaeggi, S. M., Seewer, R., Nirkko, A. C., Eckstein, D., Schroth, G., Groner, R., et al. (2003). Does excessive memory load attenuate activation in the prefrontal cortex? Load-dependent processing in single and dual tasks: functional magnetic resonance imaging study. *Neuroimage, 19*, 210–225.

Johnson, M. K., Kounios, J., & Nolde, S. F. (1997). Electrophysiological brain activity and memory source monitoring. *NeuroReport, 8*, 1317–1320.

Johnson, M. K., O'Connor, M., & Cantor, J. (1997). Confabulation, memory deficits, and frontal dysfunction. *Brain and Cognition, 34*, 189–206.

Kao, A. W., Racine, C. A., Quitania, L. C., Kramer, J. H., Christine, C. W., & Miller, B. L. (2009). Cognitive and neuropsychiatric profile of the synucleinopathies: Parkinson disease, dementia with Lewy bodies, and multiple system atrophy. *Alzheimer's Disease & Associated Disorders, 23*, 365–370.

Klingberg, T., Forssberg, H., & Westerberg, H. (2002). Training of working memory in children with ADHD. *Journal of Clinical and Experimental Neuropsychology, 24*, 781–791.

Kopelman, M. D., Stanhope, N., & Kingsley, D. (1997). Temporal and spatial contex memory in patients with focal frontal, temporal lobe, and diencephalic lesions. *Neuropsychologia, 35*, 1533–1545.

Kubat-Silman, A. K., Dagenbach, D., & Absher, J. R. (2002). Patterns of impaired verbal, spatial, and object working memory after thalamic lesions. *Brain and Cognition, 50*, 178–193.

Lidstrom, A. M., Bogdanovic, N., Hesse, C., Volkman, I., Davidsson, P., & Blennow, K. (1998). Clusterin (apolipoprotein J) protein levels are increased in hippocampus and in frontal cortex in Alzheimer's disease. *Experimental Neurology, 154*, 511–521.

Longworth, C. E., Keenan, S. E., Barker, R. A., Marslen-Wilson, W. D., & Tyler, L. K. (2005). The basal ganglia and rule-governed language use: Evidence from vascular and degenerative conditions. *Brain, 128*, 584–596.

Manenti, R., Tettamanti, M., Cotelli, M., Miniussi, C., & Cappa, S. F. (2010). The neural bases of word encoding and retrieval: A fMRI-guided transcranial magnetic stimulation study. *Brain Topography, 22*, 318–332.

McKee, A. C., Au, R., Cabral, H. J., Kowall, N. W., Seshadri, S., Kubilus, C. A., et al. (2006). Visual association pathology in preclinical Alzheimer disease. *Journal of Neuropathology & Experimental Neurology, 65*, 621–630.

McKeith, I., Del Ser, T., Spano, P., Emre, M., Wesnes, K., Anand, R., et al. (2000). Efficacy of rivastigmine in dementia with Lewy bodies: A randomised, double-blind, placebo-controlled international study. *Lancet, 356,* 2031–2036.

Mehta, M. A., Goodyer, I. M., & Sahakian, B. J. (2004). Methylphenidate improves working memory and set-shifting in AD/HD: Relationships to baseline memory capacity. *Journal of Child Psychology and Psychiatry, 45,* 293–305.

Mesulam, M. -M. (2000). *Principles of behavioral and cognitive neurology.* New York: Oxford University Press.

Moretti, R., Torre, P., Antonello, R. M., Cazzato, G., & Bava, A. (2002). Use of galantamine to treat vascular dementia. *Lancet, 360,* 1512–1513.

Morita, M., Morokami, S., & Morita, H. (2010). Attribute pair-based visual recognition and memory. *PLoS One, 5,* e9571.

Newman, S. D., Carpenter, P. A., Varma, S., & Just, M. A. (2003). Frontal and parietal participation in problem solving in the Tower of London: fMRI and computational modeling of planning and high-level perception. *Neuropsychologia, 41,* 1668–1682.

O'Neill, J., Pleydell-Bouverie, B., Dupret, D., & Csicsvari, J. (2010). Play it again: Reactivation of waking experience and memory. *Trends in Neurosciences, 33*(5), 220–229.

Papez, J. W. (1937). A proposed mechanism of emotion. *Archives of Neurology and Psychiatry, 38,* 725–743.

Perani, D., Cappa, S. F., Schnur, T., Tettamanti, M., Collina, S., Rosa, M. M., et al. (1999). The neural correlates of verb and noun processing. A PET study. *Brain, 122*(Pt 12), 2337–2344.

Petrides, M. (2002). The mid-ventrolateral prefrontal cortex and active mnemonic retrieval. *Neurobiology of Learning and Memory, 78,* 528–538.

Press, D. Z. (2004). Parkinson's disease dementia – A first step? *New England Journal of Medicine, 351,* 2547–2549.

Price, J. L., & Morris, J. C. (1999). Tangles and plaques in nondemented aging and "preclinical" Alzheimer's disease. *Annals of Neurology, 45,* 358–368.

Purcell, R., Maruff, P., Kyrios, M., & Pantelis, C. (1998). Cognitive deficits in obsessive-compulsive disorder on tests of frontal-striatal function. *Biological Psychiatry, 43,* 348–357.

Ribot, T. (1881). *Les maladies de la mémoire.* Paris: Félix Alcan.

Rowe, J. B., Toni, I., Josephs, O., Frackowiak, R. S., & Passingham, R. E. (2000). The prefrontal cortex: Response selection or maintenance within working memory? *Science, 288,* 1656–1660.

Sabe, L., Jason, L., Juejati, M., Leiguarda, R., & Starkstein, S. E. (1995). Dissociation between declarative and procedural learning in dementia and depression. *Journal of Clinical and Experimental Neuropsychology, 17,* 841–848.

Salmon, D. P., & Bondi, M. W. (2009). Neuropsychological assessment of dementia. *Annual Review of Psychology, 60,* 257–282.

Salmon, D. P., Lineweaver, T. T., & Heindel, W. C. (1998). Nondeclarative memory in neurodegenerative disease. In A. I. Troster (Ed.), *Memory in neurodegenerative disease: Biological, cognitive, and clinical perspectives* (pp. 210–225). Cambridge: Cambridge University Press.

Schacter, D. L., & Tulving, E. (1994). What are the memory systems of 1994? In D. L. Schacter, & E. Tulving (Eds.), *Memory Systems 1994* (pp. 1–38). Cambridge, MA: MIT Press.

Schacter, D. L., Wagner, A. D., & Buckner, R. L. (2000). Memory systems of 1999. In E. Tulving, & F. I. M. Craik (Eds.), *The Oxford Handbook of Memory* (pp. 627–643). New York: Oxford University Press.

Schonknecht, O. D., Hunt, A., Toro, P., Henze, M., Haberkorn, U., & Schroder, J. (2009). Neural correlates of delayed episodic memory in patients with mild cognitive impairment – A FDG PET study. *Neuroscience Letters, 467*, 100–104.

Sfagos, C., Papageorgiou, C. C., Kosma, K. K., Kodopadelis, E., Uzunoglu, N. K., Vassilopoulos, D., et al. (2003). Working memory deficits in multiple sclerosis: A controlled study with auditory P600 correlates. *Journal of Neurology, Neurosurgery, & Psychiatry, 74*, 1231–1235.

Simons, J. S., Peers, P. V., Hwang, D. Y., Ally, B. A., Fletcher, P. C., & Budson, A. E. (2008). Is the parietal lobe necessary for recollection in humans? *Neuropsychologia, 46*, 1185–1191.

Simons, J. S., Peers, P. V., Mazuz, Y. S., Berryhill, M. E., & Olson, I. R. (2010). Dissociation between memory accuracy and memory confidence following bilateral parietal lesions. *Cerebral Cortex, 20*, 479–485.

Simons, J. S., & Spiers, H. J. (2003). Prefrontal and medial temporal lobe interactions in long-term memory. *Nature Reviews Neuroscience, 4*, 637–648.

Solomon, P. R., Hirschoff, A., Kelly, B., Relin, M., Brush, M., DeVeaux, R. D., et al. (1998). A 7-minute neurocognitive screening battery highly sensitive to Alzheimer's disease. *Archives of Neurology, 55*, 349–355.

Solomon, P. R., & Budson, A. E. (2003). Alzheimer's disease. *Clinical Symposia, 54*, 1–44.

Squire, L. R. (1992). Memory and the hippocampus: A synthesis from findings with rats, monkeys, and humans. *Psychological Review, 99*, 195–231.

Stickgold, R. (2005). Sleep-dependent memory consolidation. *Nature, 437*, 1272–1278.

Stickgold, R. (2006). Neuroscience: A memory boost while you sleep. *Nature, 444*, 559–560.

Tariot, P. N., Farlow, M. R., Grossberg, G. T., Graham, S. M., McDonald, S., & Gergel, I. (2004). Memantine treatment in patients with moderate to severe Alzheimer disease already receiving donepezil: A randomized controlled trial. *Journal of the American Medical Association, 291*, 317–324.

Vaidya, C. J., Zhao, M., Desmond, J. E., & Gabrieli, J. D. (2002). Evidence for cortical encoding specificity in episodic memory: Memory-induced re-activation of picture processing areas. *Neuropsychologia, 40*, 2136–2143.

Vilberg, K. L., & Rugg, M. D. (2008). Memory retrieval and the parietal cortex: A review of evidence from a dual-process perspective. *Neuropsychologia, 46*, 1787–1799.

Vilberg, K. L., & Rugg, M. D. (2009). Left parietal cortex is modulated by amount of recollected verbal information. *NeuroReport, 20*, 1295–1299.

Wagner, A. D., Schacter, D. L., Rotte, M., Koutstaal, W., Maril, A., Dale, A. M., et al. (1998). Building memories: Remembering and forgetting of verbal experiences as predicted by brain activity. *Science, 281*, 1188–1191.

Wang, X. P., Sun, B. M., & Ding, H. L. (2009). Changes of procedural learning in Chinese patients with non-demented Parkinson disease. *Neuroscience Letters, 449*, 161–163.

Welsh, K. A., Butters, N., Hughes, J. P., Mohs, R. C., & Heyman, A. (1992). Detection and staging of dementia in Alzheimer's disease. Use of the neuropsychological measures developed for the Consortium to Establish a Registry for Alzheimer's Disease. *Archives of Neurology, 49,* 448–452.

Winblad, B., Engedal, K., Soininen, H., Verhey, F., Waldemar, G., Wimo, A., et al. (2001). A 1-year, randomized, placebo-controlled study of donepezil in patients with mild to moderate AD. *Neurology, 57,* 489–495.

12

Language Processing in Dementia

Jamie Reilly, Joshua Troche, and Murray Grossman

The traditional view of dementia is that patients experience a global decline in cognition and that there is nothing particularly unique about language. This sharply contrasts with the classic position that aphasia following stroke reflects focal damage to "language-specific" processing centers in the brain (Broca, 1863; Wernicke, 1874). We argue that there is indeed something special about language processing in dementia and that specific linguistic processes are compromised. Moreover, components of language that demand executive resources such as working memory and inhibitory control are particularly vulnerable to these conditions. Here we focus our discussion on the interaction of resource-related deficits with language-specific impairment incurred in two dementia subpopulations: Alzheimer's disease (AD) and frontotemporal dementia (FTD).

Some Components of Language

Language is the uniquely human capacity that can represent concepts through an arbitrary set of acoustic symbols (☼ = "sun") and allows us to combine these symbols in a rule-governed manner, thus yielding a system of limitless generativity (Pinker & Jackendoff, 2005). Language is sufficiently flexible to reference concrete concepts (e.g., There is a dog.), as well as temporally remote events and abstract propositions (e.g., She told the truth last week). Language production and comprehension are supported by highly interactive cognitive processes. We begin by discussing key components of language followed by the neurological basis for linguistic degradation in AD and FTD.

The Handbook of Alzheimer's Disease and Other Dementias, First Edition.
Edited by Andrew E. Budson, Neil W. Kowall.
© 2011 Blackwell Publishing Ltd. Published 2011 by Blackwell Publishing Ltd.

Phonology

In most spoken languages concepts are represented by words, and words are composed of smaller units of sound called *phonemes*. Phonemes are acquired early in life and have language-specific acoustic properties. For example, *lap* and *rap* sound and mean different things to a monolingual English speaker, whereas native speakers of Japanese have difficulties perceiving this sound difference (Abramson & Lisker, 1970). Similarly, native English speakers have difficulties perceiving tonal markers of Mandarin Chinese. In addition to phonology, words are represented in written form via orthography. The orthographic system of English grossly approximates its phonological system. Yet, this sound–letter correspondence is imperfect (e.g., yacht, colonel).

Many psycholinguistic theories assume that the phonological and orthographic forms of words are stored in human memory as whole units. That is, concepts have corresponding auditory and visual word forms (i.e., lexical representations) that exist independent of their meaning (Coltheart, 2004). Lexical and phonological deficits such as acquired dyslexia and pure word deafness significantly impact language perception. Impairment within phonological and orthographic domains occurs in both AD (Biassou et al., 1995; Croot et al., 2000; Weiner et al., 2008) and FTD (Ash et al., in press; Gorno-Tempini et al., 2006; Kwok et al., 2006). We review these deficits in the respective sections to follow.

Semantics/Word meaning

Assuming intact phonology, language comprehension also demands access to one's stored conceptual knowledge via *semantic memory*. During the past two decades, our understanding of the structure of semantic memory has vastly progressed as a result of neuroimaging and patient-based studies. Both lines of research have demonstrated that temporal lobe structures are critical for knowledge representation. For example, whether one hears the word *dog* or sees a picture of a dog, shared areas of temporal cortex are active in relation to the concept, DOG. Common areas of activation include ventral temporal cortex (e.g., fusiform gyrus), anterolateral temporal cortex, and the posterior middle temporal gyrus (Bright et al., 2004; Thierry & Price, 2006). These cortical regions are prominently affected in both FTD and AD (Bonner et al., 2009; Galton et al., 2001; Mesulam et al., 2003; Patterson, Nestor et al., 2007; Rosen et al., 2002; Yi et al., 2007). We review semantic memory impairment as the second major component that affects language in dementia.

Naming

Naming engages a large-scale neural network dedicated to phonological, lexical, and semantic levels of processing. Neural structures that support the various components of naming are susceptible to different types of brain damage. It is well established that naming impairment (i.e., anomia) is among the most common diagnostic features of stroke aphasia. However, anomia has also been identified as among the most common and socially isolating aspects of dementia (Bayles & Kim, 2003; Graham et al., 2001; Grossman et al., 2004). We review naming as the third major aspect of language processing in dementia.

Syntax

Language competency demands far more than the simple concatenation of single words. Language is structured via grammar, a rule-governed system for combining individual elements of language. Agrammatism, a neurogenic language deficit that affects grammar, is characterized by diminished syntactic complexity with elimination of function words (e.g., the) and bound morphemes (e.g., -ing). There is also a concurrent reduction in phrase length (e.g., John go store) and simplification of long-distance syntactic relationships between words in a sentence. Agrammatism also affects comprehension of noncanonical sentence structures such as passives (e.g., Mary was kissed by Jane). Neuroimaging and lesion studies have long implicated inferior frontal lobe structures in grammatical processing (Friederici, 2001). Grammatical deficits have been reported in both AD (Grober & Bang, 1995) and the non-fluent variant of primary progressive aphasia (Ash et al., 2009; Peelle et al., 2008; Peelle, Cooke et al., 2007). Syntax is the fourth major component of language processing in dementia we will address here.

Narrative discourse

Narrative discourse is a resource-demanding process that is critical for human communication. "How was your day?" is an invitation for a narrative, and in order to effectively frame a response, one must accurately sequence events, convey meaningful content, and maintain a cohesive thread throughout the story. These processes tax executive resources necessary for planning, as well as episodic and working memory resources necessary to retrieve remote events. Due to the multiplicity of these demands, perhaps it is not surprising that patients have difficulties with discourse production (Ash et al., 2006; Cosentino et al., 2006). We address the integrity of narrative discourse as the final aspect of language processing in dementia.

Dementia

Dementia is perhaps most commonly associated with an impairment of episodic memory. Although this is true of AD, this particular disease also includes among its criteria a disorder of language, entailing difficulty with naming or comprehension. In addition, while AD is the most common neurodegenerative condition, there is another large group of dementias that is characterized by their generally earlier age of onset. These conditions include FTD, corticobasal degeneration (CBD), Parkinson's disease, motor neuron disease, and others. Although any one of these conditions is less common than AD, they are collectively almost as common as AD in the population of patients with dementia that are younger than 65 years of age. Common symptoms of these dementias include a social disorder involving personality change, impulsivity, agitation, visuospatial difficulty, and impaired problem solving, or primary progressive aphasia (NINDS, 2009). The hallmark of a dementia, from this perspective, is progressive decline in *any* cognitive or social domain after an adult level of competence has been acquired. Here we focus on language comprehension and production in two of the best-characterized dementias: AD and FTD.

Alzheimer's Disease

AD is the most common form of dementia in the United States, affecting an estimated five million adults (NINDS, 2009). Although a deficit in episodic memory is the most familiar symptom, language disturbance is also a core marker for AD (McKhann et al., 1984; Weiner et al., 2008). Typically, AD patients experience increasing word-finding and language comprehension difficulties as the disease progresses. The toll of these deficits has recently spurred advances in treating associated language impairment (Bayles & Kim, 2003; Gonzalez Rothi et al., 2009). Yet, much remains unclear about cognitive-linguistic functioning in AD.

Phonology in Alzheimer's disease

The dominant theoretical position is that phonological processing is well preserved until late stages of AD. Empirical support for this assumption has been derived from studies showing that speech production in AD is similar to healthy control participants on tasks such as reading orthographically regular words aloud, and producing connected speech (Bayles & Tomoeda, 1983; Lambon Ralph et al., 1995).

A number of researchers have, however, questioned the assumption of intact phonology in AD. Studies of spoken-word recognition have demonstrated lexical discrimination difficulties with frequent phonological confusions (e.g., *doll* for *dog*) that worsen during the course of the disease and become especially evident for words that have many similar-sounding neighbors (Eustache et al., 1995; Sommers, 1998). AD patients also poorly accommodate acoustic variability in their speech perception across speakers. The ability to effectively compensate for these variations, known as *talker normalization*, allows normal listeners to flexibly apply their knowledge of invariant acoustic cues in order to correctly perceive *cat* whether it is spoken by a New York cabdriver or a toddler in Georgia. The normalization deficit in AD is apparent when more advanced AD patients fail to discriminate words presented in succession produced by speakers of different ages, genders, and dialects (Sommers, 1998).

Other work has demonstrated phonological output deficits in AD that manifest as speech errors (Cuetos et al., 2003; Glosser et al., 1998; Glosser et al., 1997). In one study, AD patients repeated sentences of increasing length and syntactic complexity (Biassou, et al., 1995). Patients produced significantly more pseudoword errors (e.g., the cat *popped* the balloon → the cat *plopped* the balloon), word initial errors, and phonemic substitution errors than controls. The authors attributed this particular error pattern to a deficit in lexical-phonological retrieval.

Croot and colleagues examined repetition, naming, and connected speech in a sample of 10 AD patients selected specifically for their phonological deficits. They argued for variability in etiology, extending from phonetic encoding to degraded lexical-phonological knowledge (Croot et al., 2000). In conversational speech, phonological paraphasias composed 39.1% of all speech errors; patients also made phonemic errors in repetition and naming and in reciting overlearned material (e.g., days of the week, the alphabet). Six of the 10 patients in the Croot et al. sample had autopsy-confirmed Alzheimer's pathology with damage to perisylvian structures critical for speech production. The authors note that focal perisylvian damage is an atypical presentation for AD, and thus the extent to which these phonological errors are present in AD patients as a whole is not clear.

Semantic memory in Alzheimer's disease

Our laboratory has proposed a two-component model of semantic memory based on the dynamic interaction between knowledge and process (Koenig & Grossman, 2007). We will interpret semantic memory deficits throughout this review in terms of this model. We argue that conceptual representation depends on two overarching and at least partially neuroanatomically dissociable processes: (i) stored semantic feature knowledge, i.e., *content*; and (ii) dynamic integration of these stored features via categorization, i.e., *process* (Koenig et al., 2007).

Concrete concepts (e.g., CAT) are composed of features, and functional imaging studies suggest that semantic features are stored in or near modality-specific regions of cortex. For example, storage of visually salient semantic features such as color and form relies heavily on cortical regions proximal to the ventral temporal-occipital visual pathway (Bussey & Saksida, 2002; Humphreys & Riddoch, 2006; Martin & Chao, 2001), whereas auditory features are stored in areas of superior temporal cortex (Beauchamp, 2005; Binder et al., 1996), and manipulability/functional features are stored in inferior frontal, premotor, and parietal cortex (Grossman et al., 2008; Pulvermuller, 2001).

Semantic processing involves rapid categorization and binding of features from different sensory modalities (e.g., barking, slobbering, furry) with abstract propositional knowledge (e.g., is friendly) into a single cohesive concept (DOG). Several candidate brain regions for semantic integration include multimodal association cortex in the lateral temporal lobe (superior temporal sulcus) and posterior temporoparietal cortex (i.e., angular gyrus) (Beauchamp, 2005; Murtha et al., 1999). Other researchers have strongly argued that feature convergence occurs primarily in the temporal poles (Joubert et al., 2009; Lambon Ralph et al., 2001; Rogers, Hocking et al., 2006; Rogers et al., 2004).

Neural structures dedicated to processing, active maintenance, and inhibitory control of competing concepts include frontal lobe regions such as dorsolateral prefrontal cortex and left inferior frontal gyrus (Thompson-Schill et al., 1997; Wagner, Desmond et al., 1998). Anatomical regions critical for semantic processing are affected early during the course of AD as demonstrated through decreased resting fluorodeoxyglucose (FDG) uptake via positron emission tomography (PET) (Zahn et al., 2006). Converging evidence has been reported via voxel-based morphometry (Grossman et al., 2004; Joubert et al., 2009), perfusion imaging (Grossman, Koenig, Glosser et al., 2003), and postmortem tissue volume studies (Harasty et al., 1999). Many of the same studies have also documented damage to regions important for semantic storage, most notably the temporal neocortex, temporopolar region, posterior fusiform gyrus, and premotor cortex. Thus, one biologically plausible hypothesis based on the frontal-temporal distribution of cortical damage in AD is that semantic memory deficits reflect damage to *both* process and content in semantic memory. This process–content hypothesis remains controversial as some researchers have argued for the differential weighting of either process or content (Aronoff et al., 2006; Rogers & Friedman, 2008), whereas others have argued exclusively for process-based impairment that affects semantic access (Bayles et al., 1991; Ober & Shenaut, 1999). Yet others have argued for specific degradation of semantic content (Hornberger et al., 2009).

Substantive evidence for degraded semantic memory in AD has been derived from word association and naming tasks in which patients show disproportionate impairment in semantic category fluency (e.g., the number of animals listed in 60 seconds) relative to letter-naming fluency (e.g., the number of words beginning with the letter "F" listed in 60 seconds) (Adlam et al., 2006; Salmon et al., 1999). AD patients also show reduced semantic priming effects in word-stem fragment completion (e.g., cat → d–?) (Passafiume et al., 2006) and reduced word frequency effects in free association (e.g., bride → ?) (Gollan et al., 2006). Degraded semantic knowledge is also apparent in nonverbal domains such as demonstrating appropriate functions of common objects (Chainay et al., 2006) and sorting pictures into appropriate categories such as tool–animal or domesticated–wild (Aronoff et al., 2006; Salmon et al., 1999). In summary, there is compelling evidence to support core semantic knowledge deficits in AD. However, the organization and degradation of semantic memory remains controversial. This is especially true with respect to category-specific semantic impairment that is characterized by the apparent loss of some semantic categories (e.g., animals or tools) with relative preservation of other categories.

Items within the same superordinate category (e.g., ANIMALS) tend to have greater semantic feature intercorrelation (e.g., tail, fur, etc.) than items between semantic categories (Garrard et al., 2001; Rogers et al., 2004). For example, many TOOLS have serrated edges, whereas ANIMALS have tails and legs. High feature density has the advantage of facilitating categorization but also the disadvantage of requiring finer-grained processing of distinctive features to distinguish among coordinate category members. In the face of a neurodegenerative disease such as AD, the feature knowledge contributing to a concept may be degraded due to the progressive loss of knowledge represented in sensory-motor cortices. This could include visual-perceptual knowledge, for example. From this perspective, visual-perceptual feature knowledge plays a heavily weighted role in the meaning of categories consisting of natural kinds, and progressive loss of this kind of knowledge can mimic a category-specific semantic memory impairment. Alternately, there may be preferential degradation of feature knowledge that is distinctive. Many have theorized that distinctive features are particularly vulnerable to AD (Chertkow & Bub, 1990; Duarte et al., 2009). It follows that as distinctive features are lost, patients "average" coordinate concepts into a prototype or central tendency that is representative of the category. Thus, patients may be likely to produce coordinate naming errors such as "dog" for "cat" and may also progress toward naming at a higher taxonomic level, producing "animal" for "cat." This may lead to a category-specific semantic memory impairment because of the differential density of the concepts in these semantic fields. Both of these hierarchical error types have been reported in AD. We have argued that concepts have distributed representations within a semantic memory system that is largely undifferentiated by semantic category (Grossman et al., 2002). We return to the concept of category specificity in the section to follow.

Naming in Alzheimer's disease

The distribution of neuropathology in AD suggests multiple potential sources of disruption along the naming pathway. One hypothesis is that perceptual deficits in AD interfere with naming at a pre-semantic stage of visual object recognition. Other possibilities include lexical retrieval difficulties and "downstream" deficits that disrupt phonological encoding. Although difficulties exist at these perceptual and lexical levels of processing in AD, careful analyses of naming error distributions reveal predominance of semantic errors relative to phonemic or visual errors. Figure 12.1 represents the distribution of errors we recently found in AD relative to the two other patient groups described later in this review, progressive non-fluent aphasia (PNFA) and semantic dementia (SD). These errors reflect ratios of specific error types elicited by naming a set of 60 black-and-white line drawings within a sample of 36 AD patients. The most frequent error in this patient sample was semantic, constituting 19% of all naming errors.

A semantic basis for anomia in AD is further supported by studies that have demonstrated strong correlations between residual conceptual knowledge and

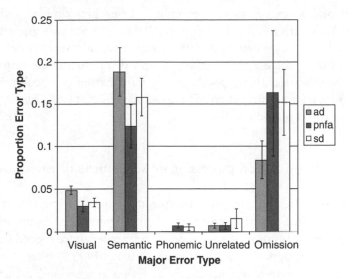

Figure 12.1 Major naming errors in SD, AD, and PNFA

naming ability. Hodges and colleagues (1996) examined the correlation between "naming and knowing" via quality of concept definitions. The majority of AD patients (76%) showed significant naming impairment relative to controls. Sixty percent of items that were correctly named were also defined in a way that the authors argued captured the core concept of the referent. In contrast, significantly fewer correct definitions were provided for items patients were unable to name (<30% correct). The correlation between naming and knowing in AD has also been demonstrated in nonverbal domains including picture sorting and semantic feature verification, thus ruling out isolated lexical impairment (Aronoff et al., 2006; Garrard Lambon Ralph et al., 2005; Salmon et al., 1999).

One of the most fiercely contested aspects of language processing is category specificity, in which items from a particular semantic category are differentially impaired. The most common category deficit in AD occurs for naming biological natural kinds such as animals and fruits relative to manufactured artifacts (Gonnerman et al., 1997; Whatmough et al., 2003). We have argued that this category effect reflects loss of distinctive feature knowledge that is necessary for distinguishing natural kinds (Grossman, Koenig et al., 2007). Support for this hypothesis is derived from double dissociations observed in naming manufactured artifacts and natural kinds in AD (Gonnerman et al., 1997).

Gonnerman and colleagues hypothesized that cortical damage in AD ultimately results in a "crossover" naming impairment, with initial deficits that present as impairment in natural kinds due to vulnerability of distinctive features, and later evolving toward deficits in artifacts due to greater resilience of shared features to brain damage. This crossover from natural kinds to artifacts awaits definitive support from a larger sample of patients. In one larger study (*n* = 72), however,

Whatmough and colleagues found that anomia for natural kinds was worse across all levels of AD severity (Whatmough et al., 2003). The authors argued in accord with *sensory-functional theory* that, rather than a specific segregation of natural kinds and artifacts, these category effects reflect disproportionate impairment to temporal lobe structures that support sensory information (e.g., color, form) relative to a frontoparietal distribution of brain structures that supports knowledge of object function and manipulability.

Grammatical processing in Alzheimer's disease

AD patients have sentence comprehension difficulties. A persistent challenge involves disentangling syntactic processing deficits from other co-morbid difficulties that affect sentence comprehension. Some researchers have argued that genuine syntactic deficits are apparent in AD (Grober & Bang, 1995). Others have hypothesized that many apparent syntactic deficits reflect methodological artifact. For example, the integrity of grammar is often probed by asking patients to make acceptability judgments of sentence structures with some syntactic violation (e.g., John go store). Such "offline" measures require a patient to hold a sentence in working memory until they can make a metalinguistic judgment of its acceptability. This process relies on a notoriously fragile memory system in AD. Thus, one strong position is that "post-interpretive" working memory deficits underlie difficulties with offline measures of grammatical ability in AD (Waters & Caplan, 1997).

Kempler and colleagues compared performance of AD patients via both offline and online measures of grammatical ability (Kempler et al., 1998). Their offline measure was a sentence–picture pointing varied by sentence type. Sentences differed in grammatical complexity from canonical (simple structures) to non-canonical (complex) structures. Sentences were either (i) active voice (e.g., The boy kicked the girl . . . Who kicked?); (ii) active voice with conjoined noun phrases (e.g., The boy kicked the girl and the dog); (iii) passive voice (e.g., The boy was kicked by the girl.); or (iv) active voice with a relative clause (e.g., The boy kicks the girl that chases the dog). AD patients performed worse than controls across all conditions; however, their performance with passive and conjoined sentences (conditions i and ii) was similar. Patients with classic agrammatism show deficits in comprehension of passive sentences. In contrast, patients with AD were not significantly more impaired on passives than with the simpler active conjoined sentences. The authors argued accordingly for a working memory locus over a specific syntactic impairment in AD. Further evidence for an underlying working memory impairment was presented by Kempler et al.'s online task, crossmodal naming. The dependent measure was reaction time for naming a target word in the presence of a syntactic violation (e.g., John go store). Healthy adults are slower to name *store*, for example, in a syntactically anomalous sentence environment. AD patients also showed reaction time differences, suggesting continued sensitivity to grammatical structure.

Another line of research has investigated the role of degraded verb knowledge in sentence processing. Verbs act as the director of a sentence, dictating argument structure and thematic relations between other elements. For this reason, verb deficits can grossly impair sentence processing. Studies have demonstrated a small but consistent disadvantage for comprehension and naming of verbs relative to nouns in AD (Cappa et al., 1998; Grossman, Koenig, DeVita et al., 2003; Grossman & White-Devine, 1998). One methodological difficulty, however, is that verbs and nouns generally differ semantically and grammatically. Naming is an insufficient index for discriminating the locus of verb impairment. We attempted to tease apart semantic from grammatical factors underlying verb deficits in AD via an online word-monitoring task in which patients responded as quickly as possible when they heard a specific word (Price & Grossman, 2005). Unbeknownst to the patient, the target word (represented in capital letters in these examples) appeared in either (i) a grammatically anomalous context in which verb transitivity was violated (e.g., The boy sleeps the CAT); (ii) a semantically anomalous context in which thematic roles were violated (e.g., The milk drinks the CAT.); or (iii) a grammatically and semantically acceptable sentence (e.g., The boy kicks the CAT). Normal adults are slower to respond when a target word appears in the presence of a semantic or grammatical violation (Marslen-Wilson & Tyler, 1980). AD patients showed similar sensitivity via reaction time differences to the transitivity violation, thus demonstrating sensitivity to grammatical properties of verbs. However, patients failed to show the same reaction time discrepancies for thematic role violations, suggesting impairment at the level of verb semantics.

We were able to validate these findings in a lexical acquisition experiment where we explicitly taught patients the novel verb, *lour*, in a naturalistic manner (Grossman, Murray et al., 2007). *Lour* is an archaic but nonetheless real English verb that denotes a frowning expression with clear disapproval. Patients were exposed to the meaning and grammatical properties of *lour* via a narrated picture story involving a badly behaved little girl. The final scene of the story linked the word with the image of an angry father, "Louise sees her father lour at her." AD patients showed significant impairment learning the semantic properties of the verb as illustrated by poor performance on word–picture matching. They were, however, not impaired in acquisition and retention of the grammatical subcategory suggesting impairment with semantics and not grammar.

Discourse Processing in Alzheimer's Disease

The most striking examples of narrative dissolution come from public figures diagnosed with AD. Perhaps the most famous study of AD narrative was reported by Gottschalk et al. (1988), who examined thematic, grammatical, and pragmatic content of Ronald Reagan's presidential debates in 1980 and 1984 via a standardized neuropsychological measure known as the *Gottschalk–Gleser Cognitive Impairment Scale* (Gottschalk et al., 1988). The authors identified cognitive impairment that worsened in the interval between Reagan's first and second terms (1980–1984), leading ultimately to the controversial claim that Reagan experienced active symptoms of AD throughout his presidency.

A more systematic opportunity to examine narrative discourse is afforded by British author, Iris Murdoch (1919–1999), who produced her final novel, *Jackson's Dilemma*, during the early stages of AD. *Jackson's Dilemma* diverged from the quality of Murdoch's previous novels and was panned by literary critics at the time of its publication in 1995. Peter Garrard and colleagues analyzed form and content of *Jackson's Dilemma* using two of Murdoch's previous novels as baselines (Garrard, Maloney et al., 2005). Interestingly, syntactic structure was similar across all three novels. However, large differences emerged in an index of lexical diversity known as type–token–ratio (TTR), a figure that reflects the number of distinct words divided by the total number of words in a given sample. TTR was significantly reduced in *Jackson's Dilemma* relative to Murdoch's previous novels, indicating repetitive use of a smaller set of words. Garrard et al. argued that this discourse pattern reflected lexical impoverishment in the context of generally preserved syntax.

Controlled analyses of AD discourse have demonstrated impairment across a number of domains. Some studies have demonstrated difficulties in maintaining global connectedness necessary for a cohesive storyline, whereas others demonstrate impairment at the level of semantic propositional knowledge (Ehrlich et al., 1997). Common themes throughout AD discourse are excessive repetition of content, poor organization and circumlocutions (i.e., describing things instead of naming them). These deficits culminate in discourse that is most often described as fluent but empty (Tomoeda & Bayles, 1993; Tomoeda et al., 1996).

Semantic Dementia

SD is a variant of FTD linked to a specific distribution of cortical atrophy that affects anterolateral and ventral temporal cortex in the left hemisphere greater than right, later spreading to posterior and lateral temporal lobe structures bilaterally (Galton et al., 2001; Mummery et al., 2000; Snowden et al., 1989). Insidious language impairment (i.e., anomia) in the absence of a focal neurological insult is one of the earliest diagnostic features of SD (Neary et al., 1998). In the early stages of SD, patients may show worse impairment for words relative to pictures. This impairment later evolves into an apparent amodal conceptual disorder that persists regardless of representational format (e.g., pictures, words, sounds, odors, etc.) (Lambon Ralph et al., 2001).

SD patients show striking conceptual loss in the context of preserved functioning in domains such as phonology, syntax, and visual-spatial perception. Our laboratory has proposed a cognitive-linguistic model of SD, hypothesizing that support for language in this population degrades in a top-down manner, beginning with semantic, extending through lexical, and ultimately impacting phonological representations (Reilly Cross et al., 2007; Reilly et al., 2005). Figure 12.2 (plate section) represents this cognitive model. Circumscribed brain damage isolated to ventral and inferolateral temporal cortex early in SD affects semantic knowledge. As atrophy compromises lateral temporal cortex and spreads posteriorly, patients experience lexical degradation. Finally, in the latest stages of SD, auditory perception and phonological storage are compromised. We reference this model in the review of SD to follow.

Phonology in semantic dementia

Patients with SD typically produce fluent, well-formed speech, as noted in many case studies (Hodges et al., 1995; Hodges et al., 1992; Neary et al., 1998; Snowden et al., 1989). Although SD patients do produce generally fluent speech, there has been little direct empirical support for preserved phonology. One line of research has inferred preserved phonology from repetition ability. That is, SD patients repeat single words with high accuracy (Knott et al., 1997). Yet, as the length of word lists increases, SD patients have been observed to make phoneme migration errors (e.g., dog, wheel, ship → dog, eel, whip), Patterson and colleagues have proposed the *lexical-semantic binding hypothesis* to account for this effect, arguing that word meaning acts as a glue that binds the constituent phonemes of words together (Knott et al., 1997). By this binding account, as conceptual support for language degrades, patients are more likely to make phoneme transposition errors. Although this phoneme migration effect has been reported in word-list recall, it is not always apparent and does not occur in spontaneous speech in SD (Reilly et al., 2005).

Another inference for preserved phonology in SD is found in patterns of reading aloud. SD patients show a consistent pattern of surface dyslexia, in which they can successfully read orthographically regular words (e.g., cat), but show marked impairment for irregular words (i.e., words with imperfect letter-sound correspondence such as yacht) (Cipolotti & Warrington, 1995; Patterson & Behrmann, 1997; Patterson & Lambon Ralph, 1999). Models of reading account for surface dyslexia in different ways. One common thread is that surface dyslexia reflects a reduced contribution of word meaning and over-reliance upon direct grapheme-to-phoneme conversion (i.e., converting letters directly to sounds). Thus, surface dyslexia has been described as "reading without semantics" (Shallice et al., 1983; Woollams et al., 2007).

Focusing on the anatomical distribution of the disease may also improve understanding of the cause of surface dyslexia in SD. One recent study measured the activation in the brains of SD patients using functional magnetic resonance imaging (fMRI) relative to controls while reading words with low-frequency atypical letter-sound correspondence (e.g., chassis) and pseudowords (e.g., doost, bonverse) (Wilson et al., 2009). During the reading of pseudowords, the left intraparietal sulcus was equally activated in both controls and SD patients. During reading of the low-frequency atypical words the same left intraparietal sulcus was activated in SD patients as with pseudowords, whereas the controls showed no significant fMRI activation in this area. This finding led the researchers to hypothesize that at a neural level SD patients were treating low-frequency atypical words as pseudowords, which indicated they were not able to access the semantics of the word. It should be noted, however, that other researchers have focused on the anatomical distribution of disease, hypothesizing that surface dyslexic errors emerge as cortical atrophy spreads posteriorly in ventral temporal cortex resulting in the compromise of high-level visual perception (Glosser et al., 2002).

Beyond repetition and surface dyslexia, there have been few systematic investigations of phonology in SD. Kwok and colleagues (2006) examined phonemic perception in SD and found that patients categorically perceive the acoustic shift in voicing that marks specific consonant boundaries (e.g., "pa" vs. "ba") similar to healthy adults (Kwok et al., 2006). Reilly et al. (2007) extended this work and examined auditory discrimination via same–different judgments for pairs of pure tones varied by frequency (1000 Hz vs. 900 Hz) and discrimination of consonant–vowel bigrams ("ba" versus "ga"). SD patients showed subtle difficulties in detecting frequency differences in pairs of pure tones. Furthermore, patients with advanced SD paradoxically performed better than milder patients in bigram discrimination, a trend the authors attributed to reduced lexical interference as the disease progresses (Reilly, Cross, et al., 2007).

Semantic memory in semantic dementia

SD presents with perhaps the strongest in vivo model for examining degraded object knowledge in the context of preserved functioning in other linguistic domains. We review several positions and ultimately interpret this impairment via our two-component model of semantic memory described earlier in this review.

SD patients show similar performance on word-versus-picture tasks and in making object decisions when features are presented in an auditory-versus-visual format (e.g., telephone ringing vs. picture of telephone) (Garrard & Carroll, 2006). Such item consistency distinguishes SD from other forms of aphasia, wherein patients show clear deficits for words over pictures, and also from visual agnosia, where patients show the opposite trend. This agnosia–aphasia double dissociation is critical, as one theoretical position holds that semantic deficits in SD mask a combination of aphasia and visual agnosia due to the dual compromise of left hemisphere language areas and ventral temporal-occipital structures that comprise the putative "what" pathway of visual object recognition (Mesulam, 2001, 2003).

Other researchers have argued that rather than a combination of agnosia and aphasia, SD presents with a modality-neutral deficit that results in the progressive degradation of amodal knowledge (Bozeat et al., 2000; Coccia et al., 2004; Patterson, Nestor et al., 2007; Rogers, Hocking, et al., 2006). One view of semantic degradation in SD is that anterior inferolateral temporal cortex acts as a binding site or convergence zone for disparate semantic features stored in modality-specific regions of cortex (Damasio et al., 1996; Jefferies & Lambon Ralph, 2006; Lambon Ralph &

Patterson, 2008). According to this view, damage to temporal cortex causes "binding" deficits that result in a progressive loss of knowledge, beginning with specific exemplars (e.g., dog) and later extending to entire superordinate categories (e.g., *animal*).

We argue that semantic deficits in SD begin with damage to visual association cortices degrading knowledge of visual features. Indeed, since visual feature knowledge plays a critical role in the representation of concepts, this may give the appearance initially of an amodal deficit or in fact may compromise semantic memory in a modality-neutral manner. This is due to the fact that conceptual meaning is heavily grounded in visual feature knowledge. We hypothesize that as the disease spreads to the homologous regions of the right hemisphere and dorsally to auditory association cortex and the superior temporal sulcus where auditory features of concepts may be represented, the semantic memory impairment in SD progresses and eventually may become amodal.

Tyler and colleagues (2004) have demonstrated that ventromedial anterior portions of the temporal lobe (i.e., perirhinal cortex) are recruited when fine-grained semantic discrimination is necessary between items, whereas only caudal structures are necessary for making superordinate distinctions between the same items ("Is this an animal or tool?"). This perspective on semantic specificity appears to fit well with both the distribution of cortical damage in SD and the hierarchical organization of semantic memory in normal adults. SD patients typically show impairment for distinguishing between basic-level concepts, tending to make coordinate and superordinate semantic naming errors (e.g., CAT→ DOG or CAT→ ANIMAL) (Grossman et al., 2004; Hodges et al., 1995). The same hierarchical taxonomic loss is evident in concept definitions and in delayed picture drawing, where SD patients have been observed to assign prototypical features to a particular exemplar (e.g., adding four legs to a duck because most category members of ANIMAL share this feature) (Bozeat et al., 2003).

Further evidence for a differential weighting of visual feature knowledge comes from performance on concrete versus abstract words in SD. Among normal adults, concrete words (e.g., dog) are earlier learned, better recalled, and more rapidly identified than abstract words (e.g., love) (Kroll & Merves, 1986). Many psycholinguists have argued that this *word concreteness effect* results from the additional visual perceptual salience associated with concrete words. SD patients show an atypical pattern known as *reversal of the concreteness effect* characterized by a selective impairment for concrete words with relative preservation of abstract words. This effect has been reported in naming (Breedin et al., 1994; Warrington, 1975), word-to-definition matching (Yi et al., 2007), narrative performance (Bird et al., 2000), lexical decision latency (Reilly et al., 2006; Reilly, Peelle et al., 2007), and single-word semantic judgments of concreteness (Reilly, Cross, et al., 2007). We and other researchers (Macoir, 2009; Vesely et al., 2007) attribute reversal of the concreteness effect in SD to the degradation of visual-perceptual feature knowledge associated with disease in visual association cortex. Difficulty with concrete relative-to-abstract concepts on a two-alternative forced-choice word associativity task correlated with right anterior temporal atrophy (Bonner et al., 2009). This is consistent with our view of the heavy weighting of visual feature knowledge in human semantic memory.

Naming in semantic dementia

It is widely acknowledged that anomia emerges early during the course of SD (Hodges et al., 1992). Yet, the nature and etiology of this naming deficit remains quite controversial. One argument holds that naming deficits in SD reflect impaired lexical retrieval from a relatively intact semantic system (Mesulam, 2003). Evidence for this hypothesis is derived from patients with early SD who demonstrate appropriate use of objects they cannot name and show discrepant performance on picture versus word versions of semantic batteries. Differential verbal versus visual performance in early SD has also been used to advance "multiple semantics" theories that assume the existence of separate verbal and visual semantic systems subject to dissociable decline in SD.

At the heart of this debate is the issue of whether naming deficits in SD are underpinned by a central semantic loss. Patterson and colleagues have advanced the theory that semantic anomia does indeed reflect degraded knowledge by demonstrating that patients produce richer concept definitions for successfully named objects over empty descriptions of objects for which they are anomic (Lambon Ralph et al., 1999). In line with this theory, a second hypothesis is that SD patients show a strong frequency-by-typicality interaction in their naming ability. That is, highly frequent words that are prototypical examples of their respective semantic categories are better named (Patterson, 2007). For example, SD patients may be more likely to correctly assign the name DOG to a Labrador Retriever, whereas they err with infrequent and atypical category exemplars, calling a Chihuahua a CAT.

By default, healthy adults name objects at a basic level of specificity (e.g., DOG), as opposed to a subordinate (e.g., LABRADOR), superordinate (e.g., ANIMAL), or a specific exemplar (e.g., FIDO). Some theorists have argued that semantic naming errors in SD demonstrate the progressive "bottom-up" loss of a hierarchically organized semantic system. Error analyses, for example, have shown a preponderance of superordinate and coordinate errors, suggesting increased reliance on residual superordinate knowledge with loss of fine-grained specificity within categories (Lambon Ralph et al., 2001). Although this hypothesis is intuitively appealing, we recently conducted a naming error analysis and found that SD patients made few superordinate semantic errors (Reilly et al., in press). Patients in our study named 60 black-and-white line drawings from the Snodgrass and Vanderwart picture series (Snodgrass & Vanderwart, 1980), and by far the most common error SD patients produced was functional associative (e.g., hammer → "I know that thing . . . you hit with it"). We hypothesize that the prevalence of this naming error reflects a reliance on residual contextual and functional knowledge, which may be represented in frontal and parietal cortices that are relatively spared during the early stages of SD (Snowden & Neary, 2002). Further evidence for contributions of preserved frontoparietal structure to naming in SD comes from a study where we correlated naming performance with regional gray matter atrophy in SD via voxel-based morphometry (Grossman et al., 2004). SD naming deficits correlated strongly with atrophy in inferior and middle temporal gyri situated posterior to the temporal pole.

Grammatical processing in semantic dementia

SD patients produce empty but nonetheless syntactically well-formed utterances, leading to the assumption that grammatical aspects of language remain intact until late stages of the disease (Snowden & Neary, 2002). Although SD patients show clear deficits in sentence comprehension, the theoretical consensus is that this impairment stems from lexical-semantic impairment. That is, if one fails to comprehend the meaning of individual words within a sentence, that person will also fail to comprehend the sentence. Further evidence for preserved syntactic knowledge is evident by the frequent use of function words (e.g., the) and high-frequency verbs (e.g., go) in spontaneous speech (Bird et al., 2000).

Empirical evidence for preserved grammatical knowledge in SD is derived from two studies conducted by our laboratory. In one of these studies, we employed an auditory word-monitoring paradigm in the context of a syntactic anomaly. Normal listeners are slower to identify a target word (e.g., ball) when it occurs in the presence of a grammatical violation (e.g., John foots the ball) (Marslen-Wilson & Tyler, 1980). SD produced the same effect, showing lengthier reaction times to recognize words in the presence of a grammatical violation, suggesting continued sensitivity to this property.

SD patients also showed evidence for grammatical preservation in a recent lexical acquisition experiment where we explicitly taught patients the novel verb, *lour*, in a naturalistic manner (Murray et al., 2007). For more detail on this experiment, we refer the reader to our earlier discussion of grammatical processing in AD. SD patients showed significant impairment learning the semantic properties of the verb as illustrated by poor performance on word–picture matching. We also probed grammatical knowledge of *lour* and found that SD patients were impaired at distinguishing between the use of *lour* as a verb or a noun, although they were somewhat better at detecting violations of thematic matrix. Patients also correctly rejected *lour* when it was presented as a closed-class word such as a preposition (e.g., He ran lour the hall). These results suggest difficulty with lexical-semantic processing in the context of sensitivity to the major grammatical distinction between closed- and open-class words.

Discourse processing in semantic dementia

SD patients experience semantic impairment that manifests as severe anomia at the single-word level. Perhaps, for this reason, studies of SD discourse are exceedingly rare. In one study, Bird and colleagues (Bird et al., 2000) examined dissolution of narrative discourse in SD via descriptions of the *Cookie Theft Picture*, a complex scene depicting a kitchen in disarray (Goodglass & Kaplan, 1983). The authors assessed performance of three SD patients at three different times during their decline. Speech rate among patients was comparable to age-matched controls. However, patients showed marked differences in the content of their production, tending to progressively lose low-frequency, high-imageability words (e.g., spatula), while retaining highly frequent closed-class words (e.g., the) and verbs (e.g., go). Thus, patients tended to produce increasingly empty and abstract narratives as SD worsened.

Sharon Ash and colleagues (2006) conducted one of the most detailed study of SD discourse published to date, asking patients ($n = 13$) to narrate the wordless children's picture book, *Frog, Where Are You?* (Mayer, 1969). Each page in this text depicts a plot twist in the adventure of a boy in search of his pet frog. This method of eliciting a narrative has many advantages over a description of a single static picture, including the ability to examine cohesion, global connectedness, and the gist of the story, referencing of temporally remote events, and conveying specific semantic content within different scenes. SD patients had difficulties narrating the story. Their verbal fluency was reduced relative to controls (SD = 81 words per minute (wpm); controls = 142 wpm), and patients often omitted or gave nonspecific references to items they could not name (e.g., "that thing"), a trend that reduced the specificity of content throughout the story. Additional naming errors were found, including the production of nonspecific pronominal references (e.g., "he" for the boy, dog, and frog) and general superordinate terms (e.g., "animal" or "critter" for "dog" or "frog"). Despite difficulties in lexical retrieval, patients were able to demonstrate reasonable global connectivity across the episodes of the story, suggesting preserved gist knowledge. In a companion study, Ash and her co-workers (2009) associated reduced fluency during narrative performance to a semantic deficit.

Meteyard and Patterson (2009) conducted a study in which they analyzed the naturally occurring speech of SD patients during interviews of autobiographical memory. They found that SD patients were more likely to make open-class word (e.g., nouns, verbs) substitution and omissions and closed-class word (e.g. the, it, is) substitutions as compared to controls. These findings led the researchers to hypothesize that a minor syntactic deficit was present. It should be noted, however, that the researchers still point to semantic degradation as the largest contributing factor to deficits in discourse.

Progressive Non-Fluent Aphasia

Arnold Pick (1892) described a patient with progressive deterioration in personality and social comportment who subsequently developed a reduction in speech fluency that eventually led to complete mutism. The next year, Serieux (1893) likely described the earliest case study of a syndrome today known as progressive non-fluent aphasia (PNFA). PNFA is currently recognized as a variant of FTD characterized by cortical atrophy that affects inferior frontal and anterior perisylvian regions critical for speech production (Nestor et al., 2003). PNFA is so named because of its phenotype, describing a progressive decline in speech fluency; however, these patients do show deficits in other aspects of language, including phonemic and grammatical processing.

Phonology in progressive non-fluent aphasia

One of the most striking behavioral features of PNFA is the presence of halting and effortful speech. PNFA patients often experience co-morbid apraxia of speech (AOS) and dysarthria, and their speech is slow, hypophonic, and dysprosodic (Brambati et al., 2009; Kertesz et al., 1994; Ogar et al., 2007; Thompson et al., 1997). As noted earlier, the progressive decline of speech in PNFA often leads to mutism. Gorno-Tempini and colleagues (2006) investigated the neural basis for early mutism in PNFA, contrasting gray matter atrophy of mute with non-mute PNFA patients via voxel-based morphometry (VBM). In this structural anatomical study, both PNFA groups showed atrophy in the left inferior frontal gyrus pars opercularis (posterior Broca's area), superior temporal gyrus, insula, and precentral gyrus. Additionally, mute PNFA patients had atrophy that extended subcortically to the basal ganglia, an area critical for timing and execution of speech (Gorno-Tempini, et al., 2006). Corroborating evidence for the disease locus of PNFA was reported by Nestor and colleagues (2003), who found FDG-PET hypometabolism (reduced metabolic activity) in left anterior insula and frontal operculum regions of a sample of non-mute PNFA patients without dementia ($n = 10$). Ogar and colleagues using VBM compared gray matter volume of PNFA patients with AOS and dysarthria to that of age-matched controls. Relative to healthy controls, there was a correlation in the PNFA patients between AOS, dysarthria, and volumetric loss in the left posterior frontal cortex and basal ganglia (Ogar et al., 2007).

A number of studies have analyzed speech production in PNFA. Croot and colleagues (1998) examined production for nouns varied by word length in two PNFA patients and found rates of phonological paraphasias (e.g., skunk → skump) in up to 46.9% of all utterances. Patients in the Croot et al. study showed benefit from phonological structure, displaying a task-by-accuracy interaction. Production was best for reading aloud (38.5% mean accuracy), followed by single-word repetition (28.75% mean accuracy), and then naming (21.55% mean accuracy). There was also a strong negative linear correlation between accuracy and word length. That is, word length negatively impacted production in these patients. In a larger and more heterogeneous patient sample, investigators reported that almost half of the utterances of these patients were distorted and/or contained paraphasic errors in a semi-structured speech sample (Ash et al., 2004). This was a significantly higher rate of phonemic paraphasic errors than was produced by either AD or SD patients on the same task.

The studies described above involved informal characterizations of speech, without providing strict criteria for categorizing the nature of the speech errors in PNFA. Ash et al. (2010) studied digitized speech in a large series of PNFA patients. She used strict criteria to distinguish between a speech-sound error that might be related to a disorder of motor planning seen in AOS, on the one hand, and a speech-sound error related to a disorder of the phonological system. These investigators found that over 80% of the speech-sound errors produced by PNFA patients are phonemic in nature, derived from a disorder of the speech-sound system of language, although about 20% of errors were distortions of speech sounds that are not part of the English speech-sound system. One patient in the Ash series had AOS, while the remaining 16 patients did not.

The nature of PNFA phonemic deficits remains controversial. Nestor and colleagues (2003) have argued that decreased speech dysfluency in PNFA reflects a combination of agrammatism and AOS (Nestor et al., 2003), whereas others have argued that PNFA patients experience degraded phonological representations that affect encoding processes earlier in the chain of motor speech programming (Croot et al., 1998). Corroborating evidence for phonological and higher level cognitive-linguistic involvement is derived from the fact that PNFA patients show agrammatism and sentence-processing deficits not typically evident in patients with an isolated apraxia of speech but is strikingly apparent in stroke aphasia. This direct comparison to stroke aphasia was recently conducted by Patterson and colleagues (2006), who contrasted PNFA with Broca's aphasia, revealing several group differences (Patterson et al., 2006). For one, PNFA patients failed to show evidence of substantial phonological/deep dyslexia, a condition wherein reading proceeds via a semantic route, resulting in severe impairment for reading pseudowords and function words aloud (Jefferies et al., 2007; Patterson et al., 2006). In contrast, Broca's aphasics showed varying levels of phonological dyslexia. In addition, PNFA patients nearly doubled their speech rate for oral reading over connected speech, whereas stroke aphasics showed relative consistency across tasks. This pattern demonstrated phonological scaffolding in PNFA that was not apparent in Broca's aphasia. The authors concluded that PNFA deficits reflect the selective compromise of self-generated speech (Patterson et al., 2006). Although there is no definitive answer, we have argued for degradation of lexical-phonological knowledge in PNFA, consistent with damage to perisylvian regions critical for phonological encoding (Grossman & Ash, 2004).

Semantic memory in progressive non-fluent aphasia

The study of semantic memory in PNFA presents unique challenges because traditional measures of semantic ability are often confounded with impairment in other cognitive-linguistic domains. The distribution of cortical damage in PNFA affects frontal and perisylvian structures critical for phonological working memory (Smith & Jonides, 1999), phonological output production (Poldrack et al., 1999), and grammatical processing (Friederici, 2001). Contributory deficits in each of these domains can potentially exaggerate the severity of semantic impairment. For example, PNFA patients have demonstrated gross impairment on semantic category fluency naming relative to healthy controls. Yet, these patients show comparable impairment on letter fluency tasks, suggesting a shared deficit in phonological production that impacts both tasks (Rogers, Ivanoiu et al., 2006). Based on mildly impaired performance relative to controls on receptive language tasks such as word-to-picture matching (Grossman et al., 1996) and semantic categorization of pictures and words (Rogers, Ivanoiu, et al., 2006), the theoretical consensus is that semantic memory is generally preserved in PNFA relative to either SD and AD.

The assumption of preserved semantic memory is tempered by poor performance of PNFA patients on learning paradigms recently employed in our laboratory. In these studies, AD, SD, and PNFA patients attempted to learn a novel category of fictional animals we refer to as *Crutters* (Koenig et al., 2007). Patients attempted to learn the category, CRUTTER, either through explicit rule-based instruction on semantic features (e.g., a CRUTTER has a short tail, tusks, and a spotted leg . . . Is this a CRUTTER?) or via similarity-based training relative to a prototype. Rule-based processing depends on executive resources necessary for attending to specific features and making comparisons to other exemplars via working memory. In addition, a critical aspect of rule-based processing is the ability to inhibit or suppress features that may be salient but do not discriminate between category members (e.g., Chihuahuas are small, but they are not cats). Alex Martin and others have argued that these components constitute a semantic working memory system that is localized in left inferior frontal cortex (Martin & Chao, 2001; Thompson-Schill, et al., 1997; Wagner, Poldrack et al., 1998), a region prominently affected in PNFA. In the rule-based condition of our *Crutter* experiment, PNFA patients attended to salient but incorrect semantic features such as size and color and were, thus, significantly impaired relative to controls (Koenig et al., 2006). This sharply contrasts with their remarkably accurate performance on similarity-based training, a condition with reduced executive resource demands.

Naming in progressive non-fluent aphasia

PNFA patients experience clear deficits in naming. In a recent study, PNFA patients ($n = 10$) showed a strong correlation between disease severity and anomia, correctly naming an average of 48.1 of 64 line drawings, whereas controls were at ceiling on the same stimuli (Patterson et al., 2006). If it is true that PNFA is associated with primary deficits in lexical-phonological processing and motor speech programming, one might expect their naming to be littered with phonemic paraphasias and articulatory distortions. A number of case studies have indeed reported this pattern, showing phonemic error rates up to 47% in single-word naming (Croot et al., 1998).

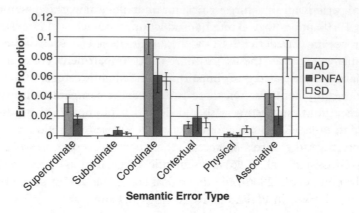

Figure 12.3   Semantic naming errors in SD, AD, and PNFA

An additional prediction is that semantic errors are unexpected in the context of grossly preserved semantic memory. This error pattern, however, was not what we found in a recent analysis of naming in PNFA (Peelle, Reilly et al., 2007). Figure 12.3 illustrates the distribution of semantic errors incurred in PNFA relative to AD and SD. Of note, PNFA patients produced similar rates of semantic error as SD patients. However, error distributions revealed a quite different pattern in PNFA compared to SD. PNFA patients showed significantly higher rates of superordinate hierarchical errors than SD patients. In contrast, SD patients produced more associative errors (e.g., hammer → "you hit with it").

Further evidence for a language-based anomia in PNFA is derived from effects of word class. Based on the frontal distribution of cortical atrophy in PNFA, one might predict naming deficits for verbs relative to nouns. Several studies have indeed reported this naming dissociation in PNFA. Hillis and colleagues demonstrated disproportionate impairment for naming verbs (54.5% accuracy) relative to nouns (81.9%) in a sample of 15 PNFA patients (Hillis et al., 2004). An additional longitudinal PNFA case study (patient M.M.L.) demonstrated a similar graded impairment of verbs relative to nouns. However, patient M.M.L. additionally showed a modality advantage with better written than oral verb naming (Hillis et al., 2002). The authors concluded that modality effects (writing better than speaking) support a grammatical component that affects verb production in PNFA.

Grammatical processing in progressive non-fluent aphasia

Much research in aphasiology has implicated areas of inferior frontal cortex (IFC) in syntactic processing. Regions of IFC are particularly vulnerable to the distribution of PNFA, suggesting a neuroanatomical basis for agrammatism in this population. As mentioned previously, a major challenge involves dissociating grammatical from executive resource and working memory deficits. To accomplish this, we have

employed a variety of online and offline measures that probe grammatical processing in PNFA. In one study we examined grammatical processing via an online
word-monitoring paradigm (Peelle, Reilly et al., 2007). That is, PNFA patients were
instructed to press a key as quickly as possible when they heard a particular cue
word. The target word was embedded in sentences that were either correct or had
a grammatical or thematic violation. Healthy adults showed longer latencies to
identify words that appear in anomalous or illegal syntactic environments. Reaction
times elicited from PNFA patients, however, demonstrated insensitivity to grammatical violations (e.g., Yesterday he go to the store). Yet, the same patients showed
reaction time disparities for thematic violations in which there was a mismatch
between the agent and the action being performed (e.g., The milk drank the cat),
a pattern that supports a preserved semantic contribution to sentence processing in
the context of a reduced grammatical contribution.

The second source of evidence for grammatical deficits in PNFA is differential
performance with respect to word class (e.g., verbs vs. nouns). Selective verb deficits
have been reported in naming in PNFA (Cappa et al., 1998; Hillis et al., 2004). As
discussed earlier, however, it is impossible to infer a pure grammatical deficit from
naming. We circumvented this confound by probing semantic and grammatical
knowledge distinctively via a lexical acquisition experiment wherein PNFA patients
acquired the novel verb, *lour*, in a naturalistic manner through a picture story
(Murray et al., 2007). For more detail on this experiment, we refer the reader to our
earlier discussion of grammatical processing in SD. After the exposure period, PNFA
patients demonstrated appropriate semantic knowledge of *lour* via accurate forced-
choice responses on a picture–word matching task. However, they showed marked
deficits relative to controls in identifying grammatical violations of lour (e.g., The
lour saw the man glancing at him), providing further empirical evidence for PNFA
syntactic impairment.

Discourse in progressive non-fluent aphasia

There have been few studies of discourse processing in PNFA, and the majority of
these have focused on phonological and grammatical aspects of production.
Patterson and colleagues, for example, examined PNFA verbal fluency via description of the *Cookie Theft Picture* from the Boston Diagnostic Examination of Aphasia
(Goodglass & Kaplan, 1983; Patterson et al., 2006). PNFA production was about
one-fifth the rate of controls, with average of 27.8 wpm (controls = 137.4 wpm).

We examined both form and content of narrative discourse by asking PNFA
patients (*n* = 10) to narrate *Frog, Where Are You?* (Ash et al., 2006; Ash et al., 2009).
In terms of speech fluency, PNFA patients produced 45 wpm, whereas controls
produced an average of 142 wpm (approximately one-third the output). Additionally,
patients produced sparse narratives with a substantially reduced mean length of
utterance (MLU) relative to controls. MLU is an index derived by dividing the total
number of words produced by the total number of utterances, thus, providing a

metric for comparing phrase length. MLU also strongly correlates with grammatical and morphological complexity (Brown, 1976). This reduction in phrase length we observed in PNFA narratives was associated with omission of function words, grammatical elements, and modifiers throughout the story (e.g., The . . . d. .boy . . . fou nd . . . um . . . muskrat). Although PNFA narratives were comparatively sparse, patients performed similar to controls on measures of global connectedness, successfully conveying the gist of the story. These findings were validated by Knibb and colleagues as they also found slowing of speech and preserved global connectedness (Knibb et al., 2009). A regression analysis specifically related reduced wpm to grammatical simplification (Gunawardena et al., submitted). A VBM analysis of performance in this study related reduced wpm to cortical thinning in dorsolateral and inferior frontal cortex as well as anterior superior temporal cortex, and this overlapped with an area of cortical thinning in inferior frontal and anterior superior temporal cortex that was related to grammatical simplification.

Conclusion

In summary, we have argued that the cognitive-linguistic profiles of AD and FTD are in many ways distinctive. These unique patterns challenge the engrained assumption that language impairment in dementia reflects a generic decline in cognition. We conclude with a brief discussion of domains in which the study of language in dementia may potentially yield clinical benefits in the near future.

Diagnostic specificity

Differential diagnosis of FTD or AD can be difficult during the early stages of dementia when symptoms are mild or nonspecific. Histopathological confirmations of these conditions are rarely conducted in vivo. Therefore, a major challenge is to establish diagnostic criteria with high sensitivity and specificity for delineating these forms of dementia. Language is one variable that in conjunction with imaging, protein biomarker assays, and other neuropsychological measures significantly improves diagnostic specificity (Forman et al., 2006; Libon et al., 2007).

Clinical management

Patterns of survival and symptomatology associated with the clinical courses of FTD and AD differ. Behavioral management of dementia subtypes can potentially improve by better characterizing the expected cognitive-linguistic courses of these diseases. For example, if mutism is an expected outcome of PNFA, preemptive use of augmentative and alternative communication devices that produce text-to-speech or picture-to-speech output may prolong communicative efficiency and functional independence in this population.

Behavioral targets for intervention

Language impairment remains one of the most debilitating aspects of dementia; yet, few options currently exist in terms of etiology-specific language therapies. Consequently, dementia remains a vastly underserved population. Improved specificity in delineating the nature of language impairment will improve outcomes by better tailoring interventions to meet the unique needs of each dementia subpopulation. This will allow us to more effectively target specific behavioral deficits underlying language difficulties. As an illustrative example, consider remediation of sentence-processing deficits in AD – if executive resource and working memory limitations underlie these sentence comprehension difficulties, it may be possible to facilitate comprehension by repeating and shortening utterances. In contrast, reducing or repeating utterances will have little effect if the impairment is genuinely grammatical. The same logic applies to retraining forgotten concepts. If loss of distinctive semantic features contributes to naming deficits, it may be possible to improve naming ability by retraining fine-grained semantic knowledge that distinguishes among category members (Kiran & Thompson, 2003). However, this approach will likely fail in the context of a more global loss of feature knowledge. At present, many of these issues remain unresolved, and the theoretical rationale for treating associated language impairment is weakened because behavioral targets remain vague. Thus, increased specificity may better inform the development and implementation of etiology-specific language treatments for dementia.

Acknowledgments

This work was supported in part by the National Institutes of Health (K23 DC010197; AG00255, AG17586, AG15116, and NS44266) and the Dana Foundation.

References

Abramson, A. S., & Lisker, L. (1970). *Discriminability along the voicing continuum: Cross-language tests.* Proceedings of the Sixth International Congress of Phonetic Sciences. Prague: Czechoslovak Academy of Sciences, 569–573.

Adlam, A., Bozeat, S., Arnold, R., Watson, P. C., & Hodges, J. R. (2006). Semantic knowledge in mild cognitive impairment and mild Alzheimer's disease. *Cortex, 42,* 675–684.

Aronoff, J. M., Gonnerman, L. M., Almor, A., Arunachalam, S., Kempler, D., & Andersen, E. S. (2006). Information content versus relational knowledge: Semantic deficits in patients with Alzheimer's disease. *Neuropsychologia, 44*(1), 21–35.

Ash, S., McMillan, C., Gunawardena, D., Avants, B., Morgan, B., Khan, A., et al. (2010). Speech errors in progressive non-fluent aphasia. *Brain and Language, 113*(1), 13–20.

Ash, S., Moore, P., Antani, S., McCawley, G., Work, M., & Grossman, M. (2006). Trying to tell a tale: Discourse impairments in progressive aphasia and frontotemporal dementia. *Neurology, 66*, 1405–1413.

Ash, S., Moore, P., Hauck, R., Antani, S., Katz, J., & Grossman, M. (2004). Quantitative analysis of paraphasic errors in frontotemporal dementia. *Neurology, 62a*, 166–183.

Ash, S., Moore, P., Vesely, L., Gunawardena, D., McMillan, C., Anderson, C., et al. (2009). Non-fluent speech in frontotemporal lobar degeneration. *Journal of Neurolinguistics, 22*(4), 370–383.

Bayles, K. A., & Kim, E. S. (2003). Improving the functioning of individuals with Alzheimer's disease: Emergence of behavioral interventions. *Journal of Communication Disorders, 36*(5), 327–343.

Bayles, K. A., & Tomoeda, C. K. (1983). Confrontation naming impairment in dementia. *Brain and Language, 19*(1), 98–114.

Bayles, K. A., Tomoeda, C. K., Kaszniak, A. W., & Trosset, M. W. (1991). Alzheimer's disease effects on semantic memory: Loss of structure or impaired processing? *Journal of Cognitive Neuroscience, 3*(2), 166–182.

Beauchamp, M. S. (2005). See me, hear me, touch me: Multisensory integration in lateral occipto-temporal cortex. *Current Opinion in Neurobiology, 15*, 145–153.

Biassou, N., Grossman, M., Onishi, K., Mickanin, J., et al. (1995). Phonologic processing deficits in Alzheimer's disease. *Neurology, 45*(12), 2165–2169.

Binder, J. R., Frost, J. A., Hammeke, T. A., Rao, S. M., & Cox, R. W. (1996). Function of the left planum temporale in auditory and linguistic processing. *Brain, 119*(4), 1239–1247.

Bird, H., Lambon Ralph, M. A., Patterson, K., & Hodges, J. R. (2000). The rise and fall of frequency and imageability: Noun and verb production in semantic dementia. *Brain and Language, 73*(1), 17–49.

Bonner, M. F., Vesely, L., Price, C., Anderson, C., Richmond, L., Farag, C., et al. (2009). Reversal of the concreteness effect in semantic dementia. *Cognitive Neuropsychology, 26*(6), 568–579.

Bozeat, S., Lambon Ralph, M. A., Graham, K. S., Patterson, K., Wilkin, H., Rowland, J., et al. (2003). A duck with four legs: Investigating the structure of conceptual knowledge using picture drawing in semantic dementia. *Cognitive Neuropsychology, 20*(1), 27–47.

Bozeat, S., Lambon Ralph, M. A., Patterson, K., Garrard, P., & Hodges, J. R. (2000). Non-verbal semantic impairment in semantic dementia. *Neuropsychologia, 38*, 1207–1215.

Brambati, S. M., Ogar, J., Neuhaus, J., Miller, B. L., & Gorno-Tempini, M. L. (2009). Reading disorders in primary progressive aphasia: A behavioral and neuroimaging study. *Neuropsychologia, 47*(8–9), 1893–1900.

Breedin, S. D., Saffran, E. M., & Coslett, H. B. (1994). Reversal of the concreteness effect in a patient with semantic dementia. *Cognitive Neuropsychology, 11*(6), 617–660.

Bright, P., Moss, H., & Tyler, L. K. (2004). Unitary vs. multiple semantics: PET studies of word and picture processing. *Brain and Language, 89*(3), 417–432.

Broca, P. (1863). Localisation des fonctions cérébrales: Siée du langage articulé. *Bulletin of the Society of Anthropology (Paris), 4*, 200–203.

Brown, R. W. (1976). *A first language: The early stages.* Hammondsworth: Penguin.

Bussey, T. J., & Saksida, L. M. (2002). The organization of visual object representations: A connectionist model of effects of lesions in perirhinal cortex. *European Journal of Neuroscience, 15*, 355–364.

Cappa, S. F., Binetti, G., Pezzini, A., Padovani, A., Rozzini, L., & Trabucchi, M. (1998). Object and action naming in Alzheimer's disease and frontotemporal dementia. *Neurology, 50*(2), 351–355.

Chainay, H., Louarn, C., & Humphreys, G. W. (2006). Ideational action impairments in Alzheimer's disease. *Brain and Cognition, 62*(3), 198–205.

Chertkow, H., & Bub, D. (1990). Semantic memory loss in dementia of Alzheimer's type. What do various measures measure? *Brain, 113*(Pt 2), 397–417.

Cipolotti, L., & Warrington, E. K. (1995). Semantic memory and reading abilities: A case report. *Journal of the International Neuropsychological Society, 1*(1), 104–110.

Coccia, M., Bartolini, M., Luzzi, S., Provinciali, L., & Lambon Ralph, M. A. (2004). Semantic memory is an amodal, dynamic system: Evidence from the interaction of naming and object use in semantic dementia. *Cognitive Neuropsychology, 21*(5), 513–527.

Coltheart, M. (2004). Are there lexicons? *Quarterly Journal of Experimental Psychology A: Human Experimental Psychology, 57A*(7), 1153–1171.

Cosentino, S., Chute, D., Libon, D., Moore, P., & Grossman, M. (2006). How does the brain represent scripts? A study of executive processes and semantic knowledge in dementia. *Neuropsychology, 20*, 307–318.

Croot, K., Hodges, J. R., Xuereb, J., & Patterson, K. (2000). Phonological and articulatory impairment in Alzheimer's disease: A case series. *Brain and Language, 75*(2), 277–309.

Croot, K., Patterson, K., & Hodges, J. R. (1998). Single word production in nonfluent progressive aphasia. *Brain and Language, 61*(2), 226–273.

Cuetos, F., Martinez, T., Martinez, C., Izura, C., & Ellis, A. W. (2003). Lexical processing in Spanish patients with probable Alzheimer's disease. *Cognitive Brain Research, 17*(3), 549–561.

Damasio, H., Grabowski, T. J., Tranel, D., Hichwa, R. D., & Damasio, A. R. (1996). A neural basis for lexical retrieval. *Nature, 380*, 499–505.

Duarte, L. R., Marquie, L., Marquie, J. C., Terrier, P., & Ousset, P. J. (2009). Analyzing feature distinctiveness in the processing of living and non-living concepts in Alzheimer's disease. *Brain and Cognition, 71*(2), 108–117.

Ehrlich, J. S., Obler, L. K., & Clark, L. (1997). Ideational and semantic contributions to narrative production in adults with dementia of the Alzheimer's type. *Journal of Communication Disorders, 30*(2), 79–99.

Eustache, F., Lambert, J., Cassier, C., Dary, M., Rossa, Y., Rioux, P., et al. (1995). Disorders of auditory identification in dementia of the Alzheimer type. *Cortex, 31*, 119–127.

Forman, M. S., Farmer, J., Johnson, J. K., Clark, C. M., Arnold, S. E., Coslett, H. B., et al. (2006). Frontotemporal dementia: Clinicopathological correlations. *Annals of Neurology, 59*(6), 952–962.

Friederici, A. D. (2001). Syntactic, prosodic, and semantic processes in the brain: Evidence from event-related neuroimaging. *Journal of Psycholinguistic Research, 30*(3), 237–250.

Galton, C. J., Patterson, K., Graham, K., Lambon Ralph, M. A., Williams, G., Antoun, N., et al. (2001). Differing patterns of temporal atrophy in Alzheimer's disease and semantic dementia. *Neurology, 57*(2), 216–225.

Garrard, P., & Carroll, E. (2006). Lost in semantic space: A multi-modal, non-verbal assessment of feature knowledge in semantic dementia. *Brain, 129*(5), 1152–1163.

Garrard, P., Lambon Ralph, M. A., Hodges, J. R., & Patterson, K. (2001). Prototypicality, distinctiveness, and intercorrelation: Analyses of the semantic attributes of living and nonliving concepts. *Cognitive Neuropsychology, 18*(2), 125–174.

Garrard, P., Lambon Ralph, M. A., Patterson, K., Pratt, K. H., & Hodges, J. R. (2005). Semantic feature knowledge and picture naming in dementia of Alzheimer's type: A new approach. *Brain and Language, 93*(1), 79–94.

Garrard, P., Maloney, L. M., Hodges, J. R., & Patterson, K. (2005). The effects of very early Alzheimer's disease on the characteristics of writing by a renowned author. *Brain, 128*(2), 250–260.

Glosser, G., Baker, K. M., de Vries, J. J., Alavi, A., Grossman, M., & Clark, C. M. (2002). Disturbed visual processing contributes to impaired reading in Alzheimer's disease. *Neuropsychologia, 40*(7), 902–909.

Glosser, G., Freidman, R., Kohn, S. E., Sands, L., & Grugan, P. (1998). Cognitive mechanisms for processing nonwords: Evidence from Alzheimer's disease. *Brain and Language, 63*(1), 32–49.

Glosser, G., Kohn, S. E., Friedman, R., Sands, L., & Grugan, P. (1997). Repetition of single words and nonwords in Alzheimer's disease. *Cortex, 33*(4), 653–666.

Gollan, T. H., Salmon, D. P., & Paxton, J. L. (2006). Word association in early Alzheimer's disease. *Brain and Language. Special Issue: Language comprehension across the life span, 99*(3), 289–303.

Gonnerman, L. M., Andersen, E. S., Devlin, J. T., Kempler, D., & Seidenberg, M. S. (1997). Double dissociation of semantic categories in Alzheimer's disease. *Brain and Language, 57*(2), 254–279.

Gonzalez Rothi, L., Fuller, R., Leon, S. A., Kendall, D. L., Moore, A., Wu, S., et al. (2009). Errorless practice as a possible adjuvant to donepazil in Alzheimer's disease. *Journal of the International Neuropsychological Society, 15*, 311–322.

Goodglass, H, & Kaplan, E (1983). *The assessment of aphasia and related disorders* (2nd edn.). Philadelphia, PA: Lea and Feibiger.

Gorno-Tempini, M. L., Ogar, J. M., Brambati, S. M., Wang, P., Jeong, J. H., Rankin, K. P., et al. (2006). Anatomical correlates of early mutism in progressive nonfluent aphasia. *Neurology, 67*(10), 1849–1851.

Gottschalk, L. A., Uliana, R., & Gilbert, R. (1988). Presidential candidates and cognitive impairment measured from behavior in campaign debates. *Public Administration Review, March/April*, 613–619.

Graham, K. S., Patterson, K., Pratt, K. H., & Hodges, J. R. (2001). Can repeated exposure to "forgotten" vocabulary help alleviate word-finding difficulties in semantic dementia? An illustrative case study. *Neuropsychological Rehabilitation, 11*(3–4), 429–454.

Grober, E., & Bang, S. (1995). Sentence comprehension in Alzheimer's disease. *Developmental Neuropsychology, 11*(1), 95–107.

Grossman, M., Anderson, C., Khan, A., Avants, B., Elman, L., & McCloskey, L. (2008). Impaired action knowledge in amyotrophic lateral sclerosis. *Neurology, 71*, 1396–1401.

Grossman, M., & Ash, S. (2004). Primary progressive aphasia: A review. *Neurocase, 10*, 3–18.

Grossman, M., Koenig, P., DeVita, C., Glosser, G., Alsop, D., Detre, J., et al. (2002). The neural basis for category-specific knowledge: An fMRI study. *Neuroimage, 15*, 936–948.

Grossman, M., Koenig, P., DeVita, C., Glosser, G., Moore, P., Gee, J., et al. (2003). Neural basis for verb processing in Alzheimer's disease: An fMRI Study. *Neuropsychology, 17*(4), 658–674.

Grossman, M., Koenig, P., Glosser, G., DeVita, C., Moore, P., Rhee, J., et al. (2003). Neural basis for semantic memory difficulty in Alzheimer's disease: An fMRI study. *Brain*, *126*(2), 292–311.

Grossman, M., Koenig, P., Troiani, V., Work, M., & Moore, P. (2007). How necessary are the stripes of a tiger? Diagnostic and characteristic features in an fMRI study of word meaning. *Neuropsychologia*, *45*, 1055–1064.

Grossman, M., McMillan, C., Moore, P., Ding, L., Glosser, G., Work, M., et al. (2004). What's in a name: Voxel-based morphometric analyses of MRI and naming difficulty in Alzheimer's disease, frontotemporal dementia and corticobasal degeneration. *Brain*, *127*(3), 628–649.

Grossman, M., Mickanin, J., Onishi, K., & Hughes, E. (1996). Progressive nonfluent aphasia: Language, cognitive, and PET measures contrasted with probable Alzheimer's disease. *Journal of Cognitive Neuroscience*, *8*(2), 135–154.

Grossman, M., Murray, R., Koenig, P., Ash, S., Cross, K., Moore, P., et al. (2007). Verb acquisition and representation in Alzheimer's disease. *Neuropsychologia*, *45*(11), 2508–2518.

Grossman, M., & White-Devine, T. (1998). Sentence comprehension in Alzheimer's disease. *Brain and Language*, *62*(2), 186–201.

Gunawardena, D., Ash, S., McMillan, C., Avants, B., Gee, J., Grossman, M. (submitted). Why are progressive non-fluent aphasics non-fluent?

Harasty, J. A., Halliday, G. M., Kril, J. J., & Code, C. (1999). Specific temporoparietal gyral atrophy reflects the pattern of language dissolution in Alzheimer's disease. *Brain*, *122*(4), 675–686.

Hillis, A. E., Sangjin, O., & Ken, L. (2004). Deterioration of naming nouns versus verbs in Primary Progressive Aphasia. *Annals of Neurology*, *55*, 268–275.

Hillis, A. E., Tuffiash, E., & Caramazza, A. (2002). Modality-specific deterioration in naming verbs in nonfluent primary progressive aphasia. *Journal of Cognitive Neuroscience*, *14*(7), 1099–1108.

Hodges, J. R., Graham, N., & Patterson, K. (1995). Charting the progression in semantic dementia: implications for the organisation of semantic memory. *Memory*, *3*, 463–495.

Hodges, J. R., Patterson, K., Graham, N. L., & Dawson, K. (1996). Naming and knowing in dementia of Alzheimer's type. *Brain and Language*, *54*(2), 302–325.

Hodges, J. R., Patterson, K., Oxbury, S., & Funnell, E. (1992). Semantic dementia: Progressive fluent aphasia with temporal lobe atrophy. *Brain*, *115*(6), 1783–1806.

Hornberger, M., Bell, B., Graham, K. S., & Rogers, T. T. (2009). Are judgments of semantic relatedness systematically impaired in Alzheimer's disease? *Neuropsychologia*, *47*(14), 3084–3094.

Humphreys, G. W., & Riddoch, M. J. (2006). Features, objects, action: The cognitive neuropsychology of visual object processing, 1984–2004. *Cognitive Neuropsychology*, *23*(1), 156–183.

Jefferies, E., & Lambon Ralph, M. A. (2006). Semantic impairment in stroke aphasia versus semantic dementia: A case-series comparison. *Brain*, *129*(8), 2132–2147.

Joubert, S., Brambati, S. M., Ansado, J., Barbeau, E. J., Felician, O., Didic, M., et al. (2009). The cognitive and neural expression of semantic memory impairment in mild cognitive impairment and early Alzheimer's disease. *Neuropsychologia*, *48*, 978–988.

Kempler, D., Almor, A., Tyler, L. K., Andersen, E. S., & MacDonald, M. C. (1998). Sentence comprehension deficits in Alzheimer's disease: A comparison of off-line vs. on-line sentence processing. *Brain and Language, 64*(3), 297–316.

Kertesz, A., Hudson, L., Mackenzie, I. R., & Munoz, D. G. (1994). The pathology and nosology of primary progressive aphasia. *Neurology, 44,* 2065–2072.

Kiran, S., & Thompson, C. K. (2003). The role of semantic complexity in treatment of naming deficits: Training semantic categories in fluent aphasia by controlling exemplar typicality. *Journal of Speech, Language, and Hearing Research, 46*(4), 773–787.

Knibb, J. A., Woollams, A. M., Hodges, J. R., & Patterson, K. (2009). Making sense of progressive non-fluent aphasia: An analysis of conversational speech. *Brain, 132*(10), 2734–2746.

Knott, R., Patterson, K., & Hodges, J. R. (1997). Lexical and semantic binding effects in short-term memory: Evidence from semantic dementia. *Cognitive Neuropsychology, 14*(8), 1165–1216.

Koenig, P., & Grossman, M. (2007). Process and content in semantic memory. In J. Hart, & M. A. Kraut (Eds.), *Neural basis of semantic memory* (pp. 247–264). Cambridge: Cambridge University Press.

Koenig, P., Smith, E. E., & Grossman, M. (2006). Semantic categorisation of novel objects in frontotemporal dementia. *Cognitive Neuropsychology, 23*(4), 541–562.

Koenig, P., Smith, E. E., Moore, P., Glosser, G., & Grossman, M. (2007). Categorization of novel animals by patients with Alzheimer's disease and corticobasal degeneration. *Neuropsychology, 21*(2), 193–206.

Kroll, J. F., & Merves, J. S. (1986). Lexical access for concrete and abstract words. *Journal of Experimental Psychology: Learning, Memory, & Cognition, 12*(1), 92–107.

Kwok, S., Reilly, J., & Grossman, M. (2006). Acoustic-phonetic processing in semantic dementia. *Brain and Language, 99,* 145–146.

Lambon Ralph, M. A., Ellis, A. W., & Franklin, S. (1995). Semantic loss without surface dyslexia. *Neurocase, 1*(4), 363–369.

Lambon Ralph, M. A., Graham, K. S., Patterson, K., & Hodges, J. R. (1999). Is a picture worth a thousand words? Evidence from concept definitions by patients with semantic dementia. *Brain and Language, 70*(3), 309–335.

Lambon Ralph, M. A., McClelland, J. L., Patterson, K., Galton, C. J., & Hodges, J. R. (2001). No right to speak? The relationship between object naming and semantic impairment: Neuropsychological evidence and a computational model. *Journal of Cognitive Neuroscience, 13*(3), 341–356.

Lambon Ralph, M. A., & Patterson, K. (2008). Generalization and differentiation in semantic memory: Insights from semantic dementia. *Annals of the New York Academy of Science, 1124,* 61–76.

Libon, D. J., Xie, S., Moore, P., Farmer, J., Antani, S., McCawley, G., et al. (2007). Patterns of neuropsychological impairment in frontotemporal dementia. *Neurology, 68,* 369–375.

Macoir, J. (2009). Is a plum a memory problem? Longitudinal study of the reversal of concreteness effect in a patient with semantic dementia. *Neuropsychologia, 47*(2), 518–535.

Marslen-Wilson, W., & Tyler, L. K. (1980). The temporal structure of spoken language understanding. *Cognition, 8*(1), 1–71.

Martin, A., & Chao, L. L. (2001). Semantic memory and the brain: Structure and processes. *Current Opinion in Neurobiology, 11,* 194–201.

Mayer, M. (1969). *Frog, Where are you?* New York: Penguin Books.

McKhann, G., Drachman, D., Folstein, M., Katzman, R., Price, D., & Stadlan, E. M. (1984). Clinical diagnosis of Alzheimer's disease: Report of the NINCDS-ADRDA work group under the auspices of Department of Health and Human Services Task Force on Alzheimer's disease. *Neurology, 34,* 939–944.

Mesulam, M., Grossman, M., Hillis, A., Kertesz, A., & Weintraub, S. (2003). The core and halo of primary progressive aphasia and semantic dementia. *Annals of Neurology, 54*(5), 1–4.

Mesulam, M. M. (2001). Primary progressive aphasia. *Annals of Neurology, 49*(4), 425–432.

Mesulam, M. M. (2003). Primary progressive aphasia: A language-based dementia. *New England Journal of Medicine, 349*(16), 1535–1542.

Meteyard, L., & Patterson, K. (2009). The relation between content and structure in language production: An analysis of speech errors in semantic dementia. *Brain and Language, 110*(3), 121–134.

Mummery, C. J., Patterson, K., Price, C. J., Ashburner, J., Frackowiak, R. S. J., & Hodges, J. R. (2000). A voxel-based morphometry study of semantic dementia: Relationship between temporal lobe atrophy and semantic memory. *Annals of Neurology, 47,* 36–45.

Murray, R. C., Koenig, P., Antani, S., McCawley, G., & Grossman, M. (2007). Lexical acquisition in progressive aphasia and frontotemporal dementia. *Cognitive Neuropsychology, 24*(1), 48–69.

Murtha, S., Chertkow, H., Beauregard, M., & Evans, A. (1999). The neural substrate of picture naming. *Journal of Cognitive Neuroscience, 11*(4), 399–423.

Neary, D., Snowden, J. S., Gustafson, L., Passant, U., Stuss, D., Black, S., et al. (1998). Frontotemporal lobar degeneration: A consensus on clinical diagnostic criteria. *Neurology, 51*(6), 1546–1554.

Nestor, P. J., Graham, N. L., Fryer, T. D., Williams, G. B., Patterson, K., & Hodges, J. R. (2003). Progressive non-fluent aphasia is associated with hypometabolism centred on the left anterior insula. *Brain, 126*(11), 2406–2418.

NINDS (2009). NINDS dementia information. Retrieved December 15, 2009, from www.ninds.nih.gov/disorders/dementias/dementia.htm.

Ober, B. A., & Shenaut, G. K. (1999). Well-organized conceptual domains in Alzheimer's disease. *Journal of the International Neuropsychological Society, 5*(7), 676–684.

Ogar, J. M., Dronkers, N. F., Brambati, S. M., Miller, B. L., & Gorno-Tempini, M. L. (2007). Progressive nonfluent aphasia and its characteristic motor speech deficits. *Alzheimer Disease & Associated Disorders, 21*(4), S23–S30.

Passafiume, D., Di Giacomo, D., & Carolei, A. (2006). Word-stem completion task to investigate semantic network in patients with Alzheimer's disease. *European Journal of Neurology, 13*(5), 460–464.

Patterson, K. (2007). The reign of typicality in semantic memory. *Philosophical transactions of the Royal Society B: Biological Sciences, 362*(1481), 813–821.

Patterson, K., & Behrmann, M. (1997). Frequency and consistency effects in a pure surface dyslexic patient. *Journal of Experimental Psychology: Human Perception and Performance, 23*(4), 1217–1231.

Patterson, K., Graham, N. L., Lambon Ralph, M. A., & Hodges, J. R. (2006). Progressive non-fluent aphasia is not a progressive form of non-fluent (post-stroke) aphasia. *Aphasiology, 20*(9–11), 1018–1034.

Patterson, K., & Lambon Ralph, M. A. (1999). Selective disorders of reading? *Current Opinion in Neurobiology, 9*(2), 235–239.

Patterson, K., Nestor, P. J., & Rogers, T. T. (2007). Where do you know what you know? The representation of semantic knowledge in the human brain. *Nature Review Neuroscience, 8*(12), 976–987.

Peelle, J. E., Cooke, A., Moore, P., Vesely, L., & Grossman, M. (2007). Syntactic and thematic components of sentence processing in progressive nonfluent aphasia and nonaphasic frontotemporal dementia. *Journal of Neurolinguistics, 20*(6), 482–494.

Peelle, J. E., Reilly, J., Anderson, C., Moore, P., Cross, K., Kwok, S., et al. (2007). Naming in progressive nonfluent aphasia and semantic dementia: Knowledge and processing impairments lead to distinct naming errors. Paper presented at the American Academy of Neurology.

Peelle, J. E., Troiani, V., Gee, J., Moore, P., McMillan, C., Vesely, L., Grossman, M. (2008). Sentence comprehension and voxel-based morphometry in progressive nonfluent aphasia, semantic dementia, and nonaphasic frontotemporal dementia. *Journal of Neurolinguistics, 21*, 418–432.

Pick, A. (1892). Uber die Beziehungen der senilen Hirnatrophie zue Aphasie. *Prager Medicinische Wochenschrift, 17*, 165–167.

Pinker, S., & Jackendoff, R. (2005). The faculty of language: What's special about it? *Cognition, 95*(2), 201–236.

Poldrack, R. A., Wagner, A. D., Prull, M. W., Desmond, J. E., Glover, G. H., & Gabrieli, J. D. E. (1999). Functional specialization for semantic and phonological processing in the left inferior frontal cortex. *Neuroimage, 10*, 15–35.

Price, C. C., & Grossman, M. (2005). Verb agreements during on-line sentence processing in Alzheimer's disease and frontotemporal dementia. *Brain and Language, 94*(2), 217–232.

Pulvermuller, F. (2001). Brain reflections of words and their meaning. *Trends in Cognitive Sciences, 5*, 517–524.

Reilly, J., Antonucci, S. M., Peelle, J. E., & Grossman, M. (in press). Anomia as a marker of distinct semantic impairments in Alzheimer's disease and semantic dementia. *Neuropsychology.*

Reilly, J., Cross, K., Troiani, V., & Grossman, M. (2007). Single word semantic judgments in semantic dementia: Do phonology and grammatical class count? *Aphasiology, 21*(6/7/8), 558–569.

Reilly, J., Grossman, M., & McCawley, G. (2006). Concreteness effects in lexical processing of semantic dementia. *Brain and Language, 99*, 218–219.

Reilly, J., Martin, N., & Grossman, M. (2005). Verbal learning in semantic dementia: Is repetition priming a useful strategy? *Aphasiology, 19*, 329–339.

Reilly, J., Peelle, J., & Grossman, M. (2007). A unitary semantics account of reverse concreteness effects in semantic dementia. *Brain and Language, 103*, 248–249.

Rogers, S. L., & Friedman, R. B. (2008). The underlying mechanisms of semantic memory loss in Alzheimer's disease and semantic dementia. *Neuropsychologia, 46*(1), 12–21.

Rogers, T. T., Hocking, J., Noppeney, U., Mechelli, A., Gorno-Tempini, M. L., Patterson, K., et al. (2006). Anterior temporal cortex and semantic memory: Reconciling findings from neuropsychology and functional imaging. *Cognitive, Affective, and Behavioral Neuroscience, 6*(3), 201–203.

Rogers, T. T., Ivanoiu, A., Patterson, K., & Hodges, J. R. (2006). Semantic memory in Alzheimer's disease and the frontotemporal dementias: A longitudinal study of 236 patients. *Neuropsychology, 20*(3), 319–335.

Rogers, T. T., Lambon Ralph, M. A., Garrard, P., Bozeat, S., McClelland, J. L., Hodges, J. R., et al. (2004). Structure and deterioration of semantic memory: A neuropsychological and computational investigation. *Psychological Review, 111*(1), 205–235.

Rosen, H. J., Gorno-Tempini, M. L., Goldman, W. P., Perry, R. J., Schuff, N., Weiner, M. W., et al. (2002). Patterns of brain atrophy in frontotemporal dementia and semantic dementia. *Neurology, 58*(2), 198–208.

Salmon, D. P., Butters, N., & Chan, A. S. (1999). The deterioration of semantic memory in Alzheimer's disease. *Canadian Journal of Experimental Psychology, 53*(1), 108–116.

Serieux, P. (1893). Sur un cas de surdite verbale pure. *Review of Medicine, 13*, 733–750.

Shallice, T., Warrington, E. K., & McCarthy, R. A. (1983). Reading without semantics. *Quarterly Journal of Experimental Psychology A: Human Experimental Psychology, 35A*(1), 111–138.

Smith, E. E., & Jonides, J. (1999). Storage and executive processes in the frontal lobes. *Science, 283*(5408), 1657–1661.

Snodgrass, J. G., & Vanderwart, M. (1980). A standardized set of 260 pictures: Norms for name agreement, image agreement, familiarity, and visual complexity. *Journal of Experimental Psychology: Human Learning & Memory, 6*(2), 174–215.

Snowden, J. S., Goulding, P. J., & Neary, D. (1989). Semantic dementia: A form of circumscribed cerebral atrophy. *Behavioural Neurology, 2*, 167–182.

Snowden, J. S., & Neary, D. (2002). Relearning of verbal labels in semantic dementia. *Neuropsychologia, 40*(10), 1715–1728.

Sommers, M. S. (1998). Spoken word recognition in individuals with dementia of the Alzheimer's type: Changes in talker normalization and lexical discrimination. *Psychology and Aging, 13*(4), 631–646.

Thierry, G., & Price, C. J. (2006). Dissociating verbal and nonverbal conceptual processing in the human brain. *Journal of Cognitive Neuroscience, 18*(6), 1018–1028.

Thompson-Schill, S. L., D'Esposito, M., Aguirre, G. K., & Farah, M. J. (1997). Role of left inferior frontal cortex in retrieval of semantic knowledge: A re-evaluation. *Proceedings of the National Academy of Sciences USA, 94*, 14792–14797.

Thompson, C. K., Ballard, K. J., Tait, M. E., Weintraub, S., & Mesulam, M. M. (1997). Patterns of language decline in non-fluent primary progressive aphasia. *Aphasiology, 11*(4–5), 297–331.

Tomoeda, C. K., & Bayles, K. A. (1993). Longitudinal effects of Alzheimer disease on discourse production. *Alzheimer Disease & Associated Disorders, 7*(4), 223–236.

Tomoeda, C. K., Bayles, K. A., Trosset, M. W., Azuma, T., et al. (1996). Cross-sectional analysis of Alzheimer disease effects on oral discourse in a picture description task. *Alzheimer Disease & Associated Disorders, 10*(4), 204–215.

Tyler, L. K., Stamatakis, E. A., Bright, P., Acres, K., Abdallah, S., Rodd, J. M., et al. (2004). Processing objects at different levels of specificity. *Journal of Cognitive Neuroscience, 16*(3), 351–362.

Vesely, L., Bonner, M., Reilly, J., & Grossman, M. (2007). Free association in semantic dementia: The importance of being abstract. *Brain and Language, 103*, 154–155.

Wagner, A. D., Desmond, J. E., Glover, G. H., & Gabrieli, J. D. E. (1998). Prefrontal cortex and recognition memory: Functional-MRI evidence for context-dependent retrieval processes. *Brain, 121*(10), 1985–2002.

Wagner, A. D., Poldrack, R. A., Eldridge, L. L., Desmond, J. E., Glover, G. H., & Gabrieli, J. D. E. (1998). Material-specific lateralization of prefrontal activation during episodic encoding and retrieval. *Neuroreport, 9*(16), 3711–3717.

Warrington, E. (1975). The selective impairment of semantic memory. *Quarterly Journal of Experimental Psychology, 27*, 635–657.

Waters, G. S., & Caplan, D. (1997). Working memory and on-line sentence comprehension in patients with Alzheimer's disease. *Journal of Psycholinguistic Research, 26*(4), 377–400.

Weiner, M. F., Neubecker, K. E., Bret, M. E., & Hynan, L. S. (2008). Language in Alzheimer's disease. *Journal of Clinical Psychiatry, 69*(8), 1223–1227.

Wernicke, C. (1874). *Der aphasische Symptomemkomplex: Eine psychologische Studie auf anatomischer Basis.* Breslau: Cohn und Weigert.

Whatmough, C., Chertkow, H., Murtha, S., Templeman, D., Babins, L., & Kelner, N. (2003). The semantic category effect increases with worsening anomia in Alzheimer's type dementia. *Brain and Language. Special Issue: Meaning in language, 84*(1), 134–147.

Wilson, S. M., Brambati, S. M., Henry, R. G., Handwerker, D. A., Agosta, F., Miller, B. L., et al. (2009). The neural basis of surface dyslexia in semantic dementia. *Brain, 132* (Pt 1), 71–86.

Woollams, A. M., Ralph, M. A., Plaut, D. C., & Patterson, K. (2007). SD-squared: On the association between semantic dementia and surface dyslexia. *Psychological Review, 114*(2), 316–339.

Yi, H., Moore, P., & Grossman, M. (2007). Reversal of the concreteness effect for verbs in semantic dementia. *Cognitive Neuropsychology, 21*(1), 1–19.

Zahn, R., Garrard, P., Talazko, J., Gondan, M., Bubrowski, P., Juengling, F., et al. (2006). Patterns of regional brain hypometabolism associated with knowledge of semantic features and categories in Alzheimer's disease. *Journal of Cognitive Neuroscience, 18*(12), 2138–2151.

13

Executive Functioning

Robert A. Stern, Stacy L. Andersen, and Brandon E. Gavett

Introduction

Executive functions have been defined as "processes [that] are part of a system that acts in a supervisory capacity in the overall hierarchy of brain processing and encompasses skills necessary for purposeful, goal-directed behavior" (Strauss et al., 2006, p.401). They allow one to plan, solve problems, and to take part in social and environmental interactions to achieve a desired result (Stern & Prohaska, 1996). In addition, they exhibit control over sensory input, internal emotional and cognitive states, and motor output, through top-down modulation, to maintain goal-directed behaviors (Gazzaley & D'Esposito, 2007). Top-down modulation may include the enhancement or suppression of the magnitude and speed of processing of information within the constraints of one's resources (Gazzaley et al., 2005). This modulation is instrumental in allowing flexibility of responses to stimuli to suit a specific context rather than constraining one to habitual or instinctual responses (Gilbert & Burgess, 2008).

Disturbances in executive functioning are common sequelae of dementia syndromes and can have wide-ranging effects on other domains of cognitive function as well as on activities of daily living. This chapter will focus on the disruptions in executive function commonly seen in the dementia syndromes. To begin, we will provide a brief conceptualization of the role of executive functions in human behavior, followed by a description of the process by which they develop. Those aspects of executive functioning that have been subject to scientific scrutiny will be described in terms of both behavioral and cognitive functions. This will be followed by an

The Handbook of Alzheimer's Disease and Other Dementias, First Edition.
Edited by Andrew E. Budson, Neil W. Kowall.
© 2011 Blackwell Publishing Ltd. Published 2011 by Blackwell Publishing Ltd.

overview of the neuroanatomical correlates of executive functioning and a description of how these functions are formally assessed in patients with dementia. Finally, the dementia syndromes will be described from a clinical and neuropathological perspective, with particular focus on the ways in which executive deficits are manifest in these disorders.

Definition

The term "executive functioning" encompasses a wide constellation of cognitive abilities that are responsible for providing a behavioral interface between the internal milieu and the external environment. These abilities provide humans with a mechanism for integrating and acting upon various divergent sources of information, ranging from primitive physiological states (e.g., hunger, thirst) to complex environmental stimuli (e.g., the topographical layout of the Rocky Mountains), as well as the information processed by other cognitive abilities (e.g., language, memory). Executive functions contribute additional levels of information processing beyond what is observed in other creatures, whose behavioral repertoires tend to include more stimulus-bound responding. This additional processing affords humans the ability to meet their needs or satisfy desires through considerable flexibility in tasks such as goal setting, inhibition of prepotent responses, prospective thinking, decision making, initiation and maintenance of behavior, continuous self-monitoring, online adaptation, and episodic learning. It is clear that proper integration of factors such as motivation, emotion, previously acquired knowledge and experiences (i.e., semantic and episodic memory, respectively), accurate perceptions, and contextual (e.g., social) information is necessary for behaving in an effective and adaptive manner.

Although executive functions are commonly thought of as "frontal lobe" functions, the frontal lobes are necessary but not sufficient for intact executive functioning. Damage to the frontal lobes, other cortical or subcortical areas, or the connections between these areas and the frontal lobes, can cause mild to severe behavioral and/or cognitive changes viewed as "executive dysfunction."

Development

Unlike more posterior aspects of the cortex, the frontal lobes continue to develop well into adolescence (Blakemore & Choudhury, 2006; St. James-Roberts, 1979). The development of the prefrontal lobe system (i.e., prefrontal association cortex and its subcortical white matter networks) is paralleled by development of higher order cognitive functions (Luna et al., 2010; Stevens et al., 2009). As gray matter density shrinks by means of synaptic pruning and apoptosis, white matter density rises due to increased myelination (Chugani, 1994). This combination of changes increases the efficiency of neuronal processing by strengthening important functional networks and improving their ability to transmit action potentials rapidly (Casey et al., 2005; Kinney et al., 1998).

Based on neuropsychological studies of the development of cognitive functioning, several conclusions can be drawn. First, there appears to be a link between cognitive and physiological development, such that with the continued development of the prefrontal lobe system, there is improvement in executive functioning. Second, performance on different neuropsychological tasks appears to change at different rates (Huizinga et al., 2006; Romine & Reynolds, 2005). Some have interpreted this to suggest that there may be specific subsystems within the prefrontal cortex and adjacent regions that become relatively specialized at mediating particular cognitive tasks, and that their asynchronous development is manifested via differences in the developmental trajectories of specific executive functions (Romine & Reynolds, 2005). However, others have pointed out that many tests of executive functioning are lacking in construct validity (e.g., Strauss et al., 2006), and that task-based approaches to measuring executive functions limits our ability to understand the relationship between physical and cognitive development, both in early and late life (Daniels et al., 2006).

This point should not be overlooked. At the present time, our understanding of executive functioning, particularly as it pertains to the stages of life that involve steady changes in both physiology and cognition (i.e., childhood development and senescence), is based primarily on neuropsychological and cognitive test performance. As stated by Daniels et al. (2006), both cognitive and neuropsychological tests provide significant barriers to interpretation. By their very nature, executive functions do not allow for the isolated measurement of specific individual abilities; rather, all tests of executive functioning require the integration of numerous cognitive abilities. As such, an intuitive approach to interpreting performance on these tasks may lead to incorrect conclusions (Daniels et al., 2006).

Specific Executive Functions: Definitions and Descriptions

As stated above, "executive functioning" is not a specific cognitive function. Rather, executive functions refer to a relatively diverse constellation of behaviors, all of which are involved, to some extent, in the maintenance of goal-directed behaviors. In this section, specific behaviors and skills typically included in the umbrella definition of executive functioning (see Table 13.1) will be described. It should be noted that there is no universally accepted definition or consensus of what the specific executive behaviors and skills are. For this chapter, we have included a relatively inclusive set of functions. It should also be noted that many of these functions are not independent of each other. That is, there can be significant overlap among the various executive functions.

Table 13.1   Specific executive functions

Executive function
Volition
Motivation
Awareness of self and environment
Social awareness
Initiation
Inhibition and impulse control
Perseverance
Generativity
Working memory
Cognitive response set
Planning and organizing
Abstraction
Judgment and decision making
Self-monitoring

Volition

Volition is the process of ascertaining one's needs or wants and forming a plan to achieve those goals (Lezak et al., 2004). A similar construct, conation, has been defined as "the ability to apply one's abilities purposefully, persistently, and effectively as required by the task at hand" (Reitan & Wolfson, 2005, p.957). Impairments in volition cause an inability to initiate activities except in relation to baser instincts. Patients with impaired volition may appear passive, withdrawn, and anergic (Lezak et al., 2004).

Motivation

Motivation is indicated by initiation in conversation and activity. Patients with motivational deficits follow routines rather than engaging with other people and participating in new and enjoyable activities (Lezak et al., 2004). Although the term "abulia" is often used to describe a lack of "drive," it can also appropriately be used to describe a lack of motivation.

Awareness of self and environment

Self-awareness involves knowledge and understanding of one's physical, psychological, cognitive, and social abilities (Lezak et al., 2004). Appreciation of one's interactions with the environment and other people, as well as the ability to read and respond to social cues, plays an integral role in intact self-awareness. A severe impairment in self-awareness can cause anosognosia, or unawareness of illness/deficits, which some have posited is due to a deficit in self-monitoring (Stuss & Benson, 1986).

Social awareness

Social awareness is the understanding of social roles and acceptable social behavior (Lezak et al., 2004). Intact social awareness ensures that goals and interactions with other people follow social norms.

Initiation

Initiation is the ability to begin goal-directed behaviors. Deficits in initiation, which have been variously termed apathy, inertia, or adynamia, may result in difficulty in executing a desired plan. External cueing can help patients overcome initiation deficits (O'Connell et al., 2003), showing that there is a dissociation between the initiation of a behavior and the actual ability to carry out the behavior.

Inhibition and impulse control

The ability to inhibit is multidimensional. The inhibition, or filtering, of irrelevant stimuli in order to channel cognitive resources to the intended stimuli also can be referred to as an aspect of selective attention. Appropriate inhibition requires contextual knowledge; that is, awareness of the expectations of behavior in a particular situation.

Difficulty exerting inhibitory control is manifest in numerous ways. Distractibility is a behavioral symptom of deficits in sustained attention and inhibition of a response to irrelevant stimuli. The term disinhibition is often used to describe abnormal impulsivity that results in socially or contextually inappropriate behaviors and/or difficulties with comportment. Socially inappropriate behavior results from the inability to inhibit instinctual responses or a lack of awareness of – or disregard for – socially accepted norms. An inability to inhibit instinctual urges can result in behavioral disturbances such as overeating and hypersexuality (Fuster, 1997). Utilization behavior is the disinhibited, uncontrolled, and inappropriate use of an object in the environment (Eslinger, 2002). A patient demonstrating utilization behavior may use the object correctly, but its use occurs without consideration of the appropriate context. Disinhibition can also be seen in the pathological replication of another person's actions or gestures (echopraxia) or vocal utterances (echolalia; Loring, 1999).

Perseverance

Perseverance is required to carry tasks through to completion successfully (Lezak et al., 2004). A lack of perseverance is associated with behavioral symptoms of impulsivity, distractibility, and difficulty completing tasks. Motor impersistence is the inability to sustain a repetitive motor task. Perseveration, or the continuation of a previously correct response or behavior after it ceases to be acceptable, may reflect difficulty shifting the focus of one's actions or intentions.

Generativity

Generativity is the ability to fluently produce responses or alternative options within a defined constraint. It relies on the ability to employ strategies for generating appropriate responses, to change strategies after exhaustion of a strategy, and to monitor responses to ensure that they fit the constraints and that they have not been previously generated. Ineffective strategies, deficits in self-monitoring, and perseveration on one concept can lead to deficits in generativity.

Working memory

Working memory has been defined as "a temporary storage system under attentional control that underpins our capacity for complex thought" (Baddeley, 2007). A four-component model has been proposed, consisting of the phonological loop, the visuospatial sketchpad, the central executive, and the episodic buffer. The phonological loop and visuospatial sketch pad serve as temporary holding centers for auditory and visual information, respectively. The episodic buffer serves to link working memory to long-term stores for the formation of stable engrams in long-term memory. The central executive coordinates the activity of the other three components, and relies heavily on intact frontal lobe functioning. It has been suggested that the central executive is involved in the tasks of focusing attention, dividing attention, switching attention, and integrating working memory and long-term memory.

Establishing, maintaining, and shifting of cognitive response set

Cognitive response set refers to the routines and rules required to carry out a task. It involves three components: establishing, maintaining, and shifting set (Stern & Prohaska, 1996). Establishing set is the ability to comprehend and effectively engage in a task to be performed. Impairments in establishing set cause difficulty in learning or performing new behaviors. Maintaining set is the ability to continue to perform an activity across time even in the presence of distractions. Deficits in maintaining set can be seen in the inability to complete a task. Shifting set is the ability to change responses in accordance with changing requirements of a task. Perseveration is a sign of impairment in shifting set, as the person is unable to switch to the new task demands and inappropriately continues the previous task.

Cognitive flexibility is the ability to change attention, actions, or cognitive processes based on changing demands. Deficits in cognitive flexibility can result in impairment in shifting set, rigidity in problem solving, the inability to alter behaviors under changing task demands, responding based only on the most salient features of a target ("stimulus pull"), perseveration of previously generated responses, and stereotyped behaviors (Lezak et al., 2004).

Planning and organizing

Planning requires the ability to think prospectively, to conceive of the various available options, and to make decisions based on those options. The components of the plan must then be organized into the proper sequential order or meaningful gestalt. Patients with frontal system dysfunction causing deficits in planning and organization are unable to formulate a plan or to modify the plan during the course of execution (Grafman, 2007). They are also inefficient, susceptible to interference, unable to allocate cognitive resources appropriately when faced with multiple task demands, and cannot integrate discrete bits of information into an organized, meaningful whole.

Abstraction

Abstraction is the ability to think in terms of concepts or generalizations as well as the ability to think about people, events, or situations of the past, future, or imagined. Patients with deficits in abstraction have impairments in concept formation and are pulled to lower level concrete qualities of objects and ideas. They are unable to make generalizations based on abstract ideas, and rely on concrete attributes, such as color or shape, to categorize items (Lezak et al., 2004).

Judgment and decision making

Judgment and decision making allow one to select the optimal action out of an array of possible routes to completing goal-directed behavior. It relies on the ability to recognize all possible options, to access memory for previous similar situations, and to analyze the resulting outcomes of those previous situations. In addition, one must predict rewards for each option as well as monitor alterations in reward values as they change over time to select the option with the highest benefit compared to risk. For lasting benefit, the reward outcome of the situation must be encoded for future decision making (O'Doherty & Dolan, 2006). Deficits in this area of functioning may result in impaired decisional capacity for specific areas of independent living (e.g., financial, medical, living situation); persons with impaired judgment and decision making may therefore be considered to have limited "competence" from a legal perspective.

Self-monitoring

Monitoring is the use of self-generated feedback about goal-directed performance to assure proper execution of a task throughout the duration of the task (Beer et al., 2004). Deficits in self-monitoring can result in inefficient and inaccurate progression to a goal as well as a lack of error correction.

Neuroanatomy

Just as the definition and conceptual framework of executive functioning is complex and diverse, the neuroanatomy underlying these functions is complex and involves numerous cortical and subcortical circuits. It is hoped that the description of the neuroanatomy of executive functioning that follows will persuade the reader that the terms "frontal lobe behavior" or "frontal lobish" do not accurately describe the complex, multifaceted behaviors and associated neuroanatomy involved in executive functioning.

Frontal cortex

Prefrontal cortex

Dorsolateral prefrontal cortex   The dorsolateral prefrontal cortex (DLPFC) consists of Brodmann's areas (BA) 9, 10, and 46 in the superior and middle frontal gyri and the frontal pole (Kaufer, 2007). It contains heteromodal association cortex and has dense bidirectional connections with most cortical areas and a number of subcortical structures (most predominantly the caudate nucleus). DLPFC is involved in planning and organization, working memory, maintaining goal-directed behaviors, and self-monitoring for the purpose of modifying behaviors in response to task demands. The posterior aspect of DLPFC is involved in modulating the allocation of attention to competing stimuli (Petrides & Pandya, 2002).

Ventrolateral prefrontal cortex The ventrolateral prefrontal cortex, BA 45 and 47, consists of heteromodal association cortex (Kaufer, 2007). It receives motivational and emotional information from the limbic system and highly integrated sensory information from both anterior and posterior association cortex. This allows for the binding of sensory information with particular emotional and visceral states for decision making based on the emotional valence and behavioral significance of stimuli (Sakagami & Pan, 2007). This area also appears to play a role in judgment, encoding, and retrieval (Petrides & Pandya, 2002).

Orbitofrontal cortex The orbitofrontal cortex, BA 11 and 12, contains heteromodal association and paralimbic cortex (Kaufer, 2007) and is primarily involved in impulse control, inhibition of responses, and regulation of comportment. It also integrates input from sensory systems and more visceral limbic and paralimbic areas to play a role in regulating emotion, reward, and punishment systems (Ogar & Gorno-Tempini, 2007), which are involved in decision making (Schoenbaum et al., 2006).

Medial frontal cortex The medial frontal cortex, BA 32, which includes the anterior cingulate gyrus and the parolfactory region (BA 24 and 25, respectively), is composed of paralimbic cortex (Kaufer, 2007). The functions of the medial frontal cortex include modulation of attention, arousal, and motivation; disruption of this area is linked to apathy and abulia (Filley, 2000; Kouneiher et al., 2009).

Frontal connectivity to other areas of the brain

Parietal lobe

The main pathway between the parietal lobes and the frontal lobes is the superior longitudinal fasciculus (SLF) which has three components – SLF I, SLF II, and SLF III (Petrides & Pandya, 2002). SLF I travels from the superior and medial aspects of the parietal lobe along the cingulate sulcus to the supplementary motor area and dorsal premotor areas. It is believed to be important for integrating body part location with higher cortical functions. SLF II connects the caudal inferior parietal lobule and occipitoparietal area via the white matter along the Sylvian fissure to the posterior dorsolateral and mid-dorsolateral prefrontal cortex. This pathway sends sensory information about visual space to the frontal lobes and the reciprocal connections modulate allocation of attentional resources in visual space. SLF III originates in the supramarginal gyrus and the parietal operculum and runs along the opercular white matter to the ventral premotor cortex, pars opercularis, frontal operculum, and ventral DLPFC. This tract sends higher order somatosensory information to the frontal lobes for abstraction of actions, imitation of actions, and gesturing, whereas the reciprocal pathway is involved in self-monitoring of facial and hand movements (Petrides & Pandya, 2002).

Occipital lobe

The occipitotemporal (ventral) stream processes visual information relevant to object recognition (Petrides & Pandya, 2002). It originates in the striate cortex in the ventrolateral occipital lobe and connects to the rostral inferotemporal area via the interior longitudinal fasciculus. Fibers then connect from the inferotemporal area to the orbitofrontal and ventrolateral frontal regions via the uncinate fasciculus. Disruption of this pathway can lead to impairments in sustained visual attention, disinhibition, and set maintenance.

The occipitoparietal (dorsal) stream is involved in spatial perception and localization. It connects the medial and dorsal occipital regions to the posterior parietal. There also appears to be a direct pathway between the dorsal and medial occipital lobes and the dorsal and ventral prefrontal areas known as the occipitofrontal fasciculus that transmits information about the peripheral visual field (Petrides & Pandya, 2002). Disruption of this pathway can result in deficits in the visual aspects of self-monitoring, awareness, motivation, and set shifting.

Temporal lobe

Similar to the occipitotemporal and occipitoparietal streams mentioned above, auditory information is also processed by ventral and dorsal streams. The ventral pathway, responsible for object recognition in the auditory modality, runs from the mid-superior temporal gyrus and multimodal superior temporal sulcus through the extreme capsule to the pars triangularis and rostral lateral prefrontal cortex (Petrides & Pandya, 2002).

The dorsal pathway, which handles information related to the spatial aspects of auditory stimuli, connects the superior temporal lobe to the frontal lobe via the arcuate fasciculus (Petrides & Pandya, 2002). This pathway originates in the superior temporal gyrus and in the cortex bounding the superior temporal sulcus. Its processes travel around the parietotemporal junction and follow the SLF II to the posterior dorsolateral prefrontal cortex. A related pathway that also processes auditory spatial information originates in the caudal superior temporal cortex and travels to the caudal dorsolateral prefrontal cortex. The behavioral manifestations of disruptions of these pathways can be viewed as auditory analogies to the visual pathways described above.

Limbic system

The ventral limbic pathways connect the rostral parahippocampal region to the orbital frontal lobe via the uncinate fasciculus; the caudal parahippocampal area to the dorsolateral prefrontal cortex via the extreme capsule; and another region of the parahippocampal area to the medial frontal cortex through the cingulum bundle. The dorsal limbic pathway connects the cingulate cortex and retrosplenial cortex to the mid-dorsolateral prefrontal region, also via the cingulum bundle (Petrides & Pandya, 2002). Links between limbic and paralimbic structures such as the amygdala and orbitofrontal cortex mediate emotional and behavioral functions such as motivation, affect, and comportment; as such, damage to these regions can produce vivid neuropsychiatric symptoms (Cummings & Mega, 2003; Mega et al., 1997; Mesulam, 2000). Links between the prefrontal cortex and medial temporal lobe limbic structures, primarily the hippocampus and entorhinal cortex, are involved in the encoding, retrieval, and recognition processes that take place during recall and recognition memory (Broadbent et al., 2002).

Frontal-subcortical circuits

All frontal-subcortical circuits originate in the frontal cortex and form loops connecting the striatum (caudate, putamen, and ventral striatum), globus pallidus, and the thalamus, and returning back to the frontal cortex. Simply stated, each circuit includes two parallel routes: a "direct" pathway that serves to agonize cortical neurons and an "indirect" pathway that is a cortical antagonist. Uninterrupted, these two pathways maintain cortical equilibrium via their balanced excitatory and inhibitory influences. Asymmetric compromise can lead to either hyper- or hypoactivation of the cortex. Neuroanatomically, each frontal-subcortical circuit is almost completely distinct from the others. Two of these circuits are primarily involved in motor functioning: a skeletomotor circuit originating in the supplementary motor area and an oculomotor circuit originating in the frontal eye fields. The other three circuits are related to aspects of executive functioning. These include the dorsolateral prefrontal-subcortical circuit, the superior medial frontal-subcortical circuit, and the orbitofrontal-subcortical circuit (Chow & Cummings, 2007).

Because these circuits modulate cortical function, the behaviors under the control of these circuits are guided by the cortical areas that they innervate. Disruption of the dorsolateral prefrontal-subcortical circuit therefore may cause an over- or under-activation of DLPFC, depending on the location of the damage, and may give rise to alterations in working memory, task setting, planning, organizing, other goal-directed behaviors, and error detection. Similarly, damage to the superior medial frontal-subcortical circuit can lead to changes in verbal or motor output, motivation, and spontaneity. Damage to the orbitofrontal-subcortical circuits can result in changes in personality, emotional regulation, impulsivity, disinhibition, social behavior, and can disrupt the attachment of emotional valence to new episodic memories (Chow & Cummings, 2007).

Neuropsychological and Neuropsychiatric Assessment of Executive Functions

Performing any act, even a simple task that ostensibly measures a seemingly well-delimited construct (e.g., visuospatial perception), requires a number of executive functions. One model of neuropsychological functioning described by Stern and White (2003) proposes a hierarchy of functions, with executive functioning at the top of this hierarchy and all other functions being subserved under executive functioning (Figure 13.1). Moreover, tests that are designed to specifically measure

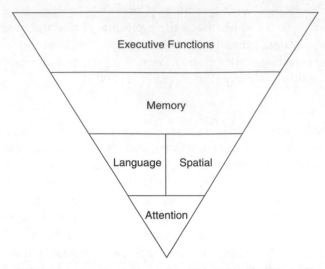

Figure 13.1   Hierarchical model of neuropsychological functions
Reproduced by special permission of the Publisher, Psychological Assessment Resources, Inc., 16204 North Florida Avenue, Lutz, Florida 33549, from the Neuropsychological Assessment Battery by Robert A. Stern, Ph.D. and Travis White, Ph.D., Copyright 2001, 2003 by PAR, Inc. Further reproduction is prohibited without permission from PAR, Inc.

executive functioning suffer from limitations to both comprehensiveness and specificity. That is, because of the diverse and multifaceted nature of the executive functions, a single test is unable to measure "executive functioning" as a unitary construct and is also unable to isolate a single subcomponent of this domain from other executive and non-executive functions. This "task impurity problem" in measuring executive functioning (e.g., Burgess, 1997; Miyake & Shah, 1999; Phillips, 1997) suggests that a single test or even a battery of tests may provide an incomplete or inaccurate picture of an individual's overall "executive functioning." Furthermore, the underlying processes used to perform a test of executive functioning may change with age (Hull et al., 2008). Another limitation of purported executive measures was addressed by Lezak et al. (2004), who argued that because executive functions are, by definition, those processes used to accomplish goal-directed behaviors in the absence of structure and direction, the structured nature of neuropsychological testing impedes the ability of the test to validly measure executive functioning. Therefore, not only must a good test of executive functioning have desirable levels of reliability and validity, it must also strike a balance between preserving standardization for proper psychometric interpretation and allowing the examinee to structure his or her environment as much as possible.

In spite of these limitations, neuropsychological assessment of executive functioning has demonstrated value in the evaluation of older adults. For example, recent studies have revealed an association between performance on tests of execu-

Table 13.2 Instruments used to measure executive functioning in dementia

Individual tests	Test batteries	Questionnaires
Wisconsin Card Sorting Test (WCST)	Behavioral Assessment of the Dysexecutive Syndrome (BADS)	Neuropsychiatric Inventory (NPI)
Rey–Osterrieth Complex Figure Test (ROCFT)	Delis–Kaplan Executive Function System (D-KEFS)	Executive Interview (EXIT25)
Halstead Category Test	Dementia Rating Scale (DRS) • initiation/perseveration • conceptualization	Frontal Systems Behavior Scale (FrSBe)
Trail Making Test	Neuropsychological Assessment Battery (NAB) • executive functions module	Behavioral Rating Inventory of Executive Function for Adults (BRIEF-A)
Verbal and Design Fluency Tests (e.g., FAS, Animal Fluency, Ruff Figural Fluency Test)	Wechsler Adult Intelligence Scales (WAIS) • block design • similarities	Dysexecutive Questionnaire (DEX)
Stroop Color-Word Test		Middelheim Frontality Score (MFS)

tive functioning and driving ability, everyday problem solving, instrumental activities of daily living (IADLs), functional decline and mortality (Amirian et al., 2010; Bell-McGinty et al., 2002; Burton et al., 2006; Cahn-Weiner et al., 2007; Giovannetti et al., 2006; Jefferson et al., 2006; Ott et al., 2003; Whelihan et al., 2005).

The formal assessment of executive functioning in dementia can range from a simple bedside examination to a comprehensive laboratory-based battery of executive function tests, to the use of informant rating scales. Below, we describe some of the most commonly used assessment tools in the neuropsychological assessment of executive functioning. This listing (Table 13.2) is not meant to be all-inclusive. The reader interested in more comprehensive descriptions of available executive functioning tests is referred to Lezak et al. (2004) and Strauss et al. (2006).

Wisconsin Card Sorting Test

The Wisconsin Card Sorting Test (WCST; Heaton et al., 1993) measures an examinee's concept formation and ability to generate, maintain, and shift strategies based on feedback from the examiner. The examinee is shown four key cards, each portraying a figure of varying shape, color, or number of objects on the card. The examinee must attempt to match additional cards that have varying combinations of the three aforementioned traits to one of the four key cards based on a matching property that is known only to the examiner. The examiner gives feedback on whether the examinee's response corresponds to the undisclosed matching rule. The examiner's rule changes throughout the course of the test without warning to the examinee. Patients with "frontal lobe damage" make more perseverative errors, lose set more often, and achieve fewer categories (Lezak et al., 2004).

Rey–Osterrieth Complex Figure Test

The Rey–Osterrieth Complex Figure Test (ROCFT) is a visuoconstructional and visual memory test that requires the examinee to copy a complex geometric line drawing and later reproduce the drawing from memory. Because of the complexity of the figure, this test, especially the copy condition, is thought to rely heavily on planning, organization, and problem-solving abilities (Strauss et al., 2006). These qualitative aspects can provide valuable information about an examinee's cognitive abilities. Along these lines, the Boston Qualitative Scoring System (BQSS; Stern et al., 1999) for the ROCFT generates five scores of executive function based on qualitative features of the examinee's drawing: fragmentation, planning, neatness, perseveration, and organization. Performance on the ROCFT, as measured by the BQSS, has been shown to correlate with other neuropsychological tests of executive function (Somerville et al., 2000).

Halstead Category Test

The Category Test, which is part of the Halstead–Reitan Neuropsychological Battery (HRNB; Reitan & Wolfson, 1993) measures a person's ability to learn a changing classification system over seven subtests. Similar to the WCST, the new classification rule for each set must be deduced by the examinee based on feedback from the examiner. This test assesses an examinee's abilities in abstraction, concept formation, cognitive flexibility, problem solving, and ability to learn from feedback. The computerized version of this test also allows for analysis of reaction time.

Trail Making Test

The Trail Making Test (Reitan & Wolfson, 1993) has two portions, Part A and Part B. Part A is primarily a test of attention, scanning, and psychomotor speed; whereas Part B is a more complex task that places demands on set maintenance abilities (i.e., maintaining the set of alternating between number and letter), and the time taken to complete these tasks is the primary variable of interest. Common errors on this test include set loss errors and sequencing errors. These errors may be interpreted as reflecting difficulties with set maintenance, impulsivity, perseveration, or reduced mental flexibility; normative data have recently been published to assist with the interpretation of errors made by older adults (Ashendorf et al., 2008).

Verbal and Design Fluency Tests

The most common verbal fluency tests assess an individual's ability to spontaneously produce words from a specified semantic category or beginning with a particular letter. In most verbal fluency tasks, the examinee is asked to generate, usually in one minute, as many words as possible from a particular category (e.g., animals; referred to as category or semantic fluency) or beginning with a certain letter (e.g., "F;" referred to as letter, phonemic, or phonological fluency). Performance on this test has been shown to be related to processing speed, initiation, working memory, and attentional control (Strauss et al., 2006). Damage to the frontal lobe system has been associated with impairments in both letter and category fluency (Henry & Crawford, 2004; Iudicello et al., 2007) due to the demands both tasks place on verbal search and retrieval processes. In contrast, temporal lobe compromise has been found to lead to greater impairment in category fluency relative to letter fluency (Henry & Crawford, 2004; Henry et al., 2004), which may reflect a breakdown in the structure or accessibility of semantic networks (Butters et al., 1987; Cerhan et al., 2002).

Tests of design fluency are also measures of generativity, and offer a nonverbal analog to tests of verbal letter fluency. For example, the Ruff Figural Fluency Test (RFFT; Ruff, 1996) requires the respondent to generate as many unique figures as possible in a specified duration by drawing lines to connect a group of dots on a page.

Stroop Color-Word Test

The Stroop is used to evaluate inhibition, mental control, working memory, and processing speed. Although administration procedures vary by publisher, it is common for the test to contain three conditions. The first requires the examinee to rapidly read color words printed in black ink (e.g., "red," "blue," "green"); the second to rapidly state the ink colors of non-word stimuli; and the third to rapidly name ink colors when written in a discordant color word (e.g., the word "red" printed in blue ink would require the response "blue"). The amount of interference produced by this third task can be predicted on the basis of performance on the word reading and color naming tasks, and substantial deviations from this prediction may reflect difficulty inhibiting a prepotent, automatized response (word reading) in favor of a less dominant response (color naming). This is often referred to as the "Stroop effect." Examinees with executive dysfunction tend to make more errors and/or complete the task less quickly.

Test batteries

Behavioral Assessment of the Dysexecutive Syndrome

The Behavioral Assessment of the Dysexecutive System (BADS; Wilson et al., 1996) is a battery of tests designed to detect subtle changes in executive functioning. Using six tests and a self- and informant-report questionnaire, (the Dysexecutive Questionnaire, see below), the BADS provides information about planning, organizing, problem solving, set shifting, and judgment of time. It yields scores for each individual test (Temporal Judgment, Rule Shift Cards, Action Program, Key Search, Zoo Map, and Modified Six Elements) as well as an overall summary score, which has been normed on individuals ranging from ages 16–87.

Delis–Kaplan Executive Function System

The Delis–Kaplan Executive Function System (D-KEFS; Delis et al., 2001) is a battery of nine tests aimed at assessing the higher level executive functions and the basic abilities that underlie them. Using a process approach, the tests in this battery attempt to isolate the various component skills thought to be important for the successful completion of the most cognitively demanding tasks. This battery includes variants of other commonly used tests, including a Trail Making Test, a Verbal Fluency Test, a Design Fluency Test, a Color-Word Test akin to the Stroop, and a Sorting Test that resembles the Neuropsychological Assessment Battery (NAB) Categories test. It also includes the Twenty Question Test, which examines problem solving based on feedback; the Word Context Test for measuring reasoning and abstraction; the Tower Test to measure planning, rule acquisition, and inhibition; and the Proverb Test to measure abstract reasoning via metaphor. Consistent with the process approach, it does not generate a single summary score of overall executive functioning.

Dementia Rating Scale

The Dementia Rating Scale (DRS; Mattis, 1988, 2004) contains a number of tests of executive functioning that comprise two scales: an Initiation/Perseveration scale, and a Conceptualization scale. The Initiation/Perseveration scale includes measures of verbal control, verbal fluency, and motor and graphomotor sequencing. Each of these tasks is intended to measure an examinee's ability to initiate and maintain a behavior without perseveration.

The Conceptualization scale from the DRS is a test of verbal abstract reasoning similar to that seen on several Wechsler scales (see below). In this test, examinees are asked to describe how two words are alike, and abstract responses are thought to reflect better verbal conceptualization abilities. Because the DRS is designed to have a very low floor for the assessment of patients at various stages of dementia, this test also includes multiple choice and priming tasks to assess this construct in low-functioning individuals who may have disturbances of communication.

Executive Functions Module from the Neuropsychological Assessment Battery

The Neuropsychological Assessment Battery (NAB; Stern & White, 2003) Executive Functions Module contains four tests: Mazes, Judgment, Categories, and Word Generation. Each of these tests has two alternate forms. The Mazes test measures aspects of visuospatial planning and may be sensitive to impulsivity and deficits in psychomotor speed. The Judgment test was designed to be an ecologically valid test of knowledge and problem-solving ability related to health and home safety. The Categories test (not to be confused with the Halstead Category Test) requires examinees to categorize pictures of six people into two groups, each containing two or more members, based on the various characteristics displayed in the pictures. The respondent is then provided with another set of pictures of six different people; the characteristics by which categorization can be made on the new set are different from those in the first. Successful performance on this task is thought to be mediated by intact conceptualization, cognitive flexibility, and generativity. An aspect of verbal generativity is measured by the NAB Word Generation test. In this test, the examinee is given a series of eight letters (printed vertically on a card), including both consonants and vowels, and is asked to produce as many different, real three-letter words as possible from these letters. It is thought to rely less on language functioning than other tests of verbal generativity and is less dependent on educational experience. Deficits in self-monitoring on this test may also lead to an increased number of perseverations (i.e., repeating the same answer more than once).

Wechsler Adult Intelligence Scales

The Wechsler Adult Intelligence Scales (WAIS, WAIS-R, WAIS-III; WAIS-IV; Wechsler, 1981, 1997, 1999, 2008) include several neuropsychological measures that can be used to investigate executive functioning.

Block Design   The Block Design subtest from the WAIS is a test of visuospatial construction. The examinee is presented with red and white blocks and asked to construct the blocks in the pattern that matches the design on the stimulus card. Although the Block Design subtest appears to rely heavily on organization, planning, and problem-solving skills, it yields only a single score that, in the WAIS-III, loads on the factors of Perceptual Organization and Performance Intelligence. As such, interpretations of executive functioning made on the basis of Block Design performance must rely on the qualitative aspects of the patient's performance or a process approach (e.g., Kaplan et al., 1991; Milberg et al., 1996; Ogden, 2005).

Similarities   The Similarities test found in the WAIS is a measure of verbal conceptualization similar to the DRS subtest described above. In this test, the examinee is given pairs of words and asked to describe how they are the same, with the correct response being a superordinate concept (Lezak et al., 2004). This open-ended test allows for the assessment of an examinee's abstract reasoning skills.

Questionnaires

Neuropsychiatric Inventory
The Neuropsychiatric Inventory (NPI; Cummings et al., 1994) is an interview conducted by a clinician with a caregiver about the presence of delusions, hallucinations, agitation, depression, anxiety, elation, apathy, disinhibition, irritability, and abnormalities of motor behavior, nighttime behaviors, and appetite/eating in the patient (Lezak et al., 2004). A briefer Neuropsychiatric Inventory Questionnaire (NPI-Q) is also available (Kaufer et al., 2000). The presence of apathy and disinhibition can be viewed as neuropsychiatric features of executive dysfunction.

Executive Interview
The Executive Interview (EXIT25) is a brief 25-item bedside assessment of "executive control" (Royall et al., 1992). It involves a series of tasks that, in patients with executive dysfunction, may result in perseveration, utilization behavior, disinhibition, imitation, echolalia, and echopraxia.

Frontal Systems Behavior Scale
Another inventory of behavioral symptoms of frontal lobe damage, the Frontal Systems Behavior Scale (FrSBe), is used to examine executive dysfunction (Grace & Malloy, 2001). This questionnaire, which allows for both self-report and informant rating, has three subscales measuring changes in apathy, disinhibition, and executive dysfunction (involving more cognitive aspects of executive function).

Behavioral Rating Inventory of Executive Function for Adults
The Behavioral Rating Inventory of Executive Function for Adults (BRIEF-A; Roth et al., 2005) is similar to the FrSBe in that it is both a self- and informant-based questionnaire of everyday behavior symptoms of executive dysfunction and impairments in self-regulation. It measures inhibition, self-monitoring, planning and organization, shifting, initiation, task monitoring, emotional control, and working memory. In addition, comparison of the self-report to the informant rating can provide information about a patient's insight into his or her deficits. A recent study found that the BRIEF-A was able to identify subtle executive function changes, particularly for working memory, that were not seen on other neuropsychological tests (Rabin et al., 2006).

Dysexecutive Questionnaire
The Dysexecutive Questionnaire (DEX), part of the Behavioral Assessment of the Dysexecutive System (BADS; Wilson et al., 1996), is given to the patient and family member or other informant to measure everyday behavioral symptoms of executive function (Strauss et al., 2006). It assesses the presence of impairments in abstract

thinking, impulse control, planning, insight, inhibition, concern for oneself and social norms, and the presence of confabulation, perseveration, apathy, and distractibility.

Middelheim Frontality Score

The Middelheim Frontality Score (MFS; De Deyn et al., 2005) is a 10-point clinician rating scale developed to differentiate between Alzheimer's disease and frontotemporal dementia based on behavioral observations that relate to the disease course of progressive dementias. The items target memory, spatial functioning, insight and judgment, eating behavior, sexual behavior, stereotyped behavior, emotional control, aspontaneity, speech disturbances, and restlessness. Patients with FTD have been shown to score significantly higher on this scale than patients with AD (DeDeyn et al., 2005).

Executive Functioning in Dementia

In the next section, we describe a number of dementia syndromes and the ways in which executive functioning is disrupted by these conditions. As more detailed information pertaining to the clinical presentation of each dementia can be found elsewhere in this volume, our discussion will focus primarily on executive functioning.

Alzheimer's disease

Alzheimer's disease (AD) is characterized primarily by episodic memory impairment; other cognitive features include deficits in language, visuospatial functioning, and executive functioning, with behavioral deficits often part of the overall profile as well (Yaari & Corey-Bloom, 2007; see Chapter 1 in current volume). AD is characterized by an insidious onset with a slow, gradual progression and a duration averaging seven years before death (Turner, 2003); it is rare before age 60. AD accounts for approximately 47–75% of all progressive neurodegenerative dementias (Costa et al., 1996; Fratiglioni et al., 1999), with the latest estimate in the United States being 70% (Plassman et al., 2007). It is estimated that there are over five million people with AD in the United States alone, with this number expected to grow to nearly eight million by 2030 (Alzheimer's Association, 2009).

The earliest changes in AD are usually observed in episodic memory, often detected by deficits in delayed recall of verbal and visual material. Although the early memory impairment is usually greater than the impairment in other domains (Reed et al., 2007), mild impairments in executive functioning may also be observed prior to the formal diagnosis of AD (Albert et al., 2007; Backman et al., 2005; Grober et al., 2008; Hodges et al., 1999; Jenner et al., 2006).

Neuropsychiatric symptoms

The behavioral and psychiatric symptoms most often exhibited by patients with AD include psychosis, disturbances in activity, and aggressiveness (Engelborghs et al., 2006). Agitation/aggression, depression, anxiety, apathy, irritability, aberrant motor behavior, and appetite disturbances may be present in at least 40% of patients with AD, with apathy occurring most often (Caputo et al., 2008; Hollingworth et al., 2006).

Awareness of self and environment

In one study, over 60% of patients with AD were found to have reduced insight (Vogel et al., 2005); this has been shown to include a lack of self-awareness of memory difficulties and lack of insight into behavioral and personality changes, such as apathy, submissiveness, and extraversion (Banks & Weintraub, 2008; Eslinger et al., 2005; Rankin et al., 2005; Souchay et al., 2003). This anosognosia can have important implications for patient safety, as a loss of insight may prevent individuals from making the compensations necessary to appropriately manage potentially dangerous situations (Starkstein et al., 2007).

Inhibition and impulse control

Studies using the Stroop test have found that, compared to controls, patients with AD take longer to complete the test (Amieva et al., 2004; Bélanger et al., 2010; Delazer et al., 2007; Graham et al., 2004) and make more errors (Amieva et al., 2004; Bélanger et al., 2010). In addition, it was found that patients with AD experience difficulty inhibiting rules from previous trials on new tasks (Amieva et al., 2004; Bélanger et al., 2010).

When comparing patients with AD to patients with other dementias, those with AD have been shown to demonstrate fewer symptoms of behavioral disinhibition (Steinberg et al., 2006). However, behavioral disinhibition becomes more common with increasing AD severity (Stout et al., 2003), and patients with AD who happen to exhibit behavioral disinhibition at any time in the course of the illness place a greater amount of burden on their caregivers than those who are not behaviorally disinhibited (Allegri et al., 2006).

Perseveration and repetition

It has been estimated that 87% of those with AD may engage in abnormally repetitive behavior, such as repetitive questioning, repetitive statements and stories, and repetitive actions. As would be expected, repetitive questioning was found to be related to memory performance; however, in one study, repetitive statements, stories, and actions were more highly correlated with the DEX, a behavioral questionnaire of dysexecutive symptoms (Cullen et al., 2005).

Individuals with AD are more likely to perseverate on tests of verbal recall (Sebastian et al., 2006), verbal fluency (Marczinski & Kertesz, 2006; Pekkala et al., 2008), and set shifting (i.e., the WCST; Traykov et al., 2005), due to deficits in working memory, self-monitoring, and mental flexibility.

Generativity

Individuals with AD and preclinical AD have been shown to perform significantly worse than elderly controls on tests of letter and category fluency (Delazer et al., 2007; Giovagnoli et al., 2008; Griffith et al., 2003; Jones et al., 2006; Levinoff et al., 2006; Marczinski & Kertesz, 2006; McGuiness et al., 2010), although this finding has not been entirely consistent in the literature (see Graham et al., 2004). Patients with AD produce fewer atypical words and fewer words overall than elderly controls on category fluency tasks, with the largest discrepancies at later serial positions (Sailor et al., 2004). A meta-analysis revealed that patients with AD suffer from greater impairment in category fluency compared to letter fluency (Henry et al., 2004), which, as a result of the significant temporal lobe pathology in AD, is thought to be due to a disruption in semantic networks (Salmon et al., 1999). Not surprisingly, category fluency has been found to be more diagnostically useful than letter fluency, with both being superior to a letter-category fluency difference score, in the detection of AD (Cerhan et al., 2002).

A qualitative analysis of verbal fluency tasks has shown that patients with mild AD utilize fewer clusters, generate smaller clusters, and perform less switching than do normal controls (Gomez & White, 2006).

Working memory

Many tests of working memory have yielded significant differences between patients with AD and healthy controls. AD often causes impairment on tests of backward digit (Delazer et al., 2007; Halpern et al., 2003; Sinz et al., 2008) and spatial spans (Giovagnoli et al., 2008; Levinoff et al., 2006), letter–number sequencing tasks (Levinoff et al., 2006; Griffith et al., 2003), n-back tests (Waltz et al., 2004), verbal and visual short-term memory tasks (McGuinness et al., 2010), and tests of multiple letter cancellation (de Jager et al., 2003). Patients with AD have also been shown to have deficits performing tests of oral calculation, which can be attributed in part to reductions in working memory; these reductions interfere with mental arithmetic by limiting the amount of information available for online processing (Halpern et al., 2003).

In regard to Baddeley's (Baddeley & Hitch, 1974) model of working memory, evidence from studies on AD patients suggests that the central executive system is disrupted in early AD, whereas the episodic buffer, visuospatial sketchpad, and phonological loop are impaired with increasing dementia severity (Huntley & Howard, 2010).

Establishing, maintaining, and shifting of cognitive response set

Studies have reported that patients with AD, even at the very mild stages, perform significantly worse than elderly controls on part B of the Trail Making Test, which requires response set maintenance, among other cognitive processes (Baudic et al., 2006; Delazer et al., 2007; Giovagnoli et al., 2008; Yuspeh et al., 2002). On a test of mental control, patients with AD were found to have difficulty maintaining cognitive set in early phases of the test (Lamar et al., 2002). And as mentioned previously, the WCST tends to elicit numerous perseverative errors from patients with AD, suggesting difficulties with response set maintenance (Traykov et al., 2005).

Planning and organizing

A recent study found that 58% of patients with AD scored below cutoff on a maze navigation task, which is thought to require problem solving, planning, and impulse control. In contrast, only 2% of controls scored below cutoff (Swanberg et al., 2004). On another task that relies heavily on organization and planning, the clock drawing task, individuals with AD performed significantly worse than older controls (Griffith et al., 2003; de Jager et al., 2003; McGuinness et al., 2010). AD patients also show impaired performance on tower tests, which requires planning and adherence to rules (Carey et al., 2008; Franceschi et al., 2007).

AD patients also have impaired decision making. In a study investigating decision making in conditions of varying risk and with or without obvious consequences, patients with mild AD failed to develop advantageous strategies and maintain beneficial response patterns compared to healthy elderly controls (Sinz et al., 2008).

Abstraction

Koenig et al. (2007) found that individuals with AD performed worse and had longer response latencies than controls on a task requiring categorization of stimuli based on rules defining category membership. In contrast, the two groups did not differ when asked to choose stimuli based on superficial (i.e., appearance) similarities. Performance on the rule-based task was found to correlate with other measures of executive function, leading the authors to suggest that intact working memory, inhibition, and selective attention are necessary for rule-based categorization.

Patients with AD, even very mild, have been found to perform worse than controls on the WCST and Modified WCST (Baudic et al., 2006; Graham et al., 2004; Souchay et al., 2003), with fewer categories and more perseverations, suggesting difficulty in the ability to generate and/or maintain the concepts necessary for correct sorting.

Vascular dementia

Vascular dementia (VaD) is the second-most common cause of dementia, accounting for approximately 10–38% of all dementias worldwide (Fratiglioni et al., 1999; Román, 2003), with the latest estimate being 17% in the United States (Plassman et al., 2007). It is a dementia syndrome that can be caused by ischemic lesions due to multiple infarcts, single isolated infarcts, ischemic changes in subcortical nuclei and white matter, chronic hypoperfusion, or hemorrhaging (Jellinger, 2008; Korczyn, 2002; Sachdev et al., 2004). Because of the wide range of events capable of producing cerebrovascular disease, the clinical picture of VaD can be quite variable, and depends on factors such as the size and location of the lesion(s). See Chapter 2 in this volume for a complete review.

Three vascular dementia syndromes are commonly described: multi-infarct, strategic single infarct, and small vessel disease with dementia (Aggarwal & DeCarli, 2007; Román et al., 1993). However, due to the nature of cerebrovascular disease, it might be argued that subtyping of VaD is likely to be misleading (Sachdev et al., 2004). So-called multi-infarct dementia is thought to occur as a result of multiple occlusions of the cerebral vasculature that leads to infarction in cortical or subcortical areas. Strategic single infarct vascular dementia involves a lesion in a distinct area that is associated with a specific cognitive function, and therefore leads to circumscribed cognitive deficits. Subcortical ischemic vascular dementia is a term used to describe the occlusion of small vessels, resulting in damage to subcortical structures and their white matter connections (Román, 2003). Whether the primary areas of infarction are cortical, subcortical, or both, may affect the clinical presentation of the dementia, both in terms of neuropsychiatric and cognitive impairments (Fuh et al., 2005; Gunstad et al., 2005; Lamar et al., 2004; Paul et al., 2001; Reed et al., 2004; Saczynski et al., 2009). Commonly, VaD causes deficits predominantly in executive functioning, with other cognitive deficits varying between patients (Desmond, 2004). However, some studies have revealed that VaD can cause global disruption of neuropsychological functioning, including deficits in executive functioning, psychomotor speed, verbal and visual memory, language, and visuospatial functioning, even in mild VaD (Paul et al., 2001).

Vascular dementia has a median age of onset of about 80 years (Knopman et al., 2003). Both multi-infarct dementia and strategic single infarct vascular dementia are characterized by an abrupt onset and stepwise progression. In contrast, small vessel disease with dementia has an insidious onset and a slow gradual progression (Aggarwal & DeCarli, 2007).

Neuropsychiatric symptoms

Vascular dementia is associated with a wide array of neuropsychiatric disturbances. Regardless of the primary site of infarction, at least 20% of patients with VaD were found to exhibit delusions, hallucinations, depression, anxiety, apathy, irritability, agitation, disinhibition, aberrant motor behavior, altered sleep, and a change in appetite. Only euphoria was manifested in fewer than 20% of patients. Among these symptoms, depression, apathy, agitation, altered sleep, and change in appetite were experienced by greater than 40% of all patients with VaD (Fuh et al., 2005).

In general, neuropsychiatric symptoms are most likely to occur following cortical infarction and least likely to occur following subcortical infarction, with mixed cortical-subcortical infarctions producing neuropsychiatric symptoms at an intermediate rate. The three most common neuropsychiatric features of cortical VaD were apathy, agitation, and altered sleep (prevalence of 60% or greater for all three); depression, apathy, and altered sleep were most typical of subcortical VaD (prevalence of 45% or greater for all three); and apathy, agitation, and altered sleep were most typical of mixed VaD (prevalence of 50% or greater for all three) (Fuh et al., 2005).

Executive dysfunction

Executive dysfunction is typically thought of as the primary cognitive deficit produced by VaD. Lamar et al. (2004) found that patients with VaD have a pronounced impairment in the ability to inhibit irrelevant stimuli, and problems with inhibition have been detected on the Stroop task (Graham et al., 2004; Yuspeh et al., 2002).

Deficits in generativity are also evident in VaD (McGuiness et al., 2010), with letter fluency typically more impaired than category fluency. Patients with VaD have been found to generate fewer words than controls on category fluency, and fewer words than controls, patients with depression, and patients with FTD on letter fluency. There have been mixed findings when comparing patients with VaD and AD on letter fluency tests (Braaten et al., 2006; Graham et al., 2004; Lamar et al., 2002; Yuspeh et al., 2002), which may be due to the heterogeneity of cerebrovascular impairment in VaD; cortical lesions may be necessary to produce lower letter fluency scores in VaD relative to AD (Yuspeh et al., 2002).

Verbal and visual working memory deficits have also been noted in patients with VaD (McGuinness et al., 2010). Graham et al. (2004) found that patients with VaD have a significantly shorter backward digit span compared to controls.

On a measure of response set maintenance, part B of the Trail Making Test, patients with subcortical ischemic VaD were found to perform worse than controls (Yuspeh et al., 2002). Compared to patients with AD, patients with VaD have been shown to make errors suggestive of difficulties establishing and maintaining set, such as a greater number of errors on the beginning of the test and more commission than omission errors overall (Lamar et al., 2002). Difficulties with organization and planning can be seen in patients with VaD on visuoconstructional tasks such as the clock drawing test (de Jager et al., 2003; McGuiness et al., 2010) and the ROCFT. On the latter test, the constructions of patients with VaD contained more fragmentation, omissions, and perseverations than did patients with AD and elderly controls (Freeman et al., 2000).

Frontotemporal dementia

Frontotemporal dementia (FTD) is a dementia syndrome that is predominantly characterized by changes in executive function and behavior. Neurodegeneration occurs in the frontal and temporal lobes, whereas the parietal and occipital lobes are generally spared (Lezak et al., 2004). The frontal variant of FTD accounts for about 70% of FTD cases (Snowden et al., 2002). It is primarily a behavioral disorder characterized by severe degeneration of the orbitofrontal cortex. Please see Chapter 4 in this volume for a complete review of FTD.

Semantic dementia (SD; Hodges et al., 1999), a variant of FTD that primarily affects the temporal lobes, accounts for about 15% of FTD cases (Snowden et al., 2002). It is characterized by a progressive loss in semantic knowledge and organization. This leads to severe naming and word comprehension impairments, in the context of otherwise preserved language, resulting in speech that is fluent but devoid of content (Grossman & Ash, 2004).

Primary progressive aphasia (PPA; Mesulam, 2003; Murman, 2003; Snowden et al., 2002), another FTD subtype, accounts for about 10% of FTD cases (Snowden et al., 2002). The fluent form of PPA is often categorized as semantic dementia because it has a similar clinical profile and usually progresses to semantic dementia. However, it does not produce agnosia, which is required for a diagnosis of semantic dementia (Adlam et al., 2006; Mesulam, 2003). The non-fluent form of PPA, progressive non-fluent aphasia (PNFA), presents as a language disorder with deficits in expressive speech and effortful speech production, phonological and grammatical errors, word retrieval deficits, and difficulties in reading and writing, but with preservation of word meaning and a lack of other cognitive and behavioral deficits for at least the first two years (Knibb et al., 2009; Mesulam, 2003; Neary et al., 1998).

Amyotrophic lateral sclerosis (ALS) is characterized by a variable combination of upper and lower motor symptoms including wasting, weakness, fasciculations, and spasticity due to degeneration of upper and lower motor neurons. ALS may be associated with frontal dysfunction similar to the frontal variant of FTD, including speech and language deficits, but cognitive decline typically progresses more rapidly (Bak & Hodges, 2001). Table 13.3 presents a succinct summary of the clinical features of each condition mentioned above.

FTD has an insidious onset, usually between age 45 and 65, and the course progresses to death in an average of eight years (Snowden et al., 2002). Disease prevalence is equal in men and women, and between 20% and 50% of cases have a family history of FTD (McKhann et al., 2001; Snowden et al., 2002). The course of ALS differs; its onset is also insidious and usually occurs in the 60s, but the decline progresses much more rapidly over a duration of approximately 2.5 years (Norris & Haines, 2003).

Neuropsychiatric symptoms

Frontotemporal dementia appears to interfere with the experience or expression of emotions. Compared to AD and VaD, a loss of emotional expressiveness was observed in most cases of FTD, but in less than 50% of cases of AD and VaD. Happiness, sadness, fear, anger, surprise, and disgust were all more likely to be disrupted in FTD than in other dementias (Bathgate et al., 2001). Apathy is common in FTD with two-thirds of patients displaying symptoms (Diehl & Kurz, 2002; (Zamboni et al., 2008), significantly more than what is seen in AD (Jenner et al.,

Table 13.3 Frontotemporal dementia subtypes and clinical features

FTD subtype	Clinical features
Frontal variant	Changes in personality and behavior including loss of empathy, apathy, socially inappropriate behavior, disinhibition, loss of insight, lack of self-awareness, presence of stereotypical behaviors and rituals
SD	Deficits in category fluency, anomia, loss of semantic knowledge, associative agnosia
PNFA	Deficits in language production and word-finding difficulties
ALS	Changes in personality and social behavior, speech and language deficits, motor symptoms of wasting, weakness, and fasciculations

FTD = Frontotemporal dementia; SD = Semantic sementia; PNFA = Progressive non-fluent aphasia; ALS = Amyotrophic Lateral Sclerosis

2006; Perri et al., 2005). Patients with FTD are likely to display a lack of social awareness and social withdrawal (Diehl & Kurz, 2002; Liscic et al., 2007). They are also less likely to display feelings of embarrassment, sympathy, and empathy for others (Bathgate et al. 2001; Eslinger et al., 2005). During neuropsychological testing, patients with FTD may be more likely to ignore personal and professional boundaries and to display unusual calm or ease compared to controls and other dementia and psychiatric groups (Rankin et al., 2008).

Displays of irritability and aggression are common in FTD (Bathgate et al., 2001; Mendez et al., 2006), but not significantly more common than in other dementias. In addition, moria, or a frivolous, childlike tendency to behave in a joking or excited manner, has been characterized as a feature of the frontal variant of FTD (Mendez et al., 2006). Depression, per se, was found to be rare in FTD patients (Diehl & Kurz, 2002), but a lack of motivation was seen in more than 30% (Hornberger et al., 2008).

Patients with FTD have been found to display less anxiety, distress, and withdrawal when completing difficult neuropsychological tasks, indicating that they may be more likely to lack insight into their deficits than patients with AD or VaD (Bathgate et al., 2001). Loss of insight is thought to be the most common behavioral disturbance of FTD, affecting approximately 90% of sufferers and with a higher frequency in men than women (Diehl & Kurz, 2002).

Patients with the frontal variant of FTD may be more likely to describe themselves based on premorbid personality characteristics, suggesting that they experience difficulty updating their self-image to reflect the personality changes caused by the dementia. Further, there may be apparent discrepancies between self-report and informant report of personality on the dimensions of dominance, submissiveness, cold heartedness, introversion, and ingenuousness. Patients with FTD may tend to overstate their positive attributes and understate their negative attributes, whereas controls tend to do the opposite (Rankin et al., 2005).

FTD can cause behavioral disinhibition and impulsivity (Hornberger et al., 2008; Liscic et al., 2007; Srikanth et al., 2005; Zamboni et al., 2008) that is more pervasive than that seen in AD (Perri et al., 2005). In patients with FTD, it is common to see a lack of personal hygiene, decreased interest in sexual activity, changes in sleep, a tendency to wander and pace, and other aberrant motor behavior, which can help distinguish FTD from AD and VaD (Bathgate et al., 2001; Diehl & Kurz, 2002; Srikanth et al., 2005). Other signs of disinhibition and poor self-monitoring in FTD include utilization behavior, as well as repetitive, ritualistic, and stereotypical behaviors. These include echolalia, repetitive clapping or humming, stereotypic facial or limb movements, verbal stereotypies, hoarding, participation in superstitious rituals, and complex repetitive behavioral routines, the latter being the most diagnostically useful of the group in distinguishing FTD from AD and VaD (Bathgate et al., 2001; Nyatsanza et al., 2003; Snowden et al., 2002). In addition, perseveration has been noted significantly more often in FTD patients than controls during a testing session (Rankin et al., 2008).

Individuals with FTD may have deficits in behavioral initiation and persistence. In more severe cases, mutism can occur in the absence of aphasia; this feature was found to be more common in FTD than AD and VaD (Bathgate et al., 2001).

Hyperorality is another common feature of FTD and can be associated with dietary changes; specifically, a tendency to overeat and a preference for sweet foods (Bathgate et al., 2001; Liscic et al., 2007; Snowden et al. 2002; Srikanth et al., 2005). Part of this change in eating behavior may be due to disinhibition, but it has also been noted that FTD is associated with changes in satiety and other dietary mechanisms as well (Bathgate et al., 2001; Jenner et al., 2006).

Neuropsychiatric differences between FTD subtypes
Patients with SD are believed to exhibit a similar behavioral profile to patients with the frontal variant of FTD, with difficulties in disinhibition, aberrant motor behavior, and eating disorders. A study of clinician ratings during a testing session found that individuals with SD perseverated, interrupted the examiner, refused to tolerate interruption, were tangential, and filled in dead space more often than controls (Rankin et al., 2008). On the other hand, the neuropsychiatric symptoms of PNFA are more similar to those seen in AD (Rosen et al., 2006). Interestingly, a study of semantic dementia patients with different asymmetrical patterns of atrophy found that patients with greater left temporal atrophy had greater rates of depression, stereotyped behaviors, and changes in eating habits, whereas patients with greater right temporal atrophy had greater deficits in affect and social conduct (Thompson et al., 2005). Some of the more common behavioral symptoms seen in ALS include perseveration, echolalia, and verbal stereotypies (Bak & Hodges, 2001).

Awareness of self and environment
Deficits in self-awareness have been found in FTD patients compared to controls; however, this ability has been shown to differ among FTD subtypes. All subtypes

of FTD are associated with reduced insight in to behavioral changes; however, only the frontal variant patients show reduced awareness of *cognitive* changes (Banks & Weintraub, 2008).

Inhibition and impulse control

Disinhibition is a characteristic feature of FTD. In addition to the behavioral disinhibition described above, patients with FTD have been shown to perform more poorly than controls, depressed individuals, and persons with other types of dementia on cognitive tasks requiring inhibitory control such as the Stroop test (Braaten et al., 2006; Libon et al., 2007; Matuszewski et al., 2006; Nedjam et al., 2004).

Generativity

Compared to controls (Giovagnoli et al., 2008; Hodges et al., 1999; Nedjam et al., 2004; Rogers et al., 2006), patients with AD (Marczinski & Kertesz, 2006; Matuszewski et al., 2006; Rascovsky et al., 2002; Thompson et al., 2005), and patients with major depressive disorder (Braaten et al., 2006), patients with FTD are more impaired on tests of verbal fluency. Patients with FTD tend to perform significantly worse on tests of letter fluency than patients with AD (Gasparini et al., 2008; Hodges et al., 1999; Perri et al., 2005; Souchay et al., 2003). In contrast to the letter-category fluency discrepancy seen in AD, patients with the frontal variant of FTD tend to perform worse on tests of letter fluency relative to category fluency (Hodges et al., 1999). However, in other variants of FTD, this letter-category fluency discrepancy is less robust. Although PNFA seems to follow the same trend as seen in the frontal variant of FTD (Mendez et al., 2006), patients with SD perform more poorly on category fluency tasks due to a breakdown in semantic knowledge (Hodges et al., 1999; Rogers et al., 2006).

Working memory

Working memory deficits have been found in FTD patients on tests such as reverse digit span (Halpern et al., 2003) and oral calculations, due to a reduction in the availability of online information for additional processing. Several studies have shown that patients with FTD have a greater tendency to commit perseverative errors on neuropsychological tests such as verbal fluency, due in part to a difficulty keeping previous responses in mind (Gregory et al., 1997).

Establishing, maintaining, and shifting of cognitive response set

The Trail Making Test-part B (TMT-B) has been shown to be a useful tool for identifying cognitive impairment in FTD, such as response set maintenance and mental flexibility (Braaten et al. , 2006; Giovagnoli et al., 2008; Matuszewski et al., 2006; Souchay et al., 2003). Compared to patients with AD, one study found that patients with FTD completed TMT-B more quickly, but at the expense of a greater number of errors, which can be interpreted as being due to difficulty maintaining set, difficulty in sequencing, impulsivity, and poor self-monitoring (Libon et al., 2007). The large number of perseverative errors made by patients with FTD on drawing tests (Thompson et al., 2005) and card sorting tests (Souchay et al., 2003) may represent an impairment in maintaining and/or shifting response set.

Planning and organizing

Both in discourse and on tasks requiring the narrative description of a visual scene, patients with FTD tend to describe items and people rather than actions. Their difficulty in organizing the information and planning a response that integrates multiple levels of information (e.g., physical descriptions, actions, themes) across scenes or across an entire story leads to a reduction in meaningful content of speech (Ash et al., 2006). Patients with FTD also have difficulty identifying sequencing errors (Moretti et al., 2005) and exhibit signs of impaired planning and organization on visuoconstructional tasks such as complex figure drawing (Gasparini et al., 2008).

Abstraction

Compared to controls, patients with FTD were found to be impaired on a number of reasoning and cognitive flexibility tests that require categorization based on featural similarities (Giovagnoli et al., 2008; Nedjam et al., 2004; Souchay et al., 2003; Wicklund et al., 2004). Conversely, patients with primary progressive aphasia were found to be unimpaired on a sorting test even in light of their language deficits (Wicklund et al., 2004).

Qualitative errors on neuropsychological tests also show cognitive differences between FTD patients and other patient groups. Thompson et al. (2005) found that FTD patients were more likely to provide concrete answers than AD patients, even on tests that did not show overall score differences between the groups.

Dementia with Lewy bodies

Dementia with Lewy bodies (DLB) is a dementia syndrome characterized by deficits in visuospatial skills, attention, and executive functioning that is associated with the presence of Lewy bodies, protein inclusions consisting of α-synuclein, most often in the form of plaques, throughout the brain (Boeve, 2005; Weisman & McKeith, 2007). There are three classifications of DLB based on clinical and neuropathological findings. Diffuse Lewy body disease consists of a syndrome with dementia and widespread Lewy body inclusions in the absence of other neuropathological changes. The Lewy body variant of AD exists when there is a clinical dementia syndrome and the presence of pathological hallmarks of both Lewy bodies and AD pathology. Parkinson's disease with dementia (PDD) refers to patients who develop dementia more than one year after the onset of parkinsonism (Weisman & McKeith, 2007); however, the cognitive and behavioral profiles of

PDD and DLB have been shown to be indistinct (Galvin et al., 2006; McKeith et al., 2005). Again, for a more comprehensive review of DLB, please see Chapter 3 in this volume.

The median age of DLB onset is approximately 78 (Knopman et al., 2003). A fluctuating course of impairments, particularly in arousal and speech, are seen in a majority of DLB cases (Ferman et al., 2004). Fluctuations in cognition, visual hallucinations, and parkinsonian features are the critical distinguishing features of DLB compared to other dementias (Ferman et al., 2004; Guidi et al., 2006). The disease has a rapid and progressive decline of 1–5 years (McKeith et al., 1996) with a loss of 3.4 to 4.5 points per year on the MMSE (Ballard et al., 2001; Burn et al., 2005; Kraybill et al., 2005). Men are more affected than women (McKeith et al., 1996).

Most DLB and PDD patients show a "subcortical" pattern of cognitive deficits with greater impairment on executive, visuoconstructional, and attention domains; however, approximately a quarter of patients have been found to have a more "cortical" pattern of impairment with greater deficits on memory tests (Janvin et al., 2006).

Neuropsychiatric symptoms

More than 40% of patients with DLB exhibit symptoms of agitation or aggression, anxiety, apathy, and irritability (Caputo et al., 2008) as well as delusions, hallucinations, disinhibition, and changes in sleep and eating behavior (Kao et al., 2009). In comparison to AD patients, DLB patients score significantly higher on the Neuropsychiatric Inventory overall as well as in the domains of hallucinations, apathy, and appetite (Ricci et al., 2009).

Executive dysfunction

Patients with DLB have been shown to have slowed reaction time on a task that required inhibition of previously learned rules (Bradshaw et al., 2006; Johns et al., 2009). Similarly, patients with PDD have demonstrated reduced performance on the Stroop test relative to controls (Bohnen et al., 2006; Johns et al., 2009), and commit more errors than patients with AD (Guidi et al., 2006).

Deficits in letter fluency are seen in DLB (Johns et al., 2009) and PDD (Levy et al., 2002); the presence of this impairment at baseline in patients with Parkinson's disease has been shown to be predictive of developing dementia (Levy et al., 2002).

Patients with DLB have significantly greater difficulty establishing and shifting mental set compared to AD patients (Doubleday et al., 2002). For example, on the Trail Making Test-part B, autopsy-confirmed patients with DLB performed worse than patients with AD, and patients with PDD performed worse than controls (Kraybill et al., 2005). Working memory tests such as holding information online and rearranging the information have also shown to be reduced in DLB relative to normal controls (Johns et al., 2009). In addition, confabulations, perseverations, and intrusions (specifically intrusions from the patients' environment), are all more common in DLB than AD (Doubleday et al., 2002).

Patients with DLB have organization and planning deficits on the clock drawing test, and make more errors related to conceptualization and number placement than other patient groups (Cahn-Weiner et al., 2003).

DLB impairs a number of attentional processes, including information processing speed, simple verbal attention span, focused attention, divided attention, and selective attention (Bohnen et al., 2006; Bradshaw et al., 2006; Guidi et al., 2006; Kraybill et al., 2005). However, relative to controls and patients with AD, patients with DLB were not found to be impaired on tests of sustained attention (Bradshaw et al., 2006). There is evidence of variable performance on attentional tasks that place heavy demands on executive and visuospatial processing, which has been attributed to the fluctuating nature of the disease (Bradshaw et al., 2006).

Other causes of dementia

Corticobasal degeneration

Corticobasal degeneration (CBD) is a syndrome characterized by an extrapyramidal motor disorder and impairments in praxis, executive functioning, language, visuospatial functioning, and social behavior, with preserved episodic memory (Graham et al., 2003; Huey et al., 2009; Murray et al., 2007). Significant tau pathology occurs in the frontal and parietal cortices and the basal ganglia (Murray et al., 2007). Loss of volume is found primarily in the dorsal frontal and parietal cortices and frontal subcortical white matter, with greater left hemisphere involvement (Boxer et al., 2006). More information on CBD may be found in Chapters 4 and 5 of this volume.

Neuropsychiatric features of CBD include depression, anxiety, and apathy, which were reported in more than 40% of the patient group (Borroni et al., 2008).

Libon et al. (2007) found that patients with CBD suffer impairment in the domains of working memory, visuoconstructional skills, processing speed, and mental flexibility, but semantic memory remains well preserved. Another study found decreased metacognitive awareness and impaired anticipatory awareness in patients with CBD (O'Keeffe et al., 2007).

A study of autopsy-confirmed patients with CBD found that 60% showed signs of impaired planning and mental search and 40% had perseverative behavior at the onset of the disease. All of the cases developed impaired executive functioning during the disease course, and 40% reportedly suffered behavioral changes based on self- or informant report (Murray et al., 2007).

On two cognitive screening tests, the DRS and Addenbrooke's Cognitive Examination, patients with CBD were more impaired than controls on all subtests, including orientation, attention, memory, verbal fluency, language, and visuospatial functioning (Bak et al., 2005). Patients with CBD are often impaired on card sorting, Trail Making, verbal fluency, backward digit span, addition, and magnitude judgment tests (see Graham et al., 2003, for a review; Halpern et al., 2003; Huey et al., 2009; Libon et al., 2007). On a naming test, patients with CBD were more impaired on action naming (thought to be heavily dependent on frontal networks) than object naming; this action-naming impairment was more pronounced than what was seen in FTD and AD (Cotelli et al., 2006). In comparison to FTD patients, CBD patients perform better on tests of abstraction and rule following but poorer on visual scanning (Huey et al., 2009).

Progressive supranuclear palsy

Patients with progressive supranuclear palsy (PSP) present with a progressive parkinsonism that typically includes vertical supranuclear gaze palsy, postural instability, contraction of facial muscles, dysarthria, dysphagia, and axial rigidity (Golbe, 2007). They also may show behavioral and cognitive changes similar to FTD (Graff-Radford & Woodruff (2007). Atrophy occurs primarily in the pons and midbrain (Boxer et al., 2006). See Chapters 4 and 5 in this volume for additional information.

Behavioral studies have shown that more than half of patients with PSP display apathy, aspontaneity, disorganization, neglect, inflexibility, and poor judgment (Cordato et al., 2006). Depression and anxiety were reported in more than 40% (Borroni et al, 2008). Other studies have also found disinhibition and indifference to be common neuropsychiatric features (see Millar et al., 2006, for a review).

The executive function deficits seen in PSP are similar to, but less severe than, FTD, and greater than those produced by other dementias (Magherini & Litvan, 2005). PSP produces deficits in conceptualization, strategy formation, problem solving, planning, sequencing, set shifting, processing speed, and metacognitive and anticipatory awareness (O'Keeffe et al., 2007). Patients with PSP have retrieval difficulties due to impaired attention and executive functioning during learning, and they show signs of perseveration and disinhibition (see Magherini & Litvan, 2005, for a review). Similar to patients with CBD, patients with PSP show a significantly greater impairment on action naming versus object naming when compared to FTD and AD patients (Cotelli et al., 2006). Individuals with PSP also have difficulties recognizing facial affect (Ghosh et al., 2009).

Multiple system atrophy

Multiple system atrophy (MSA) is a progressive neurodegenerative disorder characterized by parkinsonism, autonomic dysfunction, cerebellar ataxia, and pyramidal signs (Wenning & Geser, 2007). Cell loss, gliosis, and glial cytoplasmic inclusion are found primarily in the striatonigral and olivopontocerebellar systems.

Neuropsychiatric features of MSA include depression, apathy, and changes in sleep which were present in at least 40% in one study (Kao et al., 2009).

Patients with MSA have mild executive deficits compared to other subcortical dementias. The impairments caused by MSA include reduced letter and category fluency (Bak et al., 2005), impaired Block Design (Kawai et al., 2008), a greater number of errors on the WCST, and slow, inaccurate responding on the Stroop test (Dujardin et al., 2003). Patients with MSA affecting the cerebellum, a subtype of MSA, have cognitive deficits in verbal memory and verbal generativity, with preserved attention, visuospatial function, and no deficits on the WCST (Bürk et al., 2006) or a test requiring responses to a rule and following shifts in the rule (Kawai et al., 2008)

Conclusions

Executive dysfunction is a common feature of almost all dementia syndromes. In the case of the frontal variant of FTD, executive dysfunction is a hallmark of the disease. However, various aspects of executive functioning can be compromised in all neurodegenerative diseases. As described earlier in this chapter, the term "executive functioning" is used to describe a diverse constellation of behaviors and cognitive skills all somehow involved in the maintenance of goal-directed behaviors. Disturbances of executive functioning include behaviors as varied as the neuropsychiatric conditions of apathy and abulia, to deficits in such complex "higher order" skills of planning and organization. Many of the problems observed in executive functioning in dementia patients result in some of the most disturbing and stressful behaviors for dementia caregivers to deal with, such as poor impulse control, anosognosia, and impaired instrumental activities of daily living.

Executive functions are diverse in nature and not completely understood. As they rely heavily on other aspects of functioning and because they are integral to novel, unstructured situations, they can be difficult to formally test. Elucidation of the specific executive function impairment in a patient requires a wide range of neuropsychological testing with quantitative and qualitative analysis to begin to understand the nature of the deficit. Furthermore, because several key aspects of executive functions are more behavioral than cognitive, a complete examination of executive functions in dementia requires neuropsychological testing as well as careful observation of behavior during the examination, and a detailed history and description of behavior (either through formal questionnaire or interview) by a knowledgeable informant. With continued research in neuropsychology, neuropsychiatry, cognitive neuroscience, imaging, and pathology, we can further understand the role of executive functions in Alzheimer's disease and other dementias.

References

Adlam, A.-L. R., Patterson, K., Rogers, T. T., Nestor, P. J., Salmond, C. H., Acosta-Cabronero, J., et al. (2006). Semantic dementia and fluent primary progressive aphasia: Two sides of the same coin? *Brain, 129,* 3066–3080.

Aggarwal, N. T., & DeCarli, C. (2007). Vascular dementia: Emerging trends. *Seminars in Neurology, 27,* 66–77.

Albert, M., Blacker, D., Moss, M. B., Tanzi, R., & McArdle, J. J. (2007). Longitudinal change in cognitive performance among individuals with mild cognitive impairment. *Neuropsychology, 21,* 158–169.

Allegri, R. F., Sarasola, D., Serrano, C. M., Taragano, F. E., Arizaga, R. L., Butman, J., et al. (2006). Neuropsychiatric symptoms as a predictor of caregiver burden in Alzheimer's disease. *Neuropsychiatric Disease and Treatment, 2,* 105–110.

Alzheimer's Association (2009). *2009 Alzheimer's Disease facts and figures.* Chicago: Alzheimer's Association.

Amieva, H., Lafont, S., Rouch-Leroyer, I., Rainville, C., Dartigues, J-F., Orgogozo, J-M., et al. (2004). Evidencing inhibitory deficits in Alzheimer's disease through interference effects and shifting disabilities in the Stroop test. *Archives of Clinical Neuropsychology, 19,* 791–803.

Amirian, E., Baxter, J., Grigsby, J., Curran-Everett, D., Hokanson, J. E., & Bryant, L. L. (2010). Executive function (capacity for behavioral self-regulation) and decline predicted mortality in a longitudinal study in Southern Colorado. *Journal of Clinical Epidemiology, 63,* 307–314.

Ash, S., Moore, P., Antani, S., McCawley, G., Work, M., & Grossman, M. (2006). Trying to tell a tale: Discourse impairments in progressive aphasia and frontotemporal dementia. *Neurology, 66,* 1405–1413.

Ashendorf, L., Jefferson, A. L., O'Connor, M. K., Chaisson, C., Green, R. C., & Stern, R. A. (2008). Trail Making Test errors in normal aging, mild cognitive impairment, and dementia. *Archives of Clinical Neuropsychology, 23,* 129–137.

Backman, L., Jones, S., Berger, A-K., Jonsson Laukka, E., & Small, B. J. (2005). Cognitive impairment in preclinical Alzheimer's disease: A meta-analysis. *Neuropsychology, 19,* 520–531.

Baddeley, A. (2007). *Working memory, thought, and action.* New York: Oxford University Press.

Baddeley, A. D., & Hitch, G. (1974). Working memory. In G. H. Bower (Ed.), *The psychology of learning and motivation: Advances in research and theory* (Vol. 8, pp. 47–89). New York: Academic Press.

Bak, T. H., & Hodges, J. R. (2001). Motor neurone disease, dementia and aphasia: Coincidence, co-occurrence or continuum? *Journal of Neurology, 248,* 260–270.

Bak, T. H., Crawford, L. M., Hearn, V. C., Mathuranath, P. S., & Hodges, J. R. (2005). Subcortical dementia revisited: Similarities and differences in cognitive function between progressive supranuclear palsy (PSP), corticobasal degeneration (CBD) and multiple system atrophy (MSA). *Neurocase, 11,* 268–273.

Ballard, C., O'Brien, J., Morris, C. M., Barber, R., Swann, A., Neill, D., & McKeith, I. (2001). The progression of cognitive impairment in dementia with Lewy bodies, vascular dementia and Alzheimer's disease. *International Journal of Geriatric Psychiatry, 16,* 499–503.

Banks, S. & Weintraub, S. (2008). Self-awareness and self-monitoring of cognitive and behavioral deficits in behavioral variant frontotemporal dementia, primary progressive aphasia and probable Alzheimer's disease. *Brain and Cognition, 67,* 58–68.

Bathgate, D., Snowden, J. S., Varma, A., Blackshaw, A., & Neary, D. (2001). Behaviour in frontotemporal dementia, Alzheimer's disease and vascular dementia. *Acta Neurologica Scandinavica, 103,* 367–378.

Baudic, S., Barba, G. D., Thibaudet, M. C., Smagghe, A., Remy, P., & Traykov, L. (2006). Executive function deficits in early Alzheimer's disease and their relations with episodic memory. *Archives of Clinical Neuropsychology, 21*, 15–21.

Beer, J. S., Shimamura, A. P., & Knight, R. T. (2004). Frontal lobe contributions to executive control of cognitive and social behavior. In M. S. Gazzaniga (Ed.), *The cognitive neurosciences* (3rd edn., pp. 1091–1104). Cambridge, MA: MIT Press.

Bélanger, S., Belleville, S., & Gauthier, S. (2010). Inhibition impairments in Alzheimer's disease, mild cognitive impairment and healthy aging: Effect of congruency proportion in a Stroop task. *Neuropsychologia, 48*, 581–590.

Bell-McGinty, S., Podell, K., Franzen, M., Baird, A. D., & Williams, M. J. (2002). Standard measures of executive function in predicting instrumental activities of daily living in older adults. *International Journal of Geriatric Psychiatry, 17*, 828–834.

Blakemore, S. J., & Choudhury, S. (2006). Development of the adolescent brain: Implications for executive function and social cognition. *Journal of Child Psychology and Psychiatry, 47*, 296–312.

Boeve, B. F. (2005). Clinical, diagnostic, genetic and management issues in dementia with Lewy bodies. *Clinical Science, 109*, 343–354.

Bohnen, N. I., Kaufer, D. I., Hendrickson, R., Ivanco, L. S., Lopresti, B. J., Constantine, G. M., et al. (2006). Cognitive correlates of cortical cholinergic denervation in Parkinson's disease and parkinsonian dementia. *Journal of Neurology, 253*, 242–247.

Borroni, B., Turla, M., Bertasi, V., Agosti, C., Gilberti, N., & Padovani, A. (2008). Cognitive and behavioral assessment in the early stages of neurodegenerative extrapyramidal syndromes. *Archives of Gerontology and Geriatrics, 47*, 53–61.

Boxer, A. L., Geschwind, M. D., Belfor, N., Gorno-Tempini, M. L., Schauer, G., Miller, B. L., et al. (2006). Patterns of brain atrophy that differentiate corticobasal degeneration syndrome from progressive supranuclear palsy. *Archives of Neurology, 63*, 81–86.

Braaten, A. J., Parsons, T. D., McCue, R., Sellers, A., & Burns, W. J. (2006). Neurocognitive differential diagnosis of dementing diseases: Alzheimer's dementia, vascular dementia, frontotemporal dementia, and major depressive disorder. *International Journal of Neuroscience, 116*, 1271–1293.

Bradshaw, J. M., Saling, M., Anderson, V., Hopwood, M., & Brodtmann, A. (2006). Higher cortical deficits influence attentional processing in dementia with Lewy bodies, relative to patients with dementia of the Alzheimer's type and controls. *Journal of Neurology, Neurosurgery, and Psychiatry, 77*, 1129–1135.

Broadbent, N. J., Clark. R. E., Zola, S., & Squire, L. R. (2002). The medial temporal lobe and memory. In L. R. Squire, & D. L. Schacter (Eds.), *Neuropsychology of memory* (3rd edn., pp. 3–23). New York: Guilford Press.

Burgess, P. W. (1997). Theory and methodology in executive function research. In P. Rabbitt (Ed.), *Methodology of frontal and executive function* (pp.81–116). Hove, UK: Psychology Press.

Bürk, K., Daum, I., & Rüb, U. (2006). Cognitive function in multiple system atrophy of the cerebellar type. *Movement Disorders, 21*, 772–776.

Burn, D. J., Rowan, E. N., Allan, L. M., Molloy, S., O'Brien, J. T., & McKeith, I. G. (2005). Motor subtype and cognitive decline in Parkinson's disease, Parkinson's disease with dementia, and dementia with Lewy bodies. *Journal of Neurology, Neurosurgery, and Psychiatry, 77*, 585–589.

Burton, C. L., Strauss, E., Hultsch, D. F., & Hunter, M. A. (2006). Cognitive functioning and everyday problem solving in older adults. *Clinical Neuropsychologist, 20*, 432–452.

Butters, N., Granholm, E., Salmon, D. P., Grant, I., & Wolfe, J. (1987). Episodic and semantic memory: A comparison of amnesic and demented patients. *Journal of Clinical and Experimental Neuropsychology, 9,* 479–497.

Cahn-Weiner, D. A., Farias, S. T., Julian, L., Harvey, D. J., Kramer, J. H., Reed, B. R., et al. (2007). Cognitive and neuroimaging predictors of instrumental activities of daily living. *Journal of the International Neuropsychological Society, 13,* 747–757.

Cahn-Weiner, D. A., Williams, K., Grace, J., Tremont, G., Westervelt, H., & Stern, R. A. (2003). Discrimination of dementia with Lewy bodies from Alzheimer disease and Parkinson disease using the Clock Drawing Test. *Cognitive and Behavioral Neurology, 16,* 85–92.

Caputo, M., Monastero, R., Mariani, E., Santucci, A., Mangialasche, F., Camarda, R., et al. (2008). Neuropsychiatric symptoms in 921 elderly subjects with dementia: A comparison between vascular and neurodegenerative types. *Acta Psychiatrica Scandinavica, 117,* 455–464.

Carey, C. L., Woods, S. P., Damon, J., Halabi, C., Dean, D., Delis, D. C., et al. (2008). Discriminant validity and neuroanatomical correlates of rule monitoring in frontotemporal dementia and Alzheimer's disease. *Neuropsychologia, 46,* 1081–1087.

Casey, B. J., Tottenham, N., Liston, C., & Durston, S. (2005). Imaging the developing brain: What have we learned about cognitive development? *Trends in Cognitive Sciences, 9,* 104–110.

Cerhan, J. H., Ivnik, R. J., Smith, G. E., Tangalos, E. C., Petersen, R. C., & Boeve, B. F. (2002). Diagnostic utility of letter fluency, category fluency, and fluency difference scores in Alzheimer's disease. *Clinical Neuropsychologist, 16,* 35–42.

Chow, T. W., & Cummings, J. L. (2007). Frontal-subcortical circuits. In B. L. Miller & J. L. Cummings (Eds.), *The human frontal lobes: Functions and disorders* (pp. 25–43). New York: Guilford Press.

Chugani, H. T. (1994). Development of regional brain glucose metabolism in relation to behavior and plasticity. In G. Dawson & K. W. Fischer (Eds.), *Human behavior and the developing brain* (pp.153–175). New York: Guilford Press.

Cordato, N. J., Halliday, G. M., Caine, D., & Morris, J. G. L. (2006). Comparison of motor, cognitive, and behavioral features in progressive supranuclear palsy and Parkinson's disease. *Movement Disorders, 21,* 632–638.

Costa, P. T. Jr. et al. (1996). *Recognition and Initial Assessment of Alzheimer's Disease & Related Dementias.* Rockville, MD: US Dept of Health and Human Services, Public Health Service, Agency for Health Care Policy and Research.

Cotelli, M., Borroni, B., Manenti, R., Alberici, A., Calabria, M., Agosti, C., et al. (2006). Action and object naming in frontotemporal dementia, progressive supranuclear palsy, and corticobasal degeneration. *Neuropsychology, 20,* 558–565.

Cullen, B., Coen, R. F., Lynch, C. A., Cunningham, C. J., Coakley, D., Robertson, I. H., et al. (2005) Repetitive behaviour in Alzheimer's disease: Description, correlates, and functions. *International Journal of Geriatric Psychiatry, 20,* 686–693.

Cummings, J. L., & Mega, M. S. (2003). *Neuropsychiatry and behavioral neuroscience.* New York: Oxford University Press.

Cummings, J. L., Mega, M., Gray, K., Rosenberg-Thompson, S., Carusi, D. A., & Gornbein, J. (1994). The Neuropsychiatric Inventory: Comprehensive assessment of psychopathology in dementia. *Neurology, 44,* 2308–2314.

Daniels, K., Toth, J., & Jacoby, L. (2006). The aging of executive functions. In F. I. M. Craik, & E. Bialystok (Eds.), *Lifespan cognition: Mechanisms of change* (pp.96–111). New York: Oxford University Press.

De Deyn, P. P., Engelborghs, S., Saerens, J., Goeman, J., Mariën, P., Maertens, K., et al. (2005). The Middelheim Frontality Score: A behavioural assessment scale that discriminates frontotemporal dementia from Alzheimer's disease. *International Journal of Geriatric Psychiatry, 20*, 70–79.

de Jager, C. A., Hogervorst, E., Combrinck, M., & Budge, M. M. (2003). Sensitivity and specificity of neuropsychological tests for mild cognitive impairment, vascular cognitive impairment and Alzheimer's disease. *Psychological Medicine, 33*, 1039–1050.

Delazer, M., Sinz, H., Zamarian, L., & Benke, T. (2007). Decision-making with explicit and stable rules in mild Alzheimer's disease. *Neuropsychologia, 45*, 1632–1641.

Delis, D. C., Kaplan, E., & Kramer, J. H. (2001). *Delis-Kaplan Executive Function System (DKEFS): Examiner's manual.* San Antonio, TX: Psychological Corporation.

Desmond, D. W. (2004). The neuropsychology of vascular cognitive impairment: Is there a specific cognitive deficit? *Journal of the Neurological Sciences, 226*, 3–7.

Diehl, J., & Kurz, A. (2002). Frontotemporal dementia: Patient characteristics, cognition, and behaviour. *International Journal of Geriatric Psychiatry, 17*, 914–918.

Doubleday, E. K., Snowden, J. S., Varma, A. R., & Neary, D. (2002). Qualitative performance characteristics differentiate dementia with Lewy bodies and Alzheimer's disease. *Journal of Neurology, Neurosurgery, and Psychiatry, 72*, 602–607.

Dujardin, K., Defebvre, L., Krystkowiak, P., Degreef, J. F., & Destee, A. (2003). Executive function differences in multiple system atrophy and Parkinson's disease. *Parkinsonism and Related Disorders, 9*, 205–211.

Engelborghs, S., Maertens, K., Marien, P., Vloeberghs, E., Somers, N., Nagels, G., et al. (2006). Behavioural and neuropsychological correlates of frontal lobe features in dementia. *Psychological Medicine, 36*, 1173–1182.

Eslinger, P. J. (2002). The anatomic basis of utilization behaviour: A shift from frontal-parietal to intra-frontal mechanisms. *Cortex, 38*, 273–276.

Eslinger, P. J., Dennis, K., Moore, P., Antani, S., Hauck, R., & Grossman, M. (2005). Metacognitive deficits in frontotemporal dementia. *Journal of Neurology, Neurosurgery, and Psychiatry, 76*, 1630–1635.

Ferman, T. J., Smith, G. E., Boeve, B. F., Ivnik, R. J., Petersen, R. C., Knopman, D., et al. (2004). DLB fluctuations: Specific features that reliably differentiate DLB from AD and normal aging. *Neurology, 62*, 181–187.

Filley, C. M. (2000). Clinical neurology and executive dysfunction. *Seminars in Speech and Language, 21*, 95–108.

Franceschi, M., Caffarra, P., De Vreese, L., Pelati, O., Pradelli, S., Savarè, R., et al. (2007). Visuospatial planning and problem solving in Alzheimer's disease patients: A study with the Tower of London test. *Dementia and Geriatric Cognitive Disorders, 24*, 424–428.

Fratiglioni, L., DeRonchi, D., & Torres, A. H. (1999). Worldwide prevalence and incidence of dementia. *Drugs and Aging, 15*, 365–375.

Freeman, R. Q., Giovannetti, T., Lamar, M., Cloud, B. S., Stern, R. A., Kaplan, E., et al. (2000). Visuoconstructional problems in dementia: Contribution of executive systems functions. *Neuropsychology, 14*, 415–426.

Fuh, J. L., Wang, S. J., & Cummings, J. L. (2005). Neuropsychiatric profiles in patients with Alzheimer's disease and vascular dementia. *Journal of Neurology, Neurosurgery, and Psychiatry, 76*, 1337–1341.

Fuster, J. M. (1997). *The prefrontal cortex* (3rd edn.) New York: Lippincott-Raven.

Galvin, J. E., Pollack, J., & Morris, J. C. (2006). Clinical phenotype of Parkinson disease dementia. *Neurology, 67*, 1605–1611.

Gasparini, M., Masciarelli, G., Vanacore, N., Ottaviani, D., Salati, E., Talarico, G., et al. (2008). A descriptive study on constructional impairment in frontotemporal dementia and Alzheimer's disease. *European Journal of Neurology, 15*, 589–597.

Gazzaley, A., & D'Esposito, M. (2007). Unifying prefrontal cortex function: executive control, neural networks, and top-down modulation. In B. L. Miller, & J. L. Cummings (Eds.), *The human frontal lobes: Functions and disorders* (2nd edn., pp.44–58). New York: Guilford Press.

Gazzaley, A., Cooney, J. W., McEvoy, K., Knight, R. T., & D'Esposito, M. (2005). Top-down enhancement and suppression of the magnitude and speed of neural activity. *Journal of Cognitive Neuroscience, 17*, 507–517.

Ghosh, B. C. P., Rowe, J. B., Calder, A. J., Hodges, J. R., & Bak, T. H. (2009). Emotion recognition in progressive supranuclear palsy. *Journal of Neurology, Neurosurgery, and Psychiatry 80*, 1143–1145.

Gilbert, S. J., & Burgess, P. W. (2008). Executive function. *Current Biology, 18*, R110–R114.

Giovagnoli, A. R., Erbetta, A., Reati, F., & Bugiani, O. (2008). Differential neuropsychological patterns of frontal variant frontotemporal dementia and Alzheimer's disease in a study of diagnostic concordance. *Neuropsychologia, 46*, 1495–1504.

Giovannetti, T., Schmidt, K. S., Gallo, J. L., Sestito, N., & Libon, D. J. (2006). Everyday action in dementia: Evidence for differential deficits in Alzheimer's disease versus subcortical vascular dementia. *Journal of the International Neuropsychological Society, 12*, 45–53.

Golbe, L. I. (2007). Progressive supranuclear palsy. In J. Jankovic, & E. Tolosa (Eds.), *Parkinson's disease and movement disorders* (5th edn., pp.161–174). Philadelphia, PA: Lippincott Williams & Wilkins.

Gomez, R. G., & White, D. A. (2006). Using verbal fluency to detect very mild dementia of the Alzheimer type. *Archives of Clinical Neuropsychology, 21*, 771–775.

Grace, J., & Malloy, P. (2001). *The Frontal Systems Behavior Scale, Professional manual.* Lutz, FL: Psychological Assessment Resources.

Graff-Radford, N. R., & Woodruff, B. K. (2007). Frontotemporal dementia. *Seminars in Neurology, 27*, 48–57.

Grafman, J. (2007). Planning and the brain. In B. L. Miller & J. L. Cummings (Eds.), *The human frontal lobes: Functions and disorders* (2nd edn., pp.249–261). New York: Guilford Press.

Graham, N. L., Bak, T. H., & Hodges, J. R. (2003). Corticobasal degeneration as a cognitive disorder. *Movement Disorders, 18*, 1224–1232.

Graham, N. L., Emery, T., & Hodges, J. R. (2004). Distinctive cognitive profiles in Alzheimer's disease and subcortical vascular dementia. *Journal of Neurology, Neurosurgery, and Psychiatry, 75*, 61–71.

Gregory, C. A., Orrell, M., Sahakian, B., & Hodges, J. (1997). Can frontotemporal dementia and Alzheimer's disease be differentiated using a brief battery of tests? *International Journal of Geriatric Psychiatry, 12*, 375–383.

Griffith, H. R., Belue, K., Sicola, A., Krzywanski, S., Zamrini, E., Harrell, L., et al. (2003). Impaired financial abilities in mild cognitive impairment: a direct assessment approach. *Neurology, 60,* 449–457.

Grober, E., Hall, C. B, Lipton, R. B., Zonderman, A. B., Resnick, S. M., & Kawas, C. (2008). Memory impairment, executive dysfunction, and intellectual decline in preclinical Alzheimer's disease. *Journal of the International Neuropsychological Society, 14,* 266–278.

Grossman, M., & Ash, S. (2004). Primary progressive aphasia: A review. *Neurocase, 10,* 3–18.

Guidi, M., Paciaroni, L., Paolini, S., De Padova, S., & Scarpino, O. (2006). Differences and similarities in the neuropsychological profile of dementia with Lewy bodies and Alzheimer's disease in the early stage. *Journal of the Neurological Sciences, 248,* 120–123.

Gunstad, J., Brickman, A. M., Paul, R. H., Browndyke, J., Moser, D. J., Ott, B. R., et al. (2005). Progressive morphometric and cognitive changes in vascular dementia. *Archives of Clinical Neuropsychology, 20,* 229–241.

Halpern, C., McMillan, C., Moore, P., Dennis, K., & Grossman, M. (2003). Calculation impairment in neurodegenerative diseases. *Journal of the Neurological Sciences, 208,* 31–38.

Heaton, R. K., Chelune, G. J., Talley, J. L., Kay, G. G., & Curtis, G. (Eds.). (1993). *Wisconsin Card Sorting Test manual: Revised and expanded.* Odessa, FL: Psychological Assessment Resources.

Henry, J. D., & Crawford, J. R. (2004). A meta-analytic review of verbal fluency performance following focal cortical lesions. *Neuropsychology, 18,* 284–295.

Henry, J. D., Crawford, J. R., & Phillips, L. H. (2004). Verbal fluency performance in dementia of the Alzheimer's type: A meta-analysis. *Neuropsychologia, 42,* 1212–1222.

Hodges, J. R., Patterson, K., Ward, R., Garrard, P., Bak, T., Perry, R., & Gregory, C. (1999). The differentiation of semantic dementia and frontal lobe dementia (temporal and frontal variants of frontotemporal dementia) from early Alzheimer's disease: A comparative neuropsychological study. *Neuropsychology, 13,* 31–40.

Hollingworth, P., Hamshere, M. L., Moskvina, V., Dowzell, K., Moore, P. J., Foy, C., et al. (2006). Four components describe behavioral symptoms in 1,120 individuals with late-onset Alzheimer's disease. *Journal of the American Geriatric Society, 54,* 1348–1354.

Hornberger, M., Piguet, O., Kipps, C., & Hodges, J. R. (2008). Executive function in progressive and nonprogressive behavioral variant frontotemporal dementia. *Neurology, 71,* 1481–1488.

Huey, E. D., Goveia, E. N., Paviol, S., Pardini, M., Krueger, F., Zamboni, G., et al. (2009). Executive dysfunction in frontotemporal dementia and corticobasal syndrome. *Neurology, 72,* 453–459.

Huizinga, M., Dolan, C. V., & van der Molen, M. W. (2006). Age-related change in executive function: Developmental trends and a latent variable analysis. *Neuropsychologia, 44,* 2017–2036.

Hull, R., Martin, R. C., Beier, M. E., Lane, D., & Hamilton, A. C. (2008). Executive function in older adults: A structural equation modeling approach. *Neuropsychology, 22,* 508–522.

Huntley, J. D. & Howard, R. J. (2010). Working memory in early Alzheimer's disease: a neuropsychological review. *International Journal of Geriatric Psychiatry, 25,* 121–132.

Iudicello, J. E., Woods, S. P., Parsons, T. D., Moran, L. M., Carey, C. L., & Grant, I. (2007). Verbal fluency in HIV infection: A meta-analytic review. *Journal of the International Neuropsychological Society, 13*, 195–201.

Janvin, C. C., Larsen, J. P., Salmon, D. P., Galasko, D., Hugdahl, K., & Aarsland, D. (2006). Cognitive profiles of individual patients with Parkinson's disease and dementia: Comparison with dementia with Lewy bodies and Alzheimer's disease. *Movement Disorders, 21*, 337–342.

Jefferson, A. L., Cahn-Weiner, D., Boyle, P., Paul, R. H., Moser, D. J., Gordon, N., et al. (2006). Cognitive predictors of functional decline in vascular dementia. *International Journal of Geriatric Psychiatry, 21*, 752–754.

Jellinger, K. A. (2008). Morphologic diagnosis of "vascular dementia" – A critical update. *Journal of the Neurological Sciences, 270*, 1–12.

Jenner, C., Reali, G., Puopolo, M., & Silveri, M. C. (2006). Can cognitive and behavioural disorders differentiate frontal variant-frontotemporal dementia from Alzheimer's disease at early stages. *Behavioural Neurology, 17*, 89–95.

Johns, E. K., Phillips, N. A., Belleville, S., Goupil, D., Babins, L., Kelner, N., et al. (2009). Executive functions in frontotemporal dementia and Lewy body dementia. *Neuropsychology, 23*, 765–777.

Jones, S., Jonsson Laukka, E., & Backman, L. (2006). Differential verbal fluency deficits in the preclinical stages of Alzheimer's disease and vascular dementia. *Cortex, 42*, 347–355.

Kao, A. W., Racine, C. A., Quitania, L. C., Kramer, J. H., Christine, C. W., & Miller, B. L. (2009). Cognitive and neuropsychiatric profile of the synucleinopathies. *Alzheimer's Disease and Associated Disorders, 23*, 365–370.

Kaplan, E., Fein, D., Morris, R., & Delis D. C. (1991). *WAIS-R NI manual*. San Antonio, TX: Psychological Corporation.

Kaufer, D. I. (2007). The dorsolateral and cingulate cortex. In B. L. Miller, & J. L. Cummings (Eds.), *The human frontal lobes: Functions and disorders* (2nd edn., pp. 44–58). New York: Guilford Press.

Kaufer, D. I., Cummings, J. L., Ketchel, P., Smith, V., MacMillan, A., Shelley, T., et al. (2000). Validation of the NPI-Q, a brief clinical form of the Neuropsychiatric Inventory. *Journal of Neuropsychiatry and Clinical Neurosciences, 12*, 233–239.

Kawai, Y., Suenaga, M., Takeda, A., Ito, M., Watanabe, H., Tanaka, F., et al. (2008). Cognitive impairments in multiple system atrophy. *Neurology, 70*, 1390–1396.

Kinney, H. C., Brody, B. A., Kloman, A. S., & Gilles, F. H. (1998). Sequence of central nervous system myelination in human infancy. *Journal of Neuropathology and Experimental Neurology, 47*, 217–234.

Knibb, J. A., Woollams, A. M., Hodges, J. R., & Patterson, K. (2009). Making sense of progressive non-fluent aphasia: An analysis of conversational speech. *Brain, 132*, 2734–2746.

Knopman, D. S., Parisi, J. E., Boeve, B. F., Cha, R. H., Apaydin, H., Salviati, A., et al. (2003). Vascular dementia in a population-based autopsy study. *Archives of Neurology, 60*, 569–575.

Koenig, P., Smith, E. E., Moore, P., Glosser, G. & Grossman, M. (2007). Categorization of novel animals by patients with Alzheimer's disease and corticobasal degeneration. *Neuropsychology, 21*, 193–206.

Korczyn, A. D. (2002). The complex nosological concept of vascular dementia. *Journal of the Neurological Sciences, 203–204*, 3–6.

Kouneiher, F., Charron, S., & Koechlin, E. (2009). Motivation and cognitive control in the human prefrontal cortex. *Nature Neuroscience, 12,* 939–945.

Kraybill, M. L., Larson, E. B., Tsuang, D. W., Teri, L., McCormick, W. C., Bowen, J. D., et al. (2005). Cognitive differences in dementia patients with autopsy-verified AD, Lewy body pathology, or both. *Neurology, 64,* 2069–2073.

Lamar, M., Price, C. C., Davis., K. L., Kaplan, E., & Libon, D. J. (2002). Capacity to maintain mental set in dementia. *Neuropsychologia, 40,* 435–445.

Lamar, M., Swenson, R., Kaplan, E., & Libon, D. J. (2004). Characterizing alterations in executive functioning across distinct subtypes of cortical and subcortical dementia. *Clinical Neuropsychologist, 18,* 22–31.

Levinoff, E. J., Phillips, N. A., Verret, L., Babins, L., Kelner, N., Akerib, V., et al. (2006). Cognitive estimation impairment in Alzheimer disease and mild cognitive impairment. *Neuropsychology, 20,* 123–132.

Levy, G., Jacobs, D. M., Tang, M.-X., Côté, L. J., Louis, E. D., Alfaro, B., et al. (2002). Memory and executive function impairment predict dementia in Parkinson's disease. *Movement Disorders, 17,* 1221–1226.

Lezak, M. D., Howieson, D. B., & Loring, D. W. (2004). *Neuropsychological assessment* (4th edn). New York: Oxford University Press.

Libon, D. J., Xie, S. X., Moore, P., Farmer, J., Antani, S., McCawley, G., et al. (2007). Patterns of neuropsychological impairment in frontotemporal dementia. *Neurology, 68,* 369–375.

Liscic, R. M., Storandt, M., Cairns, N. J., & Morris, J. C. (2007). Clinical and psychometric distinction of frontotemporal and Alzheimer dementias. *Archives of Neurology, 64,* 535–540.

Loring, D. W. (Ed.). (1999). *INS dictionary of neuropsychology.* New York: Oxford University Press.

Luna, B., Padmanabhan, A., & O'Hearn, K. (2010). What has fMRI told us about the development of cognitive control through adolescence? *Brain and Cognition, 72,* 101–113.

Magherini, A., & Litvan, I. (2005). Cognitive and behavioral aspects of PSP since Steele, Richardson and Olszewski's description of PSP 40 years ago and Albert's delineation of the subcortical dementia 30 years ago. *Neurocase, 11,* 250–262.

Marczinski, C. A., & Kertesz, A. (2006). Category and letter fluency in semantic dementia, primary progressive aphasia, and Alzheimer's disease. *Brain and Language, 97,* 258–265.

Mattis, S. (1988). *Dementia Rating Scale: Professional manual.* Odessa, FL: Psychological Assessment Resources.

Mattis, S. (2004). *Dementia Rating Scale-2: Professional manual.* Psychological Assessment Resources: Odessa, FL.

Matuszewski, V., Piolino, P., de la Sayette, V., Lalevée, C., Pélerin, A., Dupuy, B., et al. (2006). Retrieval mechanisms for autobiographical memories: Insights from the frontal variant of frontotemporal dementia. *Neuropsychologia, 44,* 2386–2397.

McGuinness, B., Barrett, S. L., Craig, D., Lawson, J., & Passmore, A. P. (2010). Executive functioning in Alzheimer's disease and vascular dementia. *International Journal of Geriatric Psychiatry, 25,* 562–568.

McKeith, I. G., Dickson, D. W., Lowe, J., Emre, M., O'Brian, J. T., et al. (2005). Diagnosis and management of dementia with Lewy bodies: Third report of the DLB consortium. *Neurology, 65,* 1863–1872.

McKeith, I. G., Galasko, D., Kosaka, K., Perry, E. K., Dickson, D. W., et al. (1996). Consensus guidelines for the clinical and pathologic diagnosis of dementia with Lewy bodies (DLB): Report of the consortium on DLB international workshop. *Neurology, 47,* 1113–1124.

McKhann, G. M., Albert, M. S., Grossman, M., Miller, B., Dickson, D., & Trojanowski, J. Q. (2001). Clinical and pathological diagnosis of frontotemporal Dementia: Report of the work group on frontotemporal dementia and Pick's disease. *Archives of Neurology, 58,* 1803–1809.

Mega, M. S., Cummings, J. L., Salloway, S., & Malloy, P. (1997). The limbic system: An anatomic, phylogenetic, and clinical perspective. *Journal of Neuropsychiatry and Clinical Neuroscience, 9,* 315–330.

Mendez, M. F., McMurtray, A., Chen, A. K., Shapira, J. S., Mishkin, F., & Miller, B. L. (2006). Functional neuroimaging and presenting psychiatric features in frontotemporal dementia. *Journal of Neurology, Neurosurgery, and Psychiatry, 77,* 4–7.

Mesulam, M.-M. (2000). *Principles of behavioral and cognitive neurology* (2nd edn.). New York: Oxford University Press.

Mesulam, M.-M. (2003). Primary progressive aphasia – A language-based dementia. *New England Journal of Medicine, 349,* 1535–1542.

Milberg, W. P., Hebben, N, & Kaplan, E. (1996). The Boston Process Approach to neuropsychological assessment. In K. M. Adams, & I. Grant (Eds.), *Neuropsychological assessment of neuropsychiatric disorders* (2nd edn., pp. 58–80). New York: Oxford University Press.

Millar, D., Griffiths, P., Zermansky, A. J., & Burn, D. J. (2006). Characterizing behavioral and cognitive dysexecutive changes in progressive supranuclear palsy. *Movement Disorders, 21,* 199–207.

Miyake, A., & Shah, P. (1999). Toward unified theories of working memory: Emerging general consensus, unresolved theoretical issues, and future research directions. In A. Miyake, & P. Shah (Eds.), *Models of working memory: Mechanisms of active maintenance and executive control* (pp.442–481). New York: Cambridge University Press.

Moretti, R., Torre, P., Antonello, R. M., Cattaruzza, T., Cazzato, G., & Bava, A. (2005). Frontal lobe dementia and subcortical vascular dementia: a neuropsychological comparison. *Psychological Reports, 96,* 141–151.

Murman, D. L. (2003). Neurologic aspects of prion diseases and frontotemporal dementias. In P. A. Lichtenberg, D. L. Murman, & A. M. Mellow (Eds.), *Handbook of dementia: Psychological, neurological, and psychiatric perspectives* (pp.83–113). New Jersey: John Wiley & Sons, Inc.

Murray, R., Neumann, M., Forman, M. S., Farmer, J., Massimo, L., Rice, A., et al. (2007). Cognitive and motor assessment in autopsy-proven corticobasal degeneration. *Neurology, 68,* 1274–1283.

Neary, D., Snowden, J. S., Gustafson, L., Passant, U., Stuss, D., Black, S., et al. (1998). Frontotemporal lobar degeneration: A consensus on clinical diagnostic criteria. *Neurology, 51,* 1546–1554.

Nedjam, Z., Devouche, E., & Dalla Barba, G. (2004). Confabulation, but not executive dysfunction discriminate AD from frontotemporal dementia. *European Journal of Neurology, 11,* 728–733.

Norris, M. P. & Haines, M. E. (2003). Psychological and neuropsychological aspects of Lewy body and frontal dementia. In P. A. Lichtenberg, D. L. Murman, & A. M. Mellow (Eds.),

Handbook of dementia: Psychological, neurological, and psychiatric perspectives (pp.115–148). New Jersey: John Wiley & Sons, Inc.

Nyatsanza, S., Shetty, T., Gregory, C., Lough, S., Dawson, K., & Hodges, J. R. (2003). A study of stereotypic behaviours in Alzheimer's disease and frontal and temporal variant frontotemporal dementia. *Journal of Neurology, Neurosurgery, and Psychiatry*, 74, 1398–1402.

O'Connell, M. E., Mateer, C. A., & Kerns, K. A. (2003). Prosthetic systems for addressing problems with initiation: Guidelines for selection, training, and measuring efficacy. *NeuroRehabilitation*, 18, 9–20.

O'Doherty, J. P. & Dolan, R. J. (2006). The role of human orbitofrontal cortex in reward prediction and behavioral choice: Insights from neuroimaging. In D. H. Zald & S. L. Rauch (Eds.), *The orbitofrontal cortex* (pp.265–283). New York: Oxford University Press.

O'Keeffe, F. M., Murray, B., Coen, R. F., Dockree, P. M., Bellgrove, M. A., Garavan, H., et al. (2007). Loss of insight in frontotemporal dementia, corticobasal degeneration and progressive supranuclear palsy. *Brain*, 130, 753–764.

Ogar, J., & Gorno-Tempini, M. L. (2007). The orbitofrontal cortex and the insula. In B. L. Miller, & J. L. Cummings (Eds.), *The human frontal lobes: Functions and disorders* (2nd edn., pp.59–67). New York: Guilford Press.

Ogden, J. A. (2005). *Fractured minds: A case study approach to clinical neuropsychology* (2nd edn.). New York: Oxford University Press.

Ott, B. R., Heindel, W. C., Whelihan, W. M., Caron, M. D., Piatt, A. L., & DiCarlo, M. A. (2003). Maze test performance and reported driving ability in early dementia. *Journal of Geriatric Psychiatry and Neurology*, 16, 151–155.

Paul, R., Moser, D., Cohen, R., Browndyke, J., Zawacki, T., & Gordon, N. (2001). Dementia severity and pattern of cognitive performance in vascular dementia. *Applied Neuropsychology*, 8, 211–217.

Pekkala, S., Albert, M. L., Spiro III, A., & Erkinjuntti, T. (2008). Perseveration in Alzheimer's disease. *Dementia and Geriatric Cognitive Disorders*, 25, 109–114.

Perri, R., Koch, G., Carlesimo, G. A., Serra, L., Faada, L., Pasqualetti, P., et al. (2005). Alzheimer's disease and frontal variant of frontotemporal dementia: A very brief battery for cognitive and behavioural distinction. *Journal of Neurology*, 252, 1238–1244.

Petrides, M., & Pandya, D. N. (2002). Association pathways of the prefrontal cortex and functional observations. In D. T. Stuss, & R. T. Knight (Eds.), *Principles of frontal lobe function* (pp.31–50). New York: Oxford University Press.

Phillips, L. H. (1997). Do "frontal tests" measure executive function? Issues of assessment and evidence from fluency tests. In P. Rabbitt (Ed.), *Methodology of frontal and executive function* (pp.191–213). Hove, UK: Psychology Press.

Plassman, B. L., Langa, K. M., Fisher, G. G., Heeringa, S. G., Weir, D. R., Ofstedal, M. B., et al. (2007). Prevalence of dementia in the United States: The Aging, Demographics, and Memory Study. *Neuroepidemiology*, 29, 125–132.

Rabin, L. A., Roth, R. M., Isquith, P. K., Wishart, H. A., Nutter-Upham, K. E., Pare, N., et al. (2006). Self- and informant reports of executive function on the BRIEF-A in MCI and older adults with cognitive complaints. *Archives of Clinical Neuropsychology*, 21, 721–732.

Rankin, K. P., Baldwin, E., Pace-Savitsky, C., Kramer, J. H., & Miller, B. L. (2005). Self-awareness and personality change in dementia. *Journal of Neurology, Neurosurgery, and Psychiatry*, 76, 632–639.

Rankin, K. P., Santos-Modesitt, W., Kramer, J. H., Pavlic, D., Beckman, V., & Miller, B. L. (2008). Spontaneous social behaviors discriminate behavioral dementias from psychiatric disorders and other dementias. *Journal of Clinical Psychiatry, 69*, 60–73.

Rascovsky, K., Salmon, D. P., Ho, G. J., Galasko, D., Peavy, G. M., Hansen, L. A., et al. (2002). Cognitive profiles differ in autopsy-confirmed frontotemporal dementia and AD. *Neurology, 58*, 1801–1808.

Reed, B. R., Eberling, J. L., Mungas, D., Weiner, M., Kramer, J. H., & Jagust, W. J. (2004). Effects of white matter lesions and lacunes on cortical function. *Archives of Neurology, 61*, 1545–1550.

Reed, B. R., Mungas, D. M., Kramer, J. H., Ellis, W., Vinters, H. V., Zarow, C., et al. (2007). Profiles of neuropsychological impairment in autopsy-defined Alzheimer's disease and cerebrovascular disease. *Brain, 130*, 731–739.

Reitan, R. M., & Wolfson, D. (1993). *The Halstead–Reitan neuropsychological test battery: Theory and clinical interpretation* (2nd edn.). Tuscon, AZ: Neuropsychology Press.

Reitan, R. M., & Wolfson, D. (2005). The effect of conation in determining the differential variance among brain-damaged and nonbrain-damaged persons across a broad range of neuropsychological tests. *Archives of Clinical Neuropsychology, 20*, 957–966.

Ricci, M., Guidoni, S. V., Sepe-Monti, M., Bomboi, G., Antonini, G., Blundo, C., et al. (2009). Clinical findings, functional abilities and caregiver distress in the early stage of dementia with Lewy bodies (DLB) and Alzheimer's disease (AD). *Archives of Gerontology and Geriatrics, 49*, e101–e104.

Rogers, T. T., Ivanoiu, A., Patterson, K., & Hodges, J. R. (2006). Semantic memory in Alzheimer's disease and the frontotemporal dementias: A longitudinal study of 236 patients. *Neuropsychology, 20*, 319–335.

Román, G. C. (2003). Vascular dementia: Distinguishing characteristics, treatment, and prevention. *Journal of the American Geriatrics Society, 51*, S296–S304.

Román, G. C., Tatemichi, T. K., Erkinjuntti, T., Cummings, J. L., Masdeu, J. C., et al. (1993). Vascular dementia: Diagnostic criteria for research studies. Report of the NINDS-AIREN International Workshop. *Neurology, 43*, 250–260.

Romine, C. B., & Reynolds, C. R. (2005). A model of the development of frontal lobe functioning: Findings from a meta-analysis. *Applied Neuropsychology, 12*, 190–201.

Rosen, H. J., Allison, S. C., Ogar, J. M., Amici, S., Rose, K., Dronkers, N., et al. (2006). Behavioral features in semantic dementia vs. other forms of progressive aphasias. *Neurology, 67*, 1752–1756.

Roth, R. M., Isquith, P. K., & Gioia, G. A. (2005). *Behavioral Rating Inventory of Executive Function – Adult version*. Lutz, FL: Psychological Assessment Resources.

Royall, D. R., Mahurin, R. K., & Gray, K. F. (1992). Bedside assessment of executive cognitive impairment: The Executive Interview. *Journal of the American Geriatrics Society, 40*, 1221–1226.

Ruff, R. (1996). *Ruff Figural Fluency Test: Professional manual*. Odessa, FL: Psychological Assessment Resources.

Sachdev, P. S., Brodaty, H., Valenzuela, M. J., Lorentz, L., Looi, J. C. L., Wen, W., et al. (2004). The neuropsychological profile of vascular cognitive impairment in stroke and TIA patients. *Neurology, 62*, 912–919.

Saczynski, J. S., Sigurdsson, S., Jonsdottir, M. K., Eiriksdottir, G., Jonsson, P. V., Garcia, M. E., et al. (2009). Cerebral infarcts and cognitive performance: Importance of location and number of infarcts. *Stroke, 40*, 677–682.

Sailor, K., Antoine, M., Diaz, M., Kuslansky, G., & Kluger, A. (2004). The effects of Alzheimer's disease on item output in verbal fluency tasks. *Neuropsychology, 18*, 306–314.

Sakagami, M., & Pan., X. (2007). Functional role of the ventrolateral prefrontal cortex in decision making. *Current Opinion in Neurobiology, 17*, 228–233.

Salmon, D. P., Butters, N., & Chan, A. S. (1999). The deterioration of semantic memory in Alzheimer's disease. *Canadian Journal of Experimental Psychology, 53*, 108–116.

Schoenbaum, G., Roesch, M. R., & Stalnaker, T. A. (2006). Orbitofrontal cortex, decision-making and drug addiction. *Trends in Neurosciences, 29*, 116–124.

Sebastian, M. V., Menor, J., & Elosua, M. R. (2006). Attentional dysfunction of the central executive in AD: evidence from dual task and perseveration errors. *Cortex, 42*, 1015–1020.

Sinz, H., Zamarian, L., Benke, T., Wenning, G. K., & Delazer, M. (2008). Impact of ambiguity and risk on decision making in mild Alzheimer's disease. *Neuropsychologia, 46*, 2043–2055.

Snowden, J.S., Neary, D., & Mann, D.M.A. (2002). Frontotemporal dementia. *British Journal of Psychiatry, 180*, 140–143.

Somerville, J., Tremont, G., & Stern, R. A. (2000). The Boston Qualitative Scoring System as a measure of executive functioning in Rey–Osterrieth Complex Figure performance. *Journal of Clinical and Experimental Neuropsychology, 22*, 613–621.

Souchay, C., Isingrini, M., Pillon, B., & Gil, R. (2003). Metamemory accuracy in Alzheimer's disease and frontotemporal lobe dementia. *Neurocase, 9*, 482–492.

Srikanth, S., Nagaraja, A. V., & Ratnavalli, E. (2005). Neuropsychiatric symptoms in dementia-frequency, relationship to dementia severity and comparison in Alzheimer's disease, vascular dementia and frontotemporal dementia. *Journal of the Neurological Sciences, 236*, 43–48.

St. James-Roberts, I. (1979). Neurological plasticity, recovery from brain insult, and child development. *Advances in Child Development and Behavior, 14*, 253–319.

Starkstein, S. E., Jorge, R., Mizrahi, R., Adrian, J., & Robinson, R. G. (2007). Insight and danger in Alzheimer's disease. *European Journal of Neurology, 14*, 455–460.

Steinberg, M., Corcoran, C., Tschan, J. T., Huber, C., Welsh-Bohmer, K., Norton, M. C., et al. (2006). Risk factors for neuropsychiatric symptoms in dementia: The Cache County Study. *International Journal of Geriatric Psychiatry, 21*, 824–830.

Stern, R. A. & Prohaska, M. L. (1996). Neuropsychological evaluation of executive functioning. In L. J. Dickstein, M. B. Riba, & J. M. Oldham (Eds.), *American Psychiatric Press review of psychiatry: Vol. 15* (pp. 163–193). Washington, DC: American Psychiatric Press.

Stern, R. A., & White, T. (2003). *Neuropsychological Assessment Battery: Administration, Scoring, and Interpretation manual.* Lutz, FL: Psychological Assessment Resources.

Stern, R. A., Javorsky, D. J., Singer, E. A., Singer Harris, N. G., Somerville, J. A., Duke, L. M., et al. (1999). *The Boston Qualitative Scoring System for the Rey-Osterrieth Complex Figure.* Odessa, FL: Psychological Assessment Resources.

Stevens, M. C., Skudlarski, P., Pearlson, G. D., & Calhoun, V. D. (2009). Age-related cognitive gains are mediated by the effects of white matter development on brain network integration. *Neuroimage, 48*, 738–746.

Stout, J. C., Wyman, M. F., Johnson, S. A., Peavy, G. M., & Salmon, D. P. (2003). Frontal behavioral syndromes and functional status in probable Alzheimer disease. *American Journal of Geriatric Psychiatry, 11*, 683–686.

Strauss, E., Sherman, E. M. S., & Spreen, O. (2006). *A compendium of neuropsychological tests: Administration, norms, and commentary* (3rd edn.). New York: Oxford University Press.

Stuss, D. T., & Benson, D. F. (1986). *The frontal lobes*. New York: Raven Press.

Swanberg, M. M., Tractenberg, R. E., Mohs, R., Thal, L. J., & Cummings, J. L. (2004). Executive dysfunction in Alzheimer disease. *Archives of Neurology, 61*, 556–560.

Thompson, J. C., Stopford, C. L., Snowden, J. S., & Neary, D. (2005). Qualitative neuropsychological performance characteristics in frontotemporal dementia and Alzheimer's disease. *Journal of Neurology, Neurosurgery, and Psychiatry, 76*, 920–927.

Traykov, L., Baudic, S., Raoux, N., Latour, F., Rieu, D., Smagghe, A., et al. (2005). Patterns of memory impairment and perseverative behavior discriminate early Alzheimer's disease from subcortical vascular dementia. *Journal of the Neurological Sciences, 229–230*, 75–79.

Turner, R. S. (2003). Neurologic aspects of Alzheimer's disease. In P. A. Lichtenberg, D. L. Murman, & A. M. Mellow (Eds.), *Handbook of dementia: Psychological, neurological, and psychiatric perspectives* (pp.1–24). New Jersey: John Wiley & Sons, Inc.

Vogel, A., Hasselbach, S. G., Gade, A., Ziebell, M., & Waldemar, G. (2005). Cognitive and functional neuroimaging correlates for anosognosia in mild cognitive impairment and Alzheimer's disease. *International Journal of Geriatric Psychiatry, 20*, 238–246.

Waltz, J. A., Knowlton, B. J., Holyoak, K. J., Boone, K. B., Back-Madruga, C., McPherson, S., et al. (2004). Relational integration and executive function in Alzheimer's disease. *Neuropsychology, 18*, 296–305.

Wechsler, D. (1981). *Wechsler Adult Intelligence Scale-Revised*. San Antonio, TX: Psychological Corporation.

Wechsler, D. (1997). *Wechsler Adult Intelligence Scale* (3rd edn.). San Antonio, TX: Psychological Corporation.

Wechsler, D. (1999). *Wechsler Abbreviated Scale of Intelligence*. San Antonio, TX: Psychological Corporation.

Wechsler, D. (2008). *Wechsler Adult Intelligence Scale* (4th edn.). San Antonio, TX: Psychological Corporation.

Weisman, D., & McKeith, I. (2007). Dementia with Lewy bodies. *Seminars in Neurology, 27*, 42–47.

Wenning, G. K., & Geser, F. (2007). Multiple system atrophy. In J. Jankovic, & E. Tolosa (Eds.), *Parkinson's disease and movement disorders* (5th edn., pp.175–185). Philadelphia, PA: Lippincott Williams & Wilkins.

Whelihan, W. M., DiCarlo, M. A., & Paul, R. H. (2005). The relationship of neuropsychological functioning to driving competence in older persons with early cognitive decline. *Archives of Clinical Neuropsychology, 20*, 217–228.

Wicklund, A. H., Johnson, N., & Weintraub, S. (2004). Preservation of reasoning in primary progressive aphasia: Further differentiation from Alzheimer's disease and the behavioral presentation of frontotemporal dementia. *Journal of Clinical and Experimental Neuropsychology, 26*, 347–355.

Wilson, B. A., Alderman, N., Burgess, P. W., Emslie, H., & Evans, J. J. (1996). *Behavioral Assessment of the Dysexecutive Syndrome*. Bury St. Edmunds, UK: Thames Valley Test Company.

Yaari, R., & Corey-Bloom, J. (2007). Alzheimer's disease. *Seminars in Neurology, 27*, 32–41.

Yuspeh, R. L., Vanderploeg, R. D., Crowell, T. A., & Mullan, M. (2002). Differences in executive functioning between Alzheimer's disease and subcortical ischemic vascular dementia. *Journal of Clinical and Experimental Neuropsychology, 24,* 745–754.

Zamboni, G., Huey, E. D., Krueger, F., Nichelli, P. F., & Grafman, J. (2008). Apathy and disinhibition in frontotemporal dementia. *Neurology, 71,* 736–742.

14

Emotion and Behavior in Alzheimer's Disease and Other Dementias

Christopher I. Wright

Introduction

Although Alzheimer' disease and other dementias are often considered to be primarily cognitive disorders, it is very clear that in most cases there is a disruption of emotional systems, leading to behavioral dysregulation. This chapter hopes to give an overview of what is a rapidly expanding field – the neuroscience of emotion – initially examining some operational definitions of emotion, the neural circuitry of emotion, and how alterations in this circuitry might lead to behavioral dyscontrol. Following this more theoretical section comes an overview of the behavioral or neuropsychiatric features of Alzheimer's disease (AD) and two other illustrative dementias, frontotemporal dementia (FTD) and Lewy body dementia (LBD).

Emotions

Emotions are difficult to define. Perhaps the best way to grasp them is to look at situations where we all agree that emotion is involved. This does not refer to a description of subjective emotions or feelings per se, but to a coordinated system for processing of biologically relevant stimuli, and for generating the physiological responses and actions necessary to avoid or make the most of a particular stimulus. Thus, emotion can be viewed as relating to basic drives, for example, fear, aggression, hunger, thirst, and libido. These survival behaviors and basic drives also relate

The Handbook of Alzheimer's Disease and Other Dementias, First Edition.
Edited by Andrew E. Budson, Neil W. Kowall.
© 2011 Blackwell Publishing Ltd. Published 2011 by Blackwell Publishing Ltd.

to or are influenced by reward and punishment systems in the brain and by personality. For example, temperament (e.g. whether one is introverted or extroverted) relates to how an individual responds to emotional stimuli such as dangerous, social, or novel situations.

One definition of emotion that encompasses these complexities is that emotion is the process of an organism responding to a significant event. This process includes perception of emotional stimuli, physiological arousal, appraisal (which may lead to response inhibition or facilitation via regulatory processes), and the ultimate emotional response including motor expression or action tendencies (e.g. fight or flight mechanisms) (Lazarus, 1966; Lazarus & Folkman, 1984; Schachter & Singer, 1962). Initial rapid responses occur involving the perception of the emotional stimulus (sensory input) and the generation of physiological changes and motor tendencies (e.g., increased heart rate and preparation for flight) via specific output channels. Directly after these initial adaptive and perceptual changes, primary followed by secondary appraisals occur, as described below.

Functional Neuroanatomy of Emotion and Behavioral Regulation

The cortical circuitry involved in emotion and its regulation was probably first described by Broca in 1878, and he was the first to use the term "limbic" (Broca, 1878). He initially used this term to describe the gross anatomical similarities across species of the c-shaped medial cortical surface surrounding the corpus callosum, including the cingulate (CC) and orbitofrontal cortex (OFC), extending into the medial temporal cortex and anterior olfactory structure (Figure 14.1). Broca was

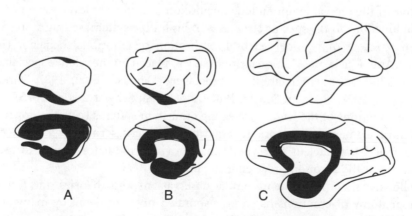

Figure 14.1   The "Grand Lobe Limbique" of Broca. (A) rodent, (B), feline, and (C) nonhuman primate brains

Source: Adapted from Broca, P. (1878). Anatomie comparée des circonvolutions cérébrales: le grand lobe limbique. *Review of Anthropology*, (1), 385–498

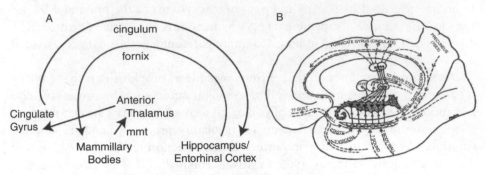

Figure 14.2   Limbic circuitry of Papez (A) and McLean (B)
Source: B is reproduced from Maclean, P. D. (1949). Psychosomatic disease and the "visceral brain"; recent developments bearing on the Papez theory of emotion. *Psychosomatic Medicine, 11*, 338–353

particularly interested in these regions as they appeared evolutionarily preserved. However, his primary interest was in their possible olfactory affiliations, and it was not until the 1930s that Papez (1937) connected these regions to emotional processes (Figure 14.2A). Papez had the benefit of current neuroanatomical studies and the works of Bard, Canon, and Penfield; and he made a connection between the "grand lobe limbique" of Broca and emotional behavior and regulation. He proposed his well-known circuitry for the cortical–subcortical control of emotion that involved connections between the hippocampus, mammillary bodies (via the fornix); and anterior nucleus of the thalamus (via the mammillothalamic tract) and the cingulate cortex. This circuit is ultimately closed via cingulate gyrus connections to the hippocampus via the cingulum bundle. MacLean (1949) expanded on these ideas, adding knowledge about the effects of lesions and Kluver and Bucy's work on the role of the medial temporal lobe in emotion. He more boldly designated emotional functions to the specific structures of his limbic system, setting a precedence for the concept of regional cerebral localization of emotional behavior (Figure 14.2B). After MacLean, additional emphasis was placed on the relative specialization of the right hemisphere in emotional processing (Davidson et al., 1987; Dimond & Farrington, 1977; Heilman & Satz, 1986; Ross, 1993; Schwartz et al. 1975) and on the contributions of the widely projecting brainstem systems (e.g., the dopaminergic ventral tegmental area, noradrenergic locus ceruleus, serotonergic raphe nuclei, cholinergic basal nucleus of Mynert) that provide modulatory input to the core structures of the emotion processing circuitry.

Following these fundamental initial observations and theories, the functional neuroanatomy of emotions has been elaborated upon in detail by many authors (e.g. Adolphs, 2002; Amaral, 2003; Davidson, 2001; LeDoux, 2000; Kringelbach & Berridge, 2009; Mesulam, 2000; Phillips et al., 2003a; Rolls, 2005). In addition, the anatomical focus has changed somewhat as it is now recognized that the hippocampus plays a primary role in memory processes (see Chapter 11, this volume) and

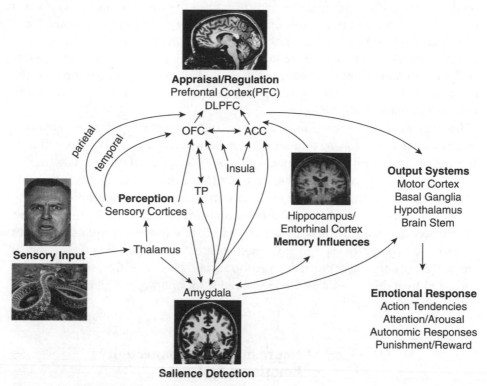

Figure 14.4   Neural circuitry of emotional processing
DLPFC = Dorsolateral prefrontal cortex; OFC = Orbitofrontal cortex; ACC = Anterior cingulate cortex; TP = Temporal pole

is less intimately connected with the medial cortical circuitry. Another medial temporal lobe structure – the amygdala (Figure 14.3, plate section) – which is closely adjacent to the hippocampus is now recognized as playing a central role in emotional processing and dysregulation. Currently, it is thought that emotion and behavioral regulation are mediated via the amygdala and the interconnected medial regions of the "grand lobe limbique" and closely adjacent structures. As will be reviewed below (Figure 14.4), the amygdala and the anterior regions of the "grand lobe limbique," encompassing the medial prefrontal cortex (PFC) – including the anterior cingulate cortex (ACC) – the OFC, the temporal pole (TP), and the insula are now considered the major structures implicated in emotional control and regulation.

The amygdala is thought to play a primary role in the early stages of emotional stimulus perception, rapidly signaling the biological relevance or salience of the stimulus (e.g., Antoniadis et al., 2009; Amaral et al., 2003; Calder et al., 2001; Davis & Whalen, 2001; LeDoux, 1996; Phan, Wager et al., 2004; Phillips et al., 2003a, 2003b; Polli et al., 2009; Rolls, 1999; Weierich et al., 2010; Weiskrantz, 1956). With respect to these rapid, early stages of emotional processing, there has been a focus on direct pathways from sensory organs (e.g., the eye or ear) to the amygdala (via the thalamus), which bypass typical unimodal sensory processing (LeDoux, 2000; Morris et al., 1999; Whalen et al., 1998). However, neuroanatomical studies in non-human primates and recent functional neuroimaging experiments raise doubts about the notion of such thalamic pathways and suggest that visual input to the amygdala even at the earliest stages passes through visual cortices (Pessoa, 2005; Pessoa et al. 2006; Rolls, 2005).

Directly following these initial adaptive and perceptual processes, appraisal mechanisms ensue involving communications between the amygdala, hippocampus/entorhinal cortex, and various regions of the PFC including the OFC, ACC, insula, and dorsolateral PFC (DLPFC) (Figure 14.4). (Note that the amygdala may influence the DLPFC mostly indirectly via effects on OFC and ACC neurons projecting into the DLPFC.) Through this circuitry, stimuli are scrutinized more carefully, past experiences are brought to bear, and the ultimate emotional response becomes refined or differentiated via regulatory mechanisms. Superimposed upon this model are also effects of widely projecting neurotransmitter systems from the brainstem and basal forebrain, as well as the specialized association of the right hemisphere with emotional processing.

Overview of Neuroanatomic Connectivity of Emotional Systems

While an extensive review of the connectivity of each region in the model above is beyond the scope of this chapter, Figure 14.4 attempts to accurately represent the major connections between the featured regions. Particularly relevant is the fact that the hippocampus and entorhinal cortex are interconnected with each other, with the DLPFC, and with the amygdala (Insausti et al., 1987; Pitkanen et al., 2000; Salvador et al., in press; Saunders et al., 1988; Van Hoesen et al., 1975). In keeping with the model above, it is thought that entorhinal/hippocampal projections to the amygdala provide relevant environmental and historical information about stimuli to which the amygdala is responsive (Kim & Fanselow, 1992; Phillips & LeDoux, 1992), while the amygdala itself enhances emotional memory storage via projections to the entorhinal cortex/hippocampus (Dolcos et al., 2005; LaBar, 2003; Phelps, 2004; Popa et al., 2010; Smith et al., 2004). Other notable projections include those from the amygdala to the ACC and OFC (De Olmos, 1990; Etkin et al., 2010; Price et al., 1987), to occipitotemporal visual cortices (e.g. fusiform cortex), to the hypothalamus, and to other autonomic centers that are involved in the visceral aspects of fear and anxiety responses (Aggleton, 1992; Amaral et al., 2003; Karlsson et al., 2010; LeDoux, 1996; Mesulam & Mufson, 1985). The occiptotemporal cortex likewise gives substantial input back to the amygdala (Updyke, 1993; Webster et al., 1991). Reciprocal connections from the ACC and OFC also reach the amygdala and emotional response output systems, thus regulating their activities (Barbas et al., 2003; Ghashghaei & Barbas, 2002; LeDoux, 1996; Rolls, 2004).

The Central Role of the Amygdala in Emotional Processing

There are now many studies in humans (and nonhuman primates) supporting a central role of the amygdala in emotional processing (Figures 14.3 and 14.4). For example, the amygdala is activated when people view fearful or angry faces (Anderson & Phelps, 2001; Breiter et al., 1996; Gur et al., 2002; Hariri, et al., 2000; Morris et al., 1996; Morris et al., 1998; Phillips et al., 2001; Whalen et al., 2004; Whalen et al., 1998; Wright et al., 2001; Wright et al., 2002), components of emotional faces (Morris et al., 2002; Whalen et al., 2004), fearful bodily gestures (Hadjikhani & de Gelder, 2003), unpleasant scenes (Irwin et al., 1996; Lane et al., 1997; Phan, Taylor et al., 2004), and aversive olfactory and gustatory stimuli (Royet et al., 2000; Zald et al., 1998; Zald & Pardo, 1997). In addition, the amygdala is engaged by positively valenced stimuli and rewards (Baxter & Murray, 2002; Breiter et al., 1996; Canli et al., 2002; Mather et al., 2004; Rolls, 1999), by novel stimuli (Dubois et al., 1999; Rolls, 1999; Schwartz, Wright, Shin, Kagan, & Rauch, 2003; Schwartz, Wright, Shin, Kagan, Whalen et al., 2003; Wright et al., 2003; Wright et al., 2006; Wright et al., 2008; Weierich et al., 2010), and by movements suggesting a living organism (Bonda et al., 1996). Not only does the amygdala respond to objects of known value, it is also instrumental in learning the value of external stimuli via mechanisms of conditioning (Büchel et al., 1999; Büchel et al., 1998; Furmark et al., 1997; LaBar et al., 1998; LeDoux, 1996; Milad et al., 2007; Morris & Dolan, 2004; Phelps, et al., 2004; Tabbert et al., 2005). Furthermore, pharmacological induction of anxiety leads to activation of the amygdala (Reiman et al., 1989).

Functional Neuroanatomy of Emotional Control and Behavioral Dysregulation

With this as background, I will review the possible roles of the circuitry of emotion and behavior regulation in the pathophysiology of the neuropsychaitric symptoms of AD and other dementias. The following sections focus primarily on AD, as this condition has been investigated to the greatest extent. In addition, the possible role of the circuitry of emotional control in FTD and LBD are also explored. Each section begins with a hypothetical case illustration typifying the behavioral manifestations of these disorders. Following this, methods of measurement, pathophysiology, epidemiology, consequences, and treatment of the behavioral manifestations of AD and other dementias are examined.

Neuropsychiatric Symptoms in Alzheimer's Disease

Illustrative case: A 79-year-old female with 2–3 years of slowly progressive memory problems came to the clinic for evaluation. She had increasingly agitated behavior, and concerns that people were coming into her house and stealing things. She thought the police were involved, as they came by several times. She was not sure why they were there, but speaking with her family revealed that she had called them several times and then forgotten. She was only oriented to self. She was able to repeat three out of three words after one trial, but with a short delay recalled zero out of three and was unable to recognize any from a list. There was mild anomia and difficulties copying pentagons. Examination was otherwise normal. MRI scan showed atrophy of the temporal lobes (Figure 14.5A, plate section), including the hippocampus and amygdala, along with regions of the paralimbic system (anterior temporal cortex, entorhinal cortex, inferior PFC) as well as the posterior parietal cortex. In concordance with this, a positron emission tomography (PET) scan (Figure 14.5B, plate section) showed hypometabolism in the parietotemporal cortices, with milder hypometabolism in regions of the frontal lobe. The patient's cognitive and behavioral syndromes progressed over several years. She ultimately contracted pneumonia and passed away. At autopsy, the brain cross-sections (Figure 14.5C, plate section) showed that generalized atrophy was present as well as more severe selective atrophy in the regions mentioned above (e.g., medial temporal lobe, paralimbic cortex, parietal cortex). Tissue studies (Figure 14.5D, plate section) demonstrated plaques and tangles, the histopathological hallmarks of AD.

Measuring neuropsychiatric symptoms in dementia

This is a typical case of AD. Although AD has been primarily considered a memory disorder, it has become increasingly apparent that significant emotional and behavioral dysregulation exist which manifests as neuropsychiatric symptomatology. Before reviewing the epidemiology of these symptoms, selected methods for assessment of behavioral and neuropsychiatric symptoms are reviewed. There are many assessments and questionnaires in use, particularly for research studies and clinical trials, but due to the time constraints in a typical clinical setting, most of these are not practical to use. However, two are reviewed that can be easily incorporated into routine clinical practice. The first is the left side of the Blessed Dementia Rating Scale (BDRS) (Blessed et al., 1968), which assesses performance of everyday activities, changes in habits, personality, interests, and drives. This is a useful instrument as it takes only a few minutes to complete and, in combination with the right side of the BDRS (the Attention, Memory and Concentration Subtests), can give a balanced view of both the behavioral and cognitive aspects of a dementia. It is a well-validated measure and determining the relative right- versus left-sided BDRS scores (with higher numbers indicating poorer performance) may help with distinguishing between different dementias early in the clinical course. For example, a greater right- versus left-sided score, indicating greater cognitive than behavioral dysregulation, is generally consistent with AD. As will be reviewed below, dementias that have major behavioral disturbance early on, with lesser cognitive decline (e.g., FTD), exhibit greater left- than right-sided Blessed scores.

The second brief tool for assessing behavioral disturbances in dementia is the Neuropsychiatric Inventory Questionnaire (NPI-Q) (Kaufer et al., 2000). This instrument, which can be completed in the waiting room, takes about 10 minutes to complete and is filled out by an informant who knows the patient well. The NPI-Q assesses 12 behavioral disturbances: delusions, hallucinations, agitation/aggression, dysphoria/depression, anxiety, euphoria/elation, apathy/indifference, disinhibition, irritability/lability, aberrant motor activity, nighttime disturbance, and appetite/eating disturbance. The severity of each behavior is rated (0 = none, 1 = mild, 2 = moderate, 3 = severe) as is the distress caused in the caregiver (0 = not distressing, 1 = minimal, 2 = mild, 3 = moderate, 4 = severe, 5 = extreme). The NPI-Q uses a screening strategy to minimize administration time, examining and scoring only those behavioral domains with positive responses to screening questions. Of note, this assessment is highly correlated with the results obtained from the longer NPI (Cummings, 1997; Cummings & McPherson, 2001; Cummings et al., 1994), which is a standard tool for research and clinical trials. Both these instruments can be used to follow the development of behavioral/neuropsychiatric disturbances as well as the responses to therapeutic interventions. If there is interest in following specific symptoms or syndromes in more detail after these more general inventories have been performed, symptom-specific instruments may also be useful, such as the Geriatric Depression Scale (GDS; Yesavage et al., 1981), the Cornell Scale for Depression in Dementia (CSDD; Alexopoulos et al., 1988) or the Cohen-Mansfield Agitation Inventory (CMAI; Cohen-Mansfield et al., 1989).

Epidemiology of Neuropsychiatric Symptoms in AD

Alois Alzheimer's initial 1907 case of AD demonstrated significant psychopathology. In his original paper he describes that the patient "initially presented at 51 yrs old with jealousy of her husband. Rapidly progressive memory loss soon followed . . . She began to believe that people wanted to kill her, and she would scream out loud." More recently a number of studies examining the neuropsychiatric symptoms of AD patients have confirmed their frequency. In fact, it has been stated that up to 90% of patients with AD manifest psychiatric signs and symptoms sometime in the course of the disease (Burns et al., 1990; Devanand et al., 1997; Mega et al., 1996; Merriam et al., 1988; Reisberg et al., 1987; Rubin & Kinscherf, 1989; Tariot et al., 1995; Teri et al., 1989; Teri et al., 1988; Vilalta-Franch et al., 2010), and that "AD is the most widely encountered cause of psychiatric pathology associated with a specific neuropathology" (Merriam et al., 1988). Depending on the stage of the disease and the study, 10–30% of AD patients have hallucinations, 20–40% depression, 30–50% delusions, 40–80% agitation and aggression, 50–90% apathy (Devanand et al., 1997; Jost & Grossberg, 1996; Merriam et al., 1988; Rubin & Kinscherf, 1989; Teri et al., 1988; Vilalta-Franch et al., 2010). These symptoms recur in 85–95% of cases on a yearly basis, and thus are a persistent problem throughout much of the disease course (at least until the terminal stages of the disease when severe mental and physical disability precludes such behaviors). They are found across the age range in AD, though older patients (vs. younger ones) may have more psychosis, while younger patients may have more depression, agitation, and personality changes (Levy et al., 1996; Rubin, Kinscherf et al., 1993; Rubin, Storandt et al., 1993). While these signs and symptoms may get worse as the disease progresses (at least until the terminal phases), they are also found early in the course of AD, and in mild cognitive impaiment (MCI) and prodromal AD, in up to 60% of cases (Devanand et al., 1997; Feldman et al., 2004; Rubin & Kinscherf, 1989; Teri et al., 1989; Teri et al., 1988). The principal psychiatric features in patients with MCI or prodromal AD include apathy, irritability, anxiety, dysphoria, and aggression (Chan et al., 2003; Copeland et al., 2003; Feldman et al., 2004; Hwang et al., 2004; Lyketsos et al., 2002; Palmer et al., in press). Excess motor activity (pacing, wandering) and psychotic features have a significantly lower frequency in MCI or mild AD as compared to later disease stages (Hwang et al., 2004).

Consequences of neuropsychiatric symptoms in AD

The presence of neuropsychiatric symptoms in AD and MCI have significant consequences for the patient and caregivers. Changes in personality have been described as one of the most distressing aspects of the disease (Fuh et al., 2001; Kaufer et al., 1998; Nagaratnam et al., 1998; Pang et al., 2002; Shin et al., 2005; Teri, 1997). Behavioral symptoms are strongly associated with caregiver distress, and may increase the likelihood of nursing home placement (Kaufer et al., 1998; O'Donnell et al., 1992; Scarmeas et al., 2005; Steele et al., 1990). Moreover, apathy, delusions, hallucinations, and agitation/aggression predict more rapid cognitive and functional decline, as well as increased mortality in patients with AD (Levy et al., 1996; Lopez & Becker, 2003; Ropacki & Jeste, 2005; Schultz et al., 2002; Starkstein et al., 2006) and MCI (Palmer et al., 2010). Neuropsychiatric symptoms may identify those with MCI or prodromal AD that will progress to AD, as irritability, agitation, depression, and apathy also predict more rapid functional and cognitive declines (Copeland et al., 2003; Elfgren et al., 2010; Feldman et al., 2004; Modrego & Ferrandez, 2004; Wilson et al., 2002; Wilson et al., 2004).

Pathophysiology of neuropsychiatric symptoms in AD

Relevance of AD pathology distribution
In his initial case, Alois Alzheimer identified abnormal nerve cells and fiber clusters in the cerebral cortex of a 55-year-old woman with a progressive dementia using

silver staining methods at autopsy. These findings, now considered to be the hallmark neuropathological lesions of AD, are known as neurofibrillary tangles (NFTs) and amyloid plaques. Currently, the beta amyloid protein, a major component of the plaques, is thought to play a central pathophysiological role in the disease (Selkoe, 2003). NFTs are found in neurons and are composed primarily of anomalous cytoskeletal proteins (Brion, 1998) and may also be of relevance for AD pathophysiology (Iqbal et al., 2005). Definitive diagnosis of AD rests upon postmortem findings of a specific distribution and number of these lesions (Hyman, 1997; Khachaturian, 1985). Particularly of interest to this chapter is the precise time course and neuroanatomical pattern of the development of AD neuropathology. Four stages of neuropathological progression have been described based primarily on the distribution of NFTs (Braak & Braak, 1991, 1995; Mesulam, 2000), as these lesions seem to best parallel cognitive decline (Arriagada et al., 1992; Bierer et al., 1995) and neuronal loss (Gomez-Isla et al., 1996), which results in a characteristic pattern of atrophy (Dickerson et al., 2009). In the earliest stage (low limbic), clusters of NFTs are found primarily in the MTL, including amygdala, the entorhinal cortex, and hippocampus (Mesulam, 2000). Notably, NFTs are seen in these regions in most brain specimens from nondemented subjects over 60 years old (Davis et al., 1999; Haroutunian et al., 1999). Their role in age-related memory or behavioral changes is uncertain, but they may relate to the development of late-life onset of neuropsychiatric disorders. The second stage (high limbic) is characterized by increased numbers of NFTs in the MTL, with spread of pathology to surrounding temporal lobe areas. This stage is associated with MCI or prodromal AD as subjects may have behavioral changes and isolated memory difficulties (Jicha et al., 2006; Markesbery et al., 2006; Mesulam, 2000; Petersen et al., 2006). The third (low neocortical) and fourth stages (high neocortical) are associated with mild-to-moderate dementia. During these stages further pathology accumulates in the temporal lobe and other brain regions that influence the circuitry of emotional processing including the parietal and prefrontal association cortices, the cingulate gyrus, fusiform gyrus, and insula, with relative sparing of the primary sensorimotor cortices until the terminal phases of dementia.

It is notable that the amygdala exhibits early and regionally selectivity pathology in AD (Braak & Braak, 1991, 1995; Haroutunian et al., 1999; Herzog & Kemper, 1980; Mesulam, 2000; Van Hoesen et al., 1999). Furthermore, neuropathological and neuroimaging studies have shown significant changes in amygdala volume in both aging and AD (DeKosky et al., 2002; Herzog & Kemper, 1980; Kovacevic et al., 1992; Smith et al., 1999; Tsuchiya & Kosaka, 1990; Van Hoesen et al., 1999; Vereecken et al., 1994). Atrophy is relatively mild and variable in early stages of AD and MCI (Bottino et al., 2002; Laakso, Partanen et al., 1995; Laakso, Soininen et al., 1995), but may increase the risk for future dementia in cognitively intact elders (den Heijer et al., 2006). Further, amygdala atrophy is related to impaired emotional memory (Mori et al., 1999), the non-cognitive features of AD (Smith et al., 1999), and with behavioral disturbances in other forms of dementia (Gorno-Tempini et al., 2004; Seeley et al., 2005).

Emotional circuitry disruption, dysregulation, and
AD neuropsychiatric symptoms

Given the distribution of AD pathology, there are multiple sites at which emotional processes could go awry in AD (Figure 14.4). As AD progresses increasing pathological involvement of the PFC (e.g., OFC, ACC, and DLPFC) and higher order sensory systems (e.g., fusiform cortex) will likely influence neuropsychiatric symptom expression. For example, PFC damage may lead to loss of appraisal/regulatory mechanisms resulting in release of 'top-down' control of amygdala activity and of emotional response output systems. Intrinsic amygdala pathology might also in itself lead to behavioral dysregulation in AD. Excessive low fidelity sensory inputs to the amygdala via the thalamus, due to sensory association cortex (e.g. fusiform gyrus) pathology, could lead to overstimulation of the amygdala. Alternatively, degraded inputs from sensory cortices (such as via the occipitotemporal stream) to the amygdala might result in aberrant behavioral responses. Loss of memory influences, in the setting of entorhinal cortex/hippocampus pathology, might result in the loss of context-dependent control of behavior via degraded signals to the connected amygdala and higher order (heteromodal) cortices. Furthermore, if there were selective right hemisphere lateralization of AD pathology a more prominent behavioral syndrome might be anticipated. Finally, there is known depletion of several widely projecting neurotransmitter systems in AD that modulate state functions of the emotional control circuitry, and this also might be anticipated to alter behavior. In the following paragraphs, data suggesting that such mechanisms hold in AD are reviewed.

Neurotransmitter disruptions and behavioral symptoms in AD

Several studies indicate that there are neurochemical abnormalities in the structures involved in emotional processing and behavioral control, suggesting that this may contribute to the neuropsychiatric features of AD (and even MCI). Changes in serotonergic and noradrenergic systems are more prominent in AD as compared to normal aging in the PFC, AC, and OFC (e.g., Meltzer et al., 1996; Versijpt et al., 2003). It is also well established that the widely projecting nuclei in the basal forebrain (nucleus basalis) and brainstem (raphe nucleus and locus ceruleus) develop significant damage in AD. Treatments that enhance cholinergic activity (e.g., rivastigmine) and have positive effects on the behavioral features of AD enhance the function of the PFC and hippocampus (Potkin et al., 2001). Interestingly, those patients who do not respond with improved behavior to the cholinesterase inhibitor, donepezil, have persistent OFC and DLPFC hypoperfusion compared to behavioral responders (Mega, Dinov et al., 2000). There is also ample evidence of neurochemical alterations in the amygdala that could represent another source of emotional dysregulation in AD. Several PET studies have demonstrated decreased acetylcholinesterase in the amygdala in patients with AD (Herholz et al., 2004; Shinotoh et al., 2003; Shinotoh, Namba, Fukushi, Nagatsuka, Tanaka, Aotsuka, Ota et al., 2000; Shinotoh, Namba, Fukushi, Nagatsuka, Tanaka, Aotsuka, Tanada et al., 2000). This occurs in both early- and late-onset AD (Shinotoh, Namba, Fukushi,

Nagatsuka, Tanaka, Aotsuka, Ota et al., 2000), and is correlated with cognitive functioning as measured by the Mini-Mental State Examination (MMSE) (Shinotoh et al., 2003). Neuropathological studies further reveal significant and parallel reductions in both acetylcholinesterase and choline acetyltransferase in the amygdala in AD (Emre et al., 1993; Esiri et al., 1990; Unger et al., 1988). While it is beyond the limits of this chapter to describe all the neurotransmitter-related findings relevant to emotional regulation, the foregoing evidence strongly suggests that these systems may contribute to behavioral alterations in AD.

Altered brain activity patterns and behavioral symptoms in AD

A number of studies have implicated specific neuropsychiatric symptoms in AD with altered function in the circuitry of emotional regulation. When a cohort of AD subjects with various neuropsychiatric symptoms was studied together, hypometabolism (as measured by PET) was found in the AC, DLPFC, and ventral striatum (without regard to the specific symptom expressed by the patients) (Mega, Lee et al., 2000). Other studies have linked specific neuropsychiatric syndromes or symptoms with hypoperfusion or hypometabolism in specific areas. For example, for patients with psychosis, delusions have been linked to right PFC and bilateral temporal lobe hypoactivity, while hallucinations have been associated with parietal hypoactivity (Staff et al., 1999; Starkstein, Federoff, et al., 1994; Starkstein, Vazquez et al., 1994). However, another study implicated the hippocampus and adjacent temporal cortices in psychosis (Zubenko et al., 1991), suggesting that multiple overlapping mechanisms may be at play. One study linked anxiety symptoms in AD to hypoactivity in the entorhinal cortex, parahippocampal gyrus, and superior temporal cortex (Hashimoto et al., 2006). Other investigators describe that apathy in AD is associated with reduced metabolic activity in the bilateral ACC and medial OFC cortex (Marshall et al., 2007). Of note, the extent of plaque and tangle pathology in the ACC is also associated with apathy (Marshall et al., 2007).

Two PET studies using memory tasks demonstrated changes in amygdala activity in AD relative to controls, but the results were disparate as one study showed decreased activity (Valladares-Neto et al., 1995) and the other increased activity (Grady et al., 2001). This may relate to differences in the clinical stage of AD studied; however, neither study related these functional activity changes specifically to neuropsychiatric symptoms. Our laboratory has used functional (f)MRI to examine amygdala function in mild AD and how this might relate to the specific neuropsychiatric features (Wright et al., 2007). In this study, young and elderly controls and patients with mild AD viewed familiar neutral faces and novel faces with fearful expressions (Figure 14.6). This work showed that there was significantly greater amygdala activation to both stimulus classes in mild AD. This effect was regionally selective, as it was not found in the calcarine cortex. Furthermore, when we examined the relationship between specific behavioral features (assessed using the NPI-Q) we found that agitation and irritability symptom severity was correlated with amygdala responses to familiar neutral, but not novel fearful, faces. No such correlations

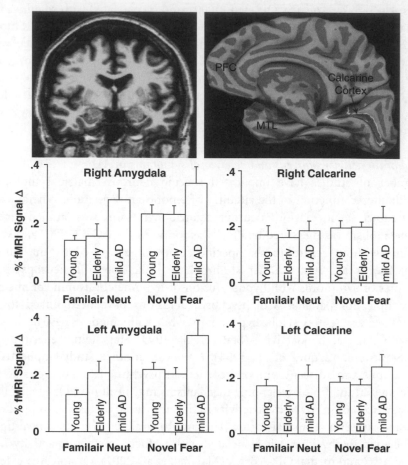

Figure 14.6 Excessive amygdala, but not calcarine cortex activation in mild AD
PFC = Medial surface of prefrontal cortex; MTL = Medial temporal lobe

between calcarine cortex activity and NPI-Q symptoms were observed. Given that the amygdala activation to familiar, neutral stimuli in healthy adults is typically weak, these results suggest that the activity–behavior relationships observed reflect an underlying amygdala hypersensitivity to stimuli that otherwise might induce a weak response.

Genetic influences on neuropsychiatric symptoms in AD
Genetic or familial factors may play an important part in establishing the predisposition for specific neurobehavioral symptoms in AD, particularly as it relates to symptoms of psychosis and aggression. For example, aggression, agitation, and delusions in AD are linked with specific dopamine and serotonin receptor polymorphisms as well as specific serotonin transporter alleles and catechol-O-methyltransferase haplotypes (Assal et al., 2004; Nacmias, Tedde, Forleo, Piacentini,

Guarnieri et al., 2001; Nacmias, Tedde, Forleo, Piacentini, Latorraca et al., 2001; Sweet et al., 2005; Sweet et al., 2002; Sweet et al., 1998; Sweet et al., 2001). In contrast, no such links were found with depression and specific serotonin receptor or transporter subtypes (Micheli et al., 2006). These genetic findings once again implicate the widely projecting brainstem nuclei in the behavioral manifestations of AD.

Focus on the relationships of depression and AD

The relationships between various forms of depression and AD (or MCI) risk with aging are complex and warrant special consideration (Steffens et al., 2006). Depression may represent a prodromal symptom of MCI or AD, indicative of underlying AD pathology (Chen et al., 1999; Devanand et al., 1996; Ganguli et al., 2006; Gatz et al., 2005; Modrego & Ferrandez, 2004). In addition, a recent study described increased hippocampal pathology in AD patients with current or past history of depression compared to those without depression (Rapp et al., 2006). Yet evidence also suggests that depressive episodes much earlier in life, including major depressive disorder (MDD) and other depressive syndromes, are independent risk factors for the later development of MCI or AD (Cannon-Spoor et al., 2005; Green et al., 2003; Kokmen et al., 1991; Ownby et al., 2006; Speck et al., 1995; The Canadian Study of Health and Aging Working Group, 2000). Based on the available data, it seems plausible that both depression earlier in life and prodromal depressive symptoms are separate and important risk factors for AD and MCI. Remote history of depression may represent a vulnerability factor increasing the lifetime risk of MCI and AD, perhaps via stress-related hippocampal damage increasing the risk of AD neuropathology (Rapp et al., 2006) in the setting of genetic modifiers, such as apolipoprotein epsilon (APOE) 4 genotype (Geda et al., 2006). Likewise, the presence of depressive symptoms in late life, particularly in the setting of MCI, may be important indicators of who with MCI will progress on to AD, and how fast this may occur (Copeland et al., 2003; Feldman et al., 2004; Modrego & Ferrandez, 2004; Wilson et al., 2002; Wilson et al., 2004). In addition, late-life depression has been associated with brain vascular disease, which is also a risk factor for AD.

Treatment of behavioral symptoms in AD

In 2010 there were approximately 5.4 million Americans with AD, by 2050 this number is predicted to swell to between 11 and 16 million (Alzheimer's Association, 2011). AD is the fifth-leading cause of death in the United States (Alzheimer's Association, 2011). Given the rising prevalence of AD, the neuropsychiatric symptoms will constitute an increasingly important public health problem, particularly given their frequency and consequences as reviewed above. While these facts are well recognized, and interests in measuring and understanding behavioral disturbances in AD (and other dementias) have increased, there are no compounds specifically approved by the U.S. Food and Drug Administration (FDA) for treating the behavioral symptoms of AD. Furthermore the available, currently approved treatments for the cognitive symptoms of AD have very modest effects on behavior. Other (non-approved) therapies used to treat agitation and aggression symptoms have significant side effects (e.g., increased mortality, strokes) (U.S. Food and Drug Administration, 2005). On this basis it is prudent to first consider behavioral and environmental interventions for treating AD neuropsychiatric symptoms. Following this discussion, the off-label pharmacological treatment of these symptoms often used in clinical practice will be reviewed.

Behavioral and environmental interventions

In many situations behavioral or environmental techniques are extremely useful for neuropsychiatric symptom management in AD. It is often the case that the unwanted behaviors are induced or exacerbated by interpersonal interactions or the environment. Periodic medical issues (e.g., urinary tract infection, pneumonia) can also be a major cause of behavioral exacerbations and should always be investigated. If these events can be identified and prevented or modified accordingly, substantial behavioral improvement can be obtained. Typical nonmedical incidents relate to misunderstandings often caused by the patient's misperception of the environment in the context of diminished emotional control. As reviewed above both of these causes may have a basis in the selective localization of brain pathology in AD. In general, it is best not to confront the patient about their forgetfulness or potentially inappropriate actions. Confrontation generally leads to escalation, exacerbating a situation that is already difficult for the patient. Thus many behavioral approaches involve various forms of diversion rather than a discussion of the problem at hand. Caregiver education is crucial in this regard. A variety of similar methods have been developed to divert the patient from the inciting incident. For example, the ADD method (Agree, Divert, and Depart) and the three Rs (Repeat, Reassure, and Redirect) (Haupt et al., 2000) may be very helpful techniques. A predictable routine and simplified environment can also be extremely helpful for patients with memory disorder. Often there are environmental complexities that lead to irritability or agitation. For example, agitation at bedtime could be due to the inability of the patient to locate their pajamas in the setting of reduced lighting. Simply improving visibility (i.e., more light), and placing pajamas in a standard place where they can easily be distinguished from the surroundings may ameliorate such difficulties. Methods for determining this and deciding how to correct such environmental irritants are extensively reviewed elsewhere (e.g., Coste, 2004). Several other types of environmental interventions may also be helpful in AD, such as music, aromatherapy, and pets for companionship (McCabe et al., 2002; Suzuki et al., 2004; Vance, 1999). Another nonpharmacological intervention of interest is morning bright light therapy, which has been demonstrated to help with sundowning or agitated behavior (Ancoli-Israel et al., 2003; Dowling et al., 2007; Skjerve et al., 2004), presumably through effects on circadian rhythms and hypothalamus (a major output structure or effector of emotional behavior).

Pharmacological interventions

In terms of pharmacological interventions, if these are necessary (as they unfortunately often are), some important general principles apply. As elderly individuals with neurodegenerative disease may be particularly sensitive to medications active in the central nervous system, all therapeutic interventions should be initiated at the lowest possible dose with gradual increases as needed (i.e., start low–go slow). As will be reviewed below, the benefits of all therapies for treatment of neuropsychiatric symptoms in AD are modest, and come with potentially concerning side effects. Along these lines, once a patient has responded and is stable on medication therapy started specifically for behavioral symptoms (i.e., this applies for therapies approved for treatment of cognition in AD), consideration should be given to tapering off the medication. Polypharmacy is best avoided. If an agent prescribed primarily for behavioral or mood control is ineffective it should be discontinued. In an acute setting when the patient is a danger to themselves or others, one may need to begin with larger doses of an antipsychotic and/or benzodiazepine. But the typical early symptoms of AD are often irritability, mild dysphoria/depression, or mild agitation, and this is where these therapeutic principles primarily apply.

In this case the initial treatment should be one of the approved therapies for AD. These include the cholinesterase inhibitors and memantine. While there is clear evidence that these medications are helpful for the cognitive symptoms of AD, their effect on behavior is often insufficient. Furthermore, not all randomized controlled trials support the benefits of these medications for behavior (Ballard & Waite, 2006; Courtney et al., 2004; Reisberg et al., 2003; Tariot et al., 2001); and reviews have highlighted the limitations of these agents for treating neuropsychiatric symptomatology (Ballard et al., 2005; Sink et al., 2005; Trinh et al., 2003). Of note, a meta-analysis of the effects of cholinesterase inhibitors points out that the effects, though statistically significant, may not be clinically meaningful (Trinh et al., 2003). For example, the effects on clinical scales are quite small across all studies, somewhere on the order of 1–2 points out of 120 on the full scale NPI (Trinh et al., 2003).

If behavioral problems persist (and are not acute or severe), the next step is probably to consider a selective serotonin reuptake inhibitor (SSRI). These medications have a fairly favorable side effect profile in elderly patients with dementias and are generally FDA indicated to treat depression. In clinical practice they appear to diminish irritability and improve mood, and these changes may help to ameliorate or reduce the risk of more agitated behavior. However, it must be noted that the results of randomized controlled trials of SSRIs are equivocal. Some trials (Pollock et al., 2002) demonstrate broader efficacy than others (Lyketsos et al., 2003; Taragano et al., 1997), and some have been negative (Petracca et al., 2001; Weintraub et al., 2010). It is also important to recognize that certain antidepressant drugs may be activating, cause somnolence, or exacerbate cognitive impairment in individual patients. Likewise, SSRIs may worsen apathy symptoms in some patients. Other antidepressants may be considered empirically, depending on the exact behavioral symptoms that require treatment. For example, bupropion, which is activating, may help with mood and motivation in patients with apathy or depression; mirtazapine may be useful for patients with depression, irritability, and sleep disturbance. The tricylic antidepressants and monoamine oxidase (MAO-A) inhibitors are best avoided because of cardiovascular risks.

If SSRIs (or other antidepressants) are not effective and significant agitation, aggression or wandering behavior persists, in may be necessary to utilize antipsychotics. In general, typical antipsychotics are best avoided because of their adverse effects profile and particularly because of the risk of drug-induced parkinsonism and QT interval prolongation on the EKG (that may predispose to ventricular arrhythmias). Furthermore, there is no strong evidence that typical antipsychotics are more effective in treating acute agitation/aggression than atypical agents. However, as has been highlighted by the FDA (U.S. Food and Drug Administration, 2005) and others, the efficacy and therapeutic index of the atypical agents is also not great. In addition to inducing a metabolic syndrome with long-term use, atypical antipsychotics received a Black Box warning in April 2005 due to excess deaths in elderly patients treated for behavioral disturbances. Fifteen of the 17 randomized controlled trials surveyed, including 5106 patients, exhibited increased mortality (relative risk = 1.6–1.7), mostly from cardiovascular events and infections. Use of typical antipsychotic drugs also increases the risk of death in the elderly (Setoguchi et al., 2008; Wang et al., 2005).

The CATIE study also highlights the limited efficacy and side effect problems that may accompany the use of atypical antipsychotics (Schneider et al., 2006). That study found no significant effect of the class on the primary outcome measure (time to discontinuation of study drug for any reason), and there was no difference between groups based on clinical symptom measures. However, time to discontinuation of treatment due to a lack of efficacy was significantly longer for the atypical antipsychotics compared to placebo. Olanzapine appeared the most effective in this regard, but also had the worst side effect profile. Risperdal was next most effective. Quetiapine was considered least effective, but the dosage utilized was quite low. Parkinsonism, sedation, and psychosis were the most common adverse events in the trial. On a positive note there were no excess deaths or cognitive decline exacerbations during the 12 weeks of treatment.

If these agents fail, others may be helpful for individual patients including anticonvulsant/mood stabilizers and anxiolytics. However, the former medication class tends to be very poorly tolerated (Herrmann et al., 2007; Sival et al., 2002; Tariot et al., 2005); the latter is bad for memory and can cause paradoxical agitation. If apathy is the main behavioral manifestation stimulants, dopamine agonists, or modafinil might be considered. Of interest, a trial comparing cyproterone (which inhibits testosterone formation) was shown to be helpful for aggression and demonstrated fewer side effects than did haloperidol (Huertas et al., 2007). Despite all these possibilities, it unfortunately remains an empirical process of trial and error to find the drug or combination of drugs that will treat the patient with resistant symptoms. Also, unfortunately, failure of treatment after multiple medications trials is an all-too common scenario in the clinic. Given the epidemiology of AD, such situations will only increase in frequency unless efficacious disease-modifying agents are discovered. As none of the agents mentioned are FDA approved for treatment of neuropsychiatric symptoms in AD, it is important to discuss this fact with the patient and caregiver, to be vigilant of adverse effects, and to be convinced that the potential benefits outweigh the potential risks to the patient.

Behavioral Dysregulation in FTD

Illustrative case: A 58-year-old man came to the office for evaluation of slowly progressive cognitive and behavior problems. He had experienced 2–3 years of increasingly less subtle personality changes. He was at some times quite jovial, but at others very apathetic. He claimed to have his own computer company, earning $100 per hour, despite having been let go from his job more than a year prior. He had taken a liking for sweets, and gained 20 lb. Throughout most of the evaluation, he repeatedly ran his fingers along the length of the desk, tapping them at the end. His examination demonstrated a jaw jerk, snout, and grasp. He was unable to perform the Luria hand–sequencing task or draw an alternating design. On the left side of the BDRS he scores a 13/37; on the right side his score was 4/28. On his NPI-Q he was described as exhibiting increased elation, apathy, disinhibition, and irritability. His MRI scan showed greater right than left frontotemporal atrophy. A PET scan (Figure 14.7A,B, plate section) demonstrated hypometabolism in the medial PFC (including the ACC and OFC) as well as portions of the DLPFC and anterior temporal lobes. At autopsy there was significant frontotemporal atrophy (Figure 14.7C), and histopathological studies (Figure 14.7D) showed tau positive inclusions consistent with Pick bodies.

FTD nosology overview

This is a typical case of the behavioral variant of FTD, with Pick's disease as the underlying cause. It is relevant to mention at this point that definitions of FTD are currently in flux (see Chapters 4 and 5). FTD may be understood as a heterogenous group of neurodegenerative disorders that involve to differing degrees regionally selective frontal and temporal degeneration (Bird et al., 2003; Forman et al., 2006; Kertesz et al., 2005). The clinical pictures and underlying pathologies are also heterogeneous. Currently subsumed under the term FTD are Pick's disease, frontotemporal lobar degeneration, primary progressive aphasia, and semantic dementia. For the purpose of this chapter, the focus is on the symptoms of the behavioral variants of FTD. Of note, FTD and other related disorders (see Chapters 4 and 5, this volume), including corticobasal degeneration (CBD) and progressive supranuclear palsy (PSP), may share overlapping pathology and may exhibit similar behavioral manifestations due to degeneration of frontotemporal systems. However, the following sections focus primarily on the behavioral variant of FTD, as it is the most illustrative of primary emotional systems degeneration.

Hallmark symptoms and their consequences

The hallmark features of this variant of FTD are behavioral and comportmental derangements, with lack of insight out of proportion to amnesia. The formal criteria include a generally slow onset followed by progressive loss of judgment, disinhibition, impulsivity, social misconduct, loss of awareness, and withdrawal. Other typical symptoms are stereotypies, excessive oral/manual exploration, hyperphagia, wanderlust, excessive joviality, sexually provocative behaviors, and inappropriate words/actions (McKhann et al., 2001).

The symptoms of FTD can be followed as with AD using similar scales such as the left side of the BDRS and the NPI-Q. Consistent with the case illustrated above, and the criteria requiring relatively spared memory, scoring worse (i.e., higher score) on the BDRS left versus right side is consistent with FTD. As FTD tends to present at a younger age than AD, there is often greater occupational and related interpersonal difficulties compared to AD. Furthermore, as in the case described above, apathy, stereotypy, compulsive behaviors, eating preference changes, disinhibition, and poor social judgment are worse in FTD versus AD (Bathgate et al., 2001; Bozeat et al., 2000; Chow et al., 2009; Ikeda et al., 2002; Mendez et al., 1997; Miller et al., 1995; Tonkonogy et al., 1994). As in AD, the behavioral consequences of FTD are hard for caregivers and patients, particularly because FTD is often accompanied by loss of insight, lack of judgment, and severe behavioral symptoms. Although supportive and long-term care is crucial for such patients, it can be extremely difficult to find a suitable setting – particularly as patients are often quite young.

Pathophysiology of emotional dysregulation in FTD

The core circuitry of emotional processing is primarily affected in FTD, including broad regions of the PFC, anterior temporal lobes, insula, and amygdala. From the clinical perspective, patients presenting with greater right than left temporal lobe involvement exhibit primarily a behavioral syndrome with emotional distance and irritability as well as disruption of sleep, appetite, and libido (Liu et al., 2004; Miller et al., 1993; Miller et al., 2001; Seeley et al., 2005). This is consistent with the notion of right hemispheric specialization for emotion. In some cases of FTD the frontal lobes may be involved to a greater extent that the temporal lobes. In these instances, patients exhibit symptoms of elation, disinhibition, apathy, and aberrant motor behavior. Interestingly, the alterations in the emotion circuitry of FTD can on occasion lead to ostensibly positive features, such as the emergence of new artistic talents (Mell et al., 2003; Miller et al., 1998). Depending on the combination of regions involved, patients with FTD exhibit specific cognitive and neuropsychiatric symptoms (Whitwell et al., 2009). As the disease progresses to involve greater expanses of the frontotemporal cortex, the clinical features become similar. The presumption is that while the atrophy and underlying pathology that initially accompanies various forms of FTD is regionally specific, it becomes more generalized as the disease progresses. Although there are fewer investigations correlating brain function and behavior in FTD versus AD, several studies have implicated the degree of frontotemporal hypoperfusion with levels of aggression in FTD (Hirono et al., 2000; Miller & Gearhart, 1999).

Treatment of behavioral symptoms in FTD

The treatment approach for FTD patients is similar to that of AD to the extent that there are no approved phamacological treatments, therefore behavioral/environmental interventions like those used in AD are crucial (Robinson, 2001; Talerico, 2001; Lough, 2002). There are no FDA-approved therapies specific for any aspect of FTD and there are similarly relatively few clinical trials available to guide off-label drug usage. Probably the most useful and best-studied agents are the antidepressants and the SSRIs in particular. Paroxetine, fluoxatine, and sertraline have been studied (Ikeda et al., 2004; Perry & Miller, 2001; Swartz et al., 1997), and can be quite helpful for reducing irritability and the repetitive obsessive-compulsive disorder-like behaviors that accompany FTD. There has been at least one study evaluating MAO-A inhibitors and suggesting their effectiveness (Adler et al., 2003), but these agents (even the reversible ones) are probably best avoided given the propensity for increased appetite in the setting of lack of insight and disinhibition. Though not well studied, clinical practice sometime includes the use of dopamine agonists or stimulants to combat apathy, but one has to be wary of exacerbating agitation in this setting. Cholinesterase inhibitors and activating depressants are also best avoided as they can likewise exacerbate agitated behaviors (Mendez et al., 2007). The role of memantine in FTD is uncertain (Boxer et al., 2009). It sometimes appears clinically helpful, but also may exacerbate agitation. Other classes of CNS active agents can sometimes be necessary depending on the nature and severity of the symptoms. With use of atypical antipsychotics and mood stabilizers, weight gain and excessive somnolence are often a problem. Anxiolytics such as the benzodiazepines may cause paradoxical disinhibition as in AD.

Behavioral Dysregulation in LBD

Illustrative case: A 78-year-old man was referred for evaluation of 3–4 years of fluctuating cognitive, mood, and motor changes. He had progressively worsening slowness and tremors over the most recent 8–12 months. He spent much of his time slouched on the couch, without enough energy to even turn on the television. He reported that fairies came to watch TV and party nightly. It was initially mildly bothersome as they would make a mess in the living room, but he covered the couches nightly with newspapers, which made their festivities bearable to him. On examination, he perseverated and was unable to perform the Luria hand-sequencing task. He was unable to draw a clock or cube. His BDRS score was 14 on the left and 12 on the right. He scored particularly high on the apathy and sleep disturbance scales of the NPI-Q. He had saccadic pursuit, mildly masked facies, and both lead pipe rigidity and Gegenhalten (involuntary resistance to passive movement). There were intermittent bilateral rest tremors and cogwheeling was present. MRI initially showed no atrophy (Figure 14.8A, plate section), but over time frontotemporal, insular, and occipital atrophy developed. A PET scan showed occipitoparietal hypometabolism (Figure 14.8B, plate section), with particularly significant metabolic reduction in the medial and lateral occipital areas. At autopsy Lewy bodies (Figure 14.8C, plate section) were found in the brain stem and cortex.

LBD behavioral symptoms and their implications

This is a typical case of LBD (McKeith et al., 2005). As in AD and FTD, symptoms of behavioral dysregulation can be measured using standard instruments as described above. In this regard, it has been reported that delusions, anxiety, psychosis, depression, and hallucinations are more common in LBD versus AD at diagnosis (Rockwell et al., 2000; Stavitsky et al., 2006), although only visual hallucinations are significantly more persistent in LBD versus AD (Ballard et al., 2001; Tiraboschi et al., 2006). This is consistent with the symptoms in the case illustration and with similar scores on both sides of the BDRS. One other important behavioral feature in LBD is sleep disorder, which is also significantly more frequent in LBD than AD (Boeve et al., 2001). As in AD and FTD, the neuropsychiatric features of LBD have significant consequences for patient and family. In fact, more major depression is found in caregivers of LBD versus AD and this was related to the severity of behavioral disturbance in LBD (Lowery et al., 2000).

Pathophysiology of behavioral symptoms in LBD

Patients with LBD may initially exhibit mild generalized atrophy, but studies suggest that as the disease progresses regions of the emotion response and control systems are preferentially affected including the frontotemporal and insular cortex, with variable atrophy in the occipital lobes (Burton et al., 2002; Gerlach et al., 2002; Middelkoop et al., 2001; Robles & Cacabelos, 1999; Uchikado et al., 2002). Though atrophy of the visual cortex may initially be very mild in LBD, patients exhibit greater medial and lateral occipital area cortical metabolism reduction versus AD. This is one of the functional imaging findings that distinguishes the two disorders, since patients with LBD may also have parietotemporal hypoperfusion as found in AD (Ishii et al., 2005).

Severe depletion of the dopaminergic system occurs in LBD, and particularly in the projection pathways of the ventral tegmental area, which include the amygdala and medial PFC. This likely contributes to the behavioral pathology in LBD (Roselli et al., 2009). Of note, patients with LBD have even more severe cholinergic depletion in early stages of the disorder than do AD patients (Tiraboschi et al., 2002), thus neurochemical contributions to abnormal behavior in LBD would be predicted. In fact, hallucinations and delusions in LBD are associated with the extent of acetylcholine depletion and nicotinic a7 receptor loss in the temporal cortex (Ballard et al., 2000; Court et al., 2000). Further, improvement of occipital hypoperfusion by donepezil correlates with improved hallucinations in DLB (Mori et al., 2006). In addition, Lewy body pathology is not uncommonly found in combination with AD pathology (Dickson, 2002; Weiner et al., 1996), thus the mechanisms of behavioral disturbance, including cholinergic depletions and alterations in sensory areas that provide input to emotional control circuits, may be similar in these two disorders.

Treatment of behavioral symptoms in LBD

The treatment considerations for LBD emotional dysregulation are quite similar to those of AD and FTD. Behavioral and environmental interventions are the first line of approach. From the neuropharmacological perspective there are no treatments specifically approved for LBD; though riviastigmine is approved for dementia associated with Parkinson's disease (Emre et al., 2004). Given the severe cholinergic depletion in LBD and evidence reviewed above that certain behavioral features, and their brain correlates, respond to cholinesterase therapy, this class of treatment is the first line of therapy for treating (non-acute) behavioral dysregulation in LBD. Although these agents are not FDA approved for this indication several clinical studies support their use in LBD (Arahata et al., 2001; Coulson et al., 2002; Emre et al., 2004; Maclean et al., 2001; McKeith, Del Ser et al., 2000; McKeith et al., 2005; McKeith, Grace et al., 2000; Rojas-Fernandez, 2001; Skjerve & Nygaard, 2000; Wesnes et al., 2005).

For more acute or persistent behavioral disturbances the atypical antipsychotics may be useful (Cummings et al., 2002; Fernandez et al., 2002; Takahashi et al., 2003). Of interest, one study suggests that clozapine may actually improve prognosis in LBD (Chacko et al., 1993), but given the logistics of prescribing this medication and the risks of agranulocytosis, it remains a difficult therapeutic choice. Risperdone, which has the greatest dopamine (receptor 2) blocking potential, and the typical antipsychotics should be strictly avoided as they are likely to significantly worsen parkinsonian symptoms in LBD.

Dopaminergic agents are usually not useful and the dopamine agonists can exacerbate hallucinations, confusion, and somnolence. However, in some cases low dose carbidopa/levodopa may be helpful and cause fewer adverse events that the more potent dopamine agonists (Frank, 2003; Kato et al., 2002). SSRIs may be helpful with depressive symptoms and irritability, but also have the potential to exacerbate motor symptoms. Anxiolytics may help sleep disorder in LBD, but can cause disinhibition and confusion. Finally, memantine is a reasonable consideration given that it is usually well tolerated and has both a mild dopaminergic and cognitive enhancing profile.

Conclusion

Emotional dysregulation and behavioral/psychiatric manifestations are common features of the dementias. These signs and symptoms relate to underlying neuropathology in frontal and temporal lobe areas (including subcortical structures such as the amygdala) involved in emotion generation and control. The right hemisphere and the widely projecting neurotransmitter systems may play an important role in this regard. Symptoms of emotional dysregulation are important and may: (i) represent premonitory signs of impending decline; (ii) help with differential diagnosis; (iii) lead to significant caregiver burden; (iv) increase the likelihood of nursing home placement; and (v) even increase the risk of mortality. Treatments exist, but are not specifically FDA approved for behavior management, are symptomatically based, are not highly effective, and may have significant adverse effects. It is clear that further clinical research and medication trials are needed in this area for the benefit of patients and their families.

References

Adler, G., Teufel, M., & Drach, L. M. (2003). Pharmacological treatment of frontotemporal dementia: Treatment response to the MAO-A inhibitor moclobemide. *International Journal of Geriatric Psychiatry, 18*(7), 653–655.

Adolphs, R. (2002). Neural systems for recognizing emotion. *Current Opinion in Neurobiology, 12*(2), 169–177.

Aggleton, J. P. (1992). *The amygdala: Neurobiological aspects of emotion, memory and mental dysfunction.* New York: Wiley-Liss.

Alexopoulos, G. S., Abrams, R. C., Young, R. C., & Shamoian, C. A. (1988). Cornell Scale for Depression in Dementia. *Biological Psychiatry, 23*(3), 271–284.

Alzheimer's Association. (2011). 2011 Alzheimer's disease facts and figures. *Alzheimers Dement, 7*(2), 208–44.

Amaral, D. G. (2003). The amygdala, social behavior, and danger detection. *Annals of the New York Academy of Science, 1000*, 337–347.

Amaral, D. G., Behniea, H., & Kelly, J. L. (2003). Topographic organization of projections from the amygdala to the visual cortex in the macaque monkey. *Neuroscience, 118*(4), 1099–1120.

Ancoli-Israel, S., Gehrman, P., Martin, J. L., Shochat, T., Marler, M., Corey-Bloom, J., et al. (2003). Increased light exposure consolidates sleep and strengthens circadian rhythms in severe Alzheimer's disease patients. *Behavioral Sleep Medicine, 1*(1), 22–36.

Anderson, A. K., & Phelps, E. A. (2001). Lesions of the human amygdala impair enhanced perception of emotionally salient events. *Nature, 411*(6835), 305–309.

Antoniadis, E. A., Winslow, J. T., Davis, M., & Amaral, D. G. (2009). The nonhuman primate amygdala is necessary for the acquisition but not the retention of fear-potentiated startle. *Biological Psychiatry, 65*, 241–248.

Arahata, H., Ohyagi, Y., Matsumoto, S., Furuya, H., Murai, H., Kuwabara, Y., et al. (2001). A patient with probable dementia with Lewy bodies, who showed improvement of dementia and parkinsonism by the administratim of donepezil. *Rinsho Shinkeigaku, 41*(7), 402–406.

Arriagada, P. V., Growdon, J. H., Hedley-Whyte, E. T., & Hyman, B. T. (1992). Neurofibrillary tangles but not senile plaques parallel duration and severity of Alzheimer's disease. *Neurology, 42*(3 Pt 1), 631–639.

Assal, F., Alarcon, M., Solomon, E. C., Masterman, D., Geschwind, D. H., & Cummings, J. L. (2004). Association of the serotonin transporter and receptor gene polymorphisms in neuropsychiatric symptoms in Alzheimer disease. *Archives of Neurology, 61*(8), 1249–1253.

Ballard, C. G., O'Brien, J. T., Swann, A. G., Thompson, P., Neill, D., & McKeith, I. G. (2001). The natural history of psychosis and depression in dementia with Lewy bodies and Alzheimer's disease: Persistence and new cases over 1 year of follow-up. *Journal of Clinical Psychiatry, 62*(1), 46–49.

Ballard, C., & Waite, J. (2006). The effectiveness of atypical antipsychotics for the treatment of aggression and psychosis in Alzheimer's disease. *Cochrane Database System Review* (*1*), CD003476.

Ballard, C., Margallo-Lana, M., Juszczak, E., Douglas, S., Swann, A., Thomas, A., et al. (2005). Quetiapine and rivastigmine and cognitive decline in Alzheimer's disease: Randomised double blind placebo controlled trial. *British Medical Journal, 330*(7496), 874.

Ballard, C., Piggott, M., Johnson, M., Cairns, N., Perry, R., McKeith, I., et al. (2000). Delusions associated with elevated muscarinic binding in dementia with Lewy bodies. *Annals of Neurology, 48*(6), 868–876.

Barbas, H., Saha, S., Rempel-Clower, N., & Ghashghaei, T. (2003). Serial pathways from primate prefrontal cortex to autonomic areas may influence emotional expression. *BMC Neuroscience, 4*(1), 25.

Bathgate, D., Snowden, J. S., Varma, A., Blackshaw, A., & Neary, D. (2001). Behaviour in frontotemporal dementia, Alzheimer's disease and vascular dementia. *Acta Neurologica Scandinavia, 103*(6), 367–378.

Baxter, M. G., & Murray, E. A. (2002). The amygdala and reward. *Nature Review Neuroscience, 3*(7), 563–573.

Bierer, L. M., Hof, P. R., Purohit, D. P., Carlin, L., Schmeidler, J., Davis, K. L., et al. (1995). Neocortical neurofibrillary tangles correlate with dementia severity in Alzheimer's disease. *Archives of Neurology, 52*(1), 81–88.

Bird, T., Knopman, D., VanSwieten, J., Rosso, S., Feldman, H., Tanabe, H., et al. (2003). Epidemiology and genetics of frontotemporal dementia/Pick's disease. *Annals of Neurology, 54*, S29–S31.

Blessed, G., Tomlinson, B. E., & Roth, M. (1968). The association between quantitative measures of dementia and of senile change in the cerebral grey matter of elderly subjects. *British Journal of Psycahitry, 114*, 797–811.

Boeve, B. F., Silber, M. H., Ferman, T. J., Lucas, J. A., & Parisi, J. E. (2001). Association of REM sleep behavior disorder and neurodegenerative disease may reflect an underlying synucleinopathy. *Movement Disorders, 16*(4), 622–630.

Bonda, E., Petrides, M., Ostry, D., & Evans, A. (1996). Specific involvement of human parietal systems and the amygdala in the perception of biological motion. *Journal of Neuroscience, 16*(11), 3737–3744.

Bottino, C. M., Castro, C. C., Gomes, R. L., Buchpiguel, C. A., Marchetti, R. L., & Neto, M. R. (2002). Volumetric MRI measurements can differentiate Alzheimer's disease, mild cognitive impairment, and normal aging. *International Psychogeriatrics, 14*(1), 59–72.

Boxer, A. L., Lipton, A. M., Womack, K., Merrilees, J., Neuhaus, J., Pavlic, D., et al. (2009). An open-label study of memantine treatment in 3 subtypes of frontotemporal lobar degeneration. *Alzheimer Disease & Associated Disorders, 23*(3), 211–217.

Bozeat, S., Gregory, C. A., Ralph, M. A., & Hodges, J. R. (2000). Which neuropsychiatric and behavioural features distinguish frontal and temporal variants of frontotemporal dementia from Alzheimer's disease? *Journal of Neurology, Neurosurgery & Psychiatry, 69*(2), 178–186.

Braak, H., & Braak, E. (1991). Neuropathological stageing of Alzheimer-related changes. *Acta Neuropathologica (Berlin), 82*(4), 239–259.

Braak, H., & Braak, E. (1995). Staging of Alzheimer's disease-related neurofibrillary changes. *Neurobiology of Aging, 16*(3), 271–278; discussion 278–284.

Breiter, H. C., Etcoff, N. L., Whalen, P. J., Kennedy, W. A., Rauch, S. L., Buckner, R. L., et al. (1996). Response and habituation of the human amygdala during visual processing of facial expression. *Neuron, 17*(5), 875–887.

Brion, J. P. (1998). Neurofibrillary tangles and Alzheimer's disease. *European Neurology, 40*(3), 130–140.

Broca, P. (1878). Anatomie comparée des circonvolutions cérébrales: le grand lobe limbique. *Review of Anthropology, (1)*, 385–498.

Büchel, C., Dolan, R., Armony, J., & Friston, K. (1999). Amygdala-hippocampal involvement in human aversive trace conditioning revealed through event-related functional magnetic resonance imaging. *Journal of Neuroscience, 19*(24), 10869–10876.

Büchel, C., Morris, J., Dolan, R. J., & Friston, K. J. (1998). Brain systems mediating aversive conditioning: an event-related fMRI study. *Neuron, 20*(5), 947–957.

Burns, A., Jacoby, R., & Levy, R. (1990). Behavioral abnormalities and psychiatric symptoms in Alzheimer's disease: Preliminary findings. *International Psychogeriatrics, 2*(1), 25–36.

Burton, E. J., Karas, G., Paling, S. M., Barber, R., Williams, E. D., Ballard, C. G., et al. (2002). Patterns of cerebral atrophy in dementia with Lewy bodies using voxel-based morphometry. *Neuroimage, 17*(2), 618–630.

Calder, A. J., Lawrence, A. D., & Young, A. W. (2001). Neuropsychology of fear and loathing. *Nature Review Neuroscience, 2*(5), 352–363.

Canli, T., Sivers, H., Whitfield, S. L., Gotlib, I. H., & Gabrieli, J. D. (2002). Amygdala response to happy faces as a function of extraversion. *Science, 296*(5576), 2191.

Cannon-Spoor, H. E., Levy, J. A., Zubenko, G. S., Zubenko, W. W., Cohen, R. M., Mirza, N., et al. (2005). Effects of previous major depressive illness on cognition in Alzheimer disease patients. *American Journal of Geriatric Psychiatry, 13*(4), 312–318.

Chacko, R. C., Hurley, R. A., & Jankovic, J. (1993). Clozapine use in diffuse Lewy body disease. *Journal of Neuropsychiatry and Clinical Neurosciences, 5*(2), 206–208.

Chan, D. C., Kasper, J. D., Black, B. S., & Rabins, P. V. (2003). Presence of behavioral and psychological symptoms predicts nursing home placement in community-dwelling elders with cognitive impairment in univariate but not multivariate analysis. *Journal of Gerontology A Biological Sciences and Medical Sciences, 58*(6), 548–554.

Chen, P., Ganguli, M., Mulsant, B. H., & DeKosky, S. T. (1999). The temporal relationship between depressive symptoms and dementia: a community-based prospective study. *Archives of General Psychiatry, 56*(3), 261–266.

Chow, T. W., Binns, M. A., Cummings, J. L., Lam, I., Black, S. E., Miller, B. L., et al. (2009). Apathy symptom profile and behavioral associations in frontotemporal dementia vs dementia of Alzheimer type. *Archives of Neurology, 66*(7), 888–893.

Cohen-Mansfield, J., Marx, M. S., & Rosenthal, A. S. (1989). A description of agitation in a nursing home. *Journal of Gerontology, 44*(3), M77–M84.

Copeland, M. P., Daly, E., Hines, V., Mastromauro, C., Zaitchik, D., Gunther, J., et al. (2003). Psychiatric symptomatology and prodromal Alzheimer's disease. *Alzheimer Disease & Associated Disorders, 17*(1), 1–8.

Coste, J. K. (2004). *Learning to speak Alzheimer's: A groundbreaking approach for everyone dealing with the disease.* New York: Houghton Mifflin.

Coulson, B. S., Fenner, S. G., & Almeida, O. P. (2002). Successful treatment of behavioural problems in dementia using a cholinesterase inhibitor: the ethical questions. *Australian and New Zealand Journal of Psychiatry, 36*(2), 259–262.

Court, J. A., Piggott, M. A., Lloyd, S., Cookson, N., Ballard, C. G., McKeith, I. G., et al. (2000). Nicotine binding in human striatum: elevation in schizophrenia and reductions in dementia with Lewy bodies, Parkinson's disease and Alzheimer's disease and in relation to neuroleptic medication. *Neuroscience, 98*(1), 79–87.

Courtney, C., Farrell, D., Gray, R., Hills, R., Lynch, L., Sellwood, E., et al. (2004). Long-term donepezil treatment in 565 patients with Alzheimer's disease (AD2000): Randomised double-blind trial. *Lancet, 363*(9427), 2105–2115.

Cummings, J. L. (1997). The Neuropsychiatric Inventory: Assessing psychopathology in dementia patients. *Neurology, 48*(5 Suppl 6), S10–S16.

Cummings, J. L., & McPherson, S. (2001). Neuropsychiatric assessment of Alzheimer's disease and related dementias. *Aging (Milano), 13*(3), 240–246.

Cummings, J. L., Mega, M., Gray, K., Rosenberg-Thompson, S., Carusi, D. A., & Gornbein, J. (1994). The Neuropsychiatric Inventory: Comprehensive assessment of psychopathology in dementia. *Neurology, 44*(12), 2308–2314.

Cummings, J. L., Street, J., Masterman, D., & Clark, W. S. (2002). Efficacy of olanzapine in the treatment of psychosis in dementia with Lewy bodies. *Dementia and Geriatric Cognitive Disorders, 13*(2), 67–73.

Davidson, R. J. (2001). Toward a biology of personality and emotion. *Annals of the New York Academy of Science, 935*, 191–207.

Davidson, R. J., Mednick, D., Moss, E., Saron, C., & Schaffer, C. E. (1987). Ratings of emotion in faces are influenced by the visual field to which stimuli are presented. *Brain and Cognitionitive, 6*(4), 403–411.

Davis, D. G., Schmitt, F. A., Wekstein, D. R., & Markesbery, W. R. (1999). Alzheimer neuropathologic alterations in aged cognitively normal subjects. *Journal of Neuropathology & Experimental Neurology, 58*(4), 376–388.

Davis, M., & Whalen, P. J. (2001). The amygdala: vigilance and emotion. *Molecular Psychiatry, 6*(1), 13–34.

De Olmos, J. (1990). Amygdaloid nuclear gray complex. In G. Paxinos (Ed.), *The human nervous system.* San Deigo: Academic Press.

DeKosky, S. T., Ikonomovic, M. D., Styren, S. D., Beckett, L., Wisniewski, S., Bennett, D. A., et al. (2002). Upregulation of choline acetyltransferase activity in hippocampus and frontal cortex of elderly subjects with mild cognitive impairment. *Annals of Neurology, 51*(2), 145–155.

den Heijer, T., Geerlings, M. I., Hoebeek, F. E., Hofman, A., Koudstaal, P. J., & Breteler, M. M. (2006). Use of hippocampal and amygdalar volumes on magnetic resonance imaging to predict dementia in cognitively intact elderly people. *Archives of General Psychiatry, 63*(1), 57–62.

Devanand, D. P., Jacobs, D. M., Tang, M. X., Del Castillo-Castaneda, C., Sano, M., Marder, K., et al. (1997). The course of psychopathologic features in mild to moderate Alzheimer disease. *Archives of General Psychiatry, 54*(3), 257–263.

Devanand, D. P., Sano, M., Tang, M. X., Taylor, S., Gurland, B. J., Wilder, D., et al. (1996). Depressed mood and the incidence of Alzheimer's disease in the elderly living in the community. *Archives of General Psychiatry, 53*(2), 175–182.

Dickerson, B. C., Bakkour, A., Salat, D. H., Feczko, E., Pacheco, J., Greve, D. N., et al. (2009). The cortical signature of Alzheimer's disease: Regionally specific cortical thinning relates to symptom severity in very mild to mild AD dementia and is detectable in asymptomatic amyloid-positive individuals. *Cerebral Cortex, 19,* 497–510.

Dickson, D. W. (2002). Dementia with Lewy bodies: Neuropathology. *Journal of Geriatric Psychiatry and Neurology, 15*(4), 210–216.

Dimond, S. J., & Farrington, L. (1977). Emotional response to films shown to the right or left hemisphere of the brain measured by heart rate. *Acta Psychologica, 41,* 255–260.

Dolcos, F., Labar, K. S., & Cabeza, R. (2005). Remembering one year later: Role of the amygdala and the medial temporal lobe memory system in retrieving emotional memories. *Proceedings of the National Academy of Sciences USA, 102*(7), 2626–2631.

Dowling, G. A., Graf, C. L., Hubbard, E. M., & Luxenberg, J. S. (2007). Light treatment for neuropsychiatric behaviors in Alzheimer's disease. *Western Journal of Nursing Research, 29*(8), 961–975.

Dubois, S., Rossion, B., Schiltz, C., Bodart, J. M., Michel, C., Bruyer, R., et al. (1999). Effect of familiarity on the processing of human faces. *Neuroimage, 9*(3), 278–289.

Elfgren, C., Gustafson, L., Vestberg, S., & Passant, U. (2010). Subjective memory complaints, neuropsychological performance and psychiatric variables in memory clinic attendees: A 3-year follow-up study. *Archives of Gerontology and Geriatrics, 51*(3), e110–e114.

Emre, M., Aarsland, D., Albanese, A., Byrne, E. J., Deuschl, G., De Deyn, P. P., et al. (2004). Rivastigmine for dementia associated with Parkinson's disease. *New England Journal of Medicine, 351*(24), 2509–2518.

Emre, M., Heckers, S., Mash, D. C., Geula, C., & Mesulam, M. M. (1993). Cholinergic innervation of the amygdaloid complex in the human brain and its alterations in old age and Alzheimer's disease. *Journal of Comparative Neurology, 336*(1), 117–134.

Esiri, M. M., Pearson, R. C., Steele, J. E., Bowen, D. M., & Powell, T. P. (1990). A quantitative study of the neurofibrillary tangles and the choline acetyltransferase activity in the cerebral cortex and the amygdala in Alzheimer's disease. *Journal of Neurology, Neurosurgery & Psychiatry*, 53(2), 161–165.

Etkin, A., Prater, K. E., Hoeft, F., Menon, V., & Schatzberg, A. F. (2010). Failure of anterior cingulate activation and connectivity with the amygdala during implicit regulation of emotional processing in generalized anxiety disorder. *American Journal of Psychiatry*, 167(5), 545–554.

Feldman, H., Scheltens, P., Scarpini, E., Hermann, N., Mesenbrink, P., Mancione, L., et al. (2004). Behavioral symptoms in mild cognitive impairment. *Neurology*, 62(7), 1199–1201.

Fernandez, H. H., Trieschmann, M. E., Burke, M. A., & Friedman, J. H. (2002). Quetiapine for psychosis in Parkinson's disease versus dementia with Lewy bodies. *Journal of Clinical Psychiatry*, 63(6), 513–515.

Forman, M. S., Farmer, J., Johnson, J. K., Clark, C. M., Arnold, S. E., Coslett, H. B., et al. (2006). Frontotemporal dementia: Clinicopathological correlations. *Annals of Neurology*, 59(6), 952–962.

Frank, C. (2003). Dementia with Lewy bodies. Review of diagnosis and pharmacologic management. *Canadian Family Physician*, 49, 1304–1311.

Fuh, J. L., Liu, C. K., Mega, M. S., Wang, S. J., & Cummings, J. L. (2001). Behavioral disorders and caregivers' reaction in Taiwanese patients with Alzheimer's disease. *International Psychogeriatrics*, 13(1), 121–128.

Furmark, T., Fischer, H., Wik, G., Larsson, M., & Fredrikson, M. (1997). The amygdala and individual differences in human fear conditioning. *Neuroreport*, 8(18), 3957–3960.

Ganguli, M., Du, Y., Dodge, H. H., Ratcliff, G. G., & Chang, C. C. (2006). Depressive symptoms and cognitive decline in late life: a prospective epidemiological study. *Archives of General Psychiatry*, 63(2), 153–160.

Gatz, J. L., Tyas, S. L., St John, P., & Montgomery, P. (2005). Do depressive symptoms predict Alzheimer's disease and dementia? *Journal of Gerontology A Biological Sciences and Medical Sciences*, 60(6), 744–747.

Geda, Y. E., Knopman, D. S., Mrazek, D. A., Jicha, G. A., Smith, G. E., Negash, S., et al. (2006). Depression, apolipoprotein E genotype, and the incidence of mild cognitive impairment: A prospective cohort study. *Archives of Neurology*, 63(3), 435–440.

Gerlach, M., Stadler, K., Aichner, F., & Ransmayr, G. (2002). Dementia with Lewy bodies and AD are not associated with occipital lobe atrophy on MRI. *Neurology*, 59(9), 1476.

Ghashghaei, H. T., & Barbas, H. (2002). Pathways for emotion: Interactions of prefrontal and anterior temporal pathways in the amygdala of the rhesus monkey. *Neuroscience*, 115(4), 1261–1279.

Gomez-Isla, T., Price, J. L., McKeel, D. W., Jr., Morris, J. C., Growdon, J. H., & Hyman, B. T. (1996). Profound loss of layer II entorhinal cortex neurons occurs in very mild Alzheimer's disease. *Journal of Neuroscience*, 16(14), 4491–4500.

Gorno-Tempini, M. L., Rankin, K. P., Woolley, J. D., Rosen, H. J., Phengrasamy, L., & Miller, B. L. (2004). Cognitive and behavioral profile in a case of right anterior temporal lobe neurodegeneration. *Cortex*, 40(4–5), 631–644.

Grady, C. L., Furey, M. L., Pietrini, P., Horwitz, B., & Rapoport, S. I. (2001). Altered brain functional connectivity and impaired short-term memory in Alzheimer's disease. *Brain*, 124(Pt 4), 739–756.

Green, R. C., Cupples, L. A., Kurz, A., Auerbach, S., Go, R., Sadovnick, D., et al. (2003). Depression as a risk factor for Alzheimer disease: the MIRAGE Study. *Archives of Neurology*, 60(5), 753–759.

Gur, R. C., Schroeder, L., Turner, T., McGrath, C., Chan, R. M., Turetsky, B. I., et al. (2002). Brain activation during facial emotion processing. *Neuroimage, 16*(3 Pt 1), 651–662.

Hadjikhani, N., & de Gelder, B. (2003). Seeing fearful body expressions activates the fusiform cortex and amygdala. *Current Biology, 13*(24), 2201–2205.

Hariri, A. R., Bookheimer, S. Y., & Mazziotta, J. C. (2000). Modulating emotional responses: Effects of a neocortical network on the limbic system. *Neuroreport, 11*(1), 43–48.

Haroutunian, V., Purohit, D. P., Perl, D. P., Marin, D., Khan, K., Lantz, M., et al. (1999). Neurofibrillary tangles in nondemented elderly subjects and mild Alzheimer disease. *Archives of Neurology, 56*(6), 713–718.

Hashimoto, H., Monserratt, L., Nguyen, P., Feil, D., Harwood, D., Mandelkern, M. A., et al. (2006). Anxiety and regional cortical glucose metabolism in patients with Alzheimer's disease. *Journal of Neuropsychiatry and Clinical Neurosciences, 18*(4), 521–528.

Haupt, M., Karger, A., & Janner, M. (2000). Improvement of agitation and anxiety in demented patients after psychoeducative group intervention with their caregivers. *International Journal of Geriatric Psychiatry, 15*(12), 1125–1129.

Heilman, K. M., & Satz, P. (1986). *Neuropsychology of human emotion.* New York: Guilford Press.

Herholz, K., Weisenbach, S., Zundorf, G., Lenz, O., Schroder, H., Bauer, B., et al. (2004). In vivo study of acetylcholine esterase in basal forebrain, amygdala, and cortex in mild to moderate Alzheimer disease. *Neuroimage, 21*(1), 136–143.

Herrmann, N., Lanctot, K. L., Rothenburg, L. S., & Eryavec, G. (2007). A placebo-controlled trial of valproate for agitation and aggression in Alzheimer's disease. *Dementia and Geriatric Cognitive Disorders, 23*(2), 116–119.

Herzog, A. G., & Kemper, T. L. (1980). Amygdaloid changes in aging and dementia. *Archives of Neurology, 37*(10), 625–629.

Hirono, N., Mega, M. S., Dinov, I. D., Mishkin, F., & Cummings, J. L. (2000). Left frontotemporal hypoperfusion is associated with aggression in patients with dementia. *Archives of Neurology, 57*(6), 861–866.

Huertas, D., Lopez-Ibor Alino, J. J., Molina, J. D., Chamorro, L., Balanza, J., Jimenez, M. P., et al. (2007). Antiaggressive effect of cyproterone versus haloperidol in Alzheimer's disease: A randomized double-blind pilot study. *Journal of Clinical Psychiatry, 68*(3), 439–444.

Hwang, T. J., Masterman, D. L., Ortiz, F., Fairbanks, L. A., & Cummings, J. L. (2004). Mild cognitive impairment is associated with characteristic neuropsychiatric symptoms. *Alzheimer Disease & Associated Disorders, 18*(1), 17–21.

Hyman, B. T. (1997). The neuropathological diagnosis of Alzheimer's disease: Clinical-pathological studies. *Neurobiology of Aging, 18*(4 Suppl), S27–S32.

Ikeda, M., Brown, J., Holland, A. J., Fukuhara, R., & Hodges, J. R. (2002). Changes in appetite, food preference, and eating habits in frontotemporal dementia and Alzheimer's disease. *Journal of Neurology, Neurosurgery & Psychiatry, 73*(4), 371–376.

Ikeda, M., Shigenobu, K., Fukuhara, R., Hokoishi, K., Maki, N., Nebu, A., et al. (2004). Efficacy of fluvoxamine as a treatment for behavioral symptoms in frontotemporal lobar degeneration patients. *Dementia and Geriatric Cognitive Disorders, 17*(3), 117–121.

Insausti, R., Amaral, D. G., & Cowan, W. M. (1987). The entorhinal cortex of the monkey: III. Subcortical afferents. *Journal of Comparative Neurology, 264*(3), 396–408.

Iqbal, K., Alonso Adel, C., Chen, S., Chohan, M. O., El-Akkad, E., Gong, C. X., et al. (2005). Tau pathology in Alzheimer disease and other tauopathies. *Biochimica et Biophysica Acta, 1739*(2–3), 198–210.

Irwin, W., Davidson, R. J., Lowe, M. J., Mock, B. J., Sorenson, J. A., & Turski, P. A. (1996). Human amygdala activation detected with echo-planar functional magnetic resonance imaging. *Neuroreport, 7*(11), 1765–1769.

Ishii, K., Sasaki, H., Kono, A. K., Miyamoto, N., Fukuda, T., & Mori, E. (2005). Comparison of gray matter and metabolic reduction in mild Alzheimer's disease using FDG-PET and voxel-based morphometric MR studies. *European Journal of Nuclear Medicine and Molecular Imaging, 32*(8), 959–963.

Jicha, G. A., Parisi, J. E., Dickson, D. W., Johnson, K., Cha, R., Ivnik, R. J., et al. (2006). Neuropathologic outcome of mild cognitive impairment following progression to clinical dementia. *Archives of Neurology, 63*(5), 674–681.

Jost, B. C., & Grossberg, G. T. (1996). The evolution of psychiatric symptoms in Alzheimer's disease: A natural history study. *Journal of the American Geriatric Society, 44*(9), 1078–1081.

Karlsson, K., Windischberger, C., Gerstl, F., Mayr, W., Siegel, J. M., & Moser, E. (2010). Modulation of hypothalamus and amygdalar activation levels with stimulus valence. *Neuroimage, 51*(1), 324–328.

Kato, K., Wada, T., Kawakatsu, S., & Otani, K. (2002). Improvement of both psychotic symptoms and Parkinsonism in a case of dementia with Lewy bodies by the combination therapy of risperidone and L-DOPA. *Progress in Neuropsychopharmacology and Biological Psychiatry, 26*(1), 201–203.

Kaufer, D. I., Cummings, J. L., Christine, D., Bray, T., Castellon, S., Masterman, D., et al. (1998). Assessing the impact of neuropsychiatric symptoms in Alzheimer's disease: The Neuropsychiatric Inventory Caregiver Distress Scale. *Journal of the American Geriatric Society, 46*(2), 210–215.

Kaufer, D. I., Cummings, J. L., Ketchel, P., Smith, V., MacMillan, A., Shelley, T., et al. (2000). Validation of the NPI-Q, a brief clinical form of the Neuropsychiatric Inventory. *Journal of Neuropsychiatry and Clinical Neurosciences, 12*(2), 233–239.

Kertesz, A., McMonagle, P., Blair, M., Davidson, W., & Munoz, D. G. (2005). The evolution and pathology of frontotemporal dementia. *Brain, 128*(9), 1996–2005.

Khachaturian, Z. S. (1985). Diagnosis of Alzheimer's disease. *Archives of Neurology, 42*(11), 1097–1105.

Kim, J. J., & Fanselow, M. S. (1992). Modality-specific retrograde amnesia of fear. *Science, 256*(5057), 675–677.

Kokmen, E., Beard, C. M., Chandra, V., Offord, K. P., Schoenberg, B. S., & Ballard, D. J. (1991). Clinical risk factors for Alzheimer's disease: A population-based case-control study. *Neurology, 41*(9), 1393–1397.

Kovacevic, S., Rafii, M. S., & Brewer, J. B. (2009). High-throughput, fully automated volumetry for prediction of MMSE and CDR decline in mild cognitive impairment. *Alzheimer Disease & Associated Disorders, 23*, 139–145.

Kringelbach, M. L., & Berridge, K. C. (2009). Towards a functional neuroanatomy of pleasure and happiness. *Trends in Cognitive Science, 13*, 479–487.

Laakso, M. P., Partanen, K., Lehtovirta, M., Hallikainen, M., Hanninen, T., Vainio, P., et al. (1995). MRI of amygdala fails to diagnose early Alzheimer's disease. *Neuroreport, 6*(17), 2414–2418.

Laakso, M. P., Soininen, H., Partanen, K., Helkala, E. L., Hartikainen, P., Vainio, P., et al. (1995). Volumes of hippocampus, amygdala and frontal lobes in the MRI-based diagnosis of early Alzheimer's disease: Correlation with memory functions. *Journal of Neural Transmission. Parkinson's Disease and Dementia Section, 9*(1), 73–86.

LaBar, K. S. (2003). Emotional memory functions of the human amygdala. *Current Neurology and Neuroscience Reports, 3*(5), 363–364.

LaBar, K. S., Gatenby, J. C., Gore, J. C., LeDoux, J. E., & Phelps, E. A. (1998). Human amygdala activation during conditioned fear acquisition and extinction: a mixed-trial fMRI study. *Neuron, 20*(5), 937–945.

Lane, R. D., Reiman, E. M., Bradley, M. M., Lang, P. J., Ahern, G. L., Davidson, R. J., et al. (1997). Neuroanatomical correlates of pleasant and unpleasant emotion. *Neuropsychologia, 35*(11), 1437–1444.

Lazarus, R. S. (1966). *Psychological stress and the coping process.* New York: McGraw-Hill.

Lazarus, R., & Folkman, S. (1984). *Stress, appraisal and coping.* New York: Springer.

LeDoux, J. E. (1996). *The emotional brain.* New York: Simon & Schuster.

LeDoux, J. E. (2000). Emotion circuits in the brain. *Annual Review of Neuroscience, 23,* 155–184.

Levy, M. L., Cummings, J. L., Fairbanks, L. A., Bravi, D., Calvani, M., & Carta, A. (1996). Longitudinal assessment of symptoms of depression, agitation, and psychosis in 181 patients with Alzheimer's disease. *American Journal of Psychiatry, 153*(11), 1438–1443.

Liu, W., Miller, B. L., Kramer, J. H., Rankin, K., Wyss-Coray, C., Gearhart, R., et al. (2004). Behavioral disorders in the frontal and temporal variants of frontotemporal dementia. *Neurology, 62*(5), 742–748.

Lopez, O. L., & Becker, J. T. (2003). Factors that modify the natural course of Alzheimer's disease. *Revista de Neurología, 37*(2), 149–155.

Lowery, K., Mynt, P., Aisbett, J., Dixon, T., O'Brien, J., & Ballard, C. (2000). Depression in the carers of dementia sufferers: a comparison of the carers of patients suffering from dementia with Lewy bodies and the carers of patients with Alzheimer's disease. *Journal of Affective Disorders, 59*(1), 61–65.

Lyketsos, C. G., DelCampo, L., Steinberg, M., Miles, Q., Steele, C. D., Munro, C., et al. (2003). Treating depression in Alzheimer disease: Efficacy and safety of sertraline therapy, and the benefits of depression reduction: the DIADS. *Archives of General Psychiatry, 60*(7), 737–746.

Lyketsos, C. G., Lopez, O., Jones, B., Fitzpatrick, A. L., Breitner, J., & DeKosky, S. (2002). Prevalence of neuropsychiatric symptoms in dementia and mild cognitive impairment: results from the cardiovascular health study. *Journal of the American Medical Association, 288*(12), 1475–1483.

Maclean, L. E., Collins, C. C., & Byrne, E. J. (2001). Dementia with Lewy bodies treated with rivastigmine: Effects on cognition, neuropsychiatric symptoms, and sleep. *International Psychogeriatrics, 13*(3), 277–288.

Maclean, P. D. (1949). Psychosomatic disease and the "visceral brain"; recent developments bearing on the Papez theory of emotion. *Psychosomatic Medicine, 11,* 338–353.

Markesbery, W. R., Schmitt, F. A., Kryscio, R. J., Davis, D. G., Smith, C. D., & Wekstein, D. R. (2006). Neuropathologic substrate of mild cognitive impairment. *Archives of Neurology, 63*(1), 38–46.

Marshall, G. A., Monserratt, L., Harwood, D., Mandelkern, M., Cummings, J. L., & Sultzer, D. L. (2007). Positron emission tomography metabolic correlates of apathy in Alzheimer disease. *Archives of Neurology, 64*(7), 1015–1020.

Mather, M., Canli, T., English, T., Whitfield, S., Wais, P., Ochsner, K., et al. (2004). Amygdala responses to emotionally valenced stimuli in older and younger adults. *Psychological Science, 15*(4), 259–263.

McCabe, B. W., Baun, M. M., Speich, D., & Agrawal, S. (2002). Resident dog in the Alzheimer's special care unit. *Western Journal of Nursing Research, 24*(6), 684–696.

McKeith, I. G., Dickson, D. W., Lowe, J., Emre, M., O'Brien, J. T., Feldman, H., et al. (2005). Diagnosis and management of dementia with Lewy bodies: Third report of the DLB Consortium. *Neurology, 65*(12), 1863–1872.

McKeith, I. G., Grace, J. B., Walker, Z., Byrne, E. J., Wilkinson, D., Stevens, T., et al. (2000). Rivastigmine in the treatment of dementia with Lewy bodies: Preliminary findings from an open trial. *International Journal of Geriatric Psychiatry, 15*(5), 387–392.

McKeith, I., Del Ser, T., Spano, P., Emre, M., Wesnes, K., Anand, R., et al. (2000). Efficacy of rivastigmine in dementia with Lewy bodies: A randomised, double-blind, placebo-controlled international study. *Lancet, 356*(9247), 2031–2036.

McKhann, G. M., Albert, M. S., Grossman, M., Miller, B., Dickson, D., & Trojanowski, J. Q. (2001). Clinical and pathological diagnosis of frontotemporal dementia: Report of the Work Group on Frontotemporal Dementia and Pick's Disease. *Archives of Neurology, 58*(11), 1803–1809.

Mega, M. S., Cummings, J. L., Fiorello, T., & Gornbein, J. (1996). The spectrum of behavioral changes in Alzheimer's disease. *Neurology, 46*(1), 130–135.

Mega, M. S., Dinov, I. D., Lee, L., O'Connor, S. M., Masterman, D. M., Wilen, B., et al. (2000). Orbital and dorsolateral frontal perfusion defect associated with behavioral response to cholinesterase inhibitor therapy in Alzheimer's disease. *Journal of Neuropsychiatry and Clinical Neurosciences, 12*(2), 209–218.

Mega, M. S., Lee, L., Dinov, I. D., Mishkin, F., Toga, A. W., & Cummings, J. L. (2000). Cerebral correlates of psychotic symptoms in Alzheimer's disease. *Journal of Neurology, Neurosurgery & Psychiatry, 69*(2), 167–171.

Mell, J. C., Howard, S. M., & Miller, B. L. (2003). Art and the brain: The influence of frontotemporal dementia on an accomplished artist. *Neurology, 60*(10), 1707–1710.

Meltzer, C. C., Zubieta, J. K., Brandt, J., Tune, L. E., Mayberg, H. S., & Frost, J. J. (1996). Regional hypometabolism in Alzheimer's disease as measured by positron emission tomography after correction for effects of partial volume averaging. *Neurology, 47*(2), 454–461.

Mendez, M. F., Perryman, K. M., Miller, B. L., Swartz, J. R., & Cummings, J. L. (1997). Compulsive behaviors as presenting symptoms of frontotemporal dementia. *Journal of Geriatric Psychiatry and Neurology, 10*(4), 154–157.

Mendez, M. F., Shapira, J. S., McMurtray, A., & Licht, E. (2007). Preliminary findings: behavioral worsening on donepezil in patients with frontotemporal dementia. *American Journal of Geriatric Psychiatry, 15*(1), 84–87.

Merriam, A. E., Aronson, M. K., Gaston, P., Wey, S. L., & Katz, I. (1988). The psychiatric symptoms of Alzheimer's disease. *Journal of the American Geriatric Society, 36*(1), 7–12.

Mesulam, M. (2000). *Principles of behavioral and cognitive neurology.* Oxford: Oxford University Press.

Mesulam, M., & Mufson, E. (1985). The insula of reil in man and monkey: Architechtonics, connectivity, and function. In E. Jones, & A. Peters (Eds.), *Cerebal cortex* (Vol. 4, pp. 179–226). New York: Plenum.

Micheli, D., Bonvicini, C., Rocchi, A., Ceravolo, R., Mancuso, M., Tognoni, G., et al. (2006). No evidence for allelic association of serotonin 2A receptor and transporter gene polymorphisms with depression in Alzheimer disease. *Journal of Alzheimer's Disease*, *10*(4), 371–378.

Middelkoop, H. A., van der Flier, W. M., Burton, E. J., Lloyd, A. J., Paling, S., Barber, R., et al. (2001). Dementia with Lewy bodies and AD are not associated with occipital lobe atrophy on MRI. *Neurology*, *57*(11), 2117–2120.

Milad, M. R., Wright, C. I., Orr, S. P., Pitman, R. K., Quirk, G. J., & Rauch, S. L. (2007). Recall of fear extinction in humans activates the ventromedial prefrontal cortex and hippocampus in concert. *Biological Psychiatry*, *62*(5), 446–445.

Miller, B. L., & Gearhart, R. (1999). Neuroimaging in the diagnosis of frontotemporal dementia. *Dementia and Geriatric Cognitive Disorders*, *10*(Suppl 1), 71–74.

Miller, B. L., Chang, L., Mena, I., Boone, K., & Lesser, I. M. (1993). Progressive right frontotemporal degeneration: clinical, neuropsychological and SPECT characteristics. *Dementia*, *4*(3–4), 204–213.

Miller, B. L., Cummings, J., Mishkin, F., Boone, K., Prince, F., Ponton, M., et al. (1998). Emergence of artistic talent in frontotemporal dementia. *Neurology*, *51*(4), 978–982.

Miller, B. L., Darby, A. L., Swartz, J. R., Yener, G. G., & Mena, I. (1995). Dietary changes, compulsions and sexual behavior in frontotemporal degeneration. *Dementia*, *6*(4), 195–199.

Miller, B. L., Seeley, W. W., Mychack, P., Rosen, H. J., Mena, I., & Boone, K. (2001). Neuroanatomy of the self: evidence from patients with frontotemporal dementia. *Neurology*, *57*(5), 817–821.

Modrego, P. J., & Ferrandez, J. (2004). Depression in patients with mild cognitive impairment increases the risk of developing dementia of Alzheimer type: A prospective cohort study. *Archives of Neurology*, *61*(8), 1290–1293.

Mori, E., Ikeda, M., Hirono, N., Kitagaki, H., Imamura, T., & Shimomura, T. (1999). Amygdalar volume and emotional memory in Alzheimer's disease. *American Journal of Psychiatry*, *156*(2), 216–222.

Mori, T., Ikeda, M., Fukuhara, R., Nestor, P. J., & Tanabe, H. (2006). Correlation of visual hallucinations with occipital rCBF changes by donepezil in DLB. *Neurology*, *66*(6), 935–937.

Morris, J. S., & Dolan, R. J. (2004). Dissociable amygdala and orbitofrontal responses during reversal fear conditioning. *Neuroimage*, *22*(1), 372–380.

Morris, J. S., deBonis, M., & Dolan, R. J. (2002). Human amygdala responses to fearful eyes. *Neuroimage*, *17*(1), 214–222.

Morris, J. S., Frith, C. D., Perrett, D. I., Rowland, D., Young, A. W., Calder, A. J., et al. (1996). A differential neural response in the human amygdala to fearful and happy facial expressions. *Nature*, *383*(6603), 812–815.

Morris, J. S., Ohman, A., & Dolan, R. J. (1998). Conscious and unconscious emotional learning in the human amygdala. *Nature*, *393*(6684), 467–470.

Morris, J. S., Ohman, A., & Dolan, R. J. (1999). A subcortical pathway to the right amygdala mediating "unseen" fear. *Proceedings of the National Academy of Sciences USA*, *96*(4), 1680–1685.

Nacmias, B., Tedde, A., Forleo, P., Piacentini, S., Guarnieri, B. M., Bartoli, A., et al. (2001). Association between 5-HT(2A) receptor polymorphism and psychotic symptoms in Alzheimer's disease. *Biological Psychiatry*, *50*(6), 472–475.

Nacmias, B., Tedde, A., Forleo, P., Piacentini, S., Latorraca, S., Guarnieri, B. M., et al. (2001). Psychosis, serotonin receptor polymorphism and Alzheimer's disease. *Archives of Gerontology and Geriatrics – Supplement, 7*, 279–283.

Nagaratnam, N., Lewis-Jones, M., Scott, D., & Palazzi, L. (1998). Behavioral and psychiatric manifestations in dementia patients in a community: Caregiver burden and outcome. *Alzheimer Disease & Associated Disorders, 12*(4), 330–334.

O'Donnell, B. F., Drachman, D. A., Barnes, H. J., Peterson, K. E., Swearer, J. M., & Lew, R. A. (1992). Incontinence and troublesome behaviors predict institutionalization in dementia. *Journal of Geriatric Psychiatry and Neurology, 5*(1), 45–52.

Ownby, R. L., Crocco, E., Acevedo, A., John, V., & Loewenstein, D. (2006). Depression and risk for Alzheimer disease: Systematic review, meta-analysis, and metaregression analysis. *Archives of General Psychiatry, 63*(5), 530–538.

Palmer, K., Di Iulio, F., Varsi, A. E., Gianni, W., Sancesario, G., Caltagirone, C., et al. (2010). Neuropsychiatric predictors of progression from amnestic-mild cognitive impairment to Alzheimer's disease: The role of depression and apathy. *Journal of Alzheimer's Disease, 20*(1), 175–178.

Pang, F. C., Chow, T. W., Cummings, J. L., Leung, V. P., Chiu, H. F., Lam, L. C., et al. (2002). Effect of neuropsychiatric symptoms of Alzheimer's disease on Chinese and American caregivers. *International Journal of Geriatric Psychiatry, 17*(1), 29–34.

Papez, J. W. (1937). A proposed mechanism of emotion. *Archives of Neurology and Psychiatry*, 725–743.

Perry, R. J., & Miller, B. L. (2001). Behavior and treatment in frontotemporal dementia. *Neurology, 56*(11 Suppl 4), S46–S51.

Pessoa, L. (2005). To what extent are emotional visual stimuli processed without attention and awareness? *Current Opinion in Neurobiology, 15*(2), 188–196.

Pessoa, L., Japee, S., Sturman, D., & Ungerleider, L. G. (2006). Target visibility and visual awareness modulate amygdala responses to fearful faces. *Cerebral Cortex, 16*(3), 366–375.

Petersen, R. C., Parisi, J. E., Dickson, D. W., Johnson, K. A., Knopman, D. S., Boeve, B. F., et al. (2006). Neuropathologic features of amnestic mild cognitive impairment. *Archives of Neurology, 63*(5), 665–672.

Petracca, G. M., Chemerinski, E., & Starkstein, S. E. (2001). A double-blind, placebo-controlled study of fluoxetine in depressed patients with Alzheimer's disease. *International Psychogeriatrics, 13*(2), 233–240.

Phan, K. L., Taylor, S. F., Welsh, R. C., Ho, S. H., Britton, J. C., & Liberzon, I. (2004). Neural correlates of individual ratings of emotional salience: A trial-related fMRI study. *Neuroimage, 21*(2), 768–780.

Phan, K. L., Wager, T. D., Taylor, S. F., & Liberzon, I. (2004). Functional neuroimaging studies of human emotions. *CNS Spectrum, 9*(4), 258–266.

Phelps, E. A. (2004). Human emotion and memory: Interactions of the amygdala and hippocampal complex. *Current Opinion in Neurobiology, 14*(2), 198–202.

Phelps, E. A., Delgado, M. R., Nearing, K. I., & LeDoux, J. E. (2004). Extinction learning in humans: Role of the amygdala and vmPFC. *Neuron, 43*(6), 897–905.

Phillips, M. L., Drevets, W. C., Rauch, S. L., & Lane, R. (2003a). Neurobiology of emotion perception I: The neural basis of normal emotion perception. *Biological Psychiatry, 54*(5), 504–514.

Phillips, M. L., Drevets, W. C., Rauch, S. L., & Lane, R. (2003b). Neurobiology of emotion perception II: Implications for major psychiatric disorders. *Biological Psychiatry, 54*(5), 515–528.

Phillips, M. L., Medford, N., Young, A. W., Williams, L., Williams, S. C., Bullmore, E. T., et al. (2001). Time courses of left and right amygdalar responses to fearful facial expressions. *Human Brain Mapping, 12*(4), 193–202.

Phillips, R. G., & LeDoux, J. E. (1992). Differential contribution of amygdala and hippocampus to cued and contextual fear conditioning. *Behavioral Neuroscience, 106*(2), 274–285.

Pitkanen, A., Pikkarainen, M., Nurminen, N., & Ylinen, A. (2000). Reciprocal connections between the amygdala and the hippocampal formation, perirhinal cortex, and postrhinal cortex in rat. A review. *Annals of the New York Academy of Science, 911*, 369–391.

Polli, F. E., Wright, C. I., Milad, M. R., Dickerson, B. C., Vangel, M., Barton, J. J., et al. (2009). Hemispheric differences in amygdala contributions to response monitoring. *Neuroreport, 20*, 398–402.

Pollock, B. G., Mulsant, B. H., Rosen, J., Sweet, R. A., Mazumdar, S., Bharucha, A., et al. (2002). Comparison of citalopram, perphenazine, and placebo for the acute treatment of psychosis and behavioral disturbances in hospitalized, demented patients. *American Journal of Psychiatry, 159*(3), 460–465.

Popa, D., Duvarci, S., Popescu, A. T., Lena, C., & Pare, D. (2010). Coherent amygdalocortical theta promotes fear memory consolidation during paradoxical sleep. *Proceedings of the National Academy of Sciences USA, 107*(14), 6516–6519.

Potkin, S. G., Anand, R., Fleming, K., Alva, G., Keator, D., Carreon, D., et al. (2001). Brain metabolic and clinical effects of rivastigmine in Alzheimer's disease. *International Journal of Neuropsychopharmacology, 4*(3), 223–230.

Price, J., Russchen, F., & Amaral, D. (1987). The limbic region. II The amygdaloid complex. In *Integrated systems of the CNS, part I. hypothalamus, hippocampus, amygdala, retina* (Vol. 4). Amsterdam: Elsevier.

Rapp, M. A., Schnaider-Beeri, M., Grossman, H. T., Sano, M., Perl, D. P., Purohit, D. P., et al. (2006). Increased hippocampal plaques and tangles in patients with Alzheimer disease with a lifetime history of major depression. *Archives of General Psychiatry, 63*(2), 161–167.

Reiman, E. M., Raichle, M. E., Robins, E., Mintun, M. A., Fusselman, M. J., Fox, P. T., et al. (1989). Neuroanatomical correlates of a lactate-induced anxiety attack. *Archives of General Psychiatry, 46*(6), 493–500.

Reisberg, B., Borenstein, J., Salob, S. P., Ferris, S. H., Franssen, E., & Georgotas, A. (1987). Behavioral symptoms in Alzheimer's disease: Phenomenology and treatment. *Journal of Clinical Psychiatry, 48*, 9–15.

Reisberg, B., Doody, R., Stoffler, A., Schmitt, F., Ferris, S., & Mobius, H. J. (2003). Memantine in moderate-to-severe Alzheimer's disease. *New England Journal of Medicine, 348*(14), 1333–1341.

Robles, A., & Cacabelos, P. (1999). [Lewy bodies dementia: New data for the understanding of neuroimaging]. *Revista de Neurología, 29*(11), 993–998.

Rockwell, E., Choure, J., Galasko, D., Olichney, J., & Jeste, D. V. (2000). Psychopathology at initial diagnosis in dementia with Lewy bodies versus Alzheimer disease: Comparison of matched groups with autopsy-confirmed diagnoses. *International Journal of Geriatric Psychiatry, 15*(9), 819–823.

Rojas-Fernandez, C. H. (2001). Successful use of donepezil for the treatment of dementia with Lewy bodies. *Annals of Pharmacotherapy, 35*(2), 202–205.

Rolls, E. T. (1999). *The brain and emotion.* Oxford: Oxford University Press.

Rolls, E. T. (2004). The functions of the orbitofrontal cortex. *Brain and Cognition, 55*(1), 11–29.

Rolls, E. T. (2005). *Emotion explained*. Oxford: Oxford University Press.

Ropacki, S. A., & Jeste, D. V. (2005). Epidemiology of and risk factors for psychosis of Alzheimer's disease: A review of 55 studies published from 1990 to 2003. *American Journal of Psychiatry, 162*(11), 2022–2030.

Roselli, F., Pisciotta, N. M., Perneczky, R., Pennelli, M., Aniello, M. S., De Caro, M. F., et al. (2009). Severity of neuropsychiatric symptoms and dopamine transporter levels in dementia with Lewy bodies: A 123I-FP-CIT SPECT study. *Movement Disorders, 24*(14), 2097–2103.

Ross, E. D. (1993). Nonverbal aspects of language. *Neurologic Clinics, 11*(1), 9–23.

Royet, J. P., Zald, D., Versace, R., Costes, N., Lavenne, F., Koenig, O., et al. (2000). Emotional responses to pleasant and unpleasant olfactory, visual, and auditory stimuli: A positron emission tomography study. *Journal of Neuroscience, 20*(20), 7752–7759.

Rubin, E. H., & Kinscherf, D. A. (1989). Psychopathology of very mild dementia of the Alzheimer type. *American Journal of Psychiatry, 146*(8), 1017–1021.

Rubin, E. H., Kinscherf, D. A., & Morris, J. C. (1993). Psychopathology in younger versus older persons with very mild and mild dementia of the Alzheimer type. *American Journal of Psychiatry, 150*(4), 639–642.

Rubin, E. H., Storandt, M., Miller, J. P., Grant, E. A., Kinscherf, D. A., Morris, J. C., et al. (1993). Influence of age on clinical and psychometric assessment of subjects with very mild or mild dementia of the Alzheimer type. *Archives of Neurology, 50*(4), 380–383.

Salvador, R., Sarro, S., Gomar, J. J., Ortiz-Gil, J., Vila, F., Capdevila, A., Bullmore, E., McKenna, P. J., & Pomarol-Clotet, E. (2010). Overall brain connectivity maps show cortico-subcortical abnormalities in schizophrenia. *Human Brain Mapping, 31*(12), 2003–2014.

Saunders, R. C., Rosene, D. L., & Van Hoesen, G. W. (1988). Comparison of the efferents of the amygdala and the hippocampal formation in the rhesus monkey: II. Reciprocal and non-reciprocal connections. *Journal of Comparative Neurology, 271*(2), 185–207.

Scarmeas, N., Brandt, J., Albert, M., Hadjigeorgiou, G., Papadimitriou, A., Dubois, B., et al. (2005). Delusions and hallucinations are associated with worse outcome in Alzheimer disease. *Archives of Neurology, 62*(10), 1601–1608.

Schachter, S., & Singer, J. E. (1962). Cognitive, social, and physiological determinants of emotional state. *Psychological Review, 69*, 379–399, errata 121.

Schneider, L. S., Tariot, P. N., Dagerman, K. S., Davis, S. M., Hsiao, J. K., Ismail, M. S., et al. (2006). Effectiveness of atypical antipsychotic drugs in patients with Alzheimer's disease. *New England Journal of Medicine, 355*(15), 1525–1538.

Schultz, S. K., Ellingrod, V. L., Moser, D. J., Kutschner, E., Turvey, C., & Arndt, S. (2002). The influence of cognitive impairment and psychiatric symptoms on daily functioning in nursing facilities: A longitudinal study. *Annals of Clinical Psychiatry, 14*(4), 209–213.

Schwartz, C. E., Wright, C. I., Shin, L. M., Kagan, J., & Rauch, S. L. (2003). Inhibited and uninhibited infants "grown up": Adult amygdalar response to novelty. *Science, 300*(5627), 1952–1953.

Schwartz, C. E., Wright, C. I., Shin, L. M., Kagan, J., Whalen, P. J., McMullin, K. G., et al. (2003). Differential amygdalar response to novel versus newly familiar neutral faces: A functional MRI probe developed for studying inhibited temperament. *Biological Psychiatry, 53*(10), 854–862.

Schwartz, G. E., Davidson, R. J., & Maer, F. (1975). Right hemisphere lateralization for emotion in the human brain: interactions with cognition. *Science*, *190*(4211), 286–288.

Seeley, W. W., Bauer, A. M., Miller, B. L., Gorno-Tempini, M. L., Kramer, J. H., Weiner, M., et al. (2005). The natural history of temporal variant frontotemporal dementia. *Neurology*, *64*(8), 1384–1390.

Selkoe, D. J. (2003). Aging, amyloid, and Alzheimer's disease: A perspective in honor of Carl Cotman. *Neurochemical Research*, *28*(11), 1705–1713.

Setoguchi, S., Wang, P. S., Alan Brookhart, M., Canning, C. F., Kaci, L., & Schneeweiss, S. (2008). Potential causes of higher mortality in elderly users of conventional and atypical antipsychotic medications. *Journal of the American Geriatric Society*, *56*(9), 1644–1650.

Shin, I. S., Carter, M., Masterman, D., Fairbanks, L., & Cummings, J. L. (2005). Neuropsychiatric symptoms and quality of life in Alzheimer disease. *American Journal of Geriatric Psychiatry*, *13*(6), 469–474.

Shinotoh, H., Fukushi, K., Nagatsuka, S., Tanaka, N., Aotsuka, A., Ota, T., et al. (2003). The amygdala and Alzheimer's disease: Positron emission tomographic study of the cholinergic system. *Annals of the New York Academy of Science*, *985*, 411–419.

Shinotoh, H., Namba, H., Fukushi, K., Nagatsuka, S., Tanaka, N., Aotsuka, A., et al. (2000). Progressive loss of cortical acetylcholinesterase activity in association with cognitive decline in Alzheimer's disease: A positron emission tomography study. *Annals of Neurology*, *48*(2), 194–200.

Shinotoh, H., Namba, H., Fukushi, K., Nagatsuka, S., Tanaka, N., Aotsuka, A., et al. (2000). Brain acetylcholinesterase activity in Alzheimer disease measured by positron emission tomography. *Alzheimer Disease & Associated Disorders*, *14*(Suppl 1), S114–S118.

Sink, K. M., Holden, K. F., & Yaffe, K. (2005). Pharmacological treatment of neuropsychiatric symptoms of dementia: a review of the evidence. *Journal of the American Medical Association*, *293*(5), 596–608.

Sival, R. C., Haffmans, P. M., Jansen, P. A., Duursma, S. A., & Eikelenboom, P. (2002). Sodium valproate in the treatment of aggressive behavior in patients with dementia – A randomized placebo controlled clinical trial. *International Journal of Geriatric Psychiatry*, *17*(6), 579–585.

Skjerve, A., & Nygaard, H. A. (2000). Improvement in sundowning in dementia with Lewy bodies after treatment with donepezil. *International Journal of Geriatric Psychiatry*, *15*(12), 1147–1151.

Skjerve, A., Holsten, F., Aarsland, D., Bjorvatn, B., Nygaard, H. A., & Johansen, I. M. (2004). Improvement in behavioral symptoms and advance of activity acrophase after short-term bright light treatment in severe dementia. *Psychiatry and Clinical Neurosciences*, *58*(4), 343–347.

Smith, A. P., Henson, R. N., Dolan, R. J., & Rugg, M. D. (2004). fMRI correlates of the episodic retrieval of emotional contexts. *Neuroimage*, *22*(2), 868–878.

Smith, C. D., Malcein, M., Meurer, K., Schmitt, F. A., Markesbery, W. R., & Pettigrew, L. C. (1999). MRI temporal lobe volume measures and neuropsychologic function in Alzheimer's disease. *Journal of Neuroimaging*, *9*(1), 2–9.

Speck, C. E., Kukull, W. A., Brenner, D. E., Bowen, J. D., McCormick, W. C., Teri, L., et al. (1995). History of depression as a risk factor for Alzheimer's disease. *Epidemiology*, *6*(4), 366–369.

Staff, R. T., Shanks, M. F., Macintosh, L., Pestell, S. J., Gemmell, H. G., & Venneri, A. (1999). Delusions in Alzheimer's disease: Spet evidence of right hemispheric dysfunction. *Cortex*, 35(4), 549–560.

Starkstein, S. E., Federoff, J. P., Price, T. R., Leiguarda, R. C., & Robinson, R. G. (1994). Neuropsychological and neuroradiologic correlates of emotional prosody comprehension. *Neurology*, 44(3 Pt 1), 515–522.

Starkstein, S. E., Jorge, R., Mizrahi, R., & Robinson, R. G. (2006). A prospective longitudinal study of apathy in Alzheimer's disease. *Journal of Neurology, Neurosurgery & Psychiatry*, 77(1), 8–11.

Starkstein, S. E., Vazquez, S., Petracca, G., Sabe, L., Migliorelli, R., Teson, A., et al. (1994). A SPECT study of delusions in Alzheimer's disease. *Neurology*, 44(11), 2055–2059.

Stavitsky, K., Brickman, A. M., Scarmeas, N., Torgan, R. L., Tang, M. X., Albert, M., et al. (2006). The progression of cognition, psychiatric symptoms, and functional abilities in dementia with Lewy bodies and Alzheimer disease. *Archives of Neurology*, 63(10), 1450–1456.

Steele, C., Rovner, B., Chase, G. A., & Folstein, M. (1990). Psychiatric symptoms and nursing home placement of patients with Alzheimer's disease. *American Journal of Psychiatry*, 147(8), 1049–1051.

Steffens, D. C., Otey, E., Alexopoulos, G. S., Butters, M. A., Cuthbert, B., Ganguli, M., et al. (2006). Perspectives on depression, mild cognitive impairment, and cognitive decline. *Archives of General Psychiatry*, 63(2), 130–138.

Suzuki, M., Kanamori, M., Watanabe, M., Nagasawa, S., Kojima, E., Ooshiro, H., et al. (2004). Behavioral and endocrinological evaluation of music therapy for elderly patients with dementia. *Nursing & Health Sciences*, 6(1), 11–18.

Swartz, J. R., Miller, B. L., Lesser, I. M., & Darby, A. L. (1997). Frontotemporal dementia: Treatment response to serotonin selective reuptake inhibitors. *Journal of Clinical Psychiatry*, 58(5), 212–216.

Sweet, R. A., Devlin, B., Pollock, B. G., Sukonick, D. L., Kastango, K. B., Bacanu, S. A., et al. (2005). Catechol-O-methyltransferase haplotypes are associated with psychosis in Alzheimer disease. *Molecular Psychiatry*, 10(11), 1026–1036.

Sweet, R. A., Nimgaonkar, V. L., Devlin, B., Lopez, O. L., & DeKosky, S. T. (2002). Increased familial risk of the psychotic phenotype of Alzheimer disease. *Neurology*, 58(6), 907–911.

Sweet, R. A., Nimgaonkar, V. L., Kamboh, M. I., Lopez, O. L., Zhang, F., & DeKosky, S. T. (1998). Dopamine receptor genetic variation, psychosis, and aggression in Alzheimer disease. *Archives of Neurology*, 55(10), 1335–1340.

Sweet, R. A., Pollock, B. G., Sukonick, D. L., Mulsant, B. H., Rosen, J., Klunk, W. E., et al. (2001). The 5-HTTPR polymorphism confers liability to a combined phenotype of psychotic and aggressive behavior in Alzheimer disease. *International Psychogeriatrics*, 13(4), 401–409.

Tabbert, K., Stark, R., Kirsch, P., & Vaitl, D. (2005). Hemodynamic responses of the amygdala, the orbitofrontal cortex and the visual cortex during a fear conditioning paradigm. *International Journal of Psychophysiolohy*, 57(1), 15–23.

Takahashi, H., Yoshida, K., Sugita, T., Higuchi, H., & Shimizu, T. (2003). Quetiapine treatment of psychotic symptoms and aggressive behavior in patients with dementia with Lewy bodies: A case series. *Progress in Neuropsychopharmacology and Biological Psychiatry*, 27(3), 549–553.

Taragano, F. E., Lyketsos, C. G., Mangone, C. A., Allegri, R. F., & Comesana-Diaz, E. (1997). A double-blind, randomized, fixed-dose trial of fluoxetine vs. amitriptyline in the treatment of major depression complicating Alzheimer's disease. *Psychosomatics, 38*(3), 246–252.

Tariot, P. N., Cummings, J. L., Katz, I. R., Mintzer, J., Perdomo, C. A., Schwam, E. M., et al. (2001). A randomized, double-blind, placebo-controlled study of the efficacy and safety of donepezil in patients with Alzheimer's disease in the nursing home setting. *Journal of the American Geriatric Society, 49*(12), 1590–1599.

Tariot, P. N., Mack, J. L., Patterson, M. B., Edland, S. D., Weiner, M. F., Fillenbaum, G., et al. (1995). The Behavior Rating Scale for Dementia of the Consortium to Establish a Registry for Alzheimer's Disease. The Behavioral Pathology Committee of the Consortium to Establish a Registry for Alzheimer's Disease. *American Journal of Psychiatry, 152*(9), 1349–1357.

Tariot, P. N., Raman, R., Jakimovich, L., Schneider, L., Porsteinsson, A., Thomas, R., et al. (2005). Divalproex sodium in nursing home residents with possible or probable Alzheimer Disease complicated by agitation: A randomized, controlled trial. *American Journal of Geriatric Psychiatry, 13*(11), 942–949.

Teri, L. (1997). Behavior and caregiver burden: Behavioral problems in patients with Alzheimer disease and its association with caregiver distress. *Alzheimer Disease & Associated Disorders, 11*(Suppl 4), S35–S38.

Teri, L., Borson, S., Kiyak, H. A., & Yamagishi, M. (1989). Behavioral disturbance, cognitive dysfunction, and functional skill. Prevalence and relationship in Alzheimer's disease. *Journal of the American Geriatric Society, 37*(2), 109–116.

Teri, L., Larson, E. B., & Reifler, B. V. (1988). Behavioral disturbance in dementia of the Alzheimer's type. *Journal of the American Geriatric Society, 36*(1), 1–6.

The Canadian Study of Health and Aging Working Group. (2000). The incidence of dementia in Canada. *Neurology, 55*(1), 66–73.

Tiraboschi, P., Hansen, L. A., Alford, M., Merdes, A., Masliah, E., Thal, L. J., et al. (2002). Early and widespread cholinergic losses differentiate dementia with Lewy bodies from Alzheimer disease. *Archives of General Psychiatry, 59*(10), 946–951.

Tiraboschi, P., Salmon, D. P., Hansen, L. A., Hofstetter, R. C., Thal, L. J., & Corey-Bloom, J. (2006). What best differentiates Lewy body from Alzheimer's disease in early-stage dementia? *Brain, 129*(Pt 3), 729–735.

Tonkonogy, J. M., Smith, T. W., & Barreira, P. J. (1994). Obsessive-compulsive disorders in Pick's disease. *Journal of Neuropsychiatry and Clinical Neurosciences, 6*(2), 176–180.

Trinh, N. H., Hoblyn, J., Mohanty, S., & Yaffe, K. (2003). Efficacy of cholinesterase inhibitors in the treatment of neuropsychiatric symptoms and functional impairment in Alzheimer disease: A meta-analysis. *Journal of the American Medical Association, 289*(2), 210–216.

Tsuchiya, K., & Kosaka, K. (1990). Neuropathological study of the amygdala in presenile Alzheimer's disease. *Journal of the Neurological Sciences, 100*(1–2), 165–173.

U.S. Food and Drug Administration. (2005). FDA Public Health Advisory: Deaths with antipsychotics in elderly patients with behavioral disturbances.

Uchikado, H., Iseki, E., Tsuchiya, K., Togo, T., Katsuse, O., Ueda, K., et al. (2002). Dementia with Lewy bodies showing advanced Lewy pathology but minimal Alzheimer pathology – Lewy pathology causes neuronal loss inducing progressive dementia. *Clinical Neuropathology, 21*(6), 269–277.

Unger, J. W., McNeill, T. H., Lapham, L. L., & Hamill, R. W. (1988). Neuropeptides and neuropathology in the amygdala in Alzheimer's disease: Relationship between somatostatin, neuropeptide Y and subregional distribution of neuritic plaques. *Brain Research*, *452*(1–2), 293–302.

Updyke, B. V. (1993). Organization of visual corticostriatal projections in the cat, with observations on visual projections to claustrum and amygdala. *Journal of Comparative Neurology*, *327*(2), 159–193.

Valladares-Neto, D. C., Buchsbaum, M. S., Evans, W. J., Nguyen, D., Nguyen, P., Siegel, B. V., et al. (1995). EEG delta, positron emission tomography, and memory deficit in Alzheimer's disease. *Neuropsychobiology*, *31*(4), 173–181.

Van Hoesen, G. W., Augustinack, J. C., & Redman, S. J. (1999). Ventromedial temporal lobe pathology in dementia, brain trauma, and schizophrenia. *Annals of the New York Academy of Science*, *877*, 575–594.

Van Hoesen, G., Pandya, D. N., & Butters, N. (1975). Some connections of the entorhinal (area 28) and perirhinal (area 35) cortices of the rhesus monkey. II. Frontal lobe afferents. *Brain Research*, *95*(1), 25–38.

Vance, D. (1999). Considering olfactory stimulation for adults with age-related dementia. *Perceptual and Motor Skills*, *88*(2), 398–400.

Vereecken, T. H., Vogels, O. J., & Nieuwenhuys, R. (1994). Neuron loss and shrinkage in the amygdala in Alzheimer's disease. *Neurobiology of Aging*, *15*(1), 45–54.

Versijpt, J., Van Laere, K. J., Dumont, F., Decoo, D., Vandecapelle, M., Santens, P., et al. (2003). Imaging of the 5-HT2A system: Age-, gender-, and Alzheimer's disease-related findings. *Neurobiology of Aging*, *24*(4), 553–561.

Vilalta-Franch, J., Lopez-Pousa, S., Turon-Estrada, A., Lozano-Gallego, M., Hernandez-Ferrandiz, M., Pericot-Nierga, I., et al. (2010). Syndromic association of behavioral and psychological symptoms of dementia in Alzheimer disease and patient classification. *American Journal of Geriatric Psychiatry*, *18*(5), 421–432.

Wang, P. S., Schneeweiss, S., Avorn, J., Fischer, M. A,, Mogun, H., Solomon, D. H., et al. (2005). Risk of death in elderly users of conventional vs. atypical antipsychotic medications. *New England Journal of Medicine*, *353*(22), 2335–2241.

Webster, M. J., Ungerleider, L. G., & Bachevalier, J. (1991). Connections of inferior temporal areas TE and TEO with medial temporal-lobe structures in infant and adult monkeys. *Journal of Neuroscience*, *11*(4), 1095–1116.

Weierich, M. R., Wright, C. I., Negreira, A., Dickerson, B. C., & Barrett, L. F. (2010). Novelty as a dimension in the affective brain. *Neuroimage*, *49*(3), 2871–2878.

Weiner, M. F., Risser, R. C., Cullum, C. M., Honig, L., White, C., 3rd, Speciale, S., et al. (1996). Alzheimer's disease and its Lewy body variant: a clinical analysis of postmortem verified cases. *American Journal of Psychiatry*, *153*(10), 1269–1273.

Weintraub, D., Rosenberg, P. B., Drye, L. T., Martin, B. K., Frangakis, C., Mintzer, J. E., et al. (2010). Sertraline for the treatment of depression in Alzheimer disease: Week-24 outcomes. *American Journal of Geriatric Psychiatry*, *18*(4), 332–340.

Wesnes, K. A., McKeith, I., Edgar, C., Emre, M., & Lane, R. (2005). Benefits of rivastigmine on attention in dementia associated with Parkinson disease. *Neurology*, *65*(10), 1654–1656.

Whalen, P. J., Kagan, J., Cook, R. G., Davis, F. C., Kim, H., Polis, S., et al. (2004). Human amygdala responsivity to masked fearful eye whites. *Science*, *306*(5704), 2061.

Whalen, P. J., Rauch, S. L., Etcoff, N. L., McInerney, S. C., Lee, M. B., & Jenike, M. A. (1998). Masked presentations of emotional facial expressions modulate amygdala activity without explicit knowledge. *Journal of Neuroscience*, *18*, 411–418.

Whitwell, J. L., Przybelski, S. A., Weigand, S. D., Ivnik, R. J., Vemuri, P., Gunter, J. L., et al. (2009). Distinct anatomical subtypes of the behavioural variant of frontotemporal dementia: A cluster analysis study. *Brain, 132*(Pt 11), 2932–2946.

Wilson, R. S., Barnes, L. L., Mendes de Leon, C. F., Aggarwal, N. T., Schneider, J. S., Bach, J., et al. (2002). Depressive symptoms, cognitive decline, and risk of AD in older persons. *Neurology, 59*(3), 364–370.

Wilson, R. S., Mendes De Leon, C. F., Bennett, D. A., Bienias, J. L., & Evans, D. A. (2004). Depressive symptoms and cognitive decline in a community population of older persons. *Journal of Neurology, Neurosurgery & Psychiatry, 75*(1), 126–129.

Wright, C. I., Dickerson, B. C., Feczko, E., Negeira, A., & Williams, D. (2007). A functional magnetic resonance imaging study of amygdala responses to human faces in aging and mild Alzheimer's disease. *Biological Psychiatry, 62*(12), 1388–1395.

Wright, C. I., Fischer, H., Whalen, P. J., McInerney, S. C., Shin, L. M., & Rauch, S. L. (2001). Differential prefrontal cortex and amygdala habituation to repeatedly presented emotional stimuli. *Neuroreport, 12*(2), 379–383.

Wright, C. I., Martis, B., Schwartz, C. E., Shin, L. M., Fischer, H. H., McMullin, K., et al. (2003). Novelty responses and differential effects of order in the amygdala, substantia innominata, and inferior temporal cortex. *Neuroimage, 18*(3), 660–669.

Wright, C. I., Martis, B., Shin, L. M., Fischer, H., & Rauch, S. L. (2002). Enhanced amygdala responses to emotional versus neutral schematic facial expressions. *Neuroreport, 13*(6), 785–790.

Wright, C. I., Negreira, A., Gold, A. L., Britton, J. C., Williams, D., Barrett, L. F. (2008). Neural correlates of novelty and face-age effects in young and elderly adults. *Neuroimage, 42*(2), 956–968.

Wright, C. I., Wedig, M. M., Williams, D., Rauch, S. L., & Albert, M. S. (2006). Novel fearful faces activate the amygdala in healthy young and elderly adults. *Neurobiology of Aging, 27*(2), 361–374.

Yesavage, J. A., Rose, T. L., & Lapp, D. (1981). *Validity of the Geriatric Depression Scale in subjects with senile dementia.* Palo Alto: Veterans Administration Medical Clinic.

Zald, D. H., & Pardo, J. V. (1997). Emotion, olfaction, and the human amygdala: Amygdala activation during aversive olfactory stimulation. *Proceedings of the National Academy of Sciences USA, 94*(8), 4119–4124.

Zald, D. H., Lee, J. T., Fluegel, K. W., & Pardo, J. V. (1998). Aversive gustatory stimulation activates limbic circuits in humans. *Brain, 121* (Pt 6), 1143–1154.

Zubenko, G. S., Moossy, J., Martinez, A. J., Rao, G., Claassen, D., Rosen, J., et al. (1991). Neuropathologic and neurochemical correlates of psychosis in primary dementia. *Archives of Neurology, 48*(6), 619–624.

15

Visuospatial Function in Alzheimer's Disease and Related Disorders

Alice Cronin-Golomb

Over a century ago, Alois Alzheimer published a case description of a 51-year-old woman whose initial behavioral abnormality was pathological jealousy of her husband. Her condition rapidly deteriorated with the accumulation of behavioral symptoms that constitute the syndrome of dementia. Besides memory loss, personality change, and agnosia, the woman described in the report exhibited visuospatial symptoms including perceptual abnormalities and dysfunction of spatial localization:

> (S)he could not find her way about her home . . . She was disoriented as to time and place . . . She suffered from serious perceptual disorders . . . While reading she would omit sentences . . . " (Alzheimer, 1907).

Though the young age of the woman in the report and her initial symptom of jealousy might cause today's neurologist to pause before offering a diagnosis of "typical" Alzheimer's disease (AD), the changes over time in memory, object recognition, and visuospatial function would lend confidence to the diagnosis. Among the cortical areas usually affected early in the disease course are the posterior regions, including the parietal lobes, which are of critical importance for normal visuospatial abilities, with involvement of the occipital lobes as well (Arnold et al., 1991; Beach & McGeer, 1988; Braak et al., 1989; Grady et al., 1993; Lewis et al., 1987; McKee et al., 2006; Pietrini et al., 1996).

The topic of the present chapter is visuospatial function in AD and related disorders. With reference to the symptoms reported in Alzheimer's original case, the focus is on spatial localization and on perceptual disorders that are related to spatial

The Handbook of Alzheimer's Disease and Other Dementias, First Edition.
Edited by Andrew E. Budson, Neil W. Kowall.
© 2011 Blackwell Publishing Ltd. Published 2011 by Blackwell Publishing Ltd.

dysfunction. We have reviewed this topic extensively in the past (Cronin-Golomb, 2001; Cronin-Golomb & Amick, 2001; Cronin-Golomb et al., 1993; Cronin-Golomb & Gilmore, 2003) and other reviews are also available (Geldmacher, 2003). Spatial memory, itself a large topic, is not discussed in detail here (see Iachini et al., 2009, for a review). The goal of this chapter is to report the most recent literature (since 2000) and to describe current conceptualizations of spatial disability in AD. These conceptualizations arise from careful behavioral and imaging studies that together permit a fresh view of spatial function in those afflicted by AD and related neuro-degenerative conditions.

Before proceeding with a discussion of the literature on spatial function, it should be noted that the potentially important factor of gender continues to be given short shrift in research studies. Gender differences are understood to be robust for certain spatial tasks (Hampson, 2000) yet are rarely examined in AD despite the fact that they have been documented for motion perception (Andersen & Atchley, 1995; Atchley & Andersen, 1998; Gilmore et al., 1994), which as shown later in the chapter is associated with visuospatial dysfunction. One more recent study has shown poorer performance by women than men with AD on a task of mental pathway generation (Millet et al., 2009) and another has shown that men and women with AD differed in predictors of navigational performance (Cushman & Duffy, 2007), providing an impetus for further investigation of potential gender differences.

In most studies of visuospatial function, individuals with AD exhibit impaired task performance relative to matched control participants. The end result of poor visuospatial function may arise from problems along several different pathways to performance, such as degraded or otherwise non-salient stimulus input, narrowing of attentional focus, suboptimal visual search strategies, and higher order cognitive disturbance. Different domains of impairment may respond to different therapeutic interventions (e.g., environmental, pharmacological), lending importance to the identification of specific causes of spatial dysfunction in individuals with AD.

The chapter sections are organized as follows:

1 Neuropsychology: findings from studies using neuropsychological, cognitive neu-roscience, and imaging techniques
2 Potential causes of visuospatial disorders:
   (a) Stimulus salience
   (b) Motion perception
   (c) Spatial exploration: scanning and attentional focus
   (d) Visual search
3 Heterogeneity of AD presentation: visual variant
4 Interventions to improve visuospatial function:
   (a) Environmental interventions
   (b) Pharmacological interventions
5 Visuospatial dysfunction arising from conditions other than AD:
   (a) Dementia with Lewy bodies
   (b) Parkinson's disease

Neuropsychology

An important problem in AD is topographic disorientation, which leads to becoming lost in familiar or unfamiliar surroundings. Cherrier and colleagues (Cherrier et al., 2001) applied a route-learning test to patients with AD who did not differ significantly from a control group on performance of a number of standard neuropsychological measures of spatial function, though they differed on memory measures. Only performance on the Standardized Road-Map Test of Direction Sense (also known as the Money Road Map) predicted the total score on the route-learning test. A novel finding of the study is that the AD patients performed relatively well on the route-learning subtest of landmark recognition, suggesting that fundamental spatial disorientation rather than failure of memory for landmarks (topographic agnosia) was the principal dysfunction leading to topographic disorientation in this sample. A similar conclusion was drawn by Monacelli and colleagues in their examination of a route-learning task, the total score on which was predicted better by map location ability than by landmark recall, though performance on both subtests was impaired in their sample of patients with AD (Monacelli et al., 2003).

Topographic orientation is especially critical for driving. Brown and Ott reviewed the literature on the use of neuropsychological measures as predictors of driving ability in demented patients and found that performance on visuospatial tasks was a factor to consider in regard to fitness to drive (Brown & Ott, 2004). Studies conducted since this review, including those of Uc and colleagues (Uc et al., 2006) and Grace and colleagues (Grace et al., 2005), are in accord with this point. In the first study (Uc et al., 2006), predictors of unsafe outcomes in a driving simulator included visual psychophysical measures (acuity, contrast sensitivity, visual attention) and measures of spatial function (Judgment of Line Orientation and visuoconstructional tests). The AD group was more likely than the control group to engage in abrupt or premature slowing, though there was no group difference for actual collisions. The second study (Grace et al., 2005) measured driving performance directly during on-road assessment rather than with a simulator, comparing performance in AD and Parkinson's disease (PD). Whereas both patient groups made more tactical driving errors than did the control group (i.e., obeying rules of the road, choice of driving speed, basic driving maneuvers), the AD group additionally committed more operational errors (such as timing of reactions to changing driving environment) and strategic errors (such as mistakes in cognitive reactions and reasoning). Unsafe drivers performed more poorly on a number of neuropsychological measures than did their safe-driving counterparts, with impaired driving predicted best by cognitive tests assessing spatial and executive function (Trail Making Test,

Rey-Osterrieth Complex Figure). Current efforts include the development of neuropsychological tests that correlate well with on-road driving skills, such as the Neuropsychological Assessment Battery's Driving Scenes test of visual attention (Brown et al., 2005), and a composite score from standardized neuropsychological tests across cognitive domains (including visuospatial and visuomotor) that identifies those patients with AD who perform poorly on on-road driving assessment (Dawson et al., 2009).

Studies combining traditional neuropsychological measures with neuroimaging are becoming increasingly common and offer new insights into the brain bases of cognitive change in AD. In a functional magnetic resonance imaging (fMRI) study, Prvulovic and colleagues (Prvulovic et al., 2002) showed patients with AD and a matched control group pairs of angles (clock hands). The task was to indicate whenever an acute angle appeared in a series of oblique angles. The AD group's performance did not differ overall from that of the control group, though it was characterized by a high variance in error rate. Despite the similarity in mean performance (and even when controlling for accuracy and reaction time of behavioral performance), imaging revealed group differences in brain processes, with the AD group showing relatively low activation of the dorsal stream's superior parietal lobule bilaterally as well as of frontal areas, basal ganglia, and thalamus. The patients also showed relatively high activation of the ventral stream's left fusiform gyrus, suggesting a reorganization of activation pattern in AD – possibly a compensatory mechanism. An important further point was that this pattern was associated with the degree of atrophy of the superior parietal lobules. That is, it is likely that the reduced parietal activation followed from parietal atrophy. This finding is further supported by a more recent fMRI study of angle judgment in AD in which it was found that dorsal pathway function was altered, indicating a failure to modulate neural responses to increasing demands of the task (Vannini et al., 2009).

A somewhat different picture was obtained through study of a visuoconstructive task, complex figure drawing (Rey-Osterrieth), performance on which was used to separate patients with AD into two groups who were otherwise matched for neuropsychological performance (Boxer et al., 2003). The more impaired group showed greater atrophy of the right inferior temporal gyrus on structural MRI than did the better-performing group. Presumably figure copying, because of its demands on form (object) perception, engages temporal cortex to a greater extent than would a test of angle orientation, which would rely more heavily on parietal-mediated processes.

Fujimori and colleagues (Fujimori et al., 2000) used positron emission tomography (PET) to measure regional cerebral glucose utilization during performance of tasks of dorsal-stream visuospatial processing (number counting) and ventral-stream object identification (overlapping figures, visual form discrimination). There were significant correlations between the metabolic rate of the bilateral inferior parietal lobules and visuospatial performance, and between the metabolic rate of the right middle temporal and right inferior parietal and object identification.

Though the AD sample size (49) was large for this type of study, there was minimal information provided on the control group (no sample characteristics or PET findings; descriptive statistics were provided for the neuropsychological tests only). The control information would have permitted comparison of the results of this study with that of Prvulovic and colleagues (2002), above, with their demonstration of reorganized activation patterns in dorsal and ventral streams in AD relative to a matched control group.

The clock drawing test (CDT) is a standard neuropsychological measure that is commonly applied to a wide variety of clinical populations. It is a sensitive index of the integrity of several cognitive domains, including spatial abilities, semantic abilities, and executive function. Its multifactorial nature makes it useful clinically but difficult to interpret in terms of brain–behavior relations. Ueda and colleagues (Ueda et al., 2002) attempted to determine the neural substrates of clock drawing in patients with AD using single photon emission computed tomography (SPECT). They used the Rouleau scoring system, which appears to be sensitive to semantic memory as well as to other cognitive abilities. Their report of a correlation of test score with left posterior temporal blood flow is consistent with the sensitivity of the scoring system to semantic dysfunction. In an fMRI study, healthy older adults showed cortical activation of intraparietal, inferior temporal, and occipital cortex during clock-time identification tasks, implicating both ventral and dorsal visual processing pathways (Leyhe et al., 2009). The task requiring identification of the placement of the clock's minute hand elicited activation of parietal areas that the investigators associated with spatial mental imagery. In patients with early AD, impaired performance on the clock tasks was associated with reduced activation of the occipital lobes and the left fusiform gyrus, the latter possibly related to this area's role in conceptual processing. Another study of AD patients, using PET and multiple CDT scoring systems, revealed consistent correlations between clock drawing performance and regional cerebral glucose metabolism in the right inferior parietal lobule (Lee et al., 2008). It is unclear why this group found right parietal to be the area correlating with test performance whereas, as noted above, Ueda et al. found the correlation with left posterior temporal, especially since both studies had a CDT scoring system in common (Rouleau).

In a qualitative assessment of clock drawing comparing individuals with AD to those with frontotemporal dementia, Blair and colleagues found the AD group committed more spatial errors as well as more stimulus-bound responses, conceptual deficits, and planning errors (Blair et al., 2006). In another study, qualitative analysis of the error patterns of patients with AD versus vascular dementia showed that it was the vascular group that made more spatial and planning errors (Kitabayashi et al., 2001), a finding that may be supported by findings from Fukui and colleagues, who reported that a group of patients with subcortical cognitive impairment (including subcortical vascular lesions, Parkinson's disease, progressive supranuclear palsy, dementia with Lewy bodies, and corticobasal degeneration) performed more poorly than patients with AD on clock tasks (drawing, reading, and matching) and figure copying (Fukui et al., 2009). This finding applied to patients with moderate to severe overall cognitive impairment. Small sample sizes did not permit subgroup analysis within the non-AD group.

A very informative approach was taken by Mosimann and colleagues (Mosimann et al., 2004), who examined eye movements in AD patients during clock reading. They found that relative to healthy age-matched adults, visual exploration in the AD group was less tightly focused on the ends of the clock hands, and fixation latency and duration were increased. The latency and duration results indicate a probable difficulty in disengaging attention from one area to move the eyes to a region of interest. Such impairments in disengagement suggest parietal dysfunction. Impaired clock reading has also been associated with poor functional status as indexed by activities of daily living scales, underscoring the importance of visuospatial ability to everyday function (Fukui & Lee, 2009).

Potential Causes of Visuospatial Disorders in AD

Stimulus salience

Stimulus salience may be reduced in AD because of impairments at the levels of basic vision (reduced signal strength leading to degraded perceptual input) and attention.

Reduced visual signal strength

A growing number of research studies are focusing on the impact of deficiencies in lower level visual processes upon higher order visuospatial function. Dysfunction occurs in multiple visual capacities in AD, including contrast sensitivity, color discrimination, depth perception, and motion perception (Cronin-Golomb, 1995). Contrast sensitivity is especially important to stimulus salience, with reductions leading to degraded perceptual input. An example may be seen in Figure 15.1. The image has been passed through an "Alzheimer filter," developed by Grover C. Gilmore and colleagues. The filter simulates the spatial contrast sensitivity deficit of a person with AD relative to a normal adult through digital reduction, thereby reflecting the proportional difference in contrast sensitivity between AD and normal groups. The image suggests how difficult spatial navigation in an environment may be for an individual with a contrast sensitivity deficit of the magnitude commonly seen in AD.

More recent work on the relation of contrast sensitivity to higher order visuo-perceptual and spatial function has come mainly from our laboratory together with that of Gilmore and his colleagues. Deficient contrast sensitivity occurs across the frequency range in AD (Neargarder et al., 2003), with low-frequency impairments especially affecting the ability to discriminate faces (Cronin-Golomb et al., 2000). We have been extending our work in the direction of enhancing stimulus strength in order to improve visual cognition in aging and AD. In one study (Cronin-

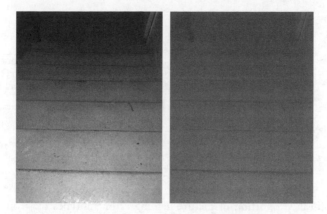

Figure 15.1   The image on the left is of a concrete staircase seen from above under normal viewing conditions. The image on the right is the same staircase passed through the "Alzheimer filter," which simulates the spatial contrast sensitivity deficit of a person with Alzheimer's disease. Source: Photographs courtesy of Thomas M. Laudate. Image filtering courtesy of Grover C. Gilmore and Cecil W. Thomas.

Golomb et al., 2007), increased signal strength was related to improved performance by the patients with AD and by healthy age-matched adults, relative to their baseline performance with stimuli of lower signal strength. This result pertained to letter and word reading, picture identification, and face discrimination. Most promising were the results with reading and picture naming. For reading, we found that increasing signal strength beyond normal levels improved AD performance to the extent that it was indistinguishable from that of healthy elderly adults. This result was similar to what was found for letter reading in a separate study (Gilmore et al., 2005). For picture naming, the percentage of perceptual-type errors (as opposed to semantic errors, or errors with no discernible basis known as "no-content" errors) decreased with increased signal strength, both for healthy elderly adults and patients with AD (Figure 15.2). It would be enlightening to examine the effect of signal strength on other standard measures of visuospatial ability, especially those that longitudinal studies suggest are sensitive to decline over the course of AD (e.g., Paxton et al., 2007, with the Hooper Visual Organization Test).

Reduced attentional salience
Traditional measures of spatial attention have used emotionally neutral stimuli that are either abstract, such as lines, letters or symbol cancellation (Liu et al., 2004) or concrete pictures that elicit verbal description, such as Cookie Theft from the Boston Diagnostic Aphasia Examination, or the Picture Description Test as in the study by Meguro and colleagues (Meguro et al., 2001). A growing trend is to examine the effect on spatial exploration of more specific stimulus components. Daffner et al. (1992) varied the novelty and complexity of emotionally neutral

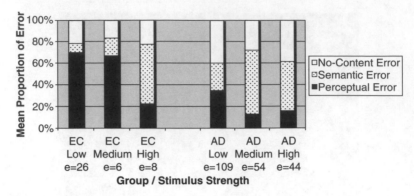

Figure 15.2   Mean proportion of picture-naming error subtypes by group and level of stimulus strength. Data are based on the combined number of errors made by all participants in each group, per condition, referred to here as "e"
EC = Elderly control; AD = Alzheimer's disease (*n* = 35/group)
Source: Cronin-Golomb, A., Gilmore, G. C., Neargarder, S., Morrison, S. R., & Laudate, T. M. (2007). Enhanced stimulus strength improves visual cognition in aging and Alzheimer's disease. *Cortex*. (Elsevier Masson)

stimuli and found that healthy adults, but not patients with AD, spent more time looking at incongruous or irregular objects and scenes than at their more congruous or regular counterparts (Daffner et al., 1992). By contrast, LaBar and colleagues (LaBar et al., 2000) varied the emotional salience of pictures (neutral-negative) and found that patients with AD were similar to healthy older adults and to young adults in the location and duration of fixations. It is unclear whether the difference in the results of the two studies arose from sample differences (with small sample sizes), from slight differences in overall cognitive status, or from a genuine difference in spatial attention as a function of the emotional salience of the viewed stimuli.

   Of relevance here is the study from our laboratory of facial emotion (Wong et al., 2005), in which we found that older and younger adults showed different topographical distributions of fixations. Older adults exhibited fewer fixations on the face overall but proportionately more fixations to the lower half of the display, with implications for accuracy of identification of specific facial emotions (Figure 15.3). Relative to the younger adults, the older adults were less accurate in identifying fear and anger in the visual modality but performed at the same level as the younger adults on an auditory test of emotion (prosody). Though this study did not examine patients with AD, the implication is that investigations of emotional salience in visual search should focus on individual emotions and should attend to where in the visual display the fixations occur. A word of caution is in order here, however, as there is a paucity of work examining facial emotion that simultaneously assesses the spatial demands of facial discrimination or recognition. A study showing

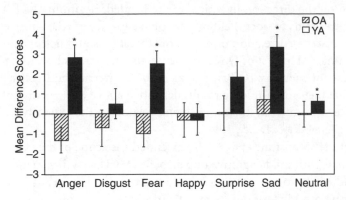

Figure 15.3   Mean difference scores for younger and older adults for individual emotions. The difference score for each participant was computed by subtracting the number of fixations made to the lower halves of the faces from the number of fixations made to the upper halves of the faces. The more positive the difference score, the more fixations the individual made to the upper half of the face, which was correlated with accuracy of emotion identification for anger, fear, and sadness. The more negative the difference score, the more fixations the individual made to the lower half of the face, which was correlated with accuracy of emotion identification for disgust. Older adults made more fixations to the bottom halves of angry, fearful, and sad faces than did younger adults. Asterisks indicate that differences between groups were significant at the *p* < .01 level
Error bars represent standard deviations. OA = Older adults; YA = Younger adults (*n* = 20/ group)
Source: Wong, B., Cronin-Golomb, A., & Neargarder, S. (2005). Patterns of visual scanning as predictors of emotion identification in normal aging. *Neuropsychology, 19*, p. 744. (American Psychological Association)

poor performance by AD patients in the perception of rotated (different orientation) or inverted faces, suggesting viewpoint dependency in AD (Adduri & Marotta, 2009), speaks to the need to address this issue more fully.

Motion perception

Mapstone, Duffy, and their colleagues have conducted a series of careful studies of the relation of deficits in motion perception to visuospatial impairments (Duffy et al., 2004; Mapstone & Weintraub, 2004; see Duffy, 2009, for a review). A specific focus of their work has been the perception of optic flow, or the apparent motion of objects in the environment as one is moving in relation to them. As an example, when we are walking, we have the sense that the visual world is moving from in front of us to behind us, on both left and right sides, which provides information on the direction in which we are headed. Beginning with a linkage of optic flow thresholds to open-field navigational capacity in AD, Duffy et al. (2000) went on to report a correlation of optic flow thresholds and performance on both the Money Road-Map Test of Direction Sense and an on-road driving test, though not with tests of memory (O'Brien et al., 2001). Cherrier and colleagues (2001) suggested that their route-finding results described above were consistent with these findings of environmental navigation being related to the integrity of optic flow perception (Tetewsky & Duffy, 1999).

A third study (Mapstone et al., 2003) extended the scope of the others by assessing individuals with mild cognitive impairment (MCI) as well as patients with AD. The AD and MCI groups performed well on a test of planar (horizontal) motion relative to one of radial motion (simulated optic flow). Those in the AD, MCI, or age-matched control group who had problems with optic flow perception were also impaired on the Road-Map Test, with much weaker correlations between optic flow performance and neuropsychological measures of memory. The implication of the results of the latter two studies is that topographical disorientation in AD arises from visuoperceptual impairments independent of memory difficulties. In addition, the studies suggest that some older normal individuals with elevated optic flow thresholds may be at risk for AD. Optic flow thresholds are correlated with temporal factors in AD, as shown through application of rapid serial visual presentation, suggesting that the temporal dynamics of perception may contribute to spatial disorientation in this disorder (Kavcic & Duffy, 2003). In further studies, this group has found that patients with AD, with their deficits in object motion and optic flow perception, were impaired at pointing or steering accurately in the direction of simulated heading (Mapstone et al., 2006), and that men and women with AD were different in regard to predictors of navigational performance (Cushman & Duffy, 2007). Though men and women were equally impaired in navigation, performance was predicted by visual motion processing in men and by verbal capacities in women.

Festa and colleagues (Festa et al., 2005) used motion perception to investigate the role of cortical connectivity in sensory integration in AD. There were two conditions within a single integration task. For one (motion and color), feature binding required more cross-cortical integration than for the other (motion and luminance). AD patients were impaired on the former but not the latter condition, whereas healthy adults as well as patients with Huntington's disease were able to effect binding under both conditions. The result accords with the disruption of cortico–cortical connections that characterizes AD.

A more recent fMRI study provides information on the neural bases of impairments in depth and motion perception, which to date had not been available in reference to AD (Thiyagesh et al., 2009). These investigators examined stereomotion and radial motion and found reduced activation in the AD group for regions that were active in the control group (e.g., V5, superior parietal lobule, parieto-occipito junction). The reductions were accompanied by greater activation for AD in inferior parietal lobule and other regions, possibly reflecting recruitment compensation.

The authors noted that the findings with stereomotion and radial motion may be relevant to understanding visuospatial disorientation, a common and debilitating visuospatial symptom of AD.

Spatial exploration: scanning and attentional focus

Spatial exploration refers to the ability to scan and search the environment, to attend to areas of interest, and to orient the body in preparation for action in this spatial realm. Neuropsychological disorders in which spatial exploration is impaired include hemineglect (unilateral) and Balint's syndrome (bilateral). Spatial exploration is conceptualized as comprising a number of abilities, including scanning or searching the environment and focusing attention on areas of interest.

Scanning

Thulborn and colleagues (Thulborn et al., 2000) administered a visually guided saccade task while recording activation patterns with fMRI. Relative to the control group, patients with AD exhibited less right parietal activation and more prefrontal activation. Whereas the age-matched control group showed right-hemisphere dominance in the intraparietal sulcus for the task (as do young adults, it is reported), the majority of the AD group showed relatively great left-parietal activation. No volumetric differences between groups were noted, by contrast with the findings of Prvulovic and colleagues (2002) described above, in which parietal deactivation was associated with regional atrophy. Other studies that used eye movement recording are described in the next section on attentional focus.

Attentional focus

Meguro and colleagues (2001) related cerebral blood flow in AD with performance on the Picture Description Test, a complex scene that has been used in studies of aphasia and verbal description capacities in AD. These investigators reported that about equal numbers of AD patients who showed some hemispatial neglect were affected on the right or left side, with 12 patients neglecting items on the right and 14 on the left. Another eight patients described elements only in the central area of the picture, neglecting both right and left peripheral regions. Frequency analysis indicated an interaction of side of hemispatial inattention and the side of the parietal lobe with relatively low blood flow as exhibited on SPECT scanning, such that the group with decreased left hemispatial attention had low flow in the right parietal whereas those with low right hemispatial attention had relatively low flow in the left parietal lobe.

There appears to be substantial heterogeneity across patients, as other investigators have reported either hemispatial neglect (Liu et al., 2004; Mendez et al., 1997) (more in left than right hemispace) or more general inattention, conceptualized as a narrowing of the zone of attentional spotlight or reduction in the useful field of view (Rösler et al., 2005). With a narrowing of the central area that one can attend to without eye movements, it becomes necessary to increase the number of relatively peripheral eye movements in order to attend across a large field, such as that presented during driving. This increase in peripheral eye movements is in fact what is seen in older relative to younger adults and in AD (Mapstone et al., 2001; Rösler et al., 2005). The findings of Mosimann and colleagues in regard to clock reading, described above, may be related to these results, in that AD patients in that study had eye movements that were less tightly focused on an area of interest (ends of clock hands) than were the eye movements of a control group (Mosimann et al., 2004).

Visual search

Liu and colleagues (Liu et al., 2004) found that patients with AD were impaired on cancellation tasks, with some patients showing unilateral and others bilateral neglect. There was a significant correlation of visual inattention on the standard measures with performance on a questionnaire of behavioral inattention, though not with other questionnaire measures of daily function, pointing perhaps to unequal sensitivity of the questionnaire measures to aspects of spatial exploration in AD. Supporting the idea of the fundamental relation of visual search to activities of daily living, it was found that impairments in visual search appeared to account for poor performance by AD patients relative to a control group on a landmark and traffic sign identification task during on-road driving assessment (Uc et al., 2005). These investigators also found a relation between scores on tests of visual perception, visual attention, visuoconstruction and other cognitive domains and the ability of AD patients to perform an on-road route-finding task, as indexed by the number of driving errors including incorrect turns, times lost, and at-fault safety errors (Uc et al., 2004).

Our laboratory has examined the influence of lower level visual characteristics of the target on the ability to search for and detect differences between naturalistic scenes in AD (Neargarder & Cronin-Golomb, 2005). We found that both reaction time and change-detection accuracy were adversely affected with increased scene complexity, and that variations in gray scale (white vs. gray vs. black) were much more difficult to detect than were changes in hue (red/green, blue/yellow). Changes in hue detection were relatively preserved in older adults as well as in patients with AD relative to a young adult group, as was the ability to note the presence of a target in one scene and its absence in an otherwise-identical scene. These findings are in line with the conceptualization of Tales and colleagues (Tales et al., 2004), who noted that targets with larger discernible differences may be processed preattentively whereas those with smaller differences may require more attention. In our study, the gray-scale changes were more difficult to discern and invoked a higher attentional load for the healthy elderly adults (targets never detected in up to 38% of trials) and especially for those with AD (targets never detected in up to 62% of trials) relative to the young adults (7% of trials). As noted earlier, visual input (e.g., contrast sensitivity) is compromised in aging and especially in AD, which may well relate to reduced ability to successfully search for items differing only in gray-scale contrast. In another study, degradation of signal strength was associated with impairments in visual search for objects in unexpected locations in AD (Stehli et al., 2003).

Applying cognitive neuroscience techniques, other groups have focused on various aspects of visual search and spatial attention. Vecera and Rizzo (2004) have invoked impairments in visual short-term memory as an important contributor to observed deficits in spatial attention. Tales and colleagues (Tales et al., 2002) examined spatial cuing with exogenous cues *versus* endogenous cues, with the former attracting attention automatically and the latter requiring voluntary shifting of attention. They found that patients with AD showed strong effects for exogenous cues but did not differ from a control group for endogenous cues, meaning that AD is associated with an impairment of automatic but not controlled visuospatial attention. They acknowledged that under other experimental conditions, controlled visuospatial attention may also be compromised. In an intriguing extension of this type of work, Greenwood, Parasuraman and colleagues (Greenwood et al., 2005) reported that apolipoprotein E (ApoE) genotype is related to cued visual search, noting that the presence of the epsilon-4 allele was associated with cognitive decline in midlife that was consistent with prodromal AD. They further found that the CHRNA4 gene is associated with attentional cuing whereas the DBH gene is associated with spatial working memory (Parasuraman & Greenwood, 2004; Parasuraman et al. 2005).

Heterogeneity of AD Presentation: Visual Variant

There is substantial heterogeneity in the symptom profile of individuals with AD, with even Alzheimer's original case being today considered atypical in presentation. Even with "typical" AD, there is extensive heterogeneity in the severity of problems that lead to visuospatial dysfunction, such as disorders of basic vision (Cronin-Golomb, 2004), as well as in extent of visuospatial difficulty (Caine & Hodges, 2001).

A subset of patients with AD present with relatively severe disorders of basic visual function (such as restricted visual fields and abnormal color discrimination and depth perception), visuoperceptual and visuocognitive problems (e.g., associative agnosia) and a variety of spatial difficulties, some of which constitute Balint's syndrome. In these individuals, impairments in the visual and spatial domains usually precede semantic deficits (Caine & Hodges, 2001; Suzuki et al., 2003). These cases are referred to as "visual variant" or posterior cortical atrophy, with AD being the usual cause. The symptoms correspond to glucose hypometabolism in the occipito-parietal regions, especially in the right hemisphere, consistent with damage to the dorsal visual processing stream (Nestor et al., 2003). It has been proposed that visual motion evoked potentials may be useful in distinguishing AD patients with more pathology in visual cortex, who showed relatively low sensitivity on a task of visual attention, from those with more pathology in higher order areas, for whom the attentional performance was relatively spared. Of note, the low-sensitivity group also had relatively impaired contrast sensitivity (Fernandez et al., 2007).

The neural substrates of atypical presentations in AD, with special emphasis on the visual variant, have been reviewed by von Gunten and colleagues (von Gunten et al., 2006) and interested readers are urged to consult this excellent reference as well as previous thorough reviews from this group (von Gunten et al., 2004) as well as from Mendez (2004).

Interventions to Improve Visuospatial Function

Environmental interventions

In an applied study, we set the goal of improving daily function in patients with AD by enhancing signal strength and thereby directing their visual attention to the important task of eating and drinking at mealtime (Dunne et al., 2004). In a dining setting of a long-term care facility, we conducted a pre-post intervention study using standard (white) and high-contrast tableware and measured the amount of food and beverage that were consumed. The intervention resulted in significant increases in ingestion of food (25% increase) and beverage (84% increase) in a severely demented AD sample (Figure 15.4). Follow-up testing indicated that the salience of the signal was of critical importance whereas hue itself was not. Specifically, red and blue tableware of saturated hues worked equally well relative to white, but pastel shades (pink, light blue) were ineffective in providing sufficient signal strength to effect behavioral change. These results are in accord with those of Koss and Gilmore, who found that modifications of the visual contrast environment improved nutritional intake in AD patients (Koss & Gilmore, 1998). An important further finding of Koss and Gilmore was that the environmental manipulation decreased agitated nighttime behavior ("sundowning") in this sample of patients.

There has been substantial interest in more general modification of the visual environment of patients with AD in order to enhance the success of spatial navigation as well as safety. Dunne has described simple environmental modifications, room by room, that are based on empirical research on visual and visuospatial dysfunction in AD, with an emphasis on color discrimination and contrast sensitivity. This review is particular helpful as it is written as a practical guide for the lay reader (Dunne, 2004).

Pharmacological interventions

Although the cholinergic hypothesis has been driving research studies of AD for many years, little attention has been paid to the cholinergic system in primary visual areas until relatively recently. Ikonomovic and colleagues examined choline

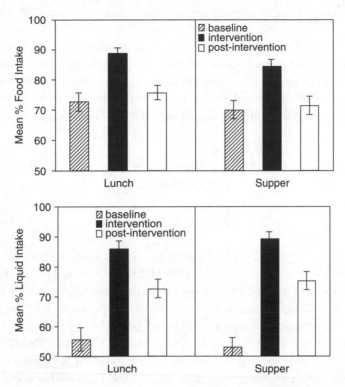

Figure 15.4   Food and liquid intake was measured under baseline and post-intervention conditions using white background (luminance 45.0 fL) and under the intervention condition using high-contrast red background (luminance 7.1 fL). Mean percent food (top) and liquid (bottom) intake is shown for the baseline, intervention, and post-intervention conditions for lunch (left) and supper (right). Error bars represent the standard error of the mean for each condition

Source: Dunne, T. E., Neargarder, S. A., Cipolloni, P. B., & Cronin-Golomb, A. (2004). Visual contrast enhances food and liquid intake in advanced Alzheimer's disease. *Clinical Nutrition 23*, p. 535. (Elsevier)

acetyltransferase (ChAT) activity in the primary visual cortex of the brains of 54 individuals with and without AD who had been enrolled in the longitudinal Religious Orders Study, who had had clinical examination within 12 months of death (Ikonomovic et al., 2005). The AD brains showed significantly less ChAT activity in this region than did brains from those with no or mild cognitive impairment. The amount of ChAT in primary visual cortex correlated significantly with the group's overall mental status as indexed by the Mini-Mental State Examination (MMSE), even when restricting AD group membership to those with only mild to moderate symptoms. As well, there was a trend for ChAT activity to correlate with an index of visuospatial ability (z score of Standard Progressive Matrices and Standard Line Orientation). The authors interpreted their results to mean that ChAT activity in primary visual cortex not only affects visuospatial function but also might interfere with the integration of visual processing to affect global cognition.

Some studies indicate the usefulness of cholinergic treatment, such as cholinesterase inhibitors, in the preservation of higher order visuospatial function in AD (clock drawing) (Almkvist et al., 2004; Fukui & Taguchi, 2005) and in improvement of performance of healthy older adults on tasks with significant visual scanning demands (tangled lines, Symbol Digit Substitution) (Wezenberg et al., 2005).

Visuospatial Dysfunction Arising from Conditions Other Than AD

Dementia with Lewy bodies

The principal dementing disorder besides AD that is associated with visuospatial impairment is Dementia with Lewy bodies (DLB). Whereas significant visual and visuospatial impairment as a prominent presenting feature is relatively rare in AD, such presentation is common in DLB. Pertinent symptoms of DLB include visual hallucinations, agnosia, delusional misidentification, and constructional impairments (Geldmacher, 2003; Kao et al., 2009; Stavitsky et al., 2006). Holroyd has effectively made the point that despite shared features such as visual hallucinations that can make differential diagnosis difficult, AD and DLB are likely distinct disorders (Holroyd, 2004).

Most studies of visual and spatial abilities in DLB provide an AD control group and regularly find that patients with AD outperform those with DLB. Developing latent constructs of verbal memory and visuospatial abilities from a comprehensive neuropsychological assessment, Johnson and colleagues found that patients with AD ($n = 66$) performed more poorly than did patients with DLB ($n = 9$) on verbal memory, whereas the opposite pattern prevailed for visuospatial ability. DLB that was co-morbid with AD, in 57 patients, was associated with poor visuospatial ability specifically (Johnson et al., 2005). In regard to spatial tests, DLB patients have been reported to perform more poorly on constructional praxis (Ala et al., 2001; Guidi et al., 2006; Stavitsky et al., 2006), size and form discrimination, identification of overlapping figures (Mori et al., 2000), and visual counting (Guidi et al., 2006; Mori et al., 2000). Those with DLB who also had visual hallucinations were especially impaired on the visuoperceptual tasks (Mori et al., 2000). These findings are consistent with AD–DLB differences in regional cerebral blood flow (Colloby et al., 2002). The latter study showed that a DLB group exhibited hypoperfusion relative to an AD group in primary visual and visual association cortices and parietal cortex (Brodmann areas 17, 18, and 7, respectively). Relative to a healthy control group, temporal perfusion deficits were seen only in AD, occipito-parietal deficits only in DLB, and frontal and parietal hypoperfusion in both groups. The importance of examining visuospatial function is underscored by a retrospective study that reported that deficits in this domain predicted the rate of cognitive decline in 22 autopsy-confirmed cases of DLB but not in AD alone (44 cases). Specifically, poor baseline performance on visuospatial tests (Block Design, Clock Drawing Copy) was associated with more rapid cognitive decline as well as with visual hallucinations (Hamilton et al., 2008).

One study has compared visuospatial performance across patients with three disorders that share the neuropathological feature of α-synuclein immunoreactivity: DLB, Parkinson's disease, and multiple system atrophy (MSA) (Kao et al., 2009). All participants in this study scored 23 or higher on the MMSE. The DLB and MSA groups performed significantly more poorly than those with PD on copying a complex figure, and the DLB group was additionally significantly worse than the others on a number location task.

Parkinson's disease

Parkinson's disease (PD) is related to DLB in that Lewy bodies are present in both disorders. Whereas in DLB these pathological entities appear in the subcortex and cortex, in PD they are mainly restricted to the subcortex. There appears to be much overlap in symptoms between DLB and PD with dementia, the criterion for differential diagnosis being whether or not motor symptoms were the presenting symptom, as they are in PD. Accordingly, one might expect similar cognitive profiles in the two disorders, including the presence of visual and visuospatial impairments. This is indeed what is found. PD is associated with multiple visual and spatial impairments, in demented patients and in those without dementia. Because the PD literature is extensive and the issue of differential diagnosis vis à vis AD is not as prominent as it is for vascular dementia and frontotemporal dementia, the present chapter has concentrated on the non-PD disorders. Reviews of the visual and spatial literature in PD appear in Cronin-Golomb (2010) and Cronin-Golomb and Amick (2001), with specific findings reported in a number of papers on vision and visuospatial function, including their relation to participant characteristics such as side of disease onset and gender (e.g., Amick et al., 2006; Clark et al., 2008 and 2010; Davidsdottir et al., 2005; Davidsdottir et al., 2008; Miller and Cronin-Golomb, 2010; Schendan et al., 2009; Young et al., 2010) as well as their relation to important daily functions such as driving (Uc, Rizzo, Anderson et al., 2009; Uc, Rizzo, Johnson et al., 2009). A neuroimaging study has linked reduction in gray matter in posterior cortices (temporal, parietal, occipital) to impaired performance on visuospatial and visuoperceptual measures (Pereira et al., 2009).

Vascular dementia

Less work has been done in the study of vascular and frontotemporal dementia than in DLB, particularly in comparison with AD. Moretti and colleagues examined clock drawing in a large sample of individuals with subcortical vascular dementia ($n = 144$) or AD ($n = 150$) (Moretti et al., 2005). The vascular group performed more poorly than did the AD group at baseline, and declined further over a 24-month period. The clock-drawing score correlated with performance on visuospatial measures, especially right–left discrimination, as well as on measures of executive function (verbal fluency). It is noteworthy that the patient group included individuals with only subcortical dementia without apparent infarcts in strategic cortical areas responsible for visuospatial abilities. As already described above, Kitabayashi and colleagues conducted a qualitative analysis of clock-drawing errors and found that patients with vascular dementia made more spatial and planning errors than did patients with AD (Kitabayashi et al., 2001).

Frontotemporal dementia

Frontotemporal dementia (FTD) is usually characterized by preservation of visuospatial abilities relative to what is commonly seen in AD. Chow and colleagues examined annualized rate of decline in both groups on subtests of the MMSE (Chow et al., 2006). They found that whereas the FTD group declined more quickly on the language subtest, the AD group showed accelerated decline on the visuospatial subtest (figure copy). The results accorded with practiced criteria for differential diagnosis of FTD and AD. As noted above, Blair and colleagues (2006) performed a qualitative assessment of clock drawing and found that a group with FTD committed fewer spatial errors as well as fewer stimulus-bound responses, conceptual deficits, and planning errors than did a group with AD.

Summary

Visuospatial dysfunction in AD is reflected in perceptual impairments as well as in deficits in higher order aspects of spatial orientation and navigation. In AD as it typically presents, visuospatial difficulties are revealed through behavioral assessments using standard neuropsychological measures and by newer tools made available by cognitive neuroscience. Neuroimaging has provided complementary findings, extending our knowledge of the relation of visuospatial behavior to particular brain areas and systems, including the possibility of compensatory mechanisms in AD relative to healthy aging.

Current studies focus not only on the phenomenology of visuospatial dysfunction but also on its sources. In regard to stimulus salience, there are some studies on aspects of stimulus novelty and incongruity as well as on emotional arousal, and there is considerable room for more work in this area. A stronger research focus in recent years is on lower level perceptual components of the stimulus, focusing either on overall visual input (e.g., contrast sensitivity, motion perception) or on actual stimulus features, especially in relation to visual search and spatial cuing. Eye-movement recording is another technique that is finding increasing use in studies of spatial function in AD, with reports of abnormal search patterns being related to general spatial abilities. An important further point of entry to understanding visuospatial problems is through study of patients with the visual variant of AD. The exceptionally severe visual and spatial disorders of this subset of patients provide more broadly relevant information on regional pathological change and its behavioral consequences. Identifying the sources of spatial dysfunction is of great importance, as it leads us to consider rational environmental and pharmacological interventions targeting one or more of the causes of impairment. Finally, it is useful to study visuospatial dysfunction in disorders besides AD, as such study helps us to narrow our hypotheses about the most likely candidate brain regions and consequent treatment strategies. Whereas there is growing interest in assessment of dementia with Lewy bodies and Parkinson's disease, a great deal more work needs to be done in the study of frontotemporal dementia, vascular dementia, and other dementing disorders.

Despite the need for more research, the current emphases on new assessment techniques, identifying the specific sources of visual, perceptual and spatial impairments, and studying the visual variant of AD and related disorders hold promise for enhancing our understanding of visuospatial dysfunction and in developing effective interventions to improve the quality of life of individuals with AD.

Acknowledgments

I am grateful to a number of colleagues for informative discussions and critiques of earlier versions of this chapter, including Melissa Amick, Grover C. Gilmore, Mark Mapstone, Sandy Neargarder, Karina Stavitsky, and Karen Sullivan. I also acknowledge the generous assistance of Tom Laudate in providing the photographs for Figure 15.1, and Grover C. Gilmore and Cecil W. Thomas for the application of the Alzheimer filter to the original image. Bruce Reese provided technical assistance. This work was conducted with the support of the National Institute of Neurological Disorders and Stroke (R01 NS052914-06).

References

Adduri, C. A., & Marotta, J. J. (2009). Mental rotation of faces in healthy aging and Alzheimer's disease. *PLoS One, 4*, e6120.

Ala, T. A., Hughes, L. F., Kyrouac, G. A., Ghobrial, M. W., & Elble, R. J. (2001). Pentagon copying is more impaired in dementia with Lewy bodies than in Alzheimer's disease. *Journal of Neurology, Neurosurgery & Psychiatry, 70*(4), 483–488.

Almkvist, O., Darreh-Shori, T., Stefanova, E., Spiegel, R., & Nordberg, A. (2004). Preserved cognitive function after 12 months of treatment with rivastigmine in mild Alzheimer's disease in comparison with untreated AD and MCI patients. *European Journal of Neurology, 11*(4), 253–261.

Alzheimer, A. (1907). A characteristic disease of the cerebral cortex. In E. Schultze, & O. Snell (Eds.), *Allgemeine Zeitschrift fur Psychiatrie und Psychisch-Gerichtliche Medizin* (Vol. 6, pp. 146–148). Berlin: Georg Relmer.

Amick, M. M., Schendan, H. E., Ganis, G., & Cronin-Golomb, A. (2006). Frontostriatal circuits are necessary for visuomotor transformation: Mental rotation in Parkinson's disease. *Neuropsychologia, 44*, 339–349.

Andersen, G. J., & Atchley, P. (1995). Age-related differences in the detection of three-dimensional surfaces from optic flow. *Psychology and Aging, 10*(4), 650–658.

Arnold, S. E., Hyman, B. T., Flory, J., Damasio, A. R., & Van Hoesen, G. W. (1991). The topographical and neuroanatomical distribution of neurofibrillary tangles and neuritic plaques in the cerebral cortex of patients with Alzheimer's disease. *Cerebral Cortex, 1*(1), 103–116.

Atchley, P., & Andersen, G. J. (1998). The effect of age, retinal eccentricity, and speed on the detection of optic flow components. *Psychology and Aging, 13*(2), 297–308.

Beach, T. G., & McGeer, E. G. (1988). Lamina-specific arrangement of astrocytic gliosis and senile plaques in Alzheimer's disease visual cortex. *Brain Research, 463*(2), 357–361.

Blair, M., Kertesz, A., McMonagle, P., Davidson, W., & Bodi, N. (2006). Quantitative and qualitative analyses of clock drawing in frontotemporal dementia and Alzheimer's disease. *Journal of the International Neuropsychological Society, 12*(2), 159–165.

Boxer, A. L., Kramer, J. H., Du, A. T., Schuff, N., Weiner, M. W., Miller, B. L., et al. (2003). Focal right inferotemporal atrophy in AD with disproportionate visual constructive impairment. *Neurology, 61*(11), 1485–1491.

Braak, H., Braak, E., & Kalus, P. (1989). Alzheimer's disease: Areal and laminar pathology in the occipital isocortex. *Acta Neuropathologica (Berlin), 77*(5), 494–506.

Brown, L. B., & Ott, B. R. (2004). Driving and dementia: A review of the literature. *Journal of Geriatric Psychiatry and Neurology, 17*(4), 232–240.

Brown, L. B., Stern, R. A., Cahn-Weiner, D. A., Rogers, B., Messer, M. A., Lannon, M. C., et al. (2005). Driving scenes test of the Neuropsychological Assessment Battery (NAB) and on-road driving performance in aging and very mild dementia. *Archives of Clinical Neuropsychology, 20*, 209–215.

Caine, D., & Hodges, J. R. (2001). Heterogeneity of semantic and visuospatial deficits in early Alzheimer's disease. *Neuropsychology, 15*(2), 155–164.

Cherrier, M. M., Mendez, M., & Perryman, K. (2001). Route learning performance in Alzheimer disease patients. *Neuropsychiatry, Neuropsychology, & Behavioral Neurology, 14*(3), 159–168.

Chow, T. W., Hynan, L. S., & Lipton, A. M. (2006). MMSE scores decline at a greater rate in frontotemporal degeneration than in AD. *Dementia and Geriatric Cognitive Disorders, 22*(3), 194–199.

Clark, U.S., Neargarder, S., Cronin-Golomb, A. (2008). Specific impairments in the recognition of emotional facial expressions in Parkinson's disease. *Neuropsychologiia, 46*, 2300–2309.

Clark, U.S., Neargarder, S., Cronin-Golomb, A. (2010). Visual exploration of emotional facial expressions in Parkinson's disease. *Neuropsychologia, 48*, 1901–1913.

Colloby, S. J., Fenwick, J. D., Williams, E. D., Paling, S. M., Lobotesis, K., Ballard, C., et al. (2002). A comparison of (99m)Tc-HMPAO SPET changes in dementia with Lewy bodies and Alzheimer's disease using statistical parametric mapping. *European Journal of Nuclear Medicine and Molecular Imaging, 29*(5), 615–622.

Cronin-Golomb, A. (1995). Vision in Alzheimer's disease. *Gerontologist, 35*(3), 370–376.

Cronin-Golomb, A. (2001). Color vision, object recognition and spatial localization in aging and Alzheimer's disease. In P. R. Hof, & C. V. Mobbs (Eds.), *Functional neurobiology of aging* (pp. 517–529). San Diego, CA: Academic Press.

Cronin-Golomb, A. (2004). Heterogeneity of visual symptom presentation in Alzheimer's disease. In A. Cronin-Golomb, & P. R. Hof (Eds.), *Vision in Alzheimer's disease.* (Vol. 34, pp. 96–111). Basel: Karger.

Cronin-Golomb, A., (2010). Parkinson's disease as a disconnection syndrome. *Neuropsychology Review, 20,* 191–208.

Cronin-Golomb, A., & Amick, M. (2001). Spatial abilities in aging, Alzheimer's disease and Parkinson's disease. In F. Boller, & S. Cappa (Eds.), *Handbook of neuropsychology* (2nd edn., Vol. 6, pp. 119–143). Amsterdam: Elsevier.

Cronin-Golomb, A., & Gilmore, G. C. (2003). Visual factors in cognitive dysfunction and enhancement in Alzheimer's disease. In S. A. Soraci, & K. Murata-Soraci (Eds.), *Visual information processing* (pp. 3–34). Westport, CT: Praeger.

Cronin-Golomb, A., Corkin, S., & Rosen, T. J. (1993). Neuropsychological assessment of dementia. In P. J. Whitehouse (Ed.), *Dementia* (pp. 130–164). Philadelphia: F.A. Davis.

Cronin-Golomb, A., Cronin-Golomb, M., Dunne, T. E., Brown, A. C., Jain, K., Cipolloni, P. B., et al. (2000). Facial frequency manipulation normalizes face discrimination in AD. *Neurology, 54*(12), 2316–2318.

Cronin-Golomb, A., Gilmore, G. C., Neargarder, S., Morrison, S. R., & Laudate, T. M. (2007). Enhanced stimulus strength improves visual cognition in aging and Alzheimer's disease. *Cortex, 43,* 952–966.

Cushman, L. A., & Duffy, C. J. (2007). The sex specificity of navigational strategies in Alzheimer disease. *Alzheimer Disease & Associated Disorders, 21*(2), 122–129.

Daffner, K. R., Scinto, L. F., Weintraub, S., Guinessey, J. E., & Mesulam, M. M. (1992). Diminished curiosity in patients with probable Alzheimer's disease as measured by exploratory eye movements. *Neurology, 42*(2), 320–328.

Davidsdottir, S., Cronin-Golomb, A., & Lee, A. C. (2005). Visual and spatial symptoms in Parkinson's disease. *Vision Research, 45,* 1285–1296.

Davidsdottir, S., Wagenaar, R., Young, D., & Cronin-Golomb, A. (2008). Visuospatial function, optic flow perception, and navigational veering in Parkinson's disease. *Brain, 131,* 2882–2893.

Dawson, J. D., Anderson, S. W., Uc, E. Y, Dastrup, E., & Rizzo, M. (2009). Predictors of driving safety in early Alzheimer disease. *Neurology, 72,* 521–527.

Duffy, C. J. (2009). Visual motion processing in aging and Alzheimer's disease: Neuronal mechanisms and behavior from monkeys to man. *Annals of the New York Academy of Science, 1170,* 736–744.

Duffy, C. J., Cushman, L., & Kavcic, V. (2004). Visuospatial disorientation in Alzheimer's disease: Impaired spatiotemporal integration in visual information processing. In A. Cronin-Golomb, & P. R. Hof (Eds.), *Vision in Alzheimer's disease* (Vol. 34, pp. 155–172). Basel: Karger.

Duffy, C. J., Tetewsky, S. J., & O'Brien, H. (2000). Cortical motion blindness in visuospatial AD. *Neurobiology of Aging, 21*(6), 867–869; discussion 875–867.

Dunne, T. (2004). Improved performance on activities of daily living in Alzheimer's disease: Practical applications of vision research. In A. Cronin-Golomb, & P. R. Hof (Eds.), *Vision in Alzheimer's disease* (Vol. 34, pp. 305–324). Basel: Karger.

Dunne, T. E., Neargarder, S. A., Cipolloni, P. B., & Cronin-Golomb, A. (2004). Visual contrast enhances food and liquid intake in advanced Alzheimer's disease. *Clinical Nutrition*, *23*(4), 533–538.

Fernandez, R., Kavcic, V., & Duffy, C. J. (2007). Neurophysiologic analyses of low- and high-level visual processing in Alzheimer disease. *Neurology*, *68*, 2066–2076.

Festa, E. K., Insler, R. Z., Salmon, D. P., Paxton, J., Hamilton, J. M., & Heindel, W. C. (2005). Neocortical disconnectivity disrupts sensory integration in Alzheimer's disease. *Neuropsychologia*, *19*, 728–738.

Fujimori, M., Imamura, T., Hirono, N., Ishii, K., Sasaki, M., & Mori, E. (2000). Disturbances of spatial vision and object vision correlate differently with regional cerebral glucose metabolism in Alzheimer's disease. *Neuropsychologia*, *38*(10), 1356–1361.

Fukui, T., & Taguchi, S. (2005). Do vascular lesions and related risk factors influence responsiveness to donepezil chloride in patients with Alzheimer's disease? *Dementia and Geriatric Cognitive Disorders*, *20*, 15–24.

Fukui, T., & Lee, E. (2009). Visuospatial function is a significant contributor to functional status in patients with Alzheimer's disease. *American Journal of Alzheimer's Disease and Other Dementias*, *24*, 313–321.

Fukui, T., Lee, E., Kitamura, M., Hosoda, H., Bokui, C., Ikusu, K., & Okita, K. (2009). Visuospatial dysfunction may be a key in the differentiation between Alzheimer's disease and subcortical cognitive impairment in moderate to severe stages. *Dementia and Geriatric Cognitive Disorders*, *28*, 288–294.

Geldmacher, D. S. (2003). Visuospatial dysfunction in the neurodegenerative diseases. *Frontiers in Bioscience*, *8*, e428–e436.

Gilmore, G. C., Cronin-Golomb, A., Neargarder, S. A., & Morrison, S. R. (2005). Enhanced stimulus contrast normalizes visual processing of rapidly presented letters in Alzheimer's disease. *Vision Research*, *45*(8), 1013–1020.

Gilmore, G. C., Wenk, H. E., Naylor, L. A., & Koss, E. (1994). Motion perception and Alzheimer's disease. *Journal of Gerontology*, *49*(2), P52–P57.

Grace, J., Amick, M. M., D'Abreu, A., Festa, E. K., Heindel, W. C., & Ott, B. R. (2005). Neuropsychological deficits associated with driving performance in Parkinson's and Alzheimer's disease. *Journal of the International Neuropsychological Society*, *11*(6), 766–775.

Grady, C. L., Haxby, J. V., Horwitz, B., Gillette, J., Salerno, J. A., Gonzalez-Aviles, A., et al. (1993). Activation of cerebral blood flow during a visuoperceptual task in patients with Alzheimer-type dementia. *Neurobiology of Aging*, *14*(1), 35–44.

Greenwood, P. M., Sunderland, T., Putnam, K., Levy, J., & Parasuraman, R. (2005). Scaling of visuospatial attention undergoes differential longitudinal change as a function of APOE genotype prior to old age: Results from the NIMH BIOCARD study. *Neuropsychology*, *19*(6), 830–840.

Guidi, M., Paciaroni, L., Paolini, S., De Padova, S., & Scarpino, O. (2006). Differences and similarities in the neuropsychological profile of dementia with Lewy bodies and Alzheimer's disease in the early stage. *Journal of the Neurological Sciences*, *248*(1–2), 120–123.

Hamilton, J. M., Salmon, D. P., Galasko, D., Raman, R., Emond, J., Hansen, L. A., et al. (2008). Visuospatial deficits predict rate of cognitive decline in autopsy-verified dementia with Lewy bodies. *Neuropsychology*, *22*, 729–737.

Hampson, E. (2000). Sexual differentiation of spatial functions in humans. In A. Matsumoto (Ed.), *Sexual differentiation of the brain* (pp. 279–300). London: CRC Press.

Holroyd, S. (2004). Visual hallucinations in Alzheimer's disease. In A. Cronin-Golomb, & P. R. Hof (Eds.), *Vision in Alzheimer's disease* (Vol. 34, pp. 126–135). Basel: Karger.

Iachini, I., Iavarone, A., Senese, V. P., Ruotolo, F., & Ruggiero, G. (2009). Visuospatial memory in healthy elderly, AD and MCI: A review. *Current Aging Science, 2*, 43–59.

Ikonomovic, M. D., Mufson, E. J., Wuu, J., Bennett, D. A., & DeKosky, S. T. (2005). Reduction of choline acetyltransferase activity in primary visual cortex in mild to moderate Alzheimer's disease. *Archives of Neurology, 62*(3), 425–430.

Johnson, D. K., Morris, J. C., & Galvin, J. E. (2005). Verbal and visuospatial deficits in dementia with Lewy bodies. *Neurology, 65*, 1232–1238.

Kao, A. W., Racine, C. A., Quitania, L. C., Kramer, J. H., Christine, C. W., & Miller, B. L. (2009). Cognitive and neuropsychiatric profile of the synucleinopathies: Parkinson's disease, dementia with Lewy bodies and multiple system atrophy. *Alzheimer Disease & Associated Disorders, 23*, 365–370.

Kavcic, V., & Duffy, C. J. (2003). Attentional dynamics and visual perception: Mechanisms of spatial disorientation in Alzheimer's disease. *Brain, 126*(Pt 5), 1173–1181.

Kitabayashi, Y., Ueda, H., Narumoto, J., Nakamura, K., Kita, H., & Fukui, K. (2001). Qualitative analyses of clock drawings in Alzheimer's disease and vascular dementia. *Psychiatry and Clinical Neurosciences, 55*(5), 485–491.

Koss, E., & Gilmore, G. C. (1998). Environmental interventions and functional ability of AD patients. In B. Vellas, J. Fitten, & G. Frisoni (Eds.), *Research and practice in Alzheimer's disease* (pp. 185–191). Paris/New York: Serdi/Springer.

LaBar, K. S., Mesulam, M., Gitelman, D. R., & Weintraub, S. (2000). Emotional curiosity: Modulation of visuospatial attention by arousal is preserved in aging and early-stage Alzheimer's disease. *Neuropsychologia, 38*(13), 1734–1740.

Lee, D. Y., Seo, E. H., Choo, I. H., Kim, S. G., Lee, J. S., Lee, D. S., et al. (2008). Neural correlates of the clock drawing test performance in Alzheimer's disease: A FDG-PET study. *Dementia and Geriatric Cognitive Disorders, 26*, 306–313.

Lewis, D. A., Campbell, M. J., Terry, R. D., & Morrison, J. H. (1987). Laminar and regional distributions of neurofibrillary tangles and neuritic plaques in Alzheimer's disease: A quantitative study of visual and auditory cortices. *Journal of Neuroscience, 7*(6), 1799–1808.

Leyhe, T., Erb, M., Milian, M., Eschweiler, G. W., Ethofer, T. Grodd, W., et al. (2009). Changes in cortical activation during retrieval of clock time representations in patients with mild cognitive impairment and early Alzheimer's disease. *Dementia and Geriatric Cognitive Disorders, 27*, 117–132.

Liu, C. J., McDowd, J., & Lin, K. C. (2004). Visuospatial inattention and daily life performance in people with Alzheimer's disease. *American Journal of Occupational Therapy, 58*(2), 202–210.

Mapstone, M., & Weintraub, S. (2004). Closing the window of spatial attention: Effects on navigational cue use in Alzheimer's disease. In A. Cronin-Golomb, & P. R. Hof (Eds.), *Vision in Alzheimer's disease* (Vol. 34, pp. 290–304). Basel: Karger.

Mapstone, M., Logan, D., & Duffy, C. J. (2006). Cue integration for the perception and control of self-movement in ageing and Alzheimer's disease. *Brain, 129*(Pt 11), 2931–2944.

Mapstone, M., Rösler, A., Hays, A., Gitelman, D. R., & Weintraub, S. (2001). Dynamic allocation of attention in aging and Alzheimer disease: Uncoupling of the eye and mind. *Archives of Neurology, 58*(9), 1443–1447.

Mapstone, M., Steffenella, T., & Duffy, C. (2003). A visuospatial variant of mild cognitive impairment. *Neurology*, *60*, 803–808.

McKee, A. C., Au, R., Cabral, H. J., Kowall, N. W., Seshadri, S., Kubilus, C. A., et al. (2006). Visual association pathology in preclinical Alzheimer disease. *Journal of Neuropathology & Experimental Neurology*, *65*(6), 621–630.

Meguro, K., Shimada, M., Someya, K., Horikawa, A., & Yamadori, A. (2001). Hemispatial visual-searching impairment correlated with decreased contralateral parietal blood flow in Alzheimer disease. *Neuropsychiatry, Neuropsychology, & Behavioral Neurology*, *14*(4), 213–218.

Mendez, M. F. (2004). Posterior cortical atrophy: A visual variant of Alzheimer's disease. In A. Cronin-Golomb, & P. R. Hof (Eds.), *Vision in Alzheimer's disease* (Vol. 34, pp. 112–125). Basel: Karger.

Mendez, M. F., Cherrier, M. M., & Cymerman, J. S. (1997). Hemispatial neglect on visual search tasks in Alzheimer's disease. *Neuropsychiatry, Neuropsychology, & Behavioral Neurology*, *10*(3), 203–208.

Miller, I. N. & Cronin-Golomb, A. (2010). Gender differences in Parkinson's disease: Clinical characteristics and cognition. *Movement Disorders*, *25*, 2695–2703.

Millet, X., Raoux, N., Le Carret, N., Bouisson, J., Dartigues, J.-F., & Amieva, H. (2009). Gender-related differences in visuospatial memory persist in Alzheimer's disease. *Archives of Clinical Neuropsychology*, *24*, 783–789.

Monacelli, A. M., Cushman, L. A., Kavcic, V., & Duffy, C. J. (2003). Spatial disorientation in Alzheimer's disease: The remembrance of things passed. *Neurology*, *61*(11), 1491–1497.

Moretti, R., Torre, P., Antonello, R. M., Cazzato, G., Bava, A., & Manos, P. J. (2005). Use of the ten-point clock test to compare executive functioning across 24 months in patients with subcortical vascular dementia. *Perceptual and Motor Skills*, *100*(1), 207–216.

Mori, E., Shimomura, T., Fujimori, M., Hirono, N., Imamura, T., Hashimoto, M., et al. (2000). Visuoperceptual impairment in dementia with Lewy bodies. *Archives of Neurology*, *57*(4), 489–493.

Mosimann, U. P., Felblinger, J., Ballinari, P., Hess, C. W., & Muri, R. M. (2004). Visual exploration behaviour during clock reading in Alzheimer's disease. *Brain*, *127*(Pt 2), 431–438.

Neargarder, S. A., Stone, E. R., Cronin-Golomb, A., & Oross, S., (2003). The impact of acuity on performance of four clinical measures of contrast sensitivity in Alzheimer's disease. *Journal of Gerontology B Psychological Sciences and Social Sciences*, *58*(1), P54–P62.

Neargarder, S., & Cronin-Golomb, A. (2005). Characteristics of visual target influence detection of change in naturalistic scenes in Alzheimer disease. *Cognitive & Behavioral Neurology*, *18*(3), 151–158.

Nestor, P. J., Caine, D., Fryer, T. D., Clarke, J., & Hodges, J. R. (2003). The topography of metabolic deficits in posterior cortical atrophy (the visual variant of Alzheimer's disease) with FDG-PET. *Journal of Neurology, Neurosurgery & Psychiatry*, *74*(11), 1521–1529.

O'Brien, H. L., Tetewsky, S. J., Avery, L. M., Cushman, L. A., Makous, W., & Duffy, C. J. (2001). Visual mechanisms of spatial disorientation in Alzheimer's disease. *Cerebral Cortex*, *11*(11), 1083–1092.

Parasuraman, R., & Greenwood, P. (2004). Visual attention, genetics and Alzheimer's disease. In A. Cronin-Golomb, & P. R. Hof (Eds.), *Vision in Alzheimer's disease* (Vol. 34, pp. 271–289). Basel: Karger.

Parasuraman, R., Greenwood, P. M., Kumar, R., & Fossella, J. (2005). Beyond heritability: Neurotransmitter genes differentially modulate visuospatial attention and working memory. *Psychological Science, 16*(3), 200–207.

Paxton, J. L., Peavy, G. M., Jenkins, C., Rice, V. A., Heindel, W. C., & Salmon, D. P. (2007). Deterioration of visual-perceptual organization ability in Alzheimer's disease. *Cortex, 43*, 967–975.

Pereira, J. B., Junque, C., Martı, M.-J., Ramirez-Ruiz, B., Bargallo, N., & Tolosa, E. (2009). Neuroanatomical substrate of visuospatial and visuoperceptual impairment in Parkinson's disease. *Movement Disorders, 24*, 1193–1199,

Pietrini, P., Furey, M. L., Graff-Radford, N., Freo, U., Alexander, G. E., Grady, C. L., et al. (1996). Preferential metabolic involvement of visual cortical areas in a subtype of Alzheimer's disease: Clinical implications. *American Journal of Psychiatry, 153*(10), 1261–1268.

Prvulovic, D., Hubl, D., Sack, A. T., Melillo, L., Maurer, K., Frolich, L., et al. (2002). Functional imaging of visuospatial processing in Alzheimer's disease. *Neuroimage, 17*(3), 1403–1414.

Rösler, A., Mapstone, M., Hays-Wicklund, A., Gitelman, D. R., & Weintraub, S. (2005). The "zoom lens" of focal attention in visual search: Changes in aging and Alzheimer's disease. *Cortex, 41*(4), 512–519.

Schendan, H. E., Amick, M., & Cronin-Golomb, A. (2009). Role of a lateralized parietal-basal ganglia circuit in hierarchical pattern perception: Evidence from Parkinson's disease. *Behavioral Neuroscience, 123*, 125–136.

Stavitsky, K., Brickman, A. M., Scarmeas, N., Torgan, R. L., Tang, M. X., Albert, M., et al. (2006). The progression of cognition, psychiatric symptoms, and functional abilities in dementia with Lewy bodies and Alzheimer disease. *Archives of Neurology, 63*(10), 1450–1456.

Stehli Nguyen, A., Chubb, C., & Huff, F. (2003). Visual identification and spatial location in Alzheimer's disease. *Brain and Cognition, 52*(2), 155–166.

Suzuki, K., Otsuka, Y., Endo, K., Ejima, A., Saito, H., Fujii, T., et al. (2003). Visuospatial deficits due to impaired visual attention: Investigation of two cases of slowly progressive visuospatial impairment. *Cortex, 39*(2), 327–341.

Tales, A., Muir, J. L., Bayer, A., & Snowden, R. J. (2002). Spatial shifts in visual attention in normal ageing and dementia of the Alzheimer type. *Neuropsychologia, 40*(12), 2000–2012.

Tales, A., Muir, J., Jones, R., Bayer, A., & Snowden, R. J. (2004). The effects of saliency and task difficulty on visual search performance in ageing and Alzheimer's disease. *Neuropsychologia, 42*(3), 335–345.

Tetewsky, S. J., & Duffy, C. J. (1999). Visual loss and getting lost in Alzheimer's disease. *Neurology, 52*(5), 958–965.

Thiyagesh, S., Farrow, T., Parks, R., Accosta-Mesa, H., Young, C., Wilkinson, I., et al. (2009). The neural basis of visuospatial perception in Alzheimer's disease and healthy elderly comparison subjects: An fMRI study. *Psychiatry Research: Neuroimaging, 172*, 109–116.

Thulborn, K. R., Martin, C., & Voyvodic, J. T. (2000). Functional MR imaging using a visually guided saccade paradigm for comparing activation patterns in patients with probable Alzheimer's disease and in cognitively able elderly volunteers. *American Journal of Neuroradiology, 21*, 524–531.

Uc, E. Y., Rizzo, M., Anderson, S. W., Dastrup, E., Sparks, J. D., & Dawson, J. D. (2009). Driving under low-contrast visibility conditions in Parkinson disease. *Neurology, 73,* 1103–1110.

Uc, E. Y., Rizzo, M., Anderson, S. W., Shi, Q., & Dawson, J. D. (2005). Driver landmark and traffic sign identification in early Alzheimer's disease. *Journal of Neurology, Neurosurgery & Psychiatry, 76,* 764–768.

Uc, E. Y., Rizzo, M., Anderson, S. W., Shi, Q., & Dawson, J. D. (2004). Driver route-following and safety errors in early Alzheimer disease. *Neurology, 63,* 832–837.

Uc, E. Y., Rizzo, M., Anderson, S. W., Shi, Q., & Dawson, J. D. (2006). Unsafe rear-end collision avoidance in Alzheimer's disease. *Journal of the Neurological Sciences, 251,* 35–43.

Uc, E. Y., Rizzo, M., Johnson, A. M., Dastrup, E., Anderson, S. W., & Dawson, J. D. (2009). Road safety in drivers with Parkinson disease. *Neurology, 73,* 2112–2119.

Ueda, H., Kitabayashi, Y., Narumoto, J., Nakamura, K., Kita, H., Kishikawa, Y., et al. (2002). Relationship between clock drawing test performance and regional cerebral blood flow in Alzheimer's disease: A single photon emission computed tomography study. *Psychiatry and Clinical Neurosciences, 56*(1), 25–29.

Vannini, P., Lehmann, C., Dierks, T., Jann, K., Viitanen, M., Wahlund, L. O., & Almkvist, O. (2008). Failure to modulate neural response to increased task demand in mild Alzheimer's disease: fMRI study of visuospatial processing. *Neurobiology of Disease, 31,* 287–297.

Vecera, S. P., & Rizzo, M. (2004). Visual attention and visual short-term memory in Alzheimer's disease. In A. Cronin-Golomb, & P. R. Hof (Eds.), *Vision in Alzheimer's disease* (Vol. 34, pp. 248–270). Basel: Karger.

von Gunten, A., Bouras, C., Kovari, E., Giannakopoulos, P., & Hof, P. R. (2006). Neural substrates of cognitive and behavioral deficits in atypical Alzheimer's disease. *Brain Research Reviews, 51*(2), 176–211.

von Gunten, A., Giannakopoulos, P., Bouras, C., & Hof, P. R. (2004). Neuropathological changes in visuospatial systems in Alzheimer's disease. In A. Cronin-Golomb, & P. R. Hof (Eds.), *Vision in Alzheimer's disease* (Vol. 34, pp. 30–61). Basel: Karger.

Wezenberg, E., Verkes, R. J., Sabbe, B. G., Ruigt, G. S., & Hulstijn, W. (2005). Modulation of memory and visuospatial processes by biperiden and rivastigmine in elderly healthy subjects. *Psychopharmacology (Berlin), 181*(3), 582–594.

Wong, B., Cronin-Golomb, A., & Neargarder, S. (2005). Patterns of visual scanning as predictors of emotion identification in normal aging. *Neuropsychology, 19*(6), 739–749.

Young, D. E., Wagenaar, R. C., Lin, C.-C., Chou, Y.-H., Davidsdottir, S. Saltzman, E., Cronin-Golomb, A. (2010). Visuospatial perception and navigation in Parkinson's disease. *Vision Research, 50,* 2495–2504.

16

Sleep and Circadian Rhythms in Dementia

David G. Harper

Patients with Alzheimer's disease (AD) and other age-associated neurodegenerative dementias experience significant sleep disturbance as a concomitant to their illness (Gabelle & Dauvilliers, 2010; Vitiello & Borson, 2001). As a result, patients and caregivers have to manage the many cognitive and behavioral sequelae resulting from this loss, which frequently leads to institutionalization (Pollak & Perlick, 1991). The nature and etiology of these disturbances are heterogeneous resulting in a confusing array of symptoms that ultimately present to the clinician. Factors such as a perturbed circadian system, degradation in systems mediating arousal, sleep initiation and maintenance, and the structure of sleep all play a role in the disturbance seen by the clinician. These symptoms develop as a result of the extent and pattern of damage that patients experience. In addition, various environmental factors such as low diurnal rhythm and high nocturnal illumination can have a profound impact on an already perturbed sleep/arousal system. The key to successful treatment of sleep disturbance in patients with dementia is an understanding of the systems governing sleep and how various dementias undermine them.

Normal Sleep

Sleep is an essential periodic function of the body and mind involving a temporary loss or reduction in sensory consciousness and a lowering of metabolic activity. While this somewhat facile definition describes the behavioral changes associated with sleep, the question of why we sleep has proven more difficult and has recently

The Handbook of Alzheimer's Disease and Other Dementias, First Edition.
Edited by Andrew E. Budson, Neil W. Kowall.
© 2011 Blackwell Publishing Ltd. Published 2011 by Blackwell Publishing Ltd.

come under intense scrutiny. Some of the answers emerging from this research would seem to have considerable relevance to the understanding of dementia. In particular, in addition to the well-known restorative properties of sleep, it appears that sleep also plays a pivotal role in cognitive processing, especially in the domain of learning and memory. These new findings provide new evidence for the importance of understanding sleep changes in patients with dementia. However, in order to contextualize these findings it would be useful first to review how sleep is regulated and the electrophysiological changes that occur during this state.

The initiation and maintenance of sleep is often conceptualized as being regulated mainly by two interacting processes, whose influence over time can be expressed as mathematical functions producing periods of consolidated sleep and wakefulness of appropriate length (Achermann, 2004; Borbely, 1982). One of these processes, generally termed homeostatic, builds need to sleep as a function of the duration of prior wakefulness. As a result, the longer wakefulness is maintained the greater the perceived need for sleep is. This urge to sleep can be resisted for a time, however, ultimately wakefulness cannot be maintained indefinitely and the urge to sleep becomes irresistible.

The second process, usually identified as circadian (from *circa* – approximately – and *dian* – day), works in humans to consolidate sleep during the nocturnal period and wakefulness during the diurnal period. As its name describes, mathematically it is expressed as a circular function with a period length of approximately one day or 24 hours and modulates propensity for sleep and wakefulness. The circadian process can be shifted according to environmental signals, like light and food availability, and therefore positions the normal sleep period to an optimal phase, which promotes maximal environmental coordination and optimal homeostatic adjustment to environmental demands.

Episodes of sleep are also highly structured comprising a specific architecture of changes in electrophysiological and neurochemical activity and accompanying behavior (Aserinsky & Kleitman, 1953; Dement & Kleitman, 1957). There are two main states that occur during sleep. These are termed rapid eye movement (REM) sleep and non-rapid eye movement (NREM) sleep. NREM sleep is generally divided into four additional stages, labeled 1–4 in order of increasing depth of sleep. During sleep, the brain oscillates between these REM and NREM states with a period of approximately 90 minutes.

Initiation of sleep occurs with entry into stage 1 NREM sleep characterized by a gradual slowing of electrophysiological activity with more synchronous theta (4–8 Hz) activity present on the electroencephalogram (EEG) and a loss of environmental awareness. Entry into stage 2 sleep is characterized by the development of two characteristic electrophysiological patterns (Rechtschaffen & Kales, 1968). The first is a high amplitude wave termed a k-complex and the second is higher frequency synchronous bursts of activity in the 7–14 Hz range termed sleep spindles. These changes occur against a background of gradually relaxing muscle activity (often measured with electromyography (EMG)) and more regular breathing. As

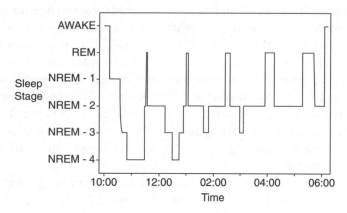

Figure 16.1 Oscillation between NREM and REM has a changing architecture through the night

the NREM period advances, electrophysiological activity gradually slows leading to a condition where arousal is more difficult and brain electrical activity occurs in high amplitude slow waves, termed delta waves (0.5–4 Hz). The increasing quantity of delta waves is what defines the transition into stage 3 and stage 4 sleep. After a period of time in these delta sleep phases, sleep begins to transition back through the stages until the major transition to REM sleep occurs.

Onset of REM sleep is characterized by a return to desynchronous EEG activity that, separate from other information, is indistinguishable from a waking EEG (Rechtschaffen & Kales, 1968). However, muscle tone, as quantified by EMG, decreases noticeably far below what would be observed in waking and along with rapid horizontal eye movements, is a defining characteristic of REM sleep. Subjects awoken during REM sleep report experiencing vivid dreams.

Observations about the electrophysiology and regulation of sleep are fascinating areas to explore, however, they doesn't answer the primary question about sleep. That is, what is its role and function? Clearly, it is extremely important, given the resources put into its regulation. One can observe the restorative function that it plays, and sleep may serve a survival function in limiting activity to certain times of the day or night. However, are there other roles that sleep has, particularly in the area of cognition?

Sleep and Memory

There are several taxonomies developing the structure and function of learning and memory with the most useful being the distinction, at least in humans, between declarative (explicit) and non-declarative (implicit) memory (Budson, 2009; Squire & Zola, 1996). Declarative memory involves learning that is conscious such as autobiographical knowledge and memorization or comprehension of textual material. Non-declarative memory in contrast is acquired without consciousness of the process and is usually performance-based. Declarative and non-declarative memories also involve different neuroanatomical structures and pathways in addition to the functional differences in their learning domains. The encoding of declarative memory involves the mesotemporal structures of the hippocampus and its proximal structures of the dentate gyrus, entorhinal cortex, and parahippocampal cortex. Non-declarative memory appears to use a diverse array of structures in information coding, including the cortex, striatum, amygdala, and cerebellum among other structures.

A simple model of memory formation can involve as few as two stages, acquisition and consolidation (Lechner et al., 1999; Muller & Pilzecker, 1900). In this two-stage model acquisition occurs during the presentation of the stimulus to learn. The memory traces formed during this initial acquisition period are labile and highly susceptible to interference from a variety of sources. Consolidation occurs over a longer period of hours to days during which time the memory trace becomes stable and no longer susceptible to interference (Brashers-Krug et al., 1996). Following consolidation, the neural representation of the task, as imaged through fMRI, is changed and no longer involves many of the structures involved in forming the trace (Shadmehr & Holcomb, 1997; see Budson, 2009, for review).

Despite the major differences in structure and function between declarative and non-declarative memory, the cellular substrate is thought to be quite similar. Synaptic plasticity is the generally accepted model of memory formation, and long-term potentiation (LTP) and long-term depression (LTD) is the key cellular substrate of synaptic plasticity. Long-term potentiation is the use-dependent ability of neurons to enhance synaptic connectivity, while long-term depression is also a use-dependent phenomenon that decreases synaptic connectivity. It appears that the timing of presynaptic and postsynaptic events are critical in this distinction with LTP involving presynaptic potentials preceding postsynaptic and LTD involving postsynaptic potential closely preceding the presynaptic. While anatomical localization may change certain features of the mechanism of LTP and LTD, it appears the same basic principles govern synaptic plasticity even if the surrounding cytoarchitecture and neurotransmitters are different, or whether it involves a cortical pyramidal cell or a hippocampal GABAergic interneuron (Kullmann & Lamsa, 2007; Morris et al., 2003).

The evidence for the enhancement of all kinds of memory consolidation by sleep has become substantial during the last two decades. The evidence is particularly strong for sleep-enhanced consolidation of non-declarative memory by REM and slow wave sleep. Positive studies have included those involving visual discrimination tasks (Karni et al., 1994; Stickgold et al., 2000), motor sequence tasks (Fischer et al., 2002; Walker et al., 2002), and a motor adaptation task (Huber et al., 2004). However, debate still continues on the role of REM sleep in the consolidation of memory (Siegel, 2001). The type of sleep also appears to be critical in the consolidation of non-declarative memory in a task-specific manner with REM sleep playing a particularly important role (Aly & Moscovitch, 2010; Gais et al., 2000; Karni, et al., 1994; O'Neill et al., 2010; Stickgold, 2005; Walker et al., 2002).

Memory, in particular declarative memory, and the encoding of new information is the cognitive domain generally affected first in patients with AD. This is likely a result of damage in the entorhinal cortex and hippocampus seen in the early stages of AD (Braak & Braak, 1991; Markesbery, 2010). Memory dysfunction in earlier stages of AD is the result of an encoding consolidation impairment that is observable as impairment on free and cued recall tests (Lowndes & Savage, 2007). Procedural and other implicit learning has been demonstrated to be relatively preserved in these patients (Budson, 2009; van Halteren-van Tilborg et al., 2007) reflecting the relative preservation of brain areas implicated in non-declarative as compared to declarative memory (Braak & Braak, 1991).

There has been substantial debate over the role of sleep in the consolidation of declarative memory (Smith, 2001). However, recent evidence has shown that, while the function of sleep in declarative memory is complex, the evidence for it playing a role in consolidation of declarative memory is impressive (Aly & Moscovitch, 2010; O'Neill et al., 2010; Stickgold, 2005). The first report of enhancement of declarative memory consolidation by sleep was made over 84 years ago in a study measuring recall of nonsense syllables after a learning session followed by either sleep or wakefulness (Jenkins & Dallenbach, 1924). During the early 1970s interest was again aroused in the consolidation of declarative memory by sleep. These initial studies were guided by the increased understanding of sleep developed from polysomnography and the finding that sleep wasn't a unitary phenomenon but instead consisted of discrete stages, which were prevalent in different amounts at different times of night or different amounts of prior sleep (Dement & Kleitman, 1957).

Selectively depriving subjects of different sleep stages led to different results in post-learning tests of declarative memory. Contrary to the prevailing hypothesis at the time, the results of these studies suggested that early sleep, rich in slow wave activity, was superior to late night sleep, which is rich in REM sleep in promoting the consolidation of declarative memory (Barrett & Ekstrand, 1972; Fowler et al., 1973; Yaroush et al., 1971). Experiments to induce REM rich sleep in subjects post learning of paired associations also failed to yield a benefit in declarative learning. However, several confounding variables are present in these studies, including different circadian conditions at learning times (Yaroush et al., 1971), assuring that the proper stage of sleep is present in the study subjects by polysomnography (Benson & Feinberg, 1977; Grosvenor & Lack, 1984; Plihal & Born, 1997), and, when polysomnography was used, a lack of examination of the intensity of the features of those stages of sleep. These difficulties rendered these results, positive and negative, suggestive but not conclusive.

More recent studies have examined the intensity of various features of sleep stages, the most prominent of these being sleep spindles associated with stage 2 sleep. Work in animal models suggests that hippocampal "ripples," short (30–200 ms) bursts of high frequency (~200 Hz) CA1 activity, selectively reactivate during sleep (Davidson et al., 2009; Ego-Stengel & Wilson, 2010; Skaggs & McNaughton, 1996; Wilson & McNaughton, 1994). In addition, these replays, by networks of hippocampal cells, are tightly associated with the appearance of sleep spindles in the neocortex (Siapas & Wilson, 1998). These findings imply transfer of hippocampal-stored information (memory traces) to cortical regions for long-term storage.

Therefore, if this correlative activity represents the substrate of the consolidation of declarative memory, the frequency of sleep spindles, occurring during stage 2 of human sleep (as opposed to the delta sleep of rodents), should be sensitive to declarative memory tasks in humans. Several recent studies have shown a significant and more convincing effect than those studies performed previously without the benefit of polysomnography and quantification of neural events during sleep. In the first study in humans to examine spindles and stage 2 sleep, spindle density increased following a paired-association word-learning task. This effect was most prominent in the first NREM episode following sleep initiation (Gais et al., 2002). Spindle density was also correlated with memory task performance following sleep and also surprisingly before sleep. It is especially interesting that sleep spindles during early sleep produced the most pronounced effect suggesting that previous results focusing on early sleep and interpreted as being delta sleep dependent may instead have been detecting this effect of early sleep spindles.

Two other studies have shown a similar polysomnographically measured, sleep spindle dependent enhancement of memory consolidation. The first study (Schabus et al., 2004) measured performance on a paired-associate word task in subjects who had enhanced spindle activity following the memory task compared to another group of subjects who did not show significant enhancement or a decline in spindles. Baseline spindle density between the groups was not significantly different. A second set of studies examined paired-associate verbal learning and visuospatial declarative memory (Clemens et al., 2006) using the Ray-Osterrieth Complex Figure task. Both studies found enhancement of spindles but with regional cortical specificity with the verbal learning task showing enhancement in the fronto-central region, whereas the visuospatial task enhanced spindles in the parietal spindles but not other cortical regions. Many recent studies are also examining the correlations between sleep spindles and memory in animals and humans (Diekelmann & Born, 2010; Johnson et al., 2010).

Finally, regional cerebral blood flow (rCBF) was measured in the hippocampal and parahippocampal regions using positron emission tomography (Peigneux et al., 2004; Noirhomme et al., 2009). The strongest associations between learning the visuospatial task and increased hippocampal rCBF was observed during NREM sleep, particularly slow wave sleep. Although polysomnography was used to measure sleep stages in this study, no measurement of sleep spindle density is reported. It will be useful to continue to apply brain imaging techniques to the problem of memory consolidation during sleep coupled with polysomnography, where spindle density and other sleep features are reported.

Pathological Sleep Changes with Aging

Circadian and homeostatic changes are generally considered a normal consequence of aging and not parasomnias. However, several primary sleep disorders also increase in frequency as a function of age. Restless legs syndrome (RLS), periodic limb movements of sleep (PLMS), sleep disordered breathing (SDB), and REM sleep behavior disorder (RSBD) are all movement disorders affecting sleep. While these disorders are symptomatically different, they share a distinctive co-morbidity that is highly suggestive of an underlying etiology (Ancoli-Israel & Cooke, 2005; Boeve, 2010; Hoque & Chesson, 2010; Hornyak & Trenkwalder, 2004).

PLMS is most prevalent in the elderly with a prevalence of 45% (Ancoli-Israel et al., 1991a). PLMS is characterized by a series of repetitive, jerking leg movements measurable by the electromyographic leg lead in a polysomnographic study. Each 0.5 to 5 second bout of >4 leg movements is separated by a period of quiescence lasting from 5 to 90 seconds. The severity of PLMS is measured by calculating a periodic leg movement index (PLMI), which is the number of bouts/hour that result in an awakening. The clinical diagnosis of PLMS is made when the PLMI is >5 bouts/hour. PLMS can occur independently, when it is called periodic leg movements disorder (PLMD) or as a symptom of another disorder including restless legs syndrome, narcolepsy, and sleep disordered breathing (Ancoli-Israel & Cooke, 2005). It can also occur as a side effect of medications (Hoque & Chesson, 2010).

Restless legs syndrome (RLS) is closely allied to PLMS. RLS is determined by reference to four essential criteria including an unpleasant or burning sensation in the legs leading to a compulsion to move them. These symptoms are worse in the evening, during periods of rest, and are alleviated by movement of the legs. The prevalence of RLS in the elderly is between 8–20% (Lavigne & Montplaisir, 1994; Ohayon & Roth, 2002), with older cohorts reporting higher incidence. Approximately 80% of patients with RLS have symptoms of PLMS (Hornyak & Trenkwalder, 2004). However, the inverse relationship of PLMS to RLS shows only 30% prevalence indicating that, while related, they are not the same disorder. RLS is frequently seen secondary to other conditions including medication side effects, iron deficiency, pregnancy, and renal disease (Ekbom & Ulfberg, 2009; Hoque & Chesson, 2010; Trenkwalder et al. 2005), the latter two possibly reflecting secondary anemia.

The symptom frequency and severity of both PLMS and RLS show a distinctive circadian rhythm and are not necessarily associated with the sleep state per se but instead the time of day (Michaud et al., 2004). The relationship between these disorders remains mysterious, however, pharmacological evidence suggests a dopaminergic or monoaminergic etiology for both since dopaminergic agents like l-DOPA can be helpful in both disorders (Chen et al., 2009).

Sleep disordered breathing (SDB) is another parasomnia that is significantly more prevalent in older (45–62%) than younger (4–9%) adults (Ancoli-Israel et al., 1991b). SDB is characterized by partial (hypopnea) or full (apnea) respiratory arrest for at least 10 seconds repeatedly during the night. Average apnea length is generally 20–30 seconds and can be as long as 2–3 minutes. These respiratory events lead to arousal and nocturnal hypoxemia resulting in sleep that is not restorative and as a result reduced daytime alertness. SDB can originate from collapse of the upper airway during sleep (obstructive sleep apnea) or from loss of central drive to the ventilatory muscles (central sleep apnea). The treatment of SDB is controversial (for a recent review see Series, 2009).

REM sleep behavior disorder (RSBD) is another sleep disorder characterized by abnormal movement (Boeve, 2010; Hoque & Chesson, 2010; Schenck et al., 1986). In RSBD, however, unlike PLMS, the motor activities are complex and associated with dream experience as a consequence of loss of muscle atonia that is a necessary component of normal REM sleep. The neural substrates involved in RSBD have not been elaborated, however, the regions of the brain involved in REM sleep atonia include regions in the pons (ventral mesopontine junction and laterodorsal and pedunculopontine tegmental nuclei), the locus coeruleus, and the medial medulla (magnocellularis, gigantocellularis and paramedianus nuclei) (Fantini et al., 2005).

Sleep Disturbance in Progressive Dementia

One of the most important findings of the last 10 years regarding sleep disturbance in neurodegenerative illnesses is that sleep disturbances may be diagnostically specific. Studies of sleep and the circadian rhythm have not to date demonstrated predictive ability to differentially diagnose dementia. However, the different patterns of sleep and circadian rhythm disturbances in the different dementias may indicate damage to different neural substrates, and may ultimately prove useful in the differential diagnosis of dementia. One prominent difficulty in understanding the contribution of neurodegenerative disease to the expression of sleep in patients with dementia is that it is only possible to confirm differential diagnosis after autopsy. This fact has complicated the study of sleep disturbance in dementia.

Alzheimer's disease

Evidence from polysomnographic recordings of patients with clinically diagnosed mild-to-moderate AD suggests that sleep changes seen in AD are similar to, but more extreme than, those seen in normal aging (Gabelle & Dauvilliers, 2010; Loewenstein et al., 1982; Prinz, Vitaliano et al., 1982; Reynolds et al., 1985). These changes include reductions of slow wave sleep beyond that seen in normal elderly.

However, some sleep variables show a discrete difference with changes seen with aging including REM latency, which is longer in AD than in age-matched controls (Bliwise et al., 1989), and mean duration of REM periods, which is significantly less than age-matched controls (Prinz, Peskind, et al., 1982). Other markers of REM sleep including intensity of REM periods and number of REM periods during the course of the night are unchanged, at least in mild AD. The increase in REM latency and decrease in REM period length is likely due to the degeneration in cholinergic neurons in the basal forebrain nucleus basalis of Meynert occurring in early stages of AD (Braak & Braak, 1991), and which exert an influence on REM sleep generation (Montplaisir et al., 1995). One study showed that patients with mild cognitive impairment (MCI) showed impaired sleep maintenance independent of depressive symptoms (Yu et al., 2009).

Patients with moderate-to-severe AD show progressive worsening of sleep along many dimensions (Gabelle & Dauvilliers, 2010) reflecting the increase in the number of brain areas involved in neurodegeneration, particularly the deeper structures involved in REM sleep (areas that are spared in mild-to-moderate AD). However, even in patients with severe AD, it is important to note that the REM–NREM oscillation remains and these patients still experience REM sleep muscle atonia. Patients with AD may also have co-morbid sleep disorders (Richards, 2009), and poor sleep in patients and caregivers can lead to cardiovascular disease in both (von Kanel et al., 2010).

Measuring sleep with polysomnography in patients with AD and other dementias can be quite difficult. Patients with behavioral disturbances and more advanced dementia such that they find it difficult to cooperate with the experimental protocol frequently are not included in these studies. One method that has been developed to quantify sleep-like behavior, without relatively intrusive polysomnography, has been to employ wrist-worn activity monitors (Naismith et al., 2010). These monitors make time series recordings and the resulting rest activity rhythm assessed for signs of disrupted sleep and abnormalities of the circadian rhythm. Nocturnal activity in patients with AD can be correlated with polysomnographic assessments of total sleep time, and the actigraphically determined sleep/wake ratio can be correlated with polysomnographically derived sleep/wake ratio (Ancoli-Israel et al., 2010).

Actigraphy, in addition to providing information about sleep and wakefulness, can also provide information about the expression of the circadian rhythm and its impact on sleep. The most commonly used, nonparametric statistics are the interdaily stability and intradaily variability (Witting et al., 1990). The interdaily stability measures the stability of the rhythm from day to day. So, for example, a patient with a high interdaily stability would have activity that is very similar at the same hour of each day. Conversely, a patient with low interdaily stability shows chaotic activity without much consistency from day to day. Intradaily variability conversely measures the hour-to-hour variability of activity. A high intradaily variability therefore suggests a great deal of fragmentation in the activity pattern with less consolidation of sleep and wakefulness. Finally, the circadian rhythm can be estimated directly by the use of cosinor analysis, which models a cosine curve to the activity data and allows for the extraction of information on amplitude and phase of the underlying circadian oscillation in the data.

Evidence for disruption of the circadian rhythm, and its impact on sleep, has been seen in institutionalized patients with clinically diagnosed AD (Neikrug & Ancoli, 2010). Interdaily stability was significantly lowered in patients with moderate-to-severe AD although not in patients with mild AD (Hatfield et al., 2004; Satlin et al., 1995; van Someren et al., 1996). Additionally patients with severe AD show several differences from normals when their activity is examined with cosinor analysis. Circadian amplitude showed significant reductions in those patients with severe clinical AD and the phase of the circadian expression of the activity was delayed (Ancoli-Israel, Klauber, et al., 1997; Satlin et al., 1995).

However, fragmentation of the activity rhythm, as measured by increased intradaily variability, was not apparent in patients with AD when comparison was made to elderly controls (Satlin et al., 1995; van Someren et al., 1996), although one study did detect an increase in fragmentation in patients with moderate probable AD (Hatfield et al., 2004). Fragmentation can also be estimated from the number of daytime naps and nocturnal awakenings inferred from locomotor activity records (Ancoli-Israel, Clopton, et al., 1997). When activity records of patients with severe dementia were examined no significant increase in naps or awakenings were observed (Ancoli-Israel, Klauber, et al., 1997). Other studies have found a correlation between sleep fragmentation and cognitive deficits (Oosterman et al., 2009).

The suggestion from the locomotor activity data that the underlying circadian rhythm is disturbed in patients with severe AD has recently been confirmed in several studies. The circadian oscillation of core body temperature reflects a more direct output of the circadian system than locomotor activity. Studies of core body temperature in patients with mild, moderate, and severe probable AD have confirmed that there is very little circadian disruption in the mild-to-moderate phase of the illness independent of institutionalization status (Harper et al., 2004; Prinz et al., 1984; Prinz et al., 1992). However, patients with severe AD, whether differentiated clinically (e.g. Mini-Mental State Examination <12) (Volicer et al., 2001) or neuropathologically (Braak Stage >4) (Harper et al., 2004) show significant circadian rhythm differences from normal controls. Since this is the phase of the illness when the hypothalamus becomes involved in the pathological process (Braak & Braak, 1991), it is likely that these changes are mediated through damage to the suprachiasmatic nucleus (SCN) and its direct efferents (Liu et al., 2000; Stopa et al., 1999; Swaab et al., 1985; Zhou et al., 1995). The sleep–wake cycle may also play a role in the pathogenesis of AD (Kang et al., 2009).

The most precise information on the state of the endogenous circadian rhythm generated in human subjects is through the use of a constant routine protocol (Mills et al., 1978). A constant routine controls for all of the influences on core body temperature except the circadian fluctuation induced by the central oscillator in the SCN. Therefore, subjects are kept awake for the duration of the 36–48 hour protocol, given their meals in hourly snacks, kept in constant low level light, and not given any time cues for the duration of the protocol (Czeisler et al., 1992). A recent study exploring the endogenous circadian rhythm in patients with severe AD found reduced amplitude in the AD patients when compared to normal young subjects but not when compared to normal elderly (Harper et al., 2005). However, endogenous phase was delayed in patients with AD compared to both normal young and elderly. In patients with AD the core body temperature nadir was frequently as late as 10 am–12 noon (compared to the normal nadir which occurs approximately two hours prior to waking).

One question that emerges as a result of this research relates to the sleep fragmentation noted in some earlier polysomnography-based studies of patients with clinically diagnosed AD, compared to later studies in samples of patients with probable AD where awakenings or activity fragmentation are not seen to the same degree. One possible explanation for this change is that the differential diagnosis of AD has improved markedly over the last 10–15 years. One reason for this change is the increased awareness of dementia diagnoses that were not well characterized until recently. Dementia with Lewy bodies (DLB), which now represents the second-largest neurodegenerative diagnosis, was only formally defined in 1996 (McKeith et al., 1996). The last 20 years has also seen increases in the availability and sophistication of imaging technologies for visualizing the central nervous system allowing for greater differential diagnostic ability. Ultimately, diagnostic differentiation can only be certain upon autopsy and several studies have employed this technique to better understand sleep and circadian disturbances in patients with age-associated neurodegenerative dementia (Harper et al., 2001; Harper et al., 2004). As it turns out, these distinctions in diagnosis can explain much of the variability seen in earlier studies.

Sleep in synucleinopathies characterized by dementia

The most significant characteristic of sleep–wake behavior in synucleinopathies (including Parkinson's disease and DLB) is the sleep fragmentation resulting from excessive daytime sleepiness and sudden-onset sleep in patients with Parkinson's disease (Naismith et al., 2010). These symptoms were originally thought to be the result of medication effects (Frucht et al., 1999) and to occur entirely without warning. However, more recent work has shown that while excessive daytime sleepiness is common (~50%) in patients with Parkinson's disease, sleep attacks, at least with no warning, are more rare (Hobson et al., 2002).

Studies of polysomnography in patients with Parkinson's disease and multiple system atrophy (MSA) show an increasing sleep fragmentation, reduction in REM sleep, and loss of sleep spindles when compared to normal elderly (Norlinah et al., 2009; Wetter et al., 2000). Reductions in REM sleep and sleep fragmentation is particularly severe in those patients who experience hallucinatory phenomena (Comella et al., 1993) suggesting a link between these two symptoms. There is also evidence that suggests that RLS and PLMS may be coincident with a diagnosis of DLB (Boeve, 2010; Boeve et al., 2002) and Parkinson's disease (Poewe & Hogl, 2004). However, RLB by itself does not seem to indicate incipient synucleinopathy (Pittock et al., 2004).

Polysomnography in DLB and Parkinson's disease dementia shows that these disorders share the sleep characteristics observed in Parkinson's disease but that the extent of the sleep disruption is more severe (Compta et al., 2009). Results from actigraphy recording in dementia patients with pathologically confirmed DLB when compared to AD patients and normal controls also suggest Parkinson's disease-like sleep fragmentation and daytime sleepiness (Harper et al., 2004) with reduced diurnal activity and reduced circadian amplitude.

Core body temperature recordings as a probe of the circadian rhythm in patients with DLB and AD with Lewy body pathology show similar dysfunction to that seen in AD alone with phase delays being most prominent (Harper et al., 2004). Patients with MSA show a significant amplitude reduction compared to DLB and Parkinson's disease accounted for by the lack of a nocturnal temperature drop (Pierangeli et al., 2001).

Finally, one of the most prominent and important features of sleep in DLB and Parkinson's disease is the presence of REM sleep behavior disorder not only as a symptom of the illness but also as a predictor of the development of DLB (Boeve, 2010; Boeve et al., 1998; Molano et al., 2010). An important consequence of RBD in patients with DLB and Parkinson's disease is that some of the hallucinatory behavior associated with DLB may be a consequence of RBD. As a result, patients may exhibit behavior that could be attributed to hallucinations that could be a consequence of RBD (Arnulf et al., 2000). In particular, attention should be paid to hallucinatory behavior that occurs around the time of apparent awakening. The patient may actually be asleep and responding to dream content as opposed to experiencing true "hallucinations."

Tauopathies

Sleep disturbance among the tauopathies, while recognized clinically and frequently characterized as more severe than that seen in AD (Harper et al., 2001; Liu et al., 2004), has not been as well studied as sleep in other forms of progressive dementia. These neurodegenerative dementias are quite rare (prevalence among progressive dementia generally in the 1–5% range) making systematic study quite difficult. In addition, differential diagnosis can frequently be difficult prior to autopsy (Varma et al., 1999) leading to considerable uncertainty. Overall, sleep in neurodegenerative dementia characterized by tauopathy is quite disturbed (Gabelle & Dauvilliers, 2010). Sleep in corticobasal degeneration, Pick's disease (Gemignani et al., 2005; Harper et al., 2001; Pawlak et al., 1986), frontotemporal dementia (Anderson et al., 2009; Harper et al., 2001), and progressive supranuclear palsy (Petit et al., 2004) has been described as highly fragmented.

Tauopathies, while sharing hyperphosporylated tau and neurofibrillary tangles as their defining lesion, are somewhat distinct in their patterns of damage in the brain leading to differences in sleep symptoms. Reports have emerged of PLMS and RBD in corticobasal degeneration and progressive supranuclear palsy (Arnulf et al., 2005; Wetter et al., 2002), whereas these parasomnias have not been reported in frontotemporal dementia and Pick's disease. Significant REM sleep disturbance has also been reported in patients with progressive supranuclear palsy (Montplaisir et al., 1997), likely reflecting the pontine damage that occurs in this diagnosis. However, one study found that RBD occurred infrequently in both corticobasal degeneration and progressive supranuclear palsy (Cooper & Josephs, 2009).

The amplitude, phase, and goodness of fit of the circadian rhythm of core body temperature in several tauopathies have been found to be remarkably similar to that seen in controls. However, the expression of this intact circadian rhythm in locomotor activity appears to be highly disrupted (Harper et al., 2001) and not under good circadian control. While the emergence of PLMS and RBD in these patients could be a factor in this observation, there are likely to be other causes at work. For example, patients with Pick's disease, who show no known signs of PLMS or RLS, are as affected as those with CBD – some of whom may show symptoms of these parasomnias.

Vascular dementia

While evidence exists that patients with vascular dementia experience clinically significant sleep disturbance, sparse data exist characterizing the forms of sleep disturbance seen in these patients. The most important finding in patients with vascular dementia relates to the fragmentation of the sleep–wake rhythm. This fragmentation is detectable with actigraphy (Mishima et al., 1997), severity dependent (Meguro et al., 1995), and likely more severe than those sleep disturbances experienced by patients with AD (Fuh et al., 2005; Mishima et al., 1997), at least in the mild-to-moderate stages.

We have found no evidence in the literature suggesting parasomnias associated with vascular dementia. However, since sleep disordered breathing is a risk factor for the development of hypertension and vascular disease, and since vascular disease is a leading risk factor for the development of vascular dementia, we strongly suspect that sleep apnea syndrome may be responsible for a significant proportion of the sleep fragmentation observed in this population.

Conclusion

It is unknown to what degree sleep disturbance in patients with AD or other neurodegenerative dementias potentiates disturbances in declarative memory. It is also not known if the loss of sleep spindles seen in AD can be associated with memory decrements in these patients. However, the evidence suggests that the sleep loss these patients frequently experience could be a significant factor in their overall memory disturbance. Further research is needed to clarify the potential linkage between sleep loss and memory disturbance in these and other patients with dementia.

References

Achermann, P. (2004). The two-process model of sleep regulation revisited. *Aviation, Space, and Environmental Medicine, 75*, A37–A43.

Aly, M., & Moscovitch, M. (2010). The effects of sleep on episodic memory in older and younger adults. *Memory*, 1–8.

Ancoli-Israel, S., & Cooke, J. R. (2005). Prevalence and comorbidity of insomnia and effect on functioning in elderly populations. *Journal of the American Geriatric Society, 53*(7 Suppl), S264–S271.

Ancoli-Israel, S., Clopton, P., Klauber, M. R., Fell, R., & Mason, W. (1997). Use of wrist activity for monitoring sleep/wake in demented nursing-home patients. *Sleep, 20*(1), 24–27.

Ancoli-Israel, S., Klauber, M. R., Jones, D. W., Kripke, D. F., Martin, J., Mason, W., et al. (1997). Variations in circadian rhythms of activity, sleep, and light exposure related to dementia in nursing-home patients. *Sleep, 20*(1), 18–23.

Ancoli-Israel, S., Kripke, D. F., Klauber, M. R., Mason, W. J., Fell, R., & Kaplan, O. (1991a). Periodic limb movements in sleep in community-dwelling elderly. *Sleep, 14*(6), 496–500.

Ancoli-Israel, S., Kripke, D. F., Klauber, M. R., Mason, W. J., Fell, R., & Kaplan, O. (1991b). Sleep-disordered breathing in community-dwelling elderly. *Sleep, 14*(6), 486–495.

Anderson, K. N., Hatfield, C., Kipps, C., Hastings, M., & Hodges, J. R. (2009). Disrupted sleep and circadian patterns in frontotemporal dementia. *European Journal of.Neurology, 16*, 317–323.

Arnulf, I., Bonnet, A. M., Damier, P., Bejjani, B. P., Seilhean, D., Derenne, J. P., et al. (2000). Hallucinations, REM sleep, and Parkinson's disease: A medical hypothesis. *Neurology, 55*(2), 281–288.

Arnulf, I., Merino-Andreu, M., Bloch, F., Konofal, E., Vidailhet, M., Cochen, V., et al. (2005). REM sleep behavior disorder and REM sleep without atonia in patients with progressive supranuclear palsy. *Sleep, 28*(3), 349–354.

Aserinsky, E., & Kleitman, N. (1953). Regularly occurring periods of eye motility, and concomitant phenomena, during sleep. *Science, 118*(3062), 273–274.

Barrett, T. R., & Ekstrand, B. R. (1972). Effect of sleep on memory. 3. Controlling for time-of-day effects. *Journal of Experimental Psychology, 96*(2), 321–327.

Benson, K., & Feinberg, I. (1977). The beneficial effect of sleep in an extended Jenkins and Dallenbach paradigm. *Psychophysiology, 14*(4), 375–384.

Bliwise, D. L., Tinklenberg, J., Yesavage, J. A., Davies, H., Pursley, A. M., Petta, D. E., et al. (1989). REM latency in Alzheimer's disease. *Biological Psychiatry, 25*(3), 320–328.

Boeve, B. F. (2010). REM sleep behavior disorder: Updated review of the core features, the REM sleep behavior disorder-neurodegenerative disease association, evolving concepts, controversies, and future directions. *Annals of the New York Academy of Science, 1184*, 15–54.

Boeve, B. F., Silber, M. H., & Ferman, T. J. (2002). Current management of sleep disturbances in dementia. *Current Neurology and Neuroscience Reports, 2*(2), 169–177.

Boeve, B. F., Silber, M. H., Ferman, T. J., Kokmen, E., Smith, G. E., Ivnik, R. J., et al. (1998). REM sleep behavior disorder and degenerative dementia: an association likely reflecting Lewy body disease. *Neurology, 51*(2), 363–370.

Borbely, A. A. (1982). A two process model of sleep regulation. *Human Neurobiology, 1*(3), 195–204.

Braak, H., & Braak, E. (1991). Neuropathological stageing of Alzheimer-related changes. *Acta Neuropathologica (Berlin), 82*(4), 239–259.

Brashers-Krug, T., Shadmehr, R., & Bizzi, E. (1996). Consolidation in human motor memory. *Nature, 382*(6588), 252–255.

Budson, A. E. (2009). Understanding memory dysfunction. *Neurologist, 15*, 71–79.

Chen, J. J., Swope, D. M., Dashtipour, K., & Lyons, K. E. (2009). Transdermal rotigotine: A clinically innovative dopamine-receptor agonist for the management of Parkinson's disease. *Pharmacotherapy, 29*, 1452–1467.

Clemens, Z., Fabo, D., & Halasz, P. (2006). Twenty-four hours retention of visuospatial memory correlates with the number of parietal sleep spindles. *Neuroscience Letters, 403*(1–2), 52–56.

Comella, C. L., Tanner, C. M., & Ristanovic, R. K. (1993). Polysomnographic sleep measures in Parkinson's disease patients with treatment-induced hallucinations. *Annals of Neurology, 34*(5), 710–714.

Compta, Y., Santamaria, J., Ratti, L., Tolosa, E., Iranzo, A., Munoz, E., et al. (2009). Cerebrospinal hypocretin, daytime sleepiness and sleep architecture in Parkinson's disease dementia. *Brain, 132*, 3308–3317.

Cooper, A. D., & Josephs, K. A. (2009). Photophobia, visual hallucinations, and REM sleep behavior disorder in progressive supranuclear palsy and corticobasal degeneration: A prospective study. *Parkinsonism and Related Disorders, 15*, 59–61.

Czeisler, C. A., Dumont, M., Duffy, J. F., Steinberg, J. D., Richardson, G. S., Brown, E. N., et al. (1992). Association of sleep-wake habits in older people with changes in output of circadian pacemaker. *Lancet, 340*(8825), 933–936.

Davidson, T. J., Kloosterman, F., & Wilson, M. A. (2009). Hippocampal replay of extended experience. *Neuron, 63*, 497–507.

Dement, W., & Kleitman, N. (1957). Cyclic variations in EEG during sleep and their relation to eye movements, body motility, and dreaming. *Electroencephalography and Clinical Neurophysiology, 9*(4), 673–690.

Diekelmann, S., & Born, J. (2010). The memory function of sleep. *Nature Reviews Neuroscience, 11*, 114–126.

Ego-Stengel, V., & Wilson, M. A. (2010). Disruption of ripple-associated hippocampal activity during rest impairs spatial learning in the rat. *Hippocampus, 20*, 1–10.

Ekbom, K., & Ulfberg, J. (2009). Restless legs syndrome. *Journal of Internal Medicine, 266*, 419–431.

Fantini, M. L., Ferini-Strambi, L., & Montplaisir, J. (2005). Idiopathic REM sleep behavior disorder: Toward a better nosologic definition. *Neurology, 64*(5), 780–786.

Fischer, S., Hallschmid, M., Elsner, A. L., & Born, J. (2002). Sleep forms memory for finger skills. *Proceedings of the National Academy of Sciences USA*, *99*(18), 11987–11991.

Fowler, M. J., Sullivan, M. J., & Ekstrand, B. R. (1973). Sleep and memory. *Science*, *179*(70), 302–304.

Frucht, S., Rogers, J. D., Greene, P. E., Gordon, M. F., & Fahn, S. (1999). Falling asleep at the wheel: motor vehicle mishaps in persons taking pramipexole and ropinirole. *Neurology*, *52*(9), 1908–1910.

Fuh, J. L., Wang, S. J., & Cummings, J. L. (2005). Neuropsychiatric profiles in patients with Alzheimer's disease and vascular dementia. *Journal of Neurology, Neurosurgery & Psychiatry*, *76*(10), 1337–1341.

Gabelle, A., & Dauvilliers, Y. (2010). Editorial: Sleep and dementia. *Journal of Nutrition, Health & Aging*, *14*, 201–202.

Gais, S., Molle, M., Helms, K., & Born, J. (2002). Learning-dependent increases in sleep spindle density. *Journal of Neuroscience*, *22*(15), 6830–6834.

Gais, S., Plihal, W., Wagner, U., & Born, J. (2000). Early sleep triggers memory for early visual discrimination skills. *Nature Neuroscience*, *3*(12), 1335–1339.

Gemignani, A., Pietrini, P., Murrell, J. R., Glazier, B. S., Zolo, P., Guazzelli, M., et al. (2005). Slow wave and rem sleep mechanisms are differently altered in hereditary pick disease associated with the TAU G389R mutation. *Archives Italiennes de Biologie*, *143*(1), 65–79.

Grosvenor, A., & Lack, L. C. (1984). The effect of sleep before or after learning on memory. *Sleep*, *7*(2), 155–167.

Harper, D. G., Stopa, E. G., McKee, A. C., Satlin, A., Fish, D., & Volicer, L. (2004). Dementia severity and Lewy bodies affect circadian rhythms in Alzheimer disease. *Neurobiology of Aging*, *25*(6), 771–781.

Harper, D. G., Stopa, E. G., McKee, A., Satlin, A., Harlan, P. C., Goldstein, R. L., et al. (2001). Differential circadian rhythm disturbances in men with Alzheimer disease and fronto-temporal degeneration. *Archives of General Psychiatry*, *58*(4), 353–360.

Harper, D. G., Volicer, L., Stopa, E. G., McKee, A. C., Nitta, M., & Satlin, A. (2005). Disturbance of endogenous circadian rhythm in aging and Alzheimer disease, *American Journal of Geriatric Psychiatry*, *13*, 359–368.

Hatfield, C. F., Herbert, J., van Someren, E. J., Hodges, J. R., & Hastings, M. H. (2004). Disrupted daily activity/rest cycles in relation to daily cortisol rhythms of home-dwelling patients with early Alzheimer's dementia. *Brain*, *127*(Pt 5), 1061–1074.

Hobson, D. E., Lang, A. E., Martin, W. R., Razmy, A., Rivest, J., & Fleming, J. (2002). Excessive daytime sleepiness and sudden-onset sleep in Parkinson disease: A survey by the Canadian Movement Disorders Group. *Journal of the American Medical Association*, *287*(4), 455–463.

Hoque, R., & Chesson, A. L., Jr. (2010). Pharmacologically induced/exacerbated restless legs syndrome, periodic limb movements of sleep, and REM behavior disorder/REM sleep without atonia: literature review, qualitative scoring, and comparative analysis. *Journal of Clinical Sleep Medicine*, *6*, 79–83.

Hornyak, M., & Trenkwalder, C. (2004). Restless legs syndrome and periodic limb movement disorder in the elderly. *Journal of Psychosomatic Research*, *56*(5), 543–548.

Huber, R., Ghilardi, M. F., Massimini, M., & Tononi, G. (2004). Local sleep and learning. *Nature*, *430*(6995), 78–81.

Jenkins, J. G., & Dallenbach, K. M. (1924). Obliviscence during sleep and waking. *American Journal of Psychology, 35*, 605–612.

Johnson, L. A., Euston, D. R., Tatsuno, M., & McNaughton, B. L. (2010). Stored-trace reactivation in rat prefrontal cortex is correlated with down-to-up state fluctuation density. *Journal of Neuroscience., 30*, 2650–2661.

Kang, J. E., Lim, M. M., Bateman, R. J., Lee, J. J., Smyth, L. P., Cirrito, J. R., et al. (2009). Amyloid-beta dynamics are regulated by orexin and the sleep-wake cycle. *Science, 326*, 1005–1007.

Karni, A., Tanne, D., Rubenstein, B. S., Askenasy, J. J., & Sagi, D. (1994). Dependence on REM sleep of overnight improvement of a perceptual skill. *Science, 265*(5172), 679–682.

Kullmann, D. M., & Lamsa, K. P. (2007). Long-term synaptic plasticity in hippocampal interneurons. *Nature Reviews Neuroscience, 8*(9), 687–699.

Lavigne, G. J., & Montplaisir, J. Y. (1994). Restless legs syndrome and sleep bruxism: Prevalence and association among Canadians. *Sleep, 17*(8), 739–743.

Lechner, H. A., Squire, L. R., & Byrne, J. H. (1999). 100 years of consolidation – Remembering Muller and Pilzecker. *Learning & Memory, 6*(2), 77–87.

Liu, R. Y., Zhou, J. N., Hoogendijk, W. J., van Heerikhuize, J., Kamphorst, W., Unmehopa, U. A., et al. (2000). Decreased vasopressin gene expression in the biological clock of Alzheimer disease patients with and without depression. *Journal of Neuropathology & Experimental Neurology, 59*(4), 314–322.

Liu, W., Miller, B. L., Kramer, J. H., Rankin, K., Wyss-Coray, C., Gearhart, R., et al. (2004). Behavioral disorders in the frontal and temporal variants of frontotemporal dementia. *Neurology, 62*(5), 742–748.

Loewenstein, R. J., Weingartner, H., Gillin, J. C., Kaye, W., Ebert, M., & Mendelson, W. B. (1982). Disturbances of sleep and cognitive functioning in patients with dementia. *Neurobiology of Aging, 3*(4), 371–377.

Lowndes, G., & Savage, G. (2007). Early detection of memory impairment in Alzheimer's disease: A neurocognitive perspective on assessment. *Neuropsychology Review, 17*(3), 193–202.

Markesbery, W. R. (2010). Neuropathologic alterations in mild cognitive impairment: A review. *Journal of Alzheimer's Disease, 19*, 221–228.

McKeith, I. G., Galasko, D., Kosaka, K., Perry, E. K., Dickson, D. W., Hansen, L. A., et al. (1996). Consensus guidelines for the clinical and pathologic diagnosis of dementia with Lewy bodies (DLB): report of the consortium on DLB international workshop. *Neurology, 47*(5), 1113–1124.

Meguro, K., Ueda, M., Kobayashi, I., Yamaguchi, S., Yamazaki, H., Oikawa, Y., et al. (1995). Sleep disturbance in elderly patients with cognitive impairment, decreased daily activity and periventricular white matter lesions. *Sleep, 18*(2), 109–114.

Michaud, M., Dumont, M., Selmaoui, B., Paquet, J., Fantini, M. L., & Montplaisir, J. (2004). Circadian rhythm of restless legs syndrome: Relationship with biological markers. *Annals of Neurology, 55*(3), 372–380.

Mills, J. N., Minors, D. S., & Waterhouse, J. M. (1978). Adaptation to abrupt time shifts of the oscillator(s) controlling human circadian rhythms. *Journal of Physiology (London), 285*(5), 455–470.

Mishima, K., Okawa, M., Satoh, K., Shimizu, T., Hozumi, S., & Hishikawa, Y. (1997). Different manifestations of circadian rhythms in senile dementia of Alzheimer's type and multi-infarct dementia. *Neurobiology of Aging, 18*(1), 105–109.

Molano, J., Boeve, B., Ferman, T., Smith, G., Parisi, J., Dickson, D., et al. (2010). Mild cognitive impairment associated with limbic and neocortical Lewy body disease: A clinicopathological study. *Brain*, *133*, 540–556.

Montplaisir, J., Petit, D., Decary, A., Masson, H., Bedard, M. A., Panisset, M., et al. (1997). Sleep and quantitative EEG in patients with progressive supranuclear palsy. *Neurology*, *49*(4), 999–1003.

Montplaisir, J., Petit, D., Lorrain, D., Gauthier, S., & Nielsen, T. (1995). Sleep in Alzheimer's disease: further considerations on the role of brainstem and forebrain cholinergic populations in sleep-wake mechanisms. *Sleep*, *18*(3), 145–148.

Morris, R. G., Moser, E. I., Riedel, G., Martin, S. J., Sandin, J., Day, M., et al. (2003). Elements of a neurobiological theory of the hippocampus: The role of activity-dependent synaptic plasticity in memory. *Philosophical Transactions of the Royal Society B: Biological Sciences*, *358*(1432), 773–786.

Muller, G. E., & Pilzecker, A. (1900). Expermentelle Beitrage zur Lehre vom Gedachtnis. *Z. Psychol. Erganzungsband*, *1*, 1–300.

Naismith, S. L., Rogers, N. L., Mackenzie, J., Hickie, I. B., & Lewis, S. J. (2010). The relationship between actigraphically defined sleep disturbance and REM sleep behaviour disorder in Parkinson's Disease. *Clinical Neurology and Neurosurgery*, *112*(5), 420–423.

Neikrug, A. B., & Ancoli, I. S. (2010). Sleep disturbances in nursing homes. *Journal of Nutrition, Health & Aging*, *14*, 207–211.

Noirhomme, Q., Boly, M., Bonhomme, V., Boveroux, P., Phillips, C., Peigneux, P., et al. (2009). Bispectral index correlates with regional cerebral blood flow during sleep in distinct cortical and subcortical structures in humans. *Archives Italiennes de Biologie*, *147*, 51–57.

Norlinah, M. I., Afidah, K. N., Noradina, A. T., Shamsul, A. S., Hamidon, B. B., Sahathevan, R., et al. (2009). Sleep disturbances in Malaysian patients with Parkinson's disease using polysomnography and PDSS. *Parkinsonism and Related Disorders*, *15*, 670–674.

Ohayon, M. M., & Roth, T. (2002). Prevalence of restless legs syndrome and periodic limb movement disorder in the general population. *Journal of Psychosomatic Research*, *53*(1), 547–554.

O'Neill, J., Pleydell-Bouverie, B., Dupret, D., & Csicsvari, J. (2010). Play it again: Reactivation of waking experience and memory. *Trends in Neuroscience*, *33*(5), 220–229.

Oosterman, J. M., van Someren, E. J., Vogels, R. L., van Harten, B., & Scherder, E. J. (2009). Fragmentation of the rest-activity rhythm correlates with age-related cognitive deficits. *Journal of Sleep Research*, *18*, 129–135.

Pawlak, C., Blois, R., Gaillard, J. M., & Richard, J. (1986). La Sommeille dans la maladie Picks. *Encephale*, *12*(6), 327–334.

Peigneux, P., Laureys, S., Fuchs, S., Collette, F., Perrin, F., Reggers, J., et al. (2004). Are spatial memories strengthened in the human hippocampus during slow wave sleep? *Neuron*, *44*(3), 535–545.

Petit, D., Gagnon, J. F., Fantini, M. L., Ferini-Strambi, L., & Montplaisir, J. (2004). Sleep and quantitative EEG in neurodegenerative disorders. *Journal of Psychosomatic Research*, *56*(5), 487–496.

Pierangeli, G., Provini, F., Maltoni, P., Barletta, G., Contin, M., Lugaresi, E., et al. (2001). Nocturnal body core temperature falls in Parkinson's disease but not in multiple-system atrophy. *Movement Disorders*, *16*(2), 226–232.

Pittock, S. J., Parrett, T., Adler, C. H., Parisi, J. E., Dickson, D. W., & Ahlskog, J. E. (2004). *Neuropathology* of primary restless leg syndrome: absence of specific tau- and alpha-synuclein pathology, *Movement Disorders, 19*, 695–699.

Plihal, W., & Born, J. (1997). Effects of early and late nocturnal sleep on declarative and procedural memory. *Journal of Cognitive Neuroscience, 9*, 534–547.

Poewe, W., & Hogl, B. (2004). Akathisia, restless legs and periodic limb movements in sleep in Parkinson's disease. *Neurology, 63*(8 Suppl 3), S12–S16.

Pollak, C. P., & Perlick, D. (1991). Sleep problems and institutionalization of the elderly. *Journal of Geriatric Psychiatry and Neurology, 4*(4), 204–210.

Prinz, P. N., Christie, C., Smallwood, R., Vitaliano, P., Bokan, J., Vitiello, M. V., et al. (1984). Circadian temperature variation in healthy aged and in Alzheimer's disease. *J Gerontol, 39*(1), 30-35.

Prinz, P. N., Moe, K. E., Vitiello, M. V., Marks, A. L., & Larsen, L. H. (1992). Entrained body temperature rhythms are similar in mild Alzheimer's disease, geriatric onset depression, and normal aging. *Journal of Geriatric Psychiatry and Neurology, 5*(2), 65–71.

Prinz, P. N., Peskind, E. R., Vitaliano, P. P., Raskind, M. A., Eisdorfer, C., Zemcuznikov, N., et al. (1982). Changes in the sleep and waking EEGs of nondemented and demented elderly subjects. *Journal of the American Geriatric Society, 30*(2), 86–93.

Prinz, P. N., Vitaliano, P. P., Vitiello, M. V., Bokan, J., Raskind, M., Peskind, E., et al. (1982). Sleep, EEG and mental function changes in senile dementia of the Alzheimer's type. *Neurobiology of Aging, 3*(4), 361–370.

Rechtschaffen, A., & Kales, A. (1968). *A manual of standardized terminology, techniques and scoring system for sleep stages of human subjects.* Los Angeles: Brain Information Service/ Brain Research Institute, UCLA.

Reynolds, C. F. d., Kupfer, D. J., Taska, L. S., Hoch, C. C., Spiker, D. G., Sewitch, D. E., et al. (1985). EEG sleep in elderly depressed, demented, and healthy subjects. *Biological Psychiatry, 20*(4), 431–442.

Richards, K. C. (2009). Comorbid Alzheimer's disease and OSAS: Does CPAP slow cognitive decline? *Journal of Clinical Sleep Medicine, 5*, 310.

Satlin, A., Volicer, L., Stopa, E. G., & Harper, D. (1995). Circadian locomotor activity and core-body temperature rhythms in Alzheimer's disease. *Neurobiology of Aging, 16*(5), 765–771.

Schabus, M., Gruber, G., Parapatics, S., Sauter, C., Klosch, G., Anderer, P., et al. (2004). Sleep spindles and their significance for declarative memory consolidation. *Sleep, 27*(8), 1479–1485.

Schenck, C. H., Bundlie, S. R., Ettinger, M. G., & Mahowald, M. W. (1986). Chronic behavioral disorders of human REM sleep: A new category of parasomnia. *Sleep, 9*(2), 293–308.

Series, F. (2009). Can improving sleep influence sleep-disordered breathing? *Drugs, 69*(Suppl 2), 77–91.

Shadmehr, R., & Holcomb, H. H. (1997). Neural correlates of motor memory consolidation. *Science, 277*(5327), 821–825.

Siapas, A. G., & Wilson, M. A. (1998). Coordinated interactions between hippocampal ripples and cortical spindles during slow-wave sleep. *Neuron, 21*(5), 1123–1128.

Siegel, J. M. (2001). The REM sleep-memory consolidation hypothesis. *Science, 294*(5544), 1058–1063.

Skaggs, W. E., & McNaughton, B. L. (1996). Replay of neuronal firing sequences in rat hippocampus during sleep following spatial experience. *Science, 271*(5257), 1870–1873.

Smith, C. (2001). Sleep states and memory processes in humans: Procedural versus declarative memory systems. *Sleep Medicine Reviews, 5*(6), 491–506.

Squire, L. R., & Zola, S. M. (1996). Structure and function of declarative and nondeclarative memory systems. *Proceedings of the National Academy of Sciences USA, 93*(24), 13515–13522.

Stickgold, R. (2005). Sleep-dependent memory consolidation. *Nature, 437*(7063), 1272–1278.

Stickgold, R., Whidbee, D., Schirmer, B., Patel, V., & Hobson, J. A. (2000). Visual discrimination task improvement: A multi-step process occurring during sleep. *Journal of Cognitive Neuroscience, 12*(2), 246–254.

Stopa, E. G., Volicer, L., Kuo-Leblanc, V., Harper, D., Lathi, D., Tate, B., et al. (1999). Pathologic evaluation of the human suprachiasmatic nucleus in severe dementia. *Journal of Neuropathology & Experimental Neurology, 58*(1), 29–39.

Swaab, D. F., Fliers, E., & Partiman, T. S. (1985). The suprachiasmatic nucleus of the human brain in relation to sex, age and senile dementia. *Brain Research, 342*(1), 37–44.

Trenkwalder, C., Paulus, W., & Walters, A. S. (2005). The restless legs syndrome. *Lancet Neurology, 4*(8), 465–475.

van Halteren-van Tilborg, I. A., Scherder, E. J., & Hulstijn, W. (2007). Motor-skill learning in Alzheimer's disease: A review with an eye to the clinical practice. *Neuropsychology Review, 17*(3), 203–212.

van Someren, E. J., Hagebeuk, E. E., Lijzenga, C., Scheltens, P., de Rooij, S. E., Jonker, C., et al. (1996). Circadian rest-activity rhythm disturbances in Alzheimer's disease. *Biological Psychiatry, 40*(4), 259–270.

Varma, A. R., Snowden, J. S., Lloyd, J. J., Talbot, P. R., Mann, D. M., & Neary, D. (1999). Evaluation of the NINCDS-ADRDA criteria in the differentiation of Alzheimer's disease and frontotemporal dementia. *Journal of Neurology, Neurosurgery & Psychiatry, 66*(2), 184–188.

Vitiello, M. V., & Borson, S. (2001). Sleep disturbances in patients with Alzheimer's disease: Epidemiology, pathophysiology and treatment. *CNS Drugs, 15*(10), 777–796.

Volicer, L., Harper, D. G., Manning, B. C., Goldstein, R., & Satlin, A. (2001). Sundowning and circadian rhythms in Alzheimer's disease. *American Journal of Psychiatry, 158*(5), 704–711.

von Kanel, R., Ancoli-Israel, S., Dimsdale, J. E., Mills, P. J., Mausbach, B. T., Ziegler, M. G., et al. (2010). Sleep and biomarkers of atherosclerosis in elderly Alzheimer caregivers and controls. *Gerontology, 56*, 41–50.

Walker, M. P., Brakefield, T., Morgan, A., Hobson, J. A., & Stickgold, R. (2002). Practice with sleep makes perfect: Sleep-dependent motor skill learning. *Neuron, 35*(1), 205–211.

Wetter, T. C., Brunner, H., Collado-Seidel, V., Trenkwalder, C., & Winkelmann, J. (2002). Sleep and periodic limb movements in corticobasal degeneration. *Sleep Medicine, 3*(1), 33–36.

Wetter, T. C., Collado-Seidel, V., Pollmacher, T., Yassouridis, A., & Trenkwalder, C. (2000). Sleep and periodic leg movement patterns in drug-free patients with Parkinson's disease and multiple system atrophy. *Sleep, 23*(3), 361–367.

Wilson, M. A., & McNaughton, B. L. (1994). Reactivation of hippocampal ensemble memories during sleep. *Science, 265*(5172), 676–679.

Witting, W., Kwa, I. H., Eikelenboom, P., Mirmiran, M., & Swaab, D. F. (1990). Alterations in the circadian rest-activity rhythm in aging and Alzheimer's disease. *Biological Psychiatry, 27*(6), 563–572.

Yaroush, R., Sullivan, M. J., & Ekstrand, B. R. (1971). Effect of sleep on memory. II. Differential effect of the first and second half of the night. *Journal of Experimental Psychology, 88*(3), 361–366.

Yu, J. M., Tseng, I. J., Yuan, R. Y., Sheu, J. J., Liu, H. C., & Hu, C. J. (2009). Low sleep efficiency in patients with cognitive impairment. *Acta Neurologica Taiwan, 18*, 91–97.

Zhou, J. N., Hofman, M. A., & Swaab, D. F. (1995). VIP neurons in the human SCN in relation to sex, age, and Alzheimer's disease. *Neurobiology of Aging, 16*(4), 571–576.

Part IV

Neuroimaging in Dementia

17

Glimpses of the Living Brain with Alzheimer's Disease

Ronald J. Killiany

Introduction

We have been given the ability to look inside the depths of the human body and view its inner workings in a minimally to non-invasive fashion by the work of the talented and dedicated scientists who developed the techniques of computed tomography and magnetic resonance imaging. Additionally, anatomists, computer scientists, physicians, and others have provided us with the tools needed to work with the images that are generated and analyze the components of the body in an effort to help us identify the earliest signs of disease. The processes of imaging and post-processing images are dynamic ones that are continuing to evolve and have the potential to provide us with ever-increasing knowledge.

Over the past 30 years investigators have been using imaging techniques to identify ways to differentiate between subjects with Alzheimer's disease (AD) and healthy controls. As this goal was accomplished these investigators set out to identify the earliest detectable changes in the brain in subjects destined to developing AD. We've learned a tremendous amount of information from the successes and failures that have taken place in these imaging studies but there is still a great deal we do not know. For the most part, imaging studies have been based on our knowledge of the neuropathology of AD, which has been provided to us by the generous donations of countless individuals who developed AD and their families.

The Handbook of Alzheimer's Disease and Other Dementias, First Edition.
Edited by Andrew E. Budson, Neil W. Kowall.

Computed Tomography (CT or CAT) Studies

The chronology of investigations targeted at uncovering the changes in the AD brain in vivo follows closely the advances that were made in the field of imaging. Most of the initial studies focused on the use of X-ray computed tomography (CT or computer assisted tomography (CAT)). The CT image is created through the measurement of the reduction in the intensity of an x-ray beam after it passes through a body section and relies on mathematical ideas about how to reconstruct an object from its projections into different directions. X-rays have been used to view the inner details of the body since around 1895 but the brain remained hidden until the development of the CT in 1971. CT scanning became widely used around the mid-1970s as whole-body systems became available on the market and replaced dedicated brain imagers. The popularity of CT can be seen in its sales that skyrocketed from around 200 units annually in the late 1970s to 5000 units annually in the early 1980s.

The introduction of CT is considered by many to be one of the major technological advances in medical investigations for the last 30 years. The importance placed on CT by the scientific community can be seen by the awarding of the Nobel Prize for the invention of CT, which was shared in 1979 by Godfrey Hounsfield, a British engineer working for the company EMI, and Allan Cormack, a physicist at Tufts University. This impact was also felt in anatomy department of medical schools across the world. The plane of section used with CT scanning of the brain differed from the standard anatomical planes (coronal, sagittal, axial) that are traditionally taught to medical students. In order to accommodate this a new anatomical plane of section, the CT plane, was introduced at medical school to many anatomy/neuroscience classes.

The impact of CT on our society was also seen in the major news events of the early 1980s. John Hinckley attempted to assassinate U.S. President Reagan and in the process shot press secretary James Brady in the head. CT scans were used by the neurosurgeons who operated on James Brady to stem the devastating effects caused by the bullet. Later on, John Hinckley's lawyer used a CT scan in an effort to convince the jury that John Hinckley had a structural defect in this brain that is typically found in CT images of schizophrenic patients.

Researchers also picked up on CT's ability to provide a non-invasive and relatively safe way to examine the structure of the brain in vivo and began to apply these techniques to the study of Alzheimer's disease (Figure 17.1A). For the most part, the goal of these researchers was to identify an objective diagnostic marker for the clinical diagnosis of AD in order to improve the accuracy of diagnosis, differential diagnosis, and identify candidates for interventions as they became available. There was a great deal of excitement associated with these investigations but unfortunately the findings did not meet these expectations mainly due to the limited ability of CT to show the details of the brain.

In general CT studies have focused on measures of general brain atrophy such as the subarachnoid space volume (SVI) that was thought to be a measure of corti-

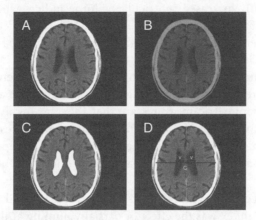

Figure 17.1   A. Example of one slice of a CT scan. In the image the bone appears as white while the tissue of the brain is in scales of gray with white matter of the brain showing a slightly darker pallor than the gray matter. B. Example of the CT subarachnoid space measure, the outer limits of the brain is outlined in black. C. Example of the CT ventricular volume measure showing the ventricle maps in white. D. Example of the CT ventricular width measure. The length of the ventricles (v) and the length of the intracranial cavity (c) are shown

cal atrophy (Figure 17.1B). The SVI was calculated by tracing the outline of the brain and the intracranial space on each of the CT images. The total volumes of the brain and intracranial space were determined by adding the slice volumes. The total brain volume was divided by the total intracranial space volume and this figure was multiplied by 100 to generate the subarachnoid space volume. Investigators used the subarachnoid space volume to differentiate between normal, aged subjects and subjects with AD. It was found in some studies that patients with AD have significantly increased subarachnoid space volume when compared with elderly controls (Arai et al., 1983; Raz et al., 1987). Further, relationships were found between the duration of AD symptoms and the subarachnoid space volume (Arai et al., 1983). There has been note of considerable overlap between the CT measure of subarachnoid space volume between the normal aged and demented groups (Huckman et al., 1975; Jacoby et al., 1980). The accuracy of the subarachnoid space volume measure in differentiating between normal, aged subjects and subjects with AD was increased when extraneous factors such as age were controlled for in the analyses.

Another measure of general brain atrophy is the ventricular volume index (Figure 17.1C). This index is calculated by outlining the ventricles and intracranial space on each of the CT slices. The total volumes are generated by adding up the slice volumes and the ventricular volume index calculated by dividing the total ventricle measure by the total intracranial volume measure and multiplying by 100. Investigators used the ventricular volume index to differentiate between normal, aged subjects and subjects with AD. It was found in some studies that patients with

AD have significantly increased ventricular volume indices when compared with elderly controls (Arai et al., 1983; Creasey et al., 1986; Gado et al., 1982; George et al., 1983; Luxenberg et al., 1987), though considerable overlap between the groups was again pointed out.

The measures made on the CT scans are either planimetric or volumetric. Planimetric measures are made on a single slice and generate a surface area. The shortcomings of planimetric measures are that they are highly sensitive to head position, slice thickness, and slice location. Volumetric measures require the measurement of the structure of interest on each image that it appears. They are less sensitive to head position, slice thickness, and slice location but are more labor intensity to employ.

One problem faced by investigators using the subarachnoid space volume and ventricular volume index was the effect of partial voluming at the edges of tissues. Partial voluming occurs on all images at the interface of two anatomical substrates (i.e., tissue and fluid, two tissue classes) making it difficult to accurately define the boundaries. Two solutions were used to overcome this problem. The first was to use a rating scale or qualitative assessment to judge the ventricular size and cortical atrophy. As with the indices, the qualitative measures found considerable overlap between normal, aged subjects and subjects with AD (Le May et al., 1986). In addition, the findings of studies using qualitative rating systems were highly dependent upon the raters' experience and training since in general there was a low inter-observer reliability (De Carli et al., 1990).

Another means of overcoming the partial voluming problem was to use linear measures, which are simply linear distances between two points (Figure 17.1D). In essence the distance between two points of interest was standardized based on the distance between two control points (i.e., inner table of the skull). Examples of linear measures include the widths of the third ventricle, lateral ventricle, and temporal horns of the lateral ventricles. These measures were found to differ between normal, aged subjects and subjects with AD in most studies (Albert et al., 1984; Colgan et al., 1986; Jacoby et al., 1980). However, instead of overcoming the problem of partial voluming the linear measures were difficult to apply because of the inaccuracies inherent at the tissue interfaces resulting in low inter-observer reliability (Jacoby et al., 1980).

A major advance in the automation of making measures on medical images was the use of Hounsfield units (HU) for describing radiodensity on CT. Essentially one could determine the appropriate HU threshold value that separates tissue from cerebral spinal fluid (CSF) and then count the number of pixels above and below this threshold to determine the volume of the CSF spaces and the brain tissue itself. Volumetric measures such as those used to determine the CSF spaces proved to be the most accurate and sensitive means of differentiating normal, aged subjects from subjects with AD (De Carli et al., 1990).

Investigators using CT to study AD also adapted the technique of densitometry for use with CT. Densitometry is a procedure that is traditionally used to quantitatively measure the optical density of materials. It has been used histologically to access the density of cells and receptors. Essentially, the methodology passes a light of known intensity through a tissue of interest and the intensity of the light is assessed once it has passed through the tissue in order to determine the "density" of the particles that block the passage of the light. With CT the x-rays serve as the light source and the CT detector assesses the passage of the x-rays. The underlying hypothesis was that densitometry measures would provide a measure of the neuropathology of AD within the brain tissue. In general, CT density measures of the whole brain and discrete brain regions failed to differentiate normal, aged subjects from subject with AD (Colgan et al., 1986; Gado et al., 1983; George et al., 1981; Luxenberg et al., 1986).

While CT densitometry did not prove to be a useful clinical tool, the findings of some investigators (Gado et al., 1983; George et al., 1981) raised a question that is still debated today. These groups found a breakdown in the normal appearance of the white matter of the brain in subjects with AD. These findings were somewhat controversial since they implied the involvement of a tissue class that had previously been thought to only play a secondary role to the gray matter of the brain. It is still being debated today whether the involvement of the white matter in AD is a primary feature of this disease or a secondary effect of the neuropathology in the gray matter.

One region of the brain that seems noteworthy in its absence in this discussion is the medial temporal lobes and more specifically the hippocampal formation. This area of the brain has been shown to be critically important for anterograde memory (Scoville & Milner, 1957) and AD has even been referred to as a hippocampal dementia (Ball et al., 1985). Unfortunately CT imaging of the temporal regions, especially the medial temporal regions, is limited by bone hardening artifacts and a limited viewing angle. Studies that were able to overcome the shortcoming of CT and measure areas in the medial temporal lobe regions were successful. In particular, it was found that the anterior temporal region and the hippocampal fissure differed in normal, aged subjects and subjects with AD (de Leon et al., 1989; George et al., 1990; Kido et al., 1989; Le May et al., 1986; Sandor et al., 1988).

On the basis of the material presented here it might be tempting to conclude that the investigations of AD using CT were largely unsuccessful. However, this conclusion would undervalue the pioneering work with medical imaging that was undertaken and the impact this work had in paving the way for investigations using magnetic resonance imaging that followed. Studies using CT worked out the principles of morphometry needed to define regions of interest and pioneered the use of segmentation procedures that were used to identify tissue classes. Both of these procedures were adopted by investigators using magnetic resonance imaging and are still in use today.

CT scanning remains a valuable tool in radiology. The scanners continue to improve in speed and resolution as the technology that is needed to operate them continues to evolve. In particular, CT imaging appears to have found a strong niche as a diagnostic tool for abdominal complaints. Interest in using CT for the study of AD diminished as it became clear that magnetic resonance imaging scans could provide more detailed images of the brain. Yet, the fundamental bases for many of the magnetic resonance imaging studies that followed were worked out by these initial CT studies.

Magnetic Resonance Imaging (MRI) Studies

The concepts that underlie MRI scanning originated somewhere in the early to mid-1900s and its innovators have been awarded with several Nobel Prizes. The first successful nuclear magnetic resonance experiments were conducted by Felix Bloch at Stanford University and Edward Purcell at Harvard in 1946 and they shared the Nobel Prize for this work in 1952. Paul Lauterbur used the principles employed in CT scanning to generate mathematical concepts on how to reconstruct the nuclear magnetic properties of materials while Peter Mansfield discovered how to analyze the nuclear magnetic resonance signals to infer the spatial arrangement of their sources. Together Lauterbur and Mansfield are credited with inventing MRI in the early 1970s and received the Nobel Prize for this work in 2003.

Essentially, MRI signals are produced by various atoms, such as the hydrogen atom, when they are excited by radiofrequency energy in the presence of a strong magnetic field. The signals that are detected by the scanner originate from these atoms as weak oscillating electrical currents that are generated when the atoms give off energy that they absorbed from the radiofrequency pulse and are returning to their equilibrium state.

The first imaging systems that were produced were rather inefficient as they were limited to the scanning of points and lines rather than whole-body sections. However, the momentum being generated by the sales of CT scanners encouraged the development of MRI techniques. A major advance took place when the process of image reconstruction changed from the use of algorithms developed for CT imaging to those developed for MRI by Richard Ernst and his colleagues who were rewarded for their efforts with the Nobel Prize in 1991.

The next major "breakthrough" took place in 1982 when it was shown that "high" field imaging was possible. Most early attempts at imaging were conducted at fields up to about $0.35\,T$ and there were concerns about an upper limit to the field strength at which imaging of the body was possible. In 1982 the research group at General Electric in Schenectady, New York were the first to show that imaging was possible at $1.5\,T$. Today, $1.5\,T$ has become the standard field strength for clinical imaging and $3.0\,T$ interest is rapidly being promoted by many of the scan vendors and users.

Since its induction into the clinical and research settings, MRI has rapidly surpassed all other tools for viewing the components of the body in vivo. MRI has been shown to be an ideal tool for the study of the nervous system because of its superior contrast. It has also become the primary imaging method of musculoskeletal soft-tissue injuries and diseases. Sales figures are difficult to obtain but growth market forecasts showed a 20.8% annual growth in 2002 indicating a rapid spread in the use of this technology.

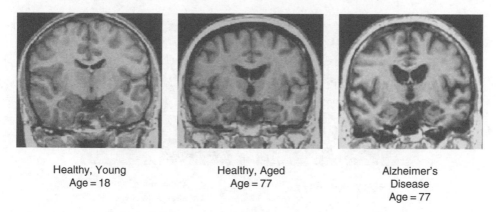

Healthy, Young
Age = 18

Healthy, Aged
Age = 77

Alzheimer's
Disease
Age = 77

Figure 17.2 Examples of three, coronal T1-weighted MRI slices illustrating the brain in a healthy, young, healthy, aged and Alzheimer's disease subjects. In these images, the gray matter is gray, white matter is white, and the bone, CSF and air are all black

In terms of the research impact that MRI has had on the early detection of AD, investigators have followed three lines of study. Using techniques originally developed for CT, one group advocated the use of linear measurements on MRI. Similarly, another group has advanced the use of volumetric measurements on MRI. Finally a third group of investigators have modified the concept of densitometry into the modern forms of automated (or semi-automated) segmentation procedures that are used to identify tissue subtypes or brain regions on MRI.

Following directly in the footsteps of investigations using CT imaging, a number of early investigations of MRI attempted to use linear measures to differentiate healthy, aged subjects from subjects with AD (Figure 17.2). The expectation at the time was that if a measure could be found it could readily be applied clinically given the ease in making these measures and minimal technical requirements. Measures were made of structures such as the ventricular system and brain, but as was found with CT scanning, considerable overlap was seen between the aged, healthy control subjects and subjects with AD. One measure that stands out focused on the medial temporal lobe by measuring the distance between the two medial temporal regions at the uncus (Figure 17.3). This interuncal distance was first proposed in 1991 (Dahlbeck et al., 1991) and it was shown to be related to cognitive performance on the Mini-Mental State Examination and Clinical Dementia Rating Scale (Howieson et al., 1993). Even though reports suggest that the interuncal distance is not a useful screening tool (Howieson et al., 1993) or a reliable diagnostic tool (Laakso, Soininen, Partanen, Hallikainen et al., 1995) its use continues to be debated today (Bersani et al., 2009; Saka et al., 2007).

While one group of MRI investigators was hoping to extend the work that was initiated with CT, another group set out to accomplish a task that was impossible with CT, i.e., directly measuring the hippocampus. The underlying belief at the time was that the profound memory impairment found in AD was the result of

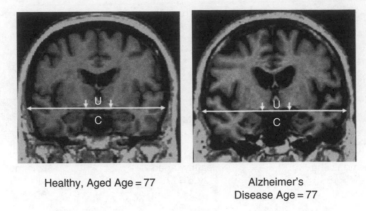

Healthy, Aged Age = 77   Alzheimer's
                               Disease Age = 77

Figure 17.3 Examples of the interuncal distance measure on coronal T1-weighted MRI slices from a healthy, aged subject and a subject with Alzheimer's disease. The distance between the two unci (U) was expressed as a percent of the intercranial distance (C).

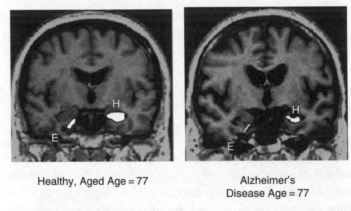

Healthy, Aged Age = 77   Alzheimer's
                               Disease Age = 77

Figure 17.4 Examples of region of interest measures on coronal T1-weighted MRI slices from a healthy, aged subject and a subject with Alzheimer's disease. This figures show an outline of the hippocampus (H) in one hemisphere and of the entorhinal cortex (E) in the other hemisphere.

hippocampal atrophy. The first studies to measure the volume of the hippocampus found about a 40% reduction in its volume with no overlap between the control group and the AD group (Seab et al., 1988) and a relationship to cognition (Kesslak et al., 1991). This seminal work was followed up quickly by other studies (Erkinjuntti et al., 1993; Jack et al., 1992; Killiany et al., 1993), which confirmed the importance of directly studying the hippocampus and highlighted means for using this measure alone or in combination with other measures as a marker for AD (Figure 17.4).

In most studies, the discrimination of AD subjects from controls ranges from 88% to 92% (Jack et al., 1992, 1997; Juottonen et al., 1999; Laakso, Soininen, Partanen, Helkala et al., 1995; Laakso et al., 1998). The hippocampal volumes of very mild AD subjects are also significantly different from healthy, control subjects though to a lesser extent, but adding information about the shape of the hippocampus improves discrimination (Csernansky et al., 2000; Yassa et al., 2010). Volumetric hippocampal measures obtained from MRI scans have been validated by demonstrating a correlation between MRI volumes and pathological assessment (Bobinski et al., 2000; Gosche et al., 2001; Jack et al. 2002; Sanchez-Benavides et al., 2010; Yassa et al., 2010). In addition, measures of the hippocampus have been shown to correlate with memory test performance in AD subjects, demonstrating that there is a functional significance to these changes in volume (de Leon et al., 1997; De Toledo-Morrell, Dickerson et al., 2000; Kohler et al., 1998; Laakso, Hallikainen et al., 2000; Loewenstein et al., 2009; Petersen et al., 2000; Storandt et al., 2009; Visser et al., 1999).

The strengths of in vivo imaging techniques such as MRI is that they are non-invasive and can be used to study longitudinal changes in the same subject. Longitudinal MRI studies focusing on volumetric measures of regions in the medial temporal lobe have demonstrated that hippocampal atrophy increases over time as AD subjects become more impaired (Fjell et al., 2010; Kaye et al., 1997; Jack et al., 1998; Laakso, Lehtovirta et al., 2000; Wang et al., 2010). The annual rate of hippocampal volume loss has been reported to be 2–3 times greater in mild AD subjects than in control subjects, ranging in value from 4–8% per year (Fjell et al., 2010; Jack et al., 1998; Laakso, Frisoni et al., 2000; Wang et al., 2010).

As the work using MRI to measure the volume of the hippocampal formation was progressing, a philosophical change took place in the way that AD was viewed. Initially, importance was place on identifying antimortem markers for AD in an effort to improve the accuracy of diagnosis and to identify subjects for potential intervention trials as compounds became available. Since AD is marked by neuronal death regionally and then globally in the brain, concern began to arise that by the time a person was diagnosed with AD too much neuronal loss would have taken place for effective interventions. Thus, the emphasis shifted from identifying individuals with AD to identifying individuals destined to develop AD. The subjects thought to be at the highest risk were those who were already showing signs of cognitive decline with respect to their peers. These subjects were deemed to have mild cognitive impairment (MCI).

Neuropathological studies in subjects with MCI have revealed neurofibrillary tangles and senile plaques in the hippocampus (Markesbery, 2010; Morris et al., 2001; Price & Morris, 1999), as found in subjects with AD. MRI studies have examined hippocampal volumes in mild cognitive impairment. These reports demonstrated that subjects with MCI have significantly smaller hippocampal volumes than elderly controls, with volume loss ranging from 10–15%, and larger volumes than patients with AD (Convit et al., 1997; De Toledo-Morrell, Dickerson et al., 2000; De Santi et al., 2001; Fjell et al., 2010; Pennanen et al., 2004; Sanchez-Benavides et al., 2010), suggesting a continuum of loss across the disease. In terms of discriminating between groups, the use of hippocampal volume alone has resulted in the ability to significantly differentiate subjects with MCI from elderly controls (accuracies range = 63–70%) and from patients with AD (accuracies range = 60–72%) (Du et al., 2001; Xu et al., 2000). Other studies found similar results (Fjell et al., 2010; Sanchez-Benavides et al., 2010). This discrimination accuracy has been shown to be subject to improvement with the addition of further information, such as the volume of other brain regions, CSF biomarkers, or PET imaging, to the volume of the hippocampus (Convit et al., 1997; Du et al., 2001; Fjell et al., 2010; Walhovd et al, 2010).

MRI-based studies have also investigated the role of the hippocampus as a predictor of eventual disease progression. A few studies have demonstrated that a measure of hippocampal volume on MRI is a significant predictor of disease progression (Devanand et al., 2007; Grundman et al., 2002; Jack et al., 1999; Risacher et al., 2009; Tapiola et al., 2006; Walhovd et al., 2010), though this remains somewhat controversial since other groups have found that hippocampal volumes do not discriminate individuals who will develop dementia within a few years from those who are not destined to do so (De Toledo-Morell et al., 2000b; Dickerson et al., 2001; Killiany et al., 2002).

Given the ambiguity associated with the MRI-based hippocampal measures in subjects with MCI, investigators have begun to look at other regions of the brain. One region associated with memory function that has received considerable attention is the entorhinal cortex. MRI studies have shown entorhinal cortex volume reductions (between 13–17.9%) in nondemented subjects who display memory problems that were significantly different than in AD subjects or control subjects (De Toledo-Morrell, Goncharova et al., 2000; Du et al., 2001; Killiany et al., 2000; Risacher et al., 2009; Xu et al., 2000). The entorhinal cortex has also been shown to be a good predictor of conversion to AD (De Toledo-Morrell, Goncharova et al., 2000; Dickerson et al., 2001; Killiany et al., 2000; Risacher et al., 2009).

To date, most studies have found that a measure of the entorhinal cortex alone shows only a modest ability to distinguish MCI patients from control subjects (i.e., 56–75%) (De Toledo-Morrell, Goncharova et al., 2000; Du et al., 2001; Risacher et al., 2009; Xu et al. 2000). My laboratory group has found that the entorhinal cortex alone, like the hippocampus, could not be used to discriminate nondemented individuals with memory problems who would not progress from those who do progress (Killiany et al., 2002). However, the combined addition of other brain regions to the entorhinal cortex did successfully discriminate between those nondemented individuals with memory problems who would not progress from those who would (Killiany et al., 2000).

In order to improve the accuracy of discrimination, investigators have also looked at the volume of other brain regions such as the amygdala (Bartzokis et al., 1993; Convit et al., 1999; Killiany et al., 1993; Risacher et al., 2009), the frontal lobe (Crespo-Facorro et al., 1999; Laakso, Soininen, Partanen, Helkala et al., 1995; Lehtovirta et al., 1995; Wible et al., 1997), the parietal lobe (Foundas et al., 1997; Risacher et al., 2009), the temporal lobe (Jack et al., 1998; Killiany et al., 1997; Risacher et al., 2009), and cerebellum (Schmahmann et al., 1999; Makris et al., 2003) with mixed results. Unlike the hippocampus and entorhinal cortex, less work has been conducted examining the role of structures outside of the medial temporal lobes in the earliest stages of AD (for a detailed review see Atiya et al., 2003; Chetelat & Baron 2003).

In a further effort to improve the accuracy in discriminating between MCI subjects and control subjects investigators have begun to look at combinations of brain regions that best predict which nondemented individuals with memory problems will develop AD. One study has found that the combined addition of the middle and inferior temporal gyri and the fusiform gyrus to the hippocampus and entorhinal cortex significantly improves the classification accuracy of MCI and predicts which individuals will eventually decline to AD (Convit et al., 2000). Another study has demonstrated that the volume of the banks of the superior temporal sulcus, together with the caudal portion of the anterior cingulate and the entorhinal cortex, significantly discriminates between subjects with memory problems destined to progress from those with memory problems that do not progress (Killiany et al., 2000).

As interest grew to measuring more and more structures in the brain, techniques were developed to subdivide the whole brain into anatomically distinct regions based on standard anatomical landmarks. Template-driven warping approaches take the whole brain and fit it to an anatomical atlas allowing one to measure the volumes of each structure represented in the atlas (Sandor & Leahy, 1997; Thompson et al., 1996). This approach has been utilized to measure anatomical structures such as the hippocampus (Csernansky et al., 1998) and the cingulate gyrus (Miller et al., 2003), and has been shown to be capable of distinguishing patients with AD from elderly controls (Csernansky et al., 2000; Miller et al., 2003).

An advance in the template-driven warping approaches has been the development of probabilistic atlases. With this technique, common information in an individual's brain is utilized by a coordinate system that can be used to reshape an anatomical atlas to fit the individual's brain (Fischl, Sereno, & Dale, 1999; Fischl, Sereno, Tootell, & Dale, 1999). The probabilistic atlas approach has also been used to differentiate patients with AD from elderly controls (Fischl et al., 2002; Sanchez-Benavides et al., 2010). It has also been shown to be important for identifying specific regions of atrophy in the parietal lobe and other brain regions and in following atrophy in these regions over time in subjects with MCI (Desikan, 2007; Sanchez-Benavides et al., 2010).

The template-driven warping approaches to post-processing MRI data are at this point in their infancy and advances in the time that these approaches take to analyze a brain and the anatomical accuracy of this analysis are improving rapidly. As these techniques mature, they offer perhaps the best way to analyze the whole brain on MRI in an anatomical manner like that found in neuropathology studies. This should allow us to identify/track diseases as they affect the various parts of the brain or more importantly target interventions to stop the spread of atrophy.

The third approach taken by investigators using MRI to study AD was to develop techniques to assess whole-brain atrophy (Simmons et al., 2010). Taken together, these methodologies tend to rely heavily on computerized processes for the analysis of the scans and often require a large degree of sophistication to run, though they have been promoted as providing a standardized method of scan analysis (Ashburner at al., 2003). Some of these methods, such as voxel-based morphometry and boundary shift integral, can trace their history back to the initial CT studies by focusing on examining the whole brain for global changes, whereas other techniques, such as the template-driven warping approaches, have developed from volumetric studies and subdivide the brain into a discreet number of regions of interest (Ashburner et al., 2003).

Voxel-based morphometry (VBM) was developed to identify areas in the whole brain that differ between two or more groups of subjects at a single time-point or within the same subjects at multiple time-points (Ashburner et al., 2003; Ashburner & Friston, 2000; Friston, 1995; Wright et al., 1995). Initial studies used this technique to detect whole-brain differences between patients with AD and elderly controls (Baron et al., 2001; Frisoni et al., 2002). More recently, this technique was used to show changes within the medial temporal lobes (Karas et al., 2004; Pennanen et al., 2005) and other brain regions (Guo et al., 2010) in subjects with MCI when compared with elderly controls and patients with AD. In addition, this technique has been used to follow differential rates of atrophy in the brain of cognitively impaired subjects as they progressed to a clinical diagnosis of AD (Chetelat et al., 2005).

Another approach for examining whole-brain atrophy on MRI scans is the boundary shift integral (Fox et al., 1996; Freeborough et al., 1996). This technique first involves the co-registration of MRI images acquired at two or more points in time from the same individual. Then, essentially the later time-point image is subtracted from the first time-point image to show the change over time (Fox et al., 1996; Freeborough & Fox 1997). These changes in an individual presumably correspond to the atrophy occurring with the disease process (Freeborough & Fox 1997). This technique has been used to confirm the presence of medial temporal lobe atrophy in the earliest stages of AD (Scahill et al., 2002). In addition, it has been employed as an outcome measure in clinical trials (Fox et al., 2005).

A direct extension of the whole-brain analysis approaches has been the study of the tissue classes (gray matter, white matter, and cerebrospinal fluid (CSF) spaces). In particular, the interest here has focused on identifying the number of regions of abnormalities in the white matter, which have been referred to generally with the term "hyperintensities" since they appear as bright spots on T2-weighted images. In order to identify the tissue classes (and abnormalities) a process like radiodensity/ densitometry on CT, referred to as segmentation, is applied. Basically the gray scale intensity of the tissue classes is determined and all areas within the brain become reclassified based upon gray scale intensity into gray matter, white matter, CSF space, and white matter hyperintensities (Figure 17.5).

The etiology of these hyperintensities is not well understood through they are often linked to the vascular system. A number of groups have been involved in the study of hyperintensities on MRI but perhaps the individual who is best known for his work with AD is Dr. DeCarli whose group has been involved in studying this form of pathology for most of the large MRI studies taking place in the United

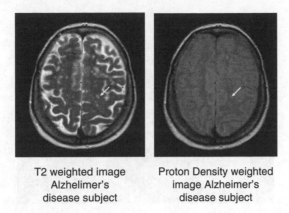

T2 weighted image
Alzhelimer's
disease subject

Proton Density weighted
image Alzheimer's
disease subject

Figure 17.5 A slice from a T2-weighted and proton density weighted image of a subject with Alzheimer's disease. In the T2-weighted image the CSF is white, and the brain tissue is in scales of gray with the white matter having a darker pallor than the gray matter. In the proton density image the CSF is black while the brain tissues retain the same scales of gray as in the T2-weighted image. The white arrow points to an example of a hyperintensity

States today. His group has found that the number of hyperintense areas increase with age and disease and may be a risk factor for cognitive decline (Yoshita et al., 2006). It is unclear how these hyperintense areas fit into the etiology of AD and whether they are a primary marker for the etiology or a secondary consequence of it.

Other forms of MRI analyses that have their origins in radiodensity/densitometry include T2 brain mapping and quantitative-MRI (Q-MRI). T2 brain mapping requires the calculation of the T2 relaxation time for each voxel in the brain usually from the echo time of two applied pulses. The T2 relaxation time is affected by the tissue iron storage (and other minerals as well) and tissue water content making it a possible early marker for subtle changes in the brain such as oxidative damage. T2 brain mapping has been used to show that iron may be a risk for age-related neurodegeneration (Bartzokis et al., 2007, 2004), age-associated memory loss (House et al., 2006), and may provide a marker for AD (Bartzokis & Tishler, 2000; Schenck et al., 2006) (Figure 17.6, plate section). T2 brain mapping is a novel technique that has not yet been fully applied to the study of AD. As this methodology is applied more to the study of AD we should be able to learn how to use this information to identify subjects at risk, follow changes over time, and assess the efficiency of potential treatments.

Q-MRI portrays the spatial distribution of a biophysical parameter of the image on a pixel-by-pixel basis. This is a very different approach from most conventional imaging (Figure 17.7). The majority of MR images are directly acquired with the only computer manipulation performed before being displayed is the image reconstruction that consists of a Fourier transform. The information (gray scale intensity value) content of directly acquired images is only relevant to pixels in the same data

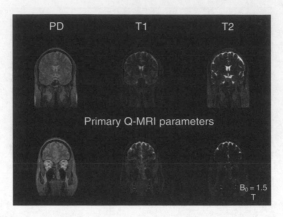

Figure 17.7   Examples of coronal proton density (PD), T1 and T2 images acquired with a quantitative MRI (Q-MRI) protocol at 1.5 T

set (not absolute values). The relationship between pixel values at different positions in directly acquired images is one of relative increase or decrease as a function of the pulse sequence used and of the tissue parameters that affect the MRI signal. On the other hand, images generated with Q-MRI techniques portray the spatial distribution of a tissue parameter on a pixel-by-pixel basis showing values that are tissue specific (see Jara et al., 2006). Q-MRI techniques offer the potential for directly identifying areas of subtle abnormalities in the brain. Such techniques have been well established and used primarily by physicists for a number of years. While Q-MRI offers the potential for revealing new information about the brain of AD subjects, this method has not yet been applied to the study of AD. As studies begin using this technique we should be able to determine how to use this new information to identify subjects at risk for AD, follow changes over time, and assess the efficiency of potential treatments.

Recently investigators have begun to turn to MRI scanning to measure cerebral blood flow using a technique called arterial spin labeling (ASL), which provides a non-invasive means of quantifying regional cerebral blood flow (Talagala & Noll, 1998). In ASL, magnetic labeling of water 1H spins in arterial blood is accomplished by perturbing the 1H magnetization so that it is no longer at equilibrium. The exchange of labeled arterial water with interstitial and intracellular water causes a reduction in the tissue MRI signal by an amount determined by cerebral blood flow and other measurable parameters. Measurement of the MRI signal with and without ASL allows quantification of the cerebral blood flow (Talagala et al., 2004). The ability to study blood flow with a non-invasive method is important since so many factors (i.e. pH, hydration) can affect blood flow and it is such a highly dynamic process that changes over time and location in the body.

To date, relatively few studies exist in the literature applying ASL techniques to the study of AD. These studies report significant reductions in blood flow in the temporal, parietal, frontal, and posterior cingulate cortices of AD subjects with respect to healthy, control subjects (Alsop et al., 2000). Clinical progression of the disease was shown to be related to reduced cerebral blood flow to the posterior parietal and posterior cingulate regions but not to the temporal regions (Alsop et al., 2000). AD subjects were more specifically found to have hypoperfusion outside of the medial temporal lobe region and in the right inferior parietal lobe that extended into the bilateral posterior cingulate gyri and left and right middle frontal gyri when compared to healthy, control subjects (Johnson, Jahng et al., 2005). MCI subjects were also reported to have regional hypoperfusion outside of the medial temporal lobe region in the inferior right parietal lobe when compared to healthy control subjects (Johnson, Schmitz et al., 2005). The pattern of hypoperfusion in AD appears to differ from that found in other dementias. When compared to subjects with frontal lobe dementia, those with AD had reduced blood flow in the parietal and posterior cingulate cortices (Du et al., 2006). One recent study found that hypoperfusion detected by ASL-MRI predicted clinical, functional, and cognitive decline (Chao et al., 2010). As more studies are completed using this technique we should be able to determine how to use this information to identify subjects at risk for AD, follow changes over time, and assess the efficacy of potential treatments.

Another set of techniques that have been developed for use with MRI are magnetic resonance spectroscopy (MRS) and diffusion tensor imaging (DTI). These techniques have generated a common response from the imaging community. Both were initially welcomed with enthusiasm but as they were applied, often incorrectly, they lost some of their initial respect and were somewhat abandoned. Both techniques are now seeing a resurgence in use as they are being more carefully applied at higher field strengths.

Proton magnetic resonance spectroscopy has been around since the early 1970s when it was first used to study metabolites in the blood. When applied to the study of the brain, four main metabolites were typically studied. N-acetylasparatate (NAA) is predominately found intraneuronally and has been used as a marker of neuronal density (Valenzuela & Sachdev, 2001). Choline is a rate-limiting precursor in the synthesis of acetylcholine and a precursor to cell membrane phosphatidylcholine. It has been readily measured and suggested as a marker for membranes, however, repeatability studies have found poor test–retest reliability (Valenzuela & Sachdev, 2001). Myo-inositol is a largely mysterious sugar-alcohol whose structure is similar to that of glucose. Myo-inositol may act as a marker of glial cells, an osmoregulator, intracellular messenger, or detoxification agent in the brain (Valenzuela & Sachdev, 2001). Creatine plus phosphocreatine acts as a reserve for high-energy phosphates and buffers cellular ATP/ADP ratios. Thus, the creatine signal reflects the health of systemic energy use and storage (Valenzuela & Sachdev, 2001).

To date, a number of studies have been conducted using MRS in AD. At first glance, the results of these studies appear to be confusing and conflicting. However, with careful scrutiny, a pattern of concordance does appear for some of the metabolites (see Valenzuela & Sachdev, 2001 for a review). For the NAA and myo-inositol

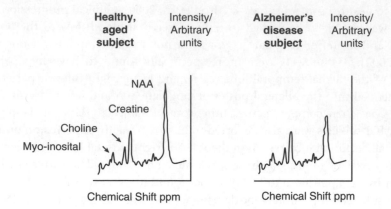

Figure 17.8   Examples of an MR spectrogram in a healthy, aged subject and a subject with Alzheimer's disease. The major peaks are labeled for the metabolite that they represent. In this illustration a reduction in the NAA peak can be seen in the AD subject. However, since the y-axis is represented in arbitrary units, ratios between the metabolites in each spectra need to be used when making a comparisons between the spectra

there appears to be a general agreement that NAA decreases throughout the cortex and myo-inositol increases in the white and gray matter in the early stages of AD (Figure 17.8). Little agreement exists in the literature for the other metabolites.

The apparent decrease in NAA and increase in myo-inositol have also been shown to relate to behavioral changes. In a study of patients with mild AD (Chantal et al., 2002), the metabolic alterations were identified in several brain regions and correlated with the level of cognitive ability. Thus, alterations in the left medial temporal lobe were related to verbal memory loss, in the left parietotemporal region with language impairment and in the right parietotemporal region with a loss of visuospatial abilities. When the range of function from healthy control to MCI to AD was studied (Kantarci et al., 2002) the NAA/myo-inositol ratio was found to be the most efficient predictor of cognitive functioning. Similarly, in a longitudinal study (Dixon et al., 2002) NAA concentration was found to be lower in cognitively impaired subjects compared to healthy, control subjects at follow-up.

The neuropathology of AD in the earliest stages can be quite difficult to distinguish from normal aging. MRS data also suggests that similar white matter biochemical changes can be found in patients with chronic hypertension and early AD. When the myo-inositol/creatine ratio was used, a significantly higher ratio was found in cognitively healthy hypertensive patients and in Alzheimer's patients than in controls (Catani et al., 2002). No differences were found in the NAA measures. This suggests that myo-inositol may be a sensitive marker for changes in the brain and that at least in the earliest stages, common brain changes are occurring in those with AD and those with chronic hypertension with respect to the myo-inositol/creatine ratio.

Most of the initial MRS studies were conducted on scanners that were 1.5 T in strength. At this field strength it is often difficult to discern the metabolite spectra from the background noise. Today, with 3.0 T scanners becoming more and more prevalent, researchers and clinicians are returning to MRS as a tool to study changes in the brain at higher field strength where greater separation between the spectra and background noise can be found. We await the findings of these studies to see what value MRS offers for identifying subjects at risk for AD (e.g., Modrego et al., 2010).

Diffusion tensor imaging (DTI) measures the directionality of molecular diffusion where the molecule of interest is typically a water molecule. When the molecule is free to diffuse in all possible directions it has "isotropic diffusion." However, when the molecule has a restriction (i.e., due to a membrane) to its direction of diffusion it has "anisotropic diffusion." A standard metric used with DTI is the measure of fractional anisotropy (FA). Highly organized white matter tracts have high FA values because the molecular diffusion is highly constrained by the tracts' cellular organization. If the white matter were to become damaged as a result of pathology such as amyloid deposition, the FA values in that region would decrease as the diffusion of the molecules become closer to isotropic due to the breakdown of the cellular organization. Studies have used DTI to show axonal damage and demyelination of the brain (Basser et al., 1994; Basser & Pierpaloi, 1996; Makris et al., 1997; Ulug et al., 1999). In addition, measures of FA have been shown to correlate with impairments of cognition in subjects with chronic head injury (Salmond et al., 2006).

Initially, DTI was touted as being an in vivo way to follow white matter tracts in the brain and many studies reported various tracts and changes in these tracts with various disease states. However, this practice quickly drew criticism mainly because the resolution of the DTI image is far beyond that needed to actually follow most white matter tracts in the brain. In addition, one only has to look at a histology slice of brain tissue (stained with a myelin marker) to realize that most "tracts" are far more theoretical in nature than discrete, discernible entities even with the resolution of a microscope. In general the philosophy changed and instead of implying that actual tracts were visualized, the relative strength of a connection between two regions of interest is emphasized. This is a unique and exciting feature to DTI since it can show the efficiency of the link between two regions even if they are known not to be directly connected to each other (i.e., separated by several synapses) (Figure 17.9, plate section).

To date, several studies have been published using DTI to show changes in subjects with either MCI or AD (Bozzali et al., 2002; Bozzao et al., 2001; Fellgiebel et al., 2004; Hanyu et al., 1999; Hanyu et al., 1998; Head et al., 2004; Kantarci et al., 2001; Medina et al., 2006; Rose et al., 2000; Sandon et al, 1999; Yoshiura et al., 2002). Because the means of acquiring and analyzing DTI scans is rapidly evolving the methodology in these studies varies widely (see Stebbins & Murphy, 2009, for review).

Finally, we're also just beginning to see an exciting merger between the MRS and DTI technologies to form the procedure called diffusion tensor spectroscopy (DTS). One problem that has plagued investigators using DTI is that the focus has mainly been on using the water molecule as the target for diffusion. Water molecules can be found throughout the brain both inside and outside of cell membranes making changes in FA somewhat difficult to interpret. For example, the breakdown in myelin would be expected to show a change in FA because of a change in intra-cellular diffusion. On the other hand, a localized edema would cause the same change in FA, but because of a change in extra-cellular diffusion. This problem can be overcome by looking at the diffusion of a molecule such as NAA, which is largely intracellular (Upadhyay et al., 2007, 2008). The combination of tools such as this expands our capacity to study disease states and helps to diminish the potential weakness in them. We await the findings of the studies using DTS to see what value it offers in identify subjects at risk for AD, follow changes over time, and assess the efficiency of potential treatments.

Conclusion

Over the past 30 years we've achieved tremendous success in our ability to diagnose and image patients with AD. As you have read through this chapter it should be clear that much of our focus has been on imaging and measuring structures such as the hippocampus in the medial temporal lobe regions. As our focus has now changed to identifying markers for individuals at risk of developing AD in the near future with imaging we've seen some limited success.

Our understanding of the neuropathology of AD has also evolved from thoughts of a "hippocampal" dementia to findings of changes early in the disease in disparate regions of the brain. The focus of our imaging studies now has to reflect this change in knowledge and look for discrete focal signs of more subtle regional injury throughout the brain. As the imaging procedures and post-processing tools continue to develop and our ability to detect more subtle changes improve, the likelihood of finding markers for disease progression increases.

The importance of using imaging techniques in helping to identify individuals at risk for developing AD, following the changes associated with the disease over time, and testing the efficacy of pharmaceutical agents can be seen by the unprecedented steps that have now been formed to standardize imaging procedures. The Alzheimer's Disease Neuroimaging Initiative was created in the United States as a cooperative agreement between the National Institutes of Health and private industry as a large-scale study designed to help standardize the procedures of image acquisition and post processing. Similar endeavors are being put together throughout the world making the search for MRI-based markers of Alzheimer's disease truly a worldwide effort.

Acknowledgments

The author would like to thank Ms. Sarah Greene for her invaluable assistance in editing and reviewing this manuscript, Dr. Carole Columbo for generously providing the CT scan, Dr. Hernan Jara for generously providing the Q-MRI figure, and Mr. Fred Powell for generously providing the DTI image. This work was supported in part by NIH/NIA P01-AG04953.

References

Albert, M., Naeser, M. A., Levine, H. L., & Garvey, A. J. (1984). Ventricular size in patients with presenile dementia of the Alzheimer's type. *Archives of Neurology, 41,* 1258–1263.

Alsop, D. C., Detre, J. A., & Grossman, M. (2000). Assessment of cerebral blood flow in Alzheimer's disease by spin-labeled magnetic resonance imaging. *Annals of Neurology, 47,* 93–100.

Arai, H., Koboyashi, K., Ikeda, K., Nagao, Y., Ogihara, R., & Kosaka, K. (1983). A computed tomography study of Alzheimer's disease. *Journal of Neurology, 229,* 69–77.

Ashburner, J., & Friston, K. J. (2000). Voxel-based morphometry – The methods. *Neuroimage, 11,* 805–821.

Ashburner, J., Csernansky, J., Davatsikos, C., Fox, N., Frisoni, G., & Thompson, P. (2003). Computer-assisted imaging to assess brain structure in healthy and diseased brains. *Lancet Neurology, 2,* 79–88.

Atiya, M., Hyman, B., Albert, M., & Killiany, R. (2003). Structural magnetic resonance imaging in established and prodromal Alzheimer's disease: A review. *Alzheimer Disease & Associated Disorders, 17,* 177–195.

Ball, M. J., Fisman, M., Hachinski, V., Blume, W., Fox, A., Kral, V. A., et al. (1985). A new definition of Alzheimer's disease: A hippocampal dementia. *Lancet, i,* 14–16.

Baron, J. C., Chetelat, G., Desgranges, B., Perchey, G., Landeau, B., de la Sayette, V., et al. (2001). In vivo mapping of gray matter loss with voxel-based morphometry in mild Alzheimer's disease. *Neuroimage, 14,* 298–309.

Bartzokis, G., & Tishler, T. A. (2000). MRI evaluation of basal ganglia ferritin iron and neurotoxicity in Alzheimer's and Huntingon's disease. *Cell and Molecular Biology, 46,* 821–833.

Bartzokis, G., Mintz, J., Marx, P., Osborn, D., Gutkind, D., Chiang, F., et al. (1993). Reliability of in vivo volume measures of hippocampus and other brain structures using MRI. *Magnetic Resonance Imaging, 11,* 993–1006.

Bartzokis, G., Tishler, T. A., Lu, P. H., Villablanca, P., Altshuler, L. L., Carter, M., et al. (2007). Brain ferritin iron may influence age- and gender-related risks of neurodegeneration. *Neurobiology of Aging, 28,* 414–423.

Bartzokis, G., Tishler, T. A., Shin, I. S., Lu, P. H., & Cummings, J. L. (2004). Brain ferritin iron as a risk factor for age at onset in neurodegenerative diseases. *Annals of the New York Academy of Science, 1012,* 224–36.

Basser, P. J., & Pierpaoli, C. (1996). Microstructural and physiological features of tissues elucidated by quantitative-diffusion-tensor MRI. *Journal of Magnetic Resonance, Series B, 111,* 209–219.

Basser, P.J., Mattiello, J., & LeBihan, D. (1994). MR diffusion tensor spectroscopy and imaging. *Biophysical Journal, 66,* 259–267.

Bersani, G., Quartini, A., Manuali, G., Iannitelli, A., Pucci, D., Conforti, F., et al. (2009). Influence of obstetric complication severity on brain morphology in schizophrenia: An MR study. *Neuroradiology, 51,* 363–371.

Bobinski, M., de Leon, M. J., Wegiel, J., Desanti, S., Convit, A., Saint Louis, L. A., et al. (2000). The histological validation of post mortem magnetic resonance imaging-determined hippocampal volume in Alzheimer's disease. *Neuroscience, 95*, 721–725.

Bozzali, M., Cercignani, M., Sormani, M. P., Comi, G., & Filippi, M. (2002). Quantification of brain gray matter damage in different MS phenotypes by use of diffusion tensor MR imaging. *American Journal of Neuroradiology, 23*, 985–988.

Bozzao, A., Floris, R., Baviera, M. E., Apruzzese, A., & Simonetti, G. (2001). Diffusion and perfusion MR imaging in cases of Alzheimer's disease: Correlations with cortical atrophy and lesion load. *American Journal of Neuroradiology, 22*, 1030–1036.

Catani, M., Howard, R. J., Pajevic, S., & Jones, D. K. (2002). Virtual in vivo interactive dissection of white matter fasciculi in the human brain. *Neuroimage, 17*, 77–94.

Chantal, S., Labelle, M., Bouchard, R. W., Braun, C. M., & Boulanger, Y. (2002). Correlation of regional proton magnetic resonance spectroscopic metabolic changes with cognitive deficits in mild Alzheimer disease. *Archives of Neurology, 59*, 955–962.

Chao, L. L., Buckley, S. T., Kornak, J., Schuff, N., Madison, C., Yaffe, K., et al. (2010). ASL perfusion MRI predicts cognitive decline and conversion from MCI to dementia. *Alzheimer Disease & Associated Disorders, 24*, 19–27.

Chetelat, G., & Baron, J. C. (2003). Early diagnosis of Alzheimer's disease: Contribution of structural neuroimaging. *Neuroimage, 18*, 525–541.

Chetelat, G., Landeau, F., Eustache, F., Mezenge, F., Viander, F., de la Sayette, V., et al. (2005). Using voxel-based morphometry to map the structural changes associated with rapid conversion from MCI: A longitudinal MRI study. *Neuroimage, 27*, 934–946.

Colgan, J., Naquib, M., & Levy, R. (1986). Computed tomographic density numbers. A comparative study of patients with senile dementia and normal elderly controls. *British Journal of Psychiatry, 149*, 716–719.

Convit, A., de Asis, J., de Leon, M. J., Tarshish, C. Y., De Santi, S., & Rusinek, H. (2000). Atrophy of the medial occipitotemporal, inferior, and middle temporal gyri in non-demented elderly predict decline to Alzheimer's disease. *Neurobiology of Aging, 21*, 19-26.

Convit, A., De Leon, M. J., Tarshish, C., De Santi, S., Tsui, W., Rusinek, H., et al. (1997). Specific hippocampal volume reductions in individuals at risk for Alzheimer's disease. *Neurobiology of Aging, 18*, 131–138.

Convit, A., McHugh, P., Wolf, O. T., de Leon, M. J., Bobinski, M., De Santi, S., et al. (1999). MRI volume of the amygdala: A reliable method allowing separation from the hippocampal formation. *Psychiatry Research, 90*, 113–123.

Creasey, H., Schwartz, M., Frederickson, H., Haxby, J. V., & Rapoport, S. I. (1986). Quantitative computed tomography in dementia of the Alzheimer's type. *Neurology, 36*, 1563–1568.

Crespo-Facorro, B., Kim, J. J., Andreasen, N. C., O'Leary, D. S., Wiser, A. K., Bailey, J. M., et al. (1999). Human frontal cortex: An MRI-based parcellation method. *Neuroimage, 10*, 500–519.

Csernansky, J. G., Joshi, S., Wang, L., Haller, J.W., Miller, J. P., et al. (1998). Hippocampal morphometry in schizophrenia by high dimensional brain mapping. *Proceedings of the National Academy of Sciences USA, 95*, 11406–11411.

Csernansky, J. G., Wang, L., Joshi, S., Miller, J. P., Gado, M., Kido, D., et al. (2000). Early DAT is distinguished from aging by high dimensional mapping of the hippocampus. *Neurology, 55*, 1636–1643.

Dahlbeck, J. W., McCluney, K. W., Yeakley, J. W., Fenstermacher, M. J., Bonmati, C., Van Horn, G., et al. (1991). The interuncal distance: A new MR measurement for the hippocampal atrophy of Alzheimer's disease. *American Journal of Neuroradiology, 12,* 931–932.

De Carli, C., Kaye, J. A., Horwitz, B. & Rapoport, S. I. (1990). Critical analysis of the use of computer assisted transverse axial tomography to study human brain in aging and dementia of the Alzheimer's type. *Neurology, 40,* 872–883.

de Leon, M. J., Convit, A., DeSanti, S., Bobinski, M., George, A. E., Wisniewski, H. M., et al. (1997). Contribution of structural neuroimaging to the early diagnosis of Alzheimer's disease. *International Psychogeriatrics,* Suppl 1, 183–190.

de Leon, M. J., George, A. E., Stylopoulos, L. A., Smith, G., & Miller, D. C. (1989). Early marker for Alzheimer's disease: The atrophic hippocampus. *Lancet, ii,* 672–673.

De Santi, S., de Leon, M. J., Rusinek, H., Convit, A., Tarshish, C. Y., Roche, A., et al. (2001). Hippocampal formation glucose metabolism and volume losses in MCI and AD. *Neurobiology of Aging, 22,* 529–539.

De Toledo-Morrell, L., Dickerson, B., Sullivan, M. P., Spanovic, C., Wilson, R., & Bennett, D. A. (2000). Hemispheric differences in hippocampal volume predict verbal and spatial memory performance in patients with Alzheimer's disease. *Hippocampus, 10,* 136–142.

De Toledo-Morrell, L., Goncharova, I., Dickerson, B., Wilson, R. S., & Bennett, D. A. (2000). From healthy aging to early Alzheimer's disease: In vivo detection of entorhinal cortex atrophy. *Annals of the New York Academy of Science, 911,* 240–245.

Desikan, R. (2007). MRI based morphometric measures of regional brain atrophy in pro-dromal Alzheimer's disease. Boston University School of Medicine Doctoral Thesis.

Devanand, D. P., Pradhaban, G., Liu, X., Khandji, A., De Santi, S., Segal, S., et al. (2007). Hippocampal and entorhinal atrophy in mild cognitive impairment: prediction of Alzheimer disease. *Neurology, 68,* 828–836.

Dickerson, B. C., Goncharova, I., Sullivan, M. P., Forchetti, C., Wilson, R. S., Bennett, D. A., et al. (2001). MRI-derived entorhinal and hippocampal atrophy in incipient and very mild Alzheimer's disease. *Neurobiology of Aging, 5,* 747–754.

Dixon, R. M., Bradley, K. M., Budge, M. M., Styles, P., & Smith, A. D. (2002). Longitudinal quantitative proton magnetic resonance spectroscopy of the hippocampus in Alzheimer's disease. *Brain, 125,* 2332–2341.

Du, A. T., Jahn, G. H., Hayasaka, S., Kramer, J. H., Rosen, H. J., Gorno-Tempini, M. L., et al. (2006). Hypoperfusion in frontotemporal dementia and Alzheimer disease by arterial spin labeling MRI. *Neurology, 67,* 1215–1220.

Du, A. T., Schuff, N., Amend, D., Laakso, M. P., Hsu, Y. Y., Jagust, W. J., et al. (2001). Magnetic resonance imaging of the entorhinal cortex and hippocampus in mild cognitive impairment and Alzheimer's disease. *Journal of Neurology, Neurosurgery & Psychiatry, 71,* 441–447.

Erkinjuntti, T., Lee, D. H., Gao, F., Steenhuis, R., Eliasziw, M., Fry, R., et al. (1993). Temporal lobe atrophy on magnetic resonance imaging in the diagnosis of early Alzheimer's disease. *Archives of Neurology, 50,* 305–310.

Fellgiebel, A., Wille, P., Muller, M. J., Winterer, G., Scheurich, A., Vucurevic, G., et al. (2004). Ultrastructural hippocampal and white matter alterations in mild cognitive impairment: A diffusion tensor imaging study. *Dementia and Geriatric Cognitive Disorders, 18,* 101–108.

Fischl, B., Salat, D. H., Busa, E., Albert, M., Dieterich, M., Haselgrove, C., et al. (2002). Whole brain segmentation: automated labeling of neuroanatomical structures in the human brain. *Neuron, 33,* 341–355.

Fischl, B., Sereno, M. I., & Dale, A. M. (1999). Cortical surface-based analysis. II: Inflation, flattening, and a surface-based coordinate system. *Neuroimage, 9,* 195–207.

Fischl, B., Sereno, M. I., Tootell, R. B., & Dale, A. M. (1999). High-resolution intersubject averaging and a coordinate system for the cortical surface. *Human Brain Mapping, 8,* 272–284.

Fjell, A. M., Walhovd, K. B., Fennema-Notestine, C., McEvoy, L. K., Hagler, D. J., Holland, D., et al. (2010). CSF biomarkers in prediction of cerebral and clinical change in mild cognitive impairment and Alzheimer's disease. *Journal of Neuroscience, 30,* 2088–2101.

Foundas, A. L., Leonard, C. M., Mohoney, S. M., Agee, O. F., & Heilman, K. M. (1997). Atrophy of the hippocampus, parietal cortex and insula in Alzheimer's disease: A volumetric magnetic resonance imaging study. *Neuropsychiatry, Neuropsychology & Behavioral Neurology, 10,* 81–89.

Fox, N. C., Black, R. S., Gilman, S., Rossor, M. N., Griffith, S. G., Jenkins, L., et al. (2005). AN1792(QS-21)-201 Study. Effects of Abeta immunization (AN1792) on MRI measures of cerebral volume in Alzheimer disease. *Neurology, 64,* 1563–1572.

Fox, N. C., Freeborough, P. A., & Rossor, M. N. (1996). Visualisation and quantification of rates of atrophy in Alzheimer's disease. *Lancet, 348,* 94–97.

Freeborough, P. A., & Fox, N. C. (1997). The boundary shift integral: An accurate and robust measure of cerebral volume changes from registered repeat MRI. *IEEE Transactions in Medical Imaging, 16,* 623–629.

Freeborough, P. A., Woods, R. P., & Fox, N. C. (1996). Accurate registration of serial 3D MR brain images and its application to visualizing change in neurodegenerative disorders. *Journal of Computer Assisted Tomography, 20*(6), 1012–1022.

Frisoni, G. B., Testa, C., Zorzan, A., Sabattoli, F., Beltramello, A., Soininen, H., et al. (2002). Detection of grey matter loss in mild Alzheimer's disease with voxel based morphometry. *Journal of Neurology, Neurosurgery & Psychiatry, 73,* 657–664.

Friston, K. J. (1995). Commentary and opinion: II. Statistical parametric mapping: ontology and current issues. *Journal of Cerebral Blood Flow and Metabolism, 15,* 361–370.

Gado, M., Danziger, W. L., Chi, D., Hughes, C. P., & Coben, L. A. (1983). Brain parenchymal density measurements by CT in demented subjects and normal controls. *Radiology, 147,* 703–710.

Gado, M., Hughes, C.P., Danziger ,W., Shi, D., Jost, G., & Berg, L. (1982). Volumetric measurements of the cerebrospinal fluid spaces in demented subjects and controls. *Radiology, 144,* 535–538.

George, A. E., de Leon, M. J., Ferris, S. h., & Kricheff, I. I. (1981). Parenchymal CT correlates of senile dementia (Alzheimer's disease): Loss of gray-white discriminability. *American Journal of Neuroradiology, 2,* 205–213.

George, A. E., de Leon, M. J., Rosenbloom, S., Ferris, S. H., Gentes, C., Emmerich, M., et al. (1983). Ventricular volume and cognitive deficit: A computed tomographic study. *Radiology, 3,* 391–394.

George, A. E., de Leon, M. J., Stylopoulos, L. A., Miller, J., Kluger, A., Smith, G., et al. (1990). CT diagnostic features of Alzheimer's disease: Importance of the choroidal/hippocampal fissure complex. *American Journal of Neuroradiology, 11,* 101–107.

Gosche, K. M., Mortimer, J. A., Smith, C. D., Markesbery, W. R., & Snowdon, D. A. (2001). An automated technique for measuring hippocampal volumes from MR imaging studies. *American Journal of Neuroradiology, 22,* 1686–1689.

Grundman, M., Sencakova, D., Jack, C. R. Jr, Petersen, R. C., Kim, H. T., Schultz, A., et al. (2002). Alzheimer's Disease Cooperative Study. Brain MRI hippocampal volume and prediction of clinical status in a mild cognitive impairment trial. *Journal of Molecular Neuroscience, 19,* 23–27.

Guo, X., Wang, Z., Li, K., Li, Z., Qi, Z., Jin, Z., et al. (2010). Voxel-based assessment of gray and white matter volumes in Alzheimer's disease. *Neuroscience Letters, 468,* 146–150.

Hanyu, H., Imon, Y., Sakurai, H., Iwamoto, T., Takasaki, M., Shindo, H., et al. (1999). Regional differences in diffusion abnormality in cerebral white matter lesions in patients with vascular dementia of the Binswanger type and Alzheimer's disease. *European Journal of Neurology, 6,* 195–203.

Hanyu, H., Sakurai, H., Iwamoto, T., Takasaki, M., Shindo, H., & Abe, K. (1998). Diffusion-weighted MR imaging of the hippocampus and temporal white matter in Alzheimer's disease. *Journal of the Neurological Sciences, 156,* 195–200.

Head, D., Buckner, R. L., Shimony, J. S., Williams, L. E., et al., (2004). Differential vulnerability of anterior white matter in nondemented aging with minimal acceleration in dementia of the Alzheimer's type: Evidence from diffusion tensor imaging. *Cerebral Cortex, 4,* 410–423.

House, M. J., St Pierre, T. G., Foster, J. K., Martins, R. N., & Clarnette, R. (2006). Quantitative MR imaging R2 relaxometry in elderly participants reporting memory loss. *American Journal of Neuroradiology, 27,* 430–439.

Howieson, J., Kaye, J. A., Holm, L. & Howieson, D. (1993). Interuncal distance: Marker of aging and Alzheimer's disease. *American Journal of Neuroradiology, 14,* 647–650.

Huckman, H.S., Fox, J., & Topel, J. (1975). The validity of criteria for evaluation of cerebral atrophy by computed tomography. *Radiology, 116,* 85–92.

Jack, C. R. Jr, Dickson, D. W., Parisi, J. E., Xu, Y. C., Cha, R. H., O'Brien, P. C., et al. (2002). Antemortem MRI findings correlate with hippocampal neuropathology in typical aging and dementia. *Neurology, 58,* 750–757.

Jack, C. R. Jr, Petersen, R. C., Xu, Y. C., O'Brien, P. C., Smith, G. E., Ivnik, R. J., et al. (1998). Rate of medial temporal lobe atrophy in typical aging and Alzheimer's disease. *Neurology, 51,* 993–999.

Jack, C. R. Jr, Petersen, R. C., Xu, Y. C., O'Brien, P. C., Smith, G. E., Ivnik, R. J., et al. (1999). Prediction of AD with MRI-based hippocampal volume in mild cognitive impairment. *Neurology, 52,* 1397–1403.

Jack, C. R., Petersen, R. C., O'Brien, P. C., & Tangalos, E. G. (1992). MR-based hippocampal volumetry in the diagnosis of Alzheimer's disease. *Neurology, 42,* 183–188.

Jacoby, R. J., Levy, R., & Dawson, J. M. (1980). Computed tomography in the elderly. 2. Senile dementia: Diagnosis and functional impairment. *British Journal of Psychiatry, 136,* 256–269.

Jara, H., Sakai, O., Mankal, P., Irving, R. P., & Norbash, A. M. (2006). Multispectral quantitative magnetic resonance imaging of brain iron stores: A theoretical perspective. *Topics in Magnetic Resonance Imaging, 17,* 19–30.

Johnson, N. A., Jahng, G., Weiner, M. W., Miller, B. L., Chui, H. C., Jagust, W. J., et al. (2005). Pattern of cerebral hypoperfustion in Alzheimer diseaes and mild cognitive impairment measured with arterial spin-labeling MR imaging: Initial experience. *Neuroradiology,* *234,* 851–859.

Johnson, S. C., Schmitz, T. W., Moritz, C. H., Meyerand, M. E., Rowley, H. A., Alexander, A. L., et al. (2006). Activation of brain regions vulnerable to Alzheimer's disease: The effect of mild cognitive impairment. *Neurobiology of Aging, 27*(11), 1604–1612.

Juottonen, K., Laakso, M. P, Partanen, K., & Soininen, H. (1999). Comparative MR analysis of the entorhinal cortex and hippocampus in diagnosing Alzheimer disease. *American* *Journal of Neuroradiology, 20,* 139–144.

Kantarci, K., Jack, C. R. Jr, Xu, Y. C., Campeau, N. G., O'Brien, P. C., Smith, G. E., et al. (2001). Mild cognitive impairment and Alzheimer disease: regional diffusivity of water. *Radiology, 219,* 101–107.

Kantarci, K., Xu, Y., Shiung, M. M., O'Brien, P. C., Cha, R. H., Smith, G. E., et al. (2002). Comparative diagnostic utility of different MR modalities in mild cognitive impairment and Alzheimer's disease. *Dementia and Geriatric Cognitive Disorders, 14*(4), 198–207.

Karas, G. B., Scheltens, P., Rombouts, S. A., Visser, P. J., van Schijndel, R. A., Fox, N. C., et al. (2004). Global and local gray matter loss in mild cognitive impairment and Alzheimer's disease. *Neuroimage, 23,* 708–716.

Kaye, J. A., Swihart, T., Howieson, D., Dame, A., Moore, M. M., Karnos, T., et al. (1997). Volume loss of the hippocampus and temporal lobe in healthy elderly persons destined to develop dementia. *Neurology, 48,* 1297–1304.

Kesslak, J. P., Nalcioglu, O., & Cotman, C. W. (1991). Quantification of magnetic resonance scans for hippocampal and parahippocampal atrophy in Alzheimer's disease. *Neurology,* *41,* 51–54.

Kido, D. K., Caine, E. D., Lemay, M., Ekholm, S., Booth, H., & Panzer, R. (1989). Temporal lobe atrophy in patients with Alzheimer's disease: A CT study. *American Journal of* *Neuroradiology, 10,* 551–555.

Killiany, R. J., Gomez-Isla, T., Moss, M. B, Kikinis, R., Sandor, T., Jolesz, F., et al. (2000). Use of structural magnetic resonance imaging to predict who will get Alzheimer's disease. *Annals of Neurology, 47,* 430–439.

Killiany, R. J., Hyman, B. T., Gomez-Isla, T., Moss, M. B, Kikinis, R., Jolesz, F., et al. (2002). MRI measures of entorhinal cortex vs. hippocampus in preclinical AD. *Neurology, 58,* 1188–1196.

Killiany, R. J., Moss, M. B, Albert, M. S., Sandor, T., Tieman, J., & Jolesz, F. (1993). Temporal lobe regions on magnetic resonance imaging identify patients with early Alzheimer's disease. *Archives of Neurology, 50,* 949–954.

Killiany, R. J., Moss, M. B, Nicholson, T., Jolesz, F., & Sandor, T. (1997). An interactive procedure for extracting features of the brain from magnetic resonance images: The lobes. *Human Brain Mapping, 5,* 355–363.

Kohler, S., Black, S. E., Sinden, M., Szekely, C., Kidron, D., Parker, J. L., et al., (1998). Memory impairments associated with hippocampal versus parahippocampal-gyrusatrophy: An MR volumetry study in Alzheimer's disease. *Neuropsychologia, 36,* 901–914.

Laakso, M. P., Hallikainen, M., Hanninen, T., Partanen, K., & Soininen, H. (2000). Diagnosis of Alzheimer's disease: MRI of the hippocampus vs. delayed recall. *Neuropsychologia,* *38,* 579–584.

Laakso, M. P., Lehtovirta, M., Partanen, K., Riekkinen, P. J., & Soininen, H. (2000). Hippocampus in Alzheimer's disease: A 3-year follow-up MRI study. *Biological* *Psychiatry, 47,* 557–561.

Laakso, M. P., Soininen, H., Partanen, K., Hallikainen, M., Lehtovirta, M., Haninen, T., et al. (1995). The interuncal distance in Alzheimer's disease and age associated memory impairment. *American Journal of Neuroradiology, 16*, 727–734.

Laakso, M. P., Soininen, H., Partanen, K., Helkala, E. L., Hartikainen, P., Vainio, P., et al. (1995). Volumes of hippocampus, amygdala and frontal lobes in the MRI-based diagnosis of early Alzheimer's disease: Correlation with memory functions. *Journal of Neural Transmission. Parkinson's Disease and Dementia Section, 9*, 73–86.

Laakso, M. P., Soininen, H., Partanen, K., Lehtovirta, M., Hallikainen, M., Hanninen, T., et al. (1998). MRI of the hippocampus in Alzheimer's disease: Sensitivity, specificity, and analysis of the incorrectly classified subjects. *Neurobiology of Aging, 19*, 23–31.

Laakso, M.P., Frisoni, G.B., Kononen, M., Mikkonen, M., Beltramello, A., Geroldi, C., et al. (2000). Hippocampus and entorhinal cortex in frontotemporal dementia and Alzheimer's disease: A morphometric MRI study. *Biological Psychiatry, 47*, 1056–1063.

Le May, M., Stafford, J. L., Sandor, T., Albert, M., Haykal, H., & Xamani, A. (1986). Statistical assessment of perceptual CT scan ratings in patients with Alzheimer's type dementia. *Journal of Computer Assisted Tomography, 10*, 802–809.

Lehtovirta, M., Laakso, M. P., Soininen, H., Helisalmi, S., Mannermaa, A., Helkala, E. L., et al. (1995). Volumes of hippocampus, amygdala and frontal lobe in Alzheimer patients with different apolipoprotein E genotypes. *Neuroscience, 67*, 65–72.

Loewenstein, D. A., Acevedo, A., Potter, E., Schinka, J. A., Raj, A., Greig, M. T., et al. (2009). Severity of medial temporal atrophy and amnestic mild cognitive impairment: Selecting type and number of memory tests. *American Journal of Geriatric Psychiatry, 17*, 1050–1058.

Luxenberg, J. S., Friedland, R. P., & Rapoport, S. I. (1986). Quantitative X-ray computed tomography (CT) in dementia of the Alzheimer's type. *Canadian Journal of Neurological Sciences, 13*, 570–572.

Luxenberg, J. S., Haxby, J. V., Creasey, H., Sundaram, M., & Rapoport, S. I. (1987). Rate of ventricular enlargement in dementia of the Alzheimer type correlates with rate of neuropsychological deterioration. *Neurology, 37*, 1135–1140.

Makris, N., Hodge, S. M., Haselgrove, C., Kennedy, D. N., Dale, A., Fischl, B., et al. (2003). Human cerebellum: Surface-assisted cortical parcellation and volumetry with magnetic resonance imaging. *Journal of Cognitive Neuroscience, 15*, 584–599.

Makris, N., Worth, A. J., Sorensen, A. G., Papadimitriou, G. M., Wu, O., Reese, T. G., et al. (1997). Morphometry of in vivo human white matter association pathways with diffusion-weighted magnetic resonance imaging. *Annals of Neurology, 42*, 951–962.

Markesbery, W. R. (2010). Neuropathologic alterations in mild cognitive impairment: A review. *Journal of Alzheimer's Disease, 19*, 221–228.

Medina, D., de Taledo-Morrell, L., Urresta, F., Gabrieli, J., Moseley, M., Fleischman, D., et al. (2006). White matter changes in mild cognitive impairment and AD: A diffusion tensor imaging study, *Neurobiology of Aging, 27*(5), 663–672.

Miller, M. I., Hosakere, M., Barker, A. R., Priebe, C. E., Lee, N., Ratnanather, J. T., et al. (2003). Labeled cortical mantle distance maps of the cingulate quantify differences between dementia of the Alzheimer type and healthy aging. *Proceedings of the National Academy of Sciences USA, 100*, 15172–15177.

Modrego, P. J., Fayed, N., Errea, J. M., Rios, C., Pina, M. A., & Sarasa, M. (2010). Memantine versus donepezil in mild to moderate Alzheimer's disease: A randomized trial with magnetic resonance spectroscopy. *European Journal of Neurology, 17*(3), 405–412.

Morris, J. C., Storandt, M., Miller, J. P., McKeel, D. W., Price, J. L., Rubin, E. H., et al. (2001). Mild cognitive impairment represents early-stage Alzheimer disease. *Archives of Neurology, 58,* 397–405.

Pennanen, C., Kivipelto, M., Tuomainen, S., Hartikainen, P., Hanninen, T., Laakso, M. P., et al. (2004). Hippocampus and entorhinal cortex in mild cognitive impairment and early AD. *Neurobiology of Aging, 25,* 303–310.

Pennanen, C., Testa, C., Laakso, M. P., Hallikainen, M., Helkala, E. L., Hanninen, T., et al. (2005). A voxel based morphometry study on mild cognitive impairment. *Journal of Neurology, Neurosurgery & Psychiatry, 76,* 11–14.

Petersen, R. C., Jack, C. R. Jr, Xu, Y. C., Waring, S. C., O'Brien, P. C., Smith, G. E., et al. (2000). Memory and MRI-based hippocampal volumes in aging and AD. *Neurology, 54,* 581–587.

Price, J. L., & Morris, J. C. (1999). Tangles and plaques in nondemented aging and "preclinical" Alzheimer's disease. *Annals of Neurology, 45,* 358–368.

Raz, N., Raz, S., Yeo, R. A., Turkheimer, E., Bigler, E. D., & Cullum, C. M. (1987). Relationship between cognitive and morphological asymmetry in dementia of the Alzheimer type: A CT scan study. *International Journal of Neuroscience, 35,* 225–232.

Risacher, S. L., Saykin, A. J., West, J. D., Shen, L., Firpi, H. A., & McDonald, B. C. (2009). Baseline MRI predictors of conversion from MCI to probable AD in the ADNI cohort. *Current Alzheimer Research, 6,* 347–361.

Rose, S. E., Chen, F., Chalk, J. B., Zelaya, F. O., Strugnell, W. E., Benson, M., et al. (2000). Loss of connectivity in Alzheimer's disease: An evaluation of white matter tract integrity with color coded MR diffusioin tensor imaging. *Journal of Neurology, Neurosurgery & Psychiatry, 69,* 528–530.

Saka, E., Dogan, E. A., Topcuoolu, M. A., Senol, U., & Balkan, S. (2007). Linear measures of temporal lobe atrophy on brain magnetic resonance imaging but not visual ratings of white matter changes can help discrimination of mild cognitive impairment and Alzheimer's disease. *Archives of Gerontology and Geriatrics, 44,* 141–151.

Salmond, C. H., Menon, D. K., Chatfield, D. A., Williams, G. B., Pena, A., Sahakian, B. J., et al. (2006). Diffusion tensor imaging in chronic head injury survivors: Correlations with learning and memory indices. *Neuroimage, 29,* 117–124.

Sanchez-Benavides, G., Gomez-Anson, B., Sainz, A., Vives, Y., Delfino, M., & Pena-Casanova, J. (2010). Manual validation of FreeSurfer's automated hippocampal segmentation in normal aging, mild cognitive impairment, and Alzheimer Disease subjects. *Psychiatry Research, 181,* 219–225.

Sandon, T. A., Felician, O., Edelman, R. R., & Warach, S. (1999). Diffusion weighted magnetic resonance imaging in Alzheimer's diseae. *Dementia, 10,* 166–171.

Sandor, S., & Leahy, R. (1997). Surface-based labeling of cortical anatomy using a deformable atlas. *IEEE Transactions in Medical Imaging, 16,* 41–54.

Sandor, T., Albert, M., Stafford, J., & Harpley, J. S. (1988). Discrimination of Alzheimer patients and normal controls using a computerized CT analysis. *American Journal of Neuroradiology, 9,* 1181–1187.

Scahill, R. I., Schott, J. M., Stevens, J. M., Rossor, M. N., & Fox, N. C. (2002). Mapping the evolution of regional atrophy in Alzheimer's disease: unbiased analysis of fluid-registered serial MRI. *Proceedings of the National Academy of Sciences USA, 99,* 4703–4707.

Schenck, J. F., Zimmerman, E. A., Li, Z., Adak, S., Saha, A., Tandon, R., et al. (2006). High-field magnetic resonance imaging of brain iron in Alzheimer disease. *Topics in Magnetic Resonance Imaging, 17,* 41–50.

Schmahmann, J. D., Doyon, J., McDonald, D., Holmes, C., Lavoie, K., Hurwitz, A. S., et al. (1999). Three-dimensional MRI atlas of the human cerebellum in proportional stereotaxic space. *Neuroimage, 10,* 233–260.

Scoville, W. B., & Milner, B. (1957). Loss of recent memory after bilateral hippocampal lesions. *Journal of Neurology, Neurosurgery & Psychiatry, 20,* 11–21.

Seab, J. P., Jagust, W. J., Wong, S. T., Roos, M. S., Reed, B. R., & Budinger, T. F. (1988). Quantitative NMR measurements of hippocampal atrophy in Alzheimer's disease. *Magnetic Resonance in Medicine, 8,* 200–208.

Simmons, A., Westman, E., Muehlboeck, S., Mecocci, P., Vellas, B., Tsolaki, M., et al. (2010). MRI measures of Alzheimer's disease and the AddNeuroMed study. *Annals of the New York Academy of Science, 1180,* 47–55.

Stebbins, G. T., & Murphy, C. M. (2009). Diffusion tensor imaging in Alzheimer's disease and mild cognitive impairment. *Behavioral Neurology, 21,* 39–49.

Storandt, M., Mintun, M. A., Head, D., & Morris, J. C. (2009). Cognitive decline and brain volume loss as signatures of cerebral amyloid-beta peptide deposition identified with Pittsburgh compound B: Cognitive decline associated with Abeta deposition. *Archives of Neurology, 66,* 1476–1481.

Talagala, S. L., & Noll, D. C. (1998). Functional MRI using steady-state arterial water labeling. *Magnetic Resonance in Medicine, 39,* 179–183.

Talagala, S. L., Ye, F. Q., Ledden, P. J., & Chesnick, S. (2004). Whole-brain 3D perfusion MRI at 3.0 T using CASAL with a separate labeling coil. *Magnetic Resonance in Medicine, 52,* 131–140.

Tapiola, T., Pennanen, C., Tapiola, M., Tervo, S., Kivipelto, M., Hanninen, T., et al. (2006). MRI of hippocampus and entorhinal cortex in mild cognitive impairment: A follow-up study. *Neurobiology of Aging,* November 9, Epub.

Thompson, P. M., Mega, M. S., Woods, R. P., Zoumalan, C. I., Lindshield, C. J., Blanton, R. E., et al. (2001). Cortical change in Alzheimer's disease detected with a disease-specific population-based brain atlas. *Cerebral Cortex, 11,* 1–16.

Ulug, A. M., Moore, D. F., Bojko, A. S., & Zimmerman, R. D. (1999). Clinical use of diffusion-tensor imaging for diseases causing neuronal and axonal damage. *American Journal of Neuroradiology, 20,* 1044–1048.

Upadhyay, J., Hallock, K., Ducros, M., Kim, D. S., & Ronen, I. (2008). Diffusion tensor spectroscopy and imaging of the arcuate fasciculas. *Neuroimage, 39*(1), 1–9.

Upadhyay, J., Hallock, K., Erb, K., Kim, D. S., & Ronen, I. (2007). Diffusion properties of NAA in human corpus calluson as studied with diffusion tensor spectroscopy. *Magnetic Resonance in Medicine, 58*(5), 1045-53.

Valenzuela, M. J., & Sachdev, P. (2001). Magnetic resonance spectroscopy in AD. *Neurology, 56,* 592–598.

Visser, P. J., Scheltens, P., Verhey, F. R., Schmand, B., Launer, L. J., Jolles, J., et al. (1999). Medial temporal lobe atrophy and memory dysfunction as predictors for dementia. *Journal of Neurology, 246,* 477–485.

Walhovd, K. B., Fjell, A. M., Brewer, J., McEvoy, L. K., Fennema-Notestine, C., Hagler, D. J., Jr., et al. (2010). Combining MR imaging, positron-emission tomography, and CSF biomarkers in the diagnosis and prognosis of Alzheimer disease. *American Journal of Neuroradiology, 31,* 347–354.

Wang, L., Harms, M. P., Staggs, J. M., Xiong, C., Morris, J. C., Csernansky, J. G., et al. (2010). Donepezil treatment and changes in hippocampal structure in very mild Alzheimer disease. *Archives of Neurology, 67,* 99–106.

Wible, C. G., Shenton, M. E., Fischer, I. A., Allard, J. E., Kikinis, R., Jolesz, F. A., et al. (1997). Parcellation of the human prefrontal cortex using MRI. *Psychiatry Research, 76,* 29–40.

Wright, I. C., McGuire, P. K., Poline, J. B., Travere, J. M., Murray, R. M., Frith, C. D., et al. (1995). A voxel-based method for the statistical analysis of gray and white matter density applied to schizophrenia. *Neuroimage, 2,* 244–252.

Xu, Y., Jack, C. R. Jr, O'Brien, P. C., Kokmen, E., Smith, G. E., Ivnik, R. J., et al. (2000). Usefulness of MRI measures of entorhinal cortex versus hippocampus in AD. *Neurology, 54,* 1760–1767.

Yassa, M. A., Stark, S. M., Bakker, A., Albert, M. S., Gallagher, M., & Stark, C. E. (2010). High-resolution structural and functional MRI of hippocampal CA3 and dentate gyrus in patients with amnestic mild cognitive impairment. *Neuroimage, 51*(3), 1242–1252.

Yoshita, M., Fletcher, E., Harvey, D., Ortega, M., Martinez, O., Mungas, D. M., et al. (2006). Extent and distribution of white matter hyperintensities in normal aging, MCI, and AD. *Neurology, 67,* 2192–2198.

Yoshiura, T., Mihara, F., Ogomori, K., Tanaka, A., Kaneko, K., & Masuda, K. (2002). Diffusion tensor in posterior cingulate gyrus: Correlation with cognitive decline in Alzheimer's disease. *Neuroreport, 13,* 2299–2302.

18

Functional MRI in Alzheimer's Disease and Other Dementias

Maija Pihlajamäki and Reisa A. Sperling

Introduction

During the past 10 years, functional MRI (fMRI) has proved to be a very useful tool in investigating the neural correlates of intact human memory and other higher cognitive functions. Clinical fMRI research into the pathophysiology of age-associated neurodegenerative diseases, in turn, has become established more recently. The neural basis of cognitive impairment characteristic of Alzheimer's disease (AD) and other neurodegenerative dementias is still largely unknown. Tools such as fMRI contribute to the common effort to solve the remaining mysteries of neurodegenerative diseases by offering a unique means to investigate function and dysfunction of the whole-brain neural networks in vivo. In combination with other imaging techniques and other types of dementia research, fMRI holds significant promise to improve diagnostic and treatment options for these devastating diseases.

Neurodegenerative dementias result in progressive brain atrophy and inevitable neurological deterioration. Structural imaging findings may, however, be relatively nonspecific in the early detection of dementias, though, for example, the presence of atrophy in the medial temporal and parietotemporal cortices supports the diagnosis of AD. Correspondingly, [18F]fluorodeoxyglucose positron emission tomography (FDG-PET) imaging has consistently revealed bilateral hypometabolism in the parietotemporal association cortices in AD patients. Routine clinical evaluation of cognitively impaired elderly subjects does include structural computed tomography (CT) or magnetic resonance imaging (MRI) but functional imaging is

The Handbook of Alzheimer's Disease and Other Dementias, First Edition.
Edited by Andrew E. Budson, Neil W. Kowall.
© 2011 Blackwell Publishing Ltd. Published 2011 by Blackwell Publishing Ltd.

currently only occasionally used in neurological everyday diagnostics. Large-scale imaging studies are, however, ongoing and there is a great hope that functional imaging would facilitate early diagnosis of dementias in the near future.

This chapter focuses on fMRI research on AD, the most common form of dementia. We will also examine the use of fMRI in investigating subjects at increased risk to develop AD, such as subjects with mild cognitive impairment (MCI) and cognitively intact elderly subjects carrying the apolipoprotein E ε4 allele (APOE ε4). To date, fMRI studies in patients with neurodegenerative dementias other than AD are few. These studies and the potential use of functional imaging in differential diagnosis of dementias will be considered, as well as the usage of fMRI in monitoring treatment effects. We will also review some earlier resting FDG-PET and PET activation studies as a basis for currently predominant trends in the field of functional neuroimaging of dementias. Finally, limitations of fMRI and goals of the future research are discussed.

Physiological Basis of fMRI in Dementia

Functional neuroimaging provides in vivo methods to investigate the integrity of resting human brain on the one hand, and mapping neural networks supporting higher cognitive functions such as memory on the other, by means of measuring regional hemodynamic changes related to underlying cellular activity (Logothetis et al., 2001; Shmuel et al., 2006). Nowadays, the majority of cognitive functional imaging is performed using fMRI, instead of PET, because unlike PET fMRI is non-invasive, radiation-free and offers a combination of good spatial and reasonable temporal resolution. The term "fMRI" is used here in a narrow sense, to encompass cerebral activation imaging but not, for example, MRI techniques used to image tissue blood flow or water diffusion.

The fMRI technique most widely used to identify cerebral activation is based on imaging of the endogenous blood-oxygen-level-dependent (BOLD) contrast (Kwong et al., 1992; Ogawa et al., 1992). As FDG-PET is principally a measure of synaptic activity, BOLD fMRI is considered to reflect the integrated synaptic activity of neurons via MRI signal changes due to changes in blood flow, blood volume, and blood oxyhemoglobin/deoxyhemoglobin ratio (Logothetis et al., 2001). In addition to observed increases in BOLD signal in activated brain areas, it has recently been shown that "negative" BOLD responses are also related to underlying neural activity and originate in decreases in neuronal activity below spontaneous activity (Shmuel et al., 2006).

Typically, fMRI experiments compare the MRI signal during one cognitive condition (e.g., memory encoding) to a control task (e.g., viewing familiar stimuli) or to a passive baseline condition (e.g., visual fixation). This can be done in a "block design" paradigm (Figure 18.1, plate section), in which stimuli of each cognitive condition are grouped together in blocks lasting 20–40 s, or in "event-related" paradigms, in which single stimuli from several different conditions are interspersed.

The peak hemodynamic response is typically observed 4–6 s after the stimulus onset. Time courses of the task-induced positive and negative BOLD responses are similar and spatially these two types of responses are typically adjacent, though segregated from each other (Shmuel et al., 2006).

In addition to functional activation studies, there has recently been considerable interest in studying the neuronal baseline activity, or the "default mode" activity, of the resting human brain using PET and fMRI (Buckner et al., 2005; Gusnard & Raichle, 2001). Cognitive processes such as self-consciousness and self-related mental representations are suggested to take place during the awake resting state and activate posterior midline cortical brain areas such as the posterior cingulate and precuneus, in particular (Cavanna & Trimble, 2006). It is very interesting that the same brain areas which show high "default mode" activity and predilection for task-induced fMRI deactivation responses, also have demonstrated the earliest hypometabolic changes in AD in previous FDG-PET studies (Buckner et al., 2005; Minoshima et al., 1997; Nestor et al., 2003).

The BOLD fMRI signal, and neurovascular coupling linking cellular activity to hemodynamic changes, is likely to undergo changes during healthy aging and during pathological processes related to neurodegenerative dementias (D'Esposito et al., 2003; Iadecola, 2004). In AD, the presence of beta amyloid (Aβ) in the brain, together with altered cholinergic activity, impairs synaptic, neuronal and glial function, and may thus lead to attenuated BOLD response (Iadecola, 2004; D'Esposito et al., 2003; Selkoe, 2002). Both increased and decreased BOLD fMRI as well as PET activation responses have, however, been reported in AD compared to elderly controls, which does not support the view of attenuation of the BOLD signal solely due to vascular reasons (Backman et al., 1999; Golby et al., 2005; Grady et al., 2003; Sperling et al., 2003a). On the other hand, it has been suggested that choline acetyl-transferase activity is upregulated in MCI in a regionally specific way (DeKosky et al., 2002), which in turn may enhance blood flow and evoke increased BOLD fMRI signal. This is in line with recent fMRI studies that have reported increased medial temporal lobe (MTL) activation in MCI subjects compared to controls (Dickerson et al., 2004; Dickerson et al., 2005; Hämäläinen et al., 2007; Kircher et al., 2007). Thus, it is possible that the differences in brain fMRI activation patterns observed between control subjects and patients with neurodegenerative dementias are both due to disease-related neuropathological changes and changes in neurovascular coupling measured by fMRI. Taken together, fMRI based on BOLD contrast offers a unique and widely available technique for the study of intact human cognition as well as alterations in neuronal function related to healthy aging and dysfunction related to neurodegenerative diseases.

FMRI Activation Studies in AD

"Memory" refers to the mind's ability to retain and retrieve past experiences. Successful memory formation is a complex cognitive process that is thought to require interplay of several large-scale neural networks, in particular, the MTL and heteromodal association cortices (Eichenbaum, 2000; Mesulam, 1998). The MTL structures, i.e., the hippocampus with the adjacent parahippocampal region, are known to be critical for encoding new events into long-term memory (Eichenbaum, 2000; Squire & Zola-Morgan 1991). Activation of the hippocampal and parahippocampal regions during (successful) memory encoding has also been demonstrated in several fMRI studies in young healthy subjects (Brewer et al., 1998; Pihlajamäki et al., 2003; Sperling et al., 2003b; Stern et al., 1996; Wagner et al., 1998).

The hallmark of early AD is the inability to form new enduring episodic memories. At the same time, mild AD patients typically present with neuropathological changes such as synaptic alterations, selective neuronal loss, and neurofibrillary tangles in the MTL structures (Braak & Braak 1991; Gomez-Isla et al., 1997; Scheff et al., 2006). Interestingly, FDG-PET imaging has described the most consistent findings in early AD not in the MTL itself but in strongly interconnected projection areas such as posterior cingulate and parietal regions (Herholz et al., 2002; Minoshima et al., 1997; Nestor et al., 2003; Rapoport, 1991). It has been demonstrated that the posterior parietal hypometabolism is positively correlated with hippocampal atrophy, that is, more atrophy is related to a more severe hypometabolism (Meguro et al., 2001) but that PET measurements of glucose metabolism begin to decrease before the onset of memory decline and before significant atrophy in structural MRI (Reiman et al., 1998). In contrast, the frontal lobes are considered to be relatively spared in early AD in terms of distribution of histopathological changes, volume loss, or perfusion deficits (Braak & Braak, 1991; Johnson & Albert, 2000; Lehtovirta et al., 1996).

Given the prominence of MTL pathology in early AD, the pioneering fMRI studies on AD focused on utilizing episodic memory tasks and investigating alterations in activation of the MTL structures (Kato et al., 2001; Machulda et al., 2003; Rombouts et al., 2000; Small et al., 1999; Sperling et al., 2003a). To date, there are several fMRI studies, which have consistently reported diminished hippocampal and/or parahippocampal activation in AD compared to healthy older controls, during encoding novel information (Dickerson et al., 2005; Golby et al., 2005; Grön & Riepe, 2004; Hämäläinen et al., 2007; Kato et al., 2001; Machulda et al., 2003; Pariente et al., 2005; Remy et al., 2005; Rombouts et al., 2000; Small et al., 1999; Sperling et al., 2003a). The studies with clinical AD patients have used a number of encoding stimuli, including faces (Rombouts et al., 2005; Small et al., 1999), face–name pairs (Pariente et al., 2005; Sperling et al., 2003a), line drawings (Hämäläinen et al., 2007; Rombouts et al., 2000), scenes (Golby et al., 2005), and geometric shapes (Kato et al., 2001). The study by Machulda et al. (2003) also included a passive sensory task into the fMRI protocol and reported, in contrast to differences in the MTL activation during memory encoding, no difference in brain activation during the sensory palm-brushing task between AD patients and normal older subjects.

Interestingly, there is also evidence of increased activation in AD during specific contrasts, primarily involving the brain response to repetitive stimuli. Golby et al. (2005) reported more MTL activation in AD patients than in older controls during processing of repeated scenes. In line with Golby et al. (2005), our recent work provides evidence that, as measured by BOLD fMRI, the normal suppression of the MTL activity to repeated face–name pairs as compared to visual fixation is impaired in AD (Pihlajamäki et al., 2008). In addition to abnormal increased MTL responses, AD patients in fact show greater activation in several areas of the "novelty detection network", including prefrontal and parietal cortices. Moreover, impaired fMRI response suppression was related to poor post-scan associative recognition memory performance in AD (Pihlajamäki et al., 2008). We suggest that intact MTL repetition suppression is part of the successful encoding/consolidation process and that failure of repetition suppression is a potential indicator of impaired MTL function early in the course of AD. Another recent study investigated repetition priming in AD during simple semantic living/nonliving decisions on words (Lustig & Buckner, 2004). These authors found that reductions in inferior frontal responses correlated with repetition-related response time reductions in AD equal to controls and thus suggested that implicit memory and corresponding cortical brain responses are well preserved in AD. Furthermore, AD patients, and also MCI subjects, have been documented to show more activation in "middle temporal" and several other brain areas during a visual working memory task compared to controls (Yetkin et al., 2006).

Thus, it can be concluded that decreased or absent MTL activation is a consistent finding in AD during episodic memory tasks and novel encoding in particular. This result is in good agreement with the known hierarchical evolution of neuropathology starting in the MTL (Braak & Braak, 1991) and the characteristic memory difficulty in early AD. Findings of decreased fMRI activation can, however, not necessarily be generalized to other kinds of cognitive tasks such as paradigms involving repetitive stimuli (Golby et al., 2005; Pihlajamäki et al., 2008) or other brain areas that are not as severely neuropathologically affected than the MTL. Altogether, the results reviewed above provide evidence that episodic memory impairment typically seen in mild AD may not only manifest as decreased but also as increased activation of the MTL memory structures under certain cognitive circumstances.

In addition to episodic memory, several fMRI studies have investigated the neural basis semantic memory difficulties in clinical AD (Grossman et al., 2003; Saykin et al., 1999). These studies revealed both similarities and differences in semantic processing between AD and controls. For example, during processing of words belonging to "animals" and "implements" categories, AD patients showed reduced temporoparietal activation compared to processing pseudowords. During processing "animals" or "implements" only, the authors found, correspondingly, dislocated ventral temporal and frontostriatal activation areas in AD compared to controls. Thus, they concluded that both category-neutral and category-specific knowledge is degraded in AD but that AD patients still are to some extent able to modulate the function of the semantic memory networks in order to maintain task performance despite neuropathology (Grossman et al., 2003). One recent multimodal functional imaging study combined PET imaging with the [^{11}C]Pittsburgh Combound B (PIB) amyloid ligand and fMRI activation imaging during associative-semantic versus visuoperceptual judgments (Nelissen et al., 2007). The fMRI response of the left posterior superior temporal sulcus was lower in AD than in controls during the semantic compared with the perceptual task. Interestingly, the BOLD response amplitude correlated inversely with PIB uptake in this region, in other words more Aβ was related to less fMRI activation in that brain area. This study indicates that regional alterations in BOLD fMRI responses may be able to reflect the Aβ burden in the AD brain. Future imaging studies combining several modalities such as PIB-PET and fMRI are likely to expand our knowledge of the relationships between cognitive impairment, neuropathological changes, and alterations in functional imaging patterns.

It is clear that not only the hippocampus but also the whole-brain neural networks, interconnected with the MTL, are critical for higher cognitive functions such as episodic memory (Buckner et al., 2005; Eichenbaum, 2000; Mesulam, 1998). It can be hypothesized that – as opposed to focal changes in the MTL only – multiple nodes within these networks and their mutual connectivity is affected already in the earliest stage of AD (Scheff et al., 2006; Selkoe, 2002). Correspondingly, in addition to consistent findings of decreased MTL activation during novel encoding, several groups have found evidence of increased fMRI or PET activation in neocortical brain regions, such as frontal and parietal cortices in mild AD patients compared to controls (Bäckman et al., 1999; Celone et al., 2006; Grady et al., 2003; Pariente et al., 2005; Sperling et al., 2003a). This may represent a compensatory process in the setting of MTL dysfunction. A series of two recent event-related fMRI studies investigated this notion of compensatory increased cortical brain responses in AD (Gould et al., 2005; Gould et al., 2006a). The authors utilized a visuospatial paired-associates task and aimed to equalize task performance between patient and control groups by giving them multiple learning trials. No significant differences in brain activations were found between AD patients who performed an easy version of the task and controls who performed a more difficult version of the task (Gould et al., 2005). Furthermore, when task performance was not equated between groups, greater recruitment of the same, rather than different, brain regions was found as a try to compensate for existing AD-related cognitive impairment (Gould et al., 2006a). In summary, there is converging functional imaging evidence that AD patients show increases in brain activity to compensate for cognitive difficulties in brain regions such as frontal areas that are less affected in early stages of the disease (Braak & Braak 1991; Johnson & Albert 2000; Lehtovirta et al., 1996).

Our own fMRI studies in AD have focused on face–name associative memory encoding tasks (Celone et al., 2006; Dickerson et al., 2005; Sperling et al., 2002; Sperling et al., 2003a; Sperling et al., 2003b). Learning the names of new individuals we encounter can be thought of as a particularly difficult cross-modal, non-contextual, paired-associate memory task. The hippocampal formation is known to be necessary in this process, acting to "bind" together items of information into a cohesive memory (Eichenbaum, 2000). Several neuropsychological studies have suggested that difficult paired-associate memory tasks may be particularly useful in detecting the earliest memory impairment in AD. Our research indicates that the MTL activation is disrupted early in the process of AD (Celone et al., 2006; Dickerson et al., 2005; Sperling et al., 2003a) but not in normal aging (Rand-Giovannetti et al., 2006; Sperling et al., 2003a). In these studies, we found that older subjects show significant activation in the hippocampal formation during novel encoding (Sperling et al., 2003a) and that they also demonstrate intact BOLD response suppression in the MTL to repeated stimuli (Rand-Giovannetti et al., 2006). In contrast, the mild AD patients did not show any evidence of hippocampal activation (Sperling et al., 2003a). In a random-effects between-group comparison, the only regions showing significantly decreased activation in the mild AD patients compared to normal older subjects, were found in the hippocampal formation (Figure 18.2, plate section). These studies are in line with the majority of fMRI studies reviewed above demonstrating failure of MTL function consonant with the characteristic inability to form new enduring episodic memories seen in early AD (Dickerson et al., 2005; Golby et al., 2005; Grön & Riepe, 2004; Hämäläinen et al., 2007; Kato et al., 2001; Machulda et al., 2003; Pariente et al., 2005; Remy et al., 2005; Rombouts et al., 2000; Small et al., 1999; Sperling et al., 2003a).

FMRI Activation Studies in MCI

The term "mild cognitive impairment" (MCI) refers to the transitional state between the cognitive changes of healthy aging and the fully developed clinical features of neurodegenerative dementia (Petersen et al., 2001). Subjects with amnestic MCI are an important group to investigate, as they are at increased risk for developing dementia, AD in particular. Most studies suggest that approximately 12–15% of MCI subjects will progress to clinical dementia within one year. On the other hand, MCI is known to be a very heterogeneous population and a subset of these subjects will not show evidence of cognitive decline, even after several years of follow-up.

Consonant with the notion of heterogeneity, results of fMRI studies published so far in MCI have been variable regarding findings of MTL activation, ranging from hyperactivation (Dickerson et al., 2004; Dickerson et al., 2005; Hämäläinen et al., 2007; Kircher et al., 2007) to hypoactivation (Johnson et al., 2006a; Machulda et al., 2003; Petrella et al., 2006). However, typically MCI subjects with significantly impaired memory have, similar to AD patients, shown decreased MTL activation compared with controls (Machulda et al., 2003; Petrella et al., 2006). The preliminary study by Small et al. (1999), at a time before the concept and criteria of MCI were widely used, examined the extent of MTL hypoactivation during encoding of novel faces in elderly subjects with isolated memory impairment compared to both healthy elderly controls and AD patients. The authors suggested that in subjects with isolated memory impairment, hypoactivation involving all the hippocampal subregions and entorhinal cortex was predictive of subsequent progression to clinical dementia, whereas hypoactivation limited to the subiculum only was not a predictor of dementia. Reduced activation in MCI subjects compared to healthy elderly has also been reported in the lateral temporal neocortex, i.e., in the superior temporal sulcus, during an associative semantic memory task (Vandenbulcke et al., 2007).

Our work, using both scene and face–name encoding stimuli, has suggested that older subjects with very mild cognitive impairment show evidence of increased MTL activation, and that this hyperactivation is related to memory performance such that MCI subjects with greater clinical impairment recruit MTL regions to a larger extent during novel encoding than less impaired subjects (Dickerson et al., 2004; Dickerson et al., 2005). Furthermore, in a recent study (Celone et al., 2006), utilizing independent component analyses, we demonstrated that "early" MCI subjects with low Clinical Dementia Rating Scale Sum of Box (CDR-SB) scores showed greater hippocampal activation than "late" MCI with high CDR-SB score consistent with studies mentioned above (Johnson et al., 2006a; Machulda et al., 2003; Petrella et al., 2006). The idea that subjects with "early" MCI are capable of showing increased MTL activation to compensate for their mild memory problems is supported by an event-related fMRI study demonstrating that MCI subjects have greater MTL activation during successful encoding of words than healthy elderly as measured by post-scan recognition test (Kircher et al., 2007). Another recent study reported that the increased and posteriorly dislocated hippocampal and parahippocampal activation during associative encoding in MCI compared to controls may be compensatory due to the incipient atrophy in the anterior parts of the MTL (Hämäläinen et al., 2007). Thus, we have hypothesized that there may be an initial phase of hyperactivation in very mildly impaired subjects, followed by decreased activation with progression of pathology and memory impairment (Figure 18.3, plate section). At the stage of clinical AD, the MTL activation during novel encoding is decreased or absent, reflecting the fact that AD patients are no longer able to compensate for their memory difficulty due to extensive dysfunction and neuronal loss. Longitudinal functional imaging studies are needed to follow-up the natural evolution of the MTL activation pattern at the level of individual subjects from normal aging via amnestic MCI to AD.

Consistent with the findings of disrupted MTL repetition suppression in AD (Golby et al., 2005; Pihlajamäki et al., 2008) and intact repetition suppression in healthy aging (Rand-Giovannetti et al., 2006), impaired adaptation of the MTL response to repeated face stimuli has been reported in MCI (Johnson et al., 2004) suggesting that the early steps of memory consolidation may be compromised already in subjects with MCI. In addition to the converging evidence that initial encoding of novel information is impaired in MCI (Dickerson et al., 2004; Dickerson et al., 2005; Hämäläinen et al., 2007; Johnson et al., 2004; Johnson et al., 2006a; Kircher et al., 2007; Machulda et al., 2003; Petrella et al., 2006), it is also possible that retrieval of recently acquired information is disrupted in MCI. One recent fMRI study examined both encoding and retrieval processes in MCI compared to healthy elderly and reported less activity in the hippocampus during encoding of novel items as well as less activity in the posterior cingulate during recognition of previously learned items (Johnson et al., 2006a). In addition to the clinical significance, this study also nicely demonstrates the capability of functional imaging, different from traditional neuropsychological methods, to investigate brain correlates of specific memory processes such as encoding and retrieval. One event-related fMRI study which utilized a verbal recognition memory task (discrimination of studied versus new words) showed more prefrontal activation in MCI than in controls during correct behavioral responses (Heun et al., 2007). In two other recent studies, a combination of a visual episodic recognition task and an autobiographical self-appraisal task was chosen to investigate the function of the posterior midline cortical regions in MCI (Ries et al., 2006; Ries et al., 2007). Interestingly, the posterior midline cortical activation was found to be decreased more in MCI during episodic retrieval than during self-appraisal (Ries et al., 2006). However, the authors also reported in a subsequent study that posterior midline cortical activation during the autobiographical self-appraisal task was related to the self-awareness of memory deficits in MCI (Ries et al., 2007), suggesting that dysfunction of the posterior midline cortices may be related to anosognosia, which may be more prevalent in MCI than previously thought.

Finally, learning, memory, and attention are closely related cognitive functions. One study investigated divided attention in amnestic MCI and found attenuated prefrontal activation compared with age-matched controls, whereas there was no difference between the MCI and control groups during a passive sensory processing task (Dannhauser et al., 2005). Additionally, two recent fMRI studies during a face-matching task also suggested that functional connectivity of the infero-temporal regions might be a sensitive indicator of emerging AD pathology in MCI (Bokde et al., 2006; Teipel et al., 2007).

Not surprisingly given the heterogeneity of the populations, fMRI results in MCI are not as consistent as findings in established clinical AD. Similar to AD, subjects with advanced MCI show decreased MTL activity and are capable in either recruiting neocortical regions to a larger extent or recruiting additional brain areas to support cognitive performance. The most interesting, important, and challenging group to investigate, however, is composed of the elderly subjects with subtle emerging cognitive impairment without significant structural atrophy. Again, combination of fMRI to other imaging modalities such as structural MRI and PIB-PET may help to understand the pathophysiology and heterogeneity of MCI and identify subjects at-risk for near future conversion to clinical dementia.

FMRI Activation Studies in Subjects at Risk for AD

The main known genetic risk factor for AD is the apolipoprotein E (APOE) ε4 allele. Similar to FDG-PET findings in AD (Herholz et al., 2002; Rapoport, 1991) and MCI (Minoshima et al., 1997; Nestor et al., 2003), posterior association cortical areas such as the posterior cingulate and precuneus have consistently shown hypometabolism already in cognitively intact carriers of APOE ε4 (Reiman et al., 1996; Small et al., 1995). As in MCI subjects, results of fMRI studies comparing activation in APOE ε4 carriers versus their non-carrier counterparts have been diverse. Increased MTL and cortical activation, which has been interpreted to reflect compensatory neural mechanisms, has been reported by several groups (Bondi et al., 2005; Bookheimer et al., 2000; Burggren et al., 2002; Dickerson et al., 2005; Fleisher et al., 2005; Han et al., 2007; Smith et al., 2002; Wishart et al., 2006). Cognitive tasks used in these studies have covered classical memory encoding tasks using novel and repeated pictures or face–name pairs (Bondi et al., 2005; Dickerson et al., 2005), encoding and retrieval of word-pairs (Bookheimer et al., 2000; Fleisher et al., 2005), a letter fluency task (Smith et al., 2002), and an auditory verbal *n*-back working memory tasks (Wishart et al., 2006). At the same time, several studies have demonstrated reduced functional brain activity, in the MTL and in other brain areas, in cognitively normal ε4 carriers (Borghesani et al., 2007; Lind et al., 2006; Smith et al., 1999; Trivedi et al., 2006) during tasks such as visuospatial encoding (Borghesani et al., 2007), visual naming and letter fluency (Smith et al., 1999), encoding novel and familiar items (Trivedi et al., 2006), and semantic categorization (Lind et al., 2006). Several of the above-mentioned studies have carefully matched the at-risk subjects with their APOE ε4 non-carrier counterparts regarding age, gender, and cognitive performance. Therefore, it is currently difficult to draw any firm conclusions of the APOE ε4 effects on BOLD fMRI activation pattern. In fact, in the most recent large-scale fMRI studies, more complex patterns of alterations in brain activation differentially affected by APOE ε4 and family history of AD (Bassett et al., 2006; Johnson et al., 2006b) have been suggested.

Regarding early-onset familial AD, Mondadori et al. (2006) recently reported findings in two nondemented carriers of the presenilin 1 mutation, in their three nondemented family members and in 21 nonrelated controls. The middle-aged mutation carrier fulfilled criteria for amnestic MCI. Parallel to the results in "early" and "late" MCI in terms of CDR-SB scores (Celone et al., 2006; Dickerson et al., 2004), the authors reported increased brain activity within memory-related neural networks during episodic encoding and retrieval in the 20-year-old presenilin 1 mutation carrier compared to controls. The increased brain activation during episodic memory, but not working memory tasks, was again suggested to reflect a compensatory effort to overcome presymptomatic neural dysfunction due to the autosomal dominant mutation causative of AD. In contrast, they found decreased brain activity in the symptomatic middle-aged mutation carrier who supposedly already has a more advanced stage of AD-related neuropathology. This again parallels the findings in more impaired MCI subjects reviewed above (Celone et al., 2006; Johnson et al., 2006a; Machulda et al., 2003; Petrella et al., 2006).

Taken together, imaging asymptomatic or very mildly impaired subjects at-risk for AD by virtue of genetics and/or family history is an intriguing and important field but more research and follow-up studies are needed to understand the interactions between the various genotypes, emerging neuropathological changes, age and several other factors and their effects on the brain activation or metabolic pattern as reflected by functional imaging.

FMRI Resting State Studies in AD and MCI

Recently, several groups have reported reduced resting state fMRI activity (He et al., 2007; Wang et al., 2006, Wang et al., 2007) or decreased task-induced deactivation responses (Celone et al., 2006; Greicius et al., 2004; Lustig et al., 2003; Pihlajamäki et al., 2009; Pihlajamäki & Sperling, 2009; Rombouts et al., 2005; Sperling et al., 2009) in AD patients or in subjects at risk for AD compared to healthy controls. The term "task-induced deactivation" refers to the tendency of a consistent set of brain areas to show relative decreases in activity (below the baseline level) when subjects are engaged in attentional, goal-directed tasks (Buckner et al., 2005; Cavanna & Trimble, 2006; Gusnard & Raichle, 2001). Regarding posterior brain areas, the posterior cingulate and precuneal cortices belong to the core regions of the "default mode" network (Buckner et al., 2005; Lustig et al., 2003). Some of these resting state/ deactivation fMRI studies in AD also included subjects with MCI, who typically show decreases in fMRI deactivation intermediate to that of older controls and AD, especially at the more advanced stage of MCI (Celone et al., 2006; Pihlajamäki et al., 2009; Pihlajamäki & Sperling, 2009; Rombouts et al., 2005). So far, results of increasingly disrupted deactivation across the continuum from healthy aging to MCI and to clinical AD are consistent (Figure 18.4, plate section) except one study reporting no differences in task-induced deactivation between AD and control subjects during successful encoding and retrieval of visuospatial paired-associates (Gould et al., 2006b). Interestingly, brain regions involved in the "default mode" network are quite comparable to those regions that typically demonstrate evidence of fibrillar Aβ deposition binding in PIB-PET studies in AD (Buckner et al., 2005; Klunk et al., 2004; Sperling et al., 2009; Sperling et al., 2010) as well as to the pattern of FDG-PET hypometabolism in AD patients (Buckner et al., 2005; Herholz et al., 2002; Rapoport, 1991) and in subjects at-risk for AD (Reiman et al., 1996; Small et al., 1995).

Our recent fMRI work suggests that the alterations in the MTL activation and posterior midline cortical deactivation over the course of MCI and AD are strongly correlated (Celone et al., 2006; Pihlajamäki et al., 2008). We have hypothesized that an interplay between several large-scale neural networks, including the hippocampal memory network, frontoparietal attentional network and the "default mode" network (Gusnard & Raichle, 2001; Mesulam, 1998), is required for successful memory performance (Celone et al., 2006; Miller et al., 2008; Pihlajamäki et al., 2008; Sperling et al., 2010). The idea of the importance of the coordination between "default mode" and active cognitive networks is supported by recent evidence in young adults (Daselaar et al., 2004) and in older adults (Grady et al., 2006; Miller et al., 2008), which suggest that the ability to suspend default mode activity, i.e., to reallocate neurocognitive resources to those brain regions optimal for the task performance, may be critical for successful memory formation. It is likely that the AD brain is no longer capable of flexibly modulating the balance of activity between neural networks, or specifically "turn off" the areas of the default mode network in order to optimally recruit other networks for task performance (Sperling et al., 2009).

FMRI in Neurodegenerative Dementias other than AD

FMRI studies on neurodegenerative dementias other AD are scarce thus far. Rombouts et al. (2003) compared seven patients with mild AD to seven patients with mild frontotemporal dementia (FTD). FMRI was performed during an n-back working memory task using letters under 1-back and 2-back conditions. The authors found bilaterally less prefrontal activation in FTD than in AD patients. Furthermore, FTD patients did not show as strong linear increase in prefrontal activation related to working memory load as the AD patients did. Consistent with PET (Ibach et al., 2004) and MRI perfusion (Du et al., 2006) studies, this study suggested that functional imaging may be helpful in early differential diagnostics between AD and FTD at a stage where significant differences in atrophy are not present.

Dementia associated with Parkinson disease (PD) is the third most common form of dementia. Compared with PD patients who are not demented, patients with dementia may show glucose hypometabolism in PET imaging in the basal ganglia and frontal regions. FDG-PET has also shown differences in the pattern of metabolic reduction between AD and PD patients with dementia (Vander Borght et al., 1997). One interesting recent fMRI study compared healthy elderly controls, 10 cognitively unimpaired patients with PD, and 11 nondemented PD patients with selective impairment of executive functions (Lewis et al., 2003). The task used in this event-related fMRI experiment was a working memory maintenance and manipulation task using letter sequences with forced-choice recognition of the correct sequence. The main finding of the study was a specific under-recruitment of the basal ganglia and frontal cortex in PD patients with cognitive impairment compared to unimpaired patients during manipulation of information within working memory. The authors speculated that fMRI may have potential in clinical assessment of PD patients and in understanding the neural correlates of cognitive impairment in PD.

Finally, fMRI activation patterns during visual color, face, and motion stimuli were investigated in patients with dementia with Lewy bodies (DLB) and compared to AD patients and controls (Sauer et al., 2006). Several significant differences in fMRI response patterns were found but most of the findings were explained by differences in behavioral performance between patients and controls or between the two patient groups. The authors found, however, also significant performance-independent differences in brain activation in the superior temporal regions during the biological motion task, that is patients with DLB showed more activation than AD. FDG-PET has, quite expectedly, shown occipital atrophy and hypometabolism in DLB as opposed to MTL atrophy and hypometabolism in AD patients (Ishii et al., 2007).

In summary, each of these dementias, i.e., AD, DLB, FTD and PDD, seems to have a somewhat characteristic pattern of functional imaging findings at the group level but future research at the level of individual subjects is warranted to develop functional imaging methods for differential diagnostics of neurodegenerative dementias.

FMRI as a Marker of Pharmacological Effects in AD

FMRI, either during cognitive paradigms or during resting state, may hold the greatest potential in the evaluation of novel pharmacological strategies to treat AD. It has been demonstrated in young subjects that fMRI can detect pharmacological effects, that is both the extent and magnitude of activation of hippocampal, fusiform and prefrontal regions were selectively decreased during pharmacologically induced memory impairment using lorazepam or scopolamine during a memory encoding task (Sperling et al., 2002).

The currently available treatments for AD are cholinesterase inhibitors (donepezil, galantamine, and rivastigmine) and an N-methyl-D-aspartate antagonist (memantine). To date, several fMRI studies have demonstrated enhanced brain activation, and also better behavioral task performance, after acute or prolonged treatment with cholinesterase inhibitors, although these studies were not conducted as typical double-blind, placebo-controlled trials. The studies were done with donepezil (Kircher et al., 2005; Saykin et al., 2004), galantamine (Goekoop et al., 2004; Goekoop et al., 2006; Grön et al., 2006; Shanks et al., 2007), and rivastigmine (Rombouts et al., 2002). Some of these studies also included MCI subjects (Goekoop et al., 2004; Goekoop et al., 2006; Grön et al., 2006; Saykin et al., 2004), who showed primarily similar kinds of effects as AD patients. Goekoop et al. (2006) also noted, however, some differences in the response pattern between MCI and AD patients such that in MCI, acute exposure to galantamine increased activation in the posterior cingulate, parietal and anterior temporal cortices, whereas in AD activation was most significantly increased in hippocampal regions. The authors speculated that observed differences in brain response to galantamine may reflect differences in the level of dysfunction of the cholinergic system between MCI and AD patients.

In 29 AD subjects we recently investigated whether the pattern of fMRI activation during an associative encoding paradigm correlated with performance on memory measures commonly used in AD clinical trials. We found that performance on the

Alzheimer's Disease Assessment Scale (ADAS-Cog) verbal memory component, the ADAS-Cog total score, and on the Free and Cued Selective Reminding Test all correlated with activation of the superior temporal and prefrontal cortices during processing of novel versus repeated face–name pairs (Diamond et al., 2007). The relationship between fMRI activation and standardized memory measures is promising when considering the potential use of fMRI in AD clinical trials. Moreover, functional imaging of pharmacologically induced neurochemical changes in whole-brain networks supporting cognitive functions has important implications for our understanding of the mechanisms by which these medications exert their effects and for the use of fMRI in treatment monitoring of AD and possibly other dementias.

Future Directions and Limitations of Functional Imaging in Dementia

The past decade has seen remarkable advances in our understanding of the pathophysiology of neurodegenerative dementias. As reviewed above, fMRI has many potential advantages in studying patients with cognitive impairment. FMRI can be acquired on a standard clinical magnet during the same session as structural imaging. Because it is non-invasive and subjects are not exposed to radiation, fMRI can be repeated many times over the course of longitudinal studies. Perhaps the greatest potential advantage of fMRI is that we can image these patients while they are attempting to do the type of cognitive process that is causing them difficulty clinically.

There are, however, several challenges in performing fMRI studies in patients with neurodegenerative dementias. It is likely that fMRI will remain quite problematic in examining patients with more severe cognitive impairment. High-field fMRI with optimized imaging parameters can offer spatial resolution as high as in the order of 1 mm, or even less. This is, however, currently not realistic with demented patients as the technique is sensitive to head motion. Inherently, the signal-to-noise ratio of BOLD signal changes between activation and baseline conditions is low, which necessitates repeated measurements and thus leads to relatively long scanning sessions. There is a need for continued technical advances, such as real-time motion correction, parallel imaging and high-speed acquisition, to fully realize the potential of this technology in dementia research. Also, if the patients are not able to adequately perform the cognitive task, one of the major advantages of fMRI activation studies is lost. Resting state fMRI can, however, be performed with less cooperative subjects and is thus better applicable to imaging more severely impaired patients.

In terms of using fMRI in longitudinal or pharmacological studies, it is critical to complete further validation experiments. BOLD fMRI response is known to be variable across subjects. The reproducibility of BOLD signal changes within young healthy individuals during memory encoding tasks across separate days is reported to be reasonable (Harrington et al., 2006; Sperling et al., 2002). However, reproducibility of fMRI activation in older and cognitively impaired subjects has not yet been well established. Longitudinal functional imaging studies are needed to track the evolution of alterations in the fMRI activation pattern over the course of the cognitive continuum from healthy aging to clinical dementias such as AD. It is also important to evaluate the contribution of structural atrophy to changes observed with functional imaging techniques in neurodegenerative diseases. A combination of structural MRI, fMRI and other imaging techniques such as PIB-PET (Julkunen et al., 2009; Miller et al., 2008; Sperling et al., 2009; Sperling et al., 2010) may eventually serve as a valuable method for the in vivo detection of AD prior to clinical dementia, at the point when disease-modifying therapies would be most efficacious.

In summary, despite the relative infancy of the field, there have already been a number of promising fMRI studies in AD, MCI, subjects at-risk for AD, and patients with neurodegenerative dementias other than AD. The greatest potential of fMRI alone and in combination with other imaging techniques likely lies in the study of very early stages of dementias, at the point of subtle neuronal dysfunction without significant macroscopic brain atrophy, and perhaps in the evaluation of pharmacological efficacy for novel therapies.

References

Bäckman, L., Andersson, J. L., Nyberg, L., Winblad, B., Nordberg, A., & Almkvist, O. (1999). Brain regions associated with episodic retrieval in normal aging and Alzheimer's disease. *Neurology*, *52*, 1861–1870.

Bassett, S. S., Yousem, D. M., Cristinzio, C., Kusevic, I., Yassa, M. A., Caffo, B. S., et al. (2006). Familial risk for Alzheimer's disease alters fMRI activation patterns. *Brain*, *129*, 1229 1239.

Bokde, A. L., Lopez-Bayo, P., Meindl, T., Pechler, S., Born, C., Faltraco, F., et al. (2006). Functional connectivity of the fusiform gyrus during a face-matching task in subjects with mild cognitive impairment. *Brain*, *129*, 1113–1124.

Bondi, M. W., Houston, W. S., Eyler, L. T., & Brown, G. G. (2005). fMRI evidence of compensatory mechanisms in older adults at genetic risk for Alzheimer disease. *Neurology*, *64*, 501–508.

Bookheimer, S. Y., Strojwas, M. H., Cohen, M. S., Saunders, A. M., Pericak-Vance, M. A., Mazziotta, J. C., et al. (2000). Patterns of brain activation in people at risk for Alzheimer's disease. *New England Journal of Medicine*, *343*, 450–456.

Borghesani, P. R., Johnson, L. C., Shelton, A. L., Peskind, E. R., Aylward, E. H., Schellenberg, G. D. et al. (2007). Altered medial temporal lobe responses during visuospatial encoding in healthy APOE*4 carriers. *Neurobiology of Aging*, *29*, 981–991.

Braak, H., & Braak, E. (1991). Neuropathological staging of Alzheimer-related changes. *Acta Neuropathologica (Berlin)*, *82*, 239–259.

Brewer, J. B., Zhao, Z., Desmond, J. E., Glover, G. H., & Gabrieli, J. D. (1998). Making memories: Brain activity that predicts how well visual experience will be remembered. *Science*, *281*, 1185–1187.

Buckner, R. L., Snyder, A. Z., Shannon, B. J., LaRossa, G., Sachs, R., Fotenos, A. F., et al. (2005). Molecular, structural, and functional characterization of Alzheimer's disease: Evidence for a relationship between default activity, amyloid, and memory. *Journal of Neuroscience, 25,* 7709–7717.

Burggren, A. C., Small, G. W., Sabb, F. W., & Bookheimer, S. Y. (2002). Specificity of brain activation patterns in people at genetic risk for Alzheimer disease. *American Journal of Geriatric Psychiatry, 10,* 44–51.

Cavanna, A. E., & Trimble, M. R. (2006). The precuneus: A review of its functional anatomy and behavioural correlates. *Brain, 129,* 564–583.

Celone, K. A., Calhoun, V. D., Dickerson, B. C., Atri, A., Chua, E. F., Miller, S., et al. (2006). Alterations in memory networks in mild cognitive impairment and Alzheimer's disease: An independent component analysis. *Journal of Neuroscience, 26,* 10222–10231.

D'Esposito, M., Deouell, L. Y., & Gazzaley, A. (2003). Alterations in the BOLD fMRI signal with aging and disease: A challenge for neuroimaging. *Nature Reviews Neuroscience, 4,* 863–872.

Dannhauser, T. M., Walker, Z., Stevens, T., Lee, L., Seal, M., & Shergill, S. S. (2005). The functional anatomy of divided attention in amnestic mild cognitive impairment. *Brain, 128,* 1418–1427.

Daselaar, S. M., Prince, S. E., & Cabeza, R. (2004). When less means more: Deactivations during encoding that predict subsequent memory. *Neuroimage, 23,* 921–927.

DeKosky, S. T., Ikonomovic, M. D., Styren, S. D., Beckett, L., Wisniewski, S., Bennett, D. A., et al. (2002). Upregulation of choline acetyltransferase activity in hippocampus and frontal cortex of elderly subjects with mild cognitive impairment. *Annals of Neurology, 51,* 145–155.

Diamond, E. L., Miller, S., Dickerson, B. C., Atri, A., DePeau, K., Fenstermacher, E., et al. (2007). Relationship of fMRI activation to clinical trial memory measures in Alzheimer's disease. *Neurology, 69,* 1331–1341.

Dickerson, B. C., Salat, D. H., Bates, J. F., Atiya, M., Killiany, R. J., Greve, D. N., et al. (2004). Medial temporal lobe function and structure in mild cognitive impairment. *Annals of Neurology, 56,* 27–35.

Dickerson, B. C., Salat, D. H., Greve, D. N., Chua, E. F., Rand-Giovannetti, E., Rentz, D. M., et al. (2005). Increased hippocampal activation in mild cognitive impairment compared to normal aging and AD. *Neurology, 65,* 404–411.

Du, A. T., Jahng, G. H., Hayasaka, S., Kramer, J. H., Rosen, H. J., Gorno-Tempini, M. L., et al. (2006). Hypoperfusion in frontotemporal dementia and Alzheimer disease by arterial spin labeling MRI. *Neurology, 67,* 1215–1220.

Eichenbaum, H. (2000). A cortical-hippocampal system for declarative memory. *Nature Reviews Neuroscience, 1,* 41–50.

Fleisher, A. S., Houston, W. S., Eyler, L. T., Frye, S., Jenkins, C., Thal, L. J., et al. (2005). Identification of Alzheimer disease risk by functional magnetic resonance imaging. *Archives of Neurology, 62,* 1881–1888.

Goekoop, R., Rombouts, S. A., Jonker, C., Hibbel, A., Knol, D. L., Truyen, L., et al. (2004). Challenging the cholinergic system in mild cognitive impairment: A pharmacological fMRI study. *Neuroimage, 23,* 1450–1459.

Goekoop, R., Scheltens, P., Barkhof, F., & Rombouts, SA. (2006). Cholinergic challenge in Alzheimer patients and mild cognitive impairment differentially affects hippocampal activation – A pharmacological fMRI study. *Brain, 129,* 141–157.

Golby, A., Silverberg, G., Race, E., Gabrieli, S., O'Shea, J., Knierim, K., et al. (2005). Memory encoding in Alzheimer's disease: An fMRI study of explicit and implicit memory. *Brain,* *128,* 773–787.

Gomez-Isla, T., Hollister, R., West, H., Mui, S., Growdon, J. H., Petersen, R. C., et al. (1997). Neuronal loss correlates with but exceeds neurofibrillary tangles in Alzheimer's disease. *Annals of Neurology, 41,* 17–24.

Gould, R. L., Arroyo, B., Brown, R. G., Owen, A. M., Bullmore, E. T., & Howard, R. J. (2006a). Brain mechanisms of successful compensation during learning in Alzheimer disease. *Neurology, 67,* 1011–1017.

Gould, R. L., Brown, R. G., Owen, A. M., Bullmore, E. T., & Howard, R. J. (2006b). Task-induced deactivations during successful paired associates learning: An effect of age but not Alzheimer's disease. *Neuroimage, 31,* 818–831.

Gould, R. L., Brown, R. G., Owen, A. M., Bullmore, E. T., Williams, S. C., & Howard, R. J. (2005). Functional neuroanatomy of successful paired associate learning in Alzheimer's disease. *American Journal of Psychiatry, 162,* 2049–2060.

Grady, C. L., McIntosh, A. R., Beig, S., Keightley, M. L., Burian, H., & Black, S. E. (2003). Evidence from functional neuroimaging of a compensatory prefrontal network in Alzheimer's disease. *Journal of Neuroscience, 23,* 986–993.

Grady, C. L., Springer, M. V., Hongwanishkul, D., McIntosh, A. R., & Winocur, G. (2006). Age-related changes in brain activity across the adult lifespan. *Journal of Cognitive Neuroscience, 18,* 227–241.

Greicius, M. D., Srivastava, G., Reiss, A. L., & Menon, V. (2004). Default-mode network activity distinguishes Alzheimer's disease from healthy aging: Evidence from functional MRI. *Proceedings of the National Academy of Sciences USA, 101,* 4637–4642.

Grön, G., & Riepe, M. W. (2004). Neural basis for the cognitive continuum in episodic memory from health to Alzheimer disease. *American Journal of Geriatric Psychiatry, 12,* 648–652.

Grön, G., Brandenburg, I., Wunderlich, A. P., & Riepe, M. W. (2006). Inhibition of hippocampal function in mild cognitive impairment: targeting the cholinergic hypothesis. *Neurobiology of Aging, 27,* 78–87.

Grossman, M., Koenig, P., Glosser, G., DeVita, C., Moore, P., Rhee, J., et al. (2003). Neural basis for semantic memory difficulty in Alzheimer's disease: An fMRI study. *Brain, 126,* 292–311.

Gusnard, D. A., & Raichle, M. E. (2001). Searching for a baseline: Functional imaging and the resting human brain. *Nature Reviews Neuroscience, 2,* 685–694.

Hämäläinen, A., Pihlajamäki, M., Tanila, H., Hänninen, T., Niskanen, E., Tervo, S., et al. (2007). Increased fMRI responses during encoding in mild cognitive impairment. *Neurobiology of Aging, 28,* 1889–1903.

Han, S. D., Houston, W. S., Jak, A. J., Eyler, L. T., Nagel, B. J., Fleisher, A. S., et al. (2007). Verbal paired-associate learning by APOE genotype in non-demented older adults: fMRI evidence of a right hemispheric compensatory response. *Neurobiology of Aging, 28,* 238–247.

Harrington, G. S., Tomaszewski Farias, S., Buonocore, M. H., & Yonelinas, A. P. (2006). The intersubject and intrasubject reproducibility of FMRI activation during three encoding tasks: Implications for clinical applications. *Neuroradiology, 48,* 495–505.

He, Y., Wang, L., Zang, Y., Tian, L., Zhang, X., Li, K., & Jiang, T. (2007). Regional coherence changes in the early stages of Alzheimer's disease: A combined structural and resting-state functional MRI study. *Neuroimage, 35,* 488–500.

Herholz, K., Salmon, E., Perani, D., Baron, J. C., Holthoff, V., Frolich, L., et al. (2002). Discrimination between Alzheimer dementia and controls by automated analysis of multicenter FDG PET. *Neuroimage, 17*, 302–316.

Heun, R., Freymann, K., Erb, M., Leube, D. T., Jessen, F., Kircher, T. T., et al. (2007). Mild cognitive impairment (MCI) and actual retrieval performance affect cerebral activation in the elderly. *Neurobiology of Aging, 28*, 404–413.

Iadecola, C. (2004). Neurovascular regulation in the normal brain and in Alzheimer's disease. *Nature Reviews Neuroscience, 5*, 347–360.

Ibach, B., Poljansky, S., Marienhagen, J., Sommer, M., Manner, P., & Hajak, G. (2004). Contrasting metabolic impairment in frontotemporal degeneration and early onset Alzheimer's disease. *Neuroimage, 23*, 739–743.

Ishii, K., Soma, T., Kono, A. K., Sofue, K., Miyamoto, N., Yoshikawa, T., et al. (2007). Comparison of regional brain volume and glucose metabolism between patients with mild dementia with Lewy bodies and those with mild Alzheimer's disease. *Journal of Nuclear Medicine, 48*, 704–711.

Johnson, K. A., & Albert, M. S. (2000). Perfusion abnormalities in prodromal AD. *Neurobiology of Aging, 21*, 289–292.

Johnson, S. C., Baxter, L. C., Susskind-Wilder, L., Connor, D. J., Sabbagh, M. N., & Caselli, R. J. (2004). Hippocampal adaptation to face repetition in healthy elderly and mild cognitive impairment. *Neuropsychologia, 42*, 980–989.

Johnson, S. C., Schmitz, T. W., Moritz, C. H., Meyerand, M. E., Rowley, H. A., Alexander, A. L., et al. (2006a). Activation of brain regions vulnerable to Alzheimer's disease: The effect of mild cognitive impairment. *Neurobiology of Aging, 27*, 1604–1612.

Johnson, S. C., Schmitz, T. W., Trivedi, M. A., Ries, M. L., Torgerson, B. M., Carlsson, C. M., et al. (2006b). The influence of Alzheimer disease family history and apolipoprotein E epsilon4 on mesial temporal lobe activation. *Journal of Neuroscience, 26*, 6069–6076.

Julkunen, V., Niskanen, E., Muehlboeck, S., Pihlajamäki, M., Könönen, M., Hallikainen, M., et al. (2009). Cortical thickness analysis to detect progressive mild cognitive impairment: A reference to Alzheimer's disease. *Dementia and Geriatric Cognitive Disorders, 28*, 404–412.

Kato, T., Knopman, D., & Liu, H. (2001). Dissociation of regional activation in mild AD during visual encoding: a functional MRI study. *Neurology, 57*, 812–816.

Kircher, T. T., Erb, M., Grodd, W., & Leube, D. T. (2005). Cortical activation during cholinesterase-inhibitor treatment in Alzheimer disease: Preliminary findings from a pharmaco-fMRI study. *American Journal of Geriatric Psychiatry, 13*, 1006–1013.

Kircher, T. T., Weis, S., Freymann, K., Erb, M., Jessen, F., Grodd, W., et al. (2007). Hippocampal activation in MCI patients is necessary for successful memory encoding. *Journal of Neurology, Neurosurgery & Psychiatry, 78*, 812–818.

Klunk, W. E., Engler, H., Nordberg, A., Wang, Y., Blomqvist, G., Holt, D. P., et al. (2004). Imaging brain amyloid in Alzheimer's disease with Pittsburgh Compound-B. *Annals of Neurology, 55*, 306–319.

Kwong, K. K., Belliveau, J. W., Chesler, D. A., Goldberg, I. E., Weisskoff, R. M., Poncelet, B. P., et al. (1992). Dynamic magnetic resonance imaging of human brain activity during primary sensory stimulation. *Proceedings of the National Academy of Sciences USA, 89*, 5675–5679.

Lehtovirta, M., Soininen, H., Laakso, M. P., Partanen, K., Helisalmi, S., Mannermaa, A., et al. (1996). SPECT and MRI analysis in Alzheimer's disease: Relation to apolipoprotein E epsilon 4 allele. *Journal of Neurology, Neurosurgery & Psychiatry, 60*, 644–649.

Lewis, S. J., Slabosz, A., Robbins, T. W., Barker, R. A., & Owen, A. M. (2003). Cognitive impairments in early Parkinson's disease are accompanied by reductions in activity in frontostriatal neural circuitry. *Journal of Neuroscience, 23*, 6351–6356.

Lind, J., Persson, J., Ingvar, M., Larsson, A., Cruts, M., Van Broeckhoven, C., et al. (2006). Reduced functional brain activity response in cognitively intact apolipoprotein E epsilon4 carriers. *Brain, 129*, 1240–1248.

Logothetis, N. K., Pauls, J., Augath, M., Trinath, T., & Oeltermann, A. (2001). Neurophysiological investigation of the basis of the fMRI signal. *Nature, 412*, 150–157.

Lustig, C., & Buckner, R. L. (2004). Preserved neural correlates of priming in old age and dementia. *Neuron, 42*(5), 865–875.

Lustig, C., Snyder, A. Z., Bhakta, M., O'Brien, K. C., McAvoy, M., Raichle, M. E., et al. (2003). Functional deactivations: change with age and dementia of the Alzheimer type. *Proceedings of the National Academy of Sciences USA, 100*, 14504–14509.

Machulda, M. M., Ward, H. A., Borowski, B., Gunter, J. L., Cha, R. H., O'Brien, P. C., et al. (2003). Comparison of memory fMRI response among normal, MCI, and Alzheimer's patients. *Neurology, 61*, 500–506.

Meguro, K., LeMestric, C., Landeau, B., Desgranges, B., Eustache, F., & Baron, J. C. (2001). Relations between hypometabolism in the posterior association neocortex and hippocampal atrophy in Alzheimer's disease: A PET/MRI correlative study. *Journal of Neurology, Neurosurgery & Psychiatry, 71*, 315–321.

Mesulam, M. M. (1998). From sensation to cognition. *Brain, 121*, 1013–1052.

Miller, S. L., Celone, K., DePeau, K., Diamond, E., Dickerson, B. C., Rentz, D., et al. (2008). Age-related memory impairment associated with loss of parietal deactivation but preserved hippocampal activation. *Proceedings of the National Academy of Sciences USA, 105*, 2181–2186.

Minoshima, S., Giordani, B., Berent, S., Frey, K. A., Foster, N. L., & Kuhl, D. E. (1997). Metabolic reduction in the posterior cingulate cortex in very early Alzheimer's disease. *Annals of Neurology, 42*, 85–94.

Mondadori, C. R., Buchmann, A., Mustovic, H., Schmidt, C. F., Boesiger, P., Nitsch, R. M., et al. (2006). Enhanced brain activity may precede the diagnosis of Alzheimer's disease by 30 years. *Brain, 129*, 2908–2922.

Nelissen, N., Vandenbulcke, M., Fannes, K., Verbruggen, A., Peeters, R., Dupont, P., et al. (2007). A{beta} amyloid deposition in the language system and how the brain responds. *Brain, 130*, 2055–2069.

Nestor, P. J., Fryer, T. D., Smielewski, P., & Hodges, J. R. (2003). Limbic hypometabolism in Alzheimer's disease and mild cognitive impairment. *Annals of Neurology, 54*, 343–351.

Ogawa, S., Tank, D. W., Menon, R., Ellermann, J. M., Kim, S. G., Merkle, H. et al. (1992). Intrinsic signal changes accompanying sensory stimulation: Functional brain mapping with magnetic resonance imaging. *Proceedings of the National Academy of Sciences USA, 89*, 5951–5955.

Pariente, J., Cole, S., Henson, R., Clare, L., Kennedy, A., Rossor, M., et al. (2005). Alzheimer's patients engage an alternative network during a memory task. *Annals of Neurology, 58*, 870–879.

Petersen, R. C., Doody, R., Kurz, A., Mohs, R. C., Morris, J. C., Rabins, P. V., et al. (2001). Current concepts in mild cognitive impairment. *Archives of Neurology, 58*, 1985–1992.

Petrella, J. R., Krishnan, S., Slavin, M. J., Tran, T. T., Murty, L., & Doraiswamy, P. M. (2006). Mild cognitive impairment: Evaluation with 4-T functional MR imaging. *Radiology, 240*, 177–186.

Pihlajamäki, M., & Sperling, R. A. (2009b). Functional MRI assessment of task-induced deactivation of the default mode network in Alzheimer's disease and at-risk older individuals. *Behavioral Neurology, 21*, 77–91.

Pihlajamäki, M., DePeau K. M., Blacker D., & Sperling R. A. (2008). Impaired medial temporal repetition suppression is related to failure of parietal deactivation in Alzheimer disease. *American Journal of Geriatric Psychiatry, 16*, 283–292.

Pihlajamäki, M., O'Keefe, K., Bertram, L., Tanzi, R. E., Dickerson, B. C., Blacker, D., et al. (2009a). Evidence of altered posteromedial cortical fMRI activity in subjects at risk for Alzheimer disease. *Alzheimer Disease and Associated Disorders* [Epub ahead of print].

Pihlajamäki, M., Tanila, H., Hänninen, T., Könönen, M., Mikkonen, M., Jalkanen, V., et al. (2003) Encoding of novel picture pairs activates the perirhinal cortex: An fMRI study. *Hippocampus, 13*, 67–80.

Rand-Giovannetti, E., Chua, E. F., Driscoll, A. E., Schacter, D. L., Albert, M. S., & Sperling, R. A. (2006). Hippocampal and neocortical activation during repetitive encoding in older persons. *Neurobiology of Aging, 27*, 173–182.

Rapoport, S. I. (1991). Positron emission tomography in Alzheimer's disease in relation to disease pathogenesis: a critical review. *Cerebrovascular and Brain Metabolism Reviews, 3*, 297–335.

Reiman, E. M., Caselli, R. J., Yun, L. S., Chen, K., Bandy, D., Minoshima, S., et al. (1996). Preclinical evidence of Alzheimer's disease in persons homozygous for the epsilon 4 allele for apolipoprotein E. *New England Journal of Medicine, 334*, 752–758.

Reiman, E. M., Uecker, A., Caselli, R. J., Lewis, S., Bandy, D., de Leon, M. J., et al. (1998). Hippocampal volumes in cognitively normal persons at genetic risk for Alzheimer's disease. *Annals of Neurology, 44*, 288–291.

Remy, F., Mirrashed, F., Campbell, B., & Richter, W. (2005). Verbal episodic memory impairment in Alzheimer's disease: A combined structural and functional MRI study. *Neuroimage, 25*, 253–266.

Ries, M. L., Jabbar, B. M., Schmitz, T. W., Trivedi, M. A., Gleason, C. E., Carlsson, C. M., et al. (2007). Anosognosia in mild cognitive impairment: Relationship to activation of cortical midline structures involved in self-appraisal. *Journal of the International Neuropsychological Society, 13*, 450–461.

Ries, M. L., Schmitz, T. W., Kawahara, T. N., Torgerson, B. M., Trivedi, M. A., & Johnson, S. C. (2006). Task-dependent posterior cingulate activation in mild cognitive impairment. *Neuroimage, 29*, 485–492.

Rombouts, S. A., Barkhof, F., Goekoop, R., Stam, C. J., & Scheltens, P. (2005). Altered resting state networks in mild cognitive impairment and mild Alzheimer's disease: An fMRI study. *Human Brain Mapping, 26*, 231–239.

Rombouts, S. A., Barkhof, F., Van Meel, C. S., & Scheltens, P. (2002). Alterations in brain activation during cholinergic enhancement with rivastigmine in Alzheimer's disease. *Journal of Neurology, Neurosurgery & Psychiatry, 73*, 665–671.

Rombouts, S. A., Barkhof, F., Veltman, D. J., Machielsen, W. C., Witter, M. P., Bierlaagh, M. A., et al. (2000). Functional MR imaging in Alzheimer's disease during memory encoding. *American Journal of Neuroradiology, 21,* 1869–1875.

Rombouts, S. A., van Swieten, J. C., Pijnenburg, Y. A., Goekoop, R., Barkhof, F., & Scheltens, P. (2003). Loss of frontal fMRI activation in early frontotemporal dementia compared to early AD. *Neurology, 60,* 1904–1908.

Sauer, J., ffytche, D. H., Ballard, C., Brown, R. G., & Howard, R. (2006). Differences between Alzheimer's disease and dementia with Lewy bodies: An fMRI study of task-related brain activity. *Brain, 129,* 1780–1788.

Saykin, A. J., Flashman, L. A., Frutiger, S. A., Johnson, S.C., Mamourian, A. C., Moritz, C. H., et al. (1999). Neuroanatomic substrates of semantic memory impairment in Alzheimer's disease: Patterns of functional MRI activation. *Journal of the International Neuropsychological Society, 5,* 377–392.

Saykin, A. J., Wishart, H. A., Rabin, L. A., Flashman, L. A., McHugh, T. L., Mamourian, A. C. et al. (2004). Cholinergic enhancement of frontal lobe activity in mild cognitive impairment. *Brain, 127,* 1574–1583.

Scheff, S. W., Price, D. A., Schmitt, F. A., & Mufson, E.J. (2006). Hippocampal synaptic loss in early Alzheimer's disease and mild cognitive impairment. *Neurobiology of Aging, 27,* 1372–1384.

Selkoe, D. J. (2002). Alzheimer's disease is a synaptic failure. *Science, 298,* 789–791.

Shanks, M. F., McGeown, W. J., Forbes-McKay, K. E., Waiter, G. D., Ries, M., & Venneri, A. (2007). Regional brain activity after prolonged cholinergic enhancement in early Alzheimer's disease. *Magnetic Resonance Imaging, 25,* 848–859.

Shmuel, A., Augath, M., Oeltermann, A., & Logothetis, N. K. (2006). Negative functional MRI response correlates with decreases in neuronal activity in monkey visual area V1. *Nature Neuroscience, 9,* 569–577.

Small, G. W., Mazziotta, J. C., Collins, M. T., Baxter, L. R., Phelps, M. E., Mandelkern, M. A., et al. (1995). Apolipoprotein E type 4 allele and cerebral glucose metabolism in relatives at risk for familial Alzheimer disease. *Jornal of the American Medical Association, 273,* 942–947.

Small, S. A., Perera, G. M., DeLaPaz, R., Mayeux, R., & Stern, Y. (1999). Differential regional dysfunction of the hippocampal formation among elderly with memory decline and Alzheimer's disease. *Annals of Neurology, 45,* 466–472.

Smith, C. D., Andersen, A. H., Kryscio, R. J., Schmitt, F. A., Kindy, M. S., Blonder, L. X. et al. (1999). Altered brain activation in cognitively intact individuals at high risk for Alzheimer's disease. *Neurology, 53,* 1391–1396.

Smith, C. D., Andersen, A. H., Kryscio, R. J., Schmitt, F. A., Kindy, M. S., Blonder, L. X., et al.. (2002). Women at risk for AD show increased parietal activation during a fluency task. *Neurology, 58,* 1197–1202.

Sperling, R., Bates, J., Chua, E., Cocchiarella, A., Schacter, D. L., Rosen, B., et al. (2003a). fMRI studies of associative encoding in young and elderly controls and mild AD patients. *Journal of Neurology, Neurosurgery & Psychiatry, 74,* 44–50.

Sperling, R., Chua, E., Cocchiarella, A., Rand-Giovannetti, E., Poldrack, R., Schacter, D. L., et al. (2003b). Putting names to faces: Successful encoding of associative memories activates the anterior hippocampal formation. *Neuroimage, 20,* 1400–1410.

Sperling, R., Dickerson, B. C., Pihlajamäki, M., Vannini, P., Laviolette, P. S., Vitolo, O. V., et al. (2010). Functional alterations in memory networks in early Alzheimer's disease. *Neuromolecular Med,* [Epub ahead of print].

Sperling, R., Greve, D., Dale, A., Killiany, R., Holmes, J., Rosas, H. D., et al. (2002). Functional MRI detection of pharmacologically induced memory impairment. *Proceedings of the National Academy of Sciences USA, 99,* 455–460.

Sperling, R., Laviolette, P. S., O'Keefe, K., O'Brien, J., Rentz, D. M., Pihlajamäki, M., et al. (2009). Amyloid deposition is associated with impaired default network function in older persons without dementia. *Neuron, 63,* 178–188.

Squire, L. R., & Zola-Morgan, S. (1991). The medial temporal lobe memory system. *Science, 253*(5026), 1380–1386.

Stern, C. E., Corkin, S., Gonzalez, R. G., Guimaraes, A. R., Baker, J. R., Jennings, P. J., et al. (1996). The hippocampal formation participates in novel picture encoding: Evidence from functional magnetic resonance imaging. *Proceedings of the National Academy of Sciences USA, 93,* 8660–8665.

Teipel, S. J., Bokde, A. L., Born, C., Meindl, T., Reiser, M., Moller, H. J., et al. (2007). Morphological substrate of face matching in healthy ageing and mild cognitive impairment: A combined MRI-fMRI study. *Brain, 130,* 1745–1758.

Trivedi, M. A., Schmitz, T. W., Ries, M. L., Torgerson, B. M., Sager, M. A., Hermann, B. P., et al. (2006). Reduced hippocampal activation during episodic encoding in middle-aged individuals at genetic risk of Alzheimer's disease: A cross-sectional study. *BMC Medicine, 4,* 1.

Vandenbulcke, M., Peeters, R., Dupont, P., Van Hecke, P., & Vandenberghe, R. (2007). Word reading and posterior temporal dysfunction in amnestic mild cognitive impairment. *Cerebral Cortex, 17,* 542–551.

Vander Borght, T., Minoshima, S., Giordani, B., Foster, N. L., Frey, K. A., Berent, S., et al. (1997). Cerebral metabolic differences in Parkinson's and Alzheimer's diseases matched for dementia severity. *Journal of Nuclear Medicine, 38,* 797–802.

Wagner, A. D., Schacter, D. L., Rotte, M., Koutstaal, W., Maril, A., Dale, A. M., et al. (1998). Building memories: remembering and forgetting of verbal experiences as predicted by brain activity. *Science, 281,* 1188–1191.

Wang, K., Liang, M., Wang, L., Tian, L., Zhang, X., Li, K. et al. (2007). Altered functional connectivity in early Alzheimer's disease: A resting-state fMRI study. *Human Brain Mapping, 28,* 967–978.

Wang, L., Zang, Y., He, Y., Liang, M., Zhang, X., Tian, L., et al. (2006). Changes in hippocampal connectivity in the early stages of Alzheimer's disease: Evidence from resting state fMRI. *Neuroimage, 31,* 496–504.

Wishart, H. A., Saykin, A. J., Rabin, L. A., Santulli, R. B., Flashman, L. A., Guerin, S. J., et al. (2006). Increased brain activation during working memory in cognitively intact adults with the APOE epsilon4 allele. *American Journal of Psychiatry, 163,* 1603–1610.

Yetkin, F. Z., Rosenberg, R. N., Weiner, M. F., Purdy, P. D., & Cullum, C. M. (2006). FMRI of working memory in patients with mild cognitive impairment and probable Alzheimer's disease. *European Radiology, 16,* 193–206.

19

Molecular Neuroimaging of the Dementias

From Scientific Insights to Clinical Applications

Bradford C. Dickerson

Introduction

The dementias, including primarily Alzheimer's disease (AD), frontotemporal dementias (FTD), vascular dementia, and Lewy body dementia and other movement disorders with dementia, are a major medical and social burden in many societies, particularly with the growth of older population segments. In many cases, these diseases involve the pathological accumulation of abnormal protein forms. As the biology of these diseases is elucidated, hope is beginning to emerge for specific treatments targeted at modification of fundamental pathophysiological processes (Bergmans & De Strooper, 2010; Bertram & Tanzi, 2005; Trojanowski, 2004). For this hope to be realized, methods for early detection of specific disease processes need to be identified. Furthermore, reliable methods for monitoring the progression of the diseases will likely be critical in demonstrating the effects of putative disease-modifying therapies. Magnetic resonance imaging (MRI), positron emission tomography (PET), single photon emission tomography (SPECT), and other neuroimaging tools offer great potential for these purposes (DeKosky & Marek, 2003; Dickerson & Sperling, 2009; Fox et al., 2009). Given the growing body of evidence that alterations in synaptic function are present very early in the course of neurodegenerative disease processes, possibly long before the development of clinical symptoms and even significant neuropathology (Coleman et al., 2004; Selkoe, 2002), functional and molecular imaging could be particularly useful for detecting alterations in brain function that may be present very early in the trajectory of neurodegenerative diseases. The uses of molecular

The Handbook of Alzheimer's Disease and Other Dementias, First Edition.
Edited by Andrew E. Budson, Neil W. Kowall.
© 2011 Blackwell Publishing Ltd. Published 2011 by Blackwell Publishing Ltd.

imaging in neurodegenerative diseases will be reviewed, with a focus on Alzheimer's disease (AD), to illustrate many points of relevance to other neurodegenerative diseases.

Before specifically discussing molecular neuroimaging, though, it is worth considering the current concepts of clinicopathological constructs of neurodegenerative diseases, since the interpretation of imaging data in patients depends critically on a detailed understanding of the clinical characteristics of the patient population(s) being studied.

Constructs of Neurodegenerative Disease: Clinical, Prodromal, and Presymptomatic Phases

Many neurodegenerative diseases are thought to arise from pathophysiological processes that take place over years, possibly decades, prior to the development of symptoms. For example, the clinical diagnosis of AD is made after a patient has developed impairment in multiple cognitive domains that is substantial enough to interfere with routine social and/or occupational function (dementia). It is only after this point that FDA-approved medications are currently indicated – that is, clinically probable AD. By this time, substantial neuronal loss and neuropathological change have damaged many brain regions. Although data from animal models suggest that it may be possible to impede this process as it is developing (Schenk et al., 1999; Weiner et al., 2000), and potentially reverse some aspects of it (Lombardo et al., 2003), it is not clear whether the pathology typically presents when patients are clinically diagnosed with AD can be reversed. Thus, it would be ideal to initiate treatment with neuroprotective medications at a time when – or even before – AD is mildly symptomatic (DeKosky & Marek, 2003; Petersen et al., 2009). This scenario is true for many neurodegenerative diseases, and is even more compelling in diseases in which known genetic abnormalities can be identified that predict future disease, as in Huntington's disease.

To approach the goal of early intervention in neurodegenerative diseases, we must improve our capability to identify individuals in the earliest symptomatic phases of the diseases prior to significant functional impairment. For example, individuals are categorized as having mild cognitive impairment (MCI) when symptoms suggestive of AD are present but mild enough that traditional diagnostic criteria (which require functional impairment consistent with dementia) are not fulfilled. This gradual transitional state may last for a number of years. Diagnostic criteria for MCI have been developed (Petersen et al., 1999; Petersen et al., 2009) and operationalized (Grundman et al., 2004) in a manner that suggests that cohorts of such individuals can be reliably identified for clinical trials. Recently, new diagnostic criteria for AD have been proposed with the goal of diagnosing probable AD prior to dementia (Dubois et al., 2007). If the pathophysiological process of AD can be slowed at this stage of the disease, then it may be possible to preserve cognitive function and delay the ultimate development of dementia for a period of time, which is clearly clinically meaningful. Therefore, MCI and other patients in the prodromal phases of neuro-degenerative diseases present excellent target populations for clinical trials of disease-modifying therapies.

Finally, the presymptomatic phase of neurodegenerative diseases is the phase when pathological alterations are developing but symptoms are not yet apparent. In the case of AD, this phase may best be studied through the identification of cohorts with particular risk factors, such as genetic determinants (e.g., amyloid precursor protein (APP) or presenilin mutations, Down syndrome) or susceptibility factors (e.g., apolipoprotein E (APOE) ε4). Ideally, it would ultimately be possible to initiate disease-modifying therapies at this point based on the presence of risk factors, much as is done in the case of primary preventive measures for cerebrovascular disease. Yet given that some of these therapies may not be benign, it would be best to have a panel of biomarkers that could be used to help guide the timing of these therapies, such that individuals at elevated risk for AD could be followed over time. When changes in biomarkers indicate the earliest phase of active pathophysiology, treatment could be initiated.

What is Molecular Neuroimaging?

Molecular neuroimaging techniques enable in vivo images to be obtained of radiolabeled compounds (radioligand) that are typically injected intravenously into the person undergoing imaging. A wide range of compounds can be labeled, and radiochemists regularly develop new compounds of use for neuroimaging (Fox et al., 2009). The two primary methods for obtaining images are PET and SPECT. In PET scanning, positrons are emitted by the radioligand, collide with electrons, and generate gamma radiation, which is ultimately detected by the sensor arrays and used to derive an image. Commonly used radioligands include carbon-11, oxygen-15, and fluorine-18 (18F). 18F is desirable because it has the longest half-life. SPECT scans work in a somewhat similar manner, but employ compounds such as technetium-99 and xenon-133, which have longer half-lives than compounds used in PET scanning. For a variety of technical reasons, PET scans are able to obtain higher resolution images than SPECT scans, but are generally less widely available.

The measures commonly obtained using these tools include blood flow, glucose metabolism, and oxygen consumption. Measures of neurotransmitter function have also been developed. Recently, new radioligands that bind to proteins associated with pathological processes (such as fibrillar beta-amyloid in AD) have been developed and are providing revolutionary insights into neurodegenerative pathology in living humans.

Since many functional neuroimaging measures assess inherently dynamic processes including blood flow and metabolism, these measures have unique characteristics that may offer both strengths and weaknesses as potential biomarkers of neurological disease. Functional neuroimaging measures may be affected by transient brain and body states at the time of imaging, such as arousal, attention, sleep deprivation, sensory processing of irrelevant stimuli, or the effects of substances with pharmacological central nervous system activity. Imaging measures of brain function may also be more sensitive than structural measures to constitutional or chronic differences between individuals, such as genetics, intelligence or educational level, learning, mood, or medication use. While these may be effects of interest in certain experimental settings, they need to be controlled when the focus is on disease-related changes and differences between subject groups or within individuals over time.

Molecular neuroimaging techniques have been used to study dynamic brain processes, such as changes in brain blood flow or metabolism with cognitive or sensorimotor task performance. These studies have provided seminal insights into normal human brain function. For the purposes of this review, however, we will focus on studies of molecular neuroimaging of dementias that have been applied toward the goals of early detection, differential diagnosis, and prediction and tracking of decline.

Identification of Abnormal Patterns of Brain Function Using Molecular Neuroimaging

Molecular neuroimaging has traditionally been applied to dementias with the goal of identifying abnormal patterns of brain function. These abnormal patterns may reveal new insights into the disruption of brain circuits by such diseases. They may also be useful in differential diagnosis. Typically, the abnormal findings involve reduced metabolism or blood flow in particular brain regions that are affected by the disease. In some situations, increased metabolism or blood flow has been identified. Molecular neuroimaging has also been used to identify abnormal patterns of brain function in individuals who are clinically normal but who carry genetic risk factors for dementias.

Patterns of abnormal regional brain function in neurodegenerative diseases

For over 20 years, these techniques have been applied to the study of dementia, and one of the most consistent findings in AD is a reduction of metabolism and perfusion in posterior temporoparietal, posterior cingulate, and frontal regions, with sparing of primary somatomotor cortices (Figure 19.1, plate section). The degree to which metabolism is reduced in these brain regions correlates with clinical severity of symptoms (Foster et al., 1984). Animal model studies suggest that posterior cingulate hypometabolism may occur after entorhinal lesions, possibly as a result of disconnection (Meguro et al., 1999). This "functional signature" of AD has been studied extensively as a potential marker of disease state – a diagnostic marker to differentiate AD from normal aging and other neurodegenerative diseases, and can do so in the proper clinical context with relatively high sensitivity and specificity when compared with clinical diagnoses in both late-onset (Jagust, 2000) and early-onset disease (Rabinovici et al., 2010). Although it does not seem surprising that metabolic abnormalities such as this would be present in more advanced AD, this signature is in fact detectable in patients with very mild AD (Johnson et al., 1998; Minoshima et al., 1997).

In previous PET or SPECT studies of AD patients followed to autopsy, the in vivo resting functional findings have also demonstrated relatively high sensitivity to detect postmortem AD neuropathology, but somewhat lower specificity (Bradley et al., 2002; Mega et al., 1997; Mega et al., 1999). However, studies suggests that the presence or absence of typical PET findings of AD are at least as sensitive and specific to the pathology of AD as an initial clinical diagnosis either by itself (Haense et al., 2009; Jagust et al., 2007) or combined with other measures (Walhovd et al., 2010). In addition, multi-center studies have demonstrated that PET data acquired using different instruments can be pooled in a manner that minimizes site-related variance and enables the detection of disease effects (Herholz et al., 1993; Herholz et al., 1999). These findings have been borne out by an international multi-center collaborative group that pooled PET and pathological data from 138 patients who had undergone dementia evaluations and been longitudinally followed at centers around the world (Silverman et al., 2001). Although these functional neuroimaging measures are diagnostically sensitive, specific, and useful for prediction of cognitive course and pathological outcome, their limitations should be kept in mind. PET and SPECT findings can be affected by subject age (Mielke et al., 1992; Rabinovici et al., 2010), analytical methods (Small et al., 2000), and atrophy (Ibanez et al., 1998). Rather than simply correcting for atrophy, it may be appropriate to use both structural and functional measures to better characterize group differences in AD (De Santi et al., 2001; Walhovd et al., 2010; Yamaguchi et al., 1997).

Abnormal metabolic or perfusion patterns of other neurodegenerative diseases have also been identified using PET and SPECT. Frontotemporal dementia (FTD) is associated with frontal or anterior temporal abnormalities (Foster et al., 2007; Panegyres et al., 2009). Dementia with Lewy bodies (DLB) is associated with occipitotemporal abnormalities (Albin et al., 1996; Lobotesis et al., 2001), and greater abnormalities in these posterior brain regions are associated with more frequent visual hallucinations. A very large study ($N = 135$) of FDG-PET metabolism illustrates abnormalities in other movement disorders (Eckert et al., 2005). In Parkinson's disease (PD), there may be hypermetabolism in globus pallidus and putamen, with reduced metabolism in parieto-occipital and prefrontal cortical regions; this contrasts with progressive supranuclear palsy, in which there is reduced metabolism in midbrain and medial prefrontal cortex. In multiple systems atrophy (MSA), there is reduced putamen/pallidal and cerebellar metabolism. Patients with corticobasal degeneration (CBD) demonstrate asymmetric basal ganglia and frontoparietal hypometabolism, contralateral to the side of prominent symptoms and signs. Huntington's disease is characterized by striatal hypometabolism (Antonini et al., 1996), while amyotrophic lateral sclerosis (ALS) is associated with sensorimotor cortical hypometabolism (Kew et al., 1994). In summary, the functional abnormalities of many neurodegenerative disorders reflect known abnormalities in brain circuits in these disorders.

Molecular imaging in the differential diagnosis of neurodegenerative diseases

The early detection and differential diagnosis of neurodegenerative disorders is a promising aim for further work using molecular imaging. Since molecular imaging is sensitive to both the character and severity of symptoms, it seems reasonable to hope that its potential capability to detect alterations in the pattern and degree of regional brain activity may provide additional useful data to complement clinical and psychometric evaluations.

In elderly individuals with cognitive symptoms, it can be difficult to distinguish a neurodegenerative process from depression – molecular imaging may be helpful in this setting. In depression, the typical pattern of AD-related hypometabolism is not seen, but prefrontal or global hypometabolism may be seen (Guze et al., 1991). In patients with AD, those with depression have greater dorsolateral prefrontal hypometabolism, while those with apathy have greater orbitofrontal hypometabolism (Holthoff et al., 2005).

Furthermore, different forms of neurodegenerative dementias may be challenging to diagnose specifically early in their course. Molecular imaging may provide helpful data to assist in differential diagnosis of the dementias. In fact, the first Medicare-approved indication for the use of FDG-PET in the diagnostic evaluation of dementias is for the differential diagnosis of FTD from AD. The value of PET in this situation, which can be difficult clinically, was recently supported by a study of patients with pathologically diagnosed FTD or AD who had been imaged with FDG-PET during life (Foster et al., 2007). Six dementia experts independently reviewed the PET and clinical data and made diagnostic decisions, and the use of the PET pattern improved the accuracy of clinical diagnoses, particularly in cases in which there was uncertainty.

The differentiation of vascular dementia (VaD) from AD has been full of challenges not only in neuroimaging but also clinically and even pathologically. FDG-PET data have suggested that vascular dementia may be characterized most prominently by reductions in frontal metabolism and blood flow (Sultzer et al., 1995), but this finding has not been universal (Duara et al., 1989). And despite some of the differences that have been reported, there is significant overlap in the hypometabolic regions in AD and VaD. In the largest study to date seeking to differentiate VaD from AD using hypometabolic FDG-PET patterns, principal component analysis was applied to 153 subjects, and was able to differentiate the groups with 100% accuracy (Kerrouche et al., 2006). The AD group showed the typical findings as described above, but the VaD group showed hypometabolism in deep gray nuclei, cerebellum, primary cortices, middle temporal gyrus, and anterior cingulate gyrus (Figure 19.2, plate section).

Further insights into the utility of molecular imaging in assisting with differential diagnosis may potentially be gained through prospective studies of patients presenting for clinical evaluation with subtle symptoms consistent with a degenerative condition who do not yet have a clear clinical diagnosis. If such individuals are scanned and then followed clinically (and ultimately pathologically), it may be possible to learn more about the predictive power of molecular imaging in differential diagnosis (Herholz, 2003).

Molecular imaging as a biomarker for monitoring or prediction of clinical status

Longitudinal studies have shown that baseline PET and SPECT measures are useful for the prediction of future cognitive decline in AD patients (Chen et al., 2010; Jagust et al., 1996; Wolfe et al., 1995) and the early detection of disease state in individuals with MCI (Arnaiz et al., 2001; Chetelat et al., 2003; Herholz et al., 1999; Johnson et al., 1998; Rinne & Nagren, 2010). Serial functional imaging studies have demonstrated that progressive metabolic decline correlates with cognitive decline in AD patients (Haxby et al., 1990; Jagust et al., 1988; Kitagawa, 2010). Power calculations suggest that PET measures may be more sensitive than cognitive measures in a one-year clinical drug trial, with estimates of 41–228 and 246–390 subjects, respectively (effect size = 25%, power = 80%) (Alexander et al., 2002).

The modulatory effects of genetic risk factors for neurological disease on brain activity

In the last few years, there has been an explosion in the literature on the basic science of genetic modulators of brain function (Hariri & Weinberger, 2003). This is an area that is ripe for study in neurological disease, with a number of studies having been done in populations at elevated genetic risk for AD and other neurodegenerative disorders.

The APOE ε4 allele is a major genetic susceptibility factor associated with increased risk for AD (Saunders, 2000). A number of studies have demonstrated that cognitively intact subjects who are carriers of the APOE ε4 allele show evidence of temporoparietal hypometabolism with a pattern similar to, but of milder severity, that of AD. In individuals in their 50s without cognitive decline, progressive metabolic decline has been observed in ε4 carriers after two years (Reiman et al., 2001). Intriguingly, this finding has been observed in carriers of the ε4 allele who are young, in their 20s and 30s (Reiman, 2007). Thus, it may be a lifelong vulnerability pattern (endophenotype) that mediates the risk effects of the gene, since it would be very unusual for young individuals to already have begun to accumulate AD pathology.

Tantalizing results are emerging from longitudinal studies with serial FDG-PET measures in subjects at elevated risk for clinical AD, but in whom symptoms are very mild or absent. Progressive metabolic abnormalities parallel cognitive decline in both older cognitively intact individuals (de Leon et al., 2001) and subjects with mild memory impairment who carry the APOE ε4 allele (Small et al., 2000).

Huntington's disease (HD) provides an excellent opportunity to study functional brain alterations in individuals who are genetically destined to develop the disease but who are not yet manifesting symptoms. Presymptomatic carriers of the genetic abnormality for HD demonstrate frontal and temporal cortical as well as striatal hypometabolism on FDG-PET scans (Ciarmiello et al., 2006).

Uses of molecular imaging in understanding and monitoring neurotherapeutics

Molecular imaging may be particularly valuable in evaluating acute and subacute effects of medications on neural activity. PET and SPECT measures of resting brain function appear to be sensitive to medication effects in clinical drug trials and relate to clinical measures in a manner that suggests their potential utility as surrogate markers. In four studies of cerebral metabolism or perfusion in AD patients given cholinesterase inhibitors, these functional brain measures paralleled clinical measures in demonstrating stability or improvement in treated vs. placebo groups or in predicting response in treated patients (Mega et al., 2001; Nakano et al., 2001; Nobili et al., 2002; Tune et al., 2003).

Molecular imaging methods have been used to monitor the effects of therapies in PD, including deep brain stimulation. Subthalamic nucleus stimulation is associated with normalization of abnormalities of cortical and basal ganglia metabolism (Hilker et al., 2004; Trost et al., 2006).

Molecular Imaging of Neurotransmitter Receptors

Molecular imaging methods can be used to visualize and quantify the distribution, density, and activity of neurotransmitter receptors in the brain. The development of tracers for specific receptors faces a number of challenges, including the need for stability of labeling, selectivity for the receptor of interest, rapid permeation of the blood–brain barrier, and relatively little in the way of metabolites that could cloud the interpretation of the signal (Heiss & Herholz, 2006).

With regard to the dopaminergic system, 18F-fluorodopa (F-DOPA) and 11C-raclopride are the most commonly used PET radiotracers. F-DOPA is typically interpreted as reflecting the amount of dopaminergic cells present (presynaptic dopamine-synthesizing cells), while raclopride reflects postsynaptic dopamine receptor (D2) density. The typical F-DOPA finding in PD is reduced tracer binding in posterior putamen, suggestive of the >50% loss of dopaminergic neurons projecting to this part of the striatum (Brooks, 1993). Furthermore, there is also a reduction of cortical F-DOPA in PD (Ito et al., 2002). In contrast, the binding capacity of postsynaptic striatal dopaminergic receptors is increased in PD (Figure 19.3, plate section). The increase is most pronounced in the posterior putamen, where the dopamine deficit is known to be most severe. As the disease progresses, striatal dopamine receptor activity declines to normal and eventually falls below normal (Figure 19.3). Dopaminergic therapy modulates these changes. Treatment with tissue grafting or subthalamic stimulation has, surprisingly, not clearly resulted in improvements in dopamine receptor density, even in situations where there are clear clinical benefits. In progressive supranuclear palsy and multiple systems atrophy, a loss of both pre- and postsynaptic dopaminergic receptors has been demonstrated. These observations support the potential value of dopaminergic receptor imaging in the differential diagnosis of Parkinson's disease from parkinsonian syndrome caused by multiple system atrophy (Figure 19.3). Abnormalities in postsynaptic striatal neurons can also be shown with dopaminergic receptor imaging in Huntington's disease, where presynaptic dopamine turnover is normal (Heiss & Herholz, 2006).

These measures may be very sensitive to subtle cognitive or motor signs. Even in PD patients without dementia and with normal FDG-PET scans, there is a correlation between F-DOPA binding in basal ganglia and memory test performance (Holthoff-Detto et al., 1997). On the other hand, there is a reduction in basal ganglia F-DOPA in DLB, even in patients without motor signs of parkinsonism (Hu et al., 2000), which contrasts with AD in which basal ganglia F-DOPA is normal.

With regard to the cholinergic system, a number of tracers have been developed relatively recently that enable the measurement of, for example, acetylcholinesterase activity (e.g., MP3A). Studies in patients with AD have shown a widespread reduction of acetylcholinesterase activity in the cerebral cortex (Herholz et al., 2000; Herholz et al., 2004; Herholz et al., 2005) (Figure 19.4, plate section) and allow differentiation from Parkinson's disease and progressive nuclear palsy. Additionally, the early loss of cholinergic transmission in the cortex could be shown with these tracers, which precedes the loss of cholinergic neurons in the nucleus basalis of Meynert (Figure 19.4). The inhibition of acetylcholinesterase, resulting from treatment with specific drugs, such as donepezil, can also be measured with these tracers (Kuhl et al., 2000). Of interest, even though the cholinergic deficit is very widespread in the cortex of AD patients including occipital cortex (Shinotoh et al., 2000), there is an even more profound occipital cholinergic deficit in patients with DLB (Heiss & Herholz, 2006), suggesting that this may be another means for differential diagnosis.

Molecular Imaging of Pathological Markers in Neurodegenerative Diseases

Our understanding of the basic mechanisms involved in the pathogenesis of AD and other neurodegenerative diseases has rapidly advanced (Walsh & Selkoe, 2004), and there are now specific disease-modifying strategies that target brain amyloid formation (Schenk et al., 1999). These dramatic advances, including preliminary evidence suggesting that such agents may be effective, have motivated intense research efforts to develop a means to accurately identify plaque pathology in vivo with neuroimaging.

Radiochemistry research has led to the development of a class of tracers that specifically bind to amyloid plaques in mouse models of AD (Mathis et al., 2002), cross the blood–brain barrier, and label plaques in vivo in humans. One such compound, known as Pittsburgh Compound B (PiB), has been tested in animal models of AD, in human AD postmortem brain tissue, in living healthy elderly subjects, and in patients with a clinical diagnosis of AD (Klunk et al., 2004). Another agent labels both fibrillar amyloid and tau (Small et al., 2006).

PiB has recently been tested in living human subjects, including normal elderly and patients with the clinical diagnosis of mild probable AD (Figure 19.5, plate section). The absolute level of PiB retention was approximately the same in the cerebellum and white matter of AD patients and normal control subjects, brain areas known to lack substantial deposits of fibrillar amyloid. In contrast, PiB retention was very high in AD patients in frontal, temporal, and parietal neocortical regions (Klunk et al., 2004; Nordberg, 2007). As expected, PiB binding similar to that of AD is seen in some subjects with mild cognitive impairment (MCI) (Forsberg et al., 2008), reflecting the presence of significant pathology even at this mild level of clinical impairment, as has also been seen in pathological studies. PiB imaging has also confirmed what has long been known from postmortem studies (Tomlinson et al., 1968): many elderly cognitively intact individuals carry a substantial burden of AD neuropathology (Mintun et al., 2006). Yet brain amyloid levels may plateau and remain fairly stable longitudinally in AD dementia (Engler et al., 2006). Thus, PET pathology markers may assist in diagnosis, but PET metabolic markers or MRI atrophy markers will likely be important for measuring changes in the rate of disease progression. Whether these findings will be useful in the prediction of the eventual development of AD dementia in nondemented individuals remains a topic of intense investigation.

The successful visualization of direct markers of AD neuropathology in living humans is a major step forward in the field, and suggests that more specific in vivo diagnostic and monitoring capabilities may be on the horizon. Furthermore, initial studies comparing AD and FTD patients suggest that it may be possible to differentiate neurodegenerative diseases using specific tracers that bind to pathological proteins (Rabinovici et al., 2007), rather than indirectly through the effects of the diseases on brain function and structure. In addition, these approaches may be very useful in the burgeoning efforts to improve translational research between animal models and humans. However, a number of issues will need to be addressed as part of the validation of these methods as surrogate markers. While visualization of a "signal of pathology" has been demonstrated, work is still in progress to refine quantitative metrics and determine the specificity of these measures. Finally, it is not yet clear how early in prodromal or presymptomatic AD these imaging pathological signals will be detectable.

Beyond Exclusion: The Use of Imaging Measures as Disease Biomarkers

At present, the potential efficacy of disease-modifying therapies for AD and other neurodegenerative diseases is evaluated primarily using clinical measures of cognition, movement, and other behaviors. In animal models, traditional behavioral assessments are often used, such as the rate at which rodents learn to navigate a maze. In clinical trials, outcome measures are typically performance-based instruments, such as the Alzheimer's Disease Assessment Scale (ADAS-Cog) (Rosen et al., 1984), or structured surveys of clinician/caregiver impression of change (Schneider et al., 1997). Although the efficacy of disease-modifying treatments for AD and other neurodegenerative diseases must ultimately be demonstrated using clinically meaningful outcome measures such as the slowing of decline in progression of symptoms or functional impairment, such trials will likely require hundreds of patients studied for a minimum of one to two years. Thus, surrogate markers of efficacy with less variability than clinical assessments are desperately needed to reduce the number of subjects. These markers may also prove particularly valuable in the early phases of drug development to detect a preliminary "signal of efficacy" over a shorter time period.

Since the pathophysiological process underlying cognitive decline in AD and other neurodegenerative diseases involves the progressive degeneration of particular brain regions, repeatable in vivo neuroimaging measures of brain anatomy, chemistry, physiology, and pathology hold promise as an important class of potential biomarkers (DeKosky & Marek, 2003). A growing body of data indicates that the natural history of gradually progressive cognitive decline in AD can be reliably related to changes in such imaging measures. Furthermore, regionally specific changes in brain anatomy, chemistry, physiology, and pathology can be detected by imaging prior to the point at which the disease is symptomatic enough to make a typical clinical diagnosis. Thus, potential disease-modifying therapies may act by impeding the accumulation of neuropathology, slowing the loss of neurons, altering neurochemistry, or preserving synaptic function; neuroimaging modalities exist to measure each of these putative therapeutic goals, and molecular imaging could potentially play a valuable role in the development of new scientific insights into functional brain abnormalities early in the course of these diseases and in the development of therapeutic agents.

As advances in research provide data to support the use of specific imaging measures as biomarkers, it becomes apparent that these measures could be useful in diagnosis, and eventually may find applications in routine clinical practice. As neurological diagnosis of neurodegenerative diseases moves beyond the simple use of imaging for the exclusion of mass lesions or other "potentially reversible" causes of dementia or other symptoms, these tools will become increasingly more important in routine practice (Scheltens et al., 2002). In fact, the American Academy of Neurology recently proposed that a structural neuroimaging study should be performed in the workup of all cases of dementia (Knopman et al., 2001). An increasing number of diagnostic criteria sets, including AD, frontotemporal, Lewy body, and cerebrovascular dementias, are including neuroimaging evidence as a core or supportive component (Dubois et al., 2007; McKeith et al., 2005; Neary et al., 1998; Neary et al., 2005; O'Brien et al., 2003). Thus, research motivated toward improving our understanding of the natural history of neurodegenerative diseases and toward the development of new therapies is also assisting in the translation of diagnostic tools from bench to bedside.

Acknowledgments

Support for this work was provided in part by grants from the National Institutes of Health (NIA K23-AG22509, R01-AG029411) and the Alzheimer's Association.

References

Albin, R. L., Minoshima, S., D'Amato, C. J., Frey, K. A., Kuhl, D. A., & Sima, A. A. (1996). Fluoro-deoxyglucose positron emission tomography in diffuse Lewy body disease. *Neurology*, *47*, 462–466.

Alexander, G. E., Chen, K., Pietrini, P., Rapoport, S. I., & Reiman, E. M. (2002). Longitudinal PET evaluation of cerebral metabolic decline in dementia: A potential outcome measure in Alzheimer's disease treatment studies. *American Journal of Psychiatry*, *159*, 738–745.

Antonini, A., Leenders, K. L., Spiegel, R., Meier, D., Vontobel, P., Weigell-Weber, M., et al. (1996). Striatal glucose metabolism and dopamine D2 receptor binding in asymptomatic gene carriers and patients with Huntington's disease. *Brain*, *119*, 2085–2095.

Arnaiz, E., Jelic, V., Almkvist, O., Wahlund, L. O., Winblad, B., Valind, S., et al. (2001). Impaired cerebral glucose metabolism and cognitive functioning predict deterioration in mild cognitive impairment. *Neuroreport*, *12*, 851–855.

Bergmans, B. A., & De Strooper, B. (2010). Gamma-secretases: From cell biology to therapeutic strategies. *Lancet Neurology*, *9*, 215–226.

Bertram, L., & Tanzi, R. E. (2005). The genetic epidemiology of neurodegenerative disease. *Journal of Clinical Investigations*, *115*, 1449–1457.

Bradley, K. M., O'Sullivan, V. T., Soper, N. D., Nagy, Z., King, E. M., Smith, A. D., et al. (2002). Cerebral perfusion SPET correlated with Braak pathological stage in Alzheimer's disease. *Brain, 125,* 1772–1781.

Brooks, D. J. (1993). PET studies on the early and differential diagnosis of Parkinson's disease. *Neurology 43,* S6–S16.

Chen, K., Langbaum, J. B., Fleisher, A. S., Ayutyanont, N., Reschke, C., Lee, W., et al. (2010). Twelve-month metabolic declines in probable Alzheimer's disease and amnestic mild cognitive impairment assessed using an empirically pre-defined statistical region-of-interest: Findings from the Alzheimer's Disease Neuroimaging Initiative. *Neuroimage, 51*(2), 654–656.

Chetelat, G., Desgranges, B., de la Sayette, V., Viader, F., Eustache, F., & Baron, J. C. (2003). Mild cognitive impairment: Can FDG-PET predict who is to rapidly convert to Alzheimer's disease? *Neurology, 60,* 1374–1377.

Ciarmiello, A., Cannella, M., Lastoria, S., Simonelli, M., Frati, L., Rubinsztein, D. C., et al. (2006). Brain white-matter volume loss and glucose hypometabolism precede the clinical symptoms of Huntington's disease. *Journal of Nuclear Medicine, 47,* 215–222.

Coleman, P., Federoff, H., & Kurlan, R. (2004). A focus on the synapse for neuroprotection in Alzheimer disease and other dementias. *Neurology, 63,* 1155–1162.

de Leon, M. J., Convit, A., Wolf, O. T., Tarshish, C. Y., DeSanti, S., Rusinek, H., et al. (2001) Prediction of cognitive decline in normal elderly subjects with 2-[(18)F]fluoro-2-deoxy-D-glucose/poitron-emission tomography (FDG/PET). *Proceedings of the National Academy of Sciences USA, 98,* 10966–10971.

De Santi, S., de Leon, M. J., Rusinek, H., Convit, A., Tarshish, C. Y., Roche, A., et al. (2001). Hippocampal formation glucose metabolism and volume losses in MCI and AD. *Neurobiology of Aging, 22,* 529–539.

DeKosky, S. T., & Marek, K. (2003). Looking backward to move forward: Early detection of neurodegenerative disorders. *Science, 302,* 830–834.

Dickerson, B. C., & Sperling, R. A. (2005). Neuroimaging biomarkers for clinical trials of disease-modifying therapies in Alzheimer's sisease. *Neurorx, 2,* 348–360.

Dickerson, B. C., & Sperling, R. A. (2009). Large-scale functional brain network abnormalities in Alzheimer's disease: Insights from functional neuroimaging. *Behavioral Neurology, 21,* 63–75.

Duara, R., Barker, W., Loewenstein, D., Pascal, S., & Bowen, B. (1989). Sensitivity and specificity of positron emission tomography and magnetic resonance imaging studies in Alzheimer's disease and multi-infarct dementia. *European Neurology, 29*(Suppl 3), 9–15.

Dubois, B., Feldman, H. H., Jacova, C., Dekosky, S. T., Barberger-Gateau, P., Cummings, J., et al. (2007). Research criteria for the diagnosis of Alzheimer's disease: Revising the NINCDS-ADRDA criteria. *Lancet Neurology, 6,* 734–746.

Eckert, T., Barnes, A., Dhawan, V., Frucht, S., Gordon, M. F., Feigin, A. S., et al. (2005). FDG PET in the differential diagnosis of parkinsonian disorders. *Neuroimage, 26,* 912–921.

Engler, H., Forsberg, A., Almkvist, O., Blomquist, G., Larsson, E., Savitcheva, I., et al. (2006). Two-year follow-up of amyloid deposition in patients with Alzheimer's disease. *Brain, 129,* 2856–2866.

Forsberg, A., Engler, H., Almkvist, O., Blomquist, G., Hagman, G., Wall, A., et al. (2008). PET imaging of amyloid deposition in patients with mild cognitive impairment. *Neurobiology of Aging, 29*(10), 1456–1465.

Foster, N. L., Chase, T. N., Mansi, L., Brooks, R., Fedio, P., Patronas, N. J., et al. (1984). Cortical abnormalities in Alzheimer's disease. *Annals of Neurology, 16*, 649–654.

Foster, N. L., Heidebrink, J. L., Clark, C. M., Jagust, W. J., Arnold, S. E., Barbas, N.R., et al. (2007). FDG-PET improves accuracy in distinguishing frontotemporal dementia and Alzheimer's disease. *Brain, 130*(Pt 10), 2616–2635.

Fox, G. B., Chin, C. L., Luo, F., Day, M., & Cox, B. F. (2009). Translational neuroimaging of the CNS: Novel pathways to drug development. *Molecular Interventions, 9*, 302–313.

Grundman, M., Petersen, R. C., Ferris, S. H., Thomas, R. G., Aisen, P. S., Bennett, D. A., et al. (2004). Mild cognitive impairment can be distinguished from Alzheimer disease and normal aging for clinical trials. *Archives of Neurology, 61*, 59–66.

Guze, B. H., Baxter, L. R., Jr., Schwartz, J. M., Szuba, M. P., Mazziotta, J. C., & Phelps, M. E. (1991). Changes in glucose metabolism in dementia of the Alzheimer type compared with depression: A preliminary report. *Psychiatry Research, 40*, 195–202.

Haense, C., Herholz, K., Jagust, W. J., & Heiss, W. D. (2009). Performance of FDG PET for detection of Alzheimer's disease in two independent multicentre samples (NEST-DD and ADNI). *Dementia and Geriatric Cognitive Disorders, 28*, 259–266.

Hariri, A. R., & Weinberger, D. R. (2003). Functional neuroimaging of genetic variation in serotonergic neurotransmission. *Genes, Brain and Behavior, 2*, 341–349.

Haxby, J. V., Grady, C. L., Koss, E., Horwitz, B., Heston, L., Schapiro, M., et al. (1990). Longitudinal study of cerebral metabolic asymmetries and associated neuropsychological patterns in early dementia of the Alzheimer type. *Archives of Neurology, 47*, 753–760.

Heiss, W.D., & Herholz, K. (2006). Brain receptor imaging. *Journal of Nuclear Medicine, 47*, 302–312.

Herholz, K. (2003). PET studies in dementia. *Annals of Nuclear Medicine, 17*, 79–89.

Herholz, K., Bauer, B., Wienhard, K., Kracht, L., Mielke, R., Lenz, M. O., et al. (2000). In vivo measurements of regional acetylcholine esterase activity in degenerative dementia: Comparison with blood flow and glucose metabolism. *Journal of Neural Transmission, 107*, 1457–1468.

Herholz, K., Nordberg, A., Salmon, E., Perani, D., Kessler, J., Mielke, R., et al. (1999). Impairment of neocortical metabolism predicts progression in Alzheimer's disease. *Dementia and Geriatric Cognitive Disorders, 10*, 494–504.

Herholz, K., Perani, D., Salmon, E., Franck, G., Fazio, F., Heiss, W.D., et al. (1993). Comparability of FDG PET studies in probable Alzheimer's disease. *Journal of Nuclear Medicine, 34*, 1460–1466.

Herholz, K., Weisenbach, S., Kalbe, E., Diederich, N. J., & Heiss, W. D. (2005). Cerebral acetylcholine esterase activity in mild cognitive impairment. *Neuroreport, 16*, 1431–1434.

Herholz, K., Weisenbach, S., Zundorf, G., Lenz, O., Schroder, H., Bauer, B., et al. (2004). In vivo study of acetylcholine esterase in basal forebrain, amygdala, and cortex in mild to moderate Alzheimer disease. *Neuroimage, 21*, 136–143.

Hilker, R., Voges, J., Weisenbach, S., Kalbe, E., Burghaus, L., Ghaemi, M., et al. (2004). Subthalamic nucleus stimulation restores glucose metabolism in associative and limbic cortices and in cerebellum: Evidence from a FDG-PET study in advanced Parkinson's disease. *Journal of Cerebral Blood Flow & Metabolism, 24*, 7–16.

Holthoff, V. A., Beuthien-Baumann, B., Kalbe, E., Ludecke, S., Lenz, O., Zundorf, G., et al. (2005). Regional cerebral metabolism in early Alzheimer's disease with clinically significant apathy or depression. *Biological Psychiatry, 57*, 412–421.

Holthoff-Detto, V. A., Kessler, J., Herholz, K., Bonner, H., Pietrzyk, U., Wurker, M., et al. (1997). Functional effects of striatal dysfunction in Parkinson disease. *Archives of Neurology, 54*, 145–150.

Hu, X. S., Okamura, N., Arai, H., Higuchi, M., Matsui, T., Tashiro, M., et al. (2000). 18F-fluorodopa PET study of striatal dopamine uptake in the diagnosis of dementia with Lewy bodies. *Neurology, 55*, 1575–1577.

Ibanez, V., Pietrini, P., Alexander, G. E., Furey, M. L., Teichberg, D., Rajapakse, J. C., et al. (1998). Regional glucose metabolic abnormalities are not the result of atrophy in Alzheimer's disease. *Neurology, 50*, 1585–1593.

Ito, K., Nagano-Saito, A., Kato, T., Arahata, Y., Nakamura, A., Kawasumi, Y., et al. (2002). Striatal and extrastriatal dysfunction in Parkinson's disease with dementia: A 6-[18F] fluoro-L-dopa PET study. *Brain, 125*, 1358–1365.

Jagust, W. J. (2000). Neuroimaging in dementia. *Neurologic Clinics, 18*, 885–902.

Jagust, W. J., Friedland, R. P., Budinger, T. F., Koss, E., & Ober, B. (1988). Longitudinal studies of regional cerebral metabolism in Alzheimer's disease. *Neurology, 38*, 909–912.

Jagust, W. J., Haan, M. N., Eberling, J. L., Wolfe, N., & Reed, B. R. (1996). Functional imaging predicts cognitive decline in Alzheimer's disease. *Journal of Neuroimaging, 6*, 156–160.

Jagust, W. J., Reed, B., Mungas, D., Ellis, W., & DeCarli, C. (2007). What does fluorodeoxy-glucose PET imaging add to a clinical diagnosis of dementia? *Neurology, 69*, 871–877.

Johnson, K. A., Jones, K., Holman, B. L., Becker, J. A., Spiers, P. A., Satlin, A., et al. (1998). Preclinical prediction of Alzheimer's disease using SPECT. *Neurology, 50*, 1563–1571.

Kerrouche, N., Herholz, K., Mielke, R., Holthoff, V., & Baron, J. C. (2006). 18FDG PET in vascular dementia: Differentiation from Alzheimer's disease using voxel-based multi-variate analysis. *Journal of Cerebral Blood Flow & Metabolism, 26*, 1213–1221.

Kew, J. J., Brooks, D. J., Passingham, R. E., Rothwell, J. C., Frackowiak, R. S., & Leigh, P. N. (1994). Cortical function in progressive lower motor neuron disorders and amyotrophic lateral sclerosis: A comparative PET study. *Neurology, 44*, 1101–1110.

Kitagawa, K. (2010). Cerebral blood flow measurement by PET in hypertensive subjects as a marker of cognitive decline. *Journal of Alzheimer's Disease, 20*(3), 855–859.

Klunk, W. E., Engler, H., Nordberg, A., Wang, Y., Blomqvist, G., Holt, D. P., et al. (2004). Imaging brain amyloid in Alzheimer's disease with Pittsburgh Compound-B. *Annals of Neurology, 55*, 306–319.

Knopman, D. S., DeKosky, S. T., Cummings, J. L., Chui, H., Corey-Bloom, J., Relkin, N., et al. (2001) Practice parameter: Diagnosis of dementia (an evidence-based review). Report of the Quality Standards Subcommittee of the American Academy of Neurology. *Neurology, 56*, 1143–1153.

Kuhl, D. E., Minoshima, S., Frey, K. A., Foster, N. L., Kilbourn, M. R., & Koeppe, R. A. (2000). Limited donepezil inhibition of acetylcholinesterase measured with positron emission tomography in living Alzheimer cerebral cortex. *Annals of Neurology, 48*, 391–395.

Lobotesis, K., Fenwick, J. D., Phipps, A., Ryman, A., Swann, A., Ballard, C., et al. (2001). Occipital hypoperfusion on SPECT in dementia with Lewy bodies but not AD. *Neurology, 56*, 643–649.

Lombardo, J. A., Stern, E. A., McLellan, M. E., Kajdasz, S. T., Hickey, G. A., Bacskai, B. J., et al. (2003). Amyloid-beta antibody treatment leads to rapid normalization of plaque-induced neuritic alterations. *Journal of Neuroscience, 23*, 10879–10883.

Mathis, C. A., Bacskai, B. J., Kajdasz, S. T., McLellan, M. E., Frosch, M. P., Hyman, B. T., et al. (2002). A lipophilic thioflavin-T derivative for positron emission tomography (PET) imaging of amyloid in brain. *Bioorganic & Medicinal Chemistry Letters, 12,* 295–298.

McKeith, I. G., Dickson, D. W., Lowe, J., Emre, M., O'Brien, J. T., Feldman, H., et al. (2005). Diagnosis and management of dementia with Lewy bodies. Third report of the DLB consortium. *Neurology, 65*(12), 1863–1872.

Mega, M. S., Chen, S. S., Thompson, P. M., Woods, R. P., Karaca, T. J., Tiwari, A., et al. (1997). Mapping histology to metabolism: Coregistration of stained whole-brain sections to premortem PET in Alzheimer's disease. *Neuroimage, 5,* 147–153.

Mega, M. S., Chu, T., Mazziotta, J. C., Trivedi, K. H., Thompson, P. M., Shah, A., et al. (1999). Mapping biochemistry to metabolism: FDG-PET and amyloid burden in Alzheimer's disease. *Neuroreport, 10,* 2911–2917.

Mega, M. S., Cummings, J. L., O'Connor, S. M., Dinov, I. D., Reback, E., Felix, J., et al. (2001). Cognitive and metabolic responses to metrifonate therapy in Alzheimer disease. *Neuropsychiatry, Neuropsychology and Behavioral Neurology, 14,* 63–68.

Meguro, K., Blaizot, X., Kondoh, Y., Le Mestric, C., Baron, J. C., & Chavoix, C. (1999). Neocortical and hippocampal glucose hypometabolism following neurotoxic lesions of the entorhinal and perirhinal cortices in the non-human primate as shown by PET. Implications for Alzheimer's disease. *Brain, 122*(Pt 8), 1519–1531.

Mielke, R., Herholz, K., Grond, M., Kessler, J., & Heiss, W. D. (1992). Differences of regional cerebral glucose metabolism between presenile and senile dementia of Alzheimer type. *Neurobiology of Aging, 13,* 93–98.

Minoshima, S., Giordani, B., Berent, S., Frey, K. A., Foster, N. L., & Kuhl, D. E. (1997). Metabolic reduction in the posterior cingulate cortex in very early Alzheimer's disease. *Annals of Neurology, 42,* 85–94.

Mintun, M. A., Larossa, G. N., Sheline, Y. I., Dence, C. S., Lee, S. Y., Mach, R. H., et al. (2006). [11C]PIB in a nondemented population: Potential antecedent marker of Alzheimer disease. *Neurology, 67,* 446–452.

Nakano, S., Asada, T., Matsuda, H., Uno, M., & Takasaki, M. (2001). Donepezil hydrochloride preserves regional cerebral blood flow in patients with Alzheimer's disease. *Journal of Nuclear Medicine, 42,* 1441–1445.

Neary, D., Snowden, J., & Mann, D. (2005). Frontotemporal dementia. *Lancet Neurology, 4,* 771–780.

Neary, D., Snowden, J., Gustafson, L., Passant, U., Stuss, D., Black, S., et al. (1998). Frontotemporal lobar degeneration: a consensus on clinical diagnostic criteria. *Neurology, 51,* 1546–1554.

Nobili, F., Koulibaly, M., Vitali, P., Migneco, O., Mariani, G., Ebmeier, K., et al. (2002). Brain perfusion follow-up in Alzheimer's patients during treatment with acetylcholinesterase inhibitors. *Journal of Nuclear Medicine, 43,* 983–990.

Nordberg, A. (2007). Amyloid imaging in Alzheimer's disease. *Current Opinion in Neurology, 20,* 398–402.

O'Brien, J.T., Erkinjuntti, T., Reisberg, B., Roman, G., Sawada, T., Pantoni, L., et al. (2003). Vascular cognitive impairment. *Lancet Neurology, 2,* 89–98.

Panegyres, P. K., Rogers, J. M., McCarthy, M., Campbell, A., & Wu, J. S. (2009). Fluorodeoxyglucose-positron emission tomography in the differential diagnosis of early-onset dementia: A prospective, community-based study. *BMC Neurology, 9,* 41.

Petersen, R. C., Roberts, R. O., Knopman, D. S., Boeve, B. F., Geda, Y. E., Ivnik, R. J., et al. (2009). Mild cognitive impairment: Ten years later. *Archives of Neurology, 66,* 1447–1455.

Petersen, R. C., Smith, G. E., Waring, S. C., Ivnik, R. J., Tangalos, E. G., & Kokmen, E. (1999). Mild cognitive impairment: clinical characterization and outcome. *Archives of Neurology, 56,* 303–308.

Rabinovici, G. D., Furst, A. J., Alkalay, A., Racine, C. A., O'Neil, J. P., Janabi, M., et al. (2010). Increased metabolic vulnerability in early-onset Alzheimer's disease is not related to amyloid burden. *Brain, 133*(Pt 2), 512–528.

Rabinovici, G. D., Furst, A. J., O'Neil, J. P., Racine, C. A., Mormino, E. C., Baker, S. L., et al. (2007). 11C-PIB PET imaging in Alzheimer disease and frontotemporal lobar degeneration. *Neurology, 68,* 1205–1212.

Reiman, E. M. (2007). Linking brain imaging and genomics in the study of Alzheimer's disease and aging. *Annals of the New York Academy of Science, 1097,* 94–113.

Reiman, E. M., Caselli, R. J., Chen, K., Alexander, G. E., Bandy, D., & Frost, J. (2001). Declining brain activity in cognitively normal apolipoprotein E epsilon 4 heterozygotes: A foundation for using positron emission tomography to efficiently test treatments to prevent Alzheimer's disease. *Proceedings of the National Academy of Sciences USA, 98,* 3334–3339.

Rinne, J. O., & Nagren, K. (2010). Positron emission tomography in at risk patients and in the progression of mild cognitive impairment to Alzheimer's disease. *Journal of Alzheimer's Disease, 19,* 291–300.

Rosen, W. G., Mohs, R. C., & Davis, K. L. (1984). A new rating scale for Alzheimer's disease. *American Journal of Psychiatry, 141,* 1356–1364.

Saunders, A. M. (2000). Apolipoprotein E and Alzheimer disease: An update on genetic and functional analyses. *Journal of Neuropathology and Experimental Neurology, 59,* 751–758.

Scheltens, P., Fox, N., Barkhof, F., & DeCarli, C. (2002). Structural magnetic resonance imaging in the practical assessment of dementia: Beyond exclusion. *Lancet Neurology, 1,* 13–21.

Schenk, D., Barbour, R., Dunn, W., Gordon, G., Grajeda, H., Guido, T., et al. (1999). Immunization with amyloid-beta attenuates Alzheimer-disease-like pathology in the PDAPP mouse. *Nature, 400,* 173–177.

Schneider, L. S., Olin, J. T., Doody, R. S., Clark, C. M., Morris, J. C., Reisberg, B., et al. (1997). Validity and reliability of the Alzheimer's Disease Cooperative Study-Clinical Global Impression of Change. The Alzheimer's Disease Cooperative Study. *Alzheimer Disease & Associated Disorders, 11*(Suppl 2), S22–S32.

Selkoe, D. J. (2002). Alzheimer's disease is a synaptic failure. *Science, 298,* 789–791.

Shinotoh, H., Namba, H., Fukushi, K., Nagatsuka, S., Tanaka, N., Aotsuka, A., et al. (2000). Brain acetylcholinesterase activity in Alzheimer disease measured by positron emission tomography. *Alzheimer Disease & Associated Disorders, 14*(Suppl 1), S114–S118.

Silverman, D. H., Small, G. W., Chang, C. Y., Lu, C. S., Kung De Aburto, M. A., Chen, W., et al. (2001). Positron emission tomography in evaluation of dementia: Regional brain metabolism and long-term outcome. *Journal of the American Medical Association, 286,* 2120–2127.

Small, G. W., Ercoli, L. M., Silverman, D. H., Huang, S. C., Komo, S., Bookheimer, S. Y., et al. (2000). Cerebral metabolic and cognitive decline in persons at genetic risk for

Alzheimer's disease. *Proceedings of the National Academy of Sciences USA*, *97*, 6037–6042.

Small, G. W., Kepe, V., Ercoli, L. M., Siddarth, P., Bookheimer, S. Y., Miller, K. J., et al. (2006). PET of brain amyloid and tau in mild cognitive impairment. *New England Journal of Medicine*, *355*, 2652–2663.

Sultzer, D. L., Mahler, M. E., Cummings, J. L., Van Gorp, W. G., Hinkin, C. H., & Brown, C. (1995). Cortical abnormalities associated with subcortical lesions in vascular dementia. Clinical and position emission tomographic findings. *Archives of Neurology*, *52*, 773–780.

Tomlinson, B. E., Blessed, G., & Roth, M. (1968). Observations on the brains of non-demented old people. *Journal of the Neurological Sciences*, *7*, 331–356.

Trojanowski, J. Q. (2004). Protein mis-folding emerges as a "drugable" target for discovery of novel therapies for neuropsychiatric diseases of aging. *American Journal of Geriatric Psychiatry*, *12*, 134–135.

Trost, M., Su, S., Su, P., Yen, R. F., Tseng, H. M., Barnes A, et al. (2006). Network modulation by the subthalamic nucleus in the treatment of Parkinson's disease. *Neuroimage*, *31*, 301–307.

Tune, L., Tiseo, P. J., Ieni, J., Perdomo, C., Pratt, R. D., Votaw, J. R., et al. (2003). Donepezil HCl (E2020) maintains functional brain activity in patients with Alzheimer disease: Results of a 24-week, double-blind, placebo-controlled study. *American Journal of Geriatric Psychiatry*, *11*, 169–177.

Walhovd, K. B., Fjell, A. M., Brewer, J., McEvoy, L. K., Fennema-Notestine, C., Hagler, D. J., Jr., et al. (2010). Combining MR imaging, positron-emission tomography, and CSF biomarkers in the diagnosis and prognosis of Alzheimer disease. *American Journal of Neuroradiology*, *31*, 347–354.

Walsh, D. M., & Selkoe, D. J. (2004). Deciphering the molecular basis of memory failure in Alzheimer's disease. *Neuron*, *44*, 181–193.

Weiner, H. L., Lemere, C. A., Maron, R., Spooner, E. T., Grenfell, T. J., Mori, C., et al. (2000) Nasal administration of amyloid-beta peptide decreases cerebral amyloid burden in a mouse model of Alzheimer's disease. *Annals of Neurology*, *48*, 567–579.

Wolfe, N., Reed, B. R., Eberling, J. L., & Jagust, W. J. (1995). Temporal lobe perfusion on single photon emission computed tomography predicts the rate of cognitive decline in Alzheimer's disease. *Archives of Neurology*, *52*, 257–262.

Yamaguchi, S., Meguro, K., Itoh, M., Hayasaka, C., Shimada, M., Yamazaki, H., et al. (1997). Decreased cortical glucose metabolism correlates with hippocampal atrophy in Alzheimer's disease as shown by MRI and PET. *Journal of Neurology, Neurosurgery & Psychiatry*, *62*, 596–600.

20

Using EEG and MEG to Understand Brain Physiology in Alzheimer's Disease and Related Dementias

Brandon A. Ally

Most of the cognitive processes that we take for granted in our daily lives, such as thinking and remembering, rely on some type of underlying brain activity. We now have several different methodologies in cognitive neuroscience to examine, measure, and understand this activity, each with its distinct advantages and drawbacks. A major distinction delineating these technologies separates those that measure *where* things happen in the brain (e.g., functional magnetic resonance imaging, positron emission tomography) versus those that measure *when* things happen in the brain (e.g., electroencephalography, magnetoencephalography). Though this is a major distinction, these methodologies converge on elucidating *how* processes happen in the brain, which may be the most interesting question for neuroscientists at present.

In an attempt to better understand how our brain activity for perceptual, cognitive, and motor functions changes over time, researchers have measured the electrical and magnetic fields generated by certain neural populations. Two specific techniques have rapidly gained interest: electroencephalography (EEG) and magnetoencephalography (MEG). EEG measures the electrical activity of the brain using electrodes or sensors placed on the scalp, whereas MEG measures the magnetic fields generated by the electrical activity using superconductive quantum interference devices (SQUIDs) placed over the head. Both techniques are noninvasive, particularly sensitive to the temporal aspects of brain function, and allow researchers to comment on the onset, duration, and interaction of certain perceptual, cognitive, or motor functions. In addition to temporal resolution on the order of milliseconds, newer technology using 128 or 256 recording sensors has

The Handbook of Alzheimer's Disease and Other Dementias, First Edition.
Edited by Andrew E. Budson, Neil W. Kowall.
© 2011 Blackwell Publishing Ltd. Published 2011 by Blackwell Publishing Ltd.

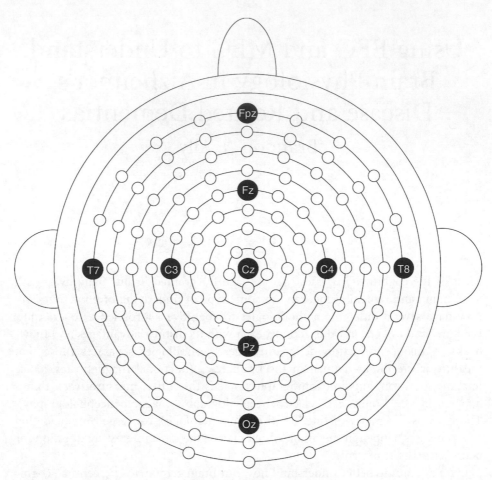

Figure 20.1 Surface head map showing electrode locations for an ActiveTwo (BioSemi, Amsterdam, Netherlands) 128-electrode array cap

realized the benefit of improved spatial resolution with these techniques. For an example of a common head cap using a 128-sensor array, see Figure 20.1. By using this type of head map, researchers can show areas of increased electrical and magnetic activity associated with a particular experimental or cognitive task.

Although research endeavors have examined a large number of dementias and related pathologies, there are several reasons why Alzheimer's disease (AD) has become the subject of intense research. Primarily, the electrical signals recorded in EEG are scalp potentials thought to reflect underlying cortical activity. AD is a cortical dementia in which EEG abnormalities are commonly seen. Although subcortical dementias do show subtle EEG changes, they exhibit rather normal patterns of activity compared to patients with AD (Verma et al., 1987). Further, EEG abnormalities seen in AD are more likely to reflect functional impairments due directly to pathology in underlying cortex (Jeong, 2004). Finally, AD is by far the most prevalent dementia, recently accounting for nearly 70% of all reported dementias (Plassman et al., 2007), and affecting nearly 50% of all individuals over the age of 85 (Vicioso, 2002). Therefore, this chapter will broadly examine research utilizing EEG and MEG techniques to better understand brain physiology in patients at risk for and in the mild-to-moderate stages of AD, as well as studies helping to differentiate AD from other dementias.

Electroencephalography

EEG recordings involving human subjects began in the early part of the 20th century, but technology has expanded the field tremendously over the past decade. Activity is typically recorded by sensors, or electrodes, placed on the scalp, that pick up very small fluctuations in the electrical activity of the brain (usually measured in microvolts). It is generally accepted that the signals that arise during EEG recording are derived from the summation of excitatory and inhibitory postsynaptic potentials rather than a summation of action potentials as once thought. Specifically, research suggests that scalp electrical potentials are due to the extracellular ionic currents caused by dendritic electrical activity. The activity recorded at the surface then reflects the summation of synchronous activity of nearly one billion cortical neurons located in a specific brain region (Kaiser & Lutzenberger, 2005). Historically, spontaneous EEG activity was recorded for short periods of time (20–40 minutes) in the clinical setting to help in the differential diagnoses between neurological and psychiatric disorders. However, its use in the clinical setting has become somewhat limited since the advent of anatomical neuroimaging techniques, such as magnetic resonance imaging (MRI) and computed tomography (CT). Although the use of EEG in the clinical setting has declined, EEG in the research arena has flourished. EEG research focuses on two general types of studies: (i) quantitative EEG and (ii) event-related potentials. These two methodologies, which will be discussed first in this chapter, have played an important role in both understanding changes in brain physiology over the course of a disease, and detecting changes in brain physiology for those at high risk for dementia.

Quantitative electroencephalography

Electroencephalography is typically reported in terms of speed, which is measured as the number of cycles from peak to peak in one second (Hz). These oscillations are thought to reflect the degree of cortical activation beneath the area of scalp covered by the electrode. For example, faster activity, such as beta (13–24 Hz) and gamma activity (24–70 Hz), is thought to indicate the increased brain activity needed for cognition, whereas alpha (8– 3 Hz), theta (4–8 Hz), and delta (0–4 Hz) activity are thought to represent states of relaxation, drowsiness, and sleep in adults, respectively. In studies of quantitative EEG (qEEG), the activity is typically converted into a digital signal from the analog EEG recordings and compared statistically to a normative sample of individuals with no known brain damage or disorder. Additionally, using a Fourier transformation, *absolute power* can then be calculated, which is a measure of the intensity, or stability over time, of activity within a series of frequency bands. Finally, researchers also examine *coherence*, which measures the consistency of two signals over time. In other words, researchers will look at correlation coefficients of the signal from two areas of the scalp to determine the extent to which they are synchronous to each other (Hughes & John, 1999). Coherence is thought to reflect the functional connectivity between brain regions. Therefore, it has been suggested that decreased coherence may reflect a loss of functional cortico–cortical interactions between certain brain regions.

Most studies involving patients with AD have shown altered spontaneous and elicited cortical activity compared to healthy age-matched peers (Holschneider & Leuchter, 1995). Conventional, visual analysis of EEG data from patients with AD reveals a general slowing of EEG activity and a decrease in the posterior dominant rhythm (Brenner et al., 1988). In general, these conventional analysis reports demonstrate that there is a strong correlation between EEG abnormalities and poor cognitive function. Work using computer-assisted spectral analysis of EEG, which provides improved quantitative analysis, has supported the notion of a general slowing of oscillatory activity in patients with AD. These studies report an increase in slow-wave activity, and a decrease in fast-wave activity (Coben et al., 1983; Huang et al., 2000; Schreiter-Gasser et al., 1993). More recent work has further suggested that the earliest changes seen in AD are an increase in theta activity accompanied by a decrease in beta activity, which are then followed by a decrease in alpha activity and an increase in delta activity as the disease progresses (see Baker et al., 2008). The significant decrement in fast-wave activity is particularly prominent in posterior and temporal regions in patients with AD (Rossini et al., 2006), areas of the brain thought to be critical to memory (Scoville & Milner, 1957; Wagner et al., 2005). Further, longitudinal studies have reported that over a two-year follow-up, patients with AD continue to demonstrate further increases in delta and theta activity as well as decreases in beta and alpha activity (Coben et al., 1985)

In addition to examination of bandwidth activity, recent work has investigated EEG coherence. Several studies have reported a general decrease in coherence of electrode sites in the alpha and beta bands (Dunkin et al., 1994; Jelles et al., 2008), with relative preservation of coherence in the slower bands (Besthorn et al., 1994). This decreased coherence in fast-wave activity has been correlated to degree of cognitive impairment (Dunkin et al., 1994), and has been particularly noted between frontal and parietal regions in patients with AD (Babiloni, Ferri et al., 2004). This loss in functional connectivity between these regions might be particularly significant with respect to impaired cognition and memory in patients with AD, as frontal and parietal regions play an important role during passive processing (i.e., the default network) (Raichle et al., 2003) and memory retrieval (Ally &

Budson, 2007; Wagner et al., 2005). The loss in functional connectivity, in combination with other neuropathology and functional neuroimaging results, has led to the hypothesis that AD is a neocortical disconnection syndrome (Jeong, 2004). However, other evidence has suggested that loss of coherence is likely due to cholinergic dysfunction in AD. Indeed, synaptic blockade of the cholinergic system using scopolamine reduces EEG coherence in healthy subjects (Kikuchi et al., 2000). Therefore, current hypotheses for decreased EEG coherence in patients with AD include both anatomical disconnections among different cortical regions, as well as reduced cholinergic coupling interactions between cortical neurons (Jeong, 2004).

Quantitative EEG work has investigated the functional significance of altered EEG patterns in patients with AD using cognitive and neuropsychological tests. Initial studies purported that a strong correlation exists between overall mean frequency and the severity of dementia. Helkala et al. (1991) further reported that patients who showed EEG abnormalities in the earliest stages of the disease exhibited rapid declines in praxic functions, confrontation naming, and language compared to those who did not show EEG abnormalities. Later studies showed that better cognitive performance is predicted by higher alpha and lower theta pre-task (Neubauer & Freudenthaler, 1995), and that successful memory encoding is dependent on tonic decreases in theta power over frontal brain regions, whereas successful retrieval is dependent on tonic increases in alpha power over posterior brain regions (Klimesch, 1999). As an example in patients with AD, Babiloni et al. (2007) showed that temporal slow-wave power at rest was negatively correlated with immediate visuospatial memory, and posterior alpha power at rest was positively correlated with digit span forward, a measure of focused attention. Data suggest that cholinergic basal forebrain neurons that project to hippocampal, frontal, and parietal regions, modulate alpha and slower EEG bands, and the disruption of these neurons in AD likely contributes to disrupted EEG patterns and worse performance on cognitive tests that rely on these brain regions (Helkala et al., 1996; Holschneider et al., 1999).

In addition to examining the relationship between qEEG and cognitive function, research has examined the relationship to structural and functional changes of the brain in patients with AD. It should be noted here, however, that whereas the relationship between the electrical activity of the brain and EEG signals measured at the scalp is generally well understood, the relationship between electrical activity of the brain and the hemodynamic response associated with fMRI is not. However, a number of pieces of converging evidence suggest there is some relationship between functional neuroimaging methods such as fMRI and PET and scalp-recorded EEG. Regional EEG changes in patients with AD, which are typically seen both in anterior and posterior brain regions, have been linked to decreased regional cerebral blood flow (Mattia et al., 2003; Rodriguez et al., 1999). Specifically, increases in theta band power have been linked with cerebral ischemia and hypoperfusion (Hughes & John, 1999; Jonkman et al., 1985). Further, increased theta activity has been associated with decreased glucose metabolism in temporal, parietal, and frontal regions (Szelies et al., 1992; Valladares-Neto et al., 1995) as well as decreased hippocampal volume (Helkala et al., 1996). Thus, it has been hypothesized that brain regions demonstrating excess slow-wave activity are under-perfused (Prichep, 2007).

Quantitative EEG techniques have also been used to differentiate AD from other types of dementia. Patients with vascular dementia (VaD) tend to show an uneven distribution of EEG abnormalities compared to patients with AD and healthy controls, likely due to differing cortical insults in vascular disease. Initial work highlighted an increase in focal abnormalities, as well as preserved occipital alpha activity compared to patients with AD (Sloan & Fenton, 1993). More recent work has shown that there is a general decline in alpha activity at central, parietal, occipital, and temporal regions for patients with AD compared to those with VaD and healthy controls (Babiloni, Binetti et al., 2004). To build on this type of work, a number of investigations have been launched to help clarify the clinical picture regarding difficult differential diagnoses. As an example, Schreiter-Gasser et al. (2008) showed that patients with a mixed AD-subcortical vascular pathology demonstrated significantly higher delta and theta power compared to the pure AD patients. Schreiter-Gasser et al. (2008) interpreted these results to suggest that the increase in slow-wave power for the patients with mixed etiology was likely due to a greater burden of subcortical vascular lesions. In another example, Lindau et al. (2003) showed that patients with both frontotemporal dementia (FTD) and AD were noted to have a decrease in fast-wave activity, whereas only the AD group demonstrated an increase in slow-wave activity. Finally, Andersson et al. (2008) showed that patients with dementia with Lewy bodies (DLB) showed a higher degree of overall coherence in the delta band and a lower degree of coherence in the alpha band at parietal electrode sites compared to patients with AD and healthy older controls. Andersson et al. (2008) suggested that this variability in cortical activity may reflect the fluctuating cognition seen in patients with DLB.

Lastly, qEEG has been used to examine individuals at high risk of converting to dementia. Specifically, patients with mild cognitive impairment (MCI) have been the subject of intense study in recent years due to the high rate of conversion to dementia (Petersen, 2004). In fact, Petersen (2004) reported that the amnestic subtype of MCI is associated with a tenfold increase in yearly conversion rate to AD compared to age-matched controls with no cognitive impairment. Finding preclinical markers and additional risk factors for AD can prospectively lead to more accurate diagnosis of those who will ultimately develop the disease, allowing treatments to be initiated earlier. Studies investigating qEEG have found some similarities between patients with MCI and those with AD. Consistent with the hypothesis that MCI is a transitional stage between healthy aging and AD (Petersen, 2004), studies report patients with MCI demonstrate increased theta power and decreased fast-wave amplitudes at ranges that fall between healthy older adults and patients with AD (Babiloni et al., 2007; Huang et al., 2000; Jelic et al., 1996; Zappoli et al., 1995). The increase in theta power for patients with MCI has been reported in regions similar to those in AD: temporal, parietal, and frontal (Grunwald et al., 2001; Kwak 2006). Additionally, Grunwald and colleagues (2001) reported a significant negative linear correlation between theta power over frontal regions and hippocampal volume in patients with MCI.

Research investigating qEEG in patients with MCI has extended into examining the ability of this measure to predict who will ultimately go on to develop dementia. Jelic et al. (2000) reported in a longitudinal study that combined alpha and theta power were predictive of patients with MCI that would ultimately convert to AD, compared to patients with MCI that remained relatively stable over a two-year period. Further, Huang et al. (2000) showed that this combined alpha and theta activity was able to discriminate between patients with MCI and AD at a fairly high rate (78% correctly classified). Huang and colleagues also found that patients with MCI who converted to AD within an average of 25 months showed overall decreased alpha activity and more anterior localization of theta, alpha, and beta frequency bands than patients with MCI who did not convert to AD within that time.

In summary, qEEG has been commonly used in clinical settings over the past 30 years in the diagnosis of dementia. It has been particularly useful in combination with other neuroimaging methods. For example, Jelic and colleagues found that the combination of EEG and PET resulted in approximately 90% of overall correct classification with a specificity of 100% (Jelic et al., 1999). Research studies examining qEEG in patients with AD find a general slowing in mean frequency. In particular, the earliest changes seen in AD are an increase in theta activity accompanied by a decrease in beta activity, which are then followed by a decrease in alpha activity and an increase in delta activity as the disease progresses. Studies of EEG coherence, or functional connectivity between brain regions, report a disconnect in the fast-wave band particularly between frontal and parietal regions. Recent hypotheses suggest that this diminished coherence reflects both cortical disconnection and cholinergic dysfunction common to AD. Further, the decrease in fast-wave activity, increase in slow-wave activity, and diminished coherence have been linked to poor performance on a range of cognitive tests. Finally, qEEG work has been critical in understanding individuals at risk for dementia. Studies report patients with MCI demonstrate decreased alpha and increased theta power at ranges that fall between healthy older adults and patients with AD, and that combined alpha and theta relative power were predictive of patients with MCI who would ultimately convert to AD. Quantitative EEG remains an interesting and cost-effective avenue for helping to diagnose and possibly predict diseases of aging.

Event-related potentials

Event-related potentials (ERPs) are *epochs* of standard EEG activity that are time-locked to the onset of sensory stimuli. These epochs, or periods of time, are typically averaged over many trials to control for movement and other artifacts such as eyeblink. The averaged ERP waveform then shows fluctuations in scalp electrical activity associated with the perception and processing of stimuli, or the engagement of certain cognitive processes. Early research referred to these recorded potentials as *evoked potentials* because it was thought that they were directly evoked by certain stimuli. However, more recent work has demonstrated that these potentials are reflective of brain activity that arises from the cognitive demands of an individual experimental task. Therefore, terminology has switched to the more appropriate *event-related potentials* when describing this type of work. ERP researchers typically examine waveform *components* with regard to both amplitude and latency of response. Though there has been some controversy as to what exactly constitutes an ERP component, for ease of use, and to compare across studies, these components are labeled according to amplitude and latency variables. For example, a positive inflection in the waveform around 300 ms is known as the P300 component, whereas a negative inflection in the waveform around 400 ms is known as the N400 component. A quick search of the literature shows that there are over 15 ERP components studied with regard to patients with dementia. Therefore, this chapter will group these components into the brain responses related to the early and mid-latency sensory/perceptual components and the late-latency cognitive components.

Early and mid-latency ERPs

Research suggests that early sensory ERP components occurring between stimulus onset and approximately 300 ms post-stimulus reflect activity of primary and secondary sensory cortices (P50, N100, P200), as well as cortical association networks (N200, P300). In general, early ERP components associated with activity of primary and secondary sensory cortices appear to remain relatively intact for patients. Indeed, initial investigations showed that N100 and P200 latencies were normal compared to healthy controls (Goodin & Aminoff, 1986). However, more recent studies have suggested possible differences within the auditory and visual domains. For example, Saito et al. (2001) recorded event-related potentials during a geometrical figure discrimination task in patients with AD. The early ERP components associated with sensory processing and pattern recognition were similar between patients and healthy age-matched controls. In contrast, research involving auditory ERPs shows that early sensory components are impaired in patients with AD (Muscoso et al., 2006). These results appear to be in line with neuropathological findings that show AD pathology first affects brain regions associated with memory, and higher level association areas, then spreading to cortical sensory areas (Braak et al., 1999). Patients with even mild AD have pathological involvement of several important components of the primary auditory pathway, including the inferior colliculus, medial geniculate body, primary auditory cortex, and secondary auditory cortex (O'Mahoney et al., 1994). However, primary visual areas remain relatively unaffected by pathology until the later stages of the disease (Braak et al., 1999). In fact, ERP and MEG work has suggested that examining brain activity of the auditory cortex may be useful in evaluating the presence and progression of AD (Pekkonen et al., 1999).

Consistent with the neuropathological picture provided by Braak et al. (1999), ERP components dependent on cortical association areas are impaired early in the AD process. A well-studied mid-latency ERP component, P300, which reflects activity of posterior association cortices, has received a great deal of attention as a biomarker for dementia. It is widely speculated that P300 *amplitude* is an index of brain processes elicited from tasks required in the maintenance of working memory (Donchin, 1981; Donchin & Coles, 1988), and research has demonstrated that larger P300 amplitudes are associated with greater memory performance (Fabiani et al., 1990; Noldy et al., 1990). Investigations involving P300 *latency* suggest that shorter latency times are related to greater cognitive performance, particularly on neuropsychological tests that assess the speed at which participants allocate and maintain attentional resources (Polich & Kok, 1995). A great deal of literature suggests that both P300 amplitudes and latencies are impaired in patients with AD and MCI (Ally et al., 2006; Frodl et al., 2002; Golob et al., 2002; Polich et al., 1990), and that P300 is a good marker of disease severity (Patterson et al., 1988). Figure 20.2 shows P300 differences between healthy older adults and patients with mild AD. It has also been shown that P300 latency increases over time at a much faster rate in patients than healthy controls in a longitudinal study (Ball et al., 1989). Further, evidence suggests that P300 is disrupted even in the biological offspring of patients with AD who are 15 to 20 years prior to typical disease onset (Ally et al., 2006; Boutros et al., 1995; Green & Levey, 1999). Ally et al. (2006) found that in a group of biological children with a mean age of 54 years, 55% showed diminished P300 amplitudes and 40% showed elongated latency times greater than one standard deviation from a group of individuals with no family history. Perhaps these neurophysiological

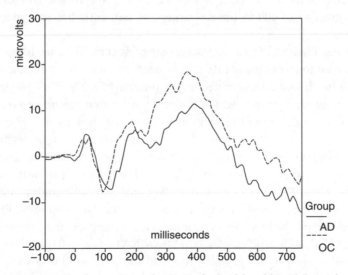

Figure 20.2 P300 amplitudes at electrode site Pz for healthy older adults and patients with mild Alzheimer's disease

abnormalities are a sensitive marker for cognitive dysfunction prior to subtle clinical manifestations seen on neuropsychological testing. Further research could be aimed at following individuals longitudinally to see what percentage of these individuals showing P300 abnormalities ultimately develop AD. It has been estimated that the cumulative risk for developing AD in first-degree relatives ranges from 23% to 67%, which is generally consistent with the percentage of individuals showing P300 abnormalities in Ally et al. (2006).

Previous work has also linked P300 abnormalities to cholinergic dysfunction (Frodl-Bauch et al., 1999; Meador, 1995; Meador et al., 1989), which tends to be disrupted in the earliest stages of the disease (Mega et al., 1999; Minger et al., 2000). Werber and colleagues completed a study examining the effect of cholineste- rase inhibitors on P300 in patients with dementia and found that after taking cholinesterase inhibitors for 26 weeks, patients with AD demonstrated significantly faster P300 latency times than at baseline and significantly improved performance on measures of neurocognitive functioning (Werber et al., 2003). Drugs that modulate the cholinergic system improve attention (Perry & Hodges, 1999), leading Werber et al. to suggest that the shortened latency times and improved cognitive performance likely reflects a cholinesterase inhibitor-induced improve- ment in attention. While P300 may be modulated by neurochemicals implicated in the progression of AD, it should be noted, however, that P300 does not appear to be particularly specific for AD. Abnormalities in this ERP component have also been reported in related disorders such as dementia with Lewy bodies, Parkinson's disease, Huntington's disease, and vascular dementia (Koberskaia et al., 2005; Nojszewska et al., 2009; Rosenberg et al., 1985; van Harten et al., 2006). Although it has been used to differentiate dementia from healthy (Frodl et al., 2002) and depressed older adults (Gordon et al., 1986), due to the lack of specificity the clinical utility of P300 in the assessment of dementia has struggled (Polich & Herbst, 2000).

While using ERPs in the clinical diagnosis of specific diseases of aging has not gained momentum, work using ERP components to understand disease process and progression has become increasingly more prevalent. Early work suggested that a disrupted cholinergic system, which is a hallmark pathological sign of AD, might be responsible for the overall slowing of EEG activity in patients with the disease (Spehlman & Norcross, 1982). Indeed, work has shown that long-term treatment with cholinesterase inhibitors increases overall mean frequencies, and decreases theta activity in patients (Kogan et al., 2001). Building on this work, researchers have begun using ERP components to understand pathophysiology and its behav- ioral and cognitive correlates in patients. For example, the component P50 has been used to understand the link between cholinergic integrity, disease progression, and cognitive and behavior problems in patients with AD. The P50 component has been associated with *sensory gating*, which refers to the inhibition of a stimulus-related neuronal response if the stimulus is preceded by a warning stimulus (Jessen et al., 2001). Data suggest that sensory gating heavily involves the cholinergic system. Studies have demonstrated that the habituation of repetitive, irrelevant sensory stimuli is an essential function of the human brain that keeps higher cortical centers from being flooded with this sensory information (Grunwald et al., 2003). Disruption in this sensory gating process could impair the brain's ability to select, process, and store important information or stimuli. In addition, it has been suggested that this disruption in sensory gating may be associated with common behavioral disturbances noted in patients with AD, such as inattention and sleep difficulties (Bohnen et al., 2005; Garcia-Alloza et al., 2005; McCool et al., 2003). Several investigations to date have revealed P50 deficits in patients with MCI and AD (Ally et al., 2007; Buchwald et al., 1989; Golob et al., 2002; Golob et al., 2005; Golob & Starr, 2000; Green et al., 1992; Jessen et al., 2001), and a recent study has linked this deficit in patients to poor performance on frontally based neuropsychological measures of inhibition (Thomas et al., 2010). Further, investigations have shown a linear pattern of decline in sensory gating as the disease progresses (Golob et al., 2001). In contrast to patients with MCI and AD, data has failed to show sensory gating deficits in the biological children of patients with AD (Ally et al., 2007). The fact that patients with MCI and AD show abnormal sensory gating, and those with biological risk for the disease do not, suggests that perhaps P50 is disrupted when AD pathology is significant enough to cause damage to the cholinergic system in the brain. Further, as Ally et al. (2007) hypothesized, it is likely disease pathology that creates cholinergic dysfunction, and not cholinergic dysfunction that causes disease pathology.

Cognitive ERPs

Studies of cognitive ERPs in patients with dementia have been relatively sparse. Significant variations in performance, and brain physiology, have been noted even in the healthy aging process (Ally et al., 2008; Wolk et al., 2009). These variations are amplified in patients with mild dementia (Ally, McKeever et al., 2009), possibly reflecting compensatory mechanisms or changes in brain structure or chemistry, making ERPs in this group difficult to assess. Further, because many cognitive studies require a significant number of trials to bin for analysis, poor behavioral performance in patients with dementia makes obtaining an adequate number of trials difficult. However, important work continues to pursue this methodology to learn about brain physiology during cognitive tasks in this group. Similar to the early and mid-latency ERP components, data has been mixed regarding the components associated with language processing, memory, and higher level cognition. The discussion will begin with the N400 component. N400 has been associated with semantic memory and processing, as well as implicit and obligate explicit memory processes. The *posterior* N400 is typically associated with language processing, as it is commonly elicited by unexpected linguistic stimuli (Hagoort, 2003). However, cognitive scientists believe that the posterior N400 is broadly related to the semantic processing of information in general (Sitnikova et al., 2003). In classic studies of word congruency, N400 amplitude is decreased for words that are semantically in the correct context, whereas N400 amplitude is increased when words occur out of context. It is believed that the N400 effect is sensitive to attention-demanding semantic integration processes and not automatic aspects of lexical access (Brown & Hagoort, 1993). These word-congruency studies have typically shown diminished N400 amplitudes and elongated latency times to incongruous words in patients with MCI and AD (Olichney et al., 2006; Olichney et al., 2002). However, N400 to congruous words appear to remain intact compared to healthy controls. This same effect is seen in studies using pictures. Here, subjects view sets of picture pairs, where the congruous stimuli retain the same category (e.g., table–chair) and the incongruous stimuli do not (baseball–guitar). Ostrosky-Solis et al. (1998) reported that patients with AD demonstrated decreased N400 amplitudes to incongruous pictures compared to healthy controls, while the amplitude to congruous pictures was similar for the two groups. Some researchers have proposed that N400 studies provide evidence for breakdown in the structure and organization of semantic memory in patients with AD (Castaneda et al., 1997; Ostrosky-Solis et al., 1998), or at the very least, less efficient processing and integration of items with semantic context (Iragui et al., 1996).

However, an interesting study by Ford and colleagues provides some evidence to the contrary. In a picture–name verification task, where patients were asked to view a picture and then its name directly after, the N400 component was similar compared to healthy controls when the picture and name were incongruous, despite a slight topographical shift from more central electrode sites to more right lateralized locations (Ford et al., 2001). Even more impressive, this effect tended to remain even when patients were unable to correctly name the object, suggesting that object knowledge was intact enough to prime cortical responses (Ford et al., 2001).

The N400 component has also been associated with studies of implicit and obligate explicit memory process. *Implicit memory* refers to memory in which previous experience aids performance on tasks without conscious awareness of the previous experience, whereas *explicit memory* refers to the conscious, effortful recollection of previously experienced information. A number of implicit processes, including conceptual fluency and conceptual priming, are thought to possibly play a role in explicit memorial familiarity (Whittlesea & Williams, 1998, 2001; Wolk et al., 2004). *Familiarity* is described as a feeling of knowing without recalling any contextual details of a previously encountered stimulus or event. The *frontal* N400, or FN400, has been linked to both conceptual implicit processes and memorial familiarity (Curran & Hancock, 2007; Stenberg et al., 2009; Voss & Paller, 2007, 2008), though the possibility that these processes engage distinct neural networks has been discussed (Voss et al., 2008). Consistent with behavioral work showing intact implicit conceptual memory processes in patients with AD, Wolk and colleagues reported intact FN400 responses associated with the use of conceptual fluency during recognition decisions in patients with AD (Wolk et al., 2005). These data are consistent with explicit memory findings by Ally, McKeever et al. (2009) that found intact FN400 responses associated with familiarity for pictures. In this study, the early frontal response (FN400) for pictures was similar between healthy older adults and patients with amnestic MCI. In contrast, the early frontal response for words was diminished in the patient group. Ally, McKeever et al. (2009) discussed the possibility of conceptual priming for visual objects playing a role in memorial familiarity, and contributing to the intact early frontal effect for pictures, but not for words. This study further highlighted the need to fully understand the interaction between implicit and explicit memory, and how patients with dementia may benefit from strategies allowing them to utilize intact implicit memory to support explicit memory.

The results of the implicit N400 work are consistent with other ERP studies of implicit memory in patients with AD. The repetition priming effect, which is associated with a broad centro-parietal positivity between 300 and 700 ms post-stimulus, appears to be similar between healthy older adults and patients with AD (Friedman et al., 1992; Kazmerski & Friedman, 1997). This is consistent with fMRI research showing that brain regions associated with repetition priming are activated in a similar pattern in patients as healthy controls (Lustig & Buckner, 2004). However, both behavioral and ERP work have shown that this is true of repetition priming only at short delays (Mitchell & Schmitt, 2006; Schnyer et al., 1999), highlighting the speed at which memory can decay in Alzheimer's.

Given this rapid rate of forgetting, studies of memorial recollection have highlighted the significant memory impairment associated with AD. *Recollection* is typically described as the retrieval of specific context-bound information about an item or event. Behavioral studies have demonstrated that patients with AD show significant impairment in recollection (Ally, Gold et al., 2009; Budson et al., 2000; Christensen et al., 1998; Dalla Barba, 1997; Gallo et al., 2004; Knight, 1998; Koivisto et al., 1998; Smith & Knight, 2002; Westerberg et al., 2006). On tests of recognition memory, ERP researchers typically associate recollection with a medial parietal old/new effect – also known as the late positive component (LPC). This parietal effect typically occurs between 500 and 800 ms post-stimulus, where studied items elicit more positive scalp activity than unstudied items (see Rugg & Curran 2007; Friedman & Johnson, 2000 for reviews). In these studies of recognition memory, the brain activity for correctly identified unstudied items (i.e., correct rejections) is subtracted from the brain activity for correctly identified studied items (i.e., hits). In this scenario, all activity associated with sensory and perception processing is subtracted out, leaving only the brain activity associated with memory. Patients with MCI and AD show a relatively nonexistent parietal effect on tasks investigating verbal (Ally, McKeever et al., 2009; Olichney et al., 2002) and visual recognition (Ally, McKeever et al., 2009), reflecting the significant impairment in episodic memory.

In summary, ERPs have been utilized in research for nearly 30 years in understanding sensory, perception, and cognition in patient populations. Pre-attentive sensory and perceptual ERP components appear to remain relatively intact in patients with AD, though some differences have been reported with respect to the auditory and visual domains. In contrast, attention-related components, and ERPs associated with higher lever association cortices, appear to be impaired. Research on P300, which is likely the most well-studied ERP component in patient populations, consistently shows decreased amplitudes and increased latency times in patients with AD. These impaired amplitudes and latencies appear to be correlated with disease severity and progression. It has been speculated that this likely reflects impaired attention and integration processes, which appear to be somewhat remediated with cholinergic drug therapy. P300 also appears to be sensitive to those at high risk for AD. Studies have shown disrupted amplitudes and latency times in the biological children of those with AD and in patients with MCI.

Studies of semantic processing and integration also show disrupted ERP-related components. Abnormalities of the posterior N400 component appear to be sensitive to cognitive dysfunction, and have been reported by numerous investigations of AD. It has been hypothesized that the disrupted N400 reflects inefficient processing and integration of items with semantic context or a breakdown in the structure and organization of semantic memory in patients with AD. In contrast, the frontal N400 appears to remain generally intact in patients with AD. Studies of implicit conceptual priming and explicit memorial familiarity for visual information have reported a similar FN400 across groups of patients with AD and healthy older controls. These studies are consistent with other work in the implicit memory domain. A number of investigations have reported intact repetition priming ERP effects in patients with AD. However, it has been highlighted that ERP components associated with both implicit and explicit memory are impaired, or even nonexistent, over long delays.

Magnetoencephalography

Magnetoencephalography (MEG) is a reference-free non-invasive imaging technique similar to EEG. Both measure the same sources of brain activity, though MEG actually measures the magnetic fields produced by the electrical activity in the brain. It has been hypothesized that whereas extracellular currents are mostly responsible for electrical fields, magnetic fields typically reflect intracellular current (Franciotti et al., 2006). In contrast to EEG, MEG tends to have a higher density of sensors and is less affected by conductivity issues related to the skull and scalp (Hämäläinen et al., 1993). It is therefore thought that MEG has better spatial resolution than traditional high-density EEG arrays, though both exhibit excellent temporal resolution. Further, recent MEG studies have used a technique called magnetic source imaging (MSI), where MEG data is superimposed on an MRI scan, to improve spatial resolution (on the order of around 1cm), and detect focal neural activity. Similar to ERP studies, MEG researchers average signals with respect to certain stimuli to give rise to components of interest. However, rather than focusing on the component generated at certain locations on the scalp, MEG studies attempt to examine *source localization*. As with ERP studies, scalp topographies can be generated to show the location of certain components. MEG researchers, however, perform mathematical calculations and modeling to estimate the most likely source in the brain responsible for the surface potentials. MEG studies involving patients with dementia are relatively novel, and like qEEG, are typically used to identify differences in brain activity in patient groups compared to healthy control groups. Recent work has mainly focused on utilizing MEG to help with diagnostic specificity.

One of the initial MEG studies to be reported in patients with AD showed a very similar pattern of results to qEEG work. Berendse et al. (2000) showed that patients with AD demonstrated increases in low-frequency magnetic power (delta and theta) and decreases in high-frequency magnetic power (alpha). This increase in slow-wave activity and decrease in fast-wave activity for patients with AD has been found in numerous subsequent MEG investigations. Further, research has suggested that the increase in low frequency band power is partial to frontal and central areas, whereas the decrease in high-frequency band power is partial to posterior and temporal regions (Criado et al., 2007; Montez et al., 2009; Osipova et al., 2005). Additionally, the initial MEG investigation by Berendse et al. (2000) reported a generalized loss of coherence between the frequencies of 2–22 Hz. This loss of functional cortico–cortical connectivity was for both far and local coherences, but was greatest for the long distance frontoparietal connections. For the most part, these coherence results were consistent with qEEG work, which typically reports a loss in functional connectivity within the higher frequency bands. It has been speculated that MEG may be a better measure of coherence than qEEG because MEG is reference-free. EEG recordings from the scalp require a reference electrode to compare activity from specific electrode channels. MEG researchers have proposed that due to the different conductivity of cranial structures, the use of reference channels may skew the interpretation of spectral coherence, and MEG is superior to EEG in examining functional connectivity of brain regions (Berendse et al., 2000; Criado et al., 2007; Fernandez et al., 2002; Franciotti et al., 2006).

Interestingly, another study examining coherence in resting-state functional connectivity in patients with AD actually showed increased coherence between parietal and occipital regions in the upper alpha and beta bands (Stam et al., 2006). These results could suggest compensatory activity in occipital regions (Stam et al., 2006). Parietal regions are activated during memory retrieval, and typically work in a network with prefrontal and medial temporal regions (Ally & Budson, 2007; Shannon & Buckner, 2004). The hypothesis that occipital regions may help to compensate for poor parietal function has been previously discussed (Ally, McKeever et al., 2009; Ally et al., 2008; Trollor et al., 2006). The results of Stam et al. (2006) are generally consistent with previous ERP work that reported increased occipital activity on tasks of recognition memory during the time interval typically associated with robust parietal activation (Ally, McKeever et al., 2009). Figure 20.3 (plate section) shows the increased occipital activity during memory retrieval for patients with very mild AD compared to the typical parietal activity seen during memory retrieval in healthy young adults.

Due to the relative novelty of using MEG in studies of dementia, there are few studies examining event-related designs, the relationship between MEG abnormalities and cognitive functioning in patient populations, or using MEG in the differential diagnosis of dementia. Fernandez et al. (2002) showed that right parietal delta activity and left temporal theta activity were significantly associated with general measures of cognitive function (CAMCOG, MMSE, respectively). These authors hypothesized that these changes in delta band power, and its related cognitive impairment, may be related to poor cholinergic function (Fernandez et al., 2002). Indeed, previous work has shown that treatment with anticholinergic drugs increase delta activity (Longo, 1966), and postmortem studies have demonstrated that patients with the highest delta activity showed diminished cortical cholinergic activity upon death (Riekkinen et al., 1990). These initial findings examining the relationship of MEG abnormalities and cognitive functioning were supported by a subsequent study of working memory (Maestu et al., 2004). Maestu et al. (2004) found that on a task of working memory, patients with AD demonstrated decreased activity in left temporal regions compared to healthy older adults with and without depression. Further, the decreased activity in left temporal regions correlated with degree of hippocampal atrophy in the patients with AD.

Event-related designs have also found differences between patients and healthy older adults. For example, Kurimoto and colleagues examined MEG activity associated with eye opening (Kurimoto et al., 2008). Eye opening and closing is an easy task for patients with dementia to complete, and it has been shown to induce a modulation in MEG power. Hans Berger first reported an abrupt suspension of alpha waveform, known as alpha desynchronization, when subjects open their eyes in a well-lit room (Berger, 1929), presumably due to the subject attending to the environment (Bohdanecky et al., 1984). Alpha desynchronization related to this task has been shown to be sensitive to neurological dysfunction in a number of patient populations (van der Hiele et al., 2007). Kurimoto et al. (2008) found that patients with AD and MCI demonstrated alpha desynchronization related to eye opening to a similar degree as healthy older adults, but patients with AD showed a shift to frontal regions as compared to the typical posterior alpha desynchronization seen in healthy adults. In another study, Maestu et al. (2001) found that patients with AD demonstrated a lower number of activity sources over parietal and temporal cortex between 400 and 700 ms post-stimulus in a target detection task compared to a control group. These results are generally consistent with a subsequent study of recognition memory in which words were studied in deep and shallow depth of encoding manipulations (Walla et al., 2005). Walla et al. (2005) found that in a similar fashion to ERP studies of recognition memory, control subjects demonstrated a significant old/new effect over posterior brain regions after deep encoding, whereas this effect was nonexistent in patients with AD. The authors suggested that this absent posterior old/new magnetoelectric effect reflected impaired conscious recollection that is commonly described in the ERP and fMRI literature.

As with qEEG, MEG has also been used to differentiate and characterize different types of dementia. Franciotti et al. (2006) used MEG to evaluate cortical rhythms during a number of tasks in patients with moderate AD, severe AD, and dementia with Lewy bodies, and a healthy older adult control group. Cortical reactivity in the alpha bandwidth (7–14 Hz) during eye-closing and eye-opening conditions differentiated the control group from the patient groups, and moderate AD from severe AD and DLB groups, respectively. In contrast, cortical reactivity in the slower bandwidths (3–7 Hz) obtained by comparing a simple mental task, and a rest condition, discriminated the severe AD group from the other groups. Franciotti et al. (2006) also reported that spectral coherence analysis in the alpha band showed loss of coherence in patients with AD and LBD, which mostly involved longer cortico–cortical connections. These differences were more pronounced for patients with AD in the left hemisphere, and for patients with DLB in the right hemisphere. Franciotti and colleagues speculated that the pronounced right hemisphere desynchronization in the patients with DLB could likely be a marker of the visuospatial deficits seen in this patient group.

Finally, MEG has been used to study individuals at high risk for dementia. An initial study of patients with MCI examined mean spectral frequency values (2–60 Hz) while patients laid at rest with eyes closed (Fernandez, Hornero et al., 2006). Fernandez et al. (2003) found mean frequency values that fell between healthy older adults and patients with AD for the patients with MCI. This finding was extended, where Maestu et al. (2005) reported that subjects who developed cognitive decline over a two-year period demonstrated a lower number of activity sources in the left medial temporal lobe between 400 and 800 ms after stimulus onset during a letter-probe task, as compared to the noncognitive decline group (Maestu et al., 2005). A subsequent study also reported a 3.5-fold increase in relative risk of conversion to AD with high levels of delta activity over left posterior regions (Fernandez, Turrero et al., 2006). Similar to studies involving qEEG, MEG studies have highlighted an increase in slow-wave activity in those at high risk for dementia. This finding has been reported in other populations, such as individuals reporting subjective cognitive complaints (Criado et al., 2007) and individuals with the apolipoprotein ε4 allele (Filbey et al., 2006).

In summary, MEG has only been recently used to study patients with dementia. Similarly to EEG, MEG provides excellent temporal resolution, but with the added benefit of greater spatial definition. Additionally, because MEG is reference-free, it is thought to be a better measure of functional cortico–cortical connectivity. In general, studies of patients with AD reveal a similar pattern of findings as qEEG. There appears to be increases in low-frequency magnetic power and decreases in high-frequency magnetic power. Research has suggested that the increase in slow-wave activity, particularly over posterior and temporal regions, is correlated with cognitive performance, and may be related to diminished cholinergic function. Investigations of coherence suggest a loss in functional cortico–cortical connectivity at both far and local brain regions, which is noted to be greatest for frontoparietal connections. MEG work has also investigated those at high risk for dementia. Studies have found mean frequency values that fall between healthy older adults and patients with AD for the patients with MCI, and that subjects who developed cognitive decline over a two-year period demonstrated a lower number of activity sources in the left medial temporal lobe as compared to the noncognitive decline group.

Summary and Perspective

Electroencephalography has been used for nearly a century to understand brain physiology. At one time, it was the first line of assessment used in the diagnosis of epilepsy, tumors, stroke, and focal brain disorders. However, due to the advent of anatomical imaging techniques, use of EEG in the clinical setting has become somewhat limited. In contrast, EEG use in the research setting has flourished over the last three decades. In addition, magnetoencephalography has become a major source of investigation in the last decade. Initial studies were aimed at using EEG and MEG in the diagnosis of dementia. Results showed patterns of changes identifiable of cognitive decline in general, but lacked high degrees of specificity for differential diagnoses. However, numerous recent investigations have reported specificities rates near 100% when EEG or MEG is used with other types of neuroimaging such as MRI and PET. These types of studies are important and may be easily transported into the clinical area, where diagnostic specificity is becoming more important with the advent of possible new disease-modifying therapies.

EEG and MEG work has also been useful in helping to quantify disease severity. In the clinical setting, these methodologies might be given in a similar manner as standard neuropsychological testing to follow changes over time. If used in combination with neuropsychological testing, EEG and MEG may provide clinicians, patients, and families a more reliable prediction of disease course. Further, it may help clinicians with decisions about medication management and planning for social and financial resources. Additionally, ERPs have been used in studies of drug treatment response. ERP assessment is an easy, cost-effective, and non-invasive method to assess response to cholinesterase inhibitors that can be conducted in the office. Many ERP paradigms can be completed in 10–15 minutes after electrode placement, and do not require overt responses from the patient. In his review of drug therapy in Alzheimer's disease, Jeffrey Cummings notes that some patients respond dramatically, some respond more moderately, while others do not show a significant response (Cummings, 2004). However, response to therapy cannot always be determined clinically. A study of cholinesterase inhibitors found that the majority of patients who were thought not to respond to therapy showed a decline in function when the medication was discontinued (Holmes et al., 2004). Since cholinesterase inhibitor therapy costs approximately $150 per month or about $1800 per year – and the monitory and societal cost of not treating patients with a therapeutic response is even higher (Neumann et al., 1999) – an inexpensive physiological method for determining the response to cholinesterase inhibitor therapy in individual patients would be extremely helpful.

One of the most exciting uses of EEG and MEG has been in risk quantification and the early detection of dementia. There have now been a host of EEG and MEG studies to show that increased slow-wave activity is predictive of conversion to AD in subjects at high risk. Further, a number of ERP studies have shown identifiable changes to particular waveforms, such as P300, that relate to the degree of one's risk. Once again, these methods in combination with other structural and functional neuroimaging methods can be implemented in the clinical setting to improve our diagnostic prediction ability. The ability to detect those at high risk for dementia or those in the very earliest stages is of great importance with respect to lifestyle changes and future planning. Further, there appears to be a number of FDA trials investigating disease-halting drugs and possibly vaccinations for those at high risk.

Finally, EEG and MEG have been critical in understanding how cognition is affected in AD and related dementias. As pointed out earlier, this can be a difficult line of research in patient populations, but remains critical to our understanding of the disease. To date, a number of ERP studies have helped us gain insight into deficits in language and memorial processing. However, possibly more important, a number of ERP studies have helped us gain insight into which cognitive processes remain intact. This understanding is critical in designing interventions to help patients live more engaged and independent lives by relying on aspects of cognition that remain relatively intact.

Acknowledgments

I am extremely thankful to my graduate school mentor and dissertation chair, Gary E. Jones, Ph.D. Gary introduced me to the world of EEG in research and has continued to support me throughout my career. I would also like to acknowledge my mentor and colleague Andrew E. Budson, M.D. for his continued dedication to my work and career. This work was completed with the support from National Institute on Aging grants F32 AG027631 and K23 AG031925. This material is also the result of work supported with resources and the use of facilities at the Bedford VA Hospital in Bedford, MA.

References

Ally, B. A., & Budson, A. E. (2007). The worth of pictures: Using high density event-related potentials to understand the memorial power of pictures and the dynamics of recognition memory. *Neuroimage, 35*, 378–395.

Ally, B. A., Gold, C. A., & Budson, A. E. (2009). An evaluation of recollection and familiarity in Alzheimer's disease and mild cognitive impairment using receiver operating characteristics. *Brain Cognition, 69*, 504–513.

Ally, B. A., Jones, G. E., Cole, J. A., & Budson, A. E. (2006). The P300 component in patients with Alzheimer's disease and their biological children. *Biological Psychology, 72,* 180–187.

Ally, B. A., Jones, G. E., Cole, J. A., & Budson, A. E. (2007). Sensory gating in patients with Alzheimer's disease and their biological children. *American Journal of Alzheimer's Disease & Other Dementias, 21,* 439–447.

Ally, B. A., McKeever, J. D., Waring, J. D., & Budson, A. E. (2009). Pictures preserve frontal memorial processes in patients with mild cognitive impairment. *Neuropsychologia, 47,* 2044–2055.

Ally, B. A., Waring, J. D., Beth, E. H., McKeever, J. D., Milberg, W. P., & Budson, A. E. (2008). Aging memory for pictures: Using high-density event-related potentials to understand the effect of aging on the picture superiority effect. *Neuropsychologia, 46,* 679–689.

Andersson, M., Hansson, O., Minthon, L., Rosen, I., & Londos, E. (2008). Electroencephalogram variability in dementia with Lewy bodies, Alzheimer's disease and controls. *Dementia and Geriatric Cognitive Disorders, 26,* 284–290.

Babiloni, C., Binetti, G., Cassetta, E., Cerboneschi, D., Dal Forno, G., Del Percio, C., et al. (2004). Mapping distributed sources of cortical rhythms in mild Alzheimer's disease. A multicentric EEG study. *Neuroimage, 22,* 57–67.

Babiloni, C., Cassetta, E., Binetti, G., Tombini, M., Del Percio, C., Ferreri, F., et al. (2007). Resting EEG sources correlate with attentional span in mild cognitive impairment and Alzheimer's disease. *European Journal of Neuroscience, 25,* 3742–3757.

Babiloni, C., Ferri, R., Moretti, D. V., Strambi, A., Binetti, G., Dal Forno, G., et al. (2004). Abnormal fronto-parietal coupling of brain rhythms in mild Alzheimer's disease: A multicentric EEG study. *European Journal of Neuroscience, 19,* 2583–2590.

Baker, M., Akrofi, K., Schiffer, R., & Boyle, M. W. (2008). EEG patterns in mild cognitive impairment (MCI) patients. *Open Neuroimaging Journal, 2,* 52–55.

Ball, S. S., Marsh, J. T., Schubarth, G., Brown, W. S., & Strandburg, R. (1989). Longitudinal P300 latency changes in Alzheimer's disease. *Journal of Gerontology, 44,* M195–M200.

Berendse, H. W., Verbunt, J. P., Scheltens, P., van Dijk, B. W., & Jonkman, E. J. (2000). Magnetoencephalographic analysis of cortical activity in Alzheimer's disease: A pilot study. *Clinical Neurophysiology, 111,* 604–612.

Berger, H. (1929). Über das elektrenkephalogramm des menchen. *Archives für Psychiatrie, 87,* 527–570.

Besthorn, C., Forstl, H., Geiger-Kabisch, C., Sattel, H., Gasser, T., & Schreiter-Gasser, U. (1994). EEG coherence in Alzheimer disease. *Electroencephalography and Clinical Neurophysiology, 90,* 242–245.

Bohdanecky, Z., Indra, M., Lansky, P., & Radil-Weiss, T. (1984). Alternation of EEG alpha and non-alpha periods does not differ in open and closed eye condition in darkness. *Acta Neurobiologiae Experimentalis (Warsaw), 44,* 229–232.

Bohnen, N. I., Kaufer, D. I., Hendrickson, R., Ivanco, L. S., Lopresti, B., Davis, J. G., et al. (2005). Cognitive correlates of alterations in acetylcholinesterase in Alzheimer's disease. *Neuroscience Letters, 380,* 127–132.

Boutros, N., Torello, M. W., Burns, E. M., Wu, S. S., & Nasrallah, H. A. (1995). Evoked potentials in subjects at risk for Alzheimer's disease. *Psychiatry Research, 57,* 57–63.

Braak, E., Griffing, K., Arai, K., Bohl, J., Bratzke, H., & Braak, H. (1999). Neuropathology of Alzheimer's disease: What is new since A. Alzheimer? *European Archives of Psychiatry and Clinical Neurosciences, 249*(Suppl 3), 14–22.

Brenner, R. P., Reynolds, C. F., 3rd, & Ulrich, R. F. (1988). Diagnostic efficacy of computerized spectral versus visual EEG analysis in elderly normal, demented and depressed subjects. *Electroencephalography and Clinical Neurophysiology, 69,* 110–117.

Brown, C. M., & Hagoort, P. (1993). The processing nature of the N400: Evidence from masked priming. *Journal of Cognitive Neuroscience, 5,* 34–44.

Buchwald, J. S., Erwin, R. J., Read, S., Van Lancker, D., & Cummings, J. L. (1989). Midlatency auditory evoked responses: Differential abnormality of P1 in Alzheimer's disease. *Electroencephalography and Clinical Neurophysiology, 74,* 378–384.

Budson, A. E., Daffner, K. R., Desikan, R., & Schacter, D. L. (2000). When false recognition is unopposed by true recognition: Gist-based memory distortion in Alzheimer's disease. *Neuropsychology, 14,* 277–287.

Castaneda, M., Ostrosky-Solis, F., Perez, M., Bobes, M. A., & Rangel, L. E. (1997). ERP assessment of semantic memory in Alzheimer's disease. *International Journal of Psychophysiology, 27,* 201–214.

Christensen, H., Kopelman, M. D., Stanhope, N., Lorentz, L., & Owen, P. (1998). Rates of forgetting in alzheimer dementia. *Neuropsychologia, 36,* 547–557.

Coben, L. A., Danziger, W. L., & Berg, L. (1983). Frequency analysis of the resting awake EEG in mild senile dementia of Alzheimer type. *Electroencephalography and Clinical Neurophysiology, 55,* 372–380.

Coben, L. A., Danziger, W., & Storandt, M. (1985). A longitudinal EEG study of mild senile dementia of Alzheimer type: Changes at 1 year and at 2.5 years. *Electroencephalography and Clinical Neurophysiology, 61,* 101–112.

Criado, J. R., Amo, C., Quint, P., Kurelowech, L., & Otis, S. M. (2007). Using magnetoencephalography to study patterns of brain magnetic activity in Alzheimer's disease. *American Journal of Alzheimer's Disease & Other Dementias, 21,* 416–423.

Cummings, J. L. (2004). Treatment of Alzheimer's disease: Current and future therapeutic approaches. *Reviews in Neurological Diseases, 1,* 60–69.

Curran, T., & Hancock, J. (2007). The FN400 indexes familiarity-based recognition of faces. *Neuroimage, 36,* 464–471.

Dalla Barba, G. (1997). Recognition memory and recollective experience in Alzheimer's disease. *Memory, 5,* 657–672.

Donchin, E. (1981). Presidential address, 1980. Surprise! . . . Surprise? *Psychophysiology, 18,* 493–513.

Donchin, E., & Coles, M. G. (1988). Is the P300 component a manifestation of context updating? *Behavioral and Brain Sciences, 11.*

Dunkin, J. J., Leuchter, A. F., Newton, T. F., & Cook, I. A. (1994). Reduced EEG coherence in dementia: State or trait marker? *Biological Psychiatry, 35,* 870–879.

Fabiani, M., Karis, D., & Donchin, E. (1990). Effects of mnemonic strategy manipulation in a von Restorff paradigm. *Electroencephalography and Clinical Neurophysiology, 75,* 22–35.

Fernandez, A., Arrazola, J., Maestu, F., Amo, C., Gil-Gregorio, P., Wienbruch, C., et al. (2003). Correlations of hippocampal atrophy and focal low-frequency magnetic activity in Alzheimer disease: Volumetric MR imaging-magnetoencephalographic study. *American Journal of Neuroradiology, 24,* 481–487.

Fernandez, A., Hornero, R., Mayo, A., Poza, J., Maestu, F., & Ortiz, A. T. (2006). Quantitative magnetoencephalography of spontaneous brain activity in Alzheimer disease: An exhaustive frequency analysis. *Alzheimer Disease & Associated Disorders, 20,* 153–159.

Fernandez, A., Maestu, F., Amo, C., Gil, P., Fehr, T., Wienbruch, C., et al. (2002). Focal tem-poroparietal slow activity in Alzheimer's disease revealed by magnetoencephalography. *Biological Psychiatry, 52*, 764–770.

Fernandez, A., Turrero, A., Zuluaga, P., Gil, P., Maestu, F., Campo, P., et al. (2006). Magnetoencephalographic parietal delta dipole density in mild cognitive impairment: Preliminary results of a method to estimate the risk of developing Alzheimer disease. *Archives of Neurology, 63*, 427–430.

Filbey, F. M., Slack, K. J., Sunderland, T. P., & Cohen, R. M. (2006). Functional magnetic resonance imaging and magnetoencephalography differences associated with apoeep-silon4 in young healthy adults. *Neuroreport, 17*, 1585–1590.

Ford, J. M., Askari, N., Mathalon, D. H., Menon, V., Gabrieli, J. D., Tinklenberg, J. R., et al. (2001). Event-related brain potential evidence of spared knowledge in Alzheimer's disease. *Psychology and Aging, 16*, 161–176.

Franciotti, R., Iacono, D., Della Penna, S., Pizzella, V., Torquati, K., Onofrj, M., et al. (2006). Cortical rhythms reactivity in AD, LBD and normal subjects: A quantitative MEG study. *Neurobiology of Aging, 27*, 1100–1109.

Friedman, D., & Johnson, R., Jr. (2000). Event-related potential (ERP) studies of memory encoding and retrieval: A selective review. *Microscopy Research and Technique, 51*, 6–28.

Friedman, D., Hamberger, M., Stern, Y., & Marder, K. (1992). Event-related potentials (ERPS) during repetition priming in Alzheimer's patients and young and older controls. *Journal of Clinical and Experimental Neuropsychology, 14*, 448–462.

Frodl, T., Hampel, H., Juckel, G., Burger, K., Padberg, F., Engel, R. R., et al. (2002). Value of event-related P300 subcomponents in the clinical diagnosis of mild cognitive impair-ment and Alzheimer's disease. *Psychophysiology, 39*, 175–181.

Frodl-Bauch, T., Bottlender, R., & Hegerl, U. (1999). Neurochemical substrates and neuroanatomical generators of the event-related P300. *Neuropsychobiology, 40*, 86–94.

Gallo, D. A., Sullivan, A. L., Daffner, K. R., Schacter, D. L., & Budson, A. E. (2004). Associative recognition in Alzheimer's disease: Evidence for impaired recall-to-reject. *Neuropsy-chology, 18*, 556–563.

Garcia-Alloza, M., Gil-Bea, F. J., Diez-Ariza, M., Chen, C. P., Francis, P. T., Lasheras, B., et al. (2005). Cholinergic-serotonergic imbalance contributes to cognitive and behavioral symptoms in Alzheimer's disease. *Neuropsychologia, 43*, 442–449.

Golob, E. J., & Starr, A. (2000). Effects of stimulus sequence on event-related potentials and reaction time during target detection in Alzheimer's disease. *Clinical Neurophysiology, 111*, 1438–1449.

Golob, E. J., Johnson, J. K., & Starr, A. (2002). Auditory event-related potentials during target detection are abnormal in mild cognitive impairment. *Clinical Neurophysiology, 113*, 151–161.

Golob, E. J., Ovasapyan, V., & Starr, A. (2005). Event-related potentials accompanying motor preparation and stimulus expectancy in the young, young-old and oldest-old. *Neurobiology of Aging, 26*, 531–542.

Goodin, D. S., & Aminoff, M. J. (1986). Electrophysiological differences between subtypes of dementia. *Brain, 109*(Pt 6), 1103–1113.

Gordon, E., Kraiuhin, C., Harris, A., Meares, R., & Howson, A. (1986). The differential diag-nosis of dementia using P300 latency. *Biological Psychiatry, 21*, 1123–1132.

Green, J. B., Flagg, L., Freed, D. M., & Schwankhaus, J. D. (1992). The middle latency auditory evoked potential may be abnormal in dementia. *Neurology, 42,* 1034–1036.

Green, J., & Levey, A. I. (1999). Event-related potential changes in groups at increased risk for Alzheimer disease. *Archives of Neurology, 56,* 1398–1403.

Grunwald, M., Busse, F., Hensel, A., Kruggel, F., Riedel-Heller, S., Wolf, H., et al. (2001). Correlation between cortical theta activity and hippocampal volumes in health, mild cognitive impairment, and mild dementia. *Journal of Clinical Neurophysiology, 18,* 178–184.

Grunwald, T., Boutros, N. N., Pezer, N., von Oertzen, J., Fernandez, G., Schaller, C., et al. (2003). Neuronal substrates of sensory gating within the human brain. *Biological Psychiatry, 53,* 511–519.

Hagoort, P. (2003). Interplay between syntax and semantics during sentence comprehension: ERP effects of combining syntactic and semantic violations. *Journal of Cognitive Neuroscience, 15,* 883–899.

Hämäläinen, M., Hari, R., Ilmoniemi, R., Knuutila, J., & Lounasmaa, O. V. (1993). Magnetoencephalography – Theory, instrumentation, and application to noninvasive studies of the working human brain. *Reviews of Modern Physics, 65,* 413–494.

Helkala, E. L., Hanninen, T., Hallikainen, M., Kononen, M., Laakso, M. P., Hartikainen, P., et al. (1996). Slow-wave activity in the spectral analysis of the electroencephalogram and volumes of hippocampus in subgroups of Alzheimer's disease patients. *Behavioral Neuroscience, 110,* 1235–1243.

Helkala, E. L., Laulumaa, V., Soikkeli, R., Partanen, J., Soininen, H., & Riekkinen, P. J. (1991). Slow-wave activity in the spectral analysis of the electroencephalogram is associated with cortical dysfunctions in patients with Alzheimer's disease. *Behavioral Neuroscience, 105,* 409–415.

Holmes, C., Wilkinson, D., Dean, C., Vethanayagam, S., Olivieri, S., Langley, A., et al. (2004). The efficacy of donepezil in the treatment of neuropsychiatric symptoms in Alzheimer disease. *Neurology, 63,* 214–219.

Holschneider, D. P., & Leuchter, A. F. (1995). Beta activity in aging and dementia. *Brain Topography, 8,* 169–180.

Holschneider, D. P., Waite, J. J., Leuchter, A. F., Walton, N. Y., & Scremin, O. U. (1999). Changes in electrocortical power and coherence in response to the selective cholinergic immunotoxin 192 IGG-saporin. *Experimental Brain Research, 126,* 270–280.

Huang, C., Wahlund, L., Dierks, T., Julin, P., Winblad, B., & Jelic, V. (2000). Discrimination of Alzheimer's disease and mild cognitive impairment by equivalent EEG sources: A cross-sectional and longitudinal study. *Clinical Neurophysiology, 111,* 1961–1967.

Hughes, J. R., & John, E. R. (1999). Conventional and quantitative electroencephalography in psychiatry. *Journal of Neuropsychiatry and Clinical Neurosciences, 11,* 190–208.

Iragui, V., Kutas, M., & Salmon, D. P. (1996). Event-related brain potentials during semantic categorization in normal aging and senile dementia of the Alzheimer's type. *Electroencephalography and Clinical Neurophysiology, 100,* 392–406.

Jelic, V., Johansson, S. E., Almkvist, O., Shigeta, M., Julin, P., Nordberg, A., et al. (2000). Quantitative electroencephalography in mild cognitive impairment: Longitudinal changes and possible prediction of Alzheimer's disease. *Neurobiology of Aging, 21,* 533–540.

Jelic, V., Shigeta, M., Julin, P., Almkvist, O., Winblad, B., & Wahlund, L. O. (1996). Quantitative electroencephalography power and coherence in Alzheimer's disease and mild cognitive impairment. *Dementia, 7*, 314–323.

Jelic, V., Walhund, L. O., AlmKvist, O., Johansson, S. E., Shigeta, M., Winblad, B., et al. (1999). Diagnostic accuracies of quantitative EEG and PET in mild Alzheimer's disease. *Alzheimer Report, 2*.

Jelles, B., Scheltens, P., van der Flier, W. M., Jonkman, E. J., da Silva, F. H., & Stam, C. J. (2008). Global dynamical analysis of the EEG in Alzheimer's disease: Frequency-specific changes of functional interactions. *Clinical Neurophysiology, 119*, 837–841.

Jeong, J. (2004). EEG dynamics in patients with Alzheimer's disease. *Clinical Neurophysiology, 115*, 1490–1505.

Jessen, F., Kucharski, C., Fries, T., Papassotiropoulos, A., Hoenig, K., Maier, W., et al. (2001). Sensory gating deficit expressed by a disturbed suppression of the P50 event-related potential in patients with Alzheimer's disease. *American Journal of Psychiatry, 158*, 1319–1321.

Jonkman, E. J., Poortvliet, D. C., Veering, M. M., De Weerd, A. W., & John, E. R. (1985). The use of neurometrics in the study of patients with cerebral ischaemia. *Electroencephalography and Clinical Neurophysiology, 61*, 333–341.

Kaiser, J., & Lutzenberger, W. (2005). Human gamma-band activity: A window to cognitive processing. *Neuroreport, 16*, 207–211.

Kazmerski, V. A., & Friedman, D. (1997). Effect of multiple presentations of words on event-related potential and reaction time repetition effects in Alzheimer's patients and young and older controls. *Neuropsychiatry, Neuropsychology, & Behavioral Neurology, 10*, 32–47.

Kikuchi, M., Wada, Y., Koshino, Y., Nanbu, Y., & Hashimoto, T. (2000). Effects of scopolamine on interhemispheric EEG coherence in healthy subjects: Analysis during rest and photic stimulation. *Clinical Electroencephalography, 31*, 109–115.

Klimesch, W. (1999). Eeg alpha and theta oscillations reflect cognitive and memory performance: A review and analysis. *Brain Research Reviews, 29*, 169–195.

Knight, R. G. (1998). Controlled and automatic memory process in Alzheimer's disease. *Cortex, 34*, 427–435.

Koberskaia, N. N., Zenkov, L. R., Zakharov, V. V., Preobrazhenskaia, I. S. (2005). Cognitive potential P300 in dementia with Levy's bodies and Alzheimer's disease. *Zh Nevrol Psikhiatr Im S S Korsakova, 105*, 61–64.

Kogan, E. A., Korczyn, A. D., Virchovsky, R. G., Klimovizky, S., Treves, T. A., & Neufeld, M. Y. (2001). EEG changes during long-term treatment with donepezil in Alzheimer's disease patients. *Journal of Neural Transmission, 108*, 1167–1173.

Koivisto, M., Portin, R., Seinela, A., & Rinne, J. (1998). Automatic influences of memory in Alzheimer's disease. *Cortex, 34*, 209–219.

Kurimoto, R., Ishii, R., Canuet, L., Ikezawa, K., Azechi, M., Iwase, M., et al. (2008). Event-related synchronization of alpha activity in early Alzheimer's disease and mild cognitive impairment: An MEG study combining beamformer and group comparison. *Neuroscience Letters, 443*, 86–89.

Kwak, Y. T. (2006). Quantitative EEG findings in different stages of Alzheimer's disease. *Journal of Clinical Neurophysiology, 23*, 456–461.

Lindau, M., Jelic, V., Johansson, S. E., Andersen, C., Wahlund, L. O., & Almkvist, O. (2003). Quantitative EEG abnormalities and cognitive dysfunctions in frontotemporal dementia and Alzheimer's disease. *Dementia and Geriatric Cognitive Disorders, 15*, 106–114.

Longo, V. G. (1966). Behavioral and electroencephalographic effects of atropine and related compounds. *Pharmacological Reviews, 18,* 965–996.

Lustig, C., & Buckner, R. L. (2004). Preserved neural correlates of priming in old age and dementia. *Neuron, 42,* 865–875.

Maestu, F., Campo, P., Gil-Gregorio, P., Fernandez, S., Fernandez, A., & Ortiz, T. (2006). Medial temporal lobe neuromagnetic hypoactivation and risk for developing cognitive decline in elderly population: A 2-year follow-up study. *Neurobiology of Aging, 27,* 32–37.

Maestu, F., Fernandez, A., Simos, P. G., Gil-Gregorio, P., Amo, C., Rodriguez, R., et al. (2001). Spatio-temporal patterns of brain magnetic activity during a memory task in Alzheimer's disease. *Neuroreport, 12,* 3917–3922.

Maestu, F., Fernandez, A., Simos, P. G., Lopez-Ibor, M. I., Campo, P., Criado, J., et al. (2004). Profiles of brain magnetic activity during a memory task in patients with Alzheimer's disease and in non-demented elderly subjects, with or without depression. *Journal of Neurology, Neurosurgery & Psychiatry, 75,* 1160–1162.

Mattia, D., Babiloni, F., Romigi, A., Cincotti, F., Bianchi, L., Sperli, F., et al. (2003). Quantitative EEG and dynamic susceptibility contrast MRI in Alzheimer's disease: A correlative study. *Clinical Neurophysiology, 114,* 1210–1216.

McCool, M. F., Varty, G. B., Del Vecchio, R. A., Kazdoba, T. M., Parker, E. M., Hunter, J. C., et al. (2003). Increased auditory startle response and reduced prepulse inhibition of startle in transgenic mice expressing a double mutant form of amyloid precursor protein. *Brain Research, 994,* 99–106.

Meador, K. J. (1995). Cholinergic, serotonergic, and gabaergic effects on the ERP. *Electroencephalography and Clinical Neurophysiology, 44,* 151–155.

Meador, K. J., Loring, D. W., Davis, H. C., Sethi, K. D., Patel, B. R., Adams, R. J., et al. (1989). Cholinergic and serotonergic effects on the p3 potential and recent memory. *Journal of Clinical and Experimental Neuropsychology, 11,* 252–260.

Mega, M. S., Masterman, D. M., O'Connor, S. M., Barclay, T. R., & Cummings, J. L. (1999). The spectrum of behavioral responses to cholinesterase inhibitor therapy in Alzheimer disease. *Archives of Neurology, 56,* 1388–1393.

Minger, S. L., Esiri, M. M., McDonald, B., Keene, J., Carter, J., Hope, T., et al. (2000). Cholinergic deficits contribute to behavioral disturbance in patients with dementia. *Neurology, 55,* 1460–1467.

Mitchell, D. B., & Schmitt, F. A. (2006). Short- and long-term implicit memory in aging and Alzheimer's disease. *Neuropsychology, Development, and Cognition. Section B, Aging, Neuropsychology and Cognition, 13,* 611–635.

Montez, T., Poil, S. S., Jones, B. F., Manshanden, I., Verbunt, J. P., van Dijk, B. W., et al. (2009). Altered temporal correlations in parietal alpha and prefrontal theta oscillations in early-stage Alzheimer disease. *Proceedings of the National Academy of Sciences USA, 106,* 1614–1619.

Muscoso, E. G., Costanzo, E., Daniele, O., Maugeri, D., Natale, E., & Caravaglios, G. (2006). Auditory event-related potentials in subcortical vascular cognitive impairment and in Alzheimer's disease. *Journal of Neural Transmission, 113,* 1779–1786.

Neubauer, A. C., & Freudenthaler, H. H. (1995). Ultradian rhythms in cognitive performance: No evidence for a 1.5-h rhythm. *Biological Psychology, 40,* 281–298.

Neumann, P. J., Hermann, R. C., Kuntz, K. M., Araki, S. S., Duff, S. B., Leon, J., et al. (1999). Cost-effectiveness of donepezil in the treatment of mild or moderate Alzheimer's disease. *Neurology, 52,* 1138–1145.

Nojszewska, M., Pilczuk, B., Zakrzewska-Pniewska, B., & Rowińska-Marcińska, K. (2009). The auditory system involvement in Parkinson disease: Electrophysiological and neuropsychological correlations. *Journal of Clinical Neurophysiology, 26*, 430–437.

Noldy, N. E., Stelmack, R. M., & Campbell, K. B. (1990). Event-related potentials and recognition memory for pictures and words: The effects of intentional and incidental learning. *Psychophysiology, 27*, 417–428.

Olichney, J. M., Iragui, V. J., Salmon, D. P., Riggins, B. R., Morris, S. K., & Kutas, M. (2006). Absent event-related potential (ERP) word repetition effects in mild Alzheimer's disease. *Clinical Neurophysiology, 117*, 1319–1330.

Olichney, J. M., Morris, S. K., Ochoa, C., Salmon, D. P., Thal, L. J., Kutas, M., et al. (2002). Abnormal verbal event related potentials in mild cognitive impairment and incipient Alzheimer's disease. *Journal of Neurology, Neurosurgery & Psychiatry, 73*, 377–384.

O'Mahony, D., Rowan, M., Feely, J., Walsh, J. B., & Coakley, D. (1994). Primary auditory pathway and reticular activating system dysfunction in Alzheimer's disease. *Neurology, 44*, 2089–2094.

Osipova, D., Ahveninen, J., Jensen, O., Ylikoski, A., & Pekkonen, E. (2005). Altered generation of spontaneous oscillations in Alzheimer's disease. *Neuroimage, 27*, 835–841.

Ostrosky-Solis, F., Castaneda, M., Perez, M., Castillo, G., & Bobes, M. A. (1998). Cognitive brain activity in Alzheimer's disease: Electrophysiological response during picture semantic categorization. *Journal of the International Neuropsychological Society, 4*, 415–425.

Patterson, J. V., Michalewski, H. J., & Starr, A. (1988). Latency variability of the components of auditory event-related potentials to infrequent stimuli in aging, Alzheimer-type dementia, and depression. *Electroencephalography and Clinical Neurophysiology, 71*, 450–460.

Pekkonen, E., Jaaskelainen, I. P., Hietanen, M., Huotilainen, M., Naatanen, R., Ilmoniemi, R. J., et al. (1999). Impaired preconscious auditory processing and cognitive functions in Alzheimer's disease. *Clinical Neurophysiology, 110*, 1942–1947.

Perry, R. J., & Hodges, J. R. (1999). Attention and executive deficits in Alzheimer's disease. A critical review. *Brain, 122*(Pt 3), 383–404.

Petersen, R. C. (2004). Mild cognitive impairment as a diagnostic entity. *Journal of Internal Medicine, 256*, 183–194.

Plassman, B. L., Langa, K. M., Fisher, G. G., Heeringa, S. G., Weir, D. R., Ofstedal, M. B., et al. (2007). Prevalence of dementia in the United States: The aging, demographics, and memory study. *Neuroepidemiology, 29*, 125–132.

Polich, J., & Herbst, K. L. (2000). P300 as a clinical assay: Rationale, evaluation, and findings. *International Journal of Psychophysiology, 38*, 3–19.

Polich, J., & Kok, A. (1995). Cognitive and biological determinants of P300: An integrative review. *Biological Psychology, 41*, 103–146.

Polich, J., Ladish, C., & Bloom, F. E. (1990). P300 assessment of early Alzheimer's disease. *Electroencephalography and Clinical Neurophysiology, 77*, 179–189.

Prichep, L. S. (2007). Quantitative EEG and electromagnetic brain imaging in aging and in the evolution of dementia. *Annals of the New York Academy of Science, 1097*, 156–167.

Raichle, M. E. (2003). Functional brain imaging and human brain function. *Journal of Neuroscience, 23*, 3959–3962.

Riekkinen, P., Jr., Sirvio, J., & Riekkinen, P. (1990). Relationship between the cortical choline acetyltransferase content and EEG delta-power. *Neuroscience Research, 8,* 12–20.

Rodriguez, G., Copello, F., Vitali, P., Perego, G., & Nobili, F. (1999). EEG spectral profile to stage Alzheimer's disease. *Clinical Neurophysiology, 110,* 1831–1837.

Rosenberg, C., Nudleman, K., & Starr, A. (1985) Cognitive evoked potentials (P300) in early Huntington's disease. *Archives of Neurology, 42,* 984–987.

Rossini, P. M., Del Percio, C., Pasqualetti, P., Cassetta, E., Binetti, G., Dal Forno, G., et al. (2006). Conversion from mild cognitive impairment to Alzheimer's disease is predicted by sources and coherence of brain electroencephalography rhythms. *Neuroscience, 143,* 793–803.

Rugg, M. D., & Curran, T. (2007). Event-related potentials and recognition memory. *Trends in Cognitive Science, 11,* 251–257.

Saito, H., Yamazaki, H., Matsuoka, H., Matsumoto, K., Numachi, Y., Yoshida, S., et al. (2001). Visual event-related potential in mild dementia of the Alzheimer's type. *Psychiatry and Clinical Neurosciences, 55,* 365–371.

Schnyer, D. M., Allen, J. J., Kaszniak, A. W., & Forster, K. I. (1999). An event-related potential examination of masked and unmasked repetition priming in alzheimer's disease: Implications for theories of implicit memory. *Neuropsychology, 13,* 323–337.

Schreiter-Gasser, U., Gasser, T., & Ziegler, P. (1993). Quantitative EEG analysis in early onset Alzheimer's disease: A controlled study. *Electroencephalography and Clinical Neurophysiology, 86,* 15–22.

Schreiter-Gasser, U., Rousson, V., Hentschel, F., Sattel, H., & Gasser, T. (2008). Alzheimer disease versus mixed dementias: An EEG perspective. *Clinical Neurophysiology, 119,* 2255–2259.

Scoville, W. B., & Milner, B. (1957). Loss of recent memory after bilateral hippocampal lesions. *Journal of Neurology, Neurosurgery & Psychiatry, 20,* 11–21.

Shannon, B. J., & Buckner, R. L. (2004). Functional-anatomic correlates of memory retrieval that suggest nontraditional processing roles for multiple distinct regions within posterior parietal cortex. *Journal of Neuroscience, 24,* 10084–10092.

Sitnikova, T., Kuperberg, G., & Holcomb, P. J. (2003). Semantic integration in videos of real-world events: An electrophysiological investigation. *Psychophysiology, 40,* 160–164.

Sloan, E. P., & Fenton, G. W. (1993). EEG power spectra and cognitive change in geriatric psychiatry: A longitudinal study. *Electroencephalography and Clinical Neurophysiology, 86,* 361–367.

Smith, J. A., & Knight, R. G. (2002). Memory processing in Alzheimer's disease. *Neuropsychologia, 40,* 666–682.

Spehlmann, R., & Norcross, K. (1982). Cholinergic mechanisms in the production of focal cortical slow waves. *Experientia, 38,* 109–111.

Stam, C. J., Jones, B. F., Manshanden, I., van Cappellen van Walsum, A. M., Montez, T., Verbunt, J. P., et al. (2006). Magnetoencephalographic evaluation of resting-state functional connectivity in Alzheimer's disease. *Neuroimage, 32,* 1335–1344.

Stenberg, G., Hellman, J., Johansson, M., & Rosén, I. (2009). Familiarity or conceptual priming: Event-related potentials in name recognition. *Journal of Cognitive Neuroscience, 21,* 447–460.

Szelies, B., Grond, M., Herholz, K., Kessler, J., Wullen, T., & Heiss, W. D. (1992). Quantitative EEG mapping and PET in Alzheimer's disease. *Journal of the Neurological Sciences, 110,* 46–56.

Thomas C, vom Berg I, Rupp A, Seidl U, Schröder J, Roesch-Ely D, Kreisel SH, Mundt C, Weisbrod M. (2010). P50 gating deficit in Alzheimer dementia correlates to frontal neuropsychological function. *Neurobiology of Aging, 31*, 416–4242

Trollor, J. N., Sachdev, P. S., Haindl, W., Brodaty, H., Wen, W., & Walker, B. M. (2006). A high-resolution single photon emission computed tomography study of verbal recognition memory in Alzheimer's disease. *Dementia and Geriatric Cognitive Disorders, 21,* 267–274.

Valladares-Neto, D. C., Buchsbaum, M. S., Evans, W. J., Nguyen, D., Nguyen, P., Siegel, B. V., et al. (1995). EEG delta, positron emission tomography, and memory deficit in Alzheimer's disease. *Neuropsychobiology, 31,* 173–181.

van der Hiele, K., Vein, A. A., van der Welle, A., van der Grond, J., Westendorp, R. G., Bollen, E. L., et al. (2007). EEG and MRI correlates of mild cognitive impairment and Alzheimer's disease. *Neurobiology of Aging, 28,* 1322–1329.

van Harten, B., Laman, D. M., van Duijn, H., Knol, D. L., Stam, C. J., Scheltens, P., et al. (2006). The auditory oddball paradigm in patients with vascular cognitive impairment: A prolonged latency of the N2 complex. *Dementia and Geriatric Cognitive Disorders, 21,* 322–327.

Verma, N. P., Nichols, C. D., Greiffenstein, M. F., Singh, R. P., & Hurst-Gordon, D. (1989). Waves earlier than p3 are more informative in putative subcortical dementias: A study with mapping and neuropsychological techniques. *Brain Topography, 1,* 183–191.

Vicioso, B. A. (2002). Dementia: When is it not Alzheimer disease? *American Journal of the Medical Sciences, 324,* 84–95.

Voss, J. L., & Paller, K. A. (2007). Neural correlates of conceptual implicit memory and their contamination of putative neural correlates of explicit memory. *Learning & Memory, 14,* 259–267.

Voss, J. L., & Paller, K. A. (2008). Brain substrates of implicit and explicit memory: The importance of concurrently acquired neural signals of both memory types. *Neuropsychologia, 46,* 3021–3029.

Voss, J. L., Reber, P. J., Mesulam, M. M., Parrish, T. B., & Paller, K. A. (2008). Familiarity and conceptual priming engage distinct cortical networks. *Cerebral Cortex, 18,* 1712–1719.

Wagner, A. D., Shannon, B. J., Kahn, I., & Buckner, R. L. (2005). Parietal lobe contributions to episodic memory retrieval. *Trends in Cognitive Science, 9,* 445–453.

Walla, P., Puregger, E., Lehrner, J., Mayer, D., Deecke, L., & Dal Bianco, P. (2005). Depth of word processing in Alzheimer patients and normal controls: A magnetoencephalographic (MEG) study. *Journal of Neural Transmission, 112,* 713–730.

Werber, E. A., Gandelman-Marton, R., Klein, C., & Rabey, J. M. (2003). The clinical use of P300 event related potentials for the evaluation of cholinesterase inhibitors treatment in demented patients. *Journal of Neural Transmission, 110,* 659–669.

Westerberg, C. E., Paller, K. A., Weintraub, S., Mesulam, M. M., Holdstock, J. S., Mayes, A. R., et al. (2006). When memory does not fail: Familiarity-based recognition in mild cognitive impairment and Alzheimer's disease. *Neuropsychology, 20,* 193–205.

Whittlesea, B. W., & Williams, L. D. (1998). Why do strangers feel familiar, but friends don't? A discrepancy-attribution account of feelings of familiarity. *Acta Psychologica (Amsterdam), 98,* 141–165.

Whittlesea, B. W., & Williams, L. D. (2001). The discrepancy-attribution hypothesis: I. The heuristic basis of feelings of familiarity. *Journal of Experimental Psychology: Human Learning and Memory, 27,* 3–13.

Wolk, D. A., Schacter, D. L., Berman, A. R., Holcomb, P. J., Daffner, K. R., & Budson, A. E. (2004). An electrophysiological investigation of the relationship between conceptual fluency and familiarity. *Neuroscience Letters, 369,* 150–155.

Wolk, D. A., Schacter, D. L., Berman, A. R., Holcomb, P. J., Daffner, K. R., & Budson, A. E. (2005). Patients with mild Alzheimer's disease attribute conceptual fluency to prior experience. *Neuropsychologia, 43,* 1662–1672.

Wolk, D. A., Sen, N. M., Chong, H., Riis, J. L., McGinnis, S. M., Holcomb, P. J., et al. (2009). ERP correlates of item recognition memory: Effects of age and performance. *Brain Research, 1250,* 218–231.

Zappoli, R., Versari, A., Paganini, M., Arnetoli, G., Muscas, G. C., Gangemi, P. F., et al. (1995). Brain electrical activity (quantitative EEG and bit-mapping neurocognitive CNV components), psychometrics and clinical findings in presenile subjects with initial mild cognitive decline or probable Alzheimer-type dementia. *Italian Journal of the Neurological Sciences, 16,* 341–376.

Index

The Handbook of Alzheimer's Disease and Other Dementias, First Edition.
Edited by Andrew E. Budson, Neil W. Kowall.
© 2011 Blackwell Publishing Ltd. Published 2011 by Blackwell Publishing Ltd.